EUROPE'S Wonderful LITTLE HOTELS & INNS 1986

"On quaint lodging places, [one of] the best."—*Harper's*

"Appeals to those who prefer to stay in small, comfortable places, surrounded by antiques, fragrant gardens, and a friendly staff."   —*Washington Post*

"Delightful.... A useful guide that's fun to read."
                                        —*Library Journal*

"The range is exciting.... An excellent idea."
                                        —*Publishers Weekly*

"Agreeably quirky.... Will well serve adventuresome Americans."   —*The Kirkus Reviews*

EUROPE'S *Wonderful* LITTLE HOTELS & INNS *1986*

Edited by Hilary Rubinstein
Eighth Edition

Published in London as THE GOOD HOTEL GUIDE 1986

Continental Editors: John Ardagh, Linda and Alex Finer,
Jeremy Round, Annasue McCleave Wilson

Managing editor: Caroline Raphael

St. Martin's Press
New York

ACKNOWLEDGEMENTS

"Tipping: The Most Odious Practice ever Invented" by Bernard Levin
and "Country House Hotels: An Opposition View" by Penny Perrick
were originally published in *The Times*, London, and are reproduced
by permission of Times Newspapers Ltd. The lines from "Bacon and
Eggs" quoted in the Introduction are reproduced by permission of
Lady Herbert. *The Accidental Traveller* by Ann Tyler, from which an
extract is also quoted in the Introduction, is published in the UK by
Chatto & Windus and, as *The Accidental Tourist*, by Alfred Knopf in
the USA.

Material published in *Europe's Wonderful Little Hotels and Inns* must
not be used in any form of advertising, sales promotion or publicity.

Library of Congress Cataloging in Publication Data
Main entry under title:

Europe's wonderful little hotels and inns, 1986.

   1. Hotels, taverns, etc.—Europe—Directories.
I. Rubinstein, Hilary.
TX910.A1E95   1986   647′.94401   85-25166
ISBN 0-312-27087-9 (pbk.)

Published in Great Britain as *The Good Hotel Guide, 1986* by
Consumers' Association and Hodder & Stoughton.

First U.S. Edition

10 9 8 7 6 5 4 3 2 1

Cover illustration by Steven Guarnaccia.

Editorial assistants: Tracey Brett, Julie Marshall, Amanda Smith

Contents

A note for new readers

This is an annual guide to hotels and inns in Britain and the continent of Western Europe that are of unusual character and quality. The entries are based on reports from readers who write to us when they come across an establishment which has given them out-of-the-ordinary satisfaction, and who also send us their comments, critical or appreciative, when they visit places already included in the Guide. Our task is to collate these reports, check and verify them, making inspections where necessary, and select those which we consider make the grade. No cash changes hands at any point: contributors are not rewarded for writing to us; hotels do not pay for their entries; the editor and his staff accept no free hospitality.

The Guide operates on the same principle as *The Good Food Guide*, but is independently owned and edited. We have no say in the hotels and restaurants chosen by our sibling publication, nor are they involved in our choices. But we are keen to share our correspondence where appropriate: we pass on to *The Good Food Guide* reports on any British hotel where the restaurant is an important feature. Hotels listed in that Guide carry the notation [GFG] after their name.

The entries in the book cover a wide range. People want different things from a hotel according to whether they are making a single night stop or spending a whole holiday in one place, whether they have young children with them, whether they are visiting a city or staying in the remote countryside, and according to their age and means. We make no claims of universal compatibility or comprehensiveness, but we hope that our descriptions will help you to find good hotels that suit your tastes, needs and purse. If an entry has misled you, we hope you will use one of the report forms at the back of the book and tell us, in order that we can do better next time; and we hope that you will also write to us if you have found the Guide useful and a hotel has fulfilled your expectations: endorsement and criticism are both essential if the Guide is to achieve its purpose. A hotel is dropped unless we get a positive feedback.

Introduction

The year 1985 has been an outstanding year for most hotels in Western Europe, since the strong dollar has brought Americans to Britain and the Continent in unprecedented numbers. The last time there was a major tourist invasion, we had evidence of hotels cashing in on the demand and raising their prices out of proportion. Regrettably, this appears to be happening again, at least in London. In May 1985, *Expotel/Caterer and Hotelkeeper* published a Hotel Tariff Survey which revealed that 2-, 3- and 5-star hotels in London had shown an increase in excess of 15% – more than twice the rate of inflation. Room shortage is at its most acute in the capital; in the provinces, average increases have been considerably less, but still above the rate of inflation. Of course, some increases can be attributed to particular schemes for refurbishment, but since Britain's largest hotel group, Trusthouse Forte, successfully contained their price rises to within the rate of inflation, it is hard to resist the conclusion that many hotels and hotel groups have taken gross advantage of the upsurge in demand.

The hotels you will find in these pages, almost all small and independently owned, are largely outside the scope of such surveys, but if the catering trade as a whole acquires a reputation for ripping off its customers, the honest and fair as well as the sharks are tarnished. One of the crucial criteria we apply in selecting a hotel is whether it offers good value for money. Some of the most famous small hotels, which regularly feature in lists of the Best Hotels of the World, disqualify themselves in our book because we don't feel they can justify their prices. We should be glad if readers would report any charges – either in the basic tariff or in optional extras – which they feel are exorbitant.

Meanwhile, the effect of the tourist boom has been felt seismically throughout the industry. Most big hotel chains are busy acquiring or building huge new properties or extending old ones to cater for the global influx of travellers expected in the late eighties and nineties. Luxury enterprises of the smaller kind are also constantly being drawn to our notice. Two years ago, in heralding the opening of the Blancs' *Manoir aux Quat' Saisons* in Great Milton, we wrote: "The risks of such an enterprise, without the benefit of a private fortune to sustain the house through its lean years, are high and getting higher. We doubt whether we shall see many new hotels of the *grand cru classé* variety in the years ahead." How wrong we were! Among the new country house hotels at or near the top of the market to have claimed an entry in 1985 and 1986 are *Middlethorpe Hall*, York, *Palé Hall*, Llandderfel, and *Ettington Park*, Alderminster, near Stratford-upon-Avon. (In passing, we should also mention the latest French super-star, the *Boyer Les Crayères* at Rheims). Next year, the major event in the British hotel calendar is bound to be the opening of *Cliveden*, the Astors' famous house spectacularly sited overlooking the Thames near Maidenhead, now being reincarnated, after a £2 million facelift, as a hotel *de grand luxe*. But there are other champagne launchings in preparation already being talked about by keen hotel-watchers, such as *Tylney Hall*, Rotherwick near Basingstoke, currently undergoing a £3 million renovation, and *Stapleford Park* in Leicestershire, recently bought by the Chicago Pizza Pie Factory magnate, Bob Payton.

Not all the interesting new developments are in the hotel category. Robert Carrier's former luxury restaurant, *Hintlesham Hall*, is now open again as a gourmet's mecca, but this time with accommodation as well. Nico Ladenis, whose two-rosetted *Chez Nico* in Battersea many gastronomes regard as London's finest restaurant, has moved down to Shinfield in Reading, taking his two rosettes along with him. *Chez Nico* at The Old Vicarage, Shinfield, will start off as a restaurant, but will become a restaurant-with-rooms in spring 1986. Book your rooms now!

These developments are of academic interest to most of our readers since prices are inevitably way beyond the means of all but the super rich. Fortunately, good hotels, offering choice and out-of-the-ordinary experiences, can be found at every price level, and we are as eager to chart the outstanding budget-priced establishment as we are to keep pace with all the intoxicating developments at the celestial end of the spectrum.

The growing range we cover

When I first conceived the notion of this Guide in the mid-seventies, I never doubted that "hotel" was the right word for the title. Now, a decade later, when I consider the wide variety of different sorts of place which the book encompasses, I am not so sure. There are still plenty of unambiguous hotels, of course, in the present edition, but alongside them is an assortment of country inns, country house homes, restaurants-with-rooms, farmhouses-with-rooms, guest-houses, and B&Bs – and their continental equivalents. Guest-houses, B&Bs and farmhouse accommodation are nothing new, but these sophisti-cated up-market variants are phenomena of the eighties. And there are some fresh hybrids too: *Wallet's Court* at West Cliffe is a B&B during the week and becomes a gourmet restaurant-with-rooms on Saturdays; *The Ceilidh Place*, Ullapool, one of this year's César winners, has its rooms as part of a complex of bookshop, café, restaurant, mini-arts centre and much else besides.

It isn't so much that our criteria have altered, but that the traditional hotel scene has changed. Mega-hotels, as we have said, are continuing to be built and expanded to meet the still growing needs of mass tourism, while conventional hotels and motels flourish and service the business trade. But more leisure, more expendable income, earlier retirement and changing tastes have encouraged the development of far more options than were dreamed of ten years ago. Tourist boards and motoring associations still stipulate much the same conditions for their various ratings, but these appear increasingly incongruous when applied to the new breed of unclassifiable places (see *Pitfalls of grading* below).

What have these heterogeneous establishments in common apart from the fact that they all come under the heading of "serviced accommodation", to use the official parlance? One response I have given before is that each is a place which I have either visited with pleasure or reckon I would enjoy if I did.

Another possible answer comes from considering the Real Ale campaign among discriminating beer-drinkers and the crusade for Real Food pursued by our sibling, *The Good Food Guide*. You could say that the common factor in all these assorted good hotels is the fact that they are run by Real People. Of course, I am not suggesting that those who look after the establishments which are outside our pale are less than human (though their behaviour may be fairly mechanical or robotic at time) any more than keg beer is less than beer or packaged convenience food is less than food. What distinguishes hotels featured in these pages is the unforced sympathetic qualities of their owners, managers and staff. One correspondent writing about *The Angel*, Bury St Edmunds, put it this way: "The staff was unusually friendly and helpful, and in the most natural way possible – ie no phrases or mannerisms that might have been taught, but all straightforward and completely sincere."

"No artificial anything" is a slogan used by the admirable New England ice cream, and I would like to think that the phrase also applies to our selection of hotels. This doesn't mean that you can expect to enjoy equally all our offerings. We provide horses for courses. Some houses are hearty and convivial: don't go if you dislike being introduced and cajoled into conversation with fellow-guests. Others are more demure and reclusive. Some are hair-singeingly expensive and provide a harvest of little extras, others are relatively basic in their accommodation. All, we hope, provide the traveller with that crucial little extra that costs nothing and is without price. . . .

Those pandering little extras

Just as airlines seek to attract more first-class customers by offering them ever more ingenious give-aways, so hotel-keepers, too, at the upper end of the price scale, vie with each other by adding to the range of exotic or extravagant freebies. Every year the list grows longer: the miniature bottle of sherry becomes a carafe; the plate of home-made biscuits becomes a tin; the two little chocolates become a box; the bowl of fruit becomes a cornucopia – we counted nine separate varieties of fruit in our room at one sybaritic establishment. Teletext is added to remote-control colour TV; bathrooms have jacuzzis these days as well as hair dryers. Bathrobes, binoculars, Scrabble – there seems no end to the possibilities. I also note, with mixed feelings, the onward march of the four-poster in country house hotels. I don't care for them personally, since they inhibit reading in bed. Are they really popular or just a passing fad? As every one of these offerings or installations is bound to be reflected in the tariff, I would be interested to know how much or how little they are appreciated by our readers.

Meanwhile, for the hotel desperate to provide its guests with something completely original, I pass on this snatch of conversation between a writer of guide books and a hotel that is being inspected, taken from Ann Tyler's new novel, *The Accidental Traveller*:

"To tell the truth," Macon said, "I've always thought a hotel ought to offer optional small animals."

"Animals?"

"I mean a cat to sleep on your bed at night, or a dog of some kind to act pleased when you come in. You ever notice how a hotel room feels so lifeless?"

"Yes, but – well, I don't see how I could – there are surely health regulations or something . . . complications, paperwork, feeding all those different . . . and allergies, of course, many guests have –"

"Oh, I understand, I understand," Macon said. "It doesn't seem that people ever take me up on that."

Thank you for not tipping

In recent issues we have railed against what we regard as two scandalous anachronisms of the catering trade – the imposition of service charges and the touting for tips. We have no wish to inhibit the generous impulses of those who have received special kindnesses beyond the call of duty, but we deplore a 10% or 15% service charge being imposed mandatorily, without reference to the nature and extent of the service provided, and before the guest has even signed the register. And we know that when service is said to be left to guests' discretion, there is often, even when the management disapproves, a powerful nudge-nudge factor at work.

We must now add a third blot on the fair name of the industry: the little-known fact that, as the law stands at the moment, there is no obligation on the part of managements to distribute any part of an obligatory service charge: they may give it all away on a *tronc* basis; they may keep a part and share out the rest; or they may hog the lot. What they do with the money is entirely their business. An attempt some years ago by George Robertson MP to introduce a Private Members' Bill which would have forced hotels and restaurants to distribute service charges among their employees failed to get a second reading. Next time your bill contains an involuntary service charge, you may care to ask where the money is going.

I put the question to the owner of an elegant Georgian country house hotel. He assured me that all the money from the service charge and the extras that came from leaving the bottom line of the credit-card slip open ("so many business users like to add something, but don't want it to come out of their own pockets") were distributed scrupulously among the staff on a strict points system according to the hours worked. So he took nothing out for himself? "Well, my wife and I work in the hotel, so we each qualify for a 42-hour week share." I doubt, though, whether many of his visitors guessed that part of their service charge and tips was going straight into their host's and hostess's pockets.

Since most of us are led to believe that a service charge goes to those who are actually supplying the service, the catering industry which connives at these charges is perpetrating a fraud. Moreover, in case you think that you can withhold a service charge from your bill if you have had appalling service, you should be warned that, providing a notice of a statutory service charge is printed on the menu or tariff card, you can be forced to pay the amount because you can be held implicitly to have accepted it as a term of contract. How little most of us know of the strange working of our laws!

Last year we invited hotels to tell us if they had a policy on tipping and service charges. Many hotels replied – and we gave their answers in italics at the end of the entry. We have done the same this year. When you stay in one of these hotels, you will at least know where you stand.

We are sure that many hoteliers who failed to answer our question, or simply said that it was left to guests' discretion, found the subject embarrassing. They may personally have disliked the practice, but knew how popular it was with staff, who naturally regard it as one of the perks of the job. One hotel-keeper, who was persuaded by our campaign to discontinue quoting his tariff "inclusive of a 10% service charge", and told guests that service was free and that the staff expected nothing, was surprised to find that his staff were taking four times more in tips than previously. Make of that what you will.

Hotel-keepers sometimes ask us what form of words they should adopt to inhibit automatic tipping while allowing free rein to those who wish to express their appreciation in the conventional manner. Last year, we printed a number of solutions to this problem from hotels opposed in principle to guests being put under an obligation to tip. This year, we commend a formula from Trusthouse Forte (whose hotels, we regret, rarely make these pages). THF has pursued an anti-tipping policy for several years and now prints on menus and tariff cards: "All prices are inclusive of service and VAT. However, if you believe that you have received exceptional service please feel free to reward staff accordingly." We also applaud the *Inn on the Lake*, Godalming, who inform their guests: "It is the policy of this Inn to maintain prices at the lowest level consistent with paying the bills and making some profit. Service and cover charges are not in keeping with this image and therefore are not charged. As in the case of the hairdresser or taxi-driver, should you particularly wish to express your personal thanks to the staff, please do this direct, but feel under no obligation to do so."

We referred last year to our surprise and delight that in Australia, no one, not even taxi-drivers, expected a tip. I imagined that taxi-drivers here took a different line; and most of us have not the nerve to defy the custom of adding 10% or 15% to what's on the meter. But one cab-driver I got talking to told me otherwise. First, he informed me that in fact taxi-drivers rarely make more than 6%-8% in tips, with the less well-off paradoxically tending to be the more generous tippers. Secondly, he said that he and most of his fellow-cabbies cordially disliked the practice and would be only too happy to add, say, 10% or 15% to the current meter charge and oppose tips on top. (Well, if taxis are at the moment only taking 7% in tips, of course they would prefer to up the meter charge by 10%.) Seeing a notice prominently displayed in the vehicle, "Thank you for not smoking", I asked the driver whether he would consider putting up a similar notice, "Thank you for not tipping". He smiled (at least so far as I could read his expression from the back of his head), and said he thought that was going a bit too far. . . .

For those who still need persuading on this subject, I recommend "Tipping: the most odious practice ever invented" by Bernard Levin to be found on page 749.

The pitfalls of grading

Ever since the Guide started, we have considered providing some sort of rudimentary grading so that readers could see at a glance, without having to read the citation, what sort of establishment was being talked about. A price guide based on the cost of B&B would be relatively simple to operate, but would be misleading when accommodation was cheap but the restaurant expensive; and the information is clear from the tariff anyway. Last year, we invited comments, and the vote was clearly for "no change". "Grading is like trying to compare a thriller with a biography" wrote a publicity director of a well-known publisher. "Any grading system would cause much controversy," wrote another.

One correspondent suggested we printed the official national classification and told us "the system of stars used by the Swiss Hotels Association is reliable in all respects". Maybe, but our investigation into the grading practices of different countries showed that systems varied enormously and could only be reproduced if accompanied by long boring explanations of their methodology.

The present British system of classification is as wayward as any. At the moment, hotels which wish to register with their national Tourist Boards are responsible for their own classifications on a one to six basis for three separate categories – bedrooms, services and meals. If you have the time to read the massive small print, you can learn a lot about what a hotel should be providing when it claims, eg, a rating of three for its accommodation. But there is at the moment no procedure, except in Wales, for establishing whether a hotel has described its facilities and services accurately – and indeed its claims are often honoured in the breach.

To be blunt, the present system, byzantine in its complexity and unregulated in its performance, is a public disgrace. We are glad to report, however, that reform is on its way. In the summer of 1985, after many years of debate and consultation, all the national Tourist Boards at last agreed on a simplified one to five classification system, with crowns as the basic symbol. More importantly, England and Scotland have agreed to follow the example of Wales in appointing a corps of verifiers who will visit all would-be classified establishments annually to make sure that the hotel's own claims can be substantiated. These visits will scarcely rank as inspections as we or the AA or *Michelin* understand the term. They will not be anonymous and will be made by appointment only; their purpose – an admirable one – will be to help establishments meet the standards their customers expect. But of course visits by appointment mean that a hotel need never be caught with its trousers down. Moreover, the ratings themselves will in no way be qualitative: a hotel may lack all cordiality, be furnished in execrable taste, be inefficient and slow in its service and provide ill-cooked meals at a rip-off price and still claim five-crown status. Nevertheless, we welcome the news that the Tourist Boards are at last beginning to put their house in order and look forward to the implementation of the scheme in 1987.

Inevitably, glaring anomalies will remain. For instance, even a single-crown hotel or guest-house (all sorts of establishments are parcelled together as "serviced accommodation") must offer a lock on a bedroom door. No doubt discretion will be used in applying its formal criteria, but, strictly speaking, that one requirement alone would disqualify many of the best country house hotels in the Guide since the presence of locks on the doors would be felt to destroy the carefully cultivated illusion of guests being in a home-from-home establishment.

Even with the new classifications, hotels will continue to be allowed to word their own copy if they choose to advertise in the Tourist Boards' *Where to Stay* publications. We are told that excessive hype is edited out, but claims of "elegant accommodation" and "a haven for lovers of good food" will continue to mislead those who believe that an entry in a Tourist Board publication contains some seal of official approval. These publications do no credit to the Boards which sponsor them. The only official handbook we can warmly recommend is the British Tourist Authority's *Commended Country Hotels, Guest Houses and Restaurants* [£2.25 in 1985], available at any tourist office. The BTA really do inspect their 400 commended establishments.

Manners, manners

You might imagine that if you are paying an innkeeper good money – and sometimes these days a small fortune – for the privilege of sleeping under his roof and eating at his table, you could expect a modicum of politeness and respect. Of course, most of the time relations between hotelier and guest are affable enough, but it is surprising how often one comes across instances of flagrant rudeness, even bare-faced effrontery.

I am talking mainly about small owner-managed hotels. Offensiveness certainly occurs in larger, more impersonal, establishments, though it tends to take a different form. Off-handedness is a besetting sin. Checking out at the *Queen's Hotel*, Leeds, not long ago, I drew the attention of the cashier to the fact that there was a charge for telephone though I had not in fact made any calls. Her indifferent response provoked me to ask – perhaps a bit pompously – whether anyone had ever taught her to apologise. She looked at me with total incomprehension. . . .

Another source of irritation or worse is the snootiness or condescension prevalent among waiters and desk staff at de luxe hotels if they feel you don't really belong; on the other hand, if they think you are a likely prospect for a fat tip, the mask of haughtiness will be replaced by another equally egregious countenence, that of intolerable obsequiousness. Ludwig Bemel-mans, who knew the inner life of the grand hotel better than anyone, once described a *maître d'hôtel* as "a type whose face is like a towel on which everyone has wiped both hands". Many of us prefer to take our chance with the uncertain congeniality of the individual landlord rather than experience yet again the machine-turned civilities or servilities of the *Hôtel Splendide*.

You run a risk, of course, whenever you venture abroad. A new criticism turned up in our correspondence recently: "The landlord's politics were inclined to bubble over." Was he ultra-right or militant left? There was no way we could warn any specific group of our readers to keep off politics: he may just have been an ardent supporter of the SDP who was keen to evangelise even the captive paying guest. The point illustrates one of the major drawbacks of the profession of hotel-keeping – namely, the need to be all things to all customers – to add to the hardship of hours no trade union would ever tolerate. The bar-tender has only to be genial during opening hours; the resident owner is never off duty. Is it better if your host has no strong convictions of his own? I doubt it. It is hard to respect insipidity. Even less agreeable are owners whom, one is instinctively aware, dislike what they are doing and secretly despise themselves for being in a service industry. There is little pleasure to be had from their company.

The most appalling piece of behaviour I have run across in a decade of editing this guide came from a well-regarded country house hotel in the south of England. A group of Jewish guests, regular seasonal visitors at the hotel for many years past, who had previously enjoyed halcyon relations with their hosts, one evening unwittingly provoked the lady of the house to a sudden pent-up explosion of anti-semitism that left every one in the restaurant in a paroxysm of embarrassment. There were explana-tions of course: the woman had had a bit too much to drink, the party had been unreasonably demanding, the husband did his best to apologise, but we doubt whether anyone who had been present at the scene that night would forget the incident.

Anti-semitism is just one of the many prejudices that can lie beneath a placid surface only to break out when incitement takes place. Anti-Americanism, deplorably, is another. Blacks, gays, fussy old people, inconsiderate young, children who are heard as well as seen, loving couples who make a public exhibition of their affections, people who complain that the helpings are gross, or grossly inadequate, or who are never satisfied with what is on the menu but always want something else: the occasions when the owner feels he has had more than enough must be innumerable. No doubt hoteliers are as frequently incensed with their guests as the other way about. Furious guests can vent their spleen by writing to the hotel guidebooks or the Tourist Boards, but hotel-keepers have to bear their grudges in silence except, no doubt, when two or three of them are gathered together. Perhaps it is not surprising that their tempers should sometimes erupt – and the victim may be relatively innocent, just the last straw.

Doubtless, there are many perfectly awful guests who reckon that paying the piper entitles them to call any tune they like – to hector and bully, to demand services at unreasonable hours (unreasonable except at five-star, 24-hour service establishments) or to disturb the midnight peace by roistering.

Inconsiderateness may also take an insidious form: booking rooms, for instance, and never turning up, or else cancelling so late that the hotel has no chance of letting the room elsewhere. Some people we know regularly double or treble book: if they don't like the look of a place when they arrive, they creep away and try the next one. No wonder hotels increasingly demand written confirmation with deposits or require telephone bookers to supply credit-card numbers in self-protection.

We were interested to read that a consortium of Scottish hotels had decided to organise a Best Guest Award – prize a week's holiday in one of the consortium's hotels. "Too much attention," said Nick Ryan of the *Crinan Hotel*, is paid in tourism to the producer and not enough to the customer, without whom we would be out of business." I applaud that line of thinking, though adjudicating a Best Guest competition can't be easy. And sometimes the best guest, from a hotel's point of view, is one who puts a good face on mishaps and discourtesies which inevitably happen even in the best-run establishments. I was reminded of a leaflet put out by the Bermuda Trades Development Board:

"I'M A NICE GUEST"

You know me, I'm a nice guest. I never complain, no matter what kind of service I get. I'll go into a hotel and stand at the front desk for a long time while the desk clerk busies himself with some books or figures and never bothers to notice me. Sometimes someone arrives after I do and gets taken care of right away, but I don't say a word. If the clerk can't find my reservation or the room isn't ready, I'm nice about it. When the bellman seems annoyed that I have checked in, I try not to take it personally.

When I go to eat, I'm thoughtful of the other person. If I get a grouchy waiter or waitress who is annoyed because I want to study the menu a bit, I'm polite as I can be. I don't believe that rudeness in return is the answer. You might say I wasn't raised that way. And it's seldom I ever send anything back to the kitchen. I've found people are just about always disagreeable to me when I do. Life is short! Too short for indulging in these unpleasant little scrimmages.

I am often too intimidated by the head waiter to complain when I order a steak medium and it is served almost raw. I never criticize. I wouldn't dream of making a scene, as I've seen some people doing in public places. I think that's awful. I'm a nice guest and I always give a tip. I'll tell you what else I am: *I'm the guest who never comes back.*

Prayers ancient and modern

Fastidious travellers have been complaining about inns – the accommodation or lack of it, the wretched food, the graceless service – for at least 2,000 years. Indeed, "no room at the inn" has a distinctly modern flavour. Every post brings us fresh complaints as well as old prayers still not answered. Here is a selection from this year's file: some new gripes, some hoary old ones.

Heating Undoubtedly the number one grievance, year in and year out, but also one most easily remedied. Occasionally, in hotels which have substantial American custom, we are told of over-heating, but almost always that heating is inadequate in cold spells. Much of this edition was written in an exceptionally unfriendly June. Inevitably, that cool wet windy summer spell was followed in July by a spate of letters telling us of hotels that, like so many foolish virgins, had not lit their lamps in time.

Lighting Probably the number two complaint, but also easy to remedy. Perhaps hotel-keepers, working such intolerably long hours, are too exhausted to want to read in bed themselves, but many of their customers would like to if lighting permitted. Bulbs are often "Scrooge-like", and the placing of bedside lighting too far from the bed to be much use; or else lights are sufficient for one partner, but not both; or heavy shades defeat the purpose. Bathroom lighting also comes in for criticism from makers-up and shavers.

Restaurant (i) *Smoking*: As more people give up smoking, the chorus of protests swells. The feeling of outrage is greatest when a master chef is displaying his art: if a heavy smoker is at the next table, the offence is similar to having your neighbour unwrap sweets at Glyndebourne. Some hotels offer exhortations to smokers to be considerate to others. But these, as at *Le Manoir aux Quat' Saisons*, may be so gently put, printed in such small type and in so inconspicuous a position on the menu, as to be virtually ineffectual. We are delighted to learn that *Gravetye Manor* has declared its restaurant a no-smoking area, and wish that all hotels would follow suit – and not just those with distinguished chefs. If the London Underground can ban smoking without causing any public disturbance, the hotel trade can surely get away with it.

(ii) *Music and musak*: "What happened to silence?" a reader asks. Less popular than it used to be is perhaps the answer, as more

Walkmanites have music wherever they go. We couldn't be sure without calling for a poll, but we think it likely that most of our readers would vote against background music at meals, whether of the live variety (as at *Thornbury Castle*) or the taped, sympathetic or antipathetic, music or musak. All very well for the lone diner, and perhaps serving a purpose when a restaurant is half empty, background music is in general an intrusion in conversation.

(iii) *Smaller appetites, shorter thirsts*: We made a pitch last year for hotels at present only offering a four- or five-course set meal to offer the option of paying less and taking only two or three courses. More vegetarian dishes on the menu would also be popular. We also wish that wine lists would offer more choice with half-bottles. Single diners, who have a drink before dinner, often prefer only a half-bottle with their meal; couples may like to share a half-bottle with a first course and split a bottle with the entrée.

Deposits   More hotels are asking for deposits – who can blame them in view of the number of no-shows and late cancellations? But they present a particular problem to visitors from overseas. An American reader told us how out of pocket she was after getting money orders from her bank ($4 apiece), and then being charged extra by some hotels for the cost of changing dollars into pounds; also, of course, the hotels had the use of her money for two months. Is there a better way? she asks. Our advice is to pay wherever possible with a credit card; if the hotel won't accept credit cards, dollar drafts are the next best alternative.

Breakfasts   (i) *Fresh orange juice*: We continue to hear of expensive hotels offering tinned or packaged fruit juice at breakfast, with the fresh sort being an optional extra – 25 francs at one avaricious French country hotel. Old readers of the Guide will know that we regard this as inexcusable, like charging extra for home-made jam or marmalade. But we think that some hotels are being unjustly accused of meanness in the orange-juice department. We once quoted a report of packaged juice at *Inverlochy Castle*, and the hotel indignantly told us that they never had and never would. However, we discover that fresh juice prepared the night before, or perhaps early in the morning, several hours before it is served, tastes like the packaged sort. Hotels please note: for the real fruit taste there is no substitute for *fresh* squeezing.

(ii) *Continental versus full*: Michael Croft of the National Youth Theatre takes us to task for recommending that hotels should provide a continental breakfast in the B&B price, and charge extra for those who want the full works. "The average traveller (which I take myself to be) wants and expects a full breakfast before we do a full day's work – especially when our working schedule may have deprived us of dinner the night before and may reduce us to a snack lunch in the day ahead. It may well be that you and your indolent chums with nothing to do all day except guzzle gourmet lunches and dinners may be incapable of facing real food in the morning, but do not imagine that, with your sensitive and clapped-out stomachs, you speak for other than a tiny part of the hotel-using population." We remain unrepentant: we think that travellers who want to eat less should pay less at breakfast, as at any other meal. (But it's ironic that the more expensive hotels charge extra, the cheaper ones always provide full breakfasts on the tariff.) In any event, we are grateful to Michael Croft for introducing us to the late A P Herbert's robust poem, "Bacon and Eggs", which opens:

> Now blest be the Briton, his beef and his beer,
> And all the strong waters that keep him in cheer,
> But blest beyond cattle and blest beyond kegs
> Is the brave British breakfast of bacon and eggs.
>
> Thus armed and thus engined, well-shaven and gay,
> We leap to our labours and conquer the day,
> While paltry pale foreigners, meagre as moles,
> Must crawl through the morning on coffee and rolls.

America's Wonderful Little Hotels and Inns

The Guide is published in the United States and Canada under the title *Europe's Wonderful Little Hotels and Inns*. Its success in North America has led to a sister publication on American and Canadian hotels based on the same principles. The US version is at present undergoing a major revision. Readers with recent experience of good hotels in North America are urged to help the cause by sending their nominations to *America's Wonderful Little Hotels and Inns*, St Martin's Press, 175 Fifth Avenue, New York, NY 10010, USA.

About this edition

1,100 hotels this year, 10% up on last, and, for those interested in our statistics, more than twice as many entries as five years ago. (Value for money note: the present edition is only one-third more expensive than the 1981 issue). Approximately 230 hotels have been dropped, and over 300 new hotels or hotels have come back after an interval. Hotels are mostly left out because the consensus of reports has gone against them, but quite a number of entries have been omitted for lack of feedback or because of a change of ownership or management.

We have introduced a new section at the start of the book, "Special hotels" which extends last year's listings of various sorts of outstanding hotels to cover Britain as well as the Continent.

No major changes in coverage this year. Northern Ireland is still disenfranchised. Our hopes of having an Icelandic section have not been realised.

John Ardagh has once again edited the French and German sections, but this year Linda and Alex Finer have taken charge of the Spanish and Swiss entries and Jeremy Round of the Turkish pages; Annasue McCleave Wilson is responsible for the rest of the Continent. As for many years past, the French section has been a major growth area. "It shows what excellent work our readers are doing in tracking down more and more of the simply enormous number of potentially Guide-worthy hotels in France," John Ardagh writes, "but it does pose a fearful space problem in the years ahead." He also tells us, having been travelling extensively in Germany this year (and helping to add to the growth of the German section), how impressed he has been by the very high standard of hotels in Germany, especially in rural districts, "far higher than in the UK or France. You can go right down-market, and still find amazing spruceness, brightness, good service and friendliness. The quality of cooking in German hotels, though rarely reaching gastronomic peaks, is far more dependable than in most other countries."

How we cope with the many new entries is the subject of much discussion. France, Germany, Austria and Switzerland are the problem areas since in those countries there is a tradition of small professional family-run hotels and inns not found so ubiquitously anywhere else in Europe or indeed in other continents. Selecting the best when standards are so consistently high becomes far more difficult. We have considered various options. We could allow the book to become still fatter or we could split the work into two volumes – the UK and the Continent. Alternatives would be for greater selectivity or shorter entries. We should welcome your views.

We have three appendices. We invited Nigel Corbett, of *Summer Lodge*, Evershot, one of last year's César winners, to tell us what, in his view, makes a good country house hotel; and, by way of contrast, Penny Perrick tells us why she far prefers an honest business hotel. And Bernard Levin gives us his trenchant views on tipping.

Good reading – and *bon voyage*.

HILARY RUBINSTEIN
London, September, 1985

The César Awards 1986

Our annual awards of Césars – called after the celebrated hotelier, César Ritz – are given for different sorts of excellence among hotels in Britain and Ireland. The categories listed below show the wide range of hotels, inns and guest-houses which appeal to us and afford some kind of definition of the scope of the Guide. As before, we have given a César for acceptable eccentricity, but otherwise categories change from year to year. Last year's Césars are indicated in the text by a small laurel wreath.

AWARD	WINNER
For classic country house excellence	**Homewood Park, Hinton Charterhouse**

By no means the most expensive country house hotel in the Guide, but providing the key quality of spacious ease. A beautiful house in attractive grounds, a fine restaurant, and owners Stephen and Penny Ross who combine professional zeal with unaffected welcome.

For country house excellence in the medium-price range	**Woodhayes, Whimple**

The welcome at *Woodhayes* is no less than at *Homewood Park*, and the attention to detail is no less assiduous in John Allen's establishment: the rooms and grounds are smaller, however, and the prices significantly lower.

For theatrical brilliance and imaginative largesse	**Miller Howe, Windermere**

A night out at *Miller Howe* is a memorable experience. John Tovey is an inspiring, innovative cook as well as a gregarious and generous master of ceremonies. The high peaks across the water provide a suitably dramatic backdrop.

For the best family hotel	**Lodore Swiss Hotel, Keswick**

One of the largest country hotels in the Guide but the Englands run the show with personal caring as well as with dependable Swiss efficiency. There is so much on offer in the way of services and entertainments that guests need never stray outside the *Lodore* grounds.

For preserving traditional values in a sporting hotel

Lake Vyrnwy Hotel, Llanwddyn

Colonel Sir John Baynes and Mrs Moir know what they are about. They make no concessions to any modern image, but maintain with conspicuous success the virtues of a comfortable old-fashioned sporting hotel.

Finest old coaching-inn

The George, Stamford

Many old coaching-inns survive in one tarted-up form or another. *The George* isn't gimcrack or pretentious: it retains the spirit as well as the fabric of a splendid old hostelry.

Most civilised bed-and-breakfast

The Old Vicarage, Rye

A fine location in the heart of the old town and two dedicated hosts in Ruth and Ernest Thompson earn for *The Old Vicarage* the B&B accolade of the year.

The pearl in the Jersey oyster

Longueville Manor, St Saviour, Jersey

Jersey has many sorts of hotel from high-rise and honky-tonk to back-street boarding. But *Longueville* is in a class apart. It has maintained its reputation for serene and sybaritic comfort through two generations of the Lewis family, and is now better than ever since chef John Dicken joined the team.

For best value

Tregony House, Tregony

You can pay wicked prices and have a sawdust experience. At this civilised guest-house, the opposite is the case: the tariff is astonishingly low, but the quality of the Locks' hospitality is dependably high. So there is an aftertaste to be savoured.

For utterly acceptable mild eccentricity

The Ceilidh Place, Ullapool

Robert and Jean Urquhart are doing their own thing in exuberant style at their life-enhancing complex of hotel, restaurant, coffee-shop, bookshop, clubhouse. . . .

Special Hotels

City hotels with luxury and grandeur

England Connaught, London; Middlethorpe, York
Austria Palais Schwarzenberg, Vienna
France Lancaster, Paris; Boyer "Les Crayères", Reims
Germany Brenner's Park, Baden-Baden; Vier Jahreszeiten, Hamburg
Hungary Gellért, Budapest
Italy Cipriani, Venice; Gritti, Venice; Residenza, Rome
Norway Continental, Oslo
Switzerland Drei Könige am Rhein, Basle; Château Gütsch, Lucerne; Trois Couronnes, Vevey

Town hotels of character and/or value

England Angel, Bury St Edmunds; Ebury Court, London; Kings Arms, Chipping Campden; Knightsbridge Green, London; Mount Royale, York; Portobello, London; Topps, Brighton
Scotland White House, Glasgow
Austria Amadeus, Vienna
Belgium Duc de Bourgogne, Bruges
France L'Abbaye St-Germain, Paris; Arlatan, Arles; Colombe, St-Paul-de-Vence; Diderot, Chinon; Scandinavia, Paris; Vieux Puits, Pont-Audemer
Germany Hanseatic, Hamburg; Mönchs Posthotel, Bad Herrenalb; Wehrle, Triberg; Posthotel Partenkirchen, Garmisch-Partenkirchen; Sankt Nepomuk, Bamberg; Westend, Frankfurt
Holland Ambassade, Amsterdam

Italy Umbra, Assisi
Spain Murillo, Seville; Suecia, Madrid

Rural charm in the luxury class

England Ettington Park, Alderminster; Hunstrete House, Hunstrete; Lainston House, Sparsholt; Sharrow Bay, Ullswater; Ston Easton Park, Ston Easton
Wales Bodysgallen, Llandudno; Palé Hall, Llandderfel
Scotland Inverlochy Castle, Fort William
Austria Schloss Dürnstein, Dürnstein
Belgium Scholteshof, Hasselt; Moulin Hideux, Noirefontaine
Denmark Falsled Kro, Falsled
France Baumanière, Les Baux; Croix Blanche, Chaumont; Mas de Chastelas, St-Tropez; Moulin du Roc, Champagnac-de-Belair; Père Bise, Talloires
Holland Kasteel Wittem, Wittem
Italy Certosa di Maggiano, Siena
Portugal Palace, Buçaco; Palácio dos Seteais, Sintra; Quinta dos Lobos, Sintra; Villa Hostilina, Lamego

Rural charm at medium price

England Downrew House, Barnstaple; Farlam Hall, Brampton; Hope End, Ledbury; Lastingham Grange, Lastingham; Manor Farm, Taynton; Old Vicarage, Witherslack; Plumber Manor, Sturminster Newton; Riber Hall, Matlock; Summer

Lodge, Evershot; Temple Sowerby
House, Temple Sowerby
Scotland Ardsheal, Kentallen
Ireland Ballymaloe, Shanagarry;
Currarevagh, Oughterard;
Marlfield House, Gorey
Denmark Steengaard Herregårds-
pension, Millinge
France Benvengudo, Les Baux;
Relais de la Magdeleine,
Gémenos; Mas Candille, Mougins;
Moulin, Flagy; Moulin de la
Gorce, La Roche-l'Abeille;
Pescalerie, Cabrerets; Trois Roses,
La Petite Pierre
Germany Adler, Gutach;
Erbguth's Landhaus, Hagnau;
Töpferhaus, Alt-Duvenstedt
Norway Utne, Utne
Portugal Casa dos Arcos, Vila
Viçosa; Quinta das Torres, Azeitão
Sweden Åkerblads, Tällberg;
Grythyttans, Grythyttan;
Rusthållargården , Arild

Rural charm,
simple style

England Hurstone, Wiveliscombe;
Langley, Wiveliscombe
Scotland Riverside, Canonbie
Belgium 't Convent, Lo
France Sans Frontières, Dégagnac;
A Pastorella, Monticello; Clos
Normand, Martin-Église;
Horizon, Cabris; Pelissaria, St-
Cirq-Lapopie; Rustica, Pons

Seaside hotels,
luxury style

England Bailiffscourt, Climping
Scotland Knockinaam Lodge,
Portpatrick
France Caribou, Porticciolo;
Maquis, Porticcio; Métropole,
Beaulieu; Voile d'Or, St-Jean-Cap-
Ferrat
Greece Akti Myrina, Lemnos
Italy Pellicano, Porto Ercole;
Pitrizza, Arzachena; Villa Balbi,
Sestri Levante; Villa Politi,
Syracuse
Malta Ta'Cenc, Sannat
Yugoslavia Sveti Stefan

Seaside hotels, medium
priced or simple

England Langleigh, Ilfracombe
Wales Porth Tocyn, Abersoch
Scotland Clifton, Nairn; Isle of
Colonsay, Colonsay
Channel Islands Island, Tresco;
White House, Herm
Belgium Fox, De Panne
France Ty-Pont, St-Jean-du-Doigt
Greece Vourlis, Hermoupolis
Italy Del Golfo, Proccio; Moderno,
Erice; Casa Albertina, Positano; La
Tonnarella, Sorrento; Villa
Athena, Agrigento
Spain Mar I Vent, Bañalbufar

Skiing or mountain
hotels

England Howtown, Ullswater;
Seatoller, Borrowdale
Wales Minffordd, Talyllyn
Austria Salome, Lech
France Roches Fleuries, Cordon;
Vieille Ferme, Serre-Chevalier
Italy Lo Bouton d'Or,
Courmayeur
Switzerland Blümlisalp,
Kandersteg; Christiania, Gstaad;
Ermitage et Golf, Schönried-
Gstaad; Flüela, Davos-Dorf

Small hotels with
outstanding cuisine

England Black Boys, Thornage;
Gidleigh Park, Chagford;
Hintlesham Hall, Hintlesham;
Hole in the Wall, Bath; Mallory
Court, Bishops Tachbrook; Manoir
aux Quat' Saisons, Great Milton;
Peacock Vane, Bonchurch; Pool
Court, Pool-in-Wharfedale;
Riverside, Helford; Rookery Hall,
Worleston
Scotland Scarista House, Scarista
France Georges Blanc, Vonnas;
Lameloise, Chagny; Pic, Valence;
Prés d'Eugénie, Eugénie-les-
Bains; Pyrénées, St-Jean-Pied-de-
Port

Friendly informality/ hotel run like a private house

England Little Hemingfold, Battle; Little Hodgeham, Bethersden; Old Millfloor, Trebarwith Strand; Stone Green, Mersham; Tregoose Old Mill
Wales Rhyd-Garn-Wen, Cardigan
Scotland Altnaharrie, Ullapool; Tiroran House, Tiroran
Belgium Groenighe, Bruges
France Arcades, Biot; Château de Roussan, St-Rémy; Prouillacs, St-Amand-de-Vergt
Holland Hoofdige Boer, Almen
Portugal Quinta da Penha de França, Funchal
Switzerland Résidence, St-Niklausen

Hotels with good amenities for children

England Crantock Bay, Crantock; Gara Rock, East Portlemouth; Knoll House, Studland; Tides Reach, Salcombe
Channel Islands La Collinette, St Peter Port, Guernsey
Austria Madrisa, Gargellan
France Étrier Camarguais, Les-Saintes-Maries-de-la-Mer

How to read the entries

As in previous editions, entries are in two parts – a citation, usually endorsed by one or several names, followed by relevant information about accommodation, amenities, location and tariffs.

We must emphasise once again that the length or brevity of an entry is not a reflection of the quality of a hotel. The size of an entry is determined in part by what we feel needs to be said to convey a hotel's special flavour and in part by the character and interest of the commendation. In general, country hotels get more space than city hotels because the atmosphere of the hotel matters more with the former and also because it is often helpful, when a hotel is in a relatively remote or little-known area, for the entry to say something about the location.

The names at the end of the citation are of those who have nominated that hotel or endorsed the entry that appeared in a previous edition. Some entries are entirely or largely quoted from one report; if several names follow such an entry, we have distinguished writers of quoted material by putting their names first. We do not give the names of those who have sent us adverse reports – though their contributions are every bit as important as the laudatory ones.

The factual material also varies in length. Some hotels provide a wide variety of facilities, others very little. But the paucity of information provided in some cases may derive from the fact that the hotel has failed to return our detailed questionnaire or send us a brochure. All hotels in the British Isles have completed our form, but the same is not true for continental hotels, even though we send out our questionnaire in five languages, and repeat the operation for the recalcitrant a month later. Around a quarter of the hotels in the second half of the book ignore our form or return it months later when the Guide has gone to press. In these instances, we have to rely on the information available from national tourist offices. The fact that no lounge or bar is mentioned in an entry is not evidence that a hotel lacks public rooms – only that we can't be sure. The same applies to availability of parking, which we aim to mention in the case of town and city hotels. As to tariffs, in those cases where we have had no communication with a hotel, or where it was unable to give next year's rates, we print the 1985 tariffs, making it clear that these are last year's terms.

Italicised entries indicate hotels on which we are particularly keen to garner reports. These hotels may be making their first appearance in the Guide (though first-timers do not appear in italics if we are confident that they make the grade); there may have been a change of ownership or management in the previous year; the character of a hotel may have changed with an extension of accommodation; we may have had ambivalent reports; or we may simply lack adequate feedback to give the hotel full backing. A hotel whose entry appears in italics need not be thought of as a half-good establishment, only one about which we are eager to have more opinions.

There is a limit to the amount of "nuts and bolts" that can be given in any guide book, and we are against providing, as some other guide books do, a lot of potted information in complicated hard-to-decipher hieroglyphic form. [GFG] after the hotel's name indicates that the hotel has an entry in the 1986 edition of our sibling publication, *The Good Food Guide*. Days and months are abbreviated, but virtually the only other shorthand we use is "B&B" for bed and breakfast and "alc" for à la carte; the "full alc" price is the hotel's estimate per person for a three-course meal and a half-bottle of modest wine, including service and taxes. The ᕃ symbol for the disabled is used in cases where we have been told enough by the hotel to be sure that it is suitable; when we know for certain that a hotel is not suitable we say so; but in all cases you should check.

There is one crucial point that must be emphasised with regard to the tariffs: their relative unreliability. We ask hotels when they complete our questionnaire in the early summer of one year to make an informed guess at their tariffs the following year. There are many reasons why this is a difficult exercise. Please don't rely on the figures printed. *You should always check at the time of booking and not blame the hotel or the Guide if the prices are wrong.*

Terms are difficult enough to cope with at the best of times. A few hotels have a standard rate for all rooms regardless of season and length of stay, but most operate a highly complicated system which varies from low season to high (and some have a medium-high season as well), according to length of stay, whether there is a bathroom *en suite* and, in the case of most British hotels, whether a room is in single or double occupancy. And on top of all that, most British hotels offer breaks of one kind or another, but rarely of the same kind. When we can, we give a room rate rather than a rate per person and hope thereby to give a reliable idea of what people, especially those travelling on their own, can expect to pay. When figures are given without mention of single or double rooms they indicate the range of tariffs per person. Lowest rates are what you pay for the simplest room, or out of season, or both; highest rates are for the "best" rooms – and in high season if the hotel has one. Meal prices are per person. In all cases we have to rely on information given by hoteliers filling in our questionnaire a considerable time before we go to press – or in the case of some foreign hotels which fail to return the questionnaire, on information gleaned from guide books and tourist offices. So we beg you to check the tariff with the hotel when you book, more especially in the case of hotels on the Continent. If you are going for two days or more to a hotel in the British Isles, it will pay you to find out the exact terms of any special offers available. Sometimes these bargain terms are amazing value, and can apply throughout the year, not just in the winter, but they may call for some adjustment in your holiday plans in order to qualify. We also strongly advise you to check whether a hotel is open before making a long detour. We try in all cases to give accurate information, but hotels, particularly small ones, do sometimes close at times when they have told us they expect to be open. And hotels on the Continent often have a weekly closing date, but fail to make this clear when returning our questionnaire. Finally, they do not always give reliable information about whether or not they take credit cards. If it is vital to you, please check.

We end with our customary exhortation: we implore readers to tell us of any errors of omission or commission in both the descriptive and the informative parts of the entries. We make constant efforts to improve our information under "Location", especially with the more out-of-the-way places, but would be very grateful if readers would let us know of any cases where they have found our directions inadequate. We recognise what an imposition it is to be asking readers to write us letters or fill in report forms, but it is essential that people do let us know their views if the Guide is to meet consumer needs as well as it can.

Part one

England
Wales
Scotland
Channel Islands
Republic of Ireland

England

THE OLD VICARAGE GUEST HOUSE RYE.

ABBERLEY Hereford and Worcester   Map 2

The Elms Hotel   *Tel* Great Witley (029 921) 666
Abberley   *Telex* 337105
Nr Worcester WR6 6AT

As *The Elms* at Abberley is invariably the first entry in any British hotel
guide that includes it – no one having yet started a hotel at Abbas Combe
in Somerset – one is glad that it should be such a worthy opener. This
exceptionally beautiful and grand Queen Anne house (though with two
well-grafted modern wings) has been a fine example of the English
country house hotel for more than a quarter of a century. It is set in 13
acres of parkland with formal gardens, croquet and putting lawns,
tennis courts, not to mention an exceptional herb garden. The
splendidly proportioned ground-floor rooms have been left exactly as
they were, and the furniture is in style. Upstairs, the bedrooms have
been kitted out with a fine array of extras. Rooms on the top floor –
presumably once the servants' quarters – tend to be on the small side;
back rooms are to be preferred, partly because the view is better and

partly as front rooms are liable to disturbance from the car park. As reported last year, Murdo MacSween has taken his *toque* off to *Oakley Court*, Windsor (q.v.), and Nigel James Lambert is now in charge of the kitchens. Reports vary on the new régime. Some have complained of small helpings, over-elaborate dishes and a major disappointment with a vegetarian meal ordered the day before. Others find the Lambert style more to their liking. There have been other staff changes, but happily Rita Mooney, the admirable manageress for many years past, is still at the helm. (*Mrs C Smith, Elaine Cole-Shear, Diana Davies, AL Gordon, Mrs M Bennett*)

Open All year.
Rooms 2 suites, 21 double, 4 single – 25 with bath, 2 with shower, all with telephone, radio, TV; some ground-floor rooms; 9 rooms in annexe.
Facilities 3 lounges opening on to garden patio; library bar, Regency dining room. Facilities for functions and conferences. 13-acre grounds with terraced gardens, large herb garden; croquet, putting and tennis court. Parking, garages.
Location On A443, 12m NW of Worcester. (Exit 5 at Droitwich off M5.)
Restriction No dogs.
Credit cards All major cards accepted.
Terms B&B: single £41, double £62; dinner B&B: single £57.50, double £95. Set lunch £11, dinner £16.50; full alc £18.50. Special breaks; Christmas programme; New Year's Eve dinner dance. Reduced rates for children sharing parents' room; special meals.

ALDERMINSTER Warwickshire   Map 2

Ettington Park Hotel [GFG]   *Tel* Stratford-upon-Avon
Alderminster   (0789) 740740
Nr Stratford-upon-Avon CV37 8BS   *Telex* 311825 ETPARK G

The latest super-star in the firmament of luxury hotels, a spectacular example of high Victorian Gothic in 40 acres of parkland, five miles south-east of Stratford-upon-Avon. It was opened in May 1985 and inspected a few weeks later by the editor of *The Good Food Guide* who sent us this elated report:

"This has to be a candidate for the hotel of the year. It is not finished yet – the trees along the drive have not all been planted, the tennis court is not yet operational, the service is rather English – not a compliment. But it promises to be one of the great hotels in creation. It is easy to see now why *maître chef* Michael Quinn left the *Ritz*. This is on the scale of *Boyer* at Rheims. It deserves a book to describe it. It is a Grade I listed building, set half a mile back from the Oxford/Stratford road, a Transylvanian-style building visible through the trees of the long gravel drive. I am still not sure which was the front door – the one at the front between abbey-style arches, through a tiled conservatory into the main lounge or the one at the side that leads into the courtyard surrounded by swimming pool, billiard room, kitchen and the reception desk. Through-out the building are patterned carpets with the finest pile and the walls are newly flock-papered to give a Gucci effect. Even the lift is carpeted.

"The swimming pool is covered by glass and looks out at one end on the garden and at the other into the soft yellow stone of another part of the house. It has a jacuzzi and a fountain. The lounge is a monster room that dwarfs a piano with light and space, connected to a long bar room with leather chairs and old books, that also populate every room. The other way and you are in a small conceit of a drawing room with another piano. My bedroom was short on fussy little trimmings – no fruit or sherry – but there was a hair dryer and a phone in the bathroom. The bed felt like a bed should – big, wide, bouncy and comfortable. Tasteful and not prissy as, say, the *Manoir aux Quat' Saisons* is.

"As to the food: Quinn is honoured in the birthday list. The menu is very sensibly short and not over-reaching – a set meal plus some carte dishes like crab-filled smoked salmon in yoghurt and chive sauce or lobster beurre blanc. Other dishes are much plainer. The strength of Quinn's cooking is that he isn't always trying to prove something with a sauce. He lets the ingredients speak for themselves, sometimes in the simplest possible way. The wine list is what you would expect – expensive and erratic in its mark-up. Commendably there is house white and claret at £6.50, though neither any great shakes. Breakfast was slow and revealed a few less good traits – pots of commercial jam, reheated croissants. My plate was blisteringly hot and had dried out the bacon and eggs. Never mind.

"Overall: A fortune has and is going to be spent. It has only been open for six weeks. All the staff are helpful, though they lose the porter from time to time. Standard rooms at £85 for two are frankly money well spent if only to stay among such history. The food is...well, Quinn once really said that he was going to be the greatest English chef ever. Of course one can't judge from one meal only, but still... An element of caution should be considered. It is early days, but I do not know of a comparable venture." *(Drew Smith)*

Open All year.
Rooms 7 suites, 42 double (also available as single) – all with bath, radio, colour TV and baby-listening.
Facilities Lift. Library bar, great drawing room/lounge, little drawing room (both with TV), dining room, indoor heated swimming pool, spa bath, sauna, billiards room; conference facilities. 40-acre grounds with tennis courts, croquet lawn, riding stables, river.
Location On A43 Oxford/Stratford road, 5 m S of Stratford.
Restrictions Not suitable for children under 7. No dogs.
Credit cards All major cards accepted.
Terms [1985 rates] B&B: single occupancy from £55, double from £85, suites from £100. Set lunch £12.50, dinner £21.50; full alc £25. Christmas programme; weekend breaks; special-event weekend breaks.

ALSTON Cumbria   **Map 4**

High Fell [GFG]   *Tel* Alston (0498) 81597
Alston CA9 3BP

Formerly a hill farm built in 1623, *High Fell* has been a remarkably civilised small hotel since it was acquired eight years ago by John and Patricia Chipman. It lies two miles south of Alston, the highest market town in England, not far from Garrigill and the slopes of Cross Fell, the highest point of the Pennines. Our latest report confirms previous good opinions: "In a lonely and remote position on wild and desolate moorland. It could be Wuthering Heights, but *High Fell* has warmth and cosiness enough to exorcise any Heathcliff. Menu most comprehensive and Mrs Chipman will vary it even more on request. Cooking is imaginative and produce markedly fresh. Bedrooms are pretty as well as warm and comfortable. A very good place to break a long north/south journey." *(Marcia Suddards; also Mrs P V A Holland, Herrick Bunney, Susan Aglionby)*

Open All year.
Rooms 5 double, 2 single – 2 with bath, 1 with shower.
Facilities Lounge, TV/games room, bar, dining room. 3½-acre grounds overlooking South Tyne Valley; river trout fishing 1m; golf, tennis, riding, bowls; walking nearby.
Location On A686, 2 m S of Alston
Restriction Not suitable for &.
Credit cards None accepted.
Terms B&B £15.50. Full alc £18.

Lovelady Shield   *Tel* Alston (0498) 81203
   Country House Hotel
Alston CA9 3LF

Two and a half miles east of Alston, in a remote and beautiful area of the High Pennines. The house itself is *c.*1830 in two and a half acres of gardens bordering the River Nent, with a hard tennis court and croquet lawn. Since last year, all bedrooms have been kitted out with colour TV. The resident owners are Barry and Annie Rosier. Mrs Rosier is French; the restaurant serves English as well as French dishes, but the French ones, we are assured, are "genuine" French. There is a long and interesting wine list, reasonably priced. "One of the best country house hotels I have visited", writes a recent visitor, endorsing last year's nomination: "A truly superb setting – an oasis of peace and quiet in beautiful countryside. The rooms are delightful – very well appointed and decorated. The cooking is excellent. The service is friendly and charming. Oh yes, and real log fires, too." *(L H Smith, J G Westmoreland)*

Open Mid-Mar–end Oct. It is necessary to book for restaurant in early season.
Rooms 10 double, 2 single – 8 with bath, 2 with shower, all with TV.
Facilities Reception/library, cocktail lounge, drawing room, dining room. 2½-acre gardens on river bank with tennis and croquet. Golf, shooting, fishing and walking nearby.
Location From Alston take road for Stanhope; after 2½ m hotel signs appear on left; hotel is down long drive.
Restrictions Not suitable for &. Very young children not allowed in dining room during dinner. Dogs by prior arrangement only; not in public rooms.
Credit cards Amex, Diners.
Terms (No service charge) B&B £20–£22; dinner, B&B £28–£31; full board £189. Set lunch (Sun only) £8.50, dinner £11.50. Reduced rates in early season (except Easter) for stays of 2 or more nights; weekly rates. Reduced rates for children sharing parents' room; special meals.

AMBLESIDE Cumbria   **Map 4**

Rothay Manor Hotel [GFG]   *Tel* Ambleside (0966) 33605
Rothay Bridge
Ambleside LA22OEH

"There are hotels which offer a particularly friendly ambience, others which are in an exhilarating location, and others again which concentrate on *haute cuisine*. Hotels which combine all three virtues are comparatively rare, but the *Rothay Manor* belongs to this class. The Nixons, who run this handsome Georgian house close to the head of Lake Windermere and within a few minutes' walk of Ambleside, have managed to preserve the atmosphere of a private house. The cooking is imaginative (though a bit on the rich side if you are staying a long time) and the service excellent. Naturally it makes a good centre for exploring the Lake District; but because of the friendly relaxed atmosphere, it is also a good place for just doing nothing.'" *(Dr P F Glenny)*

The above paragraph appeared in the first edition of the Guide in 1978. Happily, standards have not changed in the intervening years, and guests in 1985 continue to praise "the delightful service", "the delicious food" and the small attention to details, like having "proper tea brought to one in bed at the time one requests". There has been some minor nit-picking: one guest felt the dining room would be improved by the removal of the central lighting; another minded the notice at reception saying the management would prefer payment by cheque to a credit card – "one tended to feel a heel if one chose the latter"; a croissant at breakfast was "a complete disaster"; there was poor wine service on one night. How fortunate for the hotel – and its customers – when the nits are of this micro-variety.

Open 14 Feb–6 Jan.
Rooms Honeymoon suite, family suite (in annexe), 12 double, 2 single–all with bath, telephone, radio and colour TV; baby-listening in family suite, which is also suitable for &; 1 ground-floor room.
Facilities 3 lounges, 1 with bar, 2 dining rooms. 1½-acre garden with croquet. Near river Rothay and Lake Windermere (¼ m). Steamer service, sailing and water skiing nearby; also river and lake fishing, riding and golf.
Location From centre of Ambleside or Waterhead, follow signs for Coniston on A593. Hotel is on Langdale outskirts of Ambleside.
Restriction No dogs.
Credit cards All major cards accepted.
Terms (Service at guests' discretion) B&B: single £44–£46, double £63–£70; dinner, B&B: single £49–£61, double £77–101. Set buffet lunch Mon–Sat £5.50, Sun lunch £8.50, dinner £16. Winter events such as wine-tastings. Victorian Christmas dinner and party. Reduced rates Nov–Mar especially mid-week. Reduced rates for children sharing parents' room; special meals.

Wateredge Hotel [GFG]   *Tel* Ambleside (0966) 32332
Borrans Road
Ambleside LA22 OEP

Two adjoining 17th-century pebbledash fishermen's cottages with modern extensions, at the head of Windermere with views over gardens down the length of the lake – a privileged position even if lakeside traffic, heavy at weekends, passes close by. Only two rooms are on the roadside, however. The new regime of Mr and Mrs Cowap continues to please. One report mentioned an awkwardly small room, and another spoke of one of the roadside rooms where from 6 am it was "as if you were in bed on a traffic island". But these apart, all the *Wateredge* guests were unstinted in their appreciation, viz.: "The hotel's handout says: 'A relaxed homely and comfortable hotel with good food and a warm and friendly welcome.' This description was entirely borne out by our actual experience. My wife and I kept saying to each other that if we were running a hotel this is exactly how we would want it to be. It has a country house type of atmosphere, with liberal supplies of antique furniture, garden chairs and good quality magazines, tea on the lawn from really nice china and sparkling cutlery. But it is far from stuffy. There are three cheerful girls who run the reception and serve dinner with humorous aplomb. The food was simply excellent. We thought the limited choice was no drawback. Limitless good coffee available, with petits fours, in the lounge afterwards. Breakfast was no disappointment. Our room was bright and clean. The *en suite* bathroom was a good size. Top of my pops for nice touches was the soap from Woods of Windsor: a proper chunk for the bath, together with hand-washing size bars for both madame and monsieur. To sum up: we were delighted to have been directed to this hotel. We think the proprietors (who were surprisingly inconspicuous) deserve every possible encouragement to keep up the standard. With hindsight, we are amazed that we were able to book at a month's notice – this hotel deserves a waiting list!" *(Michael W Jarvis; also Ruth P Goodwin, J P Berryman, Mrs L M Sanderson, and others)*

Open 1 Feb–3 Dec.
Rooms 17 double, 3 single – 10 with bath, 2 with shower, all with tea-making facilities; 1 ground-floor room.
Facilities 3 lounges, TV room, bar, dining room. 1-acre grounds with 200-ft lake frontage, private jetty, rowing boats and sailing boat available to guests free of charge; fishing and safe bathing. Good centre for walkers and climbers.
Location ½ m of S town; just off A591 at Waterhead on Kendal/Keswick road. (Front rooms can be noisy.)
Restrictions Not ideal for &. No children under 7. No dogs in public rooms.
Credit cards Access, Visa.
Terms (No service charge) B&B £17–£30; dinner, B&B £27–£41. Set dinner £12.90. Breaks Feb–mid-May and Nov to early Dec. Half rates for children sharing parents' room; high teas.
Service/tipping: "No service charge. Any gratuities offered will be distributed equally to staff."

ASTON CLINTON Buckinghamshire   Map 2

The Bell Inn [GFG]   *Tel* Aylesbury (0296) 630252
Aston Clinton HP22 5HP   *Telex* 83252 BELINN

The Bell, at the foot of the Chilterns, has been an inn since 1650, and was once a staging post for the Duke of Buckingham between his seat at Stowe and his palace on the Mall. But the term "inn" is quite inappropriate to today's sophisticated establishment. It has been owned and run by the Harris family since 1939. Michael Harris maintains the gastronomic and oenophilic traditions of his father, Gerard. Today, it is considerably better known as a restaurant (it seats 140) than as a hotel, and the dining room, with its leather chairs, well-spaced-out mahogany tables, glass, silver and log fires, is an exceptionally lovely room in which to eat good food. We hear less about the hotel side of things – 21 rooms and suites in what were once the stables and malthouses of an old brewery just across the road from the main building. There is also a wine business, Gerard Harris Ltd – very pricey according to one consumer's report – and a conference and banqueting complex called The Pavilion which can cater for up to 250 people, including all the electronics required for simultaneous translation.

Prices are what you would expect from a luxury establishment, and perhaps because the tariff is high, flaws in the service and restaurant elicit more comment than they would elsewhere. Nevertheless, there have been more complaints than usual this year: inattentiveness by waiters, morning coffee and papers turning up half an hour later than ordered, disappointment with the standard of the full English breakfast, ditto with certain dishes in the restaurant. But for some *The Bell* continues to provide a peak experience: "Near excellence. We felt welcome as soon as we entered and upon arrival in our rooms found the owners had thought of almost everything. A bed large enough to get lost in which was super for a long person like me. Plenty of towels in the bathroom. Bathrobes in the wardrobe. Fragrant soap, bath gel and bath salts. The room was long, beautifully furnished with comfortable armchairs around the TV and near (within arm's reach) of the mini-bar. At 6 pm the telephone rang and we were asked if we had shoes for cleaning or clothes for pressing. Room service was quick and pleasant as was service in the bar and restaurant. It was so good at *The Bell* it became a challenge to fault it! Did we find any? Well, I do not like plastic toothpicks, there was no shampoo in the bathroom – oh yes! – steak at dinner was a little tough. I was so upset by these failings, I and the remainder of my family, my brothers and their families have booked for next Christmas. There was one other fault, which I suppose will occur again at Christmas. I have trouble persuading my wife to leave." *(A J Dyer)*

Open All year. Restaurant closed Sun evening and Mon (simple grill available to residents).
Rooms 6 suites, 15 double (all available as single) – all with bath, telephone, radio and colour TV; 16 in annexe around courtyard; 7 ground-floor rooms.
Facilities Drawing room, bar, smoking room, restaurant, conference/banquet facilities. 3-acre grounds at the foot of the Chilterns. Wine shop.
Location On A41, 4 m SE of Aylesbury (exit 8 off M1 for A41, or exit 11 for B489). Light sleepers should specifically request quiet rooms.
Restriction No dogs in dining room.
Credit cards Access, Visa.
Terms (Excluding VAT) B&B (continental): single occupancy from £47, double from £59. Full alc £33. Reduced rates for children sharing parents' room.

BAGSHOT Surrey   Map 2

Pennyhill Park Hotel   *Tel* (0276) 71774
College Ride, Bagshot GU19 5ET   *Telex* 858841-PHPARKG

As our map for Southern England makes only too clear, we lamentably lack recommendable hotels within a 50-mile radius of London. *Pennyhill Park* is a substantial Elizabethan-style mansion, three miles to the south-west of Bagshot. Here is the opening paragraph of our inspector's report: "*Pennyhill Park* was built in 1849, and was used as a private house until 12 years ago; it has been lavishly refurbished and converted into a truly beautiful hotel and country club. The house stands in 112 acres of glorious parkland, with immaculate gardens and terraces, a nine-hole golf course, tennis courts, stables with six horses that can be hired by guests, fishing in an enormous private lake, and there are facilities for clay pigeon shooting. If one were touring England, Windsor is only eight miles away, and places like Epsom and Guildford within easy driving distance. The hotel is used frequently for conferences, and when we visited *Pennyhill*, a group of Swedish and Norwegian bankers were staying there." The last sentence above underlines a central feature of *Pennyhill*: that it depends heavily on business and conference trade. The hotel is comfortable and well serviced by a large staff. The cooking, our inspector felt, was good though not stunning. The menu is ambitious, with flambé dishes evidently popular. Prices, both of the rooms and in the restaurant, are high in comparison with country house hotels elsewhere – but there is not much competition in this part of the Home Counties. A good hotel of its kind? Certainly. Our kind? Well . . .

Open All year.
Rooms 5 suites, 32 double, 12 single – all with bath, telephone, radio, colour TV and baby-listening. Some ground-floor rooms with wide double doors. 29 rooms in annexe.
Facilities Lounge, cocktail bar, country club bar/lounge with TV, library, dining room. 112-acre grounds with outdoor heated swimming pool, tennis, golf, trout lake with fishing, shooting, riding. &.
Location 3 m SW of Bagshot village; take exit 3 off M3.
Restriction Dogs by arrangement only.
Credit cards All major cards accepted.
Terms (No service charge) rooms: single £50, double £65. Breakfast: continental £3.60, English £4.50; full alc £20–£25. Reduced rates for children sharing parents' room; special meals on request.

BARDSEA Cumbria   Map 4

The Ship Inn   *Tel* Bardsea (022 988) 329
Bardsea
Nr Ulverston LA12 9QT

A family-run village inn, exceedingly modest in its tariff, that is recommended to Guide readers by one of our regular correspondents in the following terms: "Bardsea is a lovely village in a sublime situation, two miles from the old market town of Ulverston and with stunning views over Morecambe Bay and to sea. The Ship is very, very simple, but so out of the ordinary I thought it worth your notice. My room was spacious, a large comfy bed, excellent reading light. And a coal fire was lit in my room each night – an experience unique to me since the last war. [Editorial note: only two rooms in the inn have coal fires.] The young couple who run the place, the Cravens, are wholly delightful. I was alone. Stayed two nights. Good cooked breakfast. One supper for two – plain but good cooking. I had early tea in bed, bar drinks and a half-bottle of wine with supper – and my bill for the lot was £28." [1984] (John Hills)

Open All year.
Rooms 2 family, 4 double – all with colour TV and tea-making facilities; 2 with fireplace.
Facilities 2 lounges, one with TV, dining room. Near Morecambe Bay, 10 minutes' walk to beach, golf, and riding in village.
Location 2 m S of Ulverston, Bardsea is well signposted off the A590.
Restriction Not suitable for &.
Credit cards None accepted.
Terms B&B £8.50; dinner, B&B £12; full board £15. Set dinner £3.50; full alc £12.50. Babies free; children under 10 half-price; special meals provided.

BARNSTAPLE Devon   Map 1

Downrew House   *Tel* Barnstaple (0271) 42497
Bishops Tawton, Barnstaple EX32 0DY

"Your description in the 1983 Guide, if anything, understates the unique attraction of *Downrew House*, which we feel is the best-managed hotel we have stayed at" *(A Poliakoff)*. We were astounded to get this letter, which reached us only last year, being conscious of the fact that this vintage establishment had invariably elicited the most consistently hyperbolic entries. Here, for the record, is our 1983 entry, not significantly different from our 1981, 1982, 1984, or 1985 one:

"The aim at *Downrew*", say Desmond and Aleta Ainsworth in their mouth-watering brochure, " has always been that of perfection, whether for a family holiday in the summer months or for guests who require a quiet break out of season." When we first read those words, we thought that the Ainsworths were sticking their necks out, but now, three years on, reading our file of gratified reports, we recognise that the aim is realistic. *Downrew House* is chiefly Queen Anne (some parts older), with a lodge and a west wing. It's a few miles inland and 500 feet above Barnstaple, on the southern slopes of Codden Hill. The Ainsworths have been running the hotel for the past 18 years; they say that it is unashamedly orientated to the comfort and well-being of their adult guests, though children of seven up are welcomed and all sorts of special amenities provided for them. The nearest beaches are eight to ten miles away. Hotels that provide successfully for the welfare of children and their parents are not all that common, but *Downrew* appears to achieve this aim – as well, of course, as its target of perfection.

Open Late Mar–27 Dec. Restaurant closed to non-residents Sun and Thur evening.
Rooms 2 suites, 14 double, 8 single – all with bath, radio and colour TV; 5 rooms in West Wing, 2 in Lodge; 2 rooms on ground floor.
Facilities 2 drawing rooms, bar, dining room, billiard room, card room, games room, solarium, laundry. 15-acre grounds with golf putting course, croquet, tennis, heated outdoor pool. Free fishing within 1½ m; beaches within 8–10 m.
Location 2 m S of Barnstaple on A377, take fork just S of Bishops Tawton to Chittlehampton. Downrew is 1¼ m further on.
Restrictions Not suitable for &. No children under 7. No dogs except in Lodge.
Credit cards None accepted.
Terms (No service charge) dinner, B&B: £39.10–£41.40. Set dinner £17.25. 10% reduction for children 7–10 in own room, 35% reduction for children of any age sharing parents' room; special meal for children served at 5.30 pm July–mid-Sept.

BARWICK Somerset   Map 2

Little Barwick House [GFG]   *Tel* (0935) 23902
Yeovil BA22 9TD

Plenty of warm endorsements for Christopher and Veronica Colley's Georgian dower-house, lovingly restored and full of attractive furniture. With only three bedrooms and a restaurant seating 30, it is essentially a restaurant-with-rooms, but everything about the place – Veronica

Colley's magnificent cooking, the generous breakfasts, the sybaritic comforts of the bedrooms, not to mention the room that calls itself a lounge, but "is more like a small country house library" - is of the same high standard. "The Colleys know their stuff! Exceedingly good value for money." (*J E Genders*)

Open All year except Christmas.
Rooms 3 double – 2 with bath, 1 with shower, all with colour TV and tea-making facilities.
Facilities Lounge, cellar bar, dining room. 3½-acre garden.
Location Follow signs from Yeovil to Dorchester (A37). Turn left off A37 at the Red House pub. Hotel is ¼ m on left.
Restrictions Not suitable for &. Dogs only with advance notice and not in public rooms.
Credit cards All major cards accepted.
Terms B&B £18; dinner, B&B £31.50. Full alc £16.50. Vegetarian and special diets catered for. Winter breaks: 1 night's accommodation free in any 2 days' stay if dinner taken both nights. Reduced rates and special menus for children.

BASLOW Derbyshire   Map 2

Cavendish Hotel   *Tel* Baslow (024 688) 2311
Baslow, Bakewell DE4 1SP   *Telex* 547150 CAVTEL

Apart from one year's "sabbatical", the *Cavendish* has enjoyed an entry in the Guide from its first edition, though enjoyment has not always been the right word for some of the strictures that we have felt obliged to hand out along with compliments. A fishing inn in the 18th century, the hotel is now a thoroughly sophisticated establishment lucky to have one of the most enviable locations imaginable; although on the A619, in the centre of Baslow village, all the rooms are on the opposite side of the road overlooking Chatsworth Park – a noble vista. The bedrooms, though they vary in size, are all elegantly furnished, warm and comfortable. So are the public rooms, which have the bonus of glorious flower arrangements. ("Might not the bedrooms have some fresh flowers?" one guest queries.) The *patron* since the *Cavendish*'s translation from village pub to country house hotel has been Eric Marsh, who cares much for the reputation of the house and sets the tone for the excellent, cheerful service. Regrettably, we continue to get the odd niggle in the letter-pile: the restaurant aims high, but its performance does not always measure up to its pretensions; queries about value for money are also raised. But there is no doubt that the hotel can and often does provide its guests with the full cosseting experience hoped for in such a hotel.

Open All year.
Rooms 1 suite, 23 double – all with bath, direct-dial telephone, radio, colour TV, tea-making facilities, mini-bar, ground-floor rooms.
Facilities Lounge, bar, restaurant, private dining room for 10 people. Small grounds with golf practice (putting green and driving net); fishing in rivers Derwent and Wye.
Location On A619 in Chatsworth grounds (leave M1 at exit 29).
Restrictions Not suitable for &. No dogs.
Credit cards Amex, Diners, Visa.
Terms [1985 rates] (No service charge) single occupancy £45, double £55. Breakfast from £3; set lunch/dinner from £12. Cots/extra beds available for children; special meals by arrangement.

BASSENTHWAITE LAKE Cumbria   Map 4

The Pheasant Inn   *Tel* Bassenthwaite Lake
Bassenthwaite Lake   (059 681) 234
Cockermouth CA13 9YE

The Pheasant Inn is an old-fashioned country inn, of a kind not so easily found these days. It is 16th-century, with lots of genuine inn trimmings. The bar is thoroughly atmospheric, with oak panelling and honest pub furniture, real ale and good bar snacks, though it does have a carpet instead of spit and sawdust. It stands at the head of Bassenthwaite Lake, below Thornthwaite Forest – it does not in fact overlook the lake as there is a hill in between. Last year's entry appeared in italics: no complaints about the comfort of the rooms, but grumbles about uneven standards in the kitchen and sloppy service. Mr Barrington Wilson, who has been running the inn for many years, tells us he was aware of the problems in the service and has now appointed a new head waitress. As for the cooking, we accept that the inn is not aiming at the higher peaks of gastronomy; traditional English fare is what to expect. Our file this year has not been short of *Pheasant* lovers. One couple, who have been staying regularly twice a year for many years past, expressed their total satisfaction in negative form: "All our visits have been really happy. It is not that we are uncritical or just easily pleased, but the *Pheasant* satisfies our expectations so admirably and, in its particular charming class, it has just about got everything right. Standing as it does in comparative seclusion, backed by a pine forest and among mixed woodland, it is not a place to stay for any length of time unless you want to leave feeling completely refreshed and totally relaxed." *(LC and FE Wheeler; also Kevin Myers, K J J Bobbitt)*

Open All year except Christmas Day.
Rooms 16 double, 4 single – 12 with bath, 1 with shower, 3 rooms in bungalow on ground floor – all with ramps.
Facilities 3 lounges (2 for residents), bar, dining room; facilities for private parties and small conferences. 1½-acre grounds. Sailing, fishing, pony-trekking nearby and golf. &.
Location 6 m NW of Keswick just off A66 (on W side of Bassenthwaite Lake).
Restrictions No dogs in bedrooms. No smoking in dining room.
Credit cards None accepted.
Terms B&B: single £23, double £44; half board (min. 3 days): single £33, double £54. Weekly, dinner, B&B: single £210, double £410. Set lunch £6.40, dinner £10. Special winter rates. Reduced rates and half servings for children.

BATH Avon   Map 2

The Hole in the Wall [GFG]   *Tel* Bath (0225) 25243
16 George Street, Bath BA1 2EN

"Just as good as you say. Front bedrooms aren't noisy. Food is great. Staff very helpful. Like staying with friends in comfort and luxury." *(Alison Lurie)*

Important reminder: terms printed must be regarded as a rough guide only to the size of the bill to be expected at the end of your stay. For latest tariffs, check when booking.

The latest tribute, to add to many more this year as previously, for Sue and Tim Cumming's Georgian kitchen and coal-hole converted into a fine restaurant and reasonably elegant restaurant-with-rooms, in the centre of the city. Breakfasts are recommended as warmly as the dinners; one correspondent was excited to discover that the breakfast lady had never heard of fried bread, but you can expect most of the options of a full English breakfast. The reference to front bedrooms not being noisy refers to earlier criticism; some readers continue to report nocturnal disturbance in the front rooms, especially when a wine bar/nightclub next door spills out its midnight customers. First-timers need to be warned that rooms are up several flights of steep stairs: it's no place for the elderly or infirm. Some readers this year have reported the need for redecoration in certain rooms, including the dining room. No complaints at all about the residents' breakfast room and lounge – "delightfully proportioned rooms with a pleasant scatter of attractive magazines". *(David H Clark; also Patricia Fenn, P D Rouse, Derek Bernard, Rosemary Stewart)*

Open All year except 2 weeks Christmas/New Year. Restaurant closed on public holidays.
Rooms 8 double – all with bath, telephone, colour TV and tea-making facilities; front rooms double-glazed.
Facilities Reception, 2 lounges, 2 bars, 2 dining rooms.
Location Central. One garage – apart from that, parking could be difficult.
Restrictions Not suitable for &. No pets.
Credit cards All major cards accepted.
Terms (No service charge) B&B (continental): single occupancy from £35, double £50–£70; full board negotiable. Set dinner: 2 courses £15, 3 courses £18.50; full alc (lunch only) £21. Reduced rates for children sharing parents' room; special meals.
Service: "We do not include a service charge as all overheads are included in our price."

Paradise House Hotel
Holloway, Bath BA2 4PX

Tel Bath (0225) 317723

A civilised bed-and-breakfast establishment, seven minutes by foot from the Roman Baths, the Pump Room and the Abbey, in a quiet cul-de-sac, formerly part of the old Roman Fosse Way. The house itself is *c.*1720; it has fine views of the Georgian city, and a well-favoured three-quarter-acre garden. "Lots of Laura Ashley and Designers Guild-type wallpaper and curtains. Rooms freshly decorated. Comfortable brass bed with duvet; good chairs for watching TV. Lots of nice ornaments and mirrors. Residents' lounge with Habitat sofas and newspapers. Breakfast room has interesting wistaria wallpaper and sprigged tablecloths; excellent views of garden and Bath beyond. As a guest-house/hotel, one of the best we have stayed in. Proprietors David and Janet Cutting interested in local sights and restaurants and give good advice on things to do and see." *(Mrs K Ware; also PK Hall)*

Open Feb – Nov.
Rooms 1 for 4, 8 double, 1 single – 3 with bath, all with colour TV, tea-making facilities and baby-listening.
Facilities Sitting room, breakfast room. ¾-acre garden with patios and croquet lawn.
Location 7 minutes' walk from centre, in quiet cul-de-sac. (1) From M4 take exit 18. Take A46 to Bath. Entering city on A4 turn left at first main traffic lights onto A36, A367, Wells and Exeter ring road. At large roundabout, which is bisected by

railway viaduct, take first left (A367 Exeter road). Continue up hill, the Wellsway, about ¾ m; turn left at small shopping area near Dewhurst butcher; continue left down hill into the cul-de-sac. Hotel is 200 yds on left. (2) From city centre go S to main-line station. Follow 1-way system round to Churchill Bridge, across the Avon. Continue under the railway viaduct and round roundabout, taking A367 exit leading up the hill. Then proceed as in (1).
Restrictions Not suitable for ৬. No dogs.
Credit cards Access, Visa.
Terms B&B: single £18–£30, double £27–£40. Reduced rates for stays of 5 nights or more and for children sharing parents' room. (No restaurant; hotel can make dinner reservations in restaurants.)

The Priory Hotel [GFG]
Weston Road, Bath BA1 2XT

Tel Bath (0225) 331922
Telex 44612

The Priory has long been a favourite of discriminating hotel-users in Bath. It is not as central, nor as spectacularly sited, as the *Royal Crescent*, but some would regard its position – a mile out of the town centre – as a positive advantage; you could hardly expect to find a well-tended 2-acre garden (tea on lawn served under gigantic cedar tree) and a heated swimming pool closer in. The interior of the 1835 Gothic house also has much to recommend it: large comfortable public rooms, individually decorated bedrooms (some admittedly, on the small side), dependably courteous service and a first-rate restaurant.

The Priory has had a number of shaky years in these pages, but this year's crop of reports make more cheerful reading. Chief complaint is about the tariff – especially since prices quoted, both in the hotel and the restaurant, are, anachronistically, exclusive of VAT. "The best meal I had in England", writes a correspondent from San Francisco, but even he, paying dollars, found *The Priory* pricey.

Open All year except first 2 weeks Jan.
Rooms 18 double, 3 single – 20 with bath, 1 with shower, all with telephone, radio and colour TV; some 4-posters.
Facilities Drawing room, reception room, bar, 2 dining rooms, 2-acre grounds with croquet and swimming pool (heated May–Oct).
Location ¾ m from centre of Bath. Hotel brochure has detailed directions. Parking.
Restrictions Easy wheelchair access to public rooms, but no ground-floor bedrooms. No children under 10. No dogs.
Credit cards Access, Amex, Visa.
Terms (Excluding VAT) B&B (continental): single £40–£44, double £70–£85; dinner, B&B: single £42, double £92. Full alc £26. Weekend and mid-week breaks out of season.

The Royal Crescent Hotel
Royal Crescent, Bath BA1 2LS

Tel Bath (0225) 319090
Telex 444251

We long for the year when we can run an entry for this potentially magnificent hotel which doesn't have to be hedged round with "buts". It has, for a start, an incomparable position – at the exact centre of the famous Crescent, Bath's shining architectural glory. The decor of both the public and the private rooms by Julia Hodgess, the many splendid paintings and prints, the large and well-kept garden where afternoon tea and after-dinner drinks may be taken, the feeling of discreet luxury and comfort that emanates when you cross the door: all the ingredients are here for a winner. But for many years past The Royal Crescent *has had ambivalent entries and one year had to be missed out altogether. Last year, while printing one long sustained peal of praise from a wholly gratified guest, we also referred to complaints about the quality of cooking and the smaller rooms (over-priced and under-insulated), the quality of cooking and condescending service. In completing our questionnaire, Lord Crathorne, a director of Blakeney Hotels (which owns* The Royal Crescent *and is shortly opening* Cliveden – *see Introduction), tells us that insulation has been improved in the smaller rooms; he hopes that we have had better reports from the restaurant with the arrival of the new head chef, Michael Croft; and says that he was particularly dismayed to read of our criticism of the staff, since most visitors found them friendly and helpful. Sadly, reports continue to be mixed. One correspondent, previously an enthusiast, wrote after a return visit with a host of grievances: his room had been unacceptably small – the suitcase on the stand had to be moved for him to get into either the wardrobe or the bathroom; poor coffee and burnt toast at breakfast; two hours to serve a three-course meal, when he had particularly asked for quick service and had arrived promptly at the restaurant at its hour of opening; and other irritations besides. We are familiar with the once-something-starts-to-go-wrong-it-only-gets-worse syndrome, but his wasn't an isolated case: other readers reported a badly bungled booking, made worse by the way the complaint was dealt with, a disastrous meal, arrogance in the staff. By no means all our letters were critical, but the consensus was clear: the engine pinks. Perhaps the fact that* The Royal Crescent *is run by a London company and lacks a resident owner is responsible for these blemishes continuing to surface.*

Open All year.
Rooms 12 suites, 20 double 2 single – all with bath, telephone, radio and colour TV; 17 rooms in Pavilion annexe. Ground-floor rooms.
Facilities Lift. 2 drawing rooms, bar, dining room, restaurant, conservatory, billiards; jacuzzi, private health and beauty centre. ¼-acre garden with terrace and croquet lawn. Touring service (chauffeur available).
Location Central. Parking.
Restriction No dogs.
Credit cards All major cards accepted.
Terms B&B: single £83, double £136; dinner, B&B: single £110, double £190; full board: single £131, double £232. Full alc £34.30. Special meals for children on request.

Somerset House   *Tel* Bath (0225) 66451
35 Bathwick Hill, Bath BA2 6LD

The name on the door is the same as last year, but in fact Jane and Malcolm Seymour have moved eight houses further along Bathwick Hill, and have exchanged their three-bedroomed Georgian terraced guest-house for an altogether more imposing Regency mansion *c.*1829. They now have nine bedrooms, all with *en suite* bath or shower rooms and a 1-acre garden. In other respects, they hope that there will be no change: "Jean will still be cooking the produce from my allotment garden," writes Mr Seymour, "and the other home-made goodies which helped build up our reputation." One reader last year felt his meals had been somewhat health-foody and frugal, but others have much enjoyed "the home-made jams accompanying the home-made bread at breakfast" and their four-course dinners. *Somerset House* will still be a no-smoking establishment, but meal-times will be rather more flexible than hitherto. At the time of going to press, the new improved *Somerset House* has not yet opened its doors. We look forward to reports.

Open All year.
Rooms 8 double, 1 single – 7 with bath, 1 with shower, all with telephone and tea-making facilities.
Facilities 2 lounges, TV room, dining room. 1-acre garden with flowering trees and shrubs and 7¼-inch gauge model railway. 5 minutes from Kennet and Avon Canal – angling for temporary members at Bathampton Angling Club; canal boat trips. 15 minutes' walk from Abbey, Roman Baths, shops etc.
Location Bathwick Hill runs SE from A36 up to Claverton, University and American Museum. Car park for 12 cars.
Restrictions Not suitable for &. No children under 10. Small dogs allowed in bedrooms only. No smoking.
Credit cards Access, Visa.
Terms Dinner, B&B £25. Set lunch (Tue, Thur, and Sun only) £5.85, dinner £11. Special interest weekends: Somerset Heritage, Roman Bath, Georgian Bath, Opera etc. 4-night Christmas package. Reduced rates for children sharing parents' room; special meals. Vegetarian and simple diets catered for.

Sydney Gardens Hotel   *Tel* Bath (0225) 64818
Sydney Road, Bath BA2 6NT

Why is it that Bath can provide so many admirable hotels, guest-houses, B&Bs and the like, and other rewarding tourist cities – Oxford, Cambridge, Edinburgh, to name only three – have little or nothing to offer? Here is yet another elegant residence enjoying a fresh lease of life as a sophisticated B&B. *Sydney Gardens* is a spacious Italianate Victorian mansion, ten minutes' stroll from the city centre; you can park your car in the hotel's garden. A correspondent speaks enthusiastically about the whole set-up: the comforts of her large handsome room, its many extras, its fine view; the kindness of Mr and Mrs Smithson, her hosts; the excellence of her breakfast, with plenty of delicious coffee and hot croissants; and the delight, as a non-smoker, at finding this a non-smoking establishment. *(Gillian R Buckingham)*

Open All year except Christmas.
Rooms 6 double, 1 single – 5 with bath, all with colour TV and tea-making facilities.
Facilities Lounge, breakfast room. Spacious gardens; private gateway to park and walk along adjacent Kennet and Avon canal.
Location From M4: leave junction 18; follow A46 S to Bath; join A4 into city. Before centre, turn left at traffic lights following signs for Exeter and Wells (A36 ring road); cross Avon; gateway to *Sydney Gardens* is directly ahead. Turn right, pass Holbourne Museum on left and turn left. Hotel is 200 yards up slope on left. From South the approach road (A36) takes you past the hotel. From Bristol and West follow A367 ring road past Bathwick roundabout, turn right immediately before Holbourne Museum.
Restrictions No smoking. No dogs.
Credit cards Access, Visa.
Terms (No service charge) B&B: single £20–£22, double £35–£45.
Service/tipping: "As we run the business ourselves, we do not expect tips."

The length of an entry does not necessarily reflect the merit of a hotel. The more interesting the report or the more unusual or controversial the hotel, the longer the entry.

BATTLE East Sussex   Map 2

Little Hemingfold Farmhouse   *Tel* Battle (042 46) 2910
Telham, Battle TN33 OTT

"'Farmhouse' may suggest a much more workaday sort of place than this part 17th-century, part early Victorian house filled with books, interesting pictures and fine furniture in an exceptionally tranquil and secluded setting. The buildings – there are rooms in an old coach-house and stables as well as in the farmhouse itself, all grouped round a flowery courtyard – are reached down a fairly steep half-mile track. There are 26 acres of gardens, woods and pastures surrounding *Little Hemingfold*; ducks and moorhens breed on the two-acre lake which is used both for swimming and for fly fishing; in the fields there are cows, Jacob sheep and pigs. The grounds have direct access to the thousand acres of Battle Great Wood, with footpaths to Battle and Kent Street. The Cinque Ports and Hastings are close by. Ann Benton, the resident owner, does the cooking, grows all her own soft fruit and vegetables, including asparagus and melons, and bakes her own bread. Evening meals (four courses and a carafe of wine 'thrown in') are served communally round a large candlelit Victorian table, and guests speak warmly of her traditional English dishes. Not a hotel and rather more than a guest-house, but certainly a highly sympathetic set-up."
(Marguerite Dickinson; warmly endorsed by Elizabeth Syrett and PG Evans)

Open All year except for 2 weeks' annual holiday in Feb.
Rooms 10 double, 2 single – all doubles with bath, jack points for mobile phone, radio, colour TV, tea-making facilities and electric blankets. 6 rooms in converted coach-house and stables; 4 ground-floor rooms.
Facilities 2 lounges (1 for non-smokers), bar, TV room, dining room. 26-acre grounds with fields, woods, cows, sheep; 2-acre lake with trout fishing, swimming and dinghy; croquet and badminton.
Location 1½ m SE of Battle. From N, about 1½ m from Battle look for road sign indicating bend on left side of road. This sign is at the top of the farm lane. From S, about 1 m past Beauport park, look for sign indicating bend. Proceed round corner and the farm lane is immediately on right.
Restrictions Not suitable for &. No children under 12. Dogs in downstairs rooms only.
Credit cards None accepted.
Terms (No service charge) B&B £12–£17; dinner, B&B (including house wine) add £10. Set lunch £2.50. Spring, summer and winter rates for stays of 2, 5, or 7 nights. Christmas and New Year packages.
Service/tipping: "Any gratuity at the discretion of guests."

BEANACRE Wiltshire   Map 2

Beechfield House Hotel [GFG]   *Tel* Melksham (0225) 703700/
Beanacre, Nr Melksham SN12 7PU   706998

The area around Bath is exceptionally well provided-for with rewarding hotels. Beechfield is not as grand as some of its neighbouring rivals – *Ston Easton Park*, say, or *Homewood Park* at Hinton Charterhouse – but not as expensive either. Architecturally, the house is a gem, provided you have a taste for the ornate Victorian. And Peter Crawford-Rolt has given the same attention to the decor as he does to the preparation of his meals. An earlier visitor reported: "If *Beechfield House* had been planned for the pleasure of Guide readers it would be no surprise. It's the archetypal Guide 'find'. To begin with, it's a rarity – a Victorian house which is charming and yet has all the modern comforts. Pretty papers set off the most elegant Victoriana, from brass bedsteads to wine glasses, and there seems to be an extended family of pretty girls who tend and serve."

Beechfield has been missing from these pages for the past two years, but we are glad to welcome it back, with such warm compliments from recent guests as, "The food was exceptional, even when compared with meals we had at *Hole in the Wall, The Priory* and *Hunstrete House* (all q.v.) We forgot it was a hotel... It was like staying at our best friend's country retreat." Or, "It approaches everything with the utmost style and standard...After *Gidleigh Park* (q.v.) I think it is the nicest hotel I have stayed at in Britain." *(L Kasprowicz, Raymond Goldsmith; also A J M Frank, Dorothy and Bob Cabianca)*

Open All year except New Year.
Rooms 16 double – all with bath, telephone, radio, colour TV, baby-listening; 8 rooms in annexe, 2 on ground floor.
Facilities Residents lounge, bar, 2 dining rooms. 8-acre grounds with outdoor heated swimming pool, tennis and croquet. Coarse fishing on river Avon 300 yds away.
Location On the A530 Melksham/Chippenham road, 2 m N of Melksham. (Leave M4 at junction 17.)
Restriction No dogs.
Credit cards All major credit cards accepted.
Terms B&B: single £45–£60, double £55–£85. Set lunch £9.50; full alc £21.
Christmas programme. Winter breaks. Special meals for children.

BEERCROCOMBE Somerset   Map 2

Frog Street Farm   *Tel* Hatch Beauchamp
Beercrocombe, Taunton TA3 6AF   (0823) 480430

No hotel or inn, but a 15th-century farmhouse/guest-house of consider-able charm on a 130-acre working farm, at the end of a no-through road in a deeply rural part of Somerset, equidistant (about 21 miles) from the north and south coasts . "In the wilds of Somerset, not easy to find, but once you get there, it has a lot to offer – not least most peaceful surroundings: trees and fields on one side, lovely orchard the other; there is also a working farm with stables, a good garden with an outdoor heated pool. The house is lovely and the atmosphere as genuine as one could wish to find, with the friendliest and most generous hostess providing delicious English home cooking in ample quantities, especial-ly a marvellous traditional English breakfast in the morning, all for £16 per person [1985]. This included in our case a vast room with equally large bathroom, all adding to this feeling of lavish generosity. When full, the house can accommodate ten guests; when we were there, six others sat round a long table in the dining room and we had a round table to ourselves. There was a friendly spirit; the place is unlicensed but we were offered wine from our neighbours' table. In the lounge there is a cheerful Swedish log-burning stove. There are two young daughters who help with waiting at table and other chores. It is an ideal family place." *(ULP; warmly endorsed by Robert Ingram and family)*

Thus ran our first entry for *Frog Street* last year. A recent visitor writes: "The moment I telephoned Mrs Cole, I could tell from her friendly voice that we had made the right decision. The farm lives up to your entry, more so if that is possible." *(Paul Waring)*

Open Apr–Oct.
Rooms 1 suite, 3 double, 2 single – 1 with bath, all with tea-making facilities and baby-listening.
Facilities Lounge, TV room, dining room. Secluded garden with heated swimming pool. On 130-acre working farm; trout stream running through meadows.
Location 7 m from Taunton: take exit 25 from M5, then A358 to Ilminster; follow signs to Beercrocombe.
Restrictions Not suitable for &. No dogs.
Credit cards None accepted.
Terms B&B £10. Set dinner £6. ⅓ off for children under 11; special meals. (Unlicensed – bring your own wine.)
Service/tipping: "I don't have any problems with tipping as this is a home rather than a hotel. My visitors love the fact that there are no extras: they come as friends as much as visitors."

BETHERSDEN Kent   Map 2

Little Hodgeham   *Tel* High Halden (023 385) 323
Bull Lane, Bethersden TN26 3HE

An enchanting 500-year-old half-timbered cottage in the heart of the Kentish Weald – described by one visitor as a superior version of Snow White and the Seven Dwarfs' dwelling – has become, in the ministering hands of Erica Wallace, a distinctive sort of house-party guest-house. There are only three double bedrooms, each with its own character, one with a four-poster; the drawing room is in keeping with the house – log fire, ingle-nook fireplace, original exposed beams, and suchlike; the furnishings throughout show great flair; flowers abound. Outside, there is a beautifully kept half-acre garden with a small pool (swimsuits available if you come without). Meals are taken communally, with a set menu.

So ran our opening paragraph in a long and enthusiastic entry for *Little Hodgeham* in last year's Guide. The entry went on to quote from an inspector's report, extolling "the enchanting setting, the delightful house, the flair and panache of the vivacious hostess, the exceptional value for money of the tariff". However, we owe Erica Wallace an apology because the extract from our inspector's report also referred to her penchant for the tin opener, and may have misled readers into thinking the owner a Smash or tinned-peas addict. Not at all. Ms Wallace does use tins for things like smoked oysters, and she imports tinned passion fruit at vast expense direct from her native Australia because she prefers the taste to the cold-store "fresh" ones available in Britain. Little Hodgeham-ites have been swift to come to her defence, viz.: "The only tinned produce we ate was of the luxury variety – which we love. The only 'complaint', and purely on account of the weight you put on, is all the lashings of cream, butter and cognac Erica cooks with. We've never enjoyed eggs so much as here because the hens eat as well as the guests. No pale, insipid home-made mayonnaise; its hue is golden, and the Pavlovas wonderful." *(ES Pigdon)*

Open Mar–Oct.
Rooms 1 family, 2 double – 1 with bath, 2 with shower, all with radio, tea-making facilities and baby-listening; 2 4-poster beds.
Facilities Drawing room, TV room, bar, dining room. ½-acre garden with unheated swimming pool. Fishing in pond stocked with carp and tench. Tennis and golf nearby.
Location 10 m W of Ashford. From Bethersden take Smarden road for 2 m.
Restrictions Not suitable for &. Dogs by prior arrangement, not in public rooms.
Credit cards None accepted.
Terms (No service charge) dinner, B&B: £25–£30. Reductions for stays of 4 nights or more. Reduced rates for children depending upon age; special meals with advance warning.

BIBURY Gloucestershire   Map 2

Bibury Court   *Tel* Bibury (028 574) 337
Bibury, Nr Cirencester GL7 5NT

A splendid example of a Cotswold manor, dating from Tudor times but with its main part Jacobean, and set in six acres of parkland with the river Coln (trout fishing rights available) running along the southern boundary. There's a good deal of tangled history in these walls, including some spectacular litigation. Dickens is said to have written *Bleak House* with the *Bibury Court* case in mind. Don't miss the walk from the orchard through St Mary's churchyard, along by the river, passing the old weavers' cottages, to Bibury's famous bridge, the Old Mill and the trout hatchery.

The house has been a hotel since 1968, and has been in the hands of the Collier family for the past 15 years: four members of the family are at present employed, cooking and serving, running the bar and reception etc. "We want our guests", writes Mr Collier in his brochure, "to feel they are staying in a country home rather than a hotel, and to enjoy being in a beautiful house which has known centuries of gracious living." Prices, for a country house hotel of this calibre, are very reasonable. Our correspondents this year have been unanimously appreciative of the experience. A characteristic report: "Its beautiful grounds, its oak-panelled lounge, huge log fire, four-poster beds (my children couldn't contain their excitement!), and the good food – all help to make this an exceptional away-from-it-all hotel." *(Jane Bailey; echoed by JP Berryman, D Mansley, Graham Searle)*

Open All year except Christmas.
Rooms 1 suite (with colour TV), 13 double, 2 single–15 with bath, 5 with telephone, 1 with TV, baby-listening; 8 rooms with four-posters.
Facilities TV lounge, residents' lounge, 2 bars, dining room, 6-acre grounds with croquet and dry-fly trout fishing. Golf courses nearby.
Location On edge of village.
Restrictions Not suitable for &. No dogs in dining room.
Credit cards All major cards accepted.
Terms (No service charge) B&B (continental): single £22, double £38–£42. English breakfast £3; bar lunches from £1.50; full alc £14.50. Winter and mid-week breaks Nov–end Mar, except Cheltenham race week – £54–£58. Reduced rates and special meals for children.
Service/tipping: "In 1986 we intend to terminate service charges."

> Give the Guide positive support. Don't just leave feedback to others.

BIRTLE Greater Manchester   Map 2

Normandie Hotel [GFG]   *Tel* Manchester (061) 764 3869
Elbut Lane, Birtle   and 1170
Nr Bury BL9 6UT

"Our hotel", writes the *Normandie* with commendable candour, "caters for the requirements of gourmet businessmen who are visiting Manchester and the north-west. Our objective is to provide them with a memorable meal together with comfortable, but not formula accommodation." Our nominator writes: "The Guide needs more places in moderate price brackets, for which this qualifies, but it would justify an entry on other grounds as well. It has been in *The Good Food Guide* for many years and still well deserves its entry. The hotel is built around an older stone house, which was the original building, but now climbs up the hill behind it. It looks horrid from the outside, but is far, far nicer than it first appears. Part of the view is the Mancunian urban sprawl, but distant enough to be attractive; the rest is Pennine country. Our room was pleasant and immaculately clean, though, understandably at the price, short of luxuries. Even so, we had been staying at *Sharrow Bay* (q.v.) for the previous four nights, and this was no come-down, almost a welcome respite, from the sybarite excesses of *Sharrow*. Service was excellent – not only efficient, but friendly and warm." *(Dr HB Cardwell)*

Open All year except 26, 29 and 30 Dec and 1, 2 Jan. Restaurant closed Sun except for residents.
Rooms 1 family/honeymoon suite, 13 double, 3 single – 8 with bath, 9 with shower, all with telephone, radio, colour TV and tea-making facilities. Some ground-floor rooms.
Facilities Lift. Bar, restaurant, conference and banqueting facilities. ¾-acre grounds. Golf nearby. &.
Location Exit 2 off M66. Take Rochdale/Bury old road (B6222), look out for Birtle sign and proceed up Elbut Lane 1 m.
Restriction Dogs by arrangement; not in public rooms.
Credit cards All major cards accepted.
Terms (Excluding 10% service charge) B&B: single £31–£38, double £37–£39. Set dinner £13.50; full alc £20. Special meals for children.

BISHOPS TACHBROOK Warwickshire   Map 2

Mallory Court [GFG]   *Tel* Leamington Spa (0926) 30214
Harbury Lane, Bishops Tachbrook   *Telex* 317294
Leamington Spa CV33 9QB

"In a class of country house hotel which would be hard to match in England, or for that matter in France" *(David Wooff)*. A typical recent tribute, as in the past, for this luxurious hotel in 10 acres of manicured garden and grounds, nine miles from Stratford-upon-Avon and not much further from the National Exhibition Centre outside Birmingham. The house itself was built in the twenties, but was bought and reincarnated as a hyper-pampering hostelry 10 years ago by Allan Holland and Jeremy Mort. Their establishment is more impersonal than some other country house hotels in its class, but many visitors may be only too happy to trade a faultless service and an impeccably maintained set up for one that is more personal – and also more fallible. Allan

Holland is in charge of the kitchens, and produces *nouvelle*-inclined meals that earn their *Michelin* rosette and are worthy of all the other aspects of the house; there is an extensive wine list. Prices inevitably are high; perfection never comes cheap.

Open 2 Jan–25 Dec; Christmas Day lunch only.
Rooms 1 suite, 8 double – all with bath, telephone, radio and colour TV; 1 4-poster.
Facilities Lounge, drawing room, garden room, oak-panelled dining room. 10-acre grounds and landscaped gardens, water garden, rose garden, terraces; outdoor swimming pool, croquet and squash court; golf 2 m.
Location 2 m S of Leamington Spa off A452. Take left turning signposted Harbury.
Restrictions Not suitable for &. No children under 12. No dogs.
Credit cards Access, Amex, Visa.
Terms B&B: double £68–£110. Set lunch £15, dinner £23–£28. Mid-week breaks in winter.
Service/tipping: "We actively discourage all tipping. All prices are inclusive of VAT and service. It is stated on all our literature that all prices are inclusive of VAT and service."

BLAKENEY Norfolk   **Map 2**

The Blakeney Hotel   *Tel* Cley (0263) 740797
Quayside, Blakeney NR25 7NE

Built by the formidable Sir Henry Deterding of Shell fame in 1920, The Blakeney *has a particularly agreeable site: it is a low rambling building right on one of the more picturesque of Norfolk harbours, looking out over flotillas of small craft to Blakeney Point and the sea. A lot of people are attracted to Blakeney as a centre for sailing and fishing, but it is also a mecca for ornithologists, with three bird sanctuaries close by. The hotel is large by the standard of the Guide, but has a reputation for being well run and friendly, and sympathetic to families with children. There is a heated indoor pool and a large garden behind the hotel. No special claims to culinary distinction. The hotel changed hands two years ago and has been missing from the Guide for the past two issues. Two readers tell us it deserves a place again; some criticism of heating not being put on in a cold spell in June, but "it met our test of an away-from-it-all lazy break very well indeed" (Gwen and Peter Andrews, EV Hibbert). More reports would be welcome.*

Open All year.
Rooms 2 suites, 43 double, 9 single – 47 with bath, 2 with shower, all with telephone, radio, TV, tea-making facilities and baby-listening. 13 in annexe; some on ground floor with ramp.
Facilities 2 lounges, reading room, 3 bars, games room, restaurant. Indoor heated swimming pool. 2-acre grounds. Sailing, windsurfing, golf, birdwatching and excellent walking all available. &.
Location On the Quay. Ample free parking.
Restriction No dogs in public rooms.
Credit cards All major cards accepted.
Terms (No service charge) B&B: £21–£37. Set dinner £8.90; full alc £15. Bargain breaks (min. 2 nights) all year, any time except bank holidays. 4-day Christmas house party. Reduced rates and special meals for children.

We asked hotels to quote 1986 prices. Not all were able to predict them in the late spring of 1985. Some of our terms will be inaccurate. Do check latest tariffs at the time of booking.

BLANCHLAND Durham   Map 4

The Lord Crewe Arms Hotel [GFG]   *Tel* Blanchland (043 475) 251
Nr Consett, Durham   *Telex* 53168

Blanchland is on the River Derwent, about 30 miles south-west of
Newcastle-upon-Tyne. It is surrounded by moors, fields, forests and a
lake – some of the loneliest scenery in Britain. The name of the village
comes from the white robes of the monks who inhabited Blanchland
Abbey from its founding in the 12th century until its dissolution in the
16th. *The Lord Crewe Arms* was once the abbot's lodgings, guest-house
and kitchen, before becoming a manor house and now, its latest
transformation, a small country hotel. There is a Priest's Hole Lounge, a
Crypt Bar and, reputedly, a ghost. We consider the rooms in the main
house preferable to those in the annexe. A description given by a visitor
last year catches the flavour of *Lord Crewe*'s charms: "Approaching from
Corbridge to the north, the road winds and climbs, dips and turns
through woods, over high moors and past stone and whitewashed
farmsteads, and eventually plunges down into the Derwent Valley, with
the reservoir glinting a few miles away to the left. The bedrooms are
very individual, fitted into the old structure, and each has a name. Quite
a lot of stairs. The large dining room is at first-floor level. Thick stone
walls. Pigeons quietly talking outside the window in the morning.
Extensive garden and oddly flat meadows in the valley bottom to the
east. Ermes Oretti is a charming man, and his quiet attentiveness was
shared by his staff. Next time I'd like to stay longer." *(Don Montague;
endorsed by G G Thomas, J M Fox)*

Open Mar–Dec.
Rooms 2 honeymoon suites (1 with jacuzzi), 15 double – 13 with bath, 2 with
shower, all with direct-dial telephone, tea-making facilities, baby-listening. 9
rooms in annexe.
Facilities Lounge, TV room, cocktail bar, bar, restaurant, 1-acre garden. Sailing,
trout fishing available at nearby Derwent reservoir; golf, horse-riding 10 m away.
Location On B6306, 10 m S of Hexham. From the E you can turn off A68 – hotel is
signposted from the main road.
Restrictions Not suitable for &. No dogs in restaurant.
Credit cards None accepted.
Terms B&B: single £30–£34, double £44–£50; dinner, B&B: £30–£40 per person. Set
lunch £6.75, dinner £10. Winter and summer bargain breaks. Christmas package.
Reduced rates and special meals for children.
*Service/tipping: "All prices include service and taxes. You are not required to add a chosen
percentage for service received. If you feel you wish to reward a particular member of staff
for above-average service rendered, do feel free to do so privately."*

BLAWITH Cumbria   Map 4

Appletree Holme Farm   *Tel* Lowick Bridge (022 985) 618
Blawith, Nr Ulverston
South Lakeland LA12 8EL

"A fine example of living life the way it was meant to be lived" is the
motto on the outside of *Appletree Holme Farm*'s brochure – as beguiling a
document as we have come across this year. The host and hostess at this
unconventional establishment are Roy and Shirley Carlsen, and diligent

readers of the Guide from its first 1978 edition may recall them as *patrons* of an opulent establishment named *Leeming-on-Ullswater* at Watermillock. In 1980, they turned their backs on the admin and stress of a big 40-staff hotel, to return to what they really liked doing – cooking and being hosts. We first heard about their new set-up with a report from an American couple who wrote: "We were continually amazed at the friendliness and enthusiasm with which the Carlsens manage their house. The farm is out in the country on a single-lane road. It's very quiet and remote but there are two friendly dogs to accompany guests on walks. The cooking was excellent. We gathered before dinner with the other guests, and spent the entire evening together laughing and talking until late at night. Roy designated one of us each night as "bartender" so we could go on helping ourselves. Our most favourite place of our three-week trip, and the price very reasonable for the quality of the rooms and service" *(Mr and Mrs Richard Haier)*. Our inspector was equally enchanted with the remoteness of the location ("like being on an island with rolling waves of country coming up on all sides – delightful"); with the two collies ("a very nice extra for urbanites to have well-trained dogs laid on!"); with the solicitude with which the Carlsens prepare their menus, depending on what is in season, and discuss their guests' likes and dislikes ("visitors who have been walking all day shouldn't be embarrassed to admit their robust appetites"). He concluded: "A beautifully situated place with good food, comfortable rooms and a warm welcome."

Open All year except Christmas and New Year.
Rooms 2 suites, 2 double – all with bath and tea-making facilities.
Facilities 2 sitting rooms, TV room, dining room; 5-acre grounds with gardens, woodlands and pasture; river 1¼ m with fishing; lake with fishing and bathing 2 m.
Location 8 m N of Ulverston. Turn off A5084 up lane opposite church. ½ m turn right at farm sign.
Restrictions Not suitable for &. No children under 10. No dogs in bedrooms or public rooms.
Credit cards None accepted.
Terms Dinner, B&B £26–£34. Set dinner £11.50.
Note *Mrs Carlsen adds this note to our questionnaire:* "*Appletree is a special place with an appeal limited to country lovers and those seeking peace and seclusion. In order to safeguard our guests' privacy, casual/chance callers are not encouraged and all reservations or requests to look around must be made in advance.*"

BLICKLING Norfolk   **Map 2**

The Buckinghamshire Arms   *Tel* Aylsham (0263) 732133
Blickling
Nr Aylsham NR11 6NF

The countryside of central and north Norfolk is one of the least touristy parts of Britain and grossly under-rated. The 17th-century *Buckinghamshire Arms* lies quietly beside and with fine views of Blickling Hall, one of the country's National Trust gems (you can walk in the park for free, or pay to go round the Hall and formal gardens – well worth it). *The Arms* calls itself a hotel, but is really an inn, popular with the locals, with just three well-equipped bedrooms (each with a four-poster), though with only one bathroom between them. Nigel Elliott took the place over a few years ago, and it has prospered since. There have been some grumbles about the restaurant side, and one complaint about noise from the pub at night. But most people, unless they are expecting a pukka hotel, thoroughly enjoy their visits.

Open All year except Christmas Day.
Rooms 3 double – all with 4-poster beds, colour TV and tea-making facilities.
Facilities 2 lounges, 2 bars, restaurant. 2-acre grounds with children's play area. Bird-watching, sailing, golf, game shooting all nearby. Next door to Blickling Hall; Blickling Lake ½ m away (fishing permits available).
Location 1½ m NW of Aylsham on B1354.
Restrictions Not suitable for &. Dogs by arrangement only.
Credit cards All major cards accepted.
Terms (No service charge) B&B double £40, single occupancy £36. Set Sunday lunch £7, dinner from £12.50; full alc £15; bar lunch about £4. Special rates for 2 nights or more. Reduced rates and special meals for children.

BLOCKLEY Gloucestershire   Map 2

Lower Brook House [GFG]   *Tel* Blockley (0386) 700286
Blockley, Moreton-in-Marsh GL56 9DS

For readers unfamiliar with the name of Blockley, we should say that it is a small and delightful Cotswold village, on the way to nowhere in particular and free from the ubiquitous tourism of neighbouring showplaces, such as Broadway and Chipping Campden; but it makes an admirable centre for a Cotswold holiday and Stratford itself is only a short drive away. *Lower Brook House* is a cottagey kind of hotel, built in the local stone, with cosy rather than spacious rooms, and a terraced garden leading down to a tiny stream from which it takes its name. It has a pleasant, quiet, old-world atmosphere, and Ewan Wright and his young staff are mentioned frequently in reports for their unforced geniality and helpfulness. The standard of cooking is high if falling short of gourmet attainments: Mr Wright takes a close interest in his suppliers and uses local fresh ingredients whenever possible. A good place to unwind – and the tariff is reasonable.

Open All year except Jan.
Rooms 8 double – 6 with bath, 2 with shower, all with radio; colour TV and baby-listening on request.
Facilities Lounge, bar, restaurant. Small garden with brook. Swimming pool in village can be used by guests. & restaurant only.
Location Off A44 4m NW of Moreton-in-Marsh on B4479.
Restrictions No infants. No dogs in public rooms.
Credit card Access.
Terms (No service charge) dinner, B&B: single, £35.50–£38.50, double £68–£71. Set dinner £13.50; full alc £16. Reduced rates and special meals (on request) for children.
Service/tipping: "No service charge added. Tipping is at guests' discretion."

Hotels often book you into their most expensive rooms or suites unless you specify otherwise. Even if all room prices are the same, hotels may give you a less good room in the hope of selling their better rooms to later customers. It always pays to discuss accommodation in detail when making a reservation.

BOLTON ABBEY North Yorkshire   Map 4

The Devonshire Arms Hotel
Bolton Abbey, Skipton BD23 6AJ

Tel Skipton (075 671) 441
Telex 51218
Reservations in UK 01 937 8033
in USA (800) 288 2121

This traditional coaching inn by Bolton Bridge and within a few hundred yards of the atmospheric ruins of Bolton Abbey underwent a facelift a few years ago, and has become a sophisticated country hotel in an exceptionally beautiful position in the heart of Wharfedale. The Duchess of Devonshire herself supervised the furnishings and decor of the nine rooms in the old part, providing some further Chatsworth chattels after the Cavendish Hotel *at Baslow (q.v.) had already received part of her bequest. A modern wing, with 29 rooms, was added at the back facing the Wharfe valley with the moors as a backdrop. These modular bedrooms, with contemporary furnishings, are austere, but provide most of the amenities to be expected of a hotel of this class. The public rooms are spacious, light and comfortable. The dining room is elegant, with an expensive* nouvelle-*inspired menu. . ."Dinner was uneven: disappointing first course, an exceptional main course, and, of the sweets, one outstanding and the other indifferent. A splendid breakfast buffet, with good coffee. Service at dinner was clumsy but well meaning. That apart, the hotel gave an impression of efficient professionalism. The one missing element was any warmth of welcome: the essential difference between a manager's hotel and an owner's." (H R)*

Thus ran last year's entry (slightly truncated) written, as the initials indicate, by the Editor. The 1985 Guide appeared in November 1984. At the date of writing, we have had only one letter on The Devonshire Arms, *from a "local" who had taken umbrage at the changes made in "a once delightful hotel", dubbed the new buildings "cowsheds" and hadn't enjoyed her meal. "I know people's standards vary, but I suspect* The Devonshire Arms *only got its report because of the connection with the Duchess. We in the area are surprised that she was allowed to spoil the hotel as she seems to have done. In the past we were regulars, but not any more." We should be glad to hear from others.*

Open All year.
Rooms 1 suite, 36 double, 1 single – all with bath and shower, direct-dial telephone, radio, colour TV, tea-making facilities and baby-listening; 29 rooms in new wing; 2 ground-floor rooms equipped for partially &.
Facilities Lounge, lounge bar, public bar, restaurant; 5 rooms for private parties and business meetings. In Yorkshire Dales National Park; nearby river and fishing.
Location 5 m NE of Skipton; at junction of B6160 and A59.
Restriction Dogs in bedrooms only.
Credit cards All major cards accepted.
Terms B&B: single £48–£53.50, double £57.50–£68. Set lunch £6; full alc £22.
3-night weekend breaks. Children £10 when sharing parents' room.

Wherever possible, we have quoted prices per room. Not all hotels are prepared to quote tariffs in this way. In these cases, we have given prices per person, indicating the range of prices – the lowest is likely to be for sharing a double room out of season, the highest for a single room in the high season.

BONCHURCH Isle of Wight   Map 2

Peacock Vane [GFG]   *Tel* Ventnor (0983) 852019
Bonchurch, Nr Ventnor
Isle of Wight PO38 1RG

For more than a quarter of a century, *Peacock Vane* has been *the* hotel to recommend to Isle of Wight visitors who wished to combine the creature comforts of a well-run small hotel with what most people would agree was the best food on the island. Those who cherish *Peacock Vane* will argue over its chief attraction: whether it is the elegant Regency house nestling on the Bonchurch rock face; the finely simple English cooking and classic, inexpensive wines; or the ability of the Wolfendens to make one feel like a guest in a private house, though with no obligation save to rest, eat and listen to the twin songs of wood pigeons and the sea. The atmosphere is less that of hotel than old-fashioned manor house, growing its own vegetables, baking its own bread, bottling its own preserves – a fortress, protecting its inhabitants against all the usual hotel's homogenised impersonality. The few bedrooms, booked solid during summer weekends, are offered at even more moderate terms early in the week. To sit in the beautiful upper drawing room, sipping drinks served from a grand piano-top, before the traditionally lavish Sunday night cold table, is the quintessential *Peacock Vane* experience – taste combining with unpretentiousness, comfort with excellence, happy anticipation with absolute tranquillity of mind." *(Philip Norman)*

Philip Norman's encomium was in fact written four years ago, but readers since have subscribed to his comments, apart from one visitor this year who found the Lodge "tacky", and had a host of other minor complaints. *(Marjorie Holmes, A H, P G Evans, Professor H Richard Lamb, and others)*

Open 21 Mar–2 Nov and most weekends in winter. Restaurant closed Mon and Tue lunch.
Rooms 9 double – all with bath, mono TV and tea-making facilities; 3 rooms in annexes.
Facilities Large drawing room, dining room. 3-acre grounds with swimming pool. Sea at Bonchurch Shore, ¼ m away.
Location NE of Ventnor, 1st drive on left after pond, coming from Ventnor (1 m away). Parking.
Restrictions Not suitable for &. Children under 7 not encouraged. No dogs in dining room.
Credit cards All major cards accepted.
Terms Dinner, B&B £35 (£200 per week). 25% supplement on rooms let as singles. Set lunch £11, dinner £16. Reductions for mid-week stays of 3 days or more; weekend and weekly rates. Negotiable rates for children.

BORROWDALE Cumbria   Map 4

Seatoller House   *Tel* Borrowdale (059 684) 218
Borrowdale, Keswick CA12 5XN

An unaffectedly matey establishment and winner of a César in 1984 as most sympathetic guest-house. At the head of the Borrowdale Valley, near the Honister Pass, it is close to the starting-point of many of the most spectacular fell walks. The house itself is over 300 years old, and it has been run continuously as a guest-house for more than a 100 years – almost certainly a record. For several years past, it has been in the capable hands of David and Ann Pepper, and continues to be popular with readers. Dinner is at 7 pm, and – an attraction for some, a warning for others – meals are taken communally. One reader felt that we hadn't praised Mrs Pepper's cooking highly enough: "It constantly teeters around *The Good Food Guide* standard." "Food", writes another, "was 'real'; first courses and sweets rather more imaginative than main dishes. Breakfast: English and good." A third would have wished for more robust helpings. We also pass on the advice from one party to take your own towels, since those provided are "generally ineffectual". Prices are decidedly modest. *(P J S, T R and Sarah Mann, Harold Sheppard)*

Open Mar–Nov. Dining room closed Tue evening.
Rooms 9 double; 1 room in annexe with shower and wc; 3 rooms on ground floor.
Facilities Lounge with open fire, library, dining room, tea-bar, for guests to make hot drinks etc; picnic shop. Small conference facilities. 2-acre grounds with fish pond. 6 m from Derwent Water and Buttermere.
Location 8m S of Keswick on B5289. Regular bus service from Keswick.
Restrictions No children under 5. No dogs in public rooms.
Credit cards None accepted.
Terms (Gratuities at guests' discretion). B&B: £12–£13.50; dinner, B&B £18–£19.50. Set dinner £6 (at 7pm, not served Tue). Weekly rates available; special rates for parties of 16 or more. Reduced rates for children under 12 sharing parents' room.

BOSHAM West Sussex   Map 2

The Millstream Hotel [GFG]   *Tel* Bosham (0243) 573234
Bosham Lane, Old Bosham
Nr Chichester PO18 8HL

"We visited *The Millstream* on the night of our wedding. It was absolutely delightful. We were particularly impressed with the warm and spacious room, the most helpful and genuinely caring staff, but above all by the relaxed informal atmosphere of the place. We know several hotels in this class which are much too formal and put themselves out to increase the formality in an attempt to increase status. *The Millstream* does not need to pretend. An unreserved recommendation."

A particularly warm compliment, but one among many, for this attractive, cheerful, smartish but not oppressively trendy hotel in a small sailing village close to Chichester, about which all the above adjectives would equally apply. *The Millstream* is a harmonious conversion and blending of an early 18th-century malthouse and a row of maltsters' cottages with an Edwardian manor house: the house stands back from the road in front of a small millstream with ducks, and little bridges lead across the water into a pretty garden. *(Colin and Fiona Bocking; and many others) Note*: front rooms are preferable.

Open All year.
Rooms 19 double (incl. 2 pairs of inter-connecting rooms), 3 single – all with bath, telephone, radio, TV and tea-making facilities; 3 rooms on ground floor.
Facilities Residents' lounge, bar/lounge, cocktail bar, TV room, restaurant; conference facilities. Small garden with stream, pond and herb garden. Sailing, fishing, riding, golf nearby.
Location 4 m W of Chichester. Turn off A27 to Old Bosham, follow road to

T-junction, turn right, hotel is 200 yds on right. Car park.
Restrictions Not suitable for &. No dogs in public rooms.
Credit cards All major cards accepted.
Terms (No service charge) B&B: single £32–£34, double £58–£62; dinner, B&B (min. 2 nights) £30–£37.50 per person. Set lunch £7–£7.80, dinner £9.50; full alc £13.50. Getaway breaks at most times of year. Reduced rates and special meals for children.
Tipping: Completely at customers' discretion, although not encouraged.

BRAMPTON Cumbria   Map 4

Farlam Hall [GFG]   *Tel* Hallbankgate (069 76) 234
Brampton CA8 2NG

Once again nothing but praise for the welcome, comfort and outstanding board provided by Mr and Mrs Quinion in their part 17th-century Border manor house four miles from Hadrian's Wall. The building itself, once a farmhouse, has historical interest: Wesley is thought to have preached there, and George ("Rocket") Stephenson was a visitor. The country around – despite its castles and abbeys as well as its great scenic beauty – continues to be wonderfully unspoilt by tourist invasions even in the height of summer. "Even better than we expected despite your glowing report," was one tribute. Second-timers from California found all the expectations they had built up since their first visit in 1982 fulfilled: "The Quinions run a smooth and professional operation without sacrificing the finer elements of courtesy and warmth." Another reader wrote: "We were wrapped in a comfortable warmth." Two correspondents spoke gratefully of the welcome extended to their dog: "He was even greeted by name on the following morning." Only caveat: some of the rooms are on the small side. Perhaps prices could be reduced for these rooms? (*Beryl Crawford, Mr and Mrs Richard Haier, P Grimsdale, Doug and Diane Ginever, E Newall, Professor Charles Thomas and Jessica Mann, J & J W*)

Open Mar-Oct inclusive; second half Nov, all Dec and Jan. Closed Mon and Tue Nov to Jan inclusive.
Rooms 12 double, 1 single – 10 with bath, 3 with shower, all with colour TV; 2 ground-floor rooms.
Facilities 2 lounges, bar, dining room seating about 50; 4½-acre grounds with croquet. 2 golf courses nearby.
Location On A689, 2½ m SE of Brampton (*not* in Farlam village).
Restrictions Not suitable for &. No children under 4 in restaurant. Dogs by arrangement only.
Credit cards Access, Amex, Visa.
Terms (Service at guests' discretion) Dinner, B&B £42–£47. Set lunch £9.50; dinner £13.50. Winter breaks late Oct to mid-Apr, excluding Christmas and New Year.

BRANSCOMBE Devon   Map 1

The Mason's Arms [GFG]   *Tel* Branscombe (029 780) 300
Branscombe, Nr Seaton EX12 3DJ

An example of a disappearing species: a genuine Olde English inn, both outside with bits of thatch and creeper, and garden benches in the flowery front garden, and inside, with polished wood and brass, and ingle-nook fireplaces. The inn dates from the 14th century and is half a mile from the sea. Although this is a true local – warm and cosy, with a stone flag floor and huge open log fireplace in the bar, and a real ale pub at that – it has moved with the times: most of the bedrooms (warning – some are tiny, and the ones in the main house are said to be preferred to the dozen in the cottage) have their own bathrooms. There is also an attractive residents' lounge upstairs. Honest English fare, though one writer this year could have managed larger portions. There have been one or two other niggles as well: poor service at breakfast, electric radiators not turned on before guests arrived on a cold night, and, according to one report "profit motive a little too much in evidence". But all our correspondents enjoyed their stay and endorsed the entry. *(Mr and Mrs Beattie, B Waters, M A Goulding)*

Open All year.
Rooms 2 suites, 19 double, 3 single – 15 with bath, all with radio, colour TV and baby-listening; 12 rooms in cottages; 3 ground-floor rooms.
Facilities Lounge, bar, restaurant, ½ m from pebble beach.
Location 1½ m S of A3052, 5 m E of Sidmouth.
Restrictions Not suitable for &. No dogs in public rooms.
Credit cards Access, Visa.
Terms (No service charge) B&B £16–£24. Set lunch £6, dinner £10–£12.50. Winter breaks 1 Nov–31 Mar. Reduced rates for children sharing parents' room; high teas.

BRIGHTON East Sussex   Map 2

Topps Hotel   *Tel* Brighton (0273) 729334
17 Regency Square, Brighton BN1 2FG

"Best buy and nicest place we stayed at in England," writes an enthusiastic American visitor about this new conversion of two terraced Regency houses in a sea-front square. It is owned and run by Paul and Pauline Collins who say their aim is to provide complete rest and relaxation in a friendly casual atmosphere: "We do not appeal to people who like big hotels." In the basement is a small restaurant called *Bottoms*, offering unpretentious home-cooked English dishes. Here are extracts from one sustained paean of praise from another reader: "I believe *Topps* must be unique in Brighton. Unlike other period hotels in the area, it has been modernised from top to bottom and all the rooms are clean, modern and well appointed. The double rooms are enormous: more suites than rooms. The bedroom boasts a settee, two armchairs, a coffee-table, a desk, very comfortable beds, remote-control colour TV, radio, telephone, mini-fridge, trouser press, also flowers and plants. The bathroom has a walk-in cupboard, two basins, bidet and hair dryer, plus lots of extras. Good-night chocolates are put out at night. Single rooms are much smaller, but nevertheless most comfortable. Paul and Pauline Collins, apart from the first-class service in the hotel and restaurant, are available from early to late as counsellors, tourist guides and friends to all their guests ... About the restaurant, the first thing that must be said is that all the food is home cooked by Mrs Collins on the premises, even including the bread rolls supplied with breakfast. The second thing, which should be stated with even more emphasis, is that Pauline Collins knows how to cook!! All the food is extremely 'moreish'. Prices are extremely reasonable ... A gem." *(Harry Kahn; also Joy Bloom, D H C Hampshire)*

Open 1 Jan–23 Dec. Restaurant closed Sun and Wed.
Rooms 5 double, 3 single – 5 with bath, 3 with shower, all with telephone, radio, colour TV, tea-making facilities.
Facilities Lounge, bar, basement restaurant, conference/private dining room for 12. 100 yds from sea.
Location 200 yds from centre, opposite West Pier, but quietly situated.
Restriction Not suitable for &.
Credit cards All major cards accepted.
Terms B&B: single £27.50, double £55. Full alc £12–£14. Reduced rates and special meals for children. 10% off for any two nights Fri/Sat/Sun except public holidays.

The Twenty One [GFG]   *Tel* Brighton (0273) 686450
21 Charlotte Street
Brighton BN2 1AG

Readers support our first entry last year for Simon Ward and Stuart Farquharson's early Victorian town house in the fashionable Brighton suburb of Kemp Town (warning: no lifts and lots of stairs to the top floor), offering a sophisticated personally caring place to stay as an alternative to large impersonal hotels and mediocre look-alike guest-houses. A bonus for 21's guests is that the owners serve ambitious gastronomic dinners in the French country cooking style. "Not a hotel of great luxury and 24-hour service, nor one to do a lot of phoning from. You get the door key and there are often times when the owners are out shopping or whatever. They operate with the minimum of outside staff, so you have the odd feeling at times that it is like home when all the family are out. But it *is* comfortable and has style, which comes from personal involvement of the owners, and it doesn't take long to fall into the easy rhythm of the place. Take plenty of exercise before dinner: the menu tells only half the story!" (*D N; also P Harman, E Riley and others*)

Open Feb–Dec. Restaurant closed lunchtime, Sun and public holidays.
Rooms 6 double – 4 with shower and wc, all with radio, colour TV; 1 with 4-poster.
Facilities Lounge, dining room. Beach 1 minute's walk.
Location Central. Off Marine Parade.
Restrictions Not suitable for &. No children under 12. No dogs in public rooms.
Credit cards All major cards accepted.
Terms (No service charge on rooms) B&B: single occupancy £22–£30, double £30–£40; dinner, B&B: single occupancy £37–£45, double £45–£55. Set dinner £14.50 (plus 12½% service charge); full alc £19.50. Special 2-day breaks.

BROAD CAMPDEN Gloucestershire   Map 2

The Malt House   *Tel* Evesham (0386) 840295
Broad Campden
Chipping Campden GL55 6UU

Many owners of small country houses would like their guests to feel that they were staying in a private country house even though paying for the privilege. Mrs Pat Robinson, whose *Malt House* is a conversion of three mellow Cotswold 17th-century cottages in an unspoilt hamlet a mile from Chipping Campden, is particularly keen to foster this atmosphere: her guests normally sit together round a large refectory table for their meals, though they can opt for separate tables if they wish. One visitor this year was discomforted by the communal meal which had proved a conversation-stopper: there's always a lottery about these arrangements. Others have thoroughly enjoyed everything about the place: "the gregarious and efficient" Mrs Robinson, her "hilarious" dogs, a bed "soft as a cloud", "the lovely garden", and a special vote of thanks from an American couple for "a Thanksgiving dinner prepared for us Yankees without even asking for it ... *The Malt House* was the best place we stayed in our 12 days in the Cotswolds." *(Terry Whyte, Mr and Mrs Haier, and others)*

Open All year except Christmas week. Restaurant closed Sunday evening.
Rooms 5 double, 1 single – 4 with bath, all with TV (5 colour) and tea-making facilities.
Facilities Drawing room, dining room with log fire. 4½-acre grounds with large gazebo, small brook and pond, croquet lawn and orchard. Riding by arrangement.
Location Leave Chipping Campden by Sheep Street, turn first left after garage on left into Broad Campden; *Malt House* is second on left after Baker's Arms. Parking.
Restrictions Not suitable for &. Children over 10 preferred. No dogs (boarding at nearby kennels can be arranged).
Credit cards None accepted.
Terms (No service charge) B&B: single £22–£30, double £39–£48; dinner, B&B: single £34–£50, double £68–£100. Set dinner £12.50–£16. Reductions for children according to age; high teas.

BROADWAY Hereford and Worcester   Map 2

Collin House Hotel [GFG]   *Tel* Broadway (0386) 858354
Collin Lane, Broadway WR12 7PB

A small civilised (there are books everywhere) 16th-century Cotswold stone house in eight acres of garden and grounds a mile out of Broadway, with a high reputation for its English country cooking; but even though it only has seven bedrooms while the restaurant seats 26, it is decidedly more than a restaurant-with-rooms. It entered our lists for the first time last year with a long and enthusiastic nomination: "John and Judy Mills treat their guests as friends – but never obtrusively. Log fires in the chintzy, comfortable bar and the equally comfortable but more sedate lounge are lit at breakfast time if there is even a nip in the air. John has his own scrapbook of places to visit and things to do and is willing to sit for hours with dithering guests. Breakfasts are continental (croissants) or English (large); lunch is in the bar or garden (light snack or full meal as you wish) and dinner a three-course meal priced according to the main course. All the vegetables are fresh. The home-made ice creams and brandy bread-and-butter pudding melt in the mouth. A gentle suggestion that there wasn't a single decent lamp to read by led to an immediate improvement. *Collin House* itself is of typical Cotswold stone with lots of oak beams, and its situation just *outside* the tourist trap of Broadway is a great asset. Ideal for a short visit to the Cotswolds." *(Monica Wilson)*

Recent visitors thoroughly concur, and appreciated the wine list; only jarring note – nylon lace round their modern four-poster. *(D & A L)*

Open All year except 24–26 Dec.
Rooms 6 double (2 with 4-posters) – 1 single, 5 with bath, 2 with shower; radio and colour TV on request.
Facilities Lounge bar, TV lounge, restaurant, 8-acre grounds including ½-acre

gardens and orchard; open-air unheated swimming pool. &. bar and dining room only.
Location On A44, 1 m NW of Broadway.
Restrictions No children under 6 except by prior arrangement. Small dogs only in public rooms, not bedrooms.
Credit cards Access, Visa.
Terms (No service charge) B&B: single £28.50, double £50–£58; dinner, B&B: single £39, double £71–£79. Full alc £14. Winter breaks Nov–Mar. Special meals for children.
Service/tipping: "No service charge made. We do not forbid our staff to accept tips provided they are unsolicited."

Lygon Arms [GFG]
Broadway WR12 7DU

Tel Broadway (0386) 852255
Telex 338260 LYGON G

A show-place 16th-century hostelry in a show-place Cotswold village. Once a modest coaching-inn, it now offers luxurious hospitality to international travellers. Rooms, some in the old part and some in a new wing, are well equipped, with many fine antique pieces as well as good modern furniture. Flowers are everywhere. Service is fast and professional. The restaurant is magnificently housed in a Great Hall, with barrel-shaped ceiling and Minstrels' Gallery. Notwithstanding all these features of a visually splendid and efficient hotel, the *Lygon Arms* has often earned ambivalent entries. Last year was no exception and the entry appeared in italics. Among other matters we touched on was criticism of the Hall Porter's department, that it "was no more than a Mafia" in its pursuit of tips. We were delighted to hear from more than one recent visitor of the exemplary behaviour of porters, both at the arrival and the departure stages: no sign of "the sunburned palms", no hovering, just a natural willingness to help. In general, the *Lygon* file makes much happier reading this year, not least in respect of the kitchens. The one "disgusted" letter came from a guest who, on two successive evenings, had to dine in one of the lounges because the main dining room had been taken for a conference party. Some of his fellow-guests had come specially for a celebratory dinner. We appreciate that conference trade is important to many hotels, but unfortunately business and pleasure don't easily mix and the private-paying guests only too easily get short-changed. More reports would still be welcome.

Open All year.
Rooms 3 suites, 56 double, 3 single–all with bath, direct-dial telephone in bedroom and bathroom, radio, colour TV and baby-listening; front rooms double-glazed; 4-poster beds; 9 ground-floor rooms, ramp provided. &.
Facilities Numerous lounges with log fires, one with TV, cocktail bar, restaurant. Conference/function facilities for 100 people. 2-acre garden with tennis court.
Location In High Street. Parking for 200 cars; 6 garages.
Restriction No dogs in restaurant.
Credit cards All major cards acepted.
Terms B&B: single £50, double £86. Set lunch £9.50, dinner £16.50; full alc £25. Reduced rates May–Oct (min. 3 nights); 4-day Christmas package. Special meals for children.
Service/tipping: "Service is at the discretion of the guests."

Do you know of a good hotel in Bristol?

Do you know of a good hotel in Birmingham?

BROMSGROVE Hereford and Worcester   Map 2

Grafton Manor [GFG]   *Tel* Bromsgrove (0527) 31525/37247
Grafton Lane   *Reservations* in US (800) 323 3602
Bromsgrove B61 7HA

Formerly calling itself a restaurant-with-rooms, this architecturally splendid early 18th-century mansion now dubs itself a country house hotel, albeit a small one, with just six rooms, though one is an outsize suite occupying half of one wing on the first floor. All rooms are fitted with the mod cons appropriate to the grandeur of the house, including direct-dial telephones, colour TV and teletext. Some turbulent episodes in English history have touched this house since its pre-Norman beginnings: Jack Cade's rebellion, the Wars of the Roses, and the Gunpowder Plot, to name but three. Recently, it has enjoyed a halcyon phase in the hands of John Morris and his family (his wife, two sons and a daughter), who have been busy with restorations and improvements since they became the lords of the manor. There is a large formal herb garden and a water garden bordering the lake in their six acres of gardens. The kitchen garden provides as much as possible for the excellent restaurant in the *Manor*'s magnificent dining room. Readers endorse our summing-up last year: "There is a kind of largesse about the Morrises' enterprise, an imaginative generosity, which extends both to their dedicated work in the house and grounds, and in small details like leaving the soup tureen on the table for guests to help themselves as liberally as they wish." *(R O Marshall)*

Open All year.
Rooms 1 suite, 5 double–all with bath, direct-dial telephone, radio, colour TV and teletext.
Facilities Lounge/bar, restaurant. 7-acre grounds with gardens, 2-acre coarse fishing lake; stabling for horses. 2 golf courses nearby.
Location 1½ m from centre of Bromsgrove. From M5 (exit 4 or 5), take A38 towards Bromsgrove. Opposite Aston Fields Industrial Estate, take Charford road, turn left into Worcester Road, right into Grafton Lane.
Restrictions Not suitable for &. No children under 12. No dogs.
Credit cards All major cards accepted.
Terms (Service at guests' discretion) B&B (continental): single £45, double £60; with English breakfast: single £50.50, double £71; dinner, B&B: single £68.45, double £106.90.

BUCKDEN North Yorkshire   Map 4

Low Greenfield [GFG]   *Tel* Kettlewell (075 676) 858
Langstrothdale Chase
Nr Buckden, Skipton B23 5JN

A farmhouse, part 17th-century and part Victorian, in the heart of the Dales National Park, run as a modest-priced guest-house by Austin and Lindsay Sedgley. We had heard good things of the place, and sent along an inspector who reports: "I have never stayed in such a secluded hotel. You leave a minor road driving towards Hawes and take a 1½-mile gated road into a remote valley. Four gates to open and shut. Only the bird cry intrudes on the solitary silence. This is essentially a place for walkers, fishermen and those in search of peace and quiet. The Sedgleys' success is indubitable. On a cold April day we found a banked coal fire in the shabby, but comfy sitting room. There's a second room with piano when the hotel is full. No TV. This area is at 1,200 feet and there's a warm fire in the evenings nearly always. My husband began to purr when he looked in the bookcase. If you are interested in R H Tawney or Margaret Mead you will find *Religion and the Rise of Capitalism* and *The Coming of Age in Samoa* beside Catherine Cookson and Georgette Heyer. If you like Brahms and Mozart you can have them at dinner. We chose a clarinet concerto for after-dinner coffee beside the fire. The hotel brochure says this is not for those seeking a 'rave up', discos, or bright lights. Say that again. Dinner was the sort of meal you would ask your friends to: mushroom and bacon tart decorated with watercress, chicken breasts in a sage sauce, jacket potatoes cooked in the Aga – smeared with butter and cooked long and slow into golden balls of goodness. Bedrooms have bare spaces in them, a bit spartan, but comfortable beds and a mug of tea at 7.45 am. Plenty of hot water. Splendid breakfast."

Open 1 Apr–31 Oct. Dinner not cooked on Sun: sandwiches available 7–9 pm.
Rooms 2 3-bedded, 3 double, 1 single – all with h & c.
Facilities 2 lounges, dining room. 1-acre garden and woodland; 27-acre nature reserve with fishing in lake and beck. Fell walking, bird watching.
Location 9 m SE of Hawes: from Buckden take left fork signposted Hawes. Approx. 5 m along road, cross River Wharfe over iron bridge on tight S bend. 1 m further take small left fork signposted Greenfield. Follow gated road to Lower Greenfield.
Restriction Dogs by special arrangement, but not in public rooms.
Credit cards None accepted.
Terms (No service charge) B&B: £13.80; dinner, B&B £22.55. Set dinner £8.75 (£10.50 to non-residents). Reduced rates for children and tea in kitchen at 5.30 pm. *Tipping: Not encouraged or expected.*

BUCKLAND Hereford and Worcester   Map 2

Buckland Manor [GFG]   *Tel* Broadway (0386) 852626
Buckland
Nr Broadway WR12 7LY

"The best country house we have ever come across" (*J J Wüthrich*). "Total delight. Everything was right ... Beautiful house in magnificent setting ... Delightfully furnished bedrooms with deep-pile carpets ... You are cosseted from the time you arrive until you leave, but in an unobtrusive and elegant manner ... Wonderful food ... Excellent wine list with mark-up not excessive ... Service out of this world ... Prices on a par with top-rate hotels but in this case well worth it" (*D F Tooley*). "Impossible to believe you were only two miles from bustling tourist-ridden Broadway. The tranquillity, the decor and the staff were all the essence of relaxation. Try as I might, I could not fault it" (*Patricia Roberts*). Three tributes (the first from a Swiss hotelier of note) echoing similar ones in previous years, to this ultra-sybaritic country house hotel – a peerless pedigree Cotswold manor, in part dating from the 13th century, in 10 acres of gardens and grounds that complement the beauty of the house. The only discordant note in the chorus of praise: "Gratuities are at the discretion of guests, and they are constantly reminded of it – on the menu, on the final account and the inevitable space left on the credit card voucher ..."

Open All year except 3 weeks Jan/Feb.
Rooms 1 suite, 9 double – all with spring-fed bath (3 also with shower), direct-dial telephone, colour TV, radio on request; some ground-floor rooms; 2 4-posters.
Facilities 2 sitting rooms with log fires, writing room, dining room. 10-acre grounds with water and rose gardens, tennis court, croquet, putting greens, heated pool; stables (riding available to guests). Walks and golf nearby.
Location E of A46, 2 m SW of Broadway.
Restrictions No children under 12 in hotel, under 8 in restaurant. Dogs in kennels only.
Credit cards Access, Diners, Visa.
Terms (Service at guests' discretion) B&B: double room £79.50– £105 (single occupancy from £69.50). Full alc £18.50. Winter breaks Nov-mid-Mar. (min 2 days) except Christmas, New Year and Cheltenham Gold Cup week when there are special packages.

BURFORD Oxfordshire   Map 2

The Bay Tree [GFG]   *Tel* Burford (099 382) 3137
Sheep Street, Burford OX8 4LW

Welcome back, *Bay Tree!* Connoisseurs of country house hotels since before the last war will associate this mellow 16th-century mansion (once the home of Queen Elizabeth I's unpopular Lord Chief Baron of the Exchequer) with the name of Sylvia Gray, who ran the hotel with the help of young lady trainees for an astonishing 45 years. The house, in a quiet side street off the famous High Street, offered an old-fashioned standard of comfort, full of polished oak and chintz, which in Miss Gray's latter days became decidedly too old-fashioned and disappeared from these pages. Now it is under new owners, the Kings, who have been busy with improvements: all the bedrooms now have bathrooms *en suite* and colour TV, several have four-posters and testers, and telephones will be installed shortly. A new head chef has been engaged, aiming to produce good-quality English cooking and bake his own bread and rolls. More important than testers and TV, how is it functioning as a hotel? Pretty well, judging by recent visitors. It retains its old-world quality, the fine antiques remain, attention is still given to the silver tea services on trays around the fire at 5 pm, the house still possesses its many quiet, restful sitting places, and the garden at the back is still a haven of peace. The new owners are said to be courteous and eager to please. Of course there have been a few teething-troubles, but first reports of the new régime are more than promising. *(Ved and Lynn Mehta, Susan Riches, Eithne Scallan, Chris & Dorothy Brining)*

Open All year except Boxing Day, last week Jan and first week Feb.
Rooms 2 suites, 14 double, 3 single – all with bath, and most with shower also, telephones to be installed; 2 ground-floor rooms.
Facilities 4 public lounges, residents' bar, restaurant. Small grounds with terraced gardens, fishponds, summer house.
Location Central (but quiet). Go down hill from A40 roundabout and take first turn on left. Parking.
Restrictions Not suitable for &. Dogs only allowed in public rooms and must be closely supervised.
Terms (No service charge) B&B: single £21.50, double £45–£53; half board: single £29.50, double £61–£69. Set lunch £6.50; dinner: weekday £10.50, Sat £12.50. Special breaks Nov–Mar. Reduced rates for children sharing parents' room; special meals.

The Golden Pheasant *Tel* (099 382) 3223
The High Street, Burford OX8 4RJ *Telex* 849041 SHARET G Ref TVH 002

Timothy Rowe took over this fine 14th- or 15th-century Cotswold hotel half-way down Burford's peerless High Street in the spring of 1984, having come from a popular Guide hotel (until it changed hands) – the *Worsley Arms* at Hovingham, Yorkshire. Here is our first report:

"*The Golden Pheasant* was not my first choice in Burford. I had tried *The Bay Tree* first but was unable to get a room. *The Golden Pheasant* is on the High Street next to the very interesting Cotswold Bookshop. We received an exceptionally warm welcome from the new manager and receptionist. They were anxious that we should see our room which was gigantic, complete with vaulted beamed ceiling, Cotswold stone walls, and a beautiful old four-poster bed. It was charming. Most of the rooms are smaller, but all of them seemed friendly and comfortable, with the rooms facing the High Street especially nice (though traffic could be noisy). The food in both the bar and restaurant was cooked very well; one night I requested a special vegetarian dish, and the kitchen's solution was both creative and exceptionally well done. *The Golden Pheasant* was an altogether unexpected delight. I have rarely stayed in a place where the staff was so friendly and willing to please. Not all of the amenities are there – there are some things about the inn which are rough around the edges – but the friendly atmosphere and the energy of the young staff make it a very happy place to visit." *(J Feder)* More reports please.

Open All year.
Rooms 12 double – 5 with bath, 7 with shower, all with telephone, radio, colour TV, tea-making facilities and baby-listening. 2 with 4-posters; 2 ground-floor rooms.
Facilities 2 lounges, small bar area, dining room. Riding, walking, golf, fishing, Cotswold Wildlife Park and Country Farm nearby.
Location In town centre. (Front rooms could be noisy.) Parking.
Restriction Dogs allowed, but not in restaurant.
Credit cards Access, Visa.
Terms B&B: single £25–£30, double £37.50–£47.50; dinner, B&B: single £30–£40, double £52–£65. Sunday lunch £7, set dinner £11.50. Off-season packages (min. 2 nights); 3-day Christmas package. Reduced rates and special meals for children.
Service/tipping: "We state on our tariffs that the prices quoted include SERVICE. We do not say that they include SERVICE CHARGE. Our feelings and our policy are that the prices guests pay are quite high enough, and for the prices charged, they should expect good service without having to pay even more for it. The staff do not expect to receive any extra tips and are instructed to say to the guests that tipping is not necessary."

BURY ST EDMUNDS Suffolk Map 2

The Angel Hotel *Tel* Bury St Edmunds (0284) 3926
Angel Hill *Telex* 81630 ANGEL G
Bury St Edmunds IP33 1LT

💈 *César awarded in 1985 for best country town hotel*

The small market town of Bury St Edmunds, with its numerous fine Georgian buildings, little squares and old shop fronts, is a pleasure to visit in its own right as well as being a good touring centre for Cambridge, Newmarket and the many unspoilt villages of East Anglia.

The Angel, patronised by Dickens (who immortalised it as the place where Sam Weller first encounters Job Trotter), is an ivy-covered series of linked buildings on the main square opposite the great abbey gate, one of the glories of the town. If you are allergic to noise you should avoid the front rooms, though you will miss a splendid view. The hotel makes a lot of its Dickensian association: you can sleep in the room he actually occupied, Room 15, in a huge four-poster – one of several in the place. But it is certainly not resting on its literary – or its César – laurels. It is a thoroughly enterprising hotel, always improving this and that (the main lobby this year), and organising all kinds of special events: its bargain weekend breaks are exceptionally good value; and it earns special credit with us as the first – and perhaps the only – hotel to give an annual literary prize.

When hotels receive a César, we always worry whether next year's reports will bring a load of brickbats. There was one of sorts (see below) though compliments were more in evidence, viz.: "Top marks" *(Lady Antonia Pinter)*. "Well deserves its accolade" *(Bryan Magee)*. "Why can't all hotels be like this?" *(Richard O Whiting)*. The brickbat, or back-handed compliment, came from an American visitor: "My room was disappointing – like an untouched set from a 50s Diana Dors movie, but others I passed with open doors had been more recently smartened up. The staff was unusually friendly in the most natural way possible, ie no phrases and mannerisms that might have been taught, but all straightforward and sincere. The *maître d'* was a history buff and gave generously of his knowledge and enthusiasm. The food was of the frumpy English type, well prepared and presented, and, for this American at least, it was a treat to partake of this tradition." *(William Stephens Geffine)*

Open All year.
Rooms 2 suites, 24 double, 14 single – 37 with bath, 1 with shower, all with telephone, radio and colour TV; 5 4-poster beds.
Facilities Lounge, bar, 2 restaurants (one conventional, one in arched basement), small conference facilities. Parking for twenty cars. Large abbey gardens opposite.
Location Central (front rooms can be noisy). Parking.
Restrictions Not really suitable for &, nor young children. No dogs in restaurant; in rooms at discretion.
Credit cards All major cards accepted.
Terms [1985 rates] single rooms £39, double £46-£56; suite £66. Light breakfast £3, English breakfast £5; full alc £19. Special weekend rates. Reduced rates and special meals for children at management's discretion.

CALNE Wiltshire   Map 2

Chilvester Hill House   *Tel* Calne (0249) 813981/815785
Calne SN11 0LP

Last year we had a Calne entry for *Chilvester Lodge*, which has since closed. *Chilvester Hill House* is a similar country home "hotel" operation, 50 yards from the former *Lodge*, run by John and Gill Dilley. The house is a spacious Victorian mansion in seven acres, close to (but out of earshot of) the A4. When not entertaining their guests, Dr Dilley, recently retired from BP in Kuwait, does consultancies and Mrs Dilley breeds beef cattle. Correspondents speak warmly of the hospitality of the house – the spacious comfortable rooms, the silver, good glass, polished antiques and Mrs Dilley's excellent home cooking. "It has the best atmosphere and the most meticulous cooking of any new place I have visited in England for at least ten years." *(Maggie Clarke; also Alan Seward, A R Bradbury, B H G Sparrow)*

Open All year, except a week off-season (autumn or spring).
Rooms 3 double – all with bathroom, colour TV, tea-making facilities and baby-listening.
Facilities Drawing room, sitting room with TV, dining room. 2½-acre grounds with swimming pool; also 5 acres used for cattle; golf and riding locally.
Location ½ m W of Calne; take A4 towards Chippenham, after ½ m take the right turn signposted Bremhill and immediately turn right into the drive marked by gateposts with stone lions.
Restrictions Not suitable for &. No children under 12. No dogs.
Credit card Amex.
Terms B&B: single occupancy £23, double £36. Set dinner £10.50–£15; packed lunches or pool snacks available. Reductions for stays of a week or more.

CAMBRIDGE Cambridgeshire   Map 2

May View Guest House   *Tel* Cambridge (0223) 66018
12 Park Parade, Cambridge CB5 8AL

A pretty six-bedroomed Victorian B&B establishment in a quiet position overlooking Jesus Green and the River Cam, and only a few minutes' walk from the town centre and the colleges. Bedrooms are attractively decorated, likewise the breakfast room. The house has been in Roger Stock's family for more than half a century. He tells us that, as there is no space for a guests' lounge, he has made a point of giving rooms antique furniture and paintings so as to make visitors feel they are in their own home. "The pervading atmosphere", we said last year, in introducing *May View*, "is one of goodwill and unobtrusive comfort" – a view endorsed by *Sheila Mathieson* and *Gerhard Cohn; also Margaret Jones.*

Open All year except Christmas/New Year.
Rooms 5 double, 1 single; radio and mono TV on request.
Location Overlooking Jesus Green and river. Multi-storey car park 1 min away.
Restrictions Not suitable for &. No children under 7. No dogs.
Credit cards None accepted.
Terms B&B: single £12–£14, double £18–£24. (No restaurant.)
Service/tipping: "I discourage tipping unless the housekeeper has done washing, ironing or shopping, and only then would I approve."

CANTERBURY Kent   Map 2

Cathedral Gate Hotel   *Tel* Canterbury (0227) 464381/462800
32a Burgate CT1 2HA   *Telex* 965010 CGHLEN G

A regular correspondent recommends a modest bed-and-breakfast establishment, adjoining the ancient cathedral gate, which is said to have been used by Canterbury pilgrims since the days of Chaucer: "It could not be more central, but absolutely quiet: the only sounds are the cathedral bells and the birds. My room was on the cathedral side, and you could see the cathedral rooftops by peering out – a beautiful sight at night when floodlit. I had a really quite large twin-bedded room with my own WC and shower for £14.50 [1985]. You can't get much cheaper. And it is a nice, freshly painted, well-staffed hotel, not a dump." (Mrs M D Prodgers) More reports welcome.

Open All year, except Christmas and Boxing Day.
Rooms 21 double, 4 single – 4 with bath, 3 with shower, all with radio and tea-making facilities.
Facilities Lounge, TV lounge; breakfast served in guests' rooms.
Location Central; hotel is built in to cathedral precinct wall. Enter from ring road and top of Burgate (access only). 6-minute walk to parking place.
Restrictions Not suitable for &. No dogs.
Credit cards All major cards accepted.
Terms. (No service charge) B&B: single £16, double £28. (No restaurant.)

CARTMEL Cumbria   Map 4

Aynsome Manor Hotel [GFG]   *Tel* Cartmel (044 854) 276
Cartmel
Nr Grange-over-Sands LA11 6HH

Cartmel, though in the Lake District National Park, is away from the main tourist throng, four miles to the south of the foot of Windermere and a couple of miles inland from Grange-over-Sands (on the sea, but poor beaches). You will need a car to get into fell-walking country, but Cartmel is not without tranquil attractions of its own: its Priory Church should not be missed. *Aynsome Manor* is a handsome Georgian manor, once owned by the Earl of Pembroke and fairly recently acquired by Tony and Margaret Varley, who appear to be making a good job of restoring what had become a run-down hotel to the standards of elegance the house deserves. Much rewiring and redecorating has gone on since an inspector reported critically of his accommodation last year. Recent guests like the feel of the place: "The Varleys treat their guests in just the right way." The dining room with a fine ceiling, candle-lit, good silver and crystal, decent paintings, is mentioned in several reports. Correspondents appreciate the cooking, too, though one reported with some diffidence that the pride of the restaurant, the sweet trolley, rather overdid things with its Lucullan helpings and its cream piled on cream. But in general readers have welcomed back a beautifully peaceful country house hotel, once more in good hands. (*Robert C Sim, Eric Fricker, Herbert Lindenberger*)

Open All year except 2–23 Jan.
Rooms 12 double, 1 single – 10 with bath, 1 with shower, some with radio and colour TV. 2 rooms in annexe.
Facilities Reception, lounge, TV lounge, residents' lounge, cocktail bar, dining room, conference facilities. ¾-acre grounds. Sea 2 m, outdoor salt-water pool at Grange 2 m, lake bathing at Windermere 4 m.
Location Leave M6 at exit 36, follow A590 to Barrow for 10 m, turn left at sign for Cartmel; hotel is 2 m along on left (2 m from Grange-over-Sands).
Restrictions Not suitable for &. No children under 5 in dining room at dinner. No dogs in public rooms.
Credit cards Access, Amex, Visa.
Terms (Service optional) B&B: £27–£29.50. Set lunch £6.25, dinner £11. Winter weekend and mid-week breaks. Reduced rates for children sharing parents' room; high tea 5–6 pm.

Deadlines: nominations for the 1987 edition should reach us not later than 15 May 1986. Latest date for comments on existing entries: 30 June 1986.

Uplands Hotel [GFG]   *Tel* Cartmel (044 854) 248
Haggs Lane, Cartmel
Grange-over-Sands LA11 6HD

A transformation! Not at all like the *Uplands* that appeared last year, but a brand-new hotel, opened March 1985, that will be instantly familiar to keen hotel-watchers as an offspring of John Tovey's *Miller Howe*, with Tovey himself in partnership with Tom and Di Peter, formerly for many years chef and receptionist respectively at the famous Windermere establishment. *Uplands*, "in the Miller Howe Manner" as it says on the notepaper and menus, both in typography and in content, follows the maestro's baton; even the position – on rising ground with a view – is similar. But *Uplands* has only four rooms, and though it has a pleasant outlook towards Morecambe Bay estuary, lacks the dramatic prospect of Windermere and the high fells. The decor, too, is different: pale pastel colours on the walls and in the furnishings. The prices are decidedly modest for all that the Peters offer in the way of dependable comfort and exciting cooking. The editor, visiting the house within a few months of its opening, was much impressed with the whole set-up.

Open All year except Jan.
Rooms 4 double – 1 with bath, 3 with shower, all with telephone and colour TV.
Facilities Lounge, dining room. 2-acre garden. Golf nearby. Short drive to Windermere.
Location Leave M6 at exit 36 into Grange – past the railway station and gardens on left, up hill to Crown Hotel. Bear right then go straight across cross-road into Grange Fell Road. Proceed up hill, past golf course on right. At T-junction take right for Cartmel. *Uplands* is on this road on right.
Restrictions Not suitable for &. No children under 12. No dogs in public rooms.
Credit cards None accepted.
Terms (Excluding 10% service) dinner, B&B £30–£40. Set lunch £8, dinner £14. 3-night breaks Sun–Thur in spring and autumn.

CHADLINGTON Oxfordshire   Map 2

Chadlington House   *Tel* Chadlington (060 876) 437
Chadlington OX7 3LZ

A modest country house hotel in a tiny Oxfordshire village. "Delightfully quiet, with large, flowery garden, comfortable Victorian interior. And, most importantly, at affordable prices. Charming, friendly host and hostess, the Oxfords, who obviously care about their guests. Lounge and separate bar – reasonable prices for a short but rewarding wine list. Food is plain but interesting (if that's not a contradiction), English style: fresh asparagus Mornay, grapefruit with crème de menthe starters; steak and mushroom pie, chicken suprême with nicely cooked fresh vegetables; good choice of sweets. There are plenty of bathrooms and lavatories if your room is one of those without. It is a very comfortable small hotel, run by people who are experienced in the business, and really care about their guests." (*J C and M A Godfrey*)

Last year's entry is endorsed enthusiastically by visitors from California: "Rita and Peter Godfrey know how to run a hotel perfectly: their guests' concerns are their concerns; they are intelligent, kind, considerate and have a marvellous sense of humour. The hotel is a small-scale show-place: the rooms are lovely, spotless and, above all, romantic." (*Joanne Kinsey-Calori*)

Open Feb–Dec. Closed Christmas.
Rooms 1 suite with 4-poster, 7 double, 2 single – 3 with bath, 5 with shower, all with radio, colour TV, tea-making facilities and baby-listening.
Facilities Lounge, coffee lounge, bar, dining room. Small garden. Good centre for visiting Cotswolds, Woodstock, Oxford and Stratford-upon-Avon.
Location In village between Chipping Norton and Burford. From A34 take B4022. Parking.
Restrictions Not suitable for &. No children under 8. No dogs.
Credit cards Access, Visa.
Terms (No service charge) B&B: single £15–£25, double £35–£55; dinner, B&B: single, £23.50–£33.50, double £46–£75. Set dinner £9.50 and £12.50. 2-day winter breaks. Reduced rates and special meals for children.

CHAGFORD Devon   Map 1

Gidleigh Park Hotel [GFG]   *Tel* Chagford (064 73) 2367 or 2225
Chagford TQ13 8HH

Paul Henderson was new to the hotel business when in 1978 he bought this substantial stockbroker's Tudor country house in 40 acres of gardens and woods on the edge of Dartmoor, but he and his wife Kay served an interesting novitiate by first staying in all but three of the triple-rosetted *Michelin* restaurants in France. From the start, the Hendersons set their targets high, their aim to create in a position of great natural beauty a comprehensive sybaritic experience, with the luxurious furnishings of a spacious house complemented by an outstanding restaurant (under chef John Webber) and an exceptional (400 plus bins) wine list. Their achievement is considerable, and every year's crop of reports bring in expressions of unstinted gratitude. Moreover, we are impressed with Paul Henderson's restless search for improvements and innovations. This year, in addition to the usual round of refurbishments, he has installed a Cruvinet machine – the first, he tells us, outside London – which enables fine wines to be served by the glass. He has also pioneered throughout the winter months a series of five-day walking holidays, for £500 a couple, inclusive of dinners, wines, transport around the Moor and guides – a huge success with one correspondent, who had had the usual misgivings about joining a group but was already planning to sign up for another, along with four of the five couples who were of her party.

It is a pity that we can't leave it there. But this year, as last, there have been negative notes mixed with the compliments. Many of the complaints relate to value for money, especially in relation to the meals and to a back room deprived of a view. There have also been many small niggles about one thing or another – more than one would have expected in a hotel in this price range – and about lack of warmth in the welcome. It is difficult to find a consensus, but we end with a report from someone who listed four or five details that had disappointed him, but ended: "Nevertheless, we shall certainly go back. One of the many nice things about this essentially comfortable and pleasant hotel is the willingness and ability of the staff – chef, waitresses and stewards – to talk intelligently about the hotel, their work and the dishes they were serving; there was no profession of secrecy, no us and you."

Open All year.
Rooms 12 double – all with bath, telephone and colour TV.

Facilities Front hall, large lounge, bar loggia, 2 dining rooms. 40-acre grounds and gardens with croquet lawn and grass tennis court. North Teign river 50 yds in front of house; 14 m of trout, sea trout and salmon fishing. Golf, riding and walking nearby.
Location Approach from Chagford, *not* Gidleigh. Take the M4 or M5, then the A30 to Whiddon Down. Then go to Chagford. From Chagford Square facing Webbers with Lloyds Bank on right, turn right into Mill Street. After 200 yds fork right and go downhill to Factory Crossroad. Go straight across into Holy Street and follow lane 1½ m to end.
Restrictions Not suitable for &. No dogs in public rooms.
Credit card Amex.
Terms (Excluding VAT) B&B (continental): double £60–£110. Set lunch £15, dinner £23.50 (including 25p cover charge per meal, donated to World Wildlife Fund). 5-day winter walking holidays.

Thornworthy House [GFG] *Tel* Chagford (064 73) 3297
Chagford TQ13 8EY

A warm welcome back to *Thornworthy House*, in the Guide from 1979 to 1984, but omitted last year after a change of ownership. Our substantial dossier on *Thornworthy* this year makes it clear that Cindy and John Cull are worthy successors to the Jacksons. This hotel/guest-house, despite its address, is three miles out of Chagford, down many a twisting lane to the very edge of Dartmoor – a place of exceptional tranquillity. It is an utterly different kind of establishment to *Gidleigh Park* above, but among the tributes to the Culls came one from Paul Henderson of *Gidleigh*, who has been busy sending overflow business there after dining anonymously. Two "elderly, rather shaky ladies" found "every consideration . . . We really felt wanted and welcomed." Another report spoke of the welcome to children who were given the run of the Cull's big family playroom. "A lovely relaxed undemanding place for undemanding people needing relaxation," wrote another. "Few frills but all necessities." Other compliments: "Excellent home cooking like no one tends to cook for every day and everything beautifully served . . . Breakfasts truly gargantuan . . . Really well heated . . . Big fluffy bathrobes . . ." and much more to the same effect. Our own inspector summed up: "It is certainly more than a guest-house, even though its size and the absence of a formal bar may not qualify it to be called a country house hotel. It remains a find, however classified." (*Mrs I E Bell, D Bennett, Joan Williamson, Josephine Meakin, Graham Andrews, Mrs O J G Shelley, Jean Oliver*)

Open All year except Jan and Feb.
Rooms 4 double, 2 single – 4 with bath, all with TV, tea-making facilities and baby-listening. 2 self-catering cottages.
Facilities Drawing room, playroom, garden room, dining room; 2-acre grounds, tennis court, bicycles available for hire; fly fishing in nearby reservoir (daily permits available).
Location 3 m from Chagford; from Chagford follow signs to Kestor and Fernworthy, then follow signs to Thornworthy – then hotel.
Restrictions No dogs in public rooms.
Credit cards None accepted.
Terms B&B: £16–£17; dinner, B&B: £24–£25. Set dinner £9.50. 3-day mid-week breaks available except Jul–Sept, Easter and Whitsun. Self-catering cottages available with facility to eat in the hotel and use outdoor amenities. Reduced rates for children sharing parents' room; special meals on request.

CHAGFORD see also FRENCHBEER

CHARTHAM HATCH Kent   Map 2

Howfield Manor   *Tel* Canterbury (0227) 738294
Chartham Hatch
Canterbury CT4 7HQ

The eastern corner of Kent has been an embarrassingly blank space on our map. *Howfield Manor*, new to the Guide this year, is owned and run by the Lawrences, Clark (who is American) and his wife Janet (English). It could be a luxurious staging post for those *en route* to the Channel ports, but it would also make a centre for touring the area: Canterbury is two miles up the road, Leeds and Bodiam castles and many other tourist attractions are within easy driving distance. An inspector found all the prospects pleasing: "Amazingly beautiful . . . *Manor* is the right word for it – gabled red-brick, parts dating back to the 12th century, a monk's well, the outline of a Gothic chapel window, beams and enormous ingle-nook fireplaces, candlelight glimmering on antique furniture, the unaffectedly friendly welcome of the owners – all this contributes to the most notable feature of this hotel, its atmosphere. The bedroom accommodation is luxurious. The cooking is straightforward in its style, relying on good ingredients." It is a relaxed friendly sort of place. Guests sit family-style in the beamed dining room and pour their own drinks in the bar. Meals – their four-course set menu warmly recommended by our nominator – can be taken out of doors in fine weather. (*Charles Dewhurst*)

Open Mid-Jan–mid-Dec. Dinner by prior arrangement only.
Rooms 5 double – 3 with bath, 2 with shower, all with telephone.
Facilities Sitting room, library with TV, dining rooms. 5-acre gardens. Golf, tennis, cricket, swimming nearby.
Restrictions Not suitable for &. No children under 8. No dogs.
Location 2 m outside Canterbury on the A28 Ashford road.
Credit cards Access, Amex, Visa.
Terms B&B: single £25–£43, double £30–£50. Winter breaks 1 Nov–15 Mar. Set dinner £13.
Service/tipping: "We do not allow tipping, but since Howfield Manor *is run by us, it's an easily enforced rule."*

CHEDINGTON Dorset   Map 1

Chedington Court [GFG]   *Tel* Corscombe (093 589) 265
Chedington
Nr Beaminster DT8 3HY

"My husband and I have just returned from a two-week visit to Devon and Cornwall and both agree that, of all the hotels we stayed in (including *Ston Easton* and *The Castle*, Taunton [both q.v.]), *Chedington Court* was the best ever. Our bedroom (Dorset) was huge, our bathroom very large, both having magnificent views of the countryside and every possible comfort inside. The house is pervaded by a sense of efficient tranquillity and I can't think of a better place to get away from it all. As if the atmosphere weren't enough, the food and service were wonderful, and all such good value" *(Patricia J Sonin)*. The best of this year's crop, though the comments from *David Nutt* and *Joan Powell* were similar in spirit. *Chedington Court* is a splendid, fairly formal 1840 country house hotel in the Jacobean style, set high up in the Dorset hills, in ten acres of beautiful gardens, and with panoramic views over the Dorset countryside. Regrettably, as last year, there continues to be an opposition view – that the house lacks warmth, both literally and metaphorically, and that some things are not quite *comme il faut* for an establishment of this kind – UHT milk for tea-making, for instance, or the fittings in some of the rooms. On the warmth question, a reader comments: "Mr Chapman is extremely attentive, but somewhat retiring. He is not the genial 'mine host' type, and the hotel is not run on that sort of basis – from our point of view it was just what we wanted. Obviously, the house *is* difficult to keep warm, but there was always a big fire in the comfortable library, and our own bedroom, though vast, was always warm." In view of the lack of consensus, we should be glad to hear from other visitors.

Open All year except Christmas, 3 weeks Jan/Feb, 1 week in spring, 1 week in Aug.
Rooms 8 double – all with bath, telephone, radio, colour TV and tea-making facilities; 1 4-poster bed; baby-listening available.
Facilities Drawing room, library, bar, billiards room, dining room, conservatory. 10-acre garden with croquet and putting; golf, bird-watching, fishing nearby; coast 10 m.
Location ¼ m off A356 at Winyard's Gap, 4½ m SE of Crewkerne.
Restrictions Not suitable for &. Preferably no children under 6. Dogs discouraged.
Credit card Amex.
Terms Dinner, B&B: £35–£52 for stays of 2 nights or more (£10 extra per room for 1 night only); B&B only, 20% less. Set dinner £17.50. Winter breaks 1 Nov–24 Mar excluding Christmas and New Year. Reduced rates and special meals for children. *Service/tipping: "All prices include service and no tipping is expected."*

CHELSWORTH Suffolk   Map 2

The Peacock Inn   *Tel* Bildeston (0449) 740758
The Street
Chelsworth, Ipswich IP7 7HU

"The Peacock *does not pretend to be anything grander than it is – a country pub, dating back to the 14th century, with rooms. The rooms were charming – low-beamed, furnished individually with stripped pine furniture – it reminded me of* At the Sign of the Angel, Lacock *(q.v.), when we first went there 20 years ago. The (shared) bathrooms were spotlessly clean, as were the rooms, and there was plenty of hot water. Breakfast was excellent (home-cured bacon) and plentiful. Dinner was a mixture of good pub grub and good home cooking, served in the bar – very pleasant and generous. Many locals eating – a good sign. Cheap (and every penny well spent) and very pleasant."* (Clarissa Turner) *More reports please.*

Open All year except Christmas.
Rooms 4 double, 1 single – all with h & c, radio, colour TV and tea-making facilities.
Facilities Lounges, bar, dining room. Live music on Fri night. Small garden.

Location Near River Brett. Between villages of Monks Eleigh and Bildeston. Take B1115 Sudbury to Stowmarket road.
Restrictions Not suitable for &. No children under 10. No dogs.
Credit cards None accepted.
Terms (Service at guests' discretion) B&B: single £14.50, double £28. Set lunch £5–£6; full alc £8–£9 (excluding wine).

CHELTENHAM Gloucestershire   Map 2

Prestbury House Hotel   *Tel* Cheltenham (0242) 529533 and
The Burgage, Prestbury   30106
Cheltenham GL2 3DZ

A well-bred 18th-century house two miles from the town centre of Cheltenham and close to the racecourse. There's nothing flash about the establishment (except that more than one of the bathrooms have jacuzzis); its standards are old-fashioned in the complimentary sense. Rooms are unusually large and airy, but are properly heated when the weather is inclement; the furnishings are conservative but well appointed. The food served in the fine Regency dining room is unashamedly English in style, but excellent of its kind, with a genuine care for ingredients. The dedication of the owners, Mr and Mrs Gorrie, to run a good hotel is shown in many small ways: in the fresh fruit, shortbread and orange juice provided in the rooms, not to mention hair dryers and electric trouser presses; in the servicing of bedrooms and supply of new towels while guests are dining; in the generous flower arrangements; in the pleasant professionalism of the staff. (*N McNamara; F & I W*)

Open All year except bank holidays, 1 week at Christmas and 4 days at Easter.
Rooms 9 double, 1 single – 8 with bath (some with jacuzzi), all with telephone, colour TV and tea-making facilities.
Facilities Lounge, bar, restaurant, panelled oak room available for private functions. 2-acre garden; good base for touring the Cotswolds. & restaurant only.
Restriction No dogs in public rooms.
Location From Cheltenham take the A435 as far as the roundabout at the racecourse; turn right; the Burgage is the second turning on the left.
Credit cards None accepted.
Terms B&B single; £31.63, double £43. Set lunch £13.15, dinner £13.47; full alc £22.50 Reduced rates and special meals for children.

CHICHESTER West Sussex   Map 2

Clinchs' Hotel   *Tel* Chichester (0243) 789915
Guildhall Street
Chichester PO19 1NJ

Patrons of theatre festivals often look for a civilised hotel in the vicinity, in preference to a long drive home or a flash motel. *Clinchs'* – so called because Daphne and Tom Clinch are the resident owners – is an elegant town house in a small quiet street adjoining Priory Park and no more than 300 yards from the Festival Theatre. You can park just behind the hotel. Actors often stay: "up-market theatrical digs" was one description given to us. Chichester is a most attractive town anyway, and *Clinchs'* is right in the middle of the area one would want to explore.

Open All year except Christmas. Restaurant closed after breakfast on Sun.
Rooms 6 double – 3 with bath, 3 with shower, all with telephone, radio, tea-making facilities and safe.
Facilities Lounge bar, restaurant. Parking for 8 cars.
Location In town centre adjoining Priory Walk; 300 yds from Festival Theatre. Car park at rear (approach from Priory Road).
Restrictions Not suitable for &. No children under 12. No dogs.
Credit cards All major cards accepted.
Terms (Excluding 10% service charge) [1985 rates] B&B: single £37.50, double £49.50. Set dinner £12.

CHIPPING CAMPDEN Gloucestershire   Map 2

Kings Arms Hotel   *Tel* Evesham (0386) 840256
Market Square
Chipping Campden GL55 6AW

"An idyllic combination of old-fashioned atmosphere and service with modern comfort and convenience. I can't imagine a more restful place to enjoy a long weekend, and I spent the rest of my trip to England trying to figure out how to get back here." Thus an American enthusiast adds her tribute to this rightly popular hotel in the centre of a delectable town – the quintessence of Cotswold beauty – beside the old Market Square. (Warning: front rooms can be noisy.) It is made up of two adjoining buildings – one Georgian, the other 17th-century, both stone-built, with a pleasant garden. The interior prospect pleases as much as the outside one. It has lots of character: great open fires, winding staircases, some good pieces of furniture. It isn't one of those well-heeled Cotswold hotels, with TV, radio-clocks and tea-making facilities in the bedrooms; only two of the bedrooms have their own bathrooms, and bedroom lighting could be improved. But in other important aspects, the *Kings Arms* scores heavily: it has a first-rate restaurant, also serves outstandingly good bar lunches (in the garden when the weather is suitable, except on Sundays) and generally exudes a sense of cheerful welcome. (*Suzanne Martin; also Neil French, A R Bridbury, Maria Birch*)

Open All year.
Rooms 2 suites, 4 double, 8 single – 2 with bath.
Facilities Sitting room, bar, dining room,½-acre garden (bar meals there in summer). Golf courses nearby; horse racing during spring.
Location Central, in Market Square. Parking.
Restrictions Not suitable for &. No dogs in public rooms. Credit cards All major
Credit cards All major cards accepted.
Terms B&B: single £20, double £24. Bar lunches £1-£4.50, set dinner, £11.50; full alc £17. Winter breaks Nov-Mar. Reduced rates for children.

CHITTLEHAMHOLT Devon   Map 1

Highbullen Hotel [GFG]   *Tel* Chittlehamholt (076 94) 561
Chittlehamholt
Umberleigh EX37 9HD

Highbullen returned to these columns last year, after an interval, with the following commendation from *Frank Muir*: "Hugh and Pam Neil bought this large country house in Devon overlooking a valley with spectacular views, and steadily worked it up into a most comfortable and wholly individual country house hotel which is now much enjoyed by regulars, who appreciate its restfulness. Only 30 bedrooms, but two small, but delightful, heated indoor and outdoor swimming pools, jacuzzi, squash court, tennis court, nine-hole golf course (designed and built by Mr Neil with some fiendish holes, I am told by a golfer), herd of deer, and so on. We found a Norwegian diplomat and his wife wandering around the hall trying to find a reception desk. There is no reception desk. No waiters. No room service. Your room is cleaned by fairies while you are eating breakfast. It is like staying at rich friends' houses without any obligation at all to your host. There is only a snack lunch but a superb candle-lit dinner. This is an un-hotel-like hotel, run, very personally and efficiently, by its owners, and it might very well not be to your taste. In which case you will hate it. For those of us who like this sort of retreat it is quite superb."

Regulars have been quick to welcome its return. One, on her third visit, felt the food wasn't as good as it had been, though everything else was, including the outstanding wine list. Another, on his seventh visit, remarked that the food was good, but never changed from year to year. He ended: "Lovely place. Home from home." A third wrote: "Our fifth visit: we are ever more enamoured of its charms, and seriously wonder why we ever bother going anywhere else. Frank Muir's report leaves little to say except 'Hear, hear!' – and we don't know how they do it at the price." *(Richard and Carol Thomas, Gillian Seel, J J & C L Lovejoy, and others)*

Open All year.
Rooms 28 double, 3 single – all with bath, shower, telephone, TV and tea-making facilities; 18 rooms in converted farmhouse and cottages; some ground-floor rooms, mostly in annexe.
Facilities 2 lounges, bar with small dance floor, dining room, billiard room, hairdressing and massage facilities; indoor tennis court. 50-acre grounds with 6-acre garden, 9-hole golf course, deer park, tennis and squash courts, croquet lawn, putting green, sauna, sunbed, spa bath, exercise room. 1 indoor and 2 outdoor heated swimming pools. Fishing in River Mole ½ m.
Location Leave M5 at exit 27 – on to A373; at South Molton take B3225 for 5 m, then take right turn to Chittlehamholt; go through village for 500 yards to hotel.
Restrictions Not suitable for &. No children under 10. No dogs.
Credit cards None accepted.
Terms B & continental B: single £21.50, double £33–£47; dinner, B&B: single £32, double £50–£64. Set dinner £10.50; light lunches available. Midweek breaks Nov–Mar. Reduced rates for children sharing parents' room.

CIRENCESTER Gloucestershire   Map 2

The Fleece Hotel [GFG]   *Tel* Cirencester (0285) 68507
Market Place, Cirencester GL7 4NZ

A fine old coaching-inn, part half-timbered Tudor and part Georgian, centrally placed in one of the most attractive townscapes in the Cotswolds, enjoys a fresh lease of life under new management, who aim to provide high-quality French cooking (gastronomic festivals are a feature of *The Fleece*'s calendar) in a thoroughly comfortable English hostelry. One side of the entrance offers a traditional English reception, with plush carpeting, framed tapestries and 18th-century landscape paintings, and log fires in ingle-nooks; the other has a sawdust-floored wine bar, much favoured by locals for the good-value lunches. Rooms have been elegantly refurbished with all the mod. cons., in the way of hair dryers, trouser presses and the like, to be expected. *(E M Barsham, I W)*

Open All year except 24–26 Dec.
Rooms 2 suites, 18 double, 1 single – all with bath, direct-dial telephone, radio, colour TV and tea-making facilities.
Facilities Lounge, bar, wine bar, dining room. Courtyard.
Location Central: follow signs to town centre. Parking.
Restrictions Not suitable for &. No dogs in public rooms.
Credit cards All major cards accepted.
Terms (Service at guests' discretion) B&B £21–£22.75; half board £30.45–£32.20. Set lunch £7.50, dinner £9.45; full alc £16.85. Weekend breaks. Gastronomic festivals. Reduced rates for children sharing parents' room.

CLIMPING West Sussex   Map 2

Bailiffscourt Hotel   *Tel* Littlehampton (0903) 723511
Climping   *Telex* 877870 BLFSCT
Nr Littlehampton BN17 5RW

"The most genuine fake in England" changed hands recently, and is now personally managed by Mr and Mrs Lamming instead of being part of a small group. *Bailiffscourt* is a highly convincing wholly bogus medieval manor, five miles east of Bognor Regis, built 50 years ago at fabulous cost to satisfy a caprice of the late Lord Moyne. It is built almost entirely from genuine bits of old houses. It has other national endowments apart from its ancient stones: its secluded tranquil 23 acres, with a swimming pool, two hard tennis courts, not to mention a helipad; it is only 400 yards by private path to a stretch of unspoilt coast. First reports of the new régime are decidely encouraging. The staff are said to be as friendly and helpful as ever, and the cooking a decided improvement. We also liked this note from Fiona Lamming: "Since my husband and I took over the management of *Bailiffscourt*, it has been our strict personal policy to ensure that we spend at least one night in each bedroom. In some cases we try to spend two or three nights consecutively, to get the 'feel' of being a guest. We are more than aware of any short-comings our rooms may have; little niggles can be corrected immediately and major problems (eg the noisy plumbing) are then highlighted for our long-term plans. We also encourage our reception staff, in particular, to take advantage of guest rooms when available, and report their comments to us. Ideally, we would like every member of staff to experience the other side of the proverbial coin, and see things from the guests' point of view."

Open All year.
Rooms 4 suites, 12 double, 4 single – all with bath, direct-dial telephone, radio and colour TV; some with 4-posters; tea-making facilities in 2 suites. 4 ground-floor rooms in annexe.
Facilities 2 lounges, cocktail bar, restaurant, 3 private dining rooms/conference rooms. Guitarist/harpist in restaurant on Sat night. Barbecues, medieval banquets etc. by arrangement. Courtyard. 23-acre grounds with 2 hard tennis courts, unheated swimming pool, sauna, solarium and helipad. 400 yds by private path to coast with safe sandy bathing at low tide. Golf nearby.
Location 1 m W of Littlehampton, just S of A259.
Restrictions Not suitable for &. Children under 10 by prior arrangement.

Credit cards All major cards accepted.
Terms B&B: single £50–£60, double £80–£140. Set lunch £9, dinner £14.50; full alc £24. Mid-week breaks New Year to Easter. Christmas programme.

COATHAM MUNDEVILLE Durham   Map 4

Hall Garth Country House Hotel [GFG]   *Tel* Aycliffe (0325) 313333
Coatham Mundeville DL1 3LU

A genuine country house hotel in a part of the country poorly served by hotels of character. It is a rambling, attractive old mansion, parts dating from 1540, with Georgian and Victorian extensions, in 11 acres of grounds with a heated outdoor pool, tennis court and other amenities. Since last year, all bedrooms have been given a bath or shower *en suite*. Owners are Ernest Williamson and Janice Crocker and this year, as before, readers have appreciated their friendly hospitality, sometimes extending well beyond the call of hostly duties. The hotel prides itself on its restaurant, but, also as in the past, there have been some reluctant grumbles about individual dishes. For some, however, *Hall Garth* can do no wrong: "Top marks here – welcome, service, furnishings, food, wine all excellent, and the proprietors have just the right touch, friendly but not too much so." *(Richard O Whiting)*

Open 2 Jan–24 Dec (closed May Day Mon). Restaurant closed Sun night.
Rooms 2 suites, 13 double, 6 single – 15 with bath, 6 with shower, all with telephone, radio, colour TV and tea-making facilities; 4 4-poster beds, 11 rooms in annexe.
Facilities 3 lounges, dining room in main building, public bar (with TV), lounges in annexe. 11-acre gardens with tennis court, putting, croquet, and children's play area; heated swimming pool, sauna.
Location ½ m E of A1, 3½ m N of Darlington. Leave A1 at A167 junction, go towards Darlington, take first left at brow of hill signposted Brafferton; *Hall Garth* is 200 yds down the road.
Restrictions Only restaurant suitable for &. No dogs in public rooms.
Credit cards All major cards accepted.
Terms (No service charge) B&B (continental): single £31, double £42. English breakfast £3.25; set 2-course lunch £6.95, 4-course dinner £11.95; bar lunches also available; full alc £17. Weekend rates: 25% discount on normal rates for 2 nights; honeymoon breaks. Reduced rates for children sharing parents' room; special meals on request.

COGGESHALL Essex   Map 2

The White Hart [GFG]   *Tel* Coggeshall (0376) 61654
Coggeshall CO6 1NH

In appearance, as fine an example of an old inn as one could ask for: on the old Roman road from Verulamium (St Albans) to Camulodonum (Colchester) and once a Guildhall, it has been in the hostelry business since 1489, was a prosperous coaching-inn in the early 19th century, and has had a new lease of life in the past ten years, after restoration by Raymond Pluck. The residents' lounge, part of the old Guildhall, with its original sweet chestnut beams and large brick fireplace, is a show-piece feature. Today, it is a decidedly up-market establishment: an enormous and pricey menu (no table d'hôte), a huge wine list soaring to the giddy heights of a bottle of their finest Château d'Yquem at £325, though there are also plenty of good wines at the lower end of the scale. Rooms are expensive, too, though a lot of trouble and money had been invested in making them pretty as well as comfortable. It's a place with panache, perhaps a bit flash for some tastes, though it is clearly popular with the local business community. Some visitors recently, however, have reported wrinkles in the service – touches of condescension too – and some defects in the housekeeping. More reports please.*(N D Bruce, Bill and Betty St Leger Moore)*

Open All year except Aug and New Year. Restaurant closed Fri and Sun evenings (but room service menu available at these times).
Rooms 16 double, 2 single – 14 with bath, 4 with shower; all with direct-dial telephone, radio and colour TV.
Facilities Residents' lounge, TV room, cocktail bar, restaurant, breakfast room; private dining/conference room. Small garden.
Location In town centre (back rooms are quietest).
Restrictions Not suitable for &. No dogs.
Credit cards All major cards accepted.
Terms (No service charge) B&B: single £35, double £50. Set Sun lunch (book in advance) £9.50; full alc £17.50–£20. Smaller portions for children.

COLYFORD Devon   Map 1

The Old Manor Hotel   *Tel* Colyton (0297) 52862
Colyford, Colyton EX13 6QQ

A hotel new to us is recommended to the Guide by a regular contributor in the following terms: "I think palace-type hotels (in which surely only those on expense accounts can afford to stay) are over-represented in the Guide. This is a very well done, medium-small one, serene and comfortable, so that it seems more like a friendly private house than a hotel, in an exceptionally pleasant thatched 15th-century building. It also has delicious food and that particular air of being personally cared for by the sympathetic family owners, Neil and Judith Sarginson, which company-run hotels cannot begin to match. If guests want a contrast to the haven-like peace of the hotel, there is close by the wild Undercliff walk along the coast to Lyme Regis – an extraordinary 'lost world' caused by a huge landslip." *(Ben Whitaker)* More reports please.

Open Feb–Oct and Christmas.
Rooms 10 double, 1 single – 7 with bath, 1 with shower, all with tea-making facilities. 2 ground-floor rooms.
Facilities Lounge, library, bar/dining room. 4-acre garden with tennis court. Shingle beaches, estuary and cliff walks. 1 m. Fly fishing for trout in river; golf nearby.
Location Just off A3052 between Lyme Regis and Sidmouth.
Restriction Dogs not permitted in hotel, but can be accommodated in stables.
Credit cards None accepted.
Terms (No service charge) B&B £14.50–£24.50; dinner, B&B £23–£33. Bar lunches £2.50, set dinner £8.50; full alc £12.50. Off-season rates for stay of min. 2 nights any time up to mid-May (except Easter), and October. Reduced rates and special meals for children.
Service/tipping: "The policy is not to make any charge on the bill. If guests wish to reward extra service they may do so. Any tips are shared pro rata."

Report forms (Freepost in UK) will be found at the end of the Guide.

CONSTANTINE BAY Cornwall   Map 1

Treglos Hotel   *Tel* Padstow (0841) 520727
Padstow PL28 8JH   *Telex* 45795 WSTTLXG TGS

A traditional seaside hotel – but a superior example of its kind – blessed with a choice position overlooking Constantine Bay. Golfers will be glad to know that it is very close to Trevose Golf Club. It is about a quarter of a mile from the sea, and there is of course superb walking along the Cornish Coastal Path. The furnishing is chintzy rather than trendy, and the menus, though they carry French names, are English in conception and execution. It is one of those hotels that have a high return rate – an addictive sort of place. The owners, Ted and Barbara Barlow, are welcoming and "unfailingly helpful". The quality of service is superior: shoes are cleaned, luggage is carried, breakfast, and indeed all meals, can be served in your room if desired.

One visitor this year found the requested jacket and tie for the evening meal irksome during a hot August spell, and also complained of the standard of housekeeping; but his was the only negative note. Other correspondents appreciated especially: the three coal fires, the help-yourself hors d'oeuvre, "the punctual early morning tea with a smile", the generous packed lunches ("if you require two, then one will be sufficient") and "one of the best rooms we have enjoyed in a seaside hotel". *(David St John Thomas, John Pearson)*

Open 14 Mar–5 Nov.
Rooms 4 suites, 32 double, 8 single–all with bath and shower, direct-dial telephone, radio, colour TV and baby-listening; 1 suite on ground floor; 4 self-catering flats in grounds.
Facilities Lift, ramp. 4 lounges, cocktail bar, bridge room, snooker room, coffee lounge, tea lounge, children's den, restaurant. 3-acre garden with croquet, sunken sunbathing gardens, heated enclosed swimming pool; sandy beach (with lifeguard) 300 yds; outdoor pool and golf nearby. Fishing by boat at Padstow.
Location The hotel advises you to avoid Bodmin and Wadebridge and will send directions. (Or, from Padstow, follow signs to St Merryn, then Constantine Bay.)
Restrictions No children under 3 in restaurant. Dogs at discretion, none in public rooms.
Credit cards None accepted.
Terms (No service charge) B&B: £21.50–£33.50; dinner, B&B £28.50–£40.50. Set lunch £6.95, dinner £10.25; full alc £14.25. Reduced rates for stays of 3 days or more; special weekly rate Thur–Thur. Reductions for children sharing parents' room; special meals.

CORSE LAWN Gloucestershire   Map 2

Corse Lawn House [GFG]   *Tel* Tirley (045 278) 479
Corse Lawn GL19 4LZ

This restaurant-with-rooms appeared for the first time in the 1985 edition of the Guide, in italics, following a visit from an inspector; he had found the restaurant side of things in splendid form – excellent cooking, mainly English with French overtones, a reasonable set-price menu and a superb wine list – but with shortcomings on the accommodation front. The house itself, once a coaching-inn, dates from 1745 in the Queen Anne style. There are only four bedrooms, each with a bathroom *en suite*, named after Hine brandies (Old Vintage, Antique, VSOP etc.), large, well equipped and lit, and with plenty of agreeable extras. Denis Hine, proprietor and sprig of the brandy family, tells us that he has been busy with improvements – up-grading most of the soft furnishings and with much new furniture. He hopes to add another six bedrooms and a proper lounge area in the summer of 1986. Meanwhile, reports this year are warm in praise. One mentioned perhaps the best hotel breakfast he had known. Another, possibly under the influence of some of Mr Hine's Old Vintage, wrote: "Be welcomed into the household of the Hines. Stay, eat and be fulfilled! We stayed with them at the *Three Cocks* years ago, and found standards if anything improved. Rooms are more comfortable; food better now, or at least fewer dishes beginning with a quart of heavy cream and a pint of cognac. You can eat as well in the bar as in the dining room. Bar snacks like these should be everywhere! Mr Hine, on request, provided instruction in the higher realms of cognac. Glorious!" (*Lawrence Brown, D H C Hampshire, and others*)

Open All year except 25, 26 Dec. Restaurant closed Sun evening and all day Mon (bar meals available).
Rooms 4 double – all with bath, telephone, radio, colour TV and tea-making facilities.
Facilities Large lounge bar, restaurant. 4-acre grounds.
Location 5 m SW of Tewkesbury. From Tewkesbury, take A438 to Ledbury for 4 m. Turn left (signposted Corse Lawn) on to B4211 and continue for 1 m.
Restrictions Not suitable for &. No dogs in public rooms.
Credit cards All major cards accepted.
Terms (No service charge) B&B £22.50. Set lunch £9.50, dinner £12.75; full alc £20–£26. Reduced rates for children in parents' room; special meals.
Service/tipping: "We make no charge for service, nor do we expect tips."

CRANBROOK Kent   Map 2

Kennel Holt Hotel   *Tel* Cranbrook (0580) 712032
Cranbrook TN1 2PT

A pedigree Elizabethan beamed manor house, 300 yards from the main road in five acres of beautifully tended grounds, with large lawns, pollarded walks and a duck pond; beyond lie the orchards and hopfields of the Weald of Kent. "The exterior oozes charm" and the interior also comes in for much purring: "charming, beamed and spacious, well furnished with period pieces" and log fires "adding to the warmth and welcome". The bedrooms, just seven, also receive commendations – lots of small extras; only Room 7, twin-bedded but lacking cosiness, is a let-down. The resident owners are Patrick and Ruth Cliff; Ruth, who taught for 16 years at a Cordon Bleu residential college, is in charge of the kitchens and admirably practises what she had been teaching in her previous role. "Desserts particularly imaginative." The Cliffs clearly understand the art of running a country house hotel. The one criticism of any substance in our file is the somewhat limited fixed times for meals: breakfast from 8 – 9 a.m. (8.30 – 9.30 on Sundays), and dinner from 7.30 – 8.00 p.m. (*Mrs Patrick Kenadjian, D Jean Yeo, Dr David Clark, Patricia Purvis, Elaine Cole-Shear, Professor S Majaro*)

Open 28 Jan – 31 Dec. Restaurant closed Sun, Mon, Christmas.
Rooms 5 double, 2 single – all with bath, radio, colour TV.
Facilities 2 lounges with open fires, dining room. 5½ acre grounds with croquet lawn; coarse and fly fishing nearby, golf at local club.
Location 2 m NW of Cranbrook on A262.
Restrictions No children under 6; high tea at 6 pm for children under 8. Dogs generally not allowed in public rooms.
Credit cards All major cards accepted but in restaurant only.
Terms (No service charge) B&B £16–29; half-board £28–£45. Set lunch £5, dinner £12. Off-season weekend breaks; 3-day mid-week breaks.

CRANTOCK Cornwall — Map 1

Crantock Bay Hotel   *Tel* Crantock (0637) 830229
Crantock, Newquay TR8 5SE

An addicted regular writes of her latest holiday at this jolly family hotel in a beautiful and absolutely quiet position on the West Pentire headland, facing four-square on to the Atlantic: sandy and rocky beaches, good surfing, caves and pools easily accessible. "We rather unadventurously opted to stay at *Crantock Bay* for the third time this summer for our family summer holiday and were so glad we did. The views which we take in from our bedroom window and the reception rooms stock us up for the year ahead. The position is perfect. The company always seems good, in the summer largely families with children. (We've never been out of season but are told how lovely spring is there.) Activities, all of course voluntary, like table-tennis tournaments, a dance etc., enable guests to get to know each other – but one can also have solitude, especially in the spacious garden with its secluded bays with garden chairs. There are improvements each year like new bathrooms – the food is varied, plentiful fresh and wholesome. The hotel is spotless and the service outstanding. There is good surfing (the hotel lends its plentiful supply of surf boards), lovely walks along the National Trust headland; an ideal family holiday hotel catering for all ages." *(Susan Riches; also J M Fox)*

Open End Mar – end Oct.
Rooms 20 double, 10 single – 27 with bath, 1 with shower, all with radio, colour TV, tea-making facilities and baby-listening; 1 ground-floor room suitable for partially &.
Facilities Lounge, TV room, bar, games room, restaurant; dancing, table tennis, bar billiards (competitions held), slide shows, children's parties 2-3 nights a week. 4½-acre grounds with putting green, croquet, children's play area. Sea with sandy beach and safe bathing (lifeguard service) 200 yds from hotel, reached through grounds; tennis, riding, golf nearby.
Location On West Pentire headland, 1 m beyond Crantock; 5 m SW of Newquay. Guests met by arrangement at Newquay and Truro stations.
Restrictions Not suitable for &. No dogs in public rooms.
Credit card Visa.
Terms (No service charge) dinner, B&B: single £16–£22, double £32–£44. Bar lunch from £1, set dinner £7.25. Bargain breaks Mar – May and Oct. Reduced rates for children sharing parents' room; special meals.

If you have had recent experience of a good hotel that ought to be in the Guide, please write to us at once. Report forms are to be found at the back. Procrastination is the thief of the next edition.

CRATHORNE North Yorkshire   Map 4

Crathorne Hall Hotel   *Tel* (0642) 700398
Yarm, Cleveland TS15 0AR   *Telex* 587426

An architectural curiosity, Crathorne Hall claims to be the largest
country house built in Edwardian England. It is a substantial sandstone
mansion, neo-Georgian in its front elevation, standing in 15 acres of
woodland looking over the river Leven, with the Cleveland Hills
beyond. "The peace, quiet and beautiful views belie its position just
outside the Guide's desert of Middlesbrough. In your room you feel as
though you were a country-house guest – except that there is a
bathroom cleverly *en suite*. Panelled bar, restaurant with peaceful view
of lawns and woods and ultra-comfortable lounge make the stay
pleasant; and the staff are most friendly and helpful" *(D M Callow)*.
"Supremely comfortable ... thick carpets, fresh flowers ... the sort of
place where you'd long to stay after a dose of 'flu. I even fell in love with
the loo – truly Victorian, huge, good old-fashioned flush chain, brass
light switches and loads of space. Definitely a place to linger!" *(E B)*

Open All year, except perhaps a few days in Jan.
Rooms 1 suite, 18 double, 12 single – 25 with bath, 6 with shower, all with
telephone, radio, colour TV, tea-making facilities and baby-listening.
Facilities Public lounge, residents' lounge with TV, cocktail bar, games room with
snooker table, dining room, conference room/ballroom, private function room.
15-acre grounds.
Location Close to A19 between Stockton and Thirsk.
Restrictions Not suitable for &. No dogs.
Credit cards All major cards accepted.
Terms (Service at guests' discretion) B&B: single £40.15–£46.20, double £51.70–
£60.50; dinner, B&B: single £51.15–£57.20, double £73.70–£82.50; full board: single
£58.30–£64.35, double £88–£96.80. Set lunch £7, dinner £10.50; full alc £20.
Reduced rates for children; special meals on request.

DEDHAM Essex   Map 2

Dedham Hall   *Tel* Colchester (0206) 323027
Dedham
Nr Colchester CO7 6AD

Dedham Hall is not – would not aspire to be – a hotel, more perhaps of a
farmhouse guest-house but *sui generis*. The river Stour is a walk across
the fields, and the tower of Dedham Church rises above the trees. The
resident owners are Mr and Mrs Slingo, and one of the features of the
place is the Painting Courses, weekend and weekly, which the Slingos
run, with the help of special tutors, throughout the year. "A nice
cottagey alternative to the posher places up the road (see below), if it's
Constable that you're after. A delightful working farm. . . Mrs Slingo is
a very welcoming, brisk, organised, friendly lady. The whole house is
ancient but immaculate. There is quite a largish restaurant at the back
with its own bar in among all the rough beams. Mrs Slingo is clearly a
very interested and creative cook" *(W A)*. Last year's entry is warmly
endorsed: "Comfortable rooms and friendly staff, an exceptionally
pretty garden and cooking *con amore* guarantee a happy stay." *(Nancy
Raphael; also E H Plaut)*

Open 1 Mar – 15 Dec. Closed Christmas and New Year.
Rooms 10 double, 2 single – 3 with bath, 5 with shower (3 of which also have wc), all with tea-making facilities; 3 in annexe; 3 ground-floor rooms.
Facilities 2 lounges, bar, 2 dining rooms, 6-acre grounds; river Stour within yards, coarse fishing. Converted barn used as artists' studio in grounds. Painting courses.
Location Just outside village, but 200 yds from road, so quiet.
Restrictions Not suitable for &. Under-fives not usually catered for. No dogs.
Credit cards None accepted.
Terms B&B: single £17.50–£26, double £26–£39.50; dinner, B&B: single £26.50–£35, double £44–£57.50. Set dinner £9.50. Reduced rates for children sharing parents' room; special meals on request.

Maison Talbooth *Tel* Colchester (0206) 322367
Stratford Road, Dedham *Telex* 987083 LETALB
Colchester CO7 6HN

Dedham Vale Hotel *Tel* Colchester (0206) 322273
Stratford Road, Dedham
Colchester CO7 6HW

In previous years, we have had separate entries for these two sophisticated establishments, but they deserve to be conjoined as two related vessels of Gerald Milsom's Dedham fleet, along with the shamelessly picturesque restaurant on the banks of the Stour, *Le Talbooth,* originally a 16th-century weaver's cottage, then a tollbooth (painted by Constable), and now in its latest incarnation a rosetted restaurant. You can stay in either *Maison Talbooth* or *Dedham Vale*, but the former only serves breakfast; for other meals, these residents must take themselves to *Dedham Vale*, half a mile up the road, or *Le Talbooth*, a quarter of a mile further on, or, if they wish to travel further afield but remain under Milsom's wing, they can patronise his smart fish restaurant *The Pier* on the waterfront at Harwich.

Maison Talbooth, a luxuriously equipped Victorian house, might be called Admiral Milsom's flagship. It is a far cry from the modest connotation of a B&B: its 10 outsize bedrooms are all kitted out with virtually every pampering extra your imagination can run to; the beds are king-size and the bathrooms are often as opulent as the bedrooms, some with large sunken tubs on a raised dais. For those not accustomed to this degree of cosseting comfort, the experience of a night at the *Maison* can be a bit over-rich, but you have to admire the verve of the undertaking – the same verve which Milsom has brought to the marketing of the consortium, the Pride of Britain, of which he is the founding father.

Dedham Vale is also a fully modernised Victorian mansion set in three acres of landscaped garden, close by but out of earshot of the A12. The bedrooms are a bit smaller than at the *Maison* (the prices are £10–£15 smaller, too) but are furnished with almost as many extras as at the senior house. But the pride and joy of *Dedham Vale* is its conservatory-like rôtisserie Terrace Restaraunt, "an amazingly exotic crystal palace". One reader this year, who normally stayed at *Maison Talbooth*, complained that "to get light to read in bed at the *Vale* one would have to have been prostrate on the floor, and to make up with one's back to the light is not easy! Small moans, but why don't hoteliers give a bedroom a dummy run to find these obvious howlers." But she found the Sunday cold table at the *Vale* "superb", and ended her report: "a lovely area – a memorable stay".

Maison Talbooth

Open All year.
Rooms 1 suite, 9 double – 9 with bath, 1 with shower, all with telephone, radio on request, colour TV and baby-listening; 5 ground-floor rooms.
Facilities Large hall with French windows on to the garden, drawing room with open fire. The hotel stands in 2 acres of grounds, the restaurant in 3 acres on the banks of the River Stour; fishing. 2 yachts for private hire along the East Anglian coastline. &.
Location Off A12. 6 m NE of Colchester. Take Stratford St Mary/Dedham road.
Restrictions Not suitable for &. No dogs.
Credit cards All major cards accepted.
Terms B&B: single £45–£80, double £65–£105. Set lunch £11.25 (plus 10% service), packed lunch available; full alc £20. Sailing holidays May-Sept (book a month in advance).

Dedham Vale Hotel

Open All year. Restaurant closed Sat lunchtime.
Rooms 5 double, 1 single – all with bath, telephone and colour TV.
Facilities Drawing room, bar, restaurant; function facilities. 4-acre grounds; river 100 yards; fishing and sailing locally.
Location 5 m NE of Colchester on A12.
Restrictions Not suitable for &. No dogs.
Credit cards All major cards accepted.
Terms Rooms: single £40–£48, double £55–£70. English breakfast £3.50. Set lunch (excluding 10% service): Luncheon Club £7.50 to non-members, Sun lunch £10.50. Full alc £17. Special portions for children.

DIDDLEBURY Shropshire   Map 2

Glebe Farm   *Tel* Munslow (058 476) 221
Diddlebury, Craven Arms SY7 9DH

"Far removed from the stereotyped hotel – and far cheaper, but how much nicer." A characteristic tribute to the special charms of this Tudor farmhouse, well endowed with oak beams and inglenook fireplaces, at the centre of a quiet village close by the Saxon church with its fortified tower. Wenlock Edge (immortalised by A E Housman), Ludlow with its castle and ancient houses, and Nordy Hill, an Iron Age fort with staggering views, are all within easy driving distance. Except that some of the beds sound a bit geriatric, all our reports speak glowingly of the quality of Michael and Eileen Wilkes's hospitality: "Welcome completely unforced ... Wonderful old house ... Our room looked over the beautiful garden, complete with stream and weeping willows and ducks ... Marvellous old oak panelling in the bedroom. The peace at night was blissful. The whole house is a treasure trove of beautiful furniture, pictures and *objets d'art* collected by generations of the same family. (*J H Roberts, Sheila and Dick Jordan; also L T Frazer Mackenzie, William Pollock, Guy Milner*)

Open 1 Mar – 4 Nov except 10 days early June.
Rooms 5 double, 2 single – 2 with shower; all with tea-making facilities; 4 rooms in annexe.
Facilities Sitting room with TV, bar, dining room. 1-acre garden with stream. Fishing on nearby river Corve; riding 1 m; walks on Wenlock Edge, Clee Hill etc.

Location E of B4368, 4 m NE of Craven Arms.
Restrictions Not suitable for &. No children under 10. No dogs.
Credit cards None accepted.
Terms B&B £13–£16; dinner, B&B £23.50–£28. Set dinner £9.95. Mid-week breaks off-season. Reductions for children.

DISS Norfolk   Map 2

Salisbury House [GFG]   *Tel* Diss (0379) 4738
84 Victoria Road, Diss IP22 3JG

Diss is a delightful unworldly small town at the southern part of Norfolk with a fine pedestrianised main street along the river Waveney. *Salisbury House*, alas, is a mile from the town centre on a rather drab main road not quite out of earshot of the railway, but it has a lot of compensations. The building is Victorian, set in an acre of gardens, with a croquet lawn and pond for ornamental ducks and sundry other exotic wild life. It is a quintessential restaurant with rooms (just three) and the restaurant is really of exceptional quality. The house is owned and run by a former *Michelin* inspector Anthony Rudge (chef) and a former ballet dancer Jonathon Thompson (maître d'hôtel). The dishes on the small set menu are inventive and ambitious, and the breakfasts are as special as the dinners, with delicious home-made bread and croissants. The same care and attention to detail that is displayed in the cooking is also evident in everything else about the place. All the rooms, even the private bathrooms, are furnished in period style and decorated with individual taste: the downstairs rooms have a notable collection of fans. Recent visitors warmly endorse our own report quoted above. "Honey shampoo in bathroom, masses of magazines all over the house, beautiful and *interesting* gardens with fluffy geese etc; delicious and original food ... A delightful and memorable visit." *(Professor Frank amd Mrs Joan Harrison)*

Open All year, except 1 week spring, 1 week autumn, 2 weeks at Christmas. Restaurant closed to non-residents Sun and Mon.
Rooms 3 double – 1 with bath, 2 with shower, all with radio and TV and tea-making facilities.
Facilities 2 sitting rooms, garden room, restaurant. Garden with croquet lawn, conservatory, ornamental duck pond and aviary.
Location From Bury St Edmunds take A143 and turn left towards Diss on A1066. Turn left at T-junction; *Salisbury House* is on left just beyond railway bridge.
Restrictions Only restaurant suitable for &. No children under 12. Dogs in bedrooms only if supervised; not allowed in public rooms.
Credit cards None accepted.
Terms (Service at customers' discretion) dinner, B&B: single £56, double £77. Set lunch/dinner £16.

DOVEDALE Derbyshire   Map 2

The Izaak Walton Hotel   *Tel* Thorpe Cloud (033 529) 261
Dovedale, Ashbourne DE6 2AY

Beautifully and peacefully situated at the entrance of Dovedale, The Izaak Walton *has much to offer the walker, climber or fisherman. It is a straightforward place with no fancy extras in the bedrooms or the dining room. A recent satisfied visitor reports: "This was a 'spur-of-the-minute' booking but was dealt with in a quiet and relaxed manner which was typical of this hotel and staff. The pretty receptionist greeted us with the minimum of fuss. The table d'hôte menu (inclusive on our autumn break terms) was more than adequate with six choices right through the card. The overall impression was one of quiet calm"* (Mr and Mrs Ian S Searle).

Thus our entry in 1984. *The hotel was omitted in 1985 following reports of poor meals and surly service. Recently, however,* Professor Norman Morris *makes this case for reinstatement: "We found the service and hospitality quite exceptional. Where else can you get* The Sunday Times *and* Observer *delivered with your morning tea in the depths of the countryside? The food is excellent and there is plenty of it – only the puddings disappoint slightly. The rooms are adequate, very well heated and lit, and spotlessly clean. Truly a lovely place." More reports please.*

Open All year.
Rooms 4 family, 25 double, 4 single – all with bath, telephone, radio, colour TV and baby-listening. 2 ground-floor rooms.
Facilities 2 lounges, public bar, buttery bar, restaurant, conference room; Saturday night dinner dance. 1-acre grounds with putting green. Private fishing rights on the river Dove; walking, climbing, hang-gliding.
Location 5 m from Ashbourne, off the main Ashbourne/Buxton road.
Credit cards All major cards accepted.
Terms B&B: single £31–£33.50, double £47–£49.50; dinner, B&B: single £40–£44, double £67–£70. Set meals: lunch £8 (bar snacks also available), dinner £10; full alc £16. Special breaks in and out of season. Reduced rates for children sharing parents' room.

DULVERTON Somerset Map 2

Ashwick Country House Hotel and Restaurant
Nr Dulverton TA22 9QD

Tel Dulverton (0398) 23868

A small Edwardian country house in a well-favoured position above the valley of the River Barle, 900 feet up in the Exmoor National Park. We had an entry for *Ashwick House* in an earlier edition, but took it out after the house changed hands. We are glad to reinstate it on receipt of the nomination below:

"I never thought I should place much store by things like mineral water and a welcoming drink in the room, a bowl of pot pourri, and home-made mints placed nightly by the bed, the bed turned down and the curtains drawn, up-to-date magazines and information on things as diverse as the pleasantest way to Dulverton and the cheapest place to buy petrol – all in the bedroom. I first came here last August and then the thing I enjoyed most was breakfast served on the terrace in glorious sunshine (muesli garnished with fresh strawberries). All the rooms are light, clean, spacious, airy and most comfortably appointed. The views are marvellous. The original William Morris wallpaper in the hall is sensational. The Sherwoods (mother, father and son) are kind, helpful and quiet. The food is good – imaginative and wholesome and generous. I have been back twice since, once in March when there was snow still lying on the hills but the house was blissfully warm and welcoming. It is the sort of place where you feel welcome to stay around all day. It is the perfect base for walking and exploring Exmoor; I recommend it as a haven where the indoor comforts complement the wilds without." *(Ann Webb)*

Open All year.
Rooms 6 double – all with bath, telephone point, radio, colour TV; baby-listening if required.
Facilities Reception area, hall, lounge, library, bar, dining room. 6-acre grounds with 2 ponds and croquet.
Location 2½ m NW of Dulverton. Take the B3223 Exford/Lynton road. Drive up to moor, over cattle grid; you will find hotel signpost directing you left off the moor.
Restrictions Not suitable for &. No children under 8. No dogs.
Credit cards None accepted.
Terms (No service charge) B&B £20–£23; dinner, B&B £24.25–£30. Set lunch £6, set dinner £9.50. Special rates for 2, 5 or 7 nights.

EAST BUCKLAND Devon   Map 1

Lower Pitt Restaurant and Guest House   *Tel* Filleigh (059 86) 243
East Buckland, Barnstaple EX32 OTD

The name shows the priority of things in this picturesque 16th-century farmhouse run by Suzanne and Jerome Lyons: only three cosy bedrooms but the sophisticated well-regarded restaurant can seat 28. For one visitor, this was a plus: "The restaurant does away with the awful business of making polite conversation to perfect strangers if you don't want to ... there's no hushed atmosphere here – everything is bright, jolly and cheerful. Views and peace wherever you look." An inspector ended his report: "Length of stay? Could be indefinite – though the menu might be a bit rich for more than a week. Good value for money." *(H S, S D, M C & V H Whitting)*

Open All year except 24 – 26 Dec and New Year's Day.
Rooms 3 double – 1 with bath, 2 with shower, all with tea-making facilities.
Facilities Lounge/bar, 2 dining rooms. 2-acre grounds with gardens and terrace for drinks. Sandy beaches and North Devon coast within easy reach.
Location 3 m NW of South Molton. Turn off A361 at Stagg Head.
Restrictions Not suitable for &. No dogs.
Credit cards Access, Amex, Visa.
Terms (No service charge) B&B: single £25, double £40; dinner, B&B £30–£35 per person. Full alc £15.

EAST GRINSTEAD West Sussex   Map 2

Gravetye Manor   *Tel* Sharpthorne (0342) 810567
East Grinstead RH19 4LJ   *Telex* 957239 GRAVTY

"Well, what can I say to convey the ambience of this lovely house – except to confirm what has already been said in the Guide. Service is 'gliding' – courteous and efficient. No need to wait for attention. Waiters seemed to sense our needs. The house itself is really lovely – stone floors with lovely carpets and beautiful log fires, pictures, antiques, country house flower arrangements – and all fresh! A wonderful lack of bustle – no music at all! Peaceful – so uncrowded in lounge and dining room that privacy is easily possible." *(Wendy Hillary)*.

One visitor's homage to the qualities that have made *Gravetye Manor* a kind of emblem of the English country house hotel – a stunningly beautiful Elizabethan manor house set in 30 acres of historically important gardens (*Gravetye* was the home for more half a century of William Robinson, one of the creators of the English natural garden), and the 30 acres themselves are deep in a serenely beautiful forested area of West Sussex. We should add that the restaurant has been notable for many years past, with Allan Garth the present *chef de cuisine* winning the hotel a *Michelin* rosette. The correspondent above marked her menu with "perfection", "exquisite" and other superlatives. And we still have to mention a long and resplendent wine list.

It is a pity that we can't stop there, but *Gravetye* has good years in the Guide and some not so good. 1985 has, sadly, been one – *pace Michelin* and Ms Hillary – marked by grumbles about the restaurant. One visitor from abroad, who has been back often since her first visit in 1977, makes unfavourable comparisons with a former chef, Karl Löderer. Others, more in sorrow than in anger, have felt simply that the quality of meals failed to justify their price. Of course, the tariff that has to be charged at a show-place house like *Gravetye* is necessarily steep, but top prices inevitably create expectations of perfection. Happily, in other respects *Gravetye* is fulfilling the highest expectations for most visitors, though there have been grumbles from American visitors at not being allowed to use credit cards.

Open All year.
Rooms 12 double, 2 single – 12 with bath, 2 with shower, all with telephone, radio and colour TV.
Facilities 2 sitting rooms, club members' bar, 2 restaurants (public and private dining room separate). 30-acre grounds with croquet, clock golf; private trout fishing in nearby lake.
Location 5 m SW of East Grinstead off B2110 at West Hoathly sign. Glyndebourne 40 minutes' drive; Gatwick Airport 9 m.
Restrictions Not suitable for &. No smoking in restaurants. No children under 7. No dogs.
Credit cards None accepted.
Terms (Excluding VAT) rooms: single from £48, double from £62. Continental breakfast £4, English breakfast (alc) £6–£7; full alc £32.

EAST PORTLEMOUTH Devon   Map 1

Gara Rock Hotel   *Tel* Salcombe (054 884) 2342
East Portlemouth, Nr Salcombe
TQ8 8PH

A friendly family hotel, converted from a coastguard station, in a particularly beautiful situation on National Trust land and on cliffs overlooking the sea near Salcombe. It has a solar- and boiler-heated swimming pool, hard tennis court, adventure playground, entertainments such as guitarists and singers, table-tennis tournaments, a magic-show, "The Brain of Gara Rock" quiz, and a laundry for the use of guests. In school holidays the hotel is full of families, many of them on return visits, all enjoying the tolerant atmosphere. Rooms vary in quality and some of the partitions are thin. Don't expect too much from the set meals; but the hotel's terms allow residents, for a small surcharge, to select evening meals from the à la carte and speciality fish menus.

Open Apr–end Nov; New Year week.
Rooms 50 double, 10 single – 41 with bath, 5 with shower, 38 with colour TV, all with baby-listening; 13 self-catering flats.
Facilities Lounge, bar lounge, sun lounge, games rooms, TV room; laundry for the use of guests. 5-acre grounds with heated swimming pool and paddling pool, tennis court, adventure playground and garden games. Large beach with rocks, sand and safe bathing; boating and fishing. 10-metre motor cruiser for charter; trips round Salcombe estuary organised in hotel boats.
Location Pass through Kingsbridge; turn left at mini-roundabout on to A379 for Torcoss and Dartmouth; at Frogmore turn right over bridge; follow signs for East Portlemouth and Gara Rock.
Restriction Not suitable for &.
Credit cards Access, Visa.
Terms B&B: £22–£23; dinner, B&B £31–£33. Set dinner £10.50; full alc £13. Vegetarian meals if requested. Bar lunches, cream teas. Children under 2 free, under 6 50% reduction; special meals.

EAST STOKE Dorset   Map 1

Kemps Country House Hotel [GFG]   *Tel* Bindon Abbey (0929) 462563
East Stoke, Wareham BH20 6AL

A Victorian rectory converted into a reasonably priced small hotel (bargain breaks especially good value), run by chef/proprietor Mike Kemp and his wife Valerie, *Kemps* retains a distinct Victorian atmosphere thanks to Sanderson's wallpapers, and bric-à-brac. The recently built dining room (which does a busy non-resident trade) is very pretty, with green and white colour scheme, tables well apart, a candle on each table and lighting muted. In the evening discreet taped classical music fills the dining room, bar and sitting room. The set dinner [£9 in 1985] offers a good choice, as does the à la carte menu. Service is friendly and helpful but not fawning. There are five bedrooms in the main building and four in a converted coach house. The hotel is well situated for touring many of the Dorset sights, but as it lies on the A352 front rooms may be noisy.

Open All year except 14 Dec–1 Jan.
Rooms 1 suite, 7 double, 1 single – 5 with bath, 3 with shower, all with TV and tea-making facilities; 2 on ground floor; 4 in annexe.
Facilities 2 lounges, bar, restaurant. 1½-acre grounds with play area for children.
Location On A352 midway between Wool and Wareham. (Some rooms could be noisy.)
Restriction No dogs.
Credit cards All major cards accepted.
Terms (No service charge) B&B: single £22.50, double £40; dinner, B&B: single £30, double £57–£59. Bargain breaks of 2 nights £52–£55 per person, 3 nights £75–£78, 7 nights £160–£170.

EASTON GREY Wiltshire   Map 2

Whatley Manor   *Tel* Malmesbury (066 62) 2888
Easton Grey, Malmesbury SN16 0RB   *Telex* 449380 WHOTEL

At first glance, *Whatley Manor*, on the banks of the fledgling Avon, looks like any other venerable Cotswold manor house, but appearances in this case are deceptive. Parts of the house date from the mid-18th century, but most of the present three-storey building is the fruit of an extravagant pre-war reconstruction by one Bertie Cox, then president of the Canada Life Assurance Company. He is reputed to have spent £200,000 on his hobby, which wasn't just to turn *Whatley Manor* into a grand house, but also, with the help of 23 gardeners, to make the gardens something very special too. When Bertie Cox died the house and grounds deteriorated until the late seventies when it was rescued to enjoy a new lease of life as one of the more elegant country hotels in the book. "The house is spacious and beautiful, with a vast, comfortable lounge and bedrooms which are more than adequate, although lacking some of the cosmetic touches of grander establishments. We had a glorious view, and the bathroom was luxurious, with good big towels. But the two main reasons for this recommendation are the food and the prices. We were impressed by the set dinner menu, which had plenty of choice and changed every evening. We thought the price extremely good value – and there were no extras at all. *Whatley* more than holds its own in an area where competition is intense." *(Lady Davenport-Handley; also William Rankin)*

Since our first entry (above) for *Whatley Manor* last year, the hotel has refurbished 10 ground-floor rooms in the *Court House*, 70 yards from the manor. Further reports welcome.

Open All year.
Rooms 25 double – all with bath, telephone, radio on request, TV and baby-listening; 10 rooms in annexe.
Facilities 2 lounges, library bar, dining room. 10-acre grounds with croquet lawn, tennis court, putting green, golf practice net, heated swimming pool. Trout fishing in river Avon which forms part of boundary. Riding nearby.
Location On B4040, 3 m W of Malmesbury.
Restrictions Not suitable for &. No dogs in public rooms.
Credit cards All major cards accepted.
Terms (No service charge) B&B: single £40–£45, double £54–£64. Set lunch £8.50, dinner £14.95; vegetarian meals available. Weekend breaks except during Badminton horse trials. Christmas and New Year packages. Reduced rates for children sharing parents' room; special meals.

EVERSHOT Dorset   Map 1

Summer Lodge [GFG]   *Tel* Evershot (093 583) 424
Evershot DT2 OJR

💧 *Awarded a César in 1985 for the best country house hotel in the medium-price range*

Nigel and Margaret Corbett are the hosts at this exceptionally cosseting hotel in the heart of the Dorset countryside. They have been in business since 1979 and, from their first entry in these pages, have been drawing from their grateful guests peals of praise unequalled in the Guide. When we met Nigel, freshly laurelled, at the launching of the 1985 Guide, we asked if he would contribute a short piece explaining what, in his view, made a good country house hotel – in effect, what was the secret of his success. You can read his answer on page 752.

In the meantime, and in greater numbers than ever before, his satisfied customers – we have yet to hear from one of the other kind –

have been sending us their bread-and-butter letters. Although Nigel Corbett is too modest to say so, running a good hotel is relentlessly hard work. These letters – and we only have room to quote a fraction – are the intangible rewards of so much zeal in his vocation.

"The cooking inspired that special sort of confidence that lets you know it will always be as good, every time you go there – lamb en croûte was the main dish, pink, tender and peppery, and the first two adjectives also apply to the boss who, though a mite more effusive than he had any need to be with the old barnacle who is now writing to you, showed such genuine kindness and concern to a pair of aged patrons (the wife was in her deep 90s) that I felt the better for being in the same room with him." *(Robert Robinson)*

"I cannot imagine any way in which the Corbetts could make *Summer Lodge* any better. It is two years since our first visit, but we were welcomed like old friends and the *Guardian* was waiting for us at breakfast without a word from us. The food was as delicious, the flower arrangements as beautiful and the service even more perfect if that is possible. Long may they reign." *(Gillian Seel)*

"The glowing reports made us prepare for it not coming up to expectations, but it did in every way – indeed excelled. There seemed to be no little touch overlooked . . . even the car windscreens were cleaned every morning." *(Susan Walker)* "We can't imagine this place ever varying in standards – they seem so obviously to *like* their guests." *(Angela and David Stewart)* "They deserve their accolades. Their secret seems to be a combination of friendliness and an overriding concern for the comfort and welfare of their guests." *(Neil and Claire Butter)*

Open 1 Feb – 30 Nov.
Rooms 8 double, 1 single – all with bath, telephone and tea-making facilities.
Facilities Large drawing room with log fire, TV room, bar, dining room, heated outdoor swimming pool, stables. Golf, trout fishing nearby. 12 m from sea and pebble beach, good sea fishing; sandy beach at Weymouth and Lyme Regis, 20 m away.
Location 10 m S of Yeovil. (Note: the entrance on village street is for pedestrians only; cars must turn left on reaching village into Summer Lane and then right into drive to house.)
Restrictions Not suitable for &. No children under 8. No dogs in public rooms.
Credit cards Access, Visa.
Terms (Service at guests' discretion) B&B: £25–£37.50; dinner, B&B £35–£50. Set dinner £14. Packed lunches available. Winter breaks. 30% reduction for children sharing parents' room.
Service/tipping: "Tipping is left entirely to our guests' discretion, and is never solicited by members of our staff who are fully and properly paid."

EVESHAM Hereford and Worcester   **Map 2**

Evesham Hotel [GFG]   *Tel* Evesham (0386) 49111
Coopers Lane, off Waterside   *Telex* 339342
Evesham WR11 6DA

The enterprising Jenkinson family own the *Evesham*, certainly the most attractive place to stay in the town. The hotel looks like a Georgian Manor, though it dates from Tudor times. It is in the centre, but up a quiet alley, and has a particularly attractive two-and-a-half-acre garden, full of fine trees, including mulberries and a cedar of Lebanon. The

Jenkinsons run the show with panache: their restaurant enjoys an excellent reputation, their wine list is long and eclectic, their liqueur list is the longest and most eclectic we have come across. Their rooms are admirably maintained. They have attractive bargain breaks, the more so since they offer their bargain diners the free run of the à la carte instead of, as elsewhere, treating them as second-class citizens. Since last year, the dinner menu has been extended and taken the path of greater eclecticism like the wine list – more options, with vegetarian dishes, very hot curries and such relative rarities as smoked eel and squab joining the more conventional range. Meanwhile, Algeria, Texas and Virginia have joined the other 35 sources of wine already on the list, including Wales, Malta and Mexico (Australia and California are specially well represented). "The wine list is amusing (too amusing?)" queries one reader, who also found one of the Jenkinsons a little over-hearty for her taste. But she appreciated like the other commenders the verve of the place, and the excellent value for money. (*J A Chapman, E Walker, Richard O Whiting and others*)

Open All year except New Year.
Rooms 1 family suite, 25 double, 8 single – 28 with bath, 5 with shower, all with telephone, radio, remote control colour TV, tea-making facilities and baby-listening; 8 ground-floor rooms.
Facilities Lounge, bar, restaurant. 2½-acre garden with putting green, croquet and badminton. & (restaurant only).
Location 5 minutes' walk from town centre (but quietly situated). Ask for easy directions when booking. Large car park.
Restriction No dogs in public rooms.
Credit cards All major cards accepted.
Terms [1985 rates] B&B: single £35, double £48, suite £70; dinner, B&B £46–£55 per person (min. 2 days). Set lunch £8.40 (buffet £5.30); full alc dinner £14.60. Reduced rates and special meals for children under 12.
Service/tipping: "We advise customers that service is included in the price, and tips are down to 0.5% of turnover. The catering industry has so long shamed the customer into paying extra that some people just can't kick the habit."

FARINGDON Oxfordshire   **Map 2**

The Bell Hotel [GFG]   *Tel* Faringdon (0367) 20534
The Square, Faringdon SN7 7HP

This 16th-century post house in the very pretty market square is full of traditional inn-like features, such as stone ingle-nook seat and a carved oak panel in the bar; the old coaching yard at the rear has been decked out with flowered tubs and wooden seats; the bedrooms on the first floor are attractive and well equipped. So far, it might be any other modernised coaching inn, but *The Bell* had a culinary revolution recently with the arrival of Stephen Williams, a young chef trained by Michael Quinn. Not surprisingly, the cooking is far above the usual country-inn standard: everything is cooked to order; even the bar snacks are said to be exceptional. The lounge could perhaps do with a face-lift, but in other respects *The Bell* brightens up the Oxfordshire scene. Faringdon certainly makes a good base for exploring the Vale of the White Horse to the south or the Cotswolds to the north. The go-ahead owner, William Dreyer, tells us that he is keen to show small groups the area. More reports welcome.

Open All year.
Rooms 1 suite, 7 double, 3 single – 6 with bath, 1 with shower, all with radio and baby-listening; telephone in suite; TV in rooms with bath.
Facilities Residents' lounge with TV, 2 bars, dining room, conference/function facilities. Small courtyard. Fishing 2 m; boating 6 m. &. (restaurant and WC only).
Location Town centre in market place. Parking.
Credit cards All major cards accepted.
Terms B&B (continental): single £24, double £34.45; dinner, B&B: single £31.95, double £50.35. English breakfast £3.25; set lunch/dinner £8.95; full alc £17.80. Bar snacks. Weekend breaks.

FAUGH Cumbria Map 4

The String of Horses *Tel* Hayton (022 870) 297 or 509
Faugh, Heads Nook
Carlisle CA4 9EG

"Olde worlde" is an epithet one cannot avoid applying to *The String of Horses*. It isn't our word, but that of Eric Tasker, who describes himself as "mine host" and who calls his air-conditioned restaurant, with adjoining cocktail bar, "The Olde-Worlde Restaurant". Does that suggest something a bit self-conscious? No doubt, but mine host's 17th-century pub has a number of distinctly unusual features, in addition to conventional innish items like oak beams, copper and brass and log fires. The 13 bedrooms upstairs, three of them four-poster suites, have nothing whatever pubbish about them: they all are fitted out with a wide range of electrical conveniences from alarms to video by way of mini-bars and colour TV. But their *pièces de* (irresistible) *résistance* are their *en suite* bathrooms – most of them, we are told, by Bonsack, bathmakers to kings and queens – in different shapes, colours and sizes (many are double), with gold-plated fittings, "an experience in themselves" (Mr Tasker's words). Adjoining the hotel is a mini-leisure centre, "embracing a sauna, solarium, ergometer *(sic)*, American whirlpool, and outside heated pool. Not everyone's scene certainly; kitschy for some, but great fun for others. "We only chose to stay here because of your entry, and thought that if it was *that* awful, we could always make some excuse and leave. On the contrary, we found it so refreshingly different that we booked another night! After 25 years of marriage, I can recommend it highly for a second or third honeymoon. We had our 19-year-old daughter with us, and she loved it too. I've never spent such an energetic 48 hours, making use of all facilities available, including champagne." *(M Barr)*

Open All year. Only restaurant open Christmas Day.
Rooms 3 suites, 10 double (also let as singles) – 8 with bath, 5 with shower, all with telephone, radio, colour TV, video, tea-making facilities and baby-listening.
Facilities Residents' lounge (with TV), lounge bar, cocktail bar, restaurant, fitness room. Small grounds with heated swimming pool (all year), sunbathing facilities and bar. Leisure centre with sauna, solarium, jacuzzi and ergometer. Sailing and windsurfing on Talkin Tarn 3 m away. Fishing, golf, tennis, squash, riding and shooting nearby.
Location 7½ m E of Carlisle; from M6 exit 43 take Newcastle direction, turn right off A69 at Corby Hill garage; inn is 2 m down the road.
Restriction Dogs by arrangement only, and not in public rooms.
Credit cards All major cards accepted.
Terms (Service at guests' discretion) B&B: single occupancy £37–£48, double

£46–£64. Set dinner from £8.50; alc lunch from £8.75, alc dinner from £12.50. Bargain breaks Oct–Apr (min 2 days). Reduced rates and special meals for children.
Service/tipping: "We do not add any charge for service. If guests wish to reward staff for service we feel that is their prerogative. The staff share any gratuities."

FLITWICK Bedfordshire — Map 2

Flitwick Manor [GFG] — *Tel* Flitwick (0525) 712242
Church Road, Flitwick MK45 1AE — *Telex* 825562 FM

A new country house hotel in the upper-middle bracket, *Flitwick Manor* started trading as a restaurant-with-rooms in the summer of 1984 and introduced seven bedrooms in the spring of 1985. The *Manor* is a Grade II early 18th-century listed building, set in a 50-acre park (though only six belong to the hotel). The building is pedigree, and so, you might say, are the resident owners, Somerset and Helene Moore, who ran for the past 10 years a well-esteemed nearby restaurant, *The White Hart Inn*, at Flitton. Bedfordshire is something of a gastronomic desert, so the restaurant is clearly an oasis for the neighbouring gourmets; fish, which was a speciality at the inn, is again a feature of the restaurant at the *Manor* – and the dining rooms themselves have been admirably furnished and decorated. Restaurant prices are reasonable, and also the wine list. The hotel side is likely to be equally popular since there are so few agreeable hotels of this kind within a 50-mile radius of London, and *Flitwick Manor*, just 40 miles from Hyde Park Corner, is conveniently placed three miles from the M1 at junction 12. The rooms have been done up with "country house" elegance; shoes are cleaned when left outside the bedroom door; *The Times* and the *Daily Telegraph* are served with the splendid breakfast. A promising newcomer. *(H R)*

Open All year.
Rooms 1 suite, 4 double, 1 single – 4 with bath, 2 with shower, all with direct-dial telephone, radio, colour TV and baby-listening.
Facilities Lounge, bar, restaurant. 6½-acre grounds with lake, tennis, 2 croquet lawns, 12-century church and helipad. Set in a 50-acre park (not hotel's).
Location Take exit 12 from M1, then A5120 towards Bedford. Hotel is on outskirts of Flitwick.
Restriction Not suitable for ♿.
Credit cards All major cards accepted.
Terms B&B: single £55 – £95, double £60 – £100 (including service). Set lunch/dinner (service at guests' discretion) £8.50 and £13.50; full alc £23.50.

FRENCHBEER Devon — Map 1

Teignworthy [GFG] — *Tel* Chagford (064 73) 3355
Frenchbeer, Nr Chagford TQ13 8EX

A marked conflict of opinion on this Lutyens-influenced gentleman's residence (it was built by the same craftsmen that worked on Lutyens' famous Castle Drogo nearby) in a particularly agreeable position facing south in a sheltered horseshoe of land, 1000 feet above sea level, and within walking distance of Dartmoor. "Atmosphere completely relaxed and friendly without being pushy. Food excellent without being too rich – home cooking at the highest possible level."

"What a disappointment! This lovely house has been ruined by naff furnishing . . . mediocre food . . . breakfasts let down by presentation." These opposing views sum up readers' conflicting reports. Hence the italics. The hotel has been consistently popular with our readers for many years past. We don't think its standards have changed, though it may have hit a bad patch. Could we have more reports please?

Open All year.
Rooms 9 double – all with bath, direct-dial telephone, radio and colour TV.
Facilities Hall, drawing room with large log fire, small bar, dining room; some conference facilities; sauna and sunbed. 14-acre grounds with woodland, heathland and lawned garden; fishing in the river Teign at the bottom of the garden or in the Fernworthy Reservoir; golf at Moretonhampstead; riding available. Dartmoor on the doorstep.
Location 3 m SW of Chagford. Follow signs to Fernworthy, then Kester and Thornworthy.
Restrictions Not suitable for &. No children under 12. No dogs.
Credit cards None accepted.
Terms (No service charge) B&B: single £42.50, double £67; dinner, B&B: single £55–£60, double £92–£102. Set dinner £19.50; full alc lunch £20. Special winter rates, 2 nights minimum. Christmas house party.

GITTISHAM Devon   **Map 1**

Combe House Hotel   *Tel* Honiton (0404) 2756
Gittisham, Nr Honiton EX14 OAD

Indubitably one of the more grand, not to say stately, of England's country house hotels. Although parts date back to the 14th century, *Combe House* is essentially an Elizabethan manor. It is only a couple of miles of the A30 London/Exeter road, but set in the heart of a 3,500-acre estate, in a steep and typical Devonshire combe, it offers absolute peace and seclusion. John and Thérèse Boswell took over the house in a very run-down condition. John Boswell, a direct descendant of James, has filled the mansion with furniture, books and pictures from his own ancestral home, Auchinleck House in Ayrshire. There is riding to be had within the estate, and shooting can be arranged with a local shoot. Over the years, *Combe House* has been popular with readers not too bothered with counting their pennies, and who have appreciated the scale, opulence and undoubted comforts of the house as well as the excellence of the cooking under Mrs Boswell's supervision. Recent bulletins have been mixed. For some, every prospect pleases – the decor, the cooking, the little touches, like a small box of chocolates by the bed, the whole ambience. Others have been critical, feeling that neither the meals nor the service justify the prices. More reports welcome.

Open All year.
Rooms 1 suite, 11 double – all with bath, telephone and colour TV; 1 room near ground level.
Facilities Hall, sitting room, drawing room, cocktail bar, 2 dining rooms. 6-acre gardens in 3,500-acre estate; croquet. Trout fishing on river Otter 1½ m. Sea 8 m; sandy beach at Exmouth 16 m; golf and riding nearby; shooting can be arranged.
Location Just off A30, 3½ m S of Honiton.
Restrictions Only suitable for partially &. No children under 10 in dining room at night. No dogs in public rooms during meal-times.
Credit cards All major cards accepted.
Terms B&B: single £25 – £39, double £50 – £88. Set Sun lunch £11.50, full alc

excluding wine £16.60. Reductions out of season and for stays of over a week. Winter-break rates Nov–Mar: 2 or more nights. Reduced rates for children sharing parents' room; special meals.

GOATHLAND North Yorkshire Map 4

Mallyan Spout Hotel *Tel* Whitby (0947) 86206
Goathland, Whitby YO22 5AN

Stone-built in the 1920s and draped with creepers, the *Mallyan Spout* takes its name from the fairy-like waterfall dropping through trees below the hotel. It is set on the green of this popular but unspoiled village with fine views over the moors. It had an entry in earlier editions of the Guide, but has been missing from our pages since 1980 after undergoing various changes of management. We heard that it was in good hands again, and sent along our inspector:

"The bar lounge at the *Mallyan* has green and red tartan carpets which reminded us of Queen Victoria, Albert and Balmoral. The comfy dark-green velvet wingchairs were grouped around a log fire where we took coffee after dinner. The dining room is attractive. Long low mullioned windows look into a secluded rose garden where a truly northern tea can be taken in the summer. For those who dine at eight, candle lamps wink on each table. Dinner on the three-course menu, table d'hôte £9 [1985], three choices at each course, was a balanced, carefully thought-about meal, with an accent on fresh produce. My husband thought the fresh fruit salad vacherin the best part of his meal. It was very big – soft melt-in-the-mouth meringue and bits of fresh strawberry among grapes, orange, apple etc. I chose the ham salad; a huge serving of pinky, moist, home-baked ham, cut from the bone, garnished with care. Slices of banana had been tucked into the petals of a tomato cut to look like a water lily. The wine list was representative but expensive. The house wine was not up to much. Now we must go upstairs. I fear we did not have a good bedroom! One quarter was the bathroom. We had to organise our dressing in such cramped conditions. You had to step sideways to the hand basin beside the bed, ditto past the television to the window. No chance to look at the view here, or indeed sit in comfort. A young couple next door said they were cramped, but enjoyed the large four-poster bed. I looked at No.5A which was palatial, having a low padded window seat and wingchairs. A super spot to sit and watch outdoors. Readers would be well advised to discuss rooms because they vary a lot." More reports please.

Open Jan–Dec. Closed Christmas and New Year.
Rooms 19 double, 3 single – 18 with bath, 2 with shower, all with TV.
Facilities 3 lounges, 2 bars, restaurant, garden. Golf, tennis and riding within easy reach; salmon or trout fishing on the nearby river Esk; sea fishing at Whitby.
Location 10 m E of Whitby.
Restrictions Not suitable for &. No dogs in public rooms.
Credit cards Amex, Diners, Visa.
Terms (Excluding 10% service charge) B&B: single £14–£16, double £30–£32; dinner, B&B: single £25–£27, double £50–£52. Set lunch £6 (picnic and snack lunches available); set dinner £9.50; full alc £12. Reduced rates and high tea for children. Mini-breaks and summer breaks.

Please make a habit of sending a report if you stay at a Guide hotel.

GODALMING Surrey   Map 2

Inn on the Lake   *Tel* Godalming (048 68) 5575
Godalming GU7 1RH

Our first hotel ever in Surrey! Joy and Martin Cummings took over a run-down establishment called the Lake Hotel just over two years ago, after it had had no fewer than five owners in five years. It is still in the process of being transformed. Don't be put off by the outside; the interior is much more welcoming. At the date of going to press, we cannot comment on the restaurant side as the owners have a new chef and are changing the format of the menu. But our inspector enjoyed her visit, found her room comfortable and well equipped, and liked the friendly casual feel of the place. It was clearly thriving with local trade. We approve of the tipping policy (see below). More reports please.

Open All year.
Rooms 5 double, 4 single – 3 with bath, 2 with shower, all with telephone, radio, colour TV, tea-making facilities.
Facilities Lounge, bar, dining room, functions room. 2-acre grounds with landscaped gardens including water garden and lake.
Location ½ m from Godalming. Take A3100 S from Guildford.
Restriction Not suitable for &.
Credit cards All major cards accepted.
Terms (No service charge) B&B: single £26, double £33–£40; dinner, B&B: single £34.50, double £41.50. Set meals £8.50, £10.50 and £13.50. Weekend breaks.
Service/tipping: "It is the policy of this Inn to maintain prices at the lowest level consistent with paying the bills and making some profit. Service and cover charges are not in keeping with this image and are therefore not charged. As in the case of the hair dresser or taxi driver, should you particularly wish to express your 'personal' thanks to the staff, please do this direct, but feel under no obligation to do so."

GOLANT Cornwall   Map 1

Cormorant Hotel   *Tel* Fowey (072 683) 3426
Golant, Nr Fowey PL25 1LL

A small, personal, slightly idiosyncratic hotel in an eyrie-like position on the edge of the fishing village of Golant, three miles north of Fowey. All the rooms have a panoramic view over the Fowey river, as does the hotel's special pride – a heated swimming pool, open throughout the year, with sliding glass doors and press-button motorised roof, built above the hotel and capturing the daylong sunshine. "The hotel is beautifully situated with spectacular views from *all* bedrooms and from the spacious and very comfortable lounge with its log fire. The proprietors, Jo Henderson and her son Stephen, try to create a house-party atmosphere, but once introduced to the other guests one can avoid too intimate contact if desired. The cooking is excellent, there was real ale in the bar, and flowers in the bedrooms. The proprietors take a pre-breakfast swim in their pool and welcome company at that time or later in the day. Snags to watch: walls are thin and our visit coincided with one of the noisiest 4-year olds in Cornwall, but from the proprietors' reaction he will not be there again! The near-vertical drive can be unnerving at first, but observe the notice advising bottom gear and you should make it! These gripes are easily outweighed by the pluses." *(John Timpson; warmly endorsed by Stephen Parish)*

Open All year.
Rooms 10 double – all with bath, shower, telephone, radio, colour TV and baby-listening. 4 ground-floor rooms.
Facilities Lounge, bar, writing room, dining room. 1-acre grounds with heated swimming pool (enclosed in winter). On Fowey river estuary – fishing, sailing, water skiing, skin-diving. Near many sandy beaches and coves. Golf 3½ m.
Location 5 m N of Fowey, off B3269. Parking for 25 cars.
Restriction No dogs in public rooms.
Credit card Visa.
Terms (Service at guests' discretion) B&B (continental) £18.50; dinner, B&B £26. Full alc £10–£12. Winter breaks Oct–May; 4-day Christmas package. Reduced rates for children; special meals.
Tipping: "Tipping is left to discretion of guests – it is NOT ENCOURAGED."

GOSFORTH Cumbria   Map 4

Wasdale Head Inn   *Tel* Wasdale (094 06) 229
Wasdale Head, Gosforth CA20 1EX

"Wasdale Head in the evening can leave the observer in no doubt about the purpose of this place. The Inn lives and breathes climbing – it's the closest you can get by road to the biggest and rockiest peaks of Lakeland – and the Residents' Bar is lined with sepia photos of bewhiskered pioneers, all no doubt approving of the conversation below. But for enthusiast and amateur alike this is an excellent place to stay. Its only weakness is as a touring centre – the road is a cul de sac, and to get anywhere else in the Lakes you have to go down to Gosforth and round the edge of the mountains. My odometer made it a staggering 53 miles by road from here to the top of Borrowdale – it's only about six on foot. But staying in this wild and isolated setting dosen't require any sacrifice of creature comforts . . ." (S L)*

Thus the opening of an inspector's report on this true haven for hill-walkers and mountaineers at the head of the remote valley of Wasdale. And the report goes on to detail the comforts of the house – the well-maintained and attractive rooms, the good cooking and the solicitous service. Prices are reasonable, too – especially for stays of four nights or more. More reports please.

Open All year except 17 Nov – 28 Dec.
Rooms 8 double, 2 single – 8 with bath, 2 with shower, all with telephone and tea-making facilities.
Facilities Lounge, 2 bars, pool room, restaurant. 2-acre garden leading down to Mosedale Beck with a natural swimming pool. Drying room with spin-dryer. Wastwater Lake within walking distance. Sea with safe sandy beaches 12 m.
Location Follow signs for Wasdale Head from Gosforth or Santon Bridge.
Restrictions Not suitable for ሌ. No dogs in public rooms.
Credit cards Access, Visa.
Terms [1985 rates] (No service charge) B&B: single £22–£27, double £40; dinner, B&B: single £30–£35, double, £56. Packed lunch £2, set dinner £10. Reductions for stays of 4 nights or more. Reduced rates for children sharing parents' room; special meals.

> Details of amenities vary according to the information – or lack of it – supplied by hotels in response to our questionnaire. The fact that lounges or bars or gardens are not mentioned must not be taken to mean that a hotel lacks them.

GRASMERE Cumbria   Map 4

White Moss House [GFG]   *Tel* Grasmere (096 65) 295
Rydal Water, Grasmere LA22 9SE

"A well-run establishment which consistently maintains a high standard
of food, wine and service and an enjoyable place to visit or stay. We had
the cottage at Brockstone for four of us. Bedrooms and bathrooms can be
rather small. It is quiet and the quality of the accommodation is high.
Breakfast excellent" *(Mrs Maureen Young)*. "We stayed for three days. All
the meals were faultless and very, very enjoyable. Everything home-
made. A wonderful holiday in a friendly hotel set in a beautiful position
overlooking the fells and near Rydal Water. Service cheerful and
faultless" *(Mrs Felicity Millward)*. Words of praise in 1985 for this small
hotel (five rooms in the main house, and two in Brockstone, a cottage up
the hill) run by the Butterworths and their daughter and son-in-law, the
Dixons. Five-course dinner "at 7.30 pm for 8" [£14.95, 1985, including
coffee] offers no choice until the dessert; there is a particularly
interesting selection of English cheeses and a wide-ranging wine list.

Open Mid-Mar – early Nov.
Rooms 7 double – 6 with bath, 1 with shower, all with radio and colour TV; 2 in
cottage annexe.
Facilities Lounge, bar, dining room. 1-acre garden with hillside seats. Near Rydal
Water and river Rothay; swimming and fishing.
Location On A591 between Ambleside and Grasmere.
Restrictions Not suitable for &. No children under 10. No dogs.
Credit cards None accepted.
Terms B&B £27.50–£30; dinner, B&B £42–£45. Set dinner £14.95. Reduced rates
for stays of 3 nights or more Mar and Nov.

GRASSINGTON North Yorkshire   Map 4

Ashfield House Hotel   *Tel* Grassington (0756) 752584
Grassington, Nr Skipton BD23 5AE

Ashfield House Hotel, it says on the notepaper, and just *Ashfield House* on
the brochure, but perhaps guest-house would suit better the style of
Janet and Roy Sugden's cheerful, cosy establishment close by the square
in this village in Upper Wharfedale, described by two faithful regulars in
the following terms:
"A 17th-century tree-surrounded house, tucked away just off the
main street. From it one can walk straight up through the village into the
dales. The floors are uneven, the doorways low, the walls thick and the
atmosphere delightful. The seven rooms are all individually decorated.
A blazing fire is lit after dinner in the hall/sitting room where limitless
fresh coffee is available for guests in the evenings. A 'mini-bar', run on a
'help-yourself' system, is in the other sitting room, along with TV, and
various games and books, but in our experience most people sit round
the fire on the very uncomfortable settles and laundry baskets and
high-backed old chairs and enjoy getting to know each other. Mrs
Sugden does the cooking herself and is a real expert in the best of
English fare. The only fixed point in our day is the high spot of 7 pm
when dinner is served. This always consists of three courses, normally a

delicious home-made soup, followed by meat and fresh vegetables served in abundant proportions and cooked with originality but also very simply. The guests then start watching the door to the kitchen to see what amazing new confections are being offered as sweets. We are glad when we have worked up an appetite by walking for miles, even if we ended the mammoth breakfast (marred only by the use of uninteresting sliced bread for toast) feeling we couldn't eat another thing all day. Both Mr and Mrs Sugden make every guest feel welcome. We are by no means the only people who keep going back, because the home-like atmosphere, the sparkling cleanliness, the attention to detail, the first-class food, and yet the simplicity make this an extremely pleasant place to stay." (*Phillida Sawbridge and Hedi Argent; also Dr N Naunton Davies, Prof Laurie Taylor*)

Open Apr–Oct.
Rooms 7 double – all with tea-making facilities.
Facilities 2 lounges – 1 with open fire, 1 with bar and colour TV, dining room. ¼-acre garden.
Location Central but secluded, off main square.
Restrictions Not suitable for &. No dogs.
Credit cards None accepted.
Terms B&B £11.50–£14; dinner, B&B £19–£21.50. Set dinner £7.50. Reduced rates and special meals for children.

GREAT MILTON Oxfordshire   Map 2

Le Manoir aux Quat' Saisons [GFG]   *Tel* Great Milton (084 46)
Great Milton OX9 7PD   8881 or 230

❧ *César awarded in 1985 for most brilliant newcomer*

"As close to being the perfect country hotel as you are likely to find anywhere." "A superb hotel, the best of the so-called Country House variety that I know of. It is of course very expensive, but I have never stayed anywhere where I felt that every penny was justified as much as here." "Fantastic combination of the very best of England and France: wonderful French food, but the hotel very English with log fires and beautiful flowers everywhere." "The reason for going to the *Manoir* is to revel in the incredible artistry of Raymond Blanc: the food is beyond criticism and very nearly beyond description. The justification for staying there is the wine list: no one can do justice to the food without the wine, and thereafter driving is foolhardy. But the hotel would be well worth staying in even if there were a McDonald's downstairs. The rooms are beautiful and spacious, the views from the windows are just heaven, and the little touches – the fruit, the carafe of sherry – are for once not a substitute for style, but a complement to it. The public rooms are peace itself." "The quality of the place is seen right through to the towels and bath-robes – tops all the way. But nothing comes over as pompous. All the service we received was faultless, but smiling and relaxed."

Five tributes to Raymond and Jenny Blanc's triumphant realisation of the ideal country house hotel, incarnate in a serene country manor amid 27 acres of gardens and parkland, just off the M40, 10 miles south-east of Oxford. The quotations above are only the top of the cream; we have never had a comparable postbag. Naturally, when a hotel has received such ubiquitous acclaim, expectations of perfection are aroused which cannot always be satisfied, especially when prices are as steep as at the *Manoir*. The occasional dish disappoints, the decor in the ladies' loo may be somewhat over the top for some tastes, the pictures on the wall, which are for sale, may let the side down. We ourselves had a couple of niggles which we should like to see the Blancs rectify: having suffered from a chain-smoker at the next table, we would like to see smoking banned in the restaurant; and we wish that cars could all be parked away from the front-facing rooms. But we wholly concur with the reader who wrote: "Quite the best bargain of the lot if you can afford it."

Open All year except Christmas and New Year. Restaurant closed Sun evenings, all day Mon and Tue lunch; drinks, tea and pâtisserie available on these days.
Rooms 2 suites, 10 double – all with bath and shower, some with whirlpool bath; all with direct-dial telephone, radio and colour TV; 2 with four-posters.
Facilities 2 sitting rooms, reception lounge, restaurant. 27 acres of landscaped garden and parkland with tennis court, heated swimming pool and water garden.
Location 1 m W of M40/A40, 10 m SE of Oxford. From London take M40: exit 7, 1 mile, 2nd right. From Oxford, take A40, then A329 at Milton Common towards Wallingford, 2nd right.
Restrictions No children under 5. No dogs in building – free kennel facilities in grounds.
Credit cards Access, Amex, Visa.
Terms B&B double £95–£200. Set lunch £18.50–£20, dinner £35; full alc from £40. Special mid-week breaks Oct–Mar. Reductions for children; special meals.

GREAT SNORING Norfolk   Map 2

The Old Rectory   *Tel* Walsingham (032 872) 597
Great Snoring, Fakenham NR21 OHP

"We installed Swiss friends at *The Old Rectory*," wrote a regular correspondent, "and they – who stay only at the most comfortable and expensive places all over the world – were *very* comfortable, *very* attentively looked after, and just delighted with the ambience: totally unspoilt village, totally quiet, historic building. We dined with them: the food was suitably English and good." We sent an inspector, who confirmed the epicurean Swiss couple's good opinion: "It is much grander than your average country parsonage. It was originally a manor house, perhaps dating back to 1500, and its lofty rooms and stone mullioned windows provide a fine setting, in its 1½-acre walled garden, for a little gracious living in this peaceful Norfolk backwater ... Rooms spacious and comfortable ... Flowers everywhere ... Dining-room delightfully set out with fine silver and starched damask – not a paper serviette in sight ... Food excellently cooked and served, though only one main course offered on the 4-course set menu." Only carps: the hotel says dinner is served at 7 pm, which seemed unnecessarily restrictive, especially since other diners turned up an hour late. Also, though greeted by one of the four hosts (Mr and Mrs Tooke and Mr and Mrs Scoles) on arrival, there was no sign of any host for the rest of the evening.

Open All year except 25/26 Dec.
Rooms 5 double, 1 single – 4 with shower, all with colour TV.
Facilities Sitting room, dining room. 1½-acre walled garden. 6 m from north

Norfolk nature reserves. Bathing, fishing, sailing etc. all within ½-hour drive.
Location Great Snoring is 3 m off A148 Fakenham/Cromer road. *Old Rectory* is
behind church on Barsham road.
Restrictions Not suitable for &. Children not encouraged. No dogs.
Credit cards Amex, Diners.
Terms (No service charge) B&B: single £25–£28.50, double £36–£42; half-board:
single £35–£38.50, double £56–£62.

HAMBLETON Leicestershire   Map 2

Hambleton Hall [GFG]   *Tel* Oakham (0572) 56991
Hambleton, Oakham   *Telex* 342888 HAMBLE G
Rutland LE15 8TH

🏆 *César awarded in 1985 for comprehensive excellence in the luxury class*

An exceptionally large postbag for Tim and Stefa Hart's hyper-elegant
country house hotel on a tongue of land that leads out from Oakham
into the centre of Rutland Water: visually satisfying from the fine views
of the lake scene and from the interior decor by Nina Campbell and
gastronomically rewarding thanks to the excellent rosetted *nouvelle*-ish
cooking of chef Nicholas Gill. Compliments, as previously, have been of
the most fulsome: "The ambience beyond all criticism." *(R W Cahn)* "The
most comfortable and best-appointed of all the country houses we have
sampled, and the staff are a joy to be with." *(Cynthia McDowall)* "Meal
was sublime in all respects." *(Stephen Whittle)* And much more in the
same rosy vein.

We wish that we could leave it there, but the *Hambleton* file this year
was notable for the number of criticisms. Some were no more than
niggles: "We did think it strange to have paper napkins at breakfast, but
everything else was perfect," or "We would have difficulty faulting
anything – except smoking in the restaurant." Others contradicted each
other out – a complaint from one party that the portions were insultingly
small was countered by another who wished that there could have been
a three-course set meal for those who found the five-course one far too
much (but the hotel does offer an à la carte menu); and others again were
more serious. More than one correspondent complained of a decidedly
poky room and bathroom. Another was disappointed to find that there
was only a bar lunch available because the restaurant had been taken
over for a conference. While someone wrote that *Hambleton* was the
quietest hotel he had every stayed in, another told of the shattering of
peace at 11 am on a Sunday by a clay pigeon shoot in the garden. There
were further grumbles besides: tables too close together in the
restaurant; bathroom taps that couldn't be turned on and off without
getting into the bath; poor service at breakfast. No serious offences, but
minor blemishes matter more in hotels aspiring to "comprehensive
excellence in the luxury class".

Open All year.
Rooms 15 double–all with bath and shower, telephone, radio, colour TV, and
baby-listening.
Facilities Lift. Drawing room, bar, dining room; small conference facilities;
private dining room. 17-acre grounds overlooking lake with trout fishing and
sailing; tennis court; swimming pool planned for 1986. Riding and shooting by
arrangement.
Location Off A606 Stamford Road 1 m E of Oakham.

Restrictions No children under 9. No dogs in public rooms.
Credit cards All major cards accepted.
Terms B&B (continental): single £66, double £41–£110. Set lunch/dinner £26; full alc £26. 50% discount on room rates 1 Nov–30 Apr excluding Sat, Christmas and Easter (min. 3 nights).
Service/tipping: "Service is included in all prices, so very little tipping goes on."

HARROGATE North Yorkshire   Map 4

Russell Hotel [GFG]   *Tel* Harrogate (0423) 509866
Valley Drive, Harrogate HG2 OJN

A medium-sized hotel owned and managed by various members of the Hodgson family. Richard Hodgson is in charge of the well-regarded *Hodgsons* restaurant, adjoining the hotel. The building is a row of converted terraced houses overlooking Valley Gardens: corridors run at all sorts of angles, so you may need some navigational aid first time around. Not everyone appreciates the colourful decor of the public rooms, but much else gives satisfaction. The service seems to be consistently efficient and amiable, even when the hotel is full of conferees, but the restaurant is what tends to get singled out for special commendation. *(Tom and Angela Walford, Elspeth M Carmichael)*

Open All year except 27–30 Dec.
Rooms 2 suites, 24 double, 8 single – 23 with bath, 11 with shower, all with telephone, radio, colour TV and baby-listening.
Facilities Lift. 2 lounges, cocktail lounge, public bar, restaurant; jazz duo twice weekly in bar. Terrace and veranda where drinks and meals are served in fine weather. Golf, swimming, squash, tennis, cricket, fishing, riding, racing nearby.
Location ½ m from centre. Turn into Crescent Road at traffic lights on the Leeds/Ripon road opposite Royal Hall; Valley Drive is on left side of Valley Gardens. Unrestricted street parking.
Restrictions Not suitable for &. No dogs in public rooms.
Credit cards All major cards accepted.
Terms B&B: single £25.95–£31.50, double £37.50–£47.75; dinner, B&B: single £36.25–£41.75, double £55.50–£68.25. Set dinner £10.25; full alc £17 (no service charge for meals). Weekend and mid-week breaks min. 2 nights. Christmas package. No charge for children under 12 sharing parents' room; special meals.

HAWES North Yorkshire   Map 4

Stone House Hotel   *Tel* Hawes (096 97) 571
Sedbusk, Nr Hawes DL8 3PT

"This was the 'best buy' of our trip – well up to your standards and a bargain discovery. Stone House is in the most beautiful area imaginable and we felt as if we were stepping into Herriot's TV series All Creatures Great and Small. *The hotel is a mile outside the charming town of Hawes on a little-travelled country road. Sheep graze on the surrounding hills and the view in every direction is beautiful. The hotel, built in 1908, has comfortable, well-heated rooms and wonderfully firm mattresses. We had a huge room with a four-poster bed plus a single bed but weren't charged an additional fee for this elegantly furnished room with bath. There are three public rooms, one a large comfortable lounge with fireplace, another a snooker room with books lining the walls, and the third room the entrance lounge with a small bar, lively at night with friendly locals. The*

107

dinners are not gourmet affairs but wholesome home-cooked Yorkshire fare. Breakfast was a plentiful English one, complete with smoked fish. The owners, Jane and Peter Taplin, made us feel most welcome. All the Taplin family pitch in to help run the hotel so efficiently: Jane's father and Peter's mother are there as well as the Taplins' two teenage children. Warmly recommended." (Felice Feldstein) *More reports please.*

Open 1 Apr–31 Oct. Weekends only 1 Nov–31 Mar. Closed Jan.
Rooms 1 suite with 4 poster, 11 double, 1 single – 1 with bath, 10 with shower, all with colour TV and tea-making facilities; 4 rooms on ground floor.
Facilities Small bar/lounge, drawing room, library/snooker room, dining room. 1-acre garden with tennis lawn; golf, fishing, pony-trekking and sailing nearby. River fishing day tickets available. Ramp available for &.
Location Take Muker road from Hawes; at T-junction turn right – hotel 500 yds on left.
Restriction No dogs in public rooms.
Credit card Visa.
Terms (No service charge) B&B £13.50–£19.50; dinner, B&B £21.50–£27.50 Set dinner £8. Weekend breaks Nov–Easter: 2 nights, dinner, B&B (double room with shower) £42 per room. Christmas and New Year house party. Reduced rates and special meals for children.

HAWKRIDGE Somerset   Map 1

Tarr Steps Hotel   *Tel* Winsford (064 385) 293
Hawkridge, Dulverton TA22 9PY

"One of the most beautifully situated hotels I have ever stayed in," writes a visitor to this former Georgian rectory in the south-east corner of Exmoor, "with superb views of beautiful woods, fields and hills." *Tarr Steps* stands in eight acres of what the brochure describes as "slightly wild" gardens and grounds, 800 feet above sea level, overlooking the river Barle and its valley. Close by are the Steps which give the hotel its name, a cyclopean clapper bridge said to date from the Bronze Age. A lot of country pursuits are available from the hotel, and it is particularly popular with the fishing and riding fraternity. If you are not of the sporting persuasion, do not allow yourself to be put off by the scatter of magazines about stag hunting, horse and hound, hare coursing and suchlike. It is a splendid centre for Exmoor walkers as well. Prices are reasonable. *(Alison Foster)*

Open Mid-Mar to mid-Nov and Christmas.
Rooms 12 double, 3 single–8 with bath; 3 rooms in annexe; 1 ground-floor room with bath and wheelchair access.
Facilities Sitting room, bar, dining room. 8-acre grounds with garden; rough and clay pigeon shooting over 500 acres of privately owned land surrounding hotel. 4 m of fishing on river Barle (fly only – salmon and trout, licences from the hotel – free to guests); fox and stag hunting; stables and kennels for guests horses and dogs. River bathing 100 yds, fine walking and scenic drives over Exmoor. &.
Location W of B3223 between Dulverton and Exford but approach through Hawkridge village.
Restriction No dogs in public rooms: kennels available.
Credit cards Amex, Visa.
Terms (No service charge) B&B £20; dinner, B&B £31. Set lunch £8.50, dinner £11. Children under 8 sharing parents' room, half price; high teas.

HEADLAM Durham   **Map 4**

Headlam Hall   *Tel* Darlington (0325) 730238
Headlam, Nr Gainford
Darlington DL2 3HA

Regular correspondents tipped us off about this small Jacobean mansion in a peaceful village in South Durham, nine miles from Scotch Corner, owned by John and Ann Robinson who also run a farm close by: "It should dispel the image of a barren North-East so far as attractive hotels are concerned." We sent along an inspector who reported:

"Sensible people will use this unusual place as a stop-over to or from Scotland. They will start from London or Edinburgh, take the A1, and be here for afternoon tea. But resist sense! Start earlier and try to engineer an approach from the west along the heart-stoppingly splendid A66. Then, after the big skies of Bowes Moor, plunge into rural Teesdale – all pot-holes and single-track roads between hedges. From the road, all that can be seen is Georgian, but the entrance is at the rear where the full creeper-clad glory of the Jacobean origins can be seen at their best. There is a big lawn, ancient yew and beech hedges, odd arches and sundials, and 100 yards of brook channelled into trout pools; also a hard tennis court. All is ordered, but nothing over-organised. You feel at once that you are staying with people rather than paying for a room. The feeling is confirmed when you enter. Whoever is around – in our case the chef – takes you to your room. Help yourself to drinks from the bar before dinner. Just leave a note of what you've had. Beds are comfortable, funiture is good quality. But the public rooms are something else. The bar is a corner of the central hall, with its weighty Doric columns and a fireplace the size of a small car. There is a fine Georgian drawing room with a grand piano. The dining room is small and wood-panelled. Only the food is disappointing – all perfectly hygienic and hearty but nothing more. Breakfasts were better. There is also piped music – in our case, Japanese film soundtracks, Elton John and David Bowie. The staff are charming, friendly and efficient. There is nothing genteel about the place, and some might find it a little rough round the edges. But we thought it a real find, especially in view of the extremely reaasonable rates."

Open All year.
Rooms 2 suites, 10 double, 1 single – 11 with bath, 2 with shower, all with telephone and TV.
Facilities Hall, drawing room, snooker room, bar, restaurant. 3-acre grounds with tennis court, small trout lake; surrounded by hotel's large farm.
Location 7 m W of Darlington off A67 Darlington to Barnard Castle road.
Restrictions Not suitable for &. No dogs in bedrooms or public rooms.
Credit cards Access, Visa.
Terms B&B: single £28–£43, double £41–£56; dinner, B&B: single £38–£53, double £61–£75; full board: single £45–£60, double £75–£90. Set lunch £7–£11, dinner £10–£15; full alc £14. Special weekend rates. Reduced rates and special meals for children.

If you have difficulty in finding hotels because the location details given in the Guide are inadequate, please help us to improve directions next year.

HEDDON'S MOUTH Devon   Map 1

Heddon's Gate Hotel   *Tel* Parracombe (059 83) 313
Heddon's Mouth
Parracombe, Barnstaple EX31 4PZ

A hotel for those with a yen for spectacular locations, *Heddon's Gate* is a turn-of-the-century Swiss-Victorian lodge with various eclectic extensions, perched 400 feet over a luscious valley, with views over miles of moorland and wooded hills. The 20 acres of grounds are surrounded by National Trust and Exmoor National Park land, and several private paths thread through the gardens – one directly on the South West Peninsular coastal path. The hotel is owned by Robert and Anne De Ville, who took it over in 1967 and have been busy with improvements since. The steeply terraced gardens are clearly a source of pride; the De Villes are keen members of the National Gardens Scheme. The style of cooking has changed since our last edition: the emphasis is now on all fresh foods and some wholefoods, with everything home made, including bread, jams and cakes. First reports speak of "imaginative and delectable" meals. Breakfasts of the full English variety are strongly recommended. Rooms are comfortable with a pronounced 1920s country house character. Decor is catholic and a bit outré: some antique furniture, lots of Victorian pictures and ornaments, velvet and tapestry as well as Dralon. Not to everyone's taste, but it's a stunning place if you like nature and walks and peace and quiet. *(David H Clark)*

Open Easter – 1st week Nov.
Rooms 3 suites, 11 double, 2 single – 14 with bath, 2 with shower, all with telephone, radio, colour TV and tea-making facilities; 3 suites in annexe with wheelchair access.
Facilities Sitting room, library, bar, dining room. 20-acre grounds with terraced gardens. Access to sea (¾ m) and river (¼ m) by private and National Trust footpaths. Riding, pony trekking, fishing nearby, &.
Location 4 m W of Lynton. From A39 2 m W of Lynton take Martinhoe/Woody Bay road; turn left towards Hunter's Inn; hotel sign is at next crossroads.
Restrictions No children under 10. Dogs by arrangement.
Credit cards Access, Amex.
Terms B&B £16.90–£22.90; half-board £27.40–£33.40. Cold lunch £2.20, set dinner £10.50. Reductions for stays of 3 or more days. 50% reduction for children sharing with parents.
Service/tipping: "We never make any service charge and staff do not tout for tips."

HELFORD Cornwall   Map 1

Riverside [GFG]   *Tel* Manaccan (032 623) 443
Helford, Helston TR12 6JU

"Excellent: everything honest, attractive and friendly" *(Kenneth Bell)*. One of those places which inspire compliments (that one from the châtelain of *Thornbury Castle*), *Riverside* is an enchanting conversion of two white-washed cottages bordering a small creek winding into the Helford River. George Perry-Smith and his partner Heather Crosbie made their names in the fifties and sixties running Bath's famous restaurant *The Hole in the Wall*, and have made a fresh reputation with this tiny restaurant with rooms in deepest Cornwall. It won our César in

1984 for the best restaurant with rooms. Here is another typical salute: "White-washed cottages in terraced gardens and the abundance of flowering shrubs give it a Mediterranean feel. Small, simple but charming rooms with adequate storage space and cheerful fabrics. Small modern bathrooms with abundant hot water. (The style is in danger of becoming *too* relaxed – the housekeeping could do with stricter supervision.) But the setting is idyllic, the owners and staff pleasant and friendly without being obtrusive, the food impressive, unpretentious French cooking. Whilst being in many ways deeply English, the hotel calls to mind very strongly those French family-run country inns of quality where the daily routine revolves around the kitchen and the few staff perform cheerfully whatever jobs require to be done about the place as circumstances dictate." *(David Wooff; also Heather Sharland, Dr and Mrs D Howell)*

Open End Mar–end Oct. Restaurant open to residents only on Sun and Mon.
Rooms 6 double – all with bath, radio, colour TV and tea-making facilities; 3 rooms in cottage.
Facilities Sitting room, restaurant and bar. Small grounds on Helford creek off the Helford river and Falmouth bay, with beaches, sailing and fishing within 5 minutes' walk.
Location Take Lizard road out of Helston, through RNAS Culdrose, turn left for St Keverne left again for Helford.
Restrictions No special facilities for &, but some will find it manageable. No dogs.
Credit cards None accepted.
Terms B&B: single occupancy £38, double £62. Set 4-course dinner £24. Special meals for children.

HINTLESHAM Suffolk

Map 2

Hintlesham Hall [GFG]
Hintlesham, Ipswich IP8 3NS

Tel Hintlesham (047 387) 268

A spectacularly beautiful hall dating from the 15th century, and renowned in the 1970s as a restaurant under Robert Carrier, is reincarnated as a small luxury country house hotel. After extensive renovation four rooms were opened in December 1984, and a further six have been unveiled in the summer of 1985. The head chef is Robert Mabey, ex *Le Gavroche* and *The Connaught* (q.v.). General manager is Tim Sutherland, ex *Le Talbooth* (also q.v.). First reports speak well of this new potential super-star with some caveats about inadequate heating in a cold March: "Magnificent spacious room . . . furnishings tasteful, not over ornate and very comfortable . . . Lots of expected touches – minibar, armchairs, magazines, fruit, biscuits, chocolates, bed turned down . . . Bathroom equally comfortable . . . Lighting excellent . . . Very high-quality cooking, nicely presented with friendly efficient service. Interesting wine list, with plenty of reasonably priced house wines to complement the classics. Super breakfast – choice of virtually anything, including Bucks Fizz to start, all included in room prices." *(Pat and Jeremy Temple)*

Open All year.
Rooms 10 double – 9 with bath, 1 with shower, all with telephone, radio, colour TV, mini-bar and baby-listening.
Facilities Lounge, lounge/bar, restaurant, conference/function rooms, billiard room. 18-acre grounds with all-weather tennis court, small farm, orchard, lake

with fountain. 20 minutes to sea; golf nearby.
Location 5 m W of Ipswich on the A1071 to Hadleigh. Parking.
Restrictions No children under 10 (except small babies). No dogs in hotel; kennels provided. Only restaurant suitable for &.
Credit cards All major cards accepted.
Terms B&B: single £38–£85, double £45–£95; dinner, B&B: single £58–£105, double £85–£135. Set lunch £12.75, dinner £13.50 and *menu gastronomique* on Thur, Fri and Sat £20; full alc £22. Lunch open to children Christmas, Easter and bank holidays (supervised crèche and £5 meal for under 7s).
Tipping/service: "We too feel it [tipping] is an anachronism and we positively discourage it by virtue of all printed material, and bills especially, bearing the instruction that the total includes VAT and gratuities. Any customer who still attempts to leave a tip is advised that the bill is inclusive of all gratuities, but if they continue to insist on leaving a tip we gracefully accept, as further refusal would probably cause offence."

HINTON CHARTERHOUSE Avon   Map 2

Homewood Park [GFG]   *Tel* Limpley Stoke (022 122) 3731
Hinton Charterhouse
Nr Bath BA3 6BB

César awarded for classic country house excellence

A small family-run hotel, five miles south of Bath, opposite the ruins of the Carthusian Hinton Priory, *Homewood Park*, once the abbot's house, dates from the 18th century, but with substantial Victorian additions. It is set in 10 acres of delightful rambling gardens. For the past six years it has been a country house hotel in the exceptionally gifted hands of Stephen and Penny Ross, and for many readers it represents a Platonic ideal of that species. Reports, this year as in the past, read like extracts from the "Hallelujah Chorus". Two extracts will have to suffice:

"The bedrooms and reception rooms have an overwhelming feeling of warmth and comfort and luxury. These are exactly the qualities every hotel should aim to achieve, but such success is rarely seen. The food was excellent. It deserves every recommendation it receives. Even a one-night stay was relaxing and memorable. Full marks for luxury, style, service, decor and food." *(J C Love)*

"What a pleasure to be totally enthusiastic about somewhere! Lovely gardens, well maintained and a pleasure to stroll in. A shining clean house, staffed with pleasant and helpful girls and owned and run by a delightful and unassuming couple. Excellent food. Our bedroom right at the top of the house had decor in tones of honeysuckle ... those warm yellows and slightly peachy oranges, with touches of almost red. Not overdone, peaceful. Comfortable chairs and good colour TV if one tired of the *glorious* view. Charming bathroom, done out in pale oak, even loo seat and bath panels. Help with baggage, always somebody really interested about. Really felt like staying with good friends. This is what a lot of places pretend to be, and aren't because their owners look at profits first, people last. My nomination for top of the not-overwhelmingly-posh architectural places." *(WA; also countless others)*

Open All year except 23 Dec – 12 Jan.
Rooms 15 double – all with bath, telephone, radio and colour TV; 2 ground-floor rooms.
Facilities Bar, drawing room, 3 dining rooms. 10-acre grounds with tennis court, croquet and arboretum. &.

Location On A36, 6 m S of Bath opposite Hinton Priory.
Restriction No dogs.
Credit cards All major cards accepted.
Terms B&B (continental): single £44.50, double £64.50–£94.50. Cooked breakfast £4.50; set lunch £12.50 weekdays, £15 Sun; full alc dinner £25 (set fish menu Thur £15). 2-night winter breaks. Special meals for children by arrangement.

HOLDSWORTH West Yorkshire   Map 2

Holdsworth House   *Tel* Halifax (0422) 240024
Halifax HX2 9TG   *Telex* 51574 HOLHSE

A fortunate find for those who like a hotel that offers both character and comfort to those wishing to explore Brontë country nearby, is how Bernard Theobald *sums up on this 17th-century manor house skilfully extended to provide a sophisticated 40-bedroom hotel; his only criticism, an exiguous scrambled egg at breakfast "had to be spread very thinly to cover a very small piece of toast". It lies three miles north of Halifax. We are not well off with recommendable hotels in that conurbation. More reports welcome.*

Open 2 Jan – 23 Dec and New Year's Eve. Restaurant closed Sat and Sun for lunch.
Rooms 4 split-level suites, 24 double, 12 single – 28 with bath, 12 with shower, all with telephone, radio, colour TV, baby-listening and mini-bar; some ground-floor rooms; all rooms are in new building linked to the original house.
Facilities Entrance lounge, reception lounge, reading lounge, bar, dining room, snooker room, 2 small conference rooms. 2½-acre grounds with grade 1 listed gazebo, grade 2 listed barn and ornamental gardens. Within easy reach of Yorkshire Dales and the Pennines.
Location From Halifax go N on the A629 to Keighley, turn right at Ovenden where Holmfield Industrial Estate is indicated; continue 2 m. The hotel is set back from road on right opposite Holy Trinity school.
Restriction No dogs in bar or restaurant.
Credit cards All major cards accepted.
Terms B&B: single £32–£37, double £50–£60; dinner, B&B: single £44–£52, double £74–£90; full board: single £54–£64, double £94–£114. Full alc £18. Half-board weekend rates available. Reduced rates and special meals for children.

HOLFORD Somerset   Map 2

Combe House Hotel   *Tel* Holford (027 874) 382
Holford, Bridgwater TA5 1RZ

Readers continue to appreciate the hospitality of the Danish Richard Bjergfelt in his 17th-century house, once a tannery (the mill wheel is still *in situ*), in a particularly choice location 500 feet up in the heart of the Quantocks. "I write to express our gratitude for the entry. The building is charming – sweeties and Roger & Gallet soap in our bedrooms an extra bonus. Clean towels daily, everything spotless. Gripes might include the doors needing a spot of oil and inadequate sitting area if the hotel is really full. (The latter could be helped by better arrangement and less bulky chairs in the lounges.) The food is excellent. Fresh orange juice and good coffee, super packed lunches – one between two would have been adequate. Our dinners were astounding value. Home-made soups, delicious vegetables – coffee with mints all included. The good hard tennis court tempted us out after twenty idle years. Enthusiasts should bring their own racquets. The hotel does provide them, but of the French cricket variety. The situation of the hotel is charming, and to be able to walk on to the hills from the hotel front door was an added plus. The staff are very helpful – even Polly the pussy is a comforting knee-warmer, with an extra-loud purr." *(Mary Cross; also F and M Bowles, Gareth Rees, Derek Hill, Steven Bailey)*

Open Mid-Mar to 1st week in Nov.
Rooms 1 suite, 16 double, 6 single – 13 with bath; 3 rooms in annexe. Radio, TV and baby-listening on request.
Facilities Lounge, small non-smoking lounge, cocktail bar with open fire, dining room; indoor swimming pool. 5-acre grounds with lawns, gardens, hard tennis court and croquet lawn; riding, pony-trekking, golf, fishing nearby.
Location On A39. Coming from E, turn left at garage in village, bear left at fork; hotel is ½ m further on.
Restrictions Not suitable for &. No dogs in public rooms and only in some bedrooms.
Credit cards Access, Amex, Visa. (Not for bargain breaks.)
Terms (No service charge) B&B: single £15.50–£20.50, double £28.50–£35; dinner, B&B (weekly rates): single £145–£170, double £290–£340. Bar lunches and cream teas available; set dinner £8. 2-day autumn and spring bargain breaks. Reduced rates for children sharing parents' room; special meals on request.

HOVE East Sussex   Map 2

Courtlands Hotel   *Tel* Brighton (0273) 731055
19–27 The Drive, Hove BN3 3JE   *Telex* 87574 CHF/G

"Don't allow yourself to be put off by the look of this hotel (inside and out are no great shakes) because somewhere within, a conscientious management is trying hard – and on the whole succeeding to run a good hotel. There is a pleasant air of wishing to give good service, and it is in no way amateur or obsequious. Public rooms are rather institutionalised, but the bar and restaurant are professionally run. They don't try to over-extend themselves with the food, but what is offered is of good quality, the helpings are generous and the menu not over-priced. The hotel provides a good base for visiting the area and is a pleasant retreat in summer from the hurly-burly of the main Brighton promenade. It is 400 yards from the sea on a wide avenue, which itself carries a fair amount of traffic and might be noisy in summer. An east-facing room at the back would be quieter. In all, a warm-hearted, unpretentious establishment that rises above its somewhat old-fashioned origins." Last year we introduced *Courtlands* to these columns with the above appraisal from an inspector of a thoroughly traditional three-star hotel, which at the same time incorporates traditional virtues often hard to find. We should add a bonus: the *Courtlands'* charges are very reasonable for all that is offered. *(K C Turpin, and others)*.

Open All year.
Rooms 2 flats; 33 double, 27 single – 49 with bath, 6 with shower, all with direct-dial telephone, radio, colour TV and baby-listening; 5 rooms in grounds have mini-bar (with tea-making facilities); 8 ground-floor rooms (but with seven steps).
Facilities 3 lounges, bar, games room, restaurant, spa and whirlpool bath, conference facilities. ½-acre garden with terrace, covered swimming pool and children's playground. Sea 400 yds, private bathing hut. Leisure complex nearby.

Location 400 yds from centre. Quieter rooms at back of hotel. Parking.
Restriction No dogs in public rooms; in bedrooms by arrangement.
Credit cards All major cards accepted.
Terms B&B: single £26.50–£37.50, double £45–£47.50; half-board (min.2 days): single £27.50–£30, double £50–£60; full board £10.50 per person added to B&B rate. Set lunch £8–£9, dinner £10–£11.50; full alc £15.50. Weekend, winter and summer breaks. 4-day Christmas programme. 50% reduction for children 2–11, 25% for children 12–16; special meals.
Service: "10% service charge included in the above rates for all hotel accounts, which is distributed to our staff."

HUNSTRETE Avon   **Map 2**

Hunstrete House   *Tel* Compton Dando (076 18) 578
Chelwood, Nr Bristol   *Telex* 449540 (HUNHSE)
BS18 4NS

The interior decoration of *Hunstrete House* is the inspiration of Thea Dupays, who, eight years ago with her husband John, bought and converted this serenely beautiful Georgian mansion. The visual delight of the rooms, coupled with the sense the Dupays give of inviting you to be their country house guest, has rightly brought the house fame in the interim. In 1984 we awarded it a César for "matchless decor". The exterior scene is pretty stunning, too: the 90 acres of grounds contain not only the relatively standard provisions of expensive country house hotels – heated outdoor pool, tennis court and croquet lawn – and not only a lovingly maintained flower and herb garden, but also, something of a rarity, a deer park. The Achilles heel of this otherwise idyllic hotel has been, at least for some fastidious eaters, the restaurant. However since Martin Rowbotham assumed the head toque of *Hunstrete* in 1984 and introduced a classic French menu, reports on the kitchen front have been much more encouraging. Meanwhile everything continues sunny in other departments. *(Patsy Brandt, Jeffrey Bushell, J F Greenhough, Patricia Roberts)*

Open All year except 2 weeks mid-Jan.
Rooms 2 suites, 18 double, 1 single – all with bath, telephone, radio and colour TV; 8 rooms in annexe; 4 ground-floor rooms.
Facilities Drawing room, library, bar, dining room, 90-acre grounds, walled garden, heated outdoor swimming pool, hard tennis court, croquet lawn, deer park, coarse fishing in grounds; trout fishing, riding and golf nearby. 4 racecourses within hour's drive.
Location On A368, 8 m SW of Bath.
Restrictions No children under 9. No dogs.
Credit cards Amex, Diners, Visa (none accepted for special breaks).
Terms (Excluding VAT) B&B: single £50–£66, double £80–£115. Set dinner £22. Special winter breaks Nov–Mar (min.3 days). Christmas programme.

> We need feedback on *all* entries. Often people fail to report on the most well-known hotels, assuming that "someone else is sure to".

> If you feel we have done a hotel an injustice ⎫
> If we have failed to mention salient details ⎬ please let us know.
> If you consider we have got it about right ⎭

HUNTSHAM Devon   Map 1

Huntsham Court   *Tel* Clayhanger (039 86) 210
Huntsham, Nr Tiverton EX16 7NA

Mogens Bolwig, who is Danish, and his Greek wife Andrea have now celebrated their fourth anniversary at this popular though idiosyncratic establishment. "The odd break for individuals" is how they advertise their establishment. The oddness is partly structural: *Huntsham Court* is a choice example of high Victorian architecture, with many of the rooms, both public and bedrooms, awe-inspiring in their dimensions. It would make an admirable setting for a Gothic horror movie especially since the furnishing is equally outsize and eclectic. The Bolwigs cultivate the house-party atmosphere more effectively than most: guests dine communally by candlelight at one immense long table; the bar is a help-yourself place, in which you log your own drinks in if no one is around. The music room has over 2,000 recordings.

For some visitors, *Huntsham* is an oasis among hotels, satisfying parts other hotels never reach. *"Real* living," ran one recent report from someone who had held a business conference at *Huntsham*: "Andrea went to huge lengths to ensure our comfort – and the delegates have never stopped talking about it. The records, the trust bar, the sauna, early morning cycle rides, fires in the bathroom, hot croissants on arrival, the sunbeds, wonderful books to read, and above all the peace and quiet. May they go on for ever." But of course the oddness of this Elysium doesn't suit all comers. Serious eaters should be warned that the meals are ambitious rather than distinguished. The Bolwigs encourage house parties as well as conferences which can lead to late carousing, but expressions of appreciation far outweigh the complaints: "Our favourite hotel of the trip. Your description was enticing and accurate in every respect. Our toddlers enjoyed themselves, too, and were really welcomed" *(Mr and Mrs H U Khan)*. "The whole weekend was like living in a private country house in another age. Everything seemed to be amateur, and yet nothing was left to chance. But I hope they get a new Elgar Cello Concerto and bikes with brakes before our next visit." *(Hans and Pauline Simonis)*

Open All year.
Rooms 2 suites, 12 double, 1 single – all with bath and pre-war wirelesses.
Facilities Hall, drawing room, library, music room, games room, bar, dining room; sauna, mini-gym. 5-acre garden with croquet; bicycles; grass tennis courts. Trout fishing in private lake, riding, golf nearby.
Location M5 to Taunton, then A361 towards Bampton, then turn off left to Huntsham when signposted. Parking.
Restrictions Not suitable for &. No dogs.
Credit card Visa.
Terms B&B £25–£45; dinner, B&B £40.50–£60.50. Set dinner £15.50. House parties; mid-week and weekend breaks; occasional jazz and opera weekends, special Christmas programme. Reduced rates for children sharing parents' room.

Always let a hotel know if you have to cancel a booking, whether you have paid a deposit or not. Hotels lose thousands of pounds and dollars from 'no-shows'.

ILFRACOMBE Devon Map 1

Langleigh County Hotel *Tel* Ilfracombe (0271) 62629
Langleigh Road, Ilfracombe EX34 4BG

Langleigh became a hotel in 1980, started by David Darlow, a Granada producer, and his wife Tessa. It is, we are told, the oldest inhabited house in the town, built in 1570, but it had an extensive facelift in the early 19th century and is now effectively Regency. Although in a suburban road on the outskirts of Ilfracombe, only a few minutes' walk from the town centre and Ilfracombe's sandy and rocky coves, it has an attractive setting at the foot of a wooded valley surrounded by National Trust land. Readers have continued to express their appreciation of different aspects of the *Langleigh* experience.

Last year's entry contained particularly warm tributes from an American honeymoon couple and a German family – both parties having received from the Darlows kindnesses well beyond the normal run of hotelier's responsibilities. Here are two more from this year's postbag: "A quite extraordinary pleasant place, both in atmosphere and in the house and gardens, which form a sort of small paradise (several acres) in surroundings which, with all respect to Ilfracombe, one would not describe as such. Everything is owed, obviously, to the personality and skill of the proprietors" *(AR Walmsley)*. "The owners and their staff could not have been kinder and more welcoming to us and our two children – with the result that the children, not just ours, in this relaxed and relaxing atmosphere, behaved well. I can't find the words to describe how impressed we were. We couldn't fault anything." *(Hazel and David Orme)*

Open Feb–Nov.
Rooms 3 family, 6 double, 1 single – 8 with bath, 2 with shower, all with radio, colour TV, tea-making facilities and baby-listening; also 2 family cottages, each with 2 bedrooms, living room and bathroom.
Facilities Lounge, bar, dining room, 2 games rooms. 3-acre grounds with croquet, badminton, solarium, sandpit, ornamental stream, 10 minutes' walk from the sea.
Location On corner of Broad Park Avenue and Langleigh Rd. At W end of town. Take steep hill to left of parish church.
Restrictions Not suitable for &. No dogs in public rooms.
Credit cards None accepted.
Terms (No service charge) B&B: single £12–£20, double £24–£42; dinner, B&B: single £20–£28, double £40–£58. Set dinner £8. Substantial reductions for children sharing parents' room; special meals.

IPSWICH Suffolk Map 2

The Marlborough [GFG] *Tel* Ipswich (0473) 57677
73 Henley Road *Telex* c/o Bury St Edmunds
Ipswich IP1 3SP Angel Hotel 81630

Under the same ownership as *The Angel* at Bury St Edmunds (q.v.), *The Marlborough*, a respectable red-brick Victorian residence a few minutes' walk from Ipswich's town centre, shows the same admirable professionalism in all departments. It is also, like its angelic brother, enterprising in some novel ways. We congratulated *The Angel* two years ago on inaugurating a Literary Prize for the best work by an East Anglian author; now *The Marlborough* announces its own Prize for Journalism. If only more hotels would compete with Booker in helping writers, now that the Arts Council are cutting back . . .

Its prices are high – and one reader this year felt unjustifiably so ("Crest Motel for me next time") – but it offers a lot more dependable comforts than most establishments. "Quite enchanting. When they took my reservation, I did not know of their special Olde English weekend rate, so was most impressed to be given that rate without comment, especially after the depressing atmosphere at – . I sampled the 4-course gourmet dinner twice and to great satisfaction, and a champagne breakfast was also a bargain given the going rate at chain hotels. All the services were as good as you say. A better light in the bathroom is the only improvement I would vote." *(KH Edwards; also Shirley Williams)*

Open All year; restaurant closed to non-residents on Christmas Eve.
Rooms 1 suite, 15 double, 6 single – all with bath, telephone, radio, colour TV and baby-listening; some with electric trouser press; some ground-floor rooms, 24-hr room service.
Facilities Lounge, cocktail bar, restaurant, function room. Small landscaped garden with patio for alfresco meals. Near rivers Orwell, Deben, Stow; convenient for exploring Constable country. ↺ (ramp).
Location 1 m from centre; Henley Rd runs up W side of Christchurch Park, N of town centre. From A12 from London and Colchester follow bypass signs: Ipswich West and Bury St Edmunds. Approx 1 m after Post House Hotel cross-roads. Turn left at second roundabout (A12). Go up long gradual hill; turn right at traffic lights at cross-roads into Henley road. Hotel is 600 yds on right. From A45 Bury, Newmarket etc., after A45 dual carriageway proceed on A12/A45 mini-roundabout intersection. Turn left following Felixstowe-Lowestoft-Yarmouth A12 signs. At brow of hill turn right at traffic-light controlled cross-roads into Henley Road. Hotel 600 yds on right.
Restriction No children under 5 in restaurant in the evening.
Credit cards All major cards accepted
Terms [1985 rates] (No service charge) rooms: single £38, double £45. Breakfast: continental £3, English £5, champagne £9.50. Set 2-course lunch £7.75, 3 courses £9; 3-course dinner £10.50; full alc £18. Vegetarian menu. Reduced rates at weekend; Olde English weekends all year except Easter, Christmas and New Year. Bargain holidays in Aug. Reductions for children sharing parents' room; special meals.
Tipping: Actively discouraged.

JERVAULX North Yorkshire   Map 4

Jervaulx Hall   *Tel* Bedale (0677) 60235
Jervaulx, Masham
Ripon HG4 4PH

"We returned to *Jervaulx* after a year's absence and were not let down. Shirley and John Sharp are the best of hosts. The cooking, while not *haute* or *nouvelle*, is very good. The rooms most comfortable. And the peace and beauty of the location work wonders on the mind and body. There is a personal warmth and welcome here not found in other places" *(Mrs Paul Chinar)*. *Jervaulx Hall*, now in its seventh year as a hotel under the deservedly popular resident hosts, John and Shirley Sharp, has always, with hardly a dissenting note, inspired compliments. The hotel – early Victorian with much solid, reassuring Victorian furniture – is on the site of one of the famous Cistercian abbeys. Its ruins are less well known than Fountains and Rievaulx, but nonetheless impressive. The *Hall* adjoins the ruins, separated only by a ha-ha, and enjoys the run of the substantial Abbey Park. It makes an admirable base for a touring or walking holiday in the Yorkshire Dales. *(Frances L Perry, Edward Hibbert, J H Duffus, J B B, Felice Feldstein, Mr and Mrs A P Brick)*

Open 1 Mar–22 Dec.
Rooms 8 double – all with bath and tea-making facilities; 1 on ground floor.
Facilities 2 lounges, TV room, dining room. 8-acre garden adjoining Abbey ruins; trout and grayling fishing available in nearby river Ure (by arrangement).
Location On A6108, 12 m N of Ripon.
Restriction Dogs allowed but not to be left unattended in bedrooms.
Credit cards Access, Visa.
Terms (No service charge) B&B £21.50–£25; dinner, B&B £27.50–£35. Set dinner £11.50. Winter breaks 1 Nov–Easter. Reduced rates and special meals for children by arrangement.
Service/tipping "No service charge is made. Any gratuities offered will be distributed among the staff."

KESWICK Cumbria   **Map 4**

Lodore Swiss Hotel   *Tel* Borrowdale (059 684) 285
Keswick CA12 5UX   *Telex* 64305

César awarded for the best family hotel

With its 72 bedrooms, and its huge range of facilities (see below), the *Lodore Swiss* is one of the larger and grander hotels in the Guide, though by no means the most expensive. It has an exceptional position, standing in 40 acres of grounds including the famous Lodore Falls on Derwentwater. It has been run in an exemplary manner for close on 40 years by a Swiss family named England, and its attention to the small details of customer-cosseting represent Swiss traditions of hotelmanship at their best. All kinds of improvements have taken place since our last edition: all rooms have now been fitted with built-in hair dryers, a new all-weather surface given to the tennis court, a more generous breakfast menu has been introduced, and, instead of the traditional set menu for lunch, there is now an à la carte on offer, including light inexpensive dishes such as Bauernteller, a Swiss ploughman's lunch. From this year's file, we select one report which pulled out all the stops: "Spent many happy holidays here in the sixties and seventies, and returned on the basis of your Guide and our memories. Nothing but praise – position wonderful, amenities superb, rooms comfortable, food mouth-watering, and above all the staff and service fantastic. The value for money is incomparable. The only other hotels where I have felt so much at home – I don't wax lyrical very often! – are *The Berkeley* in Wilton Place and the *Lancaster* in Paris (q.v.); they all have that indefinable ambience which makes an outstanding hotel, regardless of stars, rosettes, tureens, wine bottles etc." *(S V Bishop; also Guy Milner)*

Open Mar – early Nov.
Rooms 1 suite, 60 double, 11 single – all with bath or shower, direct-dial telephone, colour TV (with in-house movies) and baby-listening.
Facilities Lift, 2 lounges, writing room, bar, dining room, ballroom, health and beauty suite, sauna, exercise rooms, hairdressing salon, shop, indoor swimming

pool, children's nursery with 2 nannies. Dancing every Sat; disco twice-weekly during July and Aug. 40-acre grounds going down to Derwentwater and river Derwent with rowing boats and motor launches and limited fishing, outdoor swimming pool, tennis court, squash court, children's playground. &.

Location 3 m S of Keswick.
Restriction No dogs.
Credit card Amex.
Terms (No service charge) B&B £32; dinner, B&B £44. Set dinner £12; *menu gastronomique* £19, *menu surprise* (2 persons) £44. Alc lunches. Reduced rates and special meals for children.
Service: "No extra percentages are added or included in our terms: gratuities are normally not expected but may be given if guests so desire."
Note: The Hotel also owns two smaller hotels in the area, Mary Mount Hotel *and the bed-and-breakfast* Leathes Head, *both in Borrowdale. Tariffs are considerably cheaper, but guests at either can enjoy* Lodore Swiss *facilities.*

KILVE Somerset
Map 1

Meadow House Hotel
Sea Lane, Kilve TA5 1EG

Tel Holford (027 874) 546

Opened in the spring of 1984, *Meadow House* is a restored and refurbished Georgian rectory, with just four spacious double rooms, in a truly rural situation, with views across the Bristol Channel and to the Quantock Hills. It is a short walk from the rocky beaches of Kilve, described by the owners, David and Marion Macauslan, as "a geologist's delight, full of fossils, very dramatic and unspoilt". David Macauslan is an enthusiast for wine, and the hotel (an over-formal term for such a personal establishment) has a wine list of 120 bins, with a very reasonable mark-up. Our nominator writes: "Really like being a house guest in a rather luxurious country home – lovely furniture and furnishings, good food and wine and lots of peace and quiet. David and Marion are friendly and chatty without being too obstrusive. Best of all is the cost." *(Helen Hibbert; also Rosalind Pearlman)*

Open Mid-Feb to mid-Nov, also Christmas and New Year.
Rooms 4 double – all with bath, radio, remote-control colour TV and tea-making facilities. 1 self-catering cottage.
Facilities Drawing room, study, billiard room, dining room. 8 acres grounds with croquet lawn, stream, waterfall and lovely gardens. Rocky beach nearby.
Location Off A39 from Bridgwater. Turn right in Kilve, just before pub, down Sea Lane; ½ m down lane on left.
Restrictions Not suitable for &. No children under 9. No dogs.
Credit cards Access, Amex, Visa.
Terms B&B £20–£28. Full alc £14.95.
Service/tipping: "Tips are not expected, and we do not levy a service charge. After all, if you can't get service in a hotel, where can you get it? It is not an extra, it is part and parcel of what is offered in the accommodation and meal charges."

KING'S LYNN Norfolk
Map 2

Congham Hall
Lynn Road, Grimston
King's Lynn PE32 1AH

Tel Hillington (0485) 600250
Telex 817209

"Many hotels promote themselves as country houses, but few get it exactly 'right'. At *Congham*, they do. It is so precisely the same as week-ending privately at any great country house that it is difficult to believe the cast of *Upstairs Downstairs* won't pop out of the panelling. Mr Forecast waits in the porch with a welcome. No chilly reception girls here. The house is warm and beautiful, with bedrooms and bathrooms the last word in comfort and care. Dining is a 'happening'. Later one finds invisible hands have been at work: baths and bedrooms tidied, fruit replenished, curtains drawn, beds turned down. We felt cherished." *(Marcia Suddards)*

If we awarded a prize for the most perfumed bouquet of the year, Ms Suddards' eloquent tribute to this 18th-century Georgian mansion would surely be a candidate. *Congham Hall* is set in 40 acres of grounds, complete with its own cricket field, a tennis court and a small swimming pool; the house is agreeably furnished; guests' needs are looked after attentively. But we think the notion that a stay at *Congham* is like being a guest at a great country house is a piece of hyperbole: Christine and Trevor Forecast are admirable professionals and understand how to run a first-class country house better than most, but a hotel is a hotel is a hotel. A word needs to be added about the dinner "happening": one of the features of a stay at *Congham* is an eight-course dinner menu, including an appetiser at the start, a sorbet between the soup and main course, coffee and petits fours. Last year we quoted a reader who found it all a bit too much of a good thing – "really for greedy people who like a lot of very food". The Forecasts feel this was unfair: "Our chef goes to considerable lengths to offer a varied menu and, providing the customer makes a balanced choice from the selection available, we find the majority comment as to how they feel 'just right' at the end of dinner. Of course if you choose the richest dish in each course, then you are being greedy! Our average discerning customer does not do this." Point taken, but in any event we are glad to know that a shorter menu is available to fainter-stomached residents. Here is another view of *Congham*: "Your entry was absolutely accurate and the famous eight courses not too much because the helpings are delicate. Quiet was amazing. Would be an ideal writer's retreat, with everything provided by the hotel (except the tiresome business of actually writing, I suppose)." *(Lady Antonia Pinter)*

Open All year.
Rooms 1 suite, 9 double, 1 single – 10 with bath, 1 with shower, all with telephone, radio and colour TV; some with 4-posters.
Facilities Hall with seating, lounge, bar, restaurant; board room with conference facilities for up to 12. 40-acre grounds with herb garden, heated swimming pool, jacuzzi room, tennis court, cricket pitch, parklands and orchards; stabling for visiting horses. Coast with sandy beaches 10 m; nature and bird sanctuaries, fishing, golf, riding nearby.
Location 6 m NE of King's Lynn. Turn right off A148 to Grimston; Congham is 2½ m on left.
Restrictions Not suitable for &. No children under 12. No dogs.
Credit cards All major cards accepted.
Terms (No service charge) B&B (light English): single £46, double £58; full English breakfast £2 added. Set lunch £10.50, dinner £18–£25 (lighter dinner £15.50); full alc lunch £15, dinner £25. Weekend breaks (Fri/Sat) all year.

We ask hotels to estimate their 1986 tariffs some time before publication so the rates given are not necessarily exact. Please *always* check terms with hotels when making bookings.

KINGSTON BAGPUIZE Oxfordshire   Map 2

Fallowfields
Southmoor, Kingston Bagpuize
Nr Abingdon OX13 5BH

Tel Oxford (0865) 820416
Telex 83388 KINGS TG Attn
FALLOWFIELDS

Eight miles to the south-west of Oxford, in the nondescript hamlet of Southmoor (and formerly indexed under that name in the Guide), *Fallowfields* itself in no way lacks character. A small country house, Gothic in style, it was formerly the home of the Begum Aga Khan before her marriage. For the past seven years, it has been a Wolsey Lodge member – that is, a country house home taking guests – owned and run by Alison Crowther, who is herself a woman of vivacious character. "I've hunted with the old Berks, water ski'd in a ballet circus and exhibited paintings at the Royal Watercolour Society. I'm also deaf, so you've got to yell at me," she is quoted as saying in a *Guardian* article. This year, she tells us, she has been voted one of the 10 personalities of the year in the *Oxford Mail* New Year's Honours List. The house is in 12 acres of well-kept grounds, with an attractive garden and a swimming pool heated to 70°+ from May onwards. The rooms are full of antiques, paintings, books and personal treasures. Most of her guests appreciate Mrs Crowther's cooking, with the sweet trolley coming in for special commendation.

Open 1 Apr–30 Sept. (Winter weekend house parties for not fewer than 4 people – advance booking only.) Dinner not served Wed.
Rooms 4 double, 1 single – 1 with shower, all with radio and tea-making facilities.
Facilities Drawing room, library/TV room, dining room. 12-acre garden; table tennis, croquet, heated swimming pool. Riding, golf, river and lake fishing, windsurfing, waterskiing at Stanton Harcourt Leisure Centre nearby.
Location On A420 8 m SW of Oxford, 6 m from Abingdon. Light sleepers may be disturbed by traffic on A420, in north rooms.
Restrictions Not suitable for &. No children under 10. Dogs at management's discretion and not in public rooms.
Credit cards None accepted.
Terms (No service charge) B&B: single £18, double £28; dinner, B&B: single £28, double £48. Set dinner with house wine from £10; full alc £12.75.
Service/tipping: "We do not make a service charge but if clients feel that the service is of a nature they would specifically like to acknowledge – all gratuities are divided by me amongst our part-time staff."

KINTBURY Berkshire   Map 2

Dundas Arms [GFG]
Kintbury, Newbury RG15 OUT

Tel Kintbury (0488) 58263

A first-rate restaurant providing six well-decorated rooms – each with bath and patio overlooking the Kennet and Avon Canal – to which the gourmet (or gourmand) may retire. This has been a popular retreat for Londoners since our first edition. "The restaurant exceeded our expectations: proprietor David Piper excels as a pastry chef (we were given complementary hors-d'oeuvre as we sat with our drinks in front of the fire in the lounge) and offers a superior wine list." "The rooms pass muster – cheerful and warm, offering a comfortable, quiet night within earshot of the gurging canal." But we continue to hear of indifferent service and lukewarm welcome to the residents, and last year's murmurs about costs have continued. "At these prices, one expects the bathroom to be spotless and in good working order (ours wasn't quite), the bedding choice (although the bed was new, we had only a duvet), and the service impeccable (we found it well-meaning but careless)." More reports would be welcome.

Open All year except Christmas to New Year. Restaurant closed Sun and Mon.
Rooms 6 double – all with bath, 5 with telephone, all with colour TV and tea-making facilities (all rooms in annexe on ground floor).
Facilities Lounge, bar, restaurant. Kennet and Avon canal alongside.
Location 400 yards from village.
Restriction No dogs.
Credit cards All major cards accepted
Terms (No fixed service charge) B&B: single £32, double £38. Set lunch £7; full alc £18. Discounts for 2-day stays (2 people) and dining both nights any days of week during Jan – Mar. Reduced rates for children sharing parents' room; special meals on request.

KIRKBY FLEETHAM North Yorkshire　　　　　　　　Map 4

Kirkby Fleetham Hall [GFG]　　　　　*Tel* Northallerton (0609) 748226
Kirkby Fleetham
Northallerton DL7 0SU

"Can't understand how you have missed this one. Beautiful house, elegantly decorated in gracious grounds. Best and most unobtrusive 'country house' atmosphere. Bedrooms full of antiques, luxurious beds. Roaring fires, peace and quiet. Super food, plenty of choice, served by local girls, very pleasant and helpful. Highly recommended." *(Mrs P Sachs)*

Kirkby Fleetham Hall is a fine house, Elizabethan in parts, but substantially remodelled 200 years ago to give it its present Georgian appearance. A magnificently arrogant 18th-century squire of what was then a manor house demolished the village of Kirkby in order to enjoy greater privacy, so the house now sits in isolated splendour of 30 acres of grounds, with just a 12th-century Knights Templar church adjoining. The A1 is two miles to the west, with the dales beyond; the moors lie to the east; York and Castle Howard to the south. Other readers share Mrs Sachs' enthusiasm, as did our inspector: "A pleasant country house hotel without being a luxurious one. Refurbishment and redecoration have obviously been confined within a limited budget. This kind of shabby grandeur can be rather dispiriting but wasn't here. Perhaps because the place has a light, welcoming look about it and perhaps because David and Chris Grant are such relaxed, pleasant, competent hosts who are obviously firmly in control. They show guests to their rooms, explain the location of everything, advise on local places of interest. She cooks, he takes orders for dinner, chats to guests and has produced a remarkably informative and readable wine list to advise diners about the contents of the impressive wine cellar. The meals in the traditional dining room are unpretentious and excellent, using fresh herbs and produce from their kitchen garden. The kind of food one hopes to get when invited to dinner with friends who have good taste and enjoy unusual but uncomplicated food and good wine. It's also extremely good value." *(Ron Vickers, D W, Susan Cohen, D M Callow, C M Wilmot)*

Open All year.
Rooms 15 double – all with bath, telephone, radio and colour TV.
Facilities 3 lounges, library, dining room. 30-acre grounds; lake.
Location 1 m N of village of Kirkby Fleetham: follow sign to "Kirkby Hall and Church".
Restrictions Not suitable for &. No dogs.
Credit cards Amex, Visa.
Terms B&B: single occupancy £39, double £59–£69. Set lunch £7.50; dinner £13.50. Reduced rates for children.

KNOWSTONE Devon   Map 1

Masons Arm Inn   *Tel* Anstey Mills (039 84) 231
Knowstone
South Molton EX36 4RY

An old-fashioned 13th-century thatched inn in the foothills of Exmoor, with just five smallish bedrooms furnished with antiques and books, a half-hour from the M5 (junction 27), is drawn to our attention by the editor of *The Good Pub Guide* in the following terms: "Charming hospitable Exmoor-edge inn with simple unspoilt atmosphere and good food. Our tight inspection schedule had to be abandoned in ruins after our arrival as it was far too pleasant to leave. The small main bar has big rustic furniture on its stone floor, long narrow benches built into the cream-painted stone walls decorated with old farm tools, seats by a sunny window looking across to the village church, lots of antique bottles hanging from medieval black beams, and a fine open fireplace with a bread oven. Another sitting room has cosy easy chairs, bar billiards and table skittles. Good bar food, all home cooked, and a separate restaurant offering three-course dinners at £7.50 and good-value house wines. Seats on the grass behind the house overlook the hilly pastures leading up to Exmoor. It doesn't sound so very different from many other Devon pubs, but what does make this one stand out is the thoughtful friendliness of its painstaking owners, David and Elizabeth Todd, who took it over in 1981 – not to mention the equally discreet friendliness of Charlie, their bearded collie" *(Alisdair Aird)*. More reports welcome.

Open All year except Christmas. Restaurant closed to non-residents Sun.
Rooms 1 suite, 3 double, 1 single – 2 with shower, all with radio, TV and tea-making facilities; 1 room in annexe.
Facilities Lounge-bar with TV, public bar, restaurant. Occasional music in bar. ½-acre grounds.
Location 3 m NW of Rackenford; Knowstone signposted from B3321 ½ m W of Rackenford.
Restrictions Not suitable for &. No dogs in public rooms except the public bar.
Credit cards None accepted.
Terms (No service charge) B&B £11.50–£16.50; dinner, B&B £19–£24. Set dinner £7.50 (£8.50 to non-residents); full alc £12.65. Reduced rates for children sharing parents' room; special meals.
Service/tipping: "While I, personally, am against tipping, my staff seem to be quite favourably disposed to the practice. No service charge is made, however, nor are tips expected, but our very cheerful, helpful girls do seem to attract quite a bit in gratuities nevertheless."

KNUTSFORD Cheshire   Map 2

La Belle Époque [GFG]   *Tel* Knutsford (0565) 3060
60 King Street,
Knutsford WA16 2DT

Emphatically a restaurant with rooms: the restaurant seats 100 at a
sitting, and there are five bedrooms, recently refurbished, and now all
with baths *en suite* – "clean, fresh and attractive", according to one recent
visitor. But connoisseurs of the exotic shouldn't miss the experience.
Knutsford itself (Mrs Gaskell's "Cranford") is rewarding in its own right,
especially because of the creations of the eccentric Richard Harling Watt,
who, among much else, built this Italianate curiosity, a shrine to Art
Nouveau, which achieved TV immortality in *Brideshead Revisited* as the
1920s restaurant "Palliards". The spectacular decor merits a visit in its
own right; the fact that *La Belle Époque* offers an excellent French
restaurant and comfortable rooms is a substantial bonus.

Open All year except 1 Jan and bank holidays.
Rooms 5 (all let as single or double) – all with bath and tea-making facilities.
Facilities Bar, restaurant, roof garden and courtyard; facilities for conferences,
weddings etc.
Location In town centre. Large public car park opposite.
Restrictions Not suitable for &. No children under 10. No dogs.
Credit cards All major cards accepted.
Terms Rooms: single occupancy £25, double £35. Full alc £25.

LACOCK Wiltshire   Map 2

At the Sign of the Angel [GFG]   *Tel* Lacock (024 973) 230
6 Church Street, Lacock
Chippenham SN15 2LA

To say that At the Sign of the Angel is *old worlde makes it sound phoney. But
this 14th-century half-timbered building does represent a kind of emblem of the
pure old English inn, just as Lacock itself – once a prosperous medieval wool
town and now formally part of our heritage in the hands of the National Trust –
provides precisely the picture of an English village which foreigners hanker to
capture in their Olympuses. (There is something especially apt about camera-
carrying tourists in Lacock, since William Henry Fox Talbot, inventor of
photography, lived here 150 years ago, and the Fox Talbot Museum in the
village, as well as the Abbey, is well worth a visit.)*
    At the Sign of the Angel *has been a family-run affair for more than 30 years.
The Levises are innkeepers of a traditional kind, offering high-quality English
cooking and lots of it: the main course at dinner is always a roast, and the
breakfasts are of the full English variety, with hot home-made rolls, dairy
products from their own Jersey cows, eggs from their own ducks and hens. Many
of our correspondents continue to echo a previous comment: "A quintessential
inn in a fairy-tale village. Everything was pleasing – black oak panelling, huge
log fires, polished brass and silver . . . The welcome was friendly, the food good,
and the flowers fresh." But the inn has not always had an easy ride with us, and
this year the rumble of discontent has grown louder. Slow and faulty service,
diners badly cramped into two small rooms on a busy Saturday night, uneven
cooking, beds past their best, furniture ditto, careless cleaning, flowers not*

125

always fresh, hot-water supply unreliable. Quite a list. We sent an inspector, who reported ambivalently, but summed up: "The Levises are not looking at the management of the staff with as critical an eye as they once did, and the faults, though minor, of inexperienced staff go unnoticed. It is not the place for pseudo-sophisticates, as the bedroom furnishings would give them that uncomfortable feeling of visiting poor relations. However, the historical atmosphere of the village and the hotel, and the English cooking of quality, though not cheap, provide a unique atmosphere of old-world England. Still worth an entry." But we would like more reports, please.

Open All year except 22 Dec – 1 Jan. Restaurant closed Sat lunch and Sun dinner.
Rooms 6 double – all with bath.
Facilities Lounge with TV, 2 dining rooms. Small garden.
Location 7 m S of M4 (exit 17); E of A350 between Chippenham and Melksham.
Restrictions Not suitable for &. No children under 12. No dogs in public rooms.
Credit cards None accepted.
Terms (No service charge) B&B: £48 – £50 per double room; dinner, B&B: £39.50 – £42 per person. Set lunch £12.50, dinner £16. Winter breaks Nov–Mar.

LANGAR Nottinghamshire   Map 2

Langar Hall   *Tel* Harby (0949) 60559
Langar NG13 9HG

Another member of the Wolsey Lodge consortium – or, in other words, a pedigree country house opening its doors to guests. *Langar Hall*, built in 1830, is in the Vale of Belvoir, 12 miles SE of Nottingham – an area hitherto poorly represented in the Guide. Hostess is Imogen Skirving, and *Langar Hall* is her family home; her husband is a picture dealer and the house is full of family antiques (not for sale), and paintings and prints, both old and new, on exhibit which can be bought. Mrs Skirving did a Cordon Bleu course 30 years ago and more recently has taken a refresher at *Miller Howe* (q.v.), so expect a Tovey touch or two in the cooking. No licence at the moment. Guests bring their own bottles, or else, writes Mrs Skirving, "wine (rather than plonk) comes with the compliments of the cook – perhaps a glass with dinner or even a bottle between two or three." Two correspondents write appreciatively of their first visit to *Langar*, of the attractive bedrooms and the good cooking. One described his meal thus: "First courses were curried vegetable soup and a delicate cucumber mousse. When we had difficulty in deciding, the response was 'Have both'. A rack of lamb followed, with fresh vegetables and cooked exactly *al dente*. Puds were apple pie, deep and crusty, and fresh peaches with blackcurrants. Again we were urged to have both, but there are limits! All of this, with sherry before dinner, a bottle of Sainsbury's wine and coffee afterwards for a mere £10 a head ... highly recommended. *(Dr H B Cardwell; also Hope Swift)*

Open All year.
Rooms 1 suite, 2 double, 2 single – 4 with bath and shower, all with telephone, radio, TV, tea-making facilities and baby-listening.
Facilities Drawing room, reception room, TV room, dining room. 4-acre grounds with croquet lawn. Car hire (self-drive or with chauffeur arranged).
Location 12 m SE of Nottingham. From A52 turn off by Bingham traffic lights, signposted from there. From A46 turn at crossroads to Cropwell Bishop and Langar is signposted. *Langar Hall* is behind Langar Church.
Restrictions Not suitable for &. Dogs by arrangement, not in public rooms.

Credit cards None accepted.
Terms (No service charge) B&B £15-£22.50; dinner, B&B £25-£27.50. Set lunch £6, dinner £10. Christmas party of 6 negotiable. No charge for 3 year-olds and under; special meals.
Service/tipping: "No tipping policy, no service expected, but appreciated by cleaning lady when a pound of two is forthcoming."

LANGRISH Hampshire   Map 2

Langrish House   *Tel* Petersfield (0730) 66941
Langrish, Nr Petersfield GU32 1RN

Once a Tudor farmhouse, then for many years a manor house, and for the past seven years a pastoral hotel in glorious countryside, with fine views from all the bedrooms. It has been in the Guide for the past two years, with unanimous agreement about the friendliness of the staff and the excellent value of the tariff. But many other features have been criticised, and continue to be: grounds rather neglected, some rooms a bit spartan, certain dishes not very successful in the restaurant. We enjoyed this description of one of the loos: "You needed to be something of an athlete to use it. It had been planted under the eaves, and in sitting one had to assume a posture common to infrequent church-goers – seated but bent forward as if in prayer. The pose for us males would please any osteopath – the body arched backwards at a frightening angle, the head raised to the ceiling." The same correspondent told us that it felt as if time had stood still here since the 1950s. We suspect that it needs more capital investment than it's getting. Notwithstanding its shortcomings, all those who wrote to us felt it deserved to keep its entry. We would still welcome more reports.

Open All year. Restaurant closed Sun and public holidays.
Rooms 11 double, 3 single – all with bath, telephone, radio and colour TV; tea-making facilities on request.
Facilities Lounge with TV, 2 small bar lounges, dining room, function room. 13-acre grounds with lake. Tennis, squash, swimming pool, sauna, golf, fishing, riding nearby.
Location 3 m from Petersfield in village, turn S off A272 to Winchester.
Restrictions Not suitable for &. Dogs only by arrangement (and not in public rooms).
Credit cards Access, Amex, Diners.
Terms (Service optional) B&B: single £25, double £35; dinner, B&B: single £34, double £53. Set dinner £9–£14; full alc £12.50. Winter breaks Oct–Mar, min. 2 nights, not Sun. Reduced rates and special meals for children.
Service/tipping: "Gratuities to staff are left to guests' discretion."

LASTINGHAM North Yorkshire   Map 4

Lastingham Grange   *Tel* Lastingham (075 15) 345
Lastingham, York YO6 6TH

The North Yorkshire Moors have not been strongly represented in the Guide, but this modest country house hotel, once a 17th-century farmhouse, has appeared here since the first edition. It's an old stone-walled creeper-covered house built round a courtyard in 10 acres of garden and fields, and it lies right on the edge of the moors; the road peters out at its entrance and becomes a bridle path, stretching across the moors to Rosedale and beyond. It has been dubbed 'the most peaceful hotel in Britain", and is ideal for those who hanker for a place where the road runs out. There is nothing flash about the hospitality or the decor here, nor anything other than honest English fare in the dining room; the breakfast toast again comes in for a reprimand. But the place scores with the old faithfuls and first-timers alike because of the genuine dedication of Dennis Wood and his wife to their guests' welfare, maintaining a tradition of hospitality from Dennis Wood's parents that extends back to the fifties. The hotel has had a predominantly middle-aged clientele in the past, but we are glad to know that the Woods, with their own young family, are busy enfranchising a new generation. Since last year, they have installed an adventure playground, away from the formal garden, with swaying bridges, swinging tyres, climbing frames and suchlike. *(Heather Sharland, Hayward Wane)*

Open Mar–Dec and winter weekends.
Rooms 10 double, 2 single – all with bath, radio, TV, tea-making facilities and baby-listening; colour TV on request.
Facilities Large entrance hall, garden, reception, spacious lounge with log fire; sheltered terrace. 10-acre grounds with garden, croquet, swings, slides. In the heart of the National Park, near moors and dales; riding, golf and swimming nearby.
Location Off A170, N of Kirkbymoorside. Turn N towards Appleton-le-Moor 2 m E of Kirkbymoorside.
Restrictions Not suitable for &. Dogs by arrangement only; not in public rooms.
Credit cards Amex, Diners.
Terms (No service charge) B&B: single £30.75–£33.75; dinner, B&B: single £36.75–£42.35, double £67.50–£77.75. Set lunch £7.50, dinner £11. Picnic lunches available. Reduced rates for long stays and winter breaks. Children under 12 sharing parents' room free; special meals.

LEAMINGTON SPA Warwickshire Map 2

The Lansdowne Hotel *Tel* Leamington Spa (0926) 21313
Clarendon Street *Telex* 337556
Leamington Spa CV32 4PF

David and Gillian Allen, both of whom had a Swiss catering education, have converted a Regency town house in this once fashionable and still delightful watering place into a smart small hotel, with the help of Laura Ashley, Sanderson and Sekers. It is convenient for Warwick Castle, but is also well placed for the National Exhibition Centre (25 minutes by car) or the National Agricultural Centre (10 minutes' drive). Readers continue to praise the comforts of the house, including its restaurant, and the general professionalism of the Allens' undertaking, though one visitor felt her room might have been rather warmer in a cool March. A lady travelling on her own particularly appreciated the courtesies of her welcome. *(Mrs M G Patterson, G I Bigg, Marjorie Davidson)*

Open All year. Limited food service Dec 26–Jan 12.
Rooms 6 double, 4 single – 2 with bath, 2 with shower, radio, all with double glazing. Baby-listening by arrangement.
Facilities Residents' lounge with TV, bar, restaurant. Small garden. & restaurant only.
Location Central. Parking.
Restriction No dogs.
Credit card Access.
Terms (No service charge) B&B £12.95–£16.95. Set lunch £7.95, dinner £8.85.

2-night packages. Reduced rates for children; special meals by arrangement.
Service/tipping: "We have always felt this to be an unnecessary impost. When guests wish to reward a particularly helpful member of staff, we explain that our charges are listed and the staff receive a realistic, above average, wage."

LEDBURY Hereford and Worcester   Map 2

Hope End Country House Hotel [GFG]   *Tel* Ledbury (0531) 3613
Hope End
Ledbury HR8 1DS

A small remote hotel tucked away in a gentle sloping valley in a 40-acre park near the Malvern Hills, owned and run by John and Patricia Hegarty. An attraction for some, a put-off for others: no children under 12, no pets, no TV, no smoking. Portions at meals are more modest than at some other establishments. As we summed up up last year, *"Hope End is far from being an orthodox hotel; it isn't bland or grand, and not everyone appreciates a virtually no-choice menu; but, to use a cant phrase, it is doing its own thing and doing it with devotion."* A reader this year echoed these sentiments: "One of the most peaceful and individual hotels in Europe. The place and its proprietors are either everything you need or not. There is no in-between. We are very pro, and try to go back at least twice a year simply to unwind and savour the excellent food and wine." Another reader expressed her gratitude thus: "From the description in other guides I had an impression that the Hegartys were health freaks who would probably serve odd food, and that the hotel would have dust in the corners and be makeshift. Wrong. I am so glad I did decide to go there. It is marvellous. The house is fascinating, but has been beautifully, artistically, tastefully and comfortably adapted. The Hegartys love being surrounded by trees, grass, birds, rabbits, and eating fresh vegetables from their own walled garden, fruit from their trees, milk from their goats, eggs from their bantams (who wouldn't?). They are also prepared to put in all the very hard work required to produce all these good things, collect them, and then do all the chopping, stirring, mixing and waiting to produce Real Food. They also find the time to keep everywhere spotlessly clean, and all the materials and workmanship used in the conversion of the house are first class. Whether it was the Malvern water on tap, the quiet, sitting by the open log fire, the digestibility of the food or the comfortable bed that I must thank, I do not know, but I slept deeper and longer there than I have done for years. Far from being freaks, the Hegartys, formerly a lawyer and a teacher, just seem people who have got all their values completely right. I am enormously grateful to be able to share the fruits of their labours!" *(P Grimsdale, W A)*

Open End Feb to end Nov.
Rooms 7 double – all with bath and telephone; tea-making facilities on request; garden suite with TV and tea-making facilities.
Facilities 2 sitting rooms, dining room. 40-acres of wooded parkland and nature reserve; walled garden. &.
Location 3 m from Malvern Hills N of Ledbury, ¼ m W of Wellington Heath.
Restrictions No children under 12. No dogs.
Credit cards All major cards accepted.
Terms B&B: single £47–£50, double £80–£94. Set dinner £16. Special breaks Mar–Nov (min. 2 nights).

LIFTON Devon   Map 1

The Arundell Arms [GFG]   *Tel* Lifton (0566) 84666 or 84244
Lifton PL16 OAA

A much-creepered early 19th-century stone building, once a coaching
inn, on the A30 (the five rooms in the front are sound-proofed and
ventilated). It is very much a sportsperson's hotel: there are snipe- and
pheasant-shooting weekends and hunting breaks in the winter, but
Lifton is, above all, a popular resort for the fishing fraternity, and *The
Arundell* has been a leading fishing hotel for the past half-century. It has
20 miles of its own water on the Tamar and four of its tributaries, and
throughout the year it offers an extensive programme of fly-fishing
courses for beginners and for the more advanced. The hotel has been
run for almost a quarter of century with devotion and flair by Anne
Voss-Bark. Although outside sports are the central feature of the hotel, it
also runs bridge weekends and photographic courses. Since the arrival
of chef Philip Burgess, gourmet dinners take place regularly throughout
the winter months. Only critical note in *The Arundell* file this year came
from an overnighter who appreciated the friendly welcome of the house,
but was much put off by the poor quality of the furnishings of his room.
More reports would be appreciated.

Open All year except 5 days over Christmas.
Rooms 20 double, 8 single – 19 with bath, 7 with shower, all with radio, colour TV
and tea-making facilities; 23 with direct-dial telephone and baby-listening. Front
rooms sound-proofed. 5 rooms in annexe opposite. 2 self-catering flats.
Facilities Sitting room, TV room, 2 bars, 2 restaurants, games room, skittle alley;
conference suite, meeting rooms. Small terraced garden. Exclusive fishing rights
on 20 m of river Tamar and tributaries for salmon, sea trout and brown trout; also
3-acre lake. Cornish coasts within ½ hour's drive. Golf, riding, walks nearby.
Location 3 m E of Launceston on A30. Parking.
Restrictions Not suitable for &. No dogs in restaurant.
Credit cards All major cards accepted.
Terms (No service charge) B&B £21–£33; dinner, B&B £31–£44. Set lunch £7–£8,
dinner £12–£13; full alc £17–£19. Bargain breaks Oct to early May. 4-day driven
snipe and pheasant shoots and rough shooting; fly-fishing courses, bridge weeks
and weekends and photographic courses. Children under 16 free in parents'
room; special meals by arrangement.
Service/tipping: "No service charge made and no tipping expected."

LINCOLN Lincolnshire   Map 2

D'Isney Place Hotel   *Tel* Lincoln (0522) 38881
Eastgate, Lincoln LN2 4AA

*"Mixed reports" we said last year about David and Judy Payne's elegant
Georgian bed-and-breakfast establishment near the cathedral, and there is a
conflict of opinion again this year. "A wonderful hotel!" writes one grateful
customer. "Beautiful rooms, friendly service, best room-service breakfast we have
known," writes another. But there has been much criticism along with the praise.
Some rooms clearly verge on the poky: one room has good hanging space, but no
drawers, a dressing-table but no mirror. "There was no room to put anything
except on the floor" was another complaint. Two readers complained about their
bogus "four-poster"; no posts at all and with unwanted curtains hanging from
the ceiling. More reports please.*

Open All year.
Rooms 1 suite with 2 bedrooms in annexe, 13 double, 2 single – 14 with bath, 3 with shower, all with telephone, radio, colour TV, tea-making facilities and baby-listening. 6 rooms on ground floor, ramps. Front rooms double-glazed.
Facilities Sitting room/billiards room. Garden with children's slide and swing. &.
Location 100 yds from Lincoln Cathedral. Parking.
Restriction No dogs in public rooms.
Credit cards All major cards accepted.
Terms (No service charge) B&B: single £29.75, double £40. (No restaurant.) Weekend breaks. Reduced rates and special meals for children.
Service/tipping: "We dislike and discourage all suggestions that tipping is expected, but when guests genuinely want to give a tip we allow this as it gives pleasure to all concerned."

LONDON   Map 2

Basil Street Hotel   *Tel* 01-581 3311
8 Basil Street, Knightsbridge   *Telex* 28379
SW3 1AH

"All the comfort and charm of its 'country house in town' atmosphere ..." "Old-fashioned and charming – slightly worn, but never in a disquieting way ..." "Truly delightful. Immaculate room, with service polite and efficient ..." Three glowing tributes, among many others, to the small (by central-city standards) hotel in a quiet side street, close to Knightsbridge underground station, and a strolling distance to Harrods and Hyde Park. An unusually large post-bag of compliments always makes us suspicious, and we were not surprised to find, on collating the evidence, that several report forms were taken from consecutive pages of last year's Guide. An example, you might argue, of the enterprise of the *Basil Street's* conscientious manager, Stephen Korany. And the hotel does give satisfaction: even those letters which reported small hiccups were written more in sorrow than in "never again" anger.

Open All year.
Rooms 1 suite, 42 double, 52 single – 70 with bath, all with telephone, radio and colour TV. 24-hour room service.
Facilities Lounge/bar, ladies' lounge/club, writing room, coffee shop, wine bar, dining room; facilities for conferences, functions and private meals.
Location Central; public car park nearby. (Underground Knightsbridge.)
Restrictions Not suitable for &. No dogs in private rooms.
Credit cards All major cards accepted.
Terms (No service charge) rooms: single without bath £33, with bath £55–£59.50; double without bath £52, with bath £74–£78.80; family accommodation £115.50. Set lunch £10.25; full alc £17. No charge for children under 16 sharing parents' room; special meals.
Service/tipping: "We make it clear to our guests that tipping is at their discretion, and to our staff that tipping is not to be expected by right." But for those guests who want to tip, the hotel suggests that it should be restricted to the moment of departure.

Blakes Hotel [GFG]   *Tel* 01-370 6701
33 Roland Gardens, SW7 3PF   *Telex* 8813500

"There must be a misprint. How can *Blake's not* be in the Guide? The constant improvements and additions to the accommodation provide ample evidence of the management's commitment. The restaurant is a delight. The staff, *almost* without exception, are charming, helpful and friendly. The female reception staff (with the *notable* exception of the marvellous Lisa) do seem to have developed an annoying tendency to school-marmly superiority, and personally I'd get a whole new lot in; but that's no real reason to exclude a very unusual and comfortable hotel, – or is it?"

A hard question to answer, and we were faced with the same problem on the last occasion we left out the hotel, and were immediately cudgelled or beguiled into reinstating it. For the uninitiated, the hotel is a stunning transformation by the interior designer/owner, Anouska Hempel, of a staid Victorian terrace in South Kensington, trendy, showbizzy and decidedly pricey. Every time we put it in, we get complaints of one sort or another, and particularly that it can't justify its tariff. Every time we leave it out, we get stick from a devotee. More reports please.

Open All year (restaurant closed Christmas/Boxing Day).
Rooms 15 suites, 25 double, 10 single – all with bath, shower, telephone and colour TV, most with radio; 10 rooms in annexe.
Facilities Lift. Lounge, lounge bar, bar, restaurant; sauna.
Location Central; no private parking. (Underground South Kensington or Gloucester Road.)
Restrictions Not suitable for &. No dogs.
Credit cards All major cards accepted.
Terms [1985 rates] (no service charge except in restaurant where 15% is added) rooms: single £85, double £110. Breakfast: continental £4.25, English £6.25; full alc £35. Special meals for children.

Capital Hotel [GFG]   *Tel* 01-589 5171
Basil Street, Knightsbridge SW3 1AT   *Telex* 919042

A few doors away from the *Basil Street* (above) and *L'Hôtel* (below), the *Capital* is different from either: a thoroughly modern, privately owned, medium-sized (by central city standards) establishment with, as a special selling feature, a distinguished restaurant, one of only four hotels in the capital to earn a *Michelin* rosette. "A most civilised place. Comfortable bedroom with tiny bathroom and individual air-conditioning unit/heater. (We usually get cooked alive in London hotels.) Many goodies in bathroom and a fresh rosebud placed in room. Towelling bathrobes (seen better days!). Some car parking available £6 per day. Keys left with porter and they juggle the cars around to let people out! Rest of hotel very attractive in a country house style (Nina Campbell). Ladies' powder room – best ever! – pink marble with large gold-plated bowls sitting on a low marble shelf with a gold swan's head coming out of the marble to deliver the water. Absolutely IMMACU-LATE and I am *fussy*! Breakfast excellent. Lovely spotless table linen and fresh flowers. Expensive, but I think well worth the extra." *(Diana Blake)*

Open All year.
Rooms 6 suites, 30 double, 20 single – all with bath and shower, telephone, radio, TV and baby-listening.
Facilities Lift. Lounge, cocktail bar, restaurant.
Location Central. (Underground Knightsbridge.) Some parking (£6 per day).
Restriction No dogs in public rooms.
Credit cards All major cards accepted.
Terms B&B: single £99.75, double £114.50. Set lunch £14.50, dinner £16.50; full alc £28. No charge for cot in parents' room; special meals for children.

The Connaught [GFG]   *Tel* 01-499 7070
Carlos Place, W1Y 6AL

"Preserved in amber, the last of the great hotels, running as smoothly as nostalgia would have us believe all such establishments did in the thirties. There seem to be more staff than guests. They appear as genii from bottles when one presses the relevant bell. They are totally obliging, endlessly helpful, extremely polite; the food is outstanding, a model for modern hotels to copy if they could, which I totally doubt. This plus a comfortable room, large bathroom, good shower, lots of big soft white towels, bed turned down at night, and linen mat placed to step one's bare foot on to, beside the bed, a courtesy rarely still found in English hotels." *(W A)*. A 1985 encomium, to add to all its predecessors of the past, for this *nonpareil* of city hotels.

Open All year.
Rooms 90, including suites – all with bath, direct-dial telephone and colour TV; 24-hour room service.
Facilities Lounge, cocktail bar, grill/restaurant (jacket and tie required; no jeans). Air conditioning. &.
Location Central. No private parking. (Underground Bond Street.)
Restriction No dogs.
Credit card Access.
Terms On application.

Duke's Hotel   *Tel* 01-491 4840
35 St James's Place, SW1A 1NY   *Telex* 28283

A sophisticated exclusive small hotel, with the special attraction of being right in the centre, a stone's throw from St James's Palace and Fortnums, but also tucked unobtrusively away in a quiet cul-de-sac off a cul-de-sac, with an entrance still lit by gaslight as it presumably was when the hotel was built in 1908. An admirer of many years' standing writes: "Partly because it is tucked away out of sight and sound and partly because it is so small, it feels more like staying in a private house than the other grand London hotels. The food here has always been especially tempting and delicious and the staff especially kind. It is easy to understand why people come back and back." *(W A; also Barbara Stanton, Vicki Turner)*

Open All year.
Rooms 15 suites, 28 double, 8 single – all with bath, telephone, radio and colour TV. 24-hour room service; baby-listening by arrangement.
Facilities Lifts. Lounge, bar, restaurant; banquet/conference facilities. Courtyard.
Location Central; off St James's Street, betwen Piccadilly and Pall Mall; 4 minutes' walk from Green Park Underground. NCP parking nearby.
Restrictions Not suitable for &. no dogs.
Credit cards All major cards accepted.
Terms [Sept 1985–Apr 1986] (No service charge) rooms: single £90–£98, double £132–£140; suites from £165–£400. Breakfast (continental) £5, (English) £7, full alc £30.

> "Full alc" means the hotel's own estimate of the price per person for a three-course dinner with half a bottle of house wine, service and taxes included. "Set meals" indicates the cost of fixed-price meals ranging from no-choice to table d'hôte.

Durrants Hotel   *Tel* 01-935 8131
George Street, W1H 6BJ   *Telex* 894919 DURHOT

A traditional, relatively inexpensive hotel, a stone's throw from the Wallace Collection in Manchester Square, Selfridge's and Marks & Spencer in Oxford Street, and many other cultural and touristic offerings of the metropolis. The hotel is housed in an 18th-century terrace, with boxes of geraniums stretching the length of the facade – a welcoming sight. Some of this year's crop of reports have come from partially dissatified customers – breakfast (indifferent); restaurant (over-priced); some of the rooms (poky, shabby); and service (surly). On balance, the ayes have it, but readers who mind about their living space should make a point of mentioning it when booking; upper floors of these old London houses are bound to be smaller. And for central location, Durrants' prices continue to be reasonable. "The full English breakfast is back on course: good value, plenty of choice and quickly and courteously served. (It is a pity that the subterranean breakfast room is so hot: male guests will be more comfortable in shirt sleeves and no tie.) And the whole organisation has subtly changed for the better . . . Most presentable and competent chambermaids, a better level of spruceness all round. The hall porter even ran after me 100 yards down the road to tell me I was wanted on the phone." *(D C Berry)*

Open All year (restaurant closed Christmas Day/Boxing Day).
Rooms 3 suites, 73 double, 24 single – 79 with bath, 5 with shower, all with telephone, radio and colour TV; 7 rooms on ground floor. Some double-glazing.
Facilities Lift. 2 lounges, bar, breakfast room, dining room, conference and banqueting room.
Location Central (some rooms could be noisy). No private parking but multi-storey 5 minutes' away. (Underground Marble Arch.)
Restrictions Not really suitable for &. No dogs.
Credit cards All major cards accepted.
Terms Rooms: single from £29, double from £40. Full alc £21. Children's meals on request.

Ebury Court   *Tel* 01-730 8147
26 Ebury Street, SW1W OLU

🔹 *Ceśar awarded in 1985 for maintaining old-fashioned hotel virtues in the metropolis*

In an area (the environs of Victoria) crowded with hotel lookalikes, *Ebury Court* has for long been a notable exception. It has been run in a thoroughly personal way for almost half a century by Diana and Romer Topham. The rooms straddle a number of the houses on either side of No 26; there is a maze of corridors, and some of the rooms are certainly poky; occasionally we get reports of poor housekeeping and cool reception. Far more often, however, we hear of kindnesses beyond the call of duty, and expressions of gratitude for the warmth of welcome from the Tophams and their staff and the very reasonable prices. There are tributes from old friends: "I've been going there since 1960. It never seems to change. It's about the only London hotel I enjoy staying in" and also from first-timers: "They provided a kind of refuge for us, complete strangers, at a very difficult time. I can't speak too highly of the welcome, service and atmosphere." *(R Erskine, P S; also Dr H E Ross, Dr P Marsh, N McNamara)*

Open All year.
Rooms 18 double – 12 with bath, 21 single – 2 with shower, all with telephone and radio; colour TV to hire. Front rooms are double-glazed.
Facilities Lift. Front sitting room, writing room with TV, Club Bar (visitors may become temporary members), restaurant, suppers served from 6.30pm for theatre-goers.
Location 3 minutes' walk from Victoria Station. Parking difficult. (Underground Victoria.)
Restrictions Not suitable for &. No children under 5 in restaurant. Small and well-behaved dogs only; not in public rooms.
Credit cards Access, Visa.
Terms (Service at guests' discretion) B&B: single £30–£35, double £50–£60; full alc £13.50. Reduced rates for winter weekends (Nov–Mar).
Service/tipping: "Service left to guests' discretion, because we find visitors really enjoy giving a little thank-you when they've been well looked after."

Hallam Hotel   *Tel* 01-580 1166
12 Hallam Street,
WIN 5LJ

We are always being asked to recommend reasonably quiet, central, budget hotels in London, and the *Hallam*, just behind Broadcasting House, appears to be filling the bill. Recent reports speak well of the new owner, Earl Baker, who runs the hotel with his son. Extensive redecorations have been carried out, and all rooms now have colour TV. It's not a luxury place – some floorboards may creak, showers may not be endowed with adequate space, the coffee at breakfast is said to be weak. But the essentials – comfortable beds, sympathetic reception, very reasonable prices – are all in its favour. *(David Blum, Sydney Downs)*

Open All year.
Rooms 10 double, 13 single – 4 with bath, 19 with shower, all with telephone, radio and colour TV.
Facilities TV lounge with bar.
Location 5 minutes from Oxford Circus, behind Broadcasting House. (Underground Oxford Circus.)
Restrictions No dogs. Not suitable for &.
Credit cards Access, Amex, Visa.
Terms B&B: single £25–£30, double £35–£40. (No restaurant.)

L'Hôtel   *Tel* 01-589 6286
28 Basil Street, SW3 1AT

A few years back, Paul Henderson, an assiduous Guide correspondent as well as *patron* of *Gidleigh Park* (see Chagford), wrote to tell us of his favourite London hotel, *Number Sixteen* (q.v.). He now introduces a new best-loved base in the metropolis. It is owned by the Levins, who also own the neighbouring *Capital* (q.v); Margaret Levin has been responsible for the decor, rustic in style, with French pine furniture and fabric wall coverings. The continental breakfast served in rooms, or in the *Metro* wine bar in the basement, is warmly recommended. The *Metro* is a less good option for lunch, unless you arrive there before 1 pm, and it gets very crowded in the evenings. *(R A Dubery)*

Open All year. Wine bar closed Sat evening, Sun and public holidays, except for residents' breakfasts.

Rooms 1 suite, 11 double – all with bath, telephone, radio, TV; 1 ground-floor room.
Facilities Lift. Wine bar/brasserie.
Location Central NCP opposite (Underground Knightsbridge.)
Credit card Amex.
Terms Double rooms £80. Alc meal in wine bar (excluding wine, but including coffee) £8.50; light meals also available.

The Knightsbridge Hotel
10 Beaufort Gardens, SW3 1PT
Tel 01-589 9271

"A comfortable, cheery little hotel at the lower end of the price scale, one of a row of similar houses on a quiet tree-lined street a few minutes' walk past Harrods from Knightsbridge underground. On checking in, you are given a room key and a front-door key, and from then on you come and go as though it were your own home. The atmosphere is bright, pleasant and casual. My room was a bit small, but comfortable and functional. I paid extra for a room with shower, but the public bathroom was so clean and inviting that next time I will take the cheaper room without private facilities. What was special about *The Knightsbridge* was the complete absence of the dreary run-down and boring atmosphere that is so often encountered in lower-priced hotels. Obviously, at these prices this is not a place of great charm or style, but for those who would rather give their money to Harrods than to a hotel, it's a nice place to return to after an exhausting day running around the city." (*Donna Cuervo*)

Open All year.
Rooms 11 double, 9 single – 9 with bath, 4 with shower, all with telephone and radio; colour TV in 4 rooms.
Facilities TV lounge, bar/coffee room.
Location Central. Near Harrods. (Underground Knightsbridge.)
Restrictions Not suitable for &. No dogs.
Credit cards Amex, Visa.
Terms B&B (continental): single £21.50–£29.50, double £30.50–£48.50.

Knightsbridge Green Hotel
159 Knightsbridge, SW1X 7PD
Tel 01-584 6274

A small family-run hotel close to Harrods and Hyde Park, unusual in having mostly suites, each with a bath; there are five single rooms, but only one has its own bath, and two have showers with WCs. It is a hotel of some character and the rates are reasonable. "Stepping into your 'suite' feels a bit like entering the young Hubert Gregg's bachelor flat in a 1950s film; I was surprised not to have an immediate telephone call from Kay Kendall. There is a lot of cream paintwork – everywhere – and my bedroom had a vast cream vanitory unit with gilt handles and a matching fitted wardrobe. There was a little sitting room with a sofa, standard lamp, dining table and chairs and a couple of Braque still lifes; the colour television seemed a bit *de trop*. The *Knightsbridge Green Hotel* is idiosyncratic, unfashionable, original and very comfortable. A delicious breakfast of scrambled eggs arrived hot on time with hot milk for the coffee. The waitress and receptionist were charming; I could have stayed for a week" (*G V*).

We unblushingly repeat the entry for the *Knightsbridge Green* which has appeared in our last two issues, partly because it has received

unanimous endorsement, and partly because of the American correspondent who wrote: "I agree with everything *GV* said about this hotel's
eccentric charm (which I thought, by the way, was one of the most
delightful descriptions of a hotel I've ever read anywhere!). The
breakfasts were wonderful, the ambience terribly cosy and English. I
could wish this part of the city were quieter, and I wouldn't call the
Knightsbridge Green cheap, but even a cost-conscious insomniac like
myself will pay a bit more and put up with a few horns to stay at a hotel
of such charm." *(Helen Wallis; also Michael Tomlinson, A D Du Toit)*

Open All year (except 4 days at Christmas).
Rooms 4 2-bedroomed suites, 11 suites with double bedroom, 5 singles – all suites
with bath, 2 singles with showers (and 2 more planned for 1986); all rooms with
telephone and colour TV; baby-listening by arrangement.
Facilities Lift. Lounge, breakfast served to order in suites. Club Room on first
floor for coffee and tea.
Location Central. National Car Park in Pavilion Road nearby. (Underground
Knightsbridge.)
Restriction No dogs.
Credit cards Access, Amex.
Terms (Excluding VAT) rooms: single £33, double suite, £46, double suite with
2 bedrooms £55. Breakfast English £5, continental £2.75. No restaurant.
*Service/tipping: "Our rates include service charge and guests are discouraged from further
tipping."*

Number Sixteen *Tel* 01-589 5232
16 Sumner Place, SW7 3EG *Telex* 266638 WATSON G

*As envisaged last year, Michael Watson has now added a fourth to his collection
of early Victorian terraced houses in South Kensington, extending the number of
rooms in his elegant bed-and-breakfast establishment and adding a lift. However,
the enclosed Winter Garden, which we also advertised last year, has had to be
postponed till his current overdraft is reduced. In the meantime, most
correspondents continue to write appreciatively of their visits though there have
been grumbles about the smallness of some of the rooms; as with all old town
houses, rooms vary from floor to floor, though* Number Sixteen, *unlike some
establishments, modifies the prices according to size. But the attic rooms here are
a let-down, and there have been other criticisms as well. We also received one
account of a visit that went badly wrong. More reports please.*

Open All year.
Rooms 28 double, 4 single – 19 with bath, 13 with shower, all with direct-dial
telephone; colour TV on request.
Facilities Lift. Lounge, reception/TV room, bar/writing room. Small garden.
Location Central. No private parking. (Underground South Kensington.)
Restrictions Not suitable for &. Children over 12 preferred. No dogs.
Credit cards All major cards accepted.
Terms B&B: single £31–£40, double £49–£74. (No restaurant.)
Tipping: Not actively discouraged, but not encouraged.

The Portobello Hotel *Tel* 01-727 2777
22 Stanley Gardens, W11 2NG *Telex* 21789 or 25247

"I used to like *The Portobello* a lot, but this trip I found the staff laid back
to the point of being comatose. Though a relaxed attitude is nice, the line
between that and don't-care is a thin one. Maybe its 60-70s heyday has

gone, with the attitudes that engendered it."

With a report like that – and it wasn't the only one to vote against *The Portobello* this year – we thought we'd be giving the hotel a miss. This six-floor Victorian terraced house, within strolling distance of the Portobello Road Market and a little further to Kensington Gardens, has always been contentious. It is one of the few hotels in London with distinctive decor and life-style. Some of the rooms, called cabins, are poky, even if they have essential elements of life-support like colour TV, tiny fridge and micro-bathroom. But there are also, as you work downwards, normal-sized rooms and ritzy suites. Some people can't take its easy-going approach to hospitality at all; others, like the reporter quoted above, find its charms pall. But, just as we were about to consign it to the reject pile, we received the following and changed our minds:

"This eccentric, romantic and very European hotel defies the usual categories. We stayed in the round bedroom, which has gauze curtains overhanging the bed, antique Chinese furniture, and a bathtub big enough for four, all in the same room. If you like unique experiences, such a room should do the trick. The dining room downstairs is cheerfully managed on a 24-hour basis. The desk service was caring, although this hotel does not provide porter service. We also stayed in a small room, which was a monument to originality in making the best of every inch. I would recommend this terrific hotel to any but the most fastidious." *(Michael V Carlisle and Dr Sally Peterson)*

Open Approx 3 Jan to just before Christmas.
Rooms 7 suites, 9 double, 9 single – 4 with bath, 21 with shower, all with telephone, radio, TV, tea-making facilities and fridge; 2 ground-floor rooms.
Facilities Lift. Lounge, bar/restaurant (open 24 hours a day to residents).
Location Central. Meter parking. (Underground Notting Hill Gate.)
Restriction Not suitable for &.
Credit cards All major cards accepted.
Terms (no service charge) B&B (continental): single £36.80–£39.10, double £57.50–£69, suites £97.75–£103.50. Full alc £17. Special meals for children.

The Sandringham Hotel
3 Holford Road, NW3 1AD

Tel 01-435 1569

For 30 years this modest friendly B&B has been run by the Dreyer family at their Victorian house in a quiet street on the edge of Hampstead Heath. Sadly, Mr Dreyer died last year, but we are happy to say that Mrs Dreyer is continuing, assisted by her daughter-in-law Victoria. Don't expect anything special in the way of decor, but it is a friendly place, has lots of flowers and plants around, offers good coffee for breakfast, and its prices are exceedingly reasonable. "Its discovery is more than worth the price of this year's guide." *(A K F Walkers; also P J Lucas, Susan Park)*

Open All year.
Rooms 10 double, 4 single – 1 with bath.
Facilities Lounge with TV, breakfast room. Small garden.
Location 15 minutes by underground from central London (4 minutes' walk from Hampstead tube station); parking in forecourt of hotel or road.
Restrictions No dogs. Not suitable for &.
Credit cards None accepted.
Terms B&B: single £18, double £30–£32.

Swiss Cottage Hotel   *Tel* 01-722 2281
4 Adamson Road, NW3 3HP   *Telex* 297232 SWISCO G

A conversion of four Victorian terraced houses in a quiet residential street, yet close to underground and bus services and thus within 15 minutes of the West End. A medium-priced and medium-sized alternative to the big flashy city hotel, and also a hotel of genuine character – mostly ornate Edwardian and Victorian in its style, but carried out with panache. Two years ago, we ran a long *con amore* appreciation of the *Swiss Cottage*, extolling its virtues but also dwelling with jokey affection on some of its endearing shortcomings – its fairly exiguous single rooms, its volatile plumbing, its slow whimsical room service. There followed a year with no reports at all. Had our tale of minor aggravations emptied the hotel? we asked. Far from it, we are assured: it is harder to get in than ever. "Everything remains the same – the rambling building with the delightful furniture, the 19th-century paintings and the widely differing bedrooms. The plumbing is as haphazard as ever – sometimes the shower in your room works and other times it cries out for the services of an experienced tradesman. The restaurant is, as ever, off-hand and slightly muddled, but the food when it does come is pleasant and wholesome; after all, that does not matter because all the Swiss Cottage and Finchley Road restaurants are within walking distance. It remains a delightful place to stay in London (unlike nearly everywhere else we have tried) and, for us, most conveniently situated. We recommend it enthusiastically to all our friends." *(David Clark; also A P Henton and others)*

Open All year.
Rooms 4 suites, 50 double, 15 single – 42 with bath, 23 with shower, all with direct-dial telephone, radio, colour TV and baby-listening; some ground-floor rooms.
Facilities Lift. Large lounge with piano, cocktail bar, large function room, dining room, sauna. Paved patio garden. Indoor public swimming pool nearby.
Location 10 minutes from Oxford Circus by Jubilee Line; from Swiss Cottage underground station take Eton Avenue exit and follow signs to hotel (2 minutes' walk). Small car park, unrestricted street parking.
Restrictions Not suitable for &. No dogs.
Credit cards All major cards accepted.
Terms (No service charge) B&B: single £33–£60, double £50–£66. Set lunch £7, dinner £10. Children under 12 free in parents' room; special meals.
Tipping: "Left to the discretion of the guest."

Wilbraham Hotel   *Tel* 01-730 8296
1 Wilbraham Place, SW1X 9AE

An old fashioned Belgravian hotel in a quiet side street off Sloane Street. Once three Victorian terraced houses, the conversion has retained the gracious staircases, panelled walls and archways of the original structure. Prices are reasonable for this location, the service is exceptionally pleasant, rooms, even the smaller ones, are elegantly furnished with good lights, a porter carries your luggage up in a tiny wooden lift, beds are turned back in the evening. Breakfasts are served in bedrooms. Lunches and suppers are served for longish hours in an oak-panelled, slightly dark bar: respectable cooking if not gastronomically special. (S R)

Thus ran our first entry for the Wilbraham *in last year's edition, endorsed by*

139

Mike Hutton *with the cryptic comment: "Shades of P G Wodehouse and Noel Coward with guests to match ... Comfortable and good value for London if a shade eccentric", and decidedly not endorsed by another who had been made to move five times in a three-week stay, claimed his breakfast was late, greasy and cold, and found the staff surly. More reports please.*

Open All year. Bar closed Sun and bank holidays.
Rooms 40 double, 12 single – 36 with bath, 6 with shower, all with telephone; TV on request (no charge); 4 ground-floor rooms.
Facilities 2 lifts, lounge, TV room, bar/lounge serving food. &.
Location Near Sloane Square underground. Public underground parking nearby.
Restriction No dogs.
Credit cards None accepted.
Terms [1985 rates] (Excluding VAT; no service charge) rooms: single £24–£31, double £33–£52. Breakfast (continental) from £2.25, (English) from £3.50; full alc £9.
Service/tipping: "Service not included – gratuities to staff at guests' discretion."

LONGHORSLEY Northumberland   Map 4

Linden Hall Hotel   *Tel* Morpeth (0670) 56611
Longhorsley, Morpeth NE65 8XF   *Telex* 538224
                                                  Reservations in USA:
                                                  (212) 535 9530 (NY)
                                          or (800) 223 5581 (nationwide)

Thirty miles north of Newcastle, in an area pitifully ill served by good hotels, *Linden Hall* looks like a winner for those seeking luxurious accommodation in a beautiful location. It is a mansion of considerable grandeur, built in 1812 in the classical style, and set in 300 acres. The house had a major refurbishment five years ago, and opened its doors in 1981. In 1984 it was voted the Best Country Hotel of the Year by *Business Executive*.

In our entry last year, while quoting from some of the impressive testimonials we had received (including "absolutely magnificent" by renowned hotel connoisseur, *R W Apple, Jr* of the *New York Times)*, we wrote of our concern that the extensive conference and function activities of the hotel were sometimes at the expense of the independent traveller. We also mentioned complaints about poor service. While we continue to get unstinting praise – "One of the most pleasurable hotels we have ever stayed in" – reports about patchy service have been raised again by several correspondents: a bowl of fresh fruit in a bedroom had turned out to be two apples and an orange; and there were other niggling disappointments of the same kind. Also prospective bookers should be warned that, while many of the rooms are grand and spacious with a fine view, there are others at the back which are far less favoured. It is a shame that a hotel which has had so much care lavished on its restoration should not be functioning on all its cylinders.

Open All year.
Rooms 44 double, 1 single – all with bath, telephone, radio, colour TV, tea-making facilities and baby-listening ; 10 ground floor-rooms – 2 equipped for & with ramps, bathroom and warning bell.
Facilities Lift. 3 lounges, 2 bars, conservatory, pub and snack bar, TV room, restaurant, billiard room, table tennis room, sauna, solarium, hair-dressing salon; functions/conference facilities, 300-acre grounds with tennis, putting, croquet,

clay pigeon shooting, children's playground and adventure woodland area. &.
Location 1 m N of Longhorsley on A697; 30 m N of Newcastle.
Restriction No dogs in bedrooms or public rooms.
Credit cards All major cards accepted.
Terms B&B: single £49–£52, double £60–£75. Full alc £15.50. 2–4 day While-a-Way breaks throughout year (Fri–Mon only Mar–Oct); special 7-day terms. Children under 12 free of charge if sharing parents' room; special meals.

LOWER SWELL Gloucestershire   Map 2

Old Farmhouse Hotel   *Tel* Cotswold (0451) 30232
Lower Swell, Stow-on-the-Wold
Cheltenham GL54 1LF

A cosy 16th-century farmhouse in the centre of a tiny unspoiled Cotswold village a mile west of Stow-on-the-Wold lives again as a cosy country house hotel. It entered our lists two years ago, but changed hands in 1985. Readers who have stayed under the new regime of Rollo and Rosie Belsham have been quick to report that the new owners are maintaining the reputation of their predecessors. "'The bubbling enthusiasm' of the service under the previous regime may have calmed down, but is still excellent, the set menu ditto. No smoking in the dining room, hurrah! Friendly attention but not over-attentive from Mr and Mrs Belsham," are typical comments. Breakfast served between 8.30 and 9.00 am was less popular, even though guests were seen to be served both before and after the curfew hours. One couple concluded their report: "This stepping stone on our tour of the West Country ended as the highlight among some far more celebrated names." *(John and Lyn Spencer, Paul and Ann McGill; also D G Randall, C D Williams, P J Page, J L Carr)*

Open All year except 5 Jan–1 Feb.
Rooms 13 double – 11 with bath, all with radio, colour TV, and tea-making facilities; 6 rooms in the annexe.
Facilities Sitting room, bar, restaurant. Small walled garden.
Location 1 m W of Stow-on-the-Wold, on the B4068 (formerly the A436).
Restrictions Not really suitable for severely &. No smoking in the dining room. Dogs by arrangement; not in public rooms.
Credit cards Access, Visa.
Terms (Service at guests' discretion) B&B £13.50–£27; dinner, B&B £22.50–£36; full board £28.50–£42. Set dinner £9; full alc £13.50. Off-season and high-season breaks. Reduced rates and special meals for children.
Service/tipping: "We have not yet done away with tipping. Much as we personally dislike the convention, we do accept that the staff see a tip as the guest saying 'thank you; you have looked after me well'."

LUDLOW Shropshire   Map 2

The Feathers [GFG]   *Tel* Ludlow (0584) 5261
Ludlow SY8 1AA   *Telex* 35637 FETHER

The good news from Ludlow is that, after many years of undistinguished cooking, *The Feathers* has acquired a new chef, Vincent Jeffers, formerly from Robert Carrier's *Hintlesham Hall* (q.v.). First reports speak well – and gratefully – of the new kitchen regime.
    The Feathers, the town's chief hotel, has been an inn since early in the

17th century. Some inn! With its spectacular half-timbered front elevation, its carved mantelpieces and elaborately ornamented plaster ceilings, its panelling and original fireplaces, it is inevitably a showcase of a hotel in a town which is one in its own right, both historically and architecturally. Only too often one finds that such an establishment has been acquired by one of the big chains and run with impersonal efficiency by absentee landlords from London. *The Feathers* is different: it is owned and run personally by Osmond Edwards and his family. Maybe it is a little self-conscious about its special attractions such as its Richard III Restaurant, its Edward IV Meeting Room, Elizabeth I Bar, Prince Charles Suite and the like. With its coach parties, conferences and banquets, it has moved far from its innish origins. It is a thoroughly modern old hotel, alert to tourists' needs. But it still maintains a reputation for caring about traditional virtues found in old-fashioned hostelries – things like friendly service. *(C M Wilmot, S G Hare)*

Open All year.
Rooms 2 suites, 30 double, 5 single – all with bath and shower, direct-dial telephone, radio, colour TV, tea-making facilities and baby-listening, most with air-conditioning, some with 4-posters.
Facilities Lift. Lounge, 2 bars, writing room, restaurant, banqueting suite. Dances, private parties, wedding receptions catered for; conference facilities: River fishing and covered swimming pool nearby.
Location In Bull Ring (town centre). Secure parking.
Credit cards All major cards accepted.
Restrictions Not suitable for &. Dogs in public rooms only.
Terms B&B: single £35–£38, double £54–£66; dinner, B&B: single £45–£50, double £74–£86; full board: single £52–£57, double £88–£100. Set lunch £8.50, dinner £13; full alc: lunch £11, dinner £15. 2-day heritage breaks all year; Christmas and New Year packages. Reduced rates and special meals for children.

LUNDY ISLAND Devon   Map 1

Millcombe House Hotel   *Tel* Woolacombe (0271) 870870
Lundy, Via Bideford, Devon   *Reservations* at Landmark Trust
EX34 8LA   head office: Littlewick Green
                                     (062 882) 5920 or 5925

For those who have never heard of Lundy Island, it rises 400 feet out of the sea in the Bristol Channel with tremendous views of England, Wales and the Atlantic. It is a paradise for naturalists: 425 different birds have been recorded here, as well as grey seals, Sika deer and Soay sheep. The island is just over three miles long by about half a mile wide, and the nearest practicable harbours are at Clovelly and Bideford, each about 24 miles away – further than England is from France. Summer sailings are normally on Tuesdays, Thursdays and Saturdays. There is also a Saturday helicopter service from Hartland Point.

You will need to be fairly fit to stay at *Millcombe House*, the only hotel (or guest-house) on the island, since it is set on a hill and there are no made-up roads or paths. Other creature comforts, basic for some, are also missing here: the hotel provides no TV or radio. Fresh milk is limited, so be prepared for UHT. "We aim", writes the hotel, "to provide an atmosphere more of a house party than an ordinary hotel. Guests sit at one table. To stay at *Millcombe House* is a mixture of mild adventure and being thoroughly spoiled. Our full-board rate – there isn't any other

– includes such things as early morning tea, afternoon tea and coffee after dinner, so once you have paid, you have no need to put your hands in your pockets again except for wines and spirits." "A gem of a hotel on a gem of an island ... I quite understand why guests return year after year – both the hotel and the island have a unique character which hopefully will not be lost. An island to get away from it all." (*Carol Godsmark; also L H, P J Haynes*)

Open All year.
Rooms 4 double, 3 single.
Facilities Lounge, dining room. 1,100-acre grounds. Sea ¼ m with rock beach and safe bathing.
Location In the Bristol Channel. 24 m by boat from Bideford, or 15 m from Clovelly; 12 m by helicopter from Hartland Point.
Restrictions Not suitable for ⅙. Dogs not allowed to land on Lundy.
Credit cards None accepted.
Terms (No service charge) full board £22–£30. Set lunch £4, dinner, £8.50. Children under 1 free; reduced rates for older children sharing parents' room.
Service/tipping: "Our staff do not ask for tips nor do they expect them."

LYME REGIS Dorset   Map 1

The Mariners Hotel   *Tel* Lyme Regis (029 74) 2753
Silver Street, Lyme Regis DT7 3HS   *Telex* 46491 ICC G.221

"Unpretentious and comfortable and the management respond exactly as hotel keepers should. I asked for China tea at breakfast on my first morning and they didn't have it – but they certainly did by the afternoon! The food can only be described as voluminous as well as delicious and again, unpretentious – none of that mucking about that passes for 'garnishing' at the sort of hotel that takes itself seriously and disregards its customers totally!" (*Claire Rayner*)

That comment was written three years ago, but readers continue to confirm its validity. *The Mariners* is an unassumingly friendly 17th-century coaching inn on the Axminster Road, at the end of the town, with fine views of the sweeping Dorset coastline from its garden and from many of the rooms. It is run with enthusiasm by Leo Featherstone, who is also the chef-patron and takes his cooking seriously – fish specially recommended. (Warning: front rooms, though double-glazed, can be noisy, and steep stairs to the upper rooms will not suit the elderly or infirm.)

Open Mar–early Nov.
Rooms 13 double, 3 single – 8 with bath, 5 with shower, all with radio, colour TV and baby-listening; 2 rooms on ground floor but some steps. Double-glazing.
Facilities 2 lounges, bar, restaurant. Small garden overlooking sea. Golf course nearby with concessions for residents.
Location Coming from London on A35 through Lyme Regis, take right fork at top of main street (Broad Street); hotel is on right. Large car park. (Some rooms on front might get traffic noise but there is very little at night.)
Restrictions Not suitable for ⅙. No children under 7 in restaurant for dinner. No dogs.
Credit cards All major cards accepted.
Terms (Service at guests' discretion) B&B £23.50–£26; dinner, B&B (2 days min.) £28.50–£33. Bar lunches; set dinner £11. Bargain breaks out of season. Reduced rates for children sharing parents' room, children's supper (under 7) at 5.30pm.
Service/tipping: "We do not approve of service charges, but leave the onus to our guests."

MATLOCK Derbyshire   Map 2

Riber Hall [GFG]   *Tel* Matlock (0629) 2795
Matlock DE4 5JU

"Mr and Mrs Biggin have created an ambience which made us feel like pampered guests at a country house weekend. Tucked away in our peaceful and comfortable bedroom suite, we wanted for nothing. The discreet, friendly and informal service is obviously based on excellent management and good teamwork, and it created just the right atmosphere to lift our jaded spirits on arrival. Add to all those qualities excellent food in an individual style accompanied by reasonably priced wine (which *could* be found on the large wine list), and our pleasure was complete." *(CN Hobson)*

A report calculated to warm a hotel-keeper's heart, and these sentiments were echoed by most visitors this year to this partly Elizabethan country manor, extensively restored and now offering a comprehensive country house experience. There are spacious public rooms in the main house, with lots of period furniture, as well as a *nouvelle*-ish restaurant that has deservedly won a reputation among neighbouring gourmets. Bedrooms are across a steep gravelled court-yard (not recommended for the disabled) and are richly kitted out with extras; many rooms have four-posters, two have whirlpool baths. What criticisms there have been are mostly of the minor kind: poor service at breakfast (how many hotels, offering splendid service in the evening, let the side down the following morning!), poor lighting in the bedrooms (that's just the trouble with four-posters!), heating not turned on soon enough on a cold wet afternoon (yet another hotel that fails the heating test). But the pleasures of a stay at *Riber* – bargain breaks specially recommended – are attested to by *David Wooff, Mrs S Cohen, Michael Wace, Elizabeth Stanton, Pat and Jeremy Temple.*

Open All year.
Rooms 11 double – all with bath (2 whirlpool), direct-dial telephone, radio, colour TV, tea-making facilities and mini-bar, most with antique 4-poster beds.
Facilities 2 lounges, bar, dining room, conference/function room. 4-acre grounds with walled garden and orchard.
Location 1 m S of A615 at Tansley.
Restrictions Not suitable for &. No children under 10. No dogs.
Credit cards All major cards accepted.
Terms (No service charge) B&B (continental): single occupancy £45, double £59. Set lunch £7.20; full alc dinner £15.75. Hideaway weekends mid-Oct to mid-April.

MERSHAM Kent   Map 2

Stone Green Hall [GFG]   *Tel* Aldington (023 372) 418
Mersham, Nr Ashford TN25 7HE

Correspondents tend to reach for their superlatives when endeavouring to describe the intense pleasure they have had at Ingrid and Rachel Kempston's country home hotel. The house is peerless Queen Anne, furnished with lovely things and profuse with flowers. There is an Edwardian conservatory, full of gardenia and camellia, extending right across the back of the house – wonderful for breakfasts or summer drinks. The five acres of well-wooded yew-hedged garden include a ha-ha, a gazebo, a grass tennis court and a croquet lawn. The only change of substance in this demi-Eden is that the Kempstons have now introduced two alternative sorts of menu for the same price, currently [1985] £11.50: a three-course menu with four choices at each course or a five-course menu with no choice. Although the restaurant can seat 30, and there are only three rooms at *Stone Green*, none of the residents has ever suggested being short-changed. On the contrary. "I wrestled with my conscience: my wife and I were tempted not to write for selfish reasons! The entries you have are totally accurate. How many places will serve your Saturday breakfast at 10 am, without batting an eyelid, in a superb conservatory? And what a view! I have never come across a better place *totally* to switch off. If you want the hotel trimmings, this is *not* for you. You are made to feel a most welcome guest in a lovely home." *(Dr and Mrs H Manuel; with similar endorsements from Jane Balfour, Mrs S Lacey, Drew Smith)*

Open All year except Feb and Christmas Eve.
Rooms 3 double – all with bath, radio and colour TV.
Facilities Writing room, drawing room, cards room, conservatory, private dining room, restaurant; Sat dinner dance every 6 weeks or so. 5-acre garden with croquet and tennis. Sissinghurst, Great Dixter and Leeds Castle nearby.
Location Turn W off A20 3 m S of Ashford, at Mersham sign. In village, take sign marked Swanton Mill. The house is ½ m on left.
Restrictions Not suitable for &. No children under 12 in hotel, under 6 in restaurant. No dogs.
Credit cards Access, Amex, Visa.
Terms (Service at guests' discretion) B&B: single £30–£45, double £40–£60. Dinner £13–£14. Mid-week breaks Jan/Feb. 2 consecutive nights, 25% off room rates Mon–Thur. Reduced rates for children, according to age; special meals.

MIDDLEHAM North Yorkshire   Map 4

Millers House
Market Place, Middleham DL8 4NR   *Tel* Wensleydale (0969) 22630

A handsome grey-stone Georgian house, formerly a finishing school for young ladies; it is just off the market square of this enchanting Dales village, now chiefly famous for its racing stables, but whose castle was once the northern seat of Richard III. We had an entry for the hotel in earlier editions, but it disappeared last year for lack of feed-back. We are glad to welcome it again, with an eloquent vote of thanks from a grateful American couple: "We love Britain and its people, and we feel particularly grateful that we found this English hotel which projects the very best of what we value most about Britain. Room accommodation was above average, and both Mr Nicholson's breakfasts and Mrs Nicholson's dinners are as good as you'll find anywhere. The Nicholsons' it's-your-home-while-here hospitality, plus their desire to be of help, made this our best stay ever in Britain. Of some 75 hotels, grand and modest, in which we have stayed in Britain in the past seven years, this is our all-time favourite." *(Rowena and Keith Cox; also Mrs M Midgley)*

Open 1 Feb–30 Nov.
Rooms 5 double, 1 single – all with bath, colour TV and tea-making facilities.
Facilities Residents' lounge, bar, dining room. Small enclosed garden. Many castles, abbeys and country houses close by.
Location Take B6267 turn-off from A1, head for Masham then Middleham; or take

A684 turn-off from A1 and head for Leyburn then Middleham. Car park.
Restrictions Not suitable for &. No dogs.
Credit card Diners.
Terms (No service charge) B&B £19; dinner, B&B £28.50. Full alc £11.50. "Let's go" breaks for 2 or more days Nov and Feb–May. Reduced rates and special meals for children.
Service/tipping: "We make no charge for service nor add cover charges; if however a tip is given to staff it is always accepted."

MINCHINHAMPTON Gloucestershire   Map 2

Burleigh Court Hotel   *Tel* Brimscombe (0453) 883804
Stroud GL5 2PF

A Pevsner-listed Georgian country house devotedly restored by Hilary and Roger Benson, and run as a hotel with the assistance of daughters Nicola and Jo, and Jo's husband, Adrian Stewart. It has a specially attractive five-acre garden designed by Clough Williams Ellis and a fine position looking over the Stroud valley. "The situation is magnificent, the house impressively elegant, and the Bensons most hospitable. There is plenty of choice and imagination in the set-price dinner menu. The bedroom had been pleasantly refurbished. We envied the 'commercials' who obviously make this a regular port of call on their travels. The only slight disappointment was the swimming pool which was of unusually modest proportions, but everything else added up to the sort of establishment that the Guide is all about." (*John Timpson; warmly endorsed by Roy and Mary Pepper, Ken Simpson*)

Since last year, the Bensons have been converting a stable block into annexe bedrooms and suites: two new rooms this year and another six expected shortly. They have also added vegetarian and slimmers' "options" to their regular menu.

Open All year except 24–30 Dec.
Rooms 1 suite, 12 double – 10 with bath, 3 with shower, all with telephone, radio, colour TV and baby-listening; tea-making facilities on request. 2 ground-floor rooms in annexe.
Facilities TV room, reception/lounge, lounge/bar, dining room; conference/function facilities. 5-acre landscaped garden with water gardens, wooded area, heated outdoor swimming pool and putting green. Riding, tennis, golf nearby. Ramps &.
Location ½m S of A419 at Brimscombe; follow signs for Minchinhampton and *Burleigh Court*.
Restriction No dogs.
Credit cards Access, Amex, Visa.
Terms (Gratuities at guests' discretion) B&B: single £35, double £45–£55; dinner, B&B: single £47, double £37–£39 per person. Set lunch £8, dinner £11.50; full alc £14. Slimmers and vegetarians catered for. Bargain breaks at most times of year (min. 2 days). Reduced rates for children sharing parents' room; special meals.

MULLION South Cornwall   Map 1

Polurrian Hotel   *Tel* Mullion (0326) 240421
Mullion TR12 7EN

An old-fashioned – in the complimentary sense – family seaside hotel, offering plenty of sporting amenities for all age-groups, with its own private sandy beach, in a scenic position on the Lizard Peninsula overlooking St Michael's Mount, is recommended to Guide readers in the following terms: "Since my wife and I were married five years ago we estimate we have stayed in 30 different kinds of hotel both at home and abroad and without doubt this is our favourite and the one we feel gives the best value for money. There are many reasons for this. First and foremost it is still a family-run hotel owned by the Francis family. The most important feature of this hotel is the friendly concern that is shown towards guests and their needs. They are treated like old friends. Phrases like 'welcome back' and 'how nice to see you again' are as far removed from the normal stereotyped greeting as is a Rembrandt from a cheap print. The food is well above the average hotel standard. Every dish that is supposed to be piping hot comes to you piping hot. The wine list is forever being expanded and Mr Francis is always looking for good wines that he can sell to his guests at between £4 and £5. There is plenty of room between the tables. The building dates back to Edwardian times and stands on top of the cliffs overlooking Polurrian Cove, one of the few surfing coves on the south coast and relatively quiet even in mid-August. The National Trust owns most of the surrounding land and there are marvellous walks in both directions. The bedrooms are all most comfortably furnished, with pre-war rather than post-war ideas of space. Within the hotel grounds there are facilities for cricket, croquet, putting and tennis and there is still plenty of room to sit about and relax and drink in the glorious view over Mount's Bay to Penzance and Land's End. The sunsets are among the most glorious in this country. On every occasion – and we have now been four times – we have found pleasant people with whom to chat after dinner and enjoy a convivial glass. If the virtues of the *Polurrian* are old fashioned we can only say 'thank God for it'. If ever there was hotel for *The Good Hotel Guide* it is the *Polurrian*." *(Gwen and Peter Andrews)*

Open Easter to mid-Oct.
Rooms 3 suites, 36 double, 4 single – 39 with bath, all with radio, colour TV and baby-listening. Some ground-floor rooms; 6 self-catering apartments.
Facilities 2 lounges, 2 restaurants, ballroom, games room with table tennis, snooker, pool, children's playroom; squash court, dancing, disco; piano and choir evenings. 12-acre grounds with putting, croquet, hard tennis court, badminton, cricket net, play area, terrace, gardens and heated swimming pool. Private sandy beach 100 yds with unusually safe bathing, sea fishing, surfing and windsurfing.
Location From Redruth take A393 to Helston (do not take Redruth bypass); fork left at Scorrier, proceed through Redruth following signs to Helston; at Helston follow signs for A3083 to The Lizard; after approx. 6 m turn right onto B3296 to Mullion. Go through village, following signs to Mullion Cove. ½ m from village centre, past cricket field on left, take Polurrian Rd on right.
Restriction No dogs in public rooms.
Credit cards Access, Diners, Visa.
Terms B&B £22–£35; dinner, B&B £28–£40. Set lunch £6, dinner £10.50; full alc £13. Off-season breaks, honeymoon packages. Children under 7 free, 7–15 years only charged for meals if sharing adult accommodation; children's suppers 5.30–6pm with advance notice.

> Most hotels have reduced rates out of season and for children, and some British hotels offer 'mini-break' rates throughout the year. If you are staying more than one night, it is always worth asking about special terms.

MUNGRISDALE Cumbria   Map 4

The Mill   *Tel* Threlkeld (059 683) 659
Mungrisdale, Penrith CA11 OXR

No shortage of compliments for the simple but civilised pleasures of this former 17th-century mill cottage, no more than a dozen miles from the Penrith exit of the M6, but well away from the tourist pack and at the foot of the fells. In addition to the accommodation in the house, the Woods also have a cottage annexe five minutes' walk away. "We wish we could have stayed longer . . . To drift off to sleep with no sound but that of the mill stream close by was utter bliss . . . Amazing value" *(Consuelo Phelan).* "Special praise for the excellent five-course dinner, and good and reasonably priced wine list . . . We booked again" *(Dr and Mrs E Jacoby).* "Excellent and imaginative cooking . . . Extremely good value . . . Most warm and friendly welcome by the Woods made us stay longer than we originally intended" *(Mr and Mrs A Linder).* "Though modest in appearance, it was everything you said it would be and the food was outstanding." *(Linda Semanisin and Mary Abrahamson)*

Open Mid-Mar–end Oct.
Rooms 9 double, 2 single – 4 with bath, 1 with shower, 2 with colour TV; all with tea-making facilities; 3 rooms in annexe.
Facilities Lounge with log fire, TV lounge, small sun lounge, games room, dining room; drying room. 3-acre grounds with garden and trout stream. Ullswater 5 m away with fishing, sailing; fell-walking, rock-climbing, pony-trekking, bird-watching, hang-gliding and golf nearby. 2 covered and 12 open parking spaces.
Location Leave M6 at Penrith (exit 40) and take A66 for Keswick. *The Mill* is 2 m N of A66; sign post for Mungrisdale is mid-way between Penrith and Keswick.
Restrictions Not suitable for &. Dogs in annexe bedrooms only.
Credit cards None accepted.
Terms (No service charge) B&B: single £14–£16, double £26–£28; dinner, B&B: single £20–£23, double £36–£44. Set dinner £9. Reductions for children sharing parents' room; special meals by arrangement.
Tipping: Gratuities left to guests' discretion.

NAYLAND Suffolk   Map 2

The Bear Country Restaurant   *Tel* Nayland (0206) 262204
and Hotel [GFG]
Bear Street, Nayland
Nr Colchester, Essex EO6 4HX

John and Katy Naismith took over this rambling, friendly, half-timbered house, half a mile from the Stour and in the heart of Constable country, in the spring of 1983. It is, as its name suggests, more of a restaurant-with-rooms than a hotel, and, like all such establishments, better suited to a one-night stop than an extended visit. The restaurant, about which all our correspondents speak with enthusiasm – everything is home made, including bread and ice cream – can seat 70, and there are just four rooms. But the resident population is not short-changed: the rooms, which are being progressively redecorated, are comfortable and characterful, with lots of flowers around, as well as fruit, home-made biscuits, books and magazines; the bathrooms are not luxurious but have deep-pile large towels and plenty of small extras. Outside, the

Naismiths are also actively improving the four-acre garden, and there are plans to heat the pool next year and to install a hard tennis court to add to the existing grass one. Most readers write with unaffected enthusiasm for the agreeableness and warmth of the Naismiths, the comforts of the house and the reasonable prices.

Open All year except Christmas Day, 2 weeks in Jan, last week Aug, 1st week Sept. Restaurant closed Sun and Mon.
Rooms 4 double – 3 with bath, 1 with shower – all with radio, colour TV and tea-making facilities.
Facilities Private lounge on first floor, bar, 2 restaurants. 4-acre grounds with swimming pool (which should be heated by 1986), bowling area, grass tennis court (hard court planned for 1986), croquet lawn. Vineyard and terraces. River Stour and golf course nearby. ໄ (restaurant only).
Location 6 m N of Colchester on A134. Hotel is central (front rooms can be noisy). Parking.
Restriction No dogs in public rooms.
Credit cards Access, Visa.
Terms (No service charge) B&B: single occupancy £25, double £35. Set dinner £8.95; full alc £15. Children under 5 free; 5–15 years £6 if sharing parents' room or ½-price in own room; special meals.
Service/tipping: "No service charge made or tips expected."

NEWLANDS Cumbria   Map 4

Swinside Lodge   *Tel* Keswick (0596) 72948
Newlands, Nr Keswick CA12 5UE

A warmly welcoming guest-house, with exceedingly modest prices, offering plenty of home comforts, in an idyllic setting at the foot of Cat Bells, one of the best easy fell walks along the edge of Derwentwater. The good news about *Swinside Lodge* was reported by an inspector last year, and visitors since then have confirmed his findings. PS: We apologise for a number of inaccuracies in last year's entry: Mr and Mrs Dickinson are in their mid-fifties, not in their sixties, and regrettably our cartographer confused Newlands near Caldbeck with *Swinside's* Newlands which is between Keswick and Borrowdale. We should also make clear that though there is no formal choice on the evening menu, the Dickinsons take much trouble to check on personal tastes and allergies and cheerfully change menus to suit.

Open Jan–Nov.
Rooms 8 double – 2 with bath.
Facilities Lounge with TV, dining room, ⅔-acre garden. 5 minutes' walk to Derwentwater.
Location 3 m SW of Keswick on A66. At Portinscale follow road to Grange.
Restrictions Not suitable for ໄ. No dogs, but kennels provided free of charge.
Credit cards None accepted.
Terms B&B £10–£12.80; dinner, B&B £16.60–£18.35; full board £101–£122.95 per week. Set dinner £6; packed lunches on request. Reduced rates for children; special meals on request.

> Set dinner refers to a fixed price meal (which may have ample, limited or no choice on the menu). Full alc is the hotel's own estimated price per person of a three-course meal taken *à la carte*, with a half-bottle of house wine.

NEWLYN Cornwall   Map 1

Higher Faugan Country House Hotel   *Tel* Penzance (0736) 62076
Newlyn, Penzance TR18 5NS

Higher Faugan was built at the turn of the century by the artist Stanhope
Forbes to accommodate the first residential art school in Newlyn. It
stands in 10 acres of grounds 300 feet up overlooking Penzance and
Mount's Bay (sea views from the first floor) with its own heated outdoor
pool. The hotel is run by Michael and Jane Young. It has an interesting
policy: the less good the view, the better the furnishing. One reader this
year, who found himself in a room without a view, would have
preferred a price reduction; he also commented on the thinness of the
partition between his room and the one next door: "We slept and woke
when they decided." Other niggles also surfaced in the mail: towels,
though plentiful, were not of good quality and were small; no help with
bags; toilet facilities for one of the rooms were "terribly small"; the
arrangement of seating in the lounge around the walls made intimate
conversations difficult. Notwithstanding these and similar minor criticisms, most guests appreciated the friendly hospitality and comforts of
the house and Mrs Young's cooking.

Open Mid-Mar to end Sept.
Rooms 10 double, 2 single – 8 with bath, 4 with shower, all with telephone, radio,
colour TV, tea-making facilities and baby-listening; 3 ground-floor rooms.
Facilities 2 sitting rooms, bar, billiard room, dining room. 10-acre grounds with
tennis court, putting; heated swimming pool. Beaches nearby. Land's End 9 m.
Location Take B3315 from Newlyn Bridge. Hotel signposted on right on hill.
Restrictions Not really suitable for &. No dogs.
Credit cards Access, Amex, Diners.
Terms (No service charge) B&B £20.50–£24.70, dinner, B&B £27.60–£32.50. Set
dinner £10.35. Weekly rates. Reduced rates for children.

NEW MILTON Hampshire   Map 2

Chewton Glen Hotel [GFG]   *Tel* Highcliffe (042 52) 5341
New Milton BH25 6QS   *Telex* 41456
                                              Reservations in UK also on
                                    01-439 2365 and in US (800) 223 6800

"From our perspective, the room service and especially the food were as
close to perfect as makes no difference. The new drive and landscaping
makes it seem part of the New Forest – we think the first impression is
tremendously important. How many hoteliers would have spent several
tens of thousands on a driveway?" *(Paul Henderson)*
    "Restaurant, hotel standards and service throughout is superb. The
constant improvements – to the drive and to the suites and rooms – send
this hotel up and up in my estimation." *(N R Hunter)*
    "As always superb . . . Travelling alone, I am quickly aware if a place is
not being caring. Here the staff could not have been nicer or better
trained or more helpful. Lunch was amazingly reasonable for a place of
this culinary standard. The food was marvellous. Everywhere was
spotless. I had not one word of fault to find, but I am sure that if I had
had a grievance, people would have *cared*." *(W A)*

How fortunate an hotel is to earn exclamatory tributes of this glowing order. *Chewton Glen* has been for many years a *prima donna assoluta* among English country house hotels. For the record, it is one of only three hotels in the British Isles to get four red turrets and a rosette in *Michelin* (the other two are the *Connaught* in London and *Inverlochy Castle*, Fort William, both q.v.). It is more expensive than almost any other English hotel in the Guide outside London and its prices have risen "more with the dollar value than with British inflation" as one reader pointed out, though perhaps the cost of the new driveway has escalated the tariff. On the other hand, as the comments above make clear, it offers matchless service and a splendid restaurant. It is like one of the great Cunard liners in the good old days, with spacious boardroom-style lounges and a large pool in keeping with the prevailing luxuriousness. And just as the opulence of the *Queen Mary* helped its passengers to forget the monotony of the ocean, so the splendours of *Chewton Glen* and its grounds effectively disguise the fact that New Milton, though on the fringes of the New Forest, is not in itself particularly picturesque.

Regrettably, alongside the compliments, minority reports on *Chewton Glen* continue to surface. While the *patron* of *Gidleigh Park*, Paul Henderson, gives the hotel his highest accolade, another distinguished hotelier writes that he found everything overdone, impersonal and the prices hard to justify. Another reader reports a mass of small niggles – flowers needed freshening or replacing, windows needed washing, exhaust fans clearly audible in the rooms over the kitchens in the new wing. A third, a connoisseur of luxury hotels, wrote a long detailed report on high spots and low spots. Her highest spot was "the loveliest picnic imaginable". Her most serious criticism was of "the conference-centre atmosphere . . . It was difficult to escape from people with badges and roped-off rooms with raucous laughter." We recognise the importance of conferences in the economy of luxury hotels and we admire the panache of Martin Skan in his running of *Chewton Glen*. It patently offers some of its guests a supreme hotel experience; sadly, it isn't going to suit all comers.

Open All year.
Rooms 11 suites, 33 double – all with bath and shower, direct-dial telephone, radio, colour TV; baby-listening by arrangement. Some ground-floor rooms.
Facilities 1 large lounge, 2 small lounges, bar, private dining room, restaurant, shop, terrace. Pianist in lounge some evenings. 30-acre grounds with tennis court, croquet lawn, putting, jogging course and heated swimming pool. Sea ½ m with safe bathing from shingle beach; the New Forest spreads to the north. Fishing, riding, sailing nearby; 12 golf courses within radius of 20 m. Chauffeur service.
Location Do not follow New Milton signs. From A35, take turning to Walkford and Highcliffe; go through Walkford, then left down Chewton Farm road. Entrance is on right hand side.
Restrictions No children under 7. No dogs; kennel facilities nearby.
Credit cards All major cards accepted.
Terms B&B (continental): single £50–£79, double £86–£132. Full breakfast £8.50; set lunch from £10, dinner from £27.50; full alc £35.
Service/tipping "Our prices are fully inclusive and all our guests are made aware of this."

Do you know of a good hotel in Manchester?

---

*The hotel listed here changed hands
as we went to press.*

Hotels are dropped if we lack positive feedback. If you can
endorse an entry, please do so.

NUNNINGTON North Yorkshire   Map 4

Ryedale Lodge   *Tel* Nunnington (043 95) 246
Nunnington
Nr Helmsley, York YO6 5XB

"*Ryedale Lodge* is Nunnington Railway Station converted into a small
hotel. It is situated in isolation and tranquillity and one can hear the
silence. There is no separate bar (personally I prefer one) but there is no
difficulty getting a drink. There is no reception desk – sign in at leisure.
No keys to bedrooms (only people of trust stay here). No bustle, just
quiet efficiency. The decor, mainly dark green, is too dark for my
personal taste, but I overheard people admiring it. The bedrooms are
individually styled. Decorative reading lamps and impressively laun-
dered bed-linen. Bathroom of adequate size with an abundance of hot
water. The dining room was a welcoming place staffed by young local
women ever anxious to be of service. The table was well laid with good
quality table-ware" (*William Lightbrown*). So begins a nominator's report
for this small hotel or restaurant-with-rooms, well-placed for York to the
south or the Yorkshire Moors to the north. Mr Lightbrown's report was
not without criticism: not much drawer space in his bedroom for more
than a night's stop, inadequate shelving in the bathroom, cooking
standards varied, though with several peaks in a three-day visit. Other
nominators had no reservations, about the food or about any other part
of the set-up: "The best part of our month's vacation in Europe . . . A
wonderful little place . . . Beautiful lounges . . . Oh joy! – marvellous
succulent food, attractively served . . . Jan and Jon Laird are lovely
people." (*Marjory Hansen*)

Open All year except 3 weeks in Jan.
Rooms 5 double – all with bath, telephone, radio, colour TV, tea-making facilities,
baby-listening.
Facilities Large lounge with small bar and TV, restaurant. 4-acre grounds. River
Rye 10 minutes' walk; trout fishing.
Location 5 m S of Helmsley along B1247, 1 m due W of Nunnington.
Restriction No dogs.
Credit cards Access, Amex, Visa.
Terms (No service charge) B&B: single occupancy £29, double £43; dinner, B&B:
single occupancy £43.25, double £71.50. Set dinner £14.25, full alc £16.75. Reduced
rates Oct–May (min. 2 nights); Christmas package. Reduced rates and special
meals for children.

OTLEY Suffolk   Map 2

Otley House   *Tel* Helmingham (047 339) 253
Ipswich IP6 9NR

A member, and a good one, of the Wolsey Lodge group, "an
Englishman's home where you are welcome to stay as a guest for a night
or more" – or, as Lise Hilton, who runs *Otley House* with her husband,
puts it more succinctly, "a country house home". The house stands well
back from the road in spacious grounds which include a lake. It presents
itself as Georgian, though it dates back from the Tudor period, and has
Tudor features such as the large open fireplace in the hall. Rooms are
large and elegantly furnished. The four-course dinner is taken com-

munally at 7.30 pm in the candlelit Regency dining room: Lise Hilton, who is Danish, is the cook, and our correspondents speak warmly of her dishes, which are cosmopolitan in style, though the Danish element is there, along with a touch of Carrier. It would make an admirable base for touring Norfolk and Suffolk – Aldeburgh, Constable country etc. Prices are very reasonable. *(E H Plaut, U L P)*

Open 1 Feb–30 Nov.
Rooms 4 double – 3 with bath, all with radio.
Facilities Large hall with seating, drawing room, TV and billiard room, dining room. 3-acre gounds, small lake, croquet lawn.
Location 7 miles N of Ipswich, on the B1079. Hotel will send directions.
Restrictions Not suitable for &. No children under 12. No dogs.
Credit cards None accepted.
Terms B&B double £30, dinner, B&B double £50. Set dinner £10 per person; vegetarian meals on request. (Lunch not served.)

PILTON Somerset   Map 1

The Long House   *Tel* Pilton (074 989) 701
Pylle Road, Pilton BA4 4BP

This is Paul Foss and Eric Swainsbury's fifteenth year at the *Long House*, an intriguing 17th-century building in a small, very peaceful village about equidistant from two touristic magnets, Wells and Glastonbury. Their establishment is a highly personal one, and some readers (but they are in the minority) have found their attentiveness at times excessive. Dinner is at 7.30 pm with a no-choice menu. Guests sit at individual tables, but are introduced to each other by their hosts. Classical music accompanies the evening meal – "so be prepared", writes one correspondent, "to like chamber music, harpsichord and the esoteric." Prices are very reasonable. We think the following report offers the majority view: "This small hotel is well concealed in a charming Somerset village, but it is well worth finding. It is comfortable, the food is simple but very well prepared and presented. The house wine is of exceptional value. BBC3 provided a splendid recording of *La Marseillaise* on 14 July. No TV was apparent. The enterprise is a very good example of what can be achieved by much effort applied by few people, and is a great credit to the two owners." *(J K Lunn; also K W Collis, J S & F Waters, J A Powell, Jean Willson)*

Open All year.
Rooms 6 double, 1 single – 6 with bath, all with radio and baby-listening.
Facilities Bar/lounge, dining room. Small garden.
Location On S edge of village from Glastonbury (A361) take first right turn in village. From Shepton Mallet B3136 (Glastonbury) and then straight on.
Restrictions Children under 6 not encouraged. No dogs in public rooms.
Credit cards All major cards accepted.
Terms B&B £15–£20.75. Set dinner £7.40. Bargain breaks 2, 5 and 7 nights; weekly reductions available. 50% reduction for children sharing parents' room. *Tipping: discouraged.*

There are many expensive hotels in the Guide. We are keen to increase our coverage at the other end of the scale. If you know of a simple place giving simple satisfaction, please write and tell us.

POOL-IN-WHARFEDALE West Yorkshire   Map 4

Pool Court Restaurant with Rooms [GFG]   *Tel* Arthington (0532)
Otley LS21 1EH   842288 or 842414

"A warm welcome", we wrote last year, "to the most exciting new
establishment in the restaurant-with-rooms category to appear in 1985."
Michael Gill's *Pool Court Restaurant* has been a gastronomic mecca for
more than two decades and needs no embellishing. Only the rooms are
new. Four at the moment, though another two are in prospect. "This is
what I call a luxury room: a nude sculpture, an alarm clock, the wine
list left in the room with 200+ bottles, Hugh Johnson's wine book to
help consider the wine list, slippers, TV, *TV Times*, dried fruit, good
books, *Harpers and Queen*, flowers, drinks fridge with champagne,
spirits, and glasses to match, pot-pourri, leather jewellery box. And then
there's the bathroom – robes, fancy taps, shower cap and even a
clockwork frog for the bath; lavender room fragrance!, talcum powder,
hair lotion, camomile soap, four spot-lights over the basin like they have
in Hollywood stars' dressing rooms, a plant, a square designer loo, a
candle. Then the breakfast in the room: 'I won't open the curtains too
much, sir, so it is not too much of a shock.' A real breakfast of kidney,
free-range egg, sausage, potato cake, tomato, bacon plus fresh brioche
and toast and home-made marmalade, strawberry jam, honey . . . and a
compote of apples and currants. Oh yes, also a choc on the pillow at
night!" (*D S; also Harry Cardwell, Pat and Jeremy Temple, and others*)

Open All year except 2 weeks July/Aug and 2 weeks from 24 Dec. Restaurant
closed Sun and Mon (limited room service menu).
Rooms 3 double, 1 single – 3 with bath, 1 with shower, all with direct-dial
telephone, radio/alarm, colour TV, bar, fridge, wall-safe.
Facilities Cocktail bar/lounge, restaurant. 1-acre grounds.
Location Equidistant (9 m) from Leeds, Bradford and Harrogate.
Restrictions No children under 12. No dogs.
Credit cards All major credit cards accepted.
Terms (No service charge) B&B: single £35–£42, double £55–£67. Set dinner
£10–£18; full alc £23. (Lunch by prior arrangement only, for private parties of 20 or
more.) Weekend breaks Fri/Sat, 18 Jan–30 Mar. Reduced rates Sun and Mon nights
when restaurant is closed. Reduced rates for children; special meals by
arrangement.
*Service/tipping: "I fully endorse your campaign against the archaic 'obligatory service
charge'."*

POOLE Dorset   Map 1

The Mansion House Hotel   *Tel* Poole (0202) 685666
Thames Street, Poole BH15 1JN   *Telex* MH 41495 SELECT G

A modified welcome for this sophisticated, recently renovated hotel in a
pretty Georgian building near the water front in the old part of Poole.
The hall with its sweeping staircase is particularly elegant. "Our
bedroom was attractive and comfortable. Two ancient beams crossed it
just below the ceiling. There were no overhead lights but plenty of
standard ones; the bedside lights were fixed to the walls, a bit too far
from the bed for comfortable reading. There was period furniture, a TV
with remote control, flowers and fruit. Excellent towels and plenty of

hot water in the bathroom. We were surprised, however, that no local information was supplied, nor was the bedroom tidied while we had dinner. You dine in the Dining Club in the basement – residents are automatically members – and it has a large local membership. There was a lot of interesting choice on the table d'hôte and à la carte menus; service was friendly and extremely good. (Mr and Mrs Leonard's staff are predominantly young and female.) Breakfast next morning (in a pretty breakfast room) was also good, though we wished some real wholewheat toast had been available." *(C R)*

Open All year except 25–30 Dec.
Rooms 10 double, 9 single – all with bath and shower, direct-dial telephone, radio and colour TV.
Facilities Lounge, 2 bars, breakfast room, Dining Club. Poole Quay 100 yds – fishing, boating, sailing.
Location Follow signs for town centre and Quay. Thames St is off Quay, between Fisheries Office and Maritime Museum – signposted to the parish church. Park in Club car park on left before the hotel.
Restrictions Not suitable for &. No children under 8. No dogs in public rooms.
Credit cards All major cards accepted.
Terms (Excluding 10% service charge) B&B: single £40–£44, double £60–£64; dinner, B&B: single £55–£59, double £90–£94; full board: single £65–£68, double £108–£112. Set lunch £9, dinner £15; full alc £23–£25. Weekend rates throughout the year. Reduced rates for children sharing parents' room; special meals provided.

POUGHILL Cornwall   Map 1

Reeds [GFG]   *Tel* Bude (0288) 2841
Poughill, Bude EX23 9EL

A thoroughly civilised, very small guest-house or country home in a tranquil turn-of-the-century building close to the dramatic north Cornish coast. "A pretty, light, airy and immaculately maintained house, elegantly furnished and filled with potted plants, set in a lovely garden a mile from the sea (which you can see from the upper windows) at Bude. *Reeds* has only three double bedrooms and only residents can dine there, so you feel very much that you are on a private visit. The vivacious and friendly owner, Margaret Jackson, is never too busy for a chat with her visitors. Guests are consulted in advance about what they would like for dinner, and fresh local produce is served. There is a short, very reasonably priced wine list, and there are no hidden extras in the tariffs: we were not even charged for our morning coffees and afternoon teas." *(C E; also C K, and Jean Willson).*

Open All year Fri–Tue. Closed Christmas Day.
Rooms 3 double – all with bath and tea-making facilities.
Facilities Drawing room, hall with bar facilities, TV room. 4-acre grounds with landscaped garden and woodlands, sun terrace. Sea 1¼ m away with sandy beaches and cliff walks. Fishing and golf nearby.
Location Take Poughill Road from Bude. Turn left at Post Office signposted to Northcott Mount. *Reeds* is 400 yds on left beyond garden centre.
Restrictions No children under 16. No pets.
Credit cards None accepted.
Terms (No VAT or service charge) B&B £20–£25; dinner, B&B £35–£40.
Service/tipping: "I am totally opposed to the idea of tipping and actively (and I hope, politely) discourage it when the subject is raised."

POWBURN Northumberland   Map 4

Breamish House Hotel [GFG]   *Tel* Powburn (066 578) 266
Powburn, Alnwick NE66 4LL

New to the Guide, this Georgian-style country house hotel at the foot of the Cheviot Hills is recommended to us in the following terms: "A large country house set back from the main A697. Here attention to detail and quiet concern for one's well-being are paramount. Recently opened – the telephone just installed in bedrooms – but everything else is there. Colour TV, tea-making facilities, fresh fruit and flowers, also chocolates. But, most important of all, extremely comfortable beds with quality linen and good lighting in spacious rooms. Enormous trouble is taken over the food, which is perfectly cooked, interesting and varied, and not overlaid with a mish-mash of sauces so often used to hide indifferent meat. Somewhere in the kitchen lurks a Cordon Blue trained cook – but with presentation *almost* to a fault, for one can wait rather too long between the five courses." *(Dilys Pinion)* More reports please.

Open All year except Jan.
Rooms 9 double, 1 single – 8 with bath, 2 with shower, all with telephone, radio, colour TV and tea-making facilities.
Facilities Drawing room, sitting room, dining room. 5-acre garden.
Location Turn W off A1 at Alnwick on A697. Hotel is in centre of Powburn village.
Restrictions Not suitable for &. No children under 12. Dogs only by special arrangement.
Credit cards None accepted.
Terms (No service charge) B&B: single £25–£30, double £40–£45; dinner, B&B: single £37.43, double £64.69. Reduced rates for children over 12 by arrangement. Set lunch £8, dinner £13. Vegetarian meals provided. Mini-breaks Oct–Apr inclusive.

RAVENSTONEDALE Cumbria   Map 4

The Black Swan [GFG]   *Tel* Newbiggin-on-Lune (058 73) 204
Kirkby Stephen
Ravenstonedale CA17 4NG

A small country inn on the banks of Scandal Beck in a secluded and unspoilt village in the foothills of the Eden Valley, though junction 38 of the M6 is only seven minutes by car. Ten minutes to the south lies the Yorkshire Dales National Park; half an hour to the west and you are in the heart of the Lakes. Meanwhile, for those who prefer to stay put, this untouristy area of Cumbria offers superb walking and excellent fishing (the hotel has five miles of private brown trout fishing on the River Eden, lake trout fishing on Pinfold tarn, and tuition if required). *The Black Swan* was bought two years ago by Christopher and Alison Davy, and they have been busy in major refurbishment. Christopher Davy had a big hotel background before translating himself into the more fulfilling role of individual hotelier. His guests speak warmly about the whole set-up: creature comforts, good food, and lots of helpful advice about local walks etc. *(Professor J Mandelstam, Dorothy Kilshaw, Janet Pain)*

157

Open Mar–Dec incl. Restaurant closed Sun evenings (bar suppers served).
Rooms 6 double – 3 with bath.
Facilities Residents' lounge with TV, lounge bar, "Snug" bar, dining room, ballroom (separate from main hotel – dances in winter). Garden on banks of Scandal Beck. Trout and fly fishing; tennis and golf nearby. Excellent rambling country. Shooting parties arranged.
Location About 10 minutes by car from exit 38 of M6. Take A685 from motorway towards Kirkby Stephen and Brough, then follow signs to Ravenstonedale.
Restrictions Not suitable for &. Dogs not allowed in public rooms (except bar).
Credit cards Amex, Visa.
Terms (No service charge) B&B: single £20, double £32; dinner, B&B: single £31.25, double £54.50; full board: single £36.75, double £60 (£2 per person extra for *en suite* bath). Sun lunch £6.50 (packed lunches available), dinner £11.25. Winter breaks; special 3-, 5- and 7- night rates throughout year. Walking holidays; fishing holidays with tuition. Christmas and New Year house parties. Reduced rates and special meals for children.
Service/tipping: "We do not believe in a service charge but customers sometimes insist on making some extra reward for particularly good service. It would be more offensive to refuse than accept in such circumstances."

REETH North Yorkshire   **Map 4**

The Burgoyne Hotel [GFG]   *Tel* Richmond (0748) 84292
Reeth, Richmond DL11 6SN

We had our first entry last year for Chris and Penny Cordingley's unassumingly friendly Georgian-cum-Regency-cum-1920s hotel over-looking the village green, in the heart of the Yorkshire Dales, with views over Swaledale. The Cordingleys' house is domestic and welcoming, rooms are simple, bordering on the basic, but so are the prices. The food is genuine home cooking of the best sort, not the euphemism that those words so often mean. "Far and away the best value for money of our one-night stands on a three-week holiday," writes one gratified customer. Another tells us: "Guests use the hotel as a break in a long drive to or from Scotland, but we went to walk around the hills, which fold the place all around. Lovely views from every window. Lots of space in the pretty rooms. Breakfast is substantial and efficiently served. Dinner is in one sitting and promptness is appreciated. We had nothing which was 'only so-so'; simply gorgeous summer pudding, properly made, very good vegetables, and homely and exotic dishes appeared on the menu so that there was always something surprising to look forward to. My husband had some pepper and garlic soup, which I thought lethal, but he enjoyed it a great deal. Home-made bread rolls a treat. What a friendly couple the Cordingleys are, giving very good value and comfort." (*J M Butterfield, C A O'Callaghan; also M A McDonald, J and J W, M J Selby*)

Open Week before Easter–end Oct.
Rooms 7 double, 3 single – all with tea-making facilities.
Facilities 2 lounges (1 with colour TV), dining room. Very small garden (meals served outdoors in summer). Near river Swale; fishing.
Location In village, 10 m W of Richmond. Parking.
Restrictions Not suitable for &. No dogs in dining room.
Credit cards None accepted.
Terms [1985 rates] (gratuities at guests' discretion) B&B £12.50 (weekly £80); dinner, B&B £20.50 (weekly £130). Set Sun lunch £5.25, set dinner £8.30. Weekend and mid-week breaks.

RICHMOND North Yorkshire   Map 4

Howe Villa   *Tel* Richmond (0748) 2559
Whitcliffe Mill, Richmond DL1O 4TJ

Howe Villa was built in 1800 by the owner of a paper mill. It has during the past 15 years been lovingly restored by its present owners, Tom and Anita Berry. The approach to the house could make you think you have taken the wrong turning as you drive through the old mill buildings, now a small dry-cleaning works run by Mr Berry. However, keep going, turn the corner and you are in another world. From the house all you are aware of is a large beautiful garden surrounded by trees with the river Swale rushing by – the same river which powered the mill in the 16th century.

"*Howe Villa* is Georgian with large, elegantly proportioned rooms. The bedrooms are on the ground floor, all with bath or shower. Each has been individually furnished with great attention to detail; a basket of fruit and chocolates and an arrangement of fresh flowers welcome each guest. The drawing room and dining room are on the first floor with beautiful views over the river on to the National Trust land beyond. The drawing room, with a log fire, is comfortably furnished. The ornate plasterwork on the ceiling is shown to its full advantage by the beautiful antique crystal chandelier. Anita Berry tries to make the meals enjoyed by her guests an experience they wish to repeat. Each winter she does a Cordon Bleu course to increase her repertoire. The menu changes all the time with the emphasis on fresh local produce."

The above appreciation of *Howe Villa* is not our own, but penned by the lady of the house, Anita Berry. We take such offerings with the proverbial pinch of salt, but in the present instance they are fully endorsed by a regular and trusted contributor to the Guide, *Eileen Broadbent*, who confesses that the place has long been a special secret which she feels she must now share. "The approach is *horrible!* Hard to find as you drive down to a caravan site, then across a laundry, before you find Anita and Tom Berry in their beautifully maintained house. Believe me, it's well worth the shock approach to 'press on' regardless. The reward awaits you. Anita Berry is a natural cook of a very high order. I recommend this small hotel or guest-house – can't say which – most warmly."

Open Mar–Nov.
Rooms 4 double – 2 with bath, 2 with shower, all with radio and colour TV.
Facilities Large drawing room, dining room. ½-acre garden on river Swale.
Location ½ m from centre of Richmond – take A6108 signposted Leyburn and Reeth; at the ATS Tyre service station turn left, keep left following signs to Richmond Cleaners and Howe Villa.
Restrictions Not suitable for &. No children under 5. No dogs.
Credit cards None accepted.
Terms Dinner, B&B £20–£23. Reduced rates and special meals for children.
Service/tipping: "I strongly object to service charges."

Do you know of a good hotel or country inn in the United States or Canada? Nominations please to our sibling publication, *America's Wonderful Little Hotels and Inns*, c/o St Martin's Press, 175 Fifth Avenue, New York, NY10010, USA.

ROMALDKIRK Durham   Map 4

Rose and Crown Hotel   *Tel* Teesdale (0833) 50213 or 50603
Romaldkirk, Nr Barnard Castle
DL12 9EB

"Here is that mythical find, a genuine old country inn, full of fishermen
and Dales folk, swapping tall stories, the finest honest plain cooking
outside a private house, excellent beer and comfortable but not
luxurious rooms" *(M W)*. Thus our first entry for the *Rose and Crown* four
years ago. This cheerful inn on the village green of a picturesque Dales
village, near High Force Waterfall and the rewarding Bowes Museum at
Barnard Castle, has become rather more sophisticated in the interim – all
rooms now have colour TV, for instance, and other similar modern
conveniences; there is a new lunchtime bar, and a smart restaurant. But
the place still retains its atmosphere, and is as popular with locals as
with visitors. "I warmly endorse the entry – as good a small hotel as one
could find anywhere. Our room in the modern annexe was very
comfortable and excellently equipped. The food was consistently good;
breakfast delivered to our room always on time. The staff were young,
competent and very friendly. Charges very reasonable. And Romaldkirk
is an excellent centre for expeditions in all directions." *(Sir Patrick Reilly;
also Rosamund Malpas)*

Open All year.
Rooms 1 suite with four-poster, 11 double, 2 single – 9 with bath, 3 with shower,
all with telephone, radio, colour TV and baby-listening; 6 ground-floor rooms
round courtyard with tea-making facilities. 1 of them specially designed for &.
Facilities Ramps. Lounge, 2 bars, writing room, 2 dining rooms. Fishing, golf,
squash, sailing, pony-trekking, shooting, etc. nearby. Barnard Castle 6 m; Raby
Castle and Bowes Castle within easy reach. &.
Location 6 m NW of Barnard Castle on B6277.
Restriction No dogs in public rooms.
Credit cards All major cards accepted.
Terms [1985 rates] (No service charge) B&B: single £22.50–£24, double £33–£42.
Set dinner £10

RYDAL Cumbria   Map 4

Glen Rothay Hotel   *Tel* Ambleside (0966) 32524
Rydal, Ambleside LA22 9LR

Sandra Garside is the *patronne* at this part-17th-century hotel close to
Rydal Water and in the heart of Wordsworth country, a welcoming
establishment, with the hostess and her staff making extra efforts to give
their guests a good time. It's the sort of place where you are shown
round when you arrive, your bags are carried up to your room, and your
bed is turned down at night. Guests are free to use the hotel bicycles, or
to take the hotel's boats and canoe on Rydal Water, and of course
magnificent fell-side walking is close by. "No special claim to distinction
in cooking or decor," we wrote last year. One guest felt this had been
unfair: meal-times had been a most pleasant experience, as had the
whole holiday at *Glen Rothay*. *(Dorothy Matthew)* Further reports
welcome.

Open All year except 7–18 Dec, 5–25 Jan.
Rooms 1 suite with 4-poster bed and balcony, 9 double, 1 single – 4 with bath, 7 with shower, all with tea-making facilities.
Facilities 2 lounges (1 with colour TV), public bar, dining room; 2½-acre grounds, Rydal Water across road with hotel boats, canoe, windsurfer, fishing rights, bathing.
Location On A591, 1½ m N of Ambleside. (Front rooms may have noise from traffic, but it is light at night.)
Restrictions Not suitable for &. Very young children discouraged from dinner (early tea on request). No dogs in dining room.
Credit cards Access, Diners, Visa.
Terms (No service charge) B&B £20–£25; dinner, B&B £24–£33.50. Set dinner £11.50; lunches available. Winter and spring bargain breaks, weekly rates, Christmas and New Year packages. Reduced rates for children sharing parents' room.

RYE East Sussex   Map 2

🏵 The Old Vicarage Guest House   *Tel* Rye (0797) 222119
66 Church Square, Rye TN31 7HF

César awarded for most civilised bed-and-breakfast

Ruth and Ernest Thompson are exemplary hosts at their thoroughly comfortable mostly Georgian bed-and-breakfast guest-house in a quiet secluded position looking out across Church Square and the churchyard of ancient St Mary's. Among many heart-warming tributes, we choose the following from an American couple: "We visited the Thompsons for the first time two years ago and were thoroughly taken with this charming, comfortable, well-run guest-house. Since then, despite numerous visits to many delightful spots around the UK and the Continent, we have felt drawn back to Rye and *The Old Vicarage*. We've been back five times and have found not the slightest relaxation of the Thompsons' high standards. We've stayed in most of the rooms and found them all clean, comfortable and very nicely appointed. Their location is ideal. *The Old Vicarage* is atmospherically the perfect compliment to old Rye. We'd also add our high marks for the afternoon tea which the Thompsons offer – in the garden during fair weather. All of the extra touches which the Thompsons have put into their business, and their warm personal hospitality have contributed to a truly enjoyable stay on our every visit. When we return home to the US next month, we will take back memories of Rye as one of our favourite spots in the UK and of *The Old Vicarage* as the nicest B&B we've seen anywhere – in fact, the nicest place we've stayed in for less than £60 a night." *(Anthony and Kate Pinson; also J R Lloyd, Jean Farris, D J Carver, Mr & Mrs Richard Haier, M Ward, Mr and Mrs T Graty, Vicky and Ted Coxon) Note:* Not to be confused with The Old Vicarage, East Street, Rye.

Open All year except Christmas.
Rooms 1 family, 4 double – all with h & c, 2 with shower, 2 with colour TV, 3 with mono. 1 with 4-poster.
Facilities Sitting room, dining room. Small walled garden. Safe bathing/sandy beach 2 m; golf course nearby.
Location In town centre (but quietly situated), near St Mary's Church. Parking nearby.
Restrictions Not suitable for &. No children under 12. No dogs.
Credit cards All major cards accepted.

Terms B&B £16–£26. Meals not served but arrangements made with local restaurants. Off-season breaks.
Tipping: "We do not encourage tipping at all."

ST AUSTELL Cornwall   Map 1

Boscundle Manor [GFG]   *Tel* Par (072 681) 3557
Tregrehan, St Austell PL25 3RL

"The two red crossed knives and forks from *Michelin* are very well deserved. The dining room is gracious, elegant, and the food presented with considerable style and great personal flair by Andrew Flint himself if for some reason the waitress is not about. What has not really been revealed is the enormous charm and informality of the Flints. They are so very happy to be doing what they do: they abandoned the big city life to take on this rambling old manor house, parts of it with three foot walls and beams, parts looking more Georgian. The house is furnished with a great variety of assorted objects, some very good antiques, some comfortable fat velvet chairs, but is in no way *arranged* or setting out to impress. The bedrooms are the same. Comfortable, big televisions, good bathrooms, but very informal and mildly eccentric. They both love the garden, and have brought it back from a wilderness by their own labours and filled it with flowers. Again, do not expect manicured lawns, but a *real* garden to stroll through or sit in or play croquet in, or, weather permitting, swim in. Andrew met me in his gardening clothes, trowel in hand. I so enjoyed sitting and chatting to Mary that we both forgot the time and I nearly sabotaged the whole of the dinner. Which, however, was totally under control half-an-hour later at the expected time, and both memorable and delicious. Scattered throughout the house are the delightful Lowry-esque paintings of their friend, Fred Yates, which can be purchased. Don't expect glossy plastic service. Andrew and Mary Flint are delightful, warm, friendly, intelligent, interesting *real* people." (W A)

That vignette of life *chez Boscundle* was taken from last year's Guide, but warmly endorsed by subsequent visitors. The *Manor* dates back to medieval times, with Georgian additions, and bits added on later still. The Flints have been active in their own extensions: the conservatory, mentioned last year, is now functioning as a breakfast room or as an extra lounge, and new developments include a small exercise room with bicycle, rowing machine and simple gym equipment, and two more *en suite* bathrooms, one with a spa and one with a whirlpool bath. They have also acquired an adjoining property, *Wheal Eliza*, with accommodation specially suitable for disabled people and families with children. Although *Michelin* continues to classify the *Manor* as a restaurant-with-rooms, it puts most pukka hotels to shame by the indefatigable attention shown to the comfort of its residents.

Open 4 Feb–23 Dec. Restaurant closed on Sun to non-residents.
Rooms 7 double, 2 single – 4 with bath (1 with a spa, 1 with a whirlpool bath), 5 with shower, all with telephone, radio and colour TV.
Facilities Sitting room, cocktail bar, lounge/breakfast room, 2 dining rooms, exercise room. 2-acre gardens plus 7 acres of woodland including an old tin mine, croquet lawn and heated swimming pool. Beaches 1 m and 6 m; golf, riding, fishing nearby; coastal walks. &.
Location 2 m E of St Austell, 100 yds off A390 on road signposted "Tregrehan".

Restrictions Not suitable for ♿. No dogs in public rooms.
Credit cards Access, Amex, Visa.
Terms B&B: single £33–£40, double £50–£60. Set dinner £15. Special meals for children by arrangement. Weekly half-board rates.
Service/tipping: "We actively discourage anyone leaving extra money."

ST IVES Cambridgeshire   Map 2

Slepe Hall Hotel   *Tel* St Ives (0480) 62824
Ramsey Road, St Ives   *Telex* 32339 ref SSH (RODDIS G)
Huntingdon PE17 4RB

The area north of Cambridge is singularly empty on our map, and we wish that we could recommend unreservedly this Victorian mansion, once a girls' school, on the outskirts of a placid Fenland market-town beside the Ouse. "First class in every respect," writes one satisfied customer. "Cooking outstandingly good, also an extremely well-run snack bar. Smiling and pleasing service by charming local girls." Another tells us of the kindness of the hotel to his family of four. A third praised the hotel's efficiency in passing on messages and its tolerance of a late arrival. A fourth, who has stayed at Slepe Hall *seven times in the past two years, dubs it simply as "the most civilised small hotel I have stayed in in this country". Sadly, there have been reports too of dreary rooms and disappointing experiences in both the restaurant and the snack bar. No consensus. Hence the italics.*

Open All year except 25 and 26 Dec.
Rooms 12 double, 2 single – 10 with bath, all with telephone, radio, colour TV and baby-listening.
Facilities Bar/lounge, lounge, restaurant. Small garden (barbecue meals June/July/Aug), river Ouse 300 yds from hotel, riverside walks.
Location 15 minutes from centre of St Ives: follow signs to town centre (W) and St Ivo recreation centre: hotel is nearby.
Restrictions Not suitable for ♿. No dogs allowed in public rooms.
Credit cards All major cards accepted.
Terms (No service charge) B&B: single £26–£38, double £37–£48; dinner, B&B: single £35–£48, double £57–£68. Set lunch £9.50, set dinner £10.50; full alc £15.50. Bargain breaks all year. Reduced rates for children; special meals on request.
Service/tipping: "We do not make any service charge. This is left entirely to the discretion of the customer."

ST MARY'S Isles of Scilly   Map 1

Star Castle Hotel   *Tel* Scillonia (0720) 22317
St Mary's
Isles of Scilly, Cornwall TR21 0JA

A former fortress, built in 1593 in the reign of Queen Elizabeth for the defence of the Isles of Scilly, the *Star Castle* enjoys a spectacular position overlooking the town and harbour. It is a modest, reasonably priced and welcoming hotel. The most characterful bedrooms are in the castle and there is a "honeymoon bedroom" (without private bath) in a former guardroom on the ramparts. On the lawn behind the castle are sixteen larger but rather ordinary bedrooms (some of them suitable for families) and a heated covered swimming pool. Behind are further lawns enclosed in hedges, and a tennis court. Snack lunches are served in the Dungeon Bar or on the ramparts; dinner (good straightforward cooking and an extensive wine list) is in the former officers' mess. Breakfast is of the tinned grapefruit segments and packaged jams variety, but with perseverance you can get them to toast some of their excellent home-made brown bread. Do not miss the walk around the battery surrounding the castle at sunset. *(A & C R, L H)*

Open Mar–Oct.
Rooms 5 suites, 21 double, 3 single – 21 with bath, all with tea-making facilities and baby-listening; TV available on request; 16 rooms in annexe.
Facilities Reading lounge, TV lounge, games room, Dungeon Bar, restaurant. 4½-acre grounds with tennis court and covered heated swimming pool. Sandy beaches, safe bathing and fishing nearby.
Location Central, overlooking town and harbour, but in large grounds so not noisy. Parking. Regular boats and helicopter flights from Penzance.
Restrictions Not suitable for &. Dogs not allowed in public rooms.
Credit cards None accepted.
Terms (No service charge) B&B £19–£21; dinner, B&B, £23–£30. Set dinner £9.50. Vegetarian meals on request. Reduced rates and special meals for children.

ST MAWES Cornwall **Map 1**

The Rising Sun *Tel* St Mawes (0326) 270233
St Mawes TR2 5DT

A reasonably priced Cornish hotel which has the disadvantage of having no grounds apart from a small terrace in the front, separated from the sea by a road. But it is warmly recommended by a regular: "Some twenty years ago I used to stay regularly at *The Rising Sun*, and it was certainly the best inn I have ever stayed at. I returned last week and little has changed. They now call themselves a hotel but they're not really. They still have the rare ability to attract a genuine local trade in the 'front' bar, a place where visitors really are welcome, whilst at the same time providing more sophisticated facilities for those who want them. It remains a family-run establishment and I'm glad to say one doesn't feel like a country-house guest when staying there. I'm not a difficult person but I like to feel cosseted when I'm paying. I cannot expect that at friends' houses. *The Rising Sun* knows about service right down to the card index that tells them, from your first visit, of the morning papers you favour so that no ordering is required. Nowadays two chefs provide extremely good food served by attentive girls under the watchful eye of a head waiter who has been there over twenty years." *(Robert Cowan)*

Open All year except Dec.
Rooms 10 double, 6 single – 9 with bath, 2 with shower, all with tea-making facilities; 3 rooms in annexe.
Facilities Cocktail bar, public bar, lounge with TV, dining room; terrace in the front of hotel where drinks and snacks are served; near the sea – safe bathing, sailing, windsurfing.
Location In centre of village; car park.
Restriction Not suitable for &.
Credit cards All major cards accepted.
Terms (No service charge) B&B: single £17.50–£20, double £40–£53; dinner, B&B: single £26.50–£29, double £58–£71. Set dinner £9.50. Special meals for children, to order.

We are particularly keen to have reports on italicised entries.

SALCOMBE Devon   Map 1

Castle Point Hotel   *Tel* Salcombe (054 884) 2167 or
Sandhills Road, Salcombe TQ8 87J   2456

*"During our holiday in the South-West, we found a number of pleasant hotels,
but this was one we particularly felt ought to be in your Guide, for position,
all-round enjoyment and value"* (David and Barbara Nuttall). Castle Point,
an Edwardian residence with modest extensions, has a choice situation close to
Salcombe's ancient castle, with superb views over the estuary and sea. Bedrooms
vary in size and facilities, and some are a bit cramped. There is nothing chi-chi
about Castle Point, but the Nuttalls warmly commend the friendly service and
the food. On the latter subject, the resident owners, Mr and Mrs Statters, tell us
that their four-course table d'hôte dinner menu (only bar snacks at lunch-time)
with four choices at each course, changing daily according to season and the best
fresh food available, "is far better value than an à la carte menu which comes
straight from the deep freeze". More reports welcome.

Open Easter to mid-Oct.
Rooms 16 double, 4 single – 7 with bath, 4 with shower, all with radio, most with
colour TV.
Facilities Lounge, TV room, bar, dining room, 2-acre grounds adjoining castle.
Sandy beach 3 minutes' walk from hotel, fishing in estuary; two sailing clubs
providing instruction and hire facilities nearby.
Location 10 minutes' walk from the centre of Salcombe – take Main Road to Castle
Point. Hotel is on right (indicated by sign). Parking.
Restrictions Not suitable for &. No children under 6. No dogs.
Credit cards Access, Diners, Visa.
Terms (Service at guests' discretion) rooms £9–£20 B&B £12–£21; dinner, B&B
£16–£28. Bar snack lunches. Set dinner £8.95. Vegetarian meals on request. 3-day
and 5-day rates except bank holidays; off-season rates. Reduced rates for children
sharing parents' room.
*Service/tipping: "There is no service charge. The matter of gratuities is left to guests'
discretion."*

Tides Reach Hotel   *Tel* Salcombe (054 884) 3466
South Sands, Salcombe TQ8 8LJ

"It would be hard to find fault with this excellent hotel. If one is looking
for peace, quiet and comfort in beautiful surroundings with a first-rate
standard of service, *Tides Reach* is where you will find it. The atmosphere
is warm, friendly and personal. The food is outstandingly good, and one
gets splendid value for one's money. The owner, Mr Edwards, has
worked out what people need for a good rest away from home and has
got it just right." *(Rosemary Spens; also Conrad Dehn, D C Berry, Susan
Park)*

A generous tribute, but by no means an isolated one, for this
admirable family hotel – would that there were more like it! – with many
of the facilities (see below) one would expect to find only in much larger
establishments. It's singularly blessed in its position. South Sands is a
mile to the south of Salcombe itself, away from the crowded summer
scene, facing east across the estuary, and surrounded by spectacular
National Trust land. Only grumble in this year's mail: car-parking
facilities are barely adequate on a busy holiday weekend.

Open 1 Mar–mid-Nov.
Rooms 2 suites, 34 double, 4 single – 36 with bath, 4 with shower, all with telephone, radio and colour TV – some with sea view and balcony.
Facilities Lift and ramps (but disabled guests may find access to some facilities and movement outside hotel difficult). Lounge, sun lounge, reading lounge, restaurant, cocktail bar with aquarium, pool bar, health and beauty salon, sauna, jacuzzi, hairdressing salon, games room, squash court with spectator lounge. Heated swimming pool with sliding glass doors. Grounds with garden, pond, tea lawn. 10 yds from beach with safe bathing, windsurfing school, sea fishing, sailing and moorings for boats. &
Location 1 mile S of Salcombe; follow signs to Bolt Head and South Sands.
Restrictions No children under 8. No dogs in public rooms.
Credit cards All major cards accepted.
Terms (No fixed service charge) B&B £32.30–£41.50, dinner, B&B £38–£49. Set dinner £13.50; full alc £18.25. Spring into summer bargain breaks; autumn breaks; 50% reduction for children sharing parents' room.

SCOTSDYKE Cumbria   Map 4

The March Bank Country House   *Tel* Longtown (0228) 791325
Hotel [GFG]
Scotsdyke, via Longtown
Carlisle CA6 5XP

"Unpretentiously friendly" and "super food" are repeated refrains in reports on this small family-run hotel, set well back from the scenic A7, three miles north of Longtown overlooking the Esk river. Mr Grant, the owner, writes to us: "We are not a luxury establishment, but offer peace, quiet and outstanding food. My wifes makes everything in the food line from the soups down to the home-made ice cream. The breakfast marmalades and jams are all made here. We use only the best and dearest ingredients to justify the 'Real Food' award in *The Good Food Guide*." One correspondent mentions the Grants' solicitude when a booking had to be cancelled at the last moment because of illness, and trouble taken beyond the call of duty when their car broke down: "We have never before met such generous hospitality as we did at *March Bank*." *(Mrs M A Leyland and others)*

Open 5 Mar–26 Jan (closed Christmas).
Rooms 1 suite, 5 double, 1 single – 3 with shower, 1 ground-floor room.
Facilities Sitting room with TV, bar/dining room; 3-acre gardens, overlooking river Esk. Salmon and trout fishing, and golf nearby.
Location On the A7, 3 m N of Longtown.
Restriction No dogs in public rooms.
Credit cards None accepted.
Terms B&B: single £20–£27; double £36–£38; dinner, B&B £58–£60 for 2. Set lunch £6.50, set dinner £12; alc lunch £8. Reduced rates and special meals for children.
Service/tipping: "We add 10% to all bills in lieu of gratuities and make this clear on menus and notices – although people often insist on leaving something for the staff."

SEAVIEW Isle of Wight   Map 1

Seaview Hotel   *Tel* Seaview (098 371) 2711
High Street, Seaview PO34 5EX

A promising addition to the all-too-small class of reasonably priced seaside family hotels that offer good food and wine. *Seaview Hotel* is a three-storey bay-windowed Edwardian house at the foot of the High Street in this picturesque unspoilt small sailing village. Front rooms have a fine view of the sea and coast. It was bought five years ago by Nicholas Hayward, formerly Deputy General Manager of the Atheneum Hotel, London, and his wife Nicola, who herself comes from a hotel background and who has worked for city wine merchants. "It is not a grand and impressive building," writes Mrs Hayward, "and will only ever have two stars. But we would like to think the rooms are exceptional for a hotel of this standard. We have a wonderful supply of delicious local fish, especially lobsters, crabs and prawns. The AA awarded us a rosette for the food last year (the only one on the island). I do all the cooking myself and can only say that very few women win the AA rosette. Our wine list caters for the more discerning palate as one would expect from an ex-wine merchant." Two nominators, including a former Chairman of *Grosvenor House*, as well as our inspector, speak warmly of the Haywards' enterprise. *(Sir Charles Taylor, D M Farquhar)*

Open All year.
Rooms 1 suite, 14 double – 11 with bath, all with radio and baby-listening.
Facilities Lounge, bar/lounge, public bar, restaurant, private dining/conference room. Sea and sandy beaches nearby.
Location In centre of village and shops near sea. Follow signs for sea front.
Restrictions Not suitable for &. No dogs in public rooms.
Credit cards Access, Amex, Visa.
Terms (No service charge) B&B: single £15–£22, double £27–£40. Set lunch £5.95, dinner £7.95; full alc £12.50. Breakaway, weekend and weekly tariffs all year. Reduced rates and special meals for children.

SHEPTON MALLET Somerset   Map 2

Bowlish House Restaurant [GFG]   *Tel* Shepton Mallet (0749) 2022
Wells Road, Shepton Mallet BA4 5JD

A spectacular Palladian Georgian country house, in a National Conservancy Area, scheduled Grade II, with a considerable reputation as a restaurant and a remarkable wine list. The Jordans make a point of stressing that they are no more than a restaurant with rooms (just four), but correspondents speak warmly of the accommodation as well as the fare. One called his room "stylish". Another, in contrast, described his bedroom as "something out of a country farmhouse in 1890; plain honest, bare wood, very warm, and breakfast on a Sunday morning until a shameless 10 am." *(R Hughes, Fred Inglis)*

Open All year except Christmas.
Rooms 4 double – all with bath, radio, colour TV.
Facilities Sitting room, bar, conservatory, restaurant. Walled garden, croquet.
Location On main A371 Shepton Mallet to Wells road, ½ m from Shepton Mallet centre.
Restrictions Not suitable for &. No dogs in public rooms.
Credit cards None accepted.
Terms B&B: £29; dinner, B&B £41. Set dinner £12.
Service/tipping: "We discourage it. We did have a policy of refusing tips, but then suffered the embarrassment of having people send us cheques by post after returning home."

Please make a habit of sending a report if you stay at a Guide hotel.

SHIPTON GORGE Dorset   Map 1

Innsacre Farmhouse Hotel   *Tel* Bridport (0308) 56137
Shipton Gorge, Bridport DT6 4LJ

Hotel is too grand a name; inn would be more appropriate for this small stone farmhouse and barn – the former incorporating an excellent but unpretentious and very reasonable restaurant catering for 40 and the latter five modest bedrooms. "You approach it down one of those winding, steep Dorset lanes. Once a working farm, it still has a few chickens, plenty of ducks and some pigs roaming around. The feel is one of genuine relaxation – no locks on the door, so people can and do drop into the wrong room by mistake. There is a residents' lounge with TV and jigsaws. A good family bolt-hole, well placed for the sea two miles away, run by the Smith family, parents and daughters, with both professionalism and a congenial openness." *(D S; also Michael Horniman, J R C Hamilton)*

Open All year.
Rooms 3 double, 2 single – 1 with bath, all with tea-making facilities.
Facilities Lounge with TV, bar, restaurant, games room, 10-acre grounds with farm animals; 2 m from sea with shingle beach and good bathing.
Location 2 m E of Bridport, off A35.
Restrictions Not suitable for &. No dogs in public rooms.
Credit cards All major cards accepted.
Terms B&B £14–£16; dinner, B&B £25.25–£27.25; full board £32.50–£34.50. Set lunch £7.25, dinner £11.25. Reduced rates and special meals for children.

SLAIDBURN Lancashire   Map 4

Parrock Head Farm [GFG]   *Tel* Slaidburn (020 06) 614
Slaidburn, Nr Clitheroe BB7 3AH

Witnesses continue to testify to the attractions and excellent value of this small country house hotel that is also a working farm, functioning well in all departments, in a remote and beautiful location. One recent visitor writes: "It excels in every particular. Mrs Holt is a gifted and inspired cook of great artistry and professionalism. One of our happiest experiences of recent years, here or abroad." Last year's nominator has been back since, as warm in praise as ever. Of his *Parrock Head* breakfast, he writes: "The best-cooked breakfast I have had anywhere, even better than at *Sharrow Bay* (q.v.) which held my record previously. How about a Great British Breakfast César Award?" We repeat his nomination: "*Parrock Head Farm* is a 17th-century building with most of the amenities you find in a good hotel, but with really friendly, personal but not intrusive service. It is run by Richard Holt, formerly a barrister, and his wife Pat, who is the chef. It is in a very lovely spot on the edge of Lancashire and Yorkshire, dales on one side, majestic moorland on the other. The house is warm and comfortable even in the depths of winter, with a log fire in the spacious upstairs sitting room (which has a magnificent view over the moors) and good central heating everywhere. Upstairs also on a gallery is a library with plenty of books and magazines, maps and loads of tourist information. Downstairs there is a small but efficient bar (moderate prices) and the roomy dining room.

The Holts provide magnificent value for money – £17 for B&B [1985]; breakfast alone is worth more than half of this. Dinners (à la carte) are often really excellent, but just slightly more variable than the totally excellent breakfasts. Fairly small but representative wine list with *very low* mark-up. Sorry if this is a bit of a gush, but it's written with real enthusiasm since I've had such fantastic value here." *(Dr H B Cardwell; also M F and C J E Hunter, Mr and Mrs James Bourn)*

Open 1 Feb–30 Nov.
Rooms 1 family suite, 8 double – all with bath, colour TV and tea-making facilities, 5 rooms in annexe, some ground-floor rooms.
Facilities Lounge, cocktail bar, library, dining room; large garden. On working farm in remote area surrounded by fields and parklands. Excellent bird-watching.
Location 10 m N of Clitheroe. Take B6478 from Clitheroe to Slaidburn; hotel is 1 m NW of village on un-signposted road.
Restriction No dogs in public rooms.
Credit card Amex.
Terms B&B £18–£19. Full alc £11. Bar and packed lunches available. Reduced rates and special meals for children.
Service/tipping: "We include a 10% service charge in the quoted prices. Unless a customer is insistent we refuse anything extra offered as a tip."

SOUTHMOOR see KINGSTON BAGPUIZE

SOUTH ZEAL Devon
Map 1

The Oxenham Arms *Tel* (0837) 840244
South Zeal, Okehampton EX20 2JT

A genuinely old inn on the edge of Dartmoor which is recommended to the Guide in the following beguiling terms: "The inn is thought to have been a monastery *c*. 12th century and has been a hostelry since the 15th century. There is therefore a long record of welcoming and unobtrusive service which is still carried on by the present incumbents. You are so much at home that you feel you can come in with wet muddy boots and a wet muddy dog without causing comment! Despite the age of the building it has been discreetly modernised without spoiling any of the charm. Most of the bedrooms have private bathrooms with constant piping hot water (very comforting when you come in tired and aching from a long walk over the moor). Colour televisions have been installed in the bedrooms if you wish to indulge in such things. I'm happy to say, however, that there is no television in the residents' lounge where you can settle down after an excellent dinner to drink your coffee in front of an enormous log fire. On a summer's evening you can sit out in the beautiful walled garden with a mug of local cider or other refreshments and look out to the moor, smelling the scent of rose and honeysuckle, relaxed and at peace. The food is homecooked, fresh and delicious with delicacies such as local salmon and strawberries in summer and served in a dining room of great charm and character. *The Oxenham's* atmosphere is quite unique." *(Fleur Broadbent; also Mr and Mrs N P Jupp)*

Open All year (restaurant closed to non-residents Christmas Eve).
Rooms 10 double – 8 with bath, all with colour TV and tea-making facilities; 2 rooms in annexe.

Facilities Lounge-bar, residents' lounge, dining room, 2nd dining room/family room with TV. ½-acre garden. 1 hour's drive to S Devon and W Cornwall beaches. River and reservoir trout fishing in immediate vicinity – day permits available.
Location Centre of village. South Zeal lies just off main Exeter/Okehampton road (A30), 18 m W of Exeter.
Restrictions Not suitable for &. Dogs allowed in public rooms only with specific permission.
Credit cards All major cards accepted.
Terms B&B: single £28, double £40; full board: single £43, double £70. Set lunch £6.50, dinner £10. Special winter rates (1 Nov–31 Mar) for 2 nights or more. Christmas tariff – add 15% to above rates. Reduced rates for children sharing parents' room; special meals.
Tipping: "We neither encourage nor discourage tipping."

SPARK BRIDGE Cumbria   Map 4

Bridgefield House [GFG]   *Tel* Lowick Bridge (022 985) 239
Spark Bridge
Nr Ulverston LA12 8DA

An attractive newcomer to our Lakelands register, even if Spark Bridge, on the banks of the river Crake, is a car's drive to the fells and the Lakes themselves: but the scenery round *Bridgefield House* is beautiful if less dramatic than further north, and has the advantage of being well away from the tourist hordes. The Glisters, David and Rosemary, bought this gentleman's residence of the late 19th century six years ago, and have been busy with improvements in the interim. The five bedrooms are agreeably furnished. The standard of cooking – the house has a growing reputation as a restaurant in the neighbourhood – is high and ambitious. Children are made particularly welcome. All our reporters speak with enthusiasm of the Glisters' enterprise and commitment and the relaxed friendly atmosphere they engender. Only one serious criticism recurs in several reports: the house does have central heating, but it isn't adequate in cool weather. *(Ann Leeming, M R West, and others)*

Open All year, but only for lunch on Christmas Day.
Rooms 1 suite, 4 double – 3 with bath, all with radio.
Facilities Drawing room, dining room and adjoining bar. 3-acre garden. Sea bathing 3 m; salmon and trout fishing and good fell walking nearby.
Location Off A5092. On back road (signposted) from Spark Bridge to Lowick Bridge.
Restrictions Not suitable for &. No dogs in public rooms.
Credit cards Access, Amex, Diners.
Terms (No service charge) B&B from £15; dinner, B&B from £28.50. Packed lunches available on request; set dinner £13.50. Children aged 3 and under free, 50% reduction for under 12s; special meals; free laundry service for children and babies.
Tipping/service: "The inclusion of a service charge is iniquitous and should be banned by law – whatever the fatuous excuses forwarded by the hotel industry as a whole for its retention. Let's face it, it is only an extra increase in the tariff."

> Hotels often book you into their most expensive rooms or suites unless you specify otherwise. Even if all room prices are the same, hotels may give you a less good room in the hope of selling their better rooms to later customers. It always pays to discuss accommodation in detail when making a reservation.

SPARSHOLT Hampshire   Map 2

Lainston House Hotel   *Tel* Winchester (0962) 63588
Sparsholt, Nr Winchester SO21 2LT   *Telex* 477375

After a bumpy start, this beautiful early 17th-century mansion, set in its
63 acres of parkland, and approached by a mile-long avenue of limes,
appears to be settling down and becoming one of the more dependable
country house hotels in the luxury bracket. Sparsholt is 2½ miles west of
Winchester, and the success of *Lainston House* is the more welcome
because of the absence of any comparable good hotel in the area. Last
year's entry was in italics, since the hotel had only recently changed
hands after the previous owners, who had spent a fortune on
renovation, had gone bankrupt. Also, we had had reports of poor
service in the reception and restaurant – slow and dour. The general
manager, Richard Fannon – "an enthusiastic and warmly welcoming
professional hotelier", to quote one correspondent – tells us that the
dourness problem has been solved. Not altogether, we fear, to judge
from recent reports. But no complaints about the restaurant itself: the
excellence of the cooking has been commended, with a splendid buffet
lunch getting a special mention. Since last year, new suites and luxury
rooms have been added to one of the wings. Rooms come in three
categories here: suites, luxury and standard. One reader felt disappointed with his standard room in the other older wing, and we also
heard from a guest who had thoroughly enjoyed her stay but had found
her pleasure in a luxury room diminished by poor insulation. Here, in
contrast, is a report from someone who was enchanted with her
standard room in the attic: "I had a bedroom under the eaves, with a
beam from the ceiling across the room to the floor, a marble fireplace and
a dark blue and cream bathroom. The furniture was very clever repro. (I
was almost fooled at first sight); the wallpaper was charming, probably
an exact Morris copy. The blankets were fluffy, pillows soft but firm.
Lovely china and napkins, with a breakfast tray that I coveted
enormously – old wickerwork and like having a basket of breakfast.
Everything delighted the eye." (*Gillian Vincent; also Iain C Baillie, D J C
Bernard, Mary McCleary Posner, M A R*)

Open All year.
Rooms 3 suite, 22 double, 7 single – 31 with bath, 1 with shower, all with
telephone, radio and colour TV. 18 rooms in wings, 7 ground-floor rooms.
Facilities Drawing room, cocktail bar, restaurant. 63-acre grounds with croquet
lawn, and tennis; trout fishing, golf, riding nearby. &.
Location On A272, 2½ m W of Winchester. Hotel is clearly signposted.
Restriction No dogs in public rooms.
Credit cards All major cards accepted.
Terms Rooms: single £45–£50, double £65–£85. Breakfast: continental £4, English
£6. Set lunch £5–£13, dinner £15.50–£22.50; full alc £20. Winter breaks, Christmas
and Easter breaks; special Delegate weekends (can accommodate up to 140
people). Reduced rates for children sharing parents' room; special meals on
request.

> Most hotels have reduced rates out of season and for children,
> and some British hotels offer 'mini-break' rates throughout the
> year. If you are staying more than one night, it is always worth
> asking about special terms.

STAMFORD Lincolnshire — Map 2

The George of Stamford [GFG]
High Street, St Martins
Stamford PE9 2LB

Tel Stamford (0780) 55171
Telex 32578

César awarded for finest old coaching-inn

Stamford is a remarkably unspoilt medieval town, and *The George* is the old coaching-inn, and as fine an example of its kind as you may come across, preserving plenty of innish features such as a flower-tubbed cobbled courtyard, but neither prettified nor self-conscious. We have had partly critical entries for the past few years, but it is clear from this year's reports that an energetic management is busy in a programme of refurbishing the rooms, that the cooking has improved (especially recommended are the joints and the cold buffet), that the substantial breakfasts are as good as ever; "the very well-trained young staff, interested, helpful, thoughtful and friendly" come in for special commendation – "their desire to please comes from an earlier century". Front rooms are still inclined to be noisy despite double-glazing. As for the back rooms, as reported last year: "The generous foliage on the walls of the lovely inner courtyard provides a habitat for lots of bird who wake very early and very noisily." But as readers have been quick to point out, it is perverse to be complaining about the noise of birds in a town hotel, and "their awakening song is appreciated by a majority of guests and seriously disliked only by the poor chap who scrubs the courtyard several times a day". (*Dr H B Cardwell, Thomas Koralek, John H Moore, Martin Huggins, Mrs P A Warwick*)

Open All year.
Rooms 2 suites, 31 double, 11 single – 42 with bath, 2 with shower, all with direct-dial telephone, radio, colour TV with teletext, baby-listening, 24-hour room service. Double-glazing.
Facilities Lounge, garden lounge, cocktail lounge and bars, restaurant, sun room; 4 function rooms, courtyard/patio. Small grounds – Monastery Garden with gravel walks and sunken lawn. Golf ½ m; fly fishing and sailing at Rutland Water 5 m.
Location In town centre (front rooms tend to be noisy); parking for 150 cars.
Restriction No dogs in public rooms.
Credit cards All major cards accepted.
Terms B&B: single £42.50–£48, double £58–£68. Full alc £20. Reduced rates for children sharing parents' accommodation; special meals.

STON EASTON Somerset — Map 2

Ston Easton Park [GFG]
Ston Easton, Nr Bath BA3 4DF

Tel Chewton Mendip (076 121) 631
Telex 444738

After some vicissitudes this immaculately restored Palladian house, filled with lovely antiques and fresh flowers, is now firing on all cylinders and this year's postbag contains almost nothing but compliments. "The taste, discrimination and love lavished by Peter and Christine Smedley on this amazing building leaves the other Bath area hotels for dead . . . a house-party feel . . . great furnishings . . . food fine by any standards. The chef produced dishes which couldn't be simply classified by style or nationality but they were all *right*, while never facile" *(Andrew Hunt)*. "An exceptional hotel – no hotel guide could possibly be without it ... excellent service, not obsequious, just very, very good" *(D J Dunter)*. "This is a special occasion place, just right for a marriage proposal ... A really memorable evening. Best in England so far" *(Catherine Downing)*. The grounds, too, 26 acres of parkland, with the river Somer running through over a series of cascades, come in for awed comment – "mind-blowing", according to one commentator; and the Smedleys are now replanting the gardens to the plans drawn by Humphrey Repton in 1792. One correspondent had a couple of mild grumbles about the food – a mint sorbet over-sweet and too strongly flavoured, and a stuffing which drowned the taste of the duck – but she, like the rest, was full of praise, particularly for the service, mainly by local village girls, and the "marvellous bathrooms, the heaps of fat white towels".

Open All year.
Rooms 1 suite, 18 double, 1 single – 19 with bath, 1 with shower, all with direct-dial telephone, radio and colour TV.
Facilities Drawing room, library, salon, 2 restaurants, private dining room, billiards room, servants' room for chauffeurs etc. Recitals, entertainment groups occasionally. Terrace. 26-acre grounds with croquet, bowls, archery, riding, helicopter pad, river with fishing.
Location On A37 from Bristol to Wells. Turn left at sign "Ston Easton Park" on A39 to Shepton Mallet.
Restrictions No children under 12. No dogs.
Credit cards All major cards accepted.
Terms (Service at guests' discretion) B&B (continental): single £50, double £70–£140. Set lunch £14; full alc £25. Vegetarian and low-fat meals on request. 4-day Christmas programme; winter breaks.

STRATFORD-UPON-AVON Warwickshire   Map 2

Ashburton House   *Tel* Stratford-upon-Avon (0789)
27 Evesham Place   292444
Stratford-upon-Avon CV37 6HT

Mr and Mrs Downer took over this guest-house, 10 minutes' walk from the centre of town and the Festival Theatre, early in 1984. Under its previous owners, it had been noted for the high quality of its cooking and its modest tariff. The Downers may not be quite in the gastronomic class of their predecessors, but they appear to be making a very good job of it, and their prices are still remarkably competitive. They offer both a six-course and a four-course dinner, and are happy to cater for vegetarians. And they make a special feature of their breakfasts, with a huge variety of options, including home-made wholemeal bread. "After breakfast at *Ashburton*," they say, "lunch need not be a priority of the day." Here is how one reporter summed up: "Rooms are basic (no baths *en suite*), but warm, clean and comfortable. Breakfast almost unlimited ... very difficult to stand vertical afterwards. Dinners thankfully flexible as to time. Excellent fare, far better than you would expect in a small guest-house. Well-balanced wine list. Unlimited coffee. Prices very reasonable." *(Geoff Barratt; also M A Goulding, Gerhard Cohn)*

Open All year except Christmas. Restaurant closed Sun.
Rooms 3 double, 2 single – portable mono TV set available; double-glazing. Baby-sitting by arrangement.

Facilities Lounge, dining room (no smoking). Boating on river Avon; theatre tickets can be obtained for guests in advance (10% commission charged).
Location On A439, 500 yds from centre (front rooms may be noisy when windows open); 8 minutes' walk to Royal Shakespeare Theatre. Limited parking.
Restriction No dogs.
Credit cards Amex, Visa.
Terms (No service charge) B&B £11; dinner, B&B £22. Set dinner (4-course) £11, (6-course) £15. Reduced weekly rate; weekend breaks. Reduced rates according to age and special meals for children.

Billesley Manor Hotel
Billesley, Nr Alcester
Stratford-upon-Avon B49 6NF

Tel Alcester (0789) 763737
Telex 312599

This magnificent stone 16th-century mansion four miles to the west of Stratford in its eleven acres of parkland, with topiary hedges and two all-weather tennis courts, not to mention an indoor pool and a sophisticated nouvelle-*ish restaurant, was until this year the most elegant base for a Shakespeare-country vacation to be found within close range of the city. Now,* Ettington Park, Alderminster *(q.v.), is giving them a run for their money. Twelve rooms are in the venerable part of the house, but the sixteen rooms in the modern extension have been well grafted. The marriage of the old manorial with American style comfort has been well achieved. Service is another matter. Two readers this year, while appreciating other features of the place, commented on slow, inefficient – and in one case thoroughly boorish – service. Hence these italics. Further reports please.*

Open All year.
Rooms 2 suites, 26 double – all with bath, telephone, radio and colour TV and baby-listening; 3 ground-floor rooms.
Facilities Lounge with open fire, bar, minstrels' gallery, dining room; conference room. 11-acre grounds with indoor heated swimming pool, sauna, 2 all-weather tennis courts, croquet lawn, topiary gardens. &.
Location 4 m W of Stratford on A422; turn N off main road to Billesley.
Restrictions Children under 7 must take dinner in bedroom. No dogs.
Credit cards All major cards accepted.
Terms B&B: single £43–£50, double £55–£75. Set lunch £12.50, dinner £18.50; full alc £30. 2-day breaks except at Christmas. Reduced rates for children sharing parents' room; special meals.

Stratford House
Sheep Street
Stratford-upon-Avon CV37 6EF

Tel Stratford-upon-Avon (0789) 68288
Telex 312522 ref: STRATFORD HOUSE

Peter and Pamela Wade have been running this bed-and-breakfast hotel for the past six years with conspicuous success. In the winter of 1985/86 they are building on a restaurant at the back of the house, and from May 1986 onwards will be providing lunches and dinners both to their residents and to others. As a B&B it has been relatively expensive considering the size of the rooms and the single lounge, but it faces a quiet back alley, and has the great advantage of being no more than a 100-yard stroll to the theatre. The more characterful rooms are in the older part of the house facing the road, and there is an attractive family room at the top of the original house. The rooms facing the alley are a later extension and more basic in their furnishings. The "extremely helpful and personable" owners, to quote one satisfied customer, will do their best to help guests obtain theatre tickets. Generous breakfasts. Not recommended for a long stay, but highly convenient for a play or two – but closed in winter 1985/86 till May 1986. *(Roger Tandrell, Sandy Smith)* We look forward to reports on the restaurant.

Open Normally all year except one week at Christmas but closed in winter 1985/86 till May 1986.
Rooms 1 4-bedded, 7 double, one single – 7 with bath, one with shower, 6 with telephone, all with colour TV and tea-making facilities. 3 ground-floor rooms.
Facilities Lounge; no bar but residential licence; restaurant from spring 1986. Some small conference facilities. Small garden and courtyard.
Location In town centre. No private parking but car park nearby. 100 yds from Royal Shakespeare Theatre (the hotel can help you get tickets).
Restrictions Not suitable for &. Not really suitable for children, though they are not excluded. Dogs allowed if small; not in public rooms.
Credit cards All major cards accepted.
Terms B&B £19–£35. 2- and 3-night winter breaks.

STUDLAND Dorset   Map 1

Knoll House Hotel   *Tel* Studland (092 944) 251
Studland, Swanage BH19 3AH

"A perfect family hotel, catering for all ages. It has the most wonderful facilities for children which include a children's dining room for under-eights serving a full range of the foods children like from tinned purée to fish fingers; a playroom, supervised between 1 and 2 pm for children whose parents wish to lunch in peace; a games room fully equipped with Space Invaders, slot machines, pool table and table tennis; an adventure playground complete with spectacular full-scale pirate ship and plank; a large swimming pool and a small children's paddling pool. There is a refreshment kiosk serving drinks, ices and snacks. The beach is five minutes' walk from the hotel; it is sandy, but somewhat crowded in summer. Other activities include family quizzes on Monday – great fun – and discos for teenagers. Spacious lounges, TV rooms and cocktail bar add to the atmosphere, and tea on the front lawn overlooking the sea is a particularly agreeable part of the day. Rooms are small but adequate, and service is friendly and helpful. The food is adequate; excellent salads at lunch and a splendid spread of puddings in the evenings." *(Gillian Hawser)*

The above earlier verdict has been warmly endorsed by many visitors since. One wrote specially to tell us how enjoyable had been a holiday for three generations. *(Vivian Frayling, Sheila Lindsay, Keith Cole)*

Open 20 Mar–20 Oct approx.
Rooms 30 family suites (ie pairs of communicating rooms), 20 double, 29 single – all with bath, phone, baby-listening; 7 rooms in annexe; 48 ground-floor rooms.
Facilities 6 lounges, including TV room and bridge room, 3 games rooms, bar, main restaurant, junior restaurant; function facilities; fitness centre containing jacuzzi, sauna, steam-room, plunge pool, solarium, relaxation area; boutique; detached Garden Room with weekly discos, quiz etc. in high season, Easter, public holidays. Ramps to public rooms and pool. 100-acre grounds with children's playground, 9-acre golf course, 2 hard tennis courts, swimming pool (heated end May–mid-Sept) and paddling pool. Riding, squash nearby; direct access to 3-mile beach with sand; safe bathing, sailing, windsurfing, pedalos and beach huts. &.

Location 2 m N of Swanage, off B3351, on road leading to Sandbanks Ferry; or via Sandbanks car ferry from Bournemouth.
Restrictions No young children in main restaurant. Under-8s have supper and under-5s have all meals in Children's Dining Room. No dogs in restaurant.
Credit cards None accepted.
Terms B&B £25–£40; dinner, B&B (or full board for longer stays) £30–£45; full board (for shorter stays) £35–£50. (Very few people come 1 night only.) Set lunch £8.40, dinner £8.80. Reductions for children according to age.

STURMINSTER NEWTON Dorset   Map 1

Plumber Manor [GFG]   *Tel* Sturminster Newton (0258)
Sturminster Newton DT10 2AF   72507

This handsome Jacobean house, in the heart of Hardy countryside, has a number of special attributes. It has been the family home of the Prideaux-Brunes since the early 17th century; we know of no other hotel in England with a similar pedigree where the family are still in residence and actively involved in running their hotel. It insists on calling itself a restaurant-with-rooms, but though the restaurant under Brian Prideaux-Brune's direction is admirable, the number and comfort of the rooms (six in a converted stable block) make it a far more attractive hotel than many others which boast that name. It contrives to be dependably professional while effortlessly maintaining a laid-back air. Also, perhaps because it has not had to pay back some huge mortgage, its prices are low for what is being offered. We had one "disgusted" letter in this year's file: a storm had drenched this correspondent in the 100 yards walk from the annexe to the main house, and after that nothing seemed to go right. Otherwise, compliments abounded as usual, viz: "The situation was superb, with no damned noise at all. Our room in the annexe was just about faultless, as good as any room we have ever had. The standard of food was high all round. One niggle: the continental breakfast served in our room was definitely sub-standard. The one really worrying thing about *Plumber Manor* is that the proprietors work too hard." (*Paul Grotrian; Mrs M D Prodgers, T and R Rose, C Roberts*)

Open All year except Feb and first two weeks Nov. Restaurant closed for lunch and Mon; also Sun in low season (but set dinner provided for residents).
Rooms 12 double – all with bath, telephone, colour TV and tea-making facilities. 6 ground-floor rooms.
Facilities 2 bar/sitting rooms and portrait gallery, restaurant in main house; sitting/meeting room in converted barn. 4-acre gardens with tennis court, croquet lawn, trout stream running through grounds; 600-acre farm. Several golf courses, fishing on river Stour, riding and clay pigeon shooting nearby; within easy motoring distance of coast, Bath, Salisbury, Dorchester, Longleat, Stourhead, Wilton.
Location 2 m SW of Sturminster Newton, on Hazelbury Bryan road, which is a southward turn off A356.
Restrictions No children under 12. No dogs.
Credit card Visa.
Terms B&B: single £30–£35, double £40–£55. Set dinner £14–£15 (excluding service, which is at guests' discretion). 10% discount Oct–Mar and further discount in mid-week out of season.

> Don't keep your favourite hotel to yourself. The Guide supports: it doesn't spoil.

SWAY Hampshire   Map 2

Pine Trees Hotel [GFG]   *Tel* Lymington (0590) 682288
Mead End Road, Sway
Nr Lymington SO4 OEE

"We aim", write Betty and John David on our questionnaire, "to offer visitors a relaxing break completely divorced from the modern type of hotel. Probably appreciated most by the person seeking peaceful surroundings, unostentatious but excellent service, with good honest food." The Davids bought their old Victorian house in the New Forest some ten years ago, and have been running it honestly but unostentatiously ever since. It made a brief appearance in an earlier edition, but came out because of readers' complaints of shabbiness. No doubt the decor is below the standards of the modern type of hotel, but we were beguiled by the correspondent, a devoted regular, who wrote: "The charm of *Pine Trees* is unique, eccentric and batty. You have to be of a certain disposition to drive 100 miles from London to what can sometimes be a trappist retreat: two visits ago we had the place entirely to ourselves. But appearances may deceive. An almost cultivated shabbiness hides exceptional cleanliness in the rooms. Simplicity in all John David's menus does not exclude imaginative creations. The wine list prices are ridiculously low. Breakfasts are as large or small as you wish – croissants first rate, and all his own bread. Picnic lunches are so reasonable and good that one would be hard pushed to better them oneself." *(R C S Hill)*

Open All year.
Rooms 6 double – 1 with bath, 4 with shower.
Facilities Lounge with TV, bar, dining room. 4-acre grounds. 5 m from sea. Riding nearby (instruction can be arranged).
Location Off B3055 Brockenhurst to New Milton road.
Restrictions Not suitable for &. No children under 12. No dogs.
Credit cards All major cards accepted.
Terms B&B: single £18–£23, double £34–£38; dinner, B&B: single £32–£37, double £60–£66. Set lunch £8.50, dinner, £14. Vegetarian meals. Bargain breaks (2 days) Nov–Mar. ⅔ reduction for under-16s; special meals by arrangement.

TAUNTON Somerset   Map 1

The Castle Hotel [GFG]   *Tel* Taunton (0823) 72671
Castle Green, Taunton TA1 1NF   *Telex* 46488

A celebrated 300-year hostelry, creepered and castellated, in the centre of the city, though in a quiet oasis of higher ground on the site of the old castle, and with pleasant gardens at the back. For many years past, it has appeared in these pages as a kind of model of a thriving, really well-run town hotel. It has an energetic family, the Chapmans, running the show, who are assiduous in telling us of all the latest developments: refurbishing of lounges, creation of four new Garden Suites, the conversion of the Moat Room into a private dining room. It sets an example to other hotels, too, in its many enterprising "events": Musical Weekends, Wine Weekends, West Country Weekends, Gastronomic Breaks. Additionally, as reported last year, its chef, Christopher Oakes, has brought to the hotel's restaurant the distinction of a *Michelin* rosette

– the only town hotel outside London to be so honoured. In previous years, it has attracted excellent notices in these pages, with scarcely a dissenting voice. This year's file has had its share of rave reviews, for example: "This hotel and its restaurant fulfils, if not exceeds, every expectation" *(J B Miners)*; and "One of the best hotels we have ever visited" *(Dr and Mrs Richard Neville)*. There have however, been several voices heard in opposition: there has been disappointment in the restaurant, both about individual dishes and the quality of the service; and there have also been eyebrows raised at the room prices, which range from £66 for the cheapest double room to £175 for the Suite. No one suggests that the accommodation is other than utterly comfortable, but the hoary question of value for money is being raised, even by those who have formerly been staunch champions of *The Castle*.

Open All year.
Rooms 1 suite, 21 double, 13 single – all with bath and shower, telephone, radio, colour TV and baby-listening.
Facilities Lift. Lounge, bar/lounge, bar, restaurant; some rooms for functions, conference and private dining. ½-acre grounds with Norman moat, keep and square well. &.
Location Central, but quietly situated. Parking for 45 cars.
Restriction Dogs by arrangement; no dogs in dining room.
Credit cards All major cards accepted.
Terms (Service at guests' discretion) B&B: single from £48.25, double from £82; dinner, B&B: single from £57, double from £104. Set lunch £9.75, dinner £17; full alc £28.

TAYNTON Oxfordshire   Map 2

Manor Farm Barn   *Tel* Burford (099 382) 2069
Taynton, Burford OX8 4UH

Manor Farm Barn is a truly rural bed-and-breakfast in a typical unspoilt Cotswold hamlet one and a half miles from Burford – a lovely old church, but no shop, pub or post office. Our inspector's report last year was warmly commending: "Mrs Florey is a charming hostess of the perfectionist type, and she runs the establishment in a most generous way. You are immediately aware that this is a home and not a hotel, and having said this, I can think of few hotels offering such comfort and facilities. An ideal base for touring the Cotswolds." Recent visitors endorse the entry: "The Floreys make their guests feel as much at home as family or friends. The warmth of the Cotswold stone of their modernised farmhouse is reflected in their welcome, in the grateful comforts of the furnishings, in the dish of fresh fruit and serried toiletries in the rooms and in the large and varied breakfast served at the long table in the sunlit dining room. (Mrs Florey more than compensates in acceptable bonhomie and careful attention, for any apprehension engendered at the sight of strange companions at the table.)" *(Helen and Jack Thornton)*

Open All year, except Christmas and New Year.
Rooms 3 double – all with bath, radio, colour TV and tea-making facilities.
Facilities Lounge with TV, breakfast room. 8-acre garden and paddocks.
Location 1½ m NW of Burford; from Burford, go towards Stow-on-the-Wold on A361; turn left towards Taynton at roundabout, then left by church (car or personal transport essential).

Restrictions Not suitable for &. No children under 5. No dogs.
Credit cards None accepted.
Terms (No vat or service charge) B&B £13.50–£15. (No restaurant.)
Tipping: "Not required or looked for."

TEMPLE SOWERBY Cumbria   Map 4

Temple Sowerby House [GFG]   *Tel* Kirkby Thore (0930) 61578
Temple Sowerby CA10 1RZ

Last year's entry was in italics because the Hartley family (John and Eva, parents, and their two sons, Ian from the *Royal Crescent*, Bath, and Andrew) had just taken over this pedigree Georgian house on the A66 between Penrith and Appleby. The previous owners, who had lovingly restored the house and its fine two-acre walled garden, were renowned for their culinary skills and had built up a devoted clientele. A hard act to follow, we reckoned, but happily the Hartleys, to judge by our substantial and unanimously enthusiastic fan-mail, are making a first-rate job of it. "It has lost none of its excellence" is the refrain. Items which come in for special commendation are: breakfasts – "truly an Englishman's feast, particularly if you have the Sowerby Grill"; decor – "in immaculate condition and interestingly bold"; extras – "a complete set of Woods of Windsor soap, bubble bath and shampoo in a bottle – the latter the one thing I often forget and never seems to be in the bathroom freebie section"; restaurant – "superbly cooked food and a reasonably priced wine list". *(Mrs P Cornwell, R Medcalf, A & P N, I S Young, Dr G C Sen, J G Hamlin and others)*

Open All year except Christmas and New Year.
Rooms 12 double – all with bath, direct-dial telephone, radio, remote-control colour tv and tea-making facilities; 2 4-poster beds; 4 rooms in Coach House annexe; 2 ground-floor rooms. 3 front rooms which might get traffic noise are double-glazed.
Facilities 2 lounges, bar/lounge, dining room, conservatory and terrace; ramps for &. 2-acre walled Georgian garden. Fishing on river Eden; Ullswater 20 minutes.
Location 6 m E of M6 (junction 40) on A66, 6 m NW of Appleby.
Restriction No dogs.
Credit cards Amex, Visa.
Terms (No service charge) B&B: single £26, double £38. Set dinner £9.50. 10% discount for 3 nights or more. Winter breaks Oct–May, any 2 nights–approx £50. Reduced rates and special meals for children.
Service/tipping: "We believe that good service is an essential part of any stay in a hotel and therefore we do not levy a service charge or expect gratuities."

TETBURY Gloucestershire   Map 2

Calcot Manor   *Tel* Leighterton (066689) 227 or 355
Beverston, Nr Tetbury GL8 8YJ

A promising newcomer – doors opened August 1984 – to the constellation of Cotswold country houses. Brian and Barbara Ball, with their son Richard, are professionals and they have renovated their 15th-century manor house in a tranquil setting, three miles to the west of Tetbury, to a high style of elegance, equipping it with jacuzzis, a heated swimming pool and other similar conveniences. Their restaurant is in the hands of John Redmond Hayward, until recently chef of *Anna's Place* in London. One visitor found the reception and service a little cool, but most reports speak enthusiastically about the whole set-up, not least the congenial welcome of the hosts. "Barbara and Brian Ball", wrote one, "have a genius for entertaining without intrusiveness and their influence has spread throughout their staff. An American guest said to me, 'This is England as it ought to be.' I myself felt it was like taking part in a house party in a novel." We look forward to more reports. *(Mary Lewis; also Mr and Mrs E G Brown, Gordon Wrigley)*

Open All year. Restaurant closed Sun evenings.
Rooms 2 suites, 10 double, 1 single – 11 with bath (2 have whirlpool baths), all with telephone, radio and TV. 1 4-poster. 5 rooms in annexe. Ground-floor rooms in annexe fully equipped for &.
Facilities Lounge, drawing room, dining room, private dining room, conference facilities. 4-acre grounds with croquet lawn, heated outdoor swimming pool. 12th-century tithe barn and Cotswold barns. Fishing, golf and riding nearby. &.
Location 3 m W of Tetbury on A4135. Parking.
Restrictions No children under 12. No dogs.
Credit cards All major cards accepted.
Terms B&B £22–£45. Set lunch £7.50–£12.50, dinner £14.50–£17.95. Reduced rates for longer stays; weekend or mid-week breaks; Christmas packages.
Service/tipping: "All our prices include service and VAT so that our customers know exactly the cost."

THORNAGE Norfolk   Map 2

The Black Boys [GFG]   *Tel* Melton Constable (0263) 861218
Thornage, Nr Holt NR25 7QG

Five years ago, Ann Carr and Martin McKeown received rave notices in these pages for their *sui generis* establishment in the Preseli Hills, *Penlan Oleu* at Llanychaer (now once again with an entry under new management). We are delighted to welcome the Carr/McKeown team back in their new enterprise which, as before, offers quixotic enchantment. They themselves describe their transformed pub in an unspoiled pretty village as an ideal doll's house restaurant-with-rooms, and that description will do as well as any. Only two rooms at the moment, but there are plans for at least two more – though not necessarily in 1986. Everything about the place pleases. Breakfasts, though not cooked, rank high in our extensive breakfast dossier. Ann Carr's unpretentious excellence as a cook won her a reputation years ago at the *Peacock* in Islington and will win her another in this unfashionable but rewarding area of north Norfolk. This may be the smallest hotel in the Guide but it offers a kind of perfection in miniature. *(H R)*

Open Beginning Mar–end Oct. Restaurant closed Sun and Mon. Even residents must make dinner reservations, as dining rooms are small.
Rooms 2 double – 1 with bath *en suite*, 1 with bath across corridor.
Facilities Residents' lounge, bar, 2 dining rooms. ½-acre garden, 5 m from sea with bathing and sailing; birdwatching and golf nearby.
Location In centre of village on B1110, 2½ m S of Holt on the Dereham road.
Restrictions Not suitable for &. No children under 12. No dogs.
Credit cards All major cards accepted.
Terms (No service charge) B&B double £40–£44. Full alc £17. Packed lunches available.
Service/tipping: "We make no service charge at all and tips are not expected."

THORNBURY Avon   Map 2

Thornbury Castle [GFG]   *Tel* Thornbury (0454) 418511
Thornbury, Bristol BS12 1HH   *Telex* 449986 CASTLE G

There are not many genuine castle hotels in Britain; *Thornbury Castle* will appeal to those who like to sleep as well as eat like a lord. The building mostly dates from the early 15th century when the third Duke of Buckingham got permission to extend and castellate his manor. The castle as such was never finished, but the remains, renovated in appropriately luxurious style, provide an impressive backcloth to the *Thornbury* experience. And you may be sleeping in a room previously occupied by Henry VIII and Anne Boleyn, or by Mary, Queen of Scots. The pleasures of a stay here are enhanced by the excellent restaurant under Timothy Cheevers, a remarkable wine list (expensive, but there is a good selection of interesting wines at less than £10) and beautiful gardens which include Kenneth Bell's vineyards and "lovely smelly" wild boars. Some minor grumbles recur: pre-dinner drinks are taken in the library, "a curiously dead room which did not come to life even when full of guests who all spoke in whispers. It could have done with the pianist who was overpowering at dinner – and we were not given any option of not paying extra for him." Warning: bedrooms vary a lot in size and price; you should discuss the options when booking. Also, if you don't care for a pianist over dinner and paying for the privilege, you should ask for the second dining room. *(John Levy, W A, R O Marshall, and others)*

Open All year except Christmas.
Rooms 1 suite, 9 double, 2 single – all with bath, telephone, radio and colour TV.
Facilities Residents' lounge, reception room for restaurant customers, 2 dining rooms (1 with pianist). 10-acre grounds with walled garden, vineyard and farm.
Location 12 m N of Bristol, at N side of Thornbury, just off B4061; lodge gate is beside parish church (St Mary's).
Restrictions Not suitable for &. No children under 12 ("unless known to us"). No dogs.
Credit cards All major cards accepted.
Terms B&B (continental): single £45–£53, double £68–£130, suite £145. Set lunch £16; full alc £23.
Service/tipping: service is included in tariffs; tips are not expected.

TREBARWITH STRAND Cornwall   Map 1

The Old Millfloor [GFG]   *Tel* Camelford (0840) 770234
Trebarwith Strand, Tintagel PL34 0HA

No hotel, but a small secluded guest-house – three rooms in the house and a couple of self-catering chalet/bungalows in a picturesque location by a mill stream. Not for the disabled, since there is a steep path down from the road, but perfect for families: lots of pets, 10 acres of grounds and the beach 10 minutes' walk away; and the prices are remarkably low.
"What a delightful place! We spent a week there, partly prompted by the Guide and partly because it is so cheap. But we had no sense of self-denial – just repeated amazement that they could be making any profit at all. £65 per week for B&B [1985] would be a snip anywhere, let

alone in such a pretty house in a justifiably popular area; but there were no signs of corners being cut to make it feasible. Janice Waddon-Martyn runs the place with relaxed efficiency. Breakfast is 9–10.30 am, and we consistently turned up at 10.25. Breakfasts were semi-Edwardian in style and scope; a large jug of orange juice, fresh grapefruit halves, home-made yoghurt, an impressive range of cereals, a generous freshly cooked plate of eggs, bacon, sausage etc, and excellent coffee. Dinner, too, was excellent, with plenty of choice: you could choose any combination of starters, main courses (almost always a vegetarian dish among the options) and puddings to suit your appetite. Always about five kinds of vegetables. Bedrooms are quite charming. The public rooms, too, give the impression of relaxed comfort. If you are looking for a comfortable hotel in quiet rural surroundings near the coast, with good food and service, and at a very modest price – well, the *Millfloor* is difficult to beat." *(Brigid Avison)*

Open Mar–Dec.
Rooms 3 double, also 2 self-catering family bungalows, with TV.
Facilities Lounge/dining room. 10-acre grounds with stream and orchard. Beach with sand and rock pools 10 minutes' walk.
Location 2 m S of Tintagel.
Restriction Not suitable for &.
Credit cards None accepted.
Terms (No VAT or service charge) B&B £11 (£65 per week). Set dinner £8.50 (bring your own wine); cream teas and snacks served. Bungalows £80–£120 per week. Children sharing parents' room half-price; special meals.

TREGONY Cornwall   **Map 1**

Tregony House [GFG]   *Tel* Tregony (087 253) 671
Tregony, Truro TR2 5RN

César awarded for best value

"A small, quiet country hotel with a *very* friendly atmosphere, individual and personal attention from the management, and *excellent* food – *extremely* reasonable prices for B&B and a *superb* four-course evening meal." Thus the original commendation for this typical hybrid Cornish village house, part 17th-century and part Victorian, in a village at the entrance of the Roseland Peninsula, about five miles inland from the sea. It is a guest-house rather than a hotel, with books (more than 1,000), pictures, china and glass filling all the available space. Recent visitors have all endorsed the entry. "The Locks are friendly but not pushy. The food was superb – beautifully presented and inventive – and we had really comfortable beds in a cosy bedroom. For sheer value, it could not be beaten" *(Diana Rogers)*. An American visitor writes: "We were amazed that one of the favourite places we stayed at in England during a two-week visit was also the least expensive. It's the sort of simple country place you hope to discover but never do. Mr Lock has a wry sense of humour and enjoys his role as erudite host. Mrs Lock is the wonder in the kitchen. Good food, good night's sleep, good prices." *(Mrs Patrick Kenadjian; also Margaret Mann, Ronald Lowe, J A Cushman)*

Open Mar–Oct inclusive.
Rooms 5 doubles (2 can form a family suite), 1 single – 1 with bath. Front rooms double-glazed.

Facilities Lounge with TV, bar area with seating, dining room; cottage garden with seats on terrace. Beaches and Cornish coastal path 6 m.
Location In centre of village main street. Private car park.
Restrictions Not suitable for &. No children under 5. Dogs by arrangement, but not in public rooms.
Credit cards None accepted.
Terms (No VAT or service charge) dinner, B&B £17; dinner for non-residents £8. Reduced rates for stays of 7 days or more. Half price for children 5-12; special meals on request.

TREGOOSE Cornwall   Map 1

Tregoose Old Mill House   *Tel* St Columb (0637) 880559
Tregoose, St Columb Major
Nr Newquay

One way of describing the special set-up at this lovingly restored 15th-century mill is to quote what its owner and presiding genius Sue Cameron, formerly for 22 years in TV, has to say: "The *Mill* is run along the lines of a 1930s country house party. I defer to guests; they don't work round me. If someone eats out and is hungry by 10 pm I'll cook a meal; meals 24 hours a day if required. By having one dining-room table and sometimes combining residents and non-residents the meal becomes a private dinner party. I suppose you could equate the *Mill* with staying with a 'friend' but without the hassle of cooking. Most people coming to the *Mill* work in high-pressure jobs, so none of the clocks in the public areas works (all standing at 8 o'clock); this way I find that people forget time and relax. There are plenty of animals around (not in the public areas of course), so the *Mill* combines good food and wine, plus – without being oppressive – a country house ambience. The *Mill* is (I think) something unique which provides pleasure for guests and if they enjoy themselves then I do too!"

Most guests do indeed appreciate it. Here is one panegyric, but all the names at the end of this entry would subscribe in similar grateful terms: "I 'discovered' the *Old Mill House* from your pages – thank heaven! Having stayed at this idyllic retreat last summer for only one night I have subsequently returned with friends on two further occasions and fully intend to continue doing so. It's a marvellous place at the very centre of Cornwall – nestling in a quiet, warm valley amongst spectacular scenery and alongside a charming mill stream and ford. Goats, dogs, cats, geese and donkeys live in tranquil neighbourliness in the eight acres of orchard, woodland and meadow. Sue Cameron is a truly remarkable character. Almost single-handedly she maintains the grounds, the *Mill* and the animals and still has an apparently unlimited amount of time to joke with and pamper her guests and to cook for them the very best food. The bedrooms are comfortable, quiet and full of thoughtful extras – flowers, fruit, books, shampoo – the list is endless. The *Mill* is run on deceptively simple and flexible lines – breakfast 'whenever you're up'; cream tea? 'certainly – any time'; dinner – 'whatever time you're ready' and the warmth of Sue's hospitality really gives one the illusion of staying with a good friend at her country house. Perhaps it is not an illusion. Of all the charming places I have encountered through your excellent pages this is quite certainly the best." *(Mervyn Lloyd; also Mr and Mrs Mark Hill, Mr and Mrs Simon Hillier, David and Barbara Nuttall, Mary Rayner, Mr and Mrs C J Burton)*

Open All year.
Rooms 4 double – 1 with bath. Up to 4 beds available in holiday flat at *Tregoose Farm* 250 yds away.
Facilities Lounge/hall, lounge with colour TV, dining room with ingle-nook fireplace. 8-acre grounds with orchard. The *Mill* owns fishing rights (brown/rainbow trout in season) on river Porth. Close to sandy beaches, golf, riding; shark fishing on N and S coasts.
Location Off A3059 Newquay road; turning is opposite main turning for St Columb Major – follow lane, bearing left for 1½ m. The *Mill* is last house before river.
Restrictions Not suitable for &. Children and dogs by arrangement.
Credit cards None accepted.
Terms (No service charge) B&B £15–£18. All meals by arrangement: set lunch/dinner from £12; full alc from £14. (Packed lunches also provided.) Reduced rates for children under 7; special meals.
Tipping: "I leave this to guests; if they've enjoyed their stay and would like to leave a tip, it's up to them."

TRESCO Isles of Scilly   Map 1

The Island Hotel   *Tel* Scillonia (0720) 22883
Tresco, Isles of Scilly
Cornwall TR24 0PU

Tresco is a private island, two miles by one. It is renowned for the Abbey Gardens, filled with exotic plants from all over the world. No cars are allowed – there are bicycles for hire, and guests of *The Island Hotel* are met on arrival (by boat or helicopter) by a tractor and trailer – so Tresco is exceptionally peaceful. *The Island Hotel* is a modern building with five acres of grounds beside the sea, and a private beach. It enjoys dramatic views of the rocky coast and other islands. "On arrival at the hotel, a warm welcome; on leaving, a friendly farewell. In between a peaceful, comfortable stay, a most relaxing atmosphere, in a hotel run most efficiently, though unobtrusively. Nothing is too much trouble for John and Wendy Pyatt or their staff (who could not be bettered). The food is first class – the menu has a vast choice and always a very fine selection of desserts – and the Sunday cold buffet dinner has to be seen to be believed (we are told some people plan their holidays to include Sunday for that reason)." The bar lunches are also applauded. The only criticism, voiced by two readers, is of the "small cheap paper napkins" at meals. *(Dr and Mrs D Howell, Rosemary and Tom Rose)*

Open Mid-Mar to mid-Oct
Rooms 1 suite, 26 double, 7 single – all with telephone, radio and baby-listening, 22 with colour TV, 3 with tea-making facilities; some rooms arranged in groups of 1 double and 1 single, sharing a bathroom; 3 rooms on ground floor.
Facilities Lounge, bar lounge, TV room, bar, dining room, games room for adults with table tennis and bar billiards, children's playroom, laundry facilities. 5-acre grounds with heated swimming pool, bowls and croquet; private beach with safe bathing. The hire of rowing boats, sailing dinghies and small motor boats can be arranged.
Location You reach Tresco by scheduled British Airways helicopter flight (approx. 20 minutes) or by boat (approx. 2½ hours) from Penzance; not Sun. It is essential to book in good time. Hotel meets guests on arrival.
Restrictions Not suitable for &. No dogs allowed on Tresco.
Credit cards Access, Visa.
Terms (No service charge) dinner, B&B £38–£74. Set dinner £15; alc lunch from

£3. Discounts for pre-booked stays of over 5 nights. Tresco gardeners' holidays in spring and autumn. Reduced rates for children in bunk beds or cots; special meals provided.
Service/tipping: "No service charge is made or tips expected. If guests wish to reward courtesy and good service it is entirely voluntary."

TWO BRIDGES Devon   Map 1

Cherrybrook Hotel   *Tel* Tavistock (0822) 88260
Two Bridges, Yelverton PL20 6SP

This early 19th-century family-run, modest-priced hotel, formerly a farmhouse, has a splendidly central position for a Dartmoor holiday. "The view of Dartmoor from the front of the house is magnificent. The far horizon offers the purest line imaginable with eleven valleys, so I was told, folded between it and *Cherrybrook*. The house was built by a friend of the Prince Regent, which doubtless accounts for its rural elegance. Today it is pleasantly and comfortably furnished. The four-course dinner menu is good and straightforward, with just enough choice to leave no one out in the cold. It is a tremendously welcoming place, to which country-loving people return year after year." *(Frances Howell)*

Several enthusiasts for Cherrybrook hospitality have endorsed the above entry *(A Mowles, M J Dancy, W N Baker, R G S Johnston, H V White, E Humphreys, Mrs C Darvall)*." At last, recognition of a good family hotel with excellent value for money", writes one. "Why did it take you so long to find *Cherrybrook*?" asks another. But we have dissenting reports too: uneven meals, shortcomings in the service; poor packed lunches; heating coming on too late on a cold May afternoon. More reports please.

Open All year except Christmas and New Year and proprietor's holiday in winter.
Rooms 6 double, 2 single – 5 with shower, all with tea-making facilities.
Facilities Lounge, bar, dining room. 4-acre grounds with access to open moorland. Golf. Trout fishing in moorland rivers and in 4 reservoirs. Riding and pony-trekking available.
Location On B3212, ½ m NE of Two Bridges crossroads.
Restrictions Not suitable for &. No dogs in public rooms.
Credit cards None accepted.
Terms (No service charge) B&B £12–£14; dinner, B&B £19–£21. Set dinner £7. Off-season breaks and activity breaks. Reductions for children sharing parents' room; special meals.
Tipping: tips are not accepted.

ULLINGSWICK Hereford and Worcester   Map 2

The Steppes Country House Hotel   *Tel* Burley Gate (043 278) 424
Ullingswick   [may change to Hereford
Nr Hereford HR1 3JG   (0432) 820424 in autumn 1985]

Ullingswick is a tiny Domesday-old hamlet in the Wye valley. *The Steppes* is a pedigree Grade II listed 17th-century country house, well endowed with oak beams, ingle-nook fireplaces and the like. With only three bedrooms, it can hardly rate as a hotel, but it offers more than the term guesthouse would suggest, including ambitious and imaginative cooking on its four-course evening menu. Last year we carried a long

185

appreciation of the delights of a stay at *The Steppes*; this year, sadly, reports have been more mixed. A reader reported a very cold bedroom, admittedly on one of the coldest nights of the year. Some of the criticism was directed at the richness of Tricia Howland's cooking; we are glad to know that she has now introduced an à la carte menu of plainer dishes in addition to her no-choice gourmet menu. The self-consciousness engendered by a small dining room also came in for comment in several reports: classical music at meal-times helped, but whispered conversation and silence is a problem in these small establishments if the guests don't find themselves able to be matey. Some readers were enchanted by the set-up, however – "I truly felt I was a guest in Tricia's own house ... Everything I asked for was answered with a smile ... A friendly hotel in a friendly village" *(Andrena Woodhams)*. We think one reader got it right when she wrote: "Not for everyone, but a pleasure if you are on the right wavelength."

Open All year except 2 weeks before Christmas and 1 week after New Year.
Rooms 3 double – all with shower and WC, radio, colour TV and tea-making facilities; mobile telephone available. 1 ground-floor room.
Facilities Lounge with open fire and TV, dining room/bar with open fire. 1½-acre garden with sheep, rabbits and chickens; riding nearby; fishing arranged locally. Tours round Royal Worcester porcelain works arranged. Suitable for partially &.
Location 7 m NE of Hereford off A417 Leominster to Gloucester road.
Restrictions No children under 12. No dogs in public rooms.
Credit cards None accepted.
Terms B&B £14–£16; dinner, B&B £25–£28. Set dinner £13.50. Bargain breaks Mar–Nov, Christmas and New Year 3-day house parties; mid-week or weekend golfing breaks.

ULLSWATER Cumbria   Map 4

Howtown Hotel   *Tel* Pooley Bridge (085 36) 514
Ullswater, Penrith CA10 2ND

An inspector reports on this long-popular modestly priced hotel: "There are few lakeshores as unspoilt and as quiet as the southern shore of Ullswater, reached as it is by a twisting and inconvenient cul-de-sac road from Pooley Bridge. And the scenery immediately around *Howtown* is delectable – in a 10-mile round walk from Patterdale, I enjoyed a microcosm of everything the Lakes have to offer: a high-seeming mountain pass over rough fells at the top of Boredale; a superb walk down the valley through fields lined with well-kept dry-stone walls, and through neat stone farmyards; a superlative lakeshore with fine old oak woodland.

"There could hardly be a greater contrast between this and *Sharrow Bay* (see below) only a couple of miles along the shore. A long, low building set a hundred yards back from the road, and a bit further from the lake, with fells rising steeply behind, it looks like an extended farmhouse. You couldn't call it elegant: it is heavily furnished, with darkish public rooms. But, in the evening at least, it's cheerful and relaxed – particularly when it's full. The dining room is conspicuously smarter than the rest of the hotel; large but with every corner thought about and carefully furnished. There was no menu and choice was restricted. But the food was quite excellent all round: there was plenty of it, and there were no obvious weaknesses at any point in the meal. The 'compulsory' starter, waiting when we sat down, was fresh salmon with mayonnaise. Vegetable soup was clearly home made. Roast lamb and mint sauce was first-rate, a generous helping of unfatty meat in a good clear gravy. Then a creamy lemon mousse. Coffee was served in one of the numerous small lounges; with its rabbit warren of public rooms, the building 'loses' guests more easily than one might imagine from outside. The only shock to our system was when we got the bill. For a first-rate four-course meal, excluding wine and coffee, we were charged a mere £6 [1984] a head. Dinner, bed and breakfast – the Howtown price was around £14.25 – less than a quarter of the price of that other establishment down the road."

Open 24 Mar–1 Nov.
Rooms 13 double, 3 single; 2 cottages for renting; 4 rooms in annexe.
Facilities 4 lounges, 2 bars, dining room, TV room, 1-acre garden. 300 yds from the lake with own private foreshore; yachting, boating, fishing, walking, climbing. Riding and golf nearby.
Location *Howtown* is on E shore of lake 4 m S of Pooley Bridge.
Restrictions Not suitable for &. No children under 7. Dogs at proprietor's discretion, and not in public rooms.
Credit cards None accepted.
Terms (No fixed service charge) dinner, B&B £19 (£16.75 for 4 nights or more). Self-catering cottages £45–£120 per week. Set lunch: cold table on weekdays £4, on Sun from £5.25; dinner £7. Reduced rates for children sharing parents' room.
Tipping: "Any gratuities offered will be distributed equally amongst the staff."

Sharrow Bay Country House Hotel [GFG]
Ullswater, Penrith CA10 2LZ

Tel Pooley Bridge (085 36) 301 or 483

🏆 César awarded in 1985 for distinguished long service

Brian Sack's and Francis Coulson's celebrated country house hotel on the eastern shore of Ullswater – now in its 36th year and, for some enthusiasts, a part of our national heritage – invariably produces a correspondence as long and as packed with metaphorical calories as one of *Sharrow Bay*'s famous menus. The same superlatives and the same grumbles – about the bedrooms in the main house and the public rooms being over-cluttered, and the marathon meals – reappear each year. Here are some of the fruits of this year's harvest:

"The combination of gastronomic excellence and attention to detail in the superbly appointed rooms remains second to none in the UK. I have never experienced hotel rooms offering guests Scrabble, little sablé biscuits, electric trouser-press, hair-dryer, 2 TVs, radio and radio/cassette, mini-bar, mini-library, linen sheets and opulent antique furnishings." *(Alistair Jamieson)*

"The ultimate. A unique experience. Everything was overdone, and yet still in good taste." *(H Richard Lamb)*

"I cycled 70 miles on a hot August day to arrive in time for lunch. In spite of being alone, female, elderly, shabby and sweaty, I was treated like a queen. True professionalism to give the only lone luncher the table with the best view – having no one to talk to I was the best able to appreciate it. The food and furniture were over-stuffed, as were some of the clients, but the management was chivalry itself." *(M A Goulding)*

"My favourite hotel. Everything is just 'over the top'. There is a lovely new ladies' loo this year, garlanded and ruched in blue silk, with large pink bows. Downstairs, the loos have flowers all over them, even the basins have flowers." *(Heather Sharland)*

"After two days, I am only able to make vague unintelligible murmurings rather like a cat that has satisfied itself on cream. I will now eat nothing for three days. I mean, can you follow that?" *(Kathryn Stephen)*

Open 7 Mar to 1 Dec.
Rooms 4 cottage suites, 23 double, 7 single – 24 with bath, 2 with shower, all with telephone, radio, TV, some with tea-making facilities; 18 rooms in cottages and Bank House, 5 ground-floor rooms.
Facilities 4 lounges, breakfast room, 2 restaurants. 12-acre garden and woodlands; ½ m of lake shore with private jetty and boathouse; lake bathing (cold!) and fishing from shore; boats for hire nearby; steamer service in season across the lake; magnificent walking/climbing country.
Location On E shore of Ullswater, 2 m S of Pooley Bridge. Turn by small church in Pooley Bridge and take Howtown Lane. (M6 exit 40).
Restrictions Not suitable for &. No children under 13. No dogs.
Credit cards None accepted.
Terms (No service charge) dinner, B&B: single £56–£63, double £59–£80 per person. Set lunch £17.50 (light lunches also available weekdays), dinner £25. 10% mid-week reductions in Mar and Nov.
Service/tipping: "No tipping!"

UPPER SLAUGHTER Gloucestershire   Map 2

Lords of the Manor Hotel   *Tel* Cotswold (0451) 20243
Upper Slaughter   *Telex* via 83147 VIAOR G Ref Lords
Nr Bourton-on-the-Water
Cheltenham GL54 2JD

Another ageless Cotswold manor – in this case dating from the 17th century, though with later additions – complete with lake and trout stream in an unspoilt peaceful village, enjoys a fresh lease of life as a well-bred country hotel. The breeding has special point here: the Manor has been the home of the Witts family for 200 years. It was originally the rectory, and four generations of Witts were successively rectors from 1764 to 1913. In 1852 the Rev F E Witts (author of *The Diary of a Cotswold Parson*) bought the rectory from the church, made it the Manor House and became Lord of the Manor. In 1972 the Witts converted their Manor House into a hotel. It is still managed by members of the family.

"Mixed feelings. Charming amateurish service; pleasant owners and clientele; food unremarkable and a bit over-stretching the cook – a relaxation of ambition and concentration on tradition would be a good tip. Very relaxing in many ways, but I *hate* being knocked up by the maids when they want to change the sheets! My wife loves the place. Perhaps I'm just a natural grouch!" Other readers share the grouch's ambivalent view of the cooking, "breakfasts and bar lunches excepted", though one reader took the opposite view – "real dishes really platonically perfect". At least one of the rooms on the ground floor ("Anthony"), and perhaps its neighbour, suffers from creaky floor-boards from the room above. But despite these grumbles, most correspondents enjoyed their visits and would come again. *(Michael and Suzanna Harris, T R Mann, Ann Delugach)*

Open All year except 6–19 Jan.
Rooms 14 double, 1 single – 14 with bath, 1 with shower, all with telephone and tea-making facilities; 1 ground-floor room.
Facilities Drawing room, bar, garden room (with TV), restaurant. 7-acre grounds with walled garden, croquet, ornamental lake, dry-fly trout fishing, children's play area.
Location 2 m W of the Fosse Way (A429) between Stow-on-the-Wold and Bourton-on-the-Water. In village centre. Parking.
Restrictions Not suitable for &. No babies under 2. No dogs.
Credit cards All major cards accepted.
Terms [1985 rates] (No service charge) B&B (continental): single from £35, double £35–£75. Set lunch from £7 (bar snacks also available); full alc £14. Bargain breaks; Christmas package. Reduced rates and special meals for children.
Service/tipping: "No compulsory addition is made for 'service' as this is allowed for in the prices charged. Gratuities will be distributed as directed."

WADHURST East Sussex   Map 2

Spindlewood Hotel [GFG]   *Tel* Ticehurst (0580) 200430
Wallcrouch, Wadhurst TN5 7JG

Robert Fitzsimmons, formerly a Michelin *inspector, and his family opened the doors of* Spindlewood *six years ago. It is a turn-of-the-century stone-built residence in five acres of gardens and woodland deep in the Sussex countryside. Sussex has relatively few hotels in the Guide, considering its proximity to London, and* Spindlewood, *from its first entry in these pages, has enjoyed good notices both for the comforts of the house and the quality of the cooking. This year, too, has not been without reports which begin: "We desperately needed to get away from the rat race and everything at* Spindlewood *came up to our full expectations . . . The food was superb." But there have, for the first time, been many voices raised in protest: about inadequate heating, especially in the bedrooms, about off-hand reception, slow service at meals, poor housekeeping, dowdy furnishings. The reports are so contradictory that they might be describing different premises. Our conclusion: the hotel is still capable of giving much satisfaction, but some of the rooms badly need attention, the place may not function too well when the* patron *is absent, and heating should have higher priority than hitherto. We should be glad of more reports.*

Open All year, except Christmas.
Rooms 7 double, 2 single – 8 with bath, 1 with shower, all with direct-dial telephone, radio-alarm, colour TV, tea- and coffee-making facilities and baby-listening.
Facilities Lounge with TV, and games and toys for children; library, lounge bar, restaurant. 5-acre grounds with hard tennis court. Trout fishing and golf nearby.
Location On B2099, 2¼ m SE of Wadhurst.
Restrictions Not suitable for &. Only guide dogs allowed.
Credit cards Access, Amex, Visa.
Terms (No fixed service charge) B&B: single £25–£28.50, double £54–£60; dinner, B&B: single £34–£38, double £72–£79. Sun lunch £9.50. Set dinner £8.85; full alc £18.50.

> Wherever possible, we have quoted prices per room. Not all hotels are prepared to quote tariffs in this way. In these cases, we have given prices per person, indicating the range of prices – the lowest is likely to be for sharing a double room out of season, the highest for a single room in the high season.

WATERMILLOCK Cumbria   Map 4

The Old Church Hotel   *Tel* Pooley Bridge (085 36) 204
Watermillock, Penrith CA11 0JN

A reasonably priced hotel in a spectacular position on the edge of
Ullswater, an 18th-century house on the site of a 12th-century church.
"Situated in a quiet part of the Ullswater area and reached by way of a
third of a mile of private drive off the A592. The gardens go right down
to the water and the views are fine. It is extremely quiet. The present
owners, Mr and Mrs Whitemore, moved in about five years ago and
have clearly got considerable flair and are determined to create a
country-house atmosphere of a high order. The food is excellent,
imaginative and varied. The table d'hôte gives ample choice as does the
wine list. We have stayed three times since May 1984 and cannot fault it
in any way. The decorations are of a very high standard, Mrs Whitemore
being skilled in making curtains, cushions etc. herself. Mr Whitemore,
after qualifying as an accountant, went to a hotel school and specialises
in cooking. The staff would appear to be local girls who give you the
impression they really enjoy what they are doing; and are very pleasant
and helpful. Coffee A1. Petits fours provided. Flowers in the bedroom,
and also specially nice soap. Rowing boat for guests free of charge. I
could go on and on. Definitely a hotel for your next edition." *(P A Senn;
also enthusiastically recommended by Mrs C V Smith-Price)*

Open 21 Mar–2 Nov.
Rooms 1 family, 9 double, 2 single – 7 with bath.
Facilities 2 lounges, bar, dining room (no smoking). 4-acre grounds with
extensive lake frontage with mooring and fishing; sail boards and rowing boat
available for guests' use.
Location 3 m S of Pooley Bridge; 5 m from junction 40 on the M6.
Restrictions Not suitable for &. Dogs by prior arrangement – never to be left
unaccompanied in bedrooms.
Credit cards None accepted.
Terms B&B £20–£25; dinner, B&B £32–£37. Set dinner £12.

WEOBLEY Hereford and Worcester   Map 2

Red Lion   *Tel* (0544) 318220
Weobley, Nr Hereford HR4 8SG

*In the heart of Herefordshire, at the centre of a medieval village famous for its
many half-timbered black-and-white houses, an inn dating from the 14th
century. "The* Red Lion *is part of the delightful black-and-white architecture of
Weobley, backing rather agreeably on to the bowling green, and with (if our
accommodation was typical) small unfussy bedrooms, the pleasantest of dining
rooms and the most conventional of menus. Overnight, or for a weekend, it must
be in there with a chance."* (Robert Robinson) *An inn with a chance? More
reports please.*

Open All year.
Rooms 7 double – 2 with bath, 5 with shower, all with telephone, colour TV and
tea-making facilities.
Facilities Lounge/bar, bar, restaurant, terrace. 2-acre grounds, bowling green.
Golfing at Wormsley Golf Course nearby.
Location In centre of village, 10 miles NW of Hereford. Parking.

Restrictions Not suitable for &. Dogs in bar only.
Credit cards Access, Visa.
Terms B&B: single £26, double £38. Set lunch £3.75, dinner £12; full alc £14.
3–4 day Christmas package. Reduced rates and special meals for children.

WEST BEXINGTON Dorset — Map 1

The Manor Hotel [GFG]   *Tel* Burton Bradstock (0308)
West Bexington, Dorchester DT2 9DF   897616

We wish we had more places to recommend along the beautiful Dorset coast. *The Manor Hotel* is a 16th-century stone manor house, still preserving its Jacobean oak panelling in the hallway, and flagstone floors in the restaurant. It is 500 yards above Chesil beach, and recommended by the editor of *The Good Food Guide* in the following terms: "No frills or pretentions, and about as fashionable as a Dorset knob, but as an honest hostelry serving fresh food it scores each time. Not a star, but if every small hotel/pub with rooms fed guests like this . . . " *(Drew Smith)*

Open All year except Christmas and New Year.
Rooms 8 double, 3 single – 2 with bath, all with radio, colour TV, tea-making facilities and baby-listening.
Facilities Lounge, cellar bar, dining room. 3-acre grounds with childrens' play area. 500 yds from sea; Chesil beach is unsafe for swimming, but famous for fishing. Sandy beaches within easy reach at Weymouth, Charmouth and Lyme Regis; boating and sea fishing at nearby West Bay.
Location 5 m SE of Bridport on B3167.
Restrictions Not suitable for &. No dogs in public rooms.
Credit cards Access, Amex, Visa.
Terms (No service charge) B&B: single £16.50–£18, double £29–£32; dinner, B&B: single £25.50–£27.50, double £45–£49.50. Set lunch £8.95, dinner £10.45, Reduced rates for 2-night stay from 1 Sept. 50% reduction for under 10s; special meals.
Service/tipping: Tipping is left to customers' discretion.

WEST CLIFFE Kent — Map 2

Wallett's Court [GFG]   *Tel* Dover (0304) 852424
West Cliffe, Dover CT15 6EW

One of Kent's historic houses becomes a new sort of establishment for the Guide – what is essentially a bed-and-breakfast from Monday to Friday (though with simple farmhouse-style evening meals available at about £5) is transformed on Saturday night into a mecca for gourmets. The house itself would merit the journey: a 17th-century listed manor house, the home of Prime Minister William Pitt in 1804, set in rural surroundings on the white cliffs of Dover, a mile from St Margaret's Bay; inside, there are intricately carved honey-coloured beams, huge open fireplaces, plenty of good antiques, flowers everywhere. Major restoration has taken place under the supervision of Lea Oakley, wife of the chef/*patron*, Chris Oakley, who trained with the Roux brothers at *Le Gavroche* and was then chef at *Le Poulbot* in London and is responsible for the remarkable cooking. Our inspector was much impressed by all she saw and ate: "*Nouvelle*-ish food outshone some rosetted restaurants I visit and was also excellent value for money. The rooms – three in the main house without bathrooms and four with showers and toilets in the converted barn annexe – are simple but prettily furnished and comfortable. Service? They made you feel you were a very special person. I came as close to feeling I was the Princess of Wales as I ever will."

Open All year except Christmas. Gourmet dinner Sat; meals served to non-residents on other evenings by prior arrangement.
Rooms 2 family, 4 double, 1 single – 2 with bath, 5 with shower, all with TV and tea-making facilities. 1 on ground floor.
Facilities Lounge, dining room. 3-acre grounds with orchard. 1 m from St Margaret's Bay with bathing, windsurfing, tennis club; golf 2 m.
Location 3 m N of Dover, 1 m down B2058 off A258 Dover/Deal road. Hotel is on right.
Restriction No dogs.
Credit cards None accepted.
Terms B&B: single £15–£17, double £24. Gourmet dinner (Sat) £15; meals on other nights £5–£6. Children under 14 half-price.

WHIMPLE Devon   Map 1

🏵 Woodhayes Hotel   *Tel* Whimple (0404) 822237
Whimple, Nr Exeter EX5 2TD

César awarded for country house excellence in the medium-price range

The stops really get pulled out when guests try to find adequate expressions of gratitude for the generous hospitality they have found at John Allen's small Georgian country house in an apple orchard village close to the A30. One much-travelled correspondent voted it one of the two outstanding hotels he had come across on his journeys (the other was *Scarista House*, Scarista – q.v.): "Notable for the quality of its meals – the best we had in the UK – the quality of its appointments and the quiet efficiency and interest of its host. It is a hotel without any weakness, deserving your highest rating." Another wrote: "I have not encountered service like this in more than 35 years." A third itemised with awe the extras in her bedroom and outsize bathroom: "Sparkling water with glass on silver tray, three chairs, three lamps plus floor lamp, three tables plus one chest, armoire, remote-control TV, sewing box, books and magazines, Kleenex in bedroom and bathroom on lace doilies, live plant, live flower arrangement, telephone, radio in wall, pad and pen, full-length mirrors in bedroom and bathroom; bathroom completely carpeted, including sides of tub; slipper chair in bathroom, bath oil, wash cloth, huge towel plus two others, cotton balls, nail brush, shower spray, heated towel rack . . . etc. I was so comfortable that I could have stayed there through the winter!" (*James McCowan, Professor R J C Atkinson, Patricia Purvis; also Robin de Beaumont, R M Hilder, Stephen Parish*)

Open All year.
Rooms 6 double, 1 single – all with bath, telephone, radio and colour TV.
Facilities 2 lounges, dining room. 1½-acre paddock with lawns, arboretum, gazebo, croquet, bowls and kitchen garden. 11 m from sea; trout fishing nearby.
Location On the edge of Whimple village, which is just N of A30, 9 m E of Exeter.
Restrictions No children under 12. No dogs.
Credit cards All major cards accepted.
Terms B&B £30–£45; dinner, B&B £47.50–£62.50. Full board £59–£74. Set lunch £11.50, dinner £17.50. Reduced rates for winter breaks and longer stays in summer. Christmas programme.

WICKHAM Hampshire   Map 2

The Old House Hotel [GFG]   *Tel* Wickham (0329) 833049
The Square, Wickham PO17 5JG

A creepered early Georgian house in a picturesque, part-medieval, part-Georgian village square, converted by Richard and Annie Skipwith 16 years ago, and now a flourishing highly prized French restaurant (Annie Skipwith has spent some time with Vergé and Guérard) as well as "a splendid small hotel". We had an entry for *The Old House* two years ago, then left it out for lack of feed-back. As often happens, we were quick to be told the error of our ways. An inspector confirmed these good opinions. Every prospect pleased her: the attractive facade, polished floors, spic-and-span paintwork, the warmth in a chilly January, the comfortable fat chairs in the public rooms, the flower arrangements, the quality of the furnishings in the bedroom and bathroom, and every course of her evening meal – not to mention the sympathetic characters of the host and hostess. Her report concluded: "The food is quite expensive, and so is the wine, but where else for miles offers anything comparable? If you are getting a pleasant evening out, you can just tell yourself you are paying for the atmosphere."

Open All year, except 10 days Christmas, 2 weeks Easter, 2 weeks July/Aug. Both hotels and restaurant closed Sat and Sun.
Rooms 7 double, 3 single – all with bath, telephone, radio and colour TV. Double-glazing. & (restaurant only).
Facilities Hall, lounge, TV room, restaurant. Small garden. River Meon nearby.
Location In village centre. Parking. Wickham is at junction of A333 and A32, 3 m N of Fareham.
Restriction No dogs.
Credit cards All major cards accepted.
Terms B&B: single from £42, double from £55. Full alc £21. Reductions for children according to age; special meals.

WILLITON Somerset   Map 1

The White House Hotel [GFG]   *Tel* Williton (0984) 32306
Williton TA4 4QW

Dick and Kay Smith's handsome Georgian house on the A39 between Bridgwater and Minehead provides all the usual amenities of a country house hotel, but is specially noted for the consistent quality of its cooking (breakfast and dinner only). Light sleepers are advised to ask for one of the smaller and perhaps rather more austere rooms in the courtyard annexe at the back. Here is the latest report to reach us: "After an absence of four years, we returned to *The White House* and found it just as we had left it – friendly, relaxing, an absolute haven. The standard of decoration and of service are high indeed, and rates represent excellent value for money. The food and the wine are a rare delight. The menu changes daily, and, although short, provides a good choice: dinner at £12 [1985] is a real bargain. After a day's walking in the Quantocks, I can think of no greater pleasure than a discussion with Dick Smith about the choice of wine for dinner (the wine list is comprehensive, and the reserve list contains some real bargains). This is the sort of hotel the Guide is all about." *(John Kelly)*

Open Mid-May – end Oct.
Rooms 12 double, 1 single – 7 with bath; 5 rooms in annexe, some of which are ground-floor and suitable for disabled.
Facilities Lounge with TV, bar, dining room. 2 m from coast; shingle beach 3 m, sandy beach 4 m.
Location In centre of village (annexe rooms quieter). Parking in courtyard.
Restrictions Not suitable for &. Dogs allowed in bedrooms only by arrangement.
Credit cards None accepted.
Terms (No service charge) B&B: single £20, double £34; dinner, B&B: single £30, double £54. Set dinner £14. Bargain breaks for 3 or 4 days. Reduced rates for children.

WINDERMERE Cumbria   Map 4

Miller Howe [GFG]   *Tel* Windermere (096 62) 2536
Rayrigg Road, Windermere
LA23 1EY

César awarded for theatrical brilliance and imaginative largesse

Visitors to *Miller Howe* have constantly, for many years past, reported a kind of ultimate hotel experience here – a quintessence of cosseting. Appropriately, this elegant country house hotel has earned most of the symbolic accolades that the professional Guides can confer. The location, for a start, is as peaceful and enchanting as you could hope to find short of the Elysian Fields. Miller Howe is the name of a hill on which the building stands, at the foot of the road to Bowness, and to the Kirkstone Pass, with only path-threaded National Trust land dividing it from the lake. Across the water are the outlines of the great fells. The size of the hotel doubtless contributes to its agreeableness. With only 13 bedrooms, an intimacy of enjoyment is possible which larger estabishments cannot hope to achieve. And those bedrooms are furnished with imagination as well as taste – with binoculars and hair dryers as well as with antiques and pictures. The public rooms are no less luxurious and individual. But, for many visitors, it is the quality of the meals – particularly the dinners – that contributes most to the glow of well-being which a stay here generates.

That tribute to John Tovey's famous establishment is taken from the first edition of the Guide, written in 1977. There are few hotels that can sustain ovations for nine successive curtain calls (theatrical metaphors come only too easily in connection with *Miller Howe*), and can maintain both their form and their individual character in the face of so much international acclaim. The innovative nature of John Tovey's style of cooking, especially his audacious way with vegetables (commemorated in 1985 with the publication of his *Versatile Vegetables*), is increasingly recognised; he has many imitators, but the taste of *Miller Howe* is something else again. And, what is important for this Guide, the pleasure of a visit to his hotel is not just the enjoyment of a memorable meal, but a comprehensive experience. Of course there is the occasional dissenter: we had one letter this year from a lady who became disgruntled at not finding a telephone in her room, and at having to feed a hungry public phone with 10p pieces; who minded there not being a proper bar; and who by the time she sat down to dinner was in the mood to fret at the meal taking two and a half hours. The *Miller Howe* style doesn't suit all comers. But the following is a far more typical reaction: "... the first time I have ever walked into a hotel room and thought it was better than I had expected! Our room was lovely and the views magnificent – well worth the bit extra to get that view. The food was superb. John Tovey and his entire staff are very attentive and don't miss a trick. The whole place was incredibly manicured and profuse with flowers. I had read that the house was a bit close to the busy Bowness Road, but once in the driveway an incredible peacefulness takes over. Our visit to *Miller Howe* made our vacation extra special." *(Marna Davis)*

Open Mar–Early Dec.
Rooms 13 double – 11 with bath, 2 with shower; all with radio, TV on request.
Facilities 4 lounges, 2 dining rooms, sun-lounge terrace; conferences out of season. 4-acre grounds with landscaped garden and views over Windermere. Quick access to walking and climbing country; tennis nearby; sailing, fishing and water sports; lake steamer service.
Location On A592 N of Bowness.
Restrictions Not suitable for &. No children under 12. No dogs in public rooms.
Credit cards Access, Amex, Diners.
Terms (Excluding 12% service charge) dinner, B&B £48–£75. Set dinner £20. Weekend, spring and autumn breaks.
Service/tipping: "A surcharge of 12½% is added to all final accounts in lieu of gratuities." Note: Tom and Diane Peter, formerly of Miller Howe, *have opened* Uplands, *Cartmel (q.v.), in the* Miller Howe *manner.*

Quarry Garth Hotel　　　　　　　　　*Tel* Windermere (096 62) 3761
Windermere LA23 1LF

A hotel new to the Guide, and a relatively new conversion of a private house set back from the Windermere/Ambleside road, with a peaceful brook meandering through the eight acres of grounds. Owner-chef is Rudolf Schaefer, from Germany originally and more recently a manager of another Windermere hotel and lecturer at a catering college. "It feels as if one were calling on friends . . . A new drive leads through lawns and rhododendron bushes – past a splendid sparkling stream – to the back of the house. The door opens on to a panelled hall and open lounge with a log fire, and a view across the gardens to the lake. The adjoining dining room sparkled with silver and cut glass, while upstairs the bedrooms were spacious and prettily decorated and furnished. Bedside lights were adequate and the beds comfortable. Old-fashioned central heating was effective – but noisy in the night. Service was quiet, simple, but most efficient, and the food was excellent with a good choice, and several dishes prepared with an unexpected flair. We left with the genuine enjoyment of a peaceful and beautiful place – and it is very reasonably priced." *(Angela and David Stewart; also Donald Clarke)*

Open All year.
Rooms 8 double, 1 single [work on *en suite* bathrooms is being done in winter 1985/86 and will be completed spring 1986] – all have TV and tea-making facilities.
Facilities Reception lounge, residents' lounge, restaurant. 8½-acre grounds with stream and woodlands; ½ m from Lake Windermere.
Location 1 m N of Windermere on the main road mid-way between Windermere and Ambleside.
Restrictions Not suitable for &. No dogs in public rooms.
Credit cards None accepted.

Terms Dinner, B&B: single £20–£28, double £36–£56. Set lunch £6 (packed lunches available), set dinner £10.50; full alc £15. Mid-week breaks Nov–Mar, special full-board rate for Christmas and New Year. 50% reduction for children sharing parents' room; special meals.

WINDSOR Berkshire   Map 2

Oakley Court Hotel [GFG]   *Tel* Maidenhead (0628) 74141
Windsor Road, Windsor SL4 5UR   *Telex* 849958 OAKCT

No charming little coutry hideaway, but a real show-place mansion, built in 1859, half French château, half romantic Gothic, full of turrets, towers, castellations and crenellations, used as a set for many Hammer horror films, notably the *Dracula* series – and achieving its present incarnation as a grand hotel in 1981 after a £5 million conversion. There are 91 rooms, including 19 suites, and 30 acres of ground leading down to the Thames, on which the hotel has a quarter of a mile of fishing rights. Furnishing tends towards the ornate which admirably suits the style of the house, though there is also a modern annexe. The restaurant is in the hands of Murdo McSween, formerly of *The Elms*, Abberley (q.v.), a Master Chef of Great Britain, who has introduced a Menu Gourmand at £30 in addition to the regular set dinner menu at £17 [1985 prices]. Large expensive hotels, close to capital cities (London 28 miles) and to airports (Heathrow 15 minutes), are often much of a muchness, inevitably catering for conferences and banquets and passengers in transit. But *Oakley Court* has individuality and class: everyone speaks warmly of the welcoming staff, the food is dependably excellent. And Windsor is only three miles up the road. (*Mary McCleary Posner, D J C Bernard, W A*)

Open All year.
Rooms 19 suites, 72 double – all with bath, telephone, radio, colour TV, and baby-listening; 24-hour room service.
Facilities Residents' lounge, drawing room, reading room, library, cocktail bar, dining room, billiard room. 30-acre grounds with terrace, patio, croquet lawn, 9-hole pitch-and-putt course, exclusive fishing rights on Thames for ¼ m, landing stage; boat trips, tennis and squash nearby.
Location 3 m from Windsor and Maidenhead. Leave M4 at junction 6 then take A355 to Windsor roundabout; follow A308 to Maidenhead for 2 m. Parking for 120 cars.
Restrictions Not suitable for &. No babies in restaurant for evening meal. No dogs.
Credit cards All major cards accepted.
Terms B&B: single £57–£62, double £72–£77. Set lunch £12, dinner £18; full alc £38. Bar lunches available. Weekend dinner, B&B breaks (2 nights), 3-day Christmas package. Reduced rates for children sharing parents' room; 50% reduction in restaurant for children under 12.

Deadlines: nominations for the 1987 edition should reach us not later than 15 May 1986. Latest date for comments on existing entries: 30 June 1986.

Important reminder: terms printed must be regarded as a rough guide only to the size of the bill to be expected at the end of your stay. For latest tariffs, check when booking.

WITHERSLACK Cumbria   Map 4

The Old Vicarage [GFG]   *Tel* Witherslack (044 852) 381
Witherslack
Grange-over-Sands LA11 6RS

This little Georgian hotel is situated in beautiful walking country south
of Lake Windermere, and, though only 15 minutes from the M6, it is
quiet and secluded, away from the heart of the village. Roger and Jill
Burrington-Brown and Stanley and Irene Reeve run the hotel informally
as a joint enterprise. The rooms are delightfully furnished – William
Morris curtains, Heal's lampshades, lots of pine and cane in the
bedrooms, ample reading light. The emphasis is on quality – a few
rooms beautifully equipped and furnished; nothing flash, but first-rate
and imaginative. The hotel's cooking is warmly commended. Home-
made rolls are a speciality. There is a five-course set menu dinner – no
choice except at the dessert stage where both a hot and cold sweet are
offered, and you are warmly encouraged to have both.

Ever since *The Old Vicarage* appeared in the Guide in 1982, it has been
garnering compliments of the most unstinted kind from its grateful
parishioners. This year is no exception. Words like "flair", "dedication",
"perfection", and expressions like "haven of peace", "enjoyed every
mouthful", "experience not to be missed", constantly recur. Dinners are
"a gastronomic event". Rooms, even the smaller ones, are commended
for their harmonious decor and the many thoughtful extras. (*Dr C W
Nicholls, I Tashlick, H W Gallagher, Dr H B Cardwell, Rosamund Hebdon,
N Robertson, Eileen Chatten, The Rt Rev Peter Coleman*)

Open All year except Christmas week.
Rooms 7 double – 3 with bath, 4 with shower, all with telephone, radio, colour TV
and tea-making facilities.
Facilities Lounge, bar lounge, 2 dining rooms, breakfast room. 1-acre gardens,
3-acre woodlands, sea 5 m, Lake Windermere 6 m, river fishing 6 m. Fell-walking.
Location From M6 take exit 36; follow route to Barrow-in-Furness. Turn off A590
signposted Witherslack and take first turn left past phone-box. Hotel is ½ m along
this lane on left.
Restrictions Not suitable for ♿. Children under 10 by arrangement only. Dogs
only by arrangement and not in public rooms.
Credit cards All major cards accepted.
Terms (Service at guests' discretion) B&B: single £31.50–£39.50, double £50–£59;
dinner, B&B: single £45–£53, double £55–£86. Dinner £13.50 (£14.50 non-
residents). Special mid-week/weekend breaks; "Autumn into Spring" breaks
Nov–Mar. Reduced rates for children sharing parents' room; special meals.
*Tipping: "Our policy is that we do not encourage or expect tips from our customers.
However, it would be dishonest to say that we do not appreciate the extras we occasionally
receive."*

WITHINGTON Gloucestershire   Map 2

Halewell   *Tel* Withington (024 289) 238
Withington, Cheltenham GL54 4BN

A country home hotel or sophisticated guest-house, Halewell *is a venerable
15th-century manor house in an equally venerable village tucked away in the
folds of the Cotswolds: it has beautiful grounds with fine views, a heated*

swimming pool and a private lake stocked with trout. Rooms are very comfortable and un-hotel-like, filled with family pieces of the hostess, Mrs Carey-Wilson. Dinner is taken en famille *in a splendid panelled dining room, and coffee afterwards in the solar above. "Clearly when host and hostess eat together," we wrote last year when introducing* Halewell *to these pages, "there is an element of pot luck – for both parties – and* Halewell *does not pretend to culinary distinction." We need to repeat this message: one visitor this year found her hostess stand-offish and another, who felt the quality of the house deserved a higher standard of cooking, was disconcerted by the strongly voiced prejudices of a member of the household. More reports please.*

Open All year.
Rooms 6 double (2 with dressing rooms, suitable for families) – all with bath, colour TV, tea-making facilities and baby-listening; 1 ground-floor room specially designed for the physically handicapped; 2 self-catering units.
Facilities TV lounge, bar, study, drawing room, dining room with sitting area for coffee etc. 50-acre grounds, with swimming pool (heated Jun–Sept), trout lake, children's ponies, badminton, ping-pong. The lake covers 6 acres and is suitable for wet-and-dry-fly fishing (not safe for swimming). Table tennis available in stables for children. Tennis by arrangement in village. &.
Location 8 m E of Cheltenham, 9 m N of Cirencester. Take A40 from M5 or Oxford; take Andoversford turn-off from A40.
Restriction Dogs by arrangement and not allowed in public rooms.
Terms (No fixed service charge) B&B: single occupancy £29, double £45; dinner, B&B: single occupancy £39, double £65. £2 surcharge per room for stay of only one night; premium of £5 per person for stay of only one night the night of Cheltenham Gold Cup Race (normally second week Mar). Set dinner £10. Reduced rates and special meals for children.

WIVELISCOMBE Somerset   Map 1

Hurstone Farmhouse   *Tel* Wiveliscombe (0984) 23441
Waterrow, Wiveliscombe TA4 2AT

This far-off-the-beaten-track farmhouse hotel (or whatever) has one of the lowest tariffs to be found in our Guide, and is "really wonderful value for money". There are fine views down the combe and up the far hillside from the windows of the Georgian farmhouse, which the "tremendously courteous" John Bone has been running as a hotel for the past five years. It is a great place for walkers, both within the farm's 65 acres and beyond. "One couple had done 25 miles the day we arrived, but the three-course evening menu – hot baked courgettes and tomatoes gratiné (soup kindly offered for the children), game pie – excellent pastry – with young venison, mushrooms, parsnips, cabbage and baked potato, *fresh* fruit salad and cream – was generous enough even for their appetites. There is a wood-burning stove in the drawing room, and John Bone has this year added a charming old stripped pine bar in the dining room, rescued from a derelict pub. Most guests choose to drink his home-made cider, though the house red (no wine list) is decent enough. Friendly practical welcome. Excellent breakfasts deftly served. Not a sophisticated hotel, but it is comfortable, pleasantly decorated without ostentation and with newly appointed bathrooms. It is a gorgeous, peaceful spot, and the silence almost rings in your ears." *(A L; endorsed by Derek Hill, Dip and Charles Wheeler)*

Open All year.
Rooms 1 suite (double and single room with bath), 2 double, 1 single self-catering cottage with 2 bedrooms, kitchen, sitting room and bathroom.
Facilities Sitting room with TV and log fire, baby-listening. Bar/dining room; terrace and gardens; 65-acre farmland – nature trail in process of construction; small river borders farm. Wimbleball Lake (10 m away) provides sailing and trout fishing. Riding, tennis, golf nearby.
Location ¼ m off A361 at Waterrow.
Restrictions Not suitable for ৬. Dogs by arrangement only.
Credit cards None accepted.
Terms (No service charge) B&B £9.50–£12.50; dinner, B&B £15.50–£18.50. Set lunch £3, dinner £6. Weekend and mid-week breaks Oct–April except public holidays; off-season courses in arts and crafts. Reduced rates for children; special meals by arrangement.

Langley House [GFG]   *Tel* Wiveliscombe (0984) 23318
Langley Marsh, Wiveliscombe
TA4 2UF

A mainly Georgian country house on the peaceful outskirts of a small country town in the folds of the Brendon Hills – "at the heart", to quote the owners, Francis and Rosalind McCulloch, "of undiscovered Somerset". The McCullochs, now in their ninth year here, have filled their house with visual pleasures – good quality furnishings, fine silver and crystal tableware, and lots of fresh flowers. Rosalind McCulloch is an admirable and imaginative cook, and enthusiastic reports, this year as previously, record the pleasures of her table as well as all the other features of the house. "The personal welcome and attention are heart-warming in these days of so much uninterested impersonal service encountered in other hotels." *(D I Beddeley; also Hester Pean, P K Hall, C J Wall)*

Open Mar–Oct.
Rooms 5 double, 1 single – 4 with bath, 2 with shower, all with TV, 1 with 4-poster.
Facilities Lounge, lounge with bar, sun room, beamed dining room; small conference facilities. 3-acre landscaped grounds; stabling for 8 horses; kitchen garden. Riding nearby; trout fishing 2 m. Fine walking country.
Location ½ m W of Wiveliscombe. Take Langley Marsh and Huish Champflower road.
Restrictions Only restaurant suitable for ৬. No children under 7. No dogs in public rooms.
Credit cards None accepted.
Terms B&B: single £24.90, double £45; dinner, B&B: single £36.90, double £69. Set dinner £12–£17. 2- and 3-day mid-week breaks; gourmet weekends.

WOODSTOCK Oxfordshire   Map 2

The Feathers [GFG]   *Tel* Woodstock (0993) 812291
Market Street, Woodstock OX7 1SX   *Telex* 83138 TELKAY G

We had our first entry for *The Feathers* last year, and heralded it as a considerable asset to the region. A 17th-century building, it is in the centre of this show-place village, and within a few minutes' stroll of the breath-taking vista of Blenheim Palace. Opened in 1983, it had been extensively renovated from its previous incarnation as The Dorchester

Arms. We had encountered teething-troubles on an early visit of our own, but later reports suggested that it was settling down well. However, from an extensive postbag – an indication doubtless of how much good hotels are in demand in the Oxford area – it is clearly something of a curate's egg at the moment. Reports tend to be highly contradictory. Some have found the staff smiling and helpful, others the reverse. Almost everyone appreciates the breakfasts, but dinner dishes have pleased and disappointed in about equal degree. One guest reckoned that he had found a real bargain among the wines, but felt that the list as a whole was haphazard. Public rooms were well warmed, some bedrooms glacial in a cold spell. All the rooms are well appointed, but some are small to the point of pokiness, and one correspondent minded a flimsy lavatory seat "like the one in our garden loo which I have always regretted economising on." A bed was said to have a peculiar transverse sag, "which left us lying like a pair of supine bananas". Some rooms had noisy plumbing. At the same time, many guests have praised the hotel for its general comfort and discreet elegance, and thoroughly enjoyed their stay. It is emphatically an asset in the neighbourhood, and we hope for a less ambivalent set of reports next year.

Open All year.
Rooms 13 double, 2 single – 13 with bath, 2 with shower, all with telephone, radio and colour TV.
Facilities Residents' drawing room, lounge, bar, dining room. Courtyard garden (drinks and meals served in fine weather). & restaurant only.
Location In centre of village. Limited parking.
Restriction Dogs by prior arrangement; not in public rooms.
Credit cards All major cards accepted.
Terms B&B: single £38–£58, double £58–£88; dinner, B&B: single £53–£73, double £88–£118; full board: single £62–£82, double £106–£136. Set lunch £11.50, dinner £15.50; full alc £19.50. Mid-week and weekend rates available from Oct–April. Reduced rates and special meals for children.

WOOLACOMBE Devon   Map 1

Little Beach Hotel [GFG]   *Tel* Woolacombe (0271) 870398
The Esplanade, Woolacombe EX34 7DJ

The small resort of Woolacombe has one great natural advantage – the three-mile stretch of Woolacombe Sands that frame Morte Bay. The *Little Beach Hotel* is an Edwardian residence, carefully restored in character, run in a civilised and professional fashion by Nic Lowes and Alan Bradley. The rooms facing the bay are the ones to go for. Most guests, this year as previously, have much enjoyed their visits – "a happy place to stay", "a perfect small hotel", "one just feels at home", "hospitality with friendliness". The food, cooked by Alan Bradley, the decor, the reasonable prices all come in for commendation. However, a minority view has surfaced this year: no specific complaints of substance, only a suggestion that the hotel may not be equally sympathetic to all comers. *(Miss S A Targett, Stephen John Payne, Dr J B Stewart, J K M Swift, Hannelore Pistorius, S Stephens, Derek Gifford)*

Give the Guide positive support. Don't just leave feedback to others.

Open Feb–Oct.
Rooms 8 double, 2 single – 4 with bath, 4 with shower, all with radio and baby-listening.
Facilities Drawing room, TV lounge, sun lounge, bar, dining room; sauna, solarium. Small garden with sun terraces; swimming, surfing, safe sandy beach; riding, fishing, golf within 5 m.
Location On sea front. Parking.
Restrictions Not suitable for &. No dogs in dining room. No age limit for children but food and meal-times not always suitable for the very young.
Credit cards Access, Visa.
Terms B&B £13.50–£20.50; dinner, B&B £21.50–£28.50. Bar lunches only (from £2.50); set dinner £9.75. Reduced rates for stays of 2 days or more and for children.
Service/tipping: Service included in price; tipping not encouraged.

WOOLHOPE Hereford and Worcester   Map 2

The Butchers Arms   *Tel* Fownhope (043 277) 281
Woodhope HR1 4RF

An example of that disappearing species, an honest old-fashioned country inn. Woodhope is a small village, equidistant (eight miles each) from Hereford, Ross and Ledbury, and three miles from the river Wye. *The Butchers Arms*, a black-and-white half-timbered building, dating from the 14th century, is a popular village pub, with low beams and log fires in the bars (good bar snacks), but it also has three small but comfortable rooms, and an enterprising à la carte menu in its restaurant. In our questionnaire, we ask about nightlife. "Only the general atmosphere and hubbub of a country inn," was the answer of Mary Bailey, innkeeper. Visitors continue to enjoy the feel of *The Butchers Arms*. "I particularly liked the quiet soft approach of the proprietor, entirely in keeping with its surroundings," wrote one correspondent, "and I had the best scrambled egg for breakfast that I've had for ages." (*L T Fraser Mackenzie; also Dr and Mrs Machray*)

Open All year. Restaurant closed lunch-times and Sun–Tue though open for residents during winter months. Bar meals served every lunch-time and evening. Only breakfast served on Christmas Day.
Rooms 3 double – all with mono TV and tea-making facilities.
Facilities Lounge bar, public bar, restaurant; patio garden leading to small stream.
Location 8 m SE of Hereford, take B4224; at Mordiford turn left to Woolhope; at T-junction take left turn; *Butchers Arms* is ¼ m outside village.
Restrictions Not suitable for &. No children under 14 in bar in evenings. No dogs.
Credit cards None accepted.
Terms (No service charge) B&B £12.50–£13.50; bar lunch £4.60; full alc £11.20. Bargain breaks Oct–Mar (except Easter): any 2 days, dinner, B&B £17–£18.75. Children half-price if sharing parents' room. Special meals on request.
Service/tipping: "We do not add a separate charge to bills. But if a tip is given we do not embarrass the customer by refusing."

WORLESTON Cheshire   Map 2

Rookery Hall [GFG]   *Tel* Nantwich (0270) 626866
Worleston, Nr Nantwich CW5 6DQ   *Telex* 367169 ROOKHALL

No common-or-garden English country house hotel, but something altogether more exotic – a Victorian Gothic château, though parts date

201

back to Georgian times, set in 28 acres of garden and parkland, with fountains and statuary and a small lake thick with water lilies. Until last year it was owned and run by a flamboyant hotel-keeper, Harry Norton – endearing to some, grating on others – but the place has now been bought by Audrey and Peter Marks. They are a couple new to the hotel business, but judging by most first reports, are likely to put *Rookery Hall* in the first division of grand country establishments that also have the sympathetic qualities to earn a place in these columns. We did hear from one less-than-satisfied customer who felt the place lacked warmth and had several specific niggles: no beer on offer, except lager; breakfast distinctly less impressive than dinner; and guests sat communally at the breakfast table. Other visitors, however, would agree with the following view:

"Mr Peter Marks, his wife and son David are running a really lovely establishment. They are maintaining the old-established principles of managing a country house hotel. Either Mr Marks or his wife is always on hand in the front hallway to welcome guests. They oversee all of the hotel, not just the paperwork. They take the orders at dinner, they are available in the dining room and they say goodbye when you leave. They engender a feeling of well-being among all who enter the hotel. A small bottle of champagne was in our room upon arrival, and shortly thereafter they arrived with ice to chill it. When they discovered the next day that we had not drunk it, they put a cut-glass decanter of dry sherry in the room, since that is what they had seen us order prior to dinner. The dining room is one of the most beautiful we have ever seen. The panelling gleams with a satin finish achieved over many years. The food is very good. There is obviously an excellent relationship between Mr Marks and the chef. Every course is beautifully presented, as well as marvellous to eat. Our only complaint (and a personal one) is that we find it extremely hard to sit at a dinner table for two and a half hours. The second night, knowing what was ahead, we skipped the fish and cheese courses in order to cut down on the amount of time spent in the dining room. As we were leaving, we noticed that several boys were washing the windows of all the cars in the parking lot. Just another example of the type of service that *Rookery Hall* provides its guests." (*Mary McCleary Posner; also W A, Dr G S Sen*)

Open All year.
Rooms 1 suite, 8 double, 2 single – all with bath, telephone, radio and colour TV; 2 suites in lake-side annexe.
Facilities Hall, 2 sitting rooms, 2 dining rooms. 28-acre garden and parkland with brook, croquet, putting, hard tennis court, coarse fishing, clay pigeon shooting, riverside and woodland walks.
Location From the North, take junction 18 from M6; from the South, junction 16. Hotel is on B5074, 1½ m N of Nantwich (avoid town centre if possible).
Restrictions Not suitable for &. No children under 10. No dogs.
Credit cards All major cards accepted.
Terms (Service at guests' discretion) Dinner, B&B £62.50–£75. Set lunch £12.95, dinner £22.50; full alc £12.95. £5 reduction per person per day for minimum stay of 2 nights Oct–Mar.
Service/tipping: "There is no service charge – this is left to the discretion of our guests."

> Please write and confirm an entry when it is deserved. If you think that a hotel is not as good as we say, please write and tell us.

Middlethorpe Hall [GFG]   *Tel* York (0904) 641241
Bishopthorpe Road, York YO2 1QP   *Telex* 57802 MIDDLE G

Middlethorpe is the second noble house to be rescued from decay by Historic Houses Ltd, the company which brought us *Bodysgallen Hall* (q.v.). Built in the reign of William III, and subsequently the home of the diarist Lady Mary Wortley Montagu, it is a pedigree mansion, with gardens and parkland appropriate to its grandeur. It opened its doors in the spring of 1984 and almost at once we began to get glowing accounts of its splendour. Last year's entry was long and ecstatic. Here is a fresh view, no less entranced: "A rousing 'aye'. I would happily send anyone here. Do warn those with heavy luggage to draw up before the gates and allow the liveried footman (nice and cheerful, not intimidating, just the old family retainer type) to take in your bags. Everything here is shiny and bright and polished and cheerful. Nice big drawing room and library, comfortable chairs, prospect of smooth green lawns and distant hayfield, garden to one side. Helpful barman, pleasant head waiter, friendly manager. There are enough pot plants, settees, comfortable chairs, little tables and objects about to feel like home; none of that museum-like atmosphere you get at some of those grand houses. My pleasant smallish bedroom appeared to be papered in maroon suede trimmed with broad embroidered ribbon, all clever painting and papering. Nice prints; good bathroom, plenty of fat white towels, amusing good-quality small bits and pieces – everything charming and pleasing and thoughtful, down to the trouser press and pomander in the cupboard. Restaurant: starched white cloths, good silver, slightly slow service, good food – chef trained with Christian Delteil at *Chewton Glen* – need I say more?" *(W A; also R S Ryder, and others)*

Open All year.
Rooms 3 suites, 21 double, 6 single – all with bath and shower, direct-dial telephone, radio and colour TV; 1 4-poster. 20 rooms in annexe. Some ground-floor rooms.
Facilities Lift. 3 sitting rooms, library, drawing room, bar, cellar restaurant, dining room. Private dining facilities. 26-acre grounds with dovecote, walled garden and lake. York racecourse and golf course nearby.
Location 1½ m S of York, by racecourse.
Restrictions Children under 8 at management's discretion. No dogs.
Credit cards All major cards accepted.
Terms B&B (continental): single £50, double £70–£90; dinner, B&B: single £70, double £90–£110; full board; single £80, double £100–£120. Set lunch £10, dinner £17.50; full alc £22. 10% discount on room rate for stays of 7 nights or more.

Mount Royale Hotel   *Tel* York (0904) 28856
The Mount, York YO2 2DA

A hotel of character, Gothic in appearance, William IV in the main though with a modern extension, near the racecourse, a few minutes' walk from Micklegate Bar and three-quarters of a mile from the Minster. One of its great attractions is a one-and-a-half-acre garden with heated swimming pool. Its major drawback for light sleepers is traffic noise in front rooms, though mitigated by double-glazing. It is run with verve by

Richard and Christine Oxtoby, who tell us that the five-bedroom development, predicted last year, is now scheduled for this winter.

As in previous years, reports have been predominantly favourable, though two middle-aged professional women travelling together had a sorry tale of a bungled booking and felt the apologies had not been adequate for the inconvenience and disappointment. They also reported off-hand treatment in the restaurant. Two readers mentioned poor cooking of vegetables, overcooked and very salty in one case, almost raw in the other. But the account below is more typical of our *Royale* mail:

"I particularly asked for a quiet room – and it certainly was. A lovely large room, complete with four-poster and private bathroom, TV, suit press, hair dryer, kettle etc, overlooking the very attractive garden. I was even more impressed with the sofa and the space to move around. Everything worked, too. The garden was most attractive, as was the whole hotel. Nice bits of furniture. The staff were exceptionally pleasant – particularly at the reception. The waitresses were cheerful local ladies, but it pricked my social conscience to be served by rather elderly grannies who clearly had sore feet by the end of the evening. The food was excellent value for money – a delicious dinner, with enormous portions. Breakfast was incredible: the whole cooked breakfast bit with black pudding. Endless coffee, plus newspapers. Lunch was unnecessary after that breakfast. Not cheap perhaps, but not expensive by British standards." *(Penny Duckham; also Brain Bartram, Jane Bailey)*

Open All year except 24 Dec–7 Jan.
Rooms 1 suite, 17 double, 1 single – all with bath, telephone, radio, colour TV, baby-listening and tea-making facilities.
Facilities Residents' lounge, bar, bar lounge, dining room with conservatory. 1½-acre grounds with heated swimming pool.
Location On A64 from Tadcaster (front rooms have double-glazed windows). Hotel is on right just before traffic lights at junction with Albemarle Road opposite sign to Harrogate (A59). Parking for 24 cars.
Restrictions Not suitable for &. Dogs by arrangement.
Credit cards All major cards accepted.
Terms B&B: single £37.50–£45, double £55–£65. Set dinner £14.50. 2-day breaks (excluding bank holidays). Reduced rates for children sharing parents' room; special meals by arrangement.

PORTH TOCYN, ABERSOCH

ABERDOVEY Gwynedd Map 3

Plas Penhelig *Tel* Aberdovey (065 472) 676
Aberdovey LL35 0NA

A small Edwardian country house hotel overlooking the Dovey estuary
in the Snowdonia National Park. "*Plas Penhelig* sits on a sunny ledge on
the hill behind Aberdovey: the drive winds up through woods of
camellia and rhododendron. As you open the front door, you are aware
of fragrant wood-smoke from the open log fire; there are sofas and
armchairs set about invitingly in the spacious oak-panelled hall-lounge,
and glimpses of a pretty drawing room as you pass to the reception
desk. There are fresh flowers from the garden, and pleasant staff
discreetly there if you need them: a most attractive atmosphere. The
bedroom was large and airy, and looked out over the hotel's gardens to
the Dovey estuary and the hills beyond. Everything was immaculately
clean and fresh, though possibly the furnishings could have been more
imaginative. There is a large terrace on the side of the house with doors
opening on to it from bar and dining room which must be delightful in
the summer. Trees seclude the hotel completely from the town below,
and it is a place of utter peace and tranquillity." This earlier commendation has mostly been endorsed by subsequent visitors, with special
praise this year for the comfort of a single room. But one reader
complained of the constraint of house "rules": no early morning coffee
before 7.30 am, and the expectation that guests should come down at

7.30 pm for a drink and to order dinner. Also there was no sign of a promised radio.

Open Mar–Oct.
Rooms 12 double – 11 with bath, 1 with shower, all with direct-dial telephone; TV on request.
Facilities Hall/lounge, large drawing room, cocktail bar, dining room; banqueting/conference facilities. 14-acre grounds with 7-acre garden; tennis, putting and croquet. Overlooks Dovey Estuary and Cardigan Bay; sandy beach, fishing, sailing, bathing. Golf, pony-trekking and rock-climbing nearby.
Location ¼ m W of Aberdovey on A493 to Tywyn; hotel drive is on right just after Outward Bound school by small public car park.
Restrictions Not suitable for &. Dogs in owners' cars only.
Credit cards All major cards accepted.
Terms (No service charge) B&B: £17.50–£21; dinner, B&B £28.50–£41 per person. Bar lunches from £2.25; set dinner from £10; full alc £12.50. Golfing breaks, bargain breaks. Reductions and special meals for children on request.

ABERGAVENNY Gwent   Map 3

Crowfield   *Tel* Abergavenny (0873) 5048
Ross Road, Abergavenny ND7 8NH

A virtually derelict 17th-century farmhouse on the southern slopes of the Skirrid mountain in the Brecon Beacons National Park has been reincarnated by George and Sasha Crabb in the past few years into a smart welcoming modern inn. Readers continue to endorse an earlier report: "If you ever wished you had a country house without the problems it would entail, wish no more but spend your next weekend *chez* Crabb. *Crowfield* has a comfort and sort of *laissez-faire* rarely found in hotels. The Crabbs are welcoming but unobtrusive, ready to join musical guests in a duet on the beautiful Bechstein but vanishing to produce a delicious dinner seemingly effortlessly. They are the best kind of hosts, somewhat French in their attitude, laying down commonsense rules in the beginning – no pets in the hotel, no children under 12 – then relaxing completely. The rooms and bathrooms are warm, generous and simply furnished, perhaps from clever buys at auction sales; the colours are plain and restful." *(G V; also Eithne Scallan, Ceridwen Brown)*

Open All year except one week at Christmas.
Rooms 4 double with bath, 1 single with shower; all rooms in converted barn; 2 ground-floor rooms suitable for partially &.
Facilities Sitting room with TV, bar lounge, bar, dining room (dinner served 7 pm). 3-acre grounds in magnificent countryside with lakes and rivers.
Location 2 m NE of town centre on B4521 Skenfrith/Ross road.
Restrictions No children under 12; no dogs.
Credit cards None accepted.
Terms [1985 rates] B&B: single £24, double £36. Set dinner £10; full alc in bar (serving hours more flexible) £9.50.

ABERSOCH Gwynedd   Map 3

Porth Tocyn Hotel [GFG]   *Tel* Abersoch (075 881) 2966
Abersoch LL53 7BU

"Really lovely in every way. Unpretentious, friendly, splendid food. I recommend it without reservations." *(Roald Dahl)* Mr Dahl's vote of thanks would be encored by, among others, *John Hills, Anna Robinson, W H Cleghorn, N D Johnson and Christopher Godber*. The hotel they are extolling won a César for excellence as a family hotel in 1984. It has a particularly lovely position on a headland overlooking Cardigan Bay and Snowdonia, and is surrounded by its own 25-acre farm sloping down to the sea a few minutes' stroll away. It has a heated swimming pool and a tennis court, and has been run with conspicuous success for many years by Barbara Fletcher-Brewer and her son Nick. The quality of its cooking is one of the features of the hotel which has come in for special commendation, but the hotel really functions well on all its cylinders. As one reader put it, "Nick F-B never stops working and organising for a moment, and his constant care is reflected in the smooth-running and ultra-friendly atmosphere." Nick F-B himself writes to tell us of all his latest improvements and plans for the future: better insulation, refurbished bathrooms, new carpets etc, and direct-dial telephones shortly. He ends his letter, written in April 1985: "The weather is beautiful; the Lleyn peninsula quiet and peaceful; our prices are at the moment extremely reasonable – but the hotel just about empty ... It is just crazy! It's such a shame that folk crowd their holidays into the period between Whitsun and the end of September."

Open Easter–end Oct. Outside these times ring to check (probably open over Christmas and New Year).
Rooms 14 double, 4 single – all with bath and telephone; radio, TV and tea-making facilities (no extra charge) on request; 3 ground-floor rooms with easy access for &.
Facilities 6 lounges, bar, TV room, garden with hard tennis court and heated (mid-May to end Sept) swimming pool; rock garden, lawns set within the hotel's 25-acre farm; 3 minutes' walk from sea, Heritage coastal walk; sailing, bathing, water skiing, windsurfing, sea fishing; walks; golf and riding nearby.
Location Some 2½ m S of Abersoch, through the hamlets of Sarn Bach and Bwichtocyn. On the outskirts of Abersoch on the Sarn Bach road you will see the first of three highway information signs marked "Gwesty/hotel". These bi-lingual signs refer to Porth Tocyn and combined with the hotel signs will bring you to the door.
Restrictions No children under 7 in dining room at night. Dogs in bedrooms only – bring dog basket.
Credit cards Access, Amex.
Terms (No service charge) B&B: single £23–£30, double £37–£55.50; dinner, B&B: single £33–£44.25, double £57–£84. Set lunch £6.75, dinner £10 (2 courses) or £14.25 (4 courses). Bargain breaks out of season. Reduced rates and special meals for children.

BONTDDU Gwynedd

Map 3

Bontddu Hall *Tel* Bontddu (034 149) 661
Nr Dolgellau LL40 2SU *Telex* 35142

This imposing example of Victorian Gothic, a style more common in Scotland than in Wales, celebrated its 115th birthday last year – it was built (a recondite fact!) by Neville Chamberlain's aunt. 1985 also celebrated Bill Hall's 40th year as *patron*. Few hotel-keepers can boast such a long and successful innings. The *Hall* has a spectacular position, looking over well-landscaped gardens to the Mawddach estuary and the Cader Idris range of mountains: a large terrace provides an agreeable position from which to admire the view while fortifying oneself with drinks, bar snacks and lunch, when the weather allows. It has earned consistently appreciative comments from our readers for its friendly and efficient service, though two recent reports took a dissenting line: lodge rooms over-priced and shabby and food disappointing. A more typical response: "A splendid hotel: wonderful Victorian villa architecture refurbished in decor to provide a theatrical set on which to play out one's stay. Our bedroom was vast, with columns, and a door out to a secluded terrace on which we took our breakfast facing the incomparable view. Welcome and service exemplary. Food imaginative, well cooked and properly presented. A really nice place to stay." *(R S)*

Open Easter–early Oct.
Rooms 2 suites, 19 double, 2 single – 19 with bath, 4 with shower, all with telephone, radio and colour TV; 7 rooms in annexe; 1 double room on ground floor.
Facilities 2 lounges, 2 bars, restaurant. 3-acre grounds with putting green; private path to estuary. Beautiful walks to estuary or up the mountains behind. Quiet sandy beaches nearby; trout, salmon and sea fishing; golf, pony-trekking.
Location On A496 4 m E of Barmouth.
Restrictions No children under 3. No dogs in public rooms.
Credit cards All major cards accepted.
Terms (Service at guests' discretion) B&B: single £24.50–£34.50, double £49–£57; dinner, B&B £34.50–£44.50 per person; full board £39.75–£49.75 per person. "Eat and Eat" buffet lunch £5.45; full alc dinner £19.55. Spring and autumn reductions. Reduced rates for children sharing parents' room; half-price meals from menus.

CARDIGAN Dyfed   Map 3

Rhyd-Garn-Wen   *Tel* Cardigan (0239) 612742
Cardigan SA43 3NW

César awarded in 1985 for most civilised guest-house

A secluded Victorian house, one and a half miles from the sea in a remote and historic area of North Pembrokeshire, is the setting for this highly personal establishment run with flair and dedication by Huw and Susan Jones. Their aim, they say, is to help people to discover, as they have done, "the utter tranquillity of Pembrokeshire, the fantastic scope of its sporting facilities and its wonderful, interesting scenery". We are sure that the Joneses would assent to Nigel Corbett's requirements for running a country house hotel (see page 752), and report after report testifies to their continuing success. "We had the happiest possible time – just like a delightful visit to friends and a lovely atmosphere. We felt the Joneses really wanted us to enjoy every moment. The emphasis is on 'no extras' to an almost embarrassing extent, but what a pleasant change!" *(Anna and Philip Robinson)* "£27.50 for dinner, B&B [1985] is an absolute bargain for those on the receiving end of Susan and Huw Jones's hospitality and cookery. Financial rewards obviously come second for them, several lengths behind exacting standards ... A quite remarkable, I venture to say, unique place." *(Jeff Driver)* "If the Joneses asked me I would happily stay here for the rest of my life ... Their quiet thoughtfulness is what makes their house so special. You don't simply get a lovely place to stay with wonderful food; you get the Joneses as the icing on the cake." *(Charles Suisman)* "Ideal for us ... Quiet and comfortable and full of flowers ... Personal likes and dislikes always remembered." *(Lord Lloyd of Kilgerran)*

Open Easter to Oct.
Rooms 4 double – 2 with bath, 2 with shower. Also suite in stable block, consisting of bedroom, bathroom and sitting room with mono TV and tea-making facilities.
Facilities Drawing room, bar, dining room. 18-acre grounds. Hunting, shooting, fishing by arrangement; stabling for visiting horses, excellent walking country; 2 m from coast; safe swimming, boating, golf; historical sites, lectures and music festivals in vicinity.
Location 3 m from Cardigan, 5 m from Newport (Pemb.); at the Croft crossroad on the main A487 between Cardigan and Fishguard. Garage and outdoor parking.
Restrictions Not suitable for small children or &. No dogs.
Credit card Access.
Terms (No service charge) B&B: £18.50; dinner, B&B £30. Set dinner £12.

CRICKHOWELL Powys

Map 3

Gliffaes Country House Hotel
Crickhowell NP8 1RH

Tel Bwlch (0874) 730371

"Still superb value, and sure, we hope, of its place in the Guide! Cooking much improved, and showed some imaginative touches; there is now a choice between two main courses at dinner. We arrived in time to enjoy the magnificent spread of tea laid out in the lounge between 4 and 6 pm – though it somewhat ruins one's appetite for dinner. The place, par excellence, for us and a number of others, for complete relaxation and absence of constraint, thanks to the hardworking Brabners and their staff: this year's batch of young Antipodean waitresses are as charming as their predecessors. For some of us, a hotel of hotels – or at least a yardstick by which we judge others."

"On arrival we received no welcome; the receptionist was particularly aloof. Our rooms were adequate, but not very clean. The tea/coffee facilities had not been checked in either of our rooms and were incomplete. We were made to feel uncomfortable for mentioning omissions, and there was no apology. The evening meal offered only one main course, which had been ruined in the cooking. Breakfasts very limited. On our departure, no valedictory civilities – they took our money."

Not for the first time, we are faced with totally contradictory reports on this well-bred, slightly "county" country house hotel, Italianate in appearance, two and a half miles from Crickhowell in a choice position overlooking the Usk. Its special glory is the grandeur and beauty of its gardens, "a miniature Kew". It has been owned and run by the Brabner family for more than 35 years. It has never lacked eloquent support from faithful regulars, but the quality of the furnishings and decor, the amiability of the service and the character of the cooking have always been matters of contention. More reports please – from either camp.

Open Mid Mar–end Dec.
Rooms 18 double, 1 single – 16 with bath, 3 with shower, all with radio and tea-making facilities, baby-listening by arrangement.
Facilities 2 sitting rooms, bar, billiard room, sun room, dining room. 29-acre grounds with gardens, croquet lawn, putting green; hard tennis court (£2 per hour). Brown trout and salmon fishing in river Usk; bird-watching, riding, boating, squash and golf nearby.
Location 2½ m W of Crickhowell, 1 m S of A40. Turn left at "Gliffaes" sign.
Restrictions Not suitable for &. No dogs in hotel (kennels available).
Credit cards Access, Amex, Visa.
Terms B&B: single £18.50, double £37–£48; half-board: single £26.25, double £53–£67; full board: single £28.50, double £57–£76. Set lunch £5.80, dinner £8.90. Weekly rates.

DOLGELLAU Gwynedd   Map 3

Gwernan Lake Hotel   *Tel* Dolgellau (0314) 422488
Dolgellau LL40 1TL

"This hotel is like no other in these islands. It has something of an Austrian mountain *Gasthaus*, something of a Scottish fishing inn, something of a French family hotel!" This is the hotel's self-appraisal taken from its leaflet. Our own introduction to this hotel came from an inspector, who reported: "This hotel sounds rather grand but isn't. But it has undeniably got charm. You reach it after about a three-mile drive up a steepish lane which runs south-west from Dolgellau. That puts it some way up the northern slopes of Cader Idris. It's an excellent centre for walks up, round and towards the mountain. It's also extremely peaceful here. The hotel (and its setting) is very unpretentious indeed. No carefully manicured lawns and no grand public rooms or bedrooms. It is cosy rather than elegant: walls of the lounge and bar are covered with Victorian natural pine matchboard, and adorned with hunting trophies; furnishings are mostly 50s-ish but solid and in good taste. Mr Hall is clearly a keen model builder – big model ships get pride of place in the lounge and dining room. Which brings me to the food. It was so good it almost came as a shock after some experiences of the past few weeks. The menu has a huge choice of starters and desserts, but only a single main course. My only reservation about this place concerns the *bedrooms*, in good decorative order, but the furnishings are pretty basic. Limited lighting (just a strip light above the bed and a ceiling light). Hand basin only – no bath. Only two bathrooms for all the guests together – some queuing last thing at night. To sum up, a nice place to stay, especially for walking and fishing. Very peaceful, though not much in the way of grounds. Interior, apart from bedrooms, comfortable; food excellent of its kind. Very good value."

A correspondent fully endorses our inspector's recommendation, while also confirming shortcomings, including inadequate heating in a cool May.

Open Easter to Oct.
Rooms 3 double, 4 single.
Facilities Lounge, bar. 11-acre grounds, 13-acre trout lake; safe sandy beach 10 m.
Location Take Tywyn road from Dolgellau, fork left opposite Idris Garage, go 2 m up Cader Idris Road.
Restrictions Not suitable for &. No children under 4. No dogs.
Credit cards None accepted.
Terms (No service charge) B&B: £13.60; dinner, B&B £22.10 (4 nights or more £21).

DRUIDSTON HAVEN Dyfed   Map 3

Druidstone Hotel   *Tel* Broad Haven (043 783) 221
Druidston Haven
Nr Haverfordwest SA62 3NG

"Very informal always. Laughter is encouraged. Food snobs discouraged. Outdoor active types encouraged, especially those using National Park natural facilities. Activity holidays include climbing, canoeing, land-yachting, archery, sailing." The writer is Jane Bell, answering our question about special features. She and her husband Rod run this laid-back family hotel with its adjoining Activity Centre. The location is magnificent: 20 acres of wild garden and cliff walks on the Pembrokeshire coastal path, with two private paths down to a safe and sandy beach. Our entry last year was based on a long enthusiastic inspector's report. She took the scruffiness in her stride and appreciated Jane Bell's generous cooking and the relaxed unfussed-over atmosphere. "For good food and congenial surroundings in a stunning seaside position, the *Druidstone*," she concluded, "must be hard to beat." Not everyone's idea of a holiday hotel of course, and several reporters this year have found the degree of scruffiness a bit too much and also the cooking not as good as formerly. More reports would be welcome.

Open Dec–Oct inclusive.
Rooms 1 suite, 5 double, 2 single; 4 self-catering cottages.
Facilities Reception, sitting room with TV, bar, dining room; terraces. Occasional live music or theatre by prior arrangement with guests. 20-acre grounds with Activity Centre suitable for children over 11. Pétanque, croquet and field archery; paths to sandy beach with caves and safe bathing; riding, sailing, surfing, diving, waterskiing and squash available nearby. ᐱ (restaurant and 2 cottages).
Location In Haverfordwest take B4341 to Broad Haven; after 3 m fork right to Nolton; ignore turns for 2½ m. At T-junction at Haroldston Farm turn right. 150 yds on, by a field gate, take concealed left turn, signposted Druidston Haven. Over 2 cattle-grids, 500 yds on, hotel is on right.
Restriction No dogs in public rooms.
Credit cards Amex, Visa.
Terms (No service charge) B&B £15; dinner, B&B £25; cottages from £120 per week. Set Sun lunch £7.50; bar lunches; dinner £10.50. Big reductions out of season. Activity holidays: climbing, canoeing etc. Christmas break. Reduced rates and special meals for children.
Service/tipping: "Our policy for tipping is that no service charge is put on any bill, but we do not reject tips offered as I feel that a voluntary contribution for good service received is in order, whereas I strongly resent 12% being added to a bill automatically." •

LLANDDERFEL Gwynedd   Map 3

Palé Hall Hotel [GFG]   *Tel* Llandderfel (067 83) 285
Llandderfel, Bala LL23 7PS

Veteran reporters tell of a new "find" for the Guide in the country hall hotel class: a mansion built on the grand scale by a Scottish coal magnate in 1870, standing in 16 acres of park and grounds. Queen Victoria slept here: you can bathe in the royal bath. "The entrance and vestibule look rather large and forbidding, but once through the double doors into the main hall, all is golden oak panelling, antiques, pictures, fresh flowers, and a great ornately-carved fireplace filled with blazing logs. There are wide soft settees, comfort and warmth and harmonising colours. The main reception rooms lead by handsome doors out of the hall: there is a small room converted into a bar, using white marble from bedroom fireplaces to create the bar itself: next door is the 'boudoir', one of the most charming small rooms we've met anywhere": it is for non-smokers, with a beautiful circular painted ceiling. The dining room has a superb plaster-work ceiling, long windows to the ground, an immense mirror that reflects most of the room; spaciously set tables with attention paid to every detail: a lovely place in which to dine. There is always something different and interesting on the set menu and the choice at each course is wide. At the last meal, we had quite incredibly light soufflés and wonderful sauces and a salver of unusual vegetables, arranged in small portions like an artist's palette – a delight to the eye as well as the palate. The staff are all young and not yet fully trained or experienced, but are very pleasant and helpful. The bedrooms lead off a gallery which runs round three sides of the hall, at first-floor level, and each one is different, its individual colour scheme blending with the bathroom, always with quietly luxurious comfort, and quality in all the fittings and extras. The 'Caernarfon Suite' has a circular bed, and its own jacuzzi behind gauze drapes – no wonder it is greatly in demand. You would certainly need a car to enjoy this hotel to the full – the lovely country is all about you, and Bala Lake a mile or so away. Snowdonia is not far away, but *Palé Hall* itself is outside the main tourist routes. We do feel that it is worth a detour to stay there, and that it will become well known to the discerning – and reasonably affluent – especially as places of this kind are rare in Wales." *(Angela and David Stewart)*

Open All year.
Rooms 2 suites, 15 double, 1 single – all with bath, telephone, radio, colour TV; 2 with private jacuzzi.
Facilities Lift. Hall/lounge, boudoir (non-smoking lounge), gymnasium, sauna, solarium; musical evenings once a month Oct–Apr. 16-acre grounds, heated plunge pool-jacuzzi, close to river Dee with salmon and coarse fishing; sailing, canoeing, rowing and windsurfing available on Lake Bala.
Location 5 m from Bala village.
Restrictions Not ideal for &. No dogs.
Credit cards All major cards accepted.
Terms (No service charge) B&B: single £34.50, double £46–£86; dinner, B&B: single £48.50, double £74–£114. Set lunch £7.95, dinner £14; full alc £19. Vegetarian meals available. Special musical weekends, gourmet weekends in winter; 4-day Christmas package. Two-thirds reduction for children.

LLANDUDNO Gwynedd   Map 3

Bodysgallen Hall [GFG]   *Tel* Deganwy (0492) 84466
Llandudno LL30 1RS   *Telex* 617163 HHH

For those who collect country house hotels, *Bodysgallen* is a must. It is a building rich in architectural and horticultural delights: a 13th-century tower, splendid Elizabethan and Jacobean rooms with oak panelling, great fireplaces, mullioned windows, a 17th-century knot garden, a walled 18th-century rose garden – and many other atmospheric features too numerous to mention here. Snowdonia is a handsome backdrop. Fine castles and gardens abound in the neighbourhood. Since it opened its doors to paying guests four years ago, it has been attracting a plethora of compliments – alike for the palpable creature comforts of the house and for the attentive service. This year has been no exception. There have, it is true, been some minor criticisms: two readers have commented on vegetables being undercooked, a third on their being drowned in butter. More than one reader has stressed that accommodation in the main house is to be preferred to the cottage suites. But the consensus is strongly positive. One correspondent listed all the small touches which had given him pleasure: " . . . like towels changed after my evening bath while I was at dinner; like ginger biscuits by the bedside; like a very well-appointed clothes cupboard; like well-chosen potted plants; like a quick and willing hand with my bags on arrival *and* departure (this ought to be a norm, but is rare)." Another, telling us that our last year's enthusiastic entry had described the hotel to a tee, added, "It is quite simply the best hotel I have ever been in." *(Wendy Davies, Colin Gray; also William Rankin, and others)*

Open All year.
Rooms 9 cottage suites, 18 double, 1 single – all with bath, telephone, radio and colour TV; tea-making facilities in cottages. 2 special cottages with ramps for disabled.
Facilities Hall, drawing room, dining room, library, cocktail bar, conference centre. 42-acres of gardens and parkland with tennis and croquet. Sandy beaches 2 m away. River and sea fishing nearby. &.
Location On B5115, 1½ m S of town centre; parking. (Guests coming by train can be met at Llandudno Junction.)
Restrictions No children under 8. No dogs.
Credit cards All major cards accepted.
Terms (Excluding 10% service charge) Single room £40–£55, double £60–£75; dinner, B&B: single £59.50–£74.50, double £99–£114; full board: single £67.80–£82.80, double £115.60–£130.60. Breakfast £4; set lunch £8.30, dinner £15.50; full alc £25. Out of season champagne breaks, special interest weekends, Christmas package. 10% discount for stays of 7 nights or more.

The St Tudno Hotel   *Tel* Llandudno (0492) 74411
North Parade, Llandudno LL30 2LP

Possibly the only Guide hotel on the promenade of a popular sea-front resort. The *St Tudno*, opposite the pier and ornamental gardens, boasts of its connection with Alice Liddell, the original "Alice in Wonderland", who stayed here in what was then a private house in 1861, at the age of eight. But the hotel needs no specious literary connections: its merits are that of a thoroughly well-run, smart, attractive modern hotel. It recently won a red star from the AA, the only seaside resort hotel in Britain to receive that honour. *Michelin* also gives its entry in red as an unusually agreeable hotel. Our nominator, moving here from an indifferent Trusthouse Forte hotel, found it "excellent in every way. First-rate facilities. Good food and wine. The hotel realises that it has a good reputation and works hard to live up to it." *(Richard Whiting; also George Maddocks)*

Open All year except for 2–3 weeks in Jan. (Christmas 1986 opening not yet confirmed.)
Rooms 1 suite, 19 double, 1 single – 19 with bath, 2 with shower, all with telephone, radio, colour TV and tea-making facilities; baby-listening by telephone; ground-floor double room with shower.
Facilities Lift. Non-smoking residents' sitting room, coffee lounge, bar lounge, restaurant; indoor heated swimming pool. Hotel is on promenade; safe sandy beaches, pier, boat rides, fishing, sailing, wind-surfing; 3 golf courses close by.
Location Central, opposite pier. Free promenade parking and small car park at rear of hotel.
Restrictions Not suitable for &. Small, well-behaved dogs allowed by prior arrangement.
Credit cards All major cards accepted.
Terms (No sevice charge) B&B: £16.50–£36; dinner, B&B: £29–50. Set Sun lunch £7.25; dinner £14. Long and short breaks all year; winter weekend breaks.

Reductions according to age for children sharing parents' room; high tea.
Service/tipping: "We do feel that if customers enjoy kind, considerate and personalised service and feel inclined to tip, that they should be allowed to do so. As hoteliers, we would never dream of adding a service charge automatically."

LLANRWST Gwynedd

Map 3

Meadowsweet Hotel [GFG] *Tel* Llanrwst (0492) 640732
Station Road, Llanrwst LL26 ODS

It is now five years since John and Joy Evans, in their Victorian home on the outskirts of the tiny market town of of Llanrwst, turned themselves from first-class restaurateurs into hotel-keepers. With the river Conwy 200 yards from the hotel, and Snowdonia a few miles up the road, *Meadowsweet* would make a good base for a fishing or walking holiday. Don't be put off by the immediate environs of the house or the fact that it is right on the road; the distant prospects – of meadows and mountains – greatly please, and traffic dies away during the night. Apart from one comprehensive raspberry – a rotten room, a disappointing meal, with none of the wines ordered being available, and more frustrations besides – the *Meadowsweet* file has once again been almost entirely complimentary. The rooms are agreeably furnished, and the elegant dining room, to quote one reader, "a worthy setting for food of the highest distinction, and for wine from an extensive cellar. A changing spectrum of waitresses was on hand to attend to our needs pleasantly, without frills, and even with wit and humour. ... Breakfast presented a great range of possibilities at all stages from figs to black puddings, but more conventional tastes were well catered for. Long may Mr Evans give culinary excellence to this part of North Wales!" *(W H Bruton; also Dr D E Parry-Pritchard, J P Berryman, Nan and Lawrence Payne, Heather Kirk, H Richards)*

Open All year.
Rooms 10 double – all with shower, direct-dial telephone and colour TV.
Facilities Bar lounge, residents' lounge, both with log fire, dining room. Salmon fishing, horse-riding, golf within easy reach; Sea 10 m.
Location ¼ m N of town centre on A470. Car park. (Rooms at back are quietest.)
Restrictions Not suitable for &. Dogs allowed, but not in public rooms. No smoking in dining room.
Credit cards Access, Amex, Visa.
Terms (No service charge) B&B £15.50–£22; dinner, B&B £27–£33.50. Set lunch £6.50, dinner £12.50; full alc £14.50. Special rates for stays of 2 days or more; Christmas and New Year house parties. Reduced rates and special meals for children sharing parents' room.
Service/tipping: "We make no service charge. If guests ask we inform them that anything they leave will be shared amongst staff."

If you have had recent experience of a good hotel that ought to be in the Guide, please write to us at once. Report forms are to be found at the back. Procrastination is the thief of the next edition.

We invited all British hotels to tell us of their policy on service charges and tipping. Many hotels ignored this question. Replies, when given, are printed at the end of an entry.

LLANWDDYN Powys   Map 3

Lake Vyrnwy Hotel [GFG]   *Tel* Llanwddyn (069 173) 244
Llanwddyn, via Oswestry
Shropshire SY10 OLY

César awarded for preserving traditional values in a sporting hotel

"A comfortable old-fashioned sporting hotel that makes no concession
to any modern image" is the disarming claim made by Mrs Moir and
Colonel Sir John Baynes, about their solidly built turn-of-the-century
Tudor-style mansion standing 150 feet above the lake, and looking down
its four-and-a-half-mile length. (Note: it is in north Powys, despite the
misleading postal address.) The claim is true and helpful. Some will find
the upper- and middle-class atmosphere a bit oppressive (ties *de rigueur*
at dinner, for instance) and seek their pleasure elsewhere. Others will
relish the dependable virtues of large well-cooked unashamedly English
meals – much above the regional norm, incidentally – the attentive but
not obsequious service, the solidly comfortable deep armchairs in the
lounges, the impeccable silver and drapery in the dining room, the
abundance of flowers everywhere, the absence of anything gimcrack or
gimmicky. It's a hotel that puts itself out for country pursuits, especially
for fishing (the hotel has sole fishing rights on the whole lake and gives
priority to its residents) and shooting. But it also makes a wonderful
centre for a walking holiday or for exploring the country by car. As one
correspondent put it, "If you pick your time, you can have a wonderful
open-air holiday without the slaughtering that goes under the name of
sports impinging upon you." A man in a wheelchair wrote to express his
appreciation for the special trouble taken for his comfort. Another
contributor to this year's "vote of thanks" file came from a participant in
an embroidery weekend in January, along with a party of shooters:
"Although the hotel was busy, we had every consideration – a large
lounge for our stitchery which wasn't cleared up. As 13 ladies, we ate
well and our wines were served with care. It was ideal. We were treated
very well. One can be rather ignored you know." (*Mr and Mrs I D Lloyd,
Dorothy Brining, and others*)

Open All year except Feb.
Rooms 1 suite, consisting of 2 rooms and bathroom; 1 4-bedded, 14 double,
12 single – 11 with bath.
Facilities Lift to first floor, wide doors for &. Drawing room, smoking lounge with
TV, bar, bar billiards, nursery for small children's supper. Drying and airing
rooms, ironing room. Concerts 5 times a year. 27-acre grounds with hard tennis
court and games hut with ping-pong. Trout fishing on Lake Vyrnwy, walking and
bicycling. A wide range of shooting now available. 17 lock-up garages. &.
Location At SE corner of Lake Vyrnwy.
Restriction Dogs in cars or kennels only.
Credit cards None accepted.
Terms B&B: single £16.29, double £28–£56; dinner, B&B: single £23–£36, double
£42–£70; full board over 4 days same rates as for dinner, B&B. Set lunch £5, Sun
lunch £8.25; dinner £8.75. Bargain breaks 1 Oct–1 May (excluding Christmas).
Children under 5 free; children 5–10 half rate; children 10–16 two-thirds rate;
special meals.
*Service/tipping: "VAT and service are included in our prices. If guests want to give tips
they are asked to do so themselves, on a personal basis."*

LLANYCHAER Dyfed   Map 3

Penlan Oleu [GFG]   *Tel* Puncheston (034 882) 314
Llanychaer, Fishguard SA65 9TL

Faithful readers of the Guide from way back may recall *Penlan Oleu* from its earlier appearance on these pages when it was run by Martin McKeown and Ann Carr, now of the *The Black Boys*, Thornage (q.v.). In 1981, it featured as one of that year's Six of the Best (an earlier version of a César), and was described as "a gem of a hotel in wild, beautiful, remote surroundings". It then disappeared when the McKeown/Carr team sold out. We are delighted to welcome it back again under its new owners, Andrew and Ruth Stuart-Lyon. *Penlan Oleu* (the name means "Light above the Church") is a converted Welsh farmhouse. It is five miles above and behind Fishguard, 800 feet up in the Preseli Hills. On a clear day, you can look across Fishguard Bay to the mountains of Wicklow. No telephones, no TV, no radio. Just peace and seclusion. It may be used as a staging post for the Fishguard ferry, but also makes a fine centre for a walking hoilday; the Pembrokeshire coastal path is four miles away. "Room comfortable and spotless ... Excellent dinner ... Welcome and value both exceptional." *(Very Rev John Paterson; also Greg Powell, and others)*

Open All year, except Christmas and Boxing Day.
Rooms 4 double, 1 single – 3 with bath, 2 with shower, all with tea-making facilities. Some on ground floor; 1 in annexe.
Facilities Lounge, bar, garden room in summer, dining room. Several acres of garden. 4 m from sea and Pembrokeshire coastal path. Safe bathing and sandy beaches 4½ and 6 m.
Location Leave Fishguard by B4313 (signposted Maenclochog). Through Llanychaer beyond Bridge End Inn for 2 m. At top take road to Puncheston. Hotel drive well signposted off this road.
Restrictions No children under 11. Pets in cars only, and must be kept on a lead.
Credit cards Access, Visa.
Terms (No service charge) B&B £14–£16; dinner, B&B £23–£25. Full alc £13–£15.

MAENAN Gwynedd   Map 3

Bod Hyfryd Hall   *Tel* Dolgarrog (049 269) 210
Maenan, Llanrwst

This small hotel – though guest-house might describe it better – entered our lists for the first time last year. It lies two miles from Bodnant Gardens, within range of Snowdonia and about eight miles south of the coast at Llandudno or Colwyn Bay. It was recommended in these terms: "A comfortable Edwardian house in delightful surroundings set high above the river Conwy with beautiful views. Enormous bedrooms with equally enormous bathrooms equipped with every luxury from linen sheets, leather armchairs, to foam bath essence and bath sheets to dry with after a piping hot bath or refreshing shower in a king-size bath. Tea was served to us from Wedgwood china in a beautiful garden. For dinner there was a mouth-watering menu. Breakfast was as perfect as the previous evening's meal – including lashings of freshly squeezed orange juice, bacon, eggs, brown or white toast and freshly ground coffee. All this for a mere £22 [1984] per person is the best value for money we have ever experienced. The couple that so ably run this hotel are Sally and Roy Walker and they run it superbly." *(Nicole Gavaghan)*

We asked for more reports and readers have been quick to endorse last year's entry. One mentions slightly old-fashioned decoration of the bedrooms and rather tired furnishings, another wishes that the wine list had been a little less basic. But all the names below greatly appreciated the Walkers' hospitality and their extremely reasonable tariff. *(Tom and Alison Kerr, Mr and Mrs K G Archer, J S and I M Cumming, Mrs M J Nicholl, Sir Michael and Lady Franklin)*

Open 1 Mar–1 Oct, plus winter and early spring weekends. Open Christmas and New Year to prior bookings.
Rooms 4 double – all with bath.
Facilities Large drawing room with grand piano, dining room. 3-acre garden. River Conwy ½ m; fishing. Within easy reach of Snowdonia and coastal resorts.
Location 4 m N of Llanrwst off A470.
Restrictions Not suitable for &. Children and dogs by arrangement; no dogs in public rooms.
Credit cards None accepted.
Terms B&B £15; dinner, B&B £22–£26. Set dinner £8. Special winter weekend rates.

PENMAENPOOL Gwynedd   Map 3

George III Hotel   *Tel* Dolgellau (0341) 422525
Penmaenpool
Dolgellau LL40 1YD

"Occasionally you come across a place which feels right the moment you step inside. The hotel is, in effect, the upper two storeys of an old inn right on the river Mawddach, shortly before it broadens out to form one of the most glorious of all Britain's river estuaries. The prospect north to the wooded foothills of the Rhinogs is also very pleasant. The Victorians ran a railway line immediately in front of the place, on the narrow strip of land between the pub and the river, to add insult to injury, they then built their station immediately next door. When the line was closed in the middle '60s the old track became a driveway with some outdoor tables and chairs at the side. Some bedrooms are upstairs on the second floor of the main building, others in the 'lodge' which turns out to be no less than the old railway station. (It seems a fitting form of revenge.) The rooms are very comfortable indeed. The food was carefully prepared and attractively presented. The menu looks suspiciously long; but the reputation this place appears to have built up locally is enough, it seems, to encourage a reasonably rapid turnover. The emphasis is on seafood: Barmouth and Aberdovey are only a few miles away; my plaice was outstandingly fresh." *(S L)* More reports please.

Open All year except Christmas and New Year. Restaurant closed May Day.
Rooms 1 suite, 11 double, 1 single – 7 with bath; all with mono TV, tea-making facilities and baby-listening; 6 rooms in lodge annexe; some ground-floor rooms.
Facilities Ramps. Lounges, 2 bars, restaurant. 1½-acre garden; fishing. Safe bathing on sandy beach 6 m; golf and pony-trekking nearby. &.
Location 2 m from Dolgellau on Tywyn road (A439), next to toll bridge.
Restrictions Not suitable for &. No dogs in restaurant.
Credit cards All major cards accepted.

Terms (Excluding 10% service charge) B&B: single £16–£31, double £32–£47.50.
Set Sun lunch £5.25; full alc £15. Winter breaks 1 Nov–30 Apr excluding Easter.
Reduced rates for children sharing parents' room; special meals.

TALYLLYN Gwynedd   Map 3

Minffordd Hotel [GFG]   *Tel* Corris (065 473) 665
Talyllyn, Tywyn LL36 9AJ

César awarded in 1985 for outstanding value in a country hotel

"The bedroom and bathroom were a little small for my 6'4" frame, but
the atmosphere compensated. It is what all hotels, large or small, should
make us feel – welcomed guests not just £ signs" *(D A Lloyd)*.
"Marvellous . . . The three dinners we had were the best meals we ate
during two months in Britain" *(Alan Weinstein)*. "Real pride was evident
in everything we saw. Glassware, plateware, brass and anything else
that could shine polished to the point of positive brilliance. The food was
memorable. The hosts made a particular effort to introduce everyone
around and stimulate conversation at the pre-dinner cocktails. At the
risk of appearing a grouch, I have some reservations about the practice,
but I found myself discoursing along with the rest – a tribute to the
Pickles' professionalism as well as their undoubted warm concern" *(T C
Seoh)*.

Three typical comments on the *Minffordd* experience. Formerly a
coaching inn, the hotel lies at the foot of the Talyllyn Pass, half a mile
from the head of Talyllyn lake, and the path to the summit of Cader Idris
is 100 yards from the hotel door. Some of the grandest countryside in
Wales lies all around. The hotel is run by Mr and Mrs Pickles, and their
chef son Jonathan. Conviviality is a central feature of the place. In
returning our questionnaire, Bernard Pickles writes: "We show B&B
prices, but prefer our guests to stay *demi-pension*, as a welcoming and
friendly house-party atmosphere can only be created by these means."

Open Apr–Oct inclusive; weekends only Nov, Dec and Mar. Open Dec 24–26 but
closed New Year. Restaurant closed to non-residents Sun and Mon.
Rooms 1 family room, 5 double, 1 single – 5 with bath, 2 with shower, all with
telephone, radio and tea-making facilities; 2 ground-floor rooms.
Facilities Sun lounge, lounge, parlour, dining room. 2 acres of paddock and
garden with spectacular views of the Cader Idris southern escarpment; the peak of
Cader Idris rises from here, path to summit 100 yards away; river at the bottom of
paddock; ½ m from Talyllyn lake; sea 12 m; lake fishing by arrangement.
Location At junction of A487 with B4405.
Restrictions Not suitable for &. No children under 3. No dogs.
Credit cards Access, Diners, Visa.
Terms (No service charge) B&B £24–£27; dinner, B&B £25–£37. Set dinner £9.95;
packed lunches on request. Winter mid-week breaks; bargain break weekends
Oct–Dec, Mar– May; reductions for stays over 3 days June–Sept; Christmas
package. Children under 3: 12.50% discount if sharing parents' room, otherwise
25%; special meals on request.
Service/tipping: "We are a family-run hotel and thus do not want or expect to receive tips."

> In your own interest, always check latest tariffs with hotels when
> you make your bookings.

WOLFS CASTLE Dyfed   Map 3

Wolfscastle Country Hotel [GFG]   *Tel* Treffgarne (043 787) 225
Wolfs Castle, Nr Haverfordwest SA62 5LZ

Halfway between Haverfordwest and Fishguard, and thus very near the end of the long winding A40, *Wolfscastle* would be a good centre for touring the south-east corner of Wales if you didn't mind staying about eight miles inland from the coast. It is also of course convenient for the Fishguard ferry. "We are comparatively small," writes the resident owner, Andrew Stirling. "We are proud of our restaurant, and therefore attract people to stay with us who put an emphasis on their eating during their stay – with squash, tennis and scenic walks to prepare for the next meal." The latter refers to the hotel's two squash courts, as well as a tennis court, which can be used free of charge by hotel guests. Andrew Stirling himself is a qualified coach who is always willing to play a guest in the absence of another partner. Some rooms are above the squash courts, and although play stops at 10.30 pm, not everyone will enjoy the noise before that hour. We also had a complaint about the meals – both the cooking and the service. But one reader was much more positive: "We had excellent meals, even on the Sunday when only bar meals were available. Atmosphere and service pleasant. It was quite the best all-round hotel in our tour of Wales." *(Sheila Williams)*

Open All year except 5 days at Christmas.
Rooms 10 double, 2 single – 8 with bath, all with telephone, colour TV and tea-making facilities. 6 in annexe.
Facilities Residents' lounge, bar, dining room. Pianist once a week, jazz monthly. ½-acre grounds with 1 tennis and 2 squash courts (no charge); squash discos 4 times a year.
Location 7 m N of Haverfordwest, off A40.
Restriction Not suitable for &.
Credit cards Access, Amex, Visa.
Terms B&B £17–£22; dinner, B&B £26–£31. Bar lunches and suppers; set dinner £10.50; full alc £14. Weekend breaks; gourmet nights, jazz nights, musical nights. Reduced rates and special meals for children by arrangement.
Service/tipping: "Tips we leave totally to the discretion of the client – the menu makes no comment with regard to them."

Scotland

TULLICH LODGE, BALLATER

ACHILTIBUIE Highland   **Map 5**

Summer Isles Hotel [GFG]   *Tel* Achiltibuie (085 482) 282 and 251
Achiltibuie by Ullapool
Ross and Cromarty IV26 2YG

Some 25 miles north and west of Ullapool, with the last 15 miles being
on a single-track road, the *Summer Isles* ranks as one of the more remote
hotels in the Guide. It is surrounded by spectacular mountain- and
sea-scapes – wonderful country for walkers, climbers, deer-stalkers and
bird-watchers. But though the scenery is rugged, the hospitality of the
hotel is the reverse: the *Summer Isles* is a highly individual but
thoroughly sophisticated hostelry, with a reputation for many years past
for the quality of its cooking. Almost everything is produced locally: the

hotel has its own smokehouse, and it produces its own dairy products, quails, ducks, sucking pigs, veal-calves and rabbits. Owner Robert Irvine's great pride is his new Hydroponicum, with solar panels and windmills, providing an astonishing range of early fruit and vegetables.

Our entry for the *Summer Isles* was left out last year, as it seemed likely that Mr Irvine would forsake innkeeping for charter yachting. But he assures us that he is remaining in harness though the day-to-day running of the hotel is now in the hands of his son Mark. Meanwhile, as in the past, reports on the *Summer Isles* experience have been ambivalent: breakfast is 8.30–9.0 am, dinner is sharp at 7.30 pm, there is no written menu for the set four courses and no wine list either, though the food is certainly above average and the hotel does not lack a fine cellar. Guests are gently steered towards the wines the host feels they would enjoy and would be within their means. Not everyone has enjoyed this game, and others mind the slight regimentation of the meal hours. There is nowhere much to sit in the daytime if the weather is inclement. Perhaps the character of the hotel will change under Mark Irvine's management. We should be glad of further reports.

Literary footnote: Robert Irvine's daughter, Lucy, wrote her best-seller, *Castaway*, here. Her new book, *Runaway*, to be published in 1986, contains several behind-the-scenes episodes at the *Summer Isles*.

Open 1 Apr–mid-Oct.
Rooms 1 suite (available for self-catering Oct–May), 10 double, 3 single – 8 with bath. Suite and 7 rooms are in annexe. Ground-floor rooms.
Facilities Lounge, cocktail bar, reading room, dining room. Sea, sandy beach 4 m; loch fishing, walking nearby.
Location 10 m N of Ullapool; take twisting single-track road that skirts lochs Lurgain, Badagyle and Oscaig. After 15 m you reach Achiltibuie. Hotel is a few hundred yds past the post office.
Restrictions Not really suitable for &. No children under 8. Dogs allowed, but not in public rooms.
Credit cards None accepted.
Terms B&B: single £18, double £40–£60. Set dinner, £18. 10% reduction for stays of 6 nights or more.

ARDELVE Highland   Map 5

Loch Duich Hotel   *Tel* Dornie (059 985) 213
Ardelve, by Kyle of Lochalsh
Wester Ross IV40 DY

A hotel that appeared in the first issue of the Guide in 1978, and then sank from view, resurfaces with new owner, Rod Stenson, who writes: "There are reduced rates for any stay of two days or more. I actively seek to make people stay longer to get the benefit of the experience of being here. I love what I do and where I am, and so do the people who work for me – everybody is local. The food we serve is honest although often unexpected and exciting, and the menu changes every day which gives us great fun." Here is how one nominator made the pitch: "What a find! The magical quality of light that surrounds Eilean Donan Castle (two minutes' walk) is quite breathtaking. The views across the water to Skye are unforgettable. *Loch Duich Hotel* is run by young, enthusiastic and friendly owners. The rooms are fairly basic, but since most of the guests are tired out by long walks or climbs, the accommodation is adequate.

The dining room is an oasis: rich fabrics, carefully planned lighting, and some classical background music. Food was excellent: superb home-made pâté and bread, and vegetables cooked perfectly. Seafood was disappointingly ordinary – oh, and we both suffered the worst Normandy apple pie flan ever cooked! But we forgave them that since we had morning tea brought to the bedside (much better than fiddling around with teabags on strings!) and the breakfast was very good."
(Allison Bretherton; also S I and V Cohen, Marcia Suddards)

Open 1 Apr–31 Oct.
Rooms 13 double, 5 single.
Facilities 2 lounges, sun lounge, residents' bar, TV room, restaurant. 1-acre garden, 5-acres of fields with farmyard animals; sea on 3 sides with access to shore (very tidal and fast current); safe bathing nearby; use of boat; salmon fishing 8 m.
Location 7 m from Kyle of Lochalsh. Across the bridge from Dornie village and Eilean Donan Castle.
Restrictions Not suitable for &. Dogs allowed in bedrooms "if quiet and not moulting": not in public rooms.
Terms (No service charge) B&B £14–£15; dinner, B&B £22–£23.50. Light snack lunches; set dinner £8–£9. Reductions for stays of 2 nights or more. Reduced rates and special meals for children.
Service/tipping: "No service charge – I do not like tipping."

ARDUAINE Strathclyde   Map 5

Loch Melfort Hotel   *Tel* Kilmelford (085 22) 233
Arduaine, by Oban, Argyll PA34 4XG

What was originally a characteristic loch-side house has been converted into a small modern hotel, the windows of its motel-like extension of rooms opening on to balconies and patios with spectacular views south across to Jura and Scarba. *Loch Melfort* has been owned and run for the past 15 years by Jane and Colin Tindal; Colin Tindal is an active member of the Highland Yacht Club, and the hotel is popular with the sailing fraternity who come ashore for summer drinks and meals. The modern dining room is particularly attractive with "one of the finest views in Britain, over the loch – mile upon mile of sea and islands fading into memorable sunsets". The food is recommended, too: there are Loch Fyne kippers for breakfast and always some local seafood on offer on their three-course set dinner menu. Little feedback this year. Could we hear from recent visitors please?

Open Easter–mid-Oct.
Rooms 25 double, 1 single – 23 with bath, all with radio, tea-making facilities and baby-listening. 10-ground floor rooms. 4 self-catering cottages.
Facilities Lounge, 2 bars, TV room, restaurant, boutique. 50-acre grounds by the sea; safe bathing. Kilmelford boatyard nearby; Craobh Marina across the bay.
Location Off A816 18 m N of Lochgilphead.
Restriction Dogs allowed in some bedrooms; not in public rooms.
Credit card Access.
Terms (No fixed service charge) B&B (continental): £20–£35. English breakfast £2.50; set dinner £13.50; full alc £20. Vegetarian meals available. Reduced rates for children sharing parents' room; high tea on request.

Please make a habit of sending in a report as soon as possible after a visit when details are still fresh in your mind.

ARDVASAR Skye, Highland   Map 5

Ardvasar Hotel   *Tel* Ardvasar (047 14) 223
Ardvasar, Isle of Skye IV45 8RS

"Comfortable and friendly little hotel with magnificent view over Sound of Sleat. Had avocado in perfect condition with lots of *fresh* prawns (a vastly different dish from the usual), excellent pea soup, an enormous fresh half lobster, tasting better than any lobster I've ever known, along with fresh vegetables, melon with lemon sorbet, coffee and mints. The menu changes daily. Strongly recommend your inspectors to check."
(*J C Johnston*)

The *Ardvasar* is an early 18th-century coaching inn a mile from the Armadale Ferry. It was taken over two years ago by a young couple, Bill and Gretta Fowler, with Bill doing the cooking. Mrs Fowler writes: "We are a small cosy country inn, with truly personal caring service in warm unpretentious surroundings. So far as possible, everything, particularly the sea food, is fresh. We are very lucky that crab, lobster and most food here is really fresh." Our inspector gave the place her own seal of approval, except for the Scottish folk songs from a record player turned up rather too loudly during dinner. "A real find . . . and very reasonable charges."

Open All year except for part of Nov, 25 Dec and 1–2 Jan.
Rooms 12 – 4 with bath, all with tea-making facilities; radio and baby-listening on request.
Facilities Lounge with open fire, TV lounge, 2 bars, dining room; occasional music (ceilidhs and singing). Small garden; hotel overlooks beach and Sound of Sleat; safe but rocky bathing 1 m.
Location In tiny village. 2 ferries to island. Kyle of Lochalsh–Kyleakin and Mallaig–Armadale operate all year round but latter will not take vehicles in winter.
Restrictions Not suitable for &. Dogs at discretion of the management.
Credit card Visa.
Terms (No service charge) B&B: single, £10–£18, double £20–£30; dinner, B&B: single £19–£27, double £38–£48. Set dinner £10; full alc £15; picnic lunches and bar meals available.

ARISAIG Highland   Map 5

Arisaig Hotel   *Tel* Arisaig (068 75) 210
Arisaig, Inverness-shire PH39 4NH

This Jacobite coaching inn on the Road to the Isles has no connection whatever with *Arisaig House* below, and the two establishments could not be more different: the *Hotel* is a small family enterprise, with George and Janice Stewart assisted by their son sharing nearly all the work between them, and the tariff is accordingly modest; the *House* belongs at the opposite end of the price spectrum. "The *Arisaig Hotel* is well situated on the seashore in Arisaig village, and very well run by the Stewarts who are charming and gracious (and above all kindly) hosts. Their son Gordon does the cooking, assisted by local girls, and does it astoundingly well. The hotel was originally built about 1720, though most of the work is clearly much later. There is a large and very comfortable drawing room, devoted chiefly to conversation; there is a television set in a separate lounge, but this seems to be little used except for the news. Two things remain in my mind: the extraordinary warmth of the welcome and the excellence of the food. The breakfasts are splendid – and huge." *(George Maddocks)*

Our original entry above continues to be endorsed by recent visitors, with the occasional caveat ("a Scrooge-ish 40 W bulb in the bedroom", "dining room a bit chilly and spartan"). Two typical extracts: "The hotel is furnished in the solid old-fashioned style of years long since gone, but the lasting impression is of warmth and comfort. Mr and Mrs Stewart are charming hosts, full of ideas on how to get the best from the area whatever your interests" *(Allison Bretherton)*. "Every meal we had was superb. But it was really in the intangibles, which have nothing to do with the surprisingly modest tariff, that the hotel scores so. From the start we were able to achieve complete relaxation and thoroughly enjoy the atmosphere of the hotel." *(T W B and B M Hudson; also W G Alexander, W Ian Stewart)*

Open Mar–Oct.
Rooms 4 family suites, 9 double – 3 with bath, all with radio, tea-making facilities and baby-listening.
Facilities Residents' lounge with open fire, reception lounges, one with TV, lounge/bar, dining room. Ceilidhs and music every 2 weeks at weekend in public bar. ½ acre of garden. Rocky beach by hotel but sandy beaches 5 minutes' drive away, with safe bathing, yachting. Fishing permits arranged.
Location Take A830 for Mallaig, which is off A82 just N of Fort William. Hotel is on outskirts of village.
Restrictions Not suitable for &. No dogs in public rooms.
Credit cards None accepted.
Terms (No service charge) B&B: £18.50, dinner, B&B £30; full board charged by the month. Bar lunch £5–£6; set dinner £12.50; full alc £16–£17. 5% reduction for stays of a week or more. Reduced rates for children under 14; special meals.
Service/tipping: "We do not like tipping. If guests insist we ask them to hand the money to reception and divide it out on a points basis to each member of the staff (the more responsibility, the more points)."

Arisaig House [GFG]
Beasdale, Arisaig
Inverness-shire PH39 4NR

Tel Arisaig (068 75) 622
Telex 777279 ARISAIG

Arisaig House's file is again a pleasure to read. This distinctly grand house on the original "Road to the Isles" between Fort William and the port of Mallaig, a location of outstanding beauty, was opened as a hotel *de grand confort* four years ago by the family Smither. The exterior is traditional country house Victorian, the interior a perfect thirties period piece. Reports continue to speak enthusiastically about every aspect of the Smithers' undertaking: "Immaculate decor, care and detail. Our bedroom was colour matched peach/apricot/beige down to the tissues in the bathroom and the book-cover colour. Books lying on coffee table. A plate of fruit was discreetly placed in our room after checking in. Beautiful flowers in our room and on the hall landing. The bathroom had modern fittings, bidet and heated towel rail. Bathroom towels really thick. The rest of the house looked equally new, well polished, cleaned, painted or cared for. The lawns cut and well edged, no weeds to be seen in the well-hoed beds – lots of flowers. It was hot and sunny so the setting near the loch from the house windows was idyllic. Asked whether we would like a cup of tea on arrival – pretty bone china – and whether there was anything we did not like to eat for dinner . . . A really luxurious hotel." *(Carole Jackson; also W Ian Stewart and others)*

Open Apr–Oct 13.
Rooms 13 double, 3 single – all with bath, direct-dial telephone and colour TV.
Facilities 3 lounges, restaurant, billiard room, terraces. 20-acre grounds with woodland walks, croquet, and jetty for small landing craft. 10 minutes' walk to loch shore; sandy/rocky beach, safe bathing.
Location On A830, 3¼ m SE of Arisaig.
Restrictions Not suitable for &. No children under 10. Dogs by arrangement, but not in hotel building.
Credit card Visa.
Terms (No service charge) B&B: single £30, double £82.50; dinner, B&B: single £49, double £120.50. Set dinner £19. Light lunches available. Spring and autumn breaks of 2 nights or more. Weekly terms except Jan and Aug.
Service/tipping: "Our staff do not expect gratuities."

BALLATER Grampian   Map 5

Tullich Lodge [GFG]   *Tel* Ballater (0338) 55406
Ballater, Aberdeenshire AB3 5SB

Neil Bannister and Hector Macdonald have now been 18 years at their late 19th-century pink granite baronial mansion on a wooded knoll overlooking the river Dee, a few miles from Balmoral. It is very much their personal creation, not just in the fidelity with which they have renovated the house in high Victorian style – maintaining, for instance, period features such as bells to draw the service of a valet or huge brass-tapped baths, or their careful restoration of ornate wood carvings and the panelling in the dining room. They offer, they say, "not so much a hotel but more a way of life". As with all hotels of real character, *Tullich Lodge* isn't everyone's taste. Some feel the owners impose their wishes on the guests in too aggressive a fashion. Others complain of inappropriate xenophobia. Not everyone cares for a no-choice menu, though there are few complaints about the quality of Neil Bannister's cooking, and alternatives will be provided if asked. But those who appreciate individuality relish the house exceedingly. One reader wrote: "This is the most passionately cared-for place we have visited, and we like the way the owners sometimes snap at you instead of smirking all the time." *(Glen and Julie Jackson, John Macintyre, A J Newall)*

Open Apr–Nov inclusive.
Rooms 7 double, 3 single – 8 with bath, 2 with shower, all with telephone, colour TV on request.
Facilities Drawing room, library, bar, dining room. 6-acres of woodland garden. & (restaurant only).
Location 1½ m E of Ballater on A93.
Restrictions No children in dining room at dinner; high tea provided. No dogs in public rooms.
Credit card Amex.
Terms (No service charge) B&B £42–£47.50; dinner, B&B £50–£55; full board £346 weekly. Set lunch/dinner £15.50; light bar lunch £5.
Service/tipping: "Gratuities are not expected."

> Don't let old favourites down. Entries are dropped when there is no endorsement.

BANCHORY Grampian   Map 5

Banchory Lodge Hotel   *Tel* Banchory (033 02) 2625
Banchory, Kincardineshire AB3 3HS

A well-bred Georgian building in a felicitous position, close to the
confluence of the Dee and the Water of Feugh, and with fishing rights in
the water directly opposite the hotel. It's naturally popular with the
fishing fraternity, but there are also three good golf courses within easy
reach, and magnificent walking and climbing to be had in the vicinity of
Deeside. The house itself, full of Victorian and Edwardian furniture and
bric-à-brac lovingly collected over the years by the resident owners, Mr
and Mrs Jaffrays, is a friendly place – with flower arrangements and
open fires and other signs of welcome to guests. Food is traditional
English fare, with good local products like Dee salmon and Aberdeen
beef. It is the kind of traditional dependable hotel that attracts happy
returners. "Invariably delightful." *(S J Gassaway)*

Open 25 Jan–5 Dec.
Rooms 11 suites, 9 double, 5 single – all with bath, radio, colour TV, tea-making
facilities and baby-listening; 2 with 4-posters. 2 rooms in annexe, both with
bath/shower.
Facilities 3 lounges (1 with colour TV) overlooking the river, cocktail bar, 2 dining
rooms. 12-acre grounds with salmon and trout fishing on the river Dee (must be
booked well in advance); children's playground; table tennis. Golf course at
Banchory, Aboyne and Ballater; tennis, putting, bowling at Banchory; Glenshee
ski slopes an hour's drive W.
Location 5 minutes' walk from town on A93 E of Aboyne; 18 m from Aberdeen.
Restriction Not suitable for &.
Credit cards All major cards accepted.
Terms (Excluding VAT) B&B: single £35, double £55; half-board: single £47, double
£75; full board: single £50, double £80. Set lunch £5.50 (packed lunches available),
dinner £15. Reduced rates and special meals for children.

BLAIRGOWRIE Tayside   Map 5

Kinloch House   *Tel* Essendy (025 084) 237
By Blairgowrie, Perthshire PH10 6SG

A laconic nominator writes: "Country house hotel. Highland cattle in
field, peacocks in grounds. Caters for fishers, golfers, shooters.
Excellent dinner with wide choice. Local dishes predominate, with
interesting variations. Absolutely no chips and no frozen foods. A warm
welcome, a well-stocked bar and attentive service from David Shentall,
the owner, who trains local staff to his own high standards. Very good
bar lunches also" *(D W Ravenscroft; endorsed by W Ian Stewart).*

Hosts at *Kinloch House* are David and Sarah Shentall, who bought the
hotel in a badly run-down condition a few years ago, and have been
busy with restoration since. It is an ivy-creepered country house with
some attractive features – a fine fireplace, good oak panelling and an
imposing staircase which leads to a gallery. Newcomers to the business,
the Shentalls seem to be making a successful show of it, having won a
rosette from the AA for their cooking, and a red rocking chair from
Michelin for pleasantness and quiet location. They emphasise their
sporting activities: no fewer than 40 golf courses within an hour's drive,

including the championship courses at Gleneagles and St Andrews; shooting and stalking on neighbouring estates; coarse fishing on Marlee loch in front of the hotel, and salmon and sea trout on the Middle Tay.

Open All year except last week Jan, first 2 weeks Feb. Closed Christmas.
Rooms 10 double, 2 single – 7 with bath, 5 with shower, all with radio and tea-making facilities.
Facilities Residents' lounge with TV, cocktail bar, dining room. 25-acre grounds with croquet lawn. ½ m to loch with coarse fishing. Shooting and stalking. Golf nearby.
Location 3 m W of Blairgowrie on A923 Dunkeld road.
Restriction No dogs in public rooms.
Credit cards Access, Amex, Diners.
Terms B&B: single £24, double £38; dinner, B&B: single £35.75, double £61.50. Set dinner £11.75; bar lunches available. Reductions for stays of 3–6 nights. Reduced rates and special meals for children by arrangement.

BUNESSAN Mull (Strathclyde)   Map 5

Ardfenaig House [GFG]   *Tel* Fionnphort (068 17) 210
Bunessan, Isle of Mull PA67 6DX

"The house stands at the head of a small loch and is approached by a very long lane so the feeling of peace and remoteness is complete. The house is not distinguished architecturally, but is set in a delightful garden and inside is furnished and decorated with exquisite taste and lovely old furniture and paintings, obviously from the family home of the two owners, Robin Drummond-Hay and Ian Bowles. There are only five rooms for guests who share three bathrooms, and it all felt more like a house party than a hotel. We were reminded of childhood visits to grandparents in an age before inflation had made such luxurious living impossible." This original nomination for *Ardfenaig House* by *Lt-Cdr and Mrs R Kirby Harris* has been echoed by later visitors. Last year, *Simon Hoggart* wrote: "A delight. Breakfasts were so hearty that after two days we dispensed with lunch altogether. Our whole visit was marked by many acts of generosity which added to the general feeling of warmth, relaxation and pleasure. The house is in a most beautiful part of Mull, and the rooms are so wonderfully furnished, it is a pleasure to sit indoors when it rains. Not especially cheap, but excellent value." But we had one dissenting report this year. No dispute about cooking – "exceptionally good" – and the stay had been a success, but "wonderfully furnished" in Hoggart's report had not prepared her for threadbare carpets, creaking floorboards and unresponding radiators in a chilly June.

Open Mid-May–Sept inclusive.
Rooms 4 double, 1 single (maximum 6 guests at a time) – all with tea-making facilities.
Facilities Lounge, bar, music room, sun room, dining room. 18-acre grounds sloping down to loch with shingle beach (plenty of sandy beaches nearby). Fishing, safe bathing.
Location 3 m W of Bunessan on Iona ferry road. The hotel's long drive is on the right.
Restrictions Not suitable for &. No children under 13. No dogs in public rooms.
Credit cards None accepted.
Terms Dinner, B&B £40. Set dinner £13.

BUSTA Shetland   Map 5

Busta House [GFG]   *Tel* Brae (080 622) 506
Busta, Shetland ZE2 9QN   *Telex* 57515 Attn 36

The Guide's most northerly offering, *Busta* (pronounced "Boosta" - the Norwegian for "homestead") is one of Shetland's few listed buildings and said to be the oldest continuously inhabited house – parts date from the 16th century. It is 25 miles north of Lerwick, overlooking its own harbour and Busta Voe. There is now a bus service from Lerwick, but a car would still be advisable. For the past few years it has been in the hands of the Copes, Edwin (ex-Navy) and Rachel (ex-nurse). Theirs is the only Shetland hotel to have achieved *Michelin*'s red-chair symbol (for a specially quiet and pleasant hotel). It has a decent wine list and also offers, it is said, the largest selection of single malts of any hotel in the Northern Isles. Readers continue to appreciate the Copes' style of hospitality – the many personal touches, the welcome of the peat fires, the civilised feel of the house, the quality of the cooking. "By far the best hotel in the Shetlands." *(R W Apple Jr; echoed by Miss E Fawcett, M Green, Marjory Robertson, G M Jones)*

Open Mid Jan–mid Dec. [*Note:* the closed season may be extended in 1986. Please check.]
Rooms 19 double, 2 single – 13 with bath, 8 with shower, some non-smoking, all with telephone, radio, colour TV and tea-making facilities, 2 with 4-posters.
Facilities 2 lounges, library (no smoking), garden room, dining room (no smoking). 2-acre grounds with own harour and pebble beach; fishing can be arranged. Swimming for the hardy. Location 25 m N of Lerwick on A970; turn left in village of Brae. Busta signposted from there.
Restrictions Not suitable for &. No dogs in public rooms.
Credit cards None accepted.
Terms B&B: single £20–£48, double £25–£60. Set lunch £7.50, dinner £13.50. Mini-breaks and weekly rates. Reduced rates and special meals for children.

CALLANDER Central   Map 5

The Roman Camp Hotel [GFG]   *Tel* Callander (0877) 30003
Callander, Perthshire FK17 8BG

The Denzlers – Sami, who comes from Switzerland, and his Ulster-born wife, Pat – took over *The Roman Camp* five years ago, having previously been restaurateurs in Edinburgh. Faithful readers of the Guide will know of their successful transition to hotelmanship. The building, resembling a miniature French château, dates from the 17th century, a house of character, with a fine lounge and panelled library; but the crowning glory of the hotel is its 20 acres of beautifully maintained gardens along the banks of the River Teith. "We were immediately struck by the impeccable gardens and buildings," writes a visitor from South Africa, "and the beautiful riverside location; for us, it captures the essence of genteel country living. We were warmly greeted and led to a delightfully decorated chintzy bedroom-cum-sitting room. What a splendid surprise of muted colours, soft lighting, antiques and bric-à-brac, which made us feel instantly comfortable. We had all mod cons, and only the bathroom, stark and a little drab, seemed out of keeping." The same correspondent felt even more disappointed with the modern dining room. "Taking the lead from the sumptuous public rooms, we had expected a cosy atmosphere to dine on a cold night. Whilst obviously having cost an arm and a leg to decorate" - the room has a painted ceiling drawn from designs of Scottish ceilings in the 16th and 17th centuries – "the bright lighting and pine tables deprived it of ambience. The food was excellent, the service was efficient and polite, but we were not tempted to linger and savour it as we had hoped." We give this report at length, because it reflects other comments – with this year some suggestion of a fall in previous high standards of cooking. More reports please.

Open Mid-Feb – late Nov; sometimes closed for lunch in low season.
Rooms 3 suites, 8 double – 9 with bath, 2 with shower, all with telephone, radio, colour TV, tea-making facilities, baby-listening; 4 ground-floor rooms.
Facilities 2 lounges, cocktail bar, library with chapel, sun lounge, dining room (non-smoking). 20-acre grounds with walled and formal gardens. Trout and salmon fishing free to residents in river Teith (bring your own rod). Callander golf course ½ m; tennis, squash, pony-trekking and watersports nearby.
Location ½ m from centre of Callander; take driveway between two pink cottages on Main Street (east end).
Restriction Dogs at management's discretion, but not in public rooms.
Credit cards None accepted.
Terms B&B: single £35–£45, double £48–£64. Set lunch £10.50, dinner £17. Half-board rates for 3-day breaks in summer, 2-day breaks off-season. Reduced rates for children sharing parents' room; special meals on request.
Service/tipping: "All prices are inclusive of VAT and service. No further tipping is necessary unless you wish to reward outstanding service."

CANONBIE Dumfries and Galloway　　　　　　　　　　　Map 5

Riverside Inn [GFG]　　　　　　　　　　*Tel* Canonbie (054 15) 295 or 512
Canonbie, Dumfries DG14 0UX

◐ *César awarded in 1985 for best inn of the year*

Robert and Susan Phillips' 17th-century fisherman's retreat on the banks of the Esk (well placed for touring Hadrian's Wall and the Solway coast) happily changes little from year to year. The most important news last year was the opening of the long-needed bypass of Canonbie on the A7. This year, we welcome the news that the *Riverside* now has a residents' lounge, as well as a lounge bar. Meals in the restaurant continue to be, by inn standards, uncommonly enterprising, and the bar snacks ditto by any standard. Breakfasts are specially recommended. Some of the rooms are spacious, all but two with baths *en suite*; others are cosy or poky according to your state of mind. "*Riverside* was everything and more! A wonderful and friendly inn and very reasonable prices." (*Andrena Woodhams*)

Open All year except Christmas and two weeks in Feb. Restaurant closed Sun lunch.
Rooms 6 double – 4 with bath, 2 with shower, all with radio, colour TV and tea-making facilities; 2 rooms in annexe; 2 ground-floor rooms.
Facilities Lounge bar, residents' lounge, TV/coffee lounge, dining room. Small garden with children's play area and tennis courts nearby. River Esk 100 yds; salmon and sea trout fishing (permits available from hotel). Good centre for visiting Hadrian's Wall.

Location 10 m N of end of M6, on A7.
Restrictions Not suitable for &. No dogs.
Credit cards Access, Visa.
Terms (Service at guests discretion) B&B: single £28, double £38; dinner, B&B: single £40, double £62. Set dinner £12. Full-board rates (6% reduction) for stays of 1 week or more. 2-day bargain breaks Nov–Apr £48 per person for dinner, B&B including ½ bottle of champagne. Reduced rates and special meals for children.

COLONSAY Strathclyde   Map 5

Isle of Colonsay Hotel [GFG]   *Tel* Colonsay (095 12) 316
Argyllshire PA61 7YP

"For a really 'get away from it all' holiday, it would be hard to beat Colonsay. The ferry steamer from Oban takes two and a half hours and goes there and back three times a week (Mondays, Wednesdays and Fridays). You land at a wooden pier, and are meet by Kevin Byrne, the enthusiastic young proprietor of the only hotel on the island, though the house is only a few hundred yards up the road. It is a delightful old place. The lobby is full of gum-boots under a large Ordnance Survey map of the island. The lounge is one of the few really comfortable ones I have found in the islands, well stocked with old magazines and even a beautiful chess set for a rainy day. My bedroom, charmingly enlivened by old prints of Adam and Eve, was opposite the bar – but the cheerful clatter from it was never too loud or disturbing. The dressing stand was an old oriental table. Food was fresh and excellent – more imaginative than I've found in most hotels of such small size, though the choice was limited. Delicious porridge and home-made marmalade for breakfast. The island is quite enchanting – I went for a walk in misty rain over a small mountain pass (rocks, bracken and heather), past lovely lochs (reeds and herons) into woods (waterfalls and rhododendrons, and the pink mansion of Lord Strathcona) and down to the golden sands of Kiloran Bay. The sun only came out when I left – an ethereal island in a radiant glow on the horizon." *(Tim Brierly)*

Last year's introduction to the most isolated registered hotel in Britain has been endorsed by two subsequent visitors, *Christina Bewley* and *D R Newth*. Meanwhile, Kevin Byrne tells us that, on the strength of his having an entry in the Guide, he has raised the wind to install private showers/wcs in all but his three single rooms. Television and telephones are now available on request in the rooms – the latter through a cordless telephone with its own BT meter, dispensing with the need for coins and also available if you need to take an urgent call in your bath or a parked car. Other hotels please copy. More news from Colonsay: a drying room, a trouser press and a shoe-cleaning machine are now operational and the wine list is being extended. The hotel provides free bicycles to all adult guests, and free golf or a day's sailing to all weekly guests: "Our 200-year-old 18-hole golf course is primitive and challenging!"

Open All year except Christmas Day.
Rooms 1 suite, 7 double, 3 single – 1 with bath, 7 with shower, all with radio; TV, telephone, tea-making facilities and baby-listening on request.
Facilities Residents' lounge, cocktail bar (for lunches, bar meals etc.), public bar (centre of island life), sun room, restaurant. 1-acre grounds including 2 vegetable gardens; lawns, pleasure garden with burn; 400 yds from harbour, ½ m to sandy beach and lochs. Fishing and bicycles, free to all adult guests.

Location Access by car/passenger ferry from Oban Mon, Wed, Fri – 37 m crossing (2½ hours) – hotel courtesy car to/from all sailings.
Restrictions Not suitable for &. No dogs in public rooms.
Credit cards All major cards accepted.
Terms (No service charge) B&B £15–£22; dinner, B&B £20–£33; full board £140–£200 weekly. Set lunch £2.75, dinner £11. Vegan, vegetarian meals if requested. Reductions for long stays. Special rates Sept–Apr and Apr to mid-May. Reduced rates and special meals for children (they are normally charged for meals only when sharing parents' room, except in high season).
Service/tipping: "There is no service charge. Our staff operate a 'tronc' whereby any gratuities would be distributed fairly."

CRINAN Strathclyde   Map 5

Crinan Hotel   *Tel* Crinan (054 683) 235/243/222
Crinan, by Lochgilphead, Argyll
Argyllshire PA31 8SR

The *Crinan* is one of those fortunate hotels that can attract custom by virtue of an incomparable location: it lies at the seaward end of the eight-mile Crinan Canal looking across to the mountains of Mull and the Isle of Jura. At closer quarters, it has a ringside seat over a yacht basin and the constant movement of craft, big and small, bound for the Inner and Outer Hebrides. A major fire gutted much of the original Victorian building, so the present hotel offers all the 1980s mod cons, including a lift; and the Ryans have gone to much time and trouble to produce rooms that are in their decor a match for the views outside. The hotel also prides itself on its restaurants: relatively conventional in the main dining room, and a more expensive seafood restaurant called *Lock 16* on the top floor. For some, the *Crinan* can fully deliver the goods, viz., "A marvellous place to be . . . the meal near to perfect . . . I will be returning next year." Sadly, this year as previously, there have been adverse reports as well: noisy plumbing, an uncomfortable bed, disappointment with the food in the ground-floor restaurant, a politely frigid rather than welcoming atmosphere. We wish that one year we could return a *nem. con.* verdict.

Open Mar–Oct.
Rooms Family room, 20 double, 2 single – 20 with bath, 2 with shower, all with telephone and radio.
Facilities Lift; ramps. 2 lounges, cocktail bar, public bar, ground-floor restaurant (Telford Room), roof-top restaurant *(Lock 16)*. 1-acre grounds; sea in front of hotel, fishing, sailing, windsurfing, seal islands nearby.
Location On B841, 8 m NW of Lochgilphead. (There is a helicopter service from Glasgow airport to Lochgilphead.)
Restriction No dogs in public rooms.
Credit cards All major cards accepted.
Terms (Tipping at guests' discretion) B&B: single £30–£33, double £50–£70. Set dinner £16; bar lunches available. Reduced rates and special supper at 6.15 pm for children.

Most hotels have reduced rates out of season and for children, and some British hotels offer 'mini-break' rates throughout the year. If you are staying more than one night, it is always worth asking about special terms.

DERVAIG Mull, Strathclyde   Map 5

Druimnacroish Hotel   *Tel* Dervaig (068 84) 274 or 212
Dervaig, Isle of Mull PA75 6QW

Don and Wendy McLean bought this ruined farmstead and mill south of
Dervaig village in the beautiful Bellart Glen ten years ago, and have
lovingly restored it. Readers commend both the comforts of the house
and Mrs McLean's cooking. The playing of taped music at dinner, about
which we had complaints last year, has been discontinued. We give part
of last year's commendation, warmly endorsed by subsequent visitors:
"Let me recommend the *Druimnacroish* hotel because it is *absolutely silent*;
has magnificent valley-mountain/sky-mist views; and has excellent
British cooking with second helpings, and above all, vegetables from
their own garden perfectly cooked by the proprietress. Well placed for
the best beaches in northern Mull." *(J B B ; also Mary M Higgins, Mrs S
Cornwell)*

Open 1 May–1 Oct.
Rooms 5 double, 2 single – all with bath, radio, mono TV and tea-making facilities;
2 double rooms on ground floor.
Facilities 2 lounges (1 smoking, 1 non-smoking), sun room, dining room. 3½-acre
grounds with natural rock gardens. Boating, fishing, deer-stalking, golf, pony-
trekking, bird-watching nearby.
Location On A849 between Dervaig and Salen, 1½ m S of Dervaig. Car ferry from
Oban.
Restrictions No children under 10. Dogs by arrangement but not in public rooms.
Credit cards All major cards accepted.
Terms B&B £32; dinner, B&B £42. Set dinner £10 (£15 to non-residents), packed
lunches £4. Long weekends and 5- and 7-day package including golf and fishing
holidays.

DRUMNADROCHIT Highland   Map 5

Polmaily House [GFG]   *Tel* Drumnadrochit (045 62) 343
Drumnadrochit
Inverness-shire IV3 6XT

Some people, if they have the means, like to tour the Highlands in
baronial style, staying at one of the many Victorian castles or shooting
lodges that are enjoying a fresh lease of life as luxury hotels. *Polmaily
House* has charms of a different and less ostentatious order: it is a
rambling Edwardian mansion set in 22 acres, a few miles to the west of
Loch Ness – a tranquil rural setting, though the dramatic landscape of
Glen Affric is only a short drive away. Nicholas and Alison Parsons
bought the place three years ago, and though new to the business, have
shown that they understand the essence of running a small country
house hotel successfully. Alison Parsons is a very good cook, and enjoys
trying her hand at new dishes. Nicholas Parsons is a friendly thoughtful
host. The rooms, both the public ones and the bedrooms upstairs, have
a comfortable lived-in feeling. There is very little about the house that
suggests it is a hotel – and that, for many visitors, is the key to its
success. *(Shirley Williams, Lord Balfour of Burleigh, H R)*

Open Easter – mid-Oct.

Rooms 7 double, 2 single – all the doubles with bath, all rooms with radio; 1 with 4-poster bed.

Facilities Drawing room with log fire, bar, reading room, restaurant. 18-acre garden with hard tennis court, unheated swimming pool, croquet lawn, boating pond; game fishing, shooting, stalking and pony-trekking can be arranged nearby.

Location Take Cannich road (A831) out of Drumnadrochit. *Polmaily* is about 3 m on right.

Restrictions Not suitable for &. Dogs by arrangement (in cars only).

Credit cards All major cards accepted.

Terms (No service charge) B&B £22–£24. Alc dinner £11.50; snack lunch for residents only. Reduced rates for children sharing parents' room (under 2 free). *Service/tipping: Bills state, "There is no service charge. No tips are solicited."*

DUNBLANE Central   Map 5

Cromlix House [GFG]   *Tel* Dunblane (0786) 822125
Dunblane, Perthshire FK15 9JT

"The most magical place my husband and I have ever stayed at in England or Scotland . . . The bedroom was truly beautiful . . . Dinner was a very special meal . . . Coffee in front of a fire in the drawing room was most romantic."

"Everything comes in tiny portions including the soup which was unremarkable. To follow, salmon in hollandaise sauce, more of the latter than the former, which went in three mouthfuls . . . I sat and waited for the vegetables with the wild duck for some minutes until I realised they were on the plate: a teaspoonful of celeriac purée and a tiny bundle of haricot beans . . . The Roquefort had spent most of its time in the fridge . . . The breakfast kedgeree was so drenched in turmeric as to turn it into a curry – the flavour of salmon never got through at all."

"We have been twice and on neither occasion could we fault it at all, either on the warm welcome or on the cuisine . . . The staff go out of their way to help you and go about their work with a smile. You are surrounded by many genuine antiques and the trappings of a warm but stately home."

"Cromlix House should not be in your Guide . . . we had a deplorable lunch – the only saving graces were the beauty of the setting and the friendliness of the staff. The price was extortionate."

"Food was excellent. Beautiful countryside. I felt we had turned back the clock a hundred years. Staff very helpful and gracious."

"Pleasant setting, very good food. Did not like the communal breakfast arrangement. Had to ask three times for milk and left without ever getting it. The bedroom over the front door was noisy with arrivals and departures, not helped by the fact that the window jammed open and we couldn't shut it. Our bath and toilet were across a small passage, and although the unit was private and entered with a key it was a thoroughfare for staff going to a cupboard!! Poor-quality bed linen."

"The house is extremely ugly from the outside, but inside is another story. It is like someone's comfortable home, which it is. It was a unique experience to dine at Cromlix because of the delightful solicitous staff – plus the fabulous food. Only one complaint: portions are ridiculously small."

The hotel that has garnered such a contradictory set of reports (we have omitted the longest and most hostile) is a massive rambling mansion in 5,000 Perthshire acres, belonging to the Eden family and earlier this century patronised by Edward VII in the grouse season. It has seven magnificent suites, and other *rooms rather less favoured; also a private chapel. It opened its gates as a hotel in 1981. In its first two years in the Guide, it seemed likely to rival Inverlochy Castle (q.v.), but things took a turn for the worse last year and we printed our entry in italics. A new general manager took over in the spring of 1985. At the moment, it is impossible to establish any kind of consensus. The italics must continue, and we should be glad of further reports.*

Open All year.
Rooms 7 suites, 8 double – 13 with bath, 1 with shower, all with telephone, TV.
Facilities Lobby, morning room, library, 2 dining rooms, functions facilities, conservatory. 5,000-acre grounds with fishing, tennis, riding and shooting (advance booking advisable).
Location ½ m N of Kinbuck, 4 m S of Braco. Take A9 out of Dunblane; turn left on to B8033; go through Kinbuck village, and take second left turn after a small bridge.
Restrictions Not suitable for &. No dogs in public rooms.
Credit cards All major cards accepted.
Terms [1985 rates – could go up about 10%] (No service charge) B&B: single £48.50, double £87.50; dinner, B&B £25 per person added.
Service/tipping: "The staff do not expect to be tipped."

DUNOON Strathclyde   **Map 5**

Enmore Hotel   *Tel* Dunoon (0369) 2230
Marine Parade, Kirn, Dunoon
Argyllshire PA23 8HH

Dunoon still has the charm of the Victorian seaside resort it originally was, and is a popular base for exploring the Isles of Arran and Bute, and the Mull of Kintyre. The *Enmore*, a whitewashed turn-of-the-century house, overlooks the Clyde Estuary a mile out of Dunoon, and has its own gravel beach just across the road. David and Angela Wilson are an enterprising couple. They are keen on beds and have four four-posters and a water-bed, the latter with a whirlpool bathroom *en suite*. They organise Luxury Breaks, with "complimentary fruit, flowers, 'bubbly', and even a heart-shaped box of chocolates . . . Breakfast in bed with heart-shaped eggs", and Anytime Breaks, which would appear to come without the heart-shaped chocolate and eggs. There are two squash courts on the premises and the Cowan golf course is a mile away. Correspondents in the past have liked everything about the place – especially the warmth of hospitality and the good food. Mrs Wilson tells us that the Guide has brought her added business, but our file has been quiet. Could we hear from recent visitors please?

Open Mar–Nov.
Rooms 2 suites, 11 double, 4 single – 6 with bath, 6 with shower; radio, TV, tea-making facilities and baby-listening all available on request; 3 rooms in annexe.
Facilities Lounge/games room, TV room, cocktail bar, dining room. 2 squash courts. 1-acre grounds with private beach across road. Golf, swimming pool, tennis courts and pony-trekking nearby. Sailing and fishing on Clyde Estuary and neighbouring lochs. Trips to Isles of Mull, Bute, Arran etc.
Location On Marine Parade between 2 ferries, 1 m N of Dunoon.
Restriction Probably not suitable for &.
Credit cards Diners, Visa.
Terms B&B £16–£40; dinner, B&B £26–£50. Set dinner £11.50. Luxury Breaks and Anytime Breaks min. 3 nights. Reduced rates and special meals for children.

EDINBURGH Lothian   Map 5

Donmaree Hotel [GFG]   *Tel* (031) 667 3641 and 667 7611
21 Mayfield Gardens
Edinburgh EH9 2BX

A medium-priced hotel one and a half miles south of the city centre and
on the A7: no problem about parking, and buses stop by the door. Light
sleepers should ask for a room at the back. The house is a substantial
Victorian villa with extravagant period decor in the public rooms. The
bedrooms have less character and are comfortable rather than stylish.
The other significant feature of the hotel is its concern for good cooking:
not particularly cheap but "serious" and well presented. Breakfasts – the
full Scottish variety – also recommended.

Open All year except New Year. Restaurant closed bank holidays.
Rooms 15 double, 2 single – 9 with bath, 5 with shower, all with telephone, radio
and TV. 8 rooms in annexe.
Facilities Cocktail bar, TV lounge, lounge, restaurant. Garden.
Location 1½ m from centre. (Rear rooms are quietest.) From Waverley Bridge
station on Princes Street (A1) take The Bridges, then Nicolson St, South Clerk St
and Minto St; Hotel is on left. Parking.
Restrictions Not suitable for &. No dogs.
Credit cards All major cards accepted.
Terms B&B: single £30–£34.75, double £46–£57.50. Set lunch £6.55, dinner £10.75;
full alc £17.50. Reduced rates for children if sharing parents' room; special meals.

Prestonfield House Hotel   *Tel* Edinburgh (031) 668 3346
Priestfield Road   *Telex* 727396
Edinburgh EH16 5UT

A noble 17th-century house, two miles from the centre of the city
standing in splendid landscaped gardens complete with strutting
peacocks. Plenty of names to drop of distinguished guests of former
times: Bonnie Prince Charlie, Benjamin Franklin, Dr Johnson and
Boswell – to name but four. Nowadays, it's essentially a restaurant-with-
rooms: five bedrooms only, but at least four dining rooms, and various
other public spaces to cope with banquets, conferences, wedding
receptions and other large-scale gatherings. We carried a warm
encomium for *Prestonfield House* in earlier years, but it has been out of the
Guide for some time after criticism of both meals and the quality of
service, and our feeling that the catering side of the business was
dominant. Recently, however, an inspector reported: " . . . warts and all,
but there is no place like it." And a correspondent writes: "Public rooms
are as good as those one pays to walk round in the best of open stately
homes; blazing fires, gleaming cleanliness, a magnificent setting; a
caring attitude from staff and management; soap with 'his' and 'her'
flavours; fruit and Malvern water in all the bedrooms; pleasant formal
gardens – and all this two miles from the Scott monument. Who cares if
there are no rooms with private baths? It would ruin the shape of the
rooms to partition them. Bathrooms aren't far away, and the plumbing is
300 years younger than the house." (*Anthony Rota*)

Please make a habit of sending a report if you stay at a Guide hotel.

Open All year.
Rooms 5 double, 5 single – 2 with shower, all with telephone and tea-making facilities.
Facilities 2 bars, 2 lounges, 2 restaurants, 2 private dining rooms, conference facilities. 23-acre grounds with helipad. Golf course adjacent; indoor heated swimming pool, bird sanctuary and loch nearby.
Location 10-minute drive from town centre. Take A68 S out of Edinburgh. Turn first left at lights after Commonwealth swimming pool. Parking.
Restriction Bedrooms not suitable for &.
Credit cards None accepted.
Terms (Service at guests' discretion) B&B: single £45, double £58. Set lunch £10, dinner £15; full alc £25–£35. Reduced rates and special meals for children. For overseas visitors, traditional Scottish dinner with entertainment in summer.

Teviotdale House   *Tel* (031) 667 4376
53 Grange Loan, Edinburgh EH9 2ER

A stone-built Victorian guest-house in a quiet residential area (unlimited free street parking) south of the city, one and a half miles from Princes Street off the A7, two minutes from the bus stop, 10 minutes by bus to the down-town area. Recommended for the usual comforts, and especially for the breakfasts: proper porridge, home-made bread and scones, omelettes with mint and a concoction called the Duke of Edinburgh's Favourite Breakfast (scrambled eggs with fresh cream, in case you didn't know). Mrs Riley, proprietrix, tells us that her breakfasts "are renowned the world over", also that, in addition to the usual facilities, she has two chow-chows who have proved to be winners with her guests. More reports please.

Open All year.
Rooms 8 double – 1 with bath, 4 with shower, all with colour TV and baby-listening.
Facilities Breakfast room. 3 m to sea and sandy beach.
Location 1½ m from Princes Street off the A7 (bus stop 2 minutes).
Restriction Not suitable for &.
Credit cards Access, Amex, Visa.
Terms [1985 rates] (No service charge) B&B £12–£18.50. Reduced rates for children. Weekly rates. (No restaurant.)

ELGIN Grampian   Map 5

Mansion House Hotel   *Tel* Elgin (0343) 48811
The Haugh, Elgin, Moray IV30 1AW

Elgin is an interesting old town on the main Aberdeen/Inverness road, and a good centre for those exploring the "whisky trail" of the numerous distilleries of Speyside. Up till now, it has lacked a hotel of character, but this elegant Victorian mansion, newly renovated, should make good the deficiency. The first report we received spoke enthusiastically of the elegant bedrooms, the excellent cooking, the outstanding warmth of welcome. "The Victorian exterior has been preserved intact, and the interiors are, if anything, over-lovingly redecorated." We sent an inspector along who corroborated the report in every detail, and who also filled us in on the recent history of the house and its owners, Mr and Mrs De Oliveira, in the following uninspectorial terms:

"I have completely fallen in love with the owner, Fernando De Oliveira, he of the gap-toothed moustachioed smile, as did Mrs Oliveira, a local Scots girl, when she met him in a Portuguese hotel 10 years ago. He was a waiter then, and when they married, he came over here ('yes , I missed my country at first') and opened a shop selling children's clothes. One day, two years' ago, he was walking by the river Lossie on this spot, and saw the Victorian house, boarded up against vandals. When he heard the council intended to demolish it, he put in an offer and the town banded together, 3,000 strong, to petition against demolition. In June 1984 he opened, preceded by an open day in which everyone was invited to view the new hotel. He is obviously a popular hero. In January 1985 he was invited to give the speech for the local Burns supper and it was from all reports splendid. He is obviously touched by this honour. The Rotary Club and Junior Chamber of Commerce meet at the hotel. After 10 years, he is a fully fledged member of the community."

Open All year.
Rooms 1 suite, 11 double – all with bath, telephone, radio, colour TV, tea-making facilities and baby-listening; 2 4-poster beds.
Facilities Residents' lounge, lounge-bar, bar, dining room, conference/function room. 5-acre grounds with children's playground. Close to river, low cost fishing permits available; hotel is member of local squash club.
Location Coming E from Inverness or W from Aberdeen on A96 turn off Elgin High St into Alexander Rd, then left into Haugh Rd. Parking.
Restrictions Not suitable for &. No dogs.
Credit cards All major cards accepted.
Terms (No service charge) B&B: single £25–£33, double £40–£50; dinner, B&B: single £37–£45, double £64–£74; full board: single £42–£50, double £69–£79. Set lunch £4.90, dinner £12; full alc £18. 2-day weekend full-board breaks for 2 people Oct–Mar. 10% reduction for children under 12; special meals.

ERISKA Strathclyde   Map 5

Isle of Eriska Hotel [GFG]   *Tel* Ledaig (063 172) 371
Eriska, Ledaig, Connel
Argyllshire PA37 1SD

There are very few private island hotels in Britain, and only one isle of Eriska. This castellated sandstone and granite Victorian magnate's Highland home is on a tiny islet, linked to the mainland by a bridge, 12 miles north of Oban. The islet itself has little character, though the grounds of the hotel are impeccably maintained; but on the horizon is the island of Lismore with the hills of Morvern rising behind. In the past 10 years, the hotel has won a reputation for itself on the international circuit as well as among the native British, through the pastoral ministrations of a genial former Minister of the Church of Scotland, Robin Buchanan-Smith, and his wife Sheena. The Buchanan-Smiths succeed, where many hotel-keepers fail, in engendering a true house-party spirit in their congregation of guests. Followers of successive issues of the Guide will know that the *Eriska* has often been a source of controversy in these pages: the public rooms are warm and welcoming, but some of the bedrooms have disappointed; breakfasts and teas (exceptional home-made scones and cakes) are always appreciated, but dinners in the harmonious candle-lit dining room have been patchy. Eyebrows are raised at the prices. This year is no exception. Reports swing from the condemnatory to the extremes of hyperbole, though the latter are dominant: "One of the finest hostelries in the whole of the UK", "true enchantment", "this marvellous hotel in which comfort, food and staff are all of the highest quality". *(Charles Drew, J W A Forbes, R A Hood, Vida Bingham)*

Meanwhile, we learn of various changes in train: the season at *Eriska* is being extended from mid-February to the end of November, one of the few hotels of its kind in the Western Highlands to be open so long; the number of rooms is dropping, and existing rooms are being improved and refurbished; and, perhaps most important in view of past criticisms of the restaurant, the hotel is acquiring a new Head Chef, Simon Burns. Cooking weekends are planned for the 1985/86 season. We should be glad to hear from guests at the new improved *Eriska*.

Open Mid-Feb – end Nov.
Rooms 1 family room, 15 double, 1 single – all with bath, telephone, radio, tea-making facilities, baby-listening; colour TV on request. 2 ground-floor rooms; ramp for &.
Facilities Reception hall, hall, drawing room, dining room, library. Private bridge to mainland. 280-acre grounds with formal garden, park and moorland; croquet, hard tennis court; slipway for boats, bathing from shingle beach, sea fishing, waterskiing, windsurfing, anchorage, pony-trekking. Yacht with skipper for charter.
Location 12 m N of Oban, 4 m W of A828.
Restrictions No children under 12 at dinner – high tea at 5.45 pm. Dogs by arrangement, but not in public rooms.
Credit card Access.
Terms [1985 rates] (excluding VAT; no service charge) dinner, B&B £52–£62; full board rates for stays of 4–7 days. Buffet lunch £8.50, Sun lunch £14; set dinner £19.50. Reduced rates for children sharing parents' room; high tea provided. Winter and spring breaks, gourmet weekends, cooking holidays.
Service/tipping: Robin Buchanan Smith writes: "We actively discourage tipping and make no mention of service charge on our bills. I am so averse to tipping that I prefer to stay in a Club while I am in London. I suppose we regard Eriska *as a Club, but haven't yet got to the stage of throwing out members who dare to tip staff!"*

FORT WILLIAM Highland   Map 5

Inverlochy Castle [GFG]   *Tel* Fort William (0397) 2177
Fort William, Inverness-shire PH33 6SN   *Telex* 776229

This grandest of grand Victorian castles, built by the first Lord Abinger in 1863, in 50 acres of grounds rich in rhododendron, is sited superbly on the lower slopes of Ben Nevis in the heart of the West Highlands. "I never saw a lovelier or more romantic spot," said Queen Victoria, when she stayed here 10 years later, and guests have been repeating her remark ever since, frequently substituting "hotel" for "spot" since Grete Hobbs converted it into a luxury hotel some years ago. We gave it a César for "incomparable grandeur" in 1984 and would give it another tomorrow. Chef François Huguet's inspired cooking (rosetted in *Michelin*) is of the same order of excellence as everything else. Grandeur can often be oppressive – though not in the case of *Inverlochy*. Here is how one reader expressed her appreciation – or at least the first 200 words of a 2000-word sustained paean of praise:

"There is absolutely no question that *Inverlochy Castle* is in a class by itself. And, or course, the primary reason for that is the very lovely and professional Mrs Hobbs. We rank this hotel right up there with our other favorite, the *Hostellerie de la Poste* (q.v.) in Avallon, France. The welcome, the ambience, the staff (all of it), the rooms, the service, the food, and most of all (at the risk of being redundant) Mrs Hobbs. She really runs that castle. And it is the closest to actually living in someone's castle that we have found in 20 years of traveling in Europe. Other establishments proclaim that staying with them is like staying with the family, but Mrs Hobbs makes everyone feel like an honored guest. The manager Mr Leonard is equally charming and helpful. Those two people try very hard to make your stay as pleasant as possible. In other words, they do all the things that make a hotel successful. Why can't others?" *(Mary McCleary Posner)*

Open Mid-Mar to mid-Nov.
Rooms 2 suites, 13 double, 1 single – all with bath and shower, telephone, radio on request, colour TV, full room service.
Facilities Great hall, drawing room, restaurant, billiard room, table tennis room; facilities for small (25) conferences out of season. 500 acres of farmland and 50-acre grounds with rhododendron gardens; all-weather tennis court; trout fishing on nearby private loch; several golf courses within easy driving distance; pony-trekking; chauffeur-driven limousines can be hired.
Location Take turning to NW off A82, 3 m N of Fort William just past golf club. Guests met by arrangement at railway station or airports.
Restrictions Not suitable for &. No dogs.
Credit cards Access, Visa.
Terms (No service charge) B&B: single £80.50, double £109.50; dinner, B&B: single £106.95, double £162.15. Light lunch available on request. Reduced rates and special meals for children.
Service/tipping: "Our guests are advised that there is no charge and tipping is not expected."

GIGHA Strathclyde   Map 5

Gigha Hotel   *Tel* Gigha (058 35) 254
Isle of Gigha, Argyllshire PA41 7AD

If you have a taste for small islands off the main holiday routes, then Gigha (pronounced Gee-ah, with the first G hard), three miles off the Argyll peninsula (regular ferry services from Tayinloan) may well suit your needs. It is six miles long by one and a half miles wide, and has a mild climate, thanks to the North Atlantic drift. It has coves and caves and white sandy beaches, and a splendid garden at Achamore House. The *Gigha Hotel* is the well-modernised but friendly old inn of the island, looking out over the Sound to the hills of Kintyre. Readers appreciate the warm welcome of Mr and Mrs Roebuck, and their decent home cooking – soups, sweets and bread specially appreciated.

Open Apr–Oct inclusive.
Rooms 9 double – 3 with bath.
Facilities 2 lounges (1 with TV), public bar, restaurant; some conference facilities. Small garden. 300 yds from sea with white sand, rocks, safe bathing; sea fishing arranged with local fishermen. Achamore Gardens (open Mar–Oct) ½ m.
Location Via ferry from Tayinloan (off A83). Guests not wishing to bring cars will be met at ferry, if notice given.
Restrictions Not suitable for &. No dogs in restaurant.
Credit cards Access, Visa.
Terms (Service at guests' discretion) B&B from £17.50; dinner, B&B from £27.50. Set lunch £6; dinner, £11. Bar lunches. Reduced rates, special meals for children.

GLASGOW Strathclyde   Map 5

The White House   *Tel* 041-339 9375
12 Cleveden Crescent   *Telex* 777582 attention the White
Glasgow G12 0PA   House

Continued support – some of it, as previously, in a lyrical vein – for this
elegant small apartment hotel in a Georgian crescent, two miles from the
city centre. The hotel has always offered room service for meals in
addition to the kitchens in each apartment; this year, they have arranged
a tie-in with two down-town restaurants, *Rogano's* and the *Buttery*
(both in our sibling *Good Food Guide)*: a courtesy car is provided and
guests can charge the bill to their hotel account. One recent visitor
thought that some capital investment was needed in wiring, plumbing
and decorating; another would have appreciated a better reading lamp;
but these, like all our other correspondents, appreciated the comforts of
the accommodation and the friendly welcome. At least for one reader,
"the hotel met my total expectations on every count. I stay in many
hotels around the country, but this is top of my list." *(J P Rooney; also
Andrew Wall, Mrs J S Rodewig, Alan Heason)*

Open All year.
Rooms 12 suites, 11 double, 9 single – all with bath and shower, telephone, radio,
remote-control TV with in-house video, kitchenette; baby-sitting arranged.
4 ground-floor rooms.
Facilities Room service for meals. Conference suite. Small garden.
Location ½ m W of Glasgow town centre; 10 minutes' drive from airport. From
centre take Great Western Road (A82). From 2nd set of traffic lights past Botanic
Gardens turn right, then first left into Cleveden Crescent. From airport take A739
Clyde tunnel turn-off to Anniesland Cross. Courtesy car to town centre between
8.15 and 8.30 am Mon–Fri.
Restrictions Not suitable for &. No dogs.
Credit cards All major cards accepted.
Terms (Excluding VAT; no service charge) B&B: single £44–£50, double £58–£76.
Room service meals: lunch £7, dinner £13; full alc £14.50. Champagne weekends;
reductions for weekend stays of 2 or 3 nights; reduced Christmas rates 16 Dec–
10 Jan. No charge for children sharing parents' room.

GULLANE Lothian   Map 5

Greywalls Hotel   *Tel* Gullane (0620) 842144
Muirfield, Gullane   *Telex* 72294 GREYWL G
East Lothian EH31 2EG

A pedigree house, designed by Lutyens in 1901 with gardens by
Gertrude Jekyll. A fruity royal connection – Edward VII was a frequent
visitor to his mistress Mrs Willie James here, and the loo which Lutyens
built for the King is still extant in the garden wall. With a notable
position overlooking Lammermuir and the Firth of Forth and adjoining
Muirfield golf course, *Greywalls* has a lot going for it. Sadly, last year's
entry had to be in italics. There was praise for many features, but
concern about value for money, especially in relation to the meals. This
year's postbag is decidedly more friendly, though one reader felt sore
that a poorish room in the cottage annexe should have borne the same
high tariff as the well-appointed rooms in the main house. Another

reader sums up thus: "The public rooms are particularly attractive (largely occupied by the nicest sort of cultured American!). The bedrooms are mostly rather old-fashioned, but then they are historic. In 1983, we occupied Jack Nicklaus' bedroom, this year Edward VII's (complete with antique bath and loo, but the plumbing worked). We do have our reservations about the food, which is rather fussy. But I would not withdraw a restaurant recommendation altogether, and you surely should not italicise the hotel." *(A L Gordon)*

Open Mid Apr–mid Dec.
Rooms 17 double, 4 single – all with bath, telephone, TV, radio and baby-listening; 24-hour room service; 5 rooms in annexe; 8 ground-floor rooms.
Facilities Library, sitting room, sun room, TV room, bar, 2 dining rooms; conference facilities. 5-acre formal walled garden with tennis and croquet. Ten golf courses within easy reach; shooting and fishing nearby. Beach ¼ m with chilly but safe bathing.
Location On A198, 19 m E of Edinburgh.
Restrictions Children by arrangement. No dogs.
Credit cards All major cards accepted.
Terms (No service charge) B&B: single £35–£46, double £70–£92. Set dinner £20; full alc £25. Reduced rates for children; special meals by arrangement.

KELSO Borders   Map 5

Sunlaws House Hotel [GFG]   *Tel* Roxburgh (057 35) 331
Kelso, Roxburghshire TD5 8JZ   *Telex* 728147 SUNLAW

The Duke and Duchess of Roxburghe's elegant Scottish country house in 200 acres of grounds just outside Kelso had its première with us last year, and has been playing to good houses since. It makes an admirable centre for touring the Border country or for a fishing holiday in the season. There is no other country house hotel of its class known to us in the area. The Roxburghes are said to be "very personally concerned with the running"; no guest has reported a sighting, but one correspondent was impressed to find King Hussein at the next table at breakfast, and also told us that the *Sunlaws* breakfast passed the porridge test with flying colours. Another writer, who was pleased with a genuine welcome when he arrived at 10.15 pm, appreciated the flowers, trouser-press, bath oil and suchlike in his bedroom and liked the whole feel of the place – "warm and *homely*". *(F H Telford, Esme Walker)*

Open All year.
Rooms 1 suite, 13 double, 1 single – 14 with bath, 1 with shower, all with telephone, radio, colour TV, tea-making facilities and baby-listening. Some ground-floor rooms.
Facilities Main hall, residents' drawing room, library bar, dining room, Roxburghe room, conference suite, conservatory for light lunches, teas and drinks. 200-acre parkland with garden and woodland walks; hard tennis court, croquet lawn. Salmon and trout fishing rights on river Teviot (within grounds); clay pigeon shooting, golf nearby. & ramps and toilets for the disabled.
Location 3 m SW of Kelso. Take A698 to Heiton; turn off to *Sunlaws* E of Heiton (signposted lane).
Credit cards All major cards accepted.
Terms B&B: single from £35, double from £55. Set lunch £7, dinner £16–£17. Reduced rates and special meals for children on application.

KENTALLEN Highland   Map 5

Ardsheal House   *Tel* Duror (063 174) 227
Kentallen of Appin, Argyll PA38 4BX

Ardsheal House is the historic home of the Stewarts of Appin. Built in the 1500s, it was sacked in 1745 and rebuilt in 1760. It played a prominent part in Robert Louis Stevenson's *Kidnapped*, because the murder of Colin Campbell took place on the property and Lord Ardsheal's brother, James of the Glen, was hanged (wrongfully?) for it. Topographically, it is approached by an atmospheric mile-long private drive and stands on a high peninsula looking down over Loch Linnhe and the hills of Morvern – a noble sight. Gastronomically, on a limited-choice six-course menu, it offers cooking of genuine distinction. The house is owned and run by two Americans, an ex-banker Bob Taylor, and his ex-advertising-executive wife Jane. They spotted the house for sale when touring the region a few years back, fell in love with it, and decided to make a life-switch. Now they winter in the States and run *Ardsheal* in the summer months. They may be newcomers to the hotel business, but they understand the nub of the matter, and this year, as previously, readers pay tribute to the convivial atmosphere of the house. Guests find themselves quickly on first-name terms with their hosts. "Rooms are Victorian-like, with just the right amount of charm, but not 'cutesy'," writes an American correspondent. Many reports this year have been from America – the house is clearly on the lists of discriminating American travel agents. But *Ardsheal* has not lacked appreciation by the British, too: "One of the friendliest hotels in the West of Scotland – even if it is run by Americans!" *(W Ian Stewart; also Ted and Susan Hall, Patricia Purvis, and others)*

Open Apr–Nov.
Rooms 13 double – 6 with bath, 3 with shower.
Facilities Reception lounge, TV lounge, library with view of loch, dining room, billiard room. 900-acre grounds with tennis court; rocky beach behind hotel, trout stream nearby, coarse fishing from dinghies on loch; riding, hill-walking. & dining room only.
Location 17 m S of Fort William. From Ballachulish roundabout take A828 towards Oban; hotel is 4 m further on, on right. Parking for 18 cars.
Credit cards None accepted.
Terms (No service charge) dinner, B&B: single occupancy £56–£65, double £80–£110. Set lunch from £5, dinner £17. Discounts for long stays. Reduced rates for children sharing parents' room; high teas on request.
Service/tipping: "We make no mention of any service charge and receive it only if guests so desire."

KIDALTON Islay, Strathclyde   Map 5

The Dower House   *Tel* Port Ellen (0496) 2425
Kidalton, by Port Ellen
Isle of Islay, Argyll PA42 7EF

New to the Guide, and our first hotel on the Isle of Islay in the Inner Hebrides, recommended to the Guide in the following terms: "A picture in the 'Guide to Islay' prompted me to write to the *Dower House* that their place looked a dream. Sally Taylor replied that it was quite a dream place, which is why she and her husband dropped out of Oxfordshire three years ago. So off I went. David and Sally Taylor have made a reputation for themselves in the past few years for running one of the best and friendliest hotels in the Hebrides, and they made me feel completely at home. The ferry leaves twice daily from Kennacraig near Tarbert (good meal at the *West Loch Hotel* there) – reversing the car on board is a minor ordeal. From Islay's small town of Port Ellen, you drive for about five miles down a single-track road that follows the wooded coastline past at least two of Islay's famous distilleries till you come to the Kidalton Estate. The Dower House is in a little sandy cove looking over rocky islets to Gigha and Kintyre. It is utterly peaceful. The hotel itself is small but very comfortable, with a good lounge, unlike so many hotels in Scotland, and the fresh food is excellent (though not so 'fancy' as at the *West Loch*). Very friendly bar. Lots to do on Islay, and worth sparing a day to visit Jura." *(Tim Brierly)*

Open From the week before Easter to mid-Oct.
Rooms 5 double, 2 single (or small doubles) – 6 with bath, 1 with shower, all with tea-making facilities.
Facilities Lounge, bar, games room, dining room, conservatory. Occasional ceilidhs. 1-acre garden running down to safe sandy beach. Boating, fishing, seal/bird-watching. Golf, riding, tennis, bowling nearby. Car, moped or bicycle hire can be arranged.
Location 6 m E of village of Port Ellen, on the SE of the island, past Ardbeg. Car ferry daily from Kennacraig on West Loch Tarbert, Mull of Kintyre, to Port Ellen or Port Askaig (approx 2-hour crossing): Tel Gourock (0475) 34644/7. By air via Loganair from Glasgow Airport to Glenegedale Airport on Islay (30 minutes): Tel Glasgow (041) 8893181.
Restrictions Not suitable for &. Dogs allowed, but not in public rooms.
Credit cards None accepted.
Terms B&B: single £16, double £32–£34; dinner, B&B: single £25, double £50–£52. Bar lunches: set dinner £8.50–£9; full alc £12.15. Reduced rates and special meals for children. Package deals inclusive of ferry fares; fishing packages.

KILCHRENAN Strathclyde   Map 5

Ardanaiseig Hotel [GFG]   *Tel* Kilchrenan (086 63) 333
Kilchrenan, by Taynuilt   *Reservations* in USA (800) 323 3602
Argyllshire PA35 1HE

A noble house (built in 1834 by William Burn, pupil of Robert Adam) in a superb setting overlooking Loch Awe four winding miles beyond the nearest village of Kilchrenan, surrounded by one of the show-place gardens of the Western Highlands, with all the creature comforts expected from an expensive luxury hotel, including fine five-course dinners and a good if pricey wine list. Apart from one complaint about the master bedroom – sparse furnishing, housekeeping not quite *comme il faut* – readers have much enjoyed their visits. Singled out for special appreciation has been the congenial hostmanship of Michael Yeo and his wife Frieda "who give an added zest to a remarkable hotel". And the views are *nonpareil. (W Ian Stewart, Kevin Myers)*

Open Easter–mid-Oct.
Rooms 14 double (4 may be let as singles) – all with phone, radio and colour TV.
Facilities Lounge, library (with bar), dining room, billiard room, 30 acres of shrub and woodland garden in estate of 2,500 acres with mapped woodland trails,

highland croquet, tennis court and clay pigeon trap; fishing, boat hire at nearby Loch Awe; swimming for the hardy.
Location Turn off A85 on to B845 at Taynuit. The hotel is signposted from there for 9½ m.
Restrictions Not suitable for &. No children under 8. No dogs in public rooms and in bedrooms only by arrangement.
Credit cards All major cards accepted.
Terms (No service charge) dinner, B&B: single £55.50–£64, double £59–£69.50. Full alc dinner £23.25 (non-residents); alc lunch (brunch on Sun) also available. Special 4-day rate Easter and April. Children half-price in parents' room; special meals.
Service: "We do not charge for service."

Taychreggan Hotel [GFG]   *Tel* Kilchrenan (086 63) 211
Kilchrenan, by Taynuilt
Argyllshire PA35 1HQ

"Taychreggan really is special. I wanted comfort, peace and quiet, and got them and a lot more" *(Consuelo Phelan)*. "We like the friendly relaxed atmosphere. John and Tove Taylor are very much in evidence dispensing hospitality. The situation on the shores of Loch Awe is superb and many of the comfortable bedrooms are blessed with an uninterrupted view of the loch. There is a pleasant courtyard where drinks or lunch can be taken when weather permits, or a welcoming fire in the hall and a lively cocktail bar when it does not. Good food is served in an airy dining room" *(Rosamund Hebdon)*. Other correspondents endorse these views of the old coaching inn in an exceptionally peaceful and beautiful setting at what was once the main ferry point across Loch Awe from Inverary to Oban. Danish-born Tove Taylor's *koldt bord* lunch comes in for special praise. However we also have on our files a furious letter about the booking of a specific room which went wrong, and some lesser quibbles: a shower which didn't function properly at peak bath-time; no concession made on the bill for a child who only managed two of the four courses at dinner; cramped conditions in the only single room – but John Taylor tells us that a small double has now been converted into a good single with private bath. In an effort to attract guests early in the season the Taylors are offering a discount of a third on normal rates for all of April 1986.

Open Easter to 13 Oct.
Rooms 15 double, 2 single – 14 with bath, all with radio and baby-listening.
Facilities Lounge/hall, 2 lounges, TV lounge, all with log fires; bar overlooking courtyard, dining room. 25-acre rounds on the loch side, with fishing, bathing, boating. Riding, shooting, walking; fine scenery, gardens and historic sites within easy reach.
Location On N shore of Loch Awe, 7 m S of Taynuilt, off B845.
Restrictions Not suitable for &. No dogs in restaurant.
Credit cards All major cards accepted.
Terms (No service charge) dinner, B&B: single £32–£24, double £64–£84. 1/3 discount on these rates in Apr 1986. Lunch (Danish cold table) £7.50, dinner £12.50. Reduced rates for children.

We get less feedback from smaller and more remote hotels. But we need feedback on all hotels: big and small, far and near, famous and first-timers.

KILLIECRANKIE Tayside   Map 5

Killiecrankie Hotel and Restaurant [GFG]   *Tel* Pitlochry (0796) 3220
By Pitlochry
Perthshire PH16 5LG

Once again, nothing but grateful compliments from guests at this former
dower-house (*c*. 1930), hosted by Duncan and Jennifer Hattersley Smith,
sometimes assisted by daughter Emma. The area, close to the Pass of
Killiecrankie, is of great natural beauty – autumn tints especially
recommended – and Pitlochry, with its Festival Theatre, lies four miles
to the south. As reported last year, the A9 now bypasses the town,
leaving the hotel in its five acres of grounds and woodland with
enhanced peace and quiet. The rooms are of decent size and agreeably
furnished, with Laura Ashley much in evidence. The hosts are most
hostly, the staff attentive, and – a very important bonus – the cooking is
of a high order, with a particularly reasonable mark-up in the wine list.
(*K W Boothby, P W Taylor, Gwen and Peter Andrews, Joan Williamson*)

Open Mid-Mar to mid-Oct.
Rooms 11 double, 1 single – 4 with bath, 6 with shower; 4 gound-floor rooms.
Facilities Upstairs lounge with TV, bar-lounge, cocktail bar, dining room. 6-acre
gardens and woodlands at northern entrance of the Pass of Killiecrankie. Putting
green; croquet lawn. Golf, fishing, stalking, shooting, skiing, walking,
mountaineering nearby.
Location Just off A9 3½ m N of Pitlochry. Follow "Killiecrankie" signs.
Restriction Dogs not allowed in dining room.
Credit cards None accepted.
Terms B&B: single £17.60–£22, double £35.20–£44; dinner, B&B: single £25.60–
£32, double £51.20–£64. Set dinner £11.50; bar lunches. Reduced rate 3-day
mid-week breaks; special weekly rates. Reduced rates for children sharing
parents' room; special meals.
Service: No charges made (left to guests' discretion).

KILMORY Arran, Strathclyde   Map 5

The Lagg Hotel   *Tel* Sliddery (077 087) 255
Kilmory, Isle of Arran KA27 8PQ

*Our first entry on the Isle of Arran, an inn dating back to 1791, and still the local
for the neighbouring farmers, recommended to the Guide in the following terms:
"If you get off the afternoon ferry to Arran and turn south to encircle the island
you'll come, after riding alternately by plowed fields full of daffodils and by the
edge of the sea, to a tiny village in a glade. There you'll find amid gardens and a
tumbling burn the Lagg Hotel (lagg means hollow). It is a perfect place to settle
down for the night or a few days of total peace and an ideal place from which to
explore the rest of Arran. It was recently taken over by Ron and Barbara Stewart.
The rooms are charming, the bar inviting, the staff attentive and welcoming, the
dining room, supervised by an excellent young chef, bright and attractive. Who
could ask for more?"* (Barbara Morey) *More reports welcome.*

*Thus our entry last year. No feedback yet received. Lagg-ards, this is your
final call.*

Open 6 Mar–end Oct, also Christmas and New Year.
Rooms 3 suites, 11 double, 3 single – 8 with bath, all with radio, tea-making
facilities and baby-listening.

Facilities 2 bars, lounge with TV, coffee lounge, dining room. 2-acre gardens and 10-acre grounds with salmon river. Sea 5 minutes' walk, sandy beach and safe bathing.
Location "Ask anybody on the island." 16 m from Brodick.
Restrictions Not suitable for &. No dogs in public rooms.
Credit cards None accepted.
Terms (Service at guests' discretion) B&B £19–£21; dinner, B&B £29–£31; full board £34–£36. Lunch £5.25, set dinner £10.50; full alc £16.50. Weekly rates. Reductions and special meals for children.
Service/tipping: "No service charge is added to the account as it is believed that the majority of our patrons prefer that this matter be left to their own discretion."

KINGUSSIE Highland   Map 5

The Osprey Hotel [GFG]   *Tel* Kingussie (054 02) 510
Kingussie, Inverness-shire PH21 1EN

The Osprey has long been popular with Guide readers as a small welcoming hotel on a moderately quiet village street, very reasonable in price, and offering remarkably good cooking, an excellent wine list and the agreeable company of Duncan and Pauline Reeves as hosts. It is also well placed in the heart of the Spey Valley for all the leisure activities of the region – walking, fishing, golf, riding, skiing. Aviemore is 12 miles off, the Cairngorms 30 minutes by car. Since last year, one of the bedrooms has been converted into two bathrooms, so now two of the rooms will have a bath or shower *en suite*. More half-bottles have been added to the list. Correspondents continue to express their appreciation of the care taken by the hosts to create a convivial house-party atmosphere both at dinner and then post-prandially, and of the very reasonable prices. *(Norman Dupont, Jerry and Ruth Neild, T G R Cook, John Castle)*

Open 27 Dec–31 Oct.
Rooms 1 family room, 6 double, 1 single – 1 with bath, 1 with shower, all with baby-listening.
Facilities Lounge, TV room, dining room. Small garden. Most sports within easy reach: golf; salmon and trout fishing in river Spey ¼ m, trout fishing in loch 1 m; gliding at Glen Feshie; sailing, canoeing, windsurfing 6 m; all sports facilities at the Aviemore Centre 12 m; fine country for bird-watching, walking, hill-climbing; skiing in Cairngorms (usually Dec–May), 30 minutes by car.
Location Near A9, about 12 m SW of Aviemore and 200 yds from village centre; parking for 10 cars. Rail: on main London/Inverness line with good services.
Restrictions Not suitable for &. No dogs in public rooms.
Credit cards All major cards accepted.
Terms (No service charge) B&B £12–£22; dinner, B&B £22–£32. Set dinner £10.50–£11. Reduced rates for children.

KINLOCHBERVIE Highland   Map 5

The Kinlochbervie Hotel   *Tel* Kinlochbervie (097 182) 275
Kinlochbervie, by Lairg
Sutherland IV27 4RP

The most northern Guide hotel on the British mainland, overlooking Loch Clash and Loch Bervie fishing harbours, from which the hotel daily draws its supplies of white fish, king prawns, salmon and lobster. A fine centre for walking or pony-trekking or observing wildlife. The hotel is modern, with large picture windows looking out over the Atlantic Ocean – spectacular sunsets when the weather is right. It changed hands in 1983, and readers appreciate the new regime of David and Geraldine Gregory. Geraldine Gregory's cooking comes in for special commendation: grilled plaice for breakfast, home-cured smoked salmon, "irresistible home-made soups, delicious halibut steaks with subtle watercress sauce" ... Accommodation is "excellent", service "friendly, quiet and efficient", fresh flowers abound, and only the weather is unreliable. (*Mrs E B Schaefer, David Angwin*)

Open All year (accommodation by reservation only Nov–Easter). Closed Christmas.
Rooms 10 double – all with bath, telephone, radio, colour TV, tea-making facilities and baby-listening.
Facilities Lounge, public bar, dining room (no smoking). Sandy beach 1 m; bathing and fishing.
Location Only hotel in tiny village of Kinlochbervie, which is on B801 on N side of Loch Inchard.
Restrictions Not suitable for &. No dogs in public rooms.
Credit cards All major cards accepted.
Terms (No service charge) B&B: single £30–£60, double £50–£66; dinner, B&B: single £40–£73.95, double £78–£94. Set dinner £14.95. Reduced rates and special meals for children. Mini-breaks of 2, 3, 5 & 7 nights.

KIRKMICHAEL Tayside   Map 5

The Log Cabin Hotel [GFG]   *Tel* Strathardle (025 081) 288
Kirkmichael, Perthshire PH10 7NB   *Telex* 76277 LCH

Brochures don't always tell you very much, but sometimes they convey sharply the style of an establishment. Here is an extract from *The Log Cabin*'s leaflet advertising their Country Breaks: "*The Log Cabin Hotel* is tucked into the Perthshire mountains as remotely as in any fairy-tale with lung-gulping views across to the Peaks of Glenshee. Here Brian and Elizabeth Sandell, together with their daughters Kate and Emma, look forward to welcoming you to ... log fires, superb food, fine wines and heartwarming whiskies. Our Country Breaks fall into two categories – our Spring Fling and our Autumn Leaves. Spring Fling: just as Mother Nature throws off the cold and damp of Winter and life begins anew, we are sure you will benefit ..."

As the name suggests, the hotel is a timber-framed bungalow construction made of Norwegian whole logs, 900 feet up in the heather and forest pine. It's walking, climbing, riding, shooting and fishing country, with skiing in the winter. The hotel owns over 300 acres, and the basic tariff includes the use of the hotel ponies, the boat on the nearby loch, and the tennis court. Outdoor-orientated hotels are often negligent of those who like to eat well after a hard day's play. Not so *The Log Cabin*, which prides itself on its Scottish cooking as well as on its range of single malts. The dining room is a civilised place to eat well – something of a haven, according to one visitor, who found other *Log Cabin* rooms over-resonant. We also had complaints about poor insulation – and heating not adequate for a cold spell. But the hotel continues to be popular with readers – not least for its value for money.

Open All year except mid-Nov–mid-Dec.
Rooms 13 double (some are connecting, suitable for families) – 7 with bath, 6 with shower, all with radio and tea-making facilities; telephone sockets in all rooms, colour TV available on request; all rooms are on ground floor (with entrance ramps).
Facilities Residents' lounge, large lounge/bar with open fire, TV room, dining room. Dinner dances, folk nights. 300-acre grounds; boating on nearby loch. Trout fishing ¾ m on river Ardle; skiing at Glenshee; golf, water skiing, canoeing, sailing, windsurfing, climbing nearby; shooting, stalking and salmon fishing can be arranged. &.
Location Off A924; follow signs from Kirkmichael village.
Restriction No dogs in dining room.
Credit cards All major cards accepted.
Terms B&B £25–£31; dinner, B&B £31–£37. Set dinner £12; bar lunches available. Country Breaks; skiing holidays, golf package; Christmas programme. Reduced rates and special meals for children.

LAIRG Highland   Map 5

Achany House   *Tel* Lairg (0549) 2433
by Lairg, Sutherland IV27 4EB

"Real country-house hospitality from the distant past", writes one enthusiastic nominator for this new-to-the-Guide 18th-century Scottish mansion, with splendid turreted wings added by one of the Mathiesons of Jardine, Mathieson, the Hong Kong merchants. Once the seat of the Munro clan, with origins that go back to the 14th century, *Achany House* is now the Lady Burgh's family home "which we enjoy sharing with our guests". Here is another nominator's equally heart-warming appreciation: "We arrived in the warm light of an October evening and drank the offered tea by a warm fire lit for us in the small sitting room, cushioned in deep armchairs and surrounded by books, pictures, antique furniture and bric-à-brac. Our young hostess showed us up a wide staircase, hung with modern pictures, to our room overlooking the park and furnished with large, aged furniture and delectably comfortable beds. Our private bathroom was not *en suite* but next door to our room. Because we were the only guests Alexander Burgh laid a table in the small sitting room and with professionalism and informality served us a beautifully prepared meal of Lochinvar Smokies, loin of pork in an apple sauce, a perfect chocolate roulade and cheeses. We had an excellent dry Graves for which he credited us the undrunk third of a bottle. We went outdoors and listened to a distant owl hoot under a star-studded sky before going upstairs to find the curtains drawn, the beds turned down and an electric fire warming the softly lit room. Our Scottish breakfast, which included the best in a long line of Scottish kippers, was served at one end of the vast dining table (which can seat 16 or more guests), watched by the ancestors hanging on the walls! Then we glanced into the beautifully proportioned comfortably furnished drawing room which we hadn't used. We went on our own way into the Scotch mist warmed by the hospitality of this friendly young couple in their beautiful house." *(G & E Atkinson; also Gillian Cave)*

Open 1 Apr–31 Oct.
Rooms 5 double, 1 single – 5 with bath, 1 with shower.
Facilities Drawing room, small drawing room/smoking room, dining room. 12-acre parkland; trout and salmon fishing nearby.

Location 4 m S of Lairg, off B864. Signposted.
Restriction Not suitable for &.
Credit card Access.
Terms (No service charge) B&B £14–£22; dinner, B&B £23.50–£31.50; full board
£26.50–£34.50. Packed lunch £3, set dinner £9.50.

LANGBANK Strathclyde   Map 5

Gleddoch House Hotel   *Tel* Langbank (047 554) 711
Langbank, Renfrewshire PA14 6YE   *Telex* 779801

*If you are visiting Glasgow, and are not inconvenienced by staying outside the
city centre,* Gleddoch House *should be a natural choice. It is five miles from the
airport and 20 minutes by the M8 to the down-town area, but this substantial
residence, built in 1927 for the shipbuilding magnate Sir James Lithgow, is
tucked away from the less lovely aspects of outer Glasgow, set in a 250-acre estate
overlooking the Clyde. It has been a small luxury hotel for the past ten years. A
plus for golfers is that the Gleddoch Golf and Country Club is within the grounds
and available to hotel residents at no extra charge; there is also a squash court, a
snooker table, riding stables and trout fishing. Regrettably our* Gleddoch *file
this year has been full of complaints: disappointments in the service and in the
standard of food in the hotel's sophisticated restaurant. Hence the italics. We
should be glad of further reports.*

Open All year, except 26–27 Dec and 1–3 Jan.
Rooms 1 suite, 11 double, 8 single – 18 with bath, 2 with shower, all with
telephone, radio, colour TV, tea-making facilities and baby-listening.
Facilities Cocktail lounge, lounge bar, coffee shop, restaurant, function rooms.
250-acre grounds overlooking river Clyde, riding, 18-hole golf course, trout
fishing. Sauna, plunge pool, snooker, squash at Gleddoch Golf and Country Club
located within grounds.
Location 20 m NW of Glasgow. Take M8 towards Greenock, turn off at B789:
Langbank is signposted. Follow signs ½ mile.
Restrictions Not suitable for &. No dogs in public rooms.
Credit cards All major cards accepted.
Terms (No service charge) B&B: single £39 weekend, £53 weekday; double £58
weekend, £75 weekday. Set lunch £10, dinner £17.50; full alc £27. Golf and leisure
weekends. Reduced rates and special meals for children.
*Service/tipping: "We do not charge for service and tips are not expected, though accepted
courteously if offered so as not to offend or embarrass."*

MOFFAT Dumfries and Galloway   Map 5

Beechwood Country House Hotel [GFG]   *Tel* Moffat (0683) 20210
Moffat, Dumfriesshire DG10 9RS

An unassumingly pleasant Victorian country house just outside the
centre of Moffat in 12 acres of beech trees overlooking the Annan valley,
equally popular as a staging post and as a centre for touring Dumfries
and Galloway. Its popularity stems not just from the comforts of the
house, but also from the efforts of Keith and Sheila McIlwrick to give
added value in their service. As reported last year, the McIlwricks now
offer a substantial complimentary Scottish afternoon tea to their guests.
Flowers are in the bedrooms, along with many other little "extras", as
well as in all the public rooms. A Wayfarer's Lunch has been introduced
this year, with home-made soup, cold platter, wine and coffee at £4.15.

All bedrooms now have private bathrooms and will shortly have direct dialling. Sheila McIlwrick's cooking – a draw for many guests – continues to please; Keith McIlwrick has extended his wine list. "The McIlwrick family", as one reader puts it, "go from strength to strength." *(Irene Robertson; also T L & G Houghton, J A Clare, Margaret Owen, Heather Derbyshire)*

Open 1 Feb–31 Dec.
Rooms 6 double, 2 single – 6 with bath, 2 with shower, all with telephone, radio and tea-making facilities, baby-listening on request; 1 ground-floor room.
Facilities Lounge/bar, TV lounge, dining room. 1½-acre garden with mini-croquet lawn. Fishing in river Arran; golf, tennis and riding nearby.
Location 5 minutes from town centre. Turn into Harthope Place off A701 at St Mary's church, then turn left and follow track to hotel. Very quiet. Parking for 20 cars.
Restrictions Not suitable for &. No dogs.
Credit cards All major cards accepted.
Terms (No service charge) B&B £19–£22.50; dinner, B&B £30.50–£34; full board £36–£39.50. Set lunch £7, dinner £11.50. Weekend and mid-week terms spring and autumn. Reduced rates for children sharing parents' room; high tea for children too young to take dinner.

NAIRN Highland   Map 5

Clifton Hotel [GFG]   *Tel* Nairn (0667) 53119
Viewfield Street, Nairn
Nairnshire IV12 4HW

"A hotel hand-crafted for lovers of theatre and the theatrical. With the Moray Firth as a backdrop, impresario Gordon Macintyre has filled his old family hotel with paintings, sculptures, bas reliefs, *objets trouvés*, long-gones, bygones, fargones, the indifferent nestling happily against the tasteful, the tasteless complementing the outrageous. Centrepiece of the whole establishment is the large sea-facing dining room with tables placed upon podiums of varying heights. You feel as you climb the steps to your particular table that on some other night Macbeth may well have climbed up here or Hamlet's pa's ghost may have stalked these limelit battlements. Nor is this fancy. Mr Macintyre's principal preoccupation, apart from haunting salesrooms and country-house auctions whence the whole house has been assembled, is the production of plays. The amateur cast is assembled from a 40-mile catchment area, the grand piano is rolled aside and drama happens. There are concerts and recitals too, and you may well find Maria de la Pau Tortelier playing the piano in the dining room while Papa Paul rehearses beside her. The food is elaborate and as ambitious as the theatrical productions. 'Who does the cooking?' I enquired. 'Forbes!' replied Mr Macintyre, and one could be forgiven for feeling that it might well be the mortal ghost of the immortal Sir John Forbes Robertson himself." *(Derek Cooper)*

That description of the *Clifton*, a collector's piece for connoisseurs of the eccentric, was written in 1980, but no word needs to be altered for 1986. Forbes, now in his fourteenth year, still wears the toque. Gordon Macintyre has just been performing as Charles in *Blithe Spirit*, the play produced and directed by his wife Muriel, who is also a potter and whose studio adjoins the hotel. Not all the dishes in the restaurant are equally successful, and breakfasts have come in for some stick. But the experience of a stay at Clifton is *sui generis*, and not to be missed.

Open Mar–Nov inclusive.
Rooms 11 double, 5 single – 15 with bath, 1 with shower, beds have continental quilts, but conventional bedding available on request.
Facilities Drawing room, lounge bar, writing room with TV, cocktail bar, dining room (no smoking). Hotel licensed as theatre: concerts, plays, recitals in winter. 1-acre grounds. Fishing, shooting, riding; beach, tennis courts, swimming pool 50 yds away. 2 golf courses nearby.
Location 500 yds from town centre; turn W at roundabout; parking for 20 cars.
Restrictions Not suitable for &. No dogs in dining room.
Credit cards All major cards accepted.
Terms (Service at guests' discretion) B&B: single £30–£35, double £48.50–£62; one week half-board from £240. Full alc £15. Children's special meals by arrangement.

NEWTONMORE Highland   Map 5

Ard-Na-Coille Hotel   *Tel* Newtonmore (054 03) 214
Kingussie Road, Newtonmore
Inverness-shire PH20 1AY

The name means "High in the Woods" and this Edwardian shooting lodge stands in two acres surrounded by pines, with magnificent views over Strathspey towards the Cairngorms. The location is quiet, thanks to the A9 bypass. All the sporting facilities of Aviemore are 15 miles up the road. The hotel has only been running for the past three years, but Alastair and Annie Murchie are clearly making a successful go of it, their home cooking and wine list being well above the regional average. Apart from one correspondent, who complained of a small room and beds and pillows past their best, all our reports this year have been of the most complimentary kind. "More like staying in a well-run country house – comfortable, friendly, informal, with pictures, books, puzzles and magazines everywhere. Where else do you pick up a copy of the *Iliad* in the gent's loo?" *(Patricia Mitchell)*. "A really caring hotel. While feeding the children at high tea, a drink was sent through to my wife and myself (on the house), and the children while watching TV were sent drinks (soft!) on the house. Fresh flowers, often wild, were everywhere – also books evenly distributed throughout. Wonderful food: steak and kidney pie, fudge tart and raspberry mousse stand out" *(M McNamara)*. "We planned to stay one night and stayed seven. The style is similar to *Seatoller* in Borrowdale [q.v.] but the comfort, food and welcome are, if anything, even better." *(George Atkinson; also W A Low, K W Boothby, Fiona Mutch)*

Open Easter–end Oct; New Year and weekends during the skiing season.
Rooms 8 double, 2 single – 1 with bath, 3 with shower, all with radio and baby-listening.
Facilities Lounge, dining room, TV room, table-tennis room, drying room, terrace. 2-acre grounds. Large variety of sporting facilities within a few miles: salmon/trout fishing on river Spey (licence obtainable from local angling club), golf, pony-trekking, sailing, gliding, shooting, walking, bird-watching, skiing at Aviemore (15 m).
Location Leave A9 at Newtonmore/Kingussie signs. Hotel is at northernmost edge of Newtonmore, just outside speed restriction signs (London–Inverness trains stop at Newtonmore main line station).

Restrictions Not suitable for &. No dogs in public rooms.
Credit cards None accepted.
Terms (No service charge) B&B £12–£17.50; dinner, B&B £21–£26.50. Set dinner £9.75. Ski packages and golf breaks. 50% reduction for children sharing parents' room; special meals.
Tipping: "We make clear that nothing is expected, but quite a number of people like to leave a token of appreciation."

NEWTON STEWART Dumfries and Galloway   Map 5

Kirroughtree Hotel [GFG]   *Tel* (0671) 2141
Newton Stewart, Wigtownshire
DG8 6AN

A substantial four-storey Georgian mansion, striking rather than beautiful, in the heart of Galloway, half a mile from the A75, converted by Henry Velt and his wife into an opulently furnished, immaculately maintained hotel, with a fine restaurant in the hands of Ken MacPhee, formerly for six years head chef at *Inverlochy Castle*. Mr Velt is an enterprising landlord; he has written repeatedly to tell us of his activities and, most recently, to inform us that his hotel has been awarded the 10th International Trophy to the Tourist and Hotel Industry given by a Spanish tourist review, *Oro Verde*. His enterprise takes another form: the rooms at *Kirroughtree* contain an information folder, part of it given over to encouraging his guests to write to this and other guides. No wonder that we have been inundated with look-alike letters of appreciation. We find this form of lobbying counter-productive since it is easy to miss the spontaneous tribute among the pile of nudged offerings. This would be a pity, because in fact Mr Velt is working conscientiously to produce a well-run hotel with a superior restaurant – in fact two restaurants, one for smokers and one for the non-smoking brigade. There is an excellent and reasonably priced wine list, and the options on the set menu contain some innovative as well as more traditional dishes, all well prepared. You may not care for the ornate style of the house – lots of French reproduction furniture, and onyx coffee tables – but the rooms, both public and bed-, are extremely comfortable. It is the concern for recognition that we find off-putting.

Open 1 Mar–mid Nov.
Rooms 4 suites, 16 double, 4 single – all with bath, telephone, radio and colour TV. 2 rooms in annexe. 7 ground-floor rooms.
Facilities Bar, lounge, 2 dining rooms (one for non-smokers). 8-acre landscaped gardens with putting, bowling, tennis. River with fishing 1 m; sea with rock, sand and safe bathing 8 m.
Location ½ m from A75, 1 m from Newton Stewart.
Restrictions No children under 10 except by prior arrangement. Dogs allowed, but only in annexe bedrooms and not in public rooms.
Credit cards None accepted.
Terms (No service charge) B&B £30; dinner, B&B £48. Set dinner £18; full alc lunch (by prior arrangement) £14. Reduced rates for children sharing parents' room. 2- and 4-day breaks. Weekly rates. All terms include free golf at 2 courses.
Service/tipping: "We clearly state in our tariff and also in our room information that service is not charged for, that our staff do not expect any tips and that if guests wish to tip they should only do so provided they are entirely satisfied with the quality of food, service and friendliness."

PEEBLES Borders   Map 5

Cringletie House Hotel [GFG]   *Tel* Eddleston (072 13) 233
Peebles, Peeblesshire EH45 8PL

The postal address is Peebles, but *Cringletie* House is emphatically a country not a town house, two miles north of Peebles itself, close to the village of Eddleston. It is an imposing pink stone mansion in the Scots Baronial style, complete with turret, surrounded by well-maintained gardens and woodland, which include a hard tennis court, croquet lawn and putting green. It was once the home of the Wolfe Murray family: it was Colonel Alexander Murray from *Cringletie* who accepted the surrender of Quebec after General Wolfe had been killed. The hotel has long been appreciated by Guide readers for its kitchens and cellars as well as its civilised and welcoming atmosphere. Stanley and Aileen Maguire this year celebrate their fifteenth anniversary at *Cringletie*. As before, correspondents have been warm in their praise, though we had one complaint of a drab bedroom and a geriatric bed. Here is a characteristic report: "Your previous entry exactly encapsulates the feel of the place. Having enjoyed a well-balanced expertly served dinner and selected one of the many fine malt whiskies, the description which came to my mind was 'style'. Mr Maguire has honed himself a style which combines a certain unstated degree of formality with down-to-earth warmth. One does not need to be reminded to wear a jacket and tie to dinner. On a warm summer evening the soft hills around Peebles are different from but no less beautiful than the islands of the Western seaboard." *(Esler Crawford; H W Gallagher, Dr and Mrs James Stewart, P W Taylor, Mrs C Smith, F Tait, Dr David Clark)*

Open Mar–27 Dec.
Rooms 12 double, 4 single – 10 with bath, 1 with shower; 2 ground-floor rooms.
Facilities Small lift. 2 lounges, TV lounge, bar, dining room, occasional small conferences (8–15 people). 28-acres of gardens and woodlands with walled kitchen gardens, swings, hard tennis court, croquet and putting. Golf, and trout and salmon fishing nearby.
Location Off A703, 2½ m N of Peebles.
Restriction Not suitable for wheelchairs. No dogs in public rooms.
Credit cards None accepted
Terms (Service at guests' discretion) B&B £21–£24, dinner, B&B £34–£37; full board (5 nights min) £31–£34. Set Sun lunch £9.50, dinner £14.50. Reduced rates for children sharing parents' room; high teas.
Service/tipping: "We do not make a service charge but any gratuities are shared among the staff."

PORT APPIN Strathclyde   Map 5

The Airds Hotel [GFG]   *Tel* Appin (063 173) 236
Port Appin, Appin
Argyllshire PA38 4DF

An early 18th-century ferry inn overlooking Loch Linnhe, the islands of Lismore and the mountains of Morvern – an enchanting prospect, and *Airds* itself is a rare sort of traveller's rest, one which, year in and year out, draws from its grateful guests sustained songs of praise:
    "The nearest thing to perfection in a hotel I have ever experienced.

They didn't put a foot wrong with the food. I shall single out the wild salmon with hollandaise sauce. This was a completely new taste sensation, and I thought I *knew* what salmon was like! The service from attractively dressed and trained youngsters was impeccable. Our room was delightful with an ever-changing view. The attention to detail was superb." *(Christine Rutter)*

"A rave notice fully deserved by Mr and Mrs Allen and their charming and efficient staff. The cooking is superb. It really is a delightful hotel, so smoothly and quietly run at the highest standards. There is no TV, another mark of excellence." *(Michael Appleby)*

"A wonderful choice. Due to an emergency, Mrs Allen was manning the desk resplendent in hair rollers and towel on our arrival, and without turning a hair *(sic)* welcomed us and made us feel at home, and later on provided us with an exquisite meal. I wish I could deal with my emergencies thus! "*(Judi Jayson)*

Open Mar–Nov.
Rooms 13 double, 2 single – 6 with bath, 5 with shower;
2 rooms in annexe. 2 ground-floor rooms planned for 1986.
Facilities 2 residents' lounges, cocktail lounge, public bar, dining room. 1-acre grounds; near loch with shingle beach, bathing (not for the faint-hearted,) fishing, boating, pony-trekking, forest walks.
Location 2 m off A828, 25 m from Fort William and from Oban. Parking for 30 cars.
Restrictions Not suitable for &. No children under 5. No dogs in public rooms.
Credit cards None accepted.
Terms (No service charge) dinner, B&B: single £43, double £90. Set dinner £17.50. Reductions for children sharing parents' room; special meals.
Service/tipping: "We do not expect tips. However we find many guests still want to tip and we leave it to them."

PORTPATRICK Dumfries and Galloway   Map 5

Knockinaam Lodge Hotel   *Tel* Portpatrick (077681) 471
Portpatrick, Wigtownshire DG9 9AD

"A grand and splendid house, built in 1869, with a huge lawn and gardens running down to a private beach and with superb and tranquil views of the Irish coastline. A haven of tranquillity in an untouristy part of Scotland, and the resident proprietors, Simon and Caroline Pilkington, are charming and caring as are their delightful young staff." Only one of many similarly appreciative reports this year. Several readers mentioned the particular welcome given to their young children. A visitor from Belfast reckoned the hotel well worth a ferry trip over the Irish Sea in force 7 for a weekend. A couple on leave from Saudi Arabia, who had spent a month travelling round Scotland and Ireland, found nothing else that measured up in all categories to *Knockinaam*. Special praise was reserved for the "exquisite" meals served by chef John Henry. We are the more happy to acknowledge the hospitality of the Pilkingtons since their hotel has fared poorly in these columns these last two years. *(D Crosier, John Gagg, Mrs E M Shanks, Susan and Ted Hall, and others)*

Open Easter–end Oct, also Christmas and New Year.
Rooms 9 double, 1 single – 7 with bath, 1 with shower, all with radio, 3 with TV.
Facilities Cocktail bar, morning room, drawing room with TV, dining room.
30-acre grounds with croquet. Sea 50 yds, private sandy beach, safe bathing, sea

255

fishing, slipway for boats; 2 golf courses nearby.
Location 3 m S of Portpatrick on minor road. Turn left (coming from Stranraer) on the A77 3 m after Lochans and 3 m before Portpatrick. Hotel is signposted.
Restrictions Not suitable for &. No children under 10 in dining room. No dogs in public rooms.
Credit cards None accepted.
Terms Dinner, B&B £34–£60. Bar lunches from £4.50; table d'hôte £16.25. Spring rates between Easter and mid-May, 2-night bargain breaks during Oct, all-inclusive rates for winter weekends throughout Nov and Dec, Christmas and New Year packages, special rates for small conferences in Nov and Dec. Reduced rates and high tea at 6 pm for children.
Service/tipping: "This is entirely at the discretion of the guests. If they feel they have been well looked after during their stay, they may feel inclined to leave a tip with the staff."

PORTSONACHAN Strathclyde   Map 5

Portsonachan Hotel [GFG]   *Tel* Kilchrenan (086 63) 224
Portsonachan, by Dalmally
Argyllshire PA33 1BL

This hotel first appeared in the Guide last year after we received an enthusiastic report from *Diana Hayes*, commending in particular its lovely situation on Loch Awe and the excellent food provided by Savoy-trained Christopher Trotter who runs it with his wife, Caroline. (They took over the management of the hotel, which had become very run-down, in 1982.) An inspector, while initially taken aback by the scruffy state of some of the rooms, was soon won over by the friendliness of the young Trotters and their staff, and the outstanding meals; and made particular mention of the baking – wholemeal toast at breakfast, biscuits and scones at tea-time, pastries at dinner. Since then we have received many more letters praising the food, the situation and the service, but one very critical one, mentioning small bedrooms, paper-thin walls and uncomfortable beds. Doubtless it will take time to get everything right. Christopher Trotter tells us that they have now put more carpets in the bedrooms, redone the public bar and are rebuilding a cottage on the hill behind the hotel to take staff, which will allow all the hotel rooms to be kept for guests. Only three of the bedrooms have private baths, but bedrooms without private bath are the ones enjoying lake views, and there are plenty of public bathrooms. *(R L Mobbs, Janet and Norman Chambers, Fred Lang, and others)*

Open Mar–mid Nov, Christmas and New Year.
Rooms 16 double, 1 single – 3 with bath, all with radio, tea-making facilities and baby-listening.
Facilities 2 lounges, 1 with TV, public bar, residents' bar, dining room. Large garden. Hotel has own jetty on Loch Awe and 10 rowing boats (engines available). Safe bathing and fishing in Loch Awe. River and sea loch fishing can be arranged.
Location 10 m S of Dalmally. On B840 off A819 Dalmally – Inverary road. (Portsonachan often shown on maps as Southport.)
Restrictions Not suitable for &. No dogs allowed in public rooms.
Credit cards Access, Visa.
Terms (Service at guests' discretion) B&B £14–£23.25; dinner, B&B £22–£32.25; full board £26–£36.25, Set 3-course buffet lunch £4, 4-course dinner £10.50. Reduced rates and high teas for children. Christmas and New Year packages. Reductions for stays of 3 nights or more. Reduced rates off season.
Service/tipping: "We do not have a fixed charge and leave it to our guests should they want to leave anything. There is no attempt to compel people to tip."

RAASAY Skye, Highland   Map 5

Isle of Raasay Hotel   *Tel* Raasay (047 862) 222
by Kyle of Lochalsh, Skye IV40 8PB

Recently opened by the Highlands and Islands Development Board on
the tiny (4 miles wide by 15 miles long) island off Skye. "The hotel is
superbly situated, sheltered by wooded hills and looking across the
straits to the Cuillin mountains of Skye. It is a marvellous centre for
walking, although Raasay is big enough to make it worth bringing a car –
the ferry (10 minutes) runs three times a day from Sconser on Skye. The
bedrooms are comfortable, with private bath/wc, and the management –
Mrs Nicholson and her daughter Fiona – are quite charming. The food is
copious and wholesome. The snags are (a) the hotel serves no lunch,
though there is a bar where one can buy snacks; or one can order a
packed lunch; (b) the lounge is far too small, so the chairs are arranged
in a circle, as if for a seminar; (c) the ceilings of the downstairs bedrooms
are far from sound-proof, so if someone big is in the room above, it can
sound like a herd of elephants, just above one's head. (My advice would
be to insist on an upstairs room when booking.) On balance I strongly
recommend the place. Raasay is a very beautiful island." *(Tim Brierly;
warmly endorsed by Eric Major)*

Open April–Sept.
Rooms 11 double, 1 single – all with bath, radio, colour TV and tea-making
facilities; 6 ground-floor rooms, one specifically furnished for physically disabled.
Facilities Residents' lounge with TV, bar, dining room. Small garden at front of
hotel. Good walking country; trout fishing in lochs (hotel can arrange sea-angling
day trips) 5 minutes' walk from sea. &.
Location Travel to Kyle from Inverness or to Mallaig from Glasgow; take the ferry
to Kyleakin or Armadale respectively. Proceed to Sconser village on Loch
Sligachan; there are 3 ferries daily (except Sun) to Raasay, taking about 10
minutes. Hotel is signposted from ferry terminal.
Restriction Dogs allowed, but not in public rooms.
Credit cards None accepted.
Terms (No service charge) B&B £16.50. Bar and packed lunches available. Set
dinner £10. Weekly rates £155. Reduced rates for children.

ST OLA Orkney   Map 5

Foveran   *Tel* Kirkwall (0856) 2389
St Ola, Nr Kirkwall, Orkney KW15 1SF

Continued enthusiasm for our only entry in the Orkneys, two and a half
miles from Kirkwall and half a mile inland from the sea, at a welcoming
small hotel overlooking Scapa Flow designed by architect/owner Bashir
Hasham. The restaurant specialises in well-prepared local dishes and
enjoys a strong local following. The bedrooms are Scandinavian in
design, with pleasant accents of colour. A report last year read: "Greeted
by a be-pastried Mrs Hasham – charming in a sweet as well as efficient
cap. Food was original in conception, good quality, fair value,
attractively presented if occasionally lacking in finesse. Mr Hasham
plays a charming supportive background role." *(M R Medcalf)*

A more recent visitor, after commending "the sensible management,
delightful service and excellent food (and not a bad wine list)", adds

another picture of Norma Hasham: "It is not often in my experience that mine hostess squats before an open fire and melts marshmallows for her guests after dinner – a mind-blowing gesture." A three-timer from Oregon reaffirmed "the gracious hospitality and warmth ... a highlight of our British holiday". *Note:* a car is advisable. And another correspondent offers a warning about the local pebble beach – "a desolate, seaweedy, rubbish-strewn little corner, not worth the tramp. Far better to scarper to Scapa – an excellent sandy beach, only five minutes' drive away." *(John Timpson, Dr and Mrs James Stewart, Dr and Mrs Stanley Boyd, and others)*

Open All year except Oct. Restaurant closed Sun to non-residents.
Rooms 5 double, 3 single – 3 with bath, 5 with shower, all with radio and tea-making facilities; all rooms on ground floor but not suitable for wheelchairs.
Facilities Lounge with open fire, TV room, dining room. 15-acre grounds; small pebble beach. Loch and sea fishing, archaeological sites, bird reserve, swimming, golf and squash nearby. Parking.
Location SW of Kirkwall on A964, 2½ m from where it leaves A963. Hotel is signposted.
Restrictions Not suitable for &. No dogs in public rooms.
Credit cards Access, Visa.
Terms (No service charge) B&B: single £18–£18.50, double £26–£30. Full alc £16. Weekly rates. Reduced rates for children sharing parents' room; special meals on request.
Service/tipping: "Guests are not encouraged to tip individual staff. No obligatory service charge is made. Any gratuities given by customers are shared by all members of staff."

SALEN Mull, Strathclyde   Map 5

Glenforsa Hotel   *Tel* Aros (068 03) 377 and 379
Salen, Aros, Isle of Mull PA72 6JN

A friendly rural motel, built on the Norwegian log pattern, overlooking the adjacent airlanding strip and the Sound of Mull and the mountains of Morvern. "And you might think you were actually in Norway, so beautiful is the scenery in all parts of Mull. All rooms are on the ground floor, some with bath or shower – and there is plenty of provision for those without. The hotel has been run for many years by Mr and Mrs Howitt, helped by their son Roger and his wife Frances. We much enjoyed the excellent home cooking, both four-course dinners (sometimes venison, often Scottish salmon), and superb breakfasts." (R J Bateman; endorsed by K A McCleave, H G Wrigglesworth) Not all readers share Mr Bateman's approval, however. Several recent reports have detailed failings, most notably in the housekeeping and maintenance area. More reports welcome.

Open Easter–Oct; Christmas and New Year if sufficient demand.
Rooms 14 double – 7 with bath/shower, 2 with telephone; all on ground floor.
Facilities TV, lounge bar/cocktail bar, dining room; terrace; occasional ceilidhs. 6½-acre grounds with access to river; shingle beach 250 yds, dinghy available; 4 m of seatrout/salmon fishing on river Forsa, loch and sea fishing, pony-trekking, 2 golf courses close by. &.
Location 1¼ m from Salen village. 10 and 5½ m respectively from two Mull ferry terminals of Craignure and Fishnish, then 250 yds off Craignure – Tobermory road. (All guests given instructions and ferry timetables when booking.) Airstrip adjacent to hotel (open dawn to dusk).
Restrictions No children under 5. No dogs in public rooms.
Credit cards None accepted.

Terms B&B £14.50–£20; dinner, B&B £23.50–£28. Bar lunches and snacks from about £2.50; set dinner £9–£9.50; full alc £12.50. Special holiday Mull package (1 week), off-season reductions. Reduced rates for children according to age; children's supper at 5.45 pm.

SCARISTA Western Isles   Map 5

Scarista House Hotel [GFG]   *Tel* Scarista (085 985) 238
Scarista, Isle of Harris PA85 3HX

A correspondent who has spent a year travelling extensively throughout the UK with the help of the Guide tells us that he found two hotels outstanding. "One was *Scarista*, notable for its happy atmosphere, its warm and capable hosts, and for its meals, breakfasts second to none and dinners second only to *Woodhayes*, Whimple (q.v.); a remarkable accomplishment in a remote location. Neither hotel had any weakness. They deserve your highest ratings" (*James McCowan*). Another tribute from this year's bumper crop: "A model of a country house hotel. The Johnsons treat their clients as personal guests and are ever thoughtful of their needs without being over-bearing. This promotes the sort of atmosphere in which pre-and post-prandial conversation is enjoyable" (*Professor B D Ripley*).

Not much has altered in the past year at Andrew and Alison Johnson's Georgian manse overlooking a magnificent stretch of Atlantic beach on the western, gentler part of Harris. It won a *César* in 1984 for civilised living in the wilds, and merits that award no less two years later. Newspaper neurotics will need to drive 55 miles to get a same-day paper, but other print addicts will enjoy an extended library, particularly in the wildlife and nature-studies section. Misanthropists should be warned about those evening conversations around the peat fires in the library and sitting room – not everyone's scene of course. Otherwise, the major changes have been in the restaurant: the wine list has been much enlarged – "a list of which any hotel could be proud ... Many little-known wines well worth adventuring into as well as those from the great names. Prices very reasonable for the quality" – and the menus have become rather less carnivore orientated. The Johnsons are active in the anti-factory farming movement, and eschew all intensively farmed eggs, meat or fish. "Most Scotch salmon", says Alison Johnson, "is fishing farmed flab now – cruel to fish and foul to eat."

Open Easter – early Oct. May be closed occasional weekends.
Rooms 7 double – all with bath and tea-making facilities; 4 rooms in annexe.
Facilities Drawing room with peat fires (and central heating), well-stocked library, 2 dining rooms. 2-acre grounds. Access to miles of sandy beach; sea-fishing.
Location 15 m SW of Tarbert on A859, 50 m SW of Stornoway. Regular ferries from Ullapool to Stornoway and from Uig to Tarbert; daily flights to Stornoway from Glasgow and Inverness. The hotel will arrange car hire.
Restrictions No children under 7. Dogs by special arrangement, and not in public rooms.
Credit cards None accepted.
Terms (No service charge) B&B: single occupancy £33–£36, double £40–£50; dinner, B&B: single occupancy £45.50–£50; double £65–£78. Light or packed lunch £6; set dinner £14.
Service/tipping: "We are uncommitted on this subject, but try to avoid putting pressure on guests."

SCONE Tayside   Map 5

Balcraig House [GFG]   *Tel* Scone (0738) 51123
By Scone

Balcraig House is a distinctly luxurious small country house hotel five minutes from the centre of Perth. It is set in 130 acres of farm and market garden, run solely for the benefit of the kitchens. The restaurant offers a long and ambitious menu. The bedrooms all have elegant bathrooms *en suite*. "Enter a different world," says their tariff card, "with a view to gracious living." There is no doubt that Michael and Kitty Pearl, who acquired the hotel a few years back, have set their sights high. And at least some of the reports received this past year suggest they are fulfilling their aims. "Well above average in all aspects," writes a distinguised restaurateur from Avon. "Good rooms, excellent food, fantastic wine list, very reasonably priced. Proprietor closely involved. Would recommend without hesitation." But another resonant name in the catering business, though he appreciated the comforts of the house, took a more critical view and wished that the chef had offered a shorter menu and relied less on the freezer. Other readers echoed that view. One, who certainly favoured the hotel's entry in the Guide, but felt obliged to register a course-by-course critique of the dinner, summed up: "Scotland boasts some marvellous hotels and *Balcraig* deserves to be rated among them. The efforts of the kitchen outshine most British eating establishments. Their attitudes, ingredients, approach and presentation are exemplary. Perhaps they lack only judgement and encouragement."

Open All year.
Rooms 10 double – all with bathroom, telephone, radio and colour TV.
Facilities Drawing room, library, dining room (with wheelchair access). 130-acre grounds with 10-acre gardens, tennis, croquet, *boules*, free-range farms, stables, pony-trekking, and riding; tours round farms. Trout fishing on many lochs in the area, salmon fishing on river Tay (prior arrangement essential); game hunting (also by prior arrangment); excellent walking; many castles nearby.
Location Off A94 3½ m NE of Perth.
Restriction No dogs in public rooms.
Credit cards All major cards accepted.
Terms B&B: single occupancy £42.50–£55; double £75–£87.50; dinner, B&B: single £62.50–£75, double £115–£127.50. Lunch by arrangement; set dinner £20. Special meals available. Winter weekend breaks. Reduced rates for children.

SCOURIE Highland   Map 5

Eddrachilles Hotel   *Tel* Scourie (0971) 2080
Badcall Bay, Scourie, Sutherland IV27 4TH

A simple but well-run hotel in the far north-west of Scotland – "a haven of comfort," according to one reader. No frills in the cooking but generous helpings. "A long lonely and narrow road runs north-west from Dornoch or Lairg to a hamlet on the edge of restless waters bedecked by the myriads of islets and islands. The country which it crosses lies close to some of the oldest mountains in the world. The narrow road suddenly begins to dip downhill at a dramatic viewpoint and tiny Scourie lies ahead. Hill-walkers living in the area claim that

Eddrachilles has interest enough around it for two fully occupied weeks of hill-walking and hill-scrambling. The hotel is also ideally placed for bird-watchers and there is an important bird sanctuary on Handa Island. It has an austere location but Mr and Mr Wood provide bed and board way beyond what any traveller would be likely to expect in such a remote area." *(George Mair)*

Not all visitors have agreed with *George Mair*'s citation, and the hotel was left out last year. There have been modest refurbishments since but it is the hotel's beautiful setting which remains its prime attraction. Mrs Wood warns: "The hotel is ideally suited to those who like an outdoor holiday in a remote setting. The weather, even in summer, can be quite adverse. Previous entries in the Guide have brought us some guests who have left unhappy – it was too cold and wet for them to go outside, there is little to do in the hotel all day, and the local area has nothing in the way of sheltered leisure facilities – shops, museums or castles." *(G & E Atkinson, Mr and Mr H E Wilson)*

Open Mar–Oct.
Rooms 1 suite, 10 double – 3 with bath, 8 with shower, all with radio, colour TV on request and baby-listening; 4 ground-floor rooms.
Facilities Lounge, lounge bar, public bar, 2 dining rooms. Hotel stands in 320-acre estate at the head of Badcall Bay with woodland paths; boats for hire. 2 inland lochs with brown trout fishing. Near to sea with rocky shore and to Handa Island bird sanctuary.
Location 2½ m S of Scourie on A894. Hotel is well signposted.
Restrictions Not suitable for &. No children under 3. No dogs in public rooms.
Terms (No service charge) B&B £17.75–£22.40; dinner, B&B £24–£28.65; full board £28–£32.65. Bar snack lunch about £4 (packed lunches also available); set dinner £6.25; full alc £13.50.
Service/tipping: "Service charge is not applied. Tipping is neither actively encouraged nor discouraged, not for us to take the easy way out, but to reflect accurately the wide range of views of our guests."

SLEAT Skye, Highland   **Map 5**

Kinloch Lodge [GFG]   *Tel* Isle Ornsay (047 13) 214
Sleat, Isle of Skye IV43 8QY

Lord and Lady Macdonald, a thoroughly genial couple, have run this traditional white-painted shooting lodge at the head of the Sleat Peninsula as a hotel for many years, but it is only comparatively recently that they and their family have been living on the premises. Many improvements have been taking place since then: there are now 10 rooms, mostly on the small side, but each has its private bath *en suite*; the house has been double-glazed throughout; there are now two drawing rooms to prevent overcrowding before and after dinner. The quality of the cooking in the elegant dining room is one of the features of *Kinloch*: Lady Macdonald, cookbook writer as well as *châtelaine*, is an enthusiastic and inventive cook, and assisted by chef Peter Macpherson, continues to provide as good hotel cooking as you will get on Skye. In previous editions, we have commented on the uneven standards of decor and furnishings and the potholes on the one-mile drive from the main road. The drive has had some repairs recently, but meanwhile one reader angrily takes us to task: "How nit-picky can you get? We are talking about Skye not Central London, and to me that just adds to the charm and sense of adventure of 'The Road to the Isles'." As for the fixtures and fittings another correspondent comments: "The saving grace of the hotel is precisely that you do *not* get sumptuary fittings. Thank goodness that the rooms *are* less elegant than one would expect. It is the very contrast between the five-star reception and food and the two-star decor that makes this hotel such a haven." *(A Rampton; also B G Thomas, Henry Robb, Paul Jackson)*

Open 1 Mar – 10 Jan (except Christmas).
Rooms 10 double – all with bath and tea-making facilities. 1 ground-floor room.
Facilities 2 drawing rooms, one with TV, dining room; 200-acre grounds, superb hill-walking and climbing; sea at bottom of garden. Swimming; bird, seal and otter watching, stalking and rough shooting. Fishing (trout salmon and sea trout) available. Boats for hire. Pony-trekking, golf, sailing all within 20 m.
Location 1 m off A851, 6 m of S of Broadford, 10 m N of Armadale ferry. 4 flights weekly from Glasgow. Through-train London to Mallaig, then Armadale Ferry.
Restrictions Not really suitable for children under 8. No dogs in public rooms.
Credit cards None accepted.
Terms B&B £29–£40; dinner, B&B £46–£56. Set dinner £16.90. High teas for children under 8.
Service/tipping: "We no longer operate a service charge. The staff are adequately remunerated and do not expect tips. Any money left by clients is pooled and evenly distributed, but clients are in no way encouraged to leave anything extra."

SPEAN BRIDGE Highland   Map 5

Letterfinlay Lodge Hotel   *Tel* Invergloy (039 784) 222
Spean Bridge, Inverness-shire
PH34 4DZ

Two sets of readers – one from Chelmsford, Essex, England, and the other from Walla Walla, Washington, USA – sending in a batch of reports, often critical, from their respective holiday tourings, reserve their highest commendations for this unassumingly friendly family hotel overlooking Loch Lochy, seven miles north of Spean Bridge on the A82 to Fort Augustus and Inverness. The tariff is modest, so don't expect anything specially sophisticated in the restaurant or in the impersonal modern furnishings. But it is clear that the Family Forsyth-Allan, the father, assisted by sons Ian and Roy, succeed in the most crucial test, that of making their guests long to extend their stay and come again. Children, including babies, are welcomed. Here are a few nuggets from the comprehensive collection of compliments: "Something very exceptional ... Highland hospitality at its best ... A team whose friendliness and warm sense of humour and utter sense of dedication make this one of the finest small hotels we have ever stayed in ... Excellent local ingredients in the cooking ... Wonderful views ... We have left with the greatest reluctance ... By far the cleanest, best-appointed public bathrooms we have ever encountered ... Unsurpassed scenery ... Infinitely peaceful and infinitely pleasant." *(Gwen and Peter Andrews, Suzanne L Martin)*

Open All year.
Rooms 5 suites, 13 double, 2 single – 2 with bath, 3 with shower, all with radio and baby-listening.
Facilities Small lounge with TV, large sun-lounge, cocktail bar, dining room. 20-acre grounds. Fishing, boating and swimming (but cold!) in loch.

Location About 16 m N of Fort William, off A82, overlooking Loch Lochy.
Restrictions Not suitable for &. No dogs in dining rooms; preferably on leash in
public rooms.
Credit cards All major cards accepted
Terms B&B £12.50–£19; dinner, B&B £9.50–£10 added. Snack lunch £1–£10,
dinner £10. Reduced rates for children sharing parents' room, depending on age.
*Service/tipping: "We do not accept 'tipping' but have a service included in our rates
distributed to staff, so that 'tipping' is quite unnecessary."*

TARBERT Strathclyde   Map 5

Stonefield Castle   *Tel* Tarbert (088 02) 207
Tarbert, Loch Fyne, Argyllshire PA29 6YJ

Once a seat of the Campbells, this characteristic example of the Victorian
baronial has 60 acres of grounds in a striking position overlooking Loch
Fyne. There is a sunny sheltered terrace and an outdoor swimming pool.
Some rooms are lofty after the style of Scottish barons, others are more
modest and modern in an extension. It is a popular watering-hole for
yachtspeople, who can moor their boats in the bay at the foot of the hill
and walk up through (in May) the superb azaleas and rhododendrons.
Our inspector last year found the decor undistinguished, sometimes
jarring in its colour schemes and shabby in places, but also recognised
the solid three-star virtues of the place. A *Stonefield* regular reports some
major refurbishment had been undertaken recently, and that a new
mini-suite was "superb". He also tells us – can this be true ? – that
businessmen are now flying up from Glasgow just to lunch in "what I
still think is the most beautiful dining room in Scotland". *(P Grimsdale)*

Open Apr–Oct.
Rooms 2 suites, 24 double, 6 single – all with telephone, radio, colour TV,
tea-making facilities and baby-listening.
Facilities Lift. Drawing room, library, bar, restaurant. Pool/table tennis room.
60-acre grounds with heated swimming pool and tennis courts. Fishing in Tarbert
Loch; mooring, 5 golf courses in area.
Location 10 m S of Ardrishaig on W shore of Loch Fyne.
Restriction No dogs in public rooms
Credit cards All major cards accepted.
Terms [1985 rates] (service at guests' discretion) B&B £30–£50. Set lunch from
£2.50, dinner from £17.50. Bargain rates all year. Reduced rates and special meals
for children.

TIMSGARRY Isle of Lewis, Outer Hebrides   Map 5

Baile-Na-Cille   *Tel* Timsgary (085 05) 242
Timsgarry, Uig, Isle of Lewis PA86 9JD

Our only hotel on Lewis, a converted 18th-century manse, run with flair
by Richard and Joanna Gollin, originally recommended to Guide readers
by *G F S Shipway*: "Superb setting on sea shore . . . No fancy facilities,
and no licence, but the communal lounge has piano, TV and hi-fi, and
the accommodation is very comfortable – old-fashioned rather than
modern. The food all prepared by Joanna Gollin can only be described as
bountiful – country cooking rather than *haute cuisine*, but highly
appropriate to the setting. Very good value." Most subsequent visitors
have warmly endorsed that nomination, though not without occasional

263

niggles. Meals are taken communally, which doesn't suit everyone. There is plenty to do at Timsgarry, but the village is 34 miles from Stornoway, with the last 18 on a single track road, with many hairpin bends – not ideal if you like to do a lot of touring by car. The chief complainants were couples who had booked in the summer of 1984, and arrived to find that the Gollins were on a six-week vacation in France, and had left the hotel in the hands of two inexperienced young women, who did their best but ... We are assured that the Gollins have no intention of leaving their future guests in the lurch; otherwise Lewis would be a blank space on our map.

Open All year except 10 Dec – 10 Jan.
Rooms 3 double, 2 single – 1 with bath, all with tea-making facilities and baby-listening; 1 ground-floor room with adjacent bathroom.
Facilities Sitting room with TV and hi-fi, 2 dining rooms. 2-acre grounds with walled garden and direct access to beach. Near 7 sandy beaches with safe bathing; trout and sea fishing; sailing, trips in hotel's boat to see seals and birds.
Location 34 m W of Stornoway. Take A858 from Stornoway (or Tarbert) to Garynahine, B8011 towards Uig; at Miavaig follow signs to *Baile-Na-Cille*.
Restrictions Not suitable for &. Dogs only allowed in bedrooms if well behaved.
Credit cards None accepted.
Terms B&B £12–£14 (private bath £2 extra); dinner, B&B £21–£23. Set dinner £10. Special weekly packages for walkers, bird-watchers, trout fishermen and sea anglers. Reduced rates and special meals for children.

TIRORAN Mull, Strathclyde   Map 5

Tiroran House [GFG]   *Tel* Tiroran (068 15) 232
Tiroran, Isle of Mull PA69 6EF

The Hebrides have not only some of the most dramatic scenery in Britain, but also some of the most civilised hotels. *Tiroran House* is a modernised shooting lodge above Loch Scridain, with 12 acres of gardens and woodlands sweeping down to the loch on which the hotel has its own dinghies and a boat for day trips. Readers continue to confirm an earlier tribute: "This delightful small country house hotel is owned and managed by Wing Commander and Mrs Blockey; it is in effect their own private home which they open as a hotel in the summer. No TV, room phones, muzak, or even newspapers: perfect peace and quiet. Excellent breakfast: very fine Finnan haddock and fresh home-made bread every day. Dinner is the highlight of each day, served at one sitting at 7.45 pm. No choice of main course, but for starters and desserts there is always a choice of three dishes. Mrs Blockey is a superb cook, and we never had the same dishes twice during our week's stay." (G S Chadwick)

Open May–mid-Oct.
Rooms 8 double, 1 single – all with bath, radio and tea-making facilities; 2 rooms in annexe.
Facilities 2 drawing rooms, dining room, games room. 14-acre gardens and woodland, croquet lawn; immediate access to sea loch safe for bathing, sailing, canoeing; dinghies and boats for sea trips.
Location Oban-Craignure car ferry (45 minutes) bookable with Caledonian McBrayne, The Pier, Gourock PA19 1QP. (Lochaline–Fishnish car ferry is not bookable – but much cheaper – and necessitates a longish but superb drive through Morvern.) From Craignure ferry terminal take A849 to Fionnphort. At

head of Loch Scridain turn right on to B8035; after 5 m turn left to Tiroran (1 m).
Restrictions Not suitable for &. No children under 10. Dogs at manager's discretion, but not in public rooms.
Credit cards None accepted.
Terms B&B £33. Set (light) lunch £6.50, dinner £17. 5- and 7-day all-inclusive holidays including reimbursement of car ferry ticket. Reductions for stays of 3 nights or more.

TWEEDSMUIR Borders   Map 5

The Crook Inn [GFG]   *Tel* Tweedsmuir (089 97) 272
Tweedsmuir, Biggar
Lanarkshire ML12 6QN

A modest family-run inn dating from 1701 and claiming to be the oldest licensed inn in Scotland – a rambling white old building in the heart of John Buchan country, It also has associations with Sir Walter Scott and Burns; the latter wrote *Willie Wastle's Wife* in the old kitchen. Good walking and climbing country: Broad Law, the second highest peak in southern Scotland, is five miles from the inn. There are three golf courses within easy reach. As for fishing, hotel guests have the run of 30 miles of trout water on the Tweed; there are also seven miles of private salmon fishing six miles downstream from the hotel available to guests.

One visitor reported poor housekeeping and a surly reception, but others have continued to find *The Crook* as hospitable as previously. Debbie Masraff tells us that the geriatric mattress in Room 3, complained of last year, has been replaced and some improvements made with the sound-proofing. "After several Scottish disappointments, at last somewhere worthy of a repeat visit. The inn is miles from anywhere in splendid walking country, but, despite its isolation, well served with locals. Reception was a bit austere, but there's a most attractive residents' lounge for relaxing after dinner away from the hubbub of the main rooms. Dinner was imaginative without being too ambitious, with an emphasis on fresh herbs. All in all, a real find." *(A & J Leeming; also the Rt Revd Peter Coleman)*

Open All year except Christmas and Boxing Days. Restaurant may be closed weekdays Jan and Feb.
Rooms 7 double, 1 single – 5 with bath, 1 with shower, all with tea-making facilities.
Facilities Residents' lounge with TV, lounge, high-tea lounge, cocktail bar, restaurant, games room. 3-acre garden; river Tweed at bottom, with trout fishing. 3 golf courses nearby.
Location On A701, 1 m of Tweedsmuir. Parking.
Restrictions Not suitable for &. No children under 10 in dining room. No dogs in public rooms.
Credit cards None accepted.
Terms (No service charge) B&B: single £24–£28, double £40–£48; half-board: single £34–£38, double £54–£68. Set dinner £12. 2-day breaks all year; very reduced rates in spring. 3-day Hogmanay celebrations. Reduced rates and high tea for children.
Service/tipping: "We have no service charge and we do not encourage our staff to expect gratuities – but we are perfectly happy for them to receive them. Tips are demeaning neither to the donor nor to the recipient if they are genuinely given and genuinely received. It is a way of saying 'thank you' and as such encourages staff to greater efforts."

ULLAPOOL Highland   Map 5

Altnaharrie [GFG]   *Tel* Dundonnell (085 483) 230
Ullapool, Wester Ross IV26 2SS

"A tiny, cosy and charming inn oppposite Ullapool across Loch Broom.
As *Altnaharrie* is virtually inaccessible by land, you get ferried over the
water like Lord Ullin's daughter in the proprietor's excellent wee
motor-boat. The house is a centuries-old drovers' inn with just a handful
of bedrooms. The furnishing is comfortable and pretty, and the food
wonderful. I go quite weak when I remember the Loch Broom prawns,
large as langoustines, local fresh salmon, venison pâté, succulent roast
lamb and puddings of such creamy lightness as defy gravity. Oh, the
delight of lying in an *Altnaharrie* bath with a pre-prandial drink, relaxing
in the soft Highland water straight off the peat, of a colour somewhere
between lager and Guinness, the only noises being your companion
murmuring through the door what's on the evening menu, and Loch
Broom outside the window gently turning itself over at the edge. The
neighbourhood has splendid walks. We saw deer, seal and all sorts of
great northern sea birds. Further, at Ullapool for 20 weeks of the
summer, the mackerel catch is landed and it is an entertainment and an
education to watch the haul being transferred from ship to shore. Our
host Mr Brown was kindness itself. A very honeymoony place."

Shelley Cranshaw's original nomination of this very special place and
the hospitality of Fred Brown and his Norwegian partner, Gunn
Eriksen, have been endorsed by many subsequent visitors. Stops tend to
get pulled out even further than usual: "The most excellent dinner that
either my wife or I can every recall having had in any hotel or
restaurant." "The food was consistently the best I've eaten anywhere."
"An idyllic place. It is very small and intimate and demands that the
guests are sociable; that they become so is due to the friendliness of
Gunn and Fred and to Gunn's incredible cooking. It is absolutely
inspired and we feel cheated if we do not sample everything she offers.
Gunn uses local produce to its best possible advantage; dinners are the
high spot of the day and one is compelled to walk a lot to make room for
the next night's extravaganza. We love *Altnaharrie* as much for Gunn and
Fred as for the unique atmosphere it offers through only being reached
by Fred's ferry." (*Dr James Mair, Mrs J R Jorgensen, Judi Jayson; also Beryl
Crawford, Marcia Suddards, Mr and Mrs A Lindner*)

Open Apr–early Oct.
Rooms 4 double – 2 with bath; self-catering chalet.
Facilities Residents' lounge, bar, dining room, TV on request. 15-acre garden,
pebbled beach. Safe (but cold) bathing. Trout/lobster/deep-sea fishing; free
canoes/small dinghies.
Location By water's edge on western shore of Loch Broom. Access to hotel by
private launch from Ullapool harbour. Private parking in Ullapool. Guests
requested to telephone for launch on arrival in Ullapool.
Restrictions Not suitable for &. No children under 10. Dogs allowed by
arrangement, but not in public rooms.
Credit cards None accepted.
Terms (No service charge) B&B £25–£30. Set dinner £17; bar lunches from £1.50.
Reduced rates for children sharing parents' room; special meals.
Service/tipping: "There is no service charge, nor do we encourage tipping."

The Ceilidh Place
14 West Argyle Street, Ullapool
IV26 2TY

César awarded for utterly acceptable mild eccentricity

Jean and Robert Urquhart (he, a TV actor when not running the *Place*) are doing their own thing with splendid verve in their hotel/clubhouse/restaurant/coffee shop/bookshop complex near the centre of Ullapool. Never mind that some rooms overlook a caravan site and others a council-house back garden; raise your eyes and the scenic grandeur of Loch Broom and the mountains of Western Ross lie before you. "Ceilidh" means something like get-together, and the hotel – or whatever you like to call it – has live shows of jazz, classical and folk music at least once a week in the summer, though out of earshot of hotel rooms. Most readers have again enjoyed "the quite unusual taste and charm" of the *Ceilidh* experience, conveyed best perhaps by quoting from its brochure, a prize-winning effort in describing a zany *sui generis* establishment.

"We made a Coffee Shop in the boat-shed to play music and hang pictures, but it stretched into rooms and bathrooms really posh until up jumped the Clubhouse with its family accommodation and space for an exhibition gallery and auditorium so where are we?

"Just past the post office with jazz and folk as well as classical music and the Coffee Shop is all day forever. Write your memoirs, watch the world go by with light meals and the best selection of salads you ever saw. From four-thirty until seven o'clock bed time for the weans the tea shop is open as a shrine to the Scottish Golfer with a swing to the East. Hi Tee, ha ha, is designed for kids and devoured by dads who know how to order an egg to a haddie. There is cake and tea bread, scones and shortbread which does not notice a discreet refreshment in the lee of the teapot and the Garden Room! Hosanna in the highest! This, the big one as meals go, arises in glory about 6.30 pm or eighteen thirty-five if you wish the continental menu. Its daily miracle is table d'hôte and secular pleasure comes on a French list called Ally Cart where dishes come toujours et toute le monde in memory of an auld sang. Where are we?

"Nearly finished. We have not described a single dish in detail but this sin of omission we can only offer our modesty and if you wish to seek confirmation of your own impeccable taste, we would refer you to any of the excellent guides which make a modest fortune for their publishers by praising our arrangements. For ourselves, we cling to understatements. The catchers catch, the farmers farm and the furred, the feathered and the fish arrive, wistful but delicious at our kitchen door. The boat trips trip, the climbers tell tall tales to the hill walkers and the cook says the supernatural is nothing to do with second sight. It is simply the vegetarian perfection she also provides.

"Come stay with us and let us be where we would be, alive in your heart forever. That is the magic of Wester Ross. We will arrange sea angling for you, ski-ing tow-boats, loch fishing and pony trekking. We will tell you of and guide you in all manner of pursuits but we provide you with music, comfort and rest so that you may contemplate the madness of such strenuous activity. Come and be welcome."

Give the Guide positive support. Don't just leave feedback to others.

Open Mar–Oct.
Rooms 12 double, 3 single – 8 with bath. 11 extra rooms (simpler, with bunk beds etc.) in Clubhouse in annexe.
Facilities Lounge, Clubhouse bar, coffee shop, games room, dining room; jazz, classical and folk music evenings at least once a week. Small garden; private fishing in Ledmore Lochs; rocky beach, boat trips, sea angling, waterskiing, pony-trekking, climbing, deep-sea diving.
Location First right after Pier at W end of Main Street. Large car park.
Restrictions Not suitable for &. No dogs in public rooms.
Credit card Diners.
Terms (No service charge) B&B £19–£24.50; dinner, B&B £28.50–£35. In Clubhouse £7.50–£8.50 for bed; continental breakfast £3.50, English breakfast £4.75. Packed lunches £2.75. Special rates for 6 days or more. Reduced rates and special meals for children.

WALLS Shetland   Map 5

Burrastow House [GFG]   *Tel* Walls (059 571) 307
Walls, Shetland ZE2 9PD

"Burrastow House is at the end of the road which runs west of Lerwick, past the Voes or flat fjords of Weisdale, Sandsound and Gruting, to Walls. From there the single-track road winds past Linga island and the white-flecked Quink-blue waters of the Vaila Sound until it peters out on the shore. Here lies a listed 18th-century Haa, modernised sixty years ago by the family who owned the Black Dyke Mills. The house itself is three-storeyed but small. The silence, apart from the waves breaking on the private shingle beach, is total. Seals and otters frolic in the water, scallops and lobsters are in ample supply. *Burrastow* is noted throughout Scotland for its home-cooked food, and locals sometimes make a round trip of a hundred miles for dinner. It is a perfect bolthole amid stunning scenery for walkers, bird-fanciers, anglers and the knackered." *(Derek Cooper)*

Last year's encomium has been warmly endorsed by recent visitors, viz: "We had a holiday never to be forgotten, from the warmth of our welcome to our reluctant departure. Harry and Stella Tuckey were most charming and helpful. They are full of enthusiasm for the Shetlands which they transfer to their guests. Our bedroom was large, bright and comfortable with a superb view of the sea. Always ample hot water and fluffy towels replaced daily. The food was some of the best we have eaten anywhere, and we were amazed at the variety as the hotel is so isolated; we especially appreciated Stella Tuckey's use of wholefood in her cooking and the freshness of everything." *(A C & G Bostock; also W H Brooks, R A Farrard, Miss D C Melville)*

Open All year except 23 Dec–6 Jan.
Rooms 3 double (2 forming a connecting family unit) – all with bath, colour TV, tea-making facilities and baby-listening.
Facilities Residents' sitting room (TV available on request), diners' sitting room, dining room. 7-acre grounds laid out for golf practice and croquet; private beach with safe (but cold) swimming and pier, safe mooring; sea trout fishing, free dinghy always available.
Location 3 m W of Walls.
Restrictions Not suitable for &. Dogs not allowed in public rooms.
Credit cards None accepted.

Terms B&B £24.75; dinner, B&B £33; full board £36. Set lunch £3, dinner £12.50; full alc £15. Weekend breaks and reductions for long stays. Reduced rates and special meals for children.

Tipping: "Most of our guests know that they have been served by the proprietor and therefore the problem of tipping seldom arises."

WHITEBRIDGE Highland   Map 5

Knockie Lodge [GFG]   *Tel* Gorthleck (045 63) 276
Whitebridge, Inverness-shire IV1 2UP

Ian and Brenda Milward, new to the business, took over a shabby old hotel that inhabited this former 18th-century chieftain's hunting lodge in the spring of 1984, and have been busy with improvements since. The 10 rooms, all with private bathrooms, are thoroughly comfortable, and the public rooms are filled with antique furniture and pictures from the family. A recent addition to the house is a substantial glassed-in veranda along one side of the house, providing an agreeable sun-trap patio to both dining and drawing room. The Milwards serve a five-course meal (no choice until dessert), which we reported last year was excellent value at £10. A new chef arrived in the spring of 1985, and as we go to press we lack reports on his prowess. But we see no reason to withdraw our prediction made in the 1985 Guide that *Knockie Lodge* promises to be among the more cosseting hotels in the Highlands. It lies in a position of beautiful and isolated splendour, two miles off the deserted switchback B862 which takes the eastern route to Inverness from Fort Augustus. It has a great variety of lochs to offer the fishing fraternity, and deer-stalking in the autumn for the shooting classes. But it should also suit non-sporting folk who just want to get a bit further away from it all in sybaritic comfort.

Open Apr–Nov.
Rooms 9 double, 1 single – all with bath; tea-making facilities if required.
Facilities Drawing room, dining room, patio. 10-acre grounds. Walking; 2 lochs with free fishing for guests; deer-stalking and golf nearby.
Location 2 m down single-track private road W of B862, clearly signposted on that road 8 m N of Fort Augustus.
Restrictions Not suitable for &, nor children under 10. No dogs in public rooms.
Credit cards Access, Amex, Visa.
Terms (No service charge) B&B: single £22–£27, double £44–£70. Set dinner £14. Bar lunches. Reduced rates for 4–6 night stays out of season.
Service/tipping: A notice is put in bedrooms: "Staff Gratuities. Our policy has always been that we make no service charge as we do not believe in it. Gratuities are entirely at the discretion of guests. However, if you do feel you would like to give something to the staff, if you will leave it with us we will put it into the staff 'kitty' which we divide up amongst them at the end of every month."

Channel Islands

LONGUEVILLE MANOR HOTEL, ST SAVIOUR

LA HAULE Jersey

Map 1

La Place Hotel
Route du Coin
La Haule, St Brelade's Bay

Tel (0534) 44261
Telex 4191462

An old Jersey farmhouse dating from the 17th century has been rejuvenated with modern extensions into a four-star hotel. One of the lounges has beamed ceilings and two old Jersey-style fireplaces, and the restaurant, too, has olde-worlde features and looks out over a creepered courtyard; the bar and the bedrooms are wholly contemporary and the latter have the usual four-star mod. cons. *La Place* is in a rural situation ten minutes' walk from the sea, but the hotel has its own pool, heated from April to October. Its nominator, *David Mitchell*, wrote enthusiastically about every aspect of the hotel – "one of the most memorable and caring and comfortable establishments I have ever stayed in." His only reservation concerned the food, which he felt was adequate rather than brilliant. Subsequent visitors mostly endorse the entry, appreciating in particular "its beautiful setting close to Lady Cook's famous garden" and "the non-commercial atmosphere of intimacy and charm". Reservations about the food were also echoed: "uninspired" cooking and over-large portions – "we began to feel like over-fattened geese". One couple, who were on their honeymoon, were disconcerted to find the honeymoon suite had two single beds, admittedly pushed together; they also resented the "tie and jacket" rule in the dining room. All correspondents

271

speak well of the "more than usually helpful and amiable staff". *(Gabriele Berneck and Dr Christine Herxheimer, Katie Plowden, M I Walker)*

Open All year.
Rooms 40 double – all with bath, telephone, radio, colour TV, and baby-listening; some ground-floor rooms.
Facilities Lounge, TV lounge, cocktail bar, restaurant with pianist 2 or 3 times weekly. Garden with swimming pool and courtyard. Sea 10 minutes' walk: sandy beach, safe bathing, waterskiing, windsurfing. & can be accommodated by arrangement.
Location 4 m St Helier on good bus route. From La Haule slipway (on seaboard) third turning left up La Haule hill.
Restriction No dogs in public rooms.
Credit cards All major cards accepted.
Terms (No service charge) B&B: single £32, double £44; dinner, B&B: single £37–£45, double £53–£70; full board: single £41–£48, double £62–£74. Full alc £12.

HERM

Map 1

White House Hotel
Herm, via Guernsey

Tel Guernsey (0481) 22159

Herm, one and a half miles long by one mile wide, has a native population of 36 including children, though it has to meet an invasion of up to 2,000 day-trippers from Guernsey in August. It is a unique family-run fief, with one hotel, one pub, one church. There are no cars, no TV, no clocks on any of the buildings. An earlier visitor called Herm the most perfect island he had ever clapped eyes on, a paradise. We waited in vain for further comments, we clamoured for feedback, we gave the *White House Hotel* one final call in 1984 and sadly had to drop it from last year's edition. Now readers have responded generously to our appeal: "Our crossing from Guernsey was delayed by abnormal tides and when we arrived on Herm it was to find hundreds of visitors swarming on to a series of boats for the return crossing: so much, we thought, for tranquillity. We were given a very friendly greeting at the hotel, but the rooms we were given were fairly basic. An à la carte dinner was sadly disappointing. Mercifully first impressions are not always borne out by subsequent events and over the next seven days the island and its hotel took us over completely. Herm is a magical place, a small island of high cliffs and marvellous beaches; of gentle valleys and rich pastures grazed by Guernsey cattle; with a tiny ancient chapel nestling against its manor house on the summit, and everywhere breathtaking views. You can walk round the island in about an hour and a half and I did so regularly, sometimes twice a day. When you walk round it is impossible to believe that up to 2,000 visitors do come over from Guernsey every day; they really are only visible in any number round the harbour and between noon and 4.30 pm, just before the last boat goes, in Belvoir and Shell beach.

"As for the hotel, the food is not outstanding but you do get a reasonable breakfast and a decent three-course lunch and four-course dinner every day, and if you order in advance they will cook you lobster and cook it very well. There is none of the country house elegance of some of the new generation of fine hotels on the mainland. But the large sitting rooms are comfortable and when the sun shines you can take a chair in the garden outside and look across to Guernsey. After dinner, families tend to amuse themselves with the large supply of board games the hotel thoughtfully provides. For the first time in years we played a nightly game of Scrabble and much enjoyed it. The whole atmosphere is of unsophisticated but genuine comfort, and some of the bedrooms have quite staggeringly beautiful views over the sea.

"I have never had a more relaxing holiday. The hotel will provide newspapers, but I did not take one. I just delighted in being able to adjust my life to the slow tempo of a very beautiful place in a hotel where all the basic needs and comforts were more than adequately catered for and where the added friendliness made it seem like a very favourite personal holiday home. We have already booked for 1985." *(Patrick Cormack M P; also Adrienne Wallman, H N)*

Open 24 Mar–5 Oct.
Rooms 30 double, 1 single – all with bath, radio, tea-making facilities and baby-listening; 22 rooms in 3 cottages in grounds; 7 ground-floor rooms.
Facilities 3 lounges, 2 bars, 2 restaurants. 3-acre garden with swimming pool; tennis, badminton, croquet and table tennis. Sandy beaches and safe bathing. fishing.
Location Travel via Guernsey (hourly ferry service from St Peter Port taking 20 minutes). Hotel meets guests at airport or ferry. (No cars on Herm.)
Restriction The island is not really suitable for &.
Credit card Visa.
Terms (No service charge) dinner, B&B £25–£34; full board £28–£37. Set lunch £5.75, dinner £7.75; full alc £11. Christmas and New Year programmes. Children under 6 free in family suites (which have 2 bedrooms and a bathroom) Apr–July and after mid-Sept; special meals.

ST PETER PORT Guernsey   Map 1

La Collinette Hotel   *Tel* Guernsey (0481) 22585
St Jacques

A Georgian mansion on the outskirts of St Peter Port (10 minutes' walk down to the town centre) is nominated as an unpretentiously friendly family holiday hotel. The house itself has 22 rooms, and there are in addition seven modern self-catering cottages bordering the swimming pool. Best time to visit is mid-April to appreciate the splendid tree-size camellias which border the house and pool. Rooms have all the essentials for comfort, though housekeeping and maintenance may not be impeccable. The meals are substantial, well cooked and extremely good value – dinner £5.50 [1985]. The Chambers family set the tone for "smiling friendly service". (Mrs A S Kyrle Pope, H N). *More reports please.*

Open All year except Christmas Day, Boxing Day and New Year's Day.
Rooms 5 suites, 14 double, 3 single – 20 with bath, 2 with shower, all with telephone, radio, colour TV and baby-listening. Self-catering cottages.
Facilities Lounge, writing room, bar, TV room, restaurant. 1-acre grounds with swimming pool, sauna, solarium. 5–10 minutes from sea with sandy beaches and safe bathing; golf, riding and windsurfing nearby.
Location Central. Parking.
Restrictions Not suitable for &. No dogs.
Credit cards All major cards accepted.
Terms (No service charge for accommodation, 10% service charge for meals) B&B £17–£25; dinner, B&B £20–£28. Set lunch £4, dinner £6. Bar lunches (and poolside snacks in summer) available except Sun. Full alc £10–£12. Weekend breaks Oct–Mar. Reduced rates and special meals for children.
Service/tipping: "Tipping is not encouraged in the hotel, but is left to clients' discretion."

La Frégate Hotel   *Tel* Guernsey (0481) 24624
Les Cotils

Originally an 18th-century manor house, though with a good deal of the 20th century about its present appearance, *La Frégate* has a particularly choice location in its own terraced garden high on a hill above St Peter Port harbour about five minutes' walk from the town. Eleven of the 13 bedrooms as well as the dining room and the terrace enjoy exhilarating views over the town and neighbouring islands. Some rooms now have double-glazed patio windows leading on to private balconies. A bonus is *La Frégate*'s much-esteemed French restaurant, offering almost certainly the best hotel food to be had on the island. "Splendid outlook. Well-kept lovely garden. Perfect service with Mediterranean courtesy in the smart French restaurant. Exciting starters, fanciful desserts and some 'great' wine. At dinner, and in the bar, we enjoyed the spectacular harbour view – particularly in the later evening, when the boat lights, reflected by the water, were glittering like jewels in the darkness." *(Christine Herxheimer and Gabriele Berneck)*

Open All year.
Rooms 9 double, 4 single – all with bath, telephone and tea-making facilities; TV on request.
Facilities Residents' lounge, bar, restaurant. 2-acre grounds with terraced gardens. 5 minutes' walk to harbour fishing, 10 minutes to indoor leisure centre; easy access to all island beaches.
Location Near Candie Gardens. 5 minutes' walk from town centre. Private car park.
Restrictions Not suitable for &. No children under 14 in hotel, none under 9 in restaurant. No dogs.
Credit cards All major cards accepted.
Terms [1985 rates] rooms: single £17–£22.50, double £35–£45. Set lunch £7, dinner £10; full alc £15.

Midhurst House   *Tel* St Peter Port (0481) 24391
Candie Road

A small personal establishment, recently upgraded from a guest-house to a hotel, in an elegant Regency town house five minutes' walk up from the harbour. The hotel has a small south-facing garden, but in addition Christopher Osborne, architect of the enchanting conservatory-like terrace restaurant at *Dedham Vale* (q.v.), built last year a new lounge with a similar indoor garden atmosphere. Prices are very reasonable. Jan Goodenough, who runs the hotel with her husband Brian, writes: "We endeavour to cater for a very specific market. Typically, our visitors are middle-aged, middle-class and are either tired of large pretentious hotels or unable or unwilling to afford their high tariffs to cover the cost of facilities such as pools, head waiter etc. which they do not want. We seek high standards of food (using as much as possible of good local fresh produce), service, accommodation and personal attention." A major change since last year is that Mrs Goodenough has decided that the days of communal television are over, and has installed colour TV in all the bedrooms. The former TV lounge is now another bedroom with *en suite* bathroom. "Well deserves its place in the Guide. Meals are simple but excellently cooked. Service is efficient and friendly. The well-designed new lounge encourages social exchanges between guests.

Prices are moderate and value for money very good indeed." *(Mrs R F Mayes; also Sue and Tom Price, A J Davies)*

Open Mar–Oct and Dec.
Rooms 8 double – 2 with bath, 6 with shower, all with colour TV and tea-making facilities; 3 rooms in annexe; 4 ground-floor rooms.
Facilities Lounge, dining room. Small garden. 5 minutes' walk from bathing pools and fishing.
Location 5 minutes' walk from town centre, near Candie Museum and Cambridge Park. Parking.
Restrictions Not suitable for &. No children under 8. No dogs.
Credit cards None accepted.
Terms (No service charge) B&B £11.50–£16.50; dinner, B&B £15.50–£21.50; full board £19.50–£25.50. Set meals £4. 50% reductions for children 8–10 yrs if sharing with two adults. Enquire with hotel about special packages including transport.
Service/tipping: "To provide service is our business and is therefore part of our tariff (not an addition). Staff are not permitted to solicit tips, but sometimes visitors insist on tipping or giving a small gift and these are not refused."

ST SAVIOUR Jersey   **Map 1**

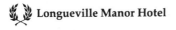 **Longueville Manor Hotel**   *Tel* Jersey (0534) 25501

César awarded to the pearl in the Jersey oyster

"A luxurious retreat run by a family whose daughters were champion riders at Wembley so there are horses and ponies. Staff absolutely devoted to their jobs – interested in people, never too much so. At the beginning of my stay, I was too tired to eat or even speak much, and was left alone albeit being cherished. Everyone was personally involved in caring for me: anything I wanted was got or done immediately. Very comfortable room. Lovely grounds, heated outdoor pool, large lounge bar with admirable barman, enthusiastic wine waiter, food very good indeed. Comfortable sitting room, several other places to sit inside, small well-chosen library. The owners said they have often seen people revive, like me, after a few days. I can't wait to go back." *(Pamela Vandyke Price)*

That tribute to the therapeutic virtues of a stay at *Longueville Manor* was taken from our first entry in 1979. Happily, the same compliments continue to be paid today. Without too much competition, the *Manor* is the most agreeable hotel in the Channel Islands – one and a half miles inland from Jersey's capital, St Helier, well away from the tourist hubbub, and, a plus for golfers, only two and a half miles from the Royal Jersey Golf Club. It has been a family-run enterprise for more than a quarter of a century. For many years, the sole complaint in these pages was that the food failed to match up to the high standards the hotel showed in all other departments. The arrival of chef John Dicken from *The Connaught* a few years ago has ended that Achilles heel: "a rising star", to quote *Derek Cooper*, "bringing the benefits of *nouvelle* to lighten the fine fresh food of the island". Now the only murmur of discontent arises over the service in the restaurant, "an insult", to quote one outraged gourmet, "to the flair and total artistry of John Dicken's creations". *(Mr and Mrs Allan Jones, A L, Paul Henderson)*

Open All year.
Rooms 9 suites (1 with 4-poster), 21 double, 3 single – all with bath, telephone, radio and colour TV. 6 ground-floor rooms suitable for &.
Facilities Lift. Hall lounge, bar/lounge, drawing room, panelled dining room. 15-acre grounds with swimming pool (heated in season), putting green, riding stables. Golf, bowls, squash, tennis within easy reach. 1½ m from sea, sandy beaches, surfing, sailing and water-skiing. Coaches call by arrangement for island drives and other excursions. &.
Location 1½ m E of St Helier; bus stops near main hotel gates. From airport, take main roads to St Helier; near harbour follow sign A17 to Georgetown. Then take A3 for 1½ m; hotel is on left.
Restrictions No children under 7. No dogs in public rooms.
Credit cards All major cards accepted.
Terms B&B: single £40–£46, double £69–£99; dinner, B&B: single £53.50–£59.50, double £96–£126. Set lunch £10.50, dinner £14.50 (excluding 10% service); full alc £26. Winter weekend breaks. Christmas–New Year package. Reductions for children sharing parents' room; special meals.

SARK   Map 1

Hotel Petit Champ   *Tel* Sark (048 183) 2046
Sark, via Guernsey

A pleasant late 19th-century granite building, in a secluded part of the island, well away from the day-trippers' tracks, but within half-an-hour's walk of any part of Sark. Most of its rooms have superb views of the sea and the neighbouring islands of Guernsey, Herm and Jethou; there's a well-tended sheltered garden and, about 50 yards from the hotel, a solar-heated and spotlessly clean swimming pool built in to a disused quarry – a fine sun-trap out of the wind. It will take you 10 minutes to walk down to a secluded bay with sand at low tide – but allow half an hour for the climb back. Reports, as in previous years, have been strongly positive. Prices extremely reasonable ... Friendly and informal ... Simply furnished but spotless rooms with marvellous views ... Superb breakfasts ... High standard of cooking. Only complaint: poor coffee. *(P E Carter, Mrs A S Kyrle Pope)*

Open Apr–Oct.
Rooms 2 suites (doubles with adjoining singles), 11 double, 3 single – 7 with bath, 4 with shower; 8 rooms in wing and some on ground floor.
Facilities 3 sun-lounges, lounge, TV lounge, bar, restaurant; forecourt. 1-acre grounds. 5 minutes' walk to sea with sandy beach and safe bathing; fishing.
Location 10 minutes' walk from centre. Head for Beau Regard and turn right just before duck pond.
Restrictions Sark not suitable for seriously &. Children must be old enough to sit with parents at dinner (children's portions of food served). No dogs in restaurant.
Credit cards Access, Diners, Visa.
Terms Dinner, B&B £21–£25; full board £25–£28.50. Set lunch £6.50, dinner £9. One-third reduction for children sharing parents' room.
Note: The hotel strongly recommends booking through Guernsey and Herm Leisure Travel Ltd – (048 183) 2046 – who will make all travel arrangements and can offer good reductions.

Republic of Ireland

CARAGH LODGE,
CARAGH LAKE

BALLINDERRY Co Tipperary Map 6

Gurthalougha House *Tel* Ballinderry 80
Ballinderry, Nenagh (through Operator)

Tipperary is one of the desert areas on our Irish map, so we are delighted to have an entry for this early 19th-century country house in 100 acres of forest, run by the Wilkinson family, on the shores of Lough Derg, the largest lake on the Shannon. Its nominator, Myrtle Allen (of *Ballymaloe House*) writes: "Very quiet and peaceful – much more attractive than the write-up in their brochure indicates. It is run by a young couple. Michael Wilkinson loves cooking and this shows through with everything that comes out of the kitchen. His wife, Bessie, is the daughter of one of Ireland's most famous hoteliers, and is perfect in the front of house. The place is very professionally run, with an authentic country house style and atmosphere. I arrived on a chilly May evening and was delighted with the warm log fires and large but cosy bedroom. The house is beautifully decorated with a lot of taste and a little money (*much* better than when things are the other way round). A lovely area for a holiday and of course excellent for fishermen."

Open All year except 16 Dec–1 Jan.
Rooms 7 double – 4 with bath.
Facilities Sitting room, library, dining room. 150-acre grounds with forest walks,

277

ornamental gardens and ½-m lake shore with private quay, safe bathing, boats for guests' use, ghillie available; windsurfing, pony-trekking.
Location On shores of Lough Derg, W of Ballinderry village, which is 16 m N of Nenagh. (Signposted from Ballinderry.)
Restriction Not suitable for ໄ.
Credit cards None acepted.
Terms B&B: IR£20; dinner, B&B IR£33. Set dinner IR£13. 33% reduction for children under 10.

BALLYLICKEY Co Cork   Map 6

Sea View House Hotel   *Tel* Bantry (027) 50073 or 50462

A comfortable friendly establishment, three miles north of Bantry and overlooking the Bay, presided over by Kathleen O'Sullivan. Recommended by our nominator "for the traveller who wants a peaceful base for touring beautiful countryside and who likes to combine quiet unsophisticated service with high standards of cooking and comfort. Everywhere is fresh, airy and bright, the back of the hotel as clean as the front. Dinner and breakfast were excellent with all those nice little things like crunchy brown bread, good marmalade, section honey, good tea and fresh fish" *(Eithne Scallan)*. Perfect for those wanting something nicer than a B&B, without the atmosphere of a large hotel. Excellent value for money." *(Diana Goodey)*

Open Easter–end Oct.
Rooms 1 suite, 10 double, 3 single – 10 with bath, 4 with shower, all with telephone, tea-making facilities and baby-listening. 3 ground-floor rooms in cottage in garden.
Facilities Lounge, TV room, cocktail bar, 2 dining rooms. 5-acre grounds. River and lake fishing 3 m; pony-trekking, boating, beaches and golf nearby.
Location 3 m N of Bantry, 70 yds off main road.
Restrictions Not suitable for ໄ.
Credit cards None accepted.
Terms B&B: single IR£17.50–IR£20, double IR£35–IR£40; dinner, B&B: single IR£25–IR£27.50, double IR£50–IR£55; full board: single IR£30–IR£32.50, double IR£60–IR£70. Set lunch IR£8, dinner, IR£15; full alc IR£18.

BALLYVAUGHAN Co Clare   Map 6

Gregans Castle   *Tel* Ennis (065) 77005
Ballyvaughan   *Telex* 70130

Gregans Castle is the only hotel in the heart of the Burren, that weird 100 square miles of lunar landscape roughly halfway between Galway and Shannon airport. The Burren is full of rare flowers and plants, both alpine and arctic, and is a paradise for botanists, as well as ornithologists, but it is also rich in historic and prehistoric remains. Yeats lovers will be attracted to Thor Ballylee, a town of great charm where he lived for a few years near Lady Gregory. But *Gregans Castle* is not only a base for cultural activity: it is also, to quote a recent report, "a country house hotel of great charm, managed by Peter and Moira Haden with a personal touch that never becomes intrusive". The Hadens' cooking comes in for special commendation (fish always on the menu), though one visitor, while appreciating the generosity and quality of the five-course dinner, would have appreciated a three-course option at a reduced price for more moderate middle-aged appetites. The Hadens tell us that they have been active in improvements this year: an extensive replanting of the garden and redecorating in the house. *(Anthony and Catherine Storr)*

Open 27 Mar–end Oct.
Rooms 1 suite, 15 double – 13 with bath; 2 rooms in annexe on ground floor.
Facilities Hall with fireplace, 2 lounges (1 with TV), Corkscrew Bar, dining room with large picture windows overlooking Galway Bay. 12-acre grounds with parkland and gardens. Safe, sandy beach 4½ m with excellent shore fishing; surfing farther off at Fanore; boat available June–Sept for sea fishing and trips to Aran Islands. &.
Location On the road N67 between Ballyvaughan and Lisdoonvarna, 3½ m SW of village, at foot of "Corkscrew Hill".
Restriction No dogs.
Credit cards Amex, Visa.
Terms B&B: single IR£32–IR£39, double IR£46–IR£58; dinner, B&B: single IR£50.50–IR£59.50, double IR£84–IR£100. Set dinner IR£19.68; full alc lunch IR£14.50.3- and 7-day packages. Reduced rates for children; special meals. *Service/tipping: "Not necessarily expected at all by staff as a service charge is on bill."*

CARAGH LAKE Co Kerry   **Map 6**

Caragh Lodge   *Tel* Caragh Lake (066) 61570
Caragh Lake

Eighteen miles due west of the tourist mêlée of Killarney, and four miles from the nearest small town, Killorglin, *Caragh Lodge* enjoys an exceptionally remote and beautiful location on Lake Caragh, ringed by the mountains of Kerry. There is unpolluted swimming in the lake itself, also good fishing; and the sea, a splendid three-mile stretch of sandy beach overlooking Dingle Bay, lies six miles further west. The nine-acre grounds of the *Lodge* itself are as serenely lovely as the outlook beyond – a garden filled with rare sub-tropical trees and shrubs, created over 20 years by the hotel's owner, Dr Schaper, with dedicated zeal and enthusiasm. The *Lodge* has twice won the Irish National Gardens Competition Award for guest-houses – a much-coveted trophy.

Guest-house or hotel? By the slightly eccentric standards of the Irish Tourist Board, *Caragh Lodge* is rated a guest-house, though it is more like what most Europeans would regard as a country house hotel. Some of the rooms – the preferred ones – are in the main house, others in an annexe, adequately comfortable though with a less attractive view and imperfect insulation. Duvets are the order of the day, but sheets and blankets are provided if asked for. There are two civilised public rooms, full of good pieces of furniture. Dinner is at 7.30 pm – with a limited choice à la carte menu. Mrs Schaper is the cook – and a caring one; the *Lodge* grows all its own vegetables and marinates its salmon.

The Schapers come from Berlin – the Doctor is by profession an ophthalmologist – and, as might be expected, the place has Germanic overtones. Aufschnitt and Apfelmus are on the breakfast menu, for instance; German books predominate on the shelves and the Germany connection also brings many visitors from the GDR. English-speaking visitors, who are looking for a truly Irish experience, may feel uncomfortable about the hybrid establishment. But the Schapers are cordial and welcoming, the setting is incomparably Irish and we know of no other country hotel in the Ring of Kerry as hospitable. *(H R)*

Open Easter–15 Sept.
Rooms 8 double, 2 single – all with bath. 7 rooms in annexe.
Facilities 2 lounges, dining room. 9-acre prize-winning gardens with lake frontage (bathing, fishing, boating) and all-weather tennis court. Sandy beach 5 m; many golf courses nearby.
Location 25 m NW of Killarney. 1 m off Ring of Kerry between Killorglin and Glenbeigh.
Restrictions Not suitable for &. No small children. No dogs in bedrooms or public rooms.
Credit cards None accepted.
Terms (Excluding 10% service charge) B&B: single IR£25–IR£30, double IR£40–IR£44. Full alc IR£20.

CASHEL BAY Co Galway   Map 6

Cashel House Hotel   *Tel* Clifden (095) 21252
Cashel, Connemara   *Telex* 28812

"A gem in a primitive part of Western Ireland. For those who love rough and rocky and volcanic country, Connemara, at least in the far west, rivals Skye. *Cashel House* is a lovely building, once a manor house. Beds are turned down at night, and many amenities seldom found in this part of the world are in evidence. Downstairs, there are three lounges with fireplaces which were kept burning brightly in late September. It is obviously very pleasant in the summer, being 100 yards from the water, with tennis court and fishing (freshwater and salt) – fishing rods are supplied as well as tennis racquets. But it is the dining room which beckons. Full Irish breakfasts are fantastic and dinners are superb. Every evening there are at least four fish courses on the menu, and as much of anything as you wish. The fish – mussels, lobster, trout, shrimps etc. – are all local, and are caught and delivered daily. A fine, extensive wine list, not expensive. Altogether a very comfortable and delightful place, and a shining beacon in an area where there is very little like it." (*Alfred A Knopf Jr*)

Agreeable compliments indeed for this handsome white-painted house at the head of Cashel Bay, with a beautiful prize-winning garden; but it is taken from last year's Guide, and followed a year with no reports at all. And now another year, and only one report from a guest who appreciated the elegance of the rooms, but found the food no more than passable and complained of "abysmal" service in the restaurant. More reports badly needed.

Open Mar–Oct inclusive.
Rooms 13 suites, 6 double 3 single – all with bath (whirlpool baths in 4 garden suites); 6 ground-floor rooms.
Facilities Bar/lounge, 3 lounges, library, dining room. 50-acre gardens with woodland walks; hard tennis court; small private sandy beach for residents; grounds lead to Cashel Hill. Many other beaches within easy reach; golf, lake and river fishing, bird-watching, riding, deep-sea fishing.
Location Take N59 from Galway. Turn left to village 1 m after Recess.
Restrictions Not suitable for &. No children under 5. No dogs in public rooms.
Credit cards All major cards accepted.
Terms (Excluding 12½% service) B&B: IR£26–IR£32; dinner, B&B (3 days min.) IR£44–IR£50. Set dinner IR£18.50; full alc IR£22. Reduced rates for children by arrangement.

CASHEL Co Tipperary   Map 6

Cashel Palace Hotel   *Tel* Tipperary (062) 61411
                                                    Telex 26938

A magnificent 18th-century episcopal palace – built in 1730 for
Archbishop Bolton by Sir Edward Lovett Pearce (the architect of the old
Parliament House in Dublin, now the Bank of Ireland), with a noble
red-brick Queen Anne façade and a garden bordering on the Rock of
Cashel, also a fine picture collection – that has been a model of a
20th-century country house hotel, albeit at the upper end of the price
spectrum. Our inspector found much to praise: really excellent dinner,
every course a success, fine napery, with the handsome dining room
overlooking a well-tended garden which had a floodlit fountain. Her
bedroom was a little small with a view of a derelict back garden, but was
wholly adequate for a single night. Quiet courteous service throughout
from the owner/manager, Ray Carroll, and all his staff.

Open All year except for a few days over Christmas. Buttery open 10am–10 pm;
Four Seasons Restaurant open for breakfast and dinner.
Rooms 3 suites, 15 double, 2 single – all with bath, most with radio; TV available
on request.
Facilities Drawing room, lounge, cellar bar, 2 restaurants. 20-acre grounds with
landscaped gardens. Golf, shooting and fishing nearby.
Location 2 minutes' walk from centre of Cashel which is on main Dublin/Cork
road.
Restriction Not suitable for &.
Credit cards None accepted.
Terms (Excluding 10% service charge) B&B: single IR£53–IR£60, double IR£73–
IR£91; dinner, B&B: single IR£74–IR£81, double IR£94–IR£133. Set dinner IR£21;
full alc IR£35.

CORK Co Cork   Map 6

Arbutus Lodge Hotel   *Tel* Cork (021) 501237
Montenotte, Cork   *Telex* 75079 ARBU

A famous Cork hotel for many years, its reputation deriving much from
the quality of its table. It lost its *Michelin* rosette a couple of years back,
but its supporters still consider the restaurant as good as ever. The *Lodge*
was once a master cooper's house, *c.*1802, in the posh suburbs of
Montenotte, 15 minutes' walk or five minutes' drive fom the city centre.
Some rooms still reflect the solid virtues of its origins, but the rooms in
the modern extension grafted on either side of the main building are no
more than functional. Many, however, have a spectacular view over the
river Lee to the city beyond; it's well worth asking for a room with a
view when booking. Downstairs there is a large comfortable bar, a
residents' lounge and the restaurant with large bay window, starched
white table cloths, good china and glass, flowers, candles and so on. The
cuisine may not be innovative, but it is serious. There is a decidedly
impressive wine list – not just because of its range and the number of
bins, but because it reflects Declan Ryan's zeal in tracing uncommonly
good wine at uncommonly low prices. The same personal flair is shown
in the public rooms, filled with the work of contemporary Irish artists. It
is a highly individual, enthusiastically run city hotel, but we think some

of the rooms badly need refurbishing, and we wish there were not so many complaints about poor service in the restaurant.

Open All year except 24–30 Dec. Restaurant closed Sun (bar meals available).
Rooms 11 double, 9 single – 15 with bath, 5 with shower, all with telephone, radio and colour TV.
Facilities Lounge, drawing room, bar, 2 dining rooms. 1-acre garden with patio.
Location 1½ m up hill from town centre. Parking.
Restrictions Not suitable for &. No dogs.
Credit cards Amex, Diners, Visa.
Terms B&B: single IR£32.50 – IR£36.50, double IR£62.50 – IR£66. Set lunch IR£15.75, dinner IR£18.95; 8-course tasting menu IR£22; full alc IR£28.

DROMAHAIR Co Leitrim   Map 6

Drumlease Glebe House   *Tel* Sligo (071) 64141
Dromahair

A welcome addition to our regrettably brief Irish section, a Georgian country house in 100 acres of grounds bordering on the river Bonet, in the heart of Yeats country, 12 miles from Sligo. It's a great place for fishing, and the hotel owns salmon and trout fishing rights on Lough Melvin and can provide boats, ghillies, tackle etc. Our inspector liked the cared-for feel of the place and the informal style of hospitality of the hosts, Patrick and Barbara Verner. The drawing room, with a log fire, is full of memorabilia and books and comfortable armchairs; you help yourself to drinks and enter the items in a book. No choice for the main course at dinner, but Mr Verner makes sure that his guests are happy with what is on offer. Mrs Verner, school of Cordon Bleu, is the cook, and the salmon served to our inspector was "outstandingly good". We look forward to more reports.

Open 15 Mar–end Sept.
Rooms 8 double, 2 single – 1 with bath, 5 with shower.
Facilities Large hall, drawing room, TV room, study, restaurant. 100 acres of wooded parkland, unheated swimming pool, private salmon and trout fishing in nearby Lough Melvin and Lough Ghill. Deep-sea fishing nearby. Ghillie, boats, engines, tackle etc. available.
Location 2 m E of Dromahair; take the school road out of Dromahair village; sign 2 m – 1 m of avenue.
Restrictions Not suitable for &. No dogs in public rooms.
Credit card Visa.
Terms (Excluding 12½% service charge) B&B: single IR£30, double IR£55; dinner, B&B: single IR£47.50, double IR£90; full board: single IR£54, double IR£102.50. Set lunch IR£6.50, dinner IR£17.50. Reduced rates and special meals for children if ordered in advance.

GOREY Co Wexford   Map 6

Marlfield House   *Tel* Gorey (055) 21124 or 21572

"The food and service were exceptional! The hotel is a delight – filled with antiques and surrounded by lovely grounds. Gracious living and dining still exist at *Marlfield House* and we applaud it!" *(Amy and Ralph Flodin).* "One of the best hotels I have ever stayed in" *(Elizabeth O'Hanlon).* "A great place to unwind, and very comfortable in all respects. What really makes it special is Mary Bowe, who seems to have enough energy for two or three people, and great natural charm. If you ever give a César for warmth of welcome, *Marlfield* should get it" *(Paul Henderson)*. Another year, much like the last in terms of warmth of praise, for Mary Bowe's noble three-storey Regency house, formerly the dower-house of the Courtown estate, and now in a particularly halcyon phase as a country house hotel. Apart from the comforts of the hotel and its acclaimed restaurant, it is in a choice position for touring – a mile from the sea with sandy beaches, close to a golf course, and with plenty of the beauty spots of Co Wicklow at hand. Only grumbles: that credit cards are not accepted and there is not enough garden furniture.

Open All year except 3 days at Christmas.
Rooms 12 double – 11 with bath and shower, 1 with shower only; all with telephone, and colour TV.
Facilities Lounge, library, bar, restaurant. 12-acre grounds with tennis court; sandy beaches and safe bathing 2 m.
Location 1 m from Gorey on the Courtown road.
Restrictions Not suitable for ♿. No children under 6. No dogs.
Credit cards None accepted.
Terms (Excluding 10% service charge) B&B: double IR£60–IR£80. Set lunch IR£13, dinner IR£19; full alc lunch IR£18.

KENMARE Co Kerry   **Map 6**

Park Hotel Kenmare   *Tel* Killarney (064) 41200
Kenmare   *Telex* 70005

What was once Kenmare's *Great Southern Hotel*, sold in 1977, has become under its new owners a formidable contender for the best country house hotel in Ireland. It is a substantial mansion, built at the turn of the century and furnished in period style, set in a large, splendidly maintained park. It is the only establishment in the Republic to earn a *Michelin* rosette. Ronay awards it 88% – only *Ashford Castle* in Cong notches up more on the elaborate and esoteric Ronay scale.

Grand hotels are not necessarily good ones, but the indications are that *Park Hotel* is giving satisfaction by the demanding standards of top-price de luxe establishments. "Absolutely first-class in every respect" was one correspondent's verdict. Another wrote: "The best part of our stay in Ireland. The public rooms are exquisite. The bedrooms are extremely comfortable, with fresh fruit among the extras. The bathroom was immaculate, with a magnificent make-up mirror. The staff is exceptionally friendly – and is truly there for you as a guest. Dinner was the best meal we had in our week's touring." *(Oliver Ward, Julie Jackson)*

Open All year.
Rooms 6 suites (1 specially adapted for ♿), 32 double, 12 single – 43 with bath, 7 with shower; all with telephone, radio and baby-listening; TV in suites.
Facilities Lift and ramps. 3 lounges, TV/games room, drawing room, cocktail bar, restaurant; harpist, piano/singer in the lounge in summer. 11-acre grounds, with all-weather tennis court and croquet; sea and river fishing available locally. ♿.
Location Adjacent to village. Parking.
Restriction No dogs.
Credit cards Access, Visa.
Terms B&B: single IR£54–IR£62, double IR£104–IR£128; dinner, B&B: single IR£80.50–IR£88.50, double IR£130.50–IR£154.50; full board: single IR£94.30–

IR£102.30, double IR£144.30–IR£168.10. Set lunch IR£13.80, dinner IR£26.50; full alc IR£30. Reduced rates and special meals for children on request.

KILLARNEY Co Kerry   Map 6

Aghadoe Heights Hotel   *Tel* Killarney (064) 31766
Killarney   *Telex* 26942

All the larger hotels in Killarney are kept in business by block bookings, and the 60-bedroom *Aghadoe Heights,* though far from the biggest in the area, is no exception. It is a spanking smart modern hotel, three miles outside the town, adjoining the ruins of Aghadoe Cathedral dating from the 7th century. Not our sort of place, really, but half the bedrooms and the dining room have a view over the lakes and mountains that no travel brochure could surpass. A previous visitor had extolled the merits of the hotel: "Architecturally unexciting though it may seem, it proved to be without fault in terms of service, pleasant atmosphere, standards of cleanliness and general comfort." The Editor and his wife, arriving (anonymously) soaked to the skin having been walking for two hours in drenching rain, would echo those sentiments. After changing in their loos, we asked the hotel if they could put our clothes in their drying room while we had lunch. Two hours later, after a modest-priced but decent meal, with the stupendous view an added bonus, we were amazed to find our togs returned dry, trousers pressed, shirt neatly folded. Service beyond the call of duty to a couple of stray soaks.

Open All year except 21 Dec–21 Jan.
Rooms 2 suites, 57 double, 1 single – all with bath and shower, telephone, radio, colour TV and baby-listening; 24 ground-floor rooms; one designed for &.
Facilities Lounge, bar (entrance with ramp), restaurant, TV room; conference facilities; entertainment and dancing nightly except Sun (Apr–Oct). 7-acre grounds with hard tennis court. Salmon and trout fishing in lake, and in river 8 m away. Golf and pony-trekking nearby.
Location 3 km W of Killarney. 1½ m off Tralee/Limerick road.
Restriction No dogs in public rooms.
Credit cards All major cards accepted.
Terms (No service charge) B&B: single IR£30.50–IR£45.50, double IR£47–IR£73; half-board: single IR£47–IR£63.25, double IR£81–IR£108; full board: single IR£55–IR£71.50, double IR£97.50–IR£124.50. Set lunch IR£8.50, dinner IR£17.25. Weekend rates. Reduced rates and special meals for children.

MALLOW Co Cork   Map 6

Longueville House   *Tel* Mallow (022) 27156/27176 and
                                                                      27306

A noble mansion set in the centre of a 500-acre wooded estate overlooking the Blackwater river, sometimes called the Irish Rhine, famous for its salmon and trout. The house is early Georgian in its central part, with two wings added later, but one of the glories of the house is its Victorian conservatory, full of graceful ironwork. It originally belonged to the O'Callaghans, but Cromwell confiscated their lands and demolished their castle. After three centuries, the estate is once more back in the family, and Michael and Jane O'Callaghan, far from being absentee landlords, are very much the present hosts. Beautiful houses are often content to settle for mediocrity in their kitchens, but *Longueville* has won accolades for its cooking under the supervision of Jane O'Callaghan.

Over the years, most visitors have appreciated the *Longueville* style, with the consensus perhaps summed up by the reader who wrote: "One of the warmest and friendliest high-class establishments we know. It isn't *perfect* – what is? We can imagine more luxurious, even more cosseting places, but not many which are more comfortable about the essential parts of an aristocratic existence. It is in no way a hotel, rather the O'Callaghans' house which some of use are privileged to share" *(Sydney Downs)*. Regrettably the Editor has to offer a dissenting view. No complaints about the dinner, taken in the splendid conservatory – filled with plants and candle-lit, and made memorable by flocks of crows wheeling overhead in the twilight. Nor about the breakfast, the best we had in an Irish tour, with a charmer of a waitress, asking at every table "Well, folks and how are you today?" and seeming genuinely to be interested in the answers. But our reception was off-hand and surly, our room no more than adequate in its decor and comfort, and the bar lunch, which came after a 40-minute delay, turned out to be Mothers Pride with tinned meat and processed cheese. More reports please.

Open Easter–late Oct.
Rooms 2 suites, 12 double, 4 single – 16 with bath, 2 with shower; 3 rooms in annexe.
Facilities Drawing room, TV room, cocktail bar, library, conservatory, President's dining room, billiards, table tennis, darts. In 500-acre wooded estate, with garden, vineyard, croquet lawn, 3 m salmon/trout fishing on river Blackwater which forms S boundary of estate. Riding nearby and free golf on Mallow course. & (restaurant only).
Location 4 m W of Mallow on Killarney road.
Restrictions No children under 10. No dogs.
Credit cards Access, Diners, Visa.
Terms B&B: single IR£30–IR£37, double IR£56–IR£73; dinner, B&B: single IR£50–IR£57, double IR£96–IR£113. Set dinner IR£20; full alc IR£25; bar lunch IR£5–IR£6.

OUGHTERARD Co Galway   Map 6

Currarevagh House   *Tel* Galway (091) 82313

"The Hodgson family have been living in this mid-Victorian country house on the banks of Lough Corrib for five generations, and June and Harry Hodgson now run it as an unstuffy, personal hotel. It is set in 150 acres of its own grounds, and there is beautiful wild country around for walks and golf and riding, but it is particularly popular with fishermen. There's a book in the hall where you can enter the number of fish caught, and that is characteristic of the 'private house' approach of the owners. There are no keys to the bedrooms – not that one would be likely to take one's diamonds to this remote spot. The decor hasn't changed much since 1900; the beds are marvellously capacious, with heavy linen sheets; splendid bathroom fittings, lots of Edwardian furniture. There are huge baskets of turf and large open fires in the two reception rooms – and the public rooms and hall are so spacious that it is easy enough to be on one's own. The food is good home cooking, such as one would get if one were lucky as a weekend guest in the country. Excellent home-made brown bread for breakfast, for instance, and first-rate coffee, kept hot over individual spirit lamps. Trout from the lough for dinner, simply cooked with melted butter." *(Mirabel Cecil)*

Mirabel Cecil's citation was written in 1976. It is a singular pleasure, 10 years later, to be able to recycle it with the confident knowledge that nothing essential has changed. Poly/cotton sheets have replaced the heavy linen ones, but a maid will still come in and put your night attire round the hot-water bottle. Chamber pots are available on request. "Every word of Mirabel Cecil's commendation is justified. For those who want real comfort, with imaginative touches and not conventional luxury, this is a hotel in a thousand. I would give it 97%, and if they would offer honey for breakfast (and/or rather better marmalade), serve butter with their potato cakes at tea and update some of the bedroom furniture, I would make it 100%." *(Professor D A Webb)*

Open Easter to early Oct.
Rooms 12 double, 3 single – 7 with bath, 5 with shower; 4 ground-floor rooms in annexe.
Facilities Drawing room, sitting room, TV room, dining room. 150-acre grounds with lakeshore fishing, boating, swimming, tennis court, croquet.
Location 4 m NW of Oughterard on lakeshore road.
Restrictions Children are tolerated but not encouraged. Dogs by arrangement and only on leads in public rooms.
Credit cards None accepted.
Terms (Excluding 10% service charge) B&B IR£24.50–IR£27.50; dinner, B&B IR£36.75–IR£39.75; full board IR£42.30–IR£45.30. Set lunch IR£6.75, dinner IR£14. 3-day rate and weekly rate. Reduced rates for children sharing parents' rooms.

RIVERSTOWN Co Sligo Map 6

Coopershill *Tel* Sligo (071) 65108

A fine Georgian house in an estate of 500 acres of woods and farmland, *Coopershill* has a spectacular position, with the Bricklieve mountains and vast peat bogs to the south, and the town of Sligo and the sea to the north. This is Yeats country, and the poet himself is buried at Drumcliff not far from Riverstown. All but one of the bedrooms have antique furniture, four-poster or canopy beds and baths *en suite.* "An extraordinary spell of weather enhanced the beauty and calm of the setting, but the spaciousness of this fine four-square 18th-century house, the friendliness, comfort and ease of the O'Haras' hospitality, and the evening fire in the drawing room after dinner, would make this a worthy entry in any weather. The food is extremely good, home cooked and graciously served. It's remarkable value. The whole place has a charming simplicity and feeling of tradition: a special place with special people." *(John and Eileen Spencer)*

This earlier evocation of *Coopershill* has been augmented by recent visitors who have fallen similarly under its spell: "One could not be other than enchanted by the house in every respect; as one rattles over wooden cattle grids on the way to the imposing entrance, it really does feel as though one is leaving the world a long way behind" *(Richard Parish).* "A gem. Mrs O'Hara is most often arranging flowers or out in front extending her hand in welcome ... The bedrooms are the biggest we have ever seen ... The playroom is a sunny warm room where our two girls gladly spent hours ... A fantastic place." *(Ted and Susan Hall; also Bridget West)*

Open Easter–Sept 30.
Rooms 5 double – 4 with bathroom, 1 with shower, most with 4-posters; tea-making facilities on request.
Facilities Hall, drawing room with colour TV, dining room, playroom for children with mono TV, piano, record-player, table tennis, etc. Large garden within 500 acres of farmland. A river runs through grounds, with coarse fishing; trout fishing nearby; sandy beach at Sligo, also golf – both 12 m.
Location 2 m from Riverstown; on Dublin/Sligo road (N4), take 2nd right turn towards Riverstown. After about 1 m, by black post and rail fence, turn left; turn right by ruined lodge, cross stone bridge and 2 cattle grids.
Restrictions Not suitable for &. No dogs in public rooms.
Credit cards Amex, Visa.
Terms (Excluding tax and service) B&B IR£20. Set dinner IR£12. Reduction for children sharing and under 12; special meals on request.

SHANAGARRY Co Cork   Map 6

Ballymaloe House   *Tel* Cork (021) 652531
Shanagarry, Nr Midleton   *Telex* 75208 BHI

Many years ago, before I had had the idea of editing the Guide, I described the *Ta' Cenc* on Gozo, Malta (q.v.) as my personal platonic idea of a holiday hotel, but *Ballymaloe* would certainly now have my vote instead. It is quite simply the most wholly sympathetic hotel I have come across.

Its natural assets are a gracious rambling house, more Georgian than anything else though somehow ageless, with its Norman keep built into the fabric on one side, and its relatively modern pink-washed cottages on the other side overlooking the courtyard. Close to the house are the swimming pool and tennis court; beyond lies a 400-acre farm; and beyond that, at two or three miles distance, is the sea with good sandy beaches, and the charming little fishing port of Ballycotton. You can borrow bicycles to roam through the countryside or get to the beach, and horses and ponies are available for riders.

The special assets of *Ballymaloe* are Myrtle and Ivan Allen, who bought the house as a family home some 40 years ago, and slowly turned it into an unique hotel – and much else besides: first a restaurant, then a hotel, then a farm shop, then a cookery school. The *Ballymaloe Cookbook* is a testament to Myrtle Allen's style of cooking based exclusively on fresh natural ingredients. Most of the Allen family – five or six children and in-laws – are engaged in one or other part of the enterprise. Virtually everything you eat, apart from the wonderful fish, is home-grown or raised on the Allen's farm. That the Allen family enjoy what they are doing is clear when you meet them – their enthusiasm is infectious. It is a very happy house and the cheerful high spirits break down the reserve of its guests. People are relaxed: they talk to each other. It doesn't feel like a hotel despite the number of rooms and the 60 people who dine every night. Characteristic of the style of the place: when I happened to let slip to a member of the staff, just as we were going in to dinner, that it was my wife's birthday, she said at once, "Do let us make a cake for her!" I didn't think they would be able to organise that at 8 pm, but a delicious meringue cake was ready, complete with candle, by the time we reached the sweet stage. There is nothing forced or synthetic in the conviviality of the place: it is a natural consequence of the Allens' confidence and pride and pleasure in what they are doing. *(H R)*

Open All year except 24–26 Dec inclusive.
Rooms 26 double, 3 single – 24 with bath, 5 with shower, all with telephone; baby-listening by arrangement; 11 rooms in annexe, 4 of which are ground-floor rooms suitable for wheelchairs. *Gate Lodge* has double-bedded room and kitchen/living room.
Facilities 2 sitting rooms, TV room, playroom, 4 dining rooms; conference facilities. Occasional folk-song evenings. 400-acre farm and grounds with tennis court, heated swimming pool, 9-hole golf course, trout pond, children's play area. Horses and ponies available for guests. Sea 3 m, with safe sandy beaches; sea and river fishing by arrangement. Shanagarry pottery is 1 m down the road, with Mr Pearse's pots (cheaper than in the shops) and his son's glass. Irish craft shop in grounds, selling tweeds, woollens, pictures; also fresh produce. &.
Location 20 m E of Cork; 2 m E of Cloyne on Ballycotton road, L35.
Restrictions No dogs in bedrooms or public rooms.
Terms [1985 rates] (excluding 10% service charge) B&B: single IR£22.50–IR£28.50, double IR£39–IR£49. Set lunch IR£9.50, dinner IR£18.50. Special weekend rates. Reduced rates and special meals for children.

Part two

Austria
Belgium
Cyprus
Denmark
Finland
France
Germany
Greece
Holland
Hungary
Italy
Luxembourg
Malta
including Gozo

Norway
Portugal
including Madeira

Spain
*including Andorra, the Balearics
and the Canaries*

Sweden
Switzerland
including Liechtenstein

Turkey
Yugoslavia

MUSEUMSVEREIN
SCHLOSS ROSENAU

ANIF 5081 Salzburg   Map 14

Hotel Friesacher   *Tel* (06246) 2075
Hellbrunn Road 58   *Telex* 632943

Anif is an all-season resort five kilometres from the centre of Salzburg,
surrounded by mountains and woods. "Finding satisfactory reasonable
accommodation with easy parking is difficult in Salzburg. By sheer luck
we found this chalet-type very modern inn, in the suburbs of the city. It
has an excellent breakfast room and a luxurious-looking dining room,
which we didn't try. Its rooms are neo-rustic, modern, very large, with
scenic-view balconies. Reception and service friendly. Everything
considered, some of the best value we have had in many years.

Charming, convenient, friendly and most reasonable." *(Nathan R Carb, Jr)* More reports welcome, especially on the restaurant.

Open All year.
Rooms 3 suites, 50 double, 12 single – 59 with bath, 6 with shower, all with telephone, radio and colour TV; many with balcony. 18 rooms in annexe. Ground-floor rooms.
Facilities Lift. Lounge, bar, dining room, conference facilities, *Heuriger* (Austrian festivities with music) every day except Tue in old farmhouses. Garden with children's play area, tennis courts and café. Swimming, skiing, skating etc. nearby. English spoken.
Location 4 km S of Salzburg. Leave *Autobahn* at Salzburg, go to the right at Anif (1 km) and turn ½ km on road to Hellbrunn. Parking.
Credit card Diners.
Terms B&B: 390–500 Sch. Set lunch 120 Sch, dinner 330 Sch; full alc 220 Sch. Reduced rates and special meals for children.

BERGHEIM 5101 Salzburg   Map 14

Hotel Gmachl   *Tel* (06222) 52180, 52124 or 52607
Telex 632771

"Bergheim is a village only two kilometres north of Salzburg in the direction of the Maria Plain Basilica. The centre consists of the church and this hotel. When it says in the *Gmachl's* brochure that they have their own butcher, they mean the butcher shop belongs to them, as indeed would have been the custom of old – we have seen it in other Austrian villages where the hotelier owns half the town! The *Gmachl* must once have been an old-fashioned *Gasthof*, but has much expanded over the years. There are several chalets interconnected by a long and airy corridor – the smaller ones containing a ground-floor apartment, and two rooms upstairs with balconies. There are 60 modern and luxurious bedrooms, double-glazed to cut out the noise of the nearby road and railway line, and completely silent when windows are shut. In a country where the main national product is wood, ample use is made of this commodity – all rooms have timber panelled ceilings and wooden panelling all round the room to waist height; even a frieze of Austrian dancers running around the top. Bathrooms are superb. There are several dining rooms and one specifically for breakfast. We enjoyed staying here. Our only reservation is the cuisine, which in our opinion is not quite up to the high standards they have set elsewhere." *(Francine and Ian Walsh)*

Open All year.
Rooms 68 rooms – 19 with bath, 21 with shower, all with telephone; many with balcony.
Facilities Lounge, TV room, bar, restaurant, conference facilities; indoor swimming pool, sauna. Garden with table-tennis, children's play area; fishing, riding and golf nearby.
Location 2 km N of Salzburg on road 156 towards Oberndorf. Take Salzburg Nord exit from motorway E14.
Credit cards Possibly some accepted.
Terms [1985 rates] B&B 650–760 Sch; full board 690–1,020 Sch.

> Hotels are dropped if we lack positive feedback. If you can endorse an entry, please do so.

BERWANG 6622 Tyrol   Map 14

Singer Sporthotel   *Tel* (05674) 8181

The Singer family's *Sporthotel* is set on a pine-studded hillside in the "enlarged but not much spoiled" summer and ski resort of Berwang, just off the main Innsbruck/Stuttgart road a few miles west of the towering Zugspitze. The *Sporthotel* is just what you might expect from its name and situation – "somewhat overblown chalet-style architecture, but we were agreeably surprised by its spacious interior, matched by the pleasant and efficient service of the Singer family and their staff. The food was excellent and everything worked; we revelled in a shamefully large room with balcony. The 'Sport' facilities of bathing, sauna, massage, jacuzzi etc. did not impinge on those looking merely to enjoy strolling in the countryside. When a 'Tyrolean evening' was held in the restaurant, it was timed for after the normal dinner time and we were specially asked whether we wished to stay at our table or go to a quieter lounge." *(Margaret and Charles Baker)* More reports please.

Open 15 Dec–10 Apr, 17 May–20 Sept.
Rooms 15 suites, 32 double, 8 single – 46 with bath, 3 with shower, all with telephone, many with balcony; radio and colour TV on request.
Facilities Lift. Lounge, 2 bars, TV room, 2 restaurants; sun terrace; fitness/sports centre with whirlpool, sauna, children's playground; heated open-air swimming pool, mini-golf, tennis; winter sports (ski-lift near hotel). Dancing in the bar each night in winter. Tyrolean evenings in summer.
Location 80 km NW of Innsbruck. Parking.
Credit card Diners.
Terms B&B 280–730 Sch; half-board 340–800 Sch; full board 380–850 Sch. Set lunch 100 Sch, dinner 160 Sch; full alc 180–260 Sch. Reduced rates and special meals for children.

BEZAU 6870 Vorarlberg   Map 14

Gasthof Gams   *Tel* (05514) 2220
                                  Telex 59144 VVWALD-GAMS

Bezau is a sleepy little town on the edge of the Bregenz forest. The road on one side winds down to the busy resorts of Lake Constance; on the other, it loops over the mountains to the big sophisticated ski-stations of Lech and St-Anton. *Gasthof Gams* is a sizeable 17th-century coaching inn, with modern additions and lots of 20th-century amenities like a lift, a swimming pool, a jacuzzi and much else – "the town's hotspot" on some evenings – but quiet enough for all but the lightest of sleepers. Despite its size, it is a genuinely personal family hotel, with one of the *Familie* Nenning always around. "Rooms vary considerably in size; the under-floor heating rather nice. The public rooms are quite *gemütlich*, particularly the dining rooms, furnished in traditional Austrian style. Dinner was very tasty with two helpings of meat and extra vegetables. The young staff were friendly despite being busy." Readers have over the years especially appreciated the warm welcome. The hotel bus takes guests to and from the ski-slopes in season. *(Kate and Steve Murray-Sykes; also Harry Robinson)*

Open All year except 1–15 Dec.
Rooms 6 suites, 24 double, 10 single – 15 with bath, 25 with shower, all with telephone; colour TV on request. Some with balcony, some ground-floor rooms.
Facilities Lift. Lounge, dining rooms, conference/functions rooms; games room, sauna, solarium, hot whirlpool; terraces. Large garden with swimming pool (heated May–Oct) and 2 tennis courts. Skiing, climbing, walking. English spoken. &.
Location 35 km SE of Bregenz, 37 km NW of Lech. Central. Parking.
Credit cards None accepted.
Terms B&B 295–440 Sch; half-board 440–590 Sch; full board 510–660 Sch. Set lunch/dinner 150–180 Sch; full alc 250 Sch. Children 4–12 half-price; special meals.

DRASSBURG 7021 Burgenland   Map 14

Schloss Drassburg   *Tel* (02686) 2220

Once the summer residence of the Barons of Esterhazy, this grand castle near the Hungarian border is, in one reader's view, "our idea of a perfect hotel". Fifth-generation Baroness Patzenhofer still owns the house, furnished in the rococo style, and manages its 25 acres of grounds designed by Le Nôtre, famous for the gardens at Versailles. "A peaceful rural setting well away from the usual tourist areas, complemented by polite and unobtrusive service. We had a modern room in the tower tastefully decorated in keeping with the elegance of the rest of the house. The many sporting facilities were well integrated so as not to spoil the layout of the gardens. The set four-course dinners (with an optional à la carte) were never repeated over our nine-day stay, and the food was of quite a high standard. This *Schloss* offers far better value for money than most English country house hotels." (*Pamela and Norman Dutson; also K Pasold*)

Although last year one reader complained about a damp and musty room, he added how charmed he'd been by the friendly service of the Baroness's family. The Baroness herself writes to us of her hotel: "Receptions for VIPs! We arrange gala dinners, seminars and wedding festivities in the castle's chapel. I keep my house in the ancient Austrian family tradition. It's the most distinguished duty for me and my staff to transmit this atmosphere to my guests, far from all mass-tourism."

Open 1 Apr–30 Nov.
Rooms 1 suite, 24 double, 9 single – 26 with bath, 8 with shower, all with telephone; some ground-floor rooms. 20 in annexe.
Facilities Large hall with fireplace, salon, glassed-in veranda; baroque dining room; conference facilities; indoor swimming pool. Wine-tasting, dances, concerts. 25-acre grounds with swimming pool, sauna, tennis courts, ice rink, riding course. English spoken.
Location Between Eisenstadt and Mattersburg; 11 km from Eisenstadt; private landing strip 6 km; bus connections from all directions; guests can be met at Wiener Neustadt railway station; Schwechat airport is about 1 hour away.
Credit card Diners.
Terms [1985 rates] Rooms: single 330–660 Sch, double 570–1,120 Sch. Breakfast 90 Sch; set lunch/dinner 150 Sch.

Deadlines: nominations for the 1987 edition should reach us not later than 15 May 1986. Latest date for comments on existing entries: 30 June 1986.

DÜRNSTEIN 3601 Lower Austria	Map 14

Richard Löwenherz   *Tel* (02711) 222
                                                   Telex 071-199 LÖWE

Dürnstein is on the northern bank of a particularly luscious stretch of the Danube, about 50 miles west of Vienna. The whole area, known as the Wachau, is steeped in the history of central Europe from the Stone and Roman Ages onwards. Richard the Lionheart was imprisoned in the town in 1192 – hence the name of the hotel. "You find this entirely delightful hotel at the end of a narrow side street in this romantic village. The main road now passes beneath the village in a tunnel, so all is quiet. The hotel is built on the site of an old abbey and incorporates some of the old buildings; there are flower-filled gardens and a shady bar-terrace on top of a cliff looking across one of the most beautiful stretches of the Danube. Good food and wine from the hotel's own vineyard." *(William Goodhart; endorsed by Nathan R Carb, and others)*

Open Mar–Nov.
Rooms 2 suites, 44 double, 4 single – 33 with bath, 3 with shower, all with telephone.
Facilities Hall, TV room, bar/terrace, dining room. Large garden with heated swimming pool. On river with bathing and fishing. English spoken.
Location 50 m W of Vienna.
Restriction Not suitable for &.
Credit cards Amex, Diners.
Terms [1985 rates] B&B: single 450–750 Sch, double 850–1,000 Sch; suites 1,100–1,500 Sch. Set dinner 240 Sch.

Schloss Dürnstein   *Tel* (02711) 212
                                                   Telex 71 147

Eulogies have been many this year for the *Schloss*. It was built in 1630 and was for centuries owned by the Princes Starhemberg; it was used as a refuge by the Emperor Leopold I when fleeing from the Turks. Some 50 years ago, it was reincarnated by the Thiery family, who still own and run it. It even has a place in modern literature as a setting for Helen MacInnes' *The Snare of the Hunter*. Rather a formal place, it has beautiful antique furniture in both the public rooms and the bedrooms, most of which have splendid views over the curving Danube. "Dressing gowns were provided and two pairs of paper slippers were by our bed on our return from dinner. Although the furnishing and some of the clientele were very elegant, we didn't feel that the atmosphere was overly formal." There is the same fine view from the lovely spacious terrace of the restaurant. Fine cooking and some of the wine comes from the castle's own vineyards. "One of Europe's great little hotels," is a claim from one reader. "Not overpriced for Austria." "A romantic sojourn." *(Kate and Steve Murray-Sykes, Chris and David Tomlinson; also Ted and Vera Baker, Susan B Hanley)*

Open 15 Mar–25 Nov.
Rooms 2 suites, 31 double, 4 single – 35 with bath, 2 with shower, all with telephone and radio, colour TV and baby-listening by request; some ground-floor rooms.
Facilities Lift. Lounge, TV room, bar, restaurant and private dining room, grill

295

room with dance floor. Courtyard with heated swimming pool. Barbecue evenings, candlelit dinners once a week. Terrace overlooking Danube; fishing and boating. English spoken.
Location At end of main street in village. Parking.
Credit cards All major cards accepted.
Terms B&B: single 700–800 Sch, double 950–1,450 Sch; dinner, B&B: single 950–1,050 Sch, double 1,450–1,850 Sch. Set lunch/dinner 225–280 Sch; full alc 400 Sch.

FIEBERBRUNN 6391 Tyrol   Map 14

Schlosshotel Rosenegg   *Tel* (0043) 5354/6201/6211
                                          Telex 51332 HOROS

A newcomer to the Guide, this castle in the heart of the Kitzbüheler Alps was built in 1555. It has been recently renovated and is connected to a modern annexe by an "original" covered tunnel. "For the past four years we have used this charming Austrian hunting lodge. With three children we can be very demanding. Ossie Eberhardt and his charming English wife, Jane, offer a unique service for families, and one of the best-appointed establishments we have found. Their attention to detail is excellent. Heated tile floors in the sparkling *en suite* bathrooms. Beautiful wooden beds, antique furniture and modern comfort. But best of all an incredible understanding of how to cater for children. The Eberhardts daily take great pains to see all their guests and personally sort out all their problems. Max's Bar is the centre for all après-ski gossip, but the hotel also has an enchanting wine bar. Service in the large restaurant is slow, but so was it everywhere we went. This hotel really is the skiing family's ideal spot." *(Nicola Hayward)*

Open All year.
Rooms 68 double (48 of which can be triple), 12 single – 77 with bath, 3 with shower, all with telephone and radio, many with balcony; baby-sitters available. 48 rooms in annexe connected by a covered bridge to main building.
Facilities 2 lifts. Hall, salon, TV room, tavern restaurant, discothèque, kindergarten with trained nanny. Evening entertainments. Winter sports (free hotel bus to main skiing areas), indoor swimming pool nearby. English spoken.
Location Leave Munich/Kufstein motorway at Kufstein, take route 173, after 6 km take route No. 112 to St Johann in Tyrol; from there it is 9 km to Fieberbrunn. Parking.
Credit cards None accepted.
Terms Half-board: summer 330–430 Sch, winter 370–595 Sch. 50 Sch supplement for full board. Set lunch 85 Sch, dinner 120 Sch; full alc 170 Sch. Reduced rates and special menus for children.

FREISTADT 4240 Upper Austria   Map 14

Gasthof Deim zum Goldenen   *Tel* (07942) 2258 or 2111
Hirschen
Böhmergasse 8

Freistadt, an old town with traces of ramparts, towers and gateways, stands on a wild granite plateau between Linz and the Czech frontier. The Deim *is a genuine old inn within the ramparts with a pretty garden. Its entry was left out two years ago, when the hotel appeared to be going through a bad patch, but readers clamoured for its return. However, we have had no reports this year, and should be glad to know whether it is again as sublime as an earlier visitor found it: "A glimpse of the flower-bedecked façade compels the weary traveller through the medieval gateway and into the gay warmth and welcome of the life within. Everything afterwards is a dream – a dream of (princesses in) canopied (but firm and comfortable) beds, of ancient walls and arched roofs (ceilings is too dull a word), of foaming (locally brewed) beer pots, of superb Upper Austrian (lighter than Viennese) cuisine and wine, of happy laughing waitresses in simple local costume. Antique furniture and etchings, and discreet hyper-efficient modern plumbing, also a beautiful garden. Ideal for refugees from Socialist reality escaping down the E14 from Prague or even from tourists in Festival-struck Salzburg. Cheap too. They speak enough English to entrance but not enough to encourage linguistic sloth. Best of all, I shall remember the gentle strains of the local chamber orchestra drifting across the castle into our bedroom."* (T J Wiseman)

Open 1 Dec–15 Nov. Closed Fri between 1 Nov–30 Apr.
Rooms 17 double, 8 single – 12 with bath, 13 with shower, all with telephone, 6 with radio and TV.
Facilities Lounge, TV lounge, breakfast room, dining room. Garden (meals can be taken outside). English spoken.
Location Central, 100 metres from square. Parking. Town is 40 km NE of Linz.
Restriction Not suitable for &.
Credit card Diners.
Terms Rooms: single 230 Sch, double 400 Sch; dinner, B&B: single 350 Sch, double 620 Sch; full board: single 380 Sch, double 720 Sch. Breakfast 50 Sch; set lunch 95 Sch, dinner 110 Sch; full alc 150 Sch. Reduced rates for children.

FUSCHL-AM-SEE Salzburg   Map 14

Pension Rupertihof   *Tel* (06226) 447
Fuschl-am-See, 5330 Salzburg

That the Fuschlsee is just a short distance east of Salzburg is not its only advantage: it also happens to lap reverently against the majestic Schober mountain. Here the *Rupertihof*, by the lakeside just outside the village, is recommended as a clean modern *pension*, within walking distance of several hotels for dinner. "Comfortable beds, many rooms with bath and/or balcony; excellent varied breakfasts (muesli, eggs, cheese etc). Hans Stollinger speaks good English." More reports please. *(David Regan)*

Open All year.
Rooms 12 double – 3 with bath, 9 with shower, some with balcony; TV on request.
Facilities 2 breakfast rooms, lounge with TV; small garden. Lake Fuschl 50 metres (beach and safe bathing, sailing etc.). English spoken.
Location 25 km E of Salzurg on road to Bad Ischl.
Restriction Not suitable for &.
Credit card Amex.
Terms B&B 160–210 Sch. Reduced rates Mar, Apr and Oct. Reduced rates for children. (No restaurant.)

> Hotels often book you into their most expensive rooms or suites unless you specify otherwise. Even if all room prices are the same, hotels may give you a less good room in the hope of selling their better rooms to later customers. It always pays to discuss accommodation in detail when making a reservation.

Hotel Schloss Fuschl   *Tel* (06229) 253
Hof bei Salzburg   *Telex* 633454
Fuschl-am-See 5322 Salzburg

"Probably the most elegant hotel in Austria" is how one visitor dubbed this former hunting lodge of the prince-archbishops of Salzburg. Still distinctly regal, but now a wholly lay establishment, it overlooks Lake Fuschl with the mountains as backdrop; Salzburg is 20 kilometres away. "Romantic, luxurious and superb", was an earlier verdict, echoed by another. "Beautifully situated, with an elegant and interesting interior. The set meals were extremely good and the staff outstandingly welcoming and helpful." Some rooms are in the main building facing the lake, but even better are the chalets in the garden. One lunches or dines overlooking the lake, and at dinner in summer there are spectacular summer sunsets. The food is Austrian international at its best. Swimming both in an indoor pool and in the lake. (*A W Berryman; also Mrs C Smith*)

Open All year.
Rooms 21 suites, 63 double, 5 single – 83 with bath, 6 with shower, all with telephone, radio, most with colour TV; 66 rooms in garden chalets; some ground-floor rooms.
Facilities Lounge, bar, TV/reading room, dining room, conservatory, conference facilities, terrace for summer meals. Indoor heated swimming pool. Large park with swimming area on lake, fishing, boating, refreshments, tennis, 9-hole golf course. English spoken.
Location Take 158 road to St Gilden; turn left 1 m after village of Hof.
Restriction Not very suitable for &. as there are many levels.
Credit cards All major cards accepted.
Terms B&B: single 900–1,200 Sch, double 1,400–3,800 Sch; dinner, B&B: single 1,200 Sch–1,580 Sch, double 2,000–4,560 Sch; full board: single 1,500–1,960 Sch, double 2,600–5,320 Sch. Set lunch/dinner 380 Sch; full alc 450 Sch. Children under 12 sharing parents' room free; special meals on request.

GARGELLEN 6787 Vorarlberg   **Map 14**

Hotel Madrisa   *Tel* (05557) 6331 or 6131
Montafon   *Telex* 52269 MADRIS

A traditional but enlarged and modernised family ski hotel "in the beautiful Montafon valley, well managed with friendly owners and a chef well above average for a small hotel in the mountains". A regular correspondent waxes lyrical about a Christmas visit: "Gargellen is a delightful friendly ski village – hard to beat for family skiers. We arrived late at the hotel but the Rhomberg family welcomed us, carried our bags and gave us extra bedding. The staff had finished for the night but a cold buffet was waiting. The hotel exuded warmth – at the end of a hard day on the slopes it was bliss to return to. Days slip away in this cosy retreat and mountains of food appear regularly. We had rooms in the old part, ample, warm, rustic. Those in the new extension have balconies. The value for money makes me blink when I think of other ski resorts." Others agree: "We have not yet found a better hotel for skiing", and "ideal for children". (*Henry Banzhaf, D H Bennett, Dr P Marsh, and others*)

Open 7 Dec–12 Apr, 20 June–20 Sept.
Rooms 5 suites, 48 double, 12 single – 47 with bath, 1 with shower, 48 with

telephone, 36 with radio; TV on request.
Facilities Lift. Hall, lounge, reading room, games room, *Stüberl*, dining room, disco; children's playroom (with children's films). Indoor swimming pool, sauna, own ski lift. Terrace and lawn. English spoken.
Location 28 km S of Bludenz. In centre of Gargellen. Parking.
Credit cards Access, Amex.
Terms Dinner, B&B 550–950 Sch; suites, half-board (3,4 and 5 people) 2,500–3,900 Sch. Set lunch 75 Sch; full alc 250–300 Sch. Reductions for children sharing parents' rooms. Weekly and Christmas packages.

HEILIGENBLUT 9844 Carinthia   Map 14

Hotel Senger   *Tel* (04824) 2215
Grossglockner

Off the beaten track, this is beautiful, adventurous territory for walkers and for skiers. "Just above the village of Heiligenblut, there is one of those rare family hotels that offer comfort, excellent food, and the kind of personal attention that makes everyone feel relaxed and good-humoured. It's a typical old mountain chalet with a new house skilfully added. Most of the rooms have balconies – two have large terraces. The telephones have the direct-dialling system and the owners, Hans and Rosi Senger, speak English. The food is so copious that almost everyone opts for breakfast and dinner, and skips lunch – though the cook bakes cheesecakes, Sachertorte and Apfelstrudel almost every day and there is always the temptation to try them warm from the oven for afternoon coffee, after a day out on the mountains *(Hella Pick)*.The Sengers have added six new suites and an extra salon to the hotel. Although there was one complaint last year about the radio in the dining room, a reader this year reports that the establishment was every bit as wonderful as last year's entry claimed it to be. *(N Richardson, Janet Merutka, Becky Sproviero)*

Open 29 May–15 Oct, 15 Dec–15 Apr.
Rooms 6 suites, 6 double, 3 single – 4 with bath, 11 with shower, most with balcony, all with direct-dial telephone; TV on request; kitchenette and fridge in suites.
Facilities 3 salons, 2 with fireplace, 1 with TV, reading room, games room, bar/restaurant with live music; sauna. Garden. Fondue grill party once a week. Walking and winter sports. English spoken.
Location On the edge of Heiligenblut, which is on 107 40 km N of Lienz. Parking.
Credit card Amex.
Terms B&B 240–390 Sch; dinner, B&B 410–520 Sch; full board 70 Sch added. Set lunch 140 Sch, dinner 160 Sch; full alc 150–190 Sch. Christmas packages. Reduced rates for children sharing parents' room; special meals.

INNSBRUCK 6020 Tyrol   Map 14

Haus Schwarz   *Tel* (05222) 85535
Lindenbuhelweg 12

A small friendly B&B in a quiet secluded position above the Inn valley, with fine views over the town and mountains. "The house has only five rooms (10 beds) but it has many advantages. None of the rooms has private facilities, but there are two WCs and one shower on the landing. Our room was a large one with a balcony with beautiful views over the mountains. The house is only a few minutes by car or frequent bus to the centre of Innsbruck. It is in a quiet position with parking and has a pleasant garden. There is an indoor pool, well heated, with huge windows opening on to the garden. Frau Schwarz, who speaks reasonable English, is most kind and helpful, and offers drinks. There is a good restaurant nearby." (N M Williamson) *More reports welcome.*

Open All year except 1 week in New Year, 1 week Sept.
Rooms 1 triple, 3 double, 1 single – all with h & c.
Facilities Lounge with TV, breakfast room, sun-terrace where breakfast can be served. Bridge evenings. Garden with heated covered swimming pool and lawns. English spoken.
Location 7 minutes by car from centre. Regular buses (A and H) from Innsbruck station. Not easy to find – telephone and you will be met anywhere in Innsbruck and shown the way.
Restrictions Not suitable for &. Children under 7 not allowed in the swimming pool.
Credit cards None accepted.
Terms B&B 180–190 Sch. 20 Sch added for stay of 1 night only. No restaurant, but you can bring your own food and eat in the breakfast room. Reduced rates for children sharing parents' room; snacks available.

KITZBÜHEL 6370 Tyrol   Map 14

Hotel Montana   *Tel* (05356) 2526
Hahnenkammstrasse 5   *Telex* 51551

A family-owned hotel, well equipped with saunas, solarium and indoor pool, close to the main cable car and only a few minutes' walk from the town centre. "This hotel was in some ways the discovery of our holiday. The *Montana* is a short distance up the hillside beyond the Hahnenkamm railway and cable car stations, where the fields start. It is well designed, spotless and functional. Our reception was a little cool but the room allocated to us was a delight. It was comfortably furnished and the bathroom was a masterpiece of ceramic and chromium plate, only marred by a brief tendency for the hot water to run to cool. Doors opened on to a wide terrace flanked by geraniums. A buffet breakfast was provided." *(W H Bruton)*

Open Mid-May–Oct, Dec–mid-Apr.
Rooms 40 double – 38 with bath, 2 with shower, all with telephone, most with balcony; TV and baby-listening on request.
Facilities Lift. TV room, salon, bar, children's playroom; terrace; sauna, solarium, heated indoor swimming pool; table tennis. Small garden. Skiing, tennis, golf, squash nearby. English spoken.
Location 3 minutes' walk from town centre, beside ski-school and close to Hahnenkamm cable car. Parking.
Restriction Not suitable for &.
Credit cards Amex, Diners.
Terms B&B 350–700 Sch; dinner, B&B 400–750 Sch; full alc 190 Sch. Reduced rates and special meals for children.

KRIMML 5743 Salzburg   Map 14

Gasthof Krimmlerfälle   *Tel* (06564) 203

"The Krimml waterfalls – about 50 kilometres east of Innsbruck – are truly spectacular, bouncing down 1,250 feet and filling the valley with iridescent mists. No photograph could do them justice and they are well worth the long, steep walk from the village. The *Familie* Schöppl own this largish hotel (also the more luxurious *Gasthaus Edelweiss*) and it has the advantage of being sufficiently distant from the cascade for the stupendous roar to be muffled. It is a typical Austrian building with timber-clad upper floors, carved wooden balconies bearing boxes filled with petunias and geraniums – a simple, unpretentious place but very spacious and full of character. Our bedroom was palatial in proportions, with unsophisticated solid pine furniture, folk-weave rugs and goat skins. It was comfortable, had a balcony with table and chairs and faced the famous falls. There are several public rooms and summer coach-tour guests are kept firmly separate from autonomous customers – the latter being fed in a characterful dining room with a striking three-foot high frieze of Tyrolean dancers. The food was straightforward and unpretentious. Please do not sneer when you read that dinner, bed and breakfast cost us £29 [1984]!" *(Francine and Ian Walsh)*

Open All year except Nov.
Rooms 6 suites, 50 double, 10 single – 30 with beds, 5 with shower. 12 rooms in annexe; some ground-floor rooms.
Facilities Lounge, TV room, 2 bars, restaurant; musical evenings. Large garden. Swimming pool, tennis courts and winter sports nearby. English spoken.
Location Central; Krimml is on A5743 between Gerlos and Mittersil.
Credit cards None accepted.
Terms B&B: 240–260 Sch; dinner B&B 320–340 Sch; full board 375–390 Sch. Set meals 95 and 110 Sch. 10% reduction for children under 12; special meals.

LANS Tyrol   Map 14

Gasthof "Zur Traube"   *Tel* (05222) 77261
Nr Innsbruck A6072

Lans is a picture-book hamlet overlooking Innsbruck with a fantastic view of the mountains. The *Zur Traube*, recorded as an inn since 1313, is as Tyrolean as they come, with traditional furnishings and cooking provided by the Raitmayr family, who have owned and cared for the *Gasthof* for fifteen generations. "The inn is picturesque with its Tyrolean white stucco and dark beams. Most rooms have flowered balconies. Local specialities served in the enchanting dining rooms were delicious. Another serendipity was a small Austrian band which gave a night-time concert in the parking lot." Plenty to do both summer and winter. *(Vicki Turner; and others)*

Open All year except 10 Oct – 4 Nov.
Rooms 21 double, 5 single – 3 with bath, 22 with shower, all with telephone, many with balcony.
Facilities Lift. Salon, dining rooms. Garden. Winter sports; golf, tennis and swimming in summer. English spoken.
Location In village centre. Parking. Lans is 6 km S of Innsbruck.
Credit cards None accepted.
Terms B&B 270–320 Sch; dinner, B&B 380–450 Sch; full board 480–560 Sch. Set lunch 130 Sch, dinner 140 Sch; full alc 240 Sch.

We ask hotels to estimate their 1986 tariffs. About a quarter of the hotels in Part Two have failed to reply, so prices in that section are more approximate in some cases than those in Part One.

LECH AM ARLBERG 6764 Vorarlberg

Map 14

Hotel-Gasthof Salome   *Tel* (05583) 2306
Oberlech

Once a small village in the Arlberg mountains, Lech is now one of Europe's finest ski resorts. The *Salome* is a comfortable, fairly pricey ski-hotel perched on the mountainside at Oberlech with wonderful mountain views all around and a nursery slope at its front door. Readers this year warn that the hotel is probably best approached in winter during daytime as you have to drive up a narrow winding snow-covered road. It is a 600-year-old farmhouse, renovated in Alpine style with wooden ceilings and carved beams. "There was an immediate warm and friendly feeling about the place and the pine cupboards, coloured rugs, ornaments and books made the hotel feel lived in. We were taken to the nicest room we have ever had in a ski hotel." Hotel guests have their own dining room ("the food we had was very pleasant without being gastronomically outstanding"), a large and comfortable sitting room and a sun terrace, and in the basement a sauna, solarium and whirlpool. Bedrooms lead off a pretty landing on the first floor with a wooden floor and kilim rugs – some of the larger ones, divided into sleeping and sitting areas, have balconies; the smaller ones do not have a sitting area. Service is friendly and helpful. *(K M-S)*

Open Dec – Apr.
Rooms 11 suites, 4 double, 1 single – 10 with bath, 6 with shower, all with telephone, radio and colour TV.
Facilities Lift. Lounge, bar, restaurant, residents' dining room, sun terrace, sauna, solarium, whirlpool, massage. Fishing 3 km, English spoken.
Location On the mountain above Lech; take road to Oberlech. Parking.
Credit cards None accepted.
Terms Half-board 1,070–1,330 Sch. 50% reduction for children sharing parents' room.

Hotel Tannbergerhof   *Tel* (05583) 2202
                                        Telex 52 39117

"The *Tannbergerhof* is right in the thick of things on the main street of Lech, looking over the little river with its bridges, and only a few minutes' walk from the ski school and many of the lifts. At five o'clock every day there is *thé dansant* in the downstairs bar, and skiers gather to drink Glühwein in front of the hotel in the sun or snow. At night there is a disco in the bar, and to watch the *joli monde* arriving in their fur coats is an entertainment in itself. But though there is much action downstairs, the bedrooms are peaceful and comfortable. We had a beautifully quiet room at the back, not elegant, but with a good bed – though the lighting was so poor it was almost impossible to read in bed. We were impressed by the consistently high standards of service. Frau Hilde Jochum keeps a close eye on things, as does the young *maître d'hôtel*. The food was consistently delicious, beautifully presented, and not too heavy: we especially liked the generous salad trolley. Meal-times were flexible. Breakfast was a generous-self-service spread – quite enough to keep us going all day without much lunch. We enjoyed using the swimming pool and whirlpool in the annexe a short walk away. Our main criticism of the hotel is of the lack of a residents' lounge – there's nowhere you can peacefully sit and read." *(Adam and Caroline Raphael)*

Open 21 June – 21 Sept, 29 Nov – 13 Apr.
Rooms 4 suites, 17 double, 9 single – 26 with bath, 4 with shower, all with telephone, radio and colour TV. Annexe *(Chalet Hilde)* with self-catering apartments.
Facilities Lift. Reception, 3 lounges, bar, 3 restaurants, downstairs bar where disco is held daily in winter; terrace. River nearby with trout fishing. Swimming pool, whirlpool in the annexe *Chalet Hilde*, 8 minutes' walk from the hotel. English spoken.
Location Central. Parking.
Credit cards None accepted.
Terms (minimum prices in summer, maximum in winter) B&B 440–1,520 Sch; half-board 570–1,610 Sch; full board 630–1,700 Sch. Set lunch 215 Sch in summer, 270 Sch in winter. Set dinner 270 Sch in summer, 480 Sch in winter.

LERMOOS 6631 Tyrol   Map 14

Sporthotel Zugspitze   *Tel* (05673) 2630
                                                      Telex 5556

"Lermoos, a long-stretched village on the Austrian side of the Zugspitze Massiv presents a welcome break on one of the main transalpine thoroughfares. The main road actually bypasses the village which has gained in peace and quietude. The *Zugspitze* is an attractively designed large chalet at the Fernpass end of the village, lacking no modern comforts. Its attractive bedrooms, though small, are tastefully furnished in rustic/baroque style, with balconies facing either the mountainside or a wide open green plain with the dramatic Zugspitze as its impressive backdrop. Comfortable public rooms, charming service (without the often tiresome Austrian exaggerations of *Küss-die-Hand-Gnä'-Frau*), good Austrian bourgeois cuisine, and a spacious outside café-terrace contribute to the pleasant ensemble for either a short transit stay, or a longer holiday." *(Arnold R Horwell)*

Open 15 Dec–7 Apr, 17 May–26 Oct
Rooms 24 double, 2 single – all with bath, shower, telephone and colour TV; many with balcony.
Facilities Lift. Hall, lounge, bar, restaurants, sauna, solarium, games room. Tyrolean meals, fondue parties; music and dancing at weekend. Garden and terrace. Winter sports, walking, tennis, riding, swimming and fishing nearby. English spoken.
Location On the Innsbruck side of the resort. Garage and parking.
Credit cards All major cards accepted.
Terms B&B 450–650 Sch; dinner, B&B 570–720 Sch; full board 660–810 Sch. Set lunch/dinner 90–300 Sch; full alc 150–400 Sch. Reduced rates and special meals for children.

MUTTERS BEI INNSBRUCK 6162   Map 14

Hotel Restaurant Muttererhof   *Tel* (05222) 27491 and 235445
Nattererstrasse 20

"The ski resort of Mutters is a picturesque village on a ledge a few kilometres south-west of Innsbruck. Every chalet turns into a *Gasthof* during the skiing season, but in the summer it is redolent of cow byres.

Most of the houses have flower-decked balconies and picturesque frescoes painted on their walls. The hotel is the last residence on the road to Natters and faces the most breathtaking landscape. The hotel obviously had simple beginnings but has been expanded at both ends. The *pièce de résistance* is their good-sized, well-heated swimming pool, solarium and sauna. Herr Egger runs the *Muttererhof* with the help of his delightful twin daughters – fine-featured, statuesque blondes. Decor and furniture of bedrooms uninspiring, though our room had a balcony (not all do). Beds were comfortable; plenty of towels but no soap. The dining room was absolutely beautiful, panelled in dark wood with ecclesiastical-style carvings. Windows were in green and white leaded glass. I loved the two long, beribboned fair-haired plaits heralding the fact that the Egger girls were now fully liberated modern women! We had enjoyed an exhilarating swim before dinner which had given us quite an appetite, well satisfied by the meal. The carte contained quite a few Austrian specialities. The wine list was reasonable and included a very decent house wine. Service was really friendly and efficient all round. A good, reasonably priced base to explore the area." *(Francine and Ian Walsh)*

Open Dec–Mar, May–Oct.
Rooms 42 beds – 14 rooms with bath, 2 with shower, all with telephone; many with balcony.
Facilities Bar, restaurant, sauna, solarium, indoor swimming pool. Garden. Tennis and winter sports nearby.
Location SSW of Innsbruck, S of Natters, E of Gotzens.
Terms [1985 rates] B&B: single 330–370 Sch, double 600–680 Sch; full board: single 450–510 Sch, double 840–960 Sch.

SALZBURG Map 14

Hotel Elefant *Tel* (0662) 43397
Sigmund-Haffnergasse 4, Salzburg 5020 *Telex* 63725 ELHOT

"The *Elefant* is conveniently situated in the historic heart of Salzburg in a quiet street near the fashionable Getreidegasse, five minutes' walk from the festival opera house. The area is pedestrian, although taxis, horse-drawn fiacres and small local buses have right of passage. You are allowed to drive your car up to the hotel to load and unload, but not without questions from the local constabulary, and it is a good five-minutes' walk back from the fiver-a-day public car park. The hotel is a typical Salzburg town house, tall, narrow and medieval. All its public parts are nicely provided with substantial inlaid furniture and old paintings.

"The first floor is indeed grandiose with checkered marble floors, gorgeous antiques and a truly classy dining room now exclusively used for breakfast. However, the quality of the hotel degenerates as you progress upwards." Rooms on upper floors can be "cramped, furnished with ordinary furniture" and readers have asked us to warn one-nighters that the hotel's policy is probably to house them in the less grand rooms. But "the staff is pleasant and the sheets are whiter than white". Also: "Dinner, taken in the cellar restaurant, was never less than enjoyable. Altogether the hotel is strongly recommended and quite modestly priced." We have been informed that the hotel is planning to redecorate its rooms. More reports welcome. *(Francine and Ian Walsh; also Mr and Mrs D Steven McGuire, W H Bruton, Dr Peter Woodford)*

Open All year. Restaurant closed Tue except during summer festival.
Rooms 4 suites, 18 double, 13 single – 16 with bath, 20 with shower, all with telephone and radio; colour TV in suites.
Facilities Lift. Hall with bar, cellar bar, TV/writing room, breakfast room, dining room; conference facilities. English spoken. &.
Location Central, but located in pedestrian precinct. 5 minutes from municipal parking. Drive along Hauptstrasse, follow Rudolfskai, go round Mozart-Platz and Alter Markt.
Credit cards None accepted.
Terms B&B: single 400–450 Sch, double 700–1,200 Sch; half-board 140 Sch per person added to B&B rate; full board 260 Sch added. Set lunch 70 Sch; full alc 220 Sch. Reduced rates for children; special meals by arrangement.

Hotel Kasererbräu *Tel* (0622) 42445
Kaigasse 33, Salzburg 5010 *Telex* 633492

In the shadow of the magnificent Hohensalzburg fortress on the hill, this small bright hotel occupies a building dated 1342. Some of its rooms are furnished in baroque and Biedermeier styles; others are, as the hotel brochure puts it, "the latest Salzburg fashion". This was translated for us by one of our readers this year: "The hotel was simply but delightfully furnished in pinewood, beautifully fresh and clean. Breakfast was adequate and pleasantly served. We had a tasteful evening meal at the Mozart Inn attached to the hotel, reasonably priced and the service was friendly. They spoke English too!" *(Gertrude and Gerhard Cohn)*

Open All year.
Rooms 50 beds – 12 rooms with bath, 6 with shower; all with telephone.
Facilities Lift. Lounge, television, restaurant. English spoken.
Location Central. Parking.
Restriction Not suitable for &.
Credit cards Some may be accepted.
Terms [1985 rates] B&B 530–750 Sch; full board 770–990 Sch.

Hotel Markus Sittikus *Tel* (0662) 71121 or 71326
Markus Sittikus Strasse 20
Salzburg 5021

Readers continue to endorse the entry for this English-speaking modest-to-medium-priced bed-and-breakfast hotel, neat, tidy and caring, near the bus station and the Kongresshaus: no special virtues, but a friendly and comfortable option in a city where accommodation can be difficult. *(R J Harborne, D & K Perry)*

Open All year except 5 days at Christmas
Rooms 23 double, 17 single – 11 with bath, 21 with shower, all with telephone.
Facilities Lift. Hall, TV room, breakfast room. Garden. English spoken.
Location Central, near Mirabell garden and Kongresshaus. Street parking.
Restriction Not suitable for &.
Credit cards All major cards accepted.
Terms B&B: single 340–590 Sch, double 560–990 Sch. 20% reduction for children. (No restaurant.)

Pension Nonntal *Tel* (0662) 41427 and 46700
Pfadfinderweg 6 and 8
Salzburg 5020

Recommended as a pleasant bed-and-breakfast *pension* in residential
south-east Salzburg, with a spectacular view of the Hohensalzburg
fortress and only ten minutes' walk from the centre. "Most gracious and
warm: an old converted house in a quiet area, with a large garden.
Rooms are spacious, windows overlook greenery; comfortable twin beds
pushed together; bath is generous size and modern. Breakfast room
overlooked the lovely garden. The people were very friendly and helpful
and will arrange for bicycles (compliments of the house), concert tickets
and ski trips." *(Janet Merutka)* More reports welcome, especially on the
Pension's new restaurant.

Open All year except Nov.
Rooms 2 suites, 8 double, 3 single – 8 with bath, 4 with shower, all with
telephone, TV on request. Some ground-floor rooms. 7 rooms in annexe.
Accommodation for 5 people in nearby house with kitchen, garden and car park.
Facilities 2 lounges, restaurant. Garden with terrace and lawns. Bicycles
available. Management help guests to get concert tickets.
Location Leave *Autobahn* at Salzburg-Süd. Turn left after information office on
Friedensstrasse, left on Hellbrunner Strasse and immediately right on Hofhaymer-
Allee, then right on Nonntaler Hauptstrasse. The *Pension* is down a small road on
right. Buses go from nearby to all parts of Salzburg.
Credit cards Access, Visa.
Terms B&B: single 380–580 Sch, double 620–1,400 Sch. Set lunch/dinner 105–185
Sch; full alc 220–380 Sch.

Hotel Schloss Mönchstein *Tel* (0662) 413630 or 41366
Am Mönchsberg 26 *Telex* 632080
Salzburg 5020

Perched on a serene mountain-top that rises directly up from central
Salzburg, this great tan *Schloss*, with its reverse crenellated overhangs
and creeper-covered walls, was once the guest-house of an archbishop.
"At first glance it seems one has returned to England. Afternoon tea
served on the patio does nothing to lessen the feeling." So writes an
American about this Victorian hotel with its big tidy garden, lawns,
flowerbeds and dense trees. "Not a hotel, an experience" writes a visitor
this year. "Not more than 15 minutes by foot from the Festspielhaus and
yet remote from the tourist hurly-burly. Thanks to an efficient lift service
which runs until two in the morning, you can be whisked to the top of
the mountain in a mere 30 seconds. It is beautifully quiet and the air is
fresher than down in town. The hotel has only 17 rooms, and is
pleasantly and efficiently run." One reader was especially pleased:
"Breakfast ranged from brioches to fruit salad to cheese and cold cuts,
and was served on our flower-filled terrace. The management provided
a complimentary course at dinner and sent bed-time sweets to our room.
I felt truly pampered!" *(G Sharp, M and M Dettrich, Vicki Turner)*

Open All year.
Rooms 7 suites, 9 double, 1 single – 15 with bath, 2 with shower, all with
direct-dial telephone, radio and colour TV, 24-hour room service; some ground-
floor rooms.
Facilities Lift. Hall, 2 salons, bar, restaurant, chapel for weddings, terrace with

café; monthly concerts; large garden with tennis court. English spoken. &.
Location Above Salzburg on Mönchsberg Hill – hotel is signposted; (3 minutes by car to the city centre, 7 minutes by the Mönchsberg lift). Parking and garages.
Credit cards All major cards accepted.
Terms B&B: single 1,200–1,400 Sch, double 2,000–3,300 Sch; half-board 400–450 Sch per person added. Set lunch 350 Sch, dinner 400 Sch; full alc 600 Sch. 3-day "Winterdream", tennis and honeymoon packages. 20% reduction for children sharing parents' room; special meals.

Hotel Schöne Aussicht　　　　　　　　*Tel* (0662) 78226 and 78449
Heuberg 3, Salzburg 5023　　　　　　　　　　　　　*Telex* 631153

From the hotel's terrace on the sunny Heuberg the view of Salzburg is *schön* indeed. The hotel itself is a big, modern, white-walled chalet, set on a green hillside, and the swimming pool, tennis, red parasols on the panoramic terrace, and cosy beamed bar, all add to the holiday ambience. "Visiting Salzburg with the car is difficult as most of the old town is pedestrianised: a better idea is to stay out of town and then drive in to one of the large car parks. This we did. The *Schöne Aussicht* is tucked away but well signed. We had a lovely room with balcony, self-service breakfast (so you can eat on and on), and every comfort and facility we needed. Service was courteous and friendly and everthing was very clean; fresh flowers in abundance. The food was delicious, with a wide selection of fresh game (October). Glorious walks in the countryside. *Note:* although the brochure mentions public transport, the walk from the bus stop is up three steep hills, so a car is advisable." *(Bettina and Sacha Dudkin; enthusiastically endorsed by Ted and Vera Baker)* A recent visitor, while appreciating the lovely setting, complains of a disturbed night in a room above the bar, subject to nocturnal wassailing. She also comments on a waitress becoming surly when a tip was not added to a bill in which service was already included. More reports please.

Open Mar – end Oct.
Rooms 5 suites, 22 double, 1 single – 11 with bath, 17 with shower, all with telephone and radio; TV on request.
Facilities Lounge, bar, TV room, restaurant, conference/function facilities; sauna; terrace. Garden with heated swimming pool and tennis court. English spoken.
Location 3 km NE of city centre, off N158 to Bad Ischl.
Restriction Not suitable for &.
Credit cards Amex, Diners.
Terms B&B: single 400–600 Sch, double 670–950 Sch. Full alc 200 Sch. Reductions for children sharing parents' room; special meals.

SCHLOSS ROSENAU Lower Austria　　　　　　　　　　**Map 14**

Museumsverein Schloss Rosenau　　　　　　*Tel* (02822) 8203
Nr Zwettl 3924

The village of Schloss Rosenau is less than two hours' drive north-west of Vienna, not far from the Czech border. The *Schloss* is a baroque palace, three-quarters of which is now a spectacular 18th-century Freemason museum. Despite its outside grandeur, the hotel, and the adjacent *pension*, offer no more than simple accommodation but at a very reasonable price. The hotel is delightfully set amidst rolling countryside, excellent for walking and cross-country skiing: no night life, just peace and wonderful views. "The *Schloss* has a close arrangment with the *Pension Weissenhofer* just across the car park and guests who book may, like us, find themselves actually sleeping in the *Pension*. Once the manager realised that we were not entirely pleased, he was very apologetic and anxious that we shouldn't be angry (and gave us an aperitif on the house). He agreed to show us some of the bedrooms in the *Schloss* and we realised we were not really missing much. All the bedrooms are plain with white walls and simple pine furniture. There is a fairly extensive dinner menu. We thought the food was tasty, plentiful, fairly imaginative and good value." *(K and S M-S; also Professor H C Robbins Landon)*

Open All year.
Rooms 1 suite, 11 double or triple, 1 single – all with shower and WC. (Guests also accommodated in *Pension Weissenhofer* nearby.)
Facilities Salon, TV room, conference and banqueting rooms, dining room; sun terrace. Freemason museum and baroque church. Park with covered heated swimming pool, hard tennis court and miniature golf. Riding and fishing available. English spoken.
Location 8 km SW of Zwettl.
Credit cards Access, Diners, Visa.
Terms B&B: 260–300 Sch; half-board 345–385 Sch; full board 420–460 Sch. Set lunch/dinner 90–150 Sch; full alc 250 Sch. Reduced rates and special meals for children.

SCHRUNS 6780 Vorarlberg   Map 14

Hotel Krone   *Tel* (05556) 2255
Montafon

The *Krone* is a *gemütlich* family hotel five minutes' walk from the centre of Schruns, a delightful market town in the Montafon valley. "The hotel had a truly local atmosphere, pleasantly furnished and beautifully clean; our room had a most modern bathroom, and outlook over the trees of the outdoor restaurant to distant peaks." A reader last year had this to say about the restaurant: "We were impressed with the courtesy shown us and the quality of the food which is excellent; the wine list likewise cannot be faulted. The restaurant is patronised by local people. *Familie* Mayer, the fourth generation of the owner family, are kindness itself." This year's readers felt much the same. "The *Familie* Mayer brought a professional touch well complemented by the skill of their staff. We found the varied local dishes well cooked and attractively presented. It is certainly a hotel we hope to return to." *(Harry Robinson, Hugh and Elsie Pryor; also D and K Perry)*

Open Mid-Dec to Apr, mid-May to mid-Oct.
Rooms 8 double, 1 single – 4 with bath and WC, 5 with shower and WC, all with telephone and radio; TV can be hired.
Facilities Lounge, bar, wine cellar, dining room. Garden terrace. English spoken.
Location Central. Parking. 12 km SE of Bludenz.
Restriction Not suitable for &.
Credit cards None accepted.
Terms B&B 260–380 Sch; half-board 390–490 Sch; full board 490–590 Sch. Set lunch 140 Sch, dinner 160 Sch. Ski packages. Reduced rates for children.

STEYR 4400 Upper Austria   Map 14

Hotel Minichmayr   *Tel* (07252) 23410
Haratzamüllerstrasse 1–3   *Telex* 028134

"Although Steyr is the industrial capital of Upper Austria, one is unaware of the fact when wandering in its picturesque old quarter. The hotel stands on the bank immediately opposite the confluence of the Enns and Steyr rivers, commanding a truly spectacular view over the weirs and riverside buildings. The place was comfortable rather than elegant. Our room was simple. Both our bedroom windows overlooked the two rivers and the only sound was that of the rushing waters below. The bathroom was modern and well equipped. Reception was friendly and effective. There is also a view from the restaurant's picture window. A riotous and merry gathering in an inner dining room was taking place when we were there, and our meal was accompanied by songs which were so harmonious they would not have disgraced *The Sound of Music*. Certainly this place offered original, copious and shades of *nouvelle cuisine* dishes that were a cut above most of the Austrian restaurant run-of-the-mill fare. Breakfast was served in a wood-panelled room adjoining the dining room, also enjoying the view. We were astounded when we realised that dinner, bed and breakfast with bathroom, plus drinks from the mini-bar in our room and a long-distance international call, cost us £48 [1984] for two!" *(Francine and Ian Walsh)*

Open All year.
Rooms 3 suites, 35 double, 12 single – 40 with bath, 5 with shower, all with telephone, radio and TV.
Facilities Lift. Lounges, bars, restaurant; conference facilities; terrace with café. Fishing. English spoken.
Location Central. Parking.
Credit cards Amex, Diners.
Terms B&B: single 485 Sch, double 680 Sch; dinner, B&B: single 595 Sch, double 900 Sch; full board: single 695 Sch, double 1,100 Sch. Set meals 140 and 220 Sch; full alc 250 Sch. Reduced rates and special meals for children.

VIENNA   Map 14

Hotel Amadeus   *Tel* (0222) 638738
Wildpretmarkt 5
Vienna 1010

"What a wonderful little hotel" says a reader about the newly elected *Amadeus*, on a small street near St Stephan's in old Vienna. "The atmosphere was purely Maria Theresa and totally charming. The hotel is entirely painted in white, furniture included, with gilt motifs in relief. Our room was very spacious with electronically controlled shutters which shut out most of the traffic noise. Smart bathroom. The girls at reception are charming, speak excellent English and gave valuable information about restaurants and parking. Consulates and embassies seem to think it offers much better value than most since they recommend it to diplomatic visitors." Another reader voices delight about breakfast, "taken in a pleasant room across from the reception desk. Upon request, a large glass of freshly squeezed orange juice; and as standard fare, first-rate coffee and a basket of newly baked rolls. These rolls explain the fame of Viennese cooking. Despite its elegance, this hotel does not put on airs – the postwoman was being served this same ambrosial coffee in the same elegant way." *(Ruth Luborsky, F and I W)*

Open All year except Christmas and New Year.
Rooms 18 double, 12 single – 19 with bath, 11 with shower, all with telephone, radio and mini-bar; some with colour TV.
Facilities Lift. Hall, breakfast room. St Stephan's Cathedral, Vienna State Opera, State Theatre and Concert House 2 minutes' walk. English spoken.
Location Central: Wildpretmarkt is a small turning off Tuchlauben, which leads towards the Hofburg. Car park nearby.
Restriction Not suitable for &.
Credit cards Amex, Diners.
Terms [1985 rates] B&B: single 740–930 Sch, double 1,320 Sch.

König von Ungarn　　　　　　　　　　　　*Tel* (0222) 5265200
Schulerstrasse 10, Vienna 1010　　　　　　　　*Telex* 116240

A stone's throw from St Stephan's, this new entry to the Guide occupies a beautifully restored 18th-century building. An inner courtyard has been converted into an attractive Art Nouveau-style lounge with natural light coming from a skylight. "The reception area is off to one side so that when you go through the beautiful bevelled glass doors you have the feeling of entering an exclusive club. Our bedroom was a delight. Large, attractively furnished with real furniture. With a double-door arrangement and two sets of windows, the room was very quiet. Two wash basins in the bathroom, a huge, well-lit mirror and the whole thing kept spotlessly clean." Another reporter had a suite. "A large entrance led into a medium-sized double bedroom and a staircase went up to quite a sizeable attic room with twin beds. The room had a large walk-in cupboard. I felt I could have lived there with all my wardrobe. We liked it so much we stayed an extra night! The restaurant is, in fact, under separate ownership. It is very elegant and a well-known place to go among the Viennese society. The service is all one could wish for and the food excellent." "The nicest hotel we've been in in a long while. First class in the best sense of the term." *(Mr and Mrs C R Safford, Anna Waley)*

Open All year.
Rooms 70 beds – 28 rooms with bath, 4 with shower, all with telephone.
Facilities Lift. Lounge, bar, restaurant, TV room, children's room. &.
Location Central, near St Stephan's Cathedral. Parking.
Credit cards Possibly some accepted.
Terms [1985 rates] B&B 675–1,100 Sch.

Hotel im Palais Schwarzenberg　　　　　　*Tel* (0222) 784515
Schwarzenbergplatz 9　　　　　　　　　　　*Telex* 136124 HPS
Vienna 1030

"Owner?" we ask in our questionnaire. "Prince Karl Johannes zu Schwarzenberg" is the imposing answer in the case of this decidedly stately home where the Schwarzenbergs have lived since the early 18th century. It was bombed during the war, but has been faithfully reconstructed. Although only 15 minutes' walk from the Opera and the

Kärntnerstrasse, the *Palais* is discreet, quiet and impressively elegant – in its rooms, in the 19-acre park and in the admirable restaurant. It is as though Buckingham Palace had been converted into an exclusive *de luxe* hotel. Not that the guests at the *Palais* stay in the palatial rooms themselves; in fact they are accommodated in what was formerly the stables and servents' quarters.

Readers this year have had mixed opinions, but all agree that the price is high. "The most expensive hotel room we have ever stayed in – and worth every penny" was one comment. Another said: "Our room was comfortably large and expensively decorated, with fabric-covered walls, antique furniture, crystal chandelier and plush carpeting. Forgetting the price, this was definitely one of the nicest rooms we have stayed in – it didn't feel impersonal or unhomely like some top-class hotels. But you don't feel you're staying in a palace, more on the periphery. Dinner is not unreasonably priced, but, surprisingly, there was no buffet at breakfast and all except the basic rolls, jam and coffee were charged as extras. This seems unnecessarily mean on the part of the hotel when bed and breakfast was already so expensive. All the staff were helpful and polite." One reader had a particularly unpleasant experience, having been asked by the hotel for an inordinately large deposit and then receiving a very poor exchange rate from them. More reports please. *(Roger Bennett, Dr H B Cardwell, K and S M-S; Susan B Hanley)*

Open All year.
Rooms 4 suites (1 with kitchenette), 39 double – all with bath, telephone and radio; colour TV on request, some ground-floor rooms.
Facilities 3 lifts. Hall, bar with open fire, restaurant with summer and winter terraces; large conference hall with function facilities. 19-acre private park with 5 tennis courts, unheated swimming pool, sauna. English spoken. Possibly suitable for &.
Location Close to centre; despite its address entrance is at bottom of Prinz-Eugen-Strasse. Unlimited parking.
Credit cards All major cards accepted.
Terms B&B: single 1,700–2,750 Sch, double 2,450–4,500 Sch. Full alc 750 Sch. Special meals for children on request.

Hotel Sacher   *Tel* (0222) 525575
Philharmonikerstrasse 4, Vienna 1015   *Telex* 112520

"Quite one of the most charming hotels I have ever stayed at," enthuses a reader this year. For him as for others with a taste for the traditional grand, the *Sacher* is the only hotel in Vienna. It's central – just off the Ringstrasse, opposite the Opera and two minutes from the Hofburg. The decor – red velvet, crystal chandeliers, brocade curtains, flock wallpaper and all – is as nostalgic for the old imperial Vienna as anyone could wish. "Service is impeccable and all the more remarkable as its cafés and terraces are much thronged by well-heeled tourists and Viennese who come to eat Sachertorte." (That legendary delicacy is reputed to taste far better here than any of its many inferior imitations.) "What a wonderful hotel . . . real linen sheets and down pillows, not the usual foam-rubber bricks. Everything seemed to work perfectly. The best hotel I've stayed in for many years." *(W Greville-Griffiths; Mrs M D Prodgers)*

Open All year.
Rooms 5 suites, 77 double, 39 single – 121 with baths, 3 with shower, all with telephone, radio and colour TV.
Facilities Lift. Lobby, lounges, Blue Bar, Red Bar, Marble Room, 3 restaurants, café; piano and zither music every evening; conference and banqueting facilities. English spoken. &.
Location Off the Ringstrasse, opposite the Opera. Garage opposite.
Credit cards None accepted.
Terms Room with breakfast: single 1,100–1,700 Sch, double 1,900–3,000 Sch. Set lunch 480 Sch, dinner 560 Sch; full alc 580 Sch (approx.). Children under 6 free.

Pension Suzanne   *Tel* (0222) 532507
Walfischgasse 4, Vienna 1010

Above a sex-shop, but don't be put off! The Walfischgasse is no sleazy Soho alley, but a respectable thoroughfare, 100 yards from the Opera House and the start of the pedestrianised Kärntnerstrasse. Like other Viennese *pensions*, the entrance is unimpressive; the bedrooms are on the upper floors, some facing the street (double-glazed) and some a parking lot in the rear. No public rooms; breakfasts (a good *café complet*) are served in your own bedroom. What distinguishes the *Suzanne* is its agreeable Viennese furnishings – handsome beds, chairs and tables, fine mirrors, decent pictures – that, and friendly efficiency on the part of the English-speaking staff. "As the great extravagance of our trip to Vienna was three visits to the *Staatsoper,* we felt honour bound to economise on accommodation. We had a very pleasant room on the eighth floor with our own balcony overlooking the opera house – very inviting to return to at lunchtime. As well as a bathroom it had a small kitchen, which could be useful. Very clean. We were slightly worried at the lack of a fire escape – are Austrian fire regulations less stringent than ours?" *(Mr and Mrs D P Weizmann)*

Open All year.
Rooms 45 beds – 19 double rooms with bath, 5 with shower.
Facilities Lift. English spoken.
Location Central, near Opera House.
Restriction Not suitable for &.
Credit cards None accepted.
Terms [1985 rates] B&B 330–500 Sch. (No restaurant.)

VILLACH 9500 Carinthia   **Map 14**

Hilde Kreibach Hotel Post   *Tel* (042 22) 26101
Hauptplatz 26   *Telex* 45-723

Being astride the main Venice to Vienna routes, Villach was a busy trading centre in earlier centuries and still has many fine Renaissance buildings. The *Post* itself was a 16th-century palace but has been a hotel for the past 250 years: its former guests include the Emperor Charles V and the Empress Marie Thérèse. "A pleasant and comfortable place, with characterful bedrooms," wrote an inspector; "you can eat in the garden. Food quite good but not cheap, and service variable. The hotel makes a good one-night stopover." *(LH, also HC and Else Robbins Landon)*

Open All year.
Rooms 140 beds – 42 rooms with bath, 35 with shower, all with telephone.
Facilities Lift. Hall, bar, TV room, salons, 2 dining rooms; facilities for conferences and private parties; courtyard with outdoor meals in fine weather. The hotel has a bathing beach at the Ossiachersee. Winter sports. &.
Location Central; 8 minutes' walk to station.
Credit cards Some may be accepted.
Terms [1985 rates] B&B: 380–560 Sch; full board 590–770 Sch.

WAGRAIN-MOADÖRFL 5602 Salzburg   Map 14

Hotel-Gasthof Moawirt   *Tel* (06413) 8818 or 8015
Schwaighof 123

Wagrain is a year-round resort, 25 miles south of Salzburg, just off the Salzburg/Villach *Autobahn*. "Very comfortable room, good food, courteous service" is a comment on the *Moawirt*, a spruce modern flower-bedecked chalet in the Moadörf district, just outside Wagrain and backed by forested hills. An earlier report ran: "We were delighed; excellent food, beautiful large rooms with balconies and everyone kind and helpful. The hotel is owned and run by the delightful *Familie* Maurer. The surrounding countryside is lovely, perfect for relaxing or walking in the summer, and an excellent resort for winter skiing (a chair lift is opposite the hotel)." *(F C Parker, Hugh and Elsie Pryor)* A recent visitor warns of traffic noise from front rooms and minor plumbing irritations.

Open All year.
Rooms 23 double, 4 single – all with bath or shower and WC, telephone, radio and baby-listening; colour TV for hire.
Facilities Lift. TV room, breakfast room, dining room; folk music once a week. Sun terrace and garden. Winter sports. English spoken.
Location About 25 m S of Salzburg, just off Salzburg/Villach *Autobahn*.
Credit cards Access, Amex, Diners.
Terms B&B: single 270–290 Sch, double 440–480 Sch; dinner, B&B: single 350–370 Sch, double 600–640 Sch; half-board terms on request. Set lunch 80 and 95 Sch, dinner 55 and 65 Sch; full alc 153–165 Sch.

WEIZ 8160 Styria   Map 14

Modersnhof   *Tel* (03172) 3747
Büchl 32

Although this hotel is a bit out of the way, it's a good stopping off place for those travelling between Vienna and northern Italy. The Modersnhof, *25 kilometres north-east of Graz, is recommended to us especially because of the outstanding, highly personalised service rendered by the Maier family. "We are frequent travellers to Europe and never before have we encountered a combination of accommodation, food and service which were so pleasing that we were motivated to express our views in a letter. Mrs Maier does all the cooking, which is better described as continental rather than Austrian. Her son, who speaks fluent English, is the host. He seems to be unusually perceptive to the needs and desires of his guests and leaves them with a sense of well-being." (John G Peetz) More reports please.*

Open 1 Apr–31 Dec. Restaurant closed Mon.
Rooms 8 double – all with bath, telephone, radio and colour TV.
Facilities Bar, club room, dining room; terrace. Large grounds with swimming pool. English spoken.
Location Weiz is 25 km NE of Graz.
Restriction Not suitable for &.
Credit cards All major cards accepted.
Terms B&B 550–700 Sch; half-board 830–980 Sch; full board 1,010—1,160 Sch. Set lunch 180 Sch, dinner 280 Sch; full alc 390 Sch.

WINDISCHGARSTEN 4580 Upper Austria   Map 14

Hotel-Pension Schwarzes-Rössl   *Tel* (07562) 311

Long a Guide favourite, this 15th-century family inn stands in the middle of a pleasant town in the Garstner valley north of Liezen. All around are woodlands, pastures, rocky hills. Most summer visitors come for walking, climbing, riding or fishing, though the hotel has the use of a heated swimming pool and a tennis court. In winter, it's a centre for skiing, both cross-country and downhill. Thick walls and double-glazing keep out local traffic noise. The hotel has all the virtues of its age. Its rooms are larger and more characterful than in many modern hotels, the beds more spacious, the bed linen better quality, lighting adequate (just). And the Baumschlagers are an exceptionally hospitable couple: Frau Baumschlager speaks good English. Don't expect any special chic in the cooking, though there are plenty of local dishes and the helpings cater for Upper Austrian-sized appetites. But you can count on a spotlessly clean inn, and an admirable centre for an inexpensive family holiday. Recent visitors, while recommending the *Schwarzes-Rössl*, also much appreciated the Baumschlagers' other Windischgarsten hotel, the *Sport Hotel* (four stars to the former's three), with tennis courts and pool. (*Dr Bill and Lisa Fuerst*)

Open All year except Nov. Closed Mon out of season.
Rooms 2 suites, 16 double, 5 single – 12 with bath, 13 with shower.
Facilities Lounge, reading room, TV/playroom for children, restaurants. Entertainment (zither and concertina playing, folklore evenings and dancing) can be arranged. Indoor and outdoor games for children. The facilities of the nearby *Sport Hotel* are all available to guests at the *Schwarzes-Rössl* – large grounds, tennis courts, heated outdoor swimming pool, riding hall, ski school, tobogganing, squash courts, and terrace where coffee, cakes and pastries are served. Gleinber lake – 5 km.
Location Central (double-glazing). Parking.
Restriction Not suitable for &.
Credit cards None accepted.
Terms B&B: 210–250 Sch; dinner B&B: 260–290 Sch; full board: 280–310 Sch. Set lunch 100 Sch; supper 90 Sch, full alc 150–200 Sch. 25% reduction for children under 12, 50% reduction for children under 6 sharing parents' room; special meals.

Belgium

SCHOLTESHOF – HASSELT-STEVOORT

AS 3668 Limburg Map 9

Hotel Mardaga *Tel* (011) 65.70.34 or 65.72.34
Stationstraat 89

"A quiet country base with excellent food", well located near the German border for visits to Maastricht, Aachen and Liège. The *Mardaga* is a solid hostelry in a five-acre wooded garden, which until recently had a *Michelin* rosette for its mainly classical cuisine. "It is small and out of the way on the edge of a forest – you have to look carefully for the signs off the dual carriageway. The owners are very friendly. The rooms are not expensive but decor varies considerably. We preferred the cheaper, smaller 'Habitat'-style rooms to the larger more expensive ones with plastic 'G-plan'-style furniture" *(K and S M-S)*. More reports please.

Open All year, except 2nd fortnight in June and end Dec–early Jan. Restaurant closed Wed.

Rooms 17 double, 1 single – 13 with bath, 5 with shower, all with telephone and colour TV.
Facilities Lift. Salon, bar, 2 restaurants, banqueting room. English spoken.
Location 3 km N of As which is 22 km NE of Hasselt, 29 km NW of Maastricht.
Credit cards All major cards accepted.
Terms B&B: single 850–1,700 Bfrs, double 1,200–2,100 Bfrs; half-board 1,800–2,300 Bfrs per person; full board 2,000–2,500 Bfrs per person. Set meals 750–1,650 Bfrs; full alc 1,300–1,950 Bfrs. Reduced rates for children.

BRUGES 8000 Flanders   Map 9

Hotel Anselmus   *Tel* (050) 34.13.74
Ridderstraat 15

A small B&B, new to the Guide, run by Lode and Yvette Dutoit-Schoore, aunt and uncle of the Hessels, who run the *Groeninghe* (q.v.). It is centrally located and street parking is available (rare in Bruges). "We were absolutely delighted to find this charming hotel. It was opened in May 1984 and combines very modern amenities with the charm of old Bruges. The first floor has a vaulted hallway and a graceful staircase. Our room was large, beautifully decorated, looking out on a 17th-century building, and had a very comfortable bed and modern bathroom with skylight. Lobby and breakfast room most attractive." Readers were especially pleased with breakfast, which included freshly squeezed orange juice, and were very complimentary about the Dutoit-Schoores' hospitality. *(Barbara Wolfe, N M Williamson)*

Open All year.
Rooms 1 suite, 8 double, 1 single – 4 with bath, 6 with shower, all with telephone, radio and TV. 2 ground-floor rooms.
Facilities Hall, lounges, breakfast room. English spoken.
Location 5 minutes' walk from the market square. Parking in street.
Credit cards Access, Amex, Visa.
Terms B&B: single 1,000–1,200 Bfrs, double 1,700–2,000 Bfrs. Suite: for 3 people 2,800 Bfrs; for 4, 3,200 Bfrs; for 5, 3,700 Bfrs. Reduced rates for children.

Hôtel Duc de Bourgogne   *Tel* (050) 33.20.38
Huidenvettersplein 12

A beautifully situated hotel, jutting out like the bow of a sleek ship into the junction of two canals. Very expensive, but the interior splendour matches the view outside – the undulating waterway, the myriad red geraniums and immaculately preserved Renaissance buildings. Some of the rooms on the upper floors, as may be expected in an old building, are on the poky side, with windows too high to catch the view. Value for money? Here is a report from someone who thinks so: "It was the setting of the hotel which attracted us to stay there. The views from the bedroom and the restaurant were lovely. The room we had was fairly small and the food very expensive without being *Michelin* rosette standard, but the atmosphere, the elegant furnishings and the helpful staff made the expense worthwhile. When we had to leave early for the ferry, the receptionist got up specially to make us breakfast." A reader this year was ill-advised by one of the staff about parking, but particularly enjoyed the restaurant, "where they kept making romantic little niches for us in the corners. Excellent food, particularly the fish soup and the pink Sancerre." *(Kate Murray-Sykes, B J Barry; also F C Parker)*

Open All year except Jan and July. Restaurant closed Mon, also Tue lunch in summer and Sun evenings in winter.
Rooms 1 suite, 5 double, 3 single – all with bath, telephone, some with TV; baby-sitting arranged.
Facilities Salon, bar, dining room. English spoken.
Location Central. Make for Grand Place after Phillipsstockstraat by the Place du Bourg, where you park – from there 2 minutes' walk.
Restriction Not suitable for &.
Credit cards All major cards accepted.
Terms B&B: single 1,900 Bfrs, double 2,250–3,750 Bfrs. Set lunch/dinner 1,675 Bfrs; full alc 1,500–2,000 Bfrs.

Hotel Groeninghe　　　　　　　　　　　　　　　　*Tel* (050) 33.64.95
Korte Vuldersstraat 29　　　　　　　　*Telex* 26937 hotex B groeninghe

We received many letters of praise again this year for this inexpensive B&B hotel, built in the mid-19th century, with a family-home atmosphere. It is run by a young brother and sister, Luk and Tine Hessels, whose extended family runs several of Bruges' better small hotels: *Hotel Anselmus* and *Die Swaene* (q.v.). "An ideal place for a visit to Bruges." "Excellent breakfast, comfortable beds, friendly and attentive care. Luk Hessels was exceptionally kind, telephoning for taxis, making restaurant reservations – and there was no extra charge. Very quiet, most important, as Bruges is an extremely noisy town, and there is almost nowhere where you are out of earshot of the Beffroi, which played excerpts from *Eine Kleine Nacht Musik* every quarter-hour (last time I was there it was *Carmen*)." Recommended Bruges restaurants include *De Snippe* (expensive), *Ghistelhof* (medium) and *De Watermolen* (cheap). *(H Richard Lamb, C R, Ernest Thomson, and many others)*

Open All year, except 5 Jan–mid-Feb.
Rooms 8 double – 11 with hipbath and shower, telephone and radio.
Facilities Lounge with TV (drinks served), breakfast room. English spoken.
Location Central, between cathedral and railway station in quiet street. By car take main shopping street (Zuid Zandstraat), turn right in front of cathedral; behind cathedral turn immediately right into Korte Vuldersstraat. Parking normally possible in front of hotel.
Restriction Not suitable for &.
Credit cards Access, Amex, Visa.
Terms B&B: single occupancy 1,500 Bfrs, double 1,800 Bfrs. Reduced rates for babies up to 3.

Die Swaene　　　　　　　　　　　　　　　　　　　　*Tel* (050) 33.96.29
Steenhouwersdijk 1　　　　　　　　　　　　　　　　　　*Telex* 82446

The *"Swan"* is a very central B&B hotel in a 15th-century house right on a canal and almost opposite the Belfry. The owners have family connections with the *Anselmus* and the *Groeninghe* (see above). "Very friendly, warm and clean. Amazingly well furnished," commends a reader this year. Another recent visitor says the hotel has a "family-home feel; sumptuous comfort, quiet and restful. Not overpriced either." "It was wonderful," writes an American visitor, "big, clean, airy rooms, very helpful service, wonderful breakfast. The rooms at the back look over an austere courtyard, unusual in this picturesque medieval city; those at the front are a little noisier (not unpleasant) and smaller, but all are modern and clean. Very nice bathrooms." For restaurants, see under *Groeninghe*. Parking outside the hotel. *(John and Priscilla Gillett, Jane Kingsley; also R Emmich)*

Open All year.
Rooms 1 suite, 25 double, 1 single – 25 with bath, 2 with shower, all with telephone, radio and colour TV, 8 with mini-bar; some ground-floor rooms.
Facilities Lift. Lounge, breakfast room. English spoken.
Location Central: signposts from the market square. Parking in street.
Credit cards Access, Amex, Visa.
Terms B&B: single 1,500 Bfrs, double 2,600–3,300 Bfrs. (No restaurant.) Reductions for children under 3.

Hotel Ter Duinen *Tel* (050) 33.04.37
Langerei 52

An enthusiastic commendation from Larchmont, NY, for *Ter Duinen*, a new entry to the Guide: "Bruges is a city that prides itself on retaining Old World traditions of friendliness, warmth and cleanliness. *Ter Duinen* delivers these qualities to the visitor in unassuming style. The owners are a young couple in their twenties who work hard to accommodate your every need. The rooms are immaculate and we were advised of possible street noise from below which never materialised. Our room looked over one of the many canals which added to the serenity. The people of Bruges are congenial and thoughtful and *Ter Duinen* displays these qualities, at very affordable prices. In short, *Ter Duinen* is the Belgian lace of inns." *(Thomas G and Philomena R Ferrara)* More reports welcome.

Open All year.
Rooms 10 (can be used as single, double or triple, some for 4) – 8 with shower, all with telephone.
Facilities Lounge with TV. English spoken.
Location On canal 10–15 minutes' walk from centre. Street parking in front of hotel; private garage available 100 Bfrs 1st night, 50 Bfrs thereafter. Windows are double-glazed, but nights are normally quiet.
Restriction Not suitable for &.
Credit cards All major cards accepted.
Terms B&B: single 1,050–1,400 Bfrs, double 1,200–1,650 Bfrs. Reduced rates for children.

BRUSSELS 1000 **Map 9**

Hôtel Amigo *Tel* (02) 511.59.10
1–3 rue de l'Amigo *Telex* 21618

"The best location in Brussels" (close to the Grand' Place) is one reason for the enduring popularity of the *Amigo*, still the first choice in the city for many visiting diplomats and marketeers as well as tourists. There's no special chic about this modern hotel, and the restaurant is wholesome rather than enterprising. There are far more exciting meals to be had in dozens of places within strolling distance of the hotel: one of the best restaurants in the city, the *Maison du Cygne*, is fifty yards up the street; and a reader recommends the *Tête d'Or* just by the hotel's garage entrance as a cheaper alternative. But the *Amigo* offers dependable efficiency and welcome.

Open All year.
Rooms 11 suites, 157 double, 26 single – 174 with bath, 9 with shower, all with telephone, radio and colour TV; baby-listening on request. Some ground-floor rooms.
Facilities Lift. Various salons, TV room, bar, restaurant, conference rooms and banqueting facilities. English spoken. &.
Location Central, behind the Grand' Place. Garage.
Credit cards All major cards accepted.
Terms B&B: single 3,750–4,800 Bfrs, double 4,400–5,400 Bfrs. Set meals 1,000 Bfrs; full alc 1,500 Bfrs. No charge for children under 12 sharing parents' room.

DE PANNE 8470 West Flanders   Map 9

Le Fox   *Tel* (058) 41.28.55
Walckierstraat 2

A very reasonably priced *hostellerie* close to the beach in a popular resort between Ostend and the French frontier. "Basically a family-run restaurant – and a very good one too, specialising in *nouvelle cuisine* and, of course, like most restaurants on the Flanders coast, in superbly fresh fish of every kind. There are half a dozen attractive bedrooms, at a mere £11 a head for B&B [1985] (this includes bathroom and even colour TV). It is quite a find, right by the sea and in the centre of the resort. Very good value for money." *(Elizabeth Cockburn)* Another reader endorses the entry, "excellent value", and recommends booking the larger front rooms if you can, despite some street noise. *(Alan Greenwood)* Our latest correspondent, however, while appreciating the quality of the rooms and the splendid value, warns of loud street noise: the main Ostend/ French frontier road is close by and a nightclub, open all night, is next door.

Open Almost all year (exact details not known at time of going to press).
Rooms 8 double – 4 with bath, 4 with shower, all with telephone, radio and colour TV.
Facilities Lift. Restaurant. Safe bathing and sandy beach 20 metres; water-skiing, surfing etc.
Location Central, hotel is signposted; De Panne is 31 km SW of Ostend. Paid garage parking.
Credit cards All major cards accepted.
Terms B&B: single 1,500 Bfrs, double 1,750 Bfrs; dinner, B&B: single 2,600 Bfrs, double 3,350 Bfrs. Set meals 1,100–1,650 Bfrs; full alc 1,250 Bfrs.

DURBUY 5480 Luxembourg Belge   Map 9

Hostellerie le Sanglier des   *Tel* (086) 21.10.88
Ardennes   *Telex* 42240 SANDUR
Rue Comte Théodule d'Ursel 99

Durbuy is an extremely pretty little village, overcrowded in summer, set amid beautiful forests in the valley of the river Ourthe. *Le Sanglier*, originally a simple restaurant-with-rooms, has burgeoned into a small tourist complex, for its owner, Maurice Caerdinael, has annexed two

319

other establishments in the village, *Aux Vieux Durbuy* and the *Cardinal*. *Le Sanglier* serves as the one restaurant for them all. Our readers have enjoyed comfort and quiet at all three: some rooms overlook the river with views to the medieval castle. "My wife and I stayed for three days. Our room was rustic but very adequate and comfortable although a little dull. The restaurant was excellent and the food, service and ambience were all of a very high standard. We shall certainly return." The *Sanglier* has a high reputation for its cooking: *Gault Millau* gives it two *toques*. "Best venison I have had in 10 years, with wild mushrooms." (*G Goodfellow, P L C*)

Open All year except Jan. Restaurant closed Thur.
Rooms 6 suites, 45 double – 23 with bath, all with colour TV; tea-making in suites; baby-listening on request. 6 suites and 12 rooms in annexe. 2 ground-floor rooms.
Facilities 2 lounges, bar, terrace, restaurant, banquet room. Lawns by the river Ourthe. Fishing, children's play area. Swimming 3 km. English spoken.
Location 45 km S of Liège. Parking.
Restriction Not suitable for &.
Credit cards All major cards accepted.
Terms B&B: double 1,445–2,200 Bfrs; dinner, B&B 1,895–2,320 Bfrs. Set lunch/dinner 995–2,450 Bfrs; full alc 1,250 Bfrs. Gastronomic weekends (3 days min.). Reduced rates for children under 10.

ESSENE 1705 Affligem   Map 9

Hostellerie Bellemolen   *Tel* (053) 66.62.38
Stationstraat 4

This "lovely mill" lies just inside Flanders, in the lush Brabant countryside, yet only 18 kilometres from Brussels – a 12th-century watermill by a stream, converted into a smart and stylish restaurant-with-rooms, with some of the best cooking (*Michelin* rosette) in the Brussels area.

"A peaceful and pleasant stop for those with an interest in old buildings and excellent food. The building is long and low and has been painstakingly restored by the owners: it has a large cobbled courtyard with a garden and trees around the mill-pond and a small terrace over the mill-race. The attractive lounge and bar are over the mill-race too. There are six comfortably furnished rooms tucked under the beams at one end of the building. The restaurant's rosette is well deserved, with original dishes as well as a seasonal menu. Fresh flowers on the tables and antiques everywhere. Enormous wine list, including some reasonably priced bottles. Owners and staff are friendly and helpful." (*Pat and Jeremy Temple*)

Open All year except July and Christmas/New Year period. Closed Sun evening and Mon.
Rooms 6 rooms – all with bath and shower and frigobar.
Facilities Lounge, bar, restaurant, conference room. Garden and courtyard.
Location 18 km NW of Brussels, just N of motorway to Ostend, and 10 km SE of Aalst. Leave motorway at Aalst turning, or take old N10 from Brussels to Aalst and turn off S. Hotel is on river at edge of village. Parking.
Credit cards Access, Amex, Diners.
Terms [1985 rates] B&B: single 1,850 Bfrs, double 2,500 Bfrs. Alc meals (excluding wine) 1,120–1,930 Bfrs.

HASSELT-STEVOORT 3512 Limburg   Map 9

Scholteshof   *Tel* (011) 25.02.02
Kemstraat 118   *Telex* 39684 TESHOF

"Quite simply the best new hotel we've stayed in for many years and
undoubtedly one of the nicest hotels in Europe. Roger Souvereyns, one
of the leading Belgian chefs, has created this luxurious venture from an
18th-century manor house built round a small inner courtyard. It is set in
green countryside just outside the pleasant town of Hasselt; the grounds
have been landscaped, and there is a large herb and vegetable garden.

"Guests are shown into the flag-stoned entrance hall with its old
beams, lit by modern spotlights. 'Would you like a glass of champagne
while you fill in this form ...?' Each room is named after a plant or
flower in Latin; all are stylish. Ours was furnished with antiques, had a
small balcony and a huge bathroom with a settee in it. Fabrics are
excellent. There is a large lounge with white cane chairs. Mr Souvereyns
practises 'open cooking', and he and his staff work in full view of
everyone. His food is fantastic (two *Michelin* rosettes but worthy of
three): we had a special menu of eight different small dishes. The
restaurant is beautifully decorated with lots of plants and flowers and
old kitchen implements – and has a country atmosphere. Staff are
friendly. Considering the quality, the hotel is not too expensive." *(P and
J Temple)*

Open All year except 26 Dec–10 Jan.
Rooms 18 double or suites – all with bath, 2 with shower, all with telephone,
radio, TV, frigobar and air-conditioning.
Facilities Lounge, bar, dining room, restaurant, conference facilities. Garden and
courtyard.
Location On edge of Stevoort village, 5 km W of Hasselt. Parking.
Restriction Not suitable for &.
Credit cards All major cards accepted.
Terms B&B: single 1,850 Bfrs, double 2,400–4,800 Bfrs. Set lunch/dinner 1,150
Bfrs, 2,200 Bfrs and 3,300 Bfrs. Reduced rates and special meals for children.

HERBEUMONT 6803 Semois   Map 9

Hostellerie du Prieuré de Conques   *Tel* (061) 41.14.17

The *Prieuré de Conques*, on the banks of the Semois in the heart of the vast
forest of the Ardennes, has a whisper of pre-World War I comfort and
atmosphere: an 18th-century priory – long, low and white – surrounded
by coiffeured gardens. "The park-like scene is helped by open fields
which stop the dark forest pressing too close. There are long lawns set
with apple trees running down to the curving Semois river. Inside are
two connected vaulted lounges. The deep comfortable armchairs
surround large tables and the lighting is kind. On the other side of the
hall with its curving staircase are two dining rooms, elegant and
comfortable. The bedrooms on the first floor are large with bathroom
and lavatory. On the second floor the rooms are a little smaller, but more
romantic with an attic ambience and exposed beams. All the bedrooms
look down on the front garden. Everything has the stamp of cleanliness
and order." Last year's report lamented, "I wish I could say the food was

dazzling, but it wasn't." Recent visitors retort: "The food is better than your report led us to expect. The thing to do is to restrict yourself to three courses and not settle for the five they are prepared to offer." It sounds as if those with big appetites – especially for Ardennes ham – might be happy here. The director, M. Florimond de Naeyer, is extremely helpful and shows spontaneous kindness and generosity; one reader says he is "straight out of a film Jacques Tati should have made". The hotel is a good station *en route* to the Black Forest and an easy day's drive after crossing the Channel. *(Dr R L Holmes and Dr M W Atkinson; also Jonathan Williams, B W Ribbons)*

Open 15 Mar–2 Jan. Restaurant closed Tue.
Rooms 11 double – all with bath, telephone and radio.
Facilities 2 salons, bar/lounge, 2 restaurants; conference facilities. 8-acre grounds; fishing on river Semois; close to Ardennes forest; walks, bird-watching. English spoken.
Location 3 km from Herbeumont, between Florenville and Bouillon.
Restriction Not suitable for &.
Credit cards Access, Amex, Visa.
Terms B&B: single 1,535 Bfrs, double 3,000–3,140 Bfrs; half-board: single 2,000 Bfrs, double 4,200–4,300 Bfrs; full board: single 2,400 Bfrs, double 5,000–5,200 Bfrs. Set lunch/dinner 950–1,600 Bfrs; full alc 2,150 Bfrs. Gastronomic weekends. Reduced rates for children.

't Convent   *Tel* (057) 40.07.71
Halve Reningestraat 1

Caesar is said to have tethered his horse to the gnarled yew tree that still stands beside one of the 14th-century gates to the Flemish village called Lo. It is half an hour's drive from Ostend, and about 90 minutes by road or rail to Brussels. A convenient first or last stop on the way to or from the main Channel ports, *'t Convent* is a peaceful restaurant-with-rooms just outside the little town of Reninge, on the plain between Ieper (Ypres) and the sea. "This long, low, timbered building provides total tranquillity (it's in the middle of a field) and delicious food, from a creative chef using good local produce. Pre-dinner drinks come with a selection of little shrimps, tiny tomatoes and radishes, and breakfast with six home-made jams from melon to blueberry. The place is more than comfortable, with panelling, tassels and Louis XIV chairs, and the Marie Antoinette appeal is enhanced by a view of a cow from every window." *(Gillian Vincent)*

Open All year except Feb.
Rooms 6 rooms – all with bath, telephone and baby-listening; some on ground floor.
Facilities Bar, restaurant and conference facilities. English spoken.
Location On edge of village, 15 km NW of Ieper (turn off N65 at Oostvieteren). Parking.
Credit cards All major cards accepted.
Terms B&B: single 1,000 Bfrs, double 1,500 Bfrs; full board 2,500 Bfrs per person. Set lunch/dinner 1,000–1,700 Bfrs.

We should like to hear about more budget-price hotels in Brussels.

LO-RENINGE 8180 West Flanders   Map 9

Oude Abdij   *Tel* (058) 28.82.65
Noordstraat 3

The *Oude Abdij* (Old Abbey), once an Augustine monastery dating back
to the 11th century, is now an elegant small hotel owned and run by Jan
and Nelly Clement; Jan is a graduate of the *Ritz* in Paris. Reports full of
warm praise come in a steady stream to the Guide. "It's truly peaceful
and civilised – a lasting memory of kindness and hospitality." "Bedrooms, with furniture made from local cherry wood, delightful with little
extra touches like fresh fruit, free mineral water, chocolates." And of the
restaurant: "We had an excellent meal. During our dinner we observed
the kitchen boy rush seven times out to gather fresh herbs, which Jan
says must never be more than minutes old before use! We were
unobstrusively cherished all through our stay." "Nelly and Jan Clement
maintain the integrity of this sacred place both in spirit and in practice."
The Clements write this year to tell us about the Lo cheese festival
beginning the last week of July. With only six bedrooms, early booking
is advisable at any time of year. *(Norma Wagner, John and Kay Savage, Alec
and May Murray; also H Richard Lamb, Dr Christine Herxheimer and Gabriele
Berneck)*

Open All year. (Closed Sun evening and Mon except public holidays.)
Rooms 1 suite, 5 double – all with bath, telephone, mono TV and baby-listening.
Facilities Salon, bar, reading room, restaurants, solarium, terrace, small garden
with orchard. Small lake (with eel-fishing); beach 15 km. English spoken.
Location 15 km S of Veurne, just off the Veurne/Ieper motorway.
Restriction Not suitable for &.
Credit cards All major cards accepted.
Terms B&B (full English): single occupancy 1,250 Bfrs, double 1,800 Bfrs. Set
lunch/dinner (including wine) 1,250–1,750 Bfrs; full alc 1,500–2,000 Bfrs.
Christmas, New Year and Easter parties. Cheese festival end Jul/early Aug.
Special meals for children; babies free, 50% reduction for under-7s.

LUSTIN-SUR-MEUSE 5160 Namur   Map 9

Le Floraire   *Tel* (081) 41.11.99
51 rue Eugène Falmagne

"A small family-run restaurant-with-rooms, three hours by road from
Calais or Ostend, in the quiet wooded valley of the Meuse. Alain and
Catherine Magis took over the restaurant about a year ago, and have
attractively converted four or five bedrooms to a comfortable standard.
The à la carte menu is extensive, but, as we intended to stay for four
nights, we opted for the *demi-pension*. Each of the dinners was
outstanding. As we were the only guests, we were asked each evening
what we would prefer the following evening. The desserts were
especially commendable. Added enjoyments were a pot of coffee rather
than a *demi-tasse*, a charming antique-furnished salon and the friendliness of the *patrons*. A glimpse of the Meuse can be seen from the
first-floor terrace where meals and drinks are taken. There is also a
terrace in the delightful garden." *(B J Woolf)*

Open All year.
Rooms 6 double, 1 single – 1 with bath, 1 with shower.
Facilities 2 lounges, dining room, 2 terraces, garden with tables, chairs, parasols and children's play area. Some English spoken.
Location 2 km from Profondeville, off Namur/Dinant road.
Restriction Not suitable for &.
Credit cards Access, Amex, Diners.
Terms B&B: single 820 Bfrs, double 1,120 Bfrs. Set meals: 695, 1,150, 1,385 and 1,650 Bfrs. Reduced rates and special meals for children.

NOIREFONTAINE 6831 Luxembourg Belge   Map 9

Auberge du Moulin Hideux   *Tel* (061) 46.70.15
                                                Telex 41989 HIDEUX

A delectable country hotel close to the French border in the heart of the Ardennes – exquisitely furnished, internationally celebrated, gastronomically memorable (two *Michelin* rosettes, two *Gault Millau toques* for inventive specialities), owned and run by a young couple, Charles and Martine Lahire, who are both steeped in the traditions of good hotel-keeping. There are thirteen luxurious bedrooms, and a spacious garden complete with floodlit waterfall. Our readers return again and again. Here is one sample from this year's crop: "We arrived tired and cold after a long wet drive and although it was 6.30 pm a tray of tea and warm biscuits was brought to our room within minutes; what heaven to wallow in a deep bath foaming with scented essence sipping a cup of tea, followed, with indecent haste, by a glass of Champagne. The rooms we have stayed in have all been furnished to the same very high standard, with long low windows overlooking the gardens and lake. Dinner is a sumptuous feast, but the wines are expensive. I really think that the breakfasts are the best I've had on the Continent, and so beautifully served." *(Padi Howard; also K & S M-S)*

Open Mid-Mar to mid Nov. Restaurant closed Wed (Sept–July).
Rooms 3 suites, 10 double – all with bath, telephone and mono TV.
Facilities Sitting room, loggia, restaurant; garden with tennis court; golf 40 km, riding 10 km. Trout fishing nearby. Fine walking country. English spoken.
Location 22 km N of Sedan, 8 km N of Bouillon.
Restriction Not suitable for &.
Credit cards Access, Visa.
Terms B&B: single occupancy 2,000 Bfrs, double 3,200–3,700 Bfrs. Set meals 1,650–1,950 Bfrs; full alc 2,500 Bfrs. Special meals for children on request.

RONSE 9681 Maarkedal   Map 9

Hostellerie Shamrock   *Tel* (055) 21.55.29
Ommegangstraat 148, Nukerke   *Telex* 86 165 SHAMRO

"The area around Ronse, a textile town, is pleasantly wooded and hilly, and supposedly inspired Wagner. The hotel – perhaps more of a restaurant-with-rooms – is up a fairly long drive, amidst a well-tended garden and is completely surrounded at the back by ancient trees. It presents the appearance of a substantial private house in 1910 mock-Tudor style. Bedrooms are large and airy, carpeted throughout and furnished in mock Louis XV furniture. Modern bathroom was exceptionally large, carpeted and exuded an atmosphere of quiet luxury. The rooms are good value for money.

"The main dining room is quietly elegant, in shades of turquoise with impeccable white napery. The main staircase with carved wooden banister descends directly into this room giving residents an opportunity for a truly spectacular entry. The food (which merits a *Michelin* rosette and *Gault-Millau toques*) is typical of modern French-style cooking with emphasis on presentation and choicest meats, fish and vegetables in moderate quantities. However we were stunned by their wine list which is fiendishly priced and one must be prepared to pay as much for one's wine as for one's food. We also found the long wait between courses rather irksome. Service is pleasant and courteous. Everyone speaks good English." *(F and I W)*

Open All year except Christmas, New Year, 15–31 July. Closed Sun evening to Tue midday.
Rooms 5 double, 1 single – 5 with bath, 1 with shower, all with telephone and radio.
Facilities Salon, bar, restaurant; small conference room. 5-acre shady garden. Swimming pool and tennis 4 km; golf 15 km; fine walking country. English spoken.
Location Ronse 4 km. Hotel is best reached from N, whether you are coming from Ostend or Brussels. Take E3 and E5, then N58 via Oudenaarde. On the Ronse–Oudenaarde road, take direction Muziekbos. The hotel is not *in* Nukerke, but close to the tiny villages of Louise-Marie and Muziekbos.
Restriction Not suitable for &.
Credit cards All major cards accepted.
Terms B&B: single 1,650 Bfrs, double 2,350 Bfrs. Set lunch/dinner 1,200, 1,800 and 2,400 Bfrs; full alc 2,100 Bfrs.

STAMBRUGES-GRANDGLISE 7980 Hainaut   Map 9

Hostellerie Le Vert Gazon   *Tel* (069) 57.59.84

This 1896 mansion, situated in its own park near the French border, has been converted into a sophisticated hotel. "Our room was enormous with antique furniture and a huge bed – we felt we were sleeping in a château. The public rooms and staircase are wood-panelled, giving a cosy atmosphere. It is obviously a family-run hotel; service is friendly and homely. Home-made jam for breakfast. The château of Beloeil, about a mile away, is worth a visit." Though it recently lost its rosette in *Michelin*, the restaurant still has a *toque* in *Gault Millau* for the mainly classic cooking ("really excellent" is our report). *(Kate and Steve Murray-Sykes)*

Open All year except 1st fortnight Jan and 2nd fortnight June. (Closed Sun night and Mon.)
Rooms 6 double – 5 with bath, 1 with shower, all with telephone and radio.
Facilities Salon, dining room; conference and banqueting facilities. 1-hectare grounds. English spoken.
Locatin Off Mons/Tournai motorway, Blaton exit, in direction of Beloeil. From there go for 1½ km in direction of Mons.
Restriction Not suitable for &.
Credit cards All major cards accepted.
Terms B&B double 1,840 Bfrs; full board (min. 3 days) 2,600 Bfrs per person. Set lunch/dinner 1,290 Bfrs; full alc 1,700 Bfrs. Beds for children 400 Bfrs; special meals on request.

STAVELOT 4970 Liège

Map 9

Hostellerie Le Val d'Amblève *Tel* (080) 86.23.53
7 route de Malmédy

Marc Focquet most amiably runs this friendly seaside hotel. Although the family house dates from 1934, Mr Focquet's indulgent father allowed his son to turn the home into a hotel in 1956. The *Val d'Amblève* now boasts one of the finest restaurants in the region (*Michelin* rosette). "Although the surrounding countryside of the Upper Ardennes is most attractive, the hotel is set firmly in middle-class suburbia on the outskirts of the town. Happily, it is reasonably screened by old-established trees – conifers and deciduous (including a magnificent weeping beech) – and the setting has a certain charm. Tennis on the doorstep. It is a good base from which excursions can be made – westwards along the Amblève valley to Comblain-au-Pont, or to the east to the desolate region of the Hautes Fagnes." The bedrooms have changed little over the years ("a little shabby") but they don't lack comfort or character. On the ground floor there is a small bar and a lounge with deep, welcoming armchairs. The large restaurant – a modern addition with huge picture windows – has views of the distant pine-clad mountains. The food and the service are of the highest quality, ranging from a simple menu for those on *pension* terms (although the proprietor had no hesitation in offering prawns as an alternative to small lobsters to one guest whose "British constitution" could not face the latter after passing their tank in the lobby), through five different fixed-price menus, to an interesting *carte*. "We enjoyed a most relaxed and civilised dinner. Apart from the normal wine list, they have a smaller list of 'bin-ends' which represents particularly good value." A reader this year commented, "Our gastronomic experience was only slightly off-put by the extreme length of time one waited on somewhat uncomfortable chairs." Excellent breakfasts with plentiful butter, cheese and ham, "and a proper pot of jam". (*Geoffrey Sharp, P Grimsdale; also J M Beaton, Dr P Marsh and B E Ribbons*)

Open Easter – 15 Nov. Restaurant closed Mon except holidays, and Thur evening.
Rooms 19 double – 11 with bath, 4 with shower, all with telephone; TV on request; 4 ground-floor rooms; 7 rooms in annexe.
Facilities Bar, lounge, restaurant. Garden with tennis court. Golf and fishing and swimming pool nearby. English spoken.
Location On outskirts of Stavelot, SW of Malmédy. Parking.
Credit cards All major cards accepted.
Terms B&B: single 1,580 Bfrs, double 2,060 Bfrs. Set lunch 1,000 Bfrs, dinner 1,200 Bfrs.

FOREST PARK HOTEL – PLATRES

PAPHOS   **Map 17**

Apollo Hotel   *Tel* (061) 33909
St Paul Avenue, P.O. Box 219   *Telex* 3689 APOLLHTL

This year's visitors to the *Apollo*, a small hotel set back about 15 minutes'
walk from the sea not far from the centre of New Paphos near Fabria
Hill, were especially pleased with the hotel's spectacular sea views from
bedroom balconies and the poolside terrace. "Low-rise as all hotels in
Paphos are – only two storeys in local style with stone walls and arches,
raftered ceilings and woven fabrics. Very tasteful, relaxing and quiet
with lots of plants, pottery lamps, stone-tiled floors, murals etc. A
pleasant taverna at the back overlooks the pool and has open views
towards the lighthouse, Greek theatre and the sea beyond. Elaborate
beehive clay ovens still used for local dishes. Bamboo awning for shade.
Public rooms are open-plan lounge, bar, reception foyer and restaurant,
all pleasantly proportioned. Rooms are carpeted, nicely furnished with
dark wood and decorated in soft but imaginative neutral colours. An
extremely agreeable little place: not luxurious, but very good value."
Another reader comments that the set menu is predominantly international but there are inexpensive Cypriot dishes on the à la carte menu. A
car is advisable, if not absolutely necessary. *(Mrs P N Robinson, Sheila
Bush; also L H, C H Cole)*

Open All year.
Rooms 30 double, 2 single – all with bath, telephone and baby-listening;
ground-floor rooms.

Facilities Ramps. Reception foyer, restaurant, taverna, café, TV room, conference room. Sun terrace with swimming pool, children's paddling pool, outdoor restaurant with charcoal grill. Folk music in restaurant and taverna once or twice a week. Sea with sandy and rocky beach 15 minutes away; safe bathing, fishing. English spoken.
Location 20 minutes' walk from town centre, near Fabria Hill. Parking.
Credit card Access
Terms B&B CY£6–£9. Set lunch CY£2.70, dinner CY£2.90; full alc CY£4.
Off-season discounts Nov–Feb. Reduced rates for children sharing parents' room; special meals.

PEDHOULAS   Map 17

Jack's Hotel   *Tel* (054) 52350

There is nothing much to do in the straggling village of Pedhoulas in the Troodos range of mountains, except walk and read and go down to the coast (not far) for a swim. It's not a place for a long stay, but *Jack's* – a small modern purpose-built hotel in the centre of the village – has a lovely view if you're less inclined to move. The manager/owner is "highly intelligent and extremely nice. The bedrooms are simple but adequate. We had an excellent and generous Greek salad and an excellent wine for lunch. We really took to the place, which has a friendly atmosphere." *(Sheila Bush)* More reports welcome.

Open All year.
Rooms 10 double – TV on request; baby-sitting service available.
Facilities Restaurant.
Location In the Troodos mountain range 6½ m S of Karavostasi which is on the Morphou bay.
Restriction Probably not suitable for ఉ.
Terms [1985 rates] B&B: single from CY£6, double from CY£11; half-board CY£2.75 supplement per person; full board CY£5 supplement. Set lunch CY£3, dinner CY£3.50. 25% reduction during the low season.

PLATRES   Map 17

Forest Park Hotel   *Tel* (054) 21 751
                                                   Telex 2920 PARKOTEL

"Cyprus is a most lovely place, with ravishing scenery once you get away from the coast. Lots of fascinating things to see in the way of Roman remains and neolithic sites. The *Forest Park Hotel*, established in the thirties and now run by the son of the man who founded it, takes package tours but still has the air of a comfortable and classy family hotel. It's refreshingly different from the modern package hotels by the coast. Masses of eminent people have stayed here, including Daphne du Maurier, King Farouk, Roy Jenkins ... The hotel is sited in the most lovely mountain scenery. You need to be a country-lover, but since Cyprus is so thin from top to bottom it doesn't take long to go down to the coast for a bathe and/or a meal. The only drawback: boring English-type menu." *(Sheila Bush)*

For North Cyprus hotels, see under Turkey.

Open All year.

Rooms 10 suites, 90 double, 6 single – 94 with bath, 12 with shower, all with telephone, radio and baby-listening; colour TV and tea-making facilities in suites, TV available in other rooms on request. 7 suites in annexe.

Facilities Lift. 2 lounges, library, TV and video room, bars, grill room, restaurant, ballroom, conference room. 15-acre grounds and woods; outdoor solar-heated swimming pool, sauna and tennis. Winter sports. English spoken.

Location On slope of Mount Troodos, 10 minutes from centre of town; hotel is well signposted.

Credit cards Amex, Diners, Visa.

Terms (Excluding 10% surcharge) B&B: single CY£17.03–CY£17.33, double CY£25.40–CY£26; dinner, B&B: single CY£19.78–CY£20.08, double CY£30.90–CY£31.50; full board: single CY£22.53–CY£22.83, double CY£36.40–CY£37. Set lunch CY£5, set dinner CY£5.50; full alc CY£7.50. Reduced rates for children sharing parents' room; special meals.

Denmark

FALSLED KRO, FALSLED

COPENHAGEN   Map 7

Hotel Ascot   *Tel* (01) 12.60.00
57 Studiestraêde   *Telex* 15730
Copenhagen 1554

"For many years I've been staying in Copenhagen, and after trying all
the likely places I long ago settled on the *Ascot* as the best value. It is
about as close to the centre of the city as one can get. It is in the midst of
everything, but on a quiet pleasant street. The facade may remind you of
Paris: it was built sometime in the 1700s and was once somebody's
home. Today it is a lovely, modern, warm hotel, with a beautiful
red-carpeted winding stairway. The rooms are extremely comfortable
and thoughtfully furnished with full-length windows tastefully cur-
tained. You can eat breakfast in the pleasant restaurant downstairs or in
your room." *(Clay Leitch; Bryan Magee, also Mr and Mrs C R Safford)*

Open All year.
Rooms 2 suites, 43 double, 16 single – 40 with bath, 21 with shower, all with
telephone, radio and TV, 14 with tea-making facilities.
Facilities Salon with TV, breakfast room, conference room. Finnish sauna,
sun-bed and health studio next door; park nearby. English spoken.
Location Central, 2 minutes' walk from Town Hall and Tivoli. Parking.
Restriction Not suitable for &.
Credit cards All major cards accepted.
Terms B&B: single 390–560 Dkr, double 530–820 Dkr. (No restaurant.)

71 Nyhavn Hotel   *Tel* (01) 11.85.85
Nyhavn 71, Copenhagen 1051   *Telex* 27558 NYHHOT

Full of character – an early 19th-century warehouse on the *Nyhavn* or
"New Harbour" in the heart of the old city – *71 Nyhavn Hotel* is steeped
in the history of the area. Hans Christian Andersen lived next door at
No. 67. The building was restored about 15 years ago as a smart hotel,
with the sea motif much in evidence. The *Pakhuskaelderen* restaurant has
an excellent reputation, with its smorgasbord specially recommended
("but it is worth trying some of the new ones which have sprung up
along the north side of the Nyhavn"). The thick walls and beams have
obviously imposed restraints on room space (though one reader points
out that is not true of the inner walls, as one night he wasn't required
to use any imagination about what was going on next door!). The
cheapest bedrooms are very small; the dearer ones do have a view over
the canal. But the staff are helpful and welcoming and the hotel is not so
big as to be impersonal. A couple this year wrote to say they
wholeheartedly endorse the hotel and "would stay again with less
luggage as closet space is minimal." *(John F Shapley, Mr and Mrs H E
Wilson, and others)*

Open All year. Restaurant closed 24–26 Dec.
Rooms 6 suites, 39 double, 37 single – 19 with bath, all with shower, all with
telephone, radio, colour TV and baby-listening.
Facilities Lift. Lounge, bar, TV room, restaurant; 2 conference/function rooms.
English spoken.
Location In town centre at waterfront, facing Nyhavn Canal and the harbour.
Parking.
Restriction Not suitable for &.
Credit cards All major cards accepted.
Terms B&B: single 770–1,080 Dkr, double 918–1,400 Dkr; half-board 230 Dkr per
person added; full board 400 Dkr per person added. Set lunch 140 Dkr, dinner 250
Dkr; full alc 325 Dkr. Christmas package. Children under 12 free in parents' room;
50% reduction on meals.

Hotel Vestersøhus   *Tel* (01) 11.38.70
Vestersøgade 58, Copenhagen 1601

A modest but useful hotel, with a friendly and helpful staff. The centre
of the old town is within ten minutes' walk; and the nearest train station,
with frequent trains to the suburbs and about half of Zeeland, is even
closer. Rooms are spacious, each with several comfortable armchairs, a
sofa and plenty of lighting; very adequate for a short stay. A few rooms
form little flatlets with separate kitchens and could be used for a
self-catering holiday. Most rooms have a delightful view over the Skt
Jørgens Lake, one of a ring of artificial lakes on the western edge of the
old town. The tree-lined Vestersøgade is in daytime a fast traffic lane.
"In winter the double-glazing would keep the noise out totally; in
summer the rooms at the back would be much quieter, but they look on
to an office block. The hotel serves only breakfast, in a pretty little
room." *(Ralph Blumenau)*

Open All year except Christmas.
Rooms 9 4-bedded apartments with bath, WC and kitchen, 38 double, 13 single
– 27 with bath, 5 with shower, all with telephone; some with radio, TV and
tea-making facilities; baby-sitting service.

Facilities Lift. Salon, breakfast room, roof garden; in front of artificial lake. English spoken.
Location 10 minutes' walk from centre, on W edge of old town. Parking.
Credit cards All major cards accepted.
Terms [1985 rates] B&B: single 300–475 Dkr, double 450–650 Dkr; apartments 7,500 Dkr per week. (No restaurant.)

FALSLED 5642 Funen   Map 7

Falsled Kro   *Tel* (09) 681111
                                                          Telex 50404

Known as a smugglers' inn in the 15th century, the *Falsled Kro* is today recommended by Danes as *the* place for stylish country weekends. It calls itself "the epitome of a cosy Danish roadside inn", but this may be misleading, for it is very swish. It is on the south-west coast of the central island of Funen. "A low white building with a thatched roof, built around a pretty courtyard with a tiny fountain. The garden leads down to a yacht harbour with an attractive view across the bay. The interior is a skilful blend of modern design in antique surroundings. A huge open fireplace in reception, a light sitting room with doors opening on to the garden, and a long dining room with beautiful modern Scandinavian glass and crockery. All bedrooms are different: some are colourfully tiled and have four-poster beds. The place is French-influenced and food is taken very seriously." Very French menu, distinctly *nouvelle cuisine*. *(N B)* More reports please.

Open 1 Mar–10 Dec. Restaurant closed Mon.
Rooms 3 suites, 9 double, 2 single – 12 with bath, 2 with shower, all with telephone and radio; some 4-poster beds. 3 suites are in the *Ryttergården* farmhouse opposite the hotel – all have bathroom, sitting room, mini-bar, and TV.
Facilities Lounge, salon with TV, bar, restaurant. Garden. Sea 100 metres. English spoken.
Location 10 km from Millinge; S of Odense on Fåborg/Assens road.
Restriction Not suitable for &.
Credit cards All major cards accepted.
Terms Rooms: single 420 Dkr, double 870 Dkr. Breakfast 90 Dkr; lunch 210 Dkr, dinner 410 Dkr. Special meals for children.

FREDENSBORG 3480 Seeland   Map 7

Store Kro   *Tel* (02) 280047
Slotsgade 6

This big comfortable inn has royal connections. Close to Fredensborg Castle (the Danish Queen's spring and autumn residence), it was built by Frederik IV in 1723 at the same time as he was putting up his royal palace next door; he was, we are told, the first innkeeper here, and one of his original buildings is still in use as a hotel annexe. The main building is more modern, and quite a grand sort of hotel, much used by conferences and package tours. "A remarkable place, but don't expect too much of the service or food," was one visitor's verdict. "Our bedroom was first-class, more like a suite, cosily furnished and recently redecorated. Double glazing ensured quiet. The dining room is immense, high-ceilinged, with a faint 1930s aura: hordes of guests, stampeding through it to the conference room at the back, destroyed any feeling of intimacy. Service was adequate but only just; the food was only fair, and pricey for what it was. Breakfast was ill-organised and inadequate, maybe due to the coachloads of German tourists." *(Ian and Francine Walsh)* We have no reason to think that standards have fallen, but sadly lack feedback. More reports would be welcome.

Open All year.
Rooms 6 suites, 20 double, 23 single – all with bath, all with telephone; 16 rooms in annexe; some ground-floor rooms. Double-glazing.
Facilities Lift. Lounges, bar, coffee room, restaurant with music Fri and Sat, games room; banqueting rooms, conference facilities. Large garden. Riding and tennis nearby; near Esrum lake with fishing, water sports and bathing; sea at Hornbaek 16 km away. English spoken.
Location 9 km NE of Hillerød. Hotel is in centre of town next to Castle. Parking for 20 cars.
Credit cards All major cards accepted.
Terms Rooms with breakfast: single 470 Dkr, double 700 Dkr. Full alc 250–350 Dkr. Reduced rates and special meals for chldren.

MARIAGER 9550 Jutland   Map 7

Hotel Postgaarden   *Tel* (08) 541012
Torvet 6

"Mariager is a tiny port some 30 kilometres inland on the Mariager Fjord in north-east Jutland. The village is charming, if a little ramshackle: in its cobbled streets the colourful timbered cottages are wonderfully warped and bowed with age. The wonkiest façade of all belongs to the *Postgaarden*, an inn dating from 1710, but surprisingly modern inside – it was refurbished in 1982. It offers the best of both worlds – antique charm and modern plumbing. There are three small connecting dining rooms, rather stylish, and a snug wood-panelled bar popular with locals. Behind is a peaceful terrace with a view of nothing in particular. Just eight bedrooms, all with bathrooms and handsome modern wood furnishings. Breakfast was the best I have had at a Danish inn and included a Danish pastry. The young staff were extremely helpful." *(N B)*

Open All year.
Rooms 8 double – all with bath and shower, telephone radio and colour TV.
Facilities Bar, dining rooms, conference room. Garden terrace. Beach 1 km, good fishing. English spoken.
Location In village which is between Hobro and Hadsund, 13 km from each.
Restriction Not suitable for &.
Credit cards Access, Diners, Visa.
Terms B&B: single 275–290 Dkr, double 410–430 Dkr. Reduced rates for children.

MILLINGE 5642 Funen   Map 7

Steensgaard Herregårdspension   *Tel* (09) 61.94.90

A half-timbered manor house dating back to 1310 and furnished with Italian rococo, Louis XIV and English antiques. It is run by Kirsten Lund and chef Bent Lillemark, two young people who clearly know what they are doing. A guest this year substantiates last year's reports: "An excellent hotel, well deserving of its Guide entry." The manor house is set in a 27-acre park on the middle island of Funen (Fyn), which native Hans Christian Andersen called the garden of Denmark. "The country-side is probably the prettiest in Denmark – an area of small hills and fields dotted with long low farmhouses. *Steensgaard* is very much a part of this countryside. It's built on three sides of a cobbled courtyard. On one side lies a working farm; on the other a garden, a tennis court and an enclosure full of deer and boar. To complete the rural idyll, a footpath leads away through venerable woodlands.

"Inside, *Steensgaard* has a delightful country house atmosphere. The grand entrance hall is decorated with hunting trophies, the library is lined with leather-bound volumes, all three lounges are spacious. And the number of guest rooms is so few that it's quite possible to have one of these grand reception rooms to yourself, even when the hotel is full. The double rooms are handsomely furnished, most with modern bathroom." Dinner is served in the candle-lit dining room promptly at 7 o'clock. Reports vary on the food. "Not outstanding but adequate . . . a superb ice-cream cake." And "breakfast a splendid buffet, food excellent. The house sometimes caters for large parties which can be noisy into the wee hours." *(Alexander Dow, NB)*

Open 14 Feb–31 Dec.
Rooms 13 double, 2 single – 8 with bath, 2 with shower, all with telephone.
Facilities Hall, 5 salons, library, dining room; billiards, piano, chess. Large park with deer and wild boar; lake (fishing), tennis and riding. Rocky beach 2 km. English spoken.
Location NW of Millinge, halfway between Assens and Faaborg on the Middlefart road.
Restriction Not suitable for &.
Credit cards Probably some accepted.
Terms [1985 rates] rooms: single 210–345 Dkr, double 360–570 Dkr. Breakfast 50 Dkr; set lunch 115 Dkr, dinner 170 Dkr. Reduced rates for 3 or more nights; 12% reduction during low season. Reduced rates for children.

ODENSE 5000 Funen   **Map 7**

Windsor Hotel   *Tel* (09) 12.06.52
Vindegade 45   *Telex* 59972

"Odense is an industrial town and if, as I did, you yearn for poetry and Hans Christian Andersen whose birthplace it is, then forget it. The *Windsor*, built in 1898 but fully modernised, stands on a busy street (but the double-glazing is effective). We were surprised and pleased by it. Our bedroom had a huge and comfortable double bed, pleasant modern furniture, a shower room with huge towels. The dining room has been done up in dramatic colours, predominantly green. Service is excellent and friendly, and against all expectations we found the best and most adventurous cuisine of our whole holiday, also excellent value for money. Far better than usual Danish hotel fare. The trainee chef's use of dill was subtle and" – adds our reporter enigmatically – "her chocolate mousse Andersen-like". *I and F W)*

Note: Since last year the proprietor of the Windsor *has acquired the* Grand Hotel, *Jerbanegade 18, Odense. Reports on both hotels welcome.*

Open All year.
Rooms 13 suites, 35 double, 22 single – all with bath, radio, some with TV and some with fridge; baby-listening.
Facilities Lounge, bar, TV room, restaurant. English spoken.
Location Central. Parking.
Restriction Not suitable for &.
Credit cards All major cards accepted.
Terms [1985 rates] B&B: single 315–485 Dkr, double 460–630 Dkr. Set lunch 135 Dkr, dinner 175 Dkr; full alc 300 Dkr. Reduced rates and special meals for children.

RIBE 6760 Jutland   Map 7

Hotel Dagmar   *Tel* (05) 42.00.33
Torvet 1

Ribe is one of Denmark's oldest and most picturesque towns. It is on the windy west coast of Jutland, in typically flat Danish countryside, and with its 800-year-old cathedral and narrow cobbled streets it has great charm. In spring you can see the celebrated storks' nests on the rooftops. The *Dagmar* too has great character. Standing opposite the cathedral, it was built in 1581 and is in keeping with the rest of the town. "Very different from the usual modern functional Danish hotel and gives a good idea of what a traditional Danish posting-inn was like before the twentieth century. The picturesque building consists on the ground floor of a series of inter-connecting rooms, hung with splendid paintings, and filled with antique and repro furniture, haphazardly blended. Front bedrooms have tiny windows overlooking the church; those at the back have had a bathroom tacked on. Ours was very drab and without a view, but it had lovely paintings and was quiet. The main restaurant is truly spectacular, candlelit. The food was good quality with copious helpings – a little better than the average Danish cooking. Self-service breakfast was one of the best tables we came across. The style in Denmark is a substantial breakfast, just a bit for lunch, then a fair-sized dinner. The *Dagmar* is nice family-run place, friendly and helpful." *(I and F W, Rev M V Bourdeaux)*

Open All year, except New Year.
Rooms 37 double, 5 single – 20 with bath, all with telephone, radio and colour TV, video and mini-bar.
Facilities Salon, bar (open until 2 am), dining rooms, conference facilities. Fishing 3 km. English spoken.
Location Central; Ribe is 34 km SE of Esbjerg.
Restriction Not suitable for &.
Credit cards All major cards accepted.
Terms B&B: 160–280 Dkr; dinner, B&B: 290–410 Dkr; full board: 355–475 Dkr.

ROSKILDE 4000 Sjælland   Map 7

Hotel Prindsen   *Tel* (02) 35.80.10
Algade 13

Roskilde is a lovely small city only 20 minutes from Copenhagen by train. The *Prindsen* is a small hotel on the main street. The open-air market is between it and the great twin-spired cathedral, built in 900 AD. To the left is the step-roofed City Hall. Within walking distance is the Viking Museum where the long ships, sunk to block the channel against invaders, are being restored. The museum is a handsome building in a lovely park where you can see films of the recovery of the ships from their resting place of centuries. The 40 rooms in the *Prindsen* are nicely furnished and reasonably priced. If you decide to keep your room in Copenhagen, yet spend a day and a night in Roskilde, the *Prindsen* is an inexpensive way to do it. *(Clay Leitch)* More reports welcome.

Open All year.
Rooms 26 double, 15 single – 8 with bath, 28 with shower, all with telephone and radio.
Facilities Bar with TV, restaurant, conference/function facilities. English spoken.
Location Central, on main street. Private parking.
Restriction Not suitable for &.
Credit cards All major cards accepted.
Terms B&B: single 295–390 Dkr, double 395–580 Dkr; dinner, B&B: single 420–515 Dkr, double 645–830 Dkr; full board: single 510–605 Dkr, double 825–1,010 Dkr. Set lunch 90 Dkr, dinner 175 Dkr; full alc 275 Dkr. Children under 12 sharing parents' rooms free; special meals.

SKØRPING 9520 Jutland   Map 7

Hotel Rold Stor Kro   *Tel* (08) 37.51.00
Vœlderskoven 13

This modern ranch-style hotel is set deep in the coniferous forest of North Jutland. "A single-floored building in impeccable Scandinavian style. It is delightfully quiet, and the dining room gives on to a panoramic view of the Rebild hills. Our bedroom had well-designed modern furniture, decorated in muted hessian. The lounges are all attractive, with interesting wood sculpture and healthy indoor plants everywhere. One lounge is candlelit at night and has an open log fire all the year; another surrounds an indoor swimming pool. There is a children's lounge and a large outdoor play area with climbing structures carved totemlike out of dead trees. The unusual dining room is very light. Service is prompt and helpful. The menu is more imaginative than most in Denmark, and the set menu good value. 'Vin de la maison' had been imported via Harrods, no less, and was excellent. Breakfast is fresh and wholesome. This place is off the main tourist beat and seems to epitomise the modern Danish hotel at its best. People come to walk in the forests, and every Saturday and Sunday morning the owner takes guests through the forest in quest of local history." *(Ian and Francine Walsh)*

Open All year.
Rooms 2 suites, 49 double, 2 single – 12 with bath, 30 with shower; all with telephone, radio and baby-listening; some with colour TV.
Facilities Lounge with open fireplace, atrium with heated swimming pool, TV room, bar, children's play area. On edge of Rold forest, Lindenborg river within walking distance; trout and salmon fishing; walks, riding, skiing. English spoken.
Location 7 km from Skørping village, 27 km S of Åalborg where the A10 enters the Rold forest.
Restriction Not suitable for &.
Credit cards Access, Amex, Diners.
Terms B&B 115–310 Dkr, half-board 250–445 Dkr; full board 320–515 Dkr. Set lunch 80 Dkr, dinner 135 Dkr; full alc 185 Dkr. 50% reductions for children under 12.

VEJLE 7100 Jutland   Map 7

Munkebjerg Hotel   *Tel* (05) 82.75.00
Munkebjergvej 125   *Telex* 61103 MUNKEN

Larger than most establishments in the Guide, Munkebjerg *is a resort hotel in a particularly lovely setting of beechwood, a few kilometres outside Vejle (free hotel bus) and 90 metres above the Vejle fjord. It is a good area for walking or cycling (free hotel bikes), and would also make a useful base for touring Jutland. Readers have spoken enthusiastically about the good value of the special breaks, the excellent food and the exceptional service. A recent visitor agrees about the attractions of the location, the comfort of the rooms and the standards of cooking, but found the pleasure of her stay impaired by coach parties, which meant long waits in the dining room. Her verdict: an admirable hotel if you are one of a party, but not so agreeable for the independent traveller. (J S) More reports please.*

Open 3 Jan–22 Dec.
Rooms 4 suites, 128 double, 16 single – 86 with bath, 62 with shower, all with telephone, radio and colour TV.
Facilities Lift. Lounge, TV room, bar with live music, restaurant, banqueting rooms, conference facilities; nightclub open nightly except Sun; billiard room; heated indoor swimming pool, sauna, solarium; large grounds with tennis court and children's playground; bicycles; hotel is adjacent to golf course; beach 5 km, fishing nearby. English spoken. Safe bathing 1 km; sandy beach 12 km.
Location 6 km from town centre. To reach hotel drive along S side of Vejle fjord from Jejle, follow serpentine road up the hill.
Restriction Not suitable for &.
Credit cards All major cards accepted.
Terms B&B: single 440–960 Dkr, double 590–1,135 Dkr; dinner, B&B 410–725 Dkr per person; full board 525–865 Dkr per person. Set lunch (cold table) 115–200 Dkr, set dinner 155–180 Dkr; full alc 90–150 Dkr. Reduced rates and special menus for children.

Finland

HOTEL TORNI, HELSINKI

HELSINKI 33,00330   **Map 7**

Hotel Kalastajatorppa   *Tel (09) 488.011*
Kalastajatorpantie 1   *Telex 121571*
Fiskatorpsvågen

"The best hotel in or outside Helsinki" was one verdict this year, though
the visitor went on to warn readers not to expect quite the same
standards of service in Finland as elsewhere in Europe. An earlier
correspondent had reported: "*Kalastajatorppa* – the name simply means
'Fisherman's Cottage', but this must be the most sophisticated cottage
I've ever seen. For, in reality, it is a large de luxe hotel offering a high
degree of sophistication and magnificent setting by the sea, yet only 20
minutes' drive from the city centre. The rooms are modern with all the
facilities one expects, and many of them have the superb sea view. The
main restaurant includes an international floor-show with dinner and
dancing nearly every night. There is an intimate nightspot for those who
want to enjoy themselves into the small hours. And one can freshen up
in the hotel's sauna bath and swimming pool complex. I found the staff
very friendly, and the standard of service high, but I especially enjoyed
the magnificent view of the setting sun reddening the sea as it slowly
crossed the sky at midsummer." (*Michael J Fitzpatrick, Heather Sharland;
also Mrs G Berneck*) Major renovations are due to begin in autumn 1985.
More reports welcome.

Open All year. Main restaurant closed 1 Sept 1985 – 31 Apr 1986 for renovations.
Rooms 8 suites, 149 double, 78 single – 157 with bath, 78 with shower, all with telephone, radio and colour TV; some rooms adapted for &.
Facilities Lifts. Bar with TV, café, 2 restaurants; conference facilities; children's playroom with nanny. Hairdresser, bank, night-club; 2 indoor swimming pools, 5 saunas. Tennis, boating, fishing, golf, bicycling and winter sports nearby. Ramps and WCS for &. English spoken.
Location 5 km from town centre towards Munkkiniemi. Garage parking.
Credit cards All major cards accepted.
Terms B&B: single 430–590 FM, double 630–750 FM; dinner, B&B: 80–145 FM per person added to room rates; full board: 160–250 FM added. Full alc 300 FM. Christmas package.

Hotel Torni *Tel* (09) 644.611
Yrjönkatu 26, Helsinki 10,00100 *Telex* 125153 TORNI SF

"I cannot understand why this beautiful country is not more widely advertised" is what we heard from a reader this year. "We stayed at the *Torni* and found everything excellent." In fact, you can't miss the *Torni*. It rises up like a squared-off lighthouse from a quiet street in the heart of Helsinki, and once served as headquarters for the Occupation Army. The hotel combines the spaciousness of a traditional hotel with all modern conveniences. The roof-top restaurant with a panoramic view serves a lavish smorgasbord. (Be sure to try the national speciality – reindeer tongue.) "Very good value for money" was one view this year, though another reader was ambivalent: "no more than OK".

Open All year (except possibly Christmas).
Rooms 9 suites, 98 double, 48 single – 32 with bath, 123 with shower, all with telephone,radio and colour TV.
Facilities Lifts. Salons, 2 bars, "pub", 2 restaurants. 4 conference rooms; 4 saunas; summer terrace. English spoken.
Credit cards All major cards accepted.
Terms B&B: single 410 FM, double 560 FM. Set lunch 80–150 FM, dinner 80–250 FM; full alc 250 FM. 50% reduction for children under 12 in parents' room; special meals on request.

France

CHÂTEAU DE MARÇAY - CHINON

L'AIGLE 61300 Orne   **Map 8**

Hôtel du Dauphin   *Tel* (33) 24.43.42
Place de la Halle   *Telex* 170979

A small south Normandy town in rolling countryside; a classic sober-fronted hostelry in its main square; a log fire blazing in the lounge; a *patron/chef* serving Norman cuisine to *Michelin* rosette standard – what better introduction to *la douce France* for anyone striking south towards the Loire from Le Havre or Dieppe? "A commercial hotel, but with outstanding cuisine," says a reader this year, endorsing earlier praise: "Magnificent, warm, comfortable, with excellent food." "Unusual rambling hotel with an old-fashioned creaky comfort. We felt that probably little has changed over the years. A dog was asleep in front of the fire. M. Bernard the owner was much in evidence and added to the easy relaxed atmosphere. Excellent dinner, as was breakfast that could be taken any time before midday. Large comfortable room with large bathroom." The front rooms have just been double-glazed, so that traffic noise is now "not too bad" (but best ask for a room at the back). *(June Goodfield, Dr and Mrs Lovejoy, P K and J M Leaver)*

Open All year. Restaurant closed 24 Dec.
Rooms 24 double – 18 with bath, 6 with shower, all with telephone and colour TV. Back rooms quietest.
Facilities Lounge, TV room, bar, brasserie, restaurant, conference and functions facilities, boutique. Near to château park; swimming pool nearby, river fishing 7 km, riding 10 km. English spoken.
Location L'Aigle is 100 km SW of Rouen. Hotel is central. Parking (private or in square).
Credit cards Amex, Diners, Visa.
Terms Rooms 177–390 frs; dinner, B&B: single 268–388 frs, double 388–552 frs; full board: single 365–482 frs, double 584–744 frs. Breakfast 27 frs; set meals 98–280 frs; full alc 200 frs. Reduced rates for children.

AIRE-SUR-LA-LYS 62120 Pas-de-Calais   Map 8

Hostellerie des Trois Mousquetaires   Tel (21) 39.01.11

A small late 19th-century château, half-timbered, in a garden beside a pond. Only 60 kilometres from Calais and close to the motorway, it remains popular as a first- or last-night stop: booking is essential in the high season and a deposit is required. There is a lounge, and a small playground for children. One recent visitor found the service perfunctory and felt that a commercialised ambience was creeping in, due maybe to over-popularity. But "the highlight of our holiday: outstanding food and marvellous atmosphere" runs another report this year, confirming earlier praise.(*K & N Varley, Kate and Steve Murray-Sykes, and Graham Grose*)

Open All year except 15 Jan–15 Feb; closed Sun evening, and Mon.
Rooms 13 double – all with bath and telephone, 11 with TV. 3 in annexe.
Facilities 2 salons, TV room, garden room in summer, 2 restaurants. 7-acre garden with lawns leading to lake, and children's playground. English spoken.
Location On N43 between St Omer and Lillers, 2 km from centre of Aire on Arras side. Private parking.
Credit card Visa.
Terms B&B: single 172–272 frs, double 194–294 frs; half-board: single 332–552 frs, double 514–794 frs. Reduced rates and special meals for children.

AIX-EN-OTHE 10160 Aube   Map 10

Auberge de la Scierie   Tel (25) 46.71.26.
La Vove

In the heart of the rolling Othe country, 31 kilometres west of Troyes and a little further from the cathedral towns of Sens and Auxerre, this unusual *auberge*, just outside the little town of Aix, has a warm rural quality all its own. It consists of four farmhouse-type buildings, two modern and two conversions, 18th- and 19th-century (one a former sawmill as the name implies). They are scattered around a big pleasant garden beside a trout-stream; there are ducks, geese, peacocks, a donkey, and horses for hire. The rooms are in chalets in the garden, round a small swimming pool.

Most reports this year are again enthusiastic: "Our evening meal was wonderful, and the children enjoyed the horses." "Extremely good value for money, service willing and efficient, glorious champagne sorbets, attractive flowery gardens, delightful countryside, and the bathroom and loo smelt so nice!" "Friendly and welcoming, but a disappointing dinner." A previous report praised the prettily decorated rooms, the rustic bar with its wooden beams, horse brasses, woodcutters' tools etc., and the food – "On a summer evening we dined out in the garden: local cured ham, rabbit pâté, fresh marinated salmon, sweetbreads in a white wine and cream sauce." *(Margaret Cox, Chris and Dorothy Brining, Padi Howard, and others)*

Open All year.
Rooms 10 double – 6 with bath, 4 with shower, all with telephone, radio and colour TV; baby-listening on request. 1 ground-floor room.
Facilities TV lounge, bar, restaurant, functions room. Large park with terrace/al fresco dining area; swimming pool. English spoken.
Location 1 km S of Aix-en-Othe on N374 after the camp site. Parking.
Credit cards All major cards accepted.
Terms Rooms 250 frs; half-board 260 frs per person. Set lunch/dinner 110 and 180 frs; full alc 250 frs. Special meals for children.

AIX-EN-PROVENCE 13090 Bouches-du-Rhône   Map 11

Hôtel le Pigonnet   *Tel* (42) 59.02.90
5 avenue du Pigonnet   *Telex* 410629

Aix's most attractive hotel – a handsome creeper-covered mansion, set in its own large garden full of chestnut trees, in a quiet residential district south of the city's historic centre. "The setting is romantic, peaceful, full of roses, bird-song and old-fashioned comfort," is this year's verdict, while an earlier report ran: "The sober elegance goes well with Aix, and we did not mind paying high prices for such quality. Our large bedroom had antique furniture, cheerful wallpaper and a balcony with views of Cézanne's Mont Ste-Victoire. We enjoyed lazing by the swimming pool which is set amid flowers. The garden is most unusual, all rose-bowers, fountains and ornamental pools – more like the garden of some romantic *fin-de-siècle* villa than of a chic hotel. We found the dining room a little formal but we enjoyed lunch under the chestnut trees. The cooking, with variations on local dishes, was mostly good." Two separate visitors this year liked the food and comfort but found the restaurant service off-hand and unhelpful. Another reader liked the hotel, but complained of a small, cramped room. *(P and S A, and others)*

Open All year. Restaurant closed Sun dinner Nov–Mar inclusive.
Rooms 1 suite, 44 double, 6 single – 39 with bath, 11 with shower, all with telephone and colour TV; 14 rooms in annexe.
Facilities Lift. Lounge with log fire, bar restaurant, terrace. Small garden with swimming pool. Rocky and sandy beach 25 km. English spoken. ᕲ.
Location Coming from Nice or Toulon, leave *autoroute* at Aix-Est exit; coming from Lyon or Paris, leave it at Aix-Sud exit. Hotel is 800 metres from city centre, in a quiet side street. Parking.
Credit cards All major cards accepted.
Terms B&B 225–280 frs; half-board 355–545 frs; full board 485–675 frs. Set meals 130 frs; full alc 190–230 frs. Children in extra bed free under 6, 50% under 12; special meals on request.

Give the Guide positive support. Don't just leave feedback to others.

AJACCIO Corse-du-Sud, Corsica   Map 11

Dolce Vita   *Tel* (95) 52.00.93
Route des Sanguinaires

The Route des Sanguinaires stretches west along the coast from Ajaccio, Corsica's lively capital and the birthplace of Napoleon. Five miles from the town is the very modern *Dolce Vita*, where the sweet life centres round a beautiful swimming pool and dining terrace right by the sea and is only somewhat soured, indoors, by some hideous loud-coloured decor. A report this year: "A low two-storey building between the road and the rocky shore, where the coastline is lovely. The better rooms on the first floor are very large and beautifully furnished, with plenty of good lighting. A large balcony overlooks the lawns and the sea sparkles through the oleander blossoms. Breakfast is perfect, eaten to the soft sound of the sea. The large terrace built over the rocks is shaded with palm-trees, and here lunch was a pleasant surprise. The hotel is popular with French families; although it lacks a sandy beach, there is a slipway for landing boats, and an iron ladder from the rocks into the sea which is superb to swim in." *(Angela and David Stewart)*

Open All year except 1–30 Nov. Restaurant closed Tue.
Rooms 33 – all with bath and wc, tv, refrigerator, terrace and air-conditioning.
Facilities Lounge, bar, restaurant, private night-club. Garden with terraces and swimming pool; bathing from rocks; slipway for boats.
Location 8 km W of Ajaccio, on the coast.
Restriction Not suitable for &.
Credit cards All major cards accepted.
Terms [1985 rates] rooms 280–473 frs. Breakfast 30 frs; set lunch/dinner 160 frs.

ALBERTVILLE 73200 Savoie   Map 10

Hôtel Million   *Tel* (79) 32.25.15
8 place de la Liberté

"Rather like *Lameloise* at Chagny" (q.v.) is the accolade lavished on Philippe Million's spruce hostelry by two of the Guide's most fastidious seekers-out of French provincial perfection, especially gastronomic. It is an old family-run hotel near the centre of a dullish town in a sub-Alpine valley south-east of Annecy. "Traditional atmosphere with modern comforts. Rooms not very large but pleasantly decorated and quiet enough at night: most are in a modern extension behind the building. There is a comfortable lounge and bar in traditional style, with special booklets about the fascinating medieval hill-village of Conflans which overlooks Albertville and is a short walk from the hotel. The restaurant is superb (two rosettes in *Michelin)* and reasonably priced for the quality: original cooking in the modern style, very light and inventive. The creamy chocolate patisserie is alone worth crossing the Alps for. Good wine list with delicious local Savoie wines at only 50–60 francs. Plentiful breakfasts." In summer you can dine in elegance on a flowery terrace facing the small and pretty garden. *(Pat and Jeremy Temple)*

Open All year except 24 Apr–2 May, 1–11 July, 25 Aug–10 Oct. Restaurant closed Sun evening and Mon (except 14 July–1 Sept).
Rooms 27 double, 2 single – 24 with bath, 1 with shower, all with telephone.

Facilities Lift. Salon/bar, TV salon, dining room. Small garden terrace for dining. English spoken.
Location Central. Parking. Albertville is 45 km SE of Annecy.
Credit cards Amex, Diners.
Terms B&B: single 250–300 frs, double 250–300 frs. Breakfast 30 frs; set meals 125 and 350 frs weekdays, 225 and 350 frs Sun and holidays; full alc 300 frs. Reduced rates for children; special meals available if ordered in advance.

ALBI 81000 Tarn   Map 10

La Réserve   *Tel* (63) 60.79.79
Route de Cordes   *Telex* 520850 LA RESERVE

"One of the nicest hotels anywhere" is a comment this year on this smart modern hotel, three kilometres out of town, owned by the Rieux family; "we had a lovely room with balcony, overlooking pool and river, a perfect setting. Superb bathrooms, splendid food, and Mme Rieux was charming." Other readers this year concur, though some found the food uninteresting (you would do better at the Rieux' other hotel, see below). "The extensive grounds slope down to the Tarn on which you may venture in a pedalo; the swimming pool is large." *(Richard and Susan Faulkner, Stanley Burnton, Mary and Rodney Milne–Day)*

Open Apr–Oct.
Rooms 1 suite, 17 double, 2 single – 16 with bath, 4 with shower, all with telephone and mini-bar; 12 with colour TV.
Facilities 2 salons, TV room, restaurant. Large garden with heated outdoor swimming pool, tennis courts; near river with pedalo and boat-fishing rights.
Location 3 km from town, on the Cordes road.
Restriction Not suitable for &.
Credit cards All major cards accepted.
Terms B&B 335–430 frs. Set lunch/dinner 130–250 frs; full alc 200 frs. Reduced rates and special meals for children.

Hostellerie Saint-Antoine   *Tel* (63) 54.04.04
17 rue St-Antoine   *Telex* 520850 MAPALBI

This former monastery, run by the Rieux family (see entry above) since 1734, lies in the town centre yet is quiet, and is only 500 metres from Albi's two glories – its stunning red-brick cathedral and the adjacent Toulouse-Lautrec museum. The rooms ("charmingly pretty") are built round "a delightful little garden", and the hotel provides elegance and comfort and "notably obliging" service. Some readers find its cooking "excellent", others less so; it is praised in *Gault Millau* for innovative dishes such as pigeon with turnips. Guests are free to use the swimming pool and tennis courts of *La Réserve* (see above). *(David Ballard, Christopher Martin, Stanley Burnton)*

Open All year.
Rooms 44 double, 12 single – 40 with bath, 16 with shower, all with telephone and tea-making facilities; 30 with colour TV.
Facilities Lift. Salon, TV room, bar, restaurant; banquet/conference facilities. Inner garden. Free tennis and swimming 3 km away at *La Réserve* (route de Cordes). English spoken.
Location In centre of Albi (but very quiet). Parking.
Restriction Not suitable for &.
Credit cards All major cards accepted.
Terms B&B 185–415 frs. Set lunch/dinner 90–250 frs; full alc 190 frs.

ALENÇON 61000 Orne   Map 10

Le Grand Saint-Michel   *Tel* (33) 26.40.77
7 rue du Temple

The town of Alençon in southern Normandy has played a special role in French post-war culinary development, for this is where Moulinex comes from. It is good therefore to learn that "the food is excellent" at *Le Grand St-Michel*, a simple family-run place in the town centre, useful as a stop-over point or excursion base. "Modest and cheap, but comfortable; central but quiet. The owner, Michel Canet, and his wife are exceptionally hospitable and have a knack of making their guests feel at home. When a couple arrived with a baby, they specially got in a cot for it. No real lounge, but a nice small bar with interesting nibbles." Good simple food: the 50.50-franc menu begins with a help-yourself hors-d'oeuvre trolley. *(Jacqui Hurst, also June Goodfield)*

Open All year except 30 Jun–25 Jul.
Rooms 12 double – 3 with bath and WC, 7 with shower, all with telephone.
Facilities TV room, bar, restaurant, functions room. English spoken.
Location Central, but quietly situated in pedestrian area near the Cornmarket and museum. Alençon is 101 km S of Caen.
Credit card Visa.
Terms Rooms 80–170 frs; half-board from 130 frs per person; full board from 137 frs per person (1 week min.). Breakfast 16.50 frs; set lunch/dinner 50.50, 77.50 and 144.50 frs; full alc 150 frs.

AMBOISE 37401 Indre-et-Loire   Map 10

Hostellerie du Château de Pray   *Tel* (47) 57.23.67

For those who like to stay in a real château when in the heart of the Loir châteaux country. This one, two kilometres outside Amboise (fine château there, too), is 13th century, quite small, turreted and part creeper-covered, and has belonged to major families of the area since 1244. It still retains that atmosphere, according to readers who have found it "delightful". It stands on rising ground 500 metres from the Loire, in its own 25-acre park. "Very pleasant and welcoming, full of character. A commanding view across terraces and the river, and a small farm that appears to have changed little since the Middle Ages. Central spiral staircase with suit of armour. Comfortable bedrooms, and quiet apart from some plumbing noises. Adequate restaurant with a five-course set dinner. Not the place for a long stay, as there was no lounge." Another report adds: "The atmosphere was friendly, with the *patronne* taking orders for dinner. In fine weather meals were taken on the outside terrace facing the river; apéritifs were served in the formal garden. Excellent food, specialities being fish from the Loire." *(Richard and E-A Pile, Kenneth Garside, John Ring)*

Open 10 Feb–31 Dec.
Rooms 16 double – 15 with bath, 1 with shower, all with telephone.
Facilities Salon, bar, restaurant. Garden with terrace on the Loire.
Location 2½ km NE of Amboise, on S bank of Loire; take D751 in direction of Chaumont-sur-Loire.
Credit cards All major cards accepted
Terms Dinner, B&B 690 frs for 2. Set meals 130–160 frs.

AMIENS 80000 Somme   Map 8

Le Grand Hôtel de L'Univers   *Tel* (22) 91.52.51
2 rue de Noyon   *Telex* 145070

"Amiens' best hotel. It is pleasantly quiet, despite a very central situation, on a main street between the station and the vast and splendid Gothic cathedral that is the jewel of this otherwise rather sombre northern city. The hotel's interior has a high central foyer with galleries running round on three floors – rather Spanish, though I doubt it's the result of the former Spanish occupation of this part of France! I had a snug room at a reasonable price; good breakfast and friendly service. No restaurant, but you can eat well in town at *Joséphine*, or just outside at *La Bonne Auberge* at Dury." (*J A*)

Open All year.
Rooms 33 double, 8 single – 25 with bath, 16 with shower, all with direct-dial telephone, colour TV and mini-bar; double-glazing. Quietest rooms at rear.
Facilities Lift. Lounge with TV, cellar bar, conference/function facilities. Public garden opposite. English spoken. &.
Location Central, 100 metres from station. Parking opposite.
Credit cards All major cards accepted.
Terms Rooms 240–290 frs. Breakfast (with newspaper) 26 frs. (No restaurant.) 10% off stays of 3 nights or more 15 July–end Aug; group rates. Children under 15 free.

LES ANDELYS 27700 Eure   Map 8

Hôtel de la Chaîne d'Or   *Tel* (32) 54.00.31
27 rue Grande

A picturesque old town on a loop of the Seine south-east of Rouen, dominated by the ruins of Richard Coeur de Lion's Château Gaillard. The *Chaîne d'Or* is an 18th-century *auberge* in the town centre, its dining room and some bedrooms looking over the river. It is quiet at night, save when big river boats pass by, but they don't go late. Reports this year, numerous, nearly all praise the bedrooms and setting but are more divided about food and service. "Excellent dinners, polite and efficient service, large and comfortable rooms facing the river, but erratic plumbing." "Our room was as big as a ballroom, with huge old bath. Watching the traffic on the river kept us happy for hours and we could hardly bear to leave it to get into bed. Dining room service was slow and off-hand and the dinner poor." However, the general verdict is favourable. (*P A Thorp, Graham Grose, Kay and Neville Varley, Mary and Rodney Milne-Day, and others*)

Open All year except Jan, Sun evening and Mon.
Rooms 12 double – 4 with bath, all with telephone.
Facilities Bar/breakfast room, restaurant, functions room; courtyard.
Location Central, on the river. Parking. (Town is 39 km SE of Rouen.)
Credit cards Access, Visa.
Terms [1985 rates] rooms 95–240 frs. Breakfast 22 frs; set lunch/dinner 60–170 frs.

If you have kept brochures and tariffs for foreign hotels, please enclose them with your reports.

347

ANDUZE 30140 Gard   Map 10

Les Trois Barbus   *Tel* (66) 61.72.12
Générargues

A modern hotel, remote in the wooded southern foothills of the
Cévennes, 47 kilometres from Nîmes. "We liked it so much that we
returned this year for a longer stay. A breathtaking situation, overlooking a gorge and a branch of the river Gardon. Lovely views in all
directions. It is on a steep slope, a series of terraced gardens, with an
excellent swimming pool on the lowest. It is a family-run affair: when I
asked the presiding matriarch who the 'three bearded gentlemen' were,
she said simply: *'Ce sont mes fils.'* Our room was comfortable, if not
spacious. Very quiet, the only sound at night being a waterfall down in
the gorge. Charming Limoges china. Good food: marvellous sauces,
light and original." A visitor this year found the food excellent but the
wines "outrageously overpriced". *(Mrs R B Richards, Eileen Atkins and Bill
Shepherd, and others)*

Open 15 Mar–5 Nov. Restaurant closed Mon.
Rooms 33 double – 28 with bath, 4 with shower, all with telephone, many with
balcony; 19 rooms in annexe; 5 ground-floor rooms.
Facilities TV room, bar/lounge, bar, grill room, restaurant, terraces, seminar
room. Small garden with unheated swimming pool and *boules*. River with fishing
rights nearby. English spoken.
Location 4 m N of Anduze on D50 at Le Roucan-Générargues.
Credit card Access.
Terms B&B: single 330 frs, double 360 frs; dinner, B&B: single 380 frs, double 600
frs; full board: single 470 frs, double 760 frs. Set meals 140–180 frs; full alc 200 frs
(excluding 15% service). Reduced rates for children.

ARDRES 62610 Pas-de-Calais   Map 8

Grand Hôtel Clément   *Tel* (21) 82.25.25
91 esplanade du Maréchal Leclerc   *Telex* 130886 (RES. CLEMENT)

Being so usefully situated on the edge of a small town only 13 kilometres
from Calais, on the way to the Paris *autoroute*, this "typically French"
little family-run hotel continues to provide many readers with their first
or last taste of "the true France" – and often, as in this case, that means
superb food and much-less-than-superb bedrooms. Again we have a full
pouch of reports, with criticism more muted than in some past years.
The cooking is now in the hands of the young son of the family, François
Coolen, who has just won a red *Gault Millau toque* for his *nouvelle*
touches, and our readers are also very pleased: "outstanding", "wonderful", "excellent" are this year's epithets. The garden, the hand-carved
furniture, the attentive service, the log fire in the bar in winter, are also
praised. But the standard of the bedrooms varies: some are quiet and
comfortable with modern bathrooms, others less adequate, and we have
reports of lumpy beds, small and dusty cupboard space, and traffic noise
in front rooms. *(Arnold R Horwell, Paul Stone, Mrs N Lampert, and others)*

Open All year except 15 Jan–15 Feb. Closed Mon. Restaurant also closed Tue
midday Oct–Mar
Rooms 17 double, 1 single – 12 with bath, 4 with shower, all with direct-dial
telephone.

Facilities Salons, bar, 2 dining rooms; conference facilities in winter. Garden with swings, terrace; ping-pong. 1 km from lake. English spoken.
Location 17 km SE of Calais on N43 to St Omer. *Autoroute* A26 is 6 km away. Parking.
Restriction Not suitable for ♿.
Credit cards All major cards accepted.
Terms Rooms 150–240 frs. Breakfast 25 frs; set lunch/dinner 100, 180, 280 frs.

ARLES 13200 Bouches-du-Rhône   Map 11

Hôtel d'Arlatan   *Tel* (90) 93.56.66
26 rue du Sauvage   *Telex* 441203 ARCATAN

A hotel of unusual charm and character, run with pride by the cultivated Desjardin family. The building, dating from the 15th century, was the ancestral home of the Counts of Arlatan; it fronts a quiet street in the heart of old Arles, and has a special secretive quality. Its idyllic little garden is enclosed on one side by the high wall of the palace of Constantine. "One of the loveliest hotels I have ever visited," writes one enthusiast; "one passes through an arched gateway into a courtyard with a lone palm . . . a cool place to sit and sip in, on a hot day. The interiors are done with great taste and care, with lovely antiques and fabrics. The owner and all the staff are charming and helpful." "Relaxed and easy atmosphere, really delightful", runs another report, though one recent visitor disliked both his room and the service. No restaurant, but you can eat well in town at the *Jules César* (expensive), *La Paillotte, Le Vaccarès* (both medium-priced). *(William Goodhart, J F L Bowles, and others)*

Open All year.
Rooms 40 double, 6 single – 37 with bath, 9 with shower, all with telephone; 5 rooms in annexe.
Facilities Reading room, Louis XIII salon, salon with TV; conference room. Garden with courtyard patio decked with trees and shrubs for outdoor refreshments. English spoken.
Location Central, near place du Forum, but quiet as rooms overlook garden and patio. Garage parking.
Credit cards Amex, Diners.
Terms Rooms: single 210–295 frs, double 295–395 frs. Breakfast 30 frs. (No restaurant.)

AUCH 32000 Gers   Map 10

Hôtel de France   *Tel* (62) 05.00.44
Place de la Libération   *Telex* 520474

Although quite close to Toulouse and the Armagnac country, not many British travellers penetrate to the old Gascon city of Auch. So we were glad to get this precise report on one of France's most renowned hotel/restaurants (two *Michelin* rosettes, three red *Gault Millau toques*): "The hotel is a large old Victorian building on the edge of an impressive market square with a colourful display of massed flowers. Just round the corner is the superb cathedral with its spectacular 15th-century choir stalls. The hotel's interior has been flamboyantly decorated by someone with a sure touch and a designer's eye – artfully arranged dried flowers and attractive antique furniture. Our bedroom was comfortable and quiet, with plush red 19th-century chairs and attractive prints. The dining room was spacious and opulent (it might have been an old ballroom); the seats at our table were red velvet love-seats. A bevy of black-suited well-trained waiters served us the 240-franc [1985] menu; some dishes were delicious but others somewhat dry. Breakfast, however, was a great success (creamy butter in a large wooden barrel), in contrast to the tired meal the night before. This hotel has great comfort, but its reputation is perhaps over-exploited," *(Robert and Gilly Jamieson)*. This year, another veteran traveller concurs: "Bedroom pleasant, restaurant elegant, service impeccable, food excellent in its genre but 'interesting' more than 'revealing', and the whole place, though very professional, lacks warmth." *(Geoffrey Sharp)*

Open All year.
Rooms 25 double, 5 single – 20 with bath, 10 with shower; all with telephone, 15 rooms with TV.
Facilities Salons, TV room, bar, conference and banqueting facilities, 3 restaurants; terrace. English spoken.
Location Auch is 78 km W of Toulouse. Central. Parking.
Restriction Not suitable for &.
Terms Rooms: single 210–290 frs, double 250–600 frs; dinner, B&B 405–580 frs per person. Breakfast 45 frs; set meals (prices differ in each of the 3 restaurants) 120, 160, 235, 350 frs; full alc 120–360 frs.

AUDIERNE 29113 Finistère   Map 8

Le Goyen   *Tel* (98) 70.08.88

Experienced travellers report on a hotel they have visited several times: "It is a modern, white-painted and shuttered building in the middle of the attractive harbour town of Audierne, in far south-west Brittany. The hotel overlooks the harbour, and the view from the best bedrooms (ours was very pretty, in shades of blue) takes in colourful fishing-boats. The hotel is more comfortable with courteous, friendly staff; the decor is pretty, though for our taste a trifle kitsch. The dining room, rather quaintly decorated, overlooks the terrace where lunches are served. We ate the fixed-price meals which were usually quite delicious, eg feuilleté de langouste sauce homard. Each time we visit, the cuisine of M. Bosser, *patron/chef*, seems to be more adventurous" *(Michelin* rosette, two red *Gault Millau toques)*. A visitor this year found the cuisine "blissful" but his room rather less than clean and pretty. Another complained of being obliged to take a disappointing set menu because he was on half-board terms; he was keen to pay a *supplément* for the "star" menu but was told this was against the rules. More reports please.

Open All year except mid-Nov to mid-Dec and Mon in low season (except public holidays).
Rooms 5 suites, 29 rooms – all with bath or shower, telephone and TV.
Facilities Lift. Salon, conference facilities, dining room; terrace.
Location Central, near harbour. Audierne is 35 km W of Quimper.
Credit cards None accepted.
Terms [1985 rates] rooms 195–224 frs, suites 224–380 frs. Breakfast 30 frs; set lunch/dinner 105–280 frs.

Before making a long detour to a small hotel, do check that it is open. Some are known to close on impulse.

AUXERRE 89000 Yonne   **Map 10**

Hôtel de Seignelay   *Tel* (86) 52.03.48
2 rue du Pont

"We were delighted," writes one recent visitor to this modest hotel in the town centre, quietly run by middle-aged Burgundians; "charming welcome, excellent dinner – almost a country atmosphere, though Auxerre is quite a large town. Nice bedroom; bathroom large but lacking ventilation." This endorses an earlier verdict: "Built around a courtyard, it has a charming setting through an arch, with contrasting cream walls and red roofs. Pleasant sitting room with open fire for cold days; some modern bedrooms with baths, the others with basins only. Strictly traditional food, and excellent choice. In a week, I can eat my way through all the Burgundian specialities and expect to see different *tartes* each evening. Good house red." *(Mr and Mrs Nigel Smith, M Wolf, John Thirlwell)*

Open All year except 4 weeks in Jan/Feb and Mon Nov–July.
Rooms 2 family (4), 1 triple, 19 double, 2 single – 4 with bath, 8 with shower, all with telephone.
Facilities Salon with TV, 2 restaurants, courtyard; conference facilities for 80 people. English spoken.
Location Near centre of old town (only 4 rooms on street). Garage parking (14 frs).
Credit cards None accepted.
Terms [1985 rates] double room: with breakfast 152–213 frs; with half-board 267–337 frs. Set lunch/dinner 60, 70, 80, and 130 frs; full alc 120 frs.

AVALLON 89200 Yonne   **Map 10**

Hostellerie du Moulin des Ruats   *Tel* (86) 34.07.14
Vallée du Cousin

Very picture-postcardy, and very well known to tourists, both French and Anglo-American, this old mill-house, creeper-covered and much-balconied, lies in a lush winding valley three kilometres from Avallon and twelve from Vézelay and its mighty abbey. In fine weather you can eat out on a terrace by the rushing mill-stream, whose waters may also lull you to sleep at night. "Thoroughly likeable and well run, hard to fault for all but those who insist on obvious luxury. Bedrooms not large but immaculate and cheerful, and gardens positively manicured. The meal was a pleasant surprise, both quality and value: an excellent four-course menu for 150 francs included a splendid coq au vin." That 1984 inspector's report is backed up this year by new praise and some dissent: "Our room overlooking the mill-stream was delightful; food good, especially breakfasts." "Food outstanding, especially escargots, but breakfast service slow." "Service friendly and helpful, excellent food (eg magret de canard), but bedroom decor garish." One visitor found the plumbing noisy and her room too small. *(P F, Joan Powell, Wynne and Brian Freeman, Dr and Mrs G Collingham)*

Open 1 Mar–30 Oct; closed Mon, and Tue midday except holidays.
Rooms 20 double – 13 with bath, 1 with shower, all with telephone.
Facilities Restaurant; garden with riverside terrace. English spoken.

Location 3 km W of Avallon by D427. Parking.
Credit cards All major cards accepted.
Terms B&B double 262–364 frs. Set lunch/dinner 162 frs + 15% service.

Le Moulin des Templiers
Vallée du Cousin

Tel (86) 34.10.80

Renewed praise this year for this idyllically situated old watermill, attractively converted into a comfortable and tranquil little hotel beside the quiet-flowing Cousin, little more than a stream. "The gardens stretch along the river, and there is a beautiful terrace at the water's edge where breakfast is served. Reception and service were friendly and efficient." "The fragrance of flowers was everywhere; rooms were small but delightful, with windows overlooking the soporific stream. Warm croissants and freshly squeezed orange juice – my best French breakfast." One visitor says the plumbing could be quieter. No restaurant: but nearby Avallon and Vézelay (q.v.) have several excellent ones. (*Vicki Turner, Rosamund Hebdon, Ann Carpenter, and others*)

Open 1 Apr–15 Oct. Closed Sat.
Rooms 12 double, 2 single – 10 with bath, 4 with shower, all with telephone.
Facilities Salon. Garden with *boules*, riverside terrace. English spoken.
Location 2 km W of Avallon in direction of Vézelay. Parking.
Credit cards None accepted.
Terms Rooms: single 130 frs, double 230 frs. Breakfast 27 frs. (No restaurant.)

Hostellerie de la Poste
13 place Vauban

Tel (86) 34.06.12

In the centre of Avallon, a famous and dignified old hostelry: Napoleon spent a night here on his way back from Elba. "We dined outdoors in the charming cobblestoned and flower-bedecked courtyard; the service was impeccable, the pâté de brochet divine." So runs a report this year, backing up earlier praise for the "beautifully appointed rooms" and "stylish service in the grand old manner". One connoisseur of hotels of this quality praises its "warm and professional atmosphere as well as its beautifully superb restaurant (*Michelin* rosette). The prices are elevated but justified." (*Vicki Turner, Geoffrey Sharp, and others*)

Open Mid-Jan to Dec. Restaurant closed Wed, and Thur midday.
Rooms 4 suites, 22 double – all with bath, all with direct-dial telephone colour TV. 1 in bungalow.
Facilities Hall, lounge, bar with TV and music, restaurant; functions room. Courtyard and garden. Lakes, fishing, swimming and tennis nearby. English spoken.
Location In town centre. Parking.
Credit cards Amex, Diners, Visa.
Terms (Excluding tax and 15% service charge) double rooms 700–800 frs; dinner, B&B 1,500 frs for 2. Breakfast 50 frs; set meals 180–320 frs; full alc 180–320 frs.

Warning: there were major changes in French telephone numbers in the autumn of 1985 after we had gone to press. It is possible, therefore, that not all our French telephone numbers, particularly those of hotels which failed to answer our questionnaire, are accurate.

AVIGNON 84000 Vaucluse   Map 11

Hôtel d'Europe   *Tel* (90) 82.66.92
12 place Crillon   *Telex* 431965

Most Avignon hotels are modern and functional; this one has classic character: a former 16th-century aristocrat's house, it was already an inn when Napoleon stayed here in 1799. It is in a small square just inside the old city walls, a mere 300 metres from the Papal Palace. "The courtyard and public rooms are a feast to the eye and spirit," says a reader this year, "cool, peaceful, filled with flowers and antiques. My comfortable room was decorated with simplicity and good taste. When there was a muddle over a booking (not the hotel's fault), the staff went out of their way to accommodate me and made me feel like a welcome guest." Others too have been impressed: "furniture and period mirrors that would make an antique dealer salivate"; "quiet, unhurried, clean and gracious". However, readers do warn that a few of the bedrooms are "poky" and badly lit, and that the hotel is "much used by up-market package tours". The classic cuisine in the hotel's *Vieille Fontaine* restaurant is admired. You can eat in a rather formal dining room or, preferably, under the plane trees beside a fountain in the graceful courtyard ("a magical experience"). *(Constance Ellison, Kate Currie, and others)*

Open All year.
Rooms 6 suites, 37 double, 10 single – 45 with bath, all with telephone and colour TV.
Facilities Lift. 2 salons, bar, TV room, restaurant; conference facilities. Courtyard. 5 minutes' walk from Papal Palace. English spoken.
Location Leave *autoroute* A9 at exit Avignon Nord; cross Pont de l'Europe and turn left. Enter city by Porte de l'Oulle; place Crillon is just inside. Private garage.
Credit cards Amex, Diners, Visa.
Terms B&B: single 340 frs, double 460 frs; dinner, B&B: single 500 frs, double 780 frs; full board: single 660 frs, double 1,100 frs. Set meals 150–210 frs; full alc 300 frs.

AZAY-LE-RIDEAU 37190 Indre-et-Loire   Map 10

Hôtel du Grand Monarque   *Tel* (47) 43.30.08 or 43.30.96
Place de la République

One of the loveliest of the smaller Loire châteaux stands serenely beside the river Indre, just a few yards from this classic hostelry in the centre of the little town. The wife of the *Monarque's* owner, Serge Jacquet, died in 1984 of a cruel illness, and of course this affected the standards for a while: but it is heartwarming to hear that in 1985 a regular visitor found it "just as charming, individual and delightful as ever". Another report: "A charming place with a relaxed atmosphere and a good, if expensive restaurant" (good for local fish); "we had a comfortable room, with slightly garish decor, overlooking the attractive courtyard. What really endeared me to the hotel was its menagerie of animals – cats, hens, dogs, tortoises roam around the yard. There were chinchillas in the reception and even a wild boar (tame) in a pen." *(John Mackintyre, Fiona Stirling)*

Open All year. Restaurant open Mar–end Nov.
Rooms 24 double, 6 single – 9 with bath, 6 with shower, all with telephone, 6 with mono TV; baby-listening on request; 12 rooms in annexe.

353

Facilities Hall, bar, 2 salons (1 with TV), restaurant. Garden and courtyard. River fishing, bathing, golf and riding nearby. English spoken.
Location Central, near château. Leave A10 *autoroute* at Tours exit. Parking.
Restriction Not suitable for &.
Credit cards Access, Amex, Visa.
Terms Rooms: single 95–240 frs, double 125–320 frs; dinner, B&B 195–360 frs per person; full board 300–470 frs per person. Breakfast 25 frs; set lunch/dinner 110, 150, 205 frs. Reduced rates for children; special meals on request.

BANNEGON 18210 Charenton de Cher   Map 10

Auberge du Moulin de Chaméron   *Tel* (48) 60.75.80

A converted 18th-century watermill, very romantic, prettily lit at night – in the geographical and spiritual heart of *la douce France*, south-east of Bourges in the rolling Berry country. American nominators have this year spent very rich hours here, adding their voice to the flurry of red-print praise in the French guides: "Yes, yes! Worth the detour for the food alone. Proprietors Jacques and Annie Candoré spent seven years in San Francisco: it was nice to seek out some kindred souls and see orange California poppies in the garden. Our room modest but bathroom large. Pool was great. Walks on country lanes. Museum of former mill implements. Outdoor terrace for lunch. Dining room charming and romantic – *nouvelle cuisine*" (eg blanquette de lotte au Sancerre). *Relais de Silence*. *(Marie Earle)*

Open 15 Mar–2 Nov. Closed Thur off-season.
Rooms 10 double – 6 with bath, 4 with shower, all with telephone; 1 room suitable for disabled guests.
Facilities Lounge, bar, restaurant in old mill. Garden, with river, unheated swimming pool and old watermill converted into museum. English spoken. &.
Location 42 km SE of Bourges; off D41; hotel is signposted.
Credit card Visa.
Terms Rooms: single 160–260 frs, double 180–260 frs. Breakfast 30 frs; set meals 100, 160 and 250 frs; full alc 180 frs.

BARAQUEVILLE 12160 Aveyron   Map 10

Hôtel Segala Plein Ciel   *Tel* (65) 69.03.45
Route d'Albi

Baraqueville is a typically dour Massif Central village, in the rolling dairy-farming Segala region, just south of the old city of Rodez whose rose-grey cathedral stands imposingly on a hilltop. "On the outskirts of the village, a surprising and welcome find – a pleasant modern hotel with good views, lovely heated pool, terraces, ping-pong, spacious bar and lounges. We had a lovely bedroom with balcony overlooking the pool; helpful staff and excellent food including exquisite foie gras and écrevisses armoricaine. Good value, and a good place for children." *(Dr and Mrs G Collingham)*

Open All year except 1 Jan–15 Feb; Fri and Sun evening and Wed out of season.
Rooms 47 – most with bath or shower; all with telephone, some with balcony.
Facilities Lounges, bar, dining room; functions facilities. Grounds with swimming pool and tennis.
Location 19 km S of Rodez.

Credit cards Access, Visa.
Terms [1985 rates] rooms 110–185 frs; full board 220–252 frs per person. Breakfast 16 frs; set lunch/dinner 53–147 frs.

BASTIA 20200 Haute-Corse, Corsica   Map 11

Pietracap   *Tel* (95) 31.64.63
Pietranera

We have few other entries for Corsica's wild and very beautiful northern peninsula, Cap Corse, so this modern bed-and-breakfast hotel three kilometres north of Bastia might be useful. "Well located up a quiet road, well run, and the most comfortable hotel we stayed at on the island. Our room had flowers in it and a big balcony overlooking the sea; there is a clean swimming pool amid trees. One super local eating place, above a tiny harbour, is the *Pirate* at Erbalunga." Or try *La Taverna* in Bastia. Oddly, *Michelin* awards the hotel its red gables for "pleasantness", while *Gault Millau* finds the decor in the public rooms "very ugly". Beach two kilometres away. *(Donald W Hammond)*

Open 1 Mar–30 Nov.
Rooms 22 – all with bath or shower and wc, direct-dial telephones; some with balcony.
Facilities Reading room, TV room, bar, tea-room. Grounds with terrace, swimming pool, table tennis, *boules*, olive grove. Sea nearby. &.
Location 2 km E of Bastia. Take RN 198 towards Pietranera.
Credit cards All major cards accepted.
Terms [1985 rates] rooms 210–325 frs. Breakfast 26 frs. (No restaurant.)

LES BAUX-DE-PROVENCE 13520 Bouches-du-Rhône   Map 11

Oustaù de Baumanière   *Tel* (90) 54.33.07
                                                                Telex 420203

The ruined hill village and castle of Les Baux, on a spur of the Alpilles, is one of the show-places of Provence. In the Middle Ages it was the seat of a great feudal family and a leading "court of love" where troubadours played. Then it came under the rule of a sadistic viscount who would kidnap his neighbours and laugh as he forced them to jump to their deaths from the clifftop. In 1632 Richelieu had the castle demolished. Today it is a ghost realm, where coachloads daily pick their way across the jagged rocks of bauxite (hence its name) and through the spooky remains of medieval grandeur. It is best visited by moonlight.

The Queen and Prince Philip dined at the *Baumanière* on their 1972 State visit to France. In the valley below the village, it is still actively owned and run by 88-year-old Raymond Thuilier, surely the doyen of great French restaurateurs: he still wins *Michelin's* top rating of three stars and five red knives and forks, and he still sticks to the classic style, eschewing *nouvelle cuisine*. He is in the very top price-bracket, and therefore vulnerable: one reader this year was seriously disappointed with food and service, but others are still reaching for their superlatives: "the most lovely hotel, bedrooms exceptional, dinner faultless"; "divine food, service magnificent, the gastronomic experience of a lifetime". *(Tessa Dahl Kelly, Constance Ellison, Alan Weinstein, and others)*

Open All year except 15 Jan–1 Mar.
Rooms 11 suites, 15 double – all with bath, telephone, and air-conditioning, 16 with TV.
16 rooms in 3 annexes; 8 ground-floor rooms.
Facilities Salon, arcaded restaurant. Garden, swimming pool, tennis courts, riding stables. English spoken.
Location 19 km SW of Arles; 60 km NW of Marseilles.
Credit cards All major cards accepted.
Terms B&B double 770–1,035 frs. Set lunch/dinner 400 frs; full alc 600 frs.

La Benvengudo   *Tel* (90) 54.32.54

This creeper-covered farmhouse, in the valley two kilometres south-west of the village, would make a good choice for those not enamoured of the *Baumanière's* prices (see above). It is a charming *bastide* in a garden – quiet, idyllic and modestly glamorous. "The finest holiday we've ever had in France," enthuses one francophile this year; "*very* comfortable beds, luxury bathroom, own patio or balcony and an extra-good swimming pool, the whole enclosed in a pretty garden where you can pick any fruit that is growing, including delicious mulberries. Dinner at night is variable and not exactly cheap, but you are not obliged to eat there. Madame Beaupied was charming." Earlier visitors enjoyed "excellent dinners served in a cosy dining room with antiques", while in summer you can dine on a lovely floodlit patio. No lunches. (*Gerald Campion, A and S Carpenter, and others*)

Open 1 Feb–1 Nov. Restaurant closed lunchtime.
Rooms 2 suites, 16 double – all with bath, WC and telephone; suites with kitchenette; 10 rooms in annexe.
Facilities Salon, TV room, restaurant. Garden with terrace, swimming pool and tennis court. Sea 60 km, rivers with fishing nearby. English spoken.
Location 2 km SW of Les Baux, off D78. Parking.
Credit cards None accepted.
Terms [1985 rates] rooms 236–370 frs. Set dinner 120–160 frs.

BEAULIEU-SUR-MER 06310 Alpes-Maritimes   **Map 11**

Le Métropole   *Tel* (93) 01.00.08
15 boulevard Maréchal Leclerc   *Telex* 470304

Beaulieu with its floodlit palms is still sedately elegant, though no longer as fashionable as in pre-war days. There is a casino, and much of interest close by, eg the Ephrussi de Rothschild museum at Cap Ferrat.

Le Métropole is a well-known hotel of the old style; set back from the road, surrounded by a pretty garden and terrace, it overlooks the glorious coast and is right by the sea. A recent visitor reports: "Old-fashioned only in the sense that standards are high, especially of service – the towels and thick white dressing-gowns are changed, it seems, every time you leave your room. Bedrooms are furnished in cool blue/white, pink/white, green/white schemes, rather Scandinavian, with bathroom tiles to match. Smart David Hicks-style carpets. In May, the gardens were immaculately ablaze, stretching down to the sea, very South of France, and the swimming pool was heated to a blissful 80 degrees. I did not try the food, but friends said it was delicious and varied, though expensive. One snag is that you have to accept *demi-pension*, and extras are outrageous. The cheapest rooms are small and face on to the town; medium-priced ones are at the side, facing over the pool; those facing the sea are de luxe price." *(Patricia Fenn)*

Earlier visitors have praised the hotel's "absolute quiet", its "excellent food and service". "Once installed by the pool, or the concrete area by the beach, your table, chair, towels etc. will be laid out for you in the same spot each day." *Michelin* star, two *Gault Millau toques*.

Open 20 Dec–20 Oct.
Rooms 3 suites, 43 double, 4 single – 48 with bath, 2 with shower, all with telephone and colour TV.
Facilities Lift. Bar, terrace restaurant, dining room, air-conditioning. Garden with terrace, swimming pool heated throughout winter, private beach. English spoken.
Location 10 km E of Nice on N559. Parking.
Credit cards None accepted.
Terms Dinner, B&B: single 1,490 frs, double 2,720 frs; full board: single 1,610 frs, double 2,960 frs. Set lunch/dinner 350 frs.

La Réserve   *Tel* (93) 01.00.01
Boulevard Maréchal Leclerc   *Telex* 470301

On the seafront beside the *Métropole*, the expensive and elegant *Réserve* was one of the most fashionable venues of pre-war Riviera society. Times may have changed, but it still keeps up its standards and an inspector has just endorsed this earlier account: "A gem. Most of the rooms open on to the Mediterranean, and the views, from Nice to the Italian border, are staggering. Like the *Ritz* in Paris, there are almost as many staff as there are guests. The sea-water swimming pool is heated in winter. The rooms are delightful, mostly facing the sea; and the place is quiet, as it is set back from the road. The restaurant has had one *Michelin* star for years and is first rate. You can and should have lunch by the pool." *(L H, A K)*

Open All year except 1 Dec–9 Jan.
Rooms 3 suites, 48 double, 2 single – all with bath, shower and air-conditioning.
Facilities Lift. Salon, restaurant. Garden with swimming pool, sauna, solarium, summer restaurant. Tennis and golf nearby. English spoken.
Location On seafront near Rade de Beaulieu. Parking.
Restrictions Not suitable for &.
Credit cards None accepted.
Terms (Excluding service) rooms: single 440–1,130 frs, double 650–1,600 frs, suite 1,900–3,700 frs. Breakfast 58 frs; set lunch/dinner 320–420 frs.

BEAUNE 21200 Côte-d'Or   **Map 10**

Hôtel le Cep   *Tel* (80) 22.35.48
27 rue Maufoux   *Telex* 351256 CEPHOTEL

Le Cep is a charming 17th-century house in the centre of this Burgundy wine capital where the famous wine auctions, banquets and festivities take place every November. Readers have again written in praise of the "beautiful furnishings", "lovely bathrooms" and "delightful caring owners", backing up an earlier report: "The entrance hall, which also serves as a lounge, is welcoming, furnished with antiques and offering a civilised atmosphere. At breakfast, fresh orange juice followed by Earl Grey tea." *(Rosamund V Hebdon, Mrs J Lattimore, C F Colt, Sandy Smith)* No restaurant, but try the *Relais de Saulx*, close by.

Open Mar–Nov.
Rooms 19 double, 2 single – 17 with bath, 3 with shower, all with telephone.
Facilities Reception lounge, courtyard. English spoken.
Location In town centre. Garage parking.
Restriction Not suitable for &.
Credit cards All major cards accepted.
Terms Rooms 400–700 frs. Breakfast 50 frs. (No restaurant.)

LE BEC-HELLOUIN 27800 Eure   Map 8

Auberge de l'Abbaye   *Tel* (32) 44.86.02

"Very good indeed", says a visitor this year, confirming our previous
entry for the *Auberge* as something close to a francophile's platonic idea
of a good French inn: simple but clean rooms, modestly priced, and a
dining room offering excellent meals at a cost considerably lower than
the English equivalent. No public rooms, except for the breakfast room.
A bonus is the inn's location. Le Bec-Hellouin was the home of one of
Europe's great Benedictine monasteries, and in fact no fewer than three
Archbishops of Canterbury came from here in medieval times. The
monastery, formerly a ruin, has now been substantially restored and
once again houses a religious community; it is only a stroll from the
Auberge across the tranquil village green. "The inn, the village, the abbey
are unassuming priceless jewels, not to be missed." Warning: expect to
be woken by resonant abbatial bells at dawn. *(Stephen Bayley, John Ring)*

Open 22 Feb–6 Jan. Closed Mon evening and Tue out of season.
Rooms 1 suite, 7 double – all with bath and telephone.
Facilities Restaurant, breakfast room, courtyard. English spoken.
Location 60 km from Deauville; 5 km from Brionne; SW of Rouen, W of N138.
Parking.
Credit card Visa.
Terms Rooms 200 frs. Breakfast 25 frs; set meals 110, 150 and 195 frs; full alc
155 frs.

BELCAIRE 11340 Aude   Map 10

Hôtel Bayle   *Tel* (68) 20.31.05

The village of Belcaire lies well off the beaten track in the wild Pyrenean
foothills where the Cathar heretics retreated to their lonely castles in the
13th century. Just along the valley is Montaillou, scene of Leroy
Ladurie's celebrated account of medieval life; tragic Montségur is a little
further off. The *Bayle* is recommended as a simple one-star *logis* with
good, cheap food (red "R" in *Michelin* for value for money): "Our room
with its adjoining bathroom was huge, sparsely furnished but comfortable. There was a lovely view to the mountains, and the place was
peaceful, but front rooms might be noisy. The emphasis is very much on
the excellent restaurant, catering mainly for locals. The staff greeted us
warmly. A good location for anyone interested in Cathar castles."

Open All year except Nov; closed Fri evening and Sat out of season, except school
holidays.
Rooms 16 double – 3 with bath, 3 with shower; some ground-floor rooms.
Facilities Salon with TV, dining room. Garden. Lake with fishing nearby. English
spoken.

Location In centre of village (front rooms might be noisy); parking. 27 km SW of Quillan, 26 km NE of Ax-les-Thermes.
Restriction Not suitable for &.
Credit card Visa.
Terms Rooms: 66–130 frs; dinner, B&B: 100–130 frs per person; full board (min. 3 days) 130-158 frs per person. Breakfast 15 frs; set lunch/dinner 53, 70, 95, 130 frs. Children under 7 half-price.

BEUZEVILLE 27210 Eure   Map 8

Auberge du Cochon d'Or   *Tel* (32) 57.76.08 or 57.70.46
and Le Petit Castel
Place du Général-de-Gaulle

An old Norman *auberge* and adjacent small modern hotel, both owned and run by the Folleau family. They are in a little town near Honfleur, only 48 km from Le Havre, and come new to the Guide this year amid warm praise: "Madame is charming, the reception was courteous and the hotel very warm, a haven in wet weather. You sleep at the *Castel* (a *Logis de France*) and eat at the *Auberge*. Our room was quite luxurious, comfy beds, pretty flowered wallpaper (the *Auberge* has rooms too, much cheaper and simpler). The food (red *Michelin* 'R' for good value) is *very* good, and generously served – truite farcie, terrine aux trois poissons, poulet vallée d'Auge, on the 80-franc menu [1985]. Cheerful table settings, a buttercup yellow; blissfully comfy seats; coffee the best of our holiday. We'll be sure to come back." *(Eileen Broadbent)*

Open 15 Jan–15 Dec, closed Mon.
Rooms 24 double – 17 with bath, 7 with shower, 16 with telephone, 5 with TV; 16 quiet rooms in *Petit Castel*.
Facilities Lounge, TV room, garden, restaurant, conference room. English spoken.
Location In centre. Beuzeville is 15 km SE of Honfleur, just N of Paris/Caen motorway.
Credit cards Access, Visa.
Terms Rooms: single 90–150 frs, double 170–250 frs. Breakfast 16 frs; set meals 80–110 and 160 frs.

BEYNAC 24220 Dordogne   Map 10

Hôtel Bonnet   *Tel* (53) 29.50.01

Not far from Domme and Sarlat, the village of Beynac is one of the classic tourist centres of the lovely Dordogne valley. It dominates a curve in the river, with four medieval castles in full view, including the Château de Beynac itself which frequently changed hands in Anglo-French battles. Much more recently, and more peacefully, the *Bonnet* too has seen regular invasions by British visitors. Some have written again this year to speak well of the friendly ambience and good varied food at this family-run inn. An earlier report ran: "A wide staircase leads up to the entrance beneath the creeper-covered terrace which is attractively arranged with tables and umbrellas. All the staff were most charming and helpful. The bedroom was small but attractively furnished; the bathroom shone with care and cleanliness." Others are enthusiastic about the "beautiful flowers" and the view of the river. One snag is that the hotel is on a busy main road: if you want quiet, you might be advised to forego the view and ask for a room at the back. *(David and Rosemary Philips, Donald Sanders, Irina Ohl, and others)*

Open 1 Apr–15 Oct.
Rooms 21 double, 1 single – 18 with bath, 2 with shower, all with telephone.
Facilities Salon, bar, restaurant, terrace for meals overlooking the river Dordogne. Garden. Beach and bathing nearby; also boating, canoeing, fishing, tennis and riding. English spoken.
Location 10 km W of Sarlat and 10 km from St-Cyprien. Free garage outside.
Credit cards None accepted.
Terms Rooms with breakfast: single 130 frs, double 244 frs; dinner, B&B 205–222 frs per person; full board 242–265 frs per person. Set meals 78, 110 and 160 frs.

LES BÉZARDS 45290 Loiret   Map 10

Auberge des Templiers   *Tel* (38) 31.80.01
Boismorand   *Telex* 780998 TEMPLIE

On the N7 about one and a half hours' drive south from Paris, this is an old posting house, gastronomically distinguished, very expensive and luxuriously renovated, with some 20 rooms and apartments scattered in the grounds in new buildings. There is an outdoor swimming pool, tennis courts, and attractive gardens. "The inn has a lovely welcoming interior, with an open fire and lots of big wooden beams," writes a visitor this year. "Our bedroom, in one of the modern bungalows, was large, comfortable and prettily decorated, with bowls of fresh flowers, real live plants, and pictures – it felt more like a home than a hotel. Everything we ate was excellent (two *Michelin* rosettes, three *Gault Millau toques*); service was deft and never obtrusive." Others concur, though some have found the staff a little off-hand. The cuisine is both classic and *nouvelle*. A terrace/dining room allows all tables a view of the garden. *(Stephan and Kate Murray-Sykes, David Wooff, and others)*

Open Mid-Feb to mid-Jan.
Rooms 6 suites, 22 double – 26 with bath, 2 with shower, all with telephone and TV; baby-sitters available. Some ground-floor rooms.
Facilities Salons, bars, smoking room, 2 restaurants; conference facilities. Garden with heated swimming pool and 2 tennis courts. English spoken.
Location 138 km S of Paris – take N7 towards Nevers (69 km E of Orange).
Credit cards All major cards accepted.
Terms Rooms: single occupancy 350–550 frs, double 750–850 frs, suite 950–1,800 frs. Breakfast 45 frs; set lunch/dinner (excluding service) 250–380 frs; full alc 400 frs.

BIOT 06410 Alpes-Maritimes   Map 11

Café des Arcades   *Tel* (93) 65.01.04
16 place des Arcades

The hill village of Biot lies inland from Antibes, with the superb Fernand Léger museum just down the road. "Here's a real oddity for you. This 'café' is in part just that: a noisy place in a small arcaded square where the villagers drink, chatter and play chess. But it's also rather more: a 15th-century inn of great character, *and* believe it or not, an art gallery. This is due to its *patron*, André Brothier, an engaging Bohemian type, who lines the inn's dining room with Braques and Miros and is a friend of Vasarely and his son Yvaral. The bedrooms are olde worlde, but the plumbing, happily, is not. The inn has a hyper-relaxed ambience which may not suit all tastes, and it can be trying to have loud pop music resounding from the café while you eat your tian provençal or tripes niçoise. Nonetheless, at least for a day or two's visit, this eccentric and endearing place is fun" (*J A*). That report, four years ago, is still entirely accurate, according to very recent visitors: "High spot of our holiday, proprietor charming, food excellent" (*J A G Stonehouse*). "Lively place, lovely bohemian atmosphere, pretty bedrooms." (*A A, L H, I M*)

Open All year. Restaurant closed Nov.
Rooms 10 double – 5 with bath, 5 with shower, all with internal telephone.
Facilities Bar/TV room, restaurant, art gallery. Beaches 3 km. Golf 1 km.
Location 8 km from Antibes.
Credit card Amex.
Terms Rooms 115–250 frs. Breakfast 19 frs; set lunch/dinner 100 frs; full alc 140 frs. Reduced rates and special meals for children.

BOUILLAND 21420 Côte d'Or   Map 10

Hostellerie du Vieux Moulin   *Tel* (80) 21.51.16

Bouilland, "a small village in the middle of nowhere, not easy to find", lies amid the little hills and valleys of the so-called "Swiss Burgundy", just west of the famous golden slope of the great vineyards and 10 miles due north of Beaune. Here, beside a rapid mill-stream, the *Vieux Moulin* is a small, elegant restaurant-with-rooms, with a big garden. You can dine out under the trees in summer. "Nice decor, and impressive attention to detail by the staff. The rooms were a little small, but comfortable and, again, elegant. We had an excellent, rather *nouvelle*, meal." Two red *toques* in *Gault Millau* for such dishes as fried frogs' legs with leaks. (*John Newnham*) Another reader reported, "the best breakfast we had in France".

Open Closed 15 Dec–22 Jan; closed Wed. Restaurant closed Thur midday.
Rooms 8 double – 7 with bath; all rooms in annexe 5 metres from restaurant.
Facilities 1 salon in hotel and 1 in restaurant. Garden with river; fishing. English spoken.
Location On edge of village, 16 km N of Beaune.
Credit cards Amex, Diners, Visa.
Terms Rooms: single 170 frs, double 220 frs. Breakfast 30 frs; set lunch/dinner 130, 190 and 250 frs; full alc 280 frs. Special meals available for children.

LA BOUILLE 76530 Seine-Maritime   Map 8

Hôtel-Restaurant le Saint-Pierre   *Tel* (35) 23.80.10

"La Bouille is a picturesque Norman hamlet on the banks of the Seine south-west of Rouen. The *Saint-Pierre*, really a restaurant-with-rooms, is next to the tow-path, with a terrace where you can eat or drink outside in summer. A ferry will take you across to the Roumare forest, delightful for walking. The hotel's owners, the Huets, are charming and have spent a lot of time in England. You enter the hotel through the bar which is very colourful, open to the public and very French in atmosphere. Our bedroom, overlooking the river, was a fair size, with oriental touches in the decor and rather odd lighting. It was quiet, but some rooms on the road side might be less so. The dining room, light and airy, had a great ambience of pure enjoyment of food and wine. The cooking, a mix of traditional and *nouvelle*, was excellent (rosette in *Michelin*), though not cheap. On the 165-franc menu [1985] we especially enjoyed the salade d'huîtres et St-Jacques, and panaché de ris de veau et rognons de veau. The place was a real breath of France." *(P H; also Else Robbins Landon, Dr F P Adler)*

Open All year except Tue evening and Wed 1 Nov–31 Mar.
Rooms 7 double – 4 with bath, 3 with shower, all with telephone, 1 with TV.
Facilities Bar, restaurant; garden terrace. English spoken.
Location 20 km SW of Rouen; take "Maison Brulée" turning off Paris/Le Havre *autoroute*.
Restriction Not suitable for &.
Credit cards Amex, Diners, Visa.
Terms Rooms: single occupancy 165–190 frs, double 190–220 frs; dinner, B&B: 150–250 frs per person. Breakfast 26.80 frs; set meals 100–174 frs; full alc 250 frs. Winter weekend breaks. Special meals for children.

BOURBON-L'ARCHAMBAULT 03160 Allier　　　　　　　Map 10

Hôtel des Thermes　　　　　　　　　　　　　　　　*Tel* (70) 67.00.15

A spruce and suitably sedate little hotel in one of the many small spa towns of the northern fringe of Auvergne: Talleyrand used to visit the spa for his rheumatism. The *Thermes* has a garden-terrace facing the cure centre, also a private lake for fishing. Its *patron-chef*, M. Barichard, tells us that his Guide entry has brought him many British visitors. He has won the First Prize for Welcome and Friendliness for the Allier *département*, as well as a *Michelin* rosette for the kind of distinctly orthodox dishes (eg tournedos Rossini) that *curistes* probably prefer. An American reader says: "The hotel has everything that personally fulfills my dream place. It is in a small pretty town in a beautiful area, off the regular tourist beat. I had a spotless room looking over a flowery patio, with a large tiled modern bathroom and good reading light. Dinner was perfect (pâté, sole, lamb, cheese, sweet) and very good value." *(R N Emmich)*

Open 22 Mar–31 Oct.
Rooms 1 suite, 16 double, 5 single – 10 with bath, 6 with shower, all with telephone; 4 rooms in annexe.
Facilities Salon with TV, dining room. Garden with terrace. Private lake; fishing.
Location 100 metres from town centre. Town is 23 km W of Moulins. Garage.
Credit cards None accepted.
Terms Rooms: single 98 frs, double 188–205 frs; full board 215–265 frs per person. Breakfast 17 frs; set meals 63, 110, 134, 240 frs.

BOURDEILLES 24310 Dordogne　　　　　　　　　　　Map 10

Hostellerie Les Griffons　　　　　　　　　　　　*Tel* (53) 75.05.61

In the heart of the Périgord Noir, one of the most historic and seductive regions of south-west France, Bourdeilles is a medieval village on the river Dronne, crowned by a feudal castle on a rocky hill; the townlet of

Brantôme, even lovelier but touristy, is only 10 kilometres away. The *Griffons*, a 16th-century building recently converted, is in the village by the river, and is recommended as "quiet, with bedrooms full of character – ours was delightful. We were given a warm welcome. There is a terrace and a rustic dining room with excellent food, such as tender veal with morilles." Another recent report: "Wonderful. Our spacious room had a large comfortable bed, beamed ceiling, a modern bathroom, while the view was postcard material. There is a lovely lounge/reading room. We had excellent salmon terrine and veal in wine sauce. Friendly and attentive owners." *(Joan A Powell, Sheila Stober and Robert Letovsky).* Another reader was less lucky with his bed – lumpy and "speared by bulging springs".

Open 1 May–30 Oct.
Rooms 10 double – all with bath.
Facilities 2 salons, bar, tea room, 2 dining rooms; 2 terraces. River fishing, swimming pool and riding nearby. English spoken.
Location Bourdeilles is 10 km SW of Brantôme and 25 km NW of Périgueux.
Credit cards Access, Diners, Visa.
Terms Rooms: single occupancy 220 frs, double 220–250 frs. Breakfast 26 frs; set lunch/dinner 90–190 frs; full alc 150 frs. Reduced rates and special meals for children.

LE BOURGET-DU-LAC 73370 Savoie   Map 10

Hôtel Ombremont   *Tel* (79) 25.00.23
                                                Telex 9808320 CHAMBERY

Le Bourget is a small resort at the southern end of the lovely Lac du Bourget, with a pleasant beach and a fine Carolingian church. The *Ombremont*, a handsome gabled hotel in country-house style, stands secluded in its big garden by the lake, just north of the town. The young owners, the Carlos, and their ambitious young chef have won a rosette from *Michelin*, a *toque* from *Gault Millau* and much praise from our own readers. "We were made most welcome and were impressed with this elegantly furnished and very peaceful hotel. The setting is lovely, with magnificent views across the lake to the mountains. The dining room has large windows opening on to a terrace for meals in warm weather, and seldom have we taken dinner in such a delightful situation. The food was delicious and service attentive, though wines were pricey." Visitors this year and last have confirmed this ("dining room really lovely"), though one reader was shocked by the piped music and warns that the climb up from the swimming pool to the hotel is very steep. *(Kate Plowden, Rosamund Hebdon, James Joll)*

Open 29 Apr–13 Oct. Restaurant closed Mon midday; also Sat midday except July and Aug.
Rooms 16 double – all with bath, radio and telephone.
Facilities 2 salons, bar, restaurant, terrace. Garden leading down to lake, with swimming pool. English spoken.
Location 2 km N of Le Bourget on N504.
Credit cards All major cards accepted.
Terms [1985 rates] rooms: single 385 frs, double 560 frs. Breakfast 38 frs; set lunch/dinner 145–250 frs.

BRANTÔME 24310 Dordogne   Map 10

Le Chatenet   *Tel* (53) 05.81.08

Brantôme is a beautiful, but consequently very trippery, little town on the river Dronne, north of Périgueux. Just outside it, away from the crowds and by the river, stands this small 17th-century manor house, recently converted by its owners to take in guests for bed and breakfast: for other meals, they have no less than three rosetted *Michelin* restaurants close by (see Champagnac-de-Belair). "A lovely old house with luxurious and comfortable bedrooms in a delightful setting", says a reader this year, himself a leading hotelier in England. "We seek to share a calm family life with our guests," say the manor's owners, the Laxtons. *(Osmond Edwards)*

Open All year.
Rooms 1 suite, 7 double – all with bath, shower, and tea-making facilities; telephones should be installed in 1986.
Facilities Lounge with bar, 10-acre grounds with heated swimming pool. English spoken. Fishing and tennis nearby.
Location ½ m W of Brantôme, off D78.
Credit cards None accepted.
Terms B&B: 250–550 frs. (No restaurant.)

BRICQUEBEC 50260 Manche   Map 8

Hôtel du Vieux Château   *Tel* (33) 52.24.49
4 cours du Château

A "charming little hotel" in a small Norman town near Cherbourg, recommended as a useful overnight stop for ferry-goers. It is housed in an old stone medieval building within the bailey of the 14th-century castle, once owned by the Dukes of Suffolk (Queen Victoria is said to have stayed here in 1857). It has been tastefully restored, and is today run by a pleasant Australian couple. "Food and service good" (rognons au cidre, that sort of thing), "large dining room, bedrooms clean and nice, and a big lawn. All beautifully quiet." Some bedrooms (notably Queen Victoria's) are said to be much better value than others, which can be poky. *(Evlyn Ritchie, Kenneth Garside, P F)*

Open All year except 20 Dec–20 Jan.
Rooms 2 suites, 20 double, 2 single – 16 with bath, 4 with shower, all with telephone; 2 ground-floor rooms.
Facilities Ramps. Sitting room, bar/TV room, 2 dining rooms. Gardens. Sea 15 km. English spoken.
Location 22 km S of Cherbourg. Hotel is within castle ramparts. Parking.
Credit cards Access, Visa.
Terms Rooms: single 95 frs, double 140–200 frs; half-board 110–175 frs per person; full board 150–198 frs per person. Breakfast 16 frs; full alc 150 frs. Reduced rates and special meals for children.

If you have difficulty in finding hotels because the location details given in the Guide are inadequate, please help us to improve directions next year.

BRINON-SUR-SAULDRE 18450 Cher Map 10

Auberge La Solognote *Tel* (48) 58.50.29
Grande Rue

Brinon is an unremarkable village by a river south-east of Orléans, on the edge of the strange haunting forests and marshlands of the Sologne. It is close to Alain-Fournier country – to his birthplace at La Chapelle-d'Angillon and the nearby château of Loroy that helped to inspire his novel *Le Grand Meaulnes*. A visitor this year endorses this earlier entry: "The inn is in the village, but quiet (it's a *Relais du Silence*), and all bedrooms face the little patio-garden at the back where drinks and breakfasts are served when it's fine. This is a typical unpretentious country *auberge*, a bit cramped, with not much of a lounge, but welcoming. Our bedroom was pretty, in semi-rustic style, and quite inexpensive. Andrée and Dominique Girard own and run the place: his excellent cuisine (*Michelin* rosette, *Gault Millau toque*) tends to the *nouvelle*, but not wildly so: it is fastidiously prepared and presented, and we much enjoyed the home-smoked salmon with pancakes and sour cream, lotte en croûte with fennel, panaché de poissons en bouillabaisse. Mediocre local cheeses, but interesting sweets and fairly priced local Loire wines. Excellent breakfasts. The dining room is attractive and spacious, with tiled floor and rustic touches. All in all, a good place for a night or two's halt. (*J A; also Harry Robinson*)

Open All year except Feb, 21 May–5 Jun and 11–26 Oct; also closed Tue evening and Wed.
Rooms 2 suites, 7 double, 1 single – all with bath and telephone; 6 rooms in annexe; 2 ground-floor rooms.
Facilities Salon, bar, dining room. Garden and terrace. Tennis 200 metres, bathing and sailing at nearby lake. English spoken. &.
Location 57 km SE of Orléans.
Credit card Amex.
Terms Double rooms with breakfast 203–250 frs; with half-board 500–600 frs. Set meals 110, 135, 175 and 235 frs.

CABRERETS 46330 Lot Map 10

La Pescalerie *Tel* (65) 31.22.55

A favourite with readers ("very superior" says one this year), *La Pescalerie* stands alone at the foot of a rocky hill, a little outside the village. It is an 18th-century Quercy country house, restored and decorated in exquisite taste. A large semi-formal garden stretches away to the wooded banks of the Célé where jays call and kingfishers arrow through the shadows. There is no lift, and the lovely wood staircase is rather steep for the less youthful – "but", says one devotee, "the luxury of the bedrooms was almost sinful, the elegance of breakfast on the terrace under a huge magnolia tree, with oleanders in bloom, was unforgettable. A quiet and very special hotel, run with true charm and kindness." The chef, René Sarre, formerly with Michel Guérard, provides regional cuisine using vegetables from the garden. "The food is wonderful, the management charming, the ambience marvellous, calm and peaceful." "Food quite ambitious and its presentation delightful.

One night's five-course dinner [175 frs, 1985] was: salade verte aux haricots verts et foie gras, thon braisé au basilic, poulet grillé aux cèpes, fromages, tarte aux poires sauce fraise – all light as a feather." A report this year: "Breakfast on the terrace, attended by a friendly cat, was a joy – fresh orange juice, honey-in-the-comb. The expensive cooking clearly uses the best-quality raw materials, but is rather unimaginative." Other possible flaws in this paradise are Dunlopillo mattresses and American tour parties. (*Mrs R B Richards, Mrs S M Gillotti, and others*)

Open 1 Apr–1 Nov.
Rooms 10 double – all with bath, telephone and colour TV.
Facilities Lounge with TV, bar, dining room. Breakfast terrace; garden running to river with swimming, fishing, boating. English spoken.
Location 35 km from Cahors, 2.5 km after Cabrerets on D19 to Figeac.
Credit cards All major cards accepted.
Terms [1985 rates] rooms 300–450 frs. Breakfast 40 frs; set lunch/dinner 175–190 frs.

CABRIS 06530 Alpes-Maritimes   Map 11

Hôtel l'Horizon   *Tel* (93) 60.51.69

Camus and Sartre used to stay at this modest country hotel, and so did Leonard Bernstein (he even composed in its garden), while Gide and Marcuse are among many other luminaries who have lived in villas in the famous hill-village of Cabris, near Grasse. There have been a few nigglers this year: one thought the food good but the lounge too small; another found the plumbing noisy and the service rushed; a third felt the bedrooms were too cramped. But at least one Guide reader has been bitten by the muse here: "Two-star *routier* in a 17-star location. Cabris has red roofs tumbling down the hillside among patches of terraced garden, fig trees and geraniums. The hotel and its terrace are on the street, with fabulous views over layers of fading hills and mountains interspersed with gleaming lakes, smoke from distant bonfires, evening mist, black silhouettes of cypresses and a tiny corner of sea. Our room, small but nice, was the last one left, and had no view save our neighbours' feet as they walked up the drive. The building is well modernised, covered in creepers; inside, a tendency towards glass and wrought iron but nothing very bad. French windows lead on to a prettily overgrown walled garden. There is a smallish bar, with lots of those fascinating French magazines full of stories on incest, Siamese twins and pictures of princesses sunbathing. Dinner was great. The guests were 30 middle-aged, middle-class intellectuals from England, France and Germany, happily discussing politics, the landscape and which soup it would be. We enjoyed our tasty lentil soup, and chicken sort of provençale with squiggly noodles. A grand old Englishman in the corner, who looked as if he ought to be a Nobel prize-winner, was always served first. M. Roustan, the owner, was courteous and allowed us to leave our revolting baggage in the hall. Final opinion? – very, very good, and good value." (*L Y; also Geoffrey Sharp, J A G Stonehouse, L H, J A*)

Open 1 Mar–15 Oct. Restaurant closed Wed evening.
Rooms 18 double – 4 with bath, 8 with shower, all with telephone, some with balcony.

Facilities Lounge/bar with TV, restaurant, functions room. Garden with tables and chairs. Swimming, tennis and riding nearby. English spoken.
Location On edge of village 5 km W of Grasse. Parking.
Restriction Not suitable for &.
Credit cards Amex, Diners.
Terms B&B: single 130 frs, double 150–260 frs; half-board: single 200 frs, double 300–400 frs; full board: single 250 frs, double 400–500 frs. Set lunch/dinner 70 frs.

LA CADIÈRE-D'AZUR 83740 Var   Map 11

Hostellerie Bérard   *Tel* (94) 29.31.43 or 29.34.98
Rue Gabriel Péri   *Telex* 400509

Though only nine kilometres from the hectic coast at Bandol, La Cadière is a still-unspoilt hill village. In its main street, perched above the valley, stands this 19th-century *auberge* of real character, with white vaulted ceilings and re-tiled floors, run most sympathetically by René and Danielle Bérard. "This home-from-home is a delight; food is out of this world," says one regular visitor this year, who previously wrote, "A magic hotel and what fun! Madame is superb as the host and 'front man', Monsieur is the cook and obviously loves it." The hotel is snug and spruce, but not trying to be 'fashionable'. Attractive swimming pool, and modern bedrooms – some are in an annexe converted from an old monastery. M. Bérard provides real Provençal cooking, such as bourride. You can take lunch on the terrace, gazing over the valley; at night the dining room is prettily lit with wicker lanterns, and suffused with the aroma of the log fire used for spit roasts" (*C Portway*). Most readers take the Portway line, but one had a different and more jaundiced view: not a bad hotel certainly, but far from nirvana – very slow service, food a bit hit and miss, housekeeping erratic. (*Dr J Steinert, Dr and Mrs P H Tattersall*)

Open All year except Nov.
Rooms 3 suites, 37 double – 32 with bath, 8 with shower, all with telephone and TV; 25 rooms in annexe. Some ground-floor rooms.
Facilities Salon/bar, garden bar, dining room, conference room; terrace. Small garden with heated swimming pool and swings. Tennis and riding nearby. Sandy/rocky beaches 6 km. English spoken.
Location 9 km N of Bandol, just off Marseilles – Toulon *autoroute* (exit St-Cyr/Bandol). Village has one-way system; follow signs for "Centre Ville". Hotel is on main road. Garage parking.
Credit cards Amex, Visa.
Terms Rooms: single 181.50–209 frs, double 242–360.80 frs. Breakfast 30 frs; set lunch/dinner 138, 187 and 264 frs; full alc 250 frs. Reduced rates and special meals for children.

CAGNES-SUR-MER 06800 Alpes-Maritimes   Map 11

Le Cagnard   *Tel* (93) 20.73.22
Rue du Pontis-Long, Haut-de-Cagnes

The sizeable town of Cagnes-sur-Mer is divided, like Caesar's Gaul, into three parts: the ugly sprawling resort of Cros-de-Cagnes; just inland, Cagnes-Ville, unremarkable save for the inspiring Renoir museum in its outskirts; and, higher up, Haut-de-Cagnes, one of the region's most sophisticated hill villages (fascinating museum in the château). Here *Le Cagnard*, a well-known and very *soigné* little hotel, has been artfully converted out of some 13th-century houses by the ramparts and virtually clings to the side of a cliff. "An oasis of medieval tranquillity", "highly romantic", "splendid views of the sea", are some comments, though one visitor found the setting "a trifle claustrophobic". Rooms vary in size and comfort – some are small suites. (Warning: the hotel is accessible only by a narrow tortuous alley, impassable to large cars.)

Some readers in the past felt that the cuisine did not quite match up to its high prices. But this year's reports are less equivocal: "Cuisine and service both delightful", says one, while experienced regular visitors to the *Cagnard* write, "The food has improved and why it does not rate a *Michelin* star we can't understand" (indeed, *Gault Millau* awards a red *toque*, for example, for gâteau d'aubergines et d'artichauts au foie gras de canard). You eat either on the terrace, with stunning views, or in a graceful candlelit room, former guardroom of the château. Very trendy clientele in high season. *(Pat and Jeremy Temple, Douglas and Mary Coleman, and others)*

Open All year except 1–15 Nov. Restaurant closed 1 Nov–15 Dec and Thur midday.
Rooms 9 suites, 8 double, 2 single – 18 with bath, 1 with shower; all with telephone and baby-listening; 12 with TV; 8 rooms in annexe.
Facilities Lift; bar, restaurant, crêperie, terrace. Night club, disco. Small garden. Sea and rocky beach 3 km, sandy beach 10 km. English spoken.
Location On the ramparts, 2 minutes from château. Parking.
Restriction Not suitable for &.
Terms [1985 rates] B&B: single 265 frs, double 440 frs; suites 500–800 frs. Set lunch/dinner 250 frs.

CALVI Haute-Corse, Corsica   Map 11

Hôtel Caravelle   *Tel* (95) 65.01.21
Calvi 20260

Today a popular summer resort, the old fortified port of Calvi has a citadel on a headland built by the Genoese in the 15th century. We were glad to hear about the *Caravelle* – "an unpretentious *Logis de France*, away from the centre of Calvi, almost on the beach. The rooms are comfortable, grouped (like linked bungalows) around a small lawn; each has its own patio with deckchairs provided. Breakfast is taken in an attractive paved area under shady trees. The hotel's main joy, apart from its air of pleasant unhurried efficiency, was the evening meal: every night was an adventure with local foods, delightfully presented in a cool quiet dining room. Attentive service, interesting wines. One snag – mosquitoes were active in our room," *(Kathleen Holmes)*. Recent visitors have not altogether shared Kathleen Holmes's enjoyment of the evening meal – some courses have disappointed and there have been complaints of meagre helpings and rushed service.

Open 1 May–30 Sept.
Rooms 20 double – 16 with bath, all with telephone; all in units in grounds, each with patio.
Facilities Salon, TV room. Dining room, garden. Sandy beach nearby with bathing and fishing. English spoken.

Location 400 m from centre of town, off N197, by the beach. Parking.
Credit cards None accepted.
Terms Rooms 135–184 frs; dinner, B&B 154–192 frs per person; full board 252–262 frs per person.

Hotel Résidence "Les Aloës" *Tel* (95) 65.01.46
Quartier Donatéo, Calvi 20250

"One of the most spectacular settings in the entire Med.", says a visitor this year to Calvi (see also above) – "a big sandy bay, guarded by an old Venetian citadel, with a backdrop of 8,000-ft mountains, some still snow-capped. An ideal spot for viewing all this is the peace and cool of *Les Aloës*, a small unpretentious modern hotel above the town and away from the noise. Small but comfortable rooms with fine views of the bay, or quieter ones at the rear facing the *maquis*. Breakfast only (delicious croissants), but service in the cool gardens is good and there is a fine choice of restaurants down by the port." *(D H Bennet; also W H Bruton)*

Open May–Oct.
Rooms 6 suites, 26 double, 1 single – 6 with bath, 21 with shower, all with telephone, 6 with tea-making facilities. 6 rooms in annexe.
Facilities Bar, salon, TV room, library; terraces and garden. Fine sandy beach 5 km, with water sports and fishing; golf, tennis, riding nearby. English spoken.
Location 1 km SW of town centre: take route d'Ajaccio or route de l'Usine Electrique; hotel is signposted. Parking.
Restriction Not suitable for &.
Credit cards Amex, Diners, Visa.
Terms B&B: single 210 frs, double 275 frs. 10% off-season reduction in May, June and September, on presentation of *GHG*. (No restaurant.)

CAMBO-LES-BAINS 64250 Pyrénées-Atlantiques Map 10

Hôtel Errobia *Tel* (59) 29.71.26
Avenue Chanteclerc

Cambo is a pleasant little spa town in a valley amid the lush green knobbly hills of the Basque hinterland; Edmond Rostand, author of *Cyrano de Bergerac*, lived here, and his villa, Arnaga, is now a museum devoted to him. Another Basque villa, the *Errobia*, is recommended as "an old house in a big untidy garden, very peaceful (and quite hard to find). An informal country house atmosphere – pretty patchwork quilts on the beds, big balconies to some rooms, ideal for breakfast on a summer morning. The hotel appeared to be run entirely by one girl who was porter, receptionist, chambermaid, telephonist (maybe breakfast cook too) and carried out all her tasks with great charm and friendly sweetness." No restaurant: but the *Bellevue* close by has a red "R" in *Michelin* for good value, and there are rosetted places in some villages nearby. *(Mrs R B Richards)*

Open Easter, and May–Oct.
Rooms 12 – most with bath and telephone, some rooms with balcony.
Facilities Reception, garden.
Location In a side street off the D932 main road to Bayonne; Cambo is 19 km SE of Bayonne. Parking.
Credit card Visa.
Terms [1985 rates] rooms: single 95 frs, double 190 frs. Breakfast 16 frs. (No restaurant.)

CARCASSONNE 11000 Aude   Map 10

Domaine d'Auriac   *Tel* (68) 25.72.22
Route St-Hilaire   *Telex* 500 385

Set peacefully amid its own woods and vineyards, this imposing old
creeper-covered mansion lies three kilometres out of hectic, dusty
modern Carcassonne; only a new motorway (out of earshot) separates it
from the vast medieval hilltop fortress, magically floodlit at night.
"Approached down impressive driveway. Beautiful house, well furnished. Our bedrooms were smallish but attractive, with balcony and
view. Swimming pool and tennis court approached down lengthy flight
of steps. Good restaurant: à la carte best. Superb local wines. All staff
made us feel welcome" *(Richard and Susan Faulkner)*. Innovative cuisine
(eg monkfish in vermouth) wins *Gault Millau* red *toque*. A blazing fire in
winter in the dining room's huge chimney-piece.

Open All year except last 2 weeks of Jan. Closed Sun and Mon until 2 pm.
Rooms 23 double – all with bath, telephone, radio, TV, tea-making facilities and
baby-listening.
Facilities Lift. Salons, restaurant, conference facilities. Garden with unheated
swimming pool and tennis court.
Location Leave *autoroute* (A61) by Carcassonne Ouest exit. 2.5 km SE of town by
D118 and D104. Parking.
Credit cards All major cards accepted.
Terms Rooms 450–900 frs. Breakfast 35 frs; set meals 170–200 frs; full alc 250 frs.
Special meals for children.

CASSIS 13260 Bouches-du-Rhône   Map 11

Hôtel Roches Blanches   *Tel* (42) 01.09.30
Route de Port-Miou

Despite trippery overcrowding and recent ugly overbuilding, the old
fishing port of Cassis has still kept much of the picturesque charm that
drew Dufy and Matisse to paint here. It is a less garish St-Tropez, with
the plus of a smart modern casino, very lively, full of Marseillais who are
great gamblers. "Comfortable, dignified, with friendly and efficient
service", runs the latest report on the *Roches Blanches*, which stands a
mile west of the town, alone on a rocky, pinewoody promontory, facing
out across the bay. An earlier account: "The Dellacase family are civilised
hosts and attract an equally civilised kind of guest. Their hotel is a
handsome creeper-covered villa with a big garden that rambles down to
the rocky shore (no sand). Here they have built a spacious stone terrace
that is good for sun-bathing – and the sea-bathing too is good if you
don't mind deep water. Our room was comfortable, with a balcony
facing the sea, but its utility modern furnishing was hardly in keeping
with the hotel's otherwise graceful tone." One reader found car parking
at the hotel "a jigsaw puzzle" as the cars were packed in too tightly. *(J A,
John Newnham)* Note: the hotel was damaged by flood in the 1984/85
winter and has been extensively redecorated. More reports welcome.

Open Feb–Nov.
Rooms 36 double – 28 with bath and WC, 8 with shower (2 with WC), all with
telephone and baby-listening; 15 with colour TV. (10 rooms suitable for &.)

Facilities Salon with TV, salon, bar, restaurant, terraces, solarium. Large garden leading to rocky shore with sun-bathing terrace; children's play area, *boules*. English spoken.
Location 1.5 km W of Cassis. Parking (difficult when hotel is full).
Credit cards Amex, Diner, Visa.
Terms [1985 rates] rooms 150–350 frs. Half-board 255–600 frs. Breakfast 25 frs; full alc 150 frs.

CENTURI PORT 20238 Corsica   Map 11

Le Vieux Moulin   *Tel* (95) 35.60.15

Centuri is a charming little fishing village near the northern tip of Cap Corse, one of the most scenic parts of the island. The *Vieux Moulin*, full of character, has a pleasant terrace with views of the village. "A lovely, quiet, friendly hotel. The main house is decorated with guns, antiques etc. Bedrooms vary in size and type: those in bungalows by the terrace are fairly plain but very comfortable. The traditional Corsican/French food is well cooked and good value, and the local wines are cheap and very drinkable, especially the red. The stylish and somewhat Gauguinesque paintings on the walls are by the *patron*." *(Roland Gant, also L H)*

Open 15 Mar–31 Oct.
Rooms 14 – all with shower.
Facilities Restaurant. Garden with tennis court.
Location Centuri Port is 59 km NW of Bastia.
Credit cards Amex, Diners, Visa.
Terms [1985 rates] rooms 110–145 frs; full board 220–250 frs per person. Breakfast 16 frs; set meals 85–155 frs.

CÉRET 66400 Pyrénées-Orientales   Map 10

La Terrasse au Soleil   *Tel* (68) 87.01.94
Route de Fontfrède

"A delightful place", runs a 1985 report on this little hotel in the wooded foothills of the Pyrenees. It is perched above the small town of Céret, and you can sit on the terrace and view the mountains on one side and the Mediterranean far away on the other. In summer the house is a tranquil retreat from the hordes on the coast. It also has a splendid pool. Architecturally, it shows its Catalan heritage with a strong Spanish influence in the design of the bar and lounge. Rooms are comfortable and also have fine views; since last year six new rooms have been added in an annexe. "The Leveillé-Nizerolle family who own and run the place are charming, and their new chef gave us an excellent dinner" *(Gault Millau toque). (R A Dubery, John Bethell)*

Open 1 Apr–1 Nov.
Rooms 18 double – 12 with bath, 6 with shower, all with telephone; some with terrace. 3 ground-floor rooms; 6 rooms in annexe.
Facilities 2 lounges (1 with TV), bar, dining room. Garden with swimming pool. Tennis in Céret, sea 25 km. English spoken.
Location 7 km N of Spanish border. 2 km SW of Céret (which is 27 km SW of Perpignan). Leave *autoroute* B9 at Le Boulou exit, direction Céret and proceed for 7 km.

Restriction No children under 7.
Credit card Visa.
Terms Rooms 280 frs; dinner, B&B (4 days min.): single occupancy 400 frs, double 615 frs. Breakfast 30 frs; full alc 140–160 frs. Special meals for children on request.

CHAGNY 71150 Saône-et-Loire   Map 10

Hôtel Lameloise   *Tel* (85) 87.08.85
36 place d'Armes

The little town of Chagny lies amid woods and vineyards in the heart of Burgundy, between Beaune and Chalon-sur-Saône. The *Lameloise*, in its main street, is an elegantly converted 15th-century mansion, renowned for its cuisine (three *Michelin* rosettes and *Gault Millau* red *toques*). Again in 1984/85 readers have spoken of it as "the best cuisine we've had in France", "the best breakfast ever in France", and so on. Earlier comments: "elegant rooms, with antiques, beamed ceilings and fireplaces"; "very comfortable, with well-equipped rooms and bathrooms, fresh flowers"; "a quietly luxurious atmosphere, attentive and courteous service". Another visitor, always fastidious, thought the rooms less than totally quiet (railway and main road are nearby), but joined in the praise for the restaurant: "The waiters were friendly, and the top *sommelier* of France is a charming and modest man." Two veteran travellers this year confessed to a slight disappointment, both with the welcome, the room and the food, and felt that "two French families with badly behaved children in jeans and jerseys" were not quite the Top People clientele that our 1985 entry had led us to expect. *(Hadley and Heather Buck, Ralph Sheldon, Mrs M D Prodgers, and others)*

Open All year except 17–25 July, 4 Dec–2 Jan, probably Tue midday and Wed.
Rooms 25 double – 23 with bath or shower, all with telephone and TV.
Facilities Salon, restaurant.
Location Central. Parking.
Credit card Visa.
Terms [1985 rates] rooms: single occupancy 200 frs, double 380 frs. Breakfast 30 frs; alc 200–250 frs (excluding wine).

CHÂLONS-SUR-MARNE 51000 Marne   Map 8

Hotel d'Angleterre and   *Tel* (26) 68.21.51
Restaurant Jacky Michel
19 place Monseigneur Tissier

Châlons is a sizeable market town on the edge of the champagne country and close to the Paris-Strasbourg motorway (fine stained glass in the Gothic cathedral and the church of Notre-Dame en Vaux). Here in the town centre stands the very traditional *Angleterre*, small but *soigné*, recommended this year by former hoteliers from Switzerland: "Excellent hotel, friendly staff, comfortable rooms, beautiful modern dining room with good food" *(Curtis and Sally Wilmot-Allistone)*. The ambitious cooking of *patron-chef* Jacky Michel wins a *Gault Millau* red *toque* for innovation (eg filet de boeuf with pears). Shady flower-terrace.

Open All year except 30 Jun–15 Jul and 20 Dec–7 Jan, hotel and restaurant closed Sun.

Rooms 18 double – 13 with bath, 1 with shower, all with telephone, most with TV. Some double-glazing; back rooms quietest.
Facilities Lounge/reading room, TV room, bar, restaurant, conference facilities; small terrace where meals are served in summer. English spoken.
Location Central, near church of Notre-Dame en Vaux. Parking.
Restriction Not suitable for &.
Credit cards All major cards accepted.
Terms Rooms 160–250 frs. Breakfast 27 frs. Set lunch/dinner 130–250 frs.

CHALON-SUR-SAÔNE 71110 Saône-et-Loire　　　Map 10

Hôtel St-Georges　　　　　　　　　　　　　　*Tel* (85) 48.27.05
32 avenue Jean-Jaurès　　　　　　　　　　　　　　*Telex* 800330

In the best French tradition, here is a three-gabled commercial hotel next to the railway station in a biggish town, splendidly refreshing the parts (ie palates) of tired businessmen that similar hotels in Britain so signally fail to reach. *Michelin* rosette, two red *Gault Millau toques* – and those verdicts are endorsed by a family of "enthusiastic eaters" who come often to Burgundy to buy their annual supply of white wine: "The hotel is clean, comfortable and inviting, the service good. Good too are the fixed menus: we especially remember the bacon salad, poached eggs in wine, chicken mousse and the local cheeses." "Enthusiastic welcome, pleasant room, superb food", adds a 1985 report. *(Gordon Thwaites, P K and J M Leaver)*

Open All year.
Rooms 48 – most with bath or shower, direct-dial telephone, TV, air-conditioning.
Facilities Lift. Salon, conference facilities, restaurant.
Location Hotel is central, near railway station; parking.
Credit cards All major cards accepted.
Terms [1985 rates] rooms: single 170 frs, double 275 frs. Breakfast 27 frs; set lunch/dinner 70–200 frs.

CHAMBORD 41250 Loir-et-Cher　　　　　　　　　Map 10

Hôtel du Grand St-Michel　　　　　　　　　　*Tel* (54) 20.31.31

Directly opposite the largest and grandest of the Loire Valley châteaux (eight bedrooms overlook it). After dinner in summer you can stroll over to the *son et lumière*, and before breakfast you can drive out to see the wild boar and deer of Chambord forest feeding. This privileged setting is the hotel's chief attraction. Visitors praise its comfort, too, and this year an American reader found the hotel "enchanting" and the food "excellent". But previously there have been criticisms of food, service and ambience. It is certainly the place to stay to enjoy Chambord but not really a hotel for an extended visit. *(Mary and Mike Dettrich)*

Open All year except 15 Nov–20 Dec. Restaurant closed Mon evening and Tue 15 Oct–1 Apr (except public holidays).
Rooms 1 suite, 38 double – 21 with bath, 3 with shower, all with telephone; 1 suite on ground floor.
Facilities Salon, restaurant; conference facilities; terrace. Grounds with tennis court; horse riding nearby. English spoken.
Location Just S of Loire valley, 18 km E of Blois; opposite château. Parking.
Credit card Visa.
Terms Rooms 200–300 frs. Breakfast 20 frs; set lunch/dinner 80 frs; full alc 130 frs.

CHAMONIX 74400 Haute-Savoie   Map 10

Hôtel Albert Premier et Milan   *Tel* (50) 53.05.09
119 impasse du Montenvers   *Telex* 380779

"The best 10 days we have spent in any hotel at home or abroad. Staff young, keen and committed; room service terrific; beautifully balanced set menus." That is one of three 1984/85 reports, all favourable, backing up our earlier entry for this big chalet-type ski-hotel: "Roomy and comfortable, full of well-heeled skiers enjoying their *après-ski*. Log fire and piano in the salon; huge bedrooms, with views from their windows of the toothy white peaks all round. A large sophisticated dining room, and ambitious, interesting cooking by the son of the *patron*, Pierre Carrier; lavish helpings. The hotel is set in its own big garden (*piscine*, tennis etc.) near the middle of the resort. When fine, it's well worth taking the *téléphérique* (the world's highest, they claim) to a point just below the summit of Mont Blanc for a roof-of-the-world view." Other readers this year also praise the food. One found the set menus dull compared to the à la carte, but another liked them: "Second helpings freely offered, which more than satisfied our hungry skiers." *(Paul Barraclough, Joan Powell, J M Butterfield, J A)*

Open All year except May, Oct and Nov.
Rooms 2 suites, 31 double, 1 single – 33 with bath, 1 with shower, all with telephone, TV and mini-bar.
Facilities Lift. 2 salons, 3 dining rooms, table tennis room. Large garden with tennis court, swimming pool (heated in summer), and children's play area. Winter sports, good walking. English spoken.
Location In side road, 150 metres from station; 500 metres from town centre. Parking and garage.
Credit cards Amex, Diners, Visa.
Terms (Excluding 3 frs tax per person) B&B: single 237–277 frs, double 337–424 frs; dinner, B&B 240–330 frs per person; full board 290–380 frs per person. Set meals 120, 160, 195 and 250 frs; full alc 250 frs. Reduced rates and special meals for children.

Auberge du Bois Prin   *Tel* (50) 53.33.51
Aux Moussoux

A smaller, more elegant–also more expensive–alternative to the *Albert I* above, owned by the same Carrier and run by senior members of the family. It has a particularly attractive location outside the main hurly-burly of the town, overlooking the Chamonix valley and close to the télécabine de Brévent. "There are 11 rooms, all with bath, TV and mini-bar. Built in the style of a chalet, the front rooms have super views of Mont Blanc. Breakfast was taken on the terrace and we could happily have spent all day there. Alternatively breakfast may be taken in bedrooms. These had fresh flowers and fruit bowl renewed every day. No lunch; dinners were good but not outstanding. Wines were not expensive and a good selection for such a small hotel. Some English spoken." *(D Carswell)*

Open 19 Dec–5 May; 14 June–6 Oct. Restaurant closed for lunch.
Rooms 11 – all with bath, telephone, TV and mini-bar.

Facilities Lift. Restaurant, terrace. Winter sports nearby. English spoken.
Location At Les Moussoux, on W side of town. Parking.
Credit cards Amex, Diners, Visa.
Terms [1985 rates] B&B: single 410 frs, double 640 frs. Set dinner 115–140 frs.

CHAMPAGNAC-DE-BELAIR 24530 Dordogne Map 10

Moulin du Roc *Tel* (53) 54.80.36

In this village in northern Périgord, six kilometres north-east of the beautiful little town of Brantôme, the *Moulin* is a gracefully converted 17th-century walnut mill, in a quiet pastoral setting beside a stream. *Michelin* (two rosettes) and *Gault Millau* (two *toques)* both consider that the cuisine of the owner's wife, Solange Gardillou, is as brilliant as any in her region: her forte is variations on local dishes, eg foie gras poêlé à la ciboulette. Visitors in 1984 were charmed, and underwrite an earlier account: "Tiny hotel, small rooms, small garden, everywhere cluttered with flowers, *objets*, old walnut-mill equipment. Small sitting areas amid the museum pieces. Our room with four-poster bed, dim lights. Lots of small courses, even an extra pudding; and M. Gardillou's smiling presence. Friendly atmosphere, and tables could speak to each other without inhibition. Silver-tray breakfast: strawberries, home-made jams. View from our window of maids and waiters crossing the yard with plates and trays and chairs; rinsing a bin in the mill stream . . ." Idyllic indeed. However, readers warn that the *Moulin*, much publicised in the glossy press, is now filling up with rich international tourists – and ambience may suffer. *(Ann Carr and Martin McKeown, Ian and Francine Walsh)*

Open All year except 15 Nov–15 Dec. Restaurant probably closed Wed midday and all Tue.
Rooms 11 double – all with bath, telephone, radio and colour TV.
Facilities Salons, restaurant. Small garden. English spoken.
Location 6 km NE by D78 and D83 of Brantôme. Parking.
Credit cards All major cards accepted.
Terms [1985 rates] rooms: single occupancy 360 frs, double 420 frs. Breakfast 40 frs; set lunch/dinner 175–230 frs.

CHAMPILLON 51160 Marne Map 9

Hôtel Royal Champagne *Tel* (26) 51.11.51
Telex 830111

An 18th-century coaching-inn, smartly modernised, set on a hillside with sweeping views over the Marne valley and the famous local vineyards. The hotel consists of a grand restaurant, and superior chalet accommodation in the grounds, each room having its own veranda and view. Readers are still mainly enthusiastic: "a balcony with a glorious view, attractive bedroom decor with fabric-covered walls, delicious food (eg warm oysters with champagne, and foie gras with grapes), but service at dinner slightly amateurish"; "lovely views, staff wonderfully friendly and attentive, huge bathroom, excellent breakfast". The cuisine has won a *Michelin* rosette, and one visitor speaks with awe of his *menu de Champagne* where each course has been created to be enhanced by the champagne with which it is served. Another reader calls the hotel "casual and formal all rolled into one, which only the French can achieve with perfection". But one critic thinks that "the mock-baronial decor does not lend atmosphere to delicate cuisine". Some front rooms may be a little noisy until traffic subsides. Advance booking essential. (*Kate and Steve Murray-Sykes, Mrs Howard L Miller, Gillian Seel, and others*)

Open All year.
Rooms 2 suites, 16 double – 16 with bath, 2 with shower, all with telephone, radio and private veranda, 3 with TV; all rooms in bungalows.
Facilities Salon, TV room, bar, restaurant; conference/functions facilities. Park and garden. Tennis, riding in the forest, swimming pool and golf in vicinity. English spoken. ♿ (ramps).
Location On N51, 7 km N of Épernay on road to Rheims.
Credit cards All major cards accepted.
Terms [1985 rates] rooms 320–600 frs. Breakfast 30 frs; set lunch/dinner

---

CHANTILLY 60500 Oise   Map 8

Pavillon St-Hubert   *Tel* (4) 457.07.39
At Toutevoie, 60270 Gouvieux

Chantilly, the Ascot of France, possesses not only an elegant and fashionable racecourse but one of the finest châteaux in the Ile de France (its museum contains the 15th-century illuminated manuscript of the *Très Riches Heures du Duc de Berry*). Pleasant hours were spent this year by a visitor to the little *St-Hubert*, south-west of the town: "It is idyllically situated on the banks of the Oise, with a flower-covered façade. Having breakfast on the terrace with the river and its barges just below makes a most enjoyable start to a French holiday. Rooms are adequate, if not luxurious, service was helpful, and dinner very good (delicious frogs' legs). The hotel is *not* for the anti-canine brigade: some guests had a chair for their dogs at their tables – much to the delight of my children." (*Mrs M Lampert*)

Open All year. Restaurant closed Aug.
Rooms 19 – most with bath or shower.
Facilities Restaurant, functions facilities. Riverside terrace.
Location At Toutevoie, 6.5 km SW of Chantilly, off D909 to Beaumont.
Credit cards None accepted.
Terms [1985 rates] rooms 105–174 frs. Breakfast 28 frs; set lunch/dinner 87–105 frs. 150–300 frs; full alc 300 frs. Reduced rates and special meals for children.

CHARTRES 28000 Eure-et-Loire   Map 8

Le Grand Monarque   *Tel* (37) 21.00.72
22 place des Épars   *Telex* 760777

This large old coaching-inn, transformed into a fairly sophisticated hotel, stands on the town's main square, some 500 metres from the cathedral. It has long been praised by readers for its comfort and "quiet elegance", but this year reports (very numerous) are much more mixed, indicating faults of management. Chefs have changed frequently, which is probably why the place has this year lost its Michelin *rosette, though some of our readers are still content ("divine meal, especially the desserts"). One visitor this year had a "quiet room with lovely furnishings", another's was "clean and pretty", a third speaks appreciatively of "faded grandeur"*. While the dining-room staff are *"friendly and expert"*, room service is no more than *"absent-mindedly good"* and two visitors have detected a run-down air and bored, inefficient service. One young reader got a *"tremendous welcome"* at 4.30 am (after a wedding party), with the night porter calling her "ma cocotte" – but this is not quite enough to redeem the faults, and we badly need yet more reports. *(Sue Swift, Marie Earl, Elizabeth Hill, and others)*

Open All year.
Rooms 45 double, 2 single – 36 with bath, 7 with shower, all with direct-dial telephone and colour TV.
Facilities Lift. Salons, bar, restaurant; functions and conference facilities; courtyard. English spoken. &.
Location Central, near the cathedral; quietest rooms overlook courtyard. Garage.
Credit cards All major cards accepted.
Terms [1985 rates] rooms: single 210 frs, double 327 frs. Breakfast 27 frs; set lunch/dinner 153–227 frs. Children under 7 free; special meals.

LA CHARTRE-SUR-LE-LOIR 72340 Sarthe   Map 10

Hôtel de France   *Tel* (43) 44.40.16

A pleasant little market town between Le Mans and Tours. Just to the east is the Ronsard country, around Montoire, where the poet lived and loved and dedicated his fountain to "la belle Hélène"; also the strange hill village of Trôo where various people, including Jane and Geoffrey Grigson, dwell in cunningly modernised caves in the tufa cliffside. The *France* is an unpretentious creeper-covered hostelry on the main square. This year's visitors again enjoyed it: friendly welcome, spacious and well-lit bedrooms, and a big bright restaurant offering fairly priced local specialities – that is the general verdict, though rooms in the annexe are less pleasant than those in the main building. "Rather beset by Brits" is a comment this year from a cyclist, who adds: "Fierce Madame mellowed as we puffed in each tea-time though she plainly thought us mildly dotty." *(Mrs F E Holmes, Norman Brangham, P L Ashton, and others)*

Open All year except 15 Nov–15 Dec.
Rooms 32 double – 11 with bath, 16 with shower, all with telephone.
Facilities 2 salons, bar, restaurant; conference/functions facilities. Fishing nearby. English spoken.
Location In main square. Parking.
Credit card Visa.
Terms [1985 rates] rooms: 100–180 frs. Breakfast 15 frs; set lunch/dinner 55–160 frs.

CHÂTEAU-ARNOUX 04160 Alpes-de-Haute-Provence   Map 11

La Bonne Étape   *Tel* (92) 64.00.09
Chemin du Lac   *Telex* ESIDIGN 430605 BONETAP

Again this year reports speak highly of this "marvellous place". "The little town is in a dull part of the Durance valley, and the *auberge* stands on the main road via Grenoble into Provence, though it looks on to open fields and hills at the back. It's a 17th-century coaching-inn, transformed into a stylish and very comfortable little hotel, owned and run by the delightful Gleize family who are strongly Anglophile – father created the restaurant at the *Capital* in London, while son Jany worked at the

Connaught. They now provide some of the best cooking in Provence. We're not always sold on so-called *nouvelle cuisine*, but were fully won over to the Gleizes' gâteau de mostèle, lapereau farci, and the local speciality, Sisteron lamb, whose subtle aromatic flavour comes from its being reared on the herbs of Provençal upland pastures. Breakfasts, too, were excellent. We had an attractive bedroom in Louis XV style, with a balcony facing the hills; and we enjoyed lazing on the pretty patio beside the swimming pool." *(Hadley and Heather Buck, Kitty and Art Chester, Jean Bates.) Michelin* rosette and three red *Gault Millau toques*.

Open All year except 5 Jan–15 Feb, and last week Nov. Closed Sun evening and Mon out of season.
Rooms 18 double, 5 single – all with bath, direct-dial telephone, radio and colour TV; some with balcony.
Facilities Salons, bar, 2 dining rooms; small conference room. Air-conditioning. Garden with heated swimming pool and patio. Lake 200 metres. English spoken.
Location Near centre of town, which is 14 km S of Sisteron. Garage and parking.
Credit cards All major cards accepted.
Terms Rooms 350–600 frs. Breakfast 55 frs; set lunch/dinner 180–320 frs; full alc 250–350 frs.

CHÂTEAU-CHINON 58120 Nièvre   Map 10

Hôtel au Vieux Morvan   *Tel* (86) 85.05.01
8 place Gudin

Before he became President, François Mitterrand was *député-maire* of this little town (it even has a Mitterrand museum!) in the wooded hills of western Burgundy, where the *Vieux Morvan* is recommended for a cut-price simplicity that no Socialist could object to in France's current austerity times: "An unpretentious, old-fashioned, slightly untidy place. Our pleasant bedroom had a window looking over tumbled roofs and the Morvan hills beyond. We sat in the evening shafts of sun enjoying Kirs at half the price we had paid anywhere else. The large restaurant soon filled up. The choice on the 55-franc menu [1985] was liberal: a fine meal. So was breakfast." You can eat on an open terrace with splendid views. *(Norman Brangham)*

Open 15 Jan–31 Nov. Restaurant closed Fri.
Rooms 6 family rooms, 17 double, 1 single – 11 with shower (5 of these with WC also) – all with telephone. 2 ground-floor rooms.
Facilities Sitting room, bar with TV, dining room. Swimming 29 km; lakes 15 km and 25 km with fishing, sailing, windsurfing. &. English spoken.
Location Central. Parking.
Credit card Access.
Terms Rooms: single 56 frs, double 115 frs; dinner, B&B 110–149 frs per person; full board 160–208 frs per person. Breakfast 16.10 frs; set meals 55–90 frs.

CHÂTEAUNEUF-DU-PAPE 84230 Vaucluse   Map 11

Hostellerie Château des Fines Roches   *Tel* (90) 83.70.23

A creeper-covered neo-Gothic mansion with crenellated towers set amid its own vineyards on a hill dominating the plain north of Avignon. "Extreme comfort, antique furniture, imaginative decor, very friendly owners", runs a report this year. An earlier verdict: "Fair taste apart from the jazz, rock and Tahitian music piped in all public rooms. Lovely lounge with leather chairs. The bedrooms were of all sizes and all nice. Mosquito netting, and mosquito exterminators in the corridors. Super breakfast served on the terrace, with breathtaking view. Two dining rooms: ours was stylish but plain, with lovely modern painting. Set menus are limited, but the food was good and *different*: first class terrine and salmon, but the fruits de mer were pickled and vinegary. Wine from their own vineyards, but it's not the best C.-du-P." "We even had an electric trouser press in our rooms. Dinner probably the best fixed-price meal we had on a month's trip." *(Hadley and Heather Buck, Ian and Francine Walsh, and others.) Michelin* rosette, *Gault Millau toque* (try the huîtres chaudes à la menthe).

Open All year except Christmas–end Feb; closed Sun evening and Mon out of season. Restaurant closed Mon.
Rooms 7 double – all with bath, telephone and TV.
Facilities Salon, 2 restaurants; conference facilities, terrace. Large grounds with vineyards.
Location 3 km S of Châteauneuf (by D17) which is 18 km N of Avignon, 13 km S of Orange.
Credit cards None accepted.
Terms [1985 rates] rooms: single occupancy 280 frs, double 450 frs. Breakfast 40 frs; set lunch/dinner 170 frs.

CHÂTEAUNEUF-EN-AUXOIS 21320 Côte d'Or　　　　　Map 10

Hostellerie du Château　　　　　　　　　　　　　　*Tel* (80) 33.00.23

"Super food, nice people; drinks in front of the blazing wood fire were an experience" – so runs one recent report on Anne-Marie and Jean-Pierre Truchot's friendly and charming little rural hotel, well modernised from an old building. It has pretty patterned wallpaper, an old wooden stairway, and a beamed ceiling in the dining room. Visitors tend to feel that these qualities, plus the good Burgundian cooking, make up for the smallness of the bedrooms. The hotel, a *Relais du Silence*, stands next to the château in a picturesque medieval fortified hill-village some seven kilometres south of Pouilly. *(John and Elizabeth Hills, and others)*

Open 15 Mar–15 Nov; also Christmas. Closed Mon evening and Tue between 15 Sept and 15 June.
Rooms 11 double – 6 with bath and WC, 5 with shower but no WC; all with telephone.
Facilities Sitting room, 2 restaurants, banqueting room. Small garden with swings for children; sailing on reservoir de Panthier 3 km away, fishing in the Burgundy canal. A little English spoken.
Location 7 km from Pouilly-en-Auxois. *Note:* Although the château is visible to the east of the motorway, one must go *west* from Pouilly exit, along road to Arnay-le-Duc; there is a signpost to Châteauneuf after a short distance.
Restriction Not suitable for &.
Credit cards Access, Amex, Visa.
Terms B&B: double 140–240 frs. Set lunch/dinner 110 and 140 frs; full alc 180 frs.

> Don't trust out-of-date Guides. Many hotels are dropped and new ones added every year.

CHÂTEAUNEUF-SUR-SARTHE 49330 Maine-et-Loire Map 10

La Sarthe *Tel* (41) 69.85.29
1 rue du Port

"Food excellent." "We spent three nights here *en pension* and have seldom been treated better." These are recent verdicts on this modest but very popular hotel at the edge of a little town north of Angers. It is really a restaurant-with-rooms, and is praised mainly for its good food and the charm of its setting – when fine, grills are served on a terrace by the river. "A lovely little place built at the turn of the century, furnished in 17th-century style"; "the stretch of the river is lovely, complete with old mill, medieval church and a weir"; "charming proprietors and staff". Rooms vary in quality: some may be a little basic for some tastes. *(Eileen Broadbent, Diana Holmes, P G Wigney, and others)*

Open All year except Oct and 1 week in Feb. Restaurant closed Sun evening and Mon (except July and Aug).
Rooms 7 double – 4 with bath, 2 with shower.
Facilities Salon, bar, rustic dining room overlooking river; riverside terrace. Public swimming pool 1 km; tennis courts 200 metres; fishing nearby.
Location 31 km N of Angers. Hotel is near bridge. Parking.
Credit cards None accepted.
Terms Rooms 70–160 frs. Breakfast 15 frs; set lunch/dinner 43, 75, 110, 160 frs; full alc 95 frs.

CHAUMONT-SUR-THARONNE 41600 Loir-et-Cher Map 10

La Croix Blanche *Tel* (54) 88.55.12
5 place Mottu

Though not far from Orléans, or from Loire châteaux such as Chambord, Chaumont itself lies deep in the Sologne, a curious flat land of forests and marshy lagoons. Readers this year are again lyrical about the "ravishingly attractive" *Croix Blanche*, which has been the local village *auberge* for 300 years. It stands in the main square, yet is a *Relais du Silence*, well modernised in rustic style, with creeper-covered walls and a flowery courtyard where you can eat or drink in fine weather. Rooms are spacious, beds comfortable and service friendly and efficient, with the Crouzier family very much in charge of a skilled staff. Guests walk through a large kitchen, all oak beams and gleaming pottery tiles, to the dining room. Here the cooking has been in feminine hands – rare in French hotels – for the past two centuries, and today Gisèle Crouzier is upholding that tradition: she wins two *Gault Millau toques*, but this year has lost her *Michelin* rosette (why?). She herself is from the Dordogne, so not surprisingly her cuisine marries the *périgourdine* with the local *solognote*. It is highly original, yet without *nouvelle cuisine* chi-chi: try, for example, the braised wild duck stuffed with turbot and served with mussel sauce. *(D Skinner, Sheila Stober and Robert Letovsky, and others)*

Open All year except 3 Jan–7 Feb; 24 June–4 July.
Rooms 3 suites, 9 double, 4 single – 10 with bath, 5 with shower, all with telephone; 5 ground-floor rooms. 7 rooms in annexe.
Facilities Hall, salon, 3 restaurants. Courtyard for refreshments; garden with ping-pong and *boules*. Handy for Loire châteaux. English spoken.

Location Midway between Romorantin and Orléans (Orléans 34 km), S of La Ferté St-Aubin by D922. In centre of village. Parking.
Credit cards All major cards accepted.
Terms Rooms: single 160–200 frs; double 250–400 frs. Breakfast 30 frs; set lunch/dinner 150, 250, 350 frs; full alc 250 frs. Reduced rates and special meals for children.

CHEFFES 49330 Maine-et-Lorie   Map 10

Château de Teildras   *Tel* (41) 42.61.08
                                                         Telex 722268 TEILDRA

Cheffes is a peaceful and untrippery village on a pretty stretch of the river Sarthe, 19 kilometres north of Angers. *Teildras*, a graceful little 16th-century château, white-walled, grey-roofed, is the family home of the Comte de Bernard du Breuil, who some years ago decided that the best way to preserve his estate was to turn it into a hotel. This he has done, meticulously. You can ride, fish or go for walks in the large park. "Peaceful and beautiful in every way; food and service excellent," is a recent verdict, echoing earlier praise: "The public rooms are beautifully decorated with tapestries, paintings and plants, and the lighting is subdued and well planned. The whole atmosphere is soothing. Our bedrooms had antiques and lovely beamed ceilings, the beds were comfortable, and our windows looked on to the park with its lovely trees and three cows munching in the sunlight." *(Mrs S R Wilkins, Kate and Steve Murray-Sykes, A and C R, and others).*

We have just heard that the Comtesse is no longer doing the cooking herself, but has handed over to a chef who may not be showing quite the same skills – so we should welcome new reports.

Open 1 Apr–15 Nov. Restaurant closed Tue midday.
Rooms 1 suite, 10 double – all with bath/shower and telephone; TV on request.
Facilities 2 salons, 2 dining rooms; conference/functions facilities. Wooded park, river within 500 metres; fishing, riding, boat hire. English spoken.
Location 19 km N of Angers; château is well signposted; turn out of Cheffes towards Juvardeil. Parking.
Credit card Visa.
Terms [1985 rates] rooms: single occupancy 390–550, double 500–750 frs; half-board: single 655–815 frs, double 1,030–1,280 frs; full board: double 1,470–1,720 frs. Breakfast 46 frs; set lunch/dinner 220–260 frs.

CHINON 37500 Indre-et-Loire   Map 10

Château de Marçay   *Tel* (47) 93.03.47
                                                         Telex 751475

Sometimes a hotel guide editor begins to wonder whether the French countryside contains much else these days besides 15th-century stone châteaux with neat pepper-pot towers, stylishly converted into smart *Relais et Châteaux* hotels, and consecrated by *Michelin* with its full insignia of rosette, red gables and red rocking chair, and by *Gault Millau* with a *toque* or two for inventive cuisine. You know the kind of place: they are legion. However, they do suit some tastes, and this one fits precisely that description. One reader had reservations: service a bit hit-and-miss and some of the decor a bit tatty. But it was also much admired by several nominators this year: "Set in open country four miles south of Chinon, and offering peace and comfort. We were captivated. Our room was large, with balcony, sitting-room recess with elegant chairs, magazines on the coffee table. The public rooms are gracefully furnished. An evening swim in the sheltered outside pool was followed by dinner by candlelight on the terrace: very good service, and food a mixture of *nouvelle* and traditional" (eg foie gras de canard aux abricots secs) *(D J Stratford)*. "Excellent food in charming restaurant" *(David Blum)*. "Expensive perhaps, but one pays no less in London, and we did have one of the best rooms in the Château." *(Dr M W Atkinson and Dr R L Holmes)*

Open All year.
Rooms 2 suites, 22 double, 2 single – 16 with bath, 10 with shower, all with telephone, radio and TV on request. 11 rooms in annexe. (12 more rooms planned for 1986.)
Facilities 2 salons, TV room, bar, terrace, restaurant, conference facilities. Gardens with tennis court and heated swimming pool. English spoken.
Location 7 km S of Chinon by D116.
Credit cards Access, Amex, Visa.
Terms Rooms: single 535–650 frs, double 650–885 frs. Breakfast 45 frs; set lunch/dinner 200 frs.

Hôtel Diderot   *Tel* (47) 93.18.87
4 rue Buffon

Joan of Arc first met the Dauphin in this lovely old town near the Loire, with its half-ruined fortified hill-top castle. Again in 1984/85 praise has poured in for the *Diderot*, an unassuming bed-and-breakfast hotel of unusual charm, run by a friendly and helpful Cypriot, M. Kazamias, and his French wife: "Exceptional value, the sort of hotel one dreams of discovering in France"; "a quiet courtyard, large bedrooms, lovely atmosphere". This backs up a previous description: "A beautiful old pale stone building, much of it covered by a vine, with an enchanting wrought-iron balcony on the second floor, reached by a spiral staircase. Inside are exposed beams, and a pretty salon where we were offered Madame's thirteen different home-made jams" (including green tomato with ginger, greengage with mint, apricot and myrtle). "Our room was fresh and clean, with good lighting. We think courtyard-facing rooms are quieter, as the other side overlooks a road. Though near to the sights, the hotel is away from night-life activity." Be warned, too, that rooms vary greatly in size. *(Nicola Hayward, Marie and Hans Haenlein, Howard Harrison, Adam and Caroline Raphael, and others)*

Open All year.
Rooms 20 double, 2 single – 10 with bath, 12 with shower (4 of these with WC), all with telephone; 4 rooms with bath on ground floor.
Facilities Salon with TV, breakfast room; bar with wine-tasting planned for 1986; limited conference facilities. Courtyard. English spoken. &.
Location Near place Jeanne d'Arc; hotel is well signposted. Parking in courtyard.
Credit cards Access, Visa.
Terms Rooms: single 105–200 frs, double 125–250 frs. Breakfast 20 frs. (No restaurant.)

Please make a habit of sending a report if you stay at a Guide hotel.

CHOLET 49300 Maine-et-Loire   **Map 10**

Le Belvédère   *Tel* (41) 62.14.02
Lac de Ribou

The lake of Ribou lies on the green pastoral plain of Anjou, five kilometres south-east of the shoe-making town of Cholet. Here the *Belvédère* stands above the lake – a modern white-fronted restaurant-with-rooms, much praised (*Michelin* rosette) for the inventive cooking of its Japanese chef and co-owner, Mr Inagaki (try his cocon de sandre aux écrevisses). "The food was marvellous," runs a report this year; "our bedroom was large and pleasant, a bit in need of redecoration, but with a fine view of the lake. Nice large bathroom. The owner is charming and modest, and next day was in jeans doing repairs." *(Gerald Campion)*

Open All year except Aug. Closed Sun evening.
Rooms 8 double – all with bath and colour TV.
Facilities Bar, restaurant; terrace where meals are served. Engish spoken.
Location 5 km SE of Cholet off D20. Follow signs for Parc de Loisirs de Ribou.
Restriction Not suitable for &.
Credit cards Amex, Diners, Visa.
Terms Rooms: single occupancy 205 frs, double 230 frs. Breakfast 21 frs; set lunch/dinner 85 and 160 frs (Sun lunch 130 and 180 frs); full alc 250 frs.

CHONAS L'AMBALLON 38121 Isère   **Map 10**

Domaine de Clairefontaine   *Tel* (74) 58.81.52

A much cheaper alternative to the *Marais St-Jean* (see below), spotted this year by a veteran correspondent: "An ideal spot to break your journey, half way between Paris and Nice, or for a longer stay to unwind for a few days and sample the many delights of the region. A solid stone building with no frills: it has large and airy rooms, somewhat temperamental plumbing and lighting, and is reasonably priced. Interesting and well-presented food served in a *salle à manger* (rather than a restaurant), with somewhat stodgy atmosphere. Tennis court, but no pool. Expansive views across open fields, and the A7 *autoroute* just far enough away not to be a nuisance," *(Geoffrey Sharp)*. Another enthusiast for the family-run *Clairefontaine* advises: "Sleep at the *Domaine* for peace, friendly service, solid comfort and excellent value; eat at the *Marais St-Jean* if you can afford it." *(Eileen Broadbent)*

Open All year, except 15 Dec–1 Feb, 1 May and 1 Nov.
Rooms 17 double – 9 with bath, 2 with shower, all with telephone. 6 rooms in annexe; 5 ground-floor rooms.
Facilities Dining room; terrace. Garden with tennis court. English spoken.
Location Off N7, 9 km S of Vienne; turn off A7 motorway at Vienne Sud. Parking.
Restrictions Not really suitable for &.
Credit card Visa.
Terms (Service not included) B&B: single 84.50 frs, double 108.50 frs. Set meals 55 frs–110 frs. Special meals for children.

If you think we have over-praised a hotel or done it an injustice, please let us know.

Hostellerie "Le Marais St-Jean"   *Tel* (74) 58.83.28

In pretty countryside above the Rhône valley south of Vienne, this is a big pink farmhouse, rather Provençal in style, recently converted into a stylish modern hotel by two enthusiasts, Christian and Suzette Heugas. "Ten bedrooms beautifully furnished and comfortable. Attentive service and food well presented – Limoges china. The cheaper menu [95 francs in 1985] was the best meal we had in France," *(H R J Taylor)*. In their cool and sober dining room, with beamed ceiling and tiled floor, the Heugas provide enterprising dishes such as fresh frogs with chives and artichoke purée.

Open All year except Feb, 1 week in Aug, Tue evening and Wed.
Rooms 10 double – all with bath and telephone; mono TV on request. 1 ground-floor room.
Facilities 3 salons, bar, restaurant, conference room. Garden. English spoken.
Location Off N7, 9 km S of Vienne; turn off A7 motorway at Vienne Sud.
Credit cards Amex, Diners, Visa.
Terms Rooms 350 frs. Breakfast 35 frs; set meals 120–250 frs; full alc 200 frs. Reduced rates and special meals for children.

CLÉCY 14570 Calvados   Map 8

Moulin du Vey   *Tel* (31) 69.71.08

Rural Normandy at its most pretty and seductive, this old creeper-covered corn-mill beside the gently flowing Orne – "a really beautiful place, tastefully converted into a hotel", says a nominator this year; "the rooms are comfortable, nicely furnished, and not expensive for this kind of place, while the table d'hôte dinner at 110 francs [1985] was really excellent, despite lack of choice." Snug period decor, a beamed dining room with wide windows opening on to a terrace by the river where you can eat out in summer. Lavish Norman cooking. The mill is in a quiet spot outside the village of Clécy, which lies 37 kilometres south of Caen in the lovely hilly "Suisse Normande" area. Nearby, the Orne cuts its way through rocky gorges. *(Richard O Whiting)*

Open All year except 1–25 Dec in the morning, restaurant closed Fri between 15 Oct–1 Apr.
Rooms 1 family suite, 10 double – all rooms with bath or shower, telephone, 7 rooms in annexe. 1 family suite and 6 doubles in annexe, *Relais de Surosne*, 3 km.
Facilities TV room, lounge bar, restaurant; garden with terrace for meals. Near river Orne, with fishing, swimming and boating, English spoken.
Location By D133 2 km E of Clécy (which is 37 km S of Caen, on D562).
Restriction Not suitable for &.
Credit cards Amex, Diners, Visa.
Terms Rooms 230–280 frs; dinner, B&B: 310–330 frs per person; full board: 350–360 frs per person. Breakfast 24 frs, set lunch/dinner 110, 165, 250 frs; full alc 200 frs. Reduced rates for children under 6.

CLERMONT-L'HÉRAULT 34800 Hérault   Map 10

Hôtel Terminus   *Tel* (67) 96.10.66
11 allées Roger-Salengro

The busy little town of Clermont lies amid rolling vineyards 41 kilometres west of Montpellier and 21 kilometres north of delightful

17th-century Pézenas where Molière worked. "A heartwarming experience is the down-to-earth *Terminus*," writes a veteran devotee of French provincial simplicity. "Bedrooms are in an annexe across a narrow side-street: you enter past the kitchens and a comically Dickensian office where the local telephone directory is years out of date. Our room was clean and comfortable. The dining room was large and bare of ornament or lampshade, and recalled some 'British Restaurant' of 40 years ago. But our critical judgement was soon swept away by the convivial atmosphere. Like every other table, ours had a litre of red wine standing at the ready: it went with the 65-franc menu [1984]. No nonsense about a wine list. A sense of benevolence enfolded us. Not much choice to each course, but it was all good and generous. Breakfast was good too, with real jam." Red *Michelin* "R" for good value. *(N Brangham)*

Open All year.
Rooms 29 double, 3 single – 1 with bath, 8 with shower.
Facilities Ramps. Bar, salon, dining room. English spoken. Suitable for some &.
Location Central, near main post office. Garage.
Credit cards Access, Amex, Visa.
Terms Rooms: single 70–85 frs, double 85–120 frs. Breakfast 20 frs; set lunch/dinner (weekdays) 70 frs; full alc 100–120 frs. Half-board rates available for stays of 3 days or more. Reduced rates and special meals for children.

CLUNY 71250 Saône-et-Loire   Map 10

Hôtel de Bourgogne   *Tel* (85) 59.00.58
Place Abbaye

The old town of Cluny contains the remains of the mighty Romanesque abbey that in the Middle Ages was one of Europe's leading religious, artistic and intellectual centres. Today little of it remains; but the medieval town of narrow streets and pink tiles is still well worth a visit. Here the *Bourgogne* stands in the main square facing the abbey – a dignified old mansion that has been an inn since the 18th century (Lamartine often stayed here and guests can still sleep in his bed). Most of the bedrooms look out on to green hills or the towers of the abbey.

Again this year readers are enthusiastic about the friendly welcome, the food *(Michelin* rosette) and the attractive bedroom decor, though there is one caveat that cupboard space and bedside reading lamps are inadequate. "Pleasant atmosphere, a warm welcome and a general feeling of being well run. About the best meal we had in two weeks in France, notably the foie de veau au vinaigre de framboises." "The personal attention that M. Gosse and his wife give to small details is what makes this a very special hotel." *(Mrs R B Richards, Mrs M D Prodgers, and others)*

Open 7 Mar–12 Nov, except Tue and Wed midday.
Rooms 18 double – 11 with bath, 5 with shower, all with telephone.
Facilities Salon with TV, bar, restaurant. Small courtyard. English spoken.
Location On N79, 27 km from Mâcon. Hotel is opposite the abbey. Garage parking.
Credit cards Amex, Diners, Visa.
Terms B&B from 180 frs; half-board 300–450 frs; full board 410–560 frs. Set lunch/dinner 110, 165 and 250 frs; full alc 220 frs. Reduced rates for children.

Hôtel Moderne *Tel* (85) 59.05.65
Le Pont de l'Étang

President Mitterand dines here *en famille* at Whitsuntide, on his annual visit to the nearby panorama point of the Rock of Solutré. He is said to be satisfied, as is one of our readers: "Less attractive externally than the *Bourgogne* (see above), and in a less central position, on the river a kilometre out of town, everything else makes the *Moderne* the place to stay. Not all the bedrooms are well decorated, but the staff are welcoming. Prices are very reasonable, notably the dinner menus." Recent visitors praise the "magnificent" cooking (*Gault Millau toque* for such dishes as ris de veau au citron) and the "friendly and helpful" staff, but one of them found the bath water lukewarm and the roadside setting not especially pleasant. We should be glad of further reports.

Open 1 Jan–4 Nov. Restaurant closed until 20 Mar.
Rooms 16 double – 7 with bath, 4 with shower; all with radio, tea-making facilities and baby-listening.
Facilities Dining room; banqueting/functions room. River, swimming pool and tennis nearby. English spoken.
Location 1 km S of centre in direction of Mâcon on D985.
Restriction Not suitable for &.
Credit cards Amex, Diners, Visa.
Terms B&B: single occupancy 110 frs, double 129–238 frs; dinner, B&B: single 185 frs, double 279–598 frs; full board: single 260 frs, double 429–838 frs. Set lunch/dinner 80, 130 and 190 frs; full alc 220 frs.

COLLIOURE 66190 Pyrénées-Orientales **Map 10**

Hostellerie La Frégate *Tel* (68) 82.06.05
24 quai de l'Amirauté

Yves Costa's well-known fish restaurant-cum-hotel/pension lies slap amid the hue-and-cry of the famous fishing-port-cum-trendy-resort of Collioure, south-east of Perpignan. "The small port at the foot of the Pyrenees is in an area renowned for the beauty of its soft natural light and for the painters such as Matisse and Braque who frequented it. The houses in the charming, narrow streets are pastel-washed in soft earth colours; the mountains enclose the town. Today it's an up-to-date seaside resort, a vibrant place. "*La Frégate* is in the middle of this activity, beside a pedestrian walkway leading to the sea. We felt at times that we had strayed into a station as the hotel serves all comers at any time of the day and practically the night. With such a vast turnover the food, though good, did not quite match up to our expectations – save for the 230-franc *menu dégustation*: tartare de la marée du jour, feuilleté de St-Pierre au beurre rouge, etc. On the normal 90-franc menu we enjoyed anchois de Collioure aux poivrons frais and terrine de poissons sauce crabe. This is only a place to visit if you enjoy all things piscine! Our room, on the fourth floor, was small and rather spartan, but adequate for an informal beach holiday. Noisy, though." (*Robert and Gilly Jamieson*) In summer you can eat out on a pleasant terrace facing the castle. *Gault Millau* give a *toque*, but find the place erratic, and it is not listed in 1985 *Michelin*. More reports, please, on this possibly leaky frigate.

Open All year. Restaurant closed Fri, and Sat midday.
Rooms 24 – all with telephone.

Facilities Salon with TV, dining room, terrace. English spoken.
Location Leave *autoroute* B9 at Le Boulou, or Perpignan south exit. *La Frégate* is in centre of Collioure opposite château (rooms can be noisy). Public parking 50 metres.
Credit cards None accepted.
Terms [1985 rates] B&B: single 186 frs, double 247 frs; dinner, B&B (obligatory in season): 200–263 frs per person. Set lunch/dinner 90, 150 and 230 frs; alc (excluding wine) 260 frs.

COLLONGES-LA-ROUGE 19500 Corrèze   Map 10

Relais de St-Jacques de Compostelle   *Tel* (55) 25.41.02

A very beautiful 16th-century village, built of local purple-red stone, carefully restored, set in lush green valleys a few miles north of the Dordogne. It was used as a weekend retreat by the courtiers of the Vicomte de Turenne, former lord of the region, whose ruined château stands just to the west. Many fine buildings, including a 12th-century church. The modest but "delightful and friendly" *Relais* is again praised by several visitors this year, notably for the warmth of welcome by M. Castera and his wife and for the excellence of his cuisine (*Michelin* red "R" for good value) – "first-class French provincial", eg carré de boeuf and "superb" terrine. "M. Castera loves to chat with his guests after dinner, even if their French is poor." "Bedrooms, some small, are OK in a simple way, but the hotel has a shortage of lavatories, I think." *(David and Rosemary Phillips, Walter Baxter, H W T Bates, and others)*

Open All year.
Rooms 11 double, 1 single – 5 with bath, 2 with shower, all with telephone; 5 rooms in annexe.
Facilities Salon, bar, dining room; terrace for summer meals.
Location 21 km SE of Brive; follow signs to Meyssac. Hotel is central. Parking.
Credit card Visa.
Terms Rooms: single 65 frs, double 80 frs. Breakfast 15.50 frs; set lunch/dinner 70, 90 and 150 frs.

COLROY-LA-ROCHE 67420 Bas-Rhin   Map 9

Hostellerie la Cheneaudière   *Tel* (88) 97.61.64
Telex 870438 CHENEAU

"Really lovely" is the 1984 verdict of two connoisseurs who stayed at this imposing and luxurious modern hostelry, built in local chalet style and set amid wooded hills on the edge of a flowery Alsatian village. A winding hill-road takes you in a few minutes to such places as Riquewihr and Colmar. An earlier account: "Very superior and most enjoyable, this 'Oak Grove'. The decor verges on kitsch-de-luxe, but the rooms are comfortable, and the hotel is run with superb professional self-confidence by a stylish and friendly Lorrain family, the François – he was a lawyer and she a hospital director. Their young son-in-law, Jean-Paul Bossée, provides cooking that we found truly delicious and inventive without being chi-chi: on the expensive à la carte (no table d'hôte) we especially enjoyed the frog soup, the unusual tartare of diced raw salmon, the roast guinea-fowl and the lavish desserts. *Michelin* star and two *Gault Millau toques* fully deserved. A pity they do no Alsatian dishes, but in season there's venison. The dining room's sophistication is matched by the high (too high?) prices of the wines; fine array of liqueurs, including home-distilled mirabelle; service assured but slow-ish. A notable feature is the copious help-yourself breakfast, including smoked ham, cheese, eggs, cereals, fruit salad – most un-French but no doubt what their affluent German clientele expect. Nice sunny terrace for drinks, but garden a bit minimal for so posh a place." *(Pat and Jeremy Temple, J A)*

Open 1 Mar–31 Dec.
Rooms 4 suites, 22 double – 25 with bath, 1 with shower, all with telephone, radio, colour TV and terrace (suites have mini-bar and video); some ground-floor rooms.
Facilities Salon, bar, restaurant. Video films. Garden with tennis court and outdoor meals in fine weather; river fishing and hunting nearby; winter sports 5 km. English spoken.
Location 62 km SW of Strasbourg on N420. Parking.
Credit cards All major cards accepted.
Terms B&B double/suites 496–1,200 frs; dinner, B&B: 484–836 frs per person; full board: 693–1,001 frs per person; full alc 380–420 frs. Reduced rates for children under 12 sharing parents' room; special meals on request.

CONDRIEU 69420 Rhône	Map 10

Hostellerie Beau Rivage *Tel* (74) 59.52.24
Telex 308 946

The *rivage* is the Rhône's. How pleasant to take drinks here on the terrace in summer, under white parasols, right by the river, or to dine out on the stone-flagged patio. Visiting in chilly January, our correspondents missed these particular delights, but nonetheless relished this classy hostelry: "An old family hotel on the edge of the village of Condrieu, in the heart of the Côte du Rhône vineyards. There is a comfortable lounge and bar, and a garden for summer use. Our room had its own terrace and view of the river: on the far bank is a petro-chemical works, but half a mile away, not obtrusive. The spacious, clean and comfortable room was pleasantly decorated. The staff are all pleasant and helpful. But the restaurant is the main attraction here and has much local custom. Attractively set tables nearly all have a view of the river. Madame Castaing, the owner, is also chef and one of the very few women in France with two *Michelin* rosettes (and two *Gault Millau toques*). Excellent cooking with some local specialities, some outstanding pâtisseries and some unusual Rhône wines, fairly priced." *(Pat and Jeremy Temple; also J Newnham, Hadley and Heather Buck)*

Open All year except 5 Jan–15 Feb.
Rooms 2 suites, 18 double, 4 single – 20 with bath, 4 with shower, 16 rooms in annexe – all with direct-dial telephone and baby-listening; 4 with TV.
Facilities Salon, bar, dining room, conference/banqueting facilities; terrace restaurant overlooking the Rhône. Garden by river, fishing. Swimming 2 km.
Location 40 km S of Lyon. Leave A7 at Condrieu exit (coming from N), or Chanas exit (coming from S). Condrieu is on N86.
Credit cards All major cards accepted.
Terms Rooms: single 330 frs, double 330–370 frs. Set meals 170 and 250 frs; full alc 346–446 frs.

CONQUES 12320 St Cyprien Aveyron   Map 10

Hôtel Sainte-Foy   *Tel* (65) 69.84.03

Ever popular with readers, the *Sainte-Foy* is the only hotel in the famous old village of Conques, which lies between Figeac and Rodez and was a leading staging-post on the pilgrimage to Santiago. The village is on a steep wooded hillside above a gorge, and its slate-roofed houses and cobbled streets surround a massive and awesome abbey church, famous for the masterly Romanesque stone carving on the west doorway and for its very rich gold and silver treasure. The *Sainte-Foy* is called after the martyred girl whose weird gold relic is still to be seen in the abbey museum. It's a fine medieval house, facing the abbey, with a shaded courtyard in the rear and handsome old furniture in the public rooms. The hotel has for many years enjoyed a well-merited *Michelin* rating for good dinners at modest price; try the local Rouergue dishes such as crêpes aux herbes. Service is friendly. It isn't a place for an extended stay, but Conques itself is so remarkable, especially in the evening when the abbey is floodlit and the sightseers have gone, that it is well worth a special visit. A warning to light sleepers: two sets of church clocks tell the time at half-hourly intervals at night. *(Dr and Mrs Tattersall, Gillian Lewis, Nancy Raphael, and others)*

Open 1 Apr–15 Oct. Restaurant open only for dinner; closed Sun.
Rooms 18 double, 2 single – 12 with bath, 8 with shower, all with telephone.
Facilities Reception, reading room, TV room, dining room; interior patio. English spoken.
Location Off D601 and not far from N662 between Figeac (54 km) and Rodez (37 km). Hotel is central, opposite cathedral. Garage and car park.
Credit cards None accepted.
Terms B&B: single 125 frs, double 270 frs; half-board: single 220 frs, double 450 frs. Set dinner 90 frs; full alc 130 frs.

CORDES 81170 Tarn   Map 10

Hôtel Le Grand Écuyer   *Tel* (63) 56.01.03

The old fortified village of Cordes was built by the Counts of Toulouse in the 13th century as a defence against Simon de Montfort and his anti-Albigensian crusade. With its ramparts, ancient houses and museums, it sits on a high spur above a valley north-west of Albi (Cordes-in-the-sky, it is called). The *Grand Écuyer* is in the heart of the old village, a former hunting-lodge of Raymond, Count of Toulouse, now a very select little hotel, with distinguished antique furniture and spacious bedrooms, many with four-poster beds. It is known above all for its cuisine which tends towards the *nouvelle* (gratin de lapereau, salade de rougets) and wins a rosette from *Michelin* and two red *toques* from *Gault Millau*. "An outstanding hotel. Food and service were admirable. The chef is one of France's first fifty – his products are celestial. The sweets are inspired. All is washed down by Gaillac, the wine of the region," *(C N Janson).* "Cordes, though very striking on its hilltop, is a little too full of chic boutiques for my taste. The *Grand Écuyer* is very superior, very seductive; lovely antique furniture, an imposing old staircase; very comfortable. Food very up-market, a bit chi-chi in presentation but merits its rosette." *(Christopher Martin)*

Open 1 Apr–15 Oct.
Rooms 16 double – all with bath and telephone; some with 4-poster beds.
Facilities 3 private salons, bar, dining room. English spoken.
Location In centre of village which is 25 km NW of Albi. Public parking nearby.
Credit cards Amex, Diners, Visa.
Terms [1985 rates] rooms: single occupancy 200 frs, double 440 frs. Breakfast 35 frs; set lunch/dinner 120–260 frs.

CORDON 74700 Haute-Savoie   Map 10

Hôtel des Roches Fleuries   *Tel* (50) 58.06.71

A pleasant, spacious and informal chalet-style hotel, in the small ski-resort of Cordon, on a hillside 32 kilometres from Chamonix. It faces across the valley to Mont Blanc, with spectacular views. Many bedrooms have their own balcony. "A pure delight", says a visitor this year; "cooking of a very high standard, and staff who genuinely seem to want to make your stay pleasant." Earlier reports were in the same vein: "There is a beautiful terrace, and a green meadow beyond giving a feeling of Alpine countryside. It is very tranquil. I would not choose it for a skiing holiday for there are better slopes at other places nearby such as Mégève: but for non-skiers and at any other time of year it is an ideal location. The staff are helpful and friendly. The beds were comfortable, and the bathroom good. We enjoyed asparagus, fillet steak au poivre, fromage blanc with sugar, and good coffee." "The grandstand view of the snow-covered Mont Blanc and nearby peaks is a sight you will never forget, especially if you watch the snow turn pink in the sunset as you take your apéritif on the balcony and later see the full moon come up over the ridge." (*T C Seoh, Jean and Eric Lace, and others*). Recent visitors, however, have had reservations: eccentric plumbing, undistinguished no-choice meals, uninterested reception and poor housekeeping. More reports please.

Open All year.
Rooms 1 suite, 28 double, 1 single – 28 with bath, 1 with shower, all with telephone and balcony; TV on request; 5 rooms in 2 annexes; 1 small suite on ground floor.
Facilities Salon with log fire, TV room, bar, dining room, fondue once a week; 2 terraces; conference facilities. Ping-pong. Garden with chalet-bar in summer, 2 lakes 4 km with bathing, windsurfing and boating. Fishing. English spoken.
Location 4 km NE of Sallanches on D1113. Garages and open parking.
Restriction Not suitable for &.
Credit cards None accepted.
Terms Rooms 250–270 frs; dinner, B&B 280–350 frs; full board 320–390 frs. Breakfast 28 frs; set lunch/dinner 100 frs; full alc 180 frs. Reduced rates and special meals for children.

COTIGNAC 83850 Var   Map 11

Hostellerie Lou Calen   *Tel* (94) 04.60.40
1 cours Gambetta

Cotignac, in the hills of the Var hinterland, is oddly situated at the foot of a brown cliff holed with caves, some of them once lived in. Potters and other craftsmen abound in the village, and their wares are on sale. Recent vistors confirm earlier praise for *Lou Calen* (Provençal for "the place of the oil-lamp"), an admirable little family-run hotel, very friendly, with rooms furnished in Provençal style and modern plumbing. Large swimming pool reached through an exquisite garden filled with exotic plants. You eat on a beautiful terrace with a wide view and here the chef has won a *Gault Millau toque* for his excellent classic Provençal cooking. "Pieds de paquets and sinful great hunks of tarte aux fraises on the 79-fr menu [1985]." Only minor drawback: there is a little traffic noise at night. Much of interest to visit in the area: the majestic Gorges du Verdon, the lovely Cistercian abbey of Thoronet and, less well known, the château at Entrecasteaux, housing a most original museum created by the Scottish surrealist artist/diplomat, the late Ian McGarvie-Munn. *(John Newnham, Mrs D Curtis, Eileen Broadbent)*

Open Apr–Sept.
Rooms 8 suites, 8 double – 15 with bath, 1 with shower, all with telephone, 5 with mono TV. (3 might have traffic noise.) 10 in annexes.
Facilities Salon with TV, bar, restaurant; conference facilities. Garden with terrace and swimming pool. Tennis 1 km. English spoken.
Location On Route des Gorges du Verdon. For Cotignac take exit Brignoles or Le Luc-Toulon off N7. Central. Parking.
Credit cards Access, Visa.
Terms B&B: single 198 frs, double 376–406 frs; half-board: single 278 frs, double 496–568 frs; full board 330–370 frs per person. Set lunch/dinner 85 frs; full alc 110 frs. Reduced rates for children.

COULANDON 03000 Allier   Map 10

Le Chalet   *Tel* (70) 44.50.08

Here is rural tranquillity at a very modest price in the very centre of France. The little village of Coulandon lies six kilometres west of the market town of Moulins and the same distance east of Savigny, noted for its priory church. *Le Chalet*, just outside the village, is a former hunting lodge set peacefully (it is a *Relais du Silence)* in its own spacious park with a pond full of fish. "Very pretty clean room in converted stable in very pretty grounds," says one reader. Another adds: "The rooms are de luxe with superb fabric wall covering. The food was good but not spectacular. One could stay for a week in a sleepy drowse. Most inexpensive hotels have rooms in which one would have no room to swing a cat. This hotel could take several cats." *(Gerald Campion, C S Nelles, E Hugo)*

Open 1 Feb–15 Nov. Restaurant closed midday all year, and evenings Oct–Mar.
Rooms 21 double – 7 with bath, 14 with shower, all with telephone and mono TV.
Facilities Lounge, functions room, dining room with terrace. Grounds with lake and fishing. English spoken.
Location Well signposted: down a side-road just off D945 towards Savigny.
Credit cards Access, Diners, Visa.
Terms Rooms: single 130, double 165. Breakfast 18 frs; set lunch/dinner 60 and 92 frs; full alc 125 frs.

Warning: there were major changes in French telephone numbers in the autumn of 1985 after we had gone to press. It is possible, therefore, that not all our French telephone numbers, particularly those of hotels which failed to answer our questionnaire, are accurate.

COURCHEVEL 73120 Savoie   Map 10

Le Tournier   *Tel* (79) 08.03.19
                                                        Telex 980014

A modern hotel close to the ski-lifts in this huge and popular Alpine resort; it is on a shopping street, but looks on to snowy slopes and woods behind. "All they could offer was two attic rooms, but we were soon won over by the charming rustic-style decor, the pleasant atmosphere and Madame Tournier's attractive personality. The food is first class, in a pleasant dining room. Comfortable bar, open fire, and space for dancing if and when desired. I'd rather stay here than at the same owner's ritzier four-star *Lana*, situated right on the ski-slopes." *(Uli Lloyd Pack)*

Open 17 Dec–7 Apr.
Rooms 30 double – 28 with bath, 2 with shower, all with direct-dial telephone; some with TV.
Facilities Salon, large bar with pianist, dining room. Dancing in the bar before and after dinner. English spoken.
Location Courchevel is up a valley 97 km E of Chambéry. Hotel is central, in Quartier de la Loze.
Credit card Visa.
Terms Half-board 430–465 frs; full board 550-580 frs. Guests on full board can lunch at *l'Altitude* restaurant on the mountain for no extra charge.

DÉGAGNAC 46340 Lot   Map 10

L'Auberge sans Frontières   *Tel* (65) 41.52.88

Here is just the kind of unspoilt rural simplicity that wins the heart of so many visitors to the Dordogne/Lot area. South-west of Gourdon, and roughly halfway between Cahors and Sarlat, Dégagnac is "a quiet sleepy village surrounded by woods, hoopoes and flowers – lovely walking country". And the *auberge*: "A village *logis* with comfortable rooms (especially the enormous double bed), furnished most charmingly. Excellent *pension* rates and so cheap that everyone comes again. Madame Hauchecorne speaks good English and is delightful, helpful, and an exciting chef, with husband and friends helping out. Bar/dining room welcomes locals, kittens, orchids and bar footballers – *sans frontières!*" *(Heather Dauncey)*. Madame says her hotel is "the family life type, and we need people enjoying walking, gathering flowers and trying to mix with the life of the village".

Open All year except 15 Jan–15 Feb. Closed Tue in winter.
Rooms 1 4-bedded, 6 double, 2 single – 1 with bath, 5 with shower.
Facilities Bar/dining room; patio for drinks and meals. Fishing nearby. English spoken.
Location Dégagnac is on main Cahors/Sarlat road, 10 km SW of Gourdon. Hotel is central. Parking in the village square.
Credit card Diners.
Terms B&B 50–60 frs; half-board 85–87.50 frs; full board 125–127.50 frs. Set lunch/dinner 40–100 frs; full alc 110 frs. Cookery lessons. Children under 6 half price.

DIEPPE 76200 Seine-Maritime   **Map 8**

Hôtel de l'Univers   *Tel* (35) 84.12.55
10 boulevard de Verdun   *Telex* 770741

The *Univers*, facing Dieppe's elegant esplanade, is a middle-class hotel with old-fashioned virtues, much patronised by Britons arriving from Newhaven. Readers tend to find the rooms quiet and comfortable, though slightly shabby, and the food excellent. Previously we had criticisms of the service, but a visitor this year found it pleasant and helpful. The hotel prefers its guests to take dinner too, but this is not essential. *(J and A Sowrey, M Slater, and others)*

Open All year except 15 Dec–1 Feb.
Rooms 30 – 28 with bath or shower, all with phone and TV; some with balcony.
Facilities Lift. Restaurant, conference facilities.
Location Central. Parking.
Credit cards All major cards accepted.
Terms [1985 rates] rooms: single 180 frs, double 350 frs; full board 280–380 frs per person. Breakfast 25 frs; set lunch/dinner 78–180 frs.

DIGOIN 71160 Saône-et-Loire   **Map 10**

Hotel Diligences et Commerce   *Tel* (85) 53.06.31.
14 rue Nationale

"The best all-round hotel I know in France" is high praise indeed from an experienced Francophile returning this year to this classic hostelry, which keeps up the old solid traditions even though Peugeots and Audis have now replaced the eponymous stagecoaches in its courtyard. "Things so often lacking today in French hotels here stand out in contrast – thick, plentiful towels, the delightful breakfast tray, the help with luggage, the turning on – unasked – of the bedroom's central heating one chill September evening. In the charming beamed dining room the food is beautifully prepared and served and well deserves its *Michelin* rosette," *(Norman Brangham)*. The hotel expects its guests to dine there. Digoin, on the upper Loire, is only nine kilometres from the majestic 12th-century basilica at Paray-le-Monial.

Open All year except 2–12 May, 4 Nov–5 Dec; closed Mon evening and Tue.
Rooms 10 double – 3 with bath, 5 with shower, all with telephone.
Facilities Salon with TV, dining room.
Location Central, between the church and the Loire. Digoin is on N79 between Moulins (60 km) and Mâcon (80 km). Parking.
Credit cards All major cards accepted.
Terms Rooms: single occupancy 80 frs, double 110 frs. Breakfast 21 frs; set meals 80, 110, 165 and 250 frs; full alc 300 frs. Reduced rates and special meals for children.

Hôtel de la Gare   *Tel* (85) 53.03.04
79 avenue Général-de-Gaulle

This being France, an ordinary little hotel opposite the station in a dull little town is indeed a likely place to find really outstanding cuisine – and Jean-Pierre Billoux, son-in-law of the owners, is one of France's most brilliant young chefs (two *Michelin* rosettes, three *Gault Millau toques*). "A bright building with terracotta pots and colourful window-boxes, it exudes an air of well-kept cheerful attention. Our simple annexe bedroom and bathroom were quiet and comfortable; breakfast, in a cool secluded garden, included delicious home-made plum jam. In the large, bright, modern and slightly garish dining room we chose the 285-franc [1985] *menu dégustation*. Flavours were fresh and original." Our reporters then treat us to a litany of delights, including a "deliciously pungent" pigeon terrine in garlic, an "ambitious and surprising" bar au vin rouge, boeuf à la crème aux morilles. *(Robert and Gilly Jamieson)*

Open All year except 19–27 June, Jan, and Wed except Jul–11 Sept.
Rooms 13 double – 8 with bath, 5 with shower; all with telephone; 4 rooms in annexe; 1 ground-floor room.
Facilities Salon, bar, restaurant. Garden with terrace. English spoken.
Location Central. Private parking in hotel courtyard.
Credit cards Amex, Diners, Visa.
Terms [1985 rates] rooms 200–250 frs. Breakfast 32 frs; set meals 195–290 frs. Reduced rates for children sharing parents' room; special meals on request.

DIJON 21000 Côte d'Or   Map 10

Le Chapeau Rouge   *Tel* (80) 30.28.10
5 rue Michelet   *Telex* 350535

This classic hotel is very central, close to the cathedral and not far from the splendid Beaux-Arts museum. The street is noisy, but front rooms have double-glazing; back ones are quiet, but may be less attractive. Again this year visitors describe the hotel as comfortable and efficient, though one thought his bedroom decor ugly and found the atmosphere (the hotel belongs to the Mapotel chain) rather impersonal. But he and others agree that, in the elegant restaurant, the ambitious *nouvelle*-ish cuisine (eg gratin d'écrevisses à la mousse d'artichauts) deserves its *Michelin* rosette and two *Gault Millau toques*. Service can be slow. The garage is 400 metres away. *(A Wright, Ralph Sheldon, and others)*

Open 10 Jan–20 Dec.
Rooms 3 suites, 26 double, 4 single – all with bath, direct-dial telephone, radio, colour TV, air-conditioning and mini-bar. Baby-listening on request.
Facilities Lift. Hall, salon, bar, restaurant; conference facilities. Winter garden. English spoken.
Location Central, near cathedral (front rooms are sound-proofed). Parking.
Credit cards All major cards accepted.
Terms [1985 rates] rooms: single 240 frs, double 460 frs, suites 700 frs. Breakfast 32 frs; set lunch/dinner 145–175 frs.

Hôtel du Nord   *Tel* (80) 30.55.20
2 rue de la Liberté   *Telex* 351554

A middle-priced hotel, centrally placed, useful for a night's halt. One reader found the food disappointing, but another says: "Dinner was all that one would expect of Burgundian food; succulent, tasty, abundant." Another ate well in the candlelit restaurant, the *Port Guillaume*, with its panelled walls and beamed ceilings, and enjoyed courteous service as well as a spacious bedroom with nice solid old furniture and a heavy brocade bedspread. *(Dr and Mrs Peter Woodford, Gary and Eileen Kilday, and others)*

Open All year except 23 Dec–15 Jan.
Rooms 2 suites, 23 double, 1 single – 9 with bath, 7 with shower; all with telephone and colour TV.
Facilities Lift. Salon, bar with TV, conference and banqueting facilities, restaurant, cellar (wine tastings). English spoken.
Location Central, near cathedral. Follow signs "Point 1". No private parking.
Credit cards None accepted.
Terms B&B: single 108.60–262 frs, double 141.20–279.20 frs. Set lunch/dinner 99 and 125 frs.

DINAN 22100 Côtes-du-Nord   **Map 8**

Hôtel d'Avaugour   *Tel* (99) 39.07.49
1 place du Champ-Clos

Dinan is a handsome medieval town on a rocky hilltop above the river Rance: it has steep cobbled streets, a beautifully laid out jardin anglais, and a sturdy 14th-century castle where Duchess Anne de Bretagne used to live. The d'Avaugour is fully worthy of this setting – a spacious Breton mansion unusually comfortable and attractive, with a flowery garden beside the summit of the ramparts. This year there is a new restaurant, open evenings only, in the 15th-century tower on the ramparts. "We liked it immensely," says a correspondent; "an excellent dinner, though not cheap." Some French guides too, rate the cuisine highly. Rooms at the front can be noisy with lorries; at the back "only the municipal peacocks would be likely to disturb one". But recent visitors complain of off-hand reception, confusion in their booking and inadequate car-parking facilities. More reports please.

Open All year.
Rooms 24 double, 3 single – 25 with bath, 2 with shower, all with telephone, TV and mini-bar. (Front rooms can be noisy.)
Facilities Lift. Drawing room, bar. Garden with terrace (meals served there in summer) and tower with restaurant for evening meals. River Rance 1 km, beach (Dinard) 20 km. English spoken.
Location In town centre; coming from Rennes, turn left after the viaduct, continue straight until you reach the Place, then left. Parking.
Restriction Not ideal for &, but salon and some rooms on ground floor.
Credit cards Access, Amex, Diners.
Terms Rooms: single 250 frs, double 300 frs. Breakfast 23 frs; bar lunch 75 frs incl. wine; set dinner 85 frs; full alc 250 frs. Reduced rates and special meals for children.

DOMME 24250 Dordogne   **Map 10**

Hôtel l'Esplanade   *Tel* (53) 28.31.41

"Domme, overlooking the Dordogne valley, is tastefully restored, in the tradition of Viollet-le-duc, and is full of expensive antique shops and foie gras. M. and Mme Gillard (he the chef, she the front-of-house manager) have refurbished this hotel which has always enjoyed a superb view. The rooms are individually decorated in a variety of floral wallpapers in the best tradition of the French country hotel, but they also have private baths or showers. Gillard's table can be recommended not only for the

skill he brings to it, but also for the size of the dishes in which that skill is revealed. The dining room is large and airy, and the hotel stands at the peak of a town on a peak." *(Frederic and Sylvia Raphael)*
  The Raphaels sent us this description a few years back, and they still visit the *Esplanade* and say it is as good as ever. Recent visitors are also mainly enthusiastic. "We spent two weeks and loved every minute. Glorious position, total comfort, fabulous cuisine – try quail stuffed with foie gras." "The whole place was fresh and attractive, the service quick and friendly. Madame was very kind to us. The *demi-pension* menu offered wide choice and all was excellent." "When you arrive in Domme at midday, it is awful – a tourist trap. But in the late afternoon it quietens. On a midsummer evening, when it is still and you stroll along the cliff-top path after dinner, magic is in the air." *(Marcia Suddards, Jane Grange, John and Elizabeth Hills.)* One dissident voice however this year: "Mr Raphael writes good fiction: regrettably his description of the hotel was also in that class, we felt. Bedroom scruffy, stale fish, dubious terrine." More reports please.

Open 10 Mar–4 Nov; 4 Dec–31 Jan. Closed Mon.
Rooms 19 double, 1 single – 16 with bath, 4 with shower, all with telephone; some rooms with balconies. 5 rooms in annexe.
Facilities Salon with TV, 2 dining rooms; terrace with panoramic views. River 2 km, swimming pool 10 km. English spoken.
Location 1 km S of the Dordogne; Sarlat 12 km. Gourdon 26 km.
Restriction Not ideal for &, but salon and some rooms on ground floor.
Credit card Amex.
Terms [1985 rates] half-board (obligatory in season) 210–320 frs; full board 340 frs. Reduced rates and special meals for children.

DUCEY 50220 Manche   Map 8

Auberge de la Selune   *Tel* (33) 48.53.62
2 rue St-Germain

A veteran traveller in France enthuses this year about the hearty Norman good cheer at this spruce little hotel, with its garden and terrace above the river, in a dullish village not far from Mont-St-Michel and Avranches with its 1944 battle souvenirs. "Bedrooms very clean and pretty: ours was Rechitto blue, with white furnishings. Best rooms are those at the back, facing garden and river. Josette Girres looks after front of house with quiet charm; her husband is chef, and his freshly made pâtisserie is perfect. Crab pie is a speciality; it comes in a deep pot, topped by pastry looking like a chef's hat. Lots of fresh fish, for example lovely garlicky moules à la crème; apple sorbet with calvados; good breakfast with Normandy butter." *(Eileen Broadbent)*

Open All year except mid-Feb to mid-Jan, Christmas Eve and Mon from Oct–Mar.
Rooms 19 double, 1 single – 19 with bath, all with telephone.
Facilities TV lounge, bar, restaurant, seminar room. Garden with terrace. Salmon fishing in river Selune; tennis nearby.
Location On N176, 11 km SE of Avranches. Private car park.
Terms Rooms: single 113 frs, double 150 frs; dinner, B&B: single 168.50 frs, double 261 frs. Breakfast 13.50 frs; set meals 42, 70 and 81 frs (excluding service charge).

ELINCOURT-SAINTE-MARGUERITE 60157 Oise   Map 8

Château de Bellinglise   *Tel* (4) 476.04.76

Each year, Guide readers bring in a harvest of new French discoveries, even from a sector as well trodden as the Compiègne district north of Paris, where two regular correspondents "strongly recommend" this "most interesting rose-coloured château, part 16th century, set in a 600-acre estate. Its commanding front looks over a large lake and down the valley. We entered through massive iron gates, and were led past beautiful lounges, up a huge stone staircase and along panelled corridors to our small suite – cheerful rugs on the wooden floor, and massive antique furniture including the comfortable bed. It was all very peaceful, and dinner in one of the panelled dining rooms was excellent, with good service. Despite its size it is very much a family-run hotel. Large stables house a conference centre, and there are pavilions amid the trees." *(Angela and David Stewart)*

Open All year except Christmas. Restaurant closed Sun evening.
Rooms 2 suites, 33 double – 17 with bath, 18 with shower, all with telephone; 12 rooms in annexe.
Facilities Lounge, TV lounge, bar, restaurant, 4 conference rooms. Large grounds with tennis court. English spoken.
Location 15 km N of Compiègne, on D142 to Lassigny. Parking.
Credit cards Access, Diners, Visa.
Terms Rooms: single occupancy 290 frs, double 380 frs. Breakfast 28 frs; set meals 80, 160 and 195 frs (excluding service charge); full alc 160 frs.

EMBRUN 05200 Hautes-Alpes   Map 10

Les Bartavelles   *Tel* (92) 43.20.69
Crots   *Telex* 401480 BARTAV

"A real find", this unusually designed and fairly smart modern holiday hotel, standing alone in glorious open sub-Alpine country, between Embrun and the big lake of Serre-Ponçon with its hydro-electric dam. "Most attractive, crescent shaped with a wavy roof; lovely gardens with pool, superb bedroom (a bit dusty) with balcony. Helpful management, and excellent food in an appealing circular restaurant. *Bartavelles* are local birds," *(Joy and Lenny Alcock)*. Interesting dishes on the set menus, eg, gibelotte de lapin and filet de rascasse.

Open All year except 30 Sept–7 Nov.
Rooms 36 double, 7 single – 26 with bath, 17 with shower, all with telephone, 4 with TV, some with balcony. 3 bungalows in grounds, each containing 2 rooms and 2 suites.
Facilities TV room with video, bar, dining room, conference room. Large grounds with unheated swimming pool. Near Serre-Ponçon lake with rock beaches, bathing in July and Aug, and fishing. Tennis 1 km. Les Orres ski resort nearby. English spoken.
Location 3 km SW of Embrun, off the RN94.
Restriction Not suitable for &.
Credit cards All major cards accepted.
Terms [1985 rates] B&B: single 268 frs, double 291 frs; dinner, B&B: single 309 frs, double 481 frs; full board: single 408 frs, double 525 frs. Set lunch from 71 frs, dinner up to 165 frs. Extra beds provided free of charge for under 4-year-olds.

ÉPERNAY 51200 Marne — Map 9

Hôtel des Berceaux *Tel* (26) 55.28.84
13 rue des Berceaux

For those who enjoy the bracing Frenchness of the Champagne capital, but would also like to talk English there with an English *hôtelière*, then just the place is the *Berceaux*, cradled into a quiet side-street yet very central. It is run by *patron-chef* Luc Maillard and his English wife Jill, who will organise visits to the local Champagne firms and their *caves*. "Our welcome from Jill Maillard was charming. The hotel looks charming, too, has no pretensions, and provides simply furnished rooms with well-equipped bathrooms at a very fair price." M. Millard's dishes are expensive, of the turbot au Champagne and tournedos au vieux marc de Champagne type. Those in search of cheaper fare could try the excellent *Terrasse*, down by the Marne. *(Simon Small)*

Open All year except Christmas and Sun.
Rooms 30 double – all with bath or shower and telephone.
Facilities Lift. Lounge, bar, wine bar with piano, TV room, dining room. Visits to nearby Champagne houses. English spoken.
Location Central, near Place de la République. No special parking facilities.
Credit cards All major cards accepted.
Terms Rooms: single 195 frs, double 203 frs. Half-board: single 340 frs, double 482 frs; full board: single 448 frs, double 896 frs. Continental breakfast 25 frs; buffet breakfast 40 frs; set lunch/dinner 130 frs; full alc 400 frs. Reduced rates and special meals for children.

L'ÉPINE 51460 Marne — Map 8

Aux Armes de Champagne *Tel* (26) 68.10.43
Telex 830 998 F

A Guide newcomer this year, well liked: "Jean-Paul Perardel and his wife Denise have restored and modernised this old coaching-inn in the village of L'Épine (east of Châlons-sur-Marne) where it stands in the square opposite the enormous basilica of Notre-Dame, a pilgrimage centre in the Middle Ages. The rooms are prettily furnished. A picturesque garden at the back, with a small stream, is an ideal spot for an apéritif. Jean-Paul's meals are excellent *(Michelin* rosette, *Gault Millau toque)* and good value. The floodlighting of the basilica makes a fine backdrop for diners at the window tables," *(K W George)*. "Clean and comfortable, without the firework-night-in-Hawaii wallpaper that usually tells you that you are in a French hotel. Staff friendly and obliging, cooking a dream. The hotel is in the champagne district and three-quarters of the long wine list is devoted to the stuff" (much of the menu too – you can have either snails or pigeon cooked in it). "The hotel is on a main road, but quiet." *(Anna and Simon Levene)*

Open All year except 8 Jan–15 Feb and Christmas.
Rooms 35 double, 2 single – 13 with bath, 16 with shower, all with telephone, some with TV. 12 rooms in 2 annexes. Ground-floor rooms.
Facilities Dining room, bar, breakfast room, functions facilities. Concerts in summer. Small garden with mini-golf. English spoken.
Location Central; village is 8.5 km E of Chalons, on N3. Parking.

Credit cards Access, Diners, Visa.
Terms [1985 rates] B&B: single 154 frs, double 328 frs. Set meals 68, 120 and 180 frs; full alc 250 frs.

ERDEVEN 56410 Morbihan   Map 8

Hostellerie Château de Keravéon   *Tel* (97) 55.68.55

A regular Guide correspondent writes briefly but mouth-wateringly about this 18th-century castle, complete with dovehouse, moat, Renaissance well and two-and-a-half-acre park. "An exquisitely restored château. Although only 20 minutes from Carnac, an oasis of peace even in mid-summer. *Demi-pension* obligatory in season. The food is plentiful, with emphasis on fish dishes. The area around is littered with prehistoric monuments. The beach of Erdeven – one of the loveliest in Brittany – with its miles of clean white sand is only 10 minutes' distance. Expensive, but an idyllic retreat for those who want to visit this part of Brittany and yet be far from the madding crowd." (*David Blum*)

Open All year.
Rooms 3 triple, 3 suites, 13 double, 1 single – 18 with bath, 2 with shower, all with telephone.
Facilities Lounge with TV, reading room, dining room, conference facilities. Garden with swimming pool. Beaches, fishing, golf nearby.
Location 1.5 km NE of Erdeven by D105.
Restriction Not suitable for &.
Terms Rooms 528–638 frs; dinner, B&B: 468–528 frs per person. Breakfast 40 frs; set lunch/dinner 170–250 frs; full alc 230–300 frs.

EU 76260 Seine-Maritime   Map 8

Pavillon Joinville   *Tel* (35) 86.24.03
Route du Tréport

This little Normandy town with a short name and a long history is where William the Conqueror met Harold; its collegiate church has a sculpture of St Lawrence O'Toole, 12th-century primate of Ireland, who died here. The *Pavillon Joinville*, outside the town, is also historic: it was built as a hunting-lodge by Louis-Philippe's son, then used similarly by the Duke of Westminster who kept a pack of hounds here before 1914. Today it is a *Relais du Silence*, a handsome red-brick building with ziggurat Flemish-style roof and period decor. "The most delightful place", says a 1985 nominator; "a lovely staircase, bedrooms prettily decorated, heating on all night in chill weather, lovely country setting. I enjoyed watching the rabbits play in the garden. The obliging owner gave me a pleasant light dinner, even on the day (Monday) the restaurant was officially closed." (*Mrs M D Prodgers*) More reports welcome.

Open All year.
Rooms 18 double, 2 single – all with bath and telephone, 10 with TV.
Facilities Large hall, 2 salons, bar, restaurant, gallery. Large garden with terrace, archery and tennis; private helipad. Sea 1 km, forest 2 km, river 1 km. English spoken.
Location 25 km from Dieppe. 1 km W of Eu on road to Le Tréport. Parking.
Restriction Not suitable for &.
Credit cards Access, Visa.

Terms Rooms 290–390 frs; dinner, B&B: single 454–554 frs, double 638–738 frs ; full board: single 554–654 frs, double 838–938 frs. Breakfast 34 frs; set lunch/dinner 95 and 155 frs; full alc 240 frs. Christmas and New Year breaks. Special meals for children on request.

EUGÉNIE-LES-BAINS 40320 Landes   Map 10

Les Prés d'Eugénie   *Tel* (58) 58.19.01
                          Telex 540470

Michel Guérard's very superior restaurant in a Second Empire mansion, 53 kilometres north of Pau, is famous as the home of *cuisine minceur*: dishes at once gastronomically delicious and low on calories. Ancillary to the restaurant is an excellent hotel, a thermal establishment and, paradoxically, a health farm where guests pay to reduce on diets devised by a three-star chef. "Magical", "cuisine and service of genius", "food theatrically presented"; "a hotel full of lovely idiosyncracies and romantic colour schemes" – so ran some earlier reports, capped this year by one of our most experienced travellers: "A superb night's stay – we lapped up the comfort. Elegant buildings in very pretty grounds where fountains play, lions lie and a semi-nude lady stands in the courtyard. Our bedroom was a gentle and luxurious dream in pale dusky pink and white, looking on to a sun-bathed terrace, blue pool and green fields. The bed with a heavy brass headboard was wide and comfortable. The decor in the public rooms was a pale champagne; fires burned brightly on a chilly day, and at the edge of each table in the elegant dining room was a unique candelabra. The menus to our minds were better than the à la carte, for one tasted more dishes: this was *cuisine gourmande* at its best, and each course arrived looking like a painting – such artistry. Soft background music." Top ratings in the French guides, needless to say. *(Jean Harding, Norman and Joan Gowin, and others)*

Rosemary Rose, endorsing earlier reports, says: "Do tell your readers they can't just turn up there expecting a *cuisine minceur* meal. For that you have to have a doctor's certificate and be staying at least several days, and you eat at different times from the other guests. The food we were given was excellent, but not at all *minceur*." One or two bedrooms, at least, are without the idyllic views claimed in the brochure.

Open 9 Mar–12 Nov.
Rooms 7 suites, 28 double – all with bath, telephone, radio and colour TV.
radio and colour TV.
Facilities Salon, smoking and billiard room, TV room, gallery, bar, dining rooms. Beauty salon, thermal baths, sauna. 2 tennis courts, *boules*, unheated swimming pool. Garden and river. Golf 25 km. English spoken.
Location Off D944 St-Sever–Aubagnan, 53 km NE of Pau.
Credit cards Amex, Diners.
Terms [1985 rates, excluding 15% service] Rooms 800–1,000 frs. Breakfast 48 frs; set lunch/dinner 370 frs.

LES EYZIES-DE-TAYAC 24620 Dordogne   Map 10

Hôtel du Centenaire   *Tel* (53) 06.97.18

Les Eyzies, France's leading "centre of prehistory", is dominated by steep cliffs riddled with paleolithic caves. The *Centenaire* is an ambitious modern hotel in the village (in summer, traffic is heavy during the day but quiet at night) and has long been celebrated for its cuisine (two *Michelin* rosettes, two *Gault Millau* red *toques*, for such inventive dishes as braised foie gras with honey and mint). It was dropped from the Guide last year for lack of feedback, but we welcome its return: "We spent a comfortable and gastronomic week, in a very comfortable suite. Breakfasts were superb, dinners excellent, and the price (out of season) unimaginably low. But the owners were not friendly." "A family affair, wholly unpretentious, and its courtesies and delights are beyond criticism," is a slightly different view. Another visitor was put in a pleasant annexe in a modern villa 1.3 kilometres away and enjoyed it: "Bluetits tapped at the windows, owls hooted at night." Better than lorries. *(Stanley Burnton, Frederic and Sylvia Raphael, and others)*

Open Apr–Nov. Restaurant closed Tue lunch-time.
Rooms 3 suites, 24 double, 3 single – 27 with bath, 3 with shower, all with telephone; 10 rooms in annexe: 4 are in an annexe 1.3 km from hotel.
Facilities Salon, TV room, bar, restaurant. Large garden with terraces. English spoken.
Location 45 km SE of Périgueux, 20 km W of Sarlat off D47. Parking.
Restriction Not suitable for &.
Credit cards All major cards accepted.
Terms Rooms: single 170–190 frs, double 220–250 frs; dinner, B&B 300–450 frs per person; full board 400–550 frs per person. Breakfast 35 frs; set lunch/dinner 130, 230 and 320 frs; full alc 300 frs. Reduced rates and special meals for children.

Hôtel Cro-Magnon   *Tel* (53) 06.97.06
                         Telex 570637

Long a favourite with readers, this creeper-covered, heavily gabled old hotel on the outskirts of a busy tourist centre is again praised this year for its comfort, service, setting and especially cuisine (*Michelin* rosette, two *Gault Millau* toques). "Marvellous – friendly and welcoming, delicious food, especially the soups and the fish in pastry; dinner in the garden." "Our annexe room was spacious and pleasant, food was exquisitely presented (lovely fresh vegetables), service was excellent and the pool a bonus." A few caveats, however: the *en pension* meals are far duller than the expensive à la carte; traffic and train noises can be heard in some front rooms; and one reader found the garden and pool area a little unkempt. Set apart from the tourist hubbub, the hotel has formal elegant decor and its special atmosphere comes from the fact that its founder was a 19th-century prehistorian who first identified Cro-Magnon man and discovered the nearby prehistoric sites. *(Rodney and Mary Milne-Day, Mimi Lloyd-Chandler, and others)*

Open End Apr–12 Oct.
Rooms 3 suites, 24 double – 25 with bath, 2 with shower, all with telephone; 12 rooms in annexe; 1 ground-floor room.
Facilities 2 lounges, 2 dining rooms, garden restaurant. 5 acres of parkland with heated swimming pool; river at foot of grounds. English spoken.
Location 600 metres W of town centre. Parking.
Restriction Not suitable for &.
Credit cards All major cards accepted.
Terms B&B double 312–444 frs; dinner, B&B 325–350 frs per person; full board 365–400 frs per person. Set lunch/dinner 100–300 frs.

FRANCE

Moulin de la Beune

Tel (53) 06.94.33

This big converted mill, newly opened as a hotel and new to the Guide, stands next to the National Museum of Prehistory and beside the river Beune which flows through its garden. "Tastefully restored. There is a large old fireplace in the lounge/reception which is attractively furnished as are the bedrooms. Decor was reminiscent of the simpler Spanish *paradores*. Inviting breakfast room, with glass doors leading out to tables by the river. Breakfast exceptional, with home-made jams, hot crois-sants, coffee ad lib. Smart chairs in the garden. Warm welcome from the owners, the Dudicourts." No restaurant, but you can eat superbly (at a price) at the *Cro-Magnon* and the *Centenaire* (see above). *(Kay and Neville Varley)*

Open 23 Mar–4 Nov.
Rooms 6 suites (5 for 3 people, 1 for 4), 14 double – 14 with bath, 6 with shower, all with telephone; 4 ground-floor rooms.
Facilities Salon, salon/bar, TV room, breakfast room. Garden with river (fishing); swimming pool and tennis nearby.
Location Central, near the National Museum of Prehistory. Parking.
Credit cards Amex, Visa.
Terms Double rooms 162–205 frs. Breakfast 20 frs. (No restaurant.)

ÈZE-BORD-DE-MER 06360 Alpes-Maritimes   Map 11

Cap Estel

Tel (93) 01.50.44

On the coast between Beaulieu and Monaco, and directly below the famous eyrie-village of Èze. A stately white Italianate villa, once the home of a prince, now an elegant if somewhat staid luxury hotel, set on a promontory in its own lovely wooded garden, and with its own small pebbly beach. Readers who again went back this year report: "We have spent our summer holidays here for the past 16 years, and it's rather like a club with the same people returning. It's also family run. We have a room with sitting room leading on to a patio – you can lie in your bath and watch boats go by. There is a comfortable public lounge and poolside bar. There's a magnificent hors-d'oeuvre table at lunch outdoors under the trees, and dinner is often served there too. Food and comfort excellent." *(Tom and Rosemary Rose; also J A)*

Open Feb–end Oct.
Rooms 10 suites, 35 double – all with bath and telephone, terrace or loggia, air-conditioning; 6 rooms in annexe.
Facilities Lift. 2 salons, cocktail bar, TV room, restaurant, sauna, solarium, indoor and outdoor swimming pools. Garden with restaurant, private beach with watersports. Tennis and sailing nearby. English spoken.
Location Just off Lower Corniche (N98), 3 km NE of Beaulieu; 4 km from Monaco.
Credit card Access.
Terms Dinner, B&B: single 850–1,150 frs, double 1,550–2,100 frs; full board 200 frs per person added. Set dinner 280 frs; full alc 350 frs.

> Details of amenities vary according to the information – or lack of it – supplied by hotels in response to our questionnaire. The fact that lounges or bars or gardens are not mentioned must not be taken to mean that a hotel lacks them.

FAVERGES-DE-LA-TOUR 38110 Isère   Map 10

Le Château de Faverges   *Tel* (74) 97.42.52
La Tour-du-Pin   *Telex* FAVTOUR 300372

In winter, hoteliers Jo and Catherine Tournier run their ski-hotel of that name at Courchevel (q.v.); in summer, they turn their attention to this imposing newly converted château topped by a high circular turreted tower – a fairly typical *Relais et Châteaux* member. It is nominated this year by experienced Francophiles: "It stands high in large grounds, just off the A43 *autoroute* between Lyon and Chambéry. There are fine views towards the Alps. Public rooms are beautifully restored, with a superb marble staircase. The lower floors, almost cellar-like, provide the restaurant, attractive, though some decor is a bit 'kitsch'. There is an outdoor terrace for summer eating, a swimming pool, sauna and tennis. Our bedroom was large, comfortable, with a mix of antiques and good French rural 'repro'. The food was very good, new style with regional overtones. Staff are friendly and efficient. The Tourniers are still busy landscaping and planting," *(Pat and Jeremy Temple).* Since this report, there has been a change of chef, so we'd welcome news on whether the food is still as good (former *Michelin* rosette and two *Gault Millau toques).*

Open 10 May–30 Oct. Restaurant closed Mon.
Rooms 37 double, 3 single – 30 with bath, 10 with shower, all with telephone, radio, colour TV and baby-listening; 20 rooms in annexe; cottage with 3 rooms.
Facilities Lounge, TV lounge, bar, dining rooms, conference/function room, gymnasium, sauna. Grounds with terrace, swimming pool, 2 tennis courts, jogging track; 9-hole golf course planned for 1986. English spoken.
Location Leave Lyon/Chambéry *autoroute* (A43) at La Tour du Pin or Abrets exits and follow signs for Faverges de la Tour on N75. Parking.
Credit cards Amex, Diners, Visa.
Terms B&B: single 450–1,050 frs, double 600–1,600 frs; dinner, B&B: single 655–1,000 frs, double 1,100–1,500 frs. Set lunch from 190 frs, dinner 370 frs; full alc 400 frs.

FAYENCE 83440 Var   Map 11

Moulin de la Camandoule   *Tel* (94) 76.00.84

Quintessential Provence, with splendid hill-villages close by, such as Mons and Seillans. "The *Moulin* is a little south of the Fayence/Seillans road and stands in its own large grounds, so there is no trouble with noise at night. It is a converted olive-mill, and much of the old machinery still stands in the large dining room. There are bedrooms in the main building and in what were, I believe, the stables. We had one in the latter – or rather, two rooms: downstairs was the bathroom and a little sitting room, upstairs the bedroom reached by a small spiral staircase. The proprietor, M. Snyers, is Belgian and spent his youth in England during the war. We found this a delightful spot with good food." *(John Newnham) Michelin* and *Gault Millau* both award red for attractive charm. However, a Guide reader this year awards a black mark for failure to reply to a booking letter sent with a reply-paid coupon.

Open 1 Apr–20 Dec. Restaurant open 1 Apr–1 Oct; closed Tue except Jul and Aug when it is open in the evening.
Rooms 2 suites, 8 double, 2 single – 9 with bath, the 2 singles with shower.
Facilities Lounges, bar, restaurant. Garden with river and swimming pool. English spoken.
Restriction Children not very welcome here.
Location 3 km SE of Fayence by D19 and road to Notre-Dame-des-Cyprès.
Credit cards None accepted.
Terms Rooms: single 155 frs, double 310–330 frs; dinner, B&B: single 290 frs, double 570–600 frs. Breakfast 33 frs; set lunch/dinner 110–115 frs; full alc 180–250 frs.

FÈRE-EN-TARDENOIS 02130 Aisne   Map 9

Hostellerie du Château   *Tel* (23) 82.21.13
                                                    Telex OTELFER 145526

Readers with a taste for grandeur continue to enjoy this luxurious manor house, part-Renaissance, part-19th-century, that stands in its own sizeable park within a forest, 45 kilometres west of Rheims. "Bedroom a bit small, but dining room elegant, and cooking superb and unusual" is a report this year. Some earlier ones: "The setting, with the ruins of an old castle reached by a Renaissance bridge, is unsurpassable. We walked there by moonlight." "Complete peace in perfect countryside." "Our room was quite large, covered with typical French flower-design silk wall hangings. The windows opened on to a superb view of the grounds, where in the morning we watched rabbits on the lawns. The service was very formal but faultless, and the food delicate and exquisitely presented" (two *Michelin* rosettes, two *Gault Millau toques* for braised hot foie gras with winkles etc). However, this idyll is queried this year by a traveller who received a sympathetic and helpful welcome but then found his room under-heated and the food disappointing, pretentiously described and ineptly served – "I have come to the conclusion", he says, "that a *Michelin* star is a sort of Kiss of Death." We should welcome more verdicts. (*Joan A Powell, Ann Copp, Dorothy Masterson, and others*)

Open All year except 1 Jan–1 Mar.
Rooms 8 suites, 13 double – all with bath and telephone; 8 with TV, some with frigo-bar; 4 ground-floor rooms.
Facilities Salon, bar, 3 restaurants; some conference facilities. Large park and formal gardens with surrounding forest, with tennis court. Fishing, riding 5 km; golf 40 km. English spoken. &.
Location 5 km N of Fère-en-Tardenois, on road to Fismes; Soissons 26 km, Reims 46 km.
Credit cards Access, Amex, Visa.
Terms [1985 rates] rooms: single occupancy 360 frs, double 550–680 frs, suites 700–900 frs. Breakfast 40 frs; set lunch/dinner 220–230 frs. Reduced rates and special meals for children.

Warning: there were major changes in French telephone numbers in the autumn of 1985 after we had gone to press. It is possible, therefore, that not all our French telephone numbers, particularly those of hotels which failed to answer our questionnaire, are accurate.

FLAGY 77156 Seine-et-Marne   Map 9

Hôtel-Restaurant au Moulin   *Tel* (6) 096.67.89
6 rue du Moulin

An enchanting 13th-century mill, beautifully converted into a restaurant-with-rooms, in a village 25 kilometres south-east of Fontainebleau. Latest visitors continue to pull out superlatives ("interesting and perfect in every way") especially about the "delightful" staff and the setting – the meals in summer under weeping willows beside a stream, the sight and sound of rushing water, the charming lounge with some of the old mill-wheels and pulleys. One reader had a bedroom at the top of the lock gates and was woken by the resident cat scratching at the door. Bedrooms are small but prettily furnished and prices modest for the Île-de-France. One recent visitor had a "marvellous" meal, but another felt that the set menus are less interesting than the à la carte. *(Dennis Johnson, Mrs S R Wilkins)*

Our readers' affection is reciprocated by the hotel owner, Claude Scheidecker, who wrote in May this year: "More than ever we are submerged by English requests for bookings – between 15 and 20 letters a day – thanks to your Guide and some others, speaking so nicely about our little mill. So we are fully booked till September by reservations from England. And English clients are much more pleasant than any other kind."

Open All year except 15–27 Sept, 19–23 Jan; closed Sun evening and Mon.
Rooms 10 double – all with bath, wc and telephone.
Facilities Lounge, bar, beamed restaurant. Large garden beside river, fishing (fishing card can be bought in the village). English spoken.
Location 23 km S of Fontainebleau by N6 (18 km), then turn right by D403, and immediately left by D120.
Restriction Not suitable for &.
Credit cards Amex, Diners, Visa.
Terms B&B: single occupancy 132–159 frs, double 188–228 frs; dinner, B&B: single 220–247 frs, double 364–404 frs; full board: single 316–342 frs, double 556–596 fr. Set lunch/ dinner 81–107 frs; full alc 160–220 frs. Reduced rates for children; special meals on request.

FLORAC 48400 Lozère   Map 10

Grand Hôtel du Parc   *Tel* (66) 45.03.05
47 avenue Jean-Monestier

The sleepy and agreeable little town of Florac, in a mountain valley, makes a good base for exploring the Cévennes and the Gorges du Tarn; Stevenson described it in his *Travels with a Donkey*. The hotel is dignified and somewhat old-fashioned, though it has recently given itself a modern extension and some rooms are in a separate building across the large garden. You can take meals on a sunny terrace facing the hills. One couple found it "quiet, cool and peaceful, although near the town centre. Dinner was excellent, notably the truite aux amandes, and the splendid cheeseboard. Service efficient and courteous." *(Brian and Elizabeth Hoyle)* More reports welcome.

Open 15 Mar–1 Dec. Closed Mon out of season, restaurant also closed Sun evening out of season.
Rooms 54 double, 4 single – 21 with bath, 21 with shower, all with telephone; 26 rooms in annexe; 4 ground-floor rooms.
Facilities Lounge with TV, conference room, restaurant. Garden. 200 metres from river, sand and rock beach; fishing, canoeing. English spoken.
Location 100 metres from town centre. Florac is on N106, 39 km S of Mende. Parking and free garage.
Credit cards Amex, Diners, Visa.
Terms Rooms 128 frs; dinner, B&B 160–220 frs per person; full board 210–250 frs per person. Breakfast 15 frs; set meals 53, 72 and 130 frs.

LA FLOTTE 17630 Ile de Ré, Charente Maritime — Map 10

Le Richelieu *Tel* (46) 09.60.70
44 avenue de la Plage

Ré, a long flat island near La Rochelle, is noted for its clear sparkling light, its sandy beaches (crowded in summer) and its asparagus; some women still wear the local white headdresses known as *quichenotte*, originally used as a defence against amorous English soldiers ("kiss not"). This year an English invader brought his wife on their wedding anniversary and stayed in October at the best hotel: "Beautiful and comfortable; de luxe. We had the best room, huge balcony, good breakfast. Lovely swimming pool, heated until Hurricane Hortense arrived and ruined the grapes. Dinner was marvellous *(Michelin* rosette, two red *Gault Millau toques)* – langoustine tails on red peppers, a large fish from the bay, a divine pudding of solid cream – that sort of thing, coupled with *no vegetables or salad at all*, just about finished us every night. A delightful island, quite impossible in season we'd imagine. Best to avoid hurricanes. The other hotels all seemed a bit smelly." *(Gerald Campion)*

Open 3 Feb–3 Jan.
Rooms 22 – most with bath or shower and balcony, all with telephone and TV.
Facilities Salon, restaurant, functions facilities. Garden with swimming pool and tennis court.
Location On N coast of island, facing bay; frequent ferry service to La Pallice/La Rochelle.
Credit cards Access, Visa.
Terms [1985 rates] rooms: single 450 frs, double 650; full board 450–700 frs per person. Breakfast 35 frs; set lunch/dinner 160–280 frs.

FOIX 09000 Ariège — Map 10

Hôtel Audoye-Lons *Tel* (61) 65.52.44
6 place Georges-Duthil

A high triple-towered medieval château rises romantically above Foix, a charming and historic little town of narrow winding streets, near the foothills of the Pyrenees and on the main Toulous/Barcelona road. The *Audoye-Lons*, new to the Guide this year, is worthy of this setting: "Delightful hotel facing a small square, with fountain and half-timbered buildings. Our room was large, overlooking the river Ariège and also (alas) the road: it might be wiser to forego this view for the peace of a room facing the square. Spotlessly clean and charming service. Restaurant was very good, built out over the river with huge sliding windows, so that you feel suspended. The fixed-price menus include magnificent help-yourself hors-d'oeuvres." *(Elizabeth Hill)*

Open All year except Sat in winter.
Rooms 35 – most with bath or shower, all with telephone.
Facilities Salon with TV, bar, snack bar, restaurant and terrace; functions facilities. Swimming, tennis, fishing, riding nearby.
Location Central (back rooms quietest). Parking.
Credit cards All major cards accepted.
Terms [1985 rates] rooms: single 109 frs, double 190 frs. Breakfast 13 frs; set lunch/dinner 48–121 frs.

FONTAINEBLEAU 77300 Seine-et-Marne   Map 8

Hôtel Aigle Noir   *Tel* (1) 64.22.32.65
27 place Napoléon Bonaparte   *Telex* 600080

Fontainebleau's grandest hotel, in the centre, facing the gardens of Napoleon's favourite palace. "A pleasant welcome and I was shown to a wonderfully Victorian room," runs a report this year; "it had all modern conveniences including a television hidden in the wall – but the bath took 15 minutes to become half full. Dinner was not disastrous but not good" (albeit *Gault Millau* awards a red *toque*). Previous visitors have admired the spacious bedrooms and efficient service, and a certain *"ambiance napoléonique"*. The hotel combines classic Louis XVI and Empire decor with all the latest mod. cons. – glass-fibre sound-proofing, etc. *(Roger Bennett, Mrs M D Prodgers)*

Open All year.
Rooms 4 suites (10 more planned for 1986), 26 double (all available as singles) – 28 with bath, 2 with shower, all with telephone, radio, colour TV, mini-bar and sound-proofing.
Facilities Lift. Salon, bar, 2 restaurant, conference and function facilities. 2 small gardens (meals served there weather permitting). Near château park; swimming pool nearby, river 7 km, riding 10 km. English spoken.
Location Central, opposite the château gardens. Parking.
Restriction Not suitable for &.
Credit cards All major cards accepted.
Terms Rooms: single occupancy 655 frs, double 785 frs; dinner, B&B: single 930 frs, double 1,335 frs; full board: single 1,145 frs, double 1,765 frs. Breakfast 60 frs; full alc 130 frs or 300 frs depending which of 2 restaurants you choose. Children up to 12 years sharing parents' room free; special meals.

FONTVIEILLE 13990 Bouches-du-Rhône   Map 11

Auberge La Régalido   *Tel* (90) 97.60.22 and 97.62.01
Rue Frédéric-Mistral

Fontvieille, a small town in the foothills of the Alpilles, makes a good excursion centre for the Arles and Les Baux areas; Daudet's famous windmill is on a hill close by. *La Régalido*, "this jewel of a hotel" in the view of one reader, is a former oil-mill in a side street, now converted into a most welcoming little *auberge*, luxurious yet unpretentious. The flowery garden with its neatly cut lawn is especially attractive. "Each bedroom, named for a plant (mine was *genévrier* – juniper), has great

407

individual charm. The *Auberge* is run by the Michel family. Madame Michel's hand is evident in the decor of the rooms and bathroom, and in the flowers which grace all the rooms. The food is memorable and the atmosphere warmly welcoming" – a report endorsed again this year. One visitor arriving in October found "a fire blazing in the sitting room fireplace". Another speaks of "excellent food, especially magret de canard". Jean-Pierre Michel's cooking wins a *Michelin* rosette, and a *Gault Millau toque*. *(Pierre Guillaud; also Maurice and Taya Zinkin)*

Open Mid Jan–30 Nov.
Rooms 1 suite, 13 double – 12 with bath, 1 with shower, all with telephone; some with TV. 1 ground-floor room.
Facilities 3 small salons (1 with TV), restaurant; salon for functions. Garden. English spoken.
Location 5 km NE of Arles. Leave *autoroute* A7 at Cavaillon, direction St-Rémy-de-Provence, or at Nîmes, direction Arles. Parking.
Credit cards All major cards accepted.
Terms Rooms: single 350 frs, double 600 frs; dinner, B&B: single 650 frs, double 1,100 frs. Breakfast 50 frs; full alc 300 frs. Special meals for children on request.

GÉMENOS 13420 Bouches-du-Rhône   Map 11

Relais de la Magdeleine   *Tel* (42) 82.20.05

"This charming 17th-century *bastide*, set in a large walled garden with lovely bathing pool and changing rooms, is a peaceful and luxurious oasis on the outskirts of the small town of Gémenos" (which is within easy reach of the coast at Cassis, Marseilles, and the wild and strange *massif* of La Sainte-Baume, well worth exploring). "The public rooms and large bedrooms were attractively furnished with antiques; the beds were high quality. The dining rooms were cool and spacious, with some walls covered with silk or damask. But in spite of this luxury there was nothing pretentious or formal about the atmosphere, which was friendly and happy. Monsieur and Madame, and all the young staff, were courteous, charming and helpful. There was an aura of peace, especially on the terrace in the early evening when drinks were served under floodlit plane trees. Provençal cooking par excellence, plus a large selection of pâtisseries and wonderful cheese. At breakfast, freshly made hot brioches, delicious home-made preserves, plenty of good coffee and real butter. In sum, we could find no fault with this beautiful country house, for us a perfect holiday." *(Dennis and Peggy Coombs)*

Open 1 Mar–1 Nov.
Rooms 4 suites, 16 double – 18 with baths, 2 with shower, all with telephone and colour TV.
Facilities Salons, library, dining room. Garden with swimming pool and terrace. Sea with sandy beach 15 km. English spoken.
Location On outskirts of Gémenos, which is 23 km from Marseilles. Exit Pont de L'Étoile from Aix-Toulon motorway.
Restriction Not suitable for &.
Credit cards None accepted.
Terms Double rooms 280–490 frs; dinner, B&B 325–450 frs per person; full board 475–620 frs per person. Breakfast 40 frs; set lunch/dinner 160–170 frs; full alc 270 frs. Off-season rates. Reduced rates and special meals for children.

> Do you know of a good hotel in Lyon?

GENNES 49350 Maine-et-Loire   Map 8

Aux Naulets d'Anjou   *Tel* (41) 51.81.88
Rue Croix-de-Mission

Gennes is a big village on the Loire in the heart of gentle Anjou, between
Angers and Saumur. Here the white-fronted *Naulets* comes new to the
Guide this year with praise from an expert hotel-watcher: "Very typical
of an average French country inn. Very modern with large airy dining
rooms and terrace overlooking the distant Loire. The rooms are in white
with large windows, pine furniture, fresh flowers. Colette Maudonnet,
co-owner and chef, is a gifted cook, offering regional dishes and a touch
of something different – her own type of *cuisine minceur*. The food is
inventive as well as honest. She also sometimes gives cookery courses.
Her husband, Paul, is a good watercolour painter (there is a gallery in
the hotel) who also gives painting courses once a year." *(Maggie
Angeloglou)*

Open 1 Apr–4 Nov. Restaurant closed Mon.
Rooms 20 – most with bath or shower, all with telephone.
Facilities Salon, dining room, picture gallery, functions facilities, garden with
terrace for al fresco meals. Tennis, riding, sailing and bathing nearby.
Location On edge of village. Parking.
Credit cards None accepted.
Terms [1985 rates] rooms: single 150 frs, double 190 frs. Full board 250 frs.
Breakfast 20 frs; set lunch/dinner 62–100 frs.

GIEN 45500 Loiret   Map 10

Hôtel du Rivage   *Tel* (38) 67.20.53
1 quai de Nice

Gien, an attractive Loireside town on one of the main routes south from
Paris, is dominated by a 15th-century castle that contains an impressive
museum of hunting. The very spruce and soigné *Rivage*, facing the river
but off the main road, wins a *Michelin* rosette for such dishes as escalope
de saumon aux morilles – "very attractive dining room overlooking the
river", runs this year's nomination; "attentive service and well-
presented dishes. The cheese trolley was the best I've every seen.
Rooms recently modernised, with bathrooms pleasantly tiled." *(B
Young)*

Open All year except 10 Feb–3 May.
Rooms 20 double, 9 single – all with bath, 1 with shower, all with telephone and
TV.
Facilities Salon, bathing, TV room, dining room, functions room. River with
fishing, bathing, riding, tennis nearby. Golf 20 km. English spoken.
Location On Briare road, on the banks of the Loire. Parking.
Restriction Not suitable for &.
Credit cards Amex, Visa, Diners.
Terms Rooms 95–230 frs. Breakfast 20 frs; lunch 75 frs, dinner 170 frs; full alc 170
frs. Special meals for children on request.

> We need feedback on *all* entries. Often people fail to report on the
> most well-known hotels, assuming that "someone else is sure to".

FRANCE

GIENS 83400 Var   Map 11

Relais du Bon Accueil   *Tel* (94) 58.20.48

This hilltop village stands on the Giens peninsular, south of Hyères. At
La Tour Fondue, two kilometres away, boats leave regularly for the
beautiful island of Porquerolles. The *Relais*, perched on a rocky headland
with lovely sea views, is recommended this year by an American reader:
"A small informal hotel with a well-kept garden, bougainvillea etc. At
first we were put in a very small rooms, but then moved to a lovely room
with painted ceiling, antiques, balcony with a view. Experimental
cuisine, every night something new for those *en pension*. Beach one
kilometre away." *(Cathryn Balk)* More reports welcome.

Open 15 Dec–5 Nov.
Rooms 3 double, 7 single – 3 with bath, 7 with shower, all with telephone and
colour TV; 1 room in annexe.
Facilities Salon, bar, restaurant; terrace, gardens. 1 km from the beach. English
spoken.
Location 12 km S of Hyères.
Restriction Not suitable for &.
Credit cards None accepted.
Terms B&B 255–315 frs; dinner, B&B 315–345 frs; full board 330–360 frs. Set lunch
85–100 frs, dinner 130–200 frs; full alc 140 frs.

GIVRY 71640 Saône-et-Loire   Map 10

Hôtel de la Halle   *Tel* (85) 44.32.45
Place de la Halle

"Charming owners, accommodation basic but cuisine first class and so
reasonably priced", runs a report this year on this modest little hotel in
the centre of a pleasant Burgundy village, nine kilometres west of
Chalon-sur-Saône. It is a venerable building with a fine spiral staircase,
and faces the former market hall. For some people's tastes the place may
be rather basic, and you must not expect any great luxury or elegance in
the rooms; but Christian Renard's regional cooking is popular with our
readers, as it is with locals. *(John and Priscilla Gillet, Dr K Perry, J S
Lawrence)*

Open All year. Closed Sun evening and Mon.
Rooms 10 double – 2 with bath, 5 with shower.
Facilities Salon, restaurant. Garden. Swimming pools 5 and 8 km, also swimming
in nearby river; walks in woods and vineyards. English spoken.
Location Givry is 9 km W of Chalon-sur-Saône on D69. Hotel is central. Parking.
Restriction Not suitable for &.
Credit cards All major cards accepted.
Terms Rooms 105–170 frs; half-board 204–230 frs per person; full board
260–290 frs per person. Breakfast 21 frs.

GOUMOIS 25470 Doubs   Map 10

Hôtel Taillard   *Tel* (81) 44.20.75

An inveterate Taillardophile continues this year to bid us share her
secret paradise. It's a spacious and gracious chalet, secluded on the

410

slope of a wooded valley, right by the Swiss border between Belfort and Neuchâtel. "We had a delightful room, large, very light and airy with a huge bed and settee, a lot of wardrobe space, very clean, decor bright and in sunny colours, and large bathroom – all for 178 frs [1984]. This year, two tame swallows flew into our room and spent an hour with us, trying to decide where to nest.

"We worked our way happily through several meals, drooling over fresh trout in Champagne, mountain ham, jugged hare, sweetbreads on spinach, and fresh salmon with cucumber that stirred my husband (a Yorkshireman not given to wild praise) to charge into the kitchen to tell Mme Taillard it was the best he'd ever had. We tried the local cheeses (Comte, Sassenage) and the lovely mild Vacherin, with to wash it down a glass of Vin Jaune, a Jura wine tasting like dry sherry. Strangest of all, we had a local 'vin de paille' where the grapes dry on straw mats and eventually produce an incredibly sweet dessert wine ... The service is always willing, cheerful, generating a happy and relaxed atmosphere. I cannot explain the magic exuded by the Taillard family – but we always leave Goumois only after booking our next visit." *(Padi Howard)* We have many other reports this year on the *Taillard*. Most agree with Mrs Howard, especially over the "delicious" food. But there have been complaints of small rooms, some in need of refurbishing, and one reader told us she found the *en pension* meals dull. *(Thomas G and Philomena R Ferrara, Rosamund V Hebdon, and others)*

Open 1 Mar–30 Oct.
Rooms 3 suites, 14 double – 11 with bath, 9 with shower, all with telephone.
Facilities Salon, TV room, bar, 2 dining rooms , terrace; river, trout fishing and canoeing; riding and winter sports nearby. English spoken.
Location 50 km SE of Montbéliard, 18 km E of Maiche on D437A and D437B.
Leave *autoroute* A36 at Montbéliard Sud exit. The hotel is near the church. Parking.
Credit cards Amex, Diners, Visa.
Terms B&B: single 123 frs, double 156 frs; half-board (3 days min.) 250 frs per person. Set lunch/dinner 90 frs; full alc 200 frs. Reductions in low season. 5% reduction for children under 8.

LA GRAVE 05320 Hautes-Alpes　　　　　　　　　　　　　**Map 10**

Hôtel La Meijette　　　　　　　　　　　　　　　　　*Tel* (76) 79.90.34

The small ski resort of La Grave stands 5,500 feet up near the Col du Lauteret, on the N91 Grenoble–Briançon road. Like other villages in this area, it is somewhat drab in aspect, but the scenery and the skiing are great. *La Meijette* is on the main road, on a ledge above the Romanche torrent: its modern restaurant, finely built in wood, has been cantilevered out over the river and has spectacular views, shared by the bedrooms, over the valley and the snow mountains. In 1985 a devotee wrote yet again to confirm his earlier report:

"This is as near a perfect hotel for us as any we know – for its combination of setting, unostentatious comfort, very good, homely food, friendly family and possibly the best area for wild flowers known to us. There are some older *chambres*, but most of our bedrooms are chalet-type and very comfortable. There is a five-course meal each evening and a different menu on a two-week cycle. The hotel is run by a delightful and efficient family, the Juges. The time to go for mountain flowers is between mid-June and mid-July – the millions (yes millions) of narcissi and violas are expected to be at their best about the end of June."

Other readers share this enthusiasm. One of them, however, warns that some of the older rooms are small and not very attractive, and that rooms close to the road can suffer from lorry traffic which stops at night but starts early in the morning.*(A H H Stow, and others)*

Open 15 Mar–15 Apr, 20 May–30 Sept. Closed Tue out of season.
Rooms 6 family, 10 double, 2 single – 16 with bath and wc, all with telephone.
Facilities Large sitting room with open fire, bar and TV, restaurant, sun terrace. Winter sports. Some English spoken.
Location On N91, 77 km from Grenoble, 39 km from Briançon. Hotel is in centre of village. Parking.
Restriction Not suitable for &.
Credit cards None accepted.
Terms [1985 rates] rooms 85–240 frs. Breakfast 20 frs; set lunch/dinner 65 and 95 frs.

GRENOBLE 38000 Isère   Map 10

Hôtel des Alpes   *Tel* (76) 87.00.71
45 avenue Félix-Viallet

"Grenoble, still France's number one boom-city, is a huge, sprawling, very modern, none-too-lovely place, redeemed by its sub-Alpine setting (rocky mountains rise from the plain all around) and by the pleasant traffic-free *vieille ville* around the Place Grenette and the Place St-André. Seven minutes' walk from here, and close to the main station, the *Alpes* is a modern and functional little hotel (very Grenoblois) but with a breezy, easy-going ambience. Comfortable beds, good breakfasts, and a sizeable lounge with nice easy chairs but garish decor. Lots of talkative Italian guests. No restaurant – and it's hard to eat well at a modest price in Grenoble, but if you want a splash, the *Pommerois* and *Escalier* are excellent and not *too* pricey." (*J A*)

Open All year.
Rooms 40 – 32 with bath, 8 with shower, all with telephone.
Facilities Lift. Lounge with TV, breakfast room.
Location Near the station. Lock-up underground garage.
Credit card Amex.
Terms Rooms: single 135–155 frs, double 135–180 frs. Breakfast 15 frs. (No restaurant.)

GRIMAUD 83360 Var   Map 11

Hostellerie du Coteau Fleuri   *Tel* (94) 43.20.17
Place des Pénitents

Grimaud, just inland from St-Tropez, is the kind of Provençal hill village that is now *à la mode:* that is, many of its old stones houses have been smartly converted as summer houses. This may have spoilt its authenticity, but at least has given it a new lease of life. The *Coteau Fleuri* is on the edge of the village, an attractive 1900-ish *auberge* in local style, with tiled floors, plenty of flowers, and a friendly atmosphere – "a lovely place, good food", reports an inspector recently. There is a piano for guests to use, and a log fire for chilly days. Bedrooms are rather small –

some are cell-like – but modern, with pretty furnishings and Provençal prints. A terrace leads to a delightful rambling garden slope, with olive trees. Bedrooms and dining room alike have fine view over the Maures mountains, but the sea is not visible. Sound local cooking (dinner only). Hot water can be haphazard. *(Mary and Gerald Prescott, John Newnham, L H)*

Open Mid–Mar to end Oct. Restaurant open mid–May to mid–Oct.
Rooms 14 double – 9 with bath, 5 with shower, all with telephone. Ground-floor room.
Facilities Lounge/bar, 3 dining rooms, terrace. Small garden with fine views. Sandy beach. English spoken.
Location 3 km from Port Grimaud; 10 km from St-Tropez; on edge of village. Parking.
Credit cards Amex, Diners, Visa.
Terms Rooms 260–360 frs. Breakfast 35 frs. Set dinner 110–150 frs. Special meals for children on request.

GUÉTHARY 64210 Pyrénées-Atlantiques   Map 10

Hôtel Briketenia   *Tel* (59) 26.51.34
Rue de l'Empereur

Praise from an inspector this year brings into the Guide this red-and-white Basque chalet on a hillside above the old fishing-port of Guéthary, between St-Jean-de-Luz and Biarritz. "A 17th-century coaching-inn run by the charming and talented Ibarboure family. Their cooking is highly thought of by the locals (dining rooms crowded) and thoroughly merits its *Michelin* rosette: delicious salmon marinaded in dill. Two sons aged 28 and 26 are the master chefs: one did his National Service at the Elysée Palace, cooking for President Giscard d'Estaing. No sitting room, except a TV lounge. Bedroom not elaborate, and smallish, but adequate. Fresh air blows in from the Atlantic, making for good sleep. Those bedrooms with balconies have views of the sea (and of electricity cables)." *(J H)*

Open All year except 31 Oct–14 Dec. Closed Tues except July–Sept.
Rooms 1 for 4, 21 double or triple – 21 with bath, all with telephone, 6 with mono TV, some with balcony. 13 rooms in annexe which is some distance away. 2 ground-floor rooms.
Facilities Dining room; 1 lounge in hotel, 1 in annexe (both with TV). Garden at annexe. Sea nearby with sandy beaches, safe bathing and fishing.
Location Rue de l'Empereur is a turning off RN10, near the church. Parking.
Restrictions Not suitable for &. No children under 7.
Credit cards Amex, Visa.
Terms Rooms: single 150–190 frs, double 180–240 frs; half-board (min. 3 days) 200–240 frs; full board (min. 3 days) 240–280 frs. Breakfast 23 frs; set lunch/dinner 100 and 150 frs; full alc 250 frs. Reduced rates for children; special meals on request.

Hotel Pereria   *Tel* (59) 26.51.68

There's something about Guéthary that seems to appeal to our readers this year, for both our French Basque coast entries are for this village, rather than the larger resorts of Biarritz and St-Jean-de-Luz that lie either side of it. The *Pereria* is another new find: "A seaside hotel where families resort in an old-fashioned way, run by youngish, good-looking and friendly owners, with an attractive and demure staff. It is an old

Basque house, in a big, rather roughly tended garden, with huge bedrooms and bathrooms *en suite*. The annexe, across a busy road, is possibly more comfortable than the hotel itself. Food is naturally good – dishes of plum jam and warm croissants at breakfast, well-cooked and varied dinner menu (for Sunday lunch they gave us lobster). The ambience in fine weather is beautiful – there are hills and the distant sea, and you can watch the sunset from the outdoor dining terrace. We've already booked for next year." *(Eileen Broadbent)*

Open 1 Mar–1 Nov.
Rooms 30 – 26 with bath, 4 with shower, all with telephone; some rooms in annexe.
Facilities Restaurant, conference facilities; terrace. Garden.
Location On the coast between Biarritz and St-Jean-de-Luz.
Restriction Not suitable for ♿.
Credit cards None accepted.
Terms [1985 rates] rooms: single 40–60 frs; double 70–90 frs; full board: 175–220 frs per person. Breakfast 18 frs.

LE HAVRE 76600 Seine-Maritime   Map 8

Hôtel de Bordeaux
147 rue Louis-Brindeau

Tel (35) 22.69.44
Telex 190428 BOROTEL

"Great value for money, a warm welcome, spotless bedroom, breakfast charmingly served in our room" runs a recent report on this modern hotel, utilitarian but much liked by readers for its cheerful service, reasonable prices and useful situation – only five minutes' drive from the car ferries. It stands right opposite the arresting new Maison de la Culture, one of the few architectural joys of a drab Communist-run city. "Super bathrooms"; "the staff speak good English and go out of their way to help." Ferry-catchers can get early breakfasts. No restaurant, but for food try *Le Monaco* or the tiny, always crowded *Mon Auberge*. *(Ann and Kelvin Price, David and Rosemary Philips, and others)*

Open All year.
Rooms 22 double, 9 single – 20 with bath, 11 with shower, all with direct-dial telephone, colour TV, and mini-bar. Rooms are sound-proofed.
Facilities Large lift. Salon, breakfast room. Beach 1 km. English spoken.
Location In town centre, opposite Niemayer centre. Underground car park opposite.
Credit cards All major cards accepted.
Terms B&B: single 270 frs, double 388–461 frs. (No restaurant.) Reduced rates in winter for long stays. Reduced rates for children out of season.

HENNEBONT 56700 Morbihan   Map 8

Château de Locguénolé
Route de Port-Louis

Tel (97) 76.29.04
Telex 950636 CHATEL

A stately home beside a quiet river estuary, not far from Lorient on the south Brittany coast. It stands in 250 acres of its own wooded parkland, with meadows stretching to the river banks. The château has been the family seat of the de la Sablières since 1200; and today, rather than sell it, the Comtesse runs it as an exclusive hotel. Praise from this year's earlier visitors ("a dream"; "truly magnificent cooking") confirms this earlier account: "On a warm, sunny afternoon, it must be one of the most restful places on earth, with only the birds in the trees to disturb the tranquillity. Much of the furniture is well over a hundred years old (I had an Empire *escritoire* in my room) as are the prints and pictures that adorn the walls. The glory of the *Château* resides in its cuisine, proudly presented and well worth its two *Michelin* stars and three *Gault Millau toques*. Some might think it expensive. Personally, for the setting, the square miles of private quiet, the (rather genteel) charm – perhaps a little frayed in places – but, above all, for the deference and imagination which they extend towards a good meal, I am happy to pay the price." However, another traveller this year thought the price exorbitantly high and the ambience too cool and formal. *(John Ring and Mark Dumont, Elaine and Thomas Greene, Yvette and Stefan Wiener)*

Open 1 Mar–16 Nov.
Rooms 4 suites, 38 double – all with bath, direct-dial telephone, baby-listening; 10 with colour TV. 12 rooms in annexe, 3 km away, 10 ground-floor rooms.
Facilities 4 salons, TV room, music room, bar, 3 dining rooms; banqueting room, conference facilities. 250-acre park with heated swimming pool. Tennis court 3 km, golf 20 km. On river; 9 km from beaches. Riding nearby. 2 night clubs and cabaret 1 km; discos nearby. English spoken.
Location 5 km S of Hennebont. Take D781 S for 4 km; sign to hotel is on right. On *autoroute* from Vannes, Auray, Nantes and Rennes take exit Port Louis.
Credit cards All major cards accepted.
Terms B&B: single 400–790 frs, double 440–1,050 frs; dinner, B&B 489–1,000 frs; full board 709–1,220 frs. Set lunch/dinner 195–380 frs; full alc 290 frs. Reduced rates and special meals for children.

HONFLEUR 14600 Calvados   **Map 10**

Hôtel l'Écrin   *Tel* (31) 89.32.39
19 rue Eugène-Boudin

Honfleur is a trippery but very picturesque old Normandy fishing port, where Corot, Monet and notably Boudin formed an artists' colony (there's a Boudin museum). The *Écrin* is recommended by an inspector this year as "up a hill 400 metres from the harbourside, so fairly quiet. The main house, built round a courtyard, has palatial bedrooms at about 400 francs, some with four-posters. Ours was in the cheaper stable block: a pretty room in pale blue with comfortable beds. Spiral stair awkward for carrying luggage, but the staff are obliging. Thin walls. Breakfast fine. The office is worth a detour: 3-feet high black teddy sitting on one chair and two life-sized stuffed fawns lying on a sideboard." *(A H, Patricia Fenn)* No restaurant but *Carlin* and *l'Absinthe*, with views of the port, are both recommended.

Open All year.
Rooms 15 – some in annexe.
Facilities Breakfast room, courtyard. Near beach.
Location Central, near old port.
Credit cards All major cards accepted.
Terms [1985 rates] rooms: single 200 frs, double 410 frs. Breakfast 22 frs. (No restaurant.)

> We depend on detailed fresh reports to keep our entries up-to-date.

IGÉ 71960 Saône-et-Loire   Map 8

Château d'Igé   *Tel* (16) 85.33.33.99
                                                    Telex 351915

This luxurious six-room hotel is a former medieval fortress and
hunting-lodge of the Dukes of Mâcon, set beside a stream on the edge of
the Mâcon hills in Burgundy. Igé itself is "a small village in the middle of
nowhere, away from main roads, with pleasant country lanes for
walking or cycling. Some of the local wines (Mâcon Viré blanc for
example) are very good". As for the hotel: "A proper castle with
rounded turrets, grey ivy-covered walls and stone-flagged floors and
staircases. It is full of character. We had a sizeable room in one of the
turrets – the bedroom was circular, which felt slightly odd at first – with
a large *en suite* bathroom. Food was good, the service was friendly and
some of the staff speak English." Another visitor praises the home
farm's goat's cheese and enjoyed being able to select his own trout from
a holding pond. Food is not cheap, but straightforward rather than fancy
modern. (*K and S M-S, Clay Leitch, Mrs M D Prodgers*)

Open 15 Mar–15 Nov.
Rooms 6 suites, 8 double – 12 with bath, 2 with shower, all with telephone.
Facilities Salon, dining room. Garden. English spoken.
Location 6.5 km N of N79; 14 km NW of Mâcon, 11 km SE of Cluny.
Restriction Not suitable for &.
Credit cards All major cards accepted.
Terms Rooms 420–700 frs. Breakfast 40 frs; set lunch 170 frs, dinner 140–250 frs;
full alc: price not available.

JARNAC 16200 Charente   Map 10

Hostellerie du Château de Fleurac   *Tel* (45) 81.78.22

A 16-century château, rebuilt in the 19th century, set quietly amid the
rolling Cognac vineyards. "Well worth a visit: quite a pretty château in
pleasant grounds; friendly welcome. Inside, it is very pretty with a
marvellous trompe l'oeil floor in the lounge (and there *is* a lounge, a
leg-up on most French hotels). Altogether very civilised, almost
luxurious. Rooms very pleasant, all different – ours, with a marvellous
bed, was newly decorated all in jet black, which sounds awful but
wasn't. Food very good, reasonably priced." (*Gerald Campion*) The
owner, Michel Guichemerre, prides himself on his collection of Cognacs:
two whole rooms are devoted to them.

Open All year except 1–15 Dec. Closed Christmas night, also Sun evening and
Mon in low season.
Rooms 1 suite, 10 double, 8 single – 15 with bath, 3 with shower, all with
telephone; the 8 singles are in the annexe.
Facilities Bar, Cognac lounge, TV room, 3 dining rooms, garden. English spoken.
Location At Fleurac, 9 km NE of Jarnac: take N141 towards Angoulême, then
D384.
Credit cards Access, Diners, Visa.
Terms Rooms: single 120–140 frs, double 250–300 frs; dinner, B&B: single 260–280
frs, double 520–600 frs. Breakfast 25 frs; set lunch/dinner 110 and 160 frs.

JOUÉ-LES-TOURS 37300 Indre-et-Loire   Map 10

Hôtel du Château de Beaulieu   *Tel* (47) 53.20.26
Route de Villandry

This modernised 18th-century château on the south-west outskirts of
Tours, run by a Frenchman, Jean-Pierre Lozay, and his Scottish wife,
has won much new praise this year: "Beautiful grounds, luxurious
rooms, a gastronomic and wine paradise with excellent service in the
best old-fashioned tradition." "Madame Lozay was charming and
helpful." "A treasure for those who want to 'do' the Loire châteaux with
their children: the trim park with large pool, ping-pong, tennis,
mini-golf, is a welcome change for them after the sight-seeing." One
visitor this year found the dining-room's ambience a bit pretentious
(waiters in bow ties) and the service slow. (*Emelyn W Patterson, P L
Aston, Mrs B P Whitehouse, and others*)

Open All year except evening of Christmas Eve.
Rooms 16 double, 1 single – 9 with bath, 7 with shower, all with telephone;
8 rooms in annexe; 3 ground-floor rooms.
Facilities 2 sitting rooms (1 with TV), bar, 2 dining rooms; conference room. Large
park with ping-pong and *boules*. Tennis, swimming and mini-golf nearby; riding,
fishing, golf, sailing a few km away. English spoken. &.
Location 4 km SW of Tours by D86 and D207.
Credit card Visa.
Terms Rooms: single 100–360 frs, double 190–360 frs. For 2 people staying 3 days
or more: half-board 500–650 frs; full board 720–860 frs. Breakfast 28 frs; set
lunch/dinner 140, 180 and 300; full alc 220–250 frs. 20–30% reduction Nov–end
Mar.

KAYSERBERG 68420 Haut-Rhin   Map 10

Hôtel Résidence Chambard   *Tel* (89) 47.10.17
13 rue du Général de Gaulle   *Telex* 880 272

"Kayserberg, one of the prettiest of Alsace's old wine villages, was the
birthplace of Albert Schweitzer and has a small museum devoted to him.
At the other end of its narrow main street is the *Chambard*, a new venture
by *patron/chef* Pierre Irrmann who has taken two old buildings and
renovated them radically, preserving the picturesque façades. His
smartish restaurant-with-rooms puts its accent on serious eating; the
bedroom annexe lacks the personality of a hotel, though the modernised
rooms are comfortable. Breakfast, served in a foyer with dubious 'repro'
decor, included freshly squeezed orange juice. It might be worth paying
the 100 francs extra to secure the one special room, which has a big
canopied bed and a quaint round salon in a 15th-century tower with
views over the wooded hills.

"M. Irrmann's cuisine, *nouvelle* but not too much so, is of a high
standard, deftly served, and deserves its *Michelin* rosette. On the
220-franc [1985] special menu, the marinated raw salmon and the
garlicky ragoût of lamb were delicious. Lavish puddings, a long wine list
with some distinguished clarets, and the Alsace wines reasonably
priced for once (many in the 50 to 70-franc range). Very comfortable.
Breakfast in a crypt. Rooms at the back have small balconies overlooking
vineyards." (*J A, Jonathan Williams*)

Open All year except 1–21 Mar and 1–15 Dec. Restaurant closed Sun evening and all day Mon.
Rooms 2 suites, 16 double, 2 single – all with bath, direct-dial telephone, radio and colour TV.
Facilities Lounge, bar, restaurant, cellar for conferences/functions. 3-acre grounds. English spoken.
Location 10 minutes NW of Colmar on D4. Hotel is central, but quietly situated. Parking.
Restriction Not suitable for &.
Credit cards All major cards accepted.
Terms (Excluding tax: 3 frs per person per day) rooms 320–420 frs. Breakfast 28 frs; set lunch 120 frs, dinner 300 frs; full alc 200–300 frs.

LACAVE 46200 Dordogne   Map 10

Le Pont de l'Ouysse   *Tel* (65) 37.87.04

This part of the Dordogne/Quercy area is as studded with good little country hotels as, say, cafés in Montmartre. This one, only 10 kilometres from Rocamadour, is a restaurant-with-rooms, new to the Guide this year, and much reputed for its regional cooking (*Gault Millau toque*, red *Michelin* "R"). "A delightful situation on a river, with a château looming above, and a chestnut-tree-covered terrace where one can dine in good weather. Family run, with a dog taking up most of the seating in the small sitting room. Some bedrooms adequate, some very simple. The *patron-chef*'s cooking is superb – but too rich for a long stay." (*Elizabeth Robey*)

Open 1 Mar–11 Nov. Closed on Mon out of season.
Rooms 10 double, 1 single – 6 with bath, 2 with shower, all with telephone.
Facilities Lounge, dining room. Garden with swings. Near river, fishing. Some English spoken.
Location 10 km NW of Rocamadour.
Credit cards Access, Visa.
Terms double rooms 150–170 frs; dinner, B&B: 172–180 frs per person. Breakfast 15 frs. Set meals 100, 150 and 160 frs.

LAMASTRE 07270 Ardèche   Map 10

Hôtel du Midi/Restaurant Barattero   *Tel* (75) 06.41.50
Place Seignobos

A pleasant little town in ravishing country on the edge of the Rhône valley, 40 kilometres west of Valence on the road to Le Puy. "Superb countryside, a warm welcome, interesting food, a comfortable bed in the annexe", is one report this year on the *Midi*, which stands in the market square. "The food and the service were wonderful," says another recent visitor; "the dining room was attractive, with fresh flowers, and our bedroom was beautiful, quiet, large and well furnished. We were in an annexe, which had two big public sitting rooms with flowers." Other reports speak of plain furnishings in the bedroom and much traffic noise in front rooms. "But the meal more than compensated for a disappointing room." Clearly, the star asset of the *Midi* is the cuisine of owner/chef Bernard Perrier, which wins a rosette in *Michelin* and *toque* in *Gault Millau*: salade tiède and poularde en vessie are among his specialities. (*Angela and David Stewart, and others*)

Open 1 Mar–15 Dec.
Rooms 20 – 12 with bath, 3 with shower, all with telephone; 1 ground-floor room.
Garden rooms are quietest.
Facilities 2 salons, 3 restaurants. Garden. Ramps for &.
Location Central. Parking.
Credit cards Access, Amex, Visa.
Terms Rooms: single 150 frs, double 200 frs. Breakfast 25 frs. Set lunch/dinner
130–300 frs. Reduced rates and special meals for children.

LANGRES 52200 Haute-Marne   Map 10

Grand Hôtel de l'Europe   *Tel* (25) 85.10.88
23–25 rue Diderot

Langres deserves to be better known: with its fine ancient ramparts, it
stands high on a ridge and has many 17th- and 18th-century buildings.
The *Europe*, a sedate stone-fronted hostelry near the town centre, offers
good value at modest prices and makes a useful *étape* on the way to
Switzerland. "Excellent – a nice room in the courtyard", "very good –
food better than the rooms, a bit basic", are two recent comments. The
cooking has a red *Michelin* "R" for quality at fair prices: "The 113-franc
menu [1985] was one of the best meals I have eaten anywhere," is one
reader's verdict. The main road bypasses the town, making it fairly quiet
at night, though front rooms may suffer from the noise from the bar
opposite. (*R S Gunn, K W George, William Goodhart, and others*)

Open All year except 28 Apr–12 May and 29 Sept–21 Oct. Restaurant closed Sun
evening and Mon lunchtime.
Rooms 3 suites, 24 double, 1 single – 8 with bath, 16 with shower, all with
direct-dial telephone; 8 rooms in annexe. Rooms overlooking garden are quietest.
Facilities Salon, restaurant, TV room, bar. English spoken.
Location Between Chaumont (35 km) and Dijon (66 km); railway station 3 km.
Take Langres Nord exit from *autoroute* (A31). 10 minutes to hotel. Central. Garage
facilities for 20 cars.
Restriction Not suitable for &.
Credit cards Access, Amex, Visa.
Terms Rooms: single 65–135 frs, double 130–150 frs. Breakfast 16 frs; set
lunch/dinner 48, 78 and 113 frs.

LAPOUTROIE 68650 Haut-Rhin   Map 10

Les Alisiers   *Tel* (89) 47.52.82

*Most of our other Alsatian entries are rather smart. This one, a new
recommendation, is simpler and more rural – an old farmhouse with beamed
ceilings, secluded, up in the Vosges where the mountain views are splendid.
Kayserberg and Colmar are close at hand. "The* patron *was pleasant and
friendly. We had very good meals, and after a week in expensive Alsace could
hardly believe the bill of a mere 225 francs for two [1984]. Some rooms are very
small, others bigger with glorious views – all good value."* (Gillian Seel) *More
reports welcome.*

Open All year except 15 Nov–15 Dec.
Rooms 13 double, 2 single – 3 with bath, 10 with shower.
Facilities Salon, bar, dining room. Garden, terrace. Walking, cross-country
skiing, tennis courts 5 minutes away: swimming pool, horse riding and trout
fishing nearby. English spoken.

Location 19 km NW of Colmar, off N 415 to St-Dié. Hotel is 3 km from centre of Lapoutroie, from church follow signs indicating Ausier.
Restriction Not suitable for &.
Credit card Visa.
Terms Double 190 frs; with full board 225 frs. Breakfast 10 frs; set meals 80 frs; full alc 79 frs. 30–50% reductions for children, depending on age, if sharing parents' room; special meals on request.

LOCHES 37600 Indre-et-Loire   Map 10

Hôtel George Sand   *Tel* (47) 59.39.74
39 rue Quintefol

Loches, a small historical town 40 kilometres south of Tours, has many remarkable buildings – notably in the *cité médiévale* with its ramparts, castle and former torture chamber. The French kings kept many of their leading prisoners here. Some 100 kilometres to the south-east is the *"pays noir"* where George Sand lived and loved – and this year her eponymous hotel is regarded by readers as the best bet in Loches: "On the main road and not very prepossessing outside, but quite charming inside, with a lovely old stone, rather tortuous, staircase. We had a pleasantly furnished room with modern bathroom: possibly, traffic noise could be a problem at the front. Two dining rooms, one with attractive open fireplace, lead to a pleasant terrace above the river where the 100-franc menu [1984] gave good choice – delicious food, bordering on *nouvelle cuisine*, but we saw bigs bowls of excellent pommes frites being carried to a table of hungry young Germans. A local told us the *George Sand* is the best place to eat in town." *(Kay and Neville Varley)*

Open All year. Restaurant closed Christmas.
Rooms 3 suites (for 4 and 5 people), 14 double – 10 with bath, 7 with shower, all with telephone.
Facilities Salon, bar, restaurant. Garden. English spoken.
Location Central, parking.
Restriction Not suitable for &.
Credit cards All major cards accepted.
Terms Rooms 160 frs. Breakfast 16 frs; set lunch/dinner 55 frs; full alc 140 frs.

LUZARCHES 95270 Val d'Oise   Map 10

Château de Chaumontel   *Tel* (3) 471.03.51 or 471.00.30

Chantilly and the lovely Abbaye de Royaumont are both quite close to this turreted and ivy-covered château in the Ile-de-France; a stream, a lake and lovely trees complete the idyll – yet Paris is quite close. "A beautiful château with a moat, gardens and flowers. Charming informality; lots of local people come for dinner in the garden. The rooms have names like 'Casanova' and 'Madame du Barry'. Some rooms are in attics reached by stairs, but all are charmingly furnished. Delicious breakfast." Food is strictly traditional. *(Dorothy Masterson)*

Open All year except 20 Dec–3 Jan and 15 July–25 Aug.
Rooms 1 suite, 19 double – 16 with bath, 1 with shower, all with telephone; 3 rooms in annexe.
Facilities Salon with TV, dining rooms, functions rooms. Garden with volley ball, ping-pong and *pétanque*. Fishing in nearby lake. English spoken.

Location At Chaumontel, 1 km N of Luzarches (off N16).
Restriction Not suitable for ఉ.
Credit card Amex.
Terms (Excluding 15% service) double rooms 230–450 frs; suite 520 frs; full board 340–450 frs (plus 100 frs for single occupancy). Breakfast 24 frs; set lunch/dinner 125 frs; full alc 250–300 frs.

LA MALÈNE 48210 Lozère   Map 10

Château de la Caze   *Tel* (66) 48.51.01

"We drove from Florac through one of France's natural wonders, the Gorges du Tarn, a fantastic landscape of wooded hills and craggy rock formations. In this wild and unique natural setting one comes upon a 15th-century château rising out of spacious grounds with the hills of the gorges surrounding it and the river rushing past its side. All the rooms are furnished in 15th-century style, with tapestries, painted ceilings. There is an annexe with a terrace where one can enjoy the view and where the bathrooms have huge sunken Roman baths. The food is extremely good and the dining room (the château's former chapel) is comfortable, with fine service." That report from last year is warmly endorsed by others this year: "A sympathetic conversion, so the castle still looks as it must have done hundreds of years ago. Our bedroom was vast, with genuine antiques, polished wood floor, modern bathroom. The sheltered terrace overlooks a moat, now a trout stream, providing one of the hotel's specialities. Light, beautifully prepared food, fully deserving its *Michelin* rosette and pleasantly served by young girls." (*Moti and Gisa Slonim, Angela and David Stewart*)

Open 1 May–mid-Oct. Restaurant closed Tue.
Rooms 6 suites, 8 double – all with bath, telephone and TV; suites in annexe.
Facilities Salons, dining room; terrace. Large grounds with garden and stream.
Location 5.5 km NE of La Malène which is equidistant from Mende and Millau.
Restriction Not suitable for ఉ.
Credit cards All major cards accepted.
Terms [1985 rates] suites 560–750 frs, double rooms 375–540 frs; half-board 470–570 frs per person. Continental breakfast 40 frs, English 50 frs; set lunch/dinner 160 frs.

LE MANS 72000 Sarthe   Map 10

Hôtel Moderne   *Tel* (43) 24.79.20
14 rue du Bourg-Belé

"To those who have always thought of Le Mans as basically a race-track for cars, a visit comes as a pleasant surprise. While most of this big town is newly built and uninspiring, the medieval part is a delight; surrounding an extraordinary cathedral, it is very much alive" (as admirers of Rohmer's *Un beau mariage* may remember). "The *Moderne* is in the modern part, near the station. It has light airy rooms, each decorated with furniture in a different French style, comfortable without the unpleasant 'contemporary' look of so many posh hotels. Quieter rooms overlook the ivy-clad courtyard, others a narrow road. One-rosette *(Michelin)* restaurant, good value, with excellent frozen nougat in raspberry sauce." (*Maria Elena de La Iglesia*) Also praised are the terrine de caneton aux pistaches and the fricassée de poulet aux morilles.

421

Open All year.
Rooms 30 double, 3 single – 17 with shower, all with direct-dial telephone and colour TV; 19 rooms in annexe.
Facilities Salon, bar, restaurant. English spoken.
Location Near centre, and station. Private parking.
Credit cards All major cards accepted.
Terms (Excluding 15% service charge) rooms: single 160frs, double 240 frs. Breakfast 24 frs; set lunch/dinner 100–160 frs. Special meals for children.

MARSEILLES   Map 11

Résidences Le Petit Nice et Marina Maldormé   *Tel* (91) 52.14.39
16 rue des Braves, Corniche Kennedy   *Telex* 401565 PASSEDA

Very small, very stylish, very select and superior, *Le Petit Nice* is the last place you might expect to find in noisy, dusty proletarian Marseilles. It stands aloof. Though well inside the conurbation, it is miraculously secluded on an isolated strip of rocky coast (access down a narrow alley is not easy if your car is large) and is recommended by a reader as "evoking indefinably the South of France of a few decades ago – comfortable, characterful and offering exquisite food" (two *Michelin* rosettes, two *Gault Millau toques*). The house was built in the last century by the Passédat family who turned it into a hotel in 1917 and still own and run it today. The restaurant is a richly decorated Hellenic-style villa with a pretty garden: a curving picture-window overlooks the sea, service is stylish, and Jean-Paul Passédat subtly adapts Provençal dishes to his own very personal and light style of cooking. The *Marina Maldormé* is a curiously named bedroom annexe with elegant classical-style rooms and luxurious bathrooms. (*David Wooff, J A*)

Open 8 Feb–31 Dec but closed 1 May. Restaurant closed Mon.
Rooms 2 suites, 16 double – all with bath, telephone and radio; some with colour TV. 8 in annexe.
Facilities Lift in annexe. 2 small lounges, bar, restaurant. Garden with sea-water swimming pool, solarium and terrace; rocky beach. English spoken.
Location 4 km SW of city centre, off Corniche Kennedy. Parking.
Restriction Not suitable for &.
Credit cards Amex, Visa.
Terms [1985 rates] rooms 450–900 frs. Breakfast 57 frs; set lunch/dinner 310 frs (alc also available).

MARTIN-ÉGLISE 76370 Seine-Maritime   Map 10

Auberge du Clos Normand   *Tel* (35) 82.71.01 and 82.71.31
22 rue Henri IV

Six kilometres inland from Dieppe, on the edge of a forest, the *Clos Normand*, a former 16th-century *relais de poste*, now a restaurant-with-rooms, is as redolent of Normandy as its name implies. The bedrooms are in a separate vine-covered building, once a stables or hayloft, with a romantic garden which has a pavilion for eating out in summer and a stream; it's very quiet except for farmyard noises. "There is something Chekhovian about the place," writes one visitor; "it's slightly decrepit, but has great charm and is not expensive." "Bedroom a caricature of the old-style French hotel room", writes *Robert Robinson*; "sinister armoire and a couple of gouty chairs lurking in the shadows. But it doesn't matter if you're not there longer than a weekend, and how excellent are the menus – variety, skill and value."

Dinner is à la carte and obligatory: helpings are generous and the food is truly Norman – lashings of cream, butter and calvados. A recent inspector admired the duck terrine, tarte aux moules and sautéed chicken, and adds: "Service is conducted with charm and aplomb by Madame." Several visitors this year have written in similar vein, one of them pointing out that children will enjoy "the selection of cats, the stick-retrieving dog and the river abounding in young frogs". But the *Auberge*'s charm is so wayward and personal that some react negatively. They find Madame's manner "off-hand", or feel that the bedrooms are just a bit too basic and primitive to suit today's needs. *(Esler Crawford, Christine Parker, and others)*

Open Hotel open 1 Feb–31 Nov. Restaurant open 1 Mar–15 Nov. Both closed Mon evening and Tue.
Rooms 1 for 4, 7 double, 1 single – 3 with bath, 2 with shower, 3 with basin and bidet, all in separate building in the garden.
Facilities Lounge, restaurant. Garden with large lawn and stream; pavilion for outdoor summer meals. Functions room/ballroom below bedroom annexe. Some English spoken.
Location 6 km from Dieppe; off D1 to Neufchatel.
Restriction Not suitable for &.
Credit cards Access, Amex, Visa.
Terms Rooms 100–240 frs. Alc meals (excluding wine) 125–180 frs.

MERCUREY 71640 Saône-et-Loire   Map 10

Hôtellerie du Val d'Or   *Tel* (85) 47.13.70
Grande Rue

Our readers enjoy this engaging hostelry in the main street of a village producing one of Burgundy's great wines (there are several *caveaux de dégustation* close by). It serves generous helpings of fine *nouvelle*-ish cuisine *(Michelin* rosette, two *Gault Millau toques)* to jovial cohorts of Burgundians. "A comfortable, well-run hotel, owned by a courteous and efficient family. Bedrooms are charmingly decorated, if a little cramped. Light and colour in the garden, armchairs in the salon, and sociable chatter in the attractive restaurant with its stone-tiled floor, flowers and lamps. The middle-priced set menu was good value (eg aiguillettes de boeuf saignant au beurre rouge), with superb sorbets. A good range of Mercurey wines." *(D and M M)* "A pleasant family hotel, not sophisticated, good value. Comfortable beds in a room with tapestry-lined walls. The dining room was very like an old farmhouse main room, with huge fireplace, antique crocks, copper utensils." *(Ian and Francine Walsh; also Michael Wace, Margaret Coleman)* One dissenter this year found the service unhelpful and the rooms by the road noisy.

Open 5 Jan–25 Aug, 5 Sept–8 Dec. Closed Mon, and Tue midday (15 Mar–15 Nov); Sun evening and Mon (15 Nov–15 Mar). Restaurant open 12.15–1 pm, 7.30–9 pm.
Rooms 11 double, 1 single – 6 with bath and WC, 5 with shower and WC, all with telephone and colour TV.
Facilities Reception, salon-bar, 2 restaurants. Garden, swings. English spoken.
Location 13 km from Chalon-sur-Saône. Leave *autoroute* at Chalon Nord and take

D978 Autun/Nevers road, then turn right to Mercurey. Parking.
Credit card Visa.
Terms [1985 rates] rooms 116–210 frs. Breakfast 20 frs. Set meals 68–198 frs.
Special meals for children.

MIMIZAN 40200 Landes   Map 10

Au Bon Coin   *Tel* (58) 09.01.55
34 avenue du Lac

The long flat Atlantic coast south-west of Bordeaux has a number of
dullish resorts lining its sandy beaches. Just inland are freshwater lakes
amid the Landes forest, also with resort facilities, and here is *Au Bon
Coin*, a restaurant-with-rooms brought to the Guide this year by an
inspector's report: "Its setting is idyllic, its accommodation spartan and
its cuisine superb. It lies by the lake shore, six kilometres inland,
surrounded by pine trees and with Monet-style bridges leading off into
forest walks – an oasis of tranquillity. The only sound to disturb us at
night was a cat fight. At first sight the hotel does resemble a seaside café
– rather off-putting! But *patron-chef* Jean-Pierre Caule's cuisine fully
merits its *Michelin* rosette" (and two *Gault Millau toques*) "especially the
fish. Best to stick to the set menus. The bedrooms are simple but clean
and adequate, and the hotel's atmosphere is excellent with a smiling
Madame Caule leading a friendly team." *(E H)*

Open All year, except Feb.
Rooms 3 suites in annexe, 5 double – 5 with bath 3 with shower, all with
telephone, radio, TV and baby-listening. Ground-floor rooms.
Facilities Ramps. Lounges, bar, dining room; terrace. Garden. Near lake with
boating and fishing facilities. Children's games. Sea 5 km. English spoken.
Location 2 km N of Mimizan, which is 111 km SW of Bordeaux. Parking.
Credit cards Amex, Visa.
Terms Double rooms 250 frs. Breakfast 50 frs; set lunch/dinner 100 frs–250 frs; full
alc 250 frs.

MIONNAY 01390 Ain   Map 10

Alain Chapel   *Tel* (7) 891.82.02
                                                         Telex 305 605

Why do readers not write to us more often about Alain Chapel,
sometimes regarded as the greatest of all the great modern French chefs?
He is still awarded *Gault Millau*'s high rating of 19 out of 20, as well as
three rosettes and four knives and forks in *Michelin*. He runs a classically
sober, stone-floored restaurant in a simple-looking building on the edge
of Mionnay village, north of Lyon. He is a serious, rather austere man, a
tireless innovator, changing his menu regularly according to the season
and what is in the market, and buying most of his materials from local
producers whom he knows and trusts. His is a light, *nouvelle cuisine*-ish
style of cooking, creating superb new tastes from simple products.
Chapel also has 13 bedrooms (usually booked out weeks ahead). They
are in the best of taste, though, for one reader, much *too* expensive and
lacking certain modern refinements such as a television set. "The
world's best breakfasts", says *Gault Millau*; but we'd rather print our
own comments: so more reports, please.

Open All year except Jan, Mon and Tue midday (except public holidays).
Rooms 13 double – all with bath and telephone, 2 with colour TV.
Facilities Salon/bar with TV, restaurant, private dining rooms. Garden (where meals are served). Swimming pool nearby. English spoken.
Location 18 km N of Lyon on N83. Coming from Paris on *autoroute* A6 take first exit after Villefranche, and take D51 S. Parking.
Restriction Not suitable for &.
Credit cards Amex, Diners.
Terms Rooms 500–740 frs. Breakfast 75 frs; set lunch/dinner 300 and 420 frs (plus 13½% service).

LE MOLAY-LITTRY 14330 Calvados   Map 8

Château du Molay   *Tel* (31) 22.90.82
Route d'Isigny   *Telex* 171 912 Le Molay

This classic 18th-century château stands in its own big wooded park, 14 kilometres west of Bayeux, and has recently been converted into a modern hotel. "Not far from the D-Day beaches which (history apart) are also good for swimming. We approached the hotel down a long drive past tennis courts, ducks on the lake, horse and deer in the paddock. The large heated swimming pool looked enticing. The public rooms are well equipped; excellent lunch in the restaurant, with a Vivaldi concerto in the background; you can also eat out on the terrace. Our room was small (many others are larger) with a short bath. But we'd go again, for the quiet, comfort and elegance: good value for money." *(Patrick Freeman)* The hotel is much used for business seminars.

Open Mar–Nov.
Rooms 1 suite, 34 double, 5 single – 38 with bath, 2 with shower, all with telephone and radio; TV on request. 6 rooms in annexe.
Facilities Lift. 4 lounges, library/billiards room, TV room, bar, dining room. Large grounds with heated swimming pool, solarium, tennis court, jogging track, children's play area, deer park, pond and river for fishing. D-Day beaches (with good swimming) nearby. English spoken.
Location 14 km W of Bayeux. From Bayeux take D5 towards Le Molay-Littry. Turn right at Le Molay-Littry village square (towards Isigny). The *Château* is 100 yds on left, after leaving the village.
Credit cards All major cards accepted.
Terms B&B: single 335 frs, double 430–530 frs; dinner, B&B: single 465 frs, double 690–790 frs; full board: single 585 frs, double 930–1,030 frs. Set lunch/dinner 135 frs–220 frs; full alc 240 frs. Group rates. Half price for children under 7 in parents' room.

MOLLANS-SUR-OUVÈZE 26170 Drôme   Map 11

Hôtel-Restaurant Le Saint-Marc   *Tel* (75) 28.70.01

This modern white-walled hotel lies in a river valley amid the green hills of north-west Provence, 12 kilometres east of Vaison (fascinating Roman remains) and within striking distance of Orange and Mont Ventoux. "Its quiet situation down a tree-lined drive off the small village street, and the cool spaciousness of the discreetly decorated public areas and the bedrooms (with well-appointed bathrooms), were very welcome after a hot and tiring drive. The *pension* meals were generous, such as a perfect melon au porto, beautifully cooked lamb with delicate haricots verts

425

(masses of them), followed by a wide-ranging cheeseboard and a good sorbet de cassis. Service was helpful. There is an open-air swimming pool (unheated) and tennis courts in the grounds." *(Eileen A Michie)*

Open All year except Jan. Restaurant closed Mon.
Rooms 30 double, 8 single – 32 with bath, 6 with shower, all with telephone and tea-making facilities; TV on request; ground-floor rooms; some self-catering studios.
Facilities Lift. Salon with TV, reading room, bar, restaurant, conference room. Occasional live folk music. Garden with tennis court and swiming pool; fishing in nearby river. English spoken.
Location 12 km E of Vaison-la-Romaine, 10 km W of Buis-les-Baronnies. Parking.
Credit card Visa.
Terms Rooms: single 148 frs, double 168 frs; dinner, B&B: single 210 frs, double 380 frs; full board: single 262 frs, double 462 frs. Breakfast 24 frs; set meals 60, 74 and 88 frs. Reduced rates and special meals for children.

MONTBAZON 37250 Indre-et-Loire   Map 10

Château d'Artigny
Tel (47) 26.24.24
Telex 750900

"Expensive but worth it; everything you'd want for the high life". "A magnificent building with elegant and attractive rooms" – two recent comments on this seigneurial hotel, standing in its own 60-acre park above the valley of the Indre, 13 kilometres from Tours. It looks like a peerless 18th-century château, but in fact is a pastiche: it was built in the 18th-century style just in 1915 by the famous *parfumier* François Coty. He spared little expense: there is a huge staircase in polished limestone, an imposing gallery, a brass-inlaid marble floor in the dining room, delicate wood-carving in the library and so on. Heated swimming pool, tennis, wooded walks; sophisticated Parisian clientele. Chamber music concerts of some quality are held from October to March. The restaurant wins a *Michelin* rosette and two *Gault Millau* red *toques* for such dishes as ravioli de homard. Visitors this year enjoyed the dinner, and a bedroom overlooking woods and river, but were not impressed by their breakfast. Another reader found the place "elegant and comfortable", but her bedroom was small. *(Kate and Steve Murray-Sykes, Tessa Dahl Kelly)*

Open 1 Jan–30 Nov.
Rooms 6 suites, 51 double, 2 single – 53 with bath, 2 with shower, all with telephone; 21 rooms in 3 annexes.
Facilities Lift. 2 salons, TV room, bar, 2 dining rooms; conference and functions facilities. Large garden with 2 tennis courts, heated swimming pool, ping-pong, putting; fishing, riding, rowing, private flying courses nearby; golf 12 km away. English spoken.
Location Leave N10 at Montbazon, 10 km S of Tours; turn right on D17 towards Azay-le-Rideau. 2 km on left is private road leading to the Château.
Credit card Visa.
Terms [1985 rates] rooms 375–875 frs, suites 600–995 frs. Half-board (min. 3 days): 490–1,140 frs per person, full board (min. 3 days) 620–1,270 frs per person. Breakfast 48 frs; set lunch/dinner 180 and 220 frs. "Anti-weekend" rates Mon–Fri all year; musical weekends Oct–Mar. Children under 6 half price, under 12 30% reduction; special meals on request.

Report forms (Freepost in UK) will be found at the end of the Guide.

Auberge du Moulin Fleuri   *Tel* (47) 26.01.12
Route de Monts

In the deep countryside south of Tours, a converted 16th-century water-mill, enthused over this year by one of our most loyal lovers of French rural simplicity, warts and all: "A beautifully run small hotel, on the banks of the Indre which swirls through the mill-race. Neatly kept gardens; nearby *autoroute* only faintly audible at night. Alain and Martine Chaplin maintain the charm of the place: his prowess in the hotel trade is attested by the diplomas that festoon the wall of the bar. Our small bedroom had no shower or wc and was somewhat cramped: but a delightful public bathroom was available, and a fresh bowl of fruit was left in the bedroom each morning. Our room was cold in May, as the central heating had by law to be turned off by 1 May, said M. Chaplin (we must have stayed at a number of lawless hotels on this trip): but an extra blanket was provided. The elegant restaurant overlooks the garden and river: meals were varied and well prepared. Gentlemen were offered a small cigar with coffee. At breakfast, food was copious but coffee bitter and tepid. *Demi-pension* at 132 francs a head [1984] – good value for such a pleasurable experience." *(Norman Brangham)* Extensive wine list, and interesting dishes such as trout in Vouvray and pigeon with goat's cheese.

Open 21 Feb–15 Oct and 30 Nov–1 Feb. Closed Mon except national holidays.
Rooms 10 double – 3 with shower, all with radio.
Facilities Salon, bar, dining room. Large garden with direct access to river Indre; fishing rights. English spoken.
Location 18 km S of Tours and 5 km E of Montbazon, along N10 and D87.
Restriction Not suitable for &.
Credit cards Amex, Visa.
Terms Rooms 58–136 frs. Breakfast 22 frs; set lunch/dinner 88 frs; full alc 170 frs. Reduced rates for children according to age; special meals.

MONTICELLO 20220 L'Île Rousse, Corsica   **Map 11**

Hôtel A Pastorella   *Tel* (95) 60.05.65

The medieval hamlet of Monticello stands high on a hill above the smart resort of L'Île Rousse. Readers are still falling under the spell of the modest *A Pastorella* ("lively atmosphere, good country cooking, friendly family owner"), to which *Frank Muir* first introduced us: "It can be a bit noisy, but it is clean, bright and happy. The food is plentiful and cheap, usually beginning with a real soup, then moving on to something small and interesting like something stuffed with something else . . . " Since then, other praise has flowed in. "A winner – we toasted Frank Muir. A cool white dining room with polished dark furniture, bright daisies on the tables and glorious views. M. Martini is a cheerful and gentle host who murmurs the menu of the day confidentially to the diners, no menu appearing on paper. The children work efficiently in the dining room and Grandfather Martini grows the vegetables, besides minding his sheep. And the silence at night was lovely – no luxury here, but a perfect base for the hill-walker." Red "R" in *Michelin* for good value. Warning: some rooms are very small; peaceful nights, we were told, can be disturbed by beds "that play music upon the lightest portion of the anatomy"; and rooms in the converted cellar annexe can be stuffy: it is

best to book early and get a room which "opens on a stupendous view".
(D Hammond, L H, and others)

Open 2 Jan–31 Oct.
Rooms 14 double – all with shower; 5 rooms in annexe.
Facilities Salon with TV, bar, restaurant. Garden. Beach 4 km. English spoken.
Location 3 km SE of L'Île Rousse.
Restriction Not suitable for &.
Credit cards None accepted.
Terms Rooms 160–220 frs; full board 235–270 frs per person. Breakfast 20 frs, set lunch 70 frs, supper 65 frs; full alc 100–120 frs. Reduced rates and special meals for children.

MONTMORILLON 86500 Vienne   Map 10

Hôtel de France, Restaurant Mercier   *Tel* (49) 91.00.51
2 boulevard de Strasbourg

Frescoes in the 11th-century crypt of the church of Notre-Dame are one reason for halting in this pleasant little town, between Limoges and Poitiers. Another is the excellent *Hôtel de France*: "Busy, clean, very popular (mainly with locals), a good example of fine old-fashioned French hospitality and, of course, family-run. The hotel has charming and courteous staff. Our bedroom was particularly clean, fresh and airy. Cosy, crowded dining room – copper shone everywhere. We enjoyed civet de langoustines, saumon frais cru, magret de canard and poires belle Hélène, all excellent." Such praise is endorsed by *Gault Millau* (*toques* for inventive regional cuisine). *(Robert and Gilly Jamieson)*

Open Feb–Dec inclusive. Closed Sunday evening and Mon.
Rooms 21 double, 4 single – 9 with bath, 6 with shower, all with telephone.
Facilities Salon, bar, TV room, dining room. English spoken.
Location Central. Town is 84 km NW of Limoges, 48 km SE of Poitiers.
Restriction Not suitable for &.
Credit cards All major cards accepted.
Terms B&B: single 160 frs, double 200 frs; dinner, B&B: single 250 frs, double 400 frs. Set lunch/dinner 95–225 frs; full alc 200 frs.

MONTPELLIER 34000 Hérault   Map 10

Hôtel de Noailles   *Tel* (67) 60.49.80
2 rue des Écoles-Centrales

This 17th-century mansion is not easy of access by car (without a good street map, at least), for it lies in the heart of the *vieille ville*, a network of quiet alleys, some closed to traffic, that forms the kernel of this graceful southern city. The hotel too is graceful, in a cool classical style, and one couple exult in its contrast with modernism: "After Frantels (an up-market utility hotel chain), the bliss and bargain of the year. Quiet. Really large bedroom and bathroom. Particularly caring staff." No restaurant, but you can eat well at the *Chandelier* (medium/upper price) or *Le Nice* (cheap). *(R G and E Tennant)*

Open Mid Jan–mid Dec.
Rooms 27 double, 3 single – 20 with bath, 10 with shower, all with telephone and colour TV; 1 ground-floor room.

Facilities Salon/TV room. English spoken.
Location Central, near church of Notre Dame de Tables. Nearby parking not easy; the hotel advises guests to use the underground car park in place de la Comédie (300 metres S).
Credit cards All major cards accepted.
Terms Rooms: single 190–220 frs, double 280–330 frs. Breakfast 25 frs. (No restaurant.)

MONTREUIL 62170 Pas-de-Calais   Map 8

Château de Montreuil   *Tel* (21) 81.53.04
4 chaussée des Capucins   *Telex* 135205 F HOTEUIL

This is the first really stylish and ambitious hotel that you come to on the main road south from Calais and Boulogne; it has again inspired a sizeable mailbag from readers eager for a first (or last) taste of *la douce France* – "a wonderful hotel for a last-night special experience or a long weekend," says one. It is a large old house set in a lovely walled garden, close to the ruined citadel in a quiet part of the medieval hilltop town of Montreuil. The rooms are furnished in a variety of styles: all have polished tiled floors with rugs, some have panelled walls and fireplaces, and one even has "a white plaster monkey over the bed and parrots here and there". The resident owners are *protégés* of the famous Roux brothers of the *Gavroche* in London and the *Waterside Inn* at Bray. Christian Germain, formerly *chef de cuisine* at Bray, runs the hotel with his English wife Lindsay, in business partnership with the Roux brothers. *Michelin* has not yet got around to starring their efforts, but *Gault Millau* gives them two red *toques*. Our readers likewise are mainly enthusiastic: "a pleasant atmosphere and welcome"; "all dishes beautifully cooked and presented, eg mousseline d'huîtres au champagne"; "our suite elegantly furnished", though some reports speak of erratic and over-complicated cooking and excessive prices for wines and extras. Off-season the Germains run week-long cookery courses, with classes in their kitchen. *(Peter Knowles, Rosamund V Hebdon, R and G Jamieson, and others)*

Open Mid-Feb to mid-Dec and for 1 week over Christmas and New Year. Restaurant closed Thur lunch-time, except July and Aug.
Rooms 11 double, 3 single – 12 with bath, 2 with shower, all with telephone; 24-hour room service. 3 ground-floor rooms in garden annexe, 1 specially adapted for &.
Facilities Sitting room, bar, breakfast room, restaurant, conference facilities. 1-acre garden. 18 km from sandy beach at Le Touquet. English spoken.
Location 38 km S of Boulogne, just off N1. Hotel is 450 metres from centre of Montreuil, opposite the citadel. Parking.
Credit cards All major cards accepted.
Terms Rooms: single 295 frs, double 395–480 frs; dinner, B&B: single 550 frs, double 950 frs. Breakfast 35 frs; set lunch Mon–Fri 120 frs; *menu dégustation* 280 frs; full alc 260 frs. 5-day masterclass cookery courses at half-board rate out of season. Reduced rates and half portions for children.

We are particularly keen to have reports on italicised entries.

When hotels fail to return their questionnaire, we have quoted 1985 prices, with a note to that effect.

MONTRICHARD 41400 Loir-et-Cher Map 10

Hôtel Bellevue *Tel* (54) 36.06.17
Quai du Cher

"An attractive small town on the Cher, nine kilometres upstream from Chenonceaux and with its own castle and medieval centre. The *Bellevue* is a modern hotel with fine panoramic views of the river. Rooms are large and well furnished, though the wallpaper is loudly French. All double rooms face the river and are double-glazed. Perhaps the best thing is Madame's welcome and helpfulness. In the dining room, for those on *pension* terms, she comes personally with a *"Je vous propose . . ."*; for us, her choice was vegetable soup in a tureen large enough for six helpings, émincée de champignons, a superbly flavoured coq au vin, cheese, and fresh cherries in kirsch. An excellent overnight stop." *(C Pilkington)*

Open All year except 15 Nov–21 Dec. Restaurant closed Sun evening and Tue Oct–Apr.
Rooms 29 – most with bath or shower, all with telephone; air-conditioning.
Facilities Lift. Dining room.
Location On the D764 9 km E of Chenonceaux.
Credit cards All major cards accepted.
Terms [1985 rates] rooms: 113–240 frs; full board 313 frs per person. Breakfast 22 frs; lunch/dinner 79–181 frs.

MONT-ST-MICHEL 50116 Manche Map 8

Hôtel La Mère Poulard *Tel* (33) 60.14.01

No other site in France outside Paris attracts more tourists than Mont-St-Michel, that offshore granite pyramid linked to the coast by a causeway at low tide and capped by a towering ramparted Benedictine monastery. An overnight stay is well worth it, for then you can appreciate the aura of the place when the milling crowds have left in the evening, and visit the abbey early the next morning before they arrive, "an unforgettable experience". *La Mère Poulard*, facing you as you pass the rampart gates, is not the only hotel, but it has the most character and tradition, also a restaurant long famous for its omelettes and praised too for its classic Norman and Breton cooking (*Michelin* rosette, two *Gault Millau toques*). It remains popular with readers: "A delightful place, with delicious food and excellent service; our large, exquisite room had an expansive view", says an American this year. Warning: Not a hotel for the elderly as the stairways to the rooms are steep and narrow. *(Mrs Howard L Miller, John Rigg, and others)*

Open Apr–Sept inclusive.
Rooms 3 triple, 24 double – 14 with bath, 8 with shower, all with telephone.
Facilities Salon with TV, restaurant, omelette room. English spoken.
Location Just inside walls of Mont St-Michel. Large car park across causeway.
Restrictions Not suitable for &. No babies in restaurant.
Credit cards Amex, Diners.
Terms [1985 rates] half-board (obligatory) 272–452 frs per person. Set lunch/dinner 165–330 frs.

MONTSALVY 15120 Cantal

Map 10

Auberge Fleurie
Place du Barry

Tel (71) 49.20.02

Montsalvy is a typical Massif Central village within easy reach of amazing Conques (q.v.), the lovely upper Lot valley and the Truyère gorges. The *Auberge*, new to the Guide, is recommended as "delightful, also cheap – a creeper-covered building in a village amid marvellous wooded country. Comfortable rooms; no private bathrooms, but we had our own shower and bidet. Charming owners and very French dining room with red check tablecloths and good bourgeois food. Breakfast in the bar where the postman drops in for a chat. For those who want not luxury but a typical French atmosphere." *(June Bullough)* In Montsalvy, Mrs Bullough recommends also the *Hotel du Nord*, slightly larger and smarter, also with a red *Michelin* "R" for its value-for-money cooking.

Open 1 Feb–15 Nov.
Rooms 17 double, 1 single – 7 with shower; 5 in annexe.
Facilities Salon with TV, bar, dining room, banqueting facilities. 5-acre garden attached to annexe. Lake 1 km for fishing and wind-surfing. English spoken.
Location 35 km of S of Aurillac by D920 towards Rodez. Hotel is near 11th-century North Gate of Montsalvy.
Restriction Not suitable for &.
Credit cards All major cards accepted.
Terms Rooms: single 55 frs, double 85–100 frs; dinner, B&B 145–160 frs per person; full board 160–170 frs per person. Breakfast 15.50 frs; set lunch/dinner 40, 60 and 88 frs; full alc 120 frs. Reduced rates for children under 5; special meals.

MOUGINS 06250 Alpes-Maritimes

Map 11

Le Mas Candille

Tel (93) 90.00.85

The fashionable hilltop village of Mougins, just inland from Cannes, has more good restaurants per square metre (including Vergé's mighty *Moulin)* than any other in France, but few good hotels. So we are glad to be able to recommend this graceful yet unsnooty *auberge*, lined with cypresses, converted from a white-walled 17th-century farmhouse. It stands peacefully in its own flowery park, on a wooded hillside, looking out across the valley – a blessed retreat from the tumult of the Côte, so near yet so far. Most recent reports are enthusiastic: "food and comfort excellent, good value for money, we had a splendid time", "comfortable though not de luxe, cuisine of a high standard" – and so on. Most rooms are "rural' in style, a bit cramped, but well appointed, with old beams and fireplaces, and balconies with views. You can eat either in the cool dining room or out in the flower garden above the valley where at night the mood is wistfully poetic, helped by light from the candles on a huge candelabrum *(candille* in Provençal – hence the name). The cuisine tends to the *nouvelle* (red *Gault Millau toque)*. The swimming pool is small but in a lovely setting, amid firs and olive trees. Recent modernisation of the hotel has brought in air-conditioning and other benefits. But the view and tranquillity have recently been slightly marred by noisy building activity down in the valley; one reader also warns that rear bedrooms lack a good view and the gardens may be unkempt. *(Anthony Jones, and others)*

Open All year except 3 Nov–27 Dec. Restaurant closed Tue midday.
Rooms 12 suites, 13 double – all with bath, telephone, TV and air-conditioning.
Facilities Dining room. 12½-acre garden with panoramic views, terrace, swimming pool, and tennis court. Golf and beaches nearby.
Location 800 m W of the village, which is 6 km N of Cannes. Parking.
Credit cards Amex, Diners, Visa.
Terms [1985 rates] rooms: 340–440 frs. Breakfast 30 frs; set lunch/dinner 195–300 frs.

MOULINS 03000 Allier   Map 10

Hôtel de Paris   *Tel* (70) 44.00.58
21 rue de Paris   *Telex* 394853

Moulins, on the river Allier north of Vichy, is an old market town with cobbled streets, noted for its fine Gothic cathedral and the curious Jacquemart bell-tower. Near the heart of town stands the *Paris*, a small, select hotel, fairly expensive, with "period" decor in variable taste and notable cooking *(Michelin* rosette, two *Gault Millau toques)*. "Comfortable rooms and personal, helpful service", runs a report this year; "not cheap, but we were well treated and had a treat: fine, inventive food, such as hot foie gras in a mushroom and banana (yes, banana!) sauce – delicious." Earlier praise: "An hotel of exceptional charm. In the elegantly panelled restaurant, busy with a surfeit of waiters, we enjoyed snails with finely ground walnuts, rabbit stew with mushrooms and cherries." What *nouvelle cuisine* nut could ask for more? *(Stanley Burnton, Don Tibbenham, P J White)*

Open All year except Jan; closed Sun and Mon out of season, except public holidays.
Rooms 8 suites, 14 double, 6 single – 21 with bath, 6 with shower, all with telephone and radio, 15 with mono TV.
Facilities Lift. Reading room, TV room, bar, restaurant. Next to park. English spoken. Ramps for ♿.
Location Leave N7 at Moulins Nord. Hotel is central, near cathedral. Garage.
Credit cards All major cards accepted.
Terms [1985 rates] rooms: 220–410 frs; suites 420–510 frs; full board 530–690 frs per person. Breakfast 30 frs; set lunch/dinner 160–310 frs.

MOYE 74150 Haute Savoie   Map 10

Relais du Clergeon   *Tel* (50) 01.23.80

Though fairly remote and very unpretentious, this small, quiet and friendly hotel has this year attracted a larger mailbag than almost any other in France. It lies amid the green hills of Savoy, in a hamlet near the town of Rumilly, 17 kilometres south-west of Annecy. Most readers, though decidedly not all, are delighted. "The owners, the Chal family, welcomed us very warmly; food was excellent, the view wonderful, the rooms well appointed." "Food very good value, and the charm and friendliness of the owners are remarkable." One visitor was present at a raclette (cheese fondue) party for residents – "a memorable evening with a wonderful atmosphere". However, two experienced travellers, while agreeing about the beauty of the setting and the friendly charm of the Chals, found the hotel in other ways unsatisfactory – a dull room in a concrete annexe, boring food, inefficient service – and felt that staff and owners were overworked, victims of their popularity. Others reports, too, stress that the cooking is simple and modest. *(Margaret Cox, Charles Shirley, Clare and Ian Godfrey, and others)*

Open All year except 2 weeks Jan and 2 weeks Oct/Nov. Closed Mon out of season.
Rooms 20 double, 2 single – 10 with bath, 6 with shower, all with telephone, 12 with balcony; baby-listening on request. 4 ground-floor rooms.
Facilities Hall, salon, TV room, bar, breakfast room, dining room. Garden with children's play area and *boules*. Peaceful country; walks, tennis, swimming nearby. English spoken.
Location Access from *autoroute* A41 at Alby-sur-Chéran; 3.2 km from Rumilly by D231 – direction Moye.
Credit cards None accepted.
Terms B&B: single 98–203 frs, double 130–256 frs; dinner, B&B (3 days min.) 145–230 frs per person; full board (3 days min.) 170–275 frs per person. Reduced rates out of season. Reduced rates for children sharing parents' room; special meals.

NAJAC 12270 Aveyron   Map 10

Hôtel Belle-Rive   *Tel* (65) 65.74.20
Au Roc du Pont, Route 039

Najac is a beautiful medieval village above the gorges of the Aveyron, with a fairy-tale medieval castle high on a hill overlooking the river. There is much to see in this remote but scenic area, such as the even more striking hill village of Cordes; Albi is 54 kilometres to the south. *La Belle-Rive* has a choice traffic-free position by a bridge two kilometres from Najac; it is run by the Mazières family, and again this year wins praise from readers for its friendliness, fair prices, and pastoral setting. A recent reports runs: "We were very pleased with our light, spacious modern room. Later we moved to a small older-style room with a view of the castle. If booking, it might be worth stating your preference. There is a lovely outdoor swimming pool, picturesquely and peacefully sited; also swings and ping-pong – children can play in safety here. The welcome is warm , the hotel is well run, and the dining room is staffed by friendly local girls with Madame efficiently in charge. More romantic, in fine weather, is to dine on the terrace facing the castle floodlit at night." Several readers concur: they praise the comfortable bar/lounge, but point out that the food is very simple: "A typical meal would be soup, pâté, salad followed by trout, then steak or duck followed by tarte or sorbet." *(Dr and Mrs G Collingham, also K and N Varley, J H D Stapleton, June Bullough)*

Open 1 Apr–15 Oct.
Rooms 39 double – 9 with bath and WC, 21 with shower and WC, all with telephone; 7 rooms in annexe; 4 ground-floor rooms.
Facilities Lift. Salon with TV, bar, 2 restaurants, terrace. Large garden with children's play area and swimming pool. River nearby; fishing. English spoken.
Location 2 km N of Najac on D39, on edge of village. Parking.
Restriction Not suitable for &.
Credit cards None accepted.
Terms Rooms: 125–145 frs; half-board 137–149 frs per person; full board 162–174 frs per person. Breakfast 16 frs; set meals 50, 78, 103, 150 frs; full alc 100–150 frs. Reduced rates and special meals for children.

Hôtel Miquel: l'Oustal del Barry
Place du Bourg

Tel (65) 65.70.80

The *Belle-Rive* above may be the better option for a long visit, but the *Miquel* or *L'Oustal del Barry* has more to recommend it for a short stay, being better placed for sight-seeing on foot. A recent visitor writes: "A welcoming bright little hotel in the corner of the village square: white chairs, with tables outside. It is a delightful spot. There is even a private, spacious, well-tended, tiered garden nearby for sunbathing and for children to let off steam, complete with climbing frame, roundabouts etc. The town is perched on a long hilltop or ridge, with the 13th-century château (floodlit at night) and church at one end, and the hotel at the other.

"Service at dinner was slow but obliging. Extremely generous helpings of well-cooked regional food and the prices are low for the quality provided. Very good breakfast, quickly served. Our bedroom was freshly decorated and well lit. The bathroom was clean and bright." *(Jean Hayward; also Kate Currie)*

Open 23 Mar–3 Nov.
Rooms 26 double, 2 single – 17 with bath or shower and WC, all with direct-dial telephone; 7 rooms in annexe.
Facilities Lift. Salon, TV room, bar, 2 restaurants; terrace. Large garden with children's play area and small swimming pool for children; *boules*; tennis courts nearby; river Aveyron 2 km with fishing and canoeing. English spoken.
Location Coming from Villefranche de Rouergue or Cordes on D122 hotel is on right at entrance of village. Parking.
Credit card Visa.
Terms Rooms: single 110 frs, double 134 frs; dinner, B&B 136 frs per person; full board 170 frs per person. Breakfast 17 frs; set meals 54.50, 84, 114 and 160 frs; full alc 105 frs. Reduced rates for children; special meals on request.

NANTILLY 70100 Haute-Saône

Map 10

Le Relais de Nantilly

Tel (84) 65.20.12
Telex 362888

An elegant *Relais*, standing quietly in its own wooded park to the west of the town of Gray, which is midway between Dijon and Besançon on a useful cross-country route from the coast to Switzerland. It has a tranquil rural setting, the trees of its gardens busy with birds and a slow stream running along its boundary. "A charming 19th-century château in beautiful countryside. Very good meal in a pretty dining room." "Comfortable rooms furnished in traditional style, an excellent dinner, and they were very welcoming in the restaurant to our three-year-old daughter." "Our dinner was served in a happy, relaxed atmosphere." The food is traditional and copious but not cheap, and one or two recent visitors have been disappointed by the lowest-priced set menu – worth paying extra for one of the others. *(Dr Bill and Lisa Fuerst, Mr and Mrs R Trotter; endorsed this year by Mrs B P Whitehouse)*

Open 15 Mar–30 Oct.
Rooms 1 suite, 23 double – all with bath, telephone and TV; 10 rooms in annexe.
Facilities Bar, breakfast room, salons, restaurant; conference facilities, terrace. Garden with outdoor swimming pool and tennis court. 4 km from river Saône with beach, boating, waterskiing and fishing. English spoken.

Location 4 km W of Gray by D2. Parking.
Credit cards All major cards accepted.
Terms [1985 rates] rooms 328–896 frs; half-board (obligatory in season) from 400 frs per person. Breakfast 38 frs; set lunch/dinner 170–250 frs.

NANTUA 01130 Ain   Map 10

Hôtel de France   *Tel* (74) 75.00.55
44 rue du Dr-Mercier

Nantua is a small town by a lovely lake, with tree-lined promenades, flowery gardens and views of the Jura hills. Many visitors think it charming, but not so one traveller who reports: "The site is claustrophobic, menaced all round by the gloomy mountains. So thank goodness for the *Hôtel de France* which does its best to atone. Originally a posting house, it still has something of that feel about it with its long narrow courtyard. The room we had was large, comfortable, quiet. There is a pleasant 1930s bar. The food is mostly excellent (*Michelin* rosette), notably poulet au morilles à la crème." Most recent reports concur: "Superb food: mousse de rascasse with lobster sauce was like eating a fishy cloud"; "charming host, French *cuisine* at its subtle best – quenelles we can never order again elsewhere, for such perfection is to be found but once." One or two other readers however have complained of imperfect service, plastic flowers and "the choice between suffocation and traffic noise" on a hot night. The hotel has double-glazing but is on the main road: best ask for a room at the back. Further reports, please.

Open 20 Dec–1 Nov. Closed Fri except Feb, Jul, Aug.
Rooms 18 double, 1 single – all with bath, direct-dial telephone and colour TV. Double-glazing.
Facilities Salon, bar, restaurant. Garden; lake 400 metres, with beach, sailing, swimming etc. English spoken.
Location 50 metres from town centre. Garage.
Credit cards Amex, Diners, Visa.
Terms Rooms: single 150 frs, double 270 frs. Breakfast 23 frs; set lunch/dinner 105 and 180 frs; full alc 220 frs.

NARBONNE 11100 Aude   Map 10

Hôtel de la Résidence   *Tel* (68) 32.19.41
6 rue du Premier Mai   *Telex* 500441 SOMARES

This unusual little hotel in Victorian boudoir style, very feminine, is the last place you might expect to find in the shadow of Narbonne's great austere fortified cathedral, so very masculine, and the massive archbishop's palace. "An early 19th-century building in a quiet street, decorated with style – Louis XV furniture, gilt mirrors, silk flowers in vases. Words like 'precious', 'delicate' spring to mind. Our room had gold draperies and comfortable beds with twee rose-spangled bedspreads." Warmly endorsed this year: "Lovely, lovely place. Beautiful room, so quiet. Breakfast, excellent, was accompanied by a rose and a newspaper." No restaurant, but you eat well at the *Alsace* and the *Floride*, both near the station. (*E Hill, I and F W, Hugh Bates*)

Open All year except 4 Jan–8 Feb.
Rooms 20 double, 6 single – 20 with bath, 6 with shower, all with telephone;
4 ground-floor rooms.
Facilities 2 lounges (1 with TV). English spoken.
Location Central, near cathedral and canal. Parking.
Credit cards Amex, Visa.
Terms B&B: single 216 frs, double 312 frs. (No restaurant.)

NICE 06300 Alpes-Maritimes   Map 11

La Pérouse   *Tel* (93) 62.34.63
11 quai Rauba-Capeù   *Telex* 461411

"I was charmed – the only hotel in Nice worth staying at" (and the resort
has over 350 of them, mostly dull). That is a 1984 inspector's grand claim
for this lively hotel of character in a fine setting, perched half-way up the
castle rock at the east end of the promenade. An earlier account: "From
our bedroom balcony we had a stunning view of the town and the Baie
des Anges. Our room had a kitchenette, too, which is useful, as the
hotel has no restaurant (but they serve you a light lunch by the heated
swimming pool in summer). The hotel is modern, but not cold or
impersonal: they even have a pretty patio with lemon trees where you
can take breakfast or a drink. The staff are quite friendly. Because of its
position it is very quiet." Not all bedrooms have sea views. (*L H, J A,
Phyllis M Carpenter*)

Open All year.
Rooms 1 suite, 34 double, 30 single – 56 with bath, 9 with shower, all with
telephone, mini-bar and air-conditioning; 50 with colour TV; 9 with kitchenette;
some with radio; many with loggia or terrace; 1 ground-floor room.
Facilities Lift. Lounge, bar, snack bar (open in summer), solarium, conference
facilities. Large garden with patio and heated swimming pool, sauna; beach 20
metres. English spoken.
Location At E end of promenade des Anglais, by the château. Parking 20 metres.
Credit cards All major cards accepted.
Terms [1985 rates] B&B: single 300 frs, double 800 frs. (No restaurant, but light
snacks served in summer.)

NIEUIL 16270 Charente   Map 10

Le Château de Nieuil   *Tel* (45) 71.36.38
                                                        Telex 791230

A grand old Renaissance château, complete with moat and 350-acre
wooded park. Between Angoulême and Limoges, it is a former
hunting-lodge of François I, full of antiques and Aubusson tapestries
and with an imposing marble staircase. It is a *Relais et Châteaux* member,
so not surprisingly is not cheap. "Excellent hotel, friendly and
welcoming," says a reader this year, echoing earlier praise: "The owner,
M. Bodinaud, insists on carrying your luggage to your room himself
and will later take you on a sort of guided tour/tutorial. *Château* a haven
of peace, really beautiful; no lounge, but a beautifully furnished salon in
which to enjoy one of the 230 different brandies – mine was the best I've
ever had. Excellent bedroom (choice of two double beds); superb
breakfast; outstanding dinner." Another enthusiast praises the "superb"

filets de pintade au parfum de framboises (Mme Bodinaud's cooking wins a *Michelin* rosette and two *Gault Millau toques*). The old stables house an art gallery, with demonstrations of tapestry weaving. The hotel runs cookery courses too. (*Dr T J David; also Pat and Jeremy Temple*)

Open 26 Apr–12 Nov. Restaurant closed Wed midday to non-residents.
Rooms 3 suites, 11 double – 12 with bath, 2 with shower, all with telephone, some with mini-bar; TV on request in some rooms. 2 ground-floor rooms; ramps.
Facilities Salon/bar with TV; restaurant; conference facilities. 350-acre wooded park with heated swimming pool, tennis court, fishing in pond, archery and art gallery. English spoken. &.
Location Off D739, between Nieuil and Fontafie; 42 km NE of Angoulême.
Credit cards Amex, Visa.
Terms [1985 rates] Rooms: single occupancy 315–430 frs, double 360–560 frs; suites: single occupancy 510–810 frs, double 565–905 frs. Breakfast 35 frs; set meals 145 and 180 frs; full alc 280 frs. Reductions in May and Oct for half-board (3 days min.).

NONTRON 24300 Dordogne   Map 10

Grand Hôtel Pélisson   *Tel* (53) 56.11.22
3 place Alfred Agard

An old walled town on a hill, roughly midway between Angoulême and Périgueux, in the so-called "Périgord vert". The *Pélisson*, a *Logis de France*, is a former coaching-inn on the main square, with a spacious rear courtyard, good for parking. "Pleasant and welcoming, excellent food, lovely countryside", runs a report this year. Earlier ones: "Not a luxury place, but it is all you expect a French hotel to be: bright, welcoming and *'correct'*. The rooms are large and sparkling, the service attentive but unfussy, the menu and wine list outstanding value (red 'R' in *Michelin*)." "Rather old-fashioned and dark, but in an agreeable way, and very well conducted. Bedrooms small, with no luxury, but very clean, lots of hot water and good reading lights. Unusually good regional food with a large choice." Front rooms can be noisy, and one dissenter this year also criticises the food. (*Mark Ottaway, Nancy Raphael, David and Angela Hudson, and others*)

Open All year except 15–31 Jan.
Rooms 15 double, 4 single – 12 with bath, 6 with shower, all with telephone.
Facilities Lift. Salon with TV, bar, dining room, functions facilities. Terrace and garden. Swimming pool, tennis courts and doll museum nearby.
Location 50 km from Périgueux, 45 km from Angoulême. Centre of town, near *Mairie*. Garage.
Credit card Visa.
Terms Rooms: single 85–120 frs, double 90–175 frs; dinner, B&B 125–170 frs per person; full board 165–220 frs per person. Breakfast 16 frs; set lunch/dinner 65 and 100 frs; full alc 115 frs.

NOUAN-LE-FUZELIER 41600 Loir-et-Cher   Map 10

Le Moulin de Villiers   *Tel* (54) 88.72.27
Route de Chaon

A connoisseur of modest French rural hotels introduces this old mill-house, lost in the silent Sologne forests yet only three kilometres from the N20 highway south of Orléans: "The woodland approach is delightful: as the drive bends, the hotel is seen in a grassy hollow, opposite its private *étang* where ducks waterski and gabble. The long low buiding is typically Solognot, a style that, until you get used to it, has a faintly cringing appearance, a reminder of past hard times. The hotel is simple and unassuming, and reception agreeable and lacka-daisical. Our bedroom, large, spotless, adequately furnished, had a lovely view over the lake and woods – what better introduction to the Sologne of Alain-Fournier? The beamed dining room was welcoming, with fresh flowers from the garden on each table. Only two menus. Cheeseboard rather sparse, but quail with grapes delightful. The house carafe red (less than 10 francs) had a rather flabby Saumur taste, but the Cheverny was good." *(Norman Brangham)*

Open All year except 5 Jan–20 Mar, 31 Aug–15 Sept; closed Wed Oct–Dec.
Rooms 20 – most with bath or shower.
Facilities Restaurant. Garden with pond.
Location 3 km NE of Nouan-le-Fuzelier (which is 44 km S of Orléans) by D44.
Credit cards None accepted.
Terms [1985 rates] rooms 90–190 frs, full board 150–240 frs per person. Breakfast 16 frs; set lunch/dinner 65–130 frs.

NOVES 13550 Bouches-du-Rhône   **Map 11**

Auberge de Noves   *Tel* (90) 94.19.21
                                                            Telex 431312

A 19th-century manor amid pleasant open country south-east of Avignon, now a stylish and luxurious hotel, famous for its cuisine (two *Michelin* rosettes, two red *Gault Millau toques*). Our earlier report, endorsed this year, ran: "We had a large and stylish bedroom with pretty decor and a bathroom with every modern gadget including movable, dimmable lights; a balcony with a pastoral view, too. The lounge with its unusual green decor is far more snug and inviting than is usual in French hotels, and we found all the staff most helpful, as was the kindly *patron*, André Lallemand. There are neat new tennis courts, but the sprawling garden is somewhat ill cared-for. Meals, served in a cheerful flower-filled room, were delicious though pricey: interesting mint-flavoured mussel soup." A report this year: "My daughter, who had been working on a film for six months, stayed here for a week with her tutor and me. We were pleased, though it was a bit formal. We had a lovely room with a balcony overlooking the fields and orchards. Service was excellent, also the food, though a bit too *nouvelle* to suit my daughter. But M. Lallemand remedied this by preparing roast chicken and chips for her." There's *noblesse oblige* for you. *(J A, Cathryn Balk)*

Open All year except Jan and Feb. Restaurant closed Wed midday.
Rooms 20 double – most with bath or shower, telephone and TV, some with balcony.
Facilities Salon, dining room; conference facilities. Garden with swimming pool and tennis courts. &.
Location Off D28, 2 km NW of Noves, which is 13 km SE of Avignon.
Credit cards All major cards accepted.
Terms [1985 rates] rooms 330–820 frs. Breakfast 42 frs; set lunch/dinner 290 frs.

ORVAULT 44700 Loire-Atlantique   Map 10

Domaine d'Orvault   *Tel* (40) 76.84.02
Chemin des Marais du Cens   *Telex* 700454

The growth of Nantes, north-west France's biggest city, has turned
Orvault village, seven kilometres to the north-west, into a residential
suburb. Here the *Domaine* is "surrounded by a tangle of dual carriage-
ways", which hardly sounds promising. But in fact this smart hostelry
stands quietly in a big wooded garden – "a good hotel, with excellent
food and pleasant staff", is this year's verdict. An earlier one: "An oasis
of tranquil greenery. The public rooms are pleasingly plush, bedrooms
are small but comfortable, looking over a garden. The hotel's supreme
virtues are its excellent kitchen and the charm of its presiding genius,
Jean-Yves Bernard. The puddings and cakes are among the best I have
had in France, served with enthusiasm." M. Bernard wins a *Michelin*
rosette and a *Gault Millau* red *toque* for his inventive fish dishes, eg
marinière de bar aux écrevisses. *(Mrs Howard L Miller, Martin Gilbert)*

Open All year. Restaurant closed some of Feb and Mon midday.
Rooms 1 suite, 29 double – all with bath, direct-dial telephone, radio, TV and
mini-bar; some ground-floor rooms.
Facilities Lift. Bar, salon, TV room, restaurant; conference facilities. Garden with
tennis court. English spoken. &.
Location 7 km NW of Nantes off N137 route de Rennes.
Credit cards Amex, Diners, Visa.
Terms [1985 rates] rooms 290–430 frs; full board 440–515 frs per person. Breakfast
33 frs; set lunch/dinner 135–285 frs.

PAIMPOL 22500 Côtes du Nord   Map 8

Le Repaire de Kerroc'h   *Tel* (96) 20.50.13
29 quai Morand

Formerly a deep-sea cod-fishing port, Paimpol today is a yachting resort
and oyster-breeding centre on the north Breton coast. *Le Repaire* stands
on its harbour front, a sturdy stone mansion built in 1793 as the home of
a wealthy local corsair, and today tamed into a select restaurant-with-
rooms, noted for the inventive fish dishes of its *patron-chef* Robert
Abraham *(toque* in *Gault Millau)*. "Overlooks harbour. Luxurious
accommodation, beautiful furnishings, thickest bath towels ever seen –
felt like a queen. Menu good haute cuisine, but many super cheap
restaurants nearby. Amazing breakfast – three types of croissant, hot (!!!)
toast." *(Ruth P Goodwin)* More reports welcome.

Open All year except Jan, closed Mon evening and Tue except school holidays
and 1 Jun–30 Sep.
Rooms 1 suite, 6 double – all with telephone, radio and TV. Double-glazing.
Facilities Lift. Bar, restaurant, 10 minutes' walk from sandy beach; fishing,
English spoken. &.
Location Central, next to the harbour. Parking.
Credit cards All major cards accepted.
Terms Room: 290 frs, dinner, B&B: single 460 frs, double 650 frs. Breakfast 38 frs;
set lunch/dinner 90, 135 and 160 frs; full alc 250 frs. Reduced rates and special
meals for children.

Hôtel de l'Abbaye St-Germain
10 rue Cassette, 75006, 6e

Tel (1) 544.38.11

"Superb value for money", "beautifully decorated, polite and efficient staff, excellent breakfasts" - so run two comments this year on this delightfully restored 18th-century residence (formerly a monastery), decorated with simple elegance. Wide windows open on to a lovely little flagged courtyard with palms, pot-plants and flowers, where breakfast or refreshments can be taken (no other meals served). The hotel is in a busy street near St-Germain-des-Prés, and though it is a *Relais du Silence*, front rooms are not entirely noise-free: best ask for one at the back. "Great ambience" says one recent visitor and adds intriguingly: "Very amusing duo, a Greek and a Spaniard, who do everything – including porter and chambermaid – and appear to share both one uniform and one wig. Very chatty, and say they are employed because 'the French won't get their hands dirty'." *(John Tovey, Gerald Campion, and others)* One reader complains of lack of soap.

Open All year.
Rooms 45 double – all with bath and telephone. Baby-sitting by arrangement.
Facilities Lift. 2 salons (1 with TV), bar, breakfast room; interior courtyard/garden for fine-weather breakfast and refreshments. English spoken.
Location Central, near St-Sulpice church. (Métro St-Sulpice.)
Restriction Not suitable for &.
Credit cards None accepted.
Terms [1985 rates] B&B 420–525 frs.

Hôtel Cambon
3 rue Cambon, 75001, 1e

Tel (1) 426.03.809
Telex 240814

Not at all cheap, but recommended as a "small, friendly hotel, perfectly located near the Place de la Concorde. Our room was small but complete with reading lamps actually bright enough for reading in bed, good modern shower. Fresh orange juice for breakfast. Helpful concierge." *(Mrs W Lewis)* The *patron* writes this year to say that bedrooms are being enlarged.

Open All year.
Rooms 34 double, 10 single – 27 with bath, 17 with shower, all with telephone, radio, colour TV and tea-making facilities. Double-glazing; back rooms quietest.
Facilities 2 salons, lounge bar. English spoken. Parking.
Location Just off Place de la Concorde, by Concorde Métro.
Credit cards All major cards accepted.
Terms B&B: single 650–750 frs, double 780–920 frs.

Hôtel des Deux-Îles
59 rue St-Louis-en-l'Île, 75004, 4e

Tel (1) 326.13.35

An elegant 17th-century house has been prettily converted into a small hotel. It is in the middle of the Île-St-Louis, so there are no views of the Seine; but it has a small flowery inner courtyard and a hall unusually decorated with bamboo. "What a find! Such mastery in interior planning – the cosiness, the good taste," enthuses one visitor. Another reports: "Our bedroom was charming, furnished with Provençal fabrics; its smallness was compensated for by the generous bathroom, which was equally attractively decorated, with Portuguese blue and white tiles. Breakfast was delicious and prettily served in blue and white china." There is also an attractive cellar-bar. Some readers have found the front rooms noisy in the early morning and the bedrooms a little airless in hot weather. More reports welcome.

Open All year.
Rooms 13 double, 4 single – 8 with bath, 9 with shower, all with telephone and baby-listening; 1 ground-floor room.
Facilities Lift. Salons, bar. Garden. English spoken.
Location Central. No parking facilities. (Métro Pont Marie.)
Credit cards None accepted.
Terms B&B: single 425 frs, double 550 frs. (No restaurant.)

Hôtel des Grands Hommes　　　　　　　　　　　*Tel* (4) 634.19.60
17 place du Panthéon, 75005, 5e　　　　　　*Telex* PANTEOM 200 185 F

The "great men" are André Breton and other surrealist painters and writers who used to stay at this little hotel of character in the heart of the Latin Quarter, owned and run by the Brethous family and recommended this year as "small and quaint, clean, helpful and friendly: our room had excellent bed, exposed beams." The place is not cheap, but has character; each room separately furnished in period style; breakfast in a stone-vaulted 18th-century cellar. The *Hotel du Panthéon*, next door, is also owned and run by the Brethous. *(Mary and Mike Dettrich)*

Open All year.
Rooms 32 double (can be used as singles) – all with bath, direct-dial telephone, radio, colour TV, mini-bar.
Facilities Hall, lounge with bar, breakfast room. Small garden. English spoken.
Location Opposite Panthéon. Métro Luxembourg. Parking in street (difficult), underground paying car park – 100 metres.
Restriction Not suitable for &.
Credit cards Amex, Diners, Visa.
Terms Rooms: single 300 frs – 520 frs, double 450 frs – 600 frs. Breakfast 26 frs. (No restaurant.)

Hôtel Lancaster　　　　　　　　　　　　　　*Tel* (1) 359.90.43
7 rue de Berri, 75008, 8e　　　　　　　　　　*Telex* 640991 LOYNE
　　　　　　　　　　　　　　Reservations in UK (01) 734 4267
　　　　　　　　　　　　　　in USA (800) 233 5581

Leading American stage and screen stars are among the regular guests at this exclusive and luxurious hotel just off the Champs-Élysées. It is owned by the Savoy group who also own London's *Connaught* (q.v.) and might be called its Paris equivalent: it lacks the latter's gastronomic prowess, but in other respects seems even nearer to absolute perfection. "Of all the hotels I've ever stayed in, this is the one I'd most like to *live* in," writes one millionairess *manquée*; "it assumes everything for your comfort but boasts about nothing. Anything you might need to feel at home is there – towelling robes, plenty of writing paper, lots of table lamps to vary the lighting. I hadn't asked for an English newspaper, it arrived with my breakfast because the hotel thought I'd like one. Breakfast included superb pain au chocolat, fruit and fragrant coffee. The service is remarkable almost by its invisibility, and when it *is* visible it is accompanied by real smiles and courtesy. Nothing jars. There are

441

paintings and flowers, and the furnishings are quietly beautiful, from the soft lounges downstairs to Louis XIV beds with linen sheets, and inlaid desks and huge mirrors in the bedrooms." *(Gillian Vincent)* "Outstanding", adds one visitor this year *(S V Bishop)*, but another complains of discourtesy when settling a muddle over extras on the bill. The dining room facing the little garden is intimate and cosy. *Note:* as we go to press we learn that manager John Sinclair has been succeeded by Mr R G Linhardt, formerly of the *Savoy*.

Open All year. Restaurant closed Sat, Sun, Aug.
Rooms 10 suites, 43 double, 14 single – all with bath, telephone and radio, colour TV; baby-sitting by arrangement; some air-conditioning. Garden rooms quietest.
Facilities Lift. Hall, large salon, small salon, small bar, restaurant; private dinner party/functions rooms; conference facilities. Delightful garden patio which many rooms overlook, used for meals in fine weather. English spoken.
Location Central (but quiet), off Champs-Élysées and near Arc de Triomphe. Parking. (Métro Georges V.)
Restriction Not suitable for &.
Credit cards All major cards accepted.
Terms [1985 rates] (Excluding 15% service charge) rooms: single 860–1,000 frs, double 1,200–1,400 frs; suites from 1,850 frs. Breakfast 60 frs; set meals 160 frs; full alc 250 frs. Special meals for children by arrangement.

Hôtel La Louisiane   *Tel* (1) 326.97.08 or 329.59.30
60 rue de Seine, 75006, 6e

This utterly unpretentious little hotel near St-Germain-des-Prés is hallowed in literary history, for Hemingway, Connolly and others used to stay here (it's mentioned in *The Unquiet Grave)* and de Beauvoir writes in *The Prime of Life* that she and Sartre both had rooms here. "One of the most distinguished cheap hotels in Europe, leftish, intellectual/arty, scruffy". "The guests are still largely Anglo-American or otherwise foreign and still wear a bohemian aura. This is not a place for those seeking chic, and you may be put off by the cramped, minuscule foyer and shabby lift: but the cosmopolitan staff are affable in a quirky, personal way, and the bedrooms, though sparsely decorated, are well modernised, serviceable, and amazing value at around 170 francs with bath [1985]. The hotel looks straight on to the colourful but noisy Buci street market; but there's double-glazing, and rooms at the back or on upper floors in front are very quiet. Help-yourself breakfast system with a kind of soft brown soda-bread, making a pleasant change from the usual croissants." *(John Thirlwell, J A)*

Open All year.
Rooms 79 – 74 with bath or shower, all with telephone.
Facilities Lift.
Location Central, near St-Germain-des-Prés. (Métro St-Germain-des-Prés, Odéon, St-Sulpice.)
Credit cards None accepted.
Terms [1985 rates] B&B: single 160 frs, double 225–240 frs.

We ask hotels to estimate their 1986 tariffs. About a quarter of the hotels in Part Two have failed to reply, so prices in that section are more approximate in some cases than those in Part One.

Hôtel de Lutèce   *Tel* (1) 326.23.52
65 rue Saint-Louis-en-l'Île, 75004, 4e

"Peace and quiet, and pleasant people." This is the sister hotel to the
St-Louis (q.v.), in the long road that runs down the middle of the Île.
Rooms are minuscule, but comfortable and very clean and warm. A
comfortable sitting area with a log fire, and a most amiable polyglot
Italian lady at the desk. No food, but an excellent restaurant *(Les
Chimères)* next door. "Excellent value – personal service by people who
will remember your name by the second day." *(Douglas and Mary
Coleman)*

Open All year.
Rooms 23 – all with bath or shower and direct-dial telephone.
Facilities Lift. Sitting room.
Location In centre of Île-St-Louis. (Métro Pont-Marie.)
Restriction Not suitable for &.
Credit cards None accepted.
Terms [1985 rates] rooms: 352–375 frs. Breakfast 24 frs. (No restaurant.)

Hôtel le Pavillon   *Tel* (1) 551.42.87 and 551.33.54
54 rue St-Dominique, 75007, 7e

Modestly priced and usefully situated, just west of the broad Esplanade
des Invalides and five minutes' walk from the river, "this little hotel (a
former nunnery) came as a pleasant surprise, set back from the street
with a tiny courtyard and plants growing round the front. Staff helpful
and friendly. No public rooms, just the reception area. Our room was
very small with little space for clothes, but was clean and cheerful and
the price was very reasonable. Excellent breakfast served promptly in
our room." *(Dr and Mrs Lovejoy)*

Open All year.
Rooms 1 with 2 double beds, 17 double, 2 single – 1 with bath, 18 with shower, all
with telephone. Some on ground floor.
Facilities Lounge with TV. Small garden where drinks and breakfast can be
served. English spoken.
Location 500 metres W of Invalides. (Métro la Tour Maubourg or Invalides.)
Public parking nearby.
Credit card Visa.
Terms Rooms 170–360 frs. Breakfast 16 frs. Reductions for children. (No
restaurant.)

Hôtel Relais Christine   *Tel* (1) 326.71.80
3 rue Christine, 75006, 6e   *Telex* 202606 RELAIS

Renewed praise this year for this small but expensive luxury hotel,
recently converted from a 16th-century abbey. It is in a side-street near
the Seine, not far from the lively food markets of the rue de Buci. The
rooms are set round a most attractive courtyard. No restaurant, but the
breakfast (served in the converted chapel in the basement) are described
as "wonderful", especially the croissants and orange juice. "So beautifully modernised that you lose the atmosphere of an old abbey except in
the breakfast room." "The service was good everywhere and the desk
staff were particularly helpful." "The basement garage is a boon." *(Roger
Bennett, Pat and Jeremy Temple, Janey and Caradoc King)*

Open All year.
Rooms 17 suites, 35 double – 47 with bath, 4 with shower, all with telephone, radio, colour TV and mini-bar.
Facilities Lift. Reception hall with lobby, lounge, breakfast room; conference room for 15. Courtyard/garden. English spoken.
Location Central. Basement garage. (Métro St-Michel.)
Restriction Not suitable for &.
Credit cards Amex, Diners, Visa.
Terms Rooms 770-920 frs. Breakfast 45 frs. (No restaurant.)

La Résidence du Bois   *Tel* (1) 500.50.59
16 rue Chalgrin, 75116, 16e

This Third Empire mansion, is near the Étoile but in a quiet position, and has a charming garden. It is small, de luxe and exclusive, with salons and spacious bedrooms tastefully furnished with period pieces. As well as breakfast, it will also serve light meals if asked. "We adored it," writes a visitor this year who came with nanny and children; "the bedrooms are wonderful, filled with silks, satins, chinoiserie etc. Breakfast in bed was delicious." "The staff were friendly and helpful, the room comfortable and quiet. We had some of their 'light meals' - excellent." (*Tessa Dahl Kelly, H Richard Lamb, and others*)

Open All year.
Rooms 3 triple, 15 double, 2 single – 18 with bath, 2 with shower, all with direct-dial telephone and colour TV; baby-listening on request; 1 room in annexe.
Facilities Salon, bar. No restaurant, but simple meals served to residents on request. Beautiful garden full of trees and flowers for fine-weather refreshments. Swimming pool nearby. English spoken.
Location Central (near Arc de Triomphe). Parking nearby. (Métro Argentine.)
Restriction Not suitable for &.
Credit cards None accepted.
Terms [1985 rates] B&B: double 680–975 frs, suites 1,030–1,200 frs. (No restaurant.)

Hôtel Roblin   *Tel* (1) 265.57.00
6 rue Chauveau-Lagarde, 75008, 8e   *Telex* 640154

A medium-priced hotel just behind the Madeleine, again praised by several visitors this year: "Outstanding value"; "the people who work there are wonderful"; "the breakfasts were good. For the price the hotel is well maintained (we had a huge room) and excellent value." A lot of people like the *fin de siècle* decor and the high, handsome scale of the place – "everything the Romantic English could hope for". (*Cathryn Balk, Neil Bannister, and others*) The hotel's restaurant, *Le Mazagran*, is next door.

Open All year. Restaurant closed Aug, Sat and Sun.
Rooms 50 double, 20 single – 60 with bath, 10 with shower, all with telephone, colour TV and baby-listening.
Facilities Lift. Large salon, small salon, TV room, bar, restaurant next door. English spoken.
Location Central. Garage next door. (Métro Madeleine.)
Restriction Not suitable for &.
Credit cards All major cards accepted.
Terms [1985 rates] B&B: single 415 frs, double 530 frs. Set meals 150–205 frs. Special meals for children.

Hôtel St-Louis *Tel* (1) 638.04.80
75 rue St-Louis-en-l'Île, 75004, 4e

A small hotel of character in a 17th-century building with a stone-flagged entrance hall, situated not on the *quais* but in the central main street of the Île St-Louis. Most visitors this year are again appreciative, supporting earlier praise: "Exposed beams, a wood-burning fireplace, a warm welcome. The rooms are not gigantic but well furnished, with modern bathrooms: try for a top-floor one, with balcony and rooftop view." One dissenter thought the place a little run down and warns that front rooms may suffer from street noise. There is no lift. *(Mrs Howard L Miller, Mary Mitchell, Clay Leitch, and others)*

Open All year.
Rooms 25 double – 17 with bath, 8 with shower, all with telephone, tea-making facilities, some with TV and balcony.
Facilities Lobby. English spoken.
Location Central. (Métro Pont Marie.)
Restriction Not suitable for &.
Credit cards Access, Visa.
Terms [1985 rates] rooms: single occupancy 285 frs, double 307–410 frs. Breakfast 22 frs. (No restaurant.)

Hôtel St-Sulpice *Tel* (1) 634.23.90
7 rue Casimir-Delavigne, 75006, 6e

This 1986 *Good Hotel Guide* was in part edited in Room 45 of this hotel, where the editor for France and Germany tapped out these lines you are reading. His view: "A typical little Left Bank hotel, clean, serviceable, friendly, moderate-priced. It's very central, close to the Théâtre de l'Odéon and to lots of good cheap restaurants such as *Polidor* in the rue Monsieur le Prince. I stay here often. Rather hideous pink-orange decor in the breakfast room, but good coffee and croissants, lively Portuguese maids, and nice receptionist girls who took terrific pains to find us another hotel when theirs was full. Bedroom and bathroom efficient if ordinary. Big desk just right for editing hotel guides on." *(J A C A)* "Convenient and charming, helpful and friendly. We slept in attic rooms with rooftop views." *(A L)*

Open All year.
Rooms 7 triple, 32 double, 3 single – 18 with bath, 24 with shower, all with telephone.
Facilities Lift. Lounge with TV. English spoken.
Location 3 minutes' walk from Odéon métro station. Parking in street; 2 underground car parks nearby.
Restriction Not suitable for &.
Credit cards None accepted.
Terms Rooms: single 190–240 frs, double 230–260 frs. Breakfast 18.60 frs. (No restaurant.)

Hôtel Scandinavia *Tel* (1) 329.67.20
27 rue de Tournon, 75006, 6e

A sympathetic and characterful hotel in a converted 17th-century building, close to the Luxembourg Gardens. Some bedrooms have Louis XIII antiques, and a few have balconies – "Delightful, the quietest hotel we've stayed in. We had a charming room with a huge balcony at the back furnished with antiques. Best maid service we have ever encountered, though a little impersonal. Breakfast is unusually lavish for France: every day we had fresh sliced ham, hard-boiled eggs, natural yoghurt, honey, jam, croissants, fresh rolls, hot coffee, fresh oranges – all for 15 frs extra. This meant we didn't need to eat again till dinner-time." "Decorated with a lot of red plush and velvet and dark oak. All medieval style (exposed beams and even a light-bulb shining through a presumably mock suit of armour!)." This visitor also remarks on slow breakfast service and an incorrect booking. Clientele mainly American. *(Jo and Michael Féat, also Dorothy Masterson, and others)*

Open All year.
Rooms 22 double – all with bath and telephone.
Facilities 2 salons. English spoken.
Location Central. No parking facilities. (Métro Odéon.)
Credit cards None accepted.
Terms Rooms 279 frs. Breakfast 20 frs. (No restaurant.)

Hôtel de Suède　　　　　　　　　　　　　*Tel* (1) 705.00.08 and 551.49.07
31 rue Vaneau, 75007, 7e　　　　　　　　　　　　　　　　*Telex* 200596

In the heart of the old Faubourg St-Germain, aristocratic in Proust's day, governmental in ours. A medium-price hotel, recommended this year as "very good value – we had a comfortable room with balcony on the fifth floor, good size, well furnished with unelaborate elegance. The rooms at the back overlook the gardens of the Hôtel Matignon, the Prime Minister's residence; ours, on the street side, was less quiet, but apart from the usual refuse wagons at dawn it is not a busy street, despite being full of armed police. Helpful and friendly staff, good breakfast, comfortable lounge." *(Charles and Jessica Thomas)*

Open All year.
Rooms 1 suite, 34 double, 6 single – 38 with bath, all with telephone.
1 ground-floor room.
Facilities Lift. Salon, bar. Garden; next to Parc de Matignon. English spoken.
Location 10 minutes' walk from Seine and St-Germain-des-Prés. (Métro Varenne.)
Credit card Amex.
Terms B&B: single 370 frs, double 405 frs, suite 630 frs. (No restaurant.)

Hôtel de l'Université　　　　　　　　　　　　　　　*Tel* (1) 261.09.39
22 rue de Université, 75007, 7e　　　　　　　　　　　　　*Telex* 260717

"Classy, tasteful and stylish – it's what I come to Paris for. It is a 17th-century town house converted into an intimate small hotel that fits in beautifully with the antique-dealing character of the neighborhood. Brass street lamps light up the entrance. Inside, the public areas are beautifully decorated with antiques and tapestries. I understand every bedroom is different, and the few I was able to see were lovely, including my own. Beautiful touches were everywhere, from the scented soaps in the shower each day to the Limoges china with breakfast. This meal is taken at small marble tables looking out on to a charming tiny courtyard. The staff were helpful and patient with requests." *(Donna Cuervo)*

Open All year.
Rooms 1 suite, 17 double, 10 single – 20 with bath, 8 with shower; all with telephone; baby-sitters available.
Facilities Lounge, bar. English spoken.
Location 5 minutes from St-Germain-des-Prés. Underground parking nearby. (Métro Rue du Bac.)
Credit cards None accepted.
Terms Rooms: single 325 frs, double 550 frs. Breakfast 28 frs. Reduced rates for children sharing parents' room. (No restaurant, but snacks served in bar.)

Hôtel de Varenne   *Tel* (1) 551.45.55
44 rue de Bourgogne, 75007, 7e

American visitors have written warmly of this "converted mansion with a pretty little courtyard", centrally situated very near the Invalides and five minutes' walk from the river at the Pont de la Concorde. "Peaceful, with a friendly and efficient staff. Nice comfortable rooms. Breakfast on patio or in lounge area. Moderate price." *(Dr Bill and Lisa Fuerst)*

Open All year.
Rooms 17 double, 7 single – 14 with bath, 10 with shower, all with direct-dial telephone and TV.
Facilities Lounge, patio. English spoken.
Location Within walking distance of the Champs-Élysées and St-Germain-des-Prés. Parking in quiet street, 5 minutes' walk away. (Métro Varenne.)
Restriction Not suitable for &.
Credit card Amex.
Terms Rooms: single 250–350 frs, double 350–375 frs. Breakfast 25 frs. (No restaurant.)

Hôtel du Vieux Marais   *Tel* (1) 278.47.22
8 rue du Platre, 75004, 4e

A little hotel near the Pompidou Centre, confirmed this year as "excellent value, clean and comfortable, warm and welcoming". Most recent reports agree, though one reader thought the comforts a little basic, and another found the breakfast on the meagre side (you are charged five francs extra for coffee after the first two cups). A third complained of a churlish reception and of having to pay cash in advance. More reports please.

Open All year.
Rooms 22 double, 8 single – 21 with bath, 9 with shower, all with telephone; some ground-floor rooms.
Facilities Lift. Breakfast room, garden. English spoken.
Location Central (in a quiet street), near Pompidou Centre and Notre Dame. (Métro Rambuteau.) Parking in streets around hotel; public parking nearby.
Restriction Not suitable for &.
Credit cards None accepted.
Terms [1985 rates] B&B: single 210 frs, double 350 frs. (No restaurant.)

> If you feel we have done a hotel an injustice }
> If we have failed to mention salient details } please let us know.
> If you consider we have got it about right   }

PÉGOMAS 06580 Alpes-Maritimes   Map 11

Hôtel le Bosquet   *Tel* (93) 42.22.87
Quartier du Château

"A real winner, very friendly, charming and good value – but don't expect smartness." So runs a 1984 inspection report on this idiosyncratic little hotel in the scruffy outskirts of a village in the mimosa country between Cannes and Grasse. This echoes earlier praise: "No matter that the Binnses and Éperons have got here first and that half the guests seem to be British. The ebullient *patronne*, Simone Bernardi, *vaut le détour*. We were beguiled by the convivial spirit, the clean and simple comfort, the happy communal breakfasts in the courtyard. We enjoyed the *piscine*, even though you pay extra for it. The garden is unkept but spacious and there are nice views of the hills." (*J A, Gerald Campion, L H*)

Open All year except Nov.
Rooms 17 double, 7 studios with kitchenette – 2 with bath, 15 with shower, all with telephone, some with TV. All rooms are in 2 annexes.
Facilities 2 salons, breakfast room with TV, courtyard. Garden with *boules* and unheated swimming pool. English spoken.
Location On road to Mouans-Sartoux, in northern outskirts of Pégomas, which is 11 km NW of Cannes.
Restrictions Not suitable for &. No children under 3.
Credit cards None accepted.
Terms Rooms 150–190 frs. Breakfast 16 frs. (No restaurant.)

PEILLON 06440 Alpes-Maritimes   Map 11

Auberge de la Madone   *Tel* (93) 79.91.17

"A winner", writes an inspector, endorsing earlier veneration of the *Madone*: "Only 10 or so miles from Nice, yet you seem in the middle of nowhere. This civilised *auberge* is just outside one of the most attractive hill villages in the area, and has super views of the valley and hills. The young owners, the Millos, manage to create a family atmosphere, without overdoing it. The food is very good (*toque* in *Gault Millau*) and quite varied, and includes some oddities such as a kind of chilled bouillabaisse. The place seems to attract the nicest kind of Parisian, and we made several French friends during our stay. If you want a really quiet room, ask for one at the back." "Our balconied room was large and comfortable. Rather than take the fixed menu, it is wise to respond to the Oral, *'Je vous propose ... c'est délicieux'* – we did, and it was." (*L H, John Newnham*)

Open 15 Dec to 15 Oct. Closed Wed.
Rooms 2 suites, 17 double – 15 with bath, 3 with shower, all with telephone, 2 with TV.
Facilities Salon, TV room, bar, dining room; conference facilities. Large garden; sea (at Nice) 15 km. English spoken.
Location 15 km NE of Nice on D21.
Credit cards None accepted.
Terms Rooms 158–320 frs; dinner, B&B 165–330 frs per person. Breakfast 25 frs; set lunch/dinner 80–140 frs; full alc 190 frs. Reduced rates and special meals for children.

PÉROUGES 01800 Ain   Map 10

Ostellerie du Vieux Pérouges   *Tel* (74) 61.00.88

The medieval hilltop of Pérouges (40 kilometres north-east of Lyon), with its ramparts, cobbles and half-timbered houses, is so perfectly preserved that historical feature films are often shot here. The hotel, converted from 13th-century buildings, is part of the decor, forming one side of the village square and dominated by a huge and ancient tree.

"To stay here is truly to step back in time," writes an American visitor; "we climbed to our spacious rooms by way of a winding stone tower staircase. The antique furnishings are both beautiful and comfortable, and modern elements like telephones are hidden in chests. The views are magnificent, and we enjoyed eating breakfast in a private garden." Another reader took to the place, but sounds a more sceptical note: "Rather gimmicky, even down to the large rolls of parchment on which menu and wine list are presented. Large restaurant in medieval style, with waitresses in local peasant costume." However, almost everyone likes the *Michelin*-starred cuisine. "Very quiet and relaxing, fantastic food." "There are mouth-watering antiques everywhere, in the dining room and bedrooms, and the town. Brace yourself for the local rooster, who starts doing his thing at 4.30 am." Those who do not salivate at the sight of an antique may instead be made to do so by the écrevisses pérougienne or the celebrated local griddle cake with raspberries. (*Dorothy Masterson*)

Open All year.
Rooms 2 suites, 22 double, 2 single – all with bath and telephone; 10 rooms in annexe; 1 ground-floor room.
Facilities Lounges, bar, dining room; conference facilities. Gardens. English spoken.
Location In town square. Parking available. For Pérouges take N84 from Lyon to Geneva; turn off on D4 at Meximieux.
Restriction Not suitable for &.
Credit card Visa.
Terms (Excluding 15% service charge) rooms: single 360–450 frs, double 360–630; half-board 580 per person. Breakfast 40 frs; set lunch/dinner 125, 165, 190, 210 and 240 frs; full alc 180 frs.

LA PETITE PIERRE 67290 Bas-Rhin   Map 9

Aux Trois Roses   *Tel* (88) 70.45.02
                                                     Telex 890308

Much enthusiasm again in 1985 for this fine old 18th-century *auberge*, white-walled, flower-bedecked, all cosy inside. It is in the main street of an ancient hill-top village (front rooms can be noisy), with remains of ramparts, and hilly forests all around; the dining room has a fine view of the castle, romantic on summer evenings when it is floodlit. "A very typical Alsatian *auberge*, sympathetic, informal and lively, slightly unkempt, run hectically by a whole bevy of Alsatians, jabbering away in their dialect. It's very much a local social centre, less in the French than the Central European tradition – several comfy salons, and a big *Stübe* where snacks are served all day, as well as a lavish array of cakes and tartlets. The food is pleasant if unexciting – good soups and fresh trout, run-of-the-mill civet de sanglier. Our bedroom, the last, was cramped but with comfy bed and a valley view. The heated indoor pool, reserved for residents, was super in chill November." "A splendid warm welcome"; "charming, excellent value, and in a marvellous walking area." (*J A, K S, Patrick Freeman, Angela and David Stewart, and others*) PS: A correspondent who knows the area well tells us that that the *Trois Roses* tends to get crowded at weekends with visitors from Germany. He recommends as alternatives in the village the *Lion D'Or* and the *Vosges*: the latter is owned by the son of a pupil of Escoffier and maintains the Escoffier tradition. (*C F Colt*)

Open 22 Dec–22 Nov.
Rooms 29 double, 8 single – 10 with bath, 26 with shower, all with telephone; 3 rooms in annexe. 16 more rooms with balcony and bath planned for Easter 1986.
Facilities Lift and ramps. 3 lounges (2 with TV), bar, restaurant, indoor swimming pool. Garden with terrace, children's play area, tennis courts. Small lake 3 km with fishing. English spoken.
Location 60 km NW of Strasbourg; hotel is central. Parking.
Credit cards Access, Visa.
Terms Rooms: single 53–218 frs, double 120–248 frs; dinner, B&B: 157 frs–238 frs: full board: 20 frs per person added to dinner, B&B rate. Breakfast 24 frs; set lunch/dinner 69–168 frs; full alc 155 frs. Jan–Easter weekly rate 20% off. Reductions for children under 8; special meals.

LE POËT-LAVAL 26160 Drôme   Map 10

Les Hospitaliers   *Tel* (75) 46.22.32

On the borders of Provence and the Dauphiné, Le Poët-Laval is a medieval village in splendid wooded countryside where the foothills of the Alps descent to the Rhône valley. *Les Hospitaliers*, a very *soigné* country hotel in the village, with a swimming pool and flowery terrace, is again admired this year. "Excellent: large comfortable rooms, very good food, helpful staff, friendly atmosphere." An earlier report was more explicit: "One of my secret paradises, and truly quiet. There are no passing cars: the streets of this former Protestant stronghold are too narrow or bumpy to accept them, though the hotel can be reached by road and has ample parking space. Cumbrian-like hills are in view from its windows. Its creator, M. Morin, has achieved great feats of building and engineering. A few years ago there was no water, electricity or telephone system in the village. He bought old stones to restore and blend his reconstruction with the 12th-century deserted chapel towering above." M. Morin's son does the cooking, and has won a *Michelin* rosette and *Gault Millau toque* for *minceur*-type cuisine. (*S J Burnton, James Shorrocks, and others*) One visitor in 1984 felt that portions were too small, failing to cater for robust appetites; M. Morin tells us the *minceur* meals are now served in bigger portions and that all his larger rooms are now equipped with antique furniture.

Open 1 Mar–15 Nov.
Rooms 1 suite, 18 double, 1 single – 19 with bath, 1 with shower, all with telephone; 9 rooms in annexe.
Facilities Salon, TV room, bar, 2 indoor restaurants, 1 terrace restaurant; conference facilities. Garden with terrace and heated swiming pool. Tennis, riding, fishing nearby. English spoken.
Location On D540, E of La Bégude-de-Mazenc; Montélimar 25 km.

Restriction Not suitable for &.
Credit cards All major cards accepted.
Terms Rooms: single 280 frs, double 310–500 frs; dinner, B&B: single 520 frs,
double 790–980 frs; full board: single 620 frs, double 990–1,180 frs. Breakfast 50 frs;
set meals 135, 210 and 300 frs; full alc 250 frs. Reduced rates for children; special
meals on request.

PONS 17800 Charente-Maritime   Map 10

Auberge Pontoise   *Tel* (46) 94.00.99
23 rue Gambetta

The old hospice used by pilgrims on their way to Compostela is still
extant, and open to sightseers, just outside this medieval town above
the river Seugne, dominated by a castle with a vast rectangular keep.
Modern gastronomic pilgrims this year found somewhere better than
the hospice: "The *Auberge*, in the town centre, is a truly excellent little
hotel, unpretentious, clean, comfortable and quiet, with attentive staff.
The plain dining room had magnificent fresh flowers and the cuisine
was first class" (red "R" in *Michelin* for good value) " ... pleurotte
mushrooms in a delicious cream sauce, fresh hake in a champagne
sauce." *(Jean Hayward)*

Open All year except 13–26 Apr and 20 Dec–19 Jan.
Rooms 1 suite, 21 double – 16 with bath, 6 with shower, all with direct-dial
telephone and TV. Some ground-floor rooms.
Facilities Lounge, bar, 2 dining rooms, conference facilities. Swimming pool and
tennis courts nearby. English spoken.
Location Central (signposted in the town). Parking.
Credit cards Access, Visa.
Terms B&B: single occupancy 177 frs, double 254 frs. Set lunch/dinner 85–140 frs.

Le Rustica   *Tel* (46) 96.91.75
St-Léger

Readers this year are again quite ecstatic about the homely simplicity
and value-for-francs at this small restaurant-with-rooms, that lies right
off the beaten track in a vineyard-girt hamlet north-west of Pons, near
the Bordeaux/La Rochelle road. "A marvellous experience, oh such
splendour! Our room was creaky, sloping and quaint but very
comfortable. The food was all that is very best in French provincial
cuisine." An earlier account: "The bar was very simple, but the dining
room was most attractive with large open fireplace, wooden beams,
tables with flowers. The dinner was one of the best we have had in that
price range [55 frs, 1985!]: first mouclade (mussels in cream sauce,
delicious) then steak au poivre with jacket potatoes filled with butter and
chopped bacon, then home-made plum tart. We had an enormous, very
comfortable bed: the loo and shower were both new. Best night's sleep
of the holiday – it was so quiet. Helpful service, incredible value for
money." *(David Tench, Catherine Edwards, Morton Sutherland, and others)*

Open All year except 3–24 Oct, 6–13 Feb, and Wed out of season.
Rooms 7 double.
Facilities TV room, public bar, 2 dining rooms. Garden.
Location In St-Léger, just W of N137, 5 km NW of Pons. Parking.

Credit cards None accepted.
Terms Rooms 75 frs. Breakfast 17 frs; set lunch/dinner 50, 60, 110 and 125 frs; full alc 130 frs.

PONT-AUDEMER 27500 Eure   Map 8

Hôtel de la Risle   *Tel* (32) 41.14.57
16 quai Robert Leblanc

Those unafraid of simplicity, or finding the *Vieux Puits* (below) full, could well try this one – "A small-town small hotel for the Francophile. Monsieur Chochin does cooking while Madame runs a tight little ship. The rooms are sparse but neat, with comfortable beds. No private bathrooms, but showers on each floor. One fixed-price menu with interesting choices; sweets not special, but a bowl of fresh cherries suited us well. Breakfast is fresh crusty bread and, miracle, *plenty* of butter and jam. No frills, and not perhaps for everyone, but excellent value. Madame, English born, speaks English. They're a pleasant friendly couple." What's more, *Michelin* awards it coveted red "R" for good value. *(E Newall)*

Open All year except 20 Dec–1 Jan, 1–15 Sept. Restaurant closed lunch-time.
Rooms 16 double, 2 single – showers on each floor.
Facilities Bar, restaurant. English spoken.
Location Pont-Audemer is 48 km SE of Le Havre. Hotel is central. Parking nearby.
Restriction Not suitable for &.
Credit cards None accepted.
Terms B&B: single 73 frs, double 92 frs; dinner, B&B single 115 frs, double 250 frs. Reduced rates for children.

Auberge du Vieux Puits   *Tel* (32) 41.01.48
6 rue Notre-Dame du Pré

Pont-Audemer lies in a valley 48 kilometres from Le Havre – an attractive town, nicknamed "Venise normande" because the river Risle has been rechannelled through it. It is full of cobbled streets and tiny bridges. The *Vieux Puits* – mentioned by Flaubert in *Madame Bovary* – is a collection of three 17th-century buidings, originally a tannery, occupy-ing three sides of a courtyard. Again this year it has found favour with our readers. "What an enchanting place," runs one report; "rooms a bit small but very nicely done. Jacques and Hélène Holtz, the owners, are charming and fun, and obviously take great pleasure in serving genuine Norman dishes the proper way." " A very special inn of great character, with superb cuisine – the timber-frame buildings round the courtyard are beautifully restored, and our small bedroom was comfortable." These views endorse an earlier description: "The specialities – truite Bovary, calvados sorbet and canard aux cerises – were a delight *(Michelin* rosette). Breakfast was equally good – generous glasses of fruit juice and freshly potted jams. Every attempt has been made to retain the building's original character. The result is charming – antiques, ancient flagstones, oak beams and large fireplaces." *(Dr F P Woodford, D and K Perry, and others)* Note: Until now, the *Auberge* has had only eight rooms overlooking the courtyard, attractively decorated but without baths *en suite*. From the summer of 1985, six new bedrooms all with bath are available, and the original rooms will only be used in the high season.

Open All year except 16 Dec–16 Jan and 1–10 July. Closed Mon evening and Tue.
Rooms 11 double, 3 single – 6 with bath, 5 with shower, all with telephone; all overlook garden. 2 ground-floor rooms, specially equipped for &.
Facilities 2 small salons, 2 restaurants. Small garden. English spoken. &.
Location 300 metres from town centre (hotel is signposted in the town), but quiet. Parking.
Credit card Visa.
Terms Rooms: single 90 frs, double 115–280 frs. Breakfast 22 frs; set meals 210 frs; full alc 200–240 frs.

PONT-DE-L'ARN 81660 Tarn   Map 10

La Métairie Neuve   *Tel* (63) 61.23.31

Carcassonne, Toulouse and Albi are all within 60 kilometres of this handsomely converted Languedoc farmhouse just north of Mazamet. It is a complex of 18th-century farm buildings, now a quiet rural restaurant-with-rooms, with an air of spacious comfort and elegance. "The bungalow suburbs of Mazamet make an unprepossessing setting and the exterior is a bit tatty: but once you step inside the picture is very different – cool rough-cast walls, gleaming tiles, old exposed beams, the 'antique rustic' style at which the French are unbeatable. Bedrooms are simple and plainly decorated, some of them more like mini-suites. Our table at dinner overlooked the inner courtyard, yet felt very cosy with its lamp, pretty Limoges china and fresh flowers. Our meal, the *menu touristique*, was good, especially the confit de foie de canard which melted in the mouth. They do a *demi-pension* which seemed excellent value. Service is efficient and the owners charming." (*I and F W*)

Open All year except 20 Dec–10 Jan and 1–15 Aug. Restaurant closed Sat.
Rooms 7 double – all with bath and telephone.
Facilities Reception/salon, salon, dining room. Garden. Golf 2 km, tennis and swimming pool 1 km; lakes with beaches and sailing 25 km. English spoken.
Location 2 km N of Mazamet on N112 Béziers–Castres road. Parking.
Credit cards Diners, Visa.
Terms [1985 rates] rooms (single occupancy) 160 frs, double 233 frs, full board 375 frs per person. Breakfast 25 frs; set meals 70–210 frs.

PORTICCIO Corse-du-Sud, Corisca   Map 11

Le Maquis   *Tel* (95) 25.05.55
                                                         Telex 460597

We had an entry for this sophisticated hotel, right on the water across the bay from Ajaccio, in earlier editions of the Guide, but took it out after criticism of the restaurant and doubt as to whether it could justify its steepish prices. We are now persuaded to reinstate it after receiving two glowing testimonials: "A lovely hotel, small, and traditionally built along its own lovely little beach – if you have a ground-floor room, your balcony literally meets the sand. Beautifully furnished in fairly simple style – quarry tiles, nice rugs, whitewashed walls, antique furniture, huge bowls of flowers. The food is good, especially the huge help-yourself hors-d'oeuvre table. One of our happiest memories will be eating lunch on the terrace – pink tablecloths, umbrellas, silver, fine china and glass and the bright blue sky and sea below, wonderful fresh seafood and delicious Corsican wines. The lady who owns it is *soignée*, elegant, courteous – but it is not the sort of hotel where anyone talks to you too much, and there's no pool or tennis court. Not cheap, but one has to pay for such perfection." *(John and Nicky Horner)*

Another enthusiast this year: "The main road through Porticcio is brash and restless, but the hotel is quiet and delightfully situated. It is a building of some charm and eccentricity, owing nothing to the packing-case school of hotel design. Nor is it pompous despite its four-star rating, and has more the feel of a comfortable country house whose owner is a keen collector of unusual bric-à-brac and nice old furniture. Our room's exposed rafters, purlins and ridge pole resembled the squared trunks of local laricio pines. The bathroom was well equipped, though as often in Corsica the flushing mechanism had a mind of its own. Service was unobtrusively comprehensive." *(W H Bruton)*

Open All year.
Rooms 22 – mostly double (some suites), with bath; all with telephone and TV.
Facilities Lounge, bar, dining room; terrace for alfresco meals. On private beach with safe bathing.
Location On the coast 15 km SE of Ajaccio, on the D55. 12 km from airport.
Credit cards None accepted.
Terms B&B 230–750 frs. Suites with half-board 750–1,650 frs per day for 2 people. Set lunch/dinner 100–140 frs.

PORTICCIOLO 20228 Corsica | Map 11

Hôtel Le Caribou | *Tel* (95) 35.02.33 or 35.00.33
Porticciolo, Cap-Corse 2B

(Correspondence between Oct and May should be addressed to the sister hotel, Le Caribou, 38 place Thiars, 13001 Marseilles)

Veteran Guide correspondents report a "find" in Corsica: "The most delightful atmospheric hotel we have found in two Corsican holidays. It lies on the road north from Bastia to Cap Corse, in a colourful garden of flowers and trees, looking more like a French hotel. As you go up the steep drive, you find a swimming pool set into the garden and an extensive restaurant overlooking both and out to sea. Outside the restaurant, splendid old trees have been interlaced with vines to make a cool shady place for apéritifs or coffee. Madame showed us our suite across the road, overlooking the sea. *"Magnifique"* she murmured modestly. It was not quite that, but interesting and different: one of several *pavillons* built in to the rocks just above the water's edge, each with a small sun-terrace.

"It was the restaurant that was the heart of the hotel. We rarely eat lunch in the heat, but it looked so inviting we decided to have one simple course – hors-d'oeuvre for one of us, a lobster for the other. The request triggered off the most amazing response: a series of generous platefuls of luscious melon, ham, platters of hors-d'oeuvre, a sunburst of moules arranged in concentric circles, generously and most delicious-ly sauced, pâtés and sausages, hot, fresh-from-the-oven feather-light feuilletés – an abundance of the most delectable food. And my lobster, when it came, was superb. Fresh flowers had been put in our room when we retired for a siesta. Later we swam from the breakwater: there are facilities for boating, fishing, wind-surfing and simple chairs for lazing in the sun.

"We thought dinner might be an anti-climax, but it was not! There is a wonderful atmosphere in the restaurant, full of noise and animated French (not a word of English here!) – long tables of families and friends spending the whole evening in the serious and most enjoyable pastime of having dinner. Monsieur ruled here, with a genial personal care, to see that everyone had what they wanted. His chefs were outstanding: we have recently dined at several places with two or three *Michelin* rosettes which didn't seem as worthy as this. And the prices were very reasonable for all we had." *(Angela and David Stewart)*

Open 15 June–1 Sept.
Rooms 10 *pavillons* (bungalows), for 3 – 8 people, 30 double rooms – all with bath or shower and telephone; some with balcony.
Facilities Lounge, bar, restaurant; terraces. Swimming pool, tennis courts, private beach with bathing, waterskiing, sailing, fishing, skin-diving and volley-ball. English spoken. &.
Location On east coast, off N198.
Credit cards All major cards accepted.
Terms [1985 rates] rooms: single occupancy 250 frs, double 500 frs; full board 380–430 frs per person. Breakfast 25 frs; lunch/dinner 180–220 frs.

PORTO VECCHIO 20137 Corse-du-Sud, Corsica   **Map 11**

Grand Hôtel de Cala Rossa   *Tel* (95) 71.61.51
Cala Rossa   *Telex* 460394

Porto Vecchio, an old harbour town, now quite a smart summer resort, lies amid cork forests at the head of a deep gulf. The modern *Cala Rossa* is in a beautiful and tranquil position by the sea, in a big flowery garden, 10 kilometres to the north-east (you would need a car). After spending a week there recently, an inspector reports: "Being modern, it is not strong on atmosphere, but the setting is superb and the garden lush. My room was spacious and practical, with an excellent bathroom. Not all rooms face the sea. Service is pleasant, and the food good though not outstanding." Lunch, served by the sandy beach under the pines, is a big buffet of salads and grills. *(L H)*

Open 11 May to 15 Oct.
Rooms 50 double – all with bath and direct-dial telephone.
Facilities TV room, bar, dining room, conference facilities, in large park with garden, with direct access to sandy beach, where lunch is served; ping-pong; bathing, windsurfing and waterskiing. English spoken. Nightclub nearby.
Location On peninsula 10 km NE of Porto Vecchio by N198, D568, D468.
Restriction Not suitable for &.
Credit cards Amex, Diners, Visa.
Terms [1985 rates] B&B 150–400 frs; half-board (obligatory for stays of 3 days or more) 250–580 frs. Set lunch/dinner 180 frs; full alc 310 frs. Reduced rates and special meals for children.

Many hotels put up their prices in the spring. Tariffs quoted in the text may be more accurate before April/May 1986 than after.

Hôtel San Giovanni *Tel* (95) 70.22.25
Route d'Arca

The *San Giovanni* is three kilometres to the south-west of the town, just inland. "A small and delightful two-star family-run hotel in rural surroundings. You need a car here, but some beautiful beaches are within ten minutes' drive. We had a pleasant bungalow room in a newly built outside block. The only noise in the daytime was the sound of the cuckoo and at night we could hear a nightjar singing. Open-air swimming pool. The lowest-priced menu seemed rather limited and we think we ate better in town." *(Pam and Len Ratoff, L H, David G Sefton)* More reports please.

Open 1 Apr–15 Oct. Restaurant closed from 1 Oct.
Rooms 26 double – all with bath or shower and telephone; some in bungalows.
Facilities Bar, restaurant, entertainment in restaurant twice a week. Garden with tennis court, sauna and swimming pool.
Location 2 km SW of Porto Vecchio on D659.
Restriction Not ideal for & but some groundfloor rooms.
Credit card Visa.
Terms [1985 rates] B&B: single 215–250 frs, double 251–330 frs; dinner, B&B: single 285–340 frs, double 462–520 frs; full board: single 355–410 frs, double 532–590 frs. Set meals 90–110 frs.

POUZAUGES 85700 Vendée **Map 10**

Auberge de la Bruyère *Tel* (51) 91.93.46

The Vendée, still the most Catholic part of France, continues to nurse its memories of the local right-wing Royalist rebellion against the Revolution in 1793 and the massacres that followed. Pouzauges, an old hill-top town, has a feudal castle and a memorial to 50 Vendéens who were shot here by the armies sent from Paris. These events are commemorated each summer (mid-June to late August) at the half-ruined château of Puy de Fou, 16 kilometres to the north, in a spectacular floodlit pageant with a cast of 600 including 300 horsemen. Not to be missed.

This is one good reason for visiting the *Auberge de la Bruyère*, a modern *Relais du Silence* on a hill. "Outstanding", wrote a visitor last year, while one knight errant seems to have lost his heart there: "A very well equipped country hotel on the edge of a charming town. Glorious views all round, especially from restaurant and terrace. The manageress, Janie Chatain, is the most beautiful hotelier I have found in 30 years' travel. As well as being most efficient, she is warm-hearted and thoughtful for the comfort of her guests; after dinner she and the staff join them in the bar. Food excellent, well prepared" – a five-course meal for 84 francs [1985]. *(Sydney W Burden; D & B Nuttall)*

Open All year.
Rooms 4 suites, 26 double – 15 with bath, 15 with shower, all with telephone, 15 with colour TV; tea-making facilities and baby-listening on request.
Facilities Lift. Lounges, TV room/library, bar, grill and restaurant; terrace. Garden with children's games; heated indoor swimming pool. Lake with sandy beach, bathing and fishing nearby. English spoken. &.
Location 81 km SE of Nantes. Turn off road to Pommeraie-sur-Sèvre at the Pouzauges exit. 300 metres from centre. Parking.
Credit cards All major cards accepted.

Terms Rooms: single occupancy 160–205 frs, double 200–273 frs; dinner, B&B: single 270–317 frs, double 426–497 frs; full board: single 324–357 frs, double 540–615 frs. Breakfast 20 frs; set lunch/dinner 40, 56, 90 and 115 frs; full alc 125 frs. Reduced rates and special meals for children.

PROPRIANO 20110 Corsica   Map 11

Hostellerie Le Miramar   *Tel* (95) 76.06.13
Route de la Corniche

The resort of Propriano, in south-west Corsica, lies in a deep and lovely bay, with miles of sandy beaches. "The *Miramar* is up-market, fairly expensive, very stylish, overlooking the Bay of Valinco. I was given a magnificent room with a large balcony facing the sea. The hotel feels very peaceful in its high position above the road, surrounded by gardens with a swimming pool. Public areas and bedrooms are spacious and elegant, furnished and decorated with real flair: my room had beams, quarry-tiled floors, pretty painted French country-style wooden furniture and a magnificent tiled bathroom." No restaurant, but the *Lido* and *Thalassa* are recommended, both medium-priced. (*L H*)

Open Apr–Oct. Restaurant closed Apr, May and Oct.
Rooms 29 double – all with bath, telephone, frigobar and balcony.
Facilities Salon with TV, bar, conference room, restaurant and grill. Garden with terrace, swimming pool and sauna. Sandy beach 50 metres. English spoken.
Location 1 km outside town which is 73 km S of Ajaccio. Parking.
Restriction Not suitable for &.
Credit card Diners.
Terms (Excluding *taxe de séjour*) rooms 165–480 frs. Breakfast 30 frs; set lunch/dinner 150 frs. Extra bed for child 100 frs. (No restaurant.)

RASTEAU 84110 Vaucluse   Map 11

Hôtel Bellerive   *Tel* (90) 46.10.20

An ultra-modern hotel, no beauty from the outside, but bright and cheerful inside. It is surrounded by Côtes du Rhône vineyards, in open country beside the river Ouvèze, with fine views of the distant hills; Orange and Vaison-la-Romaine, both famous for their Roman remains, are within easy reach. A reader has been three years running. "Excellent rooms, comfortable, clean, modern, all with balconies to breakfast on. Some have views of Mont Ventoux. The pool is pleasant and the atmosphere relaxed. The dining room is very attractive and the food has been steadily improving. Try their excellent Sauvignon blanc, grown up the road. The place gets a bit fraught at weekends and it would be a good idea to avoid the pool on Sunday afternoons." (*Gerald Campion*)

Open Mar–Dec inclusive.
Rooms 20 double – all with bath, telephone and balcony, TV on request; some with kitchenette. Ground-floor rooms.
Facilities Salon, TV room, restaurant. Large garden with swimming pool; river bathing and fishing nearby.
Location Leave *autoroute* A7 at Orange and take N575 towards Vaison-la-Romaine; then turn right on D69; left turn off D69 for hotel. Parking.
Credit cards None accepted.
Terms [1985 rates] rooms 220 frs. Breakfast 20 frs; set meals 80 frs (125 on public holidays).

REIMS 51100 Marne   Map 8

Boyer "Les Crayères"   *Tel* (26) 82.80.80
64 blvd Henry-Vasnier   *Telex* 830959

Awe inspiring. Gerard and Elyane Boyer (he is one of the greatest French chefs) have only recently moved their famous Reims restaurant into this graceful 18th-century-style château in the city's south-east outskirts and have done it up as a very stylish and civilised little hotel. Thus it comes new to the Guide this year, amid ecstatic praise from three of our most experienced correspondents, backed by top accolades in the French guides (*Michelin's* three rosettes and four red gables, *Gault Millau's* three red *toques*). "A mansion of pale creamy stone, its perfect proportions set against the mature trees and sweeping lawns of its park. The combination of luxurious rooms and superb food must, we feel, be unsurpassed anywhere: we put it at the top of our list of best hotels. The use of subtle muted colours, blending harmoniously, gives the impression of a whole scheme designed together. Our spacious and elegant bedroom overlooked the park; off it was the best-designed dressing room we've ever met. Dinner was superb: the cuisine was *nouvelle* but unfussy, with light sauces and delicate portions. All fairly expensive but value for money." (*Angela and David Stewart*)

"Truly deserves its *Michelin* rating. The Boyers, friendly and efficient, seem to be in all places at all times – *Les Crayères* is near the Parc Pommery (the house belongs to Pommery) and close to several famous champagne producers' *caves*. The beautiful building is approached through massive wrought-iron gates; entrance hall and staircase are imposing, made of pale beige marble, with huge tapestries. Our large bedroom had enormous windows giving a feeling of light and space. The bed could have slept six in comfort; the bathroom, beautifully fitted, was a positive hall of mirrors. The head waiter was charming: he suggested girolles, and when I looked doubtful he said, "It is perhaps, you are not good friends with mushrooms?" Food was excellent, sometimes sublime, notably the warm foie gras sautéed in walnut oil, though the pigeonneau rôti contained too lethal a measure of whole garlic cloves. The dining room, in a warm apricot and beige, was a perfect setting for superb food. Service was faultless and the staff very friendly, without the pomposity often found in hotels of this class." (*Padi and John Howard*)

"Thoroughly recommended, though expensive: palatial, luxurious, with a relaxing atmosphere. The list of champagnes is phenomenal, needless to say. We had a very good meal, but – even Paradise is never perfect – found the bread hard and stale." (*Pat and Jeremy Temple*). Best to book several months ahead.

Open All year except 23 Dec–12 Jan, and Mon evenings. Restaurant also closed for lunch on Tue.
Rooms 1 suite, 15 double – all with bath, direct-dial telephone, radio and TV.
Facilities Lift. Hall, bar, restaurant. Park and gardens with tennis and helipad. English spoken.
Location Leave motorway at St Rémy exit. Travel towards Luxembourg for ½ km, then towards Châlons sur Marne on N44. Hotel is 3 km from town centre. Parking.

Credit cards All major credit cards accepted.
Terms B&B: single 713–993 frs, double 816–1,096 frs. Set lunch/dinner 310 frs (service not included); full alc 500 frs.

REPLONGES 01750 Ain   Map 10

La Huchette   *Tel* (85) 31.03.55

This red-roofed *auberge*, ornately decorated in warm colours, stands on the edge of a village just east of Mâcon, and is much admired again this year: "Not just a hotel *en route* to the South, but a delightful green oasis full of civility and charm. It has lovely spacious lawns with tall trees and a large swimming pool, equipped with luxurius mattress loungers. The owner, Mme Gualdieri, soft-spoken and efficient, makes you feel welcome. Our rooms were large and attractive, in pink and dark green, with lovely airy bathrooms. Cooking was careful: *carte* somewhat limited, but included delicious local Bresse chicken and tempting sweet trolley. The large wine list has many interesting Burgundies and includes three pages of half-bottles. In the big lounge were magazines and books in various languages." *(Chris and Dorothy Brining)* "A pretty dining room with first-class food and friendly service." *(Mr and Mrs R B Tait)*

Open All year except 20 Nov–10 Dec.
Rooms 1 suite, 12 double – all with bath, telephone and colour TV; some ground-floor rooms.
Facilities Lounge, dining room. Garden with swimming pool; fishing and golf nearby. English spoken. ⅋. (Ground-floor rooms and public rooms have wide doors.)
Location 4 km E of Mâcon off N79. On edge of village. Parking.
Restriction Not ideal for ⅋ but some ground-floor rooms.
Credit cards All major cards accepted.
Terms B&B: single occupancy 340 frs, double 480 frs; dinner, B&B: single occupancy 480 frs, double 760 frs. Set lunch 130 frs. Reduced rates and special meals for children.

RIBEAUVILLÉ 68150 Haut-Rhin   Map 9

Le Clos Saint-Vincent   *Tel* (89) 73.67.65
Route de Bergheim

Energetic walkers can climb up to the three ruined castles that stand above this picturesque little Alsatian wine town. On its outskirts is the *Clos Saint-Vincent*, anything but ruined – a sophisticated chalet-style restaurant-with-rooms, garlanded with a *Michelin* rosette and praise from our own readers: "It is a long low white building, superbly set among Riesling vineyards. The interior is spacious, elegant, uncluttered, with decor in soft muted golds and browns. The staff reflected the same quiet elegance, rather cool, but efficient. Our room was large and airy, with French windows opening on to a small terrace and attractive gardens, with views of the gently rolling countryside and the lights of Colmar in the distance. The bathroom was large, the beds comfortable, with good reading lights. The dining room was again very elegant, with tables well spaced, and that same stupendous view. The food was mostly superb (foie gras de canard, ris et rognons de veau, tarte aux mirabelles etc). Fine Alsatian wines, and good breakfast on our terrace as we watched the mists rise over the little towns." *(Padi Howard)*

Open Mar to mid-Nov. Restaurant closed Tue/Wed.
Rooms 3 suites, 8 double – all with bath. TV on request.
Facilities Salon, bar, restaurant. Garden. English spoken.
Location In NE outskirts of town, which is 15 km N of Colmar. Parking.
Restriction Not suitable for &.
Credit card Visa.
Terms B&B: double 650 frs. Set meals (incl. wine) 250 frs; full alc 300 frs.

RIGNY 70100 Haute Saône   Map 10

Château de Rigny   *Tel* (84) 65.25.01
Telex 362 926

Like the nearby *Relais* at Nantilly (q.v.), this is a small and select country house hotel, with three red gables (for attractive charm) in *Michelin*: but whereas the *Relais* is a 19th-century house, the *Château* dates from 1286, rebuilt in its present form under Louis XIII. It is set quietly in its own grounds bordering the Saône and has a 12-acre *jardin anglais* and large baronial salon. Visitors returning this year had a large bedroom of character (antique clock and matching candelabra) with a view over the river, but in some other ways felt the place was no longer quite at its best: "The elegance here is more homely than sophisticated. The main salon was still very splendid, with its tapestry and fine fireplace, but in a faded kind of way; some chairs needed upholstering. The food was tasty and plentiful but not subtle, and there was some shortage of staff. The swimming pool is now finished, and we hope that the other necessary improvements will take place for the hotel to return to its original glory. Prices very reasonable." *(Kate and Steve Murray-Sykes)* More reports welcome.

Open All year except Christmas and 4 Jan–1 Feb.
Rooms 24 double – all with bath, telephone and TV; 4 ground-floor rooms. 11 rooms in annexe.
Facilities Salon, bar, dining room, conference/functions facilities. 12-acre park with tennis court, pond for fishing, access to Saône river; swimming pool. English spoken.
Location 5 km NE of Gray on Rigny road; Gray is 49 km NE of Dijon.
Restriction Not ideal for &, but 4 ground-floor rooms.
Credit cards All major cards accepted.
Terms Rooms: single occupancy 225 frs; double 280–370 frs. Breakfast 25 frs; set lunch/dinner 140–200 frs.

ROANNE 42300 Loire   Map 10

Hôtel Troisgros   *Tel* (77) 71.66.97
Place de la Gare   *Telex* 307507

Jean, the elder of the two famous brothers, died suddenly in 1983. But Pierre Troisgros, helped by his own son Michel, is successfully continuing the tradition that made this into one of the world's most brilliant and renowned restaurants. It is a small hotel opposite the railway station in a busy industrial town – an unlikely setting for such a jewel, but then this is France. Along with Bocuse and others, the

Troisgros were the leading originators of the so-called *"nouvelle cuisine"*; and even those wary of that style of cooking are usually won over by this luxurious restaurant and accept that it merits its three *Michelin* stars and four red *Gault Millau toques*. The 19 bedrooms are luxurious too, though some readers expressed reservations: "All very wonderful," is one comment on the food, decor and service, "but with lack of attention to detail in the bedroom. Dear me, thick dust on the bathroom ledges!" *(Norman and Joan Gower)*

Open All year.
Rooms 5 suites, 24 double – 22 with bath, 2 with shower, all with telephone, radio, colour TV and tea-making facilities; baby-listening on request. Sound-proofing.
Facilities Lift. Bar, 2 restaurants. English spoken.
Location 500 metres from town centre, opposite station; 86 km NW of Lyon on N7. Parking.
Credit cards Amex, Diners, Visa.
Terms Rooms: single occupancy 430 frs, double 550 frs; suite 860 frs. Breakfast 50 frs; set lunch/dinner 200, 310 and 380 frs (plus 15% service charge); full alc 350 frs. Reduced rates and special meals for children.

LA ROCHE-L'ABEILLE 87800 Nexon, Haute-Vienne   Map 10

Moulin de la Gorce   *Tel* (55) 00.70.66

The hamlet lies in pleasant hilly Limousin country between the two porcelain centres of Limoges (large and ugly) and St-Yrieix-la-Perche (small and lovely). The *Moulin*, also small and lovely, and very *soigné*, is the kind of place that draws "aahs" of ecstasy from lovers of French rural simplicity and high gastronomic complexity: "We were completely enchanted by this amazing hotel. Two very old buildings, one with the restaurant, one with six bedrooms, beside a small lake with waterfall. Very quiet and off the beaten track. The bedrooms have lovely antiques; in one is a fine old four-poster bed. Luxurious bathrooms. Remarkable value, and a first-class dinner with excellent service." The French guides agree – *Michelin's* full arsenal of red print as well as two rosettes, and two red *Gault Millau toques* for *patron/chef* Jean Betranet's dishes such as lièvre royale and blanc de turbot à l'orange. *(June Bullough)*

Open All year except 3 weeks in Jan.
Rooms 9 double – all with bath, direct-dial telephone and colour TV. 6 rooms in annexe.
Facilities Salon, dining room, garden. Near river and lake, fishing available; tennis, swimming and riding nearby. English spoken.
Location 12 km N of St-Yrieix, on the D704.
Restriction Not suitable for &.
Credit cards Amex, Diners, Visa.
Terms Rooms: single occupancy 190 frs, double 300–320 frs; dinner, B&B 680–700 frs for 2; full board 750–800 frs for 2. Breakfast 30 frs; full alc 300 frs. Reduced rates and special meals for children.

Do you know of a good hotel or country inn in the United States or Canada? Nominations please to our sibling publication, *America's Wonderful Little Hotels and Inns*, c/o St Martin's Press, 175 Fifth Avenue, New York, NY10010, USA.

LA ROCHELLE 17000 Charente-Maritime   Map 10

Hôtel les Brises   *Tel* (46) 43.89.37
Chemin de la Digue de Richelieu

"Quite expensive, but lovely" is a 1985 visitor's verdict on this stylish modern hotel in a prime position overlooking the islands, the estuary, and the outer harbour of enchanting La Rochelle (see below). Other reports speak of "pretty room overlooking the sea"; "our car windows were cleaned religiously every night of our stay", and "the best breakfast I have ever had in France. The hotel is right on the sea front, with a vast terrace on which one can sun oneself over a drink, and two luxurious lounges. A very warm welcome. Utterly quiet." One visitor this year found the manager surly in dealing with a dispute over a booking. *(Dr and Mrs G Collingham, E Hugo, and others)* No restaurant. La Rochelle has a number of clip-joints, but you do eat well at *Serge* (expensive) and at the recently opened *Le Rabelais* or *La Marmite* (upper-medium).

Open All year except 15 Dec–21 Jan.
Rooms 41 double, 5 single – 39 with bath, 7 with shower, all with telephone; colour TV on request.
Facilities Lifts. Salon, TV room/library, breakfast room, bar; terrace with direct access to sea; panoramic views over Îles d'Aix, d'Oléron and de Ré. Park and Casino nearby. English spoken.
Location On sea front 1½ km from town centre, close to the Parc F Delmas. Underground garage and car park.
Restriction Not suitable for &.
Credit card Visa.
Terms B&B: single 248–428 frs, double 426–505 frs. (No restaurant.) Reductions for children.

Hôtel de France et d'Angleterre   *Tel* (46) 41.34.66
22 rue Gargoulleau   *Telex* 790717 FRATEL ROCHL

"A recent return visit confirmed my view that La Rochelle is the most attractive town in France – a kind of maritime Bruges, with echoes too of Bremen and the less absurd aspects of St-Tropez. The narrow streets of this ancient fishing port have been beautifully paved and closed to traffic, and all summer the town is splendidly animated, especially during the avant-garde arts festival in July. The *France et Angleterre* is a hotel worthy of La Rochelle. Gracefully modernised, it is set round a small flowery garden. The fine restaurant, the *Richelieu (Gault Millau toque)*, successfully combines regional classicism with modern inventiveness. The fish is superbly fresh." *(J A)* That earlier report is confirmed again this year. "Food of *Miller Howe* style, served without fuss." "An outstanding find. Modern, but not too modern, highly comfortable, efficient and friendly service, very good value. A bustling market nearby. J A catches the charm exactly." There was a change of chef in 1984 (hence *Michelin* dropped its rosette), but the new man is said to be even better than his predecessor. *(Brian MacArthur; also Joan A Powell, David Skinner, and others)*

Open All year. Restaurant closed Sun, and Mon midday.
Rooms 76 double – 32 with bath, 35 with shower, all with telephone, radio, 36 with mono TV; some rooms in 2 annexes.

Facilities Lift. Salon, TV room, breakfast room, restaurant; conference facilities. Interior garden for meals or drinks. English spoken. & (6 rooms).
Location Central, near place de Verdun. Parking (at a price) in adjacent rue de Minage (ask for place de Verdun or place du Marché).
Credit cards All major cards accepted.
Terms Rooms 180 frs; dinner, B&B 451–594 frs; full board 561–814 frs. Breakfast 33 frs; set lunch/dinner 110–160 frs; full alc 250 frs. 30% reduction for children sharing parents' room; special meals on request.

ROQUEFORT-SUR-SOULZON 12250 Aveyron   Map 10

Grand Hôtel   *Tel* (65) 59.90.20
Rue de Lauras

The village straggles along the side of a limestone cliff, where the noblest of French cheeses are matured in their deep cool caves (well worth a visit). The *Grand* is a classic hostelry in the main street: "We were given a friendly welcome and a good-sized traditionally furnished and comfortable room. Our dinner was delicious (*Michelin* rosette), especially the truite à l'estragon and tourte au Roquefort." In summer you eat in the cool vaulted depths of a former cheese-cellar. *(D J Cheeseman)*

Open 1 Apr–30 Sept. Closed Sun night and Mon, except July and Aug.
Rooms 14 double, 2 single – 9 with bath, 3 with shower, all with telephone.
Facilities Bar, TV room, dining room, 2 functions rooms. English spoken.
Location From the D99n road (Toulouse/Montpellier), take turning to Roquefort. Hotel is central. Parking.
Restriction Not suitable for &.
Credit cards Amex, Diners, Visa.
Terms Rooms: single 85 frs, double 295 frs. Breakfast 25 frs; set lunch 105 frs; full alc 200 frs.

LES ROSIERS-SUR-LOIRE 49350 Gennes, Maine-et-Loire   Map 10

Auberge Jeanne de Laval   *Tel* (41) 51.80.71
Route d'Angers

One of the best restaurants in Anjou (*Michelin* rosette, two *Gault Millau toques*), in a village on the north bank of the Loire between Angers and Saumur. It is a handsome creeper-covered house, all very *soigné* inside, both the public rooms and bedrms; simpler, more rustic bedrooms are in a nearby annexe, the *Ducs d'Anjou*, a converted manor. "If you can persuade the rather scatty Madame that you actually *have* booked, this makes a very pleasant overnight stay. We stayed in the annexe, a short car ride from the hotel: it is a very pretty house in a big walled garden, and the rooms were prettily decorated and adequate. Breakfast was taken by an open window facing the garden. At dinner, the rillettes and asparagus were plentiful and good and the chicken in a gentle sauce was delicious." *Patron/chef* Michel Augereau specialises in local "beurre blanc" fish dishes. *(Gillian Vincent)*

Open All year except 24 Nov–28 Dec, Mon, and possibly some time in Feb or Mar.
Rooms 7 double, some with bath or shower, all with telephone. 8 double, some with bath or shower in annexe, *Ducs d'Anjou*, nearby.
Facilities Restaurant; functions facilities. Garden. Tennis, swimming, riding and golf nearby.

Location 15 km NW of Saumur, on banks of the Loire.
Credit cards Amex, Diners, Visa.
Terms [1985 rates] rooms: single occupancy 175 frs, double 280 frs (in *Ducs d'Anjou* single 100 frs, double 280 frs). Breakfast 30 frs; set lunch/dinner 140–260 frs.

ROUEN 76000 Seine-Maritime   Map 8

La Cathédrale   *Tel* (35) 71.57.95
12 rue St-Romain

Readers continue to speak well of this straightforward, modestly priced hotel, centrally situated near the cathedral. "Turning off the busy streets of Rouen into the traffic-free rue St-Romain is like stepping into another century. *La Cathédrale* is an ancient half-timbered building, entered through a large arched doorway. Madame gave us a kind welcome. The carpets are shabby and our room's decor was nothing special. But the bathroom was efficient, and the bedside lights were like in an aeroplane – useful if you want to read while your partner is asleep. It was beautifully quiet, and the curtains were thick." "Breakfast alpha plus, as French breakfasts go," adds one veteran observer of the hotel scene. No restaurant, but there are plenty of good ones nearby; the *Dufour* is recommended for its fish – and its prices. *(H W Bates)*

Open All year.
Rooms 23 double – 7 with bath, 16 with shower, all with telephone.
Facilities Hall, breakfast room, courtyard. English spoken.
Location Central, but quietly situated near Cathedral. Public car park nearby.
Restriction Not suitable for &.
Credit cards None accepted.
Terms Rooms: single 104–176 frs, double 141–215 frs. Breakfast 15.60 frs. (No restaurant.)

ROUFFACH 68250 Haut-Rhin   Map 10

Château d'Isenbourg   *Tel* (89) 49.63.53
                                                            Telex 880 815

Rouffach, south of Colmar, is one of the many picturesque old towns on the Alsatian *route de vin*. Perched on a hill outside it, overlooking the vineyards, stands the expensive and luxuriously converted *Château d'Isenbourg*, new to the Guide this year – "an impressive building, especially at night when the courtyard and ornamental lake are floodlit. *Michelin* gives the place four red gables: but it is not overly formal or stuffy. Our room, overlooking the courtyard, was beautifully furnished, with fabric-covered walls; the public rooms were pleasant too, some with panelled ceilings. Dinner was in the 15th-century vaulted cellar" (in summer, it can be taken on an outdoor terrace, with a wide view). "Food was good, if not all of it deserving its *Michelin* rosette. On the 380-franc [sic: 1985] *menu dégusation* (including a bottle of champagne) we enjoyed the foie gras and duck with fresh figs." *(Kate and Steve Murray-Sykes)* Musical weekends and soirées, March/April, October to December. Outdoor pool with view.

Open 7 Mar–5 Jan.
Rooms 40 – all with bath, telephone, baby-listening; TV on request. Some ground-floor rooms.
Facilities Lift. 2 lounges, lounge/bar, TV room; dining rooms; terrace for dining; courtyard. Large park with swimming pool heated in season, tennis court and ornamental lake. English spoken. &.
Location On hill above village. Take Rouffach Est exit from N83.
Credit card Visa.
Terms B&B: 444–763 frs; dinner, B&B 682–946 frs; full board 814–1,078 frs. Breakfast 48 frs; set lunch 205 frs, dinner 265 frs; full alc 350 frs. Musical weekend breaks Mar–Apr and Oct–Dec; New Year rate. Children under 3 free, 3–10 30% reduction.

SAILLAGOUSE 66800 Pyrénées-Orientales   Map 10

Auberge Atalaya   *Tel* (68) 04.70.04
Llo

The Cerdagne, an hour's drive from Andorra and two from Perpignan, is one of the most appealing corners of France – an upland plain of meadows and pine forests, backed by the snowy Pyrenees. It is surprisingly lush and pastoral for such an altitude (1,066 metres) and has France's highest sunshine level. Hence its choice as the site of France's leading experimental solar furnace, at Odeillo. There's much else of interest too – the fortress of Mont-Louis, the big ski-resort of Font-Romeu, and the strange black Romanesque Madonna at l'Hermitage.

The *Atalaya*, a converted farmhouse in the hamlet of Llo, two kilometres from the resort of Saillagouse, is run by Hubert Toussaint, London born and bred, and comes new to the Guide this year: "Very attractive – a stone building with dark wood but light and spacious bedrooms. Ours had a balcony looking out on the simple village. Dinner was good, breakfast excellent. The Toussaints have a civilised attitude to their guests. A quiet and relaxing place to stay – out of season at least."
(R J G)

Open 20 Dec–5 Nov. Restaurant closed Mon and Tue in low season.
Rooms 2 suites, 7 double – all with bath or shower and WC, and mini-bar; TV on request.
Facilities Lounge, bar, restaurant; large grounds. English spoken.
Location In Llo, on D33 2 km E of Saillagouse, which is 91 km W of Perpignan.
Restriction Not suitable for &.
Credit card Diners.
Terms B&B double 320–410 frs; half-board double 560–650 frs; full board double 720–800 frs. Set meals 120 and 180 frs.

Planes et Planotel   *Tel* (68) 04.72.08

In the village of Saillagouse, these two hotels are really one, with a common restaurant at the older building *(Planes)*. A visitor this year confirms his earlier praise: "Very popular with French holidaymakers and exuding an atmosphere of courteous efficiency. The restaurant offers good service with a wide choice of menus and value for money (red *Michelin* 'R'). Excellent packed lunches too, just the thing for a day walking up the nearby Vallée d'Eyne, famous for its Pyrenean flora." *(J P Berryman)* C R adds: "I ate the best ice cream (peach) of my life here."

Open All year except 15 Oct–15 Dec.
Rooms 38 double, 2 single – 31 with bath, 9 with shower, all with telephone; TV available; many rooms have balcony; 1 room specially adapted for &.
Facilities Lift, ramps. 3 salons (1 with TV), bar serving grill snacks, restaurant. Garden. River nearby. Skiing holidays. &.
Location Central. Parking.
Credit card Visa.
Terms Half-board 160–175 frs; full board 180–195 frs. Set meals 68, 85 and 160 frs; full alc 170 frs.

ST-AMAND-DE-VERGT 24380 Dordogne   Map 10

Les Prouillacs   *Tel* (53) 54.96.61

The English take-over of the Dordogne reaches a kind of apotheosis at this stone-built 18th-century manor now run as a small private hotel by Mrs Audrey Summerskill Brontë – "a house-party atmosphere prevails", she writes. Our readers are enthusiastic: "Lovely crumbly old manor, very comfortable rooms, good plumbing, swimming pool, quiet situation amid fields. English hostess cooks delicious French food. Relaxed atmosphere." And: "Evening meal was first class – a Périgord five-course dinner which in our week included frogs' legs and quail. You can join in the life of a French provincial manor if you so desire." Dinner is taken by candlelight in the stone-floored dining room; the sitting room has a piano and shelves full of books in English; several of the bedrooms are oak-beamed. Mrs Summerskill also runs a small music festival in the village church, in late July and early August. The village is on a side-road between Bergerac and Périgueux. (*T Sales, and others*)

Open Easter–Nov.
Rooms 1 suite, 4 double – 1 with bath, 4 with shower (suite is on ground floor); 1 self-catering cottage.
Facilities Lounge with piano and books (most English), dining room. Courtyard with gardens with swimming pool (unheated); lake with boats, sand, fishing, and snack bar 3 km. English spoken.
Location Just outside hamlet of St-Amand-de-Vergt, 7 km S of Vergt and 24 km both from Bergerac and Périgueux.
Restriction Children discouraged; no reductions made.
Credit cards None accepted.
Terms (Service at guests' discretion) Terms are weekly, 3 days min., but casual unbooked stays possible at last minute if room available. Half-board per person per week in room in double occupancy £140–£200.

ST-CIRQ-LAPOPIE 46330 Lot   Map 10

Hôtel de la Pelissaria   *Tel* (65) 31.25.14

St-Cirq is a famous *village perché*, set spectacularly on a cliff high above the river Lot. One of its old houses is now a tiny six-bedroomed hotel which two recent reporters have delightedly unearthed – and what a find! "It proved to be the most enchanting stay during a six-week trip – an old house on such a steep slope that you enter at the top with bedrooms on the floors below. Each has been lovingly restored by the new owner, François-Charles Matuchet, a charming man who is said to compose songs at the grand piano in the large family living room, used by guests. There's an open fireplace, and immense views. Bedrooms have tiled floors, white walls, pine doors, rough-woven white curtains and bed-spreads, beautiful linen, a ledge of lawn and flower-beds on each bedroom level – and the most wonderful peace. Madame Matuchet cooks like an angel. The only sound is birdsong, and the faint murmuring of traffic half a mile away." Other recent visitors write in the same vein: "The dining room with its rustic furniture is reached by passing through a warm country kitchen redolent with odours of robust soups and stews and the strong whiff of rice with garlic. The beamed bedrooms overlook the ancient church, and way below beyond the apple trees is the Lot river." Paradise, in one of the loveliest corners of rural France. *(Brenda and John Stapleton, Moti and Gisa Slonim)*

Open 1 Apr–3 Nov. Restaurant closed midday.
Rooms 4 double, 2 single – 3 with bath, 3 with shower, all with telephone.
Facilities Salon, dining room. Garden. English spoken.
Location Central. Parking at some distance from hotel. Village 30 km E of Cahors.
Restriction Not suitable for &.
Credit cards None accepted.
Terms Rooms: single 130 frs, double 170 frs. Breakfast 18 frs; full alc 100 frs (guests are expected to dine in the restaurant).

ST-CYPRIEN 24220 Dordogne   Map 10

Hôtel l'Abbaye   *Tel* (53) 29.20.48

St-Cyprien is a pleasant village in the Dordogne valley: Sarlat and Les Eyzies-de-Tayac are both quite close. *L'Abbaye*, a comfortable hotel on the edge of the village, has long been a favourite with readers ("Everything done beautifully, in a relaxed and friendly manner", runs a report this year). It is noted locally for its sound Périgord cooking (eg cailles aux choux verts). Madame Schaller, *la patronne*, speaks excellent English. The hotel is well appointed and has a swimming pool and garden. *(Ann Carr, John K Pettifer)*

Open 20 Mar–end Oct.
Rooms 19 double – 9 with bath, 10 with shower, all but 1 with WC, all with telephone and baby-listening; 6 rooms in annexe; 2 ground-floor rooms.
Facilities Hall, 2 salons (1 with TV), restaurant. Garden, terrace, heated swimming pool; tennis 500 metres. English spoken. &.
Location Near town centre. Parking.
Restriction Not ideal for & but some ground-floor rooms.
Credit cards All major cards accepted.
Terms Rooms: single 170–285 frs, double 180–310 frs. Breakfast 22 frs; set meals 65, 105, 155, 235 frs; full alc 161 frs. Reduced rates and special meals for children.

ST-HIPPOLYTE 68590 Haut-Rhin   Map 8

Hôtel Munsch: Aux Ducs de Lorraine   *Tel* (89) 73.00.09
16 Route du Vin

St-Hippolyte is a village on the *route du vin* north of Colmar, a serene and well-trodden sector of Alsace where standards of hostelry are high. The *Munsch*, a gabled and half-timbered mansion on the outskirts, adjoining the owner's own vineyards, lost its place in last year's Guide purely through lack of feedback, but inspectors are certain that it needs a reprieve: "It would be hard to find a better place to stay at in the area.

The bedrooms with their large wooden balconies face over the vineyards to the hill-top castle of Haut-Koenigsbourg. We arrived at 7.45 pm without a booking but met a cheerful welcome, and enjoyed excellent and substantial Alsatian food, with the *Munschs'* own good wine, in a dining room packed with locals. Bedroom and bathroom were first-class." *(D S, A S)*

Open 1 Mar–1 Dec, 17 Dec–10 Jan.
Rooms 8 suites, 30 double, 4 single – 5 with bath, 29 with shower, many with balcony. Some on ground floor.
Facilities Lift. 3 reception rooms, breakfast room, dining room, conference facilities. Garden with children's play area. English spoken. &.
Location Near centre but quietly situated. Parking.
Credit cards Amex, Diners, Visa.
Terms Rooms: single 200–280 frs, double 260–340 frs; dinner, B&B 270–310 frs. Breakfast 28 frs; set lunch/dinner 90, 110, 145 and 240 frs; full alc 180 frs. Reduced rates for children.

ST-JEAN-DU-BRUEL 12230 Aveyron   Map 10

Hôtel du Midi   *Tel* (65) 62.26.04

St-Jean is an old Cévenol village on the river Dourbie, between Millau and Le Vigan, a good centre for walking holidays in the western Cévennes, or for visiting the Roquefort cheese caves and the Gorges du Tarn. The *Midi* finds favour as a friendly and unpretentious family-run hotel; it has been modernised, but bedrooms are said to vary in quality, some being cramped. Nightingales sing. The local country cooking has long possessed a *Michelin* red "R" for good value, and this year wins a *Gault Millau toque*, too, for its regional qualities. Readers continue to be enthusiastic: "During my 18 days we had goose, duck, guinea-fowl, turkey and escargots as well as beef, veal, pork and lamb dishes and a variety of fish. The cooking was of a high standard, all vegetables were fresh and imaginatively prepared, and there was an excellent cheese-board and selection of home-made pastries and sorbets." Booking essential. *(George Steiner; endorsed by D Ball, Ben and Olivia Gould)*

Open 22 Mar–11 Nov.
Rooms 18 double, 2 single – 11 with bath, 2 with shower, all with telephone. 2 rooms in annexe.
Facilities Ramp. Salon, TV room, bar, dining room, terrace. Situated on the banks of river Dourbie, with small beaches; fishing. English spoken.
Location 45 km SE of Millau on D991; 20 km E of N9. Garage and open parking.
Restriction Only restaurant suitable for &.
Credit cards None accepted.
Terms B&B: single 69.50 frs, double 97–162 frs; half-board: single 136–146 frs, double 252–318 frs; full board: single 157–167 frs, double 294–360 frs. Set lunch/dinner 44–128 frs; full alc 88 frs. Reduced rates for under-sixes.

ST-JEAN-DU-DOIGT 29228 Finistère   Map 8

Le Ty-Pont   *Tel* (98) 67.34.06
Plougasnou

A down-to-earth holiday hotel on the North Brittany coast. "An amazing place, a very French experience and incredible value. For about £11 each (sic) [in 1984] we had full board in high season, and the food was staggering: honest cooking and the freshest possible ingredients. We had some of the best and freshest seafood we've ever eaten. Lunch might start with crab-claws and slices of melon, then a fish in a delicate sauce, then a meat course (perhaps guinea-fowl), then cheese, fromage blanc or yoghurt, then ice-cream (home-made) or a good selection of fresh fruit or crème caramel. Dinner was one course less. One Sunday lunch included slices of langouste and quails with raisins. And the scene in the dining room was amazing – working-class French families on holiday, a baby drinking potage out of its bottle, a two-year-old having fromage blanc spooned into it. It was very noisy, but the two calm young waitresses were never flustered. Breakfast was a rushed affair that could involve long waits: some of the lady guests (especially the large ones) came down to it in dressing-gowns.

"Bedrooms were adequate. At the back of the hotel is a garden by a stream, where you can sit in the sun and recover from *la bouffe*. St-Jean is a pretty village amid farmlands, with good views; the church is lovely, but its bell strikes every thirty minutes, so we had less sleep than we'd have liked. The beach at St-Jean is adequate; Primel-Tregastel nearby has a better one, really lovely, with sand and pink rocks." *(C A R)* An out-of-season visitor reports the same excellence of food and a much more peaceful atmosphere. *(E R)*

Open Easter to Oct.
Rooms 2 suites, 36 double, 1 single – 7 with bath, 9 with shower, 17 with telephone. Back rooms are quietest.
Facilities Salon, bar, restaurant. Garden with swings. Small river with trout. Near sandy beach.
Location 17 km NE of Morlaix, 1½ km E of Plougasnou village. Parking.
Restriction Not suitable for &.
Credit cards None accepted.
Terms Half-board 99–147 frs per person; full board 119–167 per person. Set meals 45–180 frs. 30% reduction for children under 7.

ST-JEAN-CAP-FERRAT 06230 Alpes Maritimes   Map 11

La Voile d'Or   *Tel* (93) 01.13.13
Port de St-Jean   *Telex* 470317

Mostly praise again this year for this "very beautiful modernised luxury hotel", set on a low promontory by the harbour, on the edge of the fishing village of St-Jean, close to the lovely Cap-Ferrat peninsula: "Paradise – roses everywhere, service luxurious and gracious, food very good, *demi-pension* a bargain"; "heaven"; "splendid, delightful" (this from a critical inspector). An earlier visitor had a pretty and spacious bedroom with views of the sea, and was delighted by the hotel's pastel decor, the "idyllic" garden terrace where meals and drinks are served, and the two swimming pools. One is down by the rocks and you can have lunch there (no sandy beaches on this part of the *Côte*). Food highly praised, especially the fish *(Michelin* rosette, two *Gault Millau toques)*. *(Constance Ellison, G M W Williams, L H, J A)* But one dissenter raised his voice this year, complaining of poor food and "tatty" swimming pool.

Open 10 Mar–31 Oct.
Rooms 4 suites, 42 double, 4 single – all with bath, shower and telephone, some

with balcony; radio, TV and baby-listening on request. Some rooms on ground floor.
Facilities Lift. Salon, TV room, bars, restaurant, air-conditioning; conference facilities. Garden with terrace; 2 swimming pools (one heated), sauna. Direct access to rock beach with safe bathing, sailing, waterskiing etc. English spoken.
Location 10 km from Nice; 1½ km from town centre, by the marina. Parking.
Restriction Not suitable for &.
Credit cards None accepted.
Terms Rooms: single 550 frs, double 610 frs; dinner, B&B: single 900 frs; double 1,310 frs–2,550 frs. Breakfast 50 frs; set lunch/dinner 250 frs–320 frs; full alc from 300 frs. Reduced rates (off-season) for children; special meals.

ST-JEAN-PIED-DE-PORT 64220 Pyrénées-Atlantiques   Map 10

Hôtel des Pyrénées   *Tel* (59) 37.01.01
Place du Général-de-Gaulle

St-Jean, at the foot of the Roncesvalles pass into Spain, used to be a major resting-place for pilgrims about to cross the Pyrenees on their way to Santiago. Today it is one of the most picturesque of Basque towns (15th-century ramparts, hilltop citadel) and a capital of Basque folklore (summer festival and *pelota* championships). Its other distinction is the *Pyrénées*, its main *auberge*, which has been owned and run by the Arrambide family for four generations and today has one of the most highly rated kitchens in the south-west, thanks to the creative skills of Firmin A, son of the house (two *Michelin* rosettes, three red *Gault Millau toques*). Our inspector this year, himself a well-known London ex-restaurateur: "Quite exceptionally good food, with interesting set menus and seasonal specialities. In October, we had: a warm first course of assorted wild mushrooms (including delicious black 'trumpets of death'), the epitome of *nouvelle cuisine*, beautifully arranged; delicious, spare to the edge of meanness; a whole hare, boned and stuffed with foie gras; noisette of roe deer; excellent local wine. There was a sense of occasion about the entire restaurant, packed with interesting and lively well-heeled locals – a strong feeling of spontaneous pleasure, helped by exceptional service." Another visitor has lyricised over "the joy of eating on the terrace on a fine day". Does it really matter that the bedrooms lag leagues behind, some quite comfortable, others less so, with poor lighting? *(W B, Maggie Angeloglou, J A, and others)*

Open All year, except 26 Nov–23 Dec and 6–26 Jan; closed Tue except July to Sept and public holidays.
Rooms 31 double – 22 with bath, 4 with shower, all with telephone.
Facilities Lift. 2 salons (1 with TV), 2 dining rooms, conference rooms; terrace. Tennis, swimming, fishing, pigeon-shooting and forest of Iraty nearby. English spoken.
Location 54 km SE of Bayonne on D933. Parking.
Credit cards None accepted.
Terms Rooms: single occupancy 92.50 frs, double 180–220 frs. Breakfast 19 frs; set lunch/dinner 150, 190 and 240 frs and alc.

If you have had recent experience of a good hotel that ought to be in the Guide, please write to us at once. Report forms are to be found at the back. Procrastination is the thief of the next edition.

ST-MALO 35400 Ille-et-Vilaine	Map 8

Le Valmarin   *Tel* (99) 81.94.76
7 rue Jean XXIII, St -Servan

"Astonishingly good" is this year's verdict on the *Valmarin*, which we
had to drop last year for lack of feedback. It is a modernised 18th-century
house, in the suburb of St-Servan, just south of St-Malo harbour and
about two kilometres from the old walled city. "Fabulously comfortable
and civilised, with a discreet atmosphere. The proprietor brings you a
glass of chilled Muscadet on a silver tray, covered with lace, while you
sit in the impressive gardens." An earlier visitor had a room beautifully
decorated in white, green and gold. No restaurant, but there are several
good cheap fish places in the harbour area. (*Stephen and Flo Bayley,
H ap R*)

Open 1 Mar–31 Dec. Closed Sun between 1 Oct and 31 Mar except public
holidays.
Rooms 10 double – all with bath, telephone, radio and TV.
Facilities Salon, bar. Garden. 100 metres from safe sandy beach; swimming,
sailing, tennis nearby. English spoken.
Location Centre of St-Servan near Port Solidor; 2 km from old St-Malo. Parking.
Restriction Not suitable for &.
Credit cards Amex, Visa.
Terms B&B: single 275–425 frs, double 300–450 frs. (No restaurant.)

ST-MARTIN-DE-LONDRES 34380 Hérault	Map 10

La Crèche   *Tel* (67) 55.00.04
Route de Frouzet

Quintessential Languedoc – a spacious 15th-century farmhouse, stylishly converted, standing alone amid the bare undulating *garrigue* country,
five kilometres from the village, with the Cévennes just to the north and
Montpellier to the south. Bedrooms are in local style, and public rooms
have genuine old rustic furniture. "Very good in almost every respect",
writes a visitor this year; "the buildings are beautiful, the dining room
comfortable and most attractive when lit by the setting sun. Swimming
pool large, clean and uncrowded. Food is very good" (two *toques* in *Gault
Millau*) "and *pensionnaires* are treated with unusual generosity: eg hot
foie gras as a main course. Two qualifications: service can be slow and
rooms were not always as clean as they should be." (*Stanley Burnton*)
"Wonderful views and walks, staff friendly and helpful, comfortable
bedrooms and a fairly luxurious restaurant." (*James Joll*)

Open All year except Feb. Closed Mon/Tue in low season.
Rooms 1 suite, 6 double – all with bath and telephone, 4 with TV.
Facilities Salon, bar, dining rooms; terrace with bar. Garden with swimming pool
and tennis court, river (fishing) and children's play area. English spoken.
Location 5 km NW of St-Martin by D122 and private road; St-Martin is 25 km NW
of Montpellier.
Restriction Not suitable for &.
Credit cards None accepted.
Terms [1985 rates] rooms: single 199 frs, double 228–258 frs; half-board 300 frs per
person; full board 350 frs per person. Breakfast 24 frs; set lunch 159 frs, dinner
206 frs; full alc 220–250 frs. Special meals and reduced rates for children.

ST-MARTIN-VALMEROUX 15140 Cantal   Map 10

Hostellerie de la Maronne   *Tel* (71) 69.20.33
Le Theil, St-Martin-Valmeroux

Auvergnat rural bliss in plenty at this simple little hotel outside the hamlet of Le Theil, midway between St-Martin-Valmeroux (on the Mauriac–Aurillac road) and the lovely Renaissance hill-village of Salers. "A *Relais du Silence* with real distinction, in the lush upper valley of the Maronne, near Salers, where rocky outcrops give promise of the volcanic mountains to come and the cowbells alone disturb the quiet. It stands in its own informal garden and grounds. Alain de Cock, his Malagasy wife and a small, well-trained staff provide comfort and a choiceless but excellent evening meal with the occasional dish of great quality (lunches only on Sunday). Good stock of wines. The accounting is wholly by computer. Walkers may dislike the lack of availability of breakfast before 8.30 am." The de Cocks recommended their rêve d'escargots and tripoux flambé au cognac, a local dish. (*Jack and Helen Thornton*) Since last year, the hotel has created a swimming pool at the top of the garden and hopes to have a tennis court ready in 1986.

Open 1 Apr–4 Nov. Restaurant closed for lunch.
Rooms 20 double – all with bath and telephone, 1 with baby-listening; 8 ground-floor rooms in annexe.
Facilities Salon, dining room. Garden with heated swimming pool, mini-golf and ping-pong; tennis court planned for 1986. River with fishing rights 200 metres. English spoken.
Location 3 km E of St-Martin-Valmeroux on CD37 to Fontanges.
Restriction Not ideal for ♿ but some ground-floor rooms.
Credit card Access.
Terms Rooms 160–180 frs; half-board 160–180 frs per person. Breakfast 15 frs; set meals 80 frs. 30% reduction for children under 8; special meals available.

ST-PAUL-DE-VENCE 06570 Alpes-Maritimes   Map 11

La Colombe d'Or   *Tel* (93) 32.80.02
                                                                Telex 970607

We are surprised to have received so few recent reports – and we badly need them, please – on this famous little luxury hotel on the edge of a show-place village behind Nice. It's an unusual establishment. For one thing, it houses a private collection of modern art that would be the envy of any museum – Braque and Calder by the swimming pool, César and Miró in the lounge, Matisse, Picasso and Utrillo in the dining room, and much else. Many of these works were given to the former owner, the late Paul Roux, in payment by artists who stayed or ate there. It's a beautiful old house, with many fine pieces of furniture, and is still owned and run by the Roux family. Each room has a distinctive character – some with original beams, others all in white stucco with window-seats overlooking gardens. Many have lovely terraces and outside bathrooms. There is a splendid veranda, decorated with a fine Léger mural, where lunch is served; dinner is taken indoors in a large sophisticated rustic dining room. The swimming pool is surrounded by cypress trees. "As far as I am concerned, this must be the best hotel in the world," raved one visitor. But the place is not going to suit everyone. Service is casual, the food is unremarkable, and not everything is maintained in 100 per cent working order.

Open All year except 3 Nov–18 Dec.
Rooms 8 suites, 14 double – all with bath, direct-dial telephone, radio and colour TV; many with terrace; 1 ground-floor room.
Facilities Salon, restaurant, terrace for lunch or refreshments, sauna. Garden with swimming pool. 10 km from sea. English spoken.
Location 10 km from Nice; take road to La Colle and Hauts de St-Paul. Parking.
Credit cards All major cards accepted.
Terms Not available.

ST-PONS-DE-THOMIÈRES 34220 Hérault　　　　　　　Map 10

Château de Ponderach　　　　　　　　　　　　　*Tel* (67) 97.02.57

St-Pons is a pleasant town, with a fine 12th-century cathedral, within easy driving distance of Carcassonne and Narbonne. The *Château de Ponderach*, a superb 17th-century château, is in lovely gardens in the Haut Languedoc Nature Reserve, and has been the owner's family home for some 300 years. "A superlative place. Complete peace and quiet. The house lies at the edge of deep, wild, heavily forested impenetrable country, above a river, at the foot of the steep rocky foothills of the Cévennes. A paradise for birds and bird lovers. Charming reception by the aristrocratic lady owner. Particularly elegant dining room. Our bedroom, up an old stone staircase, was spacious and lovely. Superb breakfast. Only complaint: water not hot." *(John Hills)*

Open 1 Apr–15 Oct.
Rooms 9 double, 2 single – 9 with bath, all with telephone.
Facilities 2 salons (1 with TV), restaurant; conference facilities. Large garden where meals are served in good weather. Small lake nearby. English spoken.
Location 1 km S of town on Narbonne road.
Credit cards Access, Amex, Diners.
Terms Rooms: single 195 francs, double 350 frs; full board 585–595 frs per person. Breakfast 38 frs; set lunch/dinner 130–300 frs.

ST-RAPHAËL 83700 Var　　　　　　　　　　　　　Map 11

La Potinière　　　　　　　　　　　　　　　　*Tel* (94) 95.21.43
Avenue de Boulouris

In the smart suburb of Boulouris, east of St-Raphaël, some 600 metres from the beach and recommended as a suitable holiday for those who like sport and an up-to-date holiday atmosphere. It is very spacious – a group of low modern buildings in their own pinewoody park. Inspectors this year have confirmed (with reservations) an earlier holidaymaker's account: "We swam in the big pool, played tennis at the club next to the hotel, and went on sea cruises in the hotel's own skippered yacht. Evenings were animated (early September) and fellow-guests mostly young. But when the jollity has died down the place is quiet at night (it's a *Relais du Silence*). We could park by the door of our room, which had a large terrace with deckchairs, but the decor was utility-modern. We enjoyed taking meals out under the pine trees." "Nice, friendly, comfortable, though food not remarkable" (best for fish). Grill by the pool, for light lunches; pleasant westerly terrace for drinks; squash court and gym classes. *(G S, L H, Mary and Gerald Prescott)*

Open 21 Dec–5 Nov. Restaurant closed Thur lunch-time Oct–Mar.
Rooms 4 suites, 21 double – all with bath, telephone, radio and colour TV; some ground-floor rooms.
Facilities Bar, dining room. Set in grounds with swimming pool (unheated), tennis, squash courts and a gym. 6/7 minutes' walk to sandy beach. English spoken.
Location At Boulouris 4 km E of St-Raphaël on Route 1. Parking available.
Credit cards Amex, Diners.
Terms B&B: single 284 frs, double 353–432 frs; dinner, B&B: single 379 frs, double 543–630 frs. Set meals 115 and 195 frs; full alc 175 frs.

ST-RÉMY-DE-PROVENCE 13210 Bouches-du-Rhône   Map 11

Hôtel les Antiques   *Tel* (90) 92.03.02
15 avenue Pasteur

St-Rémy is the quintessential small Provençal town, with the bonus of possessing some of the most curious Roman remains in France (at Glanum, just to the south); nearby is the mental home of St-Paul-de-Mausolée where Van Gogh spent a year as a patient after cutting off his ear in Arles. So, with all this going for it, maybe it is not so surprising that little St-Rémy contains no fewer than *four* hotels recommended by readers. *Les Antiques* is a 19th-century mansion, gracefully converted, and it stands by a main road near the town centre, with its own big garden at the back. "We liked the place as much as ever," says a reader returning this year; "one of the nicest hotels we've stayed in. It has a fine if slightly run-down park with a pleasant swimming pool. Our first night was in a *pavillon* across the lawn, excellently furnished, with its own little terrace where one can breakfast (also excellent – even a dish of fruit). Then we were moved to the hotel proper, where we were equally comfortable. Both rooms were very quiet." Another recent report: "Lovely people, charming atmosphere: it was like being guests in a private home. On my husband's birthday they gave him a cake. Beautiful gardens, and a grand entrance with marble floors, tapestries, Italian painted ceiling." *(Mrs R B Richards, Janet Merutka; also Kay and Neville Varley)*

Open 21 Mar–end Oct.
Rooms 26 double, 1 single – all with bath and telephone. 2 rooms in annexe. Some ground-floor rooms.
Facilities Ramps. Large salon, TV room, bridge room, functions room, veranda overlooking park. Large grounds with unheated swimming pool; riding centre. Trout fishing 2 km in lake at St-Rémy. English spoken. &.
Location 100 metres from town centre in direction of Les Baux. From pl. de la République, take av. de Maillane, then first left, and left again into av. Pasteur. Hotel is signposted in St-Rémy. Parking.
Restriction Not ideal for & but some ground-floor rooms.
Credit cards Amex, Diners, Visa.
Terms B&B: single 252.50 frs, double 345–396 frs. (No restaurant.)

> Don't keep your favourite hotel to yourself. The Guide supports: it doesn't spoil.

Hôtel Château des Alpilles   *Tel* (90) 92.03.33
Route Départementale 31   *Telex* 431 487 ALPILLE

Chateaubriand and Lamartine were among the writers and politicians who once stayed at this graceful little 19th-century manor house (just out of town on the Tarascon road) in the days when it belonged to a leading local family. It is now a modernised hotel – "a beautiful house in large shady grounds, with pool and tennis courts. Decoration distinguished, rooms well appointed; ideal for those who want quiet. Management nice in a low-profile way." *(Antony Verney)* No restaurant, but grills are served at lunch by the pool, or try *Les Arts* in town. An earlier report warned of noisy bull-frogs at the back. This year, we are delighted to say, the manager writes, "We haven't bull-frogs. So no noise." More reports please.

Open 15 Mar–15 Nov.
Rooms 1 suite, 15 double – all with bath, telephone, radio, colour TV. 2 rooms in annexe.
Facilities Lift. Bar, lounge with TV, small dining room. Garden with swimming pool, tennis court and sauna. English spoken.
Location 1½ km outside St-Rémy-de-Provence on D31.
Credit cards All major cards accepted.
Terms Rooms: single 420–480 frs, double 420–600 frs. Breakfast 38 frs; set grill lunch 85–105 frs (in summer); otherwise no restaurant. Special meals for children on request.

Hôtel du Château de Roussan   *Tel* (90) 92.11.63
Route de Tarascon

Off the Tarascon road, three kilometres west of St-Rémy, this unusual and inviting hotel stands secluded in its own big park. "A civilised experience, more like being the house-guests of cultured friends than staying in a hotel. This stately pink 18th-century château has been the country home of the Roussel family for over a century; now that times are hard, they accept bed-and-breakfast clients to keep it going. Bathrooms are modern, but in other respects the rooms are in careful period style, with real Louis XV furniture. Louis Roussel was a courteous, seigneurial host. He showed us the 16th-century farmhouse in the grounds where Nostradamus once lived, and invited us to browse in his library. The whole place is steeped in a certain poetic melancholy, especially its sprawling, rather unkempt garden, full of pools and fountains. No restaurant: but try the *Arts* in the town, a lively, inexpensive Bohemian place." Inspectors this year underwrite that earlier view: "Excellent value, relaxing and informal. Our enormous room was full of antiques; huge windows overlooked the garden which is gradually being reclaimed from its unkempt state. Good breakfast under the chestnut trees." *(J A, P and J T)*

Open 20 Mar–20 Oct.
Rooms 1 suite, 12 double – 11 with bath, 1 with shower, all with telephone; 1 ground-floor room.
Facilities 2 salons. Large park. English spoken.
Location 3 km W of centre of St-Rémy, off Tarascon road. Parking.
Credit cards None accepted.
Terms Rooms: single occupancy 270 frs, double 330–450 frs. Breakfast 35 frs. (No restaurant.)

Hôtel Van Gogh   *Tel* (90) 92.14.02
1 avenue Jean-Moulin

"The same as ever – quiet, clean and good value", says a reader
returning this year to this small modern hotel on the eastern outskirts, a
simpler and cheaper alternative to the ones listed above. Comfortable
rooms, quiet setting, shy but helpful owners. Smallish garden and
swimming pool – "Madame's geraniums in pots by the pool are as
luxuriant as ever." No restaurant, but there are lots in town. (*E Newall*)

Open 15 Feb–15 Nov.
Rooms 18 double – 7 with bath, 11 with shower, all with telephone; 8 ground-
floor rooms.
Facilities Salon with TV, breakfast room, terrace. Garden with swimming pool.
Location On outskirts of St-Rémy-de-Provence; leave *autoroute* at exit to
Cavaillon. Parking.
Restriction Not ideal for ѣ but some ground-floor rooms.
Credit card Amex.
Terms Rooms: 160 frs. Breakfast 18 frs. (No restaurant.) Reduced rates for
children sharing parents' room.

ST-SYMPHORIEN-LE-CHÂTEAU 28700 Eure-et-Loir   Map 10

Château d'Esclimont   *Tel* (37) 31.15.15
                                                     Telex 780560

Typically Île-de-France, this stately moated Renaissance château is in a
150-acre wooded park, between Chartres and Rambouillet. On its facade
is a motto of de la Rochefoucauld: "C'est mon plaisir." And ours? – "A
pleasurable spot with views over the lawns and lovely lake. The grounds
are superb and we took an apéritif under the sun umbrellas on the wide
terrace. The swimming pool was much in use. The meal, in the prettily
beamed high-ceilinged dining room was very good indeed and the
service pleasant. Two of the guests arrived and left by helicopter. The
bedrooms, also with lovely views, are spacious and well appointed.
Truly a marvellous spot for a quiet country weekend" – at a price.
Cuisine tending to the *nouvelle* (eg bar mi-cuit au poivre rose). (*Jean
Hayward*) A new chef arrived in 1985, so we'd welcome more up-to-date
verdicts.

Open All year.
Rooms 6 suites, 48 double – all with bath, telephone, colour TV. 24 rooms in
separate buildings.
Facilities Salons, bar, 4 restaurants. Wooded park with pond and river; tennis
courts and heated swimming pool. English spoken.
Location Just N of N10 and A11, 23 km SW of Rambouillet, 26 km NE of Chartres.
Leave N10 at Ablis and go towards Prunay, then left on D101.
Restriction Not suitable for ѣ.
Credit cards Access, Diners, Visa.
Terms Double rooms 490–1,790 frs. Breakfast 50 frs; set lunch/dinner 210–300 frs;
full alc 320 frs.

We ask hotels to estimate their 1986 tariffs some time before
publication so the rates given are not necessarily exact. Please
always check terms with hotels when making bookings.

ST-TROPEZ 83990 Var   Map 11

Le Mas de Chastelas   *Tel* (94) 56.09.11
P.O. Box 32   *Telex* 461516 POSTE 75

Back in form, it seems, after what may have been a bad patch, this old
Mas is again being described as perhaps *the* most sympathetic and
tasteful hotel in the St-Tropez area (where tranquil charm and good taste
are not alway in evidence). It's a converted 17th-century farmhouse,
once used for silkworm breeding, and it stands secluded in vineyards
four kilometres west of St-Tropez and 500 metres from the sea. It is run
by a cultured Parisian couple, Gérard and Dominique Racine, who are
always present: their guests tend to include many French stars of stage,
screen and fashion, fleeing the *paparazzi* of the frenzied port area.

"Probably one of the most charming hideouts in France", runs a report
this year; "we stayed a week and loved it. The food was exceptional even
for France, the rooms spotless, the attention to detail in exquisite taste
right down to the music, and M. Racine and his staff were most
hospitable." Earlier visitors have admired the pine furnishings, the
flowers in the bedrooms, the "justly famous breakfasts" and the buffet
lunches beside the heated pool. "You almost feel you are not staying in a
hotel but in a friend's country house." Last year, one visitor found the
place rather run down: but we note that in 1985 *Michelin* for the first time
granted its coveted accolade of gables in red. Besides the lovely
swimming pool and charming garden, amenities include a jacuzzi, a
children's playground, and ten luxurious duplex suites in an annexe.
(Nicola Hayward, G S, L H, J A, and others)

Open 1 Apr–30 Sept.
Rooms 10 suites, 21 double – 27 with shower, all with telephone; colour TV in
suites; all suites and 2 rooms in annexe.
Facilities Lounge, bar with TV, restaurant. 6-acre gardens with 4 tennis courts,
heated swimming pool, jacuzzi, ping-pong, *boules* and children's playground.
Golf driving range nearby. Beach 5 km. English spoken.
Location 4 km from St-Tropez, just off Gassin road to E.
Restriction Not suitable for &.
Credit cards All major cards accepted.
Terms [1985 rates, double or single occupancy] suites 1,150–1,350 frs, rooms
480–820 frs. Breakfast 50 frs; set dinner 220 frs (lunch for residents about 120 frs).

ST-VAAST-LA-HOUGUE 50550 Manche   Map 8

Hôtel de France et des Fuchsias   *Tel* (33) 54.42.26
18 rue Maréchal Foch

St-Vaast is an attractive old oyster-breeding fishing port 27 kilometres
east of Cherbourg: Edward III landed his troops here before the battle of
Crécy. The *Fuchsias* is the main holiday hotel – small, family-run,
exuberant, down-to-earth and very pretty. It was dropped from the
Guide in 1983 after some bad reports, including complaints of dresses
ruined by stains from the eponymous red blossoms which had fallen
over chairs and tables. However, the fuchsias now seem to be under
better control, and the hotel is warmly back in favour with this year's
visitors: "I had a very agreeable stay there," says one; "outside it is
charming, with the largest fuchsias I have ever seen and a thatched

canopy over the entrance to the little cobbled courtyard. The bedroom was pretty, with blue and white paper. Two nice dining rooms, one like a conservatory with plants and glass windows, the other with pink decor. No lounge, but more sitting space than in many small French hotels. We ate well, and the young waitresses were solicitous. A very professionally run hotel and there are lovely beaches nearby." An inspector praises the "superb" breakfasts and "lavish" meals, much produce coming from the hotel's own home farm. *(Evlyn Ritchie, P F)*

Open 15 Feb–2 Jan. Closed Mon except during holidays.
Rooms 18 double, 2 single – 14 with bath, 3 with shower, all with telephone. 6 in annexes.
Facilities Bar, reading room, 2 dining rooms. Garden. 200 metres from port.
Location Central. Parking facility in winter.
Restriction Not suitable for &.
Credit cards Diners, Visa.
Terms Rooms 220 frs. Breakfast 20 frs; dinner, B&B 200 frs per person; full board 230 frs per person. Children under 7 half-price in parents' room; special menu.

ST-VALLIER-DE-THIEY 06460 Alpes-Maritimes Map 11

Hôtel le Préjoly *Tel* (93) 42.60.86
Place Rougière

St-Vallier is a small summer resort on a plateau up behind Grasse; the air is fresh, and there is a fine sense of space, with forest and mountains all round – good hiking country. "Yes, yes! Lovely!" was an inspector's recent ratification of an earlier visitor's rhapsodies over the remarkable *Préjoly*: "Just the kind of country hotel/restaurant that the French contrive so superbly. It is on the main street (the Route Napoléon to Grenoble) and front bedrooms could well be noisy: but ours at the back was quiet, and very spruce, and looked out over the meadows and hills. This family-run hotel's quality derives above all from its *patron/chef* and his wife, Georges and Arlette Pallanca, hard-working professionals yet also ebullient and affable. They won a top prize at a gastromonic festival in Rome for 'authenticity of cuisine and courtesy of service', and I'm not surprised. The food, mainly local dishes with some special touches, is lavish and tasty, and the 80-franc menu [1985] outstanding value *(Gault Milau toque)*. Small wonder the big rustic-style dining room was always crowded, with locals and tourists, and service consequently slowish. Once we ate out on the shady terrace, but were put off by the noise of traffic." *(J A C A, L H)* A recent visitor found the downstairs toilet area less than clean and tidy.

Open Feb–end Nov; closed Tue Sept–June.
Rooms 20 double – 15 with bath, all with telephone, some with terrace; 1 room with bath on ground floor.
Facilities Salon with TV, restaurant, terrace restaurant; conference facilities. Garden with tennis courts and children's play area. Swimming pool, riding, fishing, skiing nearby. Sandy beaches at Cannes 29 km. English spoken. &.
Location On N85 in the village, which is 12 km NW of Grasse.
Credit cards All major cards accepted.
Terms [1985 rates] rooms: single occupancy 130 frs, double 250 frs; full board 220–280 frs per person. Breakfast 18 frs; set lunch/dinner 45–120 frs.

STE-ANNE-LA-PALUD 29127 Finistère

Map 8

Hôtel de la Plage   *Tel* (98) 92.50.12
Plomodiern   *Telex* 941377

St Anne's chapel by the beach is the venue of one of the largest and most colourful of Breton *pardons*, held on the last Sunday in August. The busy fishing port of Douarnenez and the pretty village of Locronan are both within 20 kilometres. Near the chapel is the stylish *Plage*, dropped recently from the Guide but this year again warmly approved: "Delightful, very peaceful, comfortable, and right on a big sandy beach. We had a good well-tended bedroom with a lovely view over the sands. Friendly welcome by the Le Coz family, and very good food especially the seafood." (*Michelin* rosette and two *Gault Millau* red *toques*). Other visitors have enjoyed the heated swimming pool and lovely gardens. *(Tom and Rosemary Rose)*

Open 31 Mar–8 Oct.
Rooms 3 suites, 27 rooms – most with bath or shower.
Facilities Lift. Restaurant, conference facilities. Garden with swimming pool. Tennis 4 km.
Location On coast, 16 km NE of Douarnenez.
Credit cards All major cards accepted.
Terms Rooms 380–540 frs; full board 460–650 per person. Breakfast 35 frs; set lunch/dinner 140–250 frs.

STE-MAXIME 83120 Var

Map 11

Hôtel Calidianus   *Tel* (94) 96.23.21
Blvd Jean Moulin, Quartier de la Croisette

Ste-Maxime is a biggish resort with a tree-lined promenade, good sandy beaches and lots to do – a casino, several night-clubs, waterskiing, yachting and golf. It is less exotic than St-Tropez across the bay, but nonetheless youthful and great fun – in season. The *Calidianus*, in the western outskirts, is a very modern medium-priced bed-and-breakfast hotel, recommended recently by two readers. "Excellent and good value. It is about 200 yards from the sea, on a hill overlooking the bay, with a small swimming pool and tennis courts. Bedroom of reasonable size with plenty of lighting, good bathroom. In summer the place is packed with Porsche-owning Swiss and Germans." "Even when empty, in winter, the building had great ambience. Good views from the first-floor rooms, which have balconies." *(Richard and Carol Thomas, Ian Bryant)* In town, you eat well at *La Gruppi* (expensive) and at *La Réserve* and *Sans Souci* (both cheap and lively).

Open All year.
Rooms 24 – all with bath and telephone, some with balcony.
Facilities Breakfast room. Garden with tennis court and swimming pool. Near the beach.
Location 1 km W of centre of resort, off N98.
Restriction Not suitable for &.
Credit cards None accepted.
Terms [1985 rates] single occupancy 265 frs, double 290 frs. Breakfast 27 frs. (No restaurant.)

SAINTES 17100 Charente-Maritime   Map 10

Relais du Bois St-Georges   *Tel* (46) 93.50.99
Rue de Royan

Saintes, conveniently close to the Bordeaux–Paris *autoroute*, is one of the most attractive and historic towns of south-west France. It was a big centre in Roman days, as the size of its ruined amphitheatre indicates. Later it was an important post on the pilgrim route to Santiago, and many fine Romanesque churches survive from that period. In contrast to all this, the *Bois St-Georges* is decidedly modern, but elegantly so. It is in the western outskirts, not far from the *autoroute*, and has a garden with wide lawns and views of the quiet countryside. "An enchanting hotel and a *Relais du Silence*; the rooms are simple but tastefully decorated with pretty wallpapers and the occasional antique. Bathrooms impeccable. The open-plan dining room, lounge, bar and reception are carefully divided up; several open fires add to the ambience. The food was excellent, though not cheap. The owner is very Anglophile." *(C F Colt)*

Open All year. Restaurant closed Mon lunch-time.
Rooms 1 suite, 20 double – all with bath and shower, telephone, radio, colour TV and baby-listening. Some with balcony. Ground-floor rooms.
Location On W outskirts – 1.5 km from exit 25 of *autoroute* A10. Garage and parking.
Credit card Access.
Terms Rooms: single occupancy 315 frs, double 430 frs; dinner, B&B 350–390 frs per person; full board 445–485 frs per person. Breakfast 40 frs; full alc 310 frs. Off-season rates.

LES STES-MARIES-DE-LA-MER 13460 Bouches-du-Rhône   Map 10

L'Étrier Camarguais   *Tel* (90) 47.81.14
Chemin bas des Launes, Route d'Arles

We wish we had more entries in the Carmargue, that strange flat land of lagoons and wild white horses, bulls and flamingoes. The *Étrier* stands in its own big garden, three kilometres north of the unusual seaside town of Les Saintes-Maries where the gipsies hold a festival every 23–27 May. The *Étrier* is one of several modern ranch-like hotels in the area that cater for riding enthusiasts: it has its own herd of local white horses, which it hires to guests by the hour (at a price!). "We spent a happy week here, riding, watching birds, and exploring the Camargue. It's an excellent holiday hotel, spacious and informal, with log-cabin style decor, a breezy youthful ambience, lots of children, incessant music, and jokey staff – sub-Club Méditerranée, you could say. Our bedroom, simple but serviceable, was in a chalet in the garden. Especially we enjoyed the big swimming pool and sun-terrace, prettily lit at night. Food was copious and straightforward – lots of crudités and log-fire grills – and usually we ate out by the pool. The hotel runs a lively disco just far enough away to avoid keeping us awake." Endorsed by a visitor this year: "Breakfast on our private terrace was delightful, once with chocolate croissants. I ate a sun-ripened fig from their poolside fig-tree." *(Alan and Elsie Campbell, Vicki Turner)*.

Open 1 Apr–1 Nov.
Rooms 28 double – all with bath, telephone and colour TV; 27 on ground floor.
Facilities Bar, dining room, breakfast room, terrace; night club/disco. Garden with swimming pool, tennis court and *boules*; horses for hire. Beach 3 km. English spoken.
Location 3 km N of the town, just off N570 to Arles.
Restriction Not suitable for &.
Credit cards All major cards accepted.
Terms [1985 rates] Half-board: single 470 frs, double 620 frs; full board; single 590 frs, double 860 frs. Set lunch/dinner 130 frs.

SALON-DE-PROVENCE 13300 Bouches-du-Rhône　　　　**Map 11**

Abbaye de Sainte-Croix　　　　　　　　　　　*Tel* (90) 56.24.55
Route du Val de Cuech　　　　　　　　　　　*Telex* 401247 STECROI

A venerable 12th-century abbey, on a hillside north-east of Salon by a private road and mid-way between Aix and Arles. It has been sumptuously and carefully restored after long neglect and appeals to lovers of luxury-cum-tradition: "The Cistercian monks slept in small cells and enjoyed the space of their gardens, ambulatories and refectories. And this is rather what the hotel offers: mostly small rooms (but a few with terraces), a large wooded park, and a dining room giving on to a terrace with a stunning view south across the plain of Salon. The monastic bedrooms can be claustrophobic, but one can't have it all ways. One could do without the muzak at the swimming pool. But dinner by candlelight under the mulberry trees is an unforgettable experience, especially as the service is *soigné* yet relaxed and the food of a standard worthy of the setting." Two *Gault Millau toques*, in fact, for cooking that is both inventive and classically Provençal, on which another visitor comments: "Splendid – home-smoked fish of many kinds, steak in blueberry sauce, pork in a wild mushroom sauce, a battery of cheeses, as well as that chariot of puddings." Recent reports concur with the general praise, though one criticises the service outside meal-times and another finds the food "unexciting". (*Geoffrey Sharp, endorsed by J J Wüthrich, and others*)

Open Mar–Oct inclusive. Restaurant closed Mon midday.
Rooms 4 suites, 18 double – 20 with bath, 2 with shower, all with telephone; colour TV in suites; some rooms with terrace, some on ground floor. Ramps.
Facilities Reception, salon, bar, restaurant, functions facilities. Covered terrace. Wooded grounds and garden with unheated swimming pool and summer restaurant. Tennis and riding nearby. Sea 40 km. English spoken. &.
Location 3 km NE of Salon, off D16; sign in Salon after exit from *autoroute*. Parking.
Credit cards All major cards accepted.
Terms B&B: single 502–672 frs, double 564–734 frs; dinner, B&B: single 695–865 frs, double 950–1,120 frs; full board: single 850–1,020 frs; double 1,260–1,330 frs. Set lunch 180 frs; dinner 200–230 frs; alc (without wine) 275 frs.

> *Warning*: there were major changes in French telephone numbers in the autumn of 1985 after we had gone to press. It is possible, therefore, that not all our French telephone numbers, particularly those of hotels which failed to answer our questionnaire, are accurate.

SANCY-LES-MEAUX 77580 Seine-et-Marne   Map 10

La Catournière,   *Tel* (6) 025.71.74
1 rue de l'Église

Quite a discovery this year: a handsome creeper-covered 18th-century mansion in its own big park, in the Marne valley, very rural and horsy, yet only 30 minutes from the gates of Paris by motorway. Popular with tired Parisian weekenders, it could also make a good stop for British tourists wanting to visit Paris or skirt it to the east. "It's in a beautiful and quiet village. Madame Balestier gave us a warm welcome on both our visits this year. Rooms are large and comfortable, the indoor swimming pool is warm. Dinner was delicious: but there is no set-price menu and the à la carte is fairly expensive. The grounds boast a riding school: even if you're no rider, having a horse to talk to after dinner is rather relaxing. Alas, the presence of horses does bring horse-flies into the bedrooms in high season." *(Mr and Mrs A W Barr)*

Open All year except 18–31 Aug and Christmas.
Rooms 11 double – all with bath, direct-dial telephone, colour TV and mini-bar. 6 more in annexe planned for 1986.
Facilities Lounge, bar, restaurant, games room, conference facilities. Large grounds with covered swimming pool (heated Easter to Nov), 2 tennis courts and riding school. Golf 5 km. English spoken.
Location 35 minutes by car from Paris by A4 (exit Crécy). Between Meaux and Coulommiers on D228.
Restriction Not suitable for ♿.
Credit cards Access, Diners.
Terms Rooms 220 frs. Breakfast 23 frs; full alc 200–250 frs.

SÉGURET 84110 Vaucluse   Map 11

La Table du Comtat   *Tel* (90) 36.91.49

Terraced on a hillside above the Rhône vineyards, the quaint old village of Séguret is within easy reach of Orange and Vaison-la-Romaine and has fine views of the startling jagged peaks of the Dentelles de Montmirail. *La Table du Comtat*, a 15th-century house now a fairly sophisticated restaurant-with-rooms (*Michelin* rosette), is superbly situated just above the hill and plain. One reader speaks of "magical location, outstanding views, excellent food, service just right" and "the hospitality seems more than one could hope for". A regular correspondent adds: "A most memorable meal, especially the sole with lobster mousseline, the goats' cheeses and the sweets. The dining room furniture, Provençal rustic, is very striking; reception rooms are light and airy; the bathroom was clean and modern, and from our bedroom we could gaze at the famous rock outcrops of the Dentelles. A pleasant, clean hotel, quiet at night. Madame was harrassed at first, but blossomed, and was charming by the time we left." The small curving *piscine* beneath its high rock is a delight. *(Giles Keating, I and F W, Herbert G Hawkins)*

Open End Feb to mid-Jan. Closed Tue evening and Wed except July, Aug, Easter and Christmas holidays.
Rooms 1 suite, 7 double – all with bath and direct-dial telephone.
Facilities Salon, dining room, terrace. Small garden with unheated pool.

Location 8 km S of Vaison-la-Romaine off the D23; at entrance to Séguret; hotel is signposted.
Restriction Not suitable for &.
Credit cards Access, Diners.
Terms Rooms 260–320 frs. Set meals 170 and 280 frs; full alc 300 frs. Special children's menu.

SEILLANS 83440 Var   Map 10

Hôtel des Deux Rocs   *Tel* (94) 76.87.32
Place Font d'Amont

Seillans, in a glorious setting west of Grasse, facing across a wide and verdant valley, is a splendid old hill-village with steep narrow streets and a ruined château; many writers, artists and suchlike spend the summer here. The *Deux Rocs* is an 18th-century mansion converted into a very personal little hotel, owned and run by Lise Hirsch, formerly a biochemist in Paris. It has been in the Guide for some years, and this year came under critical inspectorial scrutiny: "A fountain playing under shady plane trees in a cobbled square provides a good start. So does the warmth of welcome. Our bags were carried up two flights of stairs to a spacious bedroom with lemon and white decor. The restaurant was busy and the à la carte dishes first class: but the service was poor, and the *en pension* meals are best avoided – no choice, and a greasy ragoût d'agneau. Not much French ambience, as almost all guests are British." You can eat outside by the fountain under two big plane trees, with a fine view. *(E B, John Newnham, and others)*

Open 24 Mar–2 Nov. Restaurant closed Tue.
Rooms 15 double – 6 with bath, 9 with shower, all with telephone.
Facilities Salon, TV room, restaurant; terrace by fountain where meals are served in summer. 15 minutes from lake, 30 minutes from sea. English spoken.
Location In upper part of village. Parking.
Restriction Not suitable for &.
Credit cards None accepted.
Terms [1985 rates] B&B: single 176–281 frs, double 202–352 frs; dinner, B&B: (3 days min.) single 300–381 frs, double 402–552 frs; set lunch/dinner 75,105, 140 frs; full alc 140 frs. Reduced rates for children.

SEPT-SAULX 51400 Marne   Map 9

Hôtel du Cheval Blanc   *Tel* (26) 61.60.27
                                                                   Telex 830885

On the eastern fringe of the champagne country, between Reims and Châlons-sur-Marne, this old coaching-inn has been run by the Robert family for five generations. The hotel straddles the main road of the village – on one side a modern block of bedrooms, on the other the charming creeper-covered old inn beside a big garden. It has long been praised by many readers both for its pastoral setting (it is a Relais du Silence) *and for its food (*Michelin *rosette,* Gault Millau toque). *A report this year: "Garden lovely, rooms variable, food excellent, eg duck aux framboises. They happily gave our children half menus: the halving was in price rather than portions! Excellent house champagne." Earlier visitors have spoken of the warm welcome and comfortable beds, the "lovely dining room with open fire and seductive lighting", and the "pretty* *courtyard with garden furniture". However, we get continuing reports of extremely slow service at meals, and two out of four of this year's visitors found the food not equal to its ambitions. Is the white horse becoming a white elephant? – we should welcome more verdicts, please.* (S Burnton, E Newall, Angela and David Stewart, Martyn Goff)

Open All year except 15 Jan to 15 Feb and New Year's Eve.
Rooms 2 suites, 18 double – 9 with bath, 12 with shower, all with direct-dial telephone, colour TV and mini-bar; all rooms on ground floor in annexe on other side of street.
Facilities 2 salons, TV room, restaurant; functions room, billiards room. Hotel is situated in large park bordered by river Vesle; tennis, mini-golf, table tennis, volleyball, fishing. Heated swimming pool 12 km away. English spoken. &.
Location 20 km E of Rheims, on D37 off N44 in direction of Châlons. Parking.
Credit cards Access, Amex, Visa.
Terms B&B: single 208–253 frs, double 253–298 frs. Set lunch/dinner 120 and 200 frs; full alc 200–300 frs. Half- and full-board rates for stays of 4 days and more.

SERRE-CHEVALIER 05240 Hautes-Alpes   Map 10

Hôtel la Vieille Ferme   *Tel* (92) 24.76.44
Villeneuve La Salle

We reprint our earlier description of Serre-Chevalier: "a straggle of hamlets on the main road just west of Briançon. It is frankly an ugly place, with little of the chalet-style spruceness of the Savoy resorts to the north. Nor is there much in the way of elegance or 'disco' night-life: people come here mainly for the challenge of high-level skiing, or for mountain walking in the summer. However, *La Vieille Ferme* itself is one of the most unusual ski-hotels in France. It is a big 1722 farmhouse in the village, which Georges Carles, a local mason, bought in 1969 and modernised largely with his own hands, helped by his Parisian wife and friends. The result is intimate and graceful with red-tiled floors, bare stone walls and beamed ceilings. Our 'rustic' room was a bit cramped, and not cheap, but we were beguiled by the hotel's breezy informal atmosphere. The ebullient Carles and their staff treat their clients like friends and drink with them in the log-cabin lounge/bar. Most guests were serious skiers, oozing ruddy good health, and we felt like a Bateman cartoon – 'the English couple who came without their ski-boots'.

"The *menus pension* and other set menus are unremarkable, though copious. But it's worth paying extra to eat in the snug rustic-style *rôtisserie* where the star turn is M. Carles himself, *rôtisseur*, presiding over a blazing open fire. Here for 150 frs [1984] I had a gargantuan feast with good inexpensive wines – an array of interesting help-yourself salads, then a succession of different cuts of tender grilled meat that M. Carles presents to each diner with the panache of a circus-master." (*J A C A*) More reports welcome.

Open 15 Dec–13 Apr, 28 Jun–7 Sept.
Rooms 6 suites, 24 double – 18 with bath, 10 with shower, all with telephone.
Facilities Salon with TV and bar, games room, restaurant, *rôtisserie*; terrace in summer. 500 metres from river with fishing rights, 400 metres from chairlifts. Winter sports. English spoken.
Location Central. 100 metres from N91. 7 km from Briançon. From Briançon turn right after church; from Grenoble turn left before church. Parking.

Restriction Not suitable for &.
Credit card Visa.
Terms B&B: single occupancy 109.50–410.50 frs, double 130–431 frs; half-board: single occupancy 168–354 frs, double 280–590 frs; full board: single occupancy 237–415 frs, double 396–692 frs. Breakfast 20 frs; set lunch/dinner 72 frs; full alc 105 frs. Children occupying parents' room free; special meals.

SERRES 05700 Hautes-Alpes   Map 10

Hôtel Fifi Moulin   *Tel* (92) 67.00.01
Route de Nyons

A useful and popular halt in a village on the main road from Grenoble to Provence, the Route Napoléon. "Totally unpretentious, not everyone's cup of tea, but very good value, with pleasant, efficient staff", is the verdict of two expert hotel-watchers; "the owner is a cheerful and dynamic man who speaks good English. The hotel is on several levels, rather like a beehive, with kitchens next to guest bedrooms: for this reason, some rooms may be a little noisy in late evening. Terrace and back bedrooms on upper levels have excellent views over the mountains in the background and blocks of council flats in the foreground. Our room was very clean and the bathroom modern and spacious: but the furniture was basic, and the wallpaper of orange daisies with brown leaves – the daisy motif runs throughout the hotel – was disconcerting. The restaurant was very popular, and food was amazingly good considering how cheap it was (red *Michelin* 'R')." Visitors this year concur: "Tremendous value. Our room perhaps a little austere, but lovely dining room, excellent set menu, breakfast with good home-made jams." "Sweet trolley excellent, but likely to be demolished by generosity of waitresses. Hot soup served at 2.30 pm (and not charged for) when we arrived wet and bedraggled." *(I and F W; also K W George, P L Aston, and others)*

Open Feb–11 Nov. Closed Wed except July–Sept.
Rooms 26 double – 19 with bath, 7 with shower, all with telephone;
12 ground-floor rooms in annexe.
Facilities Lounge, bar, restaurant, patio; conference room. Small garden, near river with bathing and fishing. English spoken. &
Location 107 km S of Grenoble, 64 km from Nyons on N75.
Credit cards All major cards accepted.
Terms B&B: single 137.50 frs, double 185 frs. Set lunch/dinner 64 and 103 frs; full alc 160 frs.

SEYSSEL 01420 Ain   Map 10

Hôtel du Rhône   *Tel* (50) 59.20.30
Quai de Gaulle

Geneva, Annecy and Aix-les-Bains are all within a 50 kilometre radius of this village on the upper Rhône. The *Hôtel du Rhône* is finely situated: you can take meals out on the broad and pretty terrace by the rushing river. "The food was excellent; the lounge was small, but games and books were provided. The only drawback could be noisy traffic across the river." "We were well treated, and the food was very good, though a little too rich for our taste. We had a comfortable room overlooking the river. Breakfast was a treat, with home-made jam." *(Mrs S H Davidson, Elizabeth Crabtree)* Robert Herbelot, the *patron-chef*, wins a *Michelin* rosette for such dishes as poularde de Bresse aux morilles. He has his own landing-stage, allowing boating and windsurfing, while fishing is also possible nearby.

Open 15 Feb–15 Nov. Closed Sun evening and Mon. Restaurant open 1 Apr–15 Nov (except Sun evening and Mon).
Rooms 10 rooms – all with shower, and telephone; 5 rooms in annexe.
Facilities Salon with TV, restaurant, terrace on the Rhône; fishing, windsurfing, canoeing nearby. English spoken.
Location 100 metres outside Seyssel on left bank of Rhône, between the 2 bridges. Garage.
Restriction Not suitable for &.
Credit cards All major cards accepted.
Terms Rooms: single 95 frs, double 200–240 frs; half-board 205–230 frs per person. Breakfast 20 frs. Reductions for stays of 3 days or more. Reduced rates for children under 10; special meals.

SOSPEL 06380 Alpes-Maritimes   Map 11

Hôtel des Étrangers   *Tel* (93) 04.00.09
7 boulevard de Verdun   *Telex* 970439

This charming old town makes an ideal centre for exploring the relatively little known hinterland behind Menton – for example, the hill village of Saorge, clinging to the side of a cliff, and the Vallée des Merveilles where prehistoric graffiti cover a rocky lunar landscape. The *Étrangers*, an unpretentious but comfortable little family hotel on the edge of the town, is again praised this year for its welcome and good food. The *patron/chef*, Jean-Pierre Domérego, has written a book about Sospel and adores talking to his guests about his beloved region. He is both Anglophone and Anglo-Americophile, having worked in Bermuda and the US, and he runs his hotel with gusto as well as doing the cooking – try his bouillabaisse, made of local trout. He takes regular English package-tours, of a discreet up-market kind. This year he has opened a pool near the river, with solarium and grill. *(J A G Stonehouse, Anthony Day, H K Wane, L H)*

Open 1 Feb–30 Nov.
Rooms 33 double, 2 single – 14 with bath, 13 with shower, all with direct-dial telephone; 5 rooms with kitchenette in annexe.
Facilities Lift. Bar, TV room, 3 restaurants; conference facilities, games room. Riverside terrace, with bar in season, and pergola; swimming pool, small pool for young children; solarium and grill; fishing. English spoken.
Location 22 km N of Menton on D2204. Parking.
Restriction Not suitable for &.
Credit cards Access, Visa.
Terms Rooms: single 90–115 frs, double 100–130 frs; dinner, B&B 190–210 frs per person; full board 220–260 frs per person. Breakfast 23 frs; set lunch/dinner 60–115 frs; full alc 150 frs. Reduced rates for children sharing parents' room.

We asked hotels to quote 1986 prices. Not all were able to predict them in the late spring of 1985. Some of our terms will be inaccurate. Do check latest tariffs at the time of booking.

SOUSCEYRAC 46190 Lot   Map 10

Au Déjeuner de Sousceyrac   *Tel* (65) 33.00.56

"Just as good as ever and stunning value for money" writes a Francophile about this "quintessentially French" little inn in a fairly remote village, south of the upper Dordogne. "I have been going here for 20 years, drawn originally by its rosette in *Michelin*, and it is now better than ever. It has been run by the same family for four generations: Pierre Espinadel, the present *patron/chef*, is the great-grandson of the founder. I could write a book about it: but in the early 1930s someone did, Pierre Benoit of the Académie-Française, and called it *Au déjeuner de Sousceyrac* – and the family, flattered (and who wouldn't be?), changed the hotel's name to this. From the outside it looks like a thousand other cheap, dingy hotels in France, but inside it is brightly clean. The bedrooms are adequate, most with baths; no room is over £12 for two [1985]. In the breakfast room you can get service all day long.

"The countryside is the epitome of *La Belle France*. The food is of outstanding quality, served with sometimes overwhelming generosity (red 'R' in *Michelin*). Perhaps asparagus, fresh salmon and sorrel sauce in May, cèpes and jugged hare in October. There are also hardy perennials of their own – sweetbreads with a creamy onion sauce, duck done in many ways, and above all their 'truite soufflée' baked in cream. The local house wines are delicious and about £1 a bottle. The excellent service has always been done by well-trained girls. 'Tout passe, tout lasse, tout casse' – grab it while you can!" *(Walter Baxter)*

Open 1 Apr–31 Oct. Restaurant closed Sat except July and Aug.
Rooms 12 double, 2 single – 2 with bath, 7 with shower; 4 rooms in annexe.
Facilities TV room, salon, 2 dining rooms, 2 terraces. Swimming, fishing and tennis locally.
Location In centre of village which is between St-Cère and Aurillac on D673 and D653. Parking.
Restrictions Not suitable for &. No children under 10.
Credit cards Amex, Diners, Visa.
Terms Rooms 100 frs; half-board 150 frs per person; full board 190 frs per person. Breakfast 15 frs; set meals 60, 90, 130 and 150 frs; full alc 180 frs.

STRASBOURG 67000 Bas-Rhin   Map 9

Nouvel Hôtel Maison Rouge   *Tel* (88) 32.08.60
4 rue des Francs-Bourgeois   *Telex* 880130

In this Euro-capital where most hotels are expensive, here is a medium-priced one that is also very central, 30 metres from the main square, the place Kléber. It is recommended as "a place of Victorian comfort; for a largish hotel, the best for the Strasbourg visitor". It is much used by delegates to the European Parliament and Council of Europe and is good for access to them. The staff are multi-lingual, efficient. Booking is essential. "Magnificent furniture, lovely atmosphere", says a reader this year. No restaurant, but you can eat very well all over Strasbourg – for example, expensively at the *Crocodile*, medium-pricewise at *l'Ancien Horloge* and cheaply at *l'Ancienne Douane*. *(John Thirlwell, F G Fallows, Vicki Turner)*

Open All year.
Rooms 10 suites, 60 double, 60 single – 90 with bath, 40 with shower, all with direct-dial telephone and sound-proofing; some with radio, some with TV.
Facilities Lift. TV room, bar, breakfast room. English spoken.
Location In town centre. Paid parking in place Kléber nearby.
Restriction Not suitable for &.
Credit cards Amex, Diners, Visa.
Terms Rooms: single 320 frs, double 360 frs. Breakfast 40 frs. (No restaurant.)

Hôtel des Rohan
17 rue Maroquin

Tel (88) 32.85.11 and 32.89.43

Being a beautiful city as well as a political capital, Strasbourg is much frequented by tourists as well as business and "Euro" visitors, and its many hotels are usually full. The *Rohan* is small and upper-medium priced, that is, rather cheaper than the nearby Hiltons and Sofitels used by MEPs on their generous expenses. It is newly modernised, but lies in the heart of the old quarter, in a cobbled pedestrain area only 50 metres from the cathedral. A visitor this year found it quiet, friendly and efficient and endorses last year's praise: "A family hotel, traditional, discreet and a joy to stay in. Though modern, it has 'repro' furniture in the current French taste and is warm and comfortable; direct-dial telephone even in the bathroom." (*J A, John Thirlwell*)

Open All year.
Rooms 36 – 24 with bath, 12 with shower, all with direct-dial telephone, radio, TV and mini-bar.
Facilities Lift. Salon, breakfast room.
Location Central, near cathedral. Parking nearby.
Credit cards None accepted.
Terms [1985 rates] rooms: single 205 frs, double 340 frs. Breakfast 24 frs. (No restaurant.)

TALLOIRES 74290 Haute-Savoie
Map 10

Hôtel Beau-Site
Tel (50) 60.71.04

For those not wishing to pay the high prices of the *Père Bise* (see below), here is a simpler alternative, also set serenely by the shores of the glorious lake of Annecy. "Delightful quiet hotel in large grounds, charmingly decorated; very pretty dining room, salon and terrace; large garden running down to private lake shore. Excellent food, especially sauces. Some bedrooms are in separate buildings close to the main one." A more recent visitor found the owners delightful and cultured, the food good and plentiful, and the large flowery park well kept, but warns that some annexe rooms may be "austere" and service not always perfect. (*Mr and Mrs M Appleby, Katie Plowden*)

Open 16 May–30 Sept.
Rooms 34 double, 4 single – 25 with bath, 3 with shower, all with telephone; 20 in annexe.
Facilities 3 salons, dining room, terrace. Garden with private lakeshore front and tennis. English spoken.
Location Central, on Lake Annecy.
Credit cards Possibly some accepted.
Terms B&B: single 140 frs, double 190–410 frs; dinner, B&B: 195–310 frs per person; full board: 240–360 frs per person. Set lunch 110 frs; full alc 130 frs.

Auberge du Père Bise   *Tel* (50) 60.72.01
Au bord du Lac   *Telex* 385812

This beautiful, famous and very expensive hostelry beside lake Annecy has long been regarded as one of the best restaurants in the French provinces. It lost its third *Michelin* rosette in 1983 when its owner, the much-loved François Bise, became very ill and ceased to do the cooking. He died in 1984, and the *Auberge* is now run by his widow and daughter. The new chef, Gilles Furtin, is so good (cooking in a classic, rather than modern, genre) that *Michelin* has now restored its top rating, and a Guide reader this year concurs, "A superb hotel, cuisine and service first class". *(Robert D Hill)*

This bears out our earlier description: "The hotel is situated right on the lake. Almost all the rooms have a view of the water, and many have small balconies. The service upstairs is perfect; maids pick up laundry and pressing, and little needs are well taken care of. Breakfast is served in your room, or outside on small tables next to the lake. Lunch is on the terrace between the lakeside and the inn itself. The road traffic is behind the inn, so that you hear no noise at all. The dining room is magnificent, and the food likewise. The other real joy is the location, the stillness and quiet, and the views of the mountains across the lake. A truly beautiful place." *(Alfred Knopf Jr)*

Open All year except 20 Dec–19 Jan, 16 Apr–4 May. Restaurant closed Wed lunch-time.
Rooms 12 suites, 22 double – all with bath and direct-dial telephone; 10 with radio and TV; 22 rooms in annexes, some on ground floor.
Facilities Lift. Piano bar, salons, restaurant, terrace and garden on lake with private beach. English spoken. &.
Location On E bank of Lake Annecy. Parking.
Credit cards Amex, Diners, Visa.
Terms B&B double 1,120 frs; half-board 900 frs per person; full board 1,100 frs. Set lunch 300, 400 and 500 frs; full alc 600 frs. Reduced rates for children.

TAMNIÈS 24620 Dordogne   **Map 10**

Hôtel-Restaurant Laborderie   *Tel* (53) 29.68.59

A truly rural hotel on the edge of a tiny hilltop village between Les Eyzies and Sarlat, facing out over rolling wooded country. With its facade of rough yellowish stone, it could be in the Cotswolds (like so many buildings in this area); inside are beamed ceilings and a log fire in winter. "Together with *The Mansion* in San Francisco, my favourite hotel", is one cosmic overview; "absolute tranquillity for a song. A warm welcome from the Laborderie family, who are good with children. Bar and lovely terrace. In the large dining room, fine rustic Périgourdin food, copious menus, with delicious hors-d'oeuvre. Large swimming pool and boating lake a kilometre away." An inspector this year thought the place good value for money, though his bedroom was small. The best rooms, he says, are in the annexe, with good views. He found breakfast and dinner excellent, apart from a terrible confit de canard: "I think the Laborderies realised what a disaster this was, for Madame made us a parting gift of two tins of their own foie gras." *(R A D)*

Open 15 Mar–15 Nov.
Rooms 2 suites, 30 double – 25 with bath, 5 with shower, all with telephone;

16 rooms in annexe, some on ground floor. More rooms planned for 1986.
Facilities Bar, 2 salons, TV room, dining room and functions rooms; terrace.
100-acre grounds with swimming pool. Lake nearby with swimming, fishing,
windsurfing, sandy beach. English spoken.
Location In centre of Tamniès which is 14 km NE of Les Eyzies. Parking.
Restriction Not suitable for &.
Credit card Access.
Terms B&B 70–140 frs; half-board 150–220 frs; full board 190–260 frs. Set
lunch/dinner 60,80, 110 and 190 frs; full alc 100 frs. Reduced rates for children.

TAVEL 30126 Gard   Map 11

Auberge de Tavel   _Tel_ (66) 50.03.41

At the edge of the famous wine village, and facing on to rolling open
country, this gracefully converted old Provençal *mas* remains in favour
mainly for its "delicious" food, "well deserving its *Michelin* star". The
restaurant, elegant and high-ceilinged, has tables set well apart; a bar
looks out on to a small garden and swimming pool. "Service extremely
kind and friendly"; "pleasantly furnished rooms with modern bathrooms". However, one reader has commented on small helpings at
meals, and there are hints that accommodation is not equal to the
cuisine. Front rooms can be noisy.

Open All year except Feb. Closed Mon except July and Aug.
Rooms 11 double – 6 with bath, 5 with shower, all with direct-dial telephone, and
mini-bar; 6 with colour TV.
Facilities 2 lounges, bar terrace, restaurant; functions room. Small garden with
swimming pool. River with rocky beach and fishing 10 km. Tennis and riding
nearby. English spoken.
Restriction Not suitable for &.
Credit cards All major cards accepted.
Terms B&B: single 158–329 frs, double 214–369 frs; dinner, B&B 209–309 frs per
person; full board 407–528 frs per person. Set lunch/dinner 107, 186 and 258 frs;
full alc 260 frs. Special meals for children.

TOURNEFEUILLE 31170 Haute-Garonne   Map 10

Les Chanterelles   _Tel_ (61) 86.21.86
27 chemin du Ramelet-Moundi

Tournefeuille, the nearest the Guide has yet penetrated to remarkable
rose-pink Toulouse, is itself an unremarkable little dormitory town eight
kilometres west of the city and six from Blagnac airport. But the
Chanterelles, nominated this year, *vaut le détour*: "A motel with 10
pavilion suites in a garden: it is a *Relais du Silence* and in all France the
best value for money we've ever come across in years of extensive
touring. The architect who designed these pavilions should be congratulated for his taste and use of space. The drawing room is spacious,
beautifully furnished, with a chimney that gives it character. The superb
bedroom, with luxurious bathroom *en suite*, opens on to a private porch
where you can take breakfast (excellent). The pavilions are large enough
to house a whole family, with extra beds in the drawing room. The motel
is run by the Sada family who are helpful and courteous. The next door
restaurant, *Le Cabanon*, under separate ownership, has good service and

an idyllic setting with a garden, stream and watermill: but the cooking is below standard." *(Maurice and Taya Zinkin)* More reports welcome on these far pavilions.

Open All year. Restaurant closed Sun evening.
Rooms 10 suites – all with bath, telephone, TV and porch.
Facilities Garden. &.
Location 1 km S of Tournefeuille, which is 8 km W of Toulouse by D632. Parking.
Credit cards Amex, Diners, Visa.
Terms [1985 rates] suites 240 frs. Breakfast 17 frs; set lunch/dinner 52–156 frs.

TREBEURDEN 22560 Côtes-du-Nord   Map 8

Hôtel Ti al-Lannec   *Tel* (96) 23.57.26
Allée de Mézo-guen   *Telex* 640656

Trebeurden is one of the most appealing of North Brittany family bathing resorts, on a coast where smooth rocks in strange shapes alternate with sandy coves. Here the *Ti al-Lannec*, a handsome grey-and-white mansion, new to the Guide, stands high above the sea in its quiet garden. "Our room was beautiful, with a small sitting room between the bedroom and sliding French windows on to a balcony. The hotel faces south and our view on to the bay with its boating activities was just perfect. The owners are charming and the food good (red *Gault Millau toque*) with plenty of seafood. Trebeurden is perfect for a spring holiday but probably crowded in summer." Big light dining room with sea views; snug, elegant lounge with period decor; white tables and chairs under parasols and trees on the lawn. *(Tom and Rosemary Rose)*

Open 14 Mar–12 Nov. Restaurant closed Mon lunch-time.
Rooms 21 double, 2 single – all with telephone; colour TV on request.
Facilities Salon, TV/games room, bar, restaurant. Garden with outdoor chess and *boules*; path leading down to sandy beach, safe bathing and fishing. Tennis, sailing and windsurfing nearby. English spoken.
Location In centre of village. Signposted from Lannion.
Restriction Not suitable for &.
Credit cards Amex, Visa.
Terms Rooms: single 210–250 frs, double 320–415 frs; dinner, B&B 315–400 frs per person; full board 415–500 frs per person. Breakfast 33 frs; set lunch/dinner 135, 175 and 240 frs; full alc 240 frs. Reduced rates for chldren under 8; special menus.

TRIGANCE 83840 Var   Map 11

Château de Trigance   *Tel* (94) 76.91.18

A boldly battlemented medieval pile on a hilltop, only about 10 kilometres from the dramatic Gorges du Verdon in Upper Provence: "Trigance is a hamlet with a church (handsome polychromatic roof to its tower) perched on a rocky hill above a river. In the Middle Ages the local baron built a small castle on the crag above (and I mean 'above': you can almost spit on the roof of the church from the castle); during the Revolution the local peasantry knocked it down, but around 1965 a Paris ex-businessman, Jean-Claude Thomas, bought the site and rebuilt the castle and small hotel. The quality of the modern stonework is so-so, especially in the low barrel-vaulted dining room. But the castle is a brave sight in the middle distance (access is by a steep rocky path and stone

491

stair). From the terrace roof there are wide views over the encircling rocky hills: one evening I watched a flock of sheep being herded over the slopes and felt a great sense of pastoral peace. Rooms comfortable though not *grand luxe*; food good; proprietor very agreeable." Another visitor warmed to M. Thomas' bonhomie, but found the dining room's assertive medievalism a little oppressive. *(John Newnham, also J A)*

Open 23 Mar–2 Nov.
Rooms 1 suite, 7 double – 7 with bath, 1 with shower, all with phone, some with TV.
Facilities Salon, dining room, large terrace. English spoken.
Location 20 km SW of Castellane, 12 km NW of Comps-sur-Artuby.
Restriction Not suitable for &.
Credit cards All major cards accepted.
Terms B&B: single 230 frs, double 310–460 frs; half-board 280–360 frs per person. Set lunch/dinner 130–250 frs; full alc 200 frs. Reduced rates and special meals for children.

VAISON-LA-ROMAINE 84110 Vaucluse   Map 11

Le Beffroi   *Tel* (90) 36.04.71
Rue de l'Évêché

Vaison is a pleasant little market town in a wooded valley, between the vineyards of the Côtes du Rhône (Gigondas etc.) to the west, and the wild *massif* of Mont Ventoux to the east. It contains some of the most interesting Roman remains in France – for Vaison in Roman days was a smart residential centre. Across the river, a 12th-century château stands on a hill above the steep and narrow streets of the medieval quarter. Here is *Le Beffroi*, a rambling 16th-century mansion with bumpy tiled floors and antique furnishings: conversion into a comfortable little hotel has not destroyed its *cachet*. This year's reports confirm last year's praise: "One of the high points of our trip through France. Cobbled streets barely a Rover wide, all swept and garnished like a front parlour and with flowers bursting out of every lovely bit of stonework. Our room had solid old furniture, tiled floor (but fine modern bathroom), all adding up to a feeling of great repose. Dinner, in a courtyard transformed by vine, fig-tree and flowers, was cheap, abundant and distinguished. Piped classical music was discreet. Highly recommended." *(Dr and Mrs F P Woodford, S R Wilkins, and others)*

Open 10 Mar–15 Nov. Restaurant closed Mon out of season and Tue midday.
Rooms 1 suite, 17 double, 3 single – 6 with bath, 8 with shower, all with direct-dial telephone; 10 rooms in annexe.
Facilities Salon, bar, 2 functions rooms, restaurant. Garden with terrace and tea room. River with fishing nearby. English spoken.
Location 27 km NE of Orange, E of N7. Hotel is in upper part of town near Beffroi arch. Parking opposite hotel.
Restriction Not suitable for &.
Credit cards All major cards accepted.
Terms B&B: single 126 frs, double 221–349 frs; dinner, B&B 190–254 frs per person; full board 281–330 frs per person. Full alc 115 frs. Special meals for children.

In your own interest, always check latest tariffs with hotels when you make your bookings.

VALENCE 26000 Drôme   Map 10

Restaurant Pic   *Tel* (75) 44.15.32
285 avenue Victor-Hugo

The triple-rosetted, four-red-knife-and-fork'd *Pic* is one of Europe's most illustrious restaurants and fully worth its high prices. In the southern outskirts of dull Valence, in the Rhône valley, Jacques Pic and his charming wife offer a shady garden, just four pretty bedrooms above a flowery courtyard, and *nouvelle cuisine* at its least affected. "Everything marvellous – helpful staff, incredible (but simple) comfort in the bedrooms and total luxury in the dining room. The whole place is so undaunting, the atmosphere is charming and there's no snootiness by anyone, unlike at many other prestigious places. Breakfast a dream of warm fresh lemon brioche etc." *(Paul Henderson, Hugh and Ann Pitt)* A further big plus: the Pics served even a vegetarian with her "most delicious meal ever". *(Mrs M D Prodgers)* The cheapest of the three set menus [190 frs in 1985] is not clearly indicated as an option: but if you ask for it, you can have it and – says one reader – it is so lavish that "there would be no reason to take the more expensive choices unless you hadn't eaten for a week." *(Patricia Fenn)*

Open All year except 10 days Feb and 1–28 Aug. Closed Sun evening and all day Wed.
Rooms 1 suite and 4 double – all with bath and telephone; TV in suite.
Facilities 2 sitting rooms, dining room. Courtyard. English spoken.
Location 1 km from town centre. Take *autoroute* exit for Valence South, then go towards centre. Parking.
Restriction Not suitable for &.
Credit cards Amex, Diners.
Terms [1985 rates] rooms 300–750 frs. Breakfast 40 frs; set lunch/dinner 300 and 380 frs.

LES VANS 07140 Ardèche   Map 10

Château du Scipionnet   *Tel* (75) 37.23.84
                                                  Telex 345790 CHAMCO

We should be glad to get new reports on this quiet hotel for lovers of peaceful seclusion, set in a valley near the northern foothills of the Cévennes. White-walled and red-roofed in the local manner, it is an imposing 17th-century *mas* (manor house), re-styled under Napoleon III as a château with ornate Second Empire decor in some rooms. It lies deep in the forest, in its own big park beside a river where you can bathe or go canoeing. "Comfortable and quiet (a *Relais du Silence*), very clean, excellent service; very welcoming and hospitable owners. The food was acceptable, with some outstanding dishes and enormous helpings. Marvellous packed lunches." *(Dr and Mrs Samuel I Cohen)*

Open 15 Mar–15 Oct.
Rooms 3 suites, 21 double, 2 single – 17 with bath, 9 with shower, all with telephone; 1 apartment on ground floor.
Facilities Salon, library, music room, bar, TV room, 3 dining rooms; terraces. Park with swimming pool, tennis, *boules*, river with beach, fishing. English spoken. &.
Location Off D104 in direction of Aubenas, 3 km N of Les Vans; hotel is signposted.

Credit card Access
Terms B&B: single 250 frs, double 280 frs; dinner, B&B (min 3 days): single 375
frs, double 535 frs; half-board (min 3 days): single 435 frs, double 640 frs. Set lunch
120 and 160 frs, set meals 160 frs; full alc 200 frs. Reduced rates and special meals
for children.

VARENGEVILLE-SUR-MER 76119 Seine-Maritime   Map 8

Hôtel de la Terrasse   *Tel* (35) 85.12.54
At Vastérival

This traditional red-brick Norman building with gables and red-tiled
roof, six miles from Dieppe, is recommended as "an excellent small
hotel, useful for a stopover before or after the car ferry. Very French,
catering largely for French clientele, but welcoming to English people.
Charming position in pine wooded garden overlooking the sea amidst
very pretty countryside. Inexpensive. The de la Fontaine family
provided very good Dieppoise food." *(Mrs D Suddards)* More reports
welcome.

Open 15 Mar–1 Nov.
Rooms 22 double, 6 single – 5 with bath, 10 with shower, all with telephone.
Facilities Large reception, salon, dining room; covered terrace. Garden with
tennis. Sea 5 minutes' walk. English spoken.
Location At Vastérival. 3 km NW of Varengeville by D75 and V013, and 11 km W
of Dieppe towards St Valéry.
Credit card Access.
Terms B&B: single 77–137 frs, double 110–218 frs; half-board: single 120–150 frs,
double 110–160 frs; full board: single 160–200 frs, double 150–220 frs. Set
lunch/dinner 60 and 110 frs; full alc 100 frs. Reduced rates and special meals for
children.

VARETZ-EN-LIMOUSIN 19240 Corrèze   Map 10

Château de Castel-Novel   *Tel* (55) 85.00.01
                                                    Telex CANOVEL 590065

Colette briefly lived and wrote in this handsome old grey-turreted,
ivy-covered, stone-walled feudal castle, set on a hill above the valley of
the Vézère gorges and the château of Pompadour, former home of a
grande dame even more famous than Colette in the annals of French
amorousness. As for the *Castel-Novel*, its renown is based today on
cuisine: *Michelin* rosette, two *Gault Millau toques*. Expensive, yes, and so
is the hotel, lavishly refurbished in traditional style – some of the
grander bedrooms have canopied four-posters. It has a holiday
atmosphere, with a big swimming pool and tennis courts. A report this
year: "Truly grand, run with tremendous style. Amazing bedrooms with
beautiful wall fabrics. The swimming pool was first rate and service
willing and friendly. Not cheap, but the rosette is deserved, and the
menu has all the best Perigourdin dishes." "A very romantic hotel with
fine antique country furniture and Laura Ashley-type wallpaper and
matching drapes, bedspreads; large vases of fresh flowers. Superb food
and wine – we had a mouthwatering salmon in oil and herbs. Terrace for
pre-dinner drink." *(Richard and Susan Faulkner, Gisa and Moti Slonim)* The
Livre d'Or has been signed by David Niven, Jacques Chirac, *et al.*

Open 8 May–20 Oct.
Rooms 5 suites, 23 double – all with bath and telephone; colour TV on request; some rooms with four-poster beds; 10 rooms in annexe.
Facilities Lift. Bar/salon, TV room, dining room, conference room. 12-acre gardens with swimming pool and tennis court (no charge). English spoken.
Location 10 km NW from Brive-la-Gaillarde on D901, just outside Varetz.
Restriction Not suitable for &.
Credit cards Amex, Diners, Visa.
Terms Suite 730–1,230 frs, double room 450–730 frs; dinner, B&B (5 days min) 620–872 frs per person; full board 145 frs per person added. Breakfast 50 frs; full alc 300 frs.

VENCE 06140 Alpes-Maritimes   Map 11

Hôtel Diana   *Tel* (93) 58.28.56
Avenue des Poilus

An efficient modern hotel near the centre of this lively little Provençal town. The rooms, although small, are beautifully designed and furnished, with well-equipped *cuisinettes* (washing up is part of the hotel's service). The underground garage is "difficult". Breakfasts are "generous" with "plenty of really good hot coffee" or merely "adequate". But "good value for money" is the general verdict. The hotel has no restaurant, but downtown you should try the romantic *Les Portiques* or the more down-to-earth *Farigoule* (where a reader dined well in a courtyard under the vines, at modest cost). Do not miss Matisse's lovely Chapel of the Rosary in Vence itself; nor the mountain drive to the north, the *circuit des clues*. (*John Hills, John Newnham, Kay and Neville Varley*)

Open All year.
Rooms 25 double – all with bath, telephone, cooking facilities, and baby-listening.
Facilities Lift. Salon, TV room, bar, library. Garden. English spoken. &.
Location 6 km from beach, 200 metres from town centre. Garage.
Credit cards Amex, Diners, Visa.
Terms Rooms 230–250 frs. Breakfast 25 frs. (No restaurant.)

Hôtel le Floréal   *Tel* (93) 58.64.40
Avenue Rhin-et-Danube   *Telex* 461613

Though modern and purpose-built, with little charm in the architecture, this hotel nonetheless has a cheerful, breezy holiday spirit, and the rooms are comfortable with good bathrooms. It is in the quiet western outskirts, about 800 metres from the centre, and there are good views from the upper bedrooms. "Comfortable, with friendly atmosphere; delightful well-kept garden with sizeable swimming pool. No restaurant, but excellent snacks available at lunch-time during the high season." Endorsed by an inspector this year. (*M T Harris; also Kay and Neville Varley*) Warning: be prepared for a 20-franc [1984] "car protection" charge, which the hotel assures its guests is "very necessary".

Open Apr–Oct.
Rooms 2 suites, 41 double – all with bath, telephone and radio; colour TV on request; some ground-floor rooms.
Facilities Lift, lounge, TV room, bar, breakfast room. Garden with swimming pool. Rocky beach 9 km, sandy beach 15 km. English spoken.

Location 800 metres from centre, on road to Grasse, near fire station.
Credit card Visa.
Terms B&B: single 300–360 frs, double 360–450 frs. (No restaurant, but light meals served round the swimming pool.)

VENDEUIL 02800 Aisne   Map 9

Auberge de Vendeuil   *Tel* (23) 66.85.22

Readers this year again praise this trim white-walled modern *auberge*, on the edge of a wood and just of the main N44 to Laon, 16 kilometres south of St-Quentin – a useful stop-over for anyone on the Calais/Reims route. "Most attractive; staff friendly and helpful. Bedrooms are small but efficiently planned; ours had white rough-cast walls, pink decor, nice pictures, efficient lighting. Bed large and comfortable; bathroom very small. Not much in the way of lounge seating, but the dining room is most attractive, with heavy wooden beams, wrought-iron-work, tables well spaced. À la carte we enjoyed excellent trout with tarragon sauce, noisettes of lamb, kidneys and sweetbreads, rich chocolate mousse. Service a bit slow, owing to large family parties of locals. Breakfasts are excellent." *Gault Millau toque* for its regional cuisine. One visitor this year found his bedroom "delightful" but the food disappointing. *(Padi Howard; also M W Forrest, Joan Powell)*

Open All year.
Rooms 2 suites, 20 double – all with bath, direct-dial telephone, radio, colour TV and baby-listening. 11 ground-floor rooms – 1 specially adapted for &.
Facilities 2 salons, bar, dining room; facilities for conferences and receptions. Zoological park 100 metres. Forest, river, lakes (fishing, boating, windsurfing) nearby.
Location 16 km S of St-Quentin, 7 km N of La Fère. Car park (locked at night).
Credit cards Amex, Diners, Visa.
Terms Rooms 210–235 frs. Breakfast 20.50 frs; set meals 78, 95, and 180 frs; full alc 200 frs. Reduced rates and special menu for children.

VENIZY 89210 Yonne   Map 9

Moulin des Pommerats   *Tel* (86) 35.08.04

A converted mill, now a small *Logis de France*, outside a little village on the northern confines of Burgundy. "Being so isolated, it is delightfully quiet, apart from the pleasant rush of the millstream which flows past the side of the hotel, and its attendant population of ducks. Warblers are also present in the grounds. The hotel is a small building, with a terrace for aperitifs. Most of the bedrooms are in adjoining converted domestic buildings and they are comfortable, all with private bathrooms. It is very much a family concern, with a friendly atmosphere. The restaurant overlooks a colourful garden and the food is conventional." Venizy is not far from the market town of St-Florentin and within easy reach of Sens and Auxerre (both with fine cathedrals) and of the Chablis wine country. *(Kenneth Garside, Mr and Mrs A W Barry, Kenneth Smith)*

Open All year except Christmas. Restaurant closed Sun pm and all day Mon in Dec, Jan and Feb.
Rooms 12 double in 2 annexes – all with bath and telephone; 2 ground-floor rooms.

Facilities Restaurant. Garden bordered by river Créanton (trout fishing); tennis. Riding, swimming nearby. Close to Abbey church of Pontigny, stately homes in Tanlay and Ancy-le-Franc and caves at Arcy-sur-Cure.
Location 3 km N of St-Florentin by D 30. Parking.
Credit cards Access, Diners, Visa.
Terms Rooms 280–320 frs. Breakfast 30 frs; set lunch/dinner 80–220 frs; full alc 170 frs. Reduced rates for children according to age; special meals.

VERDUN 55100 Meuse   Map 9

Hostellerie du Coq Hardi   *Tel* (29) 86.00.68
8 avenue de la Victoire   *Telex* 860464

As strategically situated for the tourist today as it was for the generals of 1914–18, Verdun lies just off the *autoroute* from Paris to Strasbourg and Frankfurt. The main Great War battlefields, well worth a visit, are in the hills some five kilometres to the north-east; others are to the north-west, including the big American cemetery of the Romagne-sous-Montfaucon with its 14,000 white marble tombstones. The *Coq Hardi*, very central, facing the Meuse, is a solid hostelry noted for its food (*Michelin* rosette, *Gault Millau* red *toque*, for such inventive dishes as canard au vinaigre de framboises). "Seen from outside, usual French scruffy. But the picturesque quality of the public rooms is achieved by the lavish use of what a priestly friend calls 'ecclesiastical tat', including three misericord seats just outside the ground-floor loos. Our front room was comfortable, spacious, and quiet. Dinner, on our wedding anniversary, was worthy of the occasion." *(Mrs Irene Robertson)*

Open 31 Jan–23 Dec. Restaurant closed Wed except public holidays.
Rooms 3 suites, 39 double – 20 with bath, telephone and TV.
Facilities Lift. Hall, restaurant; conference facilites. &.
Location Central, near river; front rooms may be noisy. Parking.
Credit cards Amex, Diners.
Terms [1985 rates] rooms with breakfast: single 115 frs, double 290 frs, suites 500 frs. Set lunch/dinner 135–250 frs.

VERVINS 02140 Aisne   Map 9

La Tour du Roy   *Tel* (23) 98.00.11
45 rue du Général-Leclerc

Vervins, near the Belgian frontier, is the capital of the Thiérarche, a pastoral stretch of apple orchards, streams and little green hills that contrasts pleasingly with the bare plains of most of this part of France. *La Tour du Roy* is equally inviting: a converted manor house built on the ramparts, run with warmth and skill by Claude and Annie Desvignes. Several readers praise the high quality at fair prices, especially in the restaurant (star in *Michelin*). One reader warns against the "musty" room above the kitchen but another writes: "Rooms comfortable in the nicest country house style; some noise from the busy bypass road unless it is cool enough to close double glazed windows. We enthused about the food: lapin en gelée, while salades croquantes aux guénaris (little river fish) was the most delicious dish I ate in France this summer. Dining room tending towards the twee, but exquisite presentation and quietly professional service." Madame does the cooking, using quality local produce. Husband Claude, front-of-house, is much praised for his helpfulness. *(J C and M A Godfrey, Bob Emmich, R Trotter)*

Open All year except 15 Feb–15 Mar.
Rooms 14 double, 1 single – 11 with bath, 4 with shower, all with direct-dial telephone, radio, tea-making facilities and baby-listening. 7 with TV; 2 rooms in annexe; 2 ground-floor rooms. Double-glazing.
Facilities Salon, TV room, restaurant; functions rooms. Lake and river fishing nearby. English spoken.
Location Vervins is off N2, 71 km N of Reims. Hotel is central.
Credit cards All major cards accepted.
Terms B&B: single 145 frs, double 250 frs; half-board: single 265 frs, double 490 frs; full board: single 385 frs, double 730 frs. Set lunch/dinner 120 frs; full alc 250 frs. Reduced rates and special meals for chidren.

VÉZAC 24220 Dordogne   Map 10

Rochecourbe Manoir-Hôtel   *Tel* (53) 29.50.79

A small manor house amid lush meadows, backed by gentle wooded hills, in one of the loveliest parts of the Dordogne valley, between Beynac and Domme. Visitors this year have endorsed earlier praise: "The peace and tranquillity of the country setting and the comfort of the rooms and bathrooms were superb. A spiral staircase in the tower leads from the quiet garden (reclining chairs for drinks) to the large dining room, and then up again to the seven bedrooms. From our room we looked across the valley to Beynac château, and the loudest noise was the bleating of sheep and the singing of birds. We cannot speak too highly of the comfort and kindness provided by M. and Mme Roger." "Delicious evening meals", runs one very recent report. Another, "charming and hospitable owners. We had a vast bedroom and large well-equipped bathroom. It is quiet, as it stands back from the road, though alas the noise of cars still exceeded that of sheep and birds." *(Dr and Mrs P H Tattersall, John and Elizabeth Hills, Denys Brown)*

Open 21 Apr–15 Oct.
Rooms 6 double, 1 single – 5 with bath, 2 with shower, all with telephone; 2 rooms in annexe.
Facilities Salon, TV room, dining room. Garden. 1 km from river; riding, tennis and swimming nearby; excursions to château, museums, caves etc.
Location 8 km from Sarlat on D57 between Sarlat and Beynac.
Restriction Not suitable for ♿.
Credit cards None accepted.
Terms Rooms: single occupancy 110 frs, double 190–340 frs. Breakfast 25 frs. (No restaurant.)

VÉZELAY 89450 Yonne   Map 10

L'Espérance   *Tel* (86) 33.20.45
St-Père   *Telex* 800005

Three kilometres east of Vézelay on the Avallon road, this small and smart restaurant-with-rooms recently acquired a third *Michelin* rosette (it already had four *Gault Millau* red *toques*) and is justly celebrated for serving inventive new-style cuisine (eg morilles farcies au blanc de poulet) in a gracious but unpretentious setting. Damask and silver in the dining room; antique furniture, strikingly pretty bedrooms. Our own readers rate it very highly too. "We were delighted. The hotel is a beautiful manor house with superb garden and grounds, with a river running through it. Friendly and courteous service; outstanding cuisine, and Marc Meneau, the *patron/chef*, calls at your table in the most pleasing manner. Terms are not low, but worth every franc." "The French equivalent to *Sharrow Bay* (q.v.)! Very sophisticated, catering for a smart, demanding clientele. The waiters perform a sort of ballet as they lift domed covers from your dishes. Notable saumon frais sauvage au beurre blanc. Some bedrooms are small (and creaking floorboards kept us awake) but others are large antique-furnished suites (more expensive) in a converted mill half a kilometre or so away. The garden has a rose arbour, and a stream (with ducks) lit up at night." A reader this year found the dining room's ambience strangely tense, rather than relaxed, but otherwise concurs with the general praise and notes that the better wines are very fairly priced. *(John and Padi Howard, Sally and Curtis Wilmot-Allistone, and others)*

Open All year except early Jan–early Feb. Restaurant closed midday Tue and Wed.
Rooms 5 suites, 20 double – 16 with bath, 4 with shower, all with telephone; 10 rooms with TV; 5 rooms in annexe; 3 ground-floor rooms.
Facilities Salon, restaurant. Garden with river. English spoken.
Location 3 km E of Vézelay on D957. Avallon road, at St-Père. Parking.
Credit cards Amex, Visa.
Terms [1985 rates] rooms: single occupancy 400 frs, double 700 frs. Breakfast 50 frs; set lunch 180 frs, dinner 350 frs.

Hôtel de la Poste et du Lion d'Or *Tel* (86) 33.21.23
Place du Champ-de-Foire *Telex* 800949

The medieval hill town of Vézelay, 50 kilometres south of Auxerre, is one of the most rewarding night stops for those driving up or down the A6. Its glory is the basilica of Ste Madeleine, once one of the great pilgrimage churches of France, a splendidly airy Romanesque building, with a wealth of magnificent stone carvings. The *Poste et Lion d'Or*, a former 18th-century coaching-inn, is again praised by readers this year. At the foot of the hill leading to the cathedral, it is the chief hotel of the town, with something of the atmosphere of a large handsome country house. Bedrooms look out over the countryside. "A hotel of character, enhanced by beautiful fresh flowers in the public rooms." "Staff friendly and willing, good bed linen, beautiful cooking." Several readers warn that bedroom walls are thin. *(Mrs M D Prodgers)*

Open Apr–3 Nov. Closed Wed except July–Sept. Restaurant closed Wed, and midday Thur.
Rooms 3 suites, 40 double, 3 single – 39 with bath, all with telephone. 10 with mono TV; 13 rooms in annexe.
Facilities Reception, salon, 2 restaurants; conference facilities. Small garden.
Location Central, at foot of hill leading to cathedral on S side of town. 13 km SW of Avallon; parking.
Credit cards Amex, Visa.
Terms (Excluding 15% service) rooms: 200 frs, double 450 frs; half-board: single 433 frs, double 915 frs. Breakfast 35 frs; set meals 180 and 220 frs.

Résidence Hôtel Le Pontot   *Tel* (86) 33.24.40
Place de la Mairie

This large and handsome old stone house in the village has for 30 years been the home of Charles Thum, an American architect, and Christian Abadie, a Frenchman: they have recently turned it into a very select bed-and-breakfast hotel. "I cannot praise these two charming gentlemen highly enough. They were friendly and courteous, and are running a hotel that is more like a home, where you can treat the house and gardens as your own. You enter through an arched doorway into a lovely walled garden, immaculately manicured. A stone-flagged spiral stairway leads up to the bedrooms which are furnished in exquisite taste and very spacious: opposite ours was a delightful lounge with views across Vézelay and the country below. We took breakfast in the salon before a log fire – the most beautifully prepared breakfast I have ever seen, with deep purple and gold Limoges china and excellent jams resting on dainty dishes with doilies. M. Abadie was fired with enthusiasm to help us create a really artistic photograph of it. An expensive hotel, but worth it. Plenty of good restaurants in the area." *(P H)*

Open 15 Mar–15 Nov.
Rooms 3 suites, 7 double – 9 with bath, 1 with shower, all with telephone, radio, coffee-making facilities.
Facilities Bar/reception, lounge, breakfast room. Walled garden with breakfast and bar service in fine weather. English spoken.
Location Centre of the village, but quietly situated.
Restriction Not suitable for &.
Credit cards None accepted.
Terms Rooms: 550–800 frs. Breakfast 50 frs. (No restaurant.) Reduced rates for children sharing parents' room.

VILLEFRANCHE-DU-PÉRIGORD 24550 Dordogne   **Map 10**

Hôtel du Commerce   *Tel* (53) 29.90.11

This attractive village lies in wooded country between the Dordogne and Lot rivers, and would make a good base for exploring either of these glorious valleys. A recent visitor confirms earlier praise for this simple, fairly unsophisticated family-run hotel: "An old building fronted by a deep arcade as so often in this area, it has been modernised and has a new top storey of rooms surrounding a small sun room. We had one of these which was spacious, with a good-sized bathroom. M. and Mme Fays and their family are welcoming. The restaurant has a red 'R' in *Michelin*, for good value – and certainly the food is good, the number of courses and the size of the helpings prodigious. The house wine too is excellent. This hotel is a pleasure to stay in; we have found nowhere to equal it in our travels." *(Sir Douglas Franks, Brian Beves)*

Open 1 Mar–15 Nov.
Rooms 28 double – 14 with bath, 8 with shower, all with telephone.
Facilities Salon with TV, reading room, bar, 2 restaurants; terrace. Small lake nearby with fishing rights and swimming. Tennis, riding, walking nearby.
Location In village on D60 between Fumel and Sarlat. 40 km NW of Cahors. Parking.
Restriction Not suitable for &.

Credit cards None accepted.
Terms B&B: single 168 frs, double 203 frs; dinner, B&B: single 218 frs, double 250 frs. Set meals 50–180 frs. Reduced rates and special meals for children.

VILLENEUVE-LÈS-AVIGNON 30400 Gard　　　　　　Map 11

La Magnaneraie　　　　　　　　　　　　　　　*Tel* (90) 25.11.11
37 rue Camp-de-Bataille

A flower-covered 15th-century inn, elegant, cosy and inviting, set among pine trees on a hillside above fascinating Villeneuve (see *Hostellerie le Prieuré* below). "A charming spot with a beautiful garden where dinner was delightful", "comfortable beds, wonderful food", "pleasant hosts" are recent verdicts. Each bedroom is done with country antiques and flowery wallpaper, and there is a small swimming pool. *(John Newham, Mary and Jim Alexander)* Good and interesting cuisine: eg duck salad and chicken with ginger.

Open All year.
Rooms 21 double – 16 with bath, 5 with shower, all with telephone, radio and TV. Tea-making facilities and baby-listening on request; 4 ground-floor rooms.
Facilities Salon with TV, restaurant, conference facilities. Garden with swimming pool and tennis. English spoken.
Location 3 km N of Avignon on Nîmes road. 500 metres from village. Parking.
Credit cards All major cards accepted.
Terms Rooms: single occupancy 250–300 frs, double 330–450 frs; dinner, B&B: single 420–480 frs, double 700–820 frs; full board: single 540–600 frs, double 920–1,020 frs. Breakfast 30 frs; set meals 130, 150 and 180 frs.

Hostellerie le Prieuré　　　　　　　　　　　　*Tel* (90) 25.18.20
7 place du Chapitre　　　　　　　　　　　　　　*Telex* 431042

A 14th-century priory on the edge of the old part of town, superbly converted and stylishly run by the affable Mille family as an elegant and luxurious little hotel. It is quiet and looks out over fields, the only blemish being a large ugly school building on one side. You can choose between a "characterful" bedroom in the old building (antique furniture, tiled floors) or a larger, more expensive one in the new annexe (wide balconies, big sofas). Amenities include a lovely garden with rose arbours, a tennis court, and a swimming pool and lido amid trees. Food is served either on the lawn or in the lovely beamed dining room: expensive and mainly classical, it carries a *Michelin* rosette, and our own readers too have again praised it warmly this year, though one found his dinner disappointing and the service poor. The town of Villeneuve contains almost as much of interest as Avignon itself, directly across the Rhône. Relics of its great age, when the Popes held sway in their Palace, include the gigantic Chartreuse, the Fort St-André, the municipal museum (superb painting by Charenton) and the church of Notre-Dame with its remarkable carved ivory statuette of the Virgin. The *Prieuré* is next to this church. *(A B X Fenwick)*

Open 15 Mar–15 Nov. Restaurant closed 1 May.
Rooms 9 suites, 20 double, 6 single – all with bath and telephone, most with colour TV; 2 annexes with 24 rooms; 1 ground-floor room and 15 accessible by ramp or lift. &.

Facilities Lift. 2 salons, bar, breakfast room, bridge room, dining room and outside dining facilities. Garden with 2 tennis courts and swimming pool. English spoken.
Location In town centre, behind the church. Car park.
Credit cards All major cards accepted.
Terms [1985 rates] rooms: single 200–500 frs, double 400–600 frs; suites 800–1,200 frs. Breakfast 45–80 frs; set lunch/dinner 220 frs.

Hôtel Résidence les Cèdres   *Tel* (90) 25.43.92
39 boulevard Pasteur, Bellevue

A small and friendly family hotel, in a cedar-shaded garden in the town's western outskirts. A sedate mansion, furnished partly in Louis XIV style, forms the main part of the hotel; other rooms are in bungalows in the garden. "We enjoyed the pool and the peace; the bungalows are attractive; an outdoor restaurant serves a good value menu." "We were welcomed by a delightful cigar-smoking *patronne*, a real character, and had a pleasant traditonal room in the main building." So ran two reports this year. An earlier visitor enjoyed the meals by the swimming pool and the squirrels, birds and fragrant blossom. One dissenter this year found fault with food, service and furnishings. *(Eileen Broadbent, D J Cheeseman, and others)*

Open All year. Restaurant closed Sun out of season.
Rooms 1 room for 4 people, 2 triple, 21 double, 1 single – 20 with bath, 5 with shower, all with telephone; colour TV for hire (35 frs per day). 15 rooms in bungalows in garden.
Facilities Salon with TV, restaurant. Garden, swimming pool. English spoken.
Location 3 km from Avignon, 1½ km W of town centre.
Restriction Not suitable for &.
Credit card Visa.
Terms Rooms: single 110 frs, double 220 frs. Breakfast 17 frs, *Gourmand* breakfast 38 frs; set lunch/dinner 55 and 68 frs. Special out-of-season rates – check with hotel.

VONNAS 01540 Ain   **Map 10**

Georges Blanc   *Tel* (74) 50.00.10
                                                          Telex 380776 GEBLANC

M. Blanc stands pre-eminent as ever among the great *patron/chefs* of France, and our own readers fully agree with his top ratings in the French guides – three rosettes and four red gables in *Michelin*, four red *toques* in *Gault Millau*. His chic little hotel/restaurant (formerly known as *La Mère Blanc)* stands beside the river Veyle on the edge of a quiet *village fleuri* between Mâcon and Bourg-en-Bresse, in pretty countryside. "Luxurious rooms, friendly atmosphere, food unforgettable" is the tenor of most recent reports. Some readers have found the service slowish – but who wants to be hurried through such splendid gastronomy? "We enjoyed the leisurely pace of the meals" is probably the more mature judgement. The bedrooms (some small and lacking in character) overlook the river; there are gardens and terraces and a swimming pool. Georges Blanc himself advises you on the choice of wine and dishes; he also owns vineyards and sells his own bottles at a shop beside the hotel.

A visitor new to *Blanc* writes engagingly: "I admit to being suspicious of hotels that announce themselves with enormous signs serveral miles down the road. It had better be good, I think. Here, the hotel *looks* unimpressive, though the welcome is warm. I am convinced that being unprepared for the experience of eating at *Blanc* actually increased my pleasure. I have never in my life had a meal remotely to compare with the six-course *dégustation* menu. By the time I had tasted a selection of cheeses I felt strongly that the huge road signs should have started 50 miles back, and after a selection from the sweets trolley I would be much in favour of signs between London and Dover!" *(T J David: also E Allen, Pat and Jeremy Temple)*

Open All year except 2 Jan–10 Feb. Restaurant closed Wed and Thur (except 15 June–15 Sept when open Thur).
Rooms 3 suites, 18 double – 27 with bath, 3 with shower, all with telephone, TV.
Facilities Lift. 2 aperitif lounges, breakfast room, dining room; open terrace on river Veyle. 2½-acre grounds with tennis court and swimming pool; helicopter landing pad. English spoken.
Location 20 km E of Mâcon. From N leave *autoroute* at Mâcon Nord; from S leave *autoroute* at Villefranche, then direction Châtillon-sur-Chalaronne, Neuville les Dames and Vonnas.
Credit cards Amex, Diners, Visa.
Terms (Excluding 12% service charge) double rooms 320–850 frs. Breakfast 45 frs; set meals 230–350 frs; full alc 420 frs.

HOTEL-GASTHOF ZUM BÄREN   MEERSBURG

ALT-DUVENSTEDT 2371 Schleswig-Holstein   **Map 12**

Töpferhaus
Am Bistensee   *Tel* (04338) 333
                                              Restaurant (04338) 222

Amazingly, this is the Guide's first rural entry for the whole of North
Germany, and a most welcome newcomer this year. It lies in the flattish

505

Schleswig countryside just east of the Hamburg/Flensburg *Autobahn*. "What a find! – the sort of place you dream about," says an inspector. "It's a lovely white-painted building with thatched roof, on a bluff above a lake and reached down a drive through woods. Everything inside superbly chosen and arranged – Persian rugs on the floor etc. Biggish bedroom, a real charmer. A faultless meal in the restaurant, including Labskaus, the traditional sailors' dish of North Germany and very cheap – a hash of pickled meat, herring and potato with fried eggs, tasting a bit like a pickled shepherd's pie. Supremely comfortable lounge with a sort of boudoir feel." In the corridor, a serve-yourself fridge full of drinks, based on an honesty system, the only one the Guide has ever found in Germany except at the *Monopteros*, Munich (q.v.). (*S A L*)

Open All year.
Rooms 14 – all with bath or shower and WC.
Facilities Hall, lounge, breakfast room, dining room. Garden. On lake; swimming and sailing. Riding nearby.
Location 12 km N of Rendsburg; leave *Autobahn* at Rendsburg-Nord if coming from S, at Owschlag if coming from N. Hotel is at S end of Bistensee (NB: do not go towards town of Bistensee on N side of lake).
Credit cards Possibly some accepted.
Terms [1985 rates] rooms: single 65–75 DM, double 108–135 DM. Breakfast 10 DM.

BAD BERGZABERN 6748 Rheinland-Pfalz   Map 12

Hotel-Pension Pfälzer Wald   *Tel* (06343) 1056
Kurtalstrasse 77

"A real effort is being made to promote this spa as a minor Baden-Baden," writes a visitor to this neat little town in a lush valley amid the rolling wooded hills of the southern Palatinate (Pfalz). It is at the southern end of the Pfalz "wine road" along the vineyards and only 10 kilometres from Wissembourg across the border in Alsace; there are some fine old castles nearby. The *Pfalzer Wald*, a small traditional family hotel, stands serenely alone beside a lake, with green hills behind – "It is in beautiful isolation and is modestly priced. Our double room with an excellent buffet breakfast cost only 90 DM [1985] for two; our evening meal with wine was about 18 DM each. The family who run the hotel are helpful and friendly, and with really comfortable large beds to sleep in we enjoyed our short stay." (*Richard O Whiting*)

Open All year except Feb.
Rooms 15 double, 12 single – all with shower and telephone.
Facilities Lounge/TV room, wine bar, dining room, restaurant; terrace. Large garden on lake; boating. English spoken.
Location About 1 km from centre of town; 38 km NW of Karlsruhe. Parking.
Credit card Access.
Terms B&B 35–45 DM; half-board: 50–60 DM; full board: 55–65 DM. Set lunch 9–20 DM; full alc 20-30 DM. Reduced rates and special meals for children.

"Full alc" means the hotel's own estimate of the price per person for a three-course dinner with half a bottle of house wine, service and taxes included. "Set meals" indicates the cost of fixed-price meals ranging from no-choice to table d'hôte.

BADEN-BADEN 7570 Baden-Württemberg   Map 12

Brenner's Park Hotel   *Tel* (07221) 3530
Schillerstrasse 6   *Reservations* in UK: (01) 409 0814
in USA: (800) 323 7500 or (212) 838 3110
Telex 0781261 BRHO

"Enter this leafy world. This domain of noble forebears. This globe of
dignity and grace. This shelter of the civilised. This citadel of comely
tradition. This refuge from the commonplace. . ." So runs the *Brenner*'s
blurb-song, on and on through 12 pages of the glossiest brochure in our
office library. Does a hotel of such singular opulence, Germany's
grandest, have a place in our Guide? Well, it does represent one sort of
ideal of excellence, though no longer a family hotel as it was for almost a
century. It has retained a style that matches the elegance of this
celebrated 19th-century spa: there is style in the courteous service, the
luxurious bedrooms . . . as in the days when Queen Victoria and so
many other sovereigns stayed here.

So ran our earlier entry, which inspectors this year have found to be not
far short of current reality: "It's really hard to fault save on a few details –
quite the best luxury hotel we know, in our modest experience. Spacious
and gracious public rooms, opening on to lawns that stretch to the
stream beside the Lichtentaler Allee where the kings and princes rode.
Service impeccable, genuinely friendly and warm, unsubservient. We
had a suite so vast that we kept losing each other in it; masses of fresh
fruit and flowers, bathroom with every amenity including complete sets
of Davidoff toiletry and a magnifying glass for shaving and making-up.
Only flaw in this paradise: one of the umpteen cupboard doors
squeaked. The main dining room, like a ballroom, is rather formal, but
there's a more intimate 'grill' with the same menu – conventional
upper-class food (eg pheasant, saddle of venison) with imaginative
touches (eg terrine of quail), very well done, worthy of its *Michelin*
rosette. The hotel belongs to an elderly German tycoon, the famous Dr
Oetker, grown rich from making down-market custards, jellies and
blancmanges. Probably few of his smart foreign hotel guests know they
are under the roof of a blancmange billionaire." (*J A C A; also Philip and
Mary Bush, Eric and Jean Lace, and others*)

Open All year.
Rooms 28 suites, 35 double, 46 single – all with bath, telephone, radio, colour TV
and video. Some ground-floor rooms.
Facilities Lifts; lobby, lounges, TV room, 3 bars, 2 restaurants; conference and
banqueting facilities. Dancing in lobby every night; concerts, gala dinners, fashion
shows; Beauty Farm comprising indoor swimming pool with sauna, solarium,
massage, fitness studio and hairdressing salon. Schwarzwald Clinic specialising in
internal disorders. Large park with 18-hole golf course, riding, hunting, fishing,
swimming, sailing, ballooning, waterskiing. English spoken. &.
Location Quietly situated in large park in the centre of Baden-Baden; parking and
garages. Hotel is signposted.
Credit cards None accepted.
Terms B&B: single 210–390 DM, double 230–490 DM. Set lunch/dinner 75–90 DM;
full alc 130 DM.

Hotel "Der Kleine Prinz"　　　　　　　　　　　*Tel* (07221) 3464
Lichtentaler Strasse 36
(entrance Du-Russel-Strasse)

A Victorian building in the centre of the spa, now a cosy hotel nicely balancing old and new in its furnishings. The new owners, Norbert and Edeltraud Rademacher, spent 22 years in America (he was Food Director of the *New York Hilton* and the *Waldorf Astoria*) and now their cuisine wins a red "*Karte*" in the German *Michelin* for "good food at moderate cost". An American visitor this year was impressed with the hotel: "All the rooms we saw were lovely. Ours, overlooking the town and ruined *Schloss*, was large, with pine furnishings and a fireplace; prints from *The Little Prince* hung on the walls. The bed was the most comfortable I slept on in Europe, and the bath the largest I have seen outside those marvellous tubs in England. The buffet breakfast was copious and the service excellent." (*Suzanne Bingham*) "A real charmer, excellent food." (*S A L*)

Open All year.
Rooms 13 double or suites, 4 single – 15 with bath, all with telephone, radio, colour TV and mini-bar, some with tea-making facilities; each room has a "special feature" eg open fire or balcony.
Facilities Lobby, bar, restaurant. English spoken.
Location Central, near Kurpark and convention hall. On corner of Lichtentaler Strasse and Du-Russel Strasse. Parking.
Restriction Not suitable for &.
Terms B&B: single 65–110 DM, double 130–250 DM; add 35 DM per person for dinner, B&B and 70 DM for full board.

BADENWEILER 7847 Baden-Württemberg　　　　　　　　**Map 12**

Park-Hotel　　　　　　　　　　　　　　　　　*Tel* (07632) 710
Ernst-Eisenlohrstrasse 6　　　　　　　　　　*Telex* 17763210

Set on a hillside facing the Rhine valley, and surrounded by orchards and vineyards, Badenweiler is one of the leading spas of the southern Black Forest, where disorders of the circulation and breathing system are treated. It has been a major spa since Roman days, as you can see from the fairly well-preserved Roman remains; today it has a smart *Kurhaus*, and a really lovely modern glass-roofed thermal swimming pool, as elegant as Baden-Baden's. There are good woodland walks in the area, fine views and castles to visit.

Anton Tchekov stayed in 1904 at the *Park*, largest of the spa's many hotels. It is an elegant, traditional place, dating from the 18th century, with baroque mirrors, balconies, a good swimming pool, and a garden where you can eat in summer. "Excellent and spacious. The restaurant was first class – food, service, decor, atmosphere. The hotel was central and quiet. Not many young people about." (*G M Morrison; also C F Colt*)

Open 1 Mar–10 Nov.
Rooms 10 suites, 40 double, 30 single – 70 with bath, 10 with shower, all with telephone, TV and baby-listening; some ground-floor rooms. 7 self-catering flats.
Facilities Lift; salons, bar, 2 restaurants, children's play room. Large grounds with terrace for sun-bathing and lawns; covered swimming pool, solarium and massage; tennis court. Golf and pony-trekking nearby. English spoken.
Location Central; town is mid-way between Basel (to the S) and Freiburg to the N

and just E of Mullheim. Leave *Autobahn* E4 at Neuenberg/Mullheim exit. Garage and parking facilities.
Credit cards Access, Amex, Visa.
Terms B&B: single 115–155 DM, double 170–250 DM; dinner, B&B: single 175–215 DM, double 290–370 DM; full board: single 195–235 DM, double 320-410 DM. Full alc, lunch and dinner 20–60 DM. 3-week stays with half-board for the price of 2 weeks from 17 Jun–10 Aug. Tennis and golf weekends. 50% reduction for children under 12; special meals.

BAD HERRENALB 7506 Baden-Württemberg   Map 12

Mönchs Posthotel   *Tel* (07083) 2002
Doblerstrasse 2   *Telex* 7245123

Connoisseurs of South Germany are as enthusiastic as ever about this smart and stylish old half-timbered flower-decked post-hotel, at a crossroads in the centre of a sizeable Black Forest spa town. The setting is less urban than this may suggest, for the hotel also has an outdoor swimming pool and large and graceful gardens leading to a river. "Expensive and elegant, yet also quite intimate and cosy", runs one 1985 report; "our large bedroom was superbly equipped. The lovely dining room has beamed ceilings, wood panelling and several discreet alcoves. The food, beautifully prepared and presented, tended towards *nouvelle cuisine* and was worthy of its *Michelin* rosette. Service was smooth and affable but not very informed: the local girls could not explain many of the dishes, even in German. The breakfast buffet was the most lavish we have found in Germany – and that's saying something. Fruits, cream, Muesli, cheeses, meats and eggs galore. All in all, a romantic place – despite the prevalence of rich businessmen." Other visitors this year thought the breakfast not so lavish, and service, both at dinner and breakfast, deplorably slow. (*K and S M-S, R S Ryder, J A and K S*)

Open All year.
Rooms 10 suites, 25 double, 15 single – 40 with bath, 10 with shower, all with telephone and colour TV; 9 rooms in annexe.
Facilities Hall, salon, TV room, bar, restaurant, dining rooms, conference facilities, breakfast terrace; beauty parlour. Garden with heated swimming pool; tennis and 9-hole golf course close by. English spoken.
Location Central. Parking. (Warning: rooms on the road can be noisy.)
Restriction Not suitable for &.
Credit cards Amex, Diners.
Terms B&B: single 110–130 DM, double 160–170 DM; dinner, B&B: single 140–160 DM, double 220–255 DM; full board: single 150–170 DM, double 240–275 DM. Set lunch/dinner 35–60 DM; full alc 50-70 DM.

Waldhotel Sonnenblick   *Tel* (07083) 27 49
Im Wiesengrund 2, Bad Herrenalb-Gaistal

"This modern chalet-style *pension* stands on a steep slope on the edge of the hamlet of Gaistal, up a wooded valley two kilometres outside Bad Herrenalb. In October, I had breakfast in warm sun on the terrace, facing a panoramic Black Forest view. My clean, simple room cost only 30 DM [1984], inclusive of a good breakfast served by the friendly Waidner family – and when I found the next day in Munich that I'd left my new jacket in the cupboard, I phoned them and they sent it by the next post. Typical German efficiency and honesty. No meals, save cold snacks of the Abendbrot type: but you can eat well in town. Recommended for peaceful rural *Gemütlichkeit*." (*J A C A*)

Open 21 Dec–19 Oct.
Rooms 25 – all with bath or shower, many with balcony.
Facilities Lounges, TV room, breakfast room. Garden and terrace. Tennis, swimming and winter sports nearby. Bad Herrenalb is a health spa.
Location At Gaistal, 2 km S of town.
Credit cards None accepted.
Terms [1985 rates] B&B: single 30–38 DM, double 68–88 DM. (No restaurant but cold suppers available.)

BAMBERG 8600 Bavaria

Hotel Sankt Nepomuk   *Tel* (0951) 2 51 83
Obere Mühlbrücke 9

"During six months spent touring Germany in 1985, this was our happiest discovery of all – a really enchanting and unusual hotel, newly converted from a half-timbered 17th-century millhouse, standing on stilts on the river Regnitz between two rushing millraces. It is right next to the old quarter of Bamberg, one of the loveliest of Bavarian towns, its quaint narrow streets and Baroque palaces marvellously unscathed by wartime bombing. The *Sankt Nepomuk* belongs, surprisingly, to an affluent Catholic foundation which has managed the conversion with fastidious taste. Everything is open-plan, stylish and spacious, notably the big restaurant on two floors, with handsome fireplace, curving stone stairway, and picture-windows where we gazed at the river as the light faded. Here the cooking is ambitious and varied but not pretentious, and very good indeed, with the accent on local Frankish specialities – fresh Pfifferlinge (chanterelles), trout with almonds, venison with Spätzle. As well as the Frankish wines, we enjoyed Bamberg's curious 'smoky beer', made from smoked malt, and tasting, yes, very smoky.

"Mainly this is a restaurant, but the ten bedrooms are stylish too. Ours, very comfortable, was delightfully decorated with light wood and pale-green fabric wallpaper. The special glass of our bathroom window gave out a dazzling prismatic light effect; glow-worms darted and shone above the river; and we were lulled to sleep by the therapeutic roar of the millrace – to awake next day to a sumptuous buffet breakfast that included cherries, strawberries, smoked ham and Camembert, served in a lovely room with cheerful modern murals of local scenes. The young couple who run the place on a tenancy basis, the Grüners (he chef, she manageress), were most welcoming, as were all their young staff. An original, magical hotel, like a lovely dream – and with very reasonable prices, both for bed and board." (*J A C A, K S*) "Superb cooking and excellent service," adds another recent visitor (*D Quirk*)

Open All year. Restaurant closed Mon.
Rooms 10 double – all with bath or shower, telephone, radio and mini-bar.
Facilities Lift; reception, café, 2 restaurants; conference facilities.
Location Central. Do *not* try to drive car up to hotel (narrow streets); leave it in hotel's car park in Nonnenbrücke (street) 150 metres to E., across river.
Credit cards Access, Amex, Diners.
Terms [1985 rates] room with breakfast: single occupancy 65–90 DM, double 115–125 DM, 3-bedded 150 DM. Alc meals (excluding wine) 25–50DM.

BAYREUTH 8580 Bavaria	Map 12

Bayerischer Hof *Tel* (0921) 2 20 81
Bahnhofstrasse 14 *Telex* 642737

"Still a good place" is this year's verdict from faithful admirers of the *Bayerischer Hof*, confirming their earlier account: "It has probably the best facilities of Bayreuth's hotels. The staff are as full of old-fashioned courtesy as ever. We have stayed there in the summer, and in the depths of snowy winter; and have appreciated comfortable, elegant rooms, an excellent heated indoor swimming pool, the open-air terrace extension of the top-floor dining room, the magnificent help-yourself breakfast, and luncheon and dinner menus which include plenty of local dishes. Franconian wine occupies a fairly large section of the wine list, and justifiably so. The hotel is in the centre of the town and one minute's walk from Bayreuth railway station, but the trains are never heard. During the *Wagnerfest* the hotel is likely to be full of visiting notables, but at other times the town resumes its normal quiet rhythm, with music in the old churches and the baroque opera house, and its surrounding countryside of rolling hills, low mountains and forest slopes and slumbering villages." (*John and Eileen Spencer*)

Open All year. Restaurant closed Sun.
Rooms 36 double, 26 single – 34 with bath, 21 with shower, all with telephone, some with TV.
Facilities Lift. Hans Sachs Room, TV room, Spanish-style cellar restaurant, roof-garden terrace and restaurant, conference room. Indoor swimming pool, sauna. Tiny garden. English spoken.
Location Central, 50 metres from station. Garage.
Restriction Not very suitable for &.
Credit cards All major cards accepted.
Terms B&B: single 55–95 DM, double 100–160 DM. Set lunch 17.50–24 DM, dinner 45–56 DM, full alc 32 DM.

BAYREUTH-SEUBLITZ 8580 Bavaria	Map 12

Waldhotel Stein *Tel* (0921) 90 01

"Seublitz (follow the signs to Eremitage) is a pretty farming village, six kilometres east of Bayreuth and above it, so you see the floodlit *Festspielhaus* from your window. Frau Stein and her daughter run this fabulously peaceful modern hotel like a well-run private house. One chambermaid was in the *Meistersinger* chorus, and this shows the standard of all the staff. Two swimming pools and acres of grass and trees to laze in. Many rooms are bedsitters with balconies; bathrooms large and luxurious. Food excellent. We stayed a week and could have stayed for ever." Some rooms are bungalows in the big garden, with woods all round. (*D Quirk*)

Open All year except 1–24 Dec.
Rooms 8 suites, 35 double, 5 single – all with bath or shower, telephone, TV and mini-bar; many with balcony. Many in bungalows in the grounds. Some ground-floor rooms with large bathrooms.
Facilities Tea/sitting room, restaurant. Conference facilities. Indoor heated swimming pool, sauna, solarium and massage. Large grounds with unheated swimming pool, adjoining extensive forest. English spoken.

Location 6 km E of Bayreuth, near Seublitz village.
Credit cards All major cards accepted.
Terms B&B: single 58–78 DM, double 96–130 DM, suite 240 DM. Children 20 DM per day.

BEILSTEIN 5591 Rheinland-Pfalz   Map 12

Hotel Haus Lipmann   *Tel* (02673) 1573

Beilstein is a very attractive fortified village in the Mosel valley, famous for its last overlord, Metternich, whose castle stands on the hill above. To the south is the wooded plateau of the Hunsrück, where Edgar Reitz set and filmed his masterpiece, *Heimat*. "One of the most appealing small family-run hotels we have found in years," says a recent visitor to the *Lipmann;* "it was outstanding value for the comfort and the simple but delicious food offered." Others concur: "The Lipmanns' wine and hotel business was founded in 1795 and their welcome and service reflect this tradition. The house wine is superb, the food excellent, prices reasonable and the old-world charm unbeatable." Rooms in the main house are preferred to those in the modern annexe. (*Eileen Broadbent, J M Beaton, Dr Philip Evans, B W Ribbons, and others*)

Note: Frau Lipmann suggests phoning rather than writing for reservations.

Open 15 Mar to 15 Nov.
Rooms 20 double, 4 single – 1 bath, 20 with shower; 18 rooms in annexe.
Facilities Restaurant, conference/functions facilities; wine cellar (wine tastings held); terrace on Mosel. English spoken.
Location Central, near Market place. Parking.
Credit cards None accepted.
Terms [1985 rates] B&B: single 28–45 DM, double 52–75 DM. Alc meals (excluding wine) 18-45 DM.

BERLIN 1000   Map 12

Hotel Ambassador   *Tel* (030) 219 02
Bayreutherstrasse 42, Berlin 30   *Telex* 184 259

"Very central, 500 metres east of the top of the Ku'Damm and the gaunt semi-ruined memorial church that Berliners call 'the gaping tooth'. It's a large modern tourist hotel, part of a chain that takes package tours – not at first sight Guide material, but there's a real holiday ambience and amenities. We spent three weeks here in a chilly April [1985] and were thrilled by the top-floor heated swimming pool with 'tropical' foliage and decor and a potent water-blowing machine that had the effect of a jacuzzi. This machine was useful for toning up the tummy muscles which somewhat suffered under the weight of the hotel's cornucopian buffet breakfasts, complete with scrambled eggs and bacon ad lib. Our bedroom was well equipped, though on the small side and with dreadful bed lights, so that in bed you could read *Bild Zeitung*'s headlines but not its text (terrible deprivation). Service rather impersonal and mechanical but slick (the chambermaids had been taught to lay out our pyjamas in a different style each evening, sometimes shaped like a rabbit, sometimes like a dancer). Useful tray of boiled sweets in foyer.

Expensive and highly rated fish restaurant, which we didn't try; lots of good cheap *Kneipe* (pubs) all around. Rooftop views: even in fog you can see into Honecker's realm." (*J A*)

Open All year. *Conti-Fischstüben* restaurant closed Sun.
Rooms 3 suites, 155 double, 42 single – 110 with bath, 90 with shower, all with direct-dial telephone, radio, colour TV and mini-bar.
Facilities Lift; lounge/bar, TV in large entrance hall, 2 restaurants; "tropical" swimming pool on eighth floor with jetstream, solarium, sauna, poolside bar and roof garden; conference and function facilities. Hairdressing salon. Restaurants and bar suitable for &, bedrooms for partially &. English spoken.
Location Central. 2 minutes' walk from Kurfurstendamm and 5 minutes from the zoological gardens. Parking lot and underground car park.
Credit cards All major cards accepted.
Terms B&B: single 125–170 DM, double 160–220 DM; for half-board add 30 DM. Special stay and sight-seeing rates. Full alc 28 DM.

Hotel Belvedere   *Tel* (030) 826 10 77
Seebergsteig 4, Grunewald, Berlin 33

The smart residential suburb of Grunewald, aptly named, is some four kilometres from the city centre and next to a forest that leads to the Havel lake. It's a setting that puts paid to the false image of Berlin as a claustrophobic city without space or greenery. Here inspectors this year unearthed this "big turn-of-the-century villa in its own gardens, in a quiet and leafy side-street. Stylish bedrooms with antique cane and wood furniture; some wallpaper ferocious, some less so. Public rooms have the air of a bourgeois private house. Peaceful, relaxed, unpretentious. Breakfast in a funny conservatory-like annexe." (*S A L, I E R M*) Main meals, on which we have no reports, are served to residents. Visit the fabulous Dahlem museums, quite close by.

Open All year. Restaurant open to residents only.
Rooms 11 double, 6 single – some with bath, some with shower, all with direct-dial telephone and TV.
Facilities Salon, breakfast room, dining room.
Location In Grunewald, 4 km SW of city centre.
Credit cards Access, Diners.
Terms [1985 rates] B&B: single 56–96 DM, double 87–122 DM.

BOCHUM 4630 Nordrhein-Westfalen   **Map 12**

Hotel Schmidt   *Tel* (0234) 3 70 77 or 31 22 88
Drusenbergerstrasse 164

"The sprawling city of Bochum (population 415,000) is in some ways the intellectual capital of the Ruhr, with one of Europe's finest and most famous theatres, a fascinating museum of mining, and a large (and hideous) new university. Lovely green valleys meander south towards the valley of the Ruhr where the disused coal-mines have been tidied out of sight. In the leafy southern suburbs is the *Schmidt*, a welcoming little inn. Friendly Frau Schmidt has bright yellow hair and a bright green parrot ever on her shoulder – and this colour scheme rather sets the tone for the hotel's dubious kitschy decor. But the bedrooms are practical and quiet, and cheap, and the breakfast satisfactory. Good, quite elegant restaurant under separate management." (*J A*)

Open All year. Restaurant closed Sun midday.
Rooms 9 suites, 12 double, 19 single – all with shower. Some on ground floor.
Facilities Small salon, TV room, restaurant, bowling alley; terrace. Lake nearby. English spoken.
Location 2 km S of centre of Bochum which is 17 km E of Essen. Parking.
Credit card Amex.
Terms B&B: single 47 DM, double 70 DM. Full alc 20–30 DM.

BONN 5300 Nordrhein-Westfalen   Map 12

Hotel und Restaurant Mertens   *Tel* (02 28) 0 22 21 or 47 44 51
Rheindorferstrasse 134, Bonn 3 (Beuel)

"If you want to escape the diplomatic cocktail-party chatter of Bad Godesberg, and the high prices of central Bonn where government is a mono-industry, then just cross the river to the quiet suburb of Beuel and you could be in any little friendly Rhineland town. We spent 10 days here at the *Mertens* in 1985, on a journalistic mission to Bonn, and were very content. The helpful Mertens family runs a pleasant little modern hotel in a quiet street – all very clean, tidy and practical in the best German manner, and prices are modest. Local singing clubs use the back restaurant, but not late at night. Honest German home cooking, and how appetising that is: for about 12 DM, a good pork Schnitzel with egg, a mound of crispy pommes frites, salad, and good Kölsch beer, the kind they drink in millions of gallons at the Cologne carnival." (*J A*)

Open All year. Restaurant closed Tue.
Rooms 10 double, 4 single – 5 bath, 8 with shower, all with direct-dial telephone.
Facilities Salon/bar, TV room, dining room. Rhine 500 metres. English spoken.
Location In Beuel, E of Rhine; 2 km from centre of Bonn. Parking.
Restriction Not suitable for &.
Credit card Diners.
Terms B&B: single 45 DM, double 80 DM. Full alc 15–25 DM.

Hotel Schaumberger Hof   *Tel* (0228) 36 40 95 or
Am Schaumberger Hof 10, Bonn 2 (Bad Godesberg)   36 31 13

"A solid, spacious, pleasantly old-fashioned hotel, formerly a wine tavern, in a splendid position right on the Rhine at Bad Godesberg – a paved promenade along this famous stretch of river goes right past the hotel, with views of the Siebengebirge and the Drachenfels. A pity that my bed was so hard (a common German failing – they think it healthier) and the pillow so small; breakfast too was uninteresting, by German standards. Otherwise, the place makes a good choice for anyone seeking to avoid the soulless modernism and high prices of down-town Bonn. Big salons; restaurant overlooking the Rhine." (*J A C A*)

Open All year.
Rooms 34 rooms – all with bath and telephone.
Facilities Salons, conference rooms, restaurant; terrrace.
Location On river, 1½ km NE of central Bad Godesberg, 4 km SE of central Bonn. Private parking.
Restriction Probably not suitable for &.
Credit cards None accepted.
Terms Not available.

BREMEN-HORN 2800   Map 12

Landhaus Louisenthal   *Tel* (0421) 23 20 77
Leher Heerstrasse 105, Bremen 33   *Telex* 246925 HOTEL

An 18th-century mansion in a garden, with a neat white Italianate facade, has been converted into a stylish little family-run hotel. It is in Horn, a north-east suburb of Bremen, near the *Autobahn* and with bus and tram services passing the door, but quiet. "Excellent value and comfort and attractive grounds." "We ate a delicious light supper on a terrace overlooking the garden." But a note of caution this year: "Menu fairly basic (vegetables tinned) but adequate." (*Betty Hooper, Paul Harris, Iain Elliot*) Hanseatic Bremen has a splendid breezy, quirky atmosphere: don't miss the stunning Renaissance *Rathaus*, better than Bruges, and the quaint boutiques of the charming traffic-free Böttcherstrasse.

Open All year.
Rooms 1 suite, 30 double, 12 single – 3 with bath, 40 with shower, all with telephone; baby-listening; some with radio and TV. 4 rooms in annexe.
Facilities Salon, TV room, dining room; conference facilities. Garden with terrace. English spoken. & (ramps, extra-large baths).
Location 6 km NE of centre of Bremen. Garage and car park.
Restriction Not suitable for &.
Credit cards All major cards accepted.
Terms B&B: single 49.50–60 DM, double 84–130 DM; dinner, B&B 62–110 DM; full board 75–136 DM. Set lunch from 17 DM, dinner 15 DM; full alc 25 DM.

CELLE 3100 Niedersachsen   Map 12

Fürstenhof – Restaurant Endtenfang   *Tel* (05141) 20 10
Hannoversche Strasse 55–56   *Telex* 925293

North Germany is full of good hotels still unknown to the Guide, so we were glad to get word this year of the smart and rather formal *Fürstenhof*. It stands on a main road near the centre of the very historic old city of Celle where the Guelph princes ruled (imposing *Schloss*, lovely *Altstadt* of timbered houses undamaged in the war). "The hotel successfully combines traditional character and modern amenities. One part is a 17th-century palace, housing the public rooms; bedrooms are in a new glass-fronted building, and between the two is a little garden where drinks are served. Our room was pleasant, with floral wallpaper and a big balcony. The lounge, very comfortable, is in 'baroque' style. There are two restaurants – a cheaper *Stübe* and the more formal *Endtenfang* where we found excellent food and service: lots of eponymous duck dishes such as duck fillets with rhubarb sauce, very good." (*K and S M-S*)

Open All year. *Stübe* closed midday and Sun.
Rooms 75 rooms – all with bath and shower, telephone, radio, TV and baby-listening.
Facilities Lift; lounge, bar, beer-cellar, 2 restaurants; conference and functions facilities; indoor swimming pool, solarium, sauna. Garden and terrace; bowling.
Location Central. Parking.
Credit cards Amex, Diners.
Terms [1985 rates] B&B: single 90–190 DM, double 150–290 DM. Alc meals (excluding wine): *Stübe* 20–43 DM, *Endtenfang* 31–80 DM.

COLOGNE 5000 Nordrhein-Westfalen   Map 12

Hotel Bristol   *Tel* (0221) 12 01 95/96/97
Kaiser Wilhelm Ring 48, Köln 1   *Telex* 8881146 HOBR

New to the Guide, a useful hotel centrally situated, on the inner city ring road, 700 metres from the cathedral. "Remarkably good value. Family run, with helpful staff. On the fifth floor I was almost completely sheltered from noise. The bedroom had old intricately carved wooden furniture, but good modern bathroom with hair dryer. Lovely old furniture in the hall. No restaurant, but one can order soup, cold dishes etc, and eat them in the ground-floor sitting area where, alas, the TV is distracting." (*Linda Shaughnessy*) Lower front rooms may be noisy. Some rooms have *Himmelbetten* ("heaven beds" – four-posters with roofs). In Cologne, you should visit the *Kneipe*, local taverns where you eat indifferently and drink copiously in an ultra-boisterous (at least at *Karneval* time) ambience: *Alt Köln* and *Brauhaus Sion*, both near the cathedral, are among the most typical.

Open All year, except Christmas and New Year.
Rooms 15 double, 29 single – 28 with bath, 16 with shower, all with telephone, some with TV.
Facilities Lift; hall, lounge, conference room, *Bauernstube*. English spoken
Location Central, near cathedral. Garage parking adjacent.
Restrictions Not suitable for &.
Credit cards All major cards accepted.
Terms Rooms: single 95–145 DM, double 155–215 DM. Reduced rates for children. (No restaurant.)

Haus Lyskirchen   *Tel* (0221) 23 48 91
Filzengraben 26–32, Köln 1   *Telex* 08885449

A six-storey modern hotel in the centre; rooms are functional rather than elegant. "It is in a quiet side street just off the Rhine bank, within walking distance of the cathedral, yet mercifully far enough away from its bells which plague guests of the expensive Dom *hotel. The staff were exceptionally helpful. It was useful to have a restaurant (though with a limited menu) to eat at when we were too tired from sightseeing to dine out. The best thing of all was the superb swimming pool. There is also a garage and a bowling alley, and although there are rooms for conferences, it is basically a nice small hotel, useful for the businessman and visitors like ourselves." (Mrs M Libbert)*

Readers have endorsed this entry, though one arrived to find the porter drunk, and next morning a waitress had hysterics at the breakfast table. An isolated interruption in normal service? We hope and believe so.

Open All year except 23 Dec–1 Jan. Restaurant closed Sun and public holidays.
Rooms 2 suites, 59 double, 34 single – 12 with bath, 83 with shower, all with telephone and colour TV.
Facilities Reception, bar, 2 restaurants; conference facilities. Bowling alley, indoor heated swimming pool. English spoken.
Location Near river, just S of railway station; 5 minutes' walk from centre. Large garage (8 DM).
Credit cards All major cards accepted.
Terms B&B: single 89–130 DM, double 160–250 DM. Children up to 12 free.

DEIDESHEIM 6705 Rheinland-Pfalz   Map 12

Deidesheimer Hof   *Tel* (06326) 18 11
Am Marktplatz   *Telex* 0454804 HAHN

Deidesheim is a well-known wine village in the heart of the Pfalz vineyards, on the *Weinstrasse* west of Mannheim. The hotel, in the village centre, is part of the Romantik-Hotel association, full of Germanic prettiness and good cheer: "Wonderful. Its best feature is the wood-panelled wine bar/restaurant where you can sample selected local wines and eat the local food with the locals. The hotel rooms vary and you should ask for one at the back: mine was, and it was quiet and comfortable with huge double bed and enormous bathroom. The hotel is characterful and friendly." "Modern, very attractive and atmospheric." (*D M Callow, Dr Bill and Lisa Fuerst*)

Open 5 Jan–22 Dec.
Rooms 10 suites, 13 double, 3 single – 10 with bath, 16 with shower, all with telephone and radio, 10 with TV.
Facilities Salons, wine bar (occasional wine-tastings), restaurants. Skittle alley, terrace. Golf, swimming nearby. English spoken.
Location Central (back rooms quietest). Parking.
Restriction Not suitable for &.
Credit cards All major cards accepted.
Terms B&B: single 48–78 DM, double 96–190 DM. Set meals 30–100 DM; full alc 37 DM. Extra bed for child in parents' room 32 DM; special children's menu.

DORTMUND 4600 Nordrhein-Westfalen   Map 12

Romberg-Park Hotel   *Tel* 71 40 73
Am Rombergpark 67, Dortmund 50 (Brünninghausen)

"A dining-terrace facing a small lake, enclosed by neat lawns, rhododendrons and majestic copper-beeches; joggers in the May morning sunlight; birdsong, and the gentle breakfast-burble of Japanese businessmen. And where are we? Near the heart of the industrial Ruhr, in the south Dortmund suburbs, with decaying steel-mills just out of sight. The Ruhr is far more green and cultured than its image, as we found. This square modern hotel, on the edge of a muncipal park, is no architectural marvel but pleasantly family-run, with willing service by trainees from the adjacent hotel school. Our made-to-measure bedroom was light and spacious, with a wall of stripped pine and a balcony facing the lake. The dining room lacks decor and could be dull in winter, but in summer its wide French windows open on to the terrace and here we enjoyed excellent German/international cooking (eg trout in cream sauce) at fair prices with good Dortmund beer. As elsewhere, hotel school food is above average and inventive." (*J A*)

Open All year except 2 days at Christmas.
Rooms 8 double, all with bath, 24 single, all with shower. All with direct-dial telephone, radio and TV.
Facilities Lift; large lounge, dining room. Terrace for al fresco meals. &.
Location 4 km S of central Dortmund, off *Autobahn* 54.
Credit cards Amex, Diners, Visa.
Terms B&B: single 89 DM, double 139 DM. Set lunch/dinner 19 and 29 DM; full alc 30–40 DM.

DÜSSELDORF 4000   Map 12

Hotel Schnellenburg   *Tel* (0211) 43 41 33
Rotterdamerstrasse 120, Düsseldorf 30   *Telex* 8581828 BURG

"In an ugly commercial city with few hotels of character, this one at least
is a bit unusual. It's not central, being four kilometres north-west of the
centre, but it's in a fine position on the Rhine, almost next door to the
Trade Fair centre and 10 minutes' drive from the airport. It's a low white
building by the main road, with iron grilles on the windows, and it looks
more Spanish than German; a sort of superior motel. Nice quiet rooms,
some overlooking the river. Ours was fine, save for a faulty sliding door.
Cheerful service and a good buffet breakfast that included salami and
prunes." (*J A, Sam Eadie*)

The restaurant, separately managed, was closed in 1985: but you can
eat well nearby at the *Alter Exerzierplatz* in Stockum or the *Haus am Rhein*.

Open All year except Christmas to New Year.
Rooms 2 suites, 39 double, 11 single – all with bath, telephone, radio and colour
TV. Some ground-floor rooms.
Facilities Lounge, residents' bar, restaurant, garden. English spoken. Possibly
suitable for &.
Location 4 km N of centre of Düsseldorf, on the Rhine. Parking.
Credit cards All major cards accepted.
Terms B&B: single 120–150 DM, double 160–220 DM. Full alc 45 DM. 50%
reduction for children.

EISENSCHMITT-EICHELHÜTTE 5561 Rheinland-Pfalz   Map 12

Hotel Molitors Mühle   *Tel* (06567) 5 81

Eisenschmitt is a village in hilly forested country, between the Mosel
valley to the south and the Eifel massif to the north. Here the Molitor
family have owned and run their *Mühle*, a converted millhouse, for over
a hundred years – "the setting is idyllic," writes a Guide reader, "by a
small lake, with marvellous forest walks (signposted) winding their way
along a stream near the garden. The ultimate delight is to sit on the
terrace by the lake and watch the sun set and the trout rise while
enjoying a bottle of local Mosel. The food is imaginatively cooked, not
expensive, and is eaten in the former iron foundry. The owner and his
son speak English and will lend you rods for fishing. A drawback is that
a US Air Force base is 12 miles away, and the noisy overhead flights
during the day can be a nuisance." (*Duncan Graham*) Confirmed by
S A L: "Delightful and relaxed, not smart but good value."

Open Feb–end Nov, 26 Dec–10 Jan.
Rooms 3 suites, 22 double, 10 single – 3 with bath, 30 with shower and WC, 33 with
telephone, 10 with TV. 5 rooms in annexe.
Facilities Lounge, TV room, bar, dining rooms, indoor swimming pool. Garden
by lake; boating, tennis, mini-golf, barbecues in summer. English spoken.
Location In the hamlet of Eisenschmitt-Eichelhütte, 54 km N of Trier and 17 km
from Wittlich.
Restriction Not suitable for &; access to restaurant only.
Credit cards None accepted.
Terms B&B 40–49 DM; dinner, B&B 52–61 DM; full board 60–69 DM. Set lunch/
dinner 18–25 DM; full alc 30–40 DM. Reduced rates, special meals for children.

ETTLINGEN 7505 Baden-Württemberg   Map 12

Hotel Erbprinz   *Tel* (07243) 1 20 71
                                                      Telex 0782-848

Ettlingen is a pleasant little town between Karlsruhe and the foothills of the Black Forest, where the *Autobahnen* from Frankfurt and Stuttgart converge on their way to Basel. In this workaday setting, in fact in the town centre, is the anything but workaday *Erbprinz*, worthy indeed of a Crown Prince and one of South Germany's most sleek and luxurious smaller hotels – "Very comfortable, old established: our room had excellent furnishings, with a balcony and a large marble bathroom. Staff were friendly and used our name all the time; some of them are French, as are many of the guests. Excellent, beautifully presented food (*Michelin* rosette) in the large, well-known restaurant, wood-panelled, decorated with fine paintings." (*Pat and Jeremy Temple*)

Open All year.
Rooms 48 – all with bath and shower, telephone, radio and TV.
Facilities Lift; lounge, bar, restaurant; conference and function facilities. Garden with terrace restaurant. English spoken.
Location Central. Ettlingen is 8 km S of Karlsruhe. From *Autobahn* A5 take Karlsruhe-Rüppur or Karlsruhe-Rheinhafen exits. Parking.
Credit cards Access, Amex, Diners.
Terms [1985 rates] B&B: single 120–155 DM, double 170–200 DM. Alc (excluding wine) 42–88 DM.

FEUCHTWANGEN 8805 Bavaria   Map 12

Greifen-Post   *Tel* (09852) 20 02
Marktplatz 8   *Telex* 61137

"Feuchtwangen is a pleasant little north Bavarian town with some pretty houses and an interesting Frankish folk museum. It is close to medieval Rothenburg, that tourist show-piece, and lies on the so-called Romantik-strasse that runs across Bavaria, while the *Greifen-Post*, in its attractive main square, belongs to the 'Romantik-Hotels' association of old hotels of character. But there's no need to fear a surfeit of romanticism, even though Lola Montez and Catherine the Great were among past guests: today it is a solidly down-to-earth coaching inn, spacious and rambling, with parts dating back to 1450 or earlier. Wide corridors full of antiques are part of the charm, but the bedrooms are comfortably modernised. Our only complaints were poor bed lights and (in March) inadequate heating – but no doubt a 1450 building is hard to heat properly.

"The Lorentz family have owned the *Greifen* for three generations, and they provide a personal touch. Their cooking is especially good – interesting and unusual specialities, Frankish and other, served in old beamed dining rooms. Dandelion and mushroom salad, trout fillet in a wine sauce, and Feuchtwangen Bürgerteller (a lavish mixed grill, including spicy Nuremberg sausage) were all excellent. Good buffet breakfast, too. There's a sauna, 'Renaissance-style' heated swimming pool with arcades, and cosy *Stübe* with log fire." (*J A C A, Ronald A Lehman*)

Open Hotel and grill room open all year; main restaurant open 8 Feb–31 Dec.
Rooms 33 double, 9 single – 19 with bath, 16 with shower; all with telephone and
colour TV. Double-glazing.
Facilities Lift; TV room, bar with grill room (open 5 pm–1 am), 5 dining rooms,
conference facilities, indoor heated swimming pool, sauna, solarium; garden
terrace for summer use. English spoken.
Location Central. Garage parking.
Restriction Not suitable for &.
Credit cards All major cards accepted.
Terms B&B: single 75–85 DM, double 90–190 DM; dinner, B&B: add 30 DM per
person; full board add 55 DM. Set lunch/dinner 25–86 DM; full alc 60 DM. Special
weekend breaks.

FRANKFURT-AM-MAIN 6000 Hessen — Map 12

Hotel Westend   *Tel* (0611) 74 67 02 or 74 50 02
Westendstrasse 15, Frankfurt 1

"The *Westend* is the last place you might expect to find in down-town
Frankfurt, where a small hotel of charm and character is surely as much
of a rarity as a British publisher who will admit to actually *enjoying* the
Book Fair. So what a marvellous discovery this was – a select, serene,
rather old-fashioned little place, such a contrast to the modern
skyscraper banks that tower above it in this much unloved metropolis. It
is in a quiet residential area that has somehow survived the metallic
frenzy of post-war rebuilding, yet it is very central, only five minutes
walk from the Fair centre on one side and the *Hauptbahnhof* and banking
district on the other. The late 20th century has been carefully excluded
from the *Westend*, which is tastefully furnished throughout with
antiques and old pictures; no TV sets; gracious old-world service by
discreet middle-aged men in black suits who address lady guests as
'Gnädige Frau' ('Esteemed Madam'). Very comfortable rooms; lavish
German breakfasts; light evening meals on request; a leafy garden for
summer; prices very reasonable for central Frankfurt. On our visit,
fellow guests were not at all the solemn businessmen that invade this
city, but young and cultured: eg a visiting American musical group."
(*J A C A*)

Open All year.
Rooms 23, mostly double – 8 with bath or shower, all with telephone.
Facilities Hall, lounge, restaurant, conference facilities. Garden and terrace where
light meals and drinks are served.
Location Central; 5 minutes' walk from station. By car approach from Westkreuz.
Private parking.
Credit cards Possibly some accepted.
Terms [1985 rates] B&B: single 82–122 DM, double 144–184 DM.

FREIBURG IM BREISGAU 7800 Baden-Württemberg — Map 12

Hotel Victoria   *Tel* (0761) 3 18 81
Eisenbahnstrasse 54   *Telex* 17/761103

Though badly damaged in the war, Freiburg with its half-timbered
houses remains one of the most delightful of south German cities,
famous for its Romanesque cathedral and its venerable university. The
Victoria, very central, stands opposite a little park and is close both to the

railway station and the university. It has a good local reputation – a neat, sedate place, part modern in style, part "repro" (wood panelling and chandelier in the "banqueting room"). "We much enjoyed this pleasant hotel, central yet quiet. Comfortable and clean, with crisp white sheets. Friendly and willing service: dinner served at 11 pm. Nor is it expensive." (*T D Baxendale, K S*)

Open All year.
Rooms 1 suite, 35 double, 34 single – 20 with bath, 40 with shower; all with telephone and radio; TV on request.
Facilities Lift. Salon, TV room, bar, restaurant, banqueting room. English spoken.
Location Central, by the Colombi Park in a pedestrian area. Parking.
Credit cards All major cards accepted.
Terms [1985 rates] B&B: single (with shower) 60 DM, (with bath) 110 DM; double (with shower) 90 DM, (with bath) 160 DM. Set meals 22–30 DM; full alc 40 DM. Special family weekend rates Nov–Mar. Children under 6 half-price.

FREUDENSTADT 7290 Baden-Württemberg   Map 12

Hotel-Restaurant Gut Lauterbad   *Tel* (07441) 74 96 and 74 97
Dietrichstrasse 5 (in Lauterbad)

Astride the old hill-road from Stuttgart to Strasbourg, on a plateau amid pine trees, Freudenstadt is one of the larger Black Forest resorts and spa towns. The *Gut Lauterbad*, a modern building in traditional style, lies just outside the town, in a charming setting of meadows, woods and streams. "Lovely hotel. Large, modern, very comfortable rooms, all tastefully furnished. A garden terrace overlooks a trout pond and stream. Good restaurant, friendly staff and owners. Plenty of good paths for walking close by." (*Dr Bill and Lisa Fuerst; endorsed by Ted and Vera Baker*)

Open 27 Jan–23 Nov and 22 Dec–12 Jan. Restaurant closed to non-residents Mon.
Rooms 16 double, 4 single – all with shower and WC, telephone, radio and TV. 4 in annexe.
Facilities TV room, café and terrace café, restaurant with bar; conference room. Zither music once a month. Park with children's playground, small lake and stream; trout fishing (the chef will prepare your catch). English spoken.
Location At Lauterbad, 3 km SE (B294) of Freudenstadt which is 88 km SW of Stuttgart. Garage and parking.
Restriction Not suitable for &.
Credit cards All major cards accepted.
Terms B&B: single 42–48 DM, double 72–85 DM; dinner, B&B: 16 DM per person added; full board 25 DM added. Set lunch/dinner 15.80–21.50 DM; full alc 25 DM. 7-day packages. Children under 2 free; under 12, 50% reduction; special meals.

FRIEDRICHSRUHE 7111 Baden-Württemberg   Map 12

Wald und Schlosshotel Friedrichsruhe   *Tel* (07941) 70 78
Öhringer-strasse 11   *Telex* 74498 WAFRI

"The best hotel we have stayed at so far in Germany" is the verdict this year of two discriminating travellers. It is a castle in the hilly, wooded Hohenlohe country, built in 1712 by the Fürsten of that ilk and still owned today (after conversion into a very grand hotel in 1953) by the Prinz Kraft zu Hohenlohe-Öhringen. His chef/manager, Lothar Eiermann, runs it in lordly style and has also built a reputation for serving some of the best food in south Germany (*Michelin* rosette). Rooms are in the old castle or, along with the restaurant, in an extension built in 1969. "All rooms we saw were nicely decorated, some in traditional chintzy style or with country pine. Ours had a good view. On our return from dinner, everything had been tidied up, including putting the newspaper back together in the right order. Everything we ate was excellent, especially the saddle of venison. Good breakfast too. Service, food and accommodation all faultless." "Very luxurious, beautiful gardens and rural setting, two lovely swimming pools. Much used by big firms for business conferences." (*Kate and Steve Murray-Sykes, Katinka Schmitz*)

Open All year. Restaurant closed all Mon and half Tue.
Rooms 6 suites, 31 double, 10 single – 40 with bath, 3 with shower, all with telephone; radio, TV and baby-listening on request; 22 rooms in annexe.
Facilities Lift, ramps. Lounge/bar, TV room, restaurant, functions room. Large grounds with outdoor and covered swimming pools, tennis court, 9-hole golf course, playground for children. English spoken.
Location 30 km E of Heilbronn; leave the Nürnberg motorway at Öhringen exit, drive through Öhringen till Friedrichsruhe is signposted.
Credit cards All major cards accepted.
Terms B&B: single 140 DM, double 218–238 DM. Full alc 100 DM. Reduced rates for children on request; special meals.

GARMISCH-PARTENKIRCHEN 8100 Bavaria   Map 12

Posthotel Partenkirchen   *Tel* (08821) 5 10 67/68
Ludwigstrasse 49   *Telex* 59611

Garmisch is Bavaria's smartest resort; Partenkirchen, across the railway line, is decidedly less so – "but", says an inspector this year, "it's well worth crossing the line to stay at this stylish hotel in the 'wrong' half of town. There's been a hotel on this site since the 15th century and it's been in the present family for four generations. It's a smashing place – a three-storey building with paintings on the walls outside, Bavarian-style. A feeling of antiquity pervades the place – oil portraits, and dark wood furniture set on Persian carpets or stone flags. Ceilings are beamed, with stucco motifs, and bedrooms have wood panelling. Our spacious room had a balcony too. There's a roof garden, and you can see Germany's highest mountain, the Zugspitze, on a clear day. The panelled restaurant was popular, especially with Americans (there's a big US base nearby), and food and service were excellent." (*J S*)

Open All year.
Rooms 60 rooms – all with bath or shower and telephone; some with balcony.
Facilities Lift. Lounge, TV room, bar, wine bar, restaurant; conference and function facilities. Roof garden.
Location In Partenkirchen, near *Kurhaus*. Parking.
Restriction Not suitable for &.
Credit cards All major cards accepted.
Terms B&B: single 65–100 DM, double 100–180 DM; half-board add 25 DM per person; full board add 45 DM per person. Reduced rates for children.

> Don't let old favourites down. Entries are dropped when there is no endorsement.

GEISLINGEN AN DER STEIGE 7340 Baden-Württemberg   Map 12

Burghotel   *Tel* (07331) 4 10 51
Burggasse 41, Weiler ob Helfenstein

Looking like a superior motel or ski-lodge, this attractive modern two-storey hotel lies in the rolling hills of the Schwäbische Alb, between Ulm and Stuttgart, and is reached from Geislingen via two miles of hairpin bends. It has a large garden and indoor swimming pool. "Very friendly welcome, good breakfast, and a pleasant modern room with balcony. On each of our pillows was a little sack with fruit, nuts and a chocolate Father Christmas" (of course – this is South Germany and it was St Nicholas night). "No restaurant, but the hotel has an arrangement with the *Burgstübe*, 300 metres away: very warm and welcoming in a Germanic way, and delicious home cooking, for example breast of pheasant in passion-fruit sauce, and Swabian dishes such as Spätzle baked with cheese. Borders on *Michelin* rosette standard." (*K and S M-S*)

Open All year except 3 weeks in summer (check with hotel).
Rooms 11 double, 12 single – 4 with bath, 19 with shower, all with telephone, radio, colour TV and baby-listening.
Facilities Lounge, reading room/TV lounge, breakfast room; indoor swimming pool, sauna. Large garden with terrace.
Location 3 km E of Geislingen (which is 62 km E of Stuttgart), at Weiler ob Helfenstein. Garage (6 DM).
Restriction Not suitable for &.
Credit cards None accepted.
Terms [1985 rates] rooms: single 41–83 DM, double 72–120 DM; for half-board (3 days min – meals at *Burgstübe*) add 30 or 40 DM per person depending on 3- or 4-course menu. Breakfast 6–18 DM.

GÖTTINGEN 3400 Nieder-Sachsen   Map 12

Hotel zur Sonne   *Tel* (0551) 5 67 38/39, 5 78 79
Paulinerstrasse 10–12   *Telex* 96787 SONNE

"The Cambridge of Germany? – hardly: badly bombed and dully rebuilt, this renowned university city has little of architectural interest, though its leafy residential avenues are pleasant, and so is its wooded hillside setting. On the edge of the new down-town pedestrian zone, and just about accessible by car, the *Hotel zur Sonne* makes a useful budget halt: for only 98 DM [1985] including fair breakfast, we had a spacious well-equipped room with big bathroom; a broad, soft double bed, rare in Germany where even the smartest hotels usually give you hard twin beds shunted together. Pleasant Yugoslav restaurant next door." (*J A*)

Open All year, except 21 Dec–4 Jan.
Rooms 21 double, 20 single – 21 with bath, 14 with shower, all with telephone.
Facilities Lift. Hall, lounge, dining room, conference room, TV room. English spoken.
Location Central, behind old Town Hall; access is only via Golmarstrasse or Goethe Allee, through the pedestrian maze. Garage.
Credit cards Access, Diners, Visa.
Terms B&B: single 60–75 DM, double 90–104 DM; dinner, B&B: 15 DM per person added to room rate; full board 30 DM added. Set lunch 15 DM, dinner 18 DM; full alc 20-28 DM. Reduced rates for children.

GUTACH IM BREISGAU 7809 Baden-Württemberg   Map 12

Hotel-Restaurant Adler   *Tel* (07681) 70 22 or 70 23
Landstrasse 6

Black Forest hotel standards are among the very highest in Europe. The *Adler* is no exception – a splendid hostelry in a village north-east of Freiburg, extolled by two regular correspondents this year: "A new building in traditional rustic style, with oak-beamed ceilings, tiled floors. Our bedroom was airy and attractive, furnished in repro rococo style with pretty pictures and central chandelier. It was at the back, quiet, looking on to a steep pine-clad hillside with huge rocks. The gardens are well tended: patio furniture is used to serve meals outside on warm days. "One dining room has an open log fire and beautiful Victorian oil-lamps. The other has an original 19th-century mechanical organ with moving military statuettes, playing hum-pah-pah music. We had picked the place because of its *Michelin* rosette and were not disappointed: frogs' legs, wild duck, venison with Spätzle. Good Bodensee wine. Dogs permitted in restaurant: we were treated to a howling concerto for poodle, dachshund and mongrel. Breakfast buffet included two sorts of Muesli and rather dry cheeses. Dining room had bags of charm and an expensive feel – but it's the cheapest *Michelin*-rosetted hotel we've stayed at recently. We'd go back with pleasure." (*Ian and Francine Walsh*)

Open All year.
Rooms 1 3-bedded, 10 double, 3 single – 13 with bath, 2 with shower, all with telephone, single rooms with radio and TV. 1 room in annexe.
Facilities Lounge/bar, TV room, 2 restaurants, garden terrace with outdoor meals and barbecues in summer, English spoken.
Location In village, 21 km NE of Freiburg. Ample parking.
Restriction Not suitable for &.
Credit cards None accepted.
Terms B&B: single 52–55 DM, double 75–88 DM. Full alc 35 DM. Special menu for children.

HAGNAU 7759 Baden-Württemberg   Map 12

Erbguth's Landhaus   *Tel* (07532) 62 02 and 90 51
Neugartenstrasse 39   *Telex* 733811

The Lake of Constance (Bodensee) is a busy summer holiday area. Wisely, the Germans have put the accent here on smallish hotels of character rather than big lakeside palaces, and this *Landhaus* (country house) is typical, discovered for us this year by two expert observers: "A private house on the edge of a picturesque village by the lake. Only the front upper rooms have views of it. But it's a hotel of considerable personality, run by a young couple, the Erbguths, with a great deal of flair. He cooks, she hostesses. The entrance hall with its white marble floor has an aura of cool elegance, in contrast to the warm traditional interiors of the dining areas, where you dine in the glow of candlelight, amid masses of flowers and modern 'antiques'. The only flaw here is the loud piped music. Food was pleasant and original, much of it smoked and preserved in their own kitchens – we had sensational home-smoked caviar from local fish, fantastic tender Rinderfilet, good wine from local vineyards. The buffet breakfast was the best we've had this year, a Lucullan choice including cold chicken, home-made breads and jams, coffee ad lib.

"Bedrooms and bathrooms could not be faulted, either in taste or comfort, save that lighting was dimmish. Our room had smart and excellent-quality contract furniture, and original pictures and prints. There's no doubt that Frau Erbguth has panache and artistry: she dresses smartly, is charming, modern and slick, and the same could be said of her clientele – the sort who did not baulk at spending 20 DM on a single rose for their partner, when a peasant woman brought these round. As we left the hotel, a beggar came to reception asking for food, and they gave him a neat parcel of sandwiches, tomatoes and fruit. Nice. Not a cheap place, but the quality is superb." (*Francine and Ian Walsh*)

Open All year except 22 Dec–22 Jan. Restaurant closed midday and Mon.
Rooms 15 – all with bath or shower, direct-dial telephone and TV.
Facilities Salon, breakfast room, restaurant; sauna. Garden.
Location On Lake Constance, just E of Meersburg. Parking.
Credit cards Access, Amex.
Terms [1985 rates] B&B (buffet): single 77–120 DM, double 140–160 DM. Alc dinner (excluding wine) 32–60 DM.

HAMBURG 2000   Map 12

Hotel Abtei   *Tel* (040) 44 29 05 or 45 75 65
Abteistrasse 14, Hamburg 13   *Telex* 2165645 ABHA

"A real find – once you have found it, at least. It is in a suburb, just north of the centre, and just west of the Alster. But that devalues the delightfulness of the area – it is a bit like Kensington, Chelsea, Belgravia and St John's Wood all rolled into one – but greener and more relaxed. Abteistrasse is a small leafy street lined with big stucco houses. The *Abtei* itself is slightly smaller – terraced rather than semi-detached – with a modest facade, just the word 'hotel' over the door. But it is still quite big and made bigger by its spacious well-lit and immaculately decorated rooms, both the bedrooms and the delightful breakfast room where I had one of the best breakfasts I had in Germany. The whole place has a restrained elegance and charm rare in a German city hotel. It's only a few minutes by underground to the centre of the city." (*S L*)

Open All year.
Rooms 4 suites, 8 double, 6 single – 6 with bath, 8 with shower, all with telephone, radio and colour TV.
Facilities Lounge, breakfast room. Garden. Boating on Alster lake nearby.
Location Just W of Alster lake. Parking. Easy journey by underground to centre.
Credit cards All major cards accepted.
Terms B&B: single 115–160 DM, double 160–220 DM. (No restaurant.)

Hotel Hanseatic   *Tel* (040) 485 57 72/3
Sierichstrasse 150, Hamburg 60   *Telex* ABHA 216 56 45

"A rare jewel, this extremely personal and very select little 10-bedroom private hotel – said to be Hamburg's smallest – in a residential area just north of the big Alster lake, four kilometres from the city centre and four also from the airport. Wolfgang Schüler, former assistant manager of

Hamburg's huge Atlantic Hotel, knows his trade perfectly and, what's more, adores it: he seems to spend all his time cosseting his guests and keeping everything spick and span, in this pink-fronted patrician villa that he has converted with great taste: well-chosen paintings and furniture in the very comfortable bedrooms. His breakfasts, including the breads and marmalades that he makes himself, are wonderful, and he serves them personally with style: 'Good morning, Mr Ardagh, did you sleep well? – and here is a real German country egg for you cooked by me with my own two left hands.' The personal atmosphere is like that of a private house, and it's not surprising that some film, theatre and opera people visiting Hamburg prefer to stay here rather than at the *Vier Jahreszeiten* (q.v.). It's much cheaper, too. Small garden; two studio rooms. Book well ahead." (*J A, K S*)

Open All year.
Rooms 2 suites, 8 double – all with bath, telephone, radio and TV.
Facilities Lounge, breakfast room. Small garden. Alster lake and city park both 2 blocks away. English spoken.
Location In Winterhude, 4 km N of city centre. Parking in street, but difficult.
Restriction Not suitable for &.
Credit cards Access, Amex, Diners.
Terms B&B: single occupancy 175 DM, double 205–260 DM. Children under 12 in parents' room 20 DM for extra bed, no charge for breakfast.

Hotel Prem　　　　　　　　　　　　*Tel* (040) 24 17 26
An der Alster 9, Hamburg 1　　　　　　*Telex* 2163115

This smallish and elegant hotel, recently renovated, faces Hamburg's big lake, the Alster, and is ten minutes' scenic walk from the station and the start of the down-town area. It is fairly expensive, but much less so than the city's swankier palaces. "A charming flower-filled hotel with a courteous staff and superb food"; "large, airy, colourfully decorated rooms" – so run two reports this year. Some rooms look over the lake, others over gardens; some are much smaller than others; rooms facing the street are noisy. One visitor found her bedroom insufficiently aired, but enjoyed her modern bathroom. The restaurant, *La Mer*, has a new French chef and is highly thought of by Hamburg gastronomes. (*Mr and Mrs D Steven McGuire, Linda Shaughnessy*)

Open All year.
Rooms 24 double, 24 single – 41 with bath, 8 with shower, all with telephone, colour TV and sound-proofed windows; some ground-floor rooms.
Facilities Lift. Lounge, TV room, bar, café, restaurant; conference facilities. Garden with restaurant. Opposite lake with fishing and sailing. English spoken.
Location On SE shore of Alster lake. 15 minutes' walk from central Hamburg and station. Garage (10 DM).
Restriction Not suitable for &.
Credit cards All major cards accepted.
Terms B&B: single 145–195 DM, double 210–290 DM. Set lunch 60 DM; full alc 90 DM. Special weekend rates. Reduced rates for children; special meals on request.

> Set dinner refers to a fixed price meal (which may have ample, limited or no choice on the menu). Full alc is the hotel's own estimated price per person of a three-course meal taken *à la carte*, with a half-bottle of house wine.

Hotel Vier Jahreszeiten
Neuer Jungfernstieg 9–14, Hamburg 36

Tel (040) 3 49 41
Telex 211629
Reservations in UK (01) 583 3050
in USA (800) 223 6800

A superlatively gracious hotel for all seasons, recently voted "best hotel in Europe"and "sixth best in the world" (the others were all in the Far East) in a poll of 600 top world bankers made by *Institutional Investor Magazine*. It has no connection with the other Vier Jahreszeiten hotels, (eg in Munich), being privately owned, founded in 1897, and still run by the Haerlin family (mother and two daughters) who have carefully amassed its antique furnishings over the years. It is on a quay of Hamburg's graceful inner lake, the Binnenalster.

Reports this year: "Although fairly large, with conference facilities, it is neither bustly nor impersonal and has something of the calm atmosphere of a private club. The elegant main rooms have antiques and splendid tapestries. Bedrooms too have antiques, but ours was quite homely. Some, with balcony, look over the lake. Nice extras included a shoe-horn and a thermometer for checking the bathwater – but you might well expect this at £90 a night." "Super-efficient German service dished up with a smile. You have but to *think* of a cigarette and the lighter's under your nose. Huge classy rooms with glittering chandeliers and gilt carved mirrors – all thoroughly plush and decadent. Best venison I've ever eaten – the restaurant (*Michelin* rosette) is one of Hamburg's best." The restaurant is beautiful, in a modern style; so is the *Konditorei* that serves light lunches. You should step down the road to visit Hamburg's ravishing new shopping arcades, notably the Hanse-Viertel and the Galeria. (*K and S M-S, Patricia Fenn*)

Open All year.
Rooms 37 suites, 98 double, 77 single – all with bath, telephone, radio, TV.
Facilities Lounge, 2 bars, tea-room, Restaurant *Haerlin, Jahreszeiten Grill,* conference facilities; night club, barber's shop, wine shop. English spoken.
Location Central, on N side of Alster lake. Parking.
Restriction Not suitable for &.
Credit cards All major cards accepted.
Terms Rooms: single 215–295 DM, double 310–400 DM. All meals alc: lunch/dinner (excluding wine) 46–100 DM.

HEIDELBERG 6900 Baden-Württemberg   Map 12

Hotel zum Ritter
Hauptstrasse 178

Tel (06221) 2 02 03 or 2 42 72
Telex 461506 RITHD

The ornate five-storey Renaissance facade of this 1592 building, classified an historic monument, is probably the most photographed spot in Heidelberg, except for the massive *Schloss* which towers above it in the old town. It is an archetypal member of the Romantik association of "hotels of charm and character", and it pleases readers this year who enjoy this genre: "Our room had vaulted ceilings and an interior courtyard resplendent with geraniums. The restaurant combines history with charm and served us excellent venison." "Excellent, a lovely hotel"; "cosy accommodation, pleasant service". Lower front rooms may be noisy. (*Vicki Turner, Patricia Reddish*)

Open All year.
Rooms 2 suites, 20 double, 14 single – 19 with bath, 9 with shower, all with telephone, radio, some with colour TV.
Facilities Small lift. Lounge, TV room, restaurant, conference facilities. English spoken.
Location Central, near Parkhaus 12. Parking.
Credit cards All major cards accepted.
Terms B&B: single 62–130 DM, double 135–240 DM; half-board 25 DM per person added. Set lunch 15–45 DM, dinner 18–52 DM; full alc 35 DM. Reduced rates and special meals for children.

HINTERZARTEN 7824 Baden-Württemberg   Map 12

Hotel Weisses Rössle   *Tel* (07652) 14 11
Freiburgstrasse 38   *Telex* 765211

Hinterzarten is a very stylish resort set high in the Black Forest near Titisee, popular with skiers in winter and walkers all the year. Here the *Weisses Rössle*, a traditional place bedecked with flowery window-boxes, is run with personal flair by Karl-Heinz Zimmermann and his wife Urda. With some reservations, it continues to be popular with readers. "A remarkable place", says a regular visitor this year; "food prepared with imagination and finesse." Earlier reports referred to "attractive dining room with fine views", "friendly service and ambience", "splendid breakfast buffet". Delightful hostesses look after the guests, and if required will take them for walks and do gymnastics with them. However, when the "energetic and charming" Herr Zimmermann is absent, as often happens, then there are signs that standards drop and service becomes slow and slapdash. Readers also point out that rooms in the new *Sonnenflügel* annexe are far nicer than in the main building which "needs a face-lift". (*Jonathan Williams, Dr R L Holmes, Dr M W Atkinson, S A L, K S, and many others*)

Open All year except mid-Jan to mid-Feb. Restaurant closed Mon.
Rooms 67 – some with shower, some with balcony. Some in annexe.
Facilities Bar, restaurant. Garden and terrace. Winter sports, walking.
Location 9 km S of Freiburg. Garage.
Credit cards All major cards accepted.
Terms [1985 rates] B&B: single 55–122 DM, double 85–202 DM; half-board (3 days min) add 32 DM per person; full board (3 days min) add 47 DM per person.

HORBEN-LANGACKERN 7801 Baden-Württemberg   Map 12

Hotel zum Engel   *Tel* (0761) 2 91 11

This traditional inn, 600 metres up in a village 10 kilometres south of Freiburg, lies close to the valley station of the cable car up to the Schauinsland, a Black Forest high point. "Everything very clean and well kept. Cuisine excellent: salmon trout brought to table by Herr Hagenmeier before being cooked; superb béarnaise sauce. Very friendly atmosphere, a good centre for walking or for trout fishing."
  A visitor arriving late on a Friday was given a warm welcome and "a sumptuous" dinner at 10 pm, but the next night found the place crowded out with local private parties and had to make do with dull menus, so recommends avoiding weekends. (*H L Fenn, A Wallace Barr*)

Open All year except mid-Jan to mid-Feb. Restaurant closed Mon.
Rooms 26 – some with shower, some with balcony.
Facilities Bar, restaurant. Garden and terrace. Winter sports, walking.
Location 9 km S of Freiburg. Garage.
Credit cards Access, Diners.
Terms [1985 rates] B&B: single 36–45 DM, double 72–90 DM; full board 68–77 DM
per person. Alc meals (excluding wine) 27–51 DM.

ISMANING 8045 Bavaria   Map 12

Hotel Fischerwirt   *Tel* (089) 9 61 53
Schlossstrasse 17

"Ismaning is a neat and sophisticated little commuter town on the edge
of the Munich conurbation, where rural Bavaria adjoins the sprawl of
the big city – a place of river walks and old houses, with a large
handsome yellow Schloss that was once the residence of bishops. If you
don't mind the half-hour car journey, it would make an ideal alternative
to staying in the hectic down-town area. Set back in a courtyard in a
quiet street, the *Fischerwirt* is a typical modern German inn, spruce and
unpretentious, clean, friendly and efficient – a prime example of the
consistently very high standards of German hostelry in this lower-price
range. Why can't we do it in Britain? For a mere 50 DM (1985) I had a
small but pleasant single room, with a good hot shower down the
corridor. A neat lounge with picture windows gives on to a terrace and
enclosed garden with rustic chairs that must be lovely for a drink in
summer. Usual excellent buffet help-yourself breakfast – and at 7 am
sharp the *Frühstückssaal* was packed with polite young executives *grüss
Gott*-ing each other over their Würst and cheeses. The hotel has no
restaurant; but there's a rather pricey Italian place in the same building,
separately owned. You might do better, as I did, to eat a hearty Bavarian
meal at low cost – and with that marvellous Munich beer – at the
Burgenstube, five minutes' walk away." (*J A C A*)

Open All year except 22 Dec–6 Jan.
Rooms 15 double, 30 single – 10 with bath, 27 with shower, all with telephone.
Ground-floor rooms.
Facilities Lift. 2 TV rooms, bar, breakfast room; garden terrace; garden. Close to
the river Isar, swimming, bicycle hire. English spoken.
Location Ismaning is 14 km NE of Munich. Take Garching Süd (B471) exit from the
Munich/Nürnberg motorway, hotel is on the right just past the river Isar.
Restriction Not suitable for &.
Credit cards Acces, Amex.
Terms B&B: single 50 DM, double 70 DM. (No restaurant).

KETTWIG 4300 Nordrhein-Westfalen   Map 12

Hotel Schloss Hugenpoet   *Tel* (02054) 60 54
August-Thyssen-Strasse 51
Essen 18

There was praise again in 1985 for this stately, moated 16th-century
castle. It stands on the banks of the river Ruhr in a wooded valley, yet is
close to the Ruhr industrial conurbation – an unlikely place in such a
location. It is within the borders of Essen (Germany's fifth largest city)

but 11 kilometres from its centre and just outside the residential suburb of Kettwig (where you should visit the Krupp family mansion, now a museum; also, in downtown Essen, the Folkwang Museum of local history – both provide poignant reminders of the splendours and horrors of the Ruhr's mighty past). "Fresh flowers in our room, and fresh fruit including a fresh strawberry in January. Building magnificent, bedrooms delightful, food excellent, staff helpful", runs a report this year, echoing an earlier one: "The hotel and restaurant cater for meetings and functions but this never seemed to intrude during our stay. Our room was large, well furnished with antique pieces. There is a very grand entrance hall/lounge area with a magnificent black marble staircase. The main attraction is the restaurant – a rosette in *Michelin*. The food is French, superbly cooked and presented. On Sunday there was a magnificent tea-buffet packed with local ladies enjoying the rich cream pastries etc. Highly recommended." (*Kate and Steve Murray-Sykes, and others*)

Open All year except Christmas.
Rooms 1 suite, 13 double, 6 single – 19 with bath, 1 with shower – all with telephone, radio and mini-bar; doubles have TV.
Facilities Lift. Large hall, salon, restaurant; conference facilities; chapel for weddings and christenings; terrace. Large grounds with tennis court.
Location 11 km SW of Essen off A52, near A2 and A3 motorways. Parking.
Credit cards Access, Amex, Diners.
Terms B&B: single 110–180 DM, double 190–230 DM, suite 300 DM. Full alc 80 DM. Reduced rates for children's meals.

KÖNIGSTEIN IM TAUNUS 6240 Hessen   Map 12

Hotel Sonnenhof   *Tel* (06174) 30 51
Falkensteinerstrasse 7–9   *Telex* 410636

"If you really do have to go to dread Frankfurt on business – as I do every year, to the Book Fair – then it makes a lot of sense, at least if you have a car, to stay in one of the pleasant little resorts in the Taunus mountains, rather than at one of the city hotels, mostly overpriced. Königstein is a mere 23 kilometres out of town – 20 minutes' drive, rather more at rush hour. It is a small town in the Taunus foothills, just below an imposing ruined feudal fortress. The *Sonnenhof* stands attractively on a hill in its own 20-acre park, with giant trees – a big Victorian hunting-lodge, spacious and gracious, well converted, rather grand in an old-fashioned way. It used to belong to Baron Rothschild. My small bedroom was in a modern annexe: bed a bit hard and narrow in the German manner, but pleasant view of the park from my balcony. Lavish buffet breakfast with assorted meats and tomatoes, even. Nice covered swimming pool." Recent visitors report on the restaurant: "Smart, with good but not outstanding food; notable desserts." (*Jenny Towndrow, Kate and Steve Murray-Sykes*)

Open All year.
Rooms 24 double, 21 single – 35 with bath, 10 with shower, all with telephone, radio, colour TV; 9 ground-floor rooms; 20 rooms in annexe.
Facilities Hall, salons, bar, restaurant, function rooms; heated indoor swimming pool, sauna, solarium; sun terrace. Large park with gardens and tennis. Königstein spa and therapy centre nearby. English spoken. ৬.

Location On edge of town which is 23 km NW of Frankfurt.
Credit cards Access, Amex, Diners.
Terms B&B: single 91–118 DM, double 114–197 DM; dinner, B&B: single 110–147 DM, double 172–255 DM; full board: single 141–168 DM, double 214–297 DM. Set lunch 35 DM, dinner 60–75 DM; full alc 80 DM. Half- and full board terms for 3 days or more. Christmas package. Reduced rates and special meals for children.

KRONBERG IM TAUNUS 6242 Hessen   Map 12

Schlosshotel Kronberg   *Tel* (06173) 70 11
Hainstrasse 25   *Telex* 415424 SHLO

This vast grey towered and gabled *Schloss*, eminently Victorian, was built for Queen Victoria's eldest daughter after the death of her husband, Kaiser Friedrich III. It is now a classy hotel (though still sometimes also used privately by visiting royalty) and its grounds are an 18-hole golf course. It is no more expensive than the leading hotels in down-town Frankfurt, 17 kilometres away, so could make a useful bolthole for rich publishers wanting a nightly refuge from the *Buchmesse*'s agonies. "The main rooms are imposing, with wood panelling and huge tapestries. Bedrooms are individually furnished: those on the lower floors tend to be larger and grander, but upper ones could be quieter. Staff are polite and efficient; the dining rooms are attractive and the food good quality but nothing special." (*S & K M-S*)

Open All year.
Rooms 5 suites, 20 double, 29 single – 51 with bath, 1 with shower, all with telephone and colour TV.
Facilities Lounge, lounge/bar, 2 restaurants, small salon for business/private functions, library for larger conferences, red salon for banquets or receptions. Hotel set in "English" park with 18-hole golf course. English spoken.
Location 15 minutes walk from the centre of Kronberg, which is 17 km NW of Frankfurt. Parking.
Restriction Not suitable for &.
Credit cards All major cards accepted.
Terms B&B: single 200–225 DM, double 310–340 DM. Set lunch 50 DM, dinner 80 DM; full alc 65 DM. Special meals for children on request.

LIMBURG AN DER LAHN 6250 Hessen   Map 12

Hotel Zimmermann   *Tel* (06431) 4 20 30
Blumenröderstrasse 1   *Telex* 0484782

Limburg's lofty pink-and-white Gothic cathedral, on a hill above the river Lahn, is a familiar sight to motorists using the Frankfurt-Cologne motorway. The town's old quarter has quaint half-timbered houses: its best hotel, the *Zimmermann*, behind the station, is modern – dull-looking from outside, but inside richly endowed with antique furniture, and new to the Guide this year: "Extraordinary. Public and private rooms are lovely, their furnishings obviously lovingly chosen. Prices are moderate and the service very special: Herr Zimmermann, the owner, was amazingly thoughtful and efficient in enabling us to extricate our car from an over-crowded car park and then providing a 5 am breakfast." (*Jim Engiles*) Food well spoken of in the German guides.

Open All year except Christmas and New Year.
Rooms 3 suites, 12 double, 10 single – 8 with bath, 17 with shower, all with telephone and TV; 5 rooms in annexe.
Facilities Lounge, reading room, bar, dining room.
Location Central. Take Limburg exit off Cologne-Frankfurt motorway. Garage 16.50 DM, and covered parking place (2.50 DM).
Restriction Not suitable for ♿.
Credit cards All major cards accepted.
Terms B&B: single 58–80 DM, double 85–125 DM. Alc menu (prices not available). Weekend rates.

LINDAU IM BODENSEE 8990 Bavaria   Map 12

Bayerischer Hof   *Tel* (08382) 5055
Seepromenade   *Telex* 54340 HOTELI
Representative in the UK: John Walker Reservations,
35 Harrington Gardens, London SW7 RJU
in USA: Ernest J Newman Inc.
770 Broadway, New York, NY 10003

Lindau, today the smartest resort on Lake Constance (Bodensee), was a Free Imperial City from 1275 to 1802. It is a charming and ancient town on a little island just off-shore, with narrow streets and half-timbered houses including the 15th-century *Rathaus*. The *Bayerischer Hof*, new to the Guide, is a large, smart hotel on the front facing the harbour – "opposite the station, yet no train sounds reach you. My room was small, yet had plenty of space, and it looked on to the harbour where the pleasure-boats come and go – again no noise save the boat-whistles during the day. Dining room on a terrace open to the lake. Staff charming and multi-lingual." "A lovely open swimming pool/lido, surrounded by trees and flowers, where you can lounge under parasols. Good lake-fish specialities." (*Janet White, Susan B Hanley, K S*)

Open Easter–Nov.
Rooms 1 suite, 76 double, 18 single – 82 with bath, 13 with shower, all with telephone, radio, colour TV, baby-listening.
Facilities Lift, ramps. Lounge, bar, snack bar, restaurant, conference facilities; hairdresser; table tennis, billiards; large terrace. Garden with outdoor heated swimming pool. Water sports on nearby Lake Constance. English spoken. ♿.
Location Central, by the harbour. Parking.
Credit cards Amex, Diners.
Terms B&B: single 95–165 DM, double 165–300 DM; dinner, B&B: single 135–205 DM, double 245–380 DM; full board: single 175–245 DM, double 325–460 DM. Set lunch 38 DM, dinner 44 DM; full alc 40 DM; children under 5 free when sharing parents' room; special meals.

MANDERSCHEID 5562 Rheinland-Pfalz   Map 12

Hotel Zens   *Tel* (06572) 7 69
Kurfürstenstrasse 35

The old village of Manderscheid lies in the southern part of the wooded Eifel massif, close to several ruined castles and the Trier/Coblenz motorway. Here the *Zens* is recommended this year as "a delightful hotel on the main road, with a lovely courtyard, a big garden with lawns and a heated indoor swimming pool. It has various sitting rooms and is nicely decorated. It began life 150 years ago as a coaching-inn and is still run by the same family, who greeted us in a friendly way. Our simple rooms were most comfortable – even pin-cushions were provided – and dinner and breakfast were very good." (*Mrs F A Billows*)

Open 6 Feb–9 Nov.
Rooms 23 double, 24 single – 11 with bath, 15 with shower, all with telephone, TV on request; 16 rooms in annexe. Some ground-floor rooms.
Facilities Reading room, lounge with open fireplace, restaurant, indoor heated swimming pool; terraces and garden. English spoken.
Location Manderscheid is 57 km N of Trier, off *Autobahn* 1.
Credit card Access.
Terms B&B: single 48–68 DM, double 96–136 DM; dinner B&B: single 62–85 DM, double 124–170 DM; full board: single 68–92 DM, double 136–184 DM. Set lunch 19.50–26.50 DM, dinner 18.50–26.50 DM; full alc 55 DM. Reduced rates and special meals for children.

MEERSBURG 7758 Baden-Württemberg   Map 12

Hotel-Gasthof zum Bären   *Tel* (07532) 60 44
Marktplatz 11

Meersburg is the prettiest town on Lake Constance: it has half-timbered houses, a romantic old castle and a newer pink baroque castle, crowded together in the *Altstadt* on a hill above the lake. Here in the lovely market square is the *Hotel-Gasthof zum Bären*, an inn since the 17th century, a stunning old building with flower-pots and carvings on its quaint corner-tower. It was dropped from the Guide last year after a misunderstanding, but this year returns amid praise from three separate visitors: "*Gemütlich* and friendly; food homely but good." "Everything delightful, including room, view, meals and attention by the staff. Fish wonderfully prepared. We bought our own wine which they chilled and served with no corkage fee." "Rooms very nice, main restaurant charming, but overflow one lacks atmosphere." Earlier reports had admired the beamed ceilings, Alpine furniture and the charm of the owners, the Gilowsky-Karrer family. However, the stairs are fairly steep and there is no lift; also the quieter back rooms lack a view. (*Katinka Schmitz, J A C A, D R Brumley, Ronald A Lennon*)

Open 15 Mar–10 Nov. Restaurant closed Mon.
Rooms 13 double, 3 single – all with shower, all but 1 also with WC.
Facilities 2 restaurants, sailing and windsurfing on the lake. English spoken.
Location Central (back rooms quietest). Parking and garages.
Restriction Not suitable for &.
Credit cards None accepted.
Terms B&B: single 50–78 DM, double 94–98 DM. Set lunch/dinner 16–30 DM; full alc 40 DM. Extra bed for child in parents' room 18 DM; special meals.

MUNICH 8000 Bavaria   Map 12

Hotel Biederstein   *Tel* (089) 39 50 72
Keferstrasse 18, Munich 45

A small and quiet place on the edge of the Schwabing district (the Chelsea of Munich), about 4 kilometres north-east of the city centre. "The hotel is intriguingly situated amid contrasts. It stands in a pleasantly secluded residential area of little streets and villas, with on one side the lakes, meadows and willows of the Englischer Garten, Munich's huge park, and on the other – but out of earshot – the raffish night-entertainment quarter of Schwabing. The building is modern (1970) but has some good classic furniture. My bedroom was itself in modern style, but cosy and inviting, with a balcony. My only quibble is that for 85 DM [1985] they might have provided radio and TV. The whole place is solid and spruce, with stone floors so well polished they look like marble. Home-made plum jam for breakfast and efficient service.'' (*J A; also Katie Plowden, John David Morley*)

Open All year.
Rooms 3 suites, 16 double, 13 single – all with bath/shower, WC and telephone; TV by arrangement.
Facilities Lift. Breakfast room, small conference room, TV room. Small garden. English spoken.
Location Near Englischer Garten. Underground garage (8 DM).
Restriction Not suitable for &.
Credit card Amex.
Terms B&B: single 80–100 DM, double 105–145 DM. Reduced rates for children. (No restaurant but light meals available.)

Gästehaus Englischer Garten
Liebergesellstrasse 8, Munich 40

Tel (89) 39 20 34

Surely anyone's top choice for a small medium-priced bed-and-breakfast hotel in Munich – only four kilometres from the city centre, yet idyllically rural. It is a creeper-covered 18th-century millhouse, beside a stream at the edge of the big Englischer Garten and on the eastern fringe of Schwabing. Thick carpets, antiques, a quiet garden by the stream, a pretty rustic breakfast room, all complete the picture. The place is much frequented by artists and writers, who book months ahead. "Irene Schlüter-Hübscher runs it as a family concern. In summer you can enjoy a generous breakfast in the secluded garden with a view of the park, which you can also explore on a bicycle loaned by the hotel. The house has atmosphere and the rooms are cosy: but if you want a lift, ask for a room in the annexe 50 metres down the road, where all rooms have their own kitchen. The Metro line to central Munich is six minutes' walk away.'' (*John David Morley*)

Open All year.
Rooms 23 double, 6 single – 20 with bath, 1 with shower, all with telephone and TV. 15 rooms with kitchenettes (some of them on ground floor) in annexe down the road which has a lift.
Facilities Breakfast room; terrace. Small garden. Small lake 5 minutes' walk from hotel. English spoken.
Location On edge of Englischer Garten. Parking.
Credit cards None accepted.
Terms B&B: single 65–121 DM, double 98–157 DM; extra bed 30 DM. (No restaurant.)

Always let a hotel know if you have to cancel a booking, whether you have paid a deposit or not. Hotels lose thousands of pounds and dollars from 'no-shows'.

Schloss-Hotel Grünwald *Tel* (089) 64 19 35
Zeillestrasse 1, Grünwald bei München

"Wanting to find a hotel near Munich but not in the centre, we discovered this former hunting lodge of the Bavarian dukes, converted into a 20-bed inn beside the river Isar. It is in the fashionable suburb of Grünwald, south of Munich. The friendly owners are remodelling the hotel, a curious mix of museum-quality antiques and do-it-yourself modern. There is a pleasant terrace overlooking the valley on which to have a drink, and a cheerful dining room where we had a good meal." The hotel recommends its "rustic coffee shop" and claims that the *Schloss* dates from 1293. (*Connie and John Partridge*) An inspector this year admired the setting and the decor but found the service erratic. More reports please.

Open All year except Christmas.
Rooms 3 suites, 7 double, 6 single – 6 with bath, 10 with shower, all with telephone and radio; TV on request.
Facilities Salon, bar, coffee shop, restaurant, Hunters Room for functions.
2 terraces with barbecue, 1 with beer garden. River and rock beach 5 minutes' walk. English spoken.
Location Take Grünwalderstrasse S out of Munich to Grünwald for 13 km; turn R on Schlossstrasse.
Restriction Not suitable for &.
Credit card Access, Amex, Diners.
Terms B&B: single 110 DM, double 150 DM, suite 180 DM. Full alc 40 DM.
Reduced rates for children sharing parents' room; special meals.

Marienbad Hotel *Tel* (089) 59 55 85 or 59 17 03
Barer Strasse 11

A family-run bed-and-breakfast hotel, quietly situated at the back of an office block and fairly central – near the neo-Hellenic Königsplatz and the fabulous Alte Pinakothek museum, and some 10 minutes' walk from the *Rathaus* area. Readers this year find it unassuming, pleasant and friendly, with large airy rooms and good breakfasts. (*Ian and Francine Walsh, Mr and Mrs D Steven McGuire, Muriel and Bob Safford, and others*)

Open All year.
Rooms 16 double, 11 single – 22 with shower and WC, all with telephone.
Facilities Lift. Salon with TV. English spoken. Possibly suitable for &.
Location Central, but very quiet; approach from Karolinenplatz. Parking nearby.
Credit cards None accepted.
Terms B&B: single 65–110 DM, double 150–180 DM. Reduced rates for children sharing parents' room. (No restaurant.)

Gästehaus Monopteros *Tel* (089) 29 23 48
Oettingerstrasse 35, Munich 22

"The ideal small *pension*, quite central, only some two kilometres from either the city centre or Schwabing, and right next to the southern end of the Englischer Garten ('Monopteros' is the name of a Greek-style temple in the Garten). The *pension* is run with a warm personal touch by exuberant Frau Kellenbach who puts fresh flowers in the bedrooms each Saturday. More important, she has installed a public mini-bar on the main landing, with wine and soft drinks in a fridge, and trusts her guests to be honest and sign their names for what they take. Her breakfasts are excellent, too, with boiled eggs, cheese, Würst, good coffee, and silver sugar bowls. My little room, with TV set and plenty of bright lamps for reading, was a mere 43 DM with breakfast – incredible value in this expensive city. Hot baths down the corridor, for no extra charge. Telephone messages taken efficiently. The only snag: front rooms suffer from tram noise. Good Yugoslav restaurant within 200 metres. Frau Kellenbach gives you a sticker for your windscreen, enabling you to make use of residents' parking in the street by the hotel." (*J A C A*) Book months ahead.

Open All year.
Rooms 8 Double, 3 single – 3 with shower.
Facilities Breakfast room. Some English spoken.
Location Adjoining Englischer Garten, just N of Bavarian National Museum. Street parking.
Credit cards None accepted.
Terms B&B: single 45 DM, double 88–114 DM. (No restaurant.)

Hotel an der Oper   *Tel* (089) 22 87 11
2 Falkenturmstrasse 10, Munich 2   *Telex* 522588

Unobtrusively tucked away in a small side-street off the famous and very fashionable Maximilianstrasse, this bed-and-breakfast hotel, as its name suggests, is much frequented by members of the Opera House. One visitor this year found it "simply super value, excellent in every way". Another visitor much enjoyed her large, well-equipped suite. Other rooms are not large, but have every modern amenity. Attached to the hotel is an excellent though expensive restaurant, *La Bouillabaisse*. The only snag is that various night-clubs appear to be under the hotel windows. (*Bryan Magee, May Gray, Judie Lannon*)

Open All year.
Rooms 55 – all with bath, telephone and radio.
Facilities Lift. Reception-cum-lounge, TV room, breakfast room; conference facilities.
Restriction Not suitable for &.
Location Central, near the Opera House.
Credit cards Access, Amex, Diners.
Terms [1985 rates] B&B: single 90–102 DM, double 130–158 DM.

OFFENBURG 7600 Baden-Württemberg   **Map 12**

Hotel Sonne   *Tel* (0781) 7 10 39
Hauptstrasse 94

"This industrial town is so near to Strasbourg, the Black Forest and the Frankfurt/Basel *Autobahn* that it makes a useful stopover. The *Sonne*, on its main steet, a typical small-town coaching-inn, made us snug on a snowy January night. The Schimpf-Schöppner family claim to have been running an inn here since 1350 (sic): though much rebuilt in the 19th century, the hotel still has many much older antiques. Napoleon stayed here, and you are shown the pewter tureen he used. Despite this weight of history, the *Sonne* is utterly unpretentious; no foyer, the front door leads straight into the big beamed *Stübe*, which today is very much a social centre. At its big round *Stammtisch*, elderly local worthies were tippling and speechifying in true German style, while we enjoyed sound Baden cooking (pork fillet with Spätzle etc) and local wine from the Schimpfs' own vineyards. Sumptuous ices, but buffet breakfast not quite up to the usual high German level. Our room [78 DM, 1985] was modernised, with good bathroom (some older rooms have more character, but lack baths). What value! – we paid less than £40 for dinner, B&B for two." (*J A*) "You can choose a room of the 18th or 19th century if you are an early arrival. We stayed in the new wing – very quiet and comfortable, but not such a delight for our antiquarian eyes." (*H C and Else Robbins Landon*)

Open All year. Restaurant closed 3 weeks before Easter.
Rooms 2 suites, 24 double, 15 single – 7 with bath, 11 with shower. Some with telephone. 11 rooms in annexe.
Facilities TV room, 2 dining rooms. English spoken.
Location Central; in old part of town. Parking.
Restriction Not suitable for &; access to restaurant only.
Credit cards Amex, Visa.
Terms B&B: single 53 DM, double 68–110 DM. Set lunch 18.50 DM; dinner 36 DM; full alc 31 DM.

OPPENAU-RAMSBACH 7603 Baden-Württemberg   **Map 12**

Höhengasthof Kalikutt   *Tel* (07804) 6 02

A well-built modern chalet-style hotel with typical heavily beamed rustic interior: high up in the Black Forest, with fine mountain views, it lies west of the little resort of Oppenau on the old Strasbourg/Stuttgart main road. "In 10 weeks touring by car, we enjoyed our stays at quite a few Guide hotels: the *Kalikutt* in many respects ranks with the best. Three miles up a winding, climbing road off the main highway, it serves as a good point from which to explore the beauty of the entire region. The hiking trails, and the hotel's cuisine and marvellous appointments, make the place entrancing. Herr Schmiederer is thorough and gracious; he speaks no English, but his wife does." (*Lois and Arthur Hansen*)

Open All year.
Rooms 20 double, 6 single – 2 with bath, 24 with shower, all with telephone, radio, TV, many with balcony.
Facilities Lift, ramps. Lounge with open fire, TV room, bar, dining room, conference room, sauna, solarium, games room; terrace with café. English spoken. &.
Location 4 km W of Oppenau which is 40 km E of Strasbourg.
Credit card Access.
Terms [1985 rates] B&B: 32–54 DM; half-board (min 3 days) 50–72 DM; full board (min 3 days) 58–80 DM. Set lunch/dinner 24 DM; full alc 30 DM. Low season reduction of 10%. Reduced rates and special meals for children.

Wherever possible, we have quoted prices per room. Not all hotels are prepared to quote tariffs in this way. In these cases, we have given prices per person, indicating the range of prices – the lowest is likely to be for sharing a double room out of season, the highest for a single room in the high season.

PASSAU 8390 Bavaria   Map 12

Hotel Weisser Hase   *Tel* (0851) 3 40 66
Ludwigstrasse 23

"Magnificent Passau, the Venice of the Danube", enthuses one visitor; "surely one of Europe's best-preserved 17th-century cities – and the peace of the Bayerische Wald begins at the doorstep." He recommends the *Weisser Hase* as a well-modernised hotel just inside the old part of the city: its café-terrace on the roof has a good view of Passau's remarkable setting at the three-river confluence of Danube, Inn and Ilz. "My room was absolute comfort, the service swift and efficient, and the food in its Bavarian way was delicious, in a restaurant where *Gemütlichkeit* comes in full measure. The hotel's interior has lost its medieval character but is tastefully decorated; the rooms lead off a functional inner courtyard on three floors, covered by a glass roof." (*Michael Bourdeaux*)

Open All year.
Rooms 100 double, 22 single – 87 with bath, 8 with shower, all with telephone, radio and TV.
Facilities Lift. Lounge, TV room, dining rooms, café, conference facilities; sun terrace. Courtyard. English spoken.
Location Central, between station and cathedral. Garage parking.
Credit cards All major cards accepted.
Terms B&B: single 55–75 DM, double 90–120 DM. Set meals 20 DM; full alc 35 DM. Reduced rates and special meals for children.

RETTENBACH 8449 St Englmar, Bavaria   Map 12

Kurhotel Gut Schmelmerhof   *Tel* (09965) 5 17

Rettenbach, about 15 minutes' drive from the Regensburg/Passau motorway, is a small village amid the hilly, pinewooded landscapes of eastern Bavaria, between the Danube and the Czech frontier. "The *Kurhotel*", runs a 1985 report, "is a large chalet-style building on the outskirts and has been owned by the Schmelmer family since 1630. It's a nice place for a stopover on the way to Austria, with good healthy air and lovely scenery. The hotel's excellent sporting facilities include indoor and outdoor pools, jacuzzi and sauna. Our room's furnishings were typically Bavarian, with wood panelling and hand-made rugs. The interesting restaurant has a low vaulted ceiling, and the menu is extensive and fairly priced – we much enjoyed the fresh asparagus with raw ham and fillet of wild hare. The large wine list even included English wines, and the breakfast buffet was very good. Staff unfailingly courteous, as in most German hotels." (*Kate and Steve Murray-Sykes*)

Open All year.
Rooms 7 suites, 20 double, 11 single – 39 with bath, 7 with shower, all with telephone and radio, 19 with colour TV.
Facilities Drawing room, TV room, bar, 3 restaurants, "Bayerisches Buffet" once a week, swimming pools indoor and outdoor. Garden, children's playground.
Location 4.5 km SE of St Englmar, which is 31 km NE of Straubing.
Restriction Not suitable for &.
Credit cards All major cards accepted.
Terms B&B: 28–69 DM; dinner, B&B: 49–105 DM. Full alc 40 DM. Special off-season rates. Children under 4 free; special meals.

ROTHENBURG OB DER TAUBER 8803 Bavaria Map 12

Hotel Eisenhut *Tel* (09861) 20 41
Herrngasse 3–7 *Telex* 61367

Enclosed within its 14th-century ramparts above the winding river
Tauber, this famous old town of cobbled streets, fountains and tall
gabled houses is as picturesque as any in Germany – like a medieval film
set, you could say, though it is no dead museum piece, for 12,000 people
live here, many of them within the walls. It was badly bombed in the
war, but has been faultlessly reconstructed. Especially fine is the
Rathaus, part 14th-century, part Renaissance, and almost opposite it
stands the famous old *Eisenhut*, very much in character with the town.
As a hotel it is little more than 100 years old, but the four houses that
form it date from the Middle Ages. It is in a superb old street leading off
the market place, and has been developed as a luxury hotel in ways that
mostly enhance its historic nature. The public rooms are furnished with
antiques and original paintings.

It must be reported that the hotel, much in demand today with
Japanese and American package tours, may be falling victim to its
renown. Some readers this year have been very satisfied. But there have
been many complaints of "garish bedroom decor" (hardly in keeping
with the hotel's character) and one visitor found the food "very
average". (*Vicki Turner, W R Hudson, Mrs C Smith, and others*) More
reports please.

Open 1 Mar–5 Jan.
Rooms 4 suites, 56 double, 20 single – 70 with bath, 10 with shower, all with
telephone and colour tv. 20 rooms in annexe.
Facilities Lift. Salon, bar, tv room, 2 restaurants; conference room. Garden,
terrace. English spoken.
Location Central (front rooms could be noisy). Parking. Rothenburg is 62 km S of
Würzburg. Warning: the town is closed to traffic on Whit Sun and Mon 0900–1700
hours.
Restriction Not suitable for &.
Credit cards All major cards accepted.
Terms B&B: single 140–155 DM, double 195–270 DM; dinner, B&B 48 DM added to
B&B rate; full board 96 DM added. Full alc 70 DM. No charge for children under 12
in parents' room.

Hotel Goldener Hirsch *Tel* (09861) 20 51
Untere Schmiedgasse 16/25 *Telex* 61372

"This old hostelry is not as stylish or picturesque as the *Eisenhut* (see
above), but its prices are a little lower, and in its own way it too has
plenty of character. It also has the better setting of the two, being built
over the ramparts, with superb views of the deep valley below, from the
dining room and some bedrooms. It has been renovated, elegantly if
maybe too formally, in a style that is part château, part coaching inn.
Our spacious bedroom was very well equipped, yet preserved a rustic
touch. The food was a little disappointing, as so often in German hotels
of this kind. But we enjoyed the view from our table, as dusk fell over
the lovely wooded valley. In summer you can eat out on a flowery open
terrace. Dignified old-style service. The hotel is in a quaint old street just
off the central square." (*J A C A; also D Sanders*)

Open All year except Dec and Jan.
Rooms 80 – 66 with bath or shower, most with telephone, radio and TV.
Facilities Lift. Salons, TV room, bar, conference facilities, restaurant *"Die Blaue Terrasse"*, café-restaurant on terrace. Garden.
Location Central, near the Weiberturm. Garage parking.
Credit cards All major cards accepted.
Terms [1985 rates] B&B: single 72–148 DM, double 120–240 DM. Set lunch/dinner 24–68 DM. Reduced rates for children.

RÜDESHEIM-ASSMANNSHAUSEN 6220 Hessen   Map 12

Hotel Krone   *Tel* (06722) 20 36
Rheinuferstrasse 10

Many well-known German writers have stayed and worked at this old Rhineside inn, dating from 1541. It is now a sizeable hotel in two buildings; many bedrooms have balconies overlooking the gardens and the river. "Very nice" says one visitor this year, backing up our previous entry: "The hotel is most attractive and comfortable. The staff are friendly and efficient, most of them speaking some English. There is a delightful vine-covered terrace outside the oldest part of the hotel, overlooking the river. The main restaurant, slightly raised with fine views of the passing river life, serves superb food, together with excellent local wines, one a red sparkling wine drunk as an aperitif. Our room was comfortable and well furnished with a small bathroom with shower/wc. A small circular 'turret' area contained a dining table and chairs. There is an attractive garden in front of the hotel with a swimming pool and plenty of room to relax. It is an ideal centre for exploring this part of the Rhine Valley, with its vineyards and historic towns and villages." (*Pat and Jeremy Temple, also Mrs C Smith*)

Only serious drawbacks: the rumble of trains in rooms at the back, and the noise from boats on the Rhine in front.

Open 15 Mar–15 Nov.
Rooms 2 suites, 48 double, 32 single – 36 with bath, 12 with shower, all with telephone, some with colour TV, many with balcony; 55 rooms in annexe; some ground-floor rooms.
Facilities Lift. Salons, TV room, bar restaurant; riverside terrace/restaurant; conference facilities. Garden with lawn, swimming pool and bar. English spoken.
Location Central, on the Rhine; 28 km from Wiesbaden. Parking.
Restriction Not suitable for &.
Credit cards All major cards accepted.
Terms [1985 rates] rooms: single 40–95 DM, double 80–200 DM, suite 225 DM. Breakfast 12 DM; full alc 60 DM.

ST BLASIEN-MENZENSCHWAND   Map 12
7821 Baden-Württemberg

Hotel Sonnenhof   *Tel* (07675) 501
Vorderdorf 58

A small family-run hotel in a beautiful and quiet Black Forest valley, with many walking trails in the area. "It only gets better," says a devotee returning this year and echoing his earlier praise: "An excellent restaurant where ravenous German walkers attack their food with the authority of a Mercedes diesel lorry. The particular glory of *Hotel Sonnenhof* is the jovial manager, Herr Wilhelm Jalowicki, who could not possibly be more helpful to his guests. His English is so idiomatic that he can make excellent puns in both languages." Other visitors this year agree: "Comfort and good food, delightful host". (*Jonathan Williams, J M Beaton, Dr R L Holmes*) Indoor swimming pool, sauna and fitness room.

Open All year except mid-Nov to 20 Dec.
Rooms 3 apartments, 24 double, 4 single – 8 with bath, 20 with shower, telephone and radio; TV on request.
Facilities Salon, TV room, restaurant, indoor swimming pool, sauna, solarium. Garden. Horse-riding nearby. English spoken.
Location 9 km NW of St Blasien, which is 62 km SE of Freiburg. Parking.
Restriction Not suitable for &.
Credit cards Probably none accepted.
Terms B&B: single 50–65 DM, double 130 DM; dinner, B&B 69–84 DM per person; full board 82–97 DM per person. Set lunch 20 DM, dinner 25 DM; full alc 30–50 DM. 10 Jan–31 Mar weekly packages including ski parties. Reduced rates for children.

SCHLOSS WEITENBURG 7245 Baden-Württemberg　　　　Map 12

Schloss Weitenburg　　　　　　　　　　　*Tel* (07457) 80 51 or 80 52

A large 16th-century castle on a hilltop, with breathtaking views over the Neckar valley between Horb and Tübingen. Owned since 1720 by the Barons of Rassler, it is one of a number of such *Schlösser* in this area that have been turned into hotels by their baronial owners as the best way of keeping the family estates together. "Our bedrooms were sumptuously furnished with antiques; the corridors were filled with beautiful chests and the lounges were full of character. The hotel is in extensive grounds, with riding school, swimming pool and sauna. There is a balcony over the valley where you can have drinks and meals. The dining room is massive and the food very acceptable. The welcome was most genuine." (*N E Godfrey*) "The hotel is run by a manager, but Baron von Rassler himself still lives there and is very much around, a charming and cultivated man and a great hunter. He has sensibly kept the hotel in its original style, modernising only those aspects that need it (eg bathrooms). He manages to give his customers the feeling that they really are guests in a private castle. One delightfully old-fashioned feature is the dignified elderly head waiter, who looks and behaves like an old-style English butler from, say, *Kind Hearts and Coronets*. Food good. I slept in the largest hotel suite I've ever seen outside the *Brenner's Park* at Baden-Baden (q.v.)." (*Katinka Schmitz*)

Open All year except 24–25 Dec.
Rooms 1 suite, 20 double, 16 single – 13 with bath, 20 with shower, all with telephone, radio, TV on request.
Facilities Lift to be installed Mar 1986. 2 lounges, bar, TV room, dining room, conference facilities; big balcony for drinks and meals. Large grounds with riding school, heated enclosed swimming pool, sauna and solarium. Golf course planned for 1986. English spoken.
Location 12 km E of Horb; from A81 motorway take Rottenburg exit, drive 10 minutes in the direction of Ergenzingan then follow signposts to Weitenburg.
Credit cards None accepted.
Terms B&B: single 74 DM, double 134 DM; half-board: single 107 DM, double 200 DM; full board: single 150 DM, double 286 DM. Set lunch 29 DM, supper 18 DM. Reduced rates and special meals for children.

SCHWANGAU 8959 Bavaria | Map 12

Schlosshotel Lisl und Jägerhaus
Neuschwansteinstrasse 1–3
Hohenschwangau

Tel (08362) 8 10 06
Telex 541332 LISLH

Recommended as a useful stopover for visiting the royal castles in their glorious mountain setting by the Austrian frontier – Hohenschwangau, right by the hotel, and Mad Ludwig's high-pinnacled fairytale Neuschwanstein. "The staff were friendly and helpful and the evening meal quite good. Best of all, each of us had a view of one castle or other from his window. What a romantic spot to spend the night – silent Neuschwanstein bathed in light, and all the daytime crowds gone." "We had a comfortable if idiosyncratic room, with lavish use of wood, figured velvet carpet on the floor and half the walls ditto, presided over by an engraving of an impossibly handsome King Ludwig. The dining room's immense windows had Hohenschwangau castle in full, floodlit view. Breakfast was in a room with an acoustic quality that turned the other guests' conversation into an agreeable low-pitched hum. A medium-sized hotel with the 'feel' of a large one, yet not impersonal: we were comfortable there." (*Dorothy Masterson, M J and C I Robertson*)

Open All year.
Rooms 46 double, 10 single – 27 with bath, 19 with shower, all with telephone, radio and TV; 21 rooms in annexe.
Facilities Lift. Lounge, TV room, dining room, conference room. Nearby lake with safe bathing and fishing rights. English spoken.
Location 6 km S of Fussen.
Restriction Not suitable for &.
Credit cards All major cards accepted.
Terms B&B: single 30–70 DM, double 50–170 DM. Full alc 32–37 DM. Group and off-season rates. Reduced rates and special meals for children.

SCHWARZWALD-HOCHSTRASSE 7580 Baden-Württemberg | Map 12

Höhen-Hotel Unterstmatt
Bühl

Tel (07226) 2 04 and 2 09

Dropped from the Guide for lack of feedback, but now reprieved by a reporter who relished its "breezy après-ski charm": "The Black Forest High Road winds along the high hillcrest from Baden-Baden to Freudenstadt, with fine views over the Rhine plain below. Several good holiday hotels are here: the *Unterstmatt*, by no means the smartest, is one of the most appealing – a warm, informal place in the best local tradition. It's a family place, owned and run since 1905 by the local Reymann family, catering for families who come to ski in winter or hike in summer. Circled by deep pine forests, it has its own ski-slope (for beginners) rising from its back terrace: this is floodlit for night skiing and has a snow-machine using up to 100,000 litres of water a day. Ski-school, too. Bedrooms are simple, in rustic style, with bright colours: ours had a curious Baden painted wardrobe and four-poster. The lively cellar *Stübe* has harmonica music and once a month a pantomime. Joviality reigns: yet the food, starred in *Michelin*, is unusually good for a ski-hotel, pleasantly served by girls in pink dirndls. Superb local smoked ham served with kirsch and crispy country bread; good Baden white wines; Schwarzwälderkirschtorte surprisingly disappointing." (JA)

Open 15 Dec–3 Nov. Restaurant closed Mon in summer.
Rooms 1 suite, 11 double, 6 single – 6 with bath, 9 with shower, all with telephone and TV. All rooms in separate building from restaurant.
Facilities Hall, rustic bar, restaurant. Music on Fri evening. Garden with terrace and lawn. Skiing and walking. English spoken.
Location 15 km S of Baden-Baden.
Restriction Not suitable for &.
Credit cards All major cards accepted.
Terms B&B 50–55 DM; dinner, B&B 70 DM; full board 88–93 DM. Set lunch 15 DM, dinner 21 DM; full alc 48 DM. Weekend reductions.

SEEG 8959 Bavaria   Map 12

Pension Heim   *Tel* (083 64) 2 58
Aufmberg 8

"An immaculate family-run *pension* set on a small hilltop, 10 miles north of Füssen and the Ludwig II castle of Neuschwanstein. Wonderful views of the Allgäu Alps to the south, and pleasant views from the north as well, over meadows, lakes and forest. The house itself is quite new. The south-facing rooms have balconies looking across the small garden. Some of the bedrooms have furniture carved by Herr Heim himself, a real craftsman. The whole house is white-painted and immaculate with geraniums everywhere. The living/dining room is beautiful and cosy, with a lovely outlook over the garden. I thought this house a real smasher – thoroughly recommendable to anyone visiting the royal castles, away from the tourist crowds in the mountains, but near enough to be able to see them. Splendid value, too." (S L)

Open 20 Dec–1 Nov.
Rooms 14 double, 4 single – 3 with bath, 15 with shower, all with telephone; some with balcony; colour TV on request.
Facilities Salon, restaurant, sauna, terrace and lawns.
Location On hilltop outside Seeg which is 15 km NW of Füssen.
Restriction Not suitable for &.
Terms B&B: single 45–50 DM, double 80–90 DM; dinner, B&B: single 55–60 DM, double 100–110 DM. Reductions for stays of 2 days or more.

SPROCKHÖVEL 4322 Nordrhein-Westfalen   Map 12

Rotisserie Landhaus Leick   *Tel* (02324) 7 34 33
Bochumerstrasse 67

A very civilised little restaurant-with-rooms, once a manor house, quite near the Ruhr but in a quiet rural location with its own park; it is close to the Wuppertal/Bochum Autobahn *and just south of the old medieval town of Hattingen. The elegant decor is part "rustic" in style (some rooms have four-poster beds) and part modern. The cuisine, with the accent on poultry, is among the very finest in the land (Michelin rosette). "Small and excellent. Big attractively decorated bedroom in good taste. Superb but expensive dinner, attractive garden."* (Conrad Dehn) *More reports welcome.*

Open 21 Jan–31 Dec. Restaurant closed Sun, and Mon midday.
Rooms 1 suite, 5 double – 4 with bath, 2 with shower, all with telephone, radio, colour TV and mini-bar. 1 in annexe.
Facilities Hall, bar, 3 dining rooms; facilities for parties. Garden. English spoken.
Location 2 km from Sprockhövel: from Wuppertal/Recklinghausen *Autobahn* take Sprockhövel exit towards Hattingen. After 3 traffic lights turn right to Bochum; after 600 metres left in Park.
Restriction Not suitable for &.
Credit cards Access, Amex, Diners.
Terms Rooms: single occupancy 78–106 DM, double 117–156 DM. Breakfast 12 DM; set lunch/dinner 58–98 DM; full alc 68 DM.

STUTTGART 7000 Baden-Württemberg   Map 12

Gaststätte zum Muckenstüble   *Tel* (0711) 86 51 22
Solitudestrasse 25, Stuttgart 31 (Weilimdorf)

"Stuttgart is much the most attractively situated of all the larger German cities. It is not flat, like the others, but climbs up the sides of a narrow wooded valley, and its residential suburbs have spread their way into the undulating forest all around. On the edge of one of these, Weilimdorf, 10 kilometres west of the city centre, we found the delightful *Muckenstüble*, a true Swabian country pub, and a pleasant contrast to the big down-town hotels. It is a modern building in the traditional local style, red-roofed, gabled and half-timbered, with functional but comfortable rooms, all spotless, and a spacious garden with children's playground. And all so cheap! Local Swabians on a Saturday were packing the big wood-ceilinged dining room, all eating vast sticky cakes. We had lunch on the garden-terrace in the sun, a typical Swabian country meal, excellent in its lavish simplicity; Maultaschensuppe (broth with spinach ravioli), Sauerbraten with dumplings, roast sucking pig with Spätzle (crinkly flour noodles) and sweetish local wine. All this for a mere 60 DM for two. We were so close to the city, yet seemed to be in the heart of rural Swabia. The forest began at the garden's edge, and after lunch we walked up through the trees to the famous Schloss Solitude on its hilltop, built by an 18th-century Duke of Württemberg for one of his mistresses." (*J A C A*)

Open All year except 22 July–15 Aug and Christmas.
Rooms 9 double, 13 single – 14 with bath, 8 with shower, all with telephone; many with balcony.
Facilities Lift. TV room, restaurant. Garden with terrace and childrens' play area.
Location 10 km W of central Stuttgart. Parking.
Terms [1985 rates] B&B: single 40–50 DM, double 74–84 DM. Set lunch 10–30 DM, supper 6–20 DM; full alc 35–40 DM.

Hotel Royal   *Tel* (0711) 62 50 50
Sophienstrasse 35, Stuttgart 1   *Telex* 722449

"The *Royal*, a good deal smaller than the *Zeppelin* and the *Am Schlossgarten*, is generally regarded as the most agreeable of the smarter hotels in down-town Stuttgart. It lacks any special charm, but is well appointed in a modern style, with thick carpets, dark pine, soft lighting, and a general air of plushness. My room was well equipped and quiet (the hotel is in a side-street). The restaurant serves standard Swabiancum-international dishes, carefully prepared, rather rich; desserts disappointing, mainly fruit and ice coupes. For true Swabian cooking (probably Germany's best) at modest cost, try *Börse* or the *Stüble* of the *Zeppelin Hotel*. The *Royal* is 10 minutes' walk from central Stuttgart's main tourist sights – the Schillerplatz, Neues Schloss, lovely Schlossgarten with its lake, and James Stirling's controversial new museum at the Staatsgalerie. (*J A C A*)

Open All year except Christmas.
Rooms 2 suites, 30 double, 70 single – all with bath, telephone, radio, colour TV.
Facilities Lounge, TV room, bar, restaurant, conference facilities. English spoken.
Location Central, near Österreicher-Platz. Limited parking.
Credit cards All major cards accepted.
Restriction Not suitable for ₺.
Terms B&B 132.50–197.50 DM; dinner, B&B 167.50–222.50 DM; full board 187.50–242.50 DM. Set lunch/dinner 20–30 DM; full alc 60–80 DM. Reduced rates and special meals for children.

TRIBERG IM SCHWARZWALD 7740 Baden-Württemberg   Map 12

Parkhotel Wehrle   *Tel* (07722) 40 81
Gartenstrasse 24   *Telex* 792609

Triberg, in the heart of the Black Forest, is a famous watch- and cuckoo-clock-making centre as well as a popular skiing and hiking resort. The *Parkhotel*, in the town centre, is a fairly luxurious and sumptuously furnished old hostelry, one of the Romantik-Hotels group and highly reputed; it has been owned and run by the Wehrle/Blum family since 1707. Some rooms are in the old building, others in two more modern ones in a park to one side. "Klaus Blum is a warm and civilised host and imparts a cultivated atmosphere," runs one report this year; "service is skilled and stylish, and the excellent cuisine deserves its *Michelin* rosette (20 ways with trout, a speciality). Delightful outdoor and indoor swimming pools. Many rather grand people come here for special occasions, such as groups of Arab sheikhs or Stuttgart tycoons." "Real style; not unlike the *Eisenhut* at Rothenburg" (q.v.). "Scrupulously managed in old-fashioned style but with plenty of space-age plumbing and a full complement of rest and recreation facilities." (*Katinka Schmitz, Patrick Till, Jonathan Williams*)

Open All year.
Rooms 3 suites, 43 double, 14 single – 46 with bath, 9 with shower, all with direct-dial telephone, radio and mono TV (colour on request); 29 rooms in annexe.
Facilities Lounge, TV room, dining rooms, billiard room; conference room with projector and video. Indoor and outdoor heated swimming pools; sauna, solarium, massage. Large garden. English spoken. ₺ (dining rooms only).
Location Central, near market place; some rooms might be noisy (quiet ones overlook garden). Parking.
Credit cards All major cards accepted.
Terms B&B: 64.50–110.50 DM; half-board 30 DM per person added; full board another 15 DM added. Set lunch 32 DM, dinner 42–62 DM; full alc 55 DM. 15% reductions in low season. Reduced rates and special meals for children.

We get less feedback from smaller and more remote hotels. But we need feedback on all hotels: big and small, far and near, famous and first-timers.

TRIER 5500 Rheinland-Pfalz   Map 12

Petrisberg Hotel   *Tel* (0651) 4 11 81
Sickingenstrasse 11–13

"Easily the pleasantest hotel in town." "First egg-and-bacon breakfast I've had on the Continent." "Superb, with magnificent rooms, those at the front with views over this old Roman town." So run three recent comments on this modern, family-run bed-and-breakfast place (but light meals are served in the evening) that stands above the city, amid vineyards, and close to the Roman amphitheatre. Most of the rooms overlooking the city have balconies; those at the back are quieter, but darker. Personal service by the proprietor (who speaks English). Trier is rich in history: under the Emperor Diocletian it became the capital of Gaul – a lost grandeur evoked by the Porta Nigra, the finest Roman relic in Germany. Trier is the native town of Karl Marx, and his house is now a museum. The town is also the centre of the Mosel wine trade. (*D Bailley, John Hayward, S L*)

Open All year.
Rooms 2 suites, 26 double – 2 with bath, all with shower, all with telephone, many with balcony; TV on request; some ground-floor rooms, 11 in annexe.
Facilities Salon, breakfast room, TV room; terraces. English spoken.
Location 20 minutes' walk from town centre (near Roman Amphitheatre). Parking area and garages (4.50 DM).
Restriction Not suitable for &.
Credit cards None accepted.
Terms B&B: single 65–70 DM, double 95–100 DM. (No restaurant, but light evening meals available.)

TÜBINGEN 7400 Baden-Württemberg   Map 12

Hotel Krone   *Tel* (07071) 3 10 36
Uhlandstrasse 1   *Telex* 7262762 KRON

"Tübingen may lack the Oxbridge style of social and collegiate life, but it has more of the looks and feel of an old university city than most on the Continent: 29,000 students and teachers are here, in a town of 75,000. Charming old university buildings, in pastel shades of pink, yellow and blue, stand terraced on the steep slope above the Neckar, below the medieval Schloss; on the river, girls laze in punts in summer, as pretty as any on the Cherwell. The *Krone*, very central, just south of the main bridge, is the leading hostelry, solid, well appointed, very comfortable. Decor veers between modern, semi-kitsch and pleasant repro, with beamed ceilings. I did not try the cuisine, which has a fair local reputation: but I did well in the town, at modest cost, at such places as the *Mauka-Neschtle*, below the Schloss, which has 26 interesting ways of serving Maultaschen, Swabia's ubiquitous spinach ravioli." (*J A*)

Open All year except 22–30 Dec.
Rooms 5 suites, 15 double, 31 single – 48 with bath or shower, all with direct-dial telephone; TV on request. Sound-proofed windows.
Facilities Lift. Lounge, bar, restaurants. English spoken.
Location Central. Garages.
Terms B&B: single 83 DM, double 160 DM. Full alc from 25 DM. Reduced rates for children sharing parents' room; special meals.

WANGEN-IM-ALLGÄU 7988 Baden-Württemberg   Map 12

Hotel Alte Post   *Tel* (07522) 40 14
Postplatz 2   *Telex* 732774

Not far from the Allgäu alps and the eastern end of the Bodensee, Wangen is a lively and pretty little Swabian market town, with old walls and houses with figurative signs on them. The *Alte Post* belongs to the Romantik Hotels association and has all the studied *Gemütlichkeit* you might expect, as well as some true Swabian charm. "An unusual place. One mounts a marble staircase (no lift) to the second or third floor. Flowers and antiques are placed along the way. We have stayed there four times, each time in a different room, done up differently. This year we were given a room at the top where the beam read '1579'. The sitting part of the room had a sofa as well as easy chairs, and the bathroom was well equipped. Breakfast is in a handsome room – meats and cheeses, but poor coffee. What we like above all about this place is its personal, family quality." (*Ruth and Lester Luborsky*)

Open All year.
Rooms 4 suites, 16 double, 12 single – 20 with bath, 12 with shower, all with telephone, radio and colour TV; 10 rooms are in villa.
Facilities Lounge, TV room, restaurant; conference and function facilities. Large garden surrounds villa. English spoken.
Location Central. Wangen is 20 km NE of Lindau on Ulm road. Parking.
Restriction Not suitable for &.
Credit cards All major cards accepted.
Terms B&B: single 60–65 DM, double 110–125 DM, suites 140–190 DM. Set lunch 12–36 DM, dinner 15–60 DM. Reduced rates for children.

WEIKERSHEIM 6992 Baden-Württemberg   Map 12

Hotel Laurentius   *Tel* (07934) 70 07
Marktplatz 5

This attractive little town on the Romantic Road, 42 kilometres south of Würzburg, is built round a 17th-century Hohenlohe castle beside the Tauber, worth seeing for its splendid Knights' Hall and furniture collection. "An absolute winner", say nominators of the *Laurentius* this year, a newly opened hotel in an old building where Goethe's ancestors lived. "It overlooks the quiet and pretty market square, facing up to the *Schloss* entrance where there is an international music school. Frau Koch speaks fluent English, Herr Koch gave us the best food we had had in Germany." You eat in an old vaulted cellar, and can take drinks and breakfast on a flowery patio. (*D Quirk*)

Open All year except Jan.
Rooms 10 double, 2 single – 4 with bath, 6 with shower, all with telephone, radio and mono TV.
Facilities Lift. Café, restaurants; conference facilities for 50 people; terrace. Park nearby. English spoken.
Location Central, in market square, opposite castle entrance. Parking.
Credit cards Amex, Diners.
Terms B&B: single 48–60 DM, double 75–90 DM; dinner, B&B: single 68–80 DM, double 115–130 DM; full board: single 78–90 DM, double 135–150 DM. Set lunch/dinner 14–25 DM; full alc 35 DM. Reduced rates and special meals for children.

WERTHEIM 6980 Baden-Württemberg   Map 12

Hotel Schwan   *Tel* (09342) 12 78
Mainplatz 8

A turreted castle stands on the wooded slopes above this pretty town of half-timbered houses at the confluence of the Main and Tauber rivers, west of Würzburg. In the main square, the *Schwan* is an attractive traditional inn with some Good Samaritan virtues: "We arrived at 9 pm with two children, tired, and with our luggage eight kilometres away. We were given a delicious dinner, a very comfortable room with bathroom, an excellent breakfast – and the owner's son drove into the night to retrieve our luggage! We have never known service like it, and the price was very reasonable. We shall certainly go back." The large menu has some local Franconian specialities. (*Camille Sampson*)

Open All year.
Rooms 30 double, 10 single – 10 with bath, 15 with shower; all with telephone, radio, and colour TV. 10 rooms in annexe; some ground-floor rooms.
Facilities Bar, TV room, conference room, restaurant. Large terrace. River nearby; fishing rights. English spoken.
Location Central; parking. Wertheim is 42 km W of Würzburg.
Credit cards Access, Amex, Diners.
Terms B&B: single 70–80 DM, double 80–120 DM; dinner, B&B: single 95–105 DM, double 105–170 DM; full board: single 120–130 DM, double 130–220 DM. Set lunch 20 and 35 DM, dinner 20 and 40 DM; full alc 58 DM. 10% reductions for children.

XANTEN 4232 Nordrhein-Westfalen   Map 12

Limes Hotel   *Tel* (02801) 40 91
Niederstrasse 1   *Telex* 518/280131

Xanten, just north-west of the Ruhr conurbation, is a former Roman town, its remains carefully preserved. One of its attractions in early summer is a series of Handel concerts in the beautifully restored St Viktor Dom. The *Limes* was completed in 1983. "The name means 'Roman boundary', and indeed traces of Roman days emerged when the hotel was built. We found it in a quiet side-street two minutes' drive from the medieval town centre. Inside it is attractively designed, modern, stylish and airy: light-blue, white and yellow dominate. Our room was well equipped; fine linen, lovely curtains, but, surprisingly, no blankets available as an alternative to heavier duvets. The hotel's *Fünf Gulden* restaurant also has a pleasant atmosphere, as well as nostalgic showcases with old kitchen utensils and framed embroidery. Some dishes were over-salted, but most of the food was delicious, partly in French style, with fresh ingredients sent from Paris markets. Big choice on the breakfast buffet; friendly and helpful service. From here it was a short drive through meadows to the Dutch border." (*Christine Herxheimer, Gabriele Berneck*)

Open All year.
Rooms 2 suites, 40 double, 8 single – all with shower and WC, telephone, radio, colour TV and mini-bar; baby-listening on request. 6 rooms specially designed for &.

548

Facilities Lift. Lounge, bar, restaurant, conference room. Rhine 1 km; fishing, sailing, surfing, boating. Recreation centre 2 km. &. (ramps and special wcs). English spoken.
Location Xanten is 42 km NW of Duisburg, 16 km W of Wessel. Hotel is central. Underground car park (5 DM).
Credit cards All major cards accepted.
Terms B&B: single 76–86 DM, double 117–147 DM; full board: single 126–136 DM, double 217–247 DM. Set lunch 25 DM, dinner 30 DM; full alc 55 DM. Sporting and cultural programmes.

HOTEL VOURLIS
HERMOPOULIS

ATHENS **Map 17**

Museum Hotel *Tel* (01) 360.56.11/12/13
16 Bouboulinas and Tossitsa Sts

"The Museum Hotel *is perfectly placed for the Archaeological Museum on the other side of the street. Like most Athens streets, Bouboulinas is excruciatingly noisy until quite late at night. But is there such a thing as a quiet hotel in Athens? Omonia Square, five minutes away, has a trolley bus almost to the foot of the Acropolis. The hotel is modern, our room was plain but perfectly adequate, with good beds and lights, private loo and shower. Breakfast is of the teabag/coffee sachet and powdery rusk variety, which seems to be the order of the day in Greece. No restaurant, but we were recommended to the excellent taverna* Kostoyannis *in a nearby street, with a mainly Greek clientele. This saves a long trek down to the Plaka and gives one a much more genuine, less touristy meal at a remarkably reasonable price for the quality offered."* (Ian and Agathe Lewin) *More reports please.*

Open All year.
Rooms 52 double, 7 single – all with shower, telephone and radio.
Facilities Lift. Lounge with TV, bar/cafeteria. English spoken.
Location Central; near Archaeological Museum. No special parking facilities.
Credit cards Access, Amex, Diners.
Terms B&B: single 1,150–1,800 drs, double 1,700–2,400 drs.

Saint George Lykabettus Hotel
Kleomenous 2, Platia Dexamenis,
Kolonaki

Tel (01) 729.0710/19
Telex 214253 HEAM

A de luxe hotel in the fashionable Kolonaki section of the city, at the foot of Lykabettus hill and close to Constitution hill. You can walk down to the centre of things in ten minutes, but a cab (not expensive in Athens) is recommended for the return journey. There is a rooftop swimming pool, refreshing after a hot and dusty day in the city. Some of the rooms are decidedly small. Those with a view – right across the rooftops of the city to the Acropolis – can be noisy as cars driving up the hill take the hairpin bends at speed. "An excellent place for a stay in Athens", writes one visitor this year; "modern, comfortable, lovely setting, and not over-expensive for a hotel of its class" (William Goodhart). Another, retired from running a former Guide hotel in Switzerland, added these compliments: "Superb, considering the standard of hotels in Greece. The staff at reception were most helpful in every way" (Curtis Wilmot-Allistone). But there were vociferous opposition views: dark, dingy, dirty – "the pits". We need more reports please.

Open All year.
Rooms 4 suites, 124 double, 21 single – all with bath, telephone, radio, tea-making facilities and air-conditioning, some with balcony; TV on request; some ground-floor rooms.
Facilities Lift. Residents' lounge, lounges with TV, bar, snack bar, restaurants, grill room, roof garden and swimming pool; nightly entertainment in restaurant; dancing on roof. English spoken. &.
Location At foot of Lykabettus hill. Large garage.
Credit cards All major cards accepted.
Terms [1985 rates] rooms: single 3,260–5,040 drs, double 4,625–6,875 drs, suites 7,920–16,490 drs. Breakfast 350 drs; set lunch/dinner 1,050 drs.

CHANIA Crete   Map 17

Contessa
Theofanous 15R, Palio Limani

Tel (0821) 23966 or 57437

Many Crete-lovers regard Chania as by far the most attractive town on the island, a fascinating mixture of Turkish and Venetian architecture and a cheerful bustling port. The *Contessa* will suit those who like to be at the centre of things. It is an old family house, by the harbour in the heart of the old port, carefully restored by its owner into a small bed-and-breakfast hotel. Readers have stressed "the courtesy of the owner and all the staff" and "the impeccable taste of all the decor and fittings – it is essential to ask for the room with the painted ceiling, absolutely unique and a real knock-out. The only meal served is breakfast but the care, concern and attention to detail is beyond praise. The charm of the owner surpasses even that of Cretans in general." A reader this year, who lives in Crete, says: "It's certainly doing a roaring business – full, and turning people away in droves one morning when I was waiting for my visitors (with a free cup of coffee)." Booking essential. *(P Conrad Russell, Peter Bowen)*

Open 1 Apr–31 Oct.
Rooms 2 triple,4 double – all with bath, telephone and radio; baby-listening on request. All rooms are in annexe.
Facilities Bar with TV, breakfast room. Swimming pool at *Xenia* hotel nearby. 15 minutes' walk to beach. Some English spoken.
Location Overlooking old Venetian harbour; 1 km from town centre. Parking 150 metres away.
Restriction Not suitable for &.
Credit cards None accepted.
Terms [1985 rates] B&B double 3,000–3,600 drs. (No restaurant.) 10% reductions for children.

DELPHI Central Greece   Map 17

Hotel Vouzas   *Tel* (0265) 82232
1 Pavlou and Frederikis   *Reservations* in Athens:
                                  Tel (01) 7752732 *Telex* 214155

"The location is a knock-out and probably the view one gets with breakfast is worth the price of the hotel," says our inspector this year. The hotel is on the east end of town, built into the side of the mountain overlooking a deep valley circled by eagles. An earlier report ran: "You enter the lobby which is on the *top* floor, and descend by elevator to your room. The *Vouzas* was once *the* great hotel in Delphi. Its business has been somewhat eclipsed by big modern hotels, and it may be considered a touch faded, but it is a marvellous place to stay. On a non-windy day meals are served from a wonderful open veranda off the lobby, birds filling the air. Food tends to be 'continental' rather than indigenous." Our inspector continues: "The rooms can be noisy depending on your neighbours, but, given the design of the place, no street noises (rare in Greece). The place was very well heated (January). Breakfast was okay – nothing special – good service, coffee real. We had an amazing meal at a hole-in-the-wall taverna-cum-butcher shop down the street, booze ad lib, for less than a meal without wine would have cost one of us at the hotel, and I'll bet it was better, too. Nonetheless, the hotel is well worth maintaining in the Guide." *(P B, Tim Wolf)*

Open All year.
Rooms 1 suite, 52 double, 5 single – 47 with bath, 11 with shower; all with radio.
Facilities Lift. Lobby lounge, lounge, bar, roof garden with bar in summer, restaurant. English spoken.
Location On E end of town. Parking.
Credit cards All major cards accepted.
Terms [1985 rates, excluding tax] rooms: single 2,525 drs, double 3,294 drs. Breakfast 300 drs; set lunch/dinner 1,000 drs.

Can you help us extend our coverage in Greece?

Italicised entries are for hotels on which we need more feedback – either because we are short of reports or because we have had mixed or inadequate reports.

FERMA Crete   Map 17

Coriva Village   *Tel* (0842) 61263
Ierapetra   *Telex* 262508 COR

Until fairly recently, the southern coast of Crete has escaped the
leviathan of development. Now, however, new hotels have begun to
sprout around the sleepy port of Ierapetra. *Coriva Village* is an A-class
hotel and bungalow complex (not big by the standard of these
establishments), about eight kilometres from the port and one from the
village of Ferma. It has its own swimming pool, and a nearby disco. "An
exquisite hotel," writes one grateful visitor this year, endorsing last year's
entry, and mentioning in particular the exceptional restaurant and the
large spotless swimming pool. "The great delight of this hotel at the
moment is that it is quiet and many of the rooms are in bungalows
surrounded by flowering shrubs. The beach itself is not very impressive,
but if one walks about 500 yards beyond the taverna on the beach, one
finds small secluded coves which are sheltered from the wind and
excellent for swimming. Unfortunately, there are signs even here of
building, and one cannot guarantee that the peace and quiet of this hotel
will last for many more years." *(Len Ratoff, Stephanie Sowerby)*

Open Apr–Oct.
Rooms 42 double (11 in main house, 31 in bungalows) – 37 with bath, 5 with
shower; all with telephone and air-conditioning; bungalows have terraces.
Facilities Salon with TV, bar, taverna, restaurant. Lawns and swimming pool. On
beach: water-sports. Cretan evenings once a week. Nightclub nearby. English
spoken.
Location 8 km E of Ierapetra; 1 km from Ferma. Parking.
Restriction Not suitable for &.
Credit cards None accepted.
Terms Dinner, B&B: single 2,500 drs, double 4,500 drs; full board 500 drs per
person added. Lunch in taverna 500 drs, set dinner in restaurant 650 drs. Children
under 8 free.

FIRA Santorini, Cyclades   Map 17

Hotel Kavalari   *Tel* (0286) 22455

The volcanic island of Santorini is a striking crescent shape. You sail into
a wide bay, thought to be the crater of a volcano which erupted in
Minoan times, throwing up the spectacular cliffs of pumice and lava that
surround the bay. The white-washed town of Fira is perched on the
cliffs, 800 steps up from the harbour; you can ride up by mule or take a
cable car – "for those tourists who are afraid to come up by mules," says
the *Kavalari*. "The very pleasant C-class *Kavalari* is dug out of the
mountain-side. Like many of these small hotels in the Greek islands, it
only serves bed and breakfast. It is inexpensive, clean and romantic, and
in the morning has the most beautiful views." *(Lord Beaumont)*
    A recent visitor gives this advice: "Beware not to take a room sight
unseen. Some are dark with the loo down the hall." Other visitors, while
warning that rooms are damp and that hot showers have a timer – four
minutes and you get a cold douche – endorse Lord Beaumont's
commendation: "We felt that the breathtaking view from the individual

patios where we had breakfast, watched the sunset with a glass of ouzo in hand, and where we could sun ourselves when not inclined to head toward the beach, were such valuable assets that we cheerfully put up with short showers and damp rooms. A further advantage is the hotel's central location. And it will do your laundry for a fraction of the cost of the local laundry service." *(Thomas C Seoh, Carol Christensen and Fred Parker)*

Open Apr–Oct inclusive.
Rooms 5 triple, 7 double, 10 single – all with shower, many with patio.
Facilities Breakfast room. Terraces; garden. Beaches nearby. English spoken.
Location 100 metres from town centre.
Restrictions Not suitable for elderly or &. No children under 10.
Credit cards None accepted.
Terms [1985 rates] rooms: single 790–1,050 drs, double 1,720–2,000 drs. Breakfast 175–200 drs. (No restaurant.)

HERAKLION Crete   Map 17

Hotel Lato   *Tel* (081) 225001
15 Epimenidou   *Telex* 262631

The *Hotel Lato* is conveniently located – a five-minute walk up from the old Venetian harbour and about the same the other way to the town centre and its dusty archaeological museum. "You can see the neon sign when the boat pulls in. A solid, relatively large class C hotel, it boasts a pleasant rooftop garden bar and minor brasserie (try their special spaghetti, which contains everything but the kitchen sink). If you can get Room 502 as we did, which is situated on the same rooftop level as the bar, but with its own large patio balcony overlooking the Aegean blue sea, the harbour and the Venetian castle, the *Lato* has to be the best value, indeed the best full stop, in Heraklion" *(T C Seoh)*. More reports welcome.

Open All year.
Rooms 44 double, 9 single – 5 with bath, 48 with shower; all with telephone and radio. Some ground-floor rooms.
Facilities Lift. Lobby/bar with TV, writing room, breakfast room; roof garden with snack bar, overlooking old Venetian port. English spoken.
Location Central, opposite the harbour. Parking.
Credit cards Amex, Diners, Visa.
Terms B&B: single 1,680–1,890 drs, double 1,760–2,490 drs.

HERMOUPOLIS (or ERMOUPOLIS) Syros, Cyclades   Map 17

Hotel Vourlis   *Tel* (0281) 28440
Mavrogordatou 5

Syros is in the centre of the Cyclades ("circle") islands, reached by boat from Piraeus or by air to Mykonos and then on by boat. Hermoupolis is a picturesque town of predominantly neo-classical architecture with houses that rise tier after tier on the slopes of two conical hills. The *Hotel Vourlis* is a 19th-century mansion in this neo-classical style, transformed into what one reader calls "a small, superb luxury hotel. Managed by an Englishwoman, this is a hotel with a difference and a lot of class. There are seven bedrooms, individually decorated, containing original paintings by Greek artists, each with its own well-equipped bathroom. All furnishings are of the highest quality and the individual attention and service are in keeping with the hotel's class A grading. Very strongly recommended – a beautiful hotel. As yet no restaurant but English and continental breakfasts and snacks available." *(L G Trowler)*

Open All year.
Rooms 1 suite, 5 double, 1 single – all with bath and telephone; baby-listening on request. Some ground-floor rooms.
Facilities Ramp. Hall, lounge/breakfast room with bar facilities. Small front garden and patio. 100 metres from shingle beach with safe bathing and fishing. Windsurfing, waterskiing, sailing, tennis and mini-golf all available nearby. English spoken.
Location Hermoupolis is the capital of Syros, which is the capital of the Cyclades. Daily boat connections from Piraeus and Rafina. Hotel is central. Parking.
Credit cards All major cards accepted.
Terms B&B: single 2,719–3,812 drs, double 3,356–4,722 drs. (No restaurant, but snacks available.)

IMEROVIGLION Santorini, Cyclades   Map 17

Hotel Katerina   *Tel* (0286) 2.2708

Beaches on the island of Santorini are volcanic black sand, a striking contrast to the topless and/or nude bathers that often frequent them. "We were enchanted both with the island of Santorini and with the *Katerina*, and we plan to return. Built on the side of a cliff overlooking the caldera of an ancient volcano that blew away half the island in 1450 BC, this tiny E-class hotel makes up in charm for what may be lacking in luxury. The atmosphere is friendly,thanks to owner Anthony Hadjiconstantis who goes out of his way to make guests feel at home. The view of the sunset over the caldera and outer island is magnificent, and the serenity is unmatched due to the hotel's location half an hour's walk north of the island's main village, Fira, often crawling with tourists. Meals can be taken in Fira or at one of the tavernas in Imeroviglion that cater mainly for locals but always welcome tourists." *(Jan Shannon)*

Open 15 Mar–15 Dec.
Rooms 2 4-bedded, 7 double – all with h & c.
Facilities Lounges, bar with TV, restaurant, Greek nights with dancing most evenings, roof garden, verandas, swimming pool nearby, beach 9 km, fishing. English spoken.
Location 1.5 km N of Fira.
Restrictions Not suitable for &. No children under 12.
Credit cards None accepted.
Terms B&B: single occupancy 1,510–1,870 drs, double 2,420–2,980 drs.

MYRINA Lemnos   Map 17

Hotel Akti Myrina   *Tel* (0254) 22.681 or 22.310 or
Myrina Beach   23.687
                                              Telex 297173 MYRI GR

The *Akti Myrina*, the only *Relais de Campagne* hotel in Greece, overlooks a bay just outside Myrina, the small main town of the beautiful island of

Lemnos. We've had mixed, but mainly favourable, reports this year. Here is one: "The best is the hotel's setting and layout. The individual bungalows are quiet (terraced in small blocks) and stand in lovely grounds; in late May foaming with honeysuckle, roses and stephanotis. Not many have a sea view, but the beach is unusually pretty and very safe, and the salt-water pools are well laid out although not very large. We found the service willing and friendly, if slow. At capacity, the hotel might be uncomfortably crowded." Others speak in more glowing terms: "The best holiday hotel I've ever stayed in" and "the hotel's supreme attribute is the hospitality of the amicable Greek islanders and the hotel staff in particular." The local Greek MP for the area adds: "Superb – I always stay here when visiting my constituents." There are three restaurants, with lunch "an irresistible garden buffet". Views differ on the other meals. One reported: "The cuisine was generally of a very high standard and some dishes were exceptionally fine." Another, who found the table d'hôte dinners "wavered between just acceptable and disastrous" advised: "Best plan is to stay *demi-pension* and opt for the buffet lunch. It is a pleasant stroll into the village in the evening and the little restaurants round the harbour serve wonderful fish and shellfish." A third summed up: "Ideal for families to relax in a pretty place; the children can enjoy a hot, safe and sandy holiday without starchy hotel restrictions. It won't suit smart couples in search of gloss, glamour, gourmet food and wanting to be waited on hand and foot in marble halls!" *(Janey and Caradoc King, Conrad Dehn, Demetrios Nianias, Anthony Rota)*

Open 10 May–10 Oct.
Rooms 15 suites, 110 double, all in bungalows – 100 with bath, 25 with shower; all with wc, telephone, refrigerator, veranda and small garden.
Facilities Lounge, 4 bars, TV lounge, bridge room, library; 3 indoor restaurants, 3 outdoor restaurants; hairdresser, boutique; 25-acre grounds with private sandy beach, fishing, bathing, watersports, 2 tennis courts, swimming pool, pool for children, mini-golf, ping-pong and other games. Disco and Greek evenings. English spoken.
Location 2 km (about 15 minutes' walk) from Myrina Town. Lemnos is reached by direct flight from Athens, or by boat from Piraeus. Transport to and from Lemnos airport to hotel (approx 900 drs per person each way). Parking.
Restriction Not suitable for &.
Credit cards All major cards accepted.
Terms [1985 rates] double rooms 6,000– 12,000 drs, suites 11,500–17,000 drs. Breakfast 700 drs; set lunch/dinner 2,300 drs. Reduced rates for children sharing parents' room; special meals on request. *Note*: No single half- or full-board rates 2nd half of June to 1st half Sept.

MYRTIES Kalymnos, Dodecanese   Map 17

Marilena   *Tel* (0243) 47289

"Myrties is a small seaside resort about eight kilometres from Kalymnos town, 50 drs by taxi-bus. The scenery is spectacular, with a mountain-range behind and Tolendos island rising out of the sea to 400 metres. The sunsets are stunning, and it is then that the legendary island princess asleep on the side of the mountain becomes almost real. Ten minutes by boat takes you to the tiny fishing village of Tolendos, with three or four tavernas and excellent swimming. The *Marilena* is situated above a pebbly beach a few metres from the pier for Tolendos. From the road behind, you approach the 'hotel' down a pathway lined with pines and cypress trees. It is part hotel and part bungalows, meaning rooms with private facilities and veranda. We stayed in one of the front rooms in the hotel part – only cold water, but plenty of hot and cold in shared bathrooms. The main attraction of this simple, well-run and immaculate little establishment, rated D-class in the hotel listing, is the setting, the beautiful flowers and the utterly charming resident owners, Mr and Mrs Kokkinos (she is Belgian). Breakfast only is served on the veranda (with home-made marmalade). There is a restaurant three minutes away. A quiet place for a quiet holiday." *(Sydney Carpenter)*

Open Apr–Oct.
Rooms 8 – some with shower and veranda. Some rooms in bungalows.
Facilities Veranda. Private beach.
Location 4 km from Myrties.
Credit cards Probably none accepted.
Terms [1985 rates, excluding tax] B&B: single 700 drs, double 900 drs. (No restaurant.)

NAFPLION Peloponnesus   Map 17

King Otto Hotel   *Tel* (0752) 27585 or 27595
3 Farmakopoulon Street

Nafplion is a most attractive Venetian port, ideally situated for visiting Mycenae and Epidaurus. There is a string of good fish restaurants along the waterfront where the local families parade nightly. The *King Otto* is in a side street close to the harbour (front rooms noisy), a once elegant 19th-century town house with a delightful spiral staircase and painted wooden ceilings on the first floor. Rooms – not all with private showers – are clean but simply furnished. Breakfast – good home-made marmalade but powdered coffee – is served in a leafy garden, to the accompaniment of birdsong (in cages, alas). Two recent comments: "Everything that a modern package-type hotel isn't"; "plain, simple, but very friendly. The two men who manage it are absolute sweeties." *(William Plowden, Agathe Lewin)* More reports please.

Open All year.
Rooms 2 triple suites, 7 double, 3 single – 4 with shower.
Facilities Salon with TV, courtyard, garden; near sea with rocky beach. English spoken.
Location Central, near the harbour. Parking nearby.
Credit cards None accepted.
Terms [1985 rates, excluding tax] rooms: single 900 drs, double 1,100 drs. Breakfast 200 drs. (No restaurant.)

Xenia Palace Hotel   *Tel* (0752) 28981
                                                              Telex 298154

"This hotel has the most incredible location right inside the Venetian fort above the lovely town of Nafplion. It can be reached either by car, driving up through the fortifications, or by a lift rather James Bondishly ascending from a mysterious corridor off a car park. The main part, in which we stayed, is rather overwhelmingly built of grey stones; we thought that the 'bungalows' in lovely

gardens by the swimming pool looked more luscious. We were told that the Nafplion Xenia Palace is the queen of the Xenia chain, and it is certainly most elegant. The room was luxurious, and had a balcony with fabulous views. The public rooms seemed rather cold and 'airport-lounge' in decor, and the hotel suffered from having its main clients from package tours swarming in and out. All this would obviously be less evident in the 'bungalows'. Food was standard Greek hotel food – better to eat in the fish restaurants in town." (Margaret Farrell-Clark)

This entry has appeared in the last two editions of the Guide, without either endorsement or dissent. Has none of our readers tried it out?

Open All year.
Rooms 154 bungalows, 51 double – all with bath or shower, some with air-conditioning, many with balcony.
Facilities Salons, dining room. Garden with swimming pool. Private beach.
Location By Venetian fort above Nafplion. Parking.
Credit cards None accepted.
Terms [1985 rates, excluding tax] rooms: double 3,610 drs, bungalows 2,910 drs. Breakfast 300 drs; set lunch/dinner 850 drs.

OIA (or IA) Santorini, Cyclades   Map 17

Atlantis Villas   *Tel* (0286) 71214 and 71236
Nr Fira   *Telex* 293179 ATVI

Philhellenic troglodytes will be delighted to learn of this venture: at one end of the village of Oia (or Ia), near the northern tip of the island of Santorini, an Athenian couple have tastefully restored a group of twenty traditional island dwellings, some of them caves in the volcanic hillside, and equipped them as holiday homes. Last year's entry ran: "Set well away from the touristy feel of Fira town, amid blue sea and blue-domed whitewashed churches. The villas are the most up-to-date of any accommodation we saw on the island. George and Katie Koemtzopoulos, he a lawyer, are young and eager to please. Their 'cave' suites are spacious, with workable kitchenettes and up-to-date bathrooms. Our living/dining room was very adequate. The terrace above overlooks the only hotel pool we could find on the island. The only negative factor is the nature of 'cave life' itself which brings dampness. They serve a nice breakfast." *(Janet D Merutka)*

George Koemtzopoulos writes to us this year to explain that it was the fresh plastering that caused the dampness in Ms Merutka's room last year, "which by now, of course, has dried out!" No restaurant, but there are tavernas in the village.

Open 15 Mar–31 Oct.
Rooms 20 villas with 16 suites and 4 double rooms – 10 with bath, 10 with shower. All with direct-dial telephone, kitchenette and veranda.
Facilities Bar/breakfast room with TV, sea-water swimming pool and terrace overlooking the sea. 10 minutes' walk to pebble beach; 20 minutes' walk to black sand beach. English spoken.
Location On edge of village which is 10 km NW of Fira. Parking.
Credit cards None accepted.
Terms B&B: single 6,150–7,550 drs, double 7,900–9,200 drs. 20% reduction for children under 5.(No restaurant.)

OLYMPIA Peloponnesus   Map 17

Hotel Amalia   *Tel* (0624) 22190
                                                    Telex 215161 AMAL

The ancient site of Olympia lies on one side of the modern village, while
the *Amalia* is on the other, amid fields – "spanking white; looking more
like a seaside resort hotel than one for sober sight-seeing. Inside, all was
light and airy and adventurously decorated; the rooms continued so,
and our balcony looked out on a most beautiful and restful Arcadian
scene of distant hills and nearer fields with resident goats and donkey. A
swimming pool looked inviting, but alas, it wasn't open in early April.
The restaurant served the usual Greek hotel meal in the evening. So,
since they ask you to have half-board, the thing is to have the buffet
lunch, groaning with delicious salads and hot dishes – the best meal we
had in Greece. As with other Greek hotels of A or luxury class, the
service was friendly but impersonal – designed perhaps for the
'packaged' tourist – and spotlessly clean." (*Margaret Farrell-Clark*)

Open All year.
Rooms 147 – all with bath or shower, many with balcony.
Facilities Salons, dining room. Garden with swimming pool.
Location On outskirts of town.
Credit cards None accepted.
Terms [1985 rates, excluding tax] rooms: single 2,400 drs, double 3,422 drs.
Breakfast 225 drs. Set lunch/dinner 900 drs.

Hotel Kronion   *Tel* (0624) 22502 and 22188
1 Tsoureka

"If you want to visit the beautiful archaeological site at Olympia, you
can't avoid the village of Olympia which has arisen as a by-product of it.
Its many souvenir shops can be ignored, but do try the excellent
bookshop with a superb selection of guides and books on all aspects of
Greece. We found *Hotel Kronion*, C class, along the high street, opposite
the ugly church. A substantial modern building, comfortable bedroom
and the best-appointed bathroom we ever saw in Greece, with a genuine
bath-tub and lots of towels. A helpful, friendly owner, who was always
there. He was very proud of the traditional midnight Easter meal which
he offered: red-dyed hard-boiled eggs, lemon-and-herb-flavoured lamb-
offal soup and then huge hunks of Easter lamb. But we gathered from
other guests that the usual menu was monotonous, to say the least, so
probably better to eat somewhere else if you are staying more than one
night." (*Ian and Agathe Lewin*) More reports welcome.

Open All year.
Rooms 33 double, 6 single – 29 with bath, 10 with shower, 16 in annexe opposite.
Facilities Salon, bar, restaurant. Beach 17 km. English spoken.
Location Central; on high street, opposite church. Parking.
Credit cards Access, Visa.
Terms B&B: single 1,600 drs, double 2,300 drs; half-board: single 2,300 drs,
double 3,700 drs; full board: single 3,000 drs, double 5,400 drs. Set lunch/dinner
700 drs. 20% reduction for children.

PARIKIA Paros, Cyclades   Map 17

Hotel Xenia   *Tel* (0284) 21394 and 21643

The tiny seaport of Parikia is the capital of the island of Paros, famous for its windmills, its cupola'd byzantine churches and its white marble, the material used for temples on the sacred island of Delos (the main quarries are in the hills six kilometres to the east of Parikia). "The *Xenia*, part of the chain of Government-run hotels, stands on a hill above the village and the beach. Built mostly of marble, the hotel is cool and clean with a welcoming sitting room and a pretty downstairs restaurant. Our room had a private balcony overlooking the sea, as do all rooms on the seaward side. The seaport and the beach, lined with tavernas, are just down a set of gently sloping stairs, far enough away to eliminate any noise from the discos in the evening. The island offers lovely beaches, an interesting monastery and good·restaurants." *(Jan Shannon)*

Open 1 Apr–31 Oct.
Rooms 21 double, 6 single – 14 with bath, 13 with shower; many with balcony.
Facilities Lounge, TV lounge, bar, dining room. Small garden. Many safe sandy beaches nearby; watersports. English spoken.
Location Central. Parking.
Restriction Not suitable for &.
Credit cards All major cards accepted.
Terms Rooms: single 2,150–2,750 drs, double 2,700–3,800 drs. Breakfast 250 drs, dinner 700 drs.

TOLON Peloponnesus   Map 17

Hotel Minoa   *Tel* (0752) 59207 or 59416
56 Aktis Street   *Telex* 0298157 MINO

Once a simple coastal village, Tolon has grown in tourist popularity over the years and now has hotels and tavernas running the length of the narrow beach strip. About three hours' drive south-west of Athens, near Nafplion (Mycenae, Argos and Epidaurus are all within easy reach), it still retains the air of an unsophisticated little village, where local families sit in the sun, preparing meals, mending fishing nets and just gossiping. And *Minoa*, a modern family-run place, stays aloof from the mass tourism, as a recent visitor reports: "This was my 12th or so stay, and as ever I was impressed with the hard work and friendly service of the whole Georgadakis family. Despite the unwelcome tourist development at the other end of Tolon, the *Minoa* is unchanged, with its superb location at the water's edge. Rooms are simple and plainly furnished, water is always hot. Lunch has been dropped, but you can get good salads or omelettes in the bar garden. At dinner we had superb fish soup, prawns in tomato sauce, etc." Breakfast is on the beach beneath a large tent. *(Phyllis Beach, endorsed by Mr and Mrs J H Tate)* More reports please.

Open 20 Mar–1 Nov.
Rooms 56 double, 6 single – 7 with bath, 37 with shower, telephone and radio; some rooms on ground floor in annexe (*Hotel Knossos*); some self-catering villas.
Facilities Lift. 2 lounges (1 with TV), bar, restaurant, roof terrace; dancing every night; breakfast under large beach awning. Small garden with bar. On sandy

beach with safe bathing, sailing, pedalos, boating, fishing; day-trips to nearby islands (Spetsai, Hydra, etc). English spoken.
Location Near old port. Parking nearby.
Restriction Not suitable for &.
Credit cards All major cards accepted.
Terms [1985 rates, likely to go up about 20%] B&B 980–1,462 drs (low season only); half-board 1,355–2,258 drs.

XYLOKASTRON Corinth   Map 17

Apollon Hotel   *Tel* (0743) 22239/22571
105 J Ioannou

On the Gulf of Corinth, between ancient Corinth (34 kilometres) and the port of Patras (100 kilometres), this would be a useful nightstop for some travellers. This B class bed-and-breakfast hotel, part of which was once a presidential residence, though with a modern annexe, is in the town about 200 metres from the sea front. "We were in the annexe, not as interesting as the old part of the hotel, which is, indeed, a quite spectacular old house. The public rooms were comfortable, with lots of attention to details; some considerable effort was being made. The rooms on the front tend to be noisy. We were surprised to find that there was only one proper taverna in town, so we were thrown back on the resources of the hotel. The food was surprisingly good – they were trying. On the whole, a bit overpriced by Greek standards. It did seem to attract a sizeable local clientele." An earlier report ran: "The management and staff were friendly. The furnishings were somewhat mundane, but there were lovely crisp sheets on the bed. The bathroom was immaculate, with a bidet. You can have drinks in a pleasant garden terrace at the front of the hotel." *(Peter Bowen, R S M)*

Open All year.
Rooms 27 – all with bath and telephone; baby-sitting available.
Facilities Lounges, TV room, snack-bar, restaurant; air-conditioning. Garden terrace; private beach.
Location Central; 70 metres from sea front. Parking.
Credit cards None accepted.
Terms [1985 rates, excluding tax] rooms: single, 1,630 drs, double 2,200 drs. Breakfast 165 drs; set lunch/dinner 600 drs.

Holland

HOTEL LEEUWENBRUG, DELFT

ALMEN 7218 AH   Map 9

De Hoofdige Boer   *Tel* (05751) 744
Dorpsstraat 38

An old-established family-run hotel in a leafy setting with unusual beamed decor, in a small village east of Zutphen in Eastern Holland. "When you stay at *De Hoofdige Boer*, you feel you have left the busy computer age and entered an earlier time when people didn't rush and had time to smile. The owners are lovely people who make every effort to accommodate their guests." "Ideal for a quiet holday, with tennis, swimming, and attractive towns and villages nearby. Modern bedrooms, fully equipped, and comfortable lounge; and tea garden in summer. Outstanding food, the best we had in Holland, and excellent value." "With slight reservations about the food, I heartily endorse your comments on *De Hoofdige Boer*. It is charming. At the back is a pleasant garden giving on to open fields. The restaurant is professionally run even if the food is somewhat unimaginative. At least it isn't pretentious and one feels that everyone is doing their best to please. Breakfast was copious – cheese, ham, salami plus four or five different breads, as well

563

as boiled eggs and good coffee." *(Susan Hayes, Geoffrey Sharp; also B W Ribbons and Dr Christine Herxheimer and Gabriele Berneck)*

Open All year except New Year.
Rooms 18 double, 2 single – 14 with bath, 6 with shower, 12 with telephone; TV for hire; 2 ground-floor rooms.
Facilities Pub lounge with TV, TV room, dining room, functions room, table tennis. Garden with tea garden and dinner terrace. 5 minutes' walk to heated swimming pool. English spoken.
Location Central, near the church. Parking. About 1½ hrs drive from Amsterdam via E8 Deventer and Eefde.
Credit cards Amex, Diners.
Terms B&B: single 65 glds, double 100–130 glds; dinner, B&B: single 100 glds, double 170–200 glds. Set lunch 18.50 glds, dinner 45 glds. Reduced rates for children sharing parents' room; special meals.

AMSTERDAM 1016 AZ   Map 9

Hotel Ambassade   *Tel* (020) 262333
Herengracht 341   *Telex* 10158

"The charms of this hotel must be unique in a capital city – 17th-century patrician town houses, side by side, on a grand stretch of the Herengracht, Amsterdam's grandest canal. At the friendly reception you will be given the front-door key to 'your' house." Extensive renovations have been carried out at this elegant bed-and-breakfast hotel: there are now seven houses linked together, with their rooms – varying in size according to their altitude in these five-storey buildings – all furnished in period. The public rooms have many items from the owner's own collection of antiques – old china, clocks, paintings. Our mailbag is full of praise – for the generous Dutch-style breakfasts, efficient room service, quiet yet central location, and helpful and energetic manager, Mr C Van der Velden. The only common complaint is of the very steep steps to upper floors (as so often in Holland) and of the "horrendous spiral staircases everywhere" (the elderly or less than athletic should ask for ground-floor rooms). Here are two typical reports this year: "Comfortable, largish rooms, modern bathrooms; sumptuous breakfast in the 'reception' house in a magnificent room on the *piano*

there, courteous, friendly, inviting questions and apparently running the whole show without effort or tension. The relaxed friendly atmosphere is striking." *(D Pevsner, Dr B E W Mace; also Marie Earl, Ian Elliott, K and H Bender, John M Sidwick, and others)*

Open All year.
Rooms 2 suites, 36 double, 4 single – 40 with bath, 2 with shower, all with telephone and colour TV; full room service; baby sitters available; 20 rooms in annexe; 9 ground-floor rooms.
Facilities Lounge, TV lounge, breakfast/dining room; dry-cleaning/laundry service. English spoken.
Location Central, but quietly situated on Herengracht canal. No special parking facilities.
Credit cards Access, Amex, Visa.
Terms B&B: single 135 glds, double 150–170 glds. Drinks and light refreshments available all day. Reduced rates for children sharing parents' room.

Amstel Hotel   *Tel* (020) 226060
1 Prof. Tulpplein   *Telex* 11004L AMSOT NL
Amsterdam 1018 GX

"The *Amstel Hotel* is supposedly where film stars and other famous
people stay when they visit Amsterdam. The interior of the hotel is
certainly very grand and the double rooms are like suites, with very
plush furnishings. Service is good and discreet as should be expected in
this sort of establishment. Prices are high – for rooms, drinks and food –
but you are paying for the surroundings and the setting of the hotel
overlooking the river Amstel. The only drawback of the hotel is its
distance from the centre of Amsterdam, a good 20 minutes' walk. But to
some people that might be an advantage." *(Kate and Steve Murray-Sykes)*
More reports welcome.

Open All year.
Rooms 6 suites, 94 double, 11 single – all with bath, radio and TV.
Facilities Lift. Salon, TV room, bar, restaurant, terrace, garden, air-conditioning.
English spoken.
Location On the Amstel river, 20 minutes' walk (1 km) from centre.
Credit cards All major credit cards accepted.
Terms Rooms: single 275–375 glds, double 375–500 glds. Continental breakfast
from 24 glds, American breakfast from 29 glds; set lunch from 85 glds, dinner from
100 glds.

Hotel de l'Europe   *Tel* (020) 234836
Nieuwe Doelenstraat 2–4   *Telex* 12081
Amsterdam 1012 CP   *Reservations* in UK (01) 583 3050
                                      in USA (800) 223 6800

One of the grander hotels of Amsterdam, built on the Amstel in 1895.
After extensive renovation, this medium-sized hotel is back in top form.
"The decorations and general ambience are in the finest taste."
"Beautiful rooms, luxury fittings, ideal location." Front rooms can be
noisy: those at the back or overlooking the river are quieter. Recent
visitors report that the service is quite efficient. The hotel's restaurant
has a fine reputation for both food and cellar. One reader sums it up this
way: "The hotel was not cheap, but then one does not expect a top-class
hotel in a major international city to be so." *(J M Toogood, Mr and Mrs T E
Reddish; also D E Jenkins, and others)*

Open All year.
Rooms 4 suites, 42 double, 33 single – 68 with bath, 11 with shower, all with
telephone, radio and colour TV; baby-sitting on request. 24-hour room service.
Facilities Lift. Lounge, bar, 2 restaurants; banqueting, cocktail and conference
facilities. Terrace overlooking Amstel serving meals and drinks. English spoken.
Location Central, opposite the Mint Tower and Flowermarket (quiet rooms at
back of hotel). Limited private parking, public garage nearby.
Credit cards All major cards accepted.
Terms B&B: single 345–400 glds, double 470–525 glds. Set lunch 60 glds, dinner 70
glds; full alc 120 or 65 glds. Children under 6 free; under 12 half-price; special
meals on request.

> We should like to hear about more budget-price hotels in
> Amsterdam.

Het Canal House *Tel* (020) 225182 or 229987
Keizersgracht 148 *Telex* 10412
Amsterdam 1015 CX

A former merchant's house of the 17th and 18th centuries, within earshot of those same carillon bells heard by Anne Frank. "This hotel is small, but offers comfortable modern rooms furnished with local antiques and a friendliness from the owners Len and Jane Irwin which only a small hotel can offer. All the staff speak English. The hotel is situated by a canal within five minutes' walk of the city centre and central station and two minutes of the Anne Frank House. Around the corner is the café *De Bak*, a typical Dutch bar and restaurant. I thoroughly enjoyed myself." *(Steve Mole)*

Open All year.
Rooms 15 double, 2 single – 11 with bath, 6 with shower.
Facilities Bar (for guests only), breakfast room. Garden. English spoken.
Location Central. Street parking.
Restrictions Not suitable for &. No children under 12.
Credit cards All major cards accepted.
Terms B&B: single 90–110 glds, double 125–160 glds. (No restaurant.)

Hotel Pulitzer *Tel* (20) 228333
Prinsengracht 315–331 *Telex* 16508
Amsterdam 1016 GZ

One of Amsterdam's more sophisticated hotels, the *Pulitzer* straddles a terrace of 17th-century houses, some facing the Prinsengracht where the hotel has its entrance, and some facing the neighbouring canal, the Keizersgracht. The beams and brick walls have been preserved in the hotel's 195 rooms, and each of these is unique. There are lots of little corridors and half-landings. Despite its size, it is a hotel of character as well as comfort – and quiet, except for the sound of nearby church chimes. Good service. *(Roland Gelatt, Clay Leitch, and others)*

Open All year.
Rooms 5 suites, 160 double, 30 single – all with bath, direct-dial telephone, radio, colour TV and video, mini-bar; baby-listening can be arranged. Some ground-floor rooms.
Facilities Lobby, bar, restaurant, coffee shop, conference facilities; live music in bar or garden; terrace for light meals, drinks and some concerts in summer; large garden. English spoken.
Location Central, near Wester Church; garden rooms best for light sleepers. Garage 8 minutes' walk.
Credit cards None accepted.
Terms Rooms: single 250 glds, double 300 glds. Breakfast 21 glds; alc meals 75 glds. Extra bed in room 50 glds, baby cots free; special meals for children on request.

> More nominations for the Hague would be appreciated.

> Do you know of a good hotel in Gouda?

> Give the Guide positive support. Don't just leave feedback to others.

DELFT   Map 9

Hotel Leeuwenbrug   *Tel* (015) 123062 or 134640
Koornmarkt 16   *Telex* 33756 (NRC), ref. no. 013
Delft 2611 E

Readers tell us that the *Leeuwenbrug* is even better than we reported in last year's Guide. A small hotel in one of the finest parts of Delft, its prices are reasonable, its welcome friendly, its buffet breakfasts plentiful. The best rooms are in the front overlooking the canal, a picturesque footbridge and gabled houses opposite, "the loveliest view from a European hotel bedroom that I've ever had" (there is at least one large room with a delightful flower-decked balcony). Other rooms are smallish and not all have private bath, but they are warm, adequately furnished and comfortable (some at the back are a little poky). Only limited space in the lounge, but there is a pleasant little bar. There are rumours that Mr and Mrs Wubbens are building a restaurant, but the best in town for the moment is probably *Le Chevalier* (not cheap). *(Mr and Mrs G C Burton, Mr and Mrs T E Reddish, Ann Delugach)*

Open All year.
Rooms 26 double, 8 single – 7 with bath, 27 with shower, all with telephone, radio and TV; 6 ground-floor rooms.
Facilities Lift. Lounge, TV room, bar, breakfast room, conference facilities. Sandy beach 15 km. English spoken.
Location Take Delft Zuid turning off Rotterdam/Amsterdam highway, and follow signs to Centre West. Paid parking nearby.
Credit cards All major cards accepted.
Terms B&B: single 95–130 glds, double 120–150 glds.

THE HAGUE (DEN HAAG) South Holland   Map 9

Hotel des Indes   *Tel* (070) 469553
Lange Voorhout 54–56   *Reservations* in UK: (01) 236 3242
The Hague 2514 EG   in US: (800) 228 51 51
                                                  Telex 31196

Built in 1851 as a baron's residence, opposite the Lange Voorhout Palace in the centre of the city. "A very elegant hotel. My room was so attractive, cool green and relaxing, I hated to leave it for dinner. The hotel has real old-world charm and comfort." Thus a recent correspondent echoes a report from last year. "An old-fashioned hotel in the nicest sense. Our favourite rooms are the large older-style ones on the ground and first floors, but some people prefer the very modern ones in the penthouse. Service is willing but slow and room service almost non-existent." Most readers have agreed that the food is good, but not exceptional, and that there are plenty of good restaurants nearby. *(Ann Delugach, K and S Murray-Sykes)*

Open All year.
Rooms 6 suites, 61 double, 16 single – 70 with bath, 7 with shower, all with telephone, radio, colour TV and mini-bar; some ground-floor rooms.
Facilities Lift. Lounge, TV room, bar, restaurant, breakfast room, 6 conference rooms. Bar with live music (harp). English spoken.
Location Central, near Palace. Car park.

Credit cards All major cards accepted.
Terms Rooms: single 355–410 glds, double 460–515 glds. Breakfast 25 glds; set lunch 49 glds, dinner 89 glds; full alc 80 glds. Weekend packages. Reduced rates for children sharing parents' room; special meals.

LEUSDEN Utrecht   Map 9

Huize den Treek   *Tel* (03498) 1425 and 1426
Trekerweg 23

The *Huize den Treek* is a 17th-century mansion in a wooded area at the end of a longish lane off the main road running through Leusden. "From the back one looks out on a small lake, in the centre of which is a small island populated by ducks, geese, pea-hens, and one tiny white rabbit. The location is ideal for touring the area east of Amsterdam and Utrecht. Most rooms have washstands and showers, although we did spy a largish suite with a bath. The decor was simple but very clean and comfortable: in the US we would call this 'Michigan cottage' style. But what really impressed us about this hotel was that our reception was regal. We descended to the elegant lounge which was filled with many comfortable overstuffed chairs as well as antique furniture, and were served glasses of Kir as we listened to the piped-in classical music. Then we were ushered into the handsome dining room – where we were served a Dutch–French dinner that rivalled any we had been treated to elsewhere in the Netherlands. Breakfast was also served here, overlooking the lake and small island. All this time, Boris, the resident *bouvier des Flandres,* sat patiently awaiting our leftover ham and Dutch cheese titbits. Altogether a charming stop for those who wish for peace, quiet and a chance to roam lovely grounds." *(Mary Ann Hamill)*

Open All year except Christmas and New Year. Restaurant closed some of July and Aug.
Rooms 1 suite, 10 double, 8 single – 3 with bath, 15 with shower, all with telephone, radio and colour TV.
Facilities Lift. Salon with TV, restaurant, terrace, children's playground. Garden with terrace and lake.
Location On outskirts of Leusden. Garage parking behind hotel.
Credit cards Amex, Diners.
Terms B&B: single 50–65 glds, double 100–110 glds; half-board: single 85–110 glds, double 170–180 glds; full board: single 104–119 glds, double 208–218 glds. Set lunch 22 glds, dinner 37.50 glds; full alc 65 glds. Reduced rates and special meals for children.

OISTERWIJK 5061 Noord-Brabant   Map 9

De Swaen   *Tel* (04242) 19006
De Lind 47   *Telex* 52617

An elegant small hotel situated on the tree-lined main street of the pleasant shady town of Oisterwijk. *De Swaen* is a much-lauded restaurant-with-rooms with a terrace in the front and an elegant formal garden at the back – the whole place very chic and soigné. "Recently converted by a local furniture maker, from the outside it looks like many other pleasant Dutch provincial hotels. But inside it's a veritable Aladdin's cave. Rooms are smallish but very adequate, bathroom being in marble and the bath itself warm! I stay there every month; I worry what I will do if my business in that area should cease. Food is excellent and beautifully served." A reader this year continues: "Rooms are modern, comfortably furnished, each with a small balcony. Welcoming chocolates and all the other little extras. Shoes are cleaned overnight if required." And, "the bathrooms have gold-plated fittings!" Altogether "pretty self-indulgent" confesses another. "The restaurant is regarded as one of the best in Holland. Perhaps rather formal but has a nice atmosphere." "Look for the cheeseboard loaded with all Dutch cheese quite different fom the standard Edam and Gouda." *(R G Stuart-Prince, Pat and Jeremy Temple; also P G W Whybrow)* They are be-*toqu'd* in *Gault Millau*, and two-rosetted in *Michelin*.

Open 10 Jan–8 July, 20 July–29 Dec.
Rooms 18 double, 1 single – 18 with bath, 1 with shower, all with telephone, radio and colour TV.
Facilities Lift. Bar, lounge, restaurant, 2 conference rooms. Formal garden. Swimming, fishing, woods and lakes nearby. English spoken.
Location Central. Parking. Oisterwijk is 10 km NE of Tilberg.
Credit cards Access, Amex, Diners.
Terms B&B: single 175 glds, double 225 glds. Set lunch 70–100 glds, dinner 90–150 glds, full alc 100 glds. Special meals for children can be provided; babies free of charge.

OOTMARSUM 7631 HX   **Map 9**

De Wiemsel   *Tel* (05419) 2155
Winhofflaan 2   *Telex* 44667 WIWAN

About a mile east of the pretty little town of Ootmarsum, in gentle pastoral country near the German frontier, *De Wiemsel* is a rather unusual ranch-style hotel with attractive modern decor, light and spacious. "Set quietly in its own grounds, it is really a number of low bungalow-style buildings attached to the main block which houses the restaurant. Most of the rooms are in fact apartments. We arrived in the early evening to a welcoming smile and the offer of tea or coffee with fruit bread (on the house) to revive us. The room was lovely with a view of fields, and the bathroom luxurious. Service was good. The restaurant has no *Michelin* rosette but deserves one". *(K and S M-S)* The hotel has a stable of horses for the use of guests, as well as a floodlit tennis court and a big indoor pool. It is 20 minutes' drive to the German casino across the border at Bad Bentheim. The restaurant *de Wanne* in the centre of town is under the same management.

Open All year.
Rooms 42 apartments, 7 rooms all for double or single use – all with bath and shower, telephone, radio, colour TV and baby-listening. Apartments are on ground floor and have kitchenette and terrace.
Facilities Lounge, bar, 2 restaurants, 4 private or conference rooms. Indoor heated swimming pool, sauna, solarium and billiards room. Large garden with terrace, tennis court and stables. Bicycles for hire. English spoken.
Location 1 km E of Ootmarsum, which is 28 km N of Enschede.
Credit cards All major cards accepted.
Terms B&B: single occupancy 255 glds, double 235.50; dinner, B&B: single occupancy 165 glds, double 299 glds; full board: single occupancy 177.59 glds. Set lunch 48.50 glds, dinner 70 glds; full alc 82.50 glds. Reduced rates for children.

WASSENAAR 2243 South Holland   Map 9

Auberge De Kieviet   *Tel* (01751) 79403 or 79203
Stoeplaan 27

For over thirty years Luigi and Malou Gandini have been running this
sophisticated, elegant and expensive restaurant-with-rooms in the
pleasant suburb of Wassenaar, 8 km from the centre of The Hague.
Readers to a man (and woman) say that the flair with which this place
operates is due to "the personal style, care and attention of the owners,
for example the fresh flowers arranged at my wife's place at breakfast by
Madame Gandini." There are just six bedrooms (usually booked up well
ahead), as immaculately maintained as the public rooms below. "The
bedrooms are charming, as are the Gandinis." "Attention to detail of the
highest order." "A lovely place to relax, and with much more character
than the big new hotels in The Hague itself." The restaurant, with a
huge separate area for pre-dinner drinks, is much used by the
diplomatic set from The Hague, but also by local families. *Michelin*
rosette, *Gault Millau* red *toque*, for such dishes as *blanc de turbot aux fruits
de mer et truffes. (Iain Elliott, Karen and David Bashkin, Eithne Scallan)*

Open All year except Christmas and New Year. Restaurant closed Mon.
Rooms 6 double – 5 with bath, 1 with shower; all with telephone.
Facilites Lounge, restaurant, private dining room. Garden; beach 3 km; fishing,
golf, tennis, riding, cycling nearby. English spoken.
Location 8 km from centre of The Hague; 2km SW of Wassenaar.
Credit cards All major cards accepted.
Terms B&B: single 125 glds, double 195 glds. Set lunch from 60 glds, dinner from
72.60 gls.

WELLERLOOI 5856 Limburg   Map 9

Hostellerie de Hamert   *Tel* (04703) 1260
Hamert 2, route Nijmegen-Venlo

"An interesting old family-run hotel with a pleasant terrace from where
you can watch the river traffic, recommended for a self-indulgent
stopover rather than for a long stay. Its five rooms are modest, though
adequate for a night (comfortable beds). Primarily, it's a restaurant-with-
rooms, with a good reputation for its food. When we left at 10 am they
were serving apple pie with cream and coffees in the small bar area.
Cooking is excellent. In May and June people come here from all over
Holland to eat the local white asparagus: the staff get up at 5 am to dig it
for the day's meals! Wines are interesting and fairly priced, service is
efficient and friendly." *(Pat and Jeremy Temple)* More reports welcome.

Open All year, but closed Tue and Wed (Oct–Mar).
Rooms 4 double, 1 single – 2 with bath, all with radio.
Facilities Lounge, restaurant; 2 conference/functions rooms. 2 terraces (meals
served outdoors in fine weather); garden leading to river. English spoken.
Location 15 km N of Venlo on road to Nijmegen. Parking.
Restriction Not suitable for &.
Credit cards All major cards accepted.
Terms B&B: single 70–85 glds, double 117.50–145 glds. Set lunch 52.50 glds,
dinner 75 glds; full acl 80 glds. Reduced rates and special meals for children.

WITTEM Limburg 6286 AA   Map 9

Kasteel Wittem   *Tel* (04450) 1208 or 1260
Wittemerallee 3

"In the Eighty Years' War Wittem Castle played an important part, and
the eleventh couplet of the Dutch National Anthem recalls this period in
the Netherlands' battle for freedom," says the hotel's brochure. Indeed,
steeped in history and keeping its stately tradition, this medieval castle
with its 12-foot-thick walls surrounded by ancient trees has a lot to offer
– including *Michelin*-rosetted cuisine. A reader this year writes,
dreamily, "Immediately upon checking in we entered a world of
elegance, service, history, solitude and surprising economy. We
particularly enjoyed walking around the grounds, imagining the history
the castle had witnessed. The owner and his son were extremely cordial,
obviously schooled in everything proper." Another somewhat awe-
struck visitor wrote: "A real castle very impressive to drive up to and
think, 'I'm actually going to stay here!'" The dozen rooms, each with its
own bathroom, have been successfully gouged out of these cyclopean
walls, and are splendidly comfortable. One visitor was a bit alarmed by
the fire risks – "the good news is that the building has not burnt down
for all these years, but the bad news is that, if it does catch fire, it isn't
clear how one would get out." Others say, "A rare bargain. It made a
good base for a day's exploration of Limburg but I think a three-to-five-
day visit – if your waistline can take it – would be even better. It's too
good for just one night." And readers have found the food deserving of
its accolades. "My wife described her meal as possibly the best she'd
ever eaten." *(Ronald A Lehman, Ann Delugach, Iain Elliott; also Bettina
Dudkin and others)*

Open All year.
Rooms 12 double – all with bath and shower, telephone; TV on request.
Facilities Salon, 2 restaurants; conference/banqueting facilities. Park with river,
garden, terrace. Golf, bicycling, walking, tennis and trout fishing nearby. English
spoken.
Location Between Maastricht (17 km) and Aachen (15 km). 2 km SW of Gulpen on
Maastricht road.
Restriction Not suitable for &.
Credit cards All major cards accepted.
Terms B&B: double 160 glds. Set lunch 48 glds, dinner 70 glds; full alc 100 glds.
Gastronomic weekends. Reduced rates and special meals for children.

Hungary

HOTEL SYLVANUS, VISEGRÁD

BUDAPEST 1111   **Map 16**

Hotel Gellért   *Tel* (2) 46.07.00
Szt Gellért ter 1   *Telex* 22-4363

The *Gellért* lies in its baroque deco glory at the foot of the Gellért hill, overlooking the river, with trams and buses to every part of the city passing outside at almost one-minute intervals. It is well worth asking for a room in the front: the traffic and the jangle and clang of the trams are a small price to pay for the view over the city – and all rooms are double-glazed anyway. The decor and furnishings, and the style of service inside, complement the confident and the grand-and-proud-of-it stance of the facade. The furnishings may seem outmoded by Hilton standards, but the size of the rooms, the solidity of the walls between the rooms, the large towels, the splendid corridors and stairways recall the great days of grand hotels. We apologise for a *faux pas* in last year's entry: the armchairs are indeed not plastic but expensive leather. The art deco Turkish baths adjoining the hotel (guests are supplied with bathrobes and have a special lift to take them direct to the pools) are on no account to be missed. The *Gellért* was the premier hotel of the city when it was first opened, and it still scores high for impeccably attentive

573

and cheerful service, for a very good restaurant (naturally with a diligent gypsy band), a superb coffee shop replete with rich Hungarian pastries, and much else to cheer the traveller jaded with bland contemporary establishments. *(H R; also George Maddocks)*

Open All year.
Rooms 235 – all with bath and telephone.
Facilities Large foyer, lounges, bar, brasserie, coffee shop, dining room, night club, banquet hall, 6 conference rooms; indoor swimming pool and 3 outdoor pools.
Location At the foot of Gellért hill.
Credit cards All major cards accepted.
Terms [1985 rates] B&B: single 2,600 ft, double 3,500 ft, suites 5,400 ft.

VISEGRÁD 2025, P.F.24   Map 16

Hotel Sylvanus   *Tel* (136063) 2628311 or 2628136
Telex 225720

Visegrád is 48 kilometres north of Budapest. If you are driving from the capital don't miss the delightful, picturesque village of Szentendre with its many fine 18th-century houses, its art galleries, museums and boutiques. Visegrád has its touristic claims, too, but the *Sylvanus* is seven kilometres out of the town itself, and 1,000 feet up in the hills – a superb eyrie from which to view the Danube Bend, and a popular all-the-year-round holiday area: skiing in the winter, and walking, riding, tennis and much else in the summer. The *Sylvanus*, a modern purpose-built hotel, is one of the few buildings at the top of the hill, along with a ruined castle and a look-out tower. The hotel necessarily caters for much passing trade, with a large restaurant, an espresso bar, a *Bierstübe* with skittle alley and plenty of extra accommodation on the terrace in the summer. The rooms are adequate, the food is good honest Hungarian fare – better on the bourgeois items, less confident on the more ambitious dishes. The service is quick and friendly and caters well for both the casual visitor and coach parties. Not a hotel of rare character of course, but certainly worth a night's stop to or from Budapest – and not just for the view. *(H R)*

Open All year.
Rooms 4 suites, 66 double – all with bath, many with terrace. Radio and colour TV in suites. Also 9 3-bedded tourist-class rooms without bath or shower.
Facilities Bar, beer-hall, café, restaurant, conference facilities, disco and night-club; skittle alley. Sun terrace with café-bar. Park with tennis court. Forest, sports ground, riding and thermal pool nearby.
Location 48 km N of Budapest.
Restriction Not suitable for &.
Credit card Visa.
Terms: (Service at guests' discretion). B&B: US$20; dinner, B&B US$24; full board US$28. Free accommodation and half-price meals for children under 6.

Can you help us extend our coverage in Hungary?

Italy

HOTEL CERTOSA DI MAGGIANO
SIENA

AGRIGENTO 92100 Sicily Map 16

Villa Athena *Tel* (0922) 23833 or 23834 or 56288
Via dei Templi 33 *Telex* 910617

"Anyone who visits Sicily and omits the south shore – a treasury of Greek temples – is making a mistake. Agrigento is the jewel of that coast. On a long ridge running down to the sea there is stunning ruin after stunning ruin, a beautiful site. Nothing like this in Greece, they say. The *Villa Athena* is a handsome 18th-century building built on the very edge of the temple area – so close one is almost embarrassed for having intruded. Room 205 (the one to get) has six pairs of French doors 12 feet high, and in the evening, when the temples are suddenly lighted, it's an Olympus. The interiors are reasonably attractive, once the wallpaper has receded." Even the smaller rooms get glowing praise for the awesome views: "From the large glass doors of our room (106) the temple of Juno appeared to be in our backyard. We had that fantastic view even from the bathroom, which had a small oval window that reflected in the mirror over the sink (so my husband could see the temple as he shaved!). Breakfast was served on a flower-lined terrace. The hotel also has a beautiful garden and swimming pool." "Service is not the speciality. But all is forgiven; the site is glorious." (*Tom and Connie Congdon, Kathleen McCleery and Robert Martinez*)

Open All year.
Rooms 36 double 5 single – 26 with bath, 15 with shower, all with telephone, radio and TV; air-conditioning.
Facilities Bars, restaurants; terrace. Garden with swimming pool. Sea 2 km. English spoken.
Location S of Agrigento, just off the Passeggiata Archeologica, in the centre of the Valley of the Temples.
Restriction Not suitable for &.
Credit cards Access, Amex.
Terms B&B: single 60,000 L, double 95,000 L; dinner, B&B 78,000 L, double 132,000 L; full board: single 90,000 L; double 160,000 L; full alc 28,000–30,000 L. 30% reduction for children; special meals.

ALASSIO 17021 Savona   Map 16

Hotel Grand Diana   *Tel* (0182) 42701
Via Garibaldi 110   *Telex* 270655

Alassio is a Ligurian fishing village nestled into a semi-circular bay on the Riviera di Ponente, not far from the French frontier. Karl Baedeker remarked in 1913 that "it is frequented especially by English visitors". Some things never change. "After the horrors of the south of France," writes one modern-day Briton, "Alassio is really unspoilt and relatively unchanged. The *Diana* is situated right on the beach and our room looked out over this and the sea. For the Mediterranean the beach was extraordinary in that it was so clean. Our room was of good size and very pleasant as was the bathroom. We had a very good dinner indeed and the breakfast was better than most. Staff all very pleasant and cheerful and some had enough English for normal requirements. This hotel would be a good place to unwind for a few days or to spend a holiday, particularly for those with a young family." (*R A Dubery*)

Open Apr–20 Oct.
Rooms 77 – all with bath or shower and direct-dial telephone.
Facilities Lift. Dining room, indoor swimming pool, conference facilities. Garden. Beach with safe bathing. English spoken.
Location In N part of town off S1 towards Savona. Parking.
Credit cards Access, Amex, Visa.
Terms [1985 rates] rooms: single 61,000 L, double 102,000 L. Breakfast 15,000 L; alc meals (excluding wine) 29,000–47,000 L. Reduced rates and special meals for children.

ALPE FAGGETO 52033 Arezzo   Map 16

Fonte della Galletta   *Tel* (0575) 793925
Caprese Michelangelo

Whether or not you enjoy this hotel, secluded amid woodlands in the wild Apennines, depends on your expectations. It is more of a typically Italian experience than a dependably first-class hotel – nobody speaks

English, the occasional local feasters and wedding parties make a great deal of cheerful noise, the TV dominates the lounge, where the lighting is inadequate for reading, the bedrooms can be rather cold. But the advantages are correspondingly many – "the charm and friendliness of the staff, the ravishingly beautiful countryside – the road winding down to Michelangelo's birthplace between delightful woods and quantities of wild flowers". The popular *Fonte della Galletta* clearly thinks of itself as a restaurant-with-rooms. The well-named proprietor, Signor Boncompagni, is a superb award-winning cook who uses local mushrooms and fungi in a variety of fascinating and unusual ways. There is no menu but guests are asked for their approval of the night's dinner in advance. One guest had a meal of cream of mushroom soup, various pastas stuffed with truffles and mushrooms, mixed meats including pork and sparrow, salad and zuppa inglese! In summer, trout from the small lake nearby are available. The local wine is "deep purple and delicious". (*BA*) More reports please.

Open All year.
Rooms 20 double, 3 single – 14 with bath, all with telephone; 6 rooms in annexe.
Facilities Lounge with TV, bar, restaurant; banqueting facilities. Garden. Lake nearby. English spoken.
Location 6 km SW of Caprese Michelangelo; 50 km NE of Arezzo.
Restriction Not suitable for &.
Credit cards None accepted.
Terms B&B: single 18,000 L, double 35,000 L; half-board: single 30,000 L, double 57,000 L; full board: single 40,000 L, double 70,000 L. Set lunch/dinner 13,000 and 25,000 L. 40% reduction for children under 6; special meals.

ANCONA 60020   **Map 16**

Hotel Emilia   *Tel* (071) 801117 or 801145
Collina di Portonovo

Monte Conero, 12 kilometres south-east of Ancona, is an interesting hump on the otherwise mainly flat eastern coastline of Italy. Above Portonovo is the *Emilia*, a beautiful modern clifftop hotel surrounded by fields on three sides and a sheer gorse-topped cliff on the other. "The air must be almost the purest in Italy! The hotel is well run, with a rosette in *Michelin*, though this applies to those eating à la carte rather than *en pension*; but the set menu too is good. The wine, from the owner's vineyard, is very drinkable. There's a large clean swimming pool and the Portonovo beach is only a few kilometres down (and I mean down) the road. Fellow guests tend to be slightly trendy Italians, but the atmosphere is informal." Later visitors agree. "Good value" and "at the height of the season, an oasis of calm and content. Service is outstanding (the owner even drove us to the beach and collected us later). The countryside is blissfully undeveloped as yet." "Cool white bedrooms, pretty rosebud-tiled shower rooms." However, there is some criticism of "disappointing, overpriced dinners. Rather heavily concentrated on fish. On any future visit we will probably eat à la carte rather than from the set menu." (*Martyn Goff, Robert D Hill, Joy Hatwood and Sholto Cross, Phyllis Beach*)

Open Mar–Oct. Closed Sun evening and Mon.
Rooms 28 doubles, 2 single – 3 with bath, 27 with shower, all with telephone. Some on ground floor.

Facilities Lift, ramps. Lounge with TV, restaurant; conference facilities. Garden with swimming pool, bar and tennis court. Rocky beach 2 km by road – (transport by hotel's mini-bus). English spoken. &.
Location 10 km from town centre. From the N take exit Ancona Nord; follow signs for port and station; in front of station follow signs for Riviera del Conero.
Credit cards None accepted.
Terms B&B: 46,000–80,500 L; half-board 69,000–86,250 L; full alc 40,250 L. Reduced rates and special meals for children.

ARZACHENA 07020 Sassari, Sardinia   Map 16

Hotel Pitrizza   *Tel* (0789) 92000
Porto Cervo, Costa Smeralda   *Telex* 792079

The Costa Smeralda, on the north-east corner of the island, is a rugged area covered with pines and developed as a rich playground by the Aga Khan. ("Queen Elizabeth I sleeping in stately homes had nothing on the Aga Khan and Burton and Elizabeth Taylor" teases one reader this year. "They have stayed everywhere.") Rocky outcrops jut into the sea, forming isolated coves. One of these is the setting for the *Pitrizza*, a secluded cluster of rough-stone buildings, hidden from each other and from the road by a splendidly colourful garden. The main building houses the dining room, reception and a small sitting room. Other villas hold three or four bedrooms sharing an entrance lounge but each with its own balcony. The style throughout is one of rustic luxury – rough-cast white walls, lovely hand-painted tiles. "A quiet, exclusive retreat. One of the chief delights is the swimming pool. There is a sun terrace and, down through the gardens, a private beach of golden but rather coarse sand, with umbrellas and comfortable lounge chairs. Breakfast can be taken either at the main building or at your cottage – delicious coffee and croissants. We had dinner under a veranda of plaited bamboo and eucalyptus. The hors d'oeuvre table was particularly good and the service, as everywhere else in the hotel, impeccable. The only problem was the mosquitoes – incense candles burned at strategic intervals. Expensive, of course – but an experience we wouldn't have missed." (*Angela and David Stewart*)

Another reader, however, says the Costa Smeralda is rather seedy and was not so impressed with the *Pitrizza* for the money. Could we hear from other readers if this hotel is worth its enormous weight in lira?

Open 10 May–30 Sept.
Rooms 1 suite, 22 double, 5 single – in groups of 4–6 villas; 22 with bath, 6 with shower, all with air-conditioning, most with terrace or patio.
Facilities Club house with salons, bar with piano, restaurant, terrace. Park and garden. Sea-water swimming pool, sandy beach, private mooring; wind surfing; Pevero Golf-Club nearby. English spoken.
Location 19 km NE of Arzachena. Transport by mini-bus from Olbia/Costa Smeralda airport given 24 hours' notice.
Restriction Not suitable for &.
Credit cards Access, Amex, Diners.
Terms (Excluding tax and 18½% service charge) dinner, B&B: single 230,000–330,000 L, double 460,000–660,000 L; full board: single 250,000–350,000 L, double 500,000–700,000 L. Set lunch/dinner 75,000 L. 30% reduction for children under 12 sharing parents' room.

ASSISI Perugia	**Map 16**

Hotel Fontebella
Via Fontebella 25
Assisi 06082

Tel (075) 812883/812941
Telex 660122

This 17th-century *palazzo* near the centre of the city of St Francis is "the place to be – central, reasonable and well run". Another reader calls the *Fontebella* "a charming hotel. Each room has a tiny balcony affording a spectacular view of the town. We found the proprietors pleasant and eager to help. The hotel has a comfortable (and beautiful) sitting room where we played an Italian card game and drank brandy into the wee hours of the morning." Opinions vary about the restaurant: "Over-priced, but easily avoided by a few minutes' stroll", and: "We were not disappointed – the food was superb." (*N Viney, Kathleen McCleery and Robert Martinez*)

Open All year. Restaurant closed Wed.
Rooms 32 double, 6 single – 14 with bath, 24 with shower, all with telephone.
Facilities Lounge, TV room, bar, restaurant; conference facilities. Garden. English spoken.
Location Central. Private parking.
Credit cards All major cards accepted.
Terms B&B: single 48,000 L, double 67,000 L; half-board 75,000–80,000 L; full board 95,000–100,000 L. Full alc 22,000 L.

Hotel Umbra
Via degli Archi 6
Assisi 06081

Tel (075) 812240
Telex 66122 AZIENTUR

"One of our best stops" declares a reader about this small, reasonably priced family-run hotel down an old alleyway just off the main square. "Wouldn't want to have missed it" writes another. "Lovely sunny rooms; quiet, peaceful and clean." There's a touch of Italian elegance about the public rooms, and a pleasant patio at the back where you can eat out under the trees. "Food excellent" is a tribute from one of Britain's distinguished chefs; he adds: "Bedroom a bit small but adequate, very helpful staff. Would recommend without hesitation". (*Kenneth Bell, Marie Earl; warmly endorsed by H Hannah*)

Open All year except 12 Nov–17 Dec and 11 Jan–28 Feb. Restaurant closed Tue.
Rooms 22 double, 5 single – 16 with bath, 6 with shower, all with telephone; some ground-floor rooms.
Facilities 3 lounges, TV lounge, American Bar, restaurant. Garden with terraces for meals in fine weather. English spoken.
Location In town centre, near main square.
Credit cards All major cards accepted.
Terms Rooms: single 38,000 L, double 54,000 L. Breakfast 4,500 L; full alc 23,000 L. Reduced rates for children.

The length of an entry does not necessarily reflect the merit of a hotel. The more interesting the report or the more unusual or controversial the hotel, the longer the entry.

BELLAGIO 22021 Como   Map 16

Hotel du Lac   *Tel* (031) 950320
Piazza Mazzini   *Telex* 326299

Overlooking Lake Como, this Hotel Du Lac – *not the one of Booker fame – is in one reader's opinion "one of the finest hotels in Europe. In addition to a fine structure and a breathtaking view, the Leoni family create a splendid atmosphere. Arturo, June and son Luca are genuinely interested in their guests – they constantly chat with them in the dining room and in the bar – and that alone makes the hotel very special." (David E Stewart) More reports welcome.*

Open Mid-Apr–mid-Oct.
Rooms 38 double, 11 single – 40 with bath, 7 with shower, all with telephone. Some with private terrace.
Facilities Lift. Lounge, American tea room/bar, restaurant; outdoor bar, roof garden; 300 metres from beach with safe bathing. English spoken.
Location In the centre of the village, in front of landing stage.
Restriction Not suitable for &.
Credit cards All major cards accepted.
Terms B&B: single 52,000 L, double 75,000–80,000 L; dinner, B&B 50,000 L per person; full board: 56,000–64,000 L per person. Set lunch/dinner 19,000 L; full alc 30,000 L. Reduction of 50% for children under 7, 30% if under 11, and 10% for 11 years and over; special meals.

Grand Hotel Villa Serbelloni   *Tel* (031) 950216
Via Roma 1   *Telex* 380330 SERBOT

To Stendhal, the promontory dividing Lake Como, on which Bellagio is situated, offered "sublime and charming views". The *Villa Serbelloni*, which enjoys those views, is a huge, ornate villa of grand-operatic splendour, with a superb position on the lake, and is backed by a large park famous for its display of magnolias, camellias and pomegranates. Inside, the palatial public rooms are hung with gold chandeliers and decorated with original frescoes. The staircase is flanked by gilt *putti* on giant candelabra, and the bedrooms, large enough for regal *leveés*, have wonderful views over the lake or the gardens at the back. There is a heated swimming pool and a private beach. A visitor this year writes: "We found the standard rooms a bit shabby, but we moved up to a de luxe room and it was more than we could ask for. Extremely large and palatial with beautiful furnishings and with French doors overlooking the lake. The service was wonderful and hotel employees were eager to help in any way." Another reader goes so far as to say, "We would rate this as the best all-round hotel we have stayed at abroad. It's got everything – a magnificent position, splendid public rooms, excellent food." *(Dr and Mrs Charles Stratton, Ken and Mildred Edwards; and others)*

Open Apr–Oct.
Rooms 11 suites, 60 double, 14 single – 75 with bath, 10 with shower, all with telephone and mini-bar, radio and TV on request; some ground-floor rooms.
Facilities Lifts. Palatial lounges, TV room, bridge room, writing room, games room, playroom with table tennis, bar, restaurants; banqueting and conference facilities; hairdressing salon, boutique, terrace (also for meals), evening orchestra with dancing. Gardens with tennis courts, heated swimming pool with snack bar, which lead to private beach; boating, waterskiing, boating excursions. English spoken. &.

Location Bellagio is 30 km from Como. Hotel is central. Parking and garage.
Credit cards Amex, Visa.
Terms B&B 130,000–175,000 L; dinner, B&B 155,000–200,000 L; full board
180,000–225,000 L. Set lunch/dinner 50,000–60,000 L; full alc 60,000 L. Reduced
rates for children sharing parents' room; special meals on request.

BOLOGNA   Map 16

Hotel Nettuno   *Tel* (051) 260964
Via Galliera 65
Bologna 40121

In a few years this hotel could become a pilgrimage site for *aficionados* of
pure fifties design. Today, readers recommend it as a comfortable and
straightforward hotel not far from the station. "The via Galliera was once
a main road, but is now a minor street parallel to via dell'Indipendenza;
this implies that rarest of virtues in Italy, silence. Though no doubt an
old building, it has been modernised to the point that no one would
notice this, but our room was adequately large, water was abundant and
hot, and one receives pleasant presents (miniature bottles of apéritifs, a
bag of sweets) from the management, and the agreeable and competent
men behind the desk converse in English when asked, or in careful
Italian when one tries to speak Italian oneself. It is reasonably priced; no
restaurant, but many good ones nearby – and the breakfast is no worse
than elsewhere in Italy. Bologna is a delight, still inadequately known."
(*M C and V H Whiting*)

Open All year.
Rooms 38 rooms – all with bath or shower, telephone, radio and air-conditioning.
Facilities 2 lifts. Hall, lounge, tea room; conference facilities. English spoken.
Location Central, near station.
Restriction Not suitable for &.
Credit cards All major cards accepted.
Terms Rooms: single 50,000 L, double 76,000 L. Breakfast 3,500 L. (No restaurant.)

Hotel Roma   *Tel* (051) 274400
Via Massimo D'Azeglio 9, Bologna 40123

"In the heart of the medieval centre of Bologna lies a pedestrianised area
that encloses the cathedral, the Square of Neptune, and many of the best
shopping arcades and pavement cafés: with its front doors opening into
one of the most popular of these narrow strees lies the *Hotel Roma*.
Fortunately, the back entrance of the hotel is in the area open to traffic,
so access by car is easy. Reception is formal. The room we had was a
straightforward hotel room with extra large bed – all the essentials, but
nothing much else. The bathroom was almost as large as the bedroom.
All was quiet outside by 11 pm, all quiet that is, except for the deep
sonorous chimes that struck every hour throughout the night. Although
not exciting, the food was acceptable. The waiter looked like Michelangelo's David, but didn't know about wine – his only inquiry was
'white or red'." An occasional visitor to Bologna writes this year to say
that the *Roma* is still a charming old place, "despite the hectic
wallpapers". He advises to go elsewhere for breakfast, however...

"wander across the Piazza and have it in a café, at half the price and three times the speed." (*A and D Stewart, Nigel Viney*)

Open All year. Restaurant closed 1–23 Aug.
Rooms 80 – most with bath or shower, telephone, TV, and air-conditioning (4,000 L).
Facilities Lift. Restaurant; roof garden. &.
Location Central. Covered garage at rear.
Credit cards Amex, Diners, Visa.
Terms [1985 rates] Rooms: single 45,000 L, double 75,000 L; full board 84,000–96,000 L per person. Breakfast 6,000 L; set lunch/dinner 20,000–22,000 L.

BRESSANONE 39042 Bolzano   Map 16

Hotel Senoner   *Tel* (0472) 22298

The *Senoner* sits tranquilly near the river Rienz, its typically Tyrolean roof stepping up towards the surrounding mountains. The house itself dates from 1466, when it was used as a court of justice. Only in the 18th century did the clerks manage to get permission to sell beverages to those frequenting the place. The Senoner family has run the hotel since 1931. "The decoration is attractive; there is a sun terrace, plenty of sitting rooms and a friendly bar. The staff are helpful and multi-lingual. The food was good; wines are Italian or Austrian and they have pleasant draft lager. Handy for skiers as the cable car to Plose summit is about 15 minutes' walk along the road." (*H Hannah, C A Beckwith, A Hobbs*)

Open All year except 1 Nov–20 Dec.
Rooms 1 4-bedded, 1 3-bedded, 14 double, 6 single – 3 with bath, 19 with shower, all with balcony.
Facilities 2 lounges, TV room, bar, restaurant, bowling. Garden and sun terrace. Near to mountains for skiing in winter. English spoken.
Location 7 minutes' walk E of Bressanone, by the river Rienz.
Restriction Not suitable for &.
Credit cards All major cards accepted.
Terms B&B: single 32,000 L, double 54,000 L; dinner, B&B 40,000–46,000 L per person; full board 50,000–55,000 L per person. Set lunch/dinner 13,000–14,000. 20% reduction for children under 12; special meals.

CAMAIORE 55043 Tuscany   Map 16

Peralta   *Tel* (0584) 989882
Nr Lucca   *Reservations* in UK:
Harrison Stanton & Haslam Ltd
25 Studdridge Street
London SW6
Tel 01-736 5094

"*Peralta* is run along the lines of an informal house party, not a slick hotel," say the London-based managers of this cluster of old houses on a wooded Tuscan hillside, facing towards the sea high above Viareggio. First an Etruscan settlement, then a hamlet growing olives and chestnuts, *Peralta* fell into ruin but has recently been restored by the sculptress Fiore de Henriquez and turned into an out-of-the-ordinary holiday haunt. Our correspondent sampled its joys: "We went up and up, and came to *Peralta* after a hair-raising drive. The road finally runs out and you have to walk. It is a collection of houses and studios, all simple, some primitive, all with white walls and beams, and a shower of sorts – we had the only bath. Water is a problem since it has to be pumped up. You have an open bar, everyone writes down what they take. Meals are in the open (when fine). The cook is a Cordon Bleu; the food was excellent: no choice, but alternatives could be found. You are moved around at dinner to sit with different people. Breakfast is dreadful. The small swimming pool, overlooking Tuscany, has plenty of places to sit and sunbathe.

"It was one of the most beautiful places I have ever been to. Lovely walks in the country and olive groves, amid wild flowers. Our room had views as far as the sea. We had our own small garden to sit in, with lavender bushes and an orange tree. But it's an isolated place, and if the weather is poor there is nothing to do except read. It is a highly unsuitable place for the very young or elderly: a fair amount of scrambling up and down is needed. Also you may be lucky and have very pleasant fellow guests: but if you are all incompatible it could be hell. During our stay, some of the people were a bit Sloane Rangerish – a problem." (*Heather Sharland*).

Open 10 May–27 Sept. Hotel open, but no arrivals accepted on Thur. Restaurant closed Thur.
Rooms 14 double, 1 single – 1 with bath, 14 with shower. Rooms are in 4 separate buildings.
Facilities Lounge, bar, restaurant. 2-acre grounds with terraces and unheated swimming pool; *boules* court and olive groves. Safe sandy beaches 25 minutes' drive. English spoken.
Location SE of Camaiore which is 30 km NW of Lucca, 10 km NE of Viareggio. Car park is 200 metres from village.
Restrictions Not suitable for &. No children under 16.
Credit cards None accepted.
Terms (Service at guests' discretion) B&B £13.60–£20; dinner, B&B £21.60–£28; full board £25.60–£32. Set lunch £4, dinner £8. Half-board compulsory in July and Aug.

CANNERO RIVIERA 28051 Novara   **Map 16**

Hotel Cannero   *Tel* (0323) 788046/7
Lunga lago 2

The mild climate of Cannero Riviera, which encourages lemons and oranges to grow in great proliferation, also entices travellers to the health and holiday resort on Lake Maggiore, and to the hotels situated along the water's edge. "We visit Europe every year and as far as we're concerned the *Hotel Cannero* ranks amongst the best in its category. It provided us with one of the best holidays we can remember. The room, with balcony looking over the beautiful lake and mountain scenery, was spacious and the bathroom well equipped. There is a terrace overlooking the lake and a car park attached to the hotel (a car is necessary). A variety of meat, sea fish and freshwater fish was served in the dining room together with garden-fresh vegetables delivered daily – only one pasta dish was served during the whole of our stay. All was beautifully cooked and presented, and the service was highly efficient. Excellent value for money." (*A E Pow*)

Open 20 Mar–end Oct.
Rooms 26 double, 6 single – all with bath, shower and telephone; some with balcony. Some ground-floor rooms.
Facilities Lift. Lounge, TV room, bar, restaurant. Lakeside terrace, garden (swimming pool planned for 1986). English spoken.
Location Central, on Lake Maggiore. Garage and parking.
Credit cards Access, Amex, Visa.
Terms [1985 rates, all 3 days min.] B&B: single 38,000–41,000 L, double 60,000–64,000 L; dinner, B&B 42,000–48,000 L per person; full board 48,000–55,000 L per person. 30% reduction for children under 10 in parents' room.

CAPRI 80073   Map 16

Hotel Flora   *Tel* (081) 8370211
Via Federico Serena 26

Much less fashionable and exotic than in the days of Norman Douglas and Axel Munthe, Capri today is given over to mass-tourism. But its beauties remain – the lovely island, and the little town of Capri itself, rather like a vast stage set with its small squares, white houses and alleyways. Here in the town the *Flora* is recommended as "a modern *pensione* near the main square. Front rooms have fine views and all are spacious and well equipped. The lounge is mainly used as a TV room and there is no restaurant, but there is a sun-terrace. On the whole excellent value in oh-so-expensive Capri." "Beautiful antiques, tiled floors, velvet-upholstered furniture, balconies full of bougainvillea. Friendly service; best croissants we found in Europe." (*P D Scott, David Helsdon, Trudy and Neil Reid*)

Open 1 Apr–15 Oct.
Rooms 23 double, 2 single – 23 with bath, 2 with shower, all with telephone. 10 rooms in annexe. Ground-floor rooms.
Facilities Lounge with TV, bar. Garden, sun terrace. English spoken.
Location Central.
Restriction Not suitable for &.
Credit cards All major cards accepted.
Terms B&B: single 60,000 L, double 82,000–103,000 L. (No restaurant.) 30% reduction for children.

CASTELLINA IN CHIANTI 53011 Siena   Map 16

Tenuta di Ricavo   *Tel* (0577) 740221

"An admirable hamlet-turned-hotel that is a beguiling place to stay." Certainly the *Tenuta's* location is glorious, in over 300 acres of gardens and woods commanding a breathtaking view of the famous vineyards and the surrounding countryside. You can walk for miles without meeting a soul, and yet you are only 22 kilometres from Siena and 34 from Florence. The manor house forms the main building, bedrooms are scattered among a series of lovely old stone cottages and out-buildings. There are two swimming pools. Inside the furnishings are charming but simple, in tune with the old houses. The hotel is Swiss-owned. A correspondent reported enthusiastically: "Oh bliss! I loved it and wished we could have stayed longer. Our lovely room was simple, whitewashed, with dark exposed beams and polished red tiles; a large farm fireplace filled with the yellow flames of forsythia in full bloom; wrought-iron chandelier and matching bedside lamps. The bathroom *en suite* was rather spartan. In the large vaulted dining room, dinner is at 7.30 but they don't seem to mind latecomers. There is a choice only of starter (i.e. soup or pasta): main dishes just arrive. The food is well cooked but nothing special. Chianti was from their own farm. Coffee is served in the various lounges, one very large with a burning log fire. As so often in country hotels, the guests mingled happily. My husband was a little less enthusiastic than I about the place, saying that it was not very Italian in atmosphere." Other visitors agree. Some old-timers feel the place has become too commercial and expensive. But, for one regular, the *Tenuta* still earns its place: "Much of Italy has been ironed out of the *Tenuta*, but all in all an enchanting stay and, like many before us, we are looking forward to our return." (*Nigel Viney, Mrs Patricia Solomon; F W*)

Open 22 Mar–mid-Oct.
Rooms 10 suites, 13 double, 2 single – all with bath and telephone; 16 rooms in annexe; 3 ground-floor rooms, 1 suitable for wheelchairs.
Facilities 3 salons, bar, restaurant, 300-acre grounds with 2 swimming pools; hiking trails, 2 *boccia* courses. English spoken. &.
Location 22 km NW of Siena, 34 km S of Florence. Leave Siena *superstrada* at San Donato exit, then follow signs to Castellina in Chianti.
Restriction No transistor radios allowed in rooms or garden.
Credit cards None accepted.
Terms Full board 80,000–155,000 L. Min. stay 3 nights. Reduced rates for children; special meals on request.

Villa Casalecchi
Tel (0577) 740240

A weathered patrician stone villa, surrounded by ancient oak trees, the Villa Casalecchi *is a somewhat cheaper and more traditionally Italian alternative to the* Tenuta di Ricavo (above). *The view is glorious and the setting tranquil. One visitor reports: "Our room was a perfect combination of old-fashioned character and charm with modern comforts. It looked out across the hotel's terrace to a field of vines, a meadow and a wooded hill. The only sound after dark was a cuckoo deceived by the nearly full moon. They built these old villas pretty solidly, which means that they are cool in the summer heat. There was a lovely little dining room with painted wooden boxed ceiling (as in our bedroom), with its walls and curtains all in shades of honey, walnut and ochre. Dinner was a five-course affair with a choice of five dishes in the pasta, entrée and pudding courses." There have, however, been complaints this year: about the water supply, the state of the pool, uncomfortable beds, and some readers have hinted at dissatisfaction with the food. "Monotonous"; "the chef had an over-heavy hand with the salt"; "coffee at breakfast was exceptionally poor". And this mixed blessing: "Willing service from the English waiters whose Italian somewhat bemused the large number of German guests."* (B A, Mary and Rodney Milne-Day, N and C B) *We should welcome more reports.*

Open 1 Apr–1 Oct inclusive.
Rooms 3 suites, 16 double – 16 with bath, 3 suites with shower, all with telephone.
Facilities 2 lounges, bar, restaurant. Garden, swimming pool. English spoken.
Location 45 km S of Florence, 18 km E of Siena; 1 km from town centre. Parking.
Restriction Not suitable for &.
Credit cards Access, Diners, Visa.
Terms Half-board 105,000–125,000 L; full board 125,000–140,000 L per person. Full alc 50,000 L.

CEFALÙ 90015 Sicily   Map 16

Pensione Villa Belvedere   *Tel* (0921) 21593 or 23310
Via dei Mulini 43   *Telex* 910303 (COOP TUR)

Cefalù is noted for its splendid old romanesque cathedral and for the great Gibraltar-like rock that looms up behind it, one of the major landmarks of the north Sicilian coast. "This small *pensione* stands along a narrow road leading fairly steeply up from the western approach to this enchanting little town. The entrance is charming, even though some visitors may raise their eyebrows at the statues of Snow White and the Dwarfs lining the pergola'd steps and edge of the little shady patio, where breakfast is served in good weather – in other words, usually. The entrance hall has baronial overtones with its sweeping arches and potted plants; a charming little bar is set back into the wall, and a few comfortable chairs are spaced on the split-level reception area. The downstairs restaurant is airy and surprisingly large, till you come to realise that wedding parties often take place here. Bedrooms are quite spacious and most are reasonably modern, adequate rather than luxurious. Francesco Attardo, the young owner, trained at the *Ritz* in Paris, and knows how to keep his guests happy. Cooking is homely. Views from the upper rooms are beautiful, the location quiet yet not far from the old town-centre and the fine sandy beach." (*R W E Wiersum; endorsed with minor reservations by W Ian Stewart*)

Open All year. Restaurant closed Oct–Mar incl.
Rooms 25 double, 2 single – 1 with bath, 22 with shower, all with telephone.
Facilities Large reception, bar with TV, restaurant; tea-room, sun terrace with tables; table tennis. Large garden. Sandy beach with lifeguards 10 minutes' walk, fishing. English spoken.
Location 1 km W of centre. Parking.
Restriction Not suitable for &.
Credit cards None accepted.
Terms B&B: single 28,000–30,000 L, double 45,000–50,000 L; dinner, B&B 43,000–50,000 L; full board 48,000–55,000 L. Set lunch/dinner 20,000 L; full alc 25,000 L. Reductions of up to 30% for children; special meals.

COGNE 11012 Aosta   Map 16

Hotel Bellevue   *Tel* (0165) 74825
Rue Grand Paradis 20

The village of Cogne is a summer and skiing resort, high up in a mountain valley south of Aosta, facing the San Paradiso massif. The *Bellevue*, on the edge of the village, has been in the Guide for some years. Visitors last year spelled it out: "Simple but comfortably furnished, and well kept. All rooms have bathrooms, and though not large are warm, clean and well equipped. Good traditional local food. The hotel is modest, but has a warm comfortable feeling, is run by a family that cares, and is in a beautiful area." This year we hear: "The hotel has a well-established, confident feel as befits a family concern. The staff are most obliging and affable. A lovely place – wonderful walks for those who love mountains." (*Pat and Jeremy Temple, Mrs E Newall*)

Open Feb–Easter, 4 June–19 Sept, 20 Dec–5 Jan. Restaurant closed Wed.
Rooms 4 suites, 39 double, 6 single – 24 with bath, 21 with shower, all with
telephone and radio; most with balcony; tea-making facilities in suites.
Facilities Lift. TV room, pub, bar, reading room, restaurant; conference facilities;
solarium, sauna. Garden. Tennis, fishing, walking and winter sports nearby. &.
Location 27 km S of Aosta. Parking.
Credit cards None accepted.
Terms [1985 rates] rooms: single 38,000 L, double 68,000 L; full board 52,000–
66,000 L per person. Breakfast 5,000 L; set lunch/dinner 20,000–25,000 L.

COURMAYEUR 11013 Aosta   Map 16

Hotel Lo Bouton d'Or   *Tel* (0165) 842380
Strada Statale 26, n.10   *Telex* 210369 AIRSKI

Readers reaffirm the high quality of this hotel in the ski resort of
Courmayeur, which offers spotlessly clean, very comfortable accommodation. Many rooms look across to Mont Blanc, others face across the
valley to lesser mountains. Rooms are small but tastefully decorated
with hessian-lined walls, carpets and stylish bedspreads. The attached
bathrooms have bright modern tiles and new fittings. Public rooms are
again furnished in modern fashion. Terms are bed and breakfast only,
though you can, if you wish, book a half-board arrangement, eating at
the owner's restaurant, *Le Vieux Pommier*, in the village. Breakfast is a
welcome change from the standard Italian one, "really good, not
pre-packed, with delicious coffee and rolls. We enjoyed our meals
enormously at the family's restaurant and can thoroughly recommend
it." (*Mrs B A Blum, and others*)

Open All year except May and Nov.
Rooms 21 double, 3 single – 15 with bath, 9 with shower, all with telephone and
radio; TV on request.
Facilities Lift. Bar, lounge, TV room, breakfast room. Solarium, sauna. Garden,
terrace; winter sports and fishing nearby. English spoken. &.
Location 400 metres from town centre. Parking.
Credit cards All major cards accepted.
Terms B&B 41,000–48,000 L. Half-board (meal at *Le Vieux Pommier*)
60,000–67,000 L.

ERICE 91016 Sicily   Map 16

Hotel Moderno   *Tel* (0923) 869300
Via Vittorio Emanuele 67

"Erice is an incredibly atmospheric sun-bleached town at the very tip of
a breathtakingly high pinnacle of rock, a village in the clouds, with
views of the sea and, almost straight down, western Sicily. The medieval
atmosphere is stronger than virtually anywhere we've seen. The streets
are paved with stones laid in striking patterns – ribbons, basketweaves,
checkerboards. The castle and churches are marvellous. For us, Erice is
one of the great experiences of Europe. The *Moderno* is charming, snug
and friendly. It is very much a family-run hotel, whose owner fixed our
car, and with pink-cheeked lads to scamper after bags, drinks, dinner.
No bath in our room, and the showers were not completely enclosed –
but no big problem. A very pleasant place to stay in one of the most
thrilling, loveliest towns in the world." (*Tom and Connie Congdon*)

Open All year.
Rooms 20 double, 6 single – 6 with bath, 20 with shower, all with telephone.
Facilities Lift. Lounge, bar, TV room, dining room, terrace. English spoken. &.
Location Central. Parking.
Credit cards Amex, Diners, Visa.
Terms B&B: single 40,000 L, double 63,000 L; dinner, B&B 45,000–55,000 L per person; full board 60,000–70,000 L per person. Set meals 25,000 L; full alc 30,000 L; reduced rates and special meals for children.

FIESOLE 50014 Florence   **Map 16**

Hotel Villa Bonelli   *Tel* (055) 59513 or 598941 or 598942
Via F. Poeti 1

A modern and unpretentious family-run hotel, with an attractive top-floor restaurant, offering a panoramic view of the city. The No. 7 bus, frequent and dependable, obviates taking a car into the city. Rooms tend to be on the small side, and there is nowhere much to sit after dinner except in the foyer which has TV. *But correspondents feel these are small prices to pay for "the marvellous value". The hotel prefers guests to be on half-board terms from March to October, and you will need to book ahead in the high season. Readers speak well of the food – "Very varied, and by far the best I have had in an Italian* pensione.*" One reader this year wrote that the staff were "very obliging and spoke excellent English", but another was unhappy about the off-hand reception, poky rooms and board-like beds. More reports please.* (H B Hannah)

Open All year. Restaurant closed 1 Nov–15 Mar.
Rooms 1 suite, 16 double, 7 single – 1 with bath/wc, 13 with shower/wc, all with telephone; some ground-floor rooms.
Facilities Lift. Hall, TV room, bar, roof-restaurant, terrace. English spoken.
Location 300 metres from town centre, right turn 300 metres after Piazza Mino. Garage. Regular bus service to and from Florence.
Restriction Not suitable for &.
Credit cards None accepted.
Terms B&B: single 35,000–41,000 L, double 54,000–67,000 L; dinner, B&B: single 55,000–61,000 L, double 94,500–107,000. Set lunch/dinner 20,000 L; full alc 25,000 L. Reduced rates for children; special meals on request.

FLORENCE   **Map 16**

Hermitage Hotel   *Tel* (055) 287216 or 268277 or 298901
Piazza del Pesce, Pontevecchio
Florence 50122

A splendidly situated hotel, beside the Ponte Vecchio and backing on to the Uffizi. The *Hermitage* is assembled upside down – bedrooms on the first to sixth floors, lounge, reception and breakfast rooms on the fifth. Manager Vincenzo Scarcelli writes to tell us that all the rooms have been redecorated and double-glazing added to the windows in rooms overlooking the river. "A delightful and charming little gem – and quieter than one would imagine, maybe because our room faced on to the small square. Car parking is difficult. Bedrooms are smallish. Public rooms are delightfully furnished; the roof terrace in particular is a happy, relaxing and sunny place. Altogether very good value for money." The multi-lingual staff are said to be most friendly and helpful, although last year one reader complained of being cold-shouldered. No meals, but snacks are served until 10.30 pm. Reports on room renovations would be appreciated. (*Sydney Downs; also S B; endorsed by Kenneth Bell and David Helsdon*)

Open All year.
Rooms 14 double, 2 single – 13 with bath, 2 with shower; all with telephone. Front rooms double-glazed.
Facilities Lift. Reception/lounge, TV room, breakfast room, bar; roof garden.
Location Central, near Ponte Vecchio. Garage and parking facilities nearby.
Restriction Not suitable for &.
Credit cards None accepted.
Terms [1985 rates] rooms: single 49,000 L, double 78,000 L; B&B single 59,000 L, double 98,000 L. (No restaurant.)

Hotel Monna Lisa
Borgo Pinti 27
Florence 50121

Tel (055) 2479751
Telex 573300 MONLIS

A mixed bunch of reports again this year – mainly praise, but some brick-bats too on this stylish hotel, described by an inspector as "perhaps the nicest in Florence. Ceilings are vaulted, wooden or frescoed; furniture is original antique, dating back to the quattrocento, *and there's a fine collection of sculpture – including Giambologna's first study of the 'Rape of the Sabines'. All the public areas are beautifully furnished in Florentine style and beautifully maintained. The Tuscan tiles are polished daily and the furniture restorer comes in twice a week." The bedrooms, however, vary greatly – some are "large and baronial", others "uninteresting and dreary", according to recent reports, and booking seems to be an unfruitful way of securing one of the better ones. Everyone agrees that those facing the garden and courtyard are quietest; those on the street can be very noisy. The hot water in the bathrooms, though abundant, does not always keep to its proper channels of sink and shower; but the staff is extremely cheerful and helpful. Only breakfast is served here. (S B, Lyndall Hopcraft, J M Garrick, D and B Cabianca; and many others) More reports please.*

Open All year.
Rooms 1 suite, 20 double, 7 single – 15 with bath, 9 with shower, all with telephone; some ground-floor rooms.
Facilities 4 sitting rooms, one with TV, American bar with taped music, dining room. Inner courtyard/garden. English spoken.
Location Central; rooms on street are sound-proofed. Garage.
Credit cards All major cards accepted.
Terms B&B: single 95,000 L, double 150,000 L. (No restaurant.)

Hotel Porta Rossa
Via Porta Rossa 19, Florence

Tel (055) 287551
Telex 570007 PROSSA

A modestly priced and very central hotel "with the huge advantage of being five minutes away from the *Duomo* or the river, but with the problem (in some front rooms) of noise. It is a fine 19th-century building with classical public rooms and an imposing staircase. Its grandeur is somewhat faded and the service not impeccable. But the hotel has definite charm. It is between two narrow streets, surrounded by Florentine congestion and turmoil, but the higher rooms at the back are not too noisy, and the hotel leaves no doubt that you are in Florence." One visitor this year thought the atmosphere "rather gloomy"; another approved the "friendly and helpful" staff and tolerated the shabbiness and "noisy student parties". (*Anthony Sampson; also T D Baxendale, S B*)

Open All year.
Rooms 71 – 10 with bath, 47 with shower, some with telephone.
Facilities Lift. Lounge with TV, bar.
Location Central, near the *Duomo*.
Terms [1985 rates] rooms: single 37,000–47,500 L, double 54,500–69,500 L. Breakfast 7,000 L. (No restaurant.)

Hotel Pensione Tornabuoni Beacci   *Tel* (055) 268377 or 212645
Via Tornabuoni 3   *Telex* 570215-162 BEACCI
Florence 50123

"The great charm of this top-floor hotel (which is in a 14th-century palace and very well run, with a home-like and friendly atmosphere) is its superb location (central, near the Palazzo Strozzi) and its wonderful roof-terrace. This has trees, plants, tables and chairs, where just about everyone has breakfast and where you can also work during the day in peace or have cocktails before going out. The hotel is six or seven storeys up, in an old well-built building. Bedrooms are mostly large; bathrooms somewhat old-fashioned but well maintained. There is a small restaurant with a basic menu; the well-known *Doney* restaurant is across the street. The hotel is so high up that you're not likely to be bothered by street noise, and much of historic Florence is within short walking distance." (*Julian Bach*)

Open All year.
Rooms 31 double – all with bath and telephone; TV on request. 5 in annexe.
Facilities Lift. Salon, bar, restaurant; roof-terrace. English spoken.
Location Central, close to Palazzo Strozzi. Parking.
Credit cards Access, Amex.
Terms Rooms: single 62,000 L, double 92,000 L; dinner, B&B 80,000–94,000 L per person; full board 90,000–104,000 L per person. Breakfast 10,000 L; full alc 40,000 L. 20% reduction for children; special meals.

Hotel Villa Belvedere   *Tel* (055) 222501 and 223163
Via Benedetto Castelli 3
Florence 50124

The view from this modern hotel on the Poggio Imperiale hill, "which takes in the dome of the *Duomo* by day and the twinkling lights of Fiesole by night" is one of the major attractions, along with the large rambling garden with swimming pool and tennis court. The owners, Signor and Signora Perotto, are equally appreciated. The *Villa Belvedere* has a cheerful, relaxed atmosphere and the stamp of genuine care. The bedrooms are simple – whitewashed with tile floors – but they are light and cool with large windows and, in some cases, balconies on which you can breakfast. Public rooms perhaps lack Florentine character, but are spacious and welcoming and, like the whole hotel, spotlessly clean. There has been major refurbishment of the public rooms and terrace in the past 12 months. There is no real restaurant but what the hotel refers to as "snacks al bar" turn out to be a range of simple dishes such as minestrone, spaghetti and omelettes, well prepared and served with style. A reader this year, while endorsing the hotel, found the

FORTE DEI MARMI

atmosphere slightly inhibiting for children and the service in the
bar/restaurant rather fierce. (*B A, M Slater; Robert D Hill*)

Open Mar–Nov inclusive.
Rooms 2 suites, 22 double, 3 single – 25 with bath, 2 with shower, all with
telephone; some rooms with balconies overlooking the garden; ground-floor
rooms.
Facilities Lift. Sitting rooms, TV room, bar with veranda. Large garden with
swimming pool, tennis court, children's play area. English spoken.
Location 2 km S of centre; leave Florence by Porta Romana, turn E off Via Senese.
Credit cards None accepted.
Terms B&B: single 80,000 L, double 120,000–130,000 L. (No restaurant, but light
meals available.) 50% reduction for children under 7 sharing parents' room.

Villa Le Rondini *Tel* (055) 400081 and 268212
Villa Bolognese Vecchia 224
Florence 50139

The *Villa Le Rondini* is on the top of Monterinaldi, one of the emerald
hills surrounding Florence, only six kilometres from the *Duomo*, and an
alternative to the smart hotels of Fiesole, with a similar breathtaking
view of the city and the Arno valley. We had an entry some years ago,
but left it out after ambivalent reports. In addition to rooms in the
16th-century main building, there are several villas or annexes in the 80
acres of grounds. "The room we had in one of the villas made us feel like
the Medici," said one guest. And another: "All rooms are furnished with
great taste and thought. Service perfect and friendly. There is a large
heated swimming pool, a tennis court and five riding horses. The
grounds and garden are superb, set in 80 acres overlooking Florence.
The food is good but could be better." Not every one speaks well of the
accommodation in the annexes, however, and food is clearly not *Le
Rondini's* strong point. There have also been complaints of unwillingly
served late evening meals or snacks, a legitimate gripe in view of the fact
that Florence and her trattorie are a good six kilometres down the hill.
(*J W, Sally and Curtis Wilmot-Allistone*) More reports welcome.

Open All year.
Rooms 25 double, 4 single – 28 with bath, 1 with shower. Some in villas in the
grounds.
Facilities Salon, TV room, dining room, conference/banqueting facilities. 80-acre
grounds with garden, tennis court, swimming pool and riding stables. English
spoken.
Location 6 km N of town centre. From Piazza della Liberta take via Bolognese
towards Trespiano. At La Lastra take via Bolognese Vecchia (left fork). Parking.
Regular bus service from Florence main railway station.
Credit cards All major cards accepted.
Terms [1985 rates] B&B: single 62,000 L, double 92,000 L; full board 118,000–
133,000 L per person. Set lunch/dinner 25,000–30,000 L.

FORTE DEI MARMI 55042 Lucca **Map 16**

Hotel Tirreno *Tel* (0584) 83333
Viale Morin 7

Forte dei Marmi is a traditional seaside resort of villas with shady
gardens, a wide traffic-free promenade, a pier and a long golden beach –

591

one of the most attractive towns on the Versilian Riviera. It has an Italian rather than international atmosphere, and is a particular favourite with well-to-do families from central and northern Italy. The resort is probably at its best slightly off-season. One of the advantages of the *Tirreno* is its "lovely and peaceful" garden, well equipped with deckchairs and tables. Readers this year concur with last year's favourable reports. One visitor found the bedrooms "excellent – the marble bathroom was as big as a bedroom in some hotels and the balcony had a side view of the sea". The lounges have lots of comfortable armchairs. Meals are "plentiful but unexciting", and food is available from the bar or room service at any hour of the day or night. But it is the service that draws the greatest praise; from arrival – "splendid, we were particularly well-received", to departure – "the owner appeared, shook our hands, said how nice it was to be appreciated and gave us a bottle of Italian 'champagne'. We left in a haze of mutual goodwill." (*J C Gillett, Gillian Seel, David Helsdon*)

Open Easter–Oct.
Rooms 49 double, 10 single – 12 with bath, 47 with shower, all with telephone; 20 rooms have balconies with sea views; 21 rooms in annexe.
Facilities 2 lounges, TV room, games room, bar, dining room. Luxuriant garden set with garden furniture and umbrellas. 50 metres from fine, safe beach with bathing and boat rental. English spoken.
Location 200 metres from town centre. Parking.
Restriction Not suitable for &.
Credit card Amex.
Terms [1985 rates] B&B: single 50,100 L, double 78,000 L; dinner, B&B 72,000–87,000 L per person; full board 78,000–99,000 L per person. Reductions for stays of 4 days or more. 30–60% reductions, depending on age, for children sharing parents' room; special meals.

GARDONE RIVIERA 25083 Brescia Map 16

Grand Hotel *Tel* (0365) 20261
Via Zanardelli 72 *Telex* 300254

Appropriately named, this hotel is grand, in the old style, situated regally on the shores of the celebrated Lake Garda. The hotel can boast of an exclusive promenade on the lakeside and a private beach. With its 180 rooms, it is larger than most in the Guide, and is for the more escapist (or richer) traveller who likes to live in a lordly way. "A real winner. Though we were only staying one night, we were given a palatial corner room overhanging the lake with two balconies, the most beautiful furniture and bathroom appointments in the grandest style. An excellent dinner matched by perfect table appointments, and the best of service." Other reports echo the praise. "The best poached salmon we have ever tasted." "Very friendly owner, and prices reasonable for such grandeur." (*Jack and Esther Holloway, Mr and Mrs B S Carter*)

Open Easter–Oct.
Rooms 123 double, 57 single – 161 with bath, 19 with shower, all with telephone, many with balcony; 11 ground-floor rooms.
Facilities Lift. Hall, lounge, TV room, bar, writing room, restaurant, terraces; conference/functions facilities; piano in bar July/Aug. Gardens, heated outdoor swimming pool; private sandy beach on lake, safe bathing; fishing, waterskiing, boating; golf. English spoken. &.

Location In town centre, on the lake (only 20 rooms face the road). Parking.
Credit cards All major cards accepted.
Terms [1985 rates] B&B: single 48,000–80,000 L; half-board 60,000–98,000 L; full board 70,000–110,000 L. Single room supplement 8,000–10,000 L. 25% reduction for children under 10 sharing parents' room; special meals.

GARGONZA 52048 Arezzo   Map 16

Castello di Gargonza   *Tel* (0575) 847021 or 847053
Monte San Savino   *Reservations* in Florence: (055) 241020
                                                       Telex 571466 REDCO

The *Castle of Gargonza* is, in fact, an intact 13th-century walled village overlooking the Chiana valley, once visited by the exiled Dante. "An enchanting discovery in the Tuscan woodlands, recently converted into an unusual private hotel and conference centre. Count Roberto Guicciardini's family has owned the place for centuries, both the *Castello* itself with its tall turreted tower and the score of red-roofed cottages that cluster round it for ramparted protection, archetypically Tuscan. The Count has turned the village homes (*case*) into bedrooms and suites, which can be hired either for a week or more on a self-catering basis, or else per night as at a hotel. He and his wife have done the conversion most elegantly – what flair the Italians bring to these things! Clean stone walls, beamed ceilings, pretty rustic decor, neatly cobbled alleys. The temptation might have been to go for something grand and expensive in the *Relais et Châteaux* style, but instead the Count has kept prices in the medium range: the little bedrooms have a monastic simplicity, with plain white walls and terracotta floors.

"The restaurant is open to non-residents and serves interesting Tuscan dishes: boar pâté, Tuscan white beans, almost-solid minestra, roast rabbit, spicy cold roast pork, a local delicacy of biscuit in sweet liqueur, and much else. The local wine is a bit rough. There is space for parking on the edge of the village. No swimming pool, oddly. The views are superb, over the lovely woods of chestnut, oak and cypress and across the Tuscan plain; Arezzo and Siena are both within an hour's drive." (*Jenny Towndrow*)

Open All year except 10 Jan–7 Feb. Restaurant closed Mon.
Rooms 40, in 20 separate houses – 32 with bath, 8 with shower, all with telephone and self-catering facilities.
Facilities Lounge, TV room, 2 large and 4 small conference rooms, restaurant. Large grounds with children's play area, woods and farm. (Swimming pool being installed.) English spoken.
Location 8 km W of Monte San Savino on SS No 73 towards Siena (35 km). From *autostrada* A1 – exit 27, Monte San Savino is 10 km.
Restriction Not suitable for ♿.
Credit card Amex.
Terms B&B: single 55,000–65,000 L, double 80,000–100,000 L; dinner, B&B: single 80,000–90,000 L, double 130,000–150,000 L; full board: single 105,000–115,000 L, double 180,000–200,000 L. Full alc 25,000 L. 30% discount for children under 7.

If you have difficulty in finding hotels because the location details given in the Guide are inadequate, please help us to improve directions next year.

GARLENDA 17033 Savona   Map 16

La Meridiana   *Tel* (0182) 580271

The comfortable *Meridiana* lies surrounded by woods and vineyards in its own spacious garden, sharing its pleasant valley with the small village of Garlenda 12 kilometres inland from the Riviera at Albenga. It is lovely country for walking, and there are facilities for other energetic pursuits – the hotel has its own large swimming pool and tennis courts, and there is a sailing club a few minutes' drive away. But this is, first and foremost, a golfer's hotel, in the centre of the Garlenda Golf Club. It is a modern building in a traditional style with spacious, simply furnished public rooms and well-equipped bedrooms, some self-catering. Recent visitors were particularly pleased with the "excellent food and very considerate service". (*Tom and Rosemary Rose*) More reports please.

Open All year except Nov–Dec. Restaurant closed midday.
Rooms 16 suites, 19 double – all with bath and shower, telephone, colour TV and mini-bar. 10 ground-floor rooms.
Facilities Lift. Lounge, bridge room, bar, restaurant, barbecue. In centre of Garlenda Golf club, with garden and swimming pool; tennis courts, riding school, sailing, waterskiing and fishing close at hand. Sea 10 km. English spoken. &.
Location 1 km from village, NW of Alassio leaving *autostrada* A10 at Albenga.
Credit cards Amex, Diners.
Terms B&B: single 125,000–155,000 L, double 220,000–260,000 L; full board 115,000–175,000 L per person. Set dinner 48,000 L; full alc 65,000 L. Buffet lunch available in bar. Reduced rates for children; special meals on request.

GIARDINI NAXOS 98030 Messina, Sicily   Map 16

Hotel Arathena Rocks   *Tel* (0942) 51349
Via Calcide Eubea 55

The "delicious" *Arathena Rocks* is near the centre of this bustling resort but in a peaceful location at the end of a private road. It is a family-run hotel in traditional style with white plaster walls and much of the furniture and doors painted with local scenes. Fresh flowers from the large garden decorate all the rooms – Signora Arcidiacono, who speaks excellent English, also has an Englishwoman's enthusiasm for gardening! The free-form swimming pool hewn out of lava rocks is an extra luxury with "gloriously clear, warm sea swimming only 20 yards away". A return visitor says happily, "still as spotless, bright, quiet and cheerful, and far fewer mosquitoes. Slightly more interesting food (an earlier report said food ranged from the standard to the imaginative). Ask for a room overlooking the sea and garden. Excellent value." (*Duncan Wood; also Conrad Jameson*) "Children are very welcome" says the management.

Open Apr–Oct inclusive.
Rooms 2 suites, 42 double, 10 single – 42 with bath, 10 with shower, all with telephone; 3 self-contained rooms in annexe.
Facilities Lift. 2 salons, bar with folk music, restaurant. Gardens with sea-water swimming pool and café, tennis court; man-made private beach. English spoken.
Location 5 km from city. Leave by Taormina Sud, go to Porto di Naxos; after 200 metres take small road on right towards sea. Hotel has mini-bus to take guests to Taormina.

Credit cards Amex, Diners.
Terms Dinner, B&B 62,000–68,000 L. Set lunch/dinner 22,000–30,000 L. Children under 10, 30% reduction, 10–15, 20%; special meals on request.

GREVE IN CHIANTI 50022 Florence   Map 16

Villa di Pile   *Tel* (055) 857011

A private villa in the Tuscan hills where the Count and Countess Tibaldi receive paying guests in their three spare bedrooms and extend to them the kind of hospitality they might offer free of charge to close friends. The Count writes to us to say, "*Villa di Pile* is particularly suitable for people who love the peace and quietness of the country and enjoy a family atmosphere and conversation." This new venture has impressed two of our trusted regular correspondents – "a splendid place to stay and meet educated and cultured people in the best European aristocratic tradition". "*Villa di Pile* is up in the hills beyond Greve, a characterful village in the heart of the Chianti Classico vineyards, 45 minutes by car from Florence up twisting narrow roads. It looks like a largish private house, with terraced garden, and below that an orchard and rolling vineyards. Count Cesare and his Norwegian wife have modernised the villa, merging the best of modern Italian and Scandinavian styles with some fine antiques: all is cool and calmly spacious. The two guest bedrooms on the ground floor are beautifully furnished in traditional style, with spectacular *en suite* bathrooms. Our room, on the first floor, had a large private sitting room attached, soberly furnished with Scandinavian leather seats and an Aborigine totem sculpture, and with one wall lined with English paperbacks; colour TV too. The Count invited us to join him and the five cats for pre-dinner drinks. We sat down to dinner at the baronial table, the Tibaldis at each end. Conversation was easy: they are a charming couple with excellent English. There is no choice of food: all was delicious. In the morning we opened the shutters to a sunlit view over the valley and the sight of Cesare picking flowers for our breakfast table. We were offered a cooked breakfast but instead we had two sorts of fresh bread and local honey. We were the first complete strangers coming to stay and the novelty of meeting new people day after day, saying the same things over and over, may wear off in time for our hosts. But for the moment it's splendid." (*Francine and Ian Walsh*)

Open 28 Mar–2 Nov.
Rooms 1 suite, 2 double – 2 with bath, 1 with shower. The suite has telephone and colour TV.
Facilities Hall, lounge, library, dining room. Garden. Tennis and golf nearby. English spoken.
Location On road to Lamole, 7 km E of Greve which is 27 km S of Florence, 40 km N of Siena.
Restriction Not suitable for &.
Credit cards None accepted.
Terms (Min. stay 3 days) rooms: double 100,000 L, suite 240,000 L; half-board 35,000 L per person added to room price. Breakfast 8,000 L; set dinner 30,000 L. (Lunch not served.)

Do you know of a good hotel in Naples?

JESOLO PINETA 30017 Venice   Map 16

Hotel Mediterraneo   *Tel* (0421) 961175
Via Oriente 106

"There is such a bewildering number of hotels at the big noisy popular resort of Lido di Jesolo at the eastern end of the Venetian lagoon, that it is worth persevering through the town, and six kilometres beyond to Jesolo Pineta. Here the hotels are more widely spaced, set in their own gardens, where the natural belt of pine trees gives welcome shade for the cars. Although built of modern materials, the *Mediterraneo* looks attractive. The roof is just about at top-of-pine-tree height, so it seems secluded and countrified. Our room was very basic, but one wall was almost all sliding-glass door, which made it light and cool. It had no sea view or balcony but we found it clean, fresh and comfortable. The bathroom also was only basic but all worked adequately. We enjoyed a most varied and delicious buffet lunch served outside, in the company of families, mostly with young children: it seemed an ideal place for them. Dinner was a sad come-down after lunch (perhaps the chef's evening off), but breakfast was generous." The warm gestures of the owner and family impressed our readers from their tired and hot arrival to their departing breakfast. Private swimming pool and fenced beach near a fishing village; beach chairs etc. are provided free. The hotel would be more suitable for those with a car, though there is a bus stop quite near. (*A and D Stewart; also Gordon Bennett*)

Open Apr–Sept.
Rooms 55 double, 2 single – 8 with bath, 49 with shower, all with telephone, some with air-conditioning, many with balcony.
Facilities Large lounge, bar (piano music twice a week), TV room, restaurant, sauna. Garden with heated swimming pool, solarium, tennis court, children's play area, direct access to private beach; surfing. English spoken.
Location 6 km from Lido di Jesolo. Leave *autostrada* Venezia at Venezia/Mestre; go to Quarto d'Altino, take direction Pineta/Cortellazzo.
Restriction Not suitable for &.
Credit cards None accepted.
Terms B&B: single 52,000 L, double 80,000–95,000 L; half-board 55,000–80,000 L per person; full board 60,000–85,000 L per person. Set lunch/dinner 25,000 L; full alc 25,000 L. Reduced rates and special meals for children.

MANTUA 46100   Map 16

Albergo San Lorenzo   *Tel* (0376) 327044 or 327153 or 327194
Piazza Concordia 17

There is a sombre quality to the flat Mantuan countryside, which may explain the melancholy of the great poet, Virgil, who was born in a village near here. Mantua is also a rather severe city, though with its own charm, and the *San Lorenzo* is one of its two best hotels, describing itself accurately as "*un albergo nuovo ... in un ambiente antico*". It is, according to one visitor, worth its entry for location alone – being both very central and very quiet (if you don't count the ringing of church bells as noise). The rooms are pleasantly furnished and many have a view of the Piazza delle Erbe and the lovely rotunda church of San Lorenzo. A recent visitor found them "cool – even with temperatures of 90° outside –

with the finest cotton sheets I have ever slept on!'' The *San Lorenzo* has no restaurant or public rooms, but it is a comfortable, friendly place. (*Mrs M Libbert; also Roger Bennett*)

Open All year.
Rooms 1 suite, 35 double, 10 single – 26 with bath, 15 with shower, all with telephone.
Facilities 2 lifts. Reception with sitting areas leading off it, TV room, bar; terrace at top of building. English spoken.
Location Central, near San Lorenzo rotunda, in pedestrian precinct. Parking 100 metres.
Restriction Not suitable for &.
Credit cards None accepted.
Terms [1985 rates] rooms: single 60,000 L, double 92,000 L. Breakfast 10,000 L. (No restaurant.)

MERANO 39012 South Tyrol

Hotel Fragsburg (Castel Verruca)   *Tel* (0473) 44071
Via Fragsburg 3/a (PO Box 210)

Hotel Fragsburg or *Castel Verruca* (and known in German as *Schloss Fragsburg*) is 750 metres up, overlooking the Italian spa town of Merano in the South Tyrol. "A peaceful, reasonably priced hotel on the hillside'', surrounded by woods, meadows and mountains; only a 20-minute walk to the highest waterfall in the country. There is a heated, open-air swimming pool and a game preserve. Each room has a balcony and meals are served on an open-air terrace in summer. The proprietor Hubert Ortner keeps his own bees and has fresh honey on hand. He tells us that his hotel gets two hours more sunshine a day than in the valley. Good value for money if you're in the area. (*G N Hobson*) How is the food? More reports welcome.

Open Mar–Nov.
Rooms 1 suite, 13 double, 5 single – 10 with bath, 8 with shower, all with balcony, telephone, TV and baby-listening.
Facilities 6 lounges, bar, TV room, café, dining room; terrace for summer meals. Private park with heated swimming pool, children's play area, ping-pong, chess tables. Tennis nearby. English spoken.
Location 6 km NE of Merano. From Merano take road to Bozen, turn right towards Schenna; after 2.5 km turn right at Rametz. Hotel is 5.5 km along this road.
Restriction Not suitable for &.
Credit cards None accepted.
Terms B&B 40,000–45,000 L, half-board 50,000–55,000 L, full board 60,000–65,000 per person. Set lunch/dinner 15,000 L. Special rates in May, June, July and Oct.

MILAN   Map 16

Hotel Manzoni   *Tel* (02) 705700
Via Santo Spirito 20
Milan 20121

A pleasant quiet hotel, rather modern in appearance, located in a small side street a block from the Via Manzoni which leads to the Piazza della Scala, the Vittorio Emanuele shopping arcade and the cathedral. It is described as very central, comparatively cheap (hotels in Milan are expensive) and well run. "Comfortable and convenient, very little has changed in the past 25 years." (*Anne and Peter Copp, Sarah Farrell, Richard Law*)

Open All year.
Rooms 52 – most with bath or shower and telephone.
Facilities Lift. Breakfast room.
Location In central zone, not far from public garden. Garage parking.
Credit cards None accepted.
Terms [1985 rates] rooms: single 67,000 L, double 97,000 L. Breakfast 7,000 L.

NATURNO 39025 Bolzano   Map 16

Hotel Feldhof   *Tel* (0473) 87264

The Tyrolean village of Naturno is situated on the left bank of the river Adige high in the Dolomite mountains. Although it is perhaps unclear whether you are hearing Italian with a German accent here or German with an Italian one, rest assured the staff at the *Hotel Feldhof* will understand you, even if you speak in English. We add this restful hotel to the Guide after receiving good reports about very clean and generously appointed rooms, complete with real down comforters on the beds, balconies with mountain views, and large bathrooms with showers and great towels. The best word is, however, the price: about £26.50 [1985] for two including breakfast and dinner. "By far the best value of our trip and most highly recommended." (*Deborah Imershein*)

Open Mar–10 Nov, 18 Dec–15 Jan.
Rooms 26 – most with bath or shower, all with TV and air-conditioning; some with balcony.
Facilities Lift. Dining room, indoor swimming pool, garden. Riding nearby. English spoken.
Location 15 km W of Merano.
Credit cards Probably none accepted.
Terms [1985 rates] B&B: single 46,000 L, double 92,000 L; full board 52,000–60,000 L. Set lunch/dinner 12,000–14,000 L.

ORTA SAN GIULIO 28016 Novara   Map 16

Hotel La Bussola   *Tel* (0322) 90198

The popularity of the *San Rocco* (below) is such that at certain seasons it is impossible to arrive casually and get a room. The *Bussola* makes an attractive and cheaper alternative, and we reinstate it to the Guide after a year's absence. It is a comfortable hotel on a hill above Orta, well back from the road, with a beautiful panoramic view of the lake. The restaurant with its extensive terrace, and all the front rooms, enjoy this view. There is a flowery garden with a large swimming pool and a sun terrace. A visitor this year writes: "We were very pleased by it all. The rooms were very comfortable, although our children's attic room tended to get rather hot. The staff were without exception friendly, polite and helpful. The food both in presentation and taste was some of the best we had during our trip round Italy, Austria and France. We enjoyed a complete rest here." (*Sara Price, also Dr A J Watson*)

Open All year except 15–30 Jan.
Rooms 16 double – 11 with bath, 5 with shower, all with telephone and baby-listening, 7 with refrigerator.
Facilities Lift. TV room, bar, indoor and outdoor restaurants on terrace, banqueting room. Large garden with swimming pool and sun terrace. 5 minutes' walk from lake; swimming and other water sports. English spoken.
Location Central. Garage and ample parking facilities.
Credit cards Amex, Visa.
Terms B&B: single 45,000–49,000 L, double 70,000–80,000 L; dinner, B&B 55,000–59,000 L per person; full board 65,000–70,000 L per person. Set lunch/ dinner 22,000–25,000 L; full alc 28,000 L. Reduced rates and special meals for children on request.

Hotel San Rocco   *Tel* (0322) 90222

In the 17th century, this recently modernised hotel was a monastery. And, as one reader pointed out, although San Rocco was the patron saint of the plague, not much suffering goes on in this lovely place. For it is right by the water on Lake Orta, one of the smaller and least spoiled of the Italian lakes. "The situation is enchanting, the lake and view to the little island magical and the nearby village gorgeous," writes one visitor, while another this year rated it "perfect for honeymooners". The hotel's origins are now apparent only in the cell-like dimensions of some of the rooms. Readers are unanimous in their praise for the obliging management and staff: "The overall impression of the hotel is of courteous efficiency." And, "*San Rocco* was one of the most enjoyable hotels we found in Italy." The hotel has been receiving similar compliments since the first edition of the Guide, but the food has often been a matter of contention. Although some readers this year have found the meals "left nothing to be desired", others give thumbs down to "a boring, overpriced menu". One recommends ordering from the à la carte; another says, "Eat at the nearby *Sacro Monte* restaurant where both food and wine are first rate and half the price." A visitor last year issued a warning: "The hotel was half, or more, filled with British package tourists and we found the *pension* food pretentious and poor – I suspect the second follows from the first." (*Joy Hatwood, Dr B R Matthews, P Freeman, Ruth Brown; also R S Gunn, and many others*)
Note: We received word that renovations were to begin in October 1984. Can we hear from recent visitors about this?

Open Apr–Oct.
Rooms 39 double, 1 single – all with bath and shower, telephone and balcony overlooking lake; TV on request; air-conditioning.
Facilities Lift. Hall, salon, TV room, bar with piano, dining room; 2 banqueting rooms. Garden with bar, lakeside terrace. Boating, waterskiing, tennis and mini-golf nearby. English spoken.
Location 5 minutes from centre of town, signposted from main road. Parking.
Credit cards All major cards accepted.
Terms [1985 rates] rooms: single 60,000 L, double 86,000 L; full board 65,000– 75,000 L per person. Breakfast 7,500 L; alc meals (excluding wine) 27,000–41,000 L.

> Do you know of a good hotel in Pisa?

> Do you know of a good hotel in Ravenna?

ORVIETO 05018 Terni
Map 16

Hotel Virgilio
Piazza Duomo 5/6
Tel (0763) 41882

This completely modernised small hotel is recommended for its situation and very pleasant (if small) bedrooms overlooking the Piazza Duomo. Only breakfast is served and "not the best" but also "not expensive". No restaurant, but the *Maurizio*, a few metres away, is said to be "very good, especially for grilled lamb". (*Kenneth Bell*)

Open All year.
Rooms 14 double, 2 single – 2 with bath, 14 with shower, all with telephone. Some on ground floor.
Facilities. Lift. Salon.
Location Central, near *Duomo*. Parking.
Credit cards None accepted.
Terms B&B: single 47,000 L, double 77,000 L.

OSPEDALICCHIO DI BASTIA 06080 Perugia
Map 16

Lo Spedalicchio
Tel (075) 809323

"An attractive conversion of an old fortified manor house, halfway between Perugia and Assisi. We had no car but buses stop outside the door. The management are particularly friendly and helpful, and offered to drive us anywhere we liked. The decor is a combination of modern and medieval, with lots of natural stonework and no carpets. The food was good Italian and the local wines pleasant and cheap; it seemed to be a favourite eating place for Perugians. It would be a nice place to stay for a few days while visiting the many wonderful places in Umbria – less crowded than the main centres." A recent visitor praises the hotel for its "charming staff and delicious food – delightful". (*Angela Graham, Sarah Whitfield*)

Open All year.
Rooms 3 suites, 20 double, 2 single – all with bath, telephone, mono TV, and tea-making facilities.
Facilities Lift. Salon with colour TV, American bar, restaurant, garden. English spoken.
Location On the main road 12 km E of Perugia.
Restriction Not suitable for &.
Credit cards Amex, Diners, Visa.
Terms B&B 32,000–44,000 L; dinner, B&B 49,000–60,000 L; full board 66,000–78,000 L; full alc 22,000 L. Special rates for long stays negotiable. Reductions for children under 2; special children's meals.

PADERNO DI PONZANO 31050 Treviso
Map 16

El Toulà
Via Postumia 63
Tel (0422) 969023 or 969191
Telex 410005 TURANS

"Set peacefully at the end of a long driveway through tall vines, this beautiful old villa has had extensions built either side to form a superbly comfortable and stylish (though expensive) hotel. It is just north of Treviso in the Veneto region and not easy to find: best ask for directions and look carefully for the one sign at the end of the drive. At the rear of the building is a big terrace, with a swimming pool at one end. Reception is informal at a table in the corner of a large lounge area with plenty of chairs and settees. The walls are covered with old prints and modern paintings. Everywhere there are fresh flowers.

"Our bedroom was huge with two large windows overlooking the terrace. There was a separate large wardrobe and dressing area, with a mini-bar, and a huge, fully tiled bathroom. On our second day we found a large bowl of fruit left in the room, with apples, pears, oranges, kiwi fruit and strawberries! The restaurant was excellent. The recommended house white wine was reasonable in price and most enjoyable. They are proud in this area of their sparkling Prosecco wine which is drunk everywhere as an aperitif. The staff were all very pleasant and most of them spoke some English. They do have quite a number of receptions and business functions, but this does not detract from the atmosphere of peaceful, casual elegance. A lovely place to stay." (*Pat and Jeremy Temple; also M and J Alexander*)

Open All year, except Aug. Restaurant closed Tue.
Rooms 2 suites, 8 double – all with bath, telephone, TV and mini-bar.
Facilities Lounge, bar, restaurants; banqueting and conference facilities; terrace. Large grounds with swimming pool. Private beach 20 metres. Tennis 2 km; golf and riding 20 km. English spoken.
Location Just N of Treviso; 35 km from Venice Airport.
Credit cards Amex, Diners, Visa.
Terms B&B: single 183,000 L, double 256,000 L; half-board 160,000 L per person; full board 200,000 L. Set lunch 60,000 L, dinner 65,000 L.

PALERMO 90142 Sicily | Map 16

Grand Hotel Villa Igiea　　　　　　　　　　　　　　　*Tel* (091) 543744
Via Belmonte 43　　　　　　　　　　　　　　　*Telex* 910092 VILLIGEA

"Connoisseurs come from all over Europe to gaze in awe at the salon in this huge Edwardian hotel – or they would if they knew about it. This masterwork dates from 1908 and the carving and the murals are in pristine condition. The *Villa* itself has retained its style; apart from a swimming pool overlooking the sea and awnings to protect those lunching al fresco, time hasn't flawed this stately bougainvillea-clad pile. Service is impeccable and helpful and cool sea breezes rustle the palms in the several acres of garden." Rooms are spacious; there is a lot of marble around; gardens stretch down to the sea wall; there are spectacular views over the bay. The place has its detractors. Some are embarrassed by such opulence amidst the squalor of the city, and others, while appreciating its various sybaritic delights, are less than enthusiastic about the hotel's cuisine. "The food is merely all right, not really good. And it's quite expensive. It's not the most grand, the most luxurious, but overall, it's quite a place, and great fun to stay at." (*Derek and Janet Cooper, also Dr F P Woodford, Tom and Connie Congdon*)

Open All year.
Rooms 7 suites, 90 double, 26 single – all with bath and telephone, colour TV, mini-bar and air-conditioning.
Facilities Lift. Hall, writing room, reading room, bar (piano every night), restaurants, facilities for receptions and conferences; disco. Terrace for outdoor

meals in fine weather. In large park leading down to sea with salt-water swimming pool, tennis court and rocky beach; safe bathing, fishing. English spoken.
Location Near Punta Acquasanta; 3 km N of centre of Palermo, N of port. Parking.
Credit cards All major cards accepted.
Terms (excluding 1,200 L tax per person) B&B: single 121,000–146,000 L, double: 207,000–232,000 L; half-board 143,000–188,000 L per person; full board 180,000–230,000 L per person. Low season reductions for stays of more than 3 days; reductions for stays over 2 weeks. 20% discount and special meals for children.

PANZANO IN CHIANTI 50020 Siena   Map 16

Villa Le Barone   *Tel* (055) 852215
Via San Leolino 19

A small villa high on a hilltop between Florence and Siena. Spread out below is the beautiful Tuscan landscape of rolling hills, olive groves and cypress trees. The grounds are not extensive, but there is a swimming pool and a terrace. The villa is the former home of the famous Della Robbia family whose classic blue and white had been used as a theme in the decoration. The Duchess Visconti is the present owner; she only lives here from time to time, but her villa retains the atmosphere of a cared-for private home. A return visitor declares: "Three nights were not enough, though my husband still feels the *Villa* somewhat 'genteel'. I love being looked after and the feeling of absolute peace." We reported in 1985 that the rooms were elegantly furnished with good antiques, carefully arranged flowers and fine linen sheets, although a visitor this year says this is a bit of an exaggertion, describing his room as "dark and badly furnished". Another complained as well of a poorly lit room and a useless wardrobe. But most commended the high standard of accommodation and the efficiency and courtesy of the staff. "We were really grateful to the Guide for this one." Food and service in the restaurant seem to have improved, too. (*Mr and Mrs A W Barr, Margaret and Charles Baker, R A Dubery, and many others*)

Open Apr–Oct.
Rooms 24 double, 2 single – 19 with bath, 6 with shower, all with tea-making facilities; 15 rooms in annexe.
Facilities 4 sitting rooms (1 with TV), bar, dining room, 5-acre grounds with swimming pool. Golf nearby. English spoken.
Location 31 km S of Florence, 31 km N of Siena.
Credit card Amex.
Terms [1985 rates] rooms: single 44,000–57,000 L, double 64,500–83,500 L; full board 99,500–124,500 L per person. Breakfast 8,000 L. Reduced rates (according to age) and special meals for children.

PERUGIA 06100   Map 16

Hotel La Rosetta   *Tel* (075) 20841/42/43 or 20200 or 66372
Piazza Italia 19

Perugia's biggest and best hotel, with a renowned restaurant. Readers endorse our earlier commendation: "The obvious place to stay in this delightful city ... in a perfect situation at the top of the Corso Vannucci, where the evening *passeggiata* takes place, and near all the chief sights. It is a comfortable, friendly and efficient place. True, the decor is not always alluring – our bathroom in shiny bronze was a bit much first thing in the morning – but bedrooms were large and the arched dining room spacious and elegant. There is an attractive, shady courtyard where you can lunch. The food is delicious – one of the best tables in Umbria. Altogether the kind of good, reliable, reasonably priced hotel that Guide readers will be looking for." (*A G Don; also Audrey and Tom Poole, Mrs P Solomon*)

Open All year.
Rooms 64 double, 39 single – 51 with bath, 34 with shower/wc, all with telephone, radio; some ground-floor rooms.
Facilities Lift. Salons (2 with TV), bar, games room, reading room, restaurant; conference facilities. Courtyard where meals are served in fine weather. English spoken. &.
Location Central, near Giardini Carducci; some traffic noise. Parking and 2 garages (extra charge).
Credit cards All major cards accepted.
Terms B&B: single 45,000 L, double 68,000 L; dinner, B&B: 56,000–67,000 L per person; full board 78,000–89,000 L per person.

PETTENASCO 28028 Novara   Map 16

Hotel Giardinetto   *Tel* (0323) 89118 or 89219
Via Provinciale 1, Lago d'Orta

This family hotel is on the eastern shores of Lake Orta, the smallest of the northern lakes, facing the island of San Giulio, dominated by a Romanesque basilica dedicated to the saint. There are weekly open-air markets in the town square and at Omegna at the other end of the lake. We had an entry in earlier editions, but left it out after a series of poor reports. Readers now urge its reinstatement, speaking enthusiastically of the "tireless and warm-hearted" owners, Oreste and Caterina Primatesta, who speak good English. "The rooms are very nice and clean, the view from the balconies, which are directly adjoining the lake, is superb." Readers tell us the view from the restaurant is enchanting as well. There is a lakeside coffee shop for breakfast and light lunches. "The food is first class, plentiful and well served." "Local wines are interesting and inexpensive, and the Primatestas delight in providing culinary surprises and entertainments for guests. Caterina takes a keen and sympathetic interest in children's menus and her husband exhorts everyone within earshot to have a go on the hotel's latest water-sports novelties." (*F Elston, M E Wood, and others*)

Open Apr–Oct.
Rooms 34 double, 6 single – 23 with bath, 11 with shower, all with telephone and baby-listening.
Facilities Lift. Lounge, bars, coffee shop, restaurant, conference facilities. Garden with sun terrace and swimming pool; private beach with bathing facilities and water sports.
Location 4 km from Orta. Private parking.
Credit cards Access, Amex, Visa.
Terms B&B: single 39,000–49,000 L, double 54,000–69,000 L; dinner, B&B 40,000–50,000 L per person; full board 46,000–63,000 L per person. Set lunch (3 courses) 16,000 L, set dinner (4 courses) 20,000 L; full alc 25,000 L. Reduced rates for children sharing parents' room; special meals.

PORTO ERCOLE 58018 Grosseto   Map 16

Hotel Il Pellicano   *Tel* (0564) 833801
Cala Dei Santi   *Telex* 500131 PELICA

The village of Porto Ercole is crowded and hectic in summer, but the
Pellicano four kilometres away is in a world of its own – "a near-perfect
seaside hotel, though expensive," writes one regular visitor. It is a large
irregular collection of buildings on a secluded rocky promontory, with
wide and splendid views of the sea. There are gardens and terraces with
flowers in pots and colourful sun-shades around a swimming pool.
Down below there is a tiny rocky beach. The atmosphere is quiet and
peaceful. Inside the tiled floors, whitewashed walls, exposed beams and
bright, cheerful furnishings enhance the style. In the evening, dinner is
served on a terrace overlooking the sea and the floodlit grounds.

"The space, the decor, the surroundings, the privacy, the informality
and the very pleasant staff combine to make this hotel perfect for an
extended stay – one could settle down happily for a fortnight." One
devotee of the hotel says that in the dining room the international
specialities are a little dull, though he enthuses over the Tuscan
maritime dishes and the "excellent antipasto buffet". Another visitor
writes, "Alas the food in the area is primitive and expensive so one is
pleased to have *good* but expensive food at *Il Pellicano*." (*David Wooff, C F
Colt*)

Open 27 Mar–3 Nov.
Rooms 4 suites, 30 double – all with bath and telephone, sea or garden view; TV
and radio on request; 4 luxury suites with TV in cottages in the garden; 16 rooms in
annexes.
Facilities Lounge, piano bar, restaurant, terrace; conference facilities; dinner-
dance Fri nights July and Aug. Rocky beach with safe bathing and Beach Club.
Large grounds with heated swimming pool with barbecue; tennis, ping-pong,
bowls; boats available; riding, sailing and waterskiing; golf 1 hour's drive;
sightseeing to nearby Etruscan and Roman sites. English spoken.
Location 4 km S of Porto Ercole on Monte Argentario coast. Parking.
Restrictions Not suitable for &. No children under 12.
Credit cards Amex, Diners, Visa.
Terms B&B: single occupancy 172,000 L, double 191,500 L; dinner, B&B: single
occupancy 220,000–346,000 L, double 286,000–508,000 L; full board: single
occupancy 267,000–393,000 L, double 380,000–602,000 L. Set lunch/dinner 60,500
L. Reduced rates for children sharing parents' room.

PORTOVENERE 19025 La Spezia   Map 16

Hotel Royal Sporting   *Tel* (0187) 900326

Lord Byron found Portovenere sufficiently inspiring to write the lyrical
poem "Corsair". Others have been inspired as well, but perhaps to a
different tune. "Thought Portovenere, off La Spezia, would be a little
less commercial than Portofino. Well, perhaps a mite less international,
but there are well-oiled service loads of La Spezians, Genovese,
Milanese and Turinese. No question that it is picturesque, though, with
marvellous citadel arches which frame the setting sun kissing the sea.
Also a great base for taking the winding, climbing, perennially
'just-completed' single track road to the Cinqueterre villages such as

Corniglia and Vernazza, strikingly set on or under steep cliffs which fall into the sea, impossibly covered with grapes. Great place to get away from crowds, Cinqueterre, since most people seemed scared silly of the narrow road. Oh yes, the hotel – four official stars, maids who come in to put away scattered shoes, turn sheets and lay out pyjamas, supercilious (in that Latin way) bartenders, polite buffet waiters, a surprisingly romantic dining room with spacious window view of the harbour and twinkling lights; salt-water swimming pool that maddeningly closes at 7.30 pm. The hotel is Portovenere's class act. It's not exactly an inexpensive gem full of character and charm, but it's an honest four-star establishment, with many positive advantages, especially its location." (*T C Seoh*)

Open 5 Apr–Sept.
Rooms 62 rooms – all with air-conditioning.
Facilities Lift. Dining room. Garden, salt-water swimming pool, tennis; beach with safe bathing.
Location On peninsula 12 km S of La Spezia. Garage.
Credit cards All major cards accepted.
Terms [1985 rates] rooms: single 75,000 L, double 115,000 L; full board 100,000–110,000 L per person. Breakfast 11,000 L; set lunch/dinner 35,000–40,000 L.

POSITANO 84017 Salerno   Map 16

Casa Albertina   *Tel* (089) 875143
Via della Tavolozza 4

An enchanting, medium-priced *pensione* in this justly renowned but trendy and expensive resort town. The lobby and sitting rooms have cool white walls and vaulted ceilings, while the rooms and dining room are decorated in pastels (every tablecloth a different colour). There is a lovely terrace overlooking coast and sea. "I must recommend this utterly authentic family-run *pensione* with commanding views over the sea. It has style, intimacy, friendliness, great quality and good value. Grandmother cooks: no menu – 'you eat what we eat' – and it is perfect Italian *cuisine paysanne*. Quiet, the rustle of the sea, spotless tiled bedrooms, clean sheets every other day – and cheap, by Positano prices. Breakfast with squeezed orange juice and hot croissants, brought in by Maestro himself, a smiling bear-like man, whose wife helps in the kitchen and who discusses Raphael and Italian politics in the lounges with us all. I was here two weeks for a needed rest and could not bear to leave: I can't wait to come again." Maestro Michele Cinque writes to us to say he is sorry there is no swimming pool but instead "we have a beautiful sea". (*Tom Petzal*)

Open All year.
Rooms 2 suites, 18 double, 2 single – 20 with bath, 2 with shower, all with telephone.
Facilities Lift. Sitting room, TV room, bar, dining room, open-air restaurant, roof terrace; 10 minutes' walk to beach; English spoken.
Location Central, but quietly situated. Parking 200 metres.
Restriction Not suitable for &.
Credit cards None accepted.
Terms [1985 rates] rooms: single 36,000 L, double 57,000 L. Breakfast 2,400 L. 30% reduction for children under 7; special meals on request.

Hotel Montemare   *Tel* (089) 875010
Via Pasitea 113

"The Montemare has one of the best positions in Positano. It is 365 steps
up from the beach, or a lazy 30 minutes' walk up the road lined with
fashionable boutiques. This means that even at the height of the season
it is aloof from the noise and bustle of the crowds. The terrace where
breakfast and drinks are served looks over the sea and some delightful
gardens. All the rooms face the sea too: most are very large with a
balcony. There are also two or three apartments with very large terraces:
we stayed in one and the view was beautiful. A local family run the
hotel: the husband is always ready for a chat, though not in English."
(*Anna Waley; also Geoffrey Sharp*) The hotel has reopened its restaurant,
closed at the time of Mrs Waley's visit. May we have some feedback on
its culinary endeavours?

Open 1 Apr–30 Oct.
Rooms 27 double, 2 single – all with bath and telephone; 10 rooms in annexe.
Facilities Lounge, bar, restaurant; terrace with access to public beach. English
spoken.
Location 300 metres from town centre on main road. (Rooms are quiet as they are
below road level.) Parking.
Restriction Not suitable for &.
Credit cards Amex, Diners, Visa.
Terms Rooms: single 24,000–30,000 L, double 41,000–45,000 L; dinner, B&B:
42,500–48,000 L per person; full board: 45,000–55,500 L per person. Breakfast 6,000
L; set lunch/dinner 18,000 L. 20% reduction for children 3–11 years.

Villa Franca e Residence   *Tel* (089) 875035
Via Pasitea 318

"The friendly staff in this cool, spacious villa-style hotel made us feel
welcome guests without being over-attended to. The theme is white
walls and arches, with oak woodwork and, of course, tiles – the latter
throughout the public rooms and bedrooms. Our room had a private
bathroom and small terrace. Breakfast is on a bamboo-roofed terrace
overlooking the sea (plus bougainvillaea!); dinner in a candlelit, arched
room with huge windows overlooking the southern part of the town.
Food tasted freshly prepared and was traditional Italian fare. It's quite a
long climb from the beach if you take the back stairs. A bus is quicker,
and the hotel is said to have its own in season. This was one of the nicest
hotels I've ever stayed in." (*Will Peskett*)

Open All year. Restaurant (residents only) closed Nov–Mar.
Rooms 37 – most with bath or shower and telephone; some with terrace.
Facilities Lift. Salons, dining room. &.
Location 17 km E of Sorrento on coast road.
Credit cards All major cards accepted.
Terms [1985 rates] rooms: single 40,000 L, double 65,000 L; full board 60,000–
75,000 L per person. Breakfast 6,000 L; set lunch/dinner 27,000 L.

> Do you know of a good hotel in Padua?

> Do you know of a good hotel in Turin?

PROCCHIO 57030 Isle of Elba, Livorno   Map 16

Hotel del Golfo   *Tel* (0565) 907565
Telex 590690

If you are able, before you leave Elba, visit Napoleon's villa (and attendant museum), serene on its terraced hillside, aloof above the holiday hordes on this popular tourist isle. Set quietly in a pinewood by the sea, on the north coast, the sizeable *Golfo* also to an extent escapes the mob – "As good a beach hotel of its size as we have found. The name refers to the Gulf of Procchio with its long sandy beach and not to the hitting of little white balls. The 95 rooms are of decent size: most appear to have balconies and sea views. Ours was pleasantly furnished and fitted. The public rooms are very 'Apicella' – airy, light and tiled. Most tables in the dining room offer sea views. We had scarcely a disappointing dish and many a really excellent one: the hotel also encourages use of the good range of more humble restaurants in and around the village. It has its own vineyard, producing a rich dry red and a fair dry white. Service was concerned and skilled. Breakfast on the terrace was a delight, with a fine buffet. There is a huge salt-water pool, bathing huts, umbrellas and loungers galore." (*Anthony Rota*)

Open 16 May–Sept.
Rooms 95 – all with bath or shower, most with balcony.
Facilities Lounge, bar, restaurant. Park with terrace and vineyards; swimming pool, tennis courts and access to beach.
Location Procchio is 13 km W of Portoferraio, the ferry port for the mainland. Parking.
Credit cards Access, Amex, Visa.
Terms [1985 rates] rooms: single 75,000 L, double 130,000 L; full board 75,000–125,000 L per person. Breakfast 1,500 L; set lunch/dinner 25,000–35,000 L.

RAVELLO 84010 Salerno   Map 16

Hotel Caruso Belvedere   *Tel* (089) 857111
Via Toro 52

This is a Renaissance palace perched on a cliff above lemon groves that plunge down to the blue Gulf of Salerno: "The views from bedrooms and dining room were timelessly beautiful." Most readers this year continue to lavish praise, for example: "The overwhelming impression was of an old-fashioned, elegant – but not slick – family hotel." Another said, "The hotel itself is pure Noël Coward, with service to match the atmosphere – albeit with modern plumbing." Readers do complain of "decidedly basic" bedroom decor but "deserving special praise is the superb cleanliness of everything – linens, cutlery, towels ..." The majority of readers agree that the food is good, although we did hear from one or two readers who thought it "unimaginative and at times badly prepared". Summer meals are taken on a terrace, with fabulous views over the coast. In cooler weather the marble-pillared dining room is used. The Caruso family wine is strongly recommended. The one overwhelming complaint about this hotel is the unacceptably bad breakfasts. But most readers endorse the attractions of this hotel in an enchanting town. Ravello is indeed suspended "twixt sea and sky" –

1,200 feet above the sea – and it can seem as far from the modern world as it is from the hot screaming corniche road and the coastal towns below. The town has plenty of old palaces and gardens; the Cathedral Piazza is a particularly fine place for strolling in the evening. The market square and the historic Villa Rufolo (whose garden is supposed to have inspired Klingsor's in *Parsifal*) are five minutes' walk away from the *Caruso Belvedere*, which is in the old part of town on a steep street. Signor Caruso is the third generation to own the hotel and his "charming and efficient" nephew who manages it with him seems in line to be the fourth. "The film stars can keep the *Palumbo* (q.v.); we'll settle for leaning on the balcony here murmuring 'Don't quibble Sibyl!' " (*Penny Duckham, H B Hannah, Margaret and Peter Davies, C H Cole, and many others*)

Open All year, except Feb.
Rooms 22 double, 2 single – 20 with bath, 2 with shower, all with telephone; some ground-floor rooms.
Facilities Lounge, bar, restaurant. Garden with pergolas and terraces for summer meals, with magnificent views. Sandy and rocky beaches with safe bathing and fishing rights 5 km. English spoken.
Location 300 metres from town centre on Piazza S Giovanni del Toro; coming from Amalfi turn left before reaching the centre of town. Hotel has garage. Town is 25 km from Salerno, off the Salerno–Sorrento coast road. Parking.
Restriction Not suitable for &.
Credit card Amex.
Terms Rooms: single 15,000–45,000 L, double 26,000–74,000 L; dinner, B&B 71,000–86,000 L per person; full board 81,000–94,000 L per person. Breakfast 8,000 L; set lunch/dinner 33,000 L; full alc 38,000 L. Cooking courses in Nov.

Marmorata Hotel
Strada Statale 163

Tel (089) 877777

The postal address is Ravello, but the *Marmorata* is six kilometres from Ravello itself, nestled in the cliff face beneath the coastal road, three kilometres east of Amalfi. It was once a paper mill. "The cool, restful interiors designed in the style of a ship, the seafront terraces and the friendly, helpful service are simply superb. We had a comfortable bedroom with a sea view. The bathroom was small, but well fitted. The food was well cooked and presented. There is a steep slope from the road down to the hotel and many steps down to sea level, so not suitable for the infirm, but an utterly seductive hotel to which we hope to return." (*Mrs Noreen Redfern*)

Open 1 May–30 Oct.
Rooms 5 suites, 31 double, 3 single – 3 with bath, 36 with shower, all with telephone, radio, colour TV, mini-bar and air-conditioning.
Facilities Hall lounge, bar with piano, restaurant, terraces down to sea with sea-water swimming pool, private rocky beach with safe bathing, fishing. English spoken.
Location 1 km W of Minori, 3 km E of Amalfi. Parking.
Restriction Not suitable for &.
Credit cards None accepted.
Terms B&B: single 70,000–102,000 L, double 86,000–160,000 L; half-board 70,000–115,000 L per person; full board 80,000–127,000 L per person. Alc 30,000 L (excluding wine). Reductions of 25% for children under 6 and 15% for children over 6 (sharing parents' room). Special rates (exc mid-July–mid-Sept).

Hotel Palumbo
Via S. Giovanni del Toro 28

Tel (089) 857244
Telex 770101 VUILLE

A few doors down from the *Caruso Belvedere* (q.v.) lies another venerable hotel: "In the mid-19th century a Swiss hotelier bought this 12th-century episcopal residence: a mix of Moorish arches, Corinthian pillars, terraces, winding staircases and unselfconscious charm. With the property came vineyards and by 1860 M. Vuilleumier was producing wine which he called Episcopio. Wagner, who was writing bits of *Parsifal* in the nearby Villa Rufolo, suggested that it was too good a place not to share with others. 'Why not take in paying guests?' he suggested. Over the years the p.g.s have included Longfellow, Grieg, and Lawrence, who worked on *Lady Chatterley* in one of the rooms. E M Forster stayed, and starry fugitives from Hollywood – Garbo, Bogart and Bergman. Latterly the Kennedys came. M. Vuilleumier's septuagenarian grandson Pasquale has filled the old palace with antiques, ferns and paintings. His chef, Lorenzo Mansi, produces some of the best food on the Amalfi coast. There are fruits from the garden and a changing repertoire of pasta dishes – all to be enjoyed with Pasquale's award-winning wines.

"Drinks are not cheap at the *Palumbo* but the welcome of the staff is genuine and warm, there are plenty of long chairs to recline in and the tranquillity is interrupted only by the blare of distant horns as the tour coaches wind their way up to this hilltop paradise, marred only by nocturnal mosquitoes. It was slightly surprising in these impeccable surroundings to ask for fresh orange juice in the morning and be served orange squash." *(Derek and Janet Cooper)*
Note: Not all recent visitors have found the *Palumbo* paradisical. Complaints include a cramped room, underheated on a cold March night, and a particularly dreary dining room if you have to eat indoors.

Open All year.
Rooms 2 suites, 18 double – 19 with bath, 1 with shower, all with telephone; 7 rooms in annexe.
Facilities Salons, bar, solarium; restaurant, terrace. Sea 6 km.
Location Above the Amalfi Drive, overlooking Ravello. Parking.
Credit cards All major cards accepted.
Terms Not available.

ROME Map 16

Hotel Gregoriana
Via Gregoriana 18
Rome 00187

Tel (06) 6797988

A former convent, now transformed into a charming miniature hotel – it is worth booking in advance to be sure of securing accommodation. "Even though it's only a minute's walk from the top of the Spanish Steps, this hotel could well claim to be one of the quietest in Rome. Our room, with two broad windows overlooking a little courtyard, was *silent* from midnight until dawn. It was a generous and comfortable room in a mixture of Erté and American Chinese, with a big, sunny bathroom in blues and mauves. Like most small hotels in continental cities, the only place to perch outside one's room is the reception area, and a generous breakfast on a tray is the only meal served. Because it is so small, the *Hotel Gregoriana* might be a bit claustrophobic for a long stay but for a few nights it's near perfect." Others write: "The staff are extremely friendly and helpful. Breakfast would arrive in our room almost immediately after telephoning!" (*Gillian Vincent, Dorothy and Bob Cabiana; also G D Fearnehough*)

Open All year.
Rooms 16 double, 3 single – 12 with bath, 7 with shower, all with telephone, radio and colour TV; 4 ground-floor rooms.
Facilities Lift. Hall. English spoken. &.
Location Central, near Spanish Steps. Parking.
Credit cards None accepted.
Terms [1985 rates] B&B: single 142,000 L, double 209,000 L. (No restaurant.)

Hotel d'Inghilterra
Via Bocca di Leone 14
Rome 00187

Tel (06) 672161
Telex 614552 HOTING I

Originally the guest-house for the Torlonia Palace, the *d'Inghilterra* was remodelled in 1850 to become a very fashionable hotel. Since that time its clientele has included kings, popes, writers and artists, from Pope Pius IX to Ernest Hemingway. "Think of London's *Brown's* in the heart of Rome and you have the picture – unpretentious, old-fashioned, comfortable, classy. Best of all is the hotel's position, down a quiet cobbled turning off the smart Via Condotti. A yellow-jacketed porter is alert for the taxi's arrival. Floors are marble, carpets deep; elegant yellow silk couches in the lounge. The bedrooms are not so smart as the reception area, and they differ widely, so it is wise to ask to see several before choosing. But all are spacious, with real furniture. My breakfast came on a silver tray, with real china, real jam, fresh orange juice. The bar was dark, intimate chic." (*Patricia Fenn*)

Open All year.
Rooms 28 suites, 58 double, 21 single – all with bath and shower, phone, colour TV and air-conditioning.
Facilities 3 lounges, bar, breakfast room, snack bar, private dining rooms, 2 private conference rooms. English spoken.
Restriction Not suitable for &.
Location At foot of Spanish Steps. Parking facilities nearby.
Credit cards All major cards accepted.
Terms [1985 rates] rooms: single 141,000 L, double 187,000 L, suites 340,000 L; extra bed 50,000 L. Continental breakfast 12,500 L.

Hotel Raphaël
Largo Febo 2, Rome 00186

Tel (06) 6569051
Telex 680235 RHOTEL

A quiet hotel, unobtrusively hidden behind creepers in a small side street not far from the Piazza Navona, which at night is one of Rome's liveliest piazzas. (Warning: the narrow streets behind the hotel are a noted hotbed of petty crime.) Most of our readers find the *Raphaël* very good value, though one points out that – as so often in noisy urban Italy – back rooms are preferable to front ones. The hotel is air-conditioned and has an intimate atmosphere, elegantly decorated in true Italian style, with sculptures, paintings, antiques and *objets d'art*. Bedrooms, also air-conditioned, are less ornate but for the most part comfortable.

The nicest thing about the hotel is the rooftop; a tiny area squashed between the tiled roofs, chimney pots and belfries of the surrounding buildings, with a pretty garden and magnificent views – a lovely spot to escape the city's bustle. Restaurant only adequate, but there are many eating places nearby. "When the Italian Senate is in session, many politicians stay at the hotel and there are soldiers with guns in front. That can make you feel either good or bad, depending on your sensibilities." (*Carola Haller, Joan Heyman*) More reports welcome.

Open All year.
Rooms 85 – 77 with bath, 14 with shower, all with telephone and air-conditioning.
Facilities Lift. Lounge bar, restaurant. Small rooftop garden for refreshments.
Location Central, near Piazza Navona.
Credit cards Probably none accepted.
Terms Not available.

Hotel La Residenza *Tel* (06) 463271 or 460789
Via Emilia 22 *Telex* 410423 GIOTEL att. La Residenza
Rome 00187

"This small but luxurious hotel is in a great location – around the corner from the Via Veneto, near the Villa Borghese. We had a huge double room complete with refrigerator and stocked bar, a sofa, comfortable chairs and a writing desk. There were enough closets to hold all our clothes (not just the ones we had brought with us!). Our bathroom had its own telephone and a heated towel rack – warm towels after a morning shower are a luxury I could soon get accustomed to. We found the people who work at *La Residenza* to be warm, thoughtful and very helpful." The front faces a night club which can be noisy. Breakfast is served, but no other meals: good inexpensive restaurants abound in the area. (*Kathleen McCleery and Robert Martinez; and others*)

Open All year.
Rooms 24 double, 3 single – 24 with bath, 3 with shower, all with phone, radio, TV.
Facilities Lift. Hall, 2 salons, bar, breakfast room, air-conditioning. Beauty centre. Terrace. English spoken.
Location Central, near the Via Veneto and American Embassy (back rooms quietest). Parking.
Restriction Not suitable for &.
Credit cards None accepted.
Terms B&B: single 74,000 L, double 115,000 L. (No restaurant.)

Hotel Sitea *Tel* (06) 4751560
Via Vittorio Emanuele Orlando 90 *Telex* 614163 SITEA
Rome 00185

"Excellent central location" – opposite the Grand Hotel, and close to the Baths of Diocletian, the Piazza Republica and the tempting shops of the Via Nazionale. "While it doesn't have the same kind of charm as the *Raphaël* (q.v.) which you rightly praise, it does have character – with pleasant functional rooms and a welcoming staff." This year a reader was especially pleased by his "large, old-fashioned bedroom and furniture". Although last year readers warned that the front rooms could be noisy, the management has written to say that not only has double-glazing been added to all the windows, but the hotel has been completely redecorated and refurbished, including air-conditioning. Can we hear from readers about the newly renovated *Sitea*? (*Duncan Wood, Anthony Sampson, also Robert Newman, G D Fearnehough*)

Open All year.
Rooms 33 double, 4 single – 32 with bath, 3 with shower, all with telephone; radio and TV on request. Air-conditioning and double-glazing.
Facilities Sitting room with TV, bar, winter garden, breakfast room, coffee shop, roof garden. English spoken.
Location Near Piazza della Republica virtually opposite the Museo delle Terme. Garage and parking facilities.
Restriction Not suitable for &.
Credit cards Access, Amex, Diners.
Terms B&B: single 116,000 L, double 180,000 L. (No restaurant.) Reduced rates for children depending on age and only on request.

Hotel Villa Florence
Via Nomentana 28 (Porta Pia)
Rome 00161

Tel (06) 8442841
Telex 624626 FLOTEL

This medium-priced hotel is about a kilometre north-east of the Via Veneto and 15 minutes' walk from the station (but there are plenty of buses). "I'd decided I liked it before we even arrived, finding the idea of a 19th-century Roman villa in its own little garden quite irresistible. Public rooms are best ignored, but our bedroom had a dramatic modernistic Italian flavour, moodily underlit in tones of red and brown (stylish, but a bit difficult to see what one was doing). The reception clerks outdid each other in affability. The mini-bar charges were ridiculously cheap. There is no restaurant, but two good Tuscan ones, *Al Chianti* and *Il Bersagliere*, are nearby." (*Don and Di Harley; endorsed, with reservations about the breakfast coffee, by Dr N B Fintner*)

We are informed by the management that there is "an unusual collection of ancient Roman findings" in the gardens.

Open All year.
Rooms 35 double, 1 single – 4 with bath, 32 with shower, all with telephone and radio, colour TV and mini-bar. Some ground-floor rooms.
Facilities Lift. Salon, bar, TV room. Solarium. Garden; terrace. English spoken.
Location Central, near Via Veneto and Porta Pia. Parking.
Credit card Amex.
Terms B&B: single 85,000 L, double 130,000 L. (No restaurant.) 30% reduction for children.

SAN GIMIGNANO 53037 Siena   **Map 16**

Bel Soggiorno   *Tel* (0577) 940375
Via S. Giovanni 91

The town of San Gimignano seems unchanged since the Middle Ages, but although on the tourist trail, it has escaped the coyness of other "museum" towns. Its fourteen straight towers rising above the rooftops are indeed an extraordinary sight. The *Bel Soggiorno* is a lovely 13th-century building, just inside the town walls, recommended for its "remarkably low" prices, and its friendly, efficient service. The consensus among readers is that the top floor of the hotel is to be avoided if possible: hot, and noisy with plumbing. The remaining rooms, though small, are adequate, some with terraces and most (even top-floor rooms) with magnificent views. If hot water is a priority, you had better think twice; otherwise, "a good find!" "For the back rooms at least, the view over the countryside compensates for minor deficiencies," say one enthusiastic couple. Another reader reports on the restaurant: "The menu is permanently unchanged but always excellent. Best of all is risotto di Bel Soggiorno with nutmeg and cream, but it is always tempting to order pollo allo diavolo which comes aflame! One wall of the restaurant is glass and the views of the Tuscan hills and olive groves are spectacular." (*John Huntingford, Thomas and Philomena R Ferrara, Lyndall Hopcraft*)

Open All year. Restaurant closed Mon.
Rooms 25 double, 2 single – all with bath and telephone.
Facilities Salon with TV, restaurant. English spoken.
Location 30 km from Siena; cars allowed in for loading and unloading only. Car park nearby.
Restrictions Not suitable for &. No children under 8.
Credit cards None accepted.
Terms B&B: single 35,000–37,000 L, double 55,000 L; half-board 44,000–55,000 L per person.

Hotel La Cisterna   *Tel* (0577) 940328
Piazza della Cisterna 24

The *Cisterna* is a grand palazzo with a 14th-century facade facing the main square where the townsfolk gather in the evenings. The lounge is a wonderful church-like medieval hall and the view is "astounding, since one enters the hotel at ground level, walks through to the back and finds the balcony is three storeys up. My estimate is that the view took in 50 miles of Tuscany." Ask for a room with a balcony, and though those at the back are quieter, a reader this year writes, "Try to get a room overlooking the piazza and you can sit out on the balcony, sip your wine and observe the activity." Reports about the rooms vary from "simple but large" to "verging on the luxurious". The restaurant is a spacious, beamed room with a stunning view (although one reader advises that if visitors are on *pension* terms, they are "demoted" to a more modern room with the same view). Regard for the cooking is higher this year: "We think the restaurant deserves the bouquets here"; and "never less than superb". (*C Pilkington, Dorothy and Bob Cabianca; also Ruth E Brown*)

Open 15 Feb–15 Dec. Restaurant closed all Tue, and Wed lunch-time.
Rooms 40 double, 6 single – 21 with bath, 25 with shower, all with telephone; 9 double ground-floor rooms.
Facilities Lift. 14th-century salon, salon with TV, bar, 3 dining rooms. Gardens. English spoken.
Location Central (some front rooms could be noisy). Cars allowed in for loading and unloading only; car park 400 metres.
Credit cards Access, Amex, Diners.
Terms B&B: single 41,400 L, double 74,500 L; half-board 62,500–66,700 L per person; full board 87,800–92,000 L per person. Set lunch/dinner 25,000 L; full alc 32,000 L.

Do you know of a good hotel in Vicenza?

SAN MAMETE 22010 Como   Map 16

Hotel Stella d'Italia   *Tel* (0344) 68139 or 61703
Piazza Roma 1
(postal address: P.O. Box 3, 6976 Castagnola, Switzerland)

A smallish hotel right on Lake Lugano, close to the Swiss border. The English-speaking owners, Signor and Signora Ortelli, have been running it for decades, and have won a faithfully returning clientele with their concern for guests' comfort. The bedrooms, each with its own balcony on which you can breakfast, all have views across the lake to the green slopes and the mountains in the distance. There is a garden leading down to a "lido" for swimming or sunbathing. In good weather, dinner is served on the pretty trellised terrace, with the water at one's feet, but the indoor dining room also has fine views. A recent visitor reports: "A haven of peace and beauty. The friendly style of the owners impressed us, as did the prettily furnished public rooms. Two good and varied dinners including early strawberries and delicate local fish, served by pretty and charming waitresses. Lovely and well-cared-for garden, and beautiful walks in the hills to nearby villages." Other readers borrowed the hotel dinghy and rowed across the lake.

One reader this year voted against inclusion because he disliked a no-choice evening meal served at 7.30 pm, found the front rooms noisy, and parking a major problem. (Best advice is to reserve a garage space when booking, drive straight in and have your bags carried round.) Others, this year as in the past, have been whole-heartedly enthusiastic: "It is said that the perfect hotel should have a Swiss management and Italian waiters. The *Stella d'Italia* being in Italy but four miles from the Swiss border manages to combine the two virtues, which is why I have holidayed there for four consecutive years. The true test of an Italian hotel in the mountains and lakes is whether the Italians themselves go there in their annual escape from the heat of the cities and there are a dozen who spend the whole of August every year at the *Stella d'Italia*. The approach is not auspicious. The road from Lugano along the lakeside is very narrow, very crowded and very noisy, crammed into the small shelf between the mountains and the lake. The hotel however turns its back on the road and all bedrooms and public rooms face the terraced gardens and the water. Since the opposite shore is about the only stretch of lake in the area not to have a road along the water's edge, the hotel faces across a mile of water to a deserted wooded mountain side. The hotel is an oasis of peace and calm." (*C Pilkington; also P G Bourne, Catherine Balk*)

Open Apr to beginning Oct.
Rooms 31 double, 5 single – all with bath or shower and balcony and telephone.
Facilities Large sitting room, bar, 2 dining rooms. Garden with easy chairs and open-air restaurant. Lake bathing, fishing rights, boating. 18-hole golf course 10 km away. English spoken.
Location 10 km NE of Lugano on Lake Lugano between Gandria and Menaggio. Garage for 14 cars.
Restriction Not suitable for &.
Credit cards Amex, Visa.
Terms [1985 rates] B&B: single 37,000–45,500 L, double 55,000–63,500 L; dinner, B&B 39,000–52,500 L; full board 47,000–60,500 L. Set lunch/dinner 20,000 L; full alc 30,000 L. 20%–40% reductions for children; special meals.

SANTA MARGHERITA DI PULA 09010 Sardinia Map 16

Hotel Is Morus *Tel* (070) 921424
Telex 791059 MOLAS (per Is Morus)

We've had no feedback about this hotel for a long while, though its three turrets are red in *Michelin*, denoting a specially agreeable hotel. Here is our most recent report: "About half an hour south and west of Cagliari, on the coast and well away from the road. You feel an instant sense of relief from the heat and dust outside as you step into its cool, elegant, all-white interior. The bedroom was charming – also all-white, except for pretty coral bedspread and curtains. The good-sized balcony looked over the garden where oleanders and frangipani bloomed, to the sea. Everything was immaculately clean; the white fitted chair covers were changed every morning. The veranda under Moorish arches was a very pleasant place to sit before or after dinner, in low, deep, all-white furniture as the sound of the sea blended with the pianist inside . . . Food is excellent and the staff very helpful and courteous. A rocky promontory runs from the hotel, dividing the beach in two. One side is completely natural, with only the fine soft almost-white sand framed by the sea and the pine trees behind. The other has an elegant row of cabins, showers, facilities for water sports and plenty of comfortable lounge chairs and plaited leaf umbrellas. It was never crowded and everything you could possibly require was available. The extensive grounds contain a large swimming pool, separate villas for families with young children, and plenty of parking under shade. The prices were reasonable." (*Angela and David Stewart*) More reports please.

Open Apr–Oct.
Rooms 81 – all with bath or shower and mini-bar; some in detached cottages among pine trees; many with balcony or terrace.
Facilities Reading room, bridge room, bar, restaurant; solarium, hairdresser, beauty parlour; terraces. Large grounds with fresh-water swimming pool; children's playground and tennis court; sandy beach with snack bar, facilities for water sports incl. waterskiing and wind-surfing, power boats. Golf course 10 minutes (shuttle service by hotel bus).
Location 6 km S of Pula; 37 km SW of Cagliari.
Credit cards Access, Diners, Visa.
Terms Not available.

SESTRI LEVANTE 16039 Genova Map 16

Hotel Helvetia *Tel* (0185) 41175/42716
Via Cappuccini 43

"A friendly little hotel, attractively positioned overlooking the Bay of Silence – the oldest and most interesting part of an otherwise rather tatty resort. On our arrival we received a friendly welcome and two cold beers. Our room was small but adequate and clean. There are pretty terraces outside, and a private 'beach' opposite, which consisted of a very small area of dirty grey sand." Another report endorsed the friendly atmosphere and scenic situation: "Complimentary beverages of choice on arrival and a *very* drinkable bottle of wine on departure. Gardens and terrace with great view." Dinner in the *albergo* was not

615

recommended by one reader this year. "The gloom of the dining room was little alleviated by the arrival of dreary food. There are, however, several restaurants in the area, including one with a *Michelin* rosette. Breakfasts were fine." (*J and C Lovejoy, Marie Earl*)

Open 1 Apr–30 Sept.
Rooms 25 double, 3 single – 14 with bath, 14 with shower, all with telephone, radio and TV.
Facilities Lift. TV lounge, lounge, solarium, restaurant with terrace looking over the sea, large terraced garden. Private beach. English spoken.
Location 100 metres from town centre, overlooking the Bay of Silence. Some parking.
Credit cards Access, Amex.
Terms B&B: single 50,000–51,000 L, double 78,000 L; dinner, B&B 60,000–75,000 L per person; full board 70,000–80,000 L per person. Set lunch 25,000 L; full alc 30,000 L.

Grand Hotel Villa Balbi   *Tel* (0185) 42941
Viale Rimembranze 1

For those who like their seaside holidays in traditional style: a pink palace in a leafy garden, right on the seafront of this popular Riviera resort, with its own section of private beach. There is also a heated pool in the garden. The main building was the 18th-century home of a patrician Genovese family; a modern extension has been added. "Some of us (party of six) had rooms on the top floor of the palace – very large and commodious with large bathroom and very large balcony; outlook over palm-trees to the sea. The new bedrooms were also generous in size and very comfortable. Public rooms palatial. Friendly and efficient service. Not cheap, but marvellous value for money. We would gladly have stayed a fortnight – one gets used to 'dwelling in marble halls'."
(*P R Harrison*) *Pension* meals are conventional fare.

Open Apr–Oct.
Rooms 2 suites, 78 double, 20 single – 80 with bath, 20 with shower; all with telephone; 80 rooms in annexe.
Facilities Reception hall, lounge, TV room, bar, conference facilities, dining room, and open-air restaurant. Large park with heated sea-water swimming pool. Private sandy beach 30 metres. Golf, tennis, waterskiing, riding, sailing nearby.
Location Central; Sestri Levante is 50 km E of Genoa. Parking.
Restriction Not suitable for &.
Credit cards All major cards accepted.
Terms B&B 60,000–80,000 L; dinner, B&B 80,000–115,000 L; full board 90,000–125,000 L. Set lunch/dinner 40,000 L. 50% reduction for children aged 2–6, 30% 6–11.

SIENA 53100   **Map 16**

Certosa di Maggiano   *Tel* (0577) 288180
Via Certosa 82–86   *Telex* 574221 CERMAG

The cloister and tower of this, the oldest Carthusian monastery in Tuscany (built 1314), remains, and now forms part of this "well-converted small and luxurious hotel. It lies a kilometre or so outside the city walls in a typical Tuscan bucolic setting. It is so personal in its style that it feels like weekending in a rich friend's house; drinks in the cloisters or in one of the beautiful lounges; Beethoven *à volonté* on the record-player in the spectacular scarlet library; chess in a tented room; *Eau Sauvage* in the cloakroom. We breakfasted and dined in the central courtyard, but could have eaten in a ravishingly pretty dining room (only residents may dine). Our dinner was, gastronomically speaking, the best in ten days of intensive Italian eating: at 90,000 lire for two, plus wine, perhaps it should have been! The wine list was noble and not too highly priced. Our room was small but exquisitely furnished and generously equipped, down to the small wall safe. Hooded towelling robes supplemented an array of towels of all sizes and textures. While we were lounging by the pool, a bowl of freshly picked figs and grapes was put in our room; while we dined, a dish of sweets was provided by the bedside. All in all, the manners and civilised charm of an earlier epoch, bolstered by 20th-century plumbing – but alas at 20th-century prices. Our stay was a joy to remember." (*Anthony Rota; also David Wooff*)

Open Mar–Dec, but not Christmas and New Year.
Rooms 9 suites, 5 double – all with bath, telephone, radio, TV and tea-making facilities. Ground-floor rooms.
Facilities Lift. Salon, library, TV room, games room, dining room. Garden with heated swimming pool and tennis court. English spoken.
Location 1 km SE of Siena. Parking.
Credit cards Amex, Diners, Visa.
Terms B&B: single 190,000–200,000 L, double 230,000–240,000 L; suite 240,000–390,000 L. Set lunch 50,000 L, dinner 60,000 L; full alc 70,000–80,000 L. Special meals and reduced rates for children.

Villa Scacciapensieri
Via di Scacciapensieri 24

Tel (0577) 41441/2
Telex 573390 VI SCA I

This enchanting Tuscan villa on a hillside is three kilometres from the centre of Siena. "My lifelong picture of Italy will be the view of the walls of Siena from our bedroom window. I shall also remember sunsets on the rooftop sitting area, swimming in the pool, and the lovely fragrance of the countryside. Both breakfast and dinner were excellent, but we were too stuffed to try our lunch – never do I hope to eat pasta that good again! The large lounge was comfortable, and the men in the front office spoke good English. And the hotel was up to this fussy American's standards in cleanliness!" This is good to hear, we have had reports of unkemptness in the past. There is a lovely garden, where in summer you can eat out under the trees. (Susan B Hanley) More reports welcome.

Open Mar–Nov. Restaurant closed Wed.
Rooms 2 suites, 21 double, 7 single – all with bath or shower, telephone and baby-listening; some with colour TV; 10 rooms in annexe, some on ground floor.
Facilities Lift. Hall, TV room, bar, dining room. Grounds with formal gardens, tennis court and swimming pool.
Location 3 km N of Siena on side road off main road (S408) to Montevarchi. Follow directions for Camping, then Nuovo Ospedale, then Basilica Osservanza. Frequent buses to Siena.
Credit cards All major cards accepted.
Terms B & B: single 100,000 L, double 180,000 L; dinner, B&B: single 130,000 L, double 240,000 L; full board: single 155,000 L, double 290,000 L. Set lunch 35,000 L, dinner 40,000 L; full alc 40,000 L. 20% reduction for children under 6; special meals.

SORRENTO 80067 Naples   Map 16

Hotel President   *Tel* (081) 8782262 and 8782362
Via Calle Parisi 14   *Telex* 71687

Nine ancient pine trees shade the view down on to Sorrento from the lofty *Hotel President*. "I have been many times to this large first-class hotel perched on a cliff, and it remains my favourite place to stay. The views are stupendous: beneath one is the sprawling resort, and beyond are the spectacular coastline, Vesuvius and the lights of Naples. Furnishings are cool and pleasantly understated. The food is exemplary, and the table d'hôte often has specialities it would be hard to find even in a restaurant (try to secure a table on the balcony). Peace and service are the keynotes here; a fine garden houses a good-sized pool, a regular bus service takes you down to Sorrento free of charge, and a post-prandial drink in the piano-bar is a fine way to end the evening." (*R W*)

Open 15 Mar–15 Nov.
Rooms 73 double, 10 single – 53 with bath, 30 with shower, all with telephone; some ground-floor rooms.
Facilities Lift. Lounge/bar, TV room, restaurant; conference room, disco, solarium; ping-pong. Garden with swimming pool, terrace and bar. English spoken. Beach 8 km.
Location On state road 145 about 4 km from Sorrento (free bus service to and from Sorrento). Garage, parking.
Credit cards Amex, Diners, Visa.
Terms B&B: single 70,000 L, double 115,000 L; dinner, B&B 90,000–95,000 L per person; full board 105,000–110,000 L per person. Set lunch/dinner 38,000 L; full alc 25,000–40,000 L. 20% reduction for children of 12 and under; special meals on request.

Pensione La Tonnarella   *Tel* (081) 8781153
Via Capo n. 31

A spectacularly situated hotel on a cliff that falls straight into the sea, with a private lift to and from the beach below. "An enchanting 'villa'," says a New Yorker. "We enjoyed some of the most breathtaking views ever from the large-windowed dining room, as well as from the outdoor terraces. Our room and bathroom also overlooked the water. All meals were excellent, and non-residents were often seen eating in the dining room because of its good reputation. Wines were good and not expensive. Mr Carlo Gargiulo, proprietor, was always accommodating." (*Alan and Sara Feldman*)

Open 1 Mar–31 Oct.
Rooms 18 double – 6 with bath, 12 with shower. Some on ground floor.
Facilities Bar, restaurant, terrace, garden. Lift to private beach with cabins and bar; motor and rowing boats available.
Location 1 km from centre. Parking.
Credit cards Amex, Diners, Visa.
Terms Dinner, B&B 28,000–35,000 L; full board 40,000–45,000 L. Set lunch/dinner 13,000–14,000 L; full alc 15,000–22,000 L. Reduced rates and special meals for children.

SYRACUSE 96100 Sicily	Map 16

Grand Hotel Villa Politi *Tel* (0931) 32100
Via M Politi Laudien 2 *Telex* 970205

The *Villa Politi* is set directly above the deep limestone quarries where, in ancient times, thousands of invading Greeks were held captive and left to die. Today they are full of trees and flowers, but a trace of pathos remains. This hotel once must have been glorious. It reminds one of Palermo's *Villa Igiea* (q.v.). It's somewhat run-down now, but for those who care about character, and who have a sense of humour and some patience, it's acceptable. In fact, for all its faults, we loved it. Our rooms were spacious and comfortable, even if the furniture was mismatched. The bathroom was nothing short of majestic. In short, the hotel is a great possibility for the intrepid. The manager says the hotel is being redecorated. Still, if anyone knows of a better choice in Syracuse, they should certainly come forward." (*Tom and Connie Congdon*)

Open All year.
Rooms 2 suites, 51 double, 39 single – 87 with bath, 7 with shower, all with telephone, radio and colour TV; many with balcony.
Facilities Large reception hall, lounge, TV room, bar, restaurant; conference and function facilities. Large garden and park; terrace restaurant; swimming pool; rocky beach with fishing rights 200 metres; sandy beach 15 km. English spoken.
Location 800 metres N of centre, near Piazza Cappuccini. Parking.
Restriction Not suitable for &.
Credit cards Access, Visa.
Terms B&B; single 46,000 L, double 72,000 L; dinner, B&B; 54,000–68,000 L per person; full board 72,000–88,000 L per person. Set lunch/dinner 18,000 L; full alc 24,000 L. Reduced rates and special meals for children.

TAORMINA Sicily	Map 16

Ipanema Hotel *Tel* (0942) 24720
Via Nazionale, 242 *Telex* 980169
Mazzarò, Taormina 98030

Taormina stands high above the sea facing Mount Etna, which is a splendid sight from this safe distance. A reader this year (travelling with the International Wine and Food Society – surely a hard bunch to please) declares: "Although recently built, the *Ipanema* has character, its narrow ochre-hued shape enlivened by bougainvillaea and geraniums. However, most of all it was the staff and owner, Bruno Valastro, who with unfailing courtesy and kindness made our stay so memorable. The keynote of the hotel is restrained elegance and intimacy. Rooms are solidly comfortable, and have all modern facilities – including air-conditioning – and a balcony." (*R W*)

Open 1 Mar–31 Oct and 1 Dec–15 Jan.
Rooms 48 double, 2 single – 37 with bath, 13 with shower, all with telephone, radio, baby-listening and air-conditioning; some with balconies.
Facilities Lounge/bar, dining room. Sun terrace, swimming pool, solarium, tennis court; close to the sea; hotel has private sandy beach. English spoken.
Location 3 km from centre of Taormina, near main road. Garage.
Restriction Not suitable for &.
Credit cards Amex, Diners.

Terms B&B 51,500 L; dinner, B&B 72,600 L; full board 88,900 L. Full alc 20,000 L. 35% reduction for children 2–7 years, 10% reduction for children 7–11; special meals.

Mazzarò Sea Palace
Via Nazionale 147, Taormina 98030

Tel (0942) 24004
Telex 980041 MASEAP

The *Mazzarò Sea Palace* is one of this popular resort's more luxurious hotels: it receives a rare four red turrets from *Michelin*. As its name suggests, it is both palatial (though modern) and right on the sea, below the town. It has large, cool rooms and is furnished throughout with the kind of stylish simplicity that always carries a steep price tag. One reader found the prices for "extras" particularly daunting but consoled himself with the thought that "one gets a standard of food and service truly in keeping with the hotel's status. The location is excellent: immediately above the most exclusive beach in the area, on which it has ample reserved space, away from the noise, yet within a minute's walk of the cable-car to the resort high above. Front rooms have lovely terraces, everywhere are flowers, and if you don't want to walk the few steps to the beach, there is a heated sea-water pool to one side. Lunch is a lavish affair on the terrace, with such delights as spaghetti al sugo nero di Seppie." (R W)

Open Apr–Oct.
Rooms 4 suites, 63 double, 14 single – 49 with bath, 32 with shower, all with telephone, and radio.
Facilities Sitting room, bridge room, piano-bar with dancing every evening, restaurant, functions room; terraces and sun decks; heated salt-water swimming pool, private sandy beach with windsurfing and other water sports; free tennis nearby. English spoken. &.
Location On E side of Taormina, 3 minutes by cable car to old centre of Taormina. Garage parking.
Credit cards Amex, Diners, Visa.
Terms [1985 rates] rooms: single 130,000 L, double 210,000 L; full board 113,000–182,000 L per person. Breakfast 1,300 L; alc meals (excluding wine) 54,000–75,000 L. Reduced rates and special meals for children.

San Domenico Palace Hotel
Piazza San Domenico, 5
Taormina 98039

Tel (0942) 23701
Telex 980013 DOMHOT

The *San Domenico*, crowned by one reader as "the queen of Sicilian hotels", began life as a monastery, occupying a large promontory. During the war Kesselring used it as his headquarters and much of the original 15th-century building, apart from the miraculously intact cloister, was destroyed by Allied bombs. "The reception area is like a discreet Mayfair bank, but just beyond is the interior courtyard and it is here that you begin to believe this may be the world's most beautiful hotel. If you are lucky, you will be given a room or a suite from Nos. 202–218. The staircase is grand and straight; the corridor is incredibly long and wide; the rooms are smallish, austere yet comfortable; the view from the tiny balcony is sensational. Below are the gardens, ablaze with colour and punctuated by palms, and beyond is the smoky profile of Mount Etna, sometimes clear and proud, sometimes hazy and mysterious." Another reader describes the hotel as "coyly but successfully exploiting the monastery theme. The rooms are not lavish – these are monks' cells after all – but attractive and comfortable. But it's the public spaces that are the more spectacular: grand halls, high ceilings, endless paintings, statues and ecclesiastical paraphernalia. Service is first rate. It is the garden that makes the place extraordinary, flowing with flowers, and under the most astounding view – Mount Etna rising to the south, puffing vapour into beautiful skies."

Only the food disappoints – "consistently bland and stodgy" – but there are many charming restaurants in town. (*Adrian Turner, Tom and Connie Congdon*)

Open All year.
Rooms 10 suites, 80 double, 28 single – all with bath, direct-dial telephone, radio, colour TV and air-conditioning.
Facilities Hall, 4 lounges, bar, TV room, dining room, games room, conference facilities. Sicilian mandolin group plays every night in the bar. Courtyard, terrace, garden with heated swimming pool and snack bar. Private beach (car service). Tennis nearby. English spoken.
Location On promontory on W side of town.
Restriction Not suitable for &.
Terms B&B: single 132,000–174,000 L; double 240,000–304,000 L; dinner, B&B 159,000–226,000 L; full board 208,000–280,000 L. Set lunch 55,000 L, dinner 60,000 L. 20% reduction for children sharing parents' room.

Villa Belvedere   *Tel* (0942) 23791 or 23792
Via Bagnoli Croce 79, Taormina 98039

A bed-and-breakfast hotel with a lovely garden and swimming pool. It was originally nominated for the Guide as "undoubtedly the nicest place to stay in Taormina if one wants to be independent for meals". This view has since been endorsed by a visitor who praises the owners, Monsieur Pécaut and his Italian wife, for their "exceptionally charming and helpful service". Three different sorts of rooms are available. The new rooms are well equipped and face the front with "stupendous views over the flowered garden, the bay and Mount Etna", the older ones in front are more simply appointed but offer the same view; least recommended are the back rooms which tend to be noisy. There is a pleasant bar and lounge. (*David Helsdon, R W*)

Open All year except Christmas.
Rooms 38 double, 4 single – all with bath or shower. Some on ground floor.
Facilities Lift. 1 lounge, 2 sitting rooms, one with TV, lounge bar, breakfast room. Garden with terrace, swimming pool and bar. Sea 3 km away. English spoken.
Location Central, near public gardens and tennis court. Parking.
Credit cards Access, Visa.
Terms B&B: single 42,200 L, double 74,900 L. (No restaurant.) 30% reduction for children.

Villa Fiorita   *Tel* (0942) 24122
Via Pirandello 39
Taormina 98039

Just across from the *Pensione Villa Paradiso* (see below) and the cable car that takes you down to the beach. *Villa Fiorita*, new to the Guide, is a *simpatico* hotel with a large garden, sunny verandas and a small swimming pool. Inside the hotel there are several sitting rooms – plenty of nooks and crannies to hide away with a book. "Our room was a decent size and included such modern amenities as a refrigerator, TV and full bathroom. Still, the decor was somewhat quaint – we had a brass bed, and a balcony (where we had breakfast) overlooking a panoramic view of the town and the sheer cliff leading down to the water." No restaurant but the hotel serves snacks or will pack a picnic lunch for you. (*K McCleery and R Martinez*)

Open All year.
Rooms 2 suites, 22 double – 21 with bath, 3 with shower, all with telephone, radio, colour TV, mini-bar and air-conditioning; some double rooms have terrace or balcony.
Facilities Hall, lounge, lounge/bar, games room. Sauna. Large garden with terraces and heated swimming pool; 50 metres to sandy beach (cable car down). English spoken.
Location Central, near Greek theatre, but quiet. Garage (5,000 L).
Restriction Not suitable for &.
Credit cards Not known if credit cards accepted.
Terms B&B 75,000 L. (No breakfast room – breakfast served in bedroom.) Packed lunches available 10,000 L; snacks 1,000–3,500 L. Reduced rates for children sharing parents' room. (No restaurant.)

Hotel Pensione Villa Paradiso
Via Roma 2, Taormina 98039

Tel (0942) 23922
Telex 980062 ASOTELS
attn. Hotel Paradiso

A pleasant class I *pensione* close to the centre of town. The public rooms are decorated in traditional Sicilian style and the fourth-floor restaurant with its many windows takes full advantage of the view, as does the sun terrace. "This is nearly everything a small hotel should be," was one comment. "Beautifully located next to the enchanting little public park, looking out over the most spectacular view of Etna and the Aegean. Good taste carried through to nearly every detail – very pretty interiors. An accommodating staff, led by the gracious, soft-spoken Salvatore Martorana. A pleasant restaurant, with good food." A veteran guest wrote recently to concur: "I have known the *Villa Paradiso* for many years and love it – especially the food." (*Tom and Connie Congdon, Erna Low*)

Open All year except 1 Nov–20 Dec.
Rooms 9 suites, 21 double, 3 single – 28 with bath, 5 with shower, all with balcony, telephone, radio, air-conditioning and baby-listening; TV in suites on request; some ground-floor rooms.
Facilities Lifts. Lounges, TV lounge, library, bars, panoramic restaurant; facilities for small conferences; sun terraces with tables. Next door to public gardens with tennis courts (free to hotel guests). Sandy beaches with safe bathing and fishing about 1 km by foot. English spoken. &.
Location 5 minutes to town centre; hotel is signposted. Some town-view rooms are close to road. Public parking 200 metres (free to guests).
Credit cards All major cards accepted.
Terms B&B 37,000–54,000; dinner, B&B 48,000–77,000 L; full board 63,000–92,000 L. Set lunch/dinner 27,500 L; full alc 27,500–30,000 L. Discounts for stays of more than 10 days; also for honeymoons and the elderly (min. 7 days).

TELLARO DI LERICI 19030 La Spezia — Map 16

Il Nido di Fiascherino *Tel* (0187) 967286 or 966429 or 967426
Via Fiascherino 75

We're still receiving mixed reviews about this quiet, modern hotel which stands above a cove in a small village near Lerici on the Gulf of Spezia. The location is described as "nothing less than perfect, with magnificent views over beach, rocks and pine trees". The consensus is, however: do not accept an annexe room – "comfortable but sub-G-plan" and "incredibly hot". Rooms in the main building, on the other hand, receive better reviews: "Our rooms with balconies overlooked the Bay of Tellaro where waves crashed thrillingly day and night over the rocks below. One climbs downstairs to the modern comfortable reception/bar/ dining level. The dining area also overlooks the bay, and steps lead down to the water itself, with various levels where there are tables and chairs to read or relax in. The service here was impeccable – everyone eager to please." Opinions on the food vary: "Very good Italian food (not international style). Good fish, home-made pasta and delicious salads." Many readers have been disappointed with the "fast-food packaging" of breakfast; others have found both breakfast and dinner "incredibly bad". More reports please. (David Helsdon, Mary and Rodney Milne-Day; Dr P Marsh)

Open Mar–Nov.
Rooms 29 double, 7 single – 10 with bath, 26 with shower, all with telephone, and baby-listening; some with balcony. 22 rooms in annexe.
Facilities TV room, bar, 2 dining rooms, terraces. Garden. Small private beach. English spoken.
Location 2 km SE of Lerici; follow signs for Lerici and Tellaro. Parking.
Restriction Not suitable for &.
Credit cards Access, Amex, Diners.
Terms B&B: single 47,300–49,500 L; double 69,300–73,700 L; dinner, B&B 66,000–88,000 L per person; full board 77,000–99,000 L per person. Set lunch/ dinner 32,000 L; full alc 38,500 L. 40% reduction for children under 6, 25% reduction 6-12 years; special meals.

TORRI DEL BENACO 37010 Verona — Map 16

Hotel Gardesana *Tel* (045) 7225005
Piazza Calderini 20 *Telex* 48044 EURO BI

A small unspoilt resort and fishing-port, with a 14th-century castle, on the eastern shore of Lake Garda: regular boat services ply hence to Catullus' romantic Sirmione and other places around the lake. The *Gardesana* faces the little harbour, a traditional hotel with arcades and orange-brown stucco walls, but modernised inside. "Our room was large and simply but nicely furnished, with separate shower. It had a splendid view over the harbour and castle; more expensive rooms have a small balcony. Breakfast was excellent, with fruit juice and a selection of cooked meats and cheeses. Dinner was enjoyable but not outstanding. The dining room has an outdoor terrace facing the harbour, and a group of musicians generally played by the hotel each evening." The proprietor tells us that about every two weeks under his portico there are entertainments such as Tyrolean singers, rock'n' roll and parades. (*G D and E D Fearnehough*)

Open All year. Restaurant closed 10 Oct–10 Apr.
Rooms 31 double, 3 single – 4 with bath, 30 with shower, all with telephone and baby-listening; some rooms with balcony; some ground-floor rooms.
Facilities Lift. TV lounge, bar, dining room with outdoor terrace, conference room, portico with live entertainment nightly. Private cabins at Lido 300 metres from the hotel. Water sports, golf, tennis nearby. English spoken.
Location In centre of Torri del Benaco which is 45 km from Verona. Private garage; parking 300 metres.
Credit card Access.
Terms B&B: single 41,000 L, double 72,000–82,000 L; dinner, B&B 46,200–57,000 L per person. Set lunch/dinner 20,000 L; full alc 30,000 L. 30% reductions for children 3–10 years and special meals on request.

TREVISO 31100   Map 16

Le Beccherie   *Tel* (0422) 540871
Piazza G. Ancilotto 11

The town of Treviso reached its zenith in the 13th century. "Ramparts encircle it, and the narrow almost traffic-free streets are crossed with small canals. The evening stroll in the main piazza looks like a stage set as most of the population, young and old, meet for a chat or a drink outside the 13th-century town hall. The *Albergo Beccherie* is unpretentious, comfortable and good value for money. We found the rooms spacious, with well-finished furniture and fitments, but as Treviso is the centre of the Italian furniture industry this is not really surprising. They were also clean and light, with nice views over the canal and rooftops beyond. The restaurant is a well-established family-run business with a wide choice of reasonably good food, typical of the area. The house carafe, a pleasant dry Soave, was excellent value at under £1 a litre!" The hotel is surrounded by a maze of narrow one-way streets – one visitor suggests walking to it first and then finding a route for your car. (*Pat and Jeremy Temple*) More reports please.

Open All year. Restaurant closed 15–30 July, Thur evenings and all day Fri.
Rooms 12 double, 4 single – all with shower and WC, telephone and radio. All bedrooms in separate building from restaurant.
Facilities TV room, bar, restaurant (opposite), terrace with flowers, air-conditioning. English spoken.
Location 30 km N of Venice; central in one-way street leading from railway station. No private parking; garage nearby.
Restriction Not suitable for &.
Credit cards All major cards accepted.
Terms Rooms: single 30,000 L, double 55,000 L. Breakfast 4,000 L; full alc 28,000 L.

VARENNA 22050   Map 16

Hotel du Lac   *Tel* (0341) 830238 or 830588
Via del Prestino 4

Varenna is a village on the east side of Lake Como, 24 kilometres north of Lecco. In the prose of the *Lac*'s brochure, "you can enjoy the dreamy beauties where the mirror of deep water is widest, and surrounding by coasts reminding of Manzoni". The hotel is a modest but attractive place, whose main glory is its setting – right on the lake, with fine views of the water from every room. "Mrs d'Ippolito speaks English but not Mr d'I; both are most pleasant and helpful. The rooms have showers, only exceptionally a bath. The room itself was tiny, as was the shower room, but the salvation was a large terrace with magnificent views. The public rooms and terraces were spacious, clean and inviting, the situation of the hotel delightful, the food reasonable." Another visitor writes, "Most comfortable king-size bed, great reading lights, and windows that opened to the sound of Lake Como lapping." (*Patricia Solomon, Janet D Merutka*) More reports welcome.

Open Mar–Oct inclusive.
Rooms 1 suite, 13 double, 5 single – 3 with bath, 16 with shower, all with telephone; TV on request.
Facilities Lounge, tea room, TV room, breakfast room, restaurant (with music or electric organ). Garden and 2 terraces by the lake with meals served. Swimming and fishing from hotel pier; waterskiing and boat excursions available. English spoken.
Location Hotel is at end of church square, on the lake. Parking.
Restriction Not suitable for &.
Credit cards Access, Amex, Visa.
Terms B&B: single 67,000–75,000 L, double 110,000–112,000 L; dinner, B&B: 75,000–85,000 L per person; full board 85,000–95,000 L per person. Set lunch/dinner 29,000 L; full alc 40,000 L. Reduced rates and special meals for children.

VENICE   Map 16

Pensione Accademia   *Tel* (041) 5237846 or 710188
Fondementa Maravegie, Dorsoduro 1058
Venice 30123

A delightful 17th-century villa, now a popular bed and breakfast *pensione*, facing a quiet side canal only a few yards from the Grand Canal itself, at the Accademia bridge. Public rooms are furnished with restrained grandeur and there is a shady garden and a patio facing the canal. "After a hot day of canals and cathedrals, nothing is more soothing than a cool drink at one of the pink-clothed patio tables. In good weather, this is the hub of the *pensione* – coffee and rolls for breakfast in the morning sun, afternoon tea under a canal-side arbour, a late night drink under the ornate lanterns flanking the entrance. Our room was small but cool, with lovely painted wardrobes and a canal view." "A place of beguiling charm – a hodge-podge of eclectic furnishings, kept spotlessly clean by friendly staff." (*Jonathan and Stephanie Levi, Jim Engiles*)

Open All year.
Rooms 20 double, 6 single – 8 with bath, 13 with shower, all with telephone.
Facilities 2 lounges, 1 with TV, bar. 2 gardens overlooking the water. English spoken.
Location Central, near the Grand Canal.
Restriction Not suitable for &.
Credit cards All major cards accepted.
Terms B&B: single 42,000–53,000 L, double 73,000–89,000 L. (No restaurant.) Reduced rates for children.

Many hotels put up their prices in the spring. Tariffs quoted in the text may be more accurate before April/May 1986 than after.

Casa Frollo   *Tel* (041) 5222723
Giudecca 50, Venice 30123

Pamela Todd's report is too evocative not to repeat again this year: "If you
are prepared to forfeit the busy, bruising delights of a humid Piazza San
Marco filled in equal parts with crabby tourists trailing after officious
guides, and sad pigeons trailing after everything, escape across the
water to Giudecca and the elegant calm of the *Casa Frollo*: a terraced
17th-century palace with a soothing, uninterrupted view of the square
and the Doge's Palace. To gain entrance to this classical haven, night or
day, you ring a bell signalling Madame Flora – no mean concierge – to
set in motion a Heath Robinson system of pulleys which release the
catch and spill you into a cool, ordered courtyard running the whole of
the ground floor and leading into a neat, narrow garden. Take the stairs
to the right and ascend to a vast room liberally stocked with the kind of
polished Renaissance furniture you generally meet behind red ropes.
Several dozen minor modern masters' works – personally inscribed to
Madame – hang along one wall, while the facing wall props up an older
school. This is where breakfast is served and the interior competes
distractingly well with the postcard views of the Palace to be glimpsed
through the windows. Seventeenth-century swank, however, does not
always spell 20th-century comfort, and it is a brisk baronial step down
lofty corridors to the nearest virginia-creeper-veiled bathroom if you are
not in one of the rooms favoured with a private bath. Still, it is an
historical treat and remarkably reasonable: stay there!"

Recent visitors add that breakfast in the hotel is decent: "In fact, being
seated at the large flower-bedecked table with the superb view, together
with the extraordinary variety of water traffic in the foreground, is one
of the enduring memories of our all-too-brief visit." Although the
smaller rooms at the back do not enjoy the magnificent views that those
in the front do, they give on to the garden and "are, after the bustle of
Venice, thoroughly and amazingly quiet. I don't think we'll ever go
anywhere else when we visit Venice." (*G O'Reilly and B Vinson; also Rev
Michael Bourdeaux*)

Open 20 Mar–20 Nov.
Rooms 18 double, 8 single – 4 with bath, all with telephone, some with balcony.
Facilities Bar, lounge, salon, breakfast room. Garden.
Location On the waterfront on island of Giudecca.
Credit cards None accepted.
Terms B&B: single 36,000–45,000 L, double 65,000–83,000 L.

Hotel Cipriani   *Tel* (041) 707744
Giudecca 10   *Telex* 410162 CIPRVE
Venice 30123   *Reservations* in UK: (01) 583 3050
                                                   in USA: (800) 233 6800

The super-rich traveller in Venice faces a difficult choice – the *Gritti
Palace* (q.v.) or the *Cipriani*? They offer very different experiences. The
Gritti Palace is a city hotel right in the heart of things; the *Cipriani* has
turned its back on the crowds and faces serenely over the lagoon to San
Giorgio and the Lido in the distance. With its gardens and vast sea-water
swimming pool it is a welcome retreat in the summer. "This modern de
luxe hotel seems far removed from the Venice that most people know,

but there are plenty of compensations. Such are the comforts of the *Cipriani* that you may well feel inclined to laze around in luxury and forget that one of the world's most beautiful cities lies across the water. (But there's no excuse not to do the journey when the 24-hour private launch service leaves every 10 minutes for San Marco.) The hotel is plush throughout: luxurious, creamy bedrooms, with high-quality fabrics and thick carpeting, overlook either the gardens or the lagoon (behind Giudecca). Suites are decorated in a more traditional style and the best ones are by the pool. Downstairs it's mainly modern and stylish with a few concessions to the Venetian antique style such as Murano chandeliers and the occasional piece of painted *Veneziana* furniture. With the terraces, gardens and pool (where life seems to centre in summer), it's a very relaxing place to stay – almost with a seaside atmosphere. If Venice is not enough and you want a pool, tennis court, piano bar, 24-hour room service and, of course, pure luxury, then this has to be the place to go." (*S B*)

Open Mar–Nov.
Rooms 14 suites, 76 double, 4 single – all with bath, telephone, radio and colour TV; some ground-floor rooms.
Facilities Lounge/TV room, 2 bars (one with piano), 3 restaurants (indoor and outdoor), 5 functions rooms. Gardens with tennis and Olympic-size swimming pool (domed and heated in winter), sauna, Turkish baths, solarium, fitness and beauty facilities. Private yacht harbour with 10 berths (up to 23 metres). Lectures, cookery courses and guided tours. English spoken. &.
Location On Giudecca island, 5 minutes by hotel's private motor boat to city centre.
Credit card Amex.
Terms B&B: single 400,000 L, double 600,000 L. Half-board supplement 80,000 L per person. Set lunch 80,000 L, dinner 90,000 L. Children under 6 free.

La Fenice et des Artistes
Campiello de la Fenice 1936
Venice 30124

Tel (041) 32333
Telex 411150

A few readers are annoyed with this old favourite behind the Fenice opera house, in a secluded courtyard backing on to a slim canal. Rooms are elegant and comfortable, and breakfast and drinks can be taken in the courtyard which one reader prefers to the "rather posh and overstuffed" public rooms. Others, however, warn that rooms above the Taverna La Fenice *can be noisy until after midnight, and one reader angrily reported a muddle over booking. There have also been complaints about rooms not being made up until late in the day. Good restaurants nearby include* La Colomba. (Pamela Todd, Donald Saunders)

Open All year.
Rooms 2 suites, 46 double, 20 single – all with bath and telephone.
Facilities Lift. 3 lounges; courtyard. English spoken.
Location Central, behind the Teatro de Fenice.
Credit cards None accepted.
Terms [1985 rates] rooms: single 85,000 L, double 122,000 L. Breakfast 8,000 L.

Do you know of a good hotel or country inn in the United States or Canada? Nominations please to our sibling publication, *America's Wonderful Little Hotels and Inns*, c/o St Martin's Press, 175 Fifth Avenue, New York, NY10010, USA.

Hotel Flora *Tel* (041) 705844
San Marco 2283a
Venice 30124

This fresh report sorts out the somewhat conflicting stories we heard last year about the *Flora*. "Ask anyone English where to stay in Venice and they'll probably say the *Flora* (unless they're in the *Gritti/Cipriani* (q.v.)/*Danieli* league). It's quiet, central and very inviting. Perhaps its greatest attraction is the garden – ivy-clad walls, stone fountains, handsome pots of flowering shrubs, and plenty of tables and chairs for breakfasts and Camparis. Weather not permitting, you take breakfast in the salon, decorated in floral pinks and dark wood furniture. Bedrooms can be something of an anti-climax. You may be lucky and get one of the spacious, traditional doubles with pretty *Veneziana* painted furniture; the alternative is something much smaller and simpler, saved only by views of the garden. Breakfast is a lot more substantial than those in most second-class hotels." (*S B*) The management writes to say they have replaced all mattresses and their conscientiousness is praised by this reader: "From our first contact with the hotel until we left, nothing was too much trouble for the hotel staff. On Sunday when the laundry was closed, 'Mamma' did our laundry."(*E Clark*)

Open 5 Feb–15 Nov.
Rooms 39 double, 5 single – 30 with bath, 14 with shower, all with telephone; 2 ground-floor rooms.
Facilities Lift. Lounge, TV room, bar, small breakfast room. Courtyard/garden where breakfast and drinks are served. English spoken. &.
Location Central, just off the Calle Larga XXII Marzo.
Credit cards All major cards accepted.
Terms B&B: single 97,000 L, double 158,000 L. (No restaurant.)

Gritti Palace *Tel* (041) 794611
Campo Santa Maria del Giglio 2467 *Telex* 410125 GRITTI
Venice 30124

In a word: "As the old champagne ad. used to say, 'The only question is, can you afford it?' " This famous palazzo, once the home of Doge Andrea Gritti, stands on the Grand Canal facing the wonderful church of the *Salute*. Some visitors feel that it rests too comfortably on its laurels. A *Gritti* advocate of many years standing rises to its defence: "When you pass the portal you are in a different world. It's true that not everyone can have a room overlooking the Grand Canal, but in fact the side rooms are much quieter, unless you have one of the smaller attic rooms, which are marvellous with their mini-four-posters. Service is faultless and the whole hotel is run with masterly skill and professionalism. Regular guests can always be heard complaining that it isn't what it was – but of course they always come back, as Somerset Maugham did until the end." (*Antony Verney*)

Nonetheless, we still get mixed views eg: "Superb service, bathroom worthy of a princess, bed the best I've ever slept in; but some bedrooms are small, not all have a pleasant outlook, and upstairs decor is unimaginative. Worst of all, my breakfast consisted of lukewarm coffee and stale rolls and croissants – inexcusable. At the prices it charges, the hotel should be perfect: it is not." More reports please.

Open All year.
Rooms 4 suites, 74 double, 17 single – all with bath, direct-dial telephone, radio and colour TV.
Facilities Lifts. 3 salons, TV rooms, bar, restaurants; terrace-restaurant overlooking the Grand Canal; conference and functions facilities. Beauty parlour. Guitar music every night in winter. English spoken. &.
Location On the Grand Canal, 10 minutes by boat from the Lido. Parking at Piazzale Roma.
Credit cards All major cards accepted.
Terms [1985 rates] B&B: single 380,000 L, double 522,000 L. Alc meals (excluding wine) 75,000–100,000 L.

Hotel do Pozzi   *Tel* (041) 707855
Via XXII Marzo, 2373 – San Marco   *Telex* 410275 – attn. do Pozzi
Venice 30124

"This is a reliable little hotel, tucked down an alleyway of a chic and central shopping street." The *do Pozzi* receives considerable praise as a good-value, well-located place to stay. "Bedrooms are modern and comfy, some slightly small; everything bathrooms spotlessly clean." Others have commented on the immaculate bathrooms "with oodles of towels changed daily". "It's quite quiet and you can take breakfast in peace on the patio." Last year we had reports that there was pressure to take meals at the adjoining *Ristorante da Raffaele*. A reader this year says that although it is under the same management, "we had no pressure whatsoever to eat in the restaurant". Another says, "the best thing about the *Raffaele* is the open-air, canalside terrace. But the prices are high and the food disappointing."(*S B, K and C Neeham; and others*)

Open All year, except 4/5 weeks from 10 Jan.
Rooms 21 double, 14 single – 8 with bath, 27 with shower, all with direct-dial telephone, air-conditioning and frigo-bar.
Facilities Sitting room, TV room. Courtyard with plants and flowers. English spoken.
Location Central, near San Marco.
Restriction Not suitable for &.
Credit cards All major cards accepted.
Terms B&B: single 56,000–94,000 L, double 98,000–155,000 L. (No restaurant.) Reduced rates and special meals for children.

Saturnia e International   *Tel* (041) 708377
Calle Larga XXII Marzo 2398, Venice 30123   *Telex* 410355

A 14th-century *palazzo*-cum-hotel about three minutes' walk from St Mark's. The reception area makes quite an impact: a Gothic patio with an elaborate inlaid ceiling. "Bedrooms vary enormously. The best ones are baronial and warrant the price, others are about a quarter the size, modern but unexciting, and overpriced." "The bathrooms are more than adequate. Our room overlooked a small canal at the back and was quiet at all times that mattered." Service and the breakfasts are good. But recently readers have been muttering about the "exorbitant" prices at this hotel and the poor single rooms, and don't agree about its two restaurants, the rosetted *Caravella* and the more modestly priced *Il Cortile*. Of *Caravella* we hear, "in our opinion one of the best in Venice, but not cheap" to "disappointing and service off-hand". *Il Cortile*, with

629

outdoor seating in the summer, for the most part receives warmer praise. The *Campiello*, nearby, is recommended as an alternative. (*S B, Sir Charles and Lady Davis*)

Open All year.
Rooms 79 double, 19 single – 87 with bath, 11 with shower; all with telephone and air-conditioning; some with TV.
Facilities Lift. 2 lounges, bar, TV room, conference facilities. 2 restaurants. English spoken.
Location Central, W of St Mark's Square.
Restriction Not suitable for &.
Credit cards All major cards accepted.
Terms [1985 rates] B&B: single 96,000–176,000 L, double 136,000–260,000 L. Reduced meal rates for children. *Note:* These terms are subject to change during New Year and Carnival periods.

Pensione Seguso   *Tel* (041) 22340
Zattere, 779, Venice 30123

Reinstated in the Guide after two years oblivion, this moody, modest pensione *on the Zattere has as its main attraction the stunning view from the front-facing windows of the Giudecca and Venetian craft of all sizes; the side rooms have pleasing views over a small canal. It has the virtues of a high-class, old-fashioned establishment – fine old Venetian furniture, dining room with embroidered silk wall covering and friendly service. Signora Seguso speaks good English. Opinions on the* Seguso's *food vary. Prices are based on half-board, though B&B is possible in the low season. More reports please.*

Open 1 Mar–30 Nov. Restaurant closed Wed.
Rooms 31 double, 5 single – 9 with bath, 9 with shower, all with telephone.
Facilities Lift. Lounge, restaurant, breakfast terrace. English spoken.
Location 15 minutes from the centre, overlooking the Giudecca canal.
Credit cards Access, Amex, Visa.
Terms Dinner, B&B: single 62,000–72,000 L, double 117,000–132,500 L; full board: single 89,000–99,000 L, double 170,000–186,000 L. 30% reduction for children under 6; special meals.

Hotel Torino   *Tel* (041) 705222
Via XXII Marzo, Venice 30124   *Telex* 223534 Attn. TORINO

A 14th-century palace tucked into a convenient little corner between San Marco and Santa Maria del Giglio. If you know Venice you'll have passed it a thousand times, admiring its tiny wrought-iron balcony that embraces two very beautiful windows and drops baskets full of flowers. "Good value B&B, situated five minutes from San Marco. Quite a good room but no bath, only a shower. Helpful staff, good housekeeping and not expensive. Simple but well situated – no view but not to be expected at that price. No restaurant but plenty nearby." *(Kenneth Bell)*

Open All year.
Rooms 10 double, 10 single – all with shower, telephone and radio.
Facilities Lounge, breakfast room. English spoken.
Location Central, very near Piazza San Marco.
Restriction Not suitable for &.
Credit cards All major cards accepted.
Terms B&B: single 100,000 L, double 160,000 L (No restaurant.)

Pensione Villa Parco   *Tel* (041) 760015
Via Rodi 1, Lido, Venice 30126   [in winter (041) 942499]

"The *Villa Parco* is remarkable in its combination of gracious hospitality, moderate price and exceptional location. A renovated villa with full modern conveniences, the *Parco* is located one block from the Lido beach, the Casino and a remarkable restaurant, *La Argliere*. Yet it has its own gardens and is extremely quiet. It serves as an excellent alternative to any of the hotels in Venice for anyone travelling by car or with children. Best of all, it is owned and operated by wonderful and considerate people, Giulia and Enzo Cipollato, who carry on the family tradition begun by Giulia's father. This is really a terrific find – small, intimate, elegant yet unpretentious – and the best hosts you could want." (*Dr M Brian Murphy and Susan E Hoffman*)

Open 30 Mar–30 Oct.
Rooms 20 double, 2 single – 10 with bath.
Facilities Lounge. Small garden; sandy beach (with private cabin) nearby. English spoken.
Location 1 km from centre. Quiet. Garage.
Restriction Not suitable for &.
Credit cards All major cards accepted.
Terms B&B: single occupancy 29,000–34,000 L, double 48,000–54,000 L (without bath; extra charge, unspecified, for rooms with bath). Reduced rates for children. (No restaurant.)

VERONA 37121   **Map 16**

Hotel Colomba d'Oro   *Tel* (045) 595300
Via C. Cattaneo 10   *Telex* 480872 COLOMB

This medium-sized hotel, in a dignified stone building, fulfils one important requirement of a good city hotel: it is right in the centre of things – only a few minutes from the ancient Arena – while providing a peaceful retreat when the sightseeing is over. Situated on a side street in a traffic-restricted zone, it is also fully air-conditioned and double-glazed for extra quiet. Cars can safely be left in the hotel's private garage. The interior has a club-like atmosphere with lots of polished wood and comfortable armchairs. Bedrooms are large and well appointed. Guests did have quibbles this year, however: electricity somewhat erratic; breakfast very average, mostly pre-packaged, not generous with coffee, and over-priced. More reports please.

Open All year.
Rooms 2 suites, 31 double, 19 single – 37 with bath, 15 with shower, all with direct-dial telephone, air-conditioning and baby-listening; 35 with colour TV.
Facilities Bar, salon, TV room, breakfast room, conference room, 2 meeting rooms. English spoken.
Location Central, near Arena; in restricted traffic zone, so quiet; all windows double-glazed. Garage in same building as hotel. Leave *autostrada* at Verona Sud.
Credit cards All major cards accepted.
Terms [1985 rates] rooms: single 70,000 L, double 98,000 L. Breakfast 9,500 L.

Details of amenities vary according to the information – or lack of it – supplied by hotels in response to our questionnaire. The fact that lounges or bars or gardens are not mentioned must not be taken to mean that a hotel lacks them.

Villa Condulmer
Zerman, Mogliano Veneto

Tel (041) 457100

The 18th-century Venetian villa, on the misty plain between Venice and Treviso, is described as "excellent" by two of its regular visitors: "A beautiful old villa, nicely set in the countryside. A car is essential if you want to do anything other than laze by the pool or play golf. We had one of the rooms in the main building, large and grand – it is almost like staying in a stately home in England. The staff are discreet and helpful and you are made to feel special. The food is good quality: excellent strawberry risotto (savoury). Prices reasonable. No air-conditioning, so you may have to choose between the heat and the flies." (*Kate and Steve Murray-Sykes*)

Open End Mar–beginning Nov.
Rooms 20 suites, 33 double, 7 single – 33 with bath, 7 with shower; 40 with telephone, 8 with radio. 32 rooms in annexe. Some ground-floor rooms.
Facilities Salon, reading room, TV room, 3 restaurants, bar, conference room. Piano in bar. Park with unheated swimming pool, tennis court, 18-hole golf course and riding. English spoken.
Location Outside village, which is 4 km NE of Mogliano Veneto and 22 km N of Venice. Parking.
Credit cards Access, Amex, Diners.
Terms [1985 rates] rooms: single 45,000 L, double 85,000–100,000 L. Breakfast 8,500 L; full alc 33,000–38,500 L plus 10% service.

HÔTEL DE LA MOSELLE, EHNEN

BERDORF 6550   **Map 9**

Hôtel l'Ermitage   *Tel* 79.184
44 route de Grundhof

Near the German frontier west of Echternach, Berdorf is in the hilly wooded area known as "Luxembourg Suisse" with its interesting rock formations. *L'Ermitage,* a modern building in style half-chalet, half-Italianate, is in a big garden on the outskirts of Berdorf. "Family-run, with meals cooked by the owner, using fresh foods. There is no choice, but quality and cooking are good and prices reasonable. The rooms are fairly small but pleasant and the bathrooms modern. The sitting rooms are homely and this would probably be a good hotel for a family holiday. There are some self-catering family apartments in the grounds." *(Kate and Steve Murray-Sykes)*

Open 3 Apr–3 Oct. Restaurant closed for lunch on Tue.
Rooms 14 double, 2 single – 11 with bath, 2 with shower, all with telephone and mini-bar; 9 ground-floor rooms; self-catering units.
Facilities 2 lounges, bar, loggia, restaurant. Garden. Swimming, tennis, mini-golf nearby.
Location Berdorf is 6 km W of Echternach, 32km NE of Luxembourg city. Hotel is 1 km from Berdorf, towards Grundhof.
Credit cards Amex, Diners, Visa.
Terms [1985 rates] B&B: single 1,250 Lfrs, double 2,030–2,130 Lfrs; half-board 1,600–1,690 Lfrs per person. Set lunch/dinner 700–1,000 Lfrs.

ECHTERNACH 6409   **Map 9**

Hôtel Bel-Air   *Tel 729.383*
Route de Berdorf 1   *Telex 2640*

That little Luxembourg can hold its head up in the grand country-house-hotel league is amply demonstrated by the *Bel-Air*, a *Relais et Châteaux* member that stands on the edge of the popular and pretty resort town of Echternach in the wooded and hilly "Luxembourg Suisse" area near the German frontier. It is a palatial kind of place, with extensive and imposing gardens full of pools, flowering shrubs, and Doric columns. "The old hotel has been extended and most of the bedrooms are in the modern part, each with a balcony where you can take breakfast looking down over the grounds towards the river. Walks through the woods, clearly marked, start directly outside the hotel. The restaurant has a *Michelin* rosette and the food is excellent but fairly expensive." Panoramic dining room, offering such dishes as saint-pierre aux poireaux et aux truffes. *(Kate and Steve Murray-Sykes)*

Open All year. Restaurant closed mid-Nov to mid-Dec, and 6–30 Jan.
Rooms 10 suites, 32 double, 2 single – all with bath and telephone, radio and TV.
Facilities Bar, 2 salons, TV room, dining rooms; conference facilities. 1½-acre grounds with tennis and children's playground. Fishing nearby. English spoken.
Location On western side of Echternach, off Diekirch road; follow the river Sure until Berdorf turn-off. 35 km NE of Luxembourg city. Parking.
Credit cards All major cards accepted.
Terms B&B: single 2,000–3,000 Lfrs, double 3,000–4,400 Lfrs; dinner, B&B: 2,500–3,600 Lfrs per person; full board 2,800–4,100 Lfrs per person. Set lunch 1,500 and 1,250 Lfrs, dinner 1,300, 1,900 and 2,100 Lfrs; full alc 2,000 Lfrs (excluding service). Reduced rates and special meals for children.

EHNEN 5416   **Map 9**

Hôtel de la Moselle   *Tel (352) 7.60.22 or 7.67.17*
131 route du Vin

A neat modern hotel, situated on the river Moselle (though separated from it by a fairly busy road). Although there is a *Michelin*-rosetted restaurant in town *(Hôtel Simmer*, see below), the *Hôtel de la Moselle* is much appreciated for its good food. "We were delighted – comfortable rooms, delicious dinner and fine wine." "Food delicious, beautifully served, and the service most attentive; croissants light as a feather." Bedrooms, most with their own bath or shower, are well appointed. The hotel is run by the friendly Bamberg family. The restaurant, called the *Bamberg*, has views over the river from big picture windows. We warned last year that the front rooms could be noisy, but even back rooms, it seems, suffer from a church clock striking every quarter of an hour, with two clocks striking on the hour. *(Anne and Edwin Wolff, Christopher and Eleanor Hope, D Parish)*

Open 20 Jan–1 Dec; closed Tue.
Rooms 15 double, 3 single – 7 with bath, 5 with shower, all with telephone; most with radio, 3 with TV.
Facilities Lift. 2 salons (1 with TV), dining room, banqueting room. Near a public park; Moselle river 50 metres; free fishing. English spoken.
Location Luxembourg town 20 km, Trier 30 km; Ehnen is on the river 10 km from Remich and 10 km from Grevenmacher. Hotel is central: front rooms can be noisy. Parking.
Credit cards Access, Amex, Visa.
Terms B&B: single 800–1,600 Lfrs, double 1,200–2,000 Lfrs. Full alc 1,500 Lfrs. Special winter weekend rates. Reduced rates for children according to age.

Hôtel Simmer   *Tel* (352) 7.60.30 or 7.60.10
117 route du Vin

"A most delightful and agreeable place, with charming proprietors and exquisite food", wrote one commender on the rosetted *Simmer*, which stands just across the road from the Moselle river, and along the road from the *Moselle* above. "It has a 15th-century dining room, with delightful soft lighting and quiet background music. The cooking and service are both excellent and the restaurant is in great demand both with nearby residents and foreign nationals attending EEC meetings in Luxembourg. Local wine cheap and very good. There are 23 bedrooms of a good size, most with bathroom or shower, and tastefully furnished. A chest-of-drawers would have been useful, but we did take too much clothing." "Our room at the back was beautifully quiet; although those at the front have views of the river." *(W H Bailey, Anne and Edwin Wolff)*

Open All year except Jan/Feb, and Tue (Oct–Easter).
Rooms 19 double, 4 single – 14 with bath, 4 with shower, all with telephone.
Facilities Salon with TV, bar, dining room, banqueting facilities, terrace overlooking the river; garden. Watersports and fishing. English spoken.
Location 10 km N of Remich, 10 km S of Greuenmacher.
Credit cards Access, Amex, Visa.
Restriction Not suitable for &.
Terms B&B: single 1,650 Lfrs, double 2,150 Lfrs; dinner, B&B (min. 3 days): 2,150–2,500 Lfrs per person; full board (min. 3 days, 2,350–2,700 Lfrs per person. Set lunch-dinner 1,350 Lfrs; full alc 1,400 Lfrs. Reduced rates for children under 8.

ETTELBRÜCK 9010   Map 9

Hôtel Central   *Tel* 82.116
25 rue de Bastogne

Ettelbrück is a small town pleasantly situated at the confluence of the Warke and the Alzette rivers. The *Central* has an unprepossessing external appearance and a simple reception area, but good rooms ("go high to get the view over the houses to the hills"), very pleasant proprietors and staff, and best of all, a *Michelin*-rosetted restaurant to look forward to after a day's walking up the Warke valley to the Welscheid (825 feet). "Very reasonable in price." (*J W S Hearle*)

Open 19 Jan–15 Aug, 1 Sept–19 Dec. Restaurant closed Sun and public holidays.
Rooms 16 – all with bath or shower and direct-dial telephone.
Facilities Lift. Lounge-bar, restaurant.
Location Central. Ettelbrück is 28 km N of Luxembourg town.
Credit cards All major cards accepted.
Terms [1985 rates] B&B: single 1,100–1,400 Lfrs, double 1,500–2,000 Lfrs. Set lunch/dinner 700–1,800 Lfrs.

REMICH 5533   Map 9

Hôtel St Nicolas   *Tel* 698.333 or 698.888
Esplanade 31   *Telex* 3103 HRNICO

"Remich is a small town just down the wine route along the Moselle, the last before Germany, much used by the inhabitants of Luxembourg *ville* for a short trip 'to the country'. The *St Nicolas*'s restaurant enjoys an excellent reputation locally. The hotel faces the esplanade and in August the sweet aroma of limes wafts across the road. The rooms on the higher floors enjoy a lovely view over the tree tops on to the gently flowing river. There is a terrace on the first floor, also overlooking the esplanade. The road in front provides enough parking and, though very busy during the day, quietens completely at night. Our room at the back overlooked what is at present a building site to expand the hotel. It was spacious, soberly but pleasantly furnished. Our bathrom was superb with a 'volcanically' powered shower. Public rooms are somewhat gloomy. The dining room tables are laid to overlook the river. Service was rather slow but extremely pleasant, cheerful and helpful. The house specialises in fish dishes and the wine list includes a large selection of Luxembourg wines. You can drink a lot of this without ill effects. Breakfast was copious. The price of room and breakfast [about £20 for two in 1984] is unbeatable and fantastic value for money." (*Francine and Ian Walsh; Dr N B Finter*)

Open All year.
Rooms 50, all double or single (extra bed possible) – 15 with bath, 30 with shower, all with direct-dial telephone and radio, TV (mostly colour) and video; tea-making facilities and baby-listening on request.
Facilities 2 lifts. Lounge (with TV), bar, sitting room, dining room; terrace; playroom, solarium. Open-air swimming pool nearby (for summer); fishing in the Moselle. English spoken.
Location From Luxembourg city, take direction Saarbrucken; at the German border, the hotel is by the Moselle river. No special parking facilities.
Credit cards All major cards accepted.
Terms B&B: 600–1,400 Lfrs; dinner, B&B 1,000–1,850 Lfrs; full board 1,400–2,250 Lfrs. Set lunch/dinner 650, 850 and 1,100 Lfrs; full alc 950 Lfrs. Reduced rates for children sharing parents' room.

Malta

CORNUCOPIA HOTEL — XAGHRA

SANNAT Gozo   **Map 16**

Hotel Ta´Cenc   *Tel* Gozo 55.68.19 or 55.68.30 or
55.15.20 or 55.15.23
Telex 1479 REFINZ

The island of Gozo is one of two small islands off the north-eastern corner of Malta, a quarter the size of the main island. The ferry takes half an hour, but a five-kilometre strip of sea makes a world of difference. The *Ta´Cenc* is the one luxury hotel on Gozo.

The hotel is beautifully sited on a high promontory, built in the local honey-coloured limestone on a low-profile principle: it's all one storey and cunningly terraced to blend into the hillside. The rooms are individually designed bungalows, most with a private patio for breakfast or sun-worship, ranged round a central pool, with plenty of space between for oleanders, fig trees and cacti. The pool itself offers a breath-taking view of the sea and Malta beyond, and many residents are content to brown and browse there all day. But for the more adventurous, there is lots to see on Gozo – on foot, by bus or by cheap rented car. There is plenty of good rock bathing all round the island, but only one first-class sandy beach, 10 kilometres from the hotel. Reports this year stress the personal attention (birthday flowers and cake) and the friendly atmosphere, "as welcoming as ever. The food and surroundings are superb and the hotel remains unmatched anywhere on the island."

The new manager, Pinot Demuret, is a locally renowned tennis player. It has been suggested that he is less authoritarian than the previous manager, though efficient and obviously liked by both guests and staff. (*Dr D M Taub, Polly Rubinstein; also Heather Gorkin, Tim Brierly*)

Open All year.
Rooms 15 suites, 35 double – all with bath, telephone, radio, mono TV, breakfast patio and baby-listening service; all rooms on ground floor; some self-contained family bungalows.
Facilities Ramps on request; 2 lounges, one with colour TV, restaurant; conference facilities; billiards and table tennis, disco, music in bar weekly. 3-acre gardens and terrace with fresh-water heated swimming pool and bar, 2 tennis courts (1 floodlit). Chauffeur service, car and motorbike hire; riding, bowls and *bocci*. Sand and rock beach 2 km (free transport by hotel bus 3 times a day), water-skiing, boats for hire, boat excursions (incl. moonlight trips). English spoken. &
Location 5 minutes' walk from village, on the southern part of Gozo island, near Ta' Cenc cliffs. Parking.
Credit cards All major cards accepted.
Terms B&B £M13.50–£M19.50; dinner, B&B £M18–£M28; full board £M21–£M31. Set lunch £M5, dinner £M5.50; full alc £M6.50. De luxe weekend £M24 full board per day off-season. Christmas/New Year packages. Free games and tennis off-season. Reduced rates for children under 6; special meals.

XAGHRA Gozo   Map 16

Cornucopia Hotel   *Tel* Gozo 55.64.86 or 55.38.66
10 Gnien Imrik Street   *Telex* 1467 VJB

This small family hotel is a converted farmhouse two miles inland, run by Victor Borg and his family. The atmosphere is unpretentious, relaxed and friendly. The rooms are plain but there is a sunbathing terrace, breezy public rooms and an enlarged swimming-pool area. Poolside barbecues take place on Tuesday and Friday evenings in the summer and the food in the restaurant is well cooked and generously served (*Michael Rubinstein, J B*). A self-contained annexe farmhouse has been added this year, offering self-catering or half-board.

Open All year.
Rooms 3 suites, 15 double – 17 with bath, 1 with shower, 1 suite with mono TV; tea-making facilities and baby-listening on request; 5 ground-floor rooms. Annexe farmhouse with 2 bedrooms, bathroom, kitchen and living/dining room, offering self-catering or half-board accommodation.
Facilities Lounge/library with colour TV, bar/lounge, bar, restaurant, card and games room, table tennis. Patio with swimming pool; poolside barbecues Tue and Fri. Hire of bike, scooter, car. Boat trips; 2 km from fine sandy beach at Ramla (transport available), sailing, scuba diving, fishing and windsurfing. English spoken. &
Location Central; from Xaghra square follow signs to Xerri's Grotto, turn right. Parking.
Credit cards All major cards accepted.
Terms [1985 rates] (excluding 10% service charge) B&B £M4.50–£M9.05; dinner, B&B £M5.50–£M11.05; full board £M6.75–£M12.25. Set lunch £M2.25; full alc £M4.50. Reductions and special meals for children.

Norway

UTNE HOTEL, UTNE

BERGEN Map 7

Myklebust Pensjonat *Tel* (05) 311328
Rosenbergsgt 19, Bergen 5000

"Excellent value at half the price of some Bergen hotels; in a quiet street not too far from the centre (though it wouldn't suit people who can't cope with steep hills!), upstairs in what seems to be a block of private flats. Loo and shower, across a landing, a bit primitive, though spotlessly clean. The room was delightful: a large, attractively furnished bed-sitting room, complete with a pine dining table and chairs we'd love to have taken home, very comfortable, and a built-in washbasin. Walls a bit thin. Wonderful breakfast – every item one could think of from a Norwegian breakfast selection, brought to our room. Service by a most friendly and efficient young man (son of the house?) speaking near-perfect English." (J & J W) More reports welcome.

Open All year except Christmas and New Year.
Rooms 1 suite, 5 double – 2 with shower, all with colour TV.
Facilities (No public rooms.) English spoken.

639

Location Central. Parking nearby.
Restriction Not suitable for &.
Credit cards None accepted.
Terms B&B double 310 Nkr. (No restaurant.)

Hotell Neptun   *Tel* (05) 326000
Walchendorffsgate 8, P.O. Box 658,   *Telex* 40040 NEPTUN
Bergen 5001

Bergen, founded by King Olav Kyrre in 1070, is one of Norway's oldest
towns. The *Neptun* is a well-equipped, modern hotel in a central position
overlooking the harbour and the old market. It is quiet at night, and the
restaurant is one of the city's best. One visitor enjoyed the harbour
views from upper bedrooms and the cosy and intimate bar, but felt there
was nothing very Norwegian about the hotel. An earlier report ran:
"Excellent stopover. Comfortable and efficient. We thoroughly enjoyed
an excellent dinner in the attractive restaurant. Breakfasts (buffet style)
are astonishing. What a pity that Norway is in general so expensive."
The proprietor writes to inform us that his restaurant has been awarded
a prize for the largest wine list in Norway! *(Mrs E Newall; also Mr and Mrs
H E Wilson, J S)*

Open All year except Christmas/New Year.
Rooms 83 double, 26 single – 69 with bath, 30 with shower, all with telephone,
radio and colour TV; baby-listening on request. Sound-proofing.
Facilities 2 lifts. Lounge/lobby, café; snack-bar, restaurant/bar (both open till
midnight); conference facilities; English spoken.
Location Central, near old market; some traffic noise, but quiet at night.
Underground garage with lift to hotel.
Credit cards All major cards accepted.
Terms B&B single 535–635 Nkr, double 620–735 Nkr. Full alc 225 Nkr in
restaurant, 150Nkr in café. Special weekend rates 1 Oct–15 May, family rates in
summer through Inter Nor Hotels, Kronprinsensgt 5, Oslo 2. Reduced rates and
special meals for children sharing parents' room.

JELØY 1501 Moss   **Map 7**

Hotell Refsnes Gods   *Tel* (032) 70411
P.O. Box 236   *Telex* 74353

Jeløy, one of the largest of the many islands along the east coast of the
Oslofjord, is linked by a bridge to the mainland and the small town of
Moss. The island is green and leafy; the climate allows both vines and
maize to grow. At the *Refsnes Gods*, in the residential area of town, rooms
overlook either the fjord or the large swimming poool. At the bottom of
the garden a lane leads to the seashore 100 metres away: locals swim
there regularly, in unpolluted water. "With its yellow stone walls
topped by a pair of towers, the hotel looks like a French château – indeed
it belongs to the *Relais et Châteaux* association. The open-plan reception
area is welcoming; a split-level lounge looks on to the heated outdoor
pool; a second lounge, with bar, has a very luxurious feeling, with
velvet-covered sofas and oriental-looking rugs. Bedrooms are a good
size, modern and comfortable, but lack the character of the rest of the
hotel. The cooking is very good." *(J S)* One of the best art galleries in
Norway is in Jeløy, a mile from the hotel.

Open All year except Easter and Christmas; restaurant closed Sun (Oct–May).
Rooms 3 suites, 22 double, 37 single – 8 with bath, 51 with shower, all with
telephone, radio and mini-bar; 28 with TV; some ground-floor rooms.
Facilities Lift, ramps, 2 lounges, 2 dining rooms; banqueting rooms. 4-acre park,
private bathing and boating, outdoor heated swimming pool with sauna; bicycles,
fishing. English spoken. &.
Location On W side of island which is 3 km from Moss, 60 km S of Oslo.
Credit cards Access, Amex.
Terms Rooms with breakfast: single 450–500 Nkr, double 700-950 Nkr. Set lunch
95 Nkr, dinner 155 Nkr; full alc 250 Nkr. Reduced rates for children sharing
parents' room; special meals.

LOEN 6880   Map 7

Alexandra Hotel   *Tel* (057) 77660
Telex 42665

A large modern six-storey hotel, with 210 rooms, with a wonderful
setting – in a valley surrounded by majestic mountains and fjords,
waterfalls and glaciers. Not really our sort of place perhaps, but if you're
travelling as far north as Loen for summer skiing, mountain climbing or
fishing, this could be a find. A nominator scolds: "We were staggered by
the omission of this hotel. During three weeks spent touring Norway,
this was the high spot of our visit and easily surpassed any other hotel
we stayed in, offering both parents and children the facilities required.
Beautiful situation, spacious and well-equipped bedrooms and public
rooms, and friendly and helpful staff. Endless activities available and
good food." *(J E Stapleton)*

Open All year, except 3 weeks in Jan.
Rooms 10 suites, 210 double – all with bath, telephone and radio.
Facilities Lift. 3 bars, 4 lounges. Café, buffet, restaurant. Dancing with orchestra
in bar. Convention facilities, hairdresser. Heated swimming pool, sauna, gym,
mini-golf, tennis. Near sea with fishing and water sports. English spoken.
Location Loen is in NW Norway. Nearest station at Otta (200 km); bus
connection.
Credit cards All major cards accepted.
Terms [1985 rates] B&B: single 385–435 Nkr, double 510–800 Nkr. Set lunch 100
Nkr, dinner 150 Nkr. Reduced rates and special meals for children.

OSLO   Map 7

Hotel Bristol   *Tel* (02) 41.58.40
Kristian 4dges gt 7, 0130 Oslo 1   *Telex* 71668 BRIS
P.O. Box 6764

A recent visitor calls this grand hotel "not the most expensive hotel in
Oslo but perhaps the most sympathetic of the big ones". Our inspector
last year said: "The hotel has touches of genuine class. Bedrooms are
spacious and comfortable and some public rooms have kept an aura of
old-fashioned luxury. The staff were very helpful. But the food we had
was indifferently prepared and slow to appear." An earlier visitor had
been more enthusiastic: "Here I had one of my finest gastronomic
experiences – fresh trout prepared in sour cream. Next morning, I had a
long, long breakfast from a loaded buffet starting with several kinds of
pickled herring and ending with limitless coffee. That, too, was an

641

experience. To eat well in Norway one could do worse than breakfast three times a day. The dining room was dark, old-fashioned, rather like a set from an Ibsen play. In fact, the same may be said of the hotel, at least the public parts. I found the dining-room staff extremely efficient, forthright and friendly; rather like stewards on one of the now so sadly vanished ocean liners. There is character about the place, if somewhat muted." *(M Wane, N B)*

Open All year.
Rooms 5 suites, 85 double, 53 single – 81 with bath, 62 with shower, all with telephone, radio and TV; baby-listening on request.
Facilities Lift. Large lobby with winter garden, library/bar, Trafalgar Bar; restaurant, grill, TV room, conference/banqueting facilities, night club . English spoken.
Location In town centre (front rooms may be noisy). Parking nearby.
Credit cards Access, Amex, Diners.
Terms [1985 rates] B&B: single 650–720 Nkr, double 850 Nkr. Full alc 300 Nkr. Large reductions for weekend visits.

Hotel Continental   *Tel* (02) 41.90.60
Stortingsgaten 24/26   *Telex* 71012
0161 Oslo 1

"Opposite the National Theatre, a solid-looking building dating from the turn of the century, very much in the grand stye, particularly its restaurants. The most popular attraction is the Theatercaféen, a cavernous hall packed with tables. The dining room is very formal, with chandeliers and very serious waiters. The lounge is comfy, the bar cosy and attractive; bedrooms vary in size and style. Not cheap." Another visitor elaborates: "Oslo has, more than any other European capital, preserved the traditions and atmosphere of the 19th century. The *Continental* retains the grave dignity, courtesy and friendly warmth which visitors to Norway so much appreciate. Many of the Theater-caféen's habitués seem to be Ibsen's contemporaries. A three-piece 'orchestra' led by a nonagenarian pianist enhances this atmosphere. I could wax even more lyrical over the breakfast's cold table." *(J S, N B, Arnold Horwell)*

Open All year except Easter.
Rooms 12 suites, 127 double, 40 single – all with bath, telephone, radio and colour TV.
Facilities 2 lifts. Lounge, bar, conference/banqueting facilities, restaurant, grill, café, discothèque on Sat; terrace. English spoken.
Location Central, between the Royal Palace and the National Theatre.
Restriction Not suitable for &.
Credit cards All major cards accepted.
Terms B&B: single 750–800 Nkr, double 900–1,000 Nkr.

Gabelshus Hotell   *Tel* (02) 56.25.90
Gabelsgate 16, 0272 Oslo 2

A quiet, comfortable and friendly hotel on a tree-lined residential street not far from the centre of Oslo, with the city's excellent public transport only three minutes' walk away. The hotel is popular with visitors from overseas and booking is usually essential. The lobby, decorated in dark wood, is reminiscent of a hunting lodge in the country. "The restaurant offers good, reasonably priced meals, and the bedrooms are considerably cheaper than those in the large city-centre hotels." *(M Wane)*

Open All year.
Rooms 80 beds.
Facilities Lobby, salon, dining room. Garden.
Location Near centre. Bus to centre nearby.
Credit cards Probably some accepted.
Terms [1985 rates] Single rooms: 720 Nkr, double 575–600 Nkr. Lunch and dinner à la carte.

SKIEN 3700 Telemark   Map 7

Hotel Ibsen   *Tel* (035) 24990
Kverndalen 10, P.O. Box 473   *Telex* 21 136

Skien, a small town in southern Telemark, is the birthplace of Henrik Ibsen, and makes a good stop between the port of Kristiansand and Oslo. Pleasant hours can be spent wandering around the old town and its museums and you can visit Venstöp Farm, five kilometres from the town centre, where Ibsen spent his youth. The *Hotel Ibsen*, new to the Guide, is "that rare thing, a modern hotel built primarily for business travellers, which yet has a distinct charm and character. It has a good and popular restaurant, comfortable and unusually quiet rooms and a well-maintained indoor swimming pool." *(M Wane)*

Open All year.
Rooms 5 suites, 113 double – 16 with bath, 112 with shower, all with telephone, radio and TV.
Facilities Lounge, TV room, dance-bar, restaurant, conference facilities; disco 6 nights a week; indoor heated swimming pool. Garden. 10 km to river, boat rides, watersports. English spoken. &.
Location 500 metres from town centre. Garage.
Credit cards All major cards accepted.
Terms B&B 225–560 Nkr. Set lunch 90 Nkr, dinner 100 Nkr. Group rates available; low-price weekend breaks. Reduced rates and special meals for children.

SOLVORN 5815   Map 7

Walaker Hotell   *Tel* (056) 84207
Sognefjord

Solvorn is a peaceful village at the inland end of the long Sognefjord, across the water from one of Norway's finest architectural treasures, the Urnes stave church. The village is a good base for exploring the Jostedal glacier and the surrounding mountains and meadows. The *Walaker* is a small family hotel which gets rave reviews from its nominator: "This is my favourite holiday hotel – excellent food, peace and quiet and glorious views. The Walaker family have welcomed travellers to their house since the 17th century and there is a warm family atmosphere. They have become my friends. The bedrooms, most of which have a bath or shower, are comfortable and cheerful, and the cosy parlour is furnished in traditional Norwegian style. One can choose between a room in the house or a cheaper, well-equipped cabin in the orchard, doing one's own catering. But it would be a pity to miss Mr Walaker's excellent cooking – fish at its freshest, home-grown vegetables and fruit – and his wife's mouth-watering desserts. There are good bathing places near the hotel; the cool, clear water is delicious on a hot day. In Norway, an expensive country, one feels that this moderately priced hotel gives splendid value for money." *(Mary Wane)*

Open 1 May–30 Sept.
Rooms 11 family, 9 double, 5 single – 20 with bath, 17 with shower; 11 rooms with fully equipped kitchenette. 11 ground-floor rooms.
Facilities Lounge, TV room, restaurant, conference facilities. Grounds on fjord with beach and safe bathing. English spoken.
Location On the Sognefjord, 3 km off road 55, midway between Voss (150 km) and Lom (150 km).
Restriction Not suitable for &.
Credit card Amex.
Terms [1985 rates] B&B 140–300 Nkr; dinner, B&B 230–420 Nkr. Packed lunch 25 Nkr; full alc 140 Nkr. 50% reduction for children under 16 sharing parents' room.

STAVANGER 4000 Rogaland   Map 7

Victoria Hotel   *Tel* (045) 20526
Skansegate 1   *Telex* 33056

Stavanger is the Norwegian North Sea oil headquarters and since becoming an oil-boom city has become fairly expensive to visit. Still, if you're on your way along the south coast of Norway from Bergen around to Kristiansand or the picturesque town of Kragerø, and wish to stay the night in Stavanger, you could do worse than to stay at the *Victoria Hotel*. "This large, traditional hotel in the centre of town is preferred by many visitors, from Norway and abroad, to the newer hotels. It is conveniently situated by the harbour, not far from the beautiful cathedral. The quiet and cheerful restaurant offers excellent meals and the bedrooms are well furnished and comfortable. The reception staff are particularly friendly and helpful to strangers." *(M Wane)* It is normally necessary to book in advance.

Open All year.
Rooms 100 – all with bath or shower.
Facilities Cocktail lounge, grill room, restaurant. Functions/conference facilities.
Location Near hydrofoil terminal.
Credit cards Probably some accepted.
Terms B&B: single 610 Nkr, double 710 Nkr. Set lunch 95 Nkr, dinner 150 Nkr.

UTNE 5797 Hardanger   Map 7

Hotel Utne   *Tel* Grimo (054) 66.983

"Most memorable" wrote one recent visitor, endorsing many previous commendations of this little hotel on the Hardangerfjord, south of Bergen. It is a white clapboard building, lovingly maintained, with wild flowers in each bedroom, embroidered cushions and lace curtains, and lots of old painted Norwegian furniture. Only criticism in our file this year: food very plain (boiled potatoes four nights out of five). But there are many compensating attractions. "Its setting is splendid: the foot of a steep promontory where the Hardanger branches into two small fjords;

high blue mountains across the water; sheer cliffs above it; a waterfall plunging down the cliff face and rushing through the village; apple orchards on each side. There are fine walks along the fjord in both directions. Or you can climb paths to the high pastures. The village is small and tranquil. It has a folk museum, a collection of old farm buildings in the medieval style. The *Utne* has been in the same family for 200 years. It stands in the centre of the village, opposite the boat landing. Behind it, on the hillside, is a small modern annexe. Inside, the hotel is like a charming country home, with fine old furniture, painted wood, brass and copper. Meals (taken communally) are hearty and excellent. On Sundays you have a magnificent *koldtbord*. Fru Aga Blokhus and her staff, wearing the Hardanger costume, look after you with grace and enthusiasm." *(Edward W Devlin; Dr J A Acton, J E Stapleton)* The owner is proud of the fact that there is neither radio nor TV. There is a little café in the basement for guests who stay half-board and want a snack.

Open All year except Christmas, New Year and Easter.
Rooms 20 double, 4 single – 3 with bath, 19 with shower; 8 rooms (2 of them single) in nearby annexe on the hillside; 1 ground-floor room.
Facilities Sitting rooms, basement café, dining room, games room; some off-season conference facilities; badminton. Garden and terrace; safe bathing in fjord in front of hotel; sailing, fishing, boating, cycling and good walks. English spoken.
Location At tip of Folgefonn Peninsula; at Odda cross bridge on to peninsula, or take ferries fom Kvanndal or Kinsarvik.
Credit cards Access, Amex, Diners.
Terms B&B 205–290 Nkr; dinner, B&B 275–470 Nkr; full board 65–95 Nkr per person added. 50% reduction for children aged 3–12 in parents' room.

Portugal

HOTEL PALÁCIO DOS SETEAIS, SINTRA

AZEITÃO 2925 Setubal Map 15

Estalagem Quinta das Torres   *Tel* (065) 20.80.001

"For sheer mystery and old-world charm, the *Quinta das Torres* makes the top of my list. Driving up the long, curving drive to the old mansion, through the dense greenery of trees and shrubs past an ornamental lake now emptied of water, one longs to know the history of the place. Apparently the *Quinta* was the scene of many elegant parties and a gathering place for the wealthy residents of Lisbon before the Revolution. We were led to our room by a motherly concierge who took obvious pride in the high-ceilinged room with its four-poster beds, huge antique armoire and small fireplace. The windows opened on to a lovely courtyard, which in turn led to a large garden, all rather overgrown and including a non-functioning fountain, which only added to the general air of nostalgic romance. And the food was wonderful. If Isak Dinesen had been Portuguese, she surely would have come here to write *Seven Gothic Tales*." (*Helen Wallis*)

Another correspondent put it this way: "It reminds me of the sort of place lived in by some of the slightly impoverished Scottish *lairds*. Nothing spent on their houses for years but well-loved and full of antiques – with an aura of genteel decay. It was not difficult to imagine the same sort of shooting parties at *Quinta das Torres* in the old days. There were flowers everywhere and the *bacalhau dourada* (a Portuguese salt cod speciality) was the best I have ever had. Breakfast excellent – even the coffee." *(R A D, warmly endorsed by Robert Neff)*

Late news: as we go to press we learn that one of the two elderly ladies who own the Estalagem *has been in hospital and that the place is now perhaps a bit too run-down for comfort. Can we hear from other recent visitors?*

Open All year.
Rooms 2 suites, 8 double, 2 single – 12 with bath, all with tea-making facilities and baby-listening; 2 bungalows serving as annexe; some ground-floor rooms.
Facilities Lounge, TV room, bar, restaurant. 30-acre grounds; 15 km to sandy beaches. English spoken.
Location 27 km from Lisbon, 17 km from Setubal off N10; in village centre. Parking.
Restriction Not suitable for &.
Credit cards None accepted.
Terms Rooms with breakfast: single 3,215 esc, double 4,960–5,460 esc. Set lunch/dinner 1300 esc. Reduced rates for children under 8; special meals provided.

BOM JESUS DO MONTE 4700 Braga Map 15

Hotel do Elevador *Tel* (053) 250.11
Parque do Bom Jesus do Monte

"Few tourists seem to come to the Minho, though this tender green *vinho verde* country is glorious to drive through and has some interesting old towns and villages. There aren't many good places to stay if you want to avoid the ugly modern hotels that sprawl along the Costa Verde, apart from the old-style Portuguese hotels at Bom Jesus, a 19th-century religious shrine on top of the mountain at Braga. This is a gem, spectacularly designed and landscaped, with stone terraces and larger-than-life statuary, gardens and little round chapels depicting the Stations of the Cross, and at the top a church and hotels, reached either by a funicular or a winding drive through dense and dripping woods. The *Hotel do Elevador*, the best hotel, is small, comfortable, with an old-fashioned elegance and a fantastic view of mountain peaks and the valley. This is more a place for the Portuguese than for tourists, so it hasn't been gussied up and spoiled. The menu, alas, is the standard hotel type but the view makes up for uninspired eating, and there's a good selection of the regional wines." Several correspondents have written to endorse this opinion, one declaring the food to be "un-imaginative" and another finding it compared favourably with most other Portuguese hotels and restaurants. *(Jose Wilson, Angela and David Stewart, Ralph Dubery)*

Open All year.
Rooms 25 double – all with bath.
Facilities Salon, restaurant. Garden.
Location 50 km NE of Oporto, 6 km SE of Braga.
Credit card Visa.
Terms [1985 rates] rooms with breakfast: single 4,000 esc, double 5,040 esc. Set meals 1,000 esc.

BUÇACO 3050 Aveiro

Map 15

Palace Hotel do Buçaco
Mata do Buçaco

Tel (031) 921.31
Telex 53049 BUCACO

"We always stay here whenever we can and spoil ourselves by taking the Royal suite – delightful and not expensive," say veteran visitors to the luxurious *Palace*. "It was a 19th-century royal hunting lodge, built with extreme examples of Manueline architecture. It stands in a large park on the Buçaco ridge, which is planted with a magnificent selection of trees, particularly cedars of Buçaco *(Cupressus lusitanica)*, which are world-famous. Originally, the park was planted by the Carmelite monks, whose monastery stands beside the hotel. Wellington spent the night in one of the monastery cells before the battle of Buçaco when he defeated the French attempt to capture Lisbon and throw the English out of Portugal. Buçaco is only 20 kilometres from Coimbra, a lovely university city but without a good hotel. There are also a number of interesting places in the neighbourhood so it makes a good centre for exploring this part of Portugal."

This year a visitor writes beguilingly: "Superlative service, exquisite furnishings and taste; superb food and wine – bargains. Their own wines (ask to visit the cellars) are unique: natural, unfiltered and matured in casks from Buçaco forest oaks. The plumbing can misbehave but nothing can detract from the abiding nostalgic memories." And another says: "Marvellous staff, kind and considerate; excellent food and plenty of it." We did receive one report that poor food and wine marred the "really beautiful setting. It is so cheap – it might be much helped if the best chef in Portugal was hired and the price of the meal doubled." *(R A Dubery, Neil Fairlamb, J A Murray, and others)*

Open All year.
Rooms 2 suites, 58 double – all with bath and telephone; some on ground floor.
Facilities Lift. Salon, TV room, bar, restaurant; conference facilities. Garden, park, forest; tennis courts, English spoken. &.
Location 20 km N of Coimbra on N234. Parking.
Credit cards All major cards accepted.
Terms Rooms with breakfast: single 4,500 esc, double 6,250 esc; dinner, B&B: single 6,000 esc, double 9.250 esc; full board: single 7,500 esc, double 12,500 esc. Set lunch/dinner 1,500 esc; full alc 2,200 esc. Reduced rates and special meals for children.

CANIÇADA 4850 Braga

Map 15

Pousada de São Bento

Tel (053) 571.90

"After a day exploring the huge market of Barcelos, the provincial cathedral town of Braga, and the rococo gardens of the pilgrimage centre of Bom Jesus, the *Pousada de São Bento*, high above the Caniçada dam in the mountains, gives a welcome feeling of rest. It is in the south-western end of the Peneda-Geres National Park, a couple of kilometres off the Braga/Chaves road, with a stupendous view of the river valley and reservoirs below and the surrounding mountain ranges. Built as an alpine chalet, the *Pousada* is small and welcoming, and a smell of pine and eucalyptus wafts everywhere. Our room was modest in size but very clean and had a pretty view through the ivy-clad windows. The service was attentive, but the food unmemorable." *(Eleo and Peter Carson)*

Later visitors add a gloss or two: "One should ask for a room looking outwards when booking (which is essential) as the rooms facing on to the courtyard can be rather noisy. There is a pleasant terrace overlooking the lake and a comfortable sitting room; also a well-maintained garden." *(D S S)* "The view across the valley to the mountains was breathtaking, the sunset was spectacular, and coffee on the terrace overlooking the attractive garden was a moment of pure magic. Food was as dull as expected and reception staff unsmiling, but dining room staff were pleasant." *(Mrs R B Richards; endorsed by M J Wilkinson)*

Open All year.
Rooms 10 – most with bath and telephone.
Facilities Lounge with TV, restaurant, terrace. Garden with swimming pool and tennis court; sailing and riding nearby.
Location 34 km from Braga; 2 km off N103 to Chaves.
Credit cards All major cards accepted.
Terms [1985 rates] rooms with breakfast: single 5,600 esc, double 5,900 esc. Set lunch/dinner from 1,250 esc.

CASCAIS 2750 Lisbon   Map 15

Albatroz   *Tel* (01) 28.28.21
Rua Frederico Arouca   *Telex* 16052

Cascais is a relatively unspoiled fishing village sharing its peninsula with Lisbon 30 kilometres to the east. The little port is watched over by a picturesque 17th-century citadel sitting on a rocky cape above the town. If you get up early enough you can join the fishermen tinkering down at the shore and painting their small boats in bright reds and yellows. A visitor this year tells us: "The *Albatroz* is near the station but is designed in such a way that the guest is unaware of the noise that usually accompanies that kind of convenience. This is one of the most pleasant hotels we have stayed in – elegantly furnished and decorated yet extremely comfortable. The bedroom and bathrooms were well equipped and everywhere was spotlessly clean. The staff were well trained and unobtrusive. The restaurant was good but expensive." Another reader was equally pleased. "A very quiet and discreet hotel in an attractive setting. We had a lovely bedroom with three balconies in the old part of the inn, and found the service very good." Visitors should ask for rooms in the older part of the hotel, rather than those in the new wing. *(Mrs J Gunn, Mrs Leslie Purdy)*

Open All year.
Rooms 40 – most with bath or shower, telephone and TV.
Facilities Lift; salon, bar, dining room. English spoken.
Location On the bay, near the station. Parking.
Credit cards Most major cards accepted.
Terms [1985 rates] rooms with breakfast: single 6,800–8,600 esc, double 9,000–10,900 esc. A la carte meals.

In Portugal, reservations for Pousadas can be made direct or through ENATUR, Avenida Santa Joana Princesa, 10-A, 1700 – Lisbon. *Tel.* Lisbon 889070. *Telex* 13609.

ÉVORA 7000   **Map 15**

Pousada dos Lóios   *Tel* (066) 240.51
Largo Conde de Vila Flor   *Telex* 43288

Évora dates from Roman times and is one of the loveliest old towns in
Portugal, pleasantly Moorish in style, with clean white buildings,
hanging gardens and tiled patios – many of the best of Alentejo coloured
tiles come from this area. There is much to see, including a Roman
temple, a museum of ancient art, and a fine Gothic cathedral, and the
Upper Alentejo is the least spoilt and most picturesque part of Portugal.
Converted from a 16th-century monastery and decorated in grand style,
the *Pousada* is worthy of Évora. "Superb," wrote one traveller; "most
comfortable rooms all with private bath and well furnished. The lovely
dining room is in the courtyard of the monastery and the food is
excellent. Service is perfect too." *(C R Wilmot-Allistone)* A visitor this
year, however, preached moderation in his description. "Certainly the
town and monastery itself are delightful. But the rooms, in fact, are poky
– not surprising as they were originally monks' cells. The dining area in
the cloisters is attractive, less so the food, and the service not too
friendly either." Others take a more favourable view: "The rooms,
though small, are well-furnished and comfortable and the plumbing gets
more maintenance than is usual. The food is as good as you will get
anywhere in Portugal." *(R A Dubery; also C F C)* More reports would be
welcome.

Open All year.
Rooms 32 – all with bath.
Facilities Salons, bar, dining area in cloisters.
Location Central, near Cathedral. Évora is 145 km SE of Lisbon.
Credit cards All major cards accepted.
Terms [1985 rates] rooms with breakfast: single 7,200 esc, double 7,500 esc; full
board 5,500–7,650 esc per person. Set lunch/dinner 1,960 esc.

FUNCHAL 9000 Madeira   **Map 15**

Quinta de Penha de França   *Tel* (091) 290.87 or 290.80
Rua da Penha de França 2

We've had almost entirely favourable reports this year about the newly
expanded *Quinta*, an already skilfully adapted period manor house
behind a walled garden about 50 metres from the sea.

"The extension (13 rooms) is a masterpiece of design and in no way
spoils the overall beauty." And: "We stayed in the new annexe. The
room was spacious as was the bathroom with two wash basins.
Plumbing worked perfectly and we were daily given heaps of large clean
towels. We had a small terrace and it was lovely sitting there in the
evening having a glass of local wine. The hotel has a secluded garden
containing a salt-water pool. The terrace restaurant was a good place to
eat lunch. The staff were exceptionally helpful and kind. Look no further
in Madeira. The big hotels are a stone's throw if you want night life and
there are lots of charming, small local eating spots." Another reader puts
it this way: "As someone now living on the island told us, Madeira is the
eighth wonder of the world. To stay at the *Quinta* gives you more than a

651

little insight into what he means." The only negative note: breakfasts were disappointing in variety and quantity. Finally, last year's report was too persuasive not to quote in part: "It's just like someone's elegant home, which indeed it is. The beautiful Senhora Ribeiro was born here and is a charming and attentive hostess." *(P A Morgan, D Crosier, J R Lloyd; also Lady Elstub)*

Open All year.
Rooms 35 double – 31 with bath, 4 with shower, all with telephone, tea-making facilities and baby-listening; some rooms with sea view.
Facilities Lounge, 2 bars, terrace. Large garden with sea-water swimming pool; near sea and rock beach. English spoken.
Location 1 km from town centre. Parking.
Restriction Not suitable for &.
Credit cards None accepted.
Terms Double room with breakfast £29–£35. No restaurant but substantial snacks available until 9 pm. 50% reduction for children aged 2–11 sharing parents' room; under 2 free.

Reid's Hotel   *Tel* (094) 230.01
Estrada Monumental 139   *Telex* 72129

A most renowned grand hotel, Madeira's offering in the five red-turret class, and especially esteemed for its magnificent semi-tropical gardens landscaped into a steep cliff overlooking Funchal Bay. Readers this year press for its reinstatement: "Quiet, calm and discreet – rather formal," recalls a recent visitor. "Standards of service very high. The meals were excellent and imaginative." Another says: "We spent one week there and I must rank it as one of the best hotels I have stayed in. Clean linen sheets every other day! The position of the hotel is superb and the extensive garden most attractive." A third remarks: "The best thing is, you don't have to think about anything. Good service in elegant surroundings (black tie for dinner if you are so inclined). Very relaxing." *(Alan Greenwood, H F King; Catherine Wilson and Dr Tony Wilson) Note:* It is essential to ask for a sea-facing room as back ones are on a noisy road.

Open All year.
Rooms 167 – most with bath or shower.
Facilities Lift; salons, dining room. Garden with heated swimming pool and tennis.
Location On W side of town, off road towards Camara de Lobos. Sea-facing rooms are quietest.
Credit cards Access, Amex, Visa.
Terms [1985 rates] rooms with breakfast: single 10,000 esc, double 16,000 esc; full board 13,000–15,000 esc per person. Set lunch/dinner 2,700–3,700 esc.

GUIMARÃES 4000 Braga   **Map 15**

Pousada de Santa Maria   *Tel* (053) 41.21.57
da Oliveira   *Telex* 32875
Largo da Oliveira

Guimarães, located about 50 kilometres north-east of Oporto at the foot of the Sierra Santa Catarina, was the birthplace in 1109 of Alfonso Henriques, the first king of Portugal. "The *Pousada* is in the centre of this exciting town – exciting to the historical imagination, that is. The rooms are full of the most superb examples of local linen. Fine dining room, good food." *(Neil Fairlamb) Michelin* give it three red turrets, but we should be glad of more details from readers.

Open All year.
Rooms 160 – most with bath or shower.
Facilities Lift, bar, salons, dining room. Garden, terrace.
Location Central.
Credit cards Possibly some accepted.
Terms [1985 rates] rooms with breakfast: single 5,600 esc, double 5,900 esc. Set lunch/dinner from 1,250 esc.

LAMEGO 5100 Viseu   Map 15

Villa Hostilina   *Tel* (054) 623.94

New to the Guide is this former farmhouse reincarnated as a rural hotel, on a hill overlooking the attractive old town of Lamego, in a wine-growing area near the Douro Valley in northern Portugal. "From the little tiled terrace that leads off your bedroom, gentle hills covered with vines roll and fold into the blue distance. Immediately below is the house's own vineyard where, if you're up early enough, you can watch the workers tend the vines. It is the most peaceful prospect imaginable. Downstairs a breakfast awaits you not only generous but gorgeous to behold – figs, peaches, quince jelly ... Thus nourished, you may set off to explore lovely Lamego – a gem. The villa, right on the edge of town, is comfortable and up-to-date, and the welcome is very warm. There is a health centre, the Instituto Kosmos, with a gymnasium (Senhor is a karate black belt). I need not tell you you will enjoy the wines of the area. If you like tranquillity, delicious food and interesting things to see, Lamego is for you." Lots of champagne tasting in the area. No restaurant. *(Shelley Cranshaw) Note:* Shelley Cranshaw's nomination of the Villa Hostilina has won her this year's Report of the Year award. For her full report, see page 747.

Open All year.
Rooms 6 double, 1 single – 2 with bath, 5 with shower, all with telephone, radio, mono TV on request.
Facilities Sitting room with TV, bar with TV, dining room (no restaurant but light meals and snacks served). Live music in bar. Health centre with gymnasium, massage, sauna etc. Garden with swimming pool and tennis courts. River with fishing rights nearby.
Location 500 metres from centre; private parking.
Restrictions No children 2–14. Not suitable for &.
Credit cards Some may be accepted.
Terms [1985 rates] rooms with breakfast: single £19, double £23; extra bed £3. (Rates likely to go up 25% in 1986.) No restaurant.

LISBON   Map 15

Albergaria Senhora do Monte   *Tel* (01) 86.28.46
Calçada do Monte 39, Lisbon 1100

"For the price, one of the best hotels we have ever stayed in – our children loved the patio off the bedroom," asserts a reader this year

653

about this small, unassuming family hotel near the top of one of the Lisbon hills, with a panorama of the city and the river Tejo. An earlier report summed up: "The reception-cum-TV room is a bit cramped, but the guest rooms are pleasant – flowered wallpaper, and a nice old-fashioned feeling. It is located in the older part of Lisbon; it feels off the tourist beat since the area is residential – crowing roosters in the morning, lettuce in the little backyard gardens. There's a bar but no restaurant – breakfast is brought to your bedrooms; there are several small, untouristy restaurants at the end of the street as well as the wonderful Lisbon streetcars to everywhere." A recent guest adds: "There weren't many staff but they were accommodating, the view was nice and the price certainly modest." (*Cathy Park, Lucia M Atlas, Helen Wallis*)

Open All year.
Rooms 4 suites, 18 double, 5 single – all with bath and telephone; TV on request.
Facilities Lounge, bar with terrace, TV room. English spoken.
Location 10 minutes from centre by streetcar; in the Graça district.
Restriction Not suitable for &.
Credit cards All major cards accepted.
Terms B&B: single 2,500–3,500 esc, double 3,500–4,800 esc. Reduced rates for children. (No restaurant.)

Hotel Tivoli Jardim　　　　　　　　　　　　　*Tel* (01) 53.99.71
Rua Julio Cesar Machado 7　　　　　　　　*Telex* 12172 JARDIM
Lisbon 1200

A modern multi-storey hotel just off the main central avenue of Lisbon, the Avenida da Liberdade. (*Note:* it should not be confused with its sister-hotel, the *Tivoli* next door.) A frequent visitor to the *Tivoli Jardim* stresses: "Good value for money, friendly (everything is relative) by Lisbon hotel standards, but not elegant. The restaurant is quite good, though better quality can be found at a quarter of the price in restaurants five minutes' walk away." Earlier reports have been more enthusiastic: "It was four years since we'd stayed here, but the hall porter greeted us like old friends." "It has no spectacular views (other than the roofs of Lisbon), but is elegant and welcoming from the moment you come in off the bustling streets. The bedrooms are exceptionally comfortable and well provided. The service, both in the public rooms and for room service, we found prompt and helpful. Cuisine, presentation and service in the restaurant fell no way short of excellent. Fine Portuguese wines, too." (*John M Sidwick, D S Smith, Madeleine Pollard, Gordon Wrigley*) More reports welcome.

Open All year.
Rooms 119 double – all with bath, telephone, radio, air-conditioning, colour TV and mini-bar.
Facilities Lift; main hall with bar, restaurant. Gardens with Tivoli club, swimming pool, tennis and bar. 12 km to beach. English spoken.
Location 10 minutes from town centre, NW of Botanical Garden. Garage and car park.
Credit cards All major cards accepted.
Terms [1985 rates] rooms with breakfast: single 6,900 esc, double 7,200 esc; full board 9,900–13,200 esc per person. Set lunch/dinner 1,500 esc.

York House (Residencia Inglesia)   *Tel* (01) 66.24.35 or 66.73.98
Rua des Janelas Verdes, 32, Lisbon 1200

Much enthusiasm once again for "this unique place", "this lovely hotel". *York House* is a hybrid establishment astride a road that contains the National Art Museum and looks down over the docks. The location itself is unattractive; and is about two kilometres from the city centre; but trams pass frequently during the day, and Lisbon taxis are cheap. The main part of the hotel, set round a courtyard, was an early 17th-century convent. The lower dining room was the former chapel, still complete with font and marble plaques. In the building there are many *azulejos* – traditional tiles. There are polished red tile floors in the rooms and huge wooden wardrobes. Along the corridors are blue and white Arraiolos rugs. The rooms that once housed the novitiates are still the cheapest. Across the street is the other part of the hotel, decorated in *belle époque* French-style with lots of red plush. Previous reports had praised its charm and character. "The furnishings are beautiful and antique, shining and spotless. The lighting is particularly good. Breakfast, tea and drinks served under the shade of huge and beautiful trees in the delightful courtyard garden. Some bedrooms face this courtyard: if you are a light sleeper, you must on no account take a room above the road which is noisy at night." The only criticism: the food was "plain".

Two readers wrote this year disagreeing about the "plain" food – "beautifully presented" and "extremely palatable". One reader continued: "Friends who are Portuguese and regard themselves as Lisbon's answer to *The Good Food Guide* were delighted and entranced." *(Lynne and Brian Freeman, Jill and Alan Dunning, M J Wilkinson)*

Open All year.
Rooms 5 suites, 47 double, 10 single – 45 with bath, 17 with shower, all with telephone; 18 rooms in annexe.
Facilities TV room, bridge room, 2 bars (1 in annexe), restaurant. Courtyard garden where meals and drinks are served. English spoken.
Location Near National Art Museum and docks. No special parking facilities.
Restriction Not suitable for &.
Credit cards All major cards accepted.
Terms B&B: single 4,800 esc, double 6,000–7,000 esc. Set meals 1,000 esc.

MARVÃO 7330 Portalagre   Map 15

Pousada de Santa Maria   *Tel* (045) 932.01 or 932.02
Telex 42360

Marvão, near the Spanish border, is six kilometres north of the main Lisbon/Madrid road and would make a useful break on a long journey. The village, of tiny white houses and narrow cobbled streets, is entirely inside the walls of a castle over which the keep stands guard. You can walk round the ramparts, looking within at the roofs, gardens, chicken runs, kitchens and television sets, or without over the Sierra de Torrico in Spain, and the valleys below in Portugal. The *Pousada*, like everything else in Marvão, is tiny. There are nine rooms. The building is of stone with tile floors, the public rooms are well furnished, the beds comfortable, you can see to read, and the hot water is dependable. The staff are few but amiable. The view from the bar is fine, and the local wine excellent. Prices are very reasonable. A reader this year puts it plainly: "The small staff is not only amiable but also very efficient. The food is a good deal better than that of the average Portuguese hotel. Car essential. Stay as long as they will keep you." The Portuguese know their state hotels are good and use them – so make reservations. *(R A Dubery)*

Open All year.
Rooms 9 double – all with bath and telephone.
Facilities Lounge, bar, restaurant. Garden. Riding. English spoken.
Location 22 km N of Portalagre on N521.
Credit cards All major cards accepted.
Terms B&B: single occupancy 4,600–7,000 esc, double 4,900–7,500 esc. Set lunch/dinner 1,500–2,500 esc; full alc 2,000 esc. Reduced rates for children under 12; special meals.

MONCHIQUE 8550 Faro   Map 15

Estalagem Abrigo de Montanha   *Tel* (082) 921.31
Corte Dereira/Estrada de Foia

In the Algarve, halfway between the hill town of Monchique and the peak of Foia, this *Estalagem* is 500 metres up with fine views over the green hills and lush valleys. "There is a main building and a long tier of separate apartments at the other end of a pretty garden. Wonderful mixture of flowers. It is family owned and run, and good English is spoken. Hot water is more reliable in the main hotel rooms, which are also cheaper (but smaller and lacking a balcony) than the annexe suites." This year another reader coos: "I could dine on the black olives, fresh white fish and green wine at the *Estalagem* for a long, long time before I'd get bored with it. And lunch on the terrace there, under the chestnut trees with the sweeping view of the valley below, is a memorable experience. The peacefulness of the surroundings is slightly marred (but very slightly) by the rock quarry down the hillside. The staff couldn't be warmer or more hospitable, the surrounding forests of cork, chestnut, and eucalyptus trees are lovely, and the inn itself with its flower-filled garden is most beautiful. It was one of the cheapest places we have stayed in and perhaps the most wonderful." *(Helen Wallis; also Michael J Wilkinson)*

Warning: It can be cold and wet in Monchique even when blazing on the coast. And one reader last year cautioned that the peace can be shattered when coach parties arrive for lunch.

Open All year.
Rooms 3 suites, 5 double – all with bath and telephone; 2 rooms in annexe.
Facilities Bar with TV, dining room. Garden, terrace. English spoken.
Location About 25 km inland from Portimão. Hotel is 2 km on road to Foia from Monchique. Parking.
Restriction Not suitable for &.
Credit cards All major cards accepted.
Terms Rooms with breakfast 3,000–4,000 esc; half-board 4,500–5,600 esc; full board 6,000–7,200 esc. Set lunch/dinner 1,000 esc; full alc 1,200 esc.

Important reminder: terms printed must be regarded as a rough guide only to the size of the bill to be expected at the end of your stay. For latest tariffs, check when booking.

MURTOSA 3870 Aveiro   Map 15

Pousada da Ria   *Tel* (034) 483.32
Ria de Aveiro   *Telex* 37061

Down the coast from Oporto is Murtosa, a fishing village on the Aveiro
lagoon, a wide inlet full of every kind of small ocean-going vessel. The
Pousada da Ria – a restaurant with rooms, each with a covered balcony
and a good view – "is an oasis, well managed and maintained. The
design of the reception area with its indoor garden and pool is
welcoming and cool, but bedroom and bathroom walls could do with
soundproofing." *(Daphne and Frank Hodgson)* More reports welcome,
including on the restaurant.

Open All year.
Rooms 2 suites, 8 double – all with bath, telephone and balcony.
Facilities Salon, TV room, restaurant. Garden; outdoor swimming pool. Near
river with fishing; beach 2 km (but sea a bit rough). English spoken.
Location On N327 15 km SW of Murtosa. Parking.
Credit cards All major cards accepted.
Terms Rooms with breakfast: single 4,350 esc, double 4,600 esc. Set lunch/dinner
1,600 esc.

OBIDOS 2510 Leiria   Map 15

Estalagem do Convento   *Tel* (062) 952.17
Rua Dom João D'Ornelas

"Obidos is a medieval walled town, almost perfectly preserved, perched
high on a hill with a warren of cobbled alleys and flower-skirted piazzas.
On the outskirts of the wall is the *Estalagem do Convento*. When we
arrived the manager said sorry, he was full. However, he took us to a
tiny building next to the church as ancient as the hotel itself. Table and
chairs and other bits and pieces I'm sure were medieval too! The beds
turned out to be below in another tiny room reached by a delightful
18-inch wide spiral staircase. The bedroom, although small, was entirely
adequate and there was an efficient shower room attached. For sheer
novelty we have never seen the like and we really felt we were back in
medieval Portugal. The hotel itself is quite fascinating with lots of dark
rooms and pretty cobbled courtyards. The food and service generally
were good. We would not recommend this hotel to anyone preferring
light, modern, plush comfort. It was, after all, built a long time ago for
purposes very different from the pampering of today's finicky travellers,
but if, like us, you want to feel the past as much as it is possible to do
then the hotel will suit you down to the ground." *(J O Nairn)*

Open All year.
Rooms 6 suites, 20 double – 14 with bath, all with telephone.
Facilities 2 lounges, bar, TV room, dining room. Garden. English spoken.
Location In town centre. Parking.
Restriction Not suitable for &.
Credit cards Access, Visa.
Terms B&B: 5,000 esc; dinner, B&B: single 6,500 esc, double 8,000 esc; full board:
single 8,000 esc, double 11,000 esc. Set lunch 500 esc, dinner 1,500 esc; full alc
2,500 esc (excluding service). Reduced rates and special meals for children.

OLIVEIRA DO HOSPITAL 3400 Coimbra   Map 15

Pousada de Santa Bárbara   *Tel* (038) 522.52

This modern government-owned inn is on the Coimbra/Salamanca road, seven kilometres east of the small town of Oliveira do Hospital itself. It has a magnificent view of the 6,600 feet high Serra do Estrella, the highest mountain range in Portugal, and it is a good base from which to explore the area. The bedrooms are standard hotel type, with baths, and there are excellent public rooms. The service is essentially friendly and helpful and the cooking first-class. "Superb in every way – and such good value for money." *(Madeleine Westlake)*

Open All year.
Rooms 16 double – all with bath, telephone, tea-making facilities and baby-listening. 2 ground-floor rooms.
Facilities Sitting room, TV room, restaurant. Large garden with mini-tennis; lake and river fishing. English spoken.
Location On Coimbra/Salamanca road about 80 km E of Coimbra and 7 km E of Oliveira do Hospital.
Restriction Not suitable for &.
Credit cards All major cards accepted.
Terms [1985 rates] rooms with breakfast: single 4,600–5,600 esc, double 4,900–5,900 esc; dinner, B&B: single 5,800–6,800 esc, double 7,300–8,300 esc; full board: single 7,000–8,000 esc, double 9,700–10,700 esc. Set lunch 1,300 esc, dinner 2,600 esc. Reduced rates and special meals for children.

OPORTO 4000   Map 15

Malaposta   *Tel* (02) 262.78
Rua de Conceição 80

"Good hotels in Oporto seem difficult to find, so let me commend the *Malaposta*. Though very central, it is quiet and cool, with a car park around the corner. No meals, but plenty of good restaurants are at hand and the hotel provides an excellent cheap base." *(Neil Fairlamb)* More reports welcome.

Open All year.
Rooms 37 – some with bath, some with telephone.
Facilities Lift, salon, breakfast room. English spoken.
Location Central; parking.
Credit cards Most major cards accepted.
Terms [1985 rates] rooms with breakfast: single 2,100 esc, double 2,800 esc. (No restaurant.)

PALMELA 2950 Costa de Lisboa   Map 15

Pousada do Castelo de Palmela   *Tel* (01) 235.12.26 or 235.13.95
                                            Telex 42290 PPALM

Palmela, an hour's drive south from Lisbon, stands in tiers on the northern slopes of a hillside, a small and very pretty white-walled town. Here the State-run Pousada is a recently transformed monastery inside a 1,000-year-old castle. Readers this year are unanimous in their admiration for the situation and ambience of this Pousada: "A first-class hotel in a commanding position, with a sumptuous interior and good food." And: "There was no hint of discomfort. The bed, the bath, the restaurant, the cloisters – set out with flowers, deckchairs and umbrellas – were downright glamorous. The castle is on the top of a hill and you can see for miles, even sitting on the loo. The landscape is of windmills, orange groves and the distant shore. We thought the restaurant splendid. The olives on the table were to olives what Muscatel is to the grape." Sadly, readers this year are also unanimous in condemning the staff. "The reception/booking staff could not have been ruder or less helpful." Another wrote: "I shall visit here again because of the atmosphere but I did not care for the off-hand reception." Others disagree about the food, some finding it "inevitably dull". An inspector thinks that tourists often expect too much of restaurants in pousadas *and* paradores *because the settings are so magnificent, but in these government hotels it is a mistake to expect very refined meals at the prices charged.* (M J Wilkinson, Shelley Cranshaw, Mrs R B Richards, and others)

Open All year.
Rooms 2 suites, 25 double – all with bath, telephone and radio; some ground-floor rooms.
Facilities Lift, ramps; lounge, breakfast room, bar, TV room, dining room. Large grounds with heated swimming pool and children's play area. Sandy beaches with safe bathing nearby; river 7 km with fishing and sailing. English spoken. &.
Location 7 km from Setúbal in centre of village. Parking for 40 cars.
Credit cards All major cards accepted.
Terms [1985 rates] rooms with breakfast: single occupancy 7,200 esc, double 7,500 esc; full board 10,100–13,300 esc per person. Set lunch/dinner 1,450–1950 esc.

PRAIA DO GUINCHO 2750 Lisbon   **Map 15**

Hotel do Guincho   *Tel* (01) 285.04.91
                                                              Telex 43138

Our 1984 edition carried this description: "About ten minutes (nine kilometres) from Cascais, on a beautiful, practically deserted stretch of coastline is this dazzling white 15th-century fort that has been converted to a luxury hotel with great style and charm. There is a most impressive integration of old and new architecture – the vaulted brick ceilings in the old stone building must have been newly done but look as if they were always there. Even the fireplace brick is laid in interesting chevron and herringbone designs. It is one of the most beautiful buildings I've ever seen. The views are superb – a great sweep of ocean all round." (Jose Wilson) *The entry was omitted last year, after an inspector raised doubts about value for money in this five-star establishment, but a visitor this year writes: "Indeed a splendid position, on a rocky outcrop between two stunning sandy beaches in an isolated part of the coast. But because of the position the hotel is rather exposed to the wind. Whilst the atmosphere is friendly and efficient, the hotel is relatively small and sophisticated – the dining room, certainly, is quite formal. I can't imagine going there happily with children. The rooms were well decorated, clean, attractive and extremely comfortable. The best rooms are at the front, overlooking the sea. The food was excellent and particularly good value. We had small quibbles: the electrics were decidedly dubious, and if you want to swim you have to go all the way to Cascais. But it's really an outstanding hotel and we'll definitely return."* (Penny Duckham) *Another reader felt the hotel had been mean to those guests on half-board terms, giving little choice, and modest helpings. Can we hear from other visitors, please?*

Open All year.
Rooms 39 – all with bath or shower.
Facilities Lift, salons, bar, dining room, inner courtyard. Garden; golf course and beach with watersports nearby. English spoken.
Location 9 km NW of Cascais.
Credit cards All major cards accepted.
Terms Rooms with breakfast: single 8,500 esc, double 11,000 esc, half-board 1,950 esc per person.

SANTA BARBARA DE NEXE 8000 Algarve   Map 15

Hotel La Réserve   *Tel* (089) 912.34 or 914.74
Telex 56790 FUCHS

The only Portuguese member of the *Relais et Châteaux* association, the hotel – nine kilometres from Faro and the same distance from the golden Algarve beaches – is a modern, elegant establishment with 20 air-conditioned suites each with its own kitchenette and a view of the distant sea. It is well away from the coastal hubbub, surrounded by five acres of beautifully laid-out gardens with two swimming pools. Readers' impressions vary widely this year as they did last. This fresh report provides one semi-positive view of Victor and Katya Fuchs' establishment: "One must separate the hotel from the restaurant. The hotel is almost faultless, the best on the Algarve. After a day of touring it is a delight to return to such a haven of peace and good taste. We had an apartment on two levels which was without question the most pleasant accommodation I have come across. Turning to the restaurant: the food was excellent but very expensive and pretentious, and the general layout did nothing to provide a relaxed atmosphere." Other readers have been more disgruntled about the food as well as the service. As one sophisticated traveller pointed out, perhaps the well-meaning Fuchs have set over-high standards that cannot be maintained. More reports please. *(G H Ross, Dr and Mrs P M Tattersall, T G Taylor, H Bramwell, and others)*

Open All year, except Nov. Restaurant closed Tue.
Rooms 20 suites, all with bath, telephone, radio, TV and kitchenette. 6 ground-floor rooms.
Facilities Large lounge, snack bar, 2 bars, restaurant, ramps. 5-acre gardens, tennis court (no charge), table tennis, 2 unheated swimming pools. Sandy beaches, safe bathing, boating, fishing, surfing, windsurfing, waterskiing, riding, golf (15 minutes by car). English spoken. &.
Location 9 km from Faro: take main road towards Patacao, and ask at petrol station. Parking.
Restriction No children.
Credit cards None accepted.
Terms [1985 rates] B&B: single £35–£55, double £55–£75. Snack bar or terrace lunch: £10; full alc £25.

All hotel prices are approximate. Portuguese prices are more approximate than others.

Sterling and dollar equivalents of foreign currencies at the date of going to press will be found on page 787.

SINTRA 2710 Lisbon   Map 15

Hotel Palácio dos Seteais   *Tel* (01) 923.32.00
Rua Barbosa do Bocage 8   *Telex* 14410 HOPASE P

*"Lo, Sintra's glorious Eden intervenes
In variegated maze of mount and glen."*

Thus in *Childe Harold* does Byron sing of this famous hill town, set
dramatically against the north face of the *serra*. The *Palace of Seteais*, built
a year before the poet's birth, sits regally about a mile away down the
Colares road. It is one of the *few de luxe* country houses in Portugal.
"Sheer bliss here, everyone was so kind – it was paradise," extols a
recent visitor. "An enchanting place in a beautiful garden, with a
panoramic view over a tapestry countryside to the Atlantic coast. High
ceilings, delicately painted walls, and antique furniture give a feeling of
elegance and graciousness of more leisured times. Service is good and
pleasant. Bedrooms are large and comfortable. The bathrooms are as
large as many hotel bedrooms. The main salon is a superb room. The
bar, near the attractive and spacious dining room, opens on to a terrace
with tables and chairs. The dinner was excellent. The wine was a
delicious Colares white. *Seteais* is just around the corner from this
famous wine-growing area. Breakfast was generous – large orange juice,
very good coffee. It is luxurious, quiet and peaceful, and certainly value
for money." *(Mrs Leslie Purdy, R A Dubery, Neil Fairlamb, and others)*

Open All year.
Rooms 1 suite, 17 double – all with bath; some ground-floor rooms.
Facilities Lift; salons, bar, restaurant, terrace. Garden. Beach 10 km with water
sports. English spoken.
Location 1 km W of Sintra on Colares road. Parking.
Credit cards All major cards accepted.
Terms [1985 rates] rooms: single from 10,000 esc, double from 11,000 esc. Set
lunch/dinner from 2,600 esc. Reduced rates for children's meals.

Estalagem Quinta dos Lobos   *Tel* (01) 923.02.10

Estalagem Quinta da Capela   *Tel* (01) 929.01.70
Monserrate

Both the *Quinta dos Lobos* and its sister the *Quinta da Capela* (about 2
kilometres down the Colares road past Monserrate) are manor houses
rebuilt after the great earthquake of 1755. "It would be hard to choose
between these two varieties of delights. Both offer the chance to lodge in
historic buildings restored with a sense of generous proportion and
exemplary taste in the details of the bedrooms and public rooms.
Glorious views and splendid valley sunsets. Both properties are very
quiet, and the willing service is deftly unobtrusive. No meals but use of
the kitchen. Fresh flowers everywhere, rooms carefully looked after
each day. These two places restore the mind and spirits." However, one
reader's stay was marred by a mix-up over booking; he felt the *Capela*
was less than clean, noisy and in a bad state of disrepair. *(Neil Fairlamb;
endorsed by Mr M J Wilkinson and Cathy C Bassiouni; R A D)*

Estalagem Quinta dos Lobos
Open All year.
Rooms 8 double – all with bath and shower, telephone and baby-listening.
Facilities 2 lounges, bar. No restaurant but use of kitchen. 8-acre grounds with woods, gardens, small unheated swimming pool; near sandy beaches with fishing. English spoken.
Location From National Palace of Sintra take road to Seteais; take right turn for hotel.
Credit cards None accepted.
Terms B&B: single 4,500–4,800 esc, double 4,800–5,200 esc.

Estalagem Quinta da Capela
Open All year.
Rooms 2 suites, 9 double – all with bath and shower, telephone and baby-listening. Some in cottages. Ground-floor rooms.
Facilities 2 lounges, bar, gym and sauna. 15-acre grounds and woodlands with swimming pool; sandy beaches, fishing nearby. English spoken.
Location From National Palace of Sintra take road to Seteais, then follow road to Monserrate; hotel is on right.
Credit cards None accepted.
Terms B&B: single 4,500–4,800 esc, double 4,800–5,200 esc.

VALENÇA DO MINHO 4930 Viana do Castelo Map 15

Pousada de São Teotónio *Tel* (051) 222.52 or 222.42
Telex 32837 PSTEOT

"This welcoming and efficiently run *Pousada* is built on the 17th-century ramparts of a Vaubanesque frontier fortress and commands a splendid view of the Minho river-frontier with Spain, Eiffel's road and rail bridge and the Spanish cathedral citadel of Tuy. Valença itself is pretty if trippery but the Minho valley offers gentle classical landscapes and vinho verde. The pleasant modern rooms in the main hotel share the view with the airy and comfortable lounge and restaurant. The *Pousada* is well placed for a night or two's stop on the main road into Portugal from the north. A recent visitor writes: "In the Portuguese tradition, everything starts late in the morning – the hot water as well as the 8 o'clock breakfast – but we can heartily recommend this beautifully located and well-managed *Pousada*. The beautiful linen table scarves were brought here from Viana do Castelo. I especially recommend the Minho River salmon and *broa*, the local bread made with cornmeal. The Dão wines were excellent." *(Dr Jacob Brynes)*

Open All year.
Rooms 16 double – all with bath and telephone; 4 rooms in annexe.
Facilities 2 lounges, restaurant, garden. 1 km from river; fishing; 25 km from sea. English spoken.
Location On Portuguese/Spanish frontier, 37km NE of Viana do Castelo, on E50.
Restriction Not suitable for &.
Credit cards All major cards accepted.
Terms [1985 rates] B&B: single 5,600 esc, double 5,900 esc. Set lunch/dinner 1,500–2,150 esc. Children under 8 half price; special meals.

> Hotels are dropped if we lack positive feedback. If you can endorse an entry, please do so.

VILA VIÇOSA 7160 Évora

Map 15

Casa dos Arcos *Tel* (068) 425.18
Praça Martim Afonso de Sousa 16

The town of Vila Viçosa is just about due east of Lisbon near the Spanish frontier. "It is most charming with its avenues of orange trees. The dukes of Bragança had their summer palace here and it is well worth a visit." The *Casa dos Arcos* – bed and breakfast only, but the four suites have their own kitchenettes – is a renaissance palace with distinctive neo-classical wall decorations. "All the rooms have been tastefully decorated in keeping with the period. The frescoes in the living room are original. The villa is owned by Maria Ribeiro. Her mother, who helps her with the management, is very knowledgeable on Portuguese history." No meals other than breakfast are provided but there are several reasonable restaurants nearby. Senhora Ribeiro herself, sending an alluring brochure of her palace, writes: "It is not a hotel, it is a family house, or better yet, a stately home. The owner would like guests to book in advance, as it is her home. The lady normally takes breakfast with the guests." *(Dr Diana M Smith)*

Open All year except Christmas.
Rooms 4 suites, 2 double, 4 single – all with shower and interphones; kitchenettes in suites. Ground-floor rooms.
Facilities 2 sitting rooms, study, lounge, veranda, TV room; courtyard and small orchard with orange trees. English spoken.
Location Central. Parking.
Restriction Not suitable for &.
Credit cards All major cards accepted.
Terms B&B: single 3,000 esc, double 3,500 esc, suites 4,000 esc. (No restaurant.)

Spain

HOSPEDERÍA REAL MONASTERIO
GUADALUPE

ALMAGRO Ciudad Real Map 15

Parador Nacional de Almagro *Tel* (926) 86.01.00
Ronda de San Francisco

Almagro is due south of Madrid, about halfway between the capital and
Jaén – a useful stop on the way to Granada or Malaga. Several readers
nominate this recently opened *parador* in the warmest terms: "Almagro
houses a 14th-century theatre, the oldest of its kind in Europe, and if
you want to see what the Globe in London was like you will find out in
this delightful town centre. The air-conditioning is excellent, and so are
the bedrooms. We have been using *paradores* for 20 years and this
converted 15th-century convent is certainly one of the best." (*Osmond
Edwards*) "The *parador* is beautifully and imaginatively restored; the staff
are pleasant, and not effusive; and the food is marvellous. Absolutely
the best of the many *paradores* we stayed in." (*Neil French*; also *E D
Taylor*)

Open All year.
Rooms 55 rooms – all with bath or shower, some with air-conditioning.
Facilities Dining room, conference room. Garden with swimming pool.
Location Central.

665

Restriction Not suitable for &.
Credit cards Probably some accepted.
Terms [1985 rates, excluding 5% tax] rooms: single 3,200–5,200pts, double 5,000–6,500pts. Breakfast 500pts; set lunch/dinner 1,600pts.

ANTEQUERA Málaga   Map 15

Parador Nacional de Antequera   *Tel* (952) 84.00.51
Garcia del Olmo Paseo

Two visitors have written to tell us of this recently opened *parador* just off the N342 between Granada and Jerez de la Frontera. One found it no more than a comfortable night's stop, on the outskirts of an interesting town, and was unenthusiastic about the food. Another was altogether more positive: "Antequera is a splendid base from which to explore the mountainous Andalusian countryside, inland from Málaga, but well away from the ghastliness of the Costa del Sol. The *parador* is newly built, having replaced the nearby Albergo (now closed). It is furnished in modern style, without suits of armour and tapestries on the walls, and is comfortable, clean and welcoming. There is a fine view over the valley with its rows of olive trees. The town museum with Roman relics is within easy walking distance. The newly created garden contains a swimming pool and the hotel's public rooms are large and comfortably furnished. Meals are excellent and, with one exception, we found the service good." (*L B Pinnell*)

Open All year.
Rooms 55 double – all with bath and air-conditioning.
Facilities Bar, dining room, conference room. Garden with swimming pool.
Location Off N342 between Granada and Jerez de la Frontera. Hotel is on the outskirts of the town.
Restriction Probably not suitable for &.
Credit cards All major cards accepted.
Terms [1985 rates, excluding 5% tax] double rooms, 4,500–6,000pts. Breakfast 500pts; set lunch/dinner 1,600pts.

BAÑALBUFAR Mallorca   Map 15

Mar I Vent   *Tel* (71) 61.00.25
José Antonio 47–49

Popular with readers since our very first edition, this little hotel, one of the oldest on the island and in the same family for four generations, has won further laudatory reports this year: "Truly excellent" (*J Fedigan*); "A haven of tranquillity and exceptional value" (*C L Lovejoy*). Previous reports noted that it was "not for those who want bright lights and jolly bar sessions – quiet, charming, with heavenly views; though I went alone I was never lonely as its small size fosters friendliness." Run by a brother and sister, Tony and Juanita Vives, the hotel is in a small and peaceful fishing village on the rugged west coast, the most scenic part of the island. There are wonderful views of the sea and cliffs from the hotel and its swimming pool on the sun terrace below, as well as good bathing from a tiny cove about 15 minutes' stroll by winding pathways through the terraced tomato fields. The hills behind offer exhilarating walking country. The hotel was built in the 18th century, and though much modernised it still retains some older features. There is antique furniture in the public and private rooms, and the comfortable lounges have English books. Bedrooms are furnished in local style; some are smallish, but all are bright, airy and well cared for. The best are usually reserved for regular clients. All the staff speak English. The food is said to be simple Mallorcan of the best quality. One visitor this year informs us that "rooms in a delightful new annexe provide a higher standard of accommodation, but are noisier at night, and the additional numbers causes periodic congestion in the sitting rooms. But these are minor inconveniences when weighed against the overall charm of the hotel and the courtesy and professionalism of the owners." (*Dr M A McDonald*)

Open 1 Feb–5 Dec.
Rooms 16 double, 3 single – all with bath, telephone and balcony. Some ground-floor rooms.
Facilities Lift; 2 salons (1 with TV), bar/restaurant. Terrace with swimming pool; tennis court. Sea-bathing in nearby coves; fine walks. English spoken.
Location 24 km NW of Palma, at entrance of village. Parking.
Restriction Not suitable for &.
Credit cards All major cards accepted.
Terms B&B: single 2,125pts, double 3,200pts; dinner, B&B: single 3,350pts, double 5,300pts; full board: single 4,100pts, double 6,750pts. Set lunch/dinner 1,300pts; full alc 2,750pts. 10% reduction for children sharing parents' rooms; special meals.

BURGOS   Map 15

Landa Palace Hotel   *Tel* (947) 20.63.43
Carretera de Madrid Irún

A five-star hotel on the Madrid road, this is a natural for any anthology of the grandest hotels in the world. The main hall is an impressive tower reconstructed from a country castle dating from the 14th century. Above it is the King of Spain's suite, with gold fittings in the bathroom, Isabel II's bed, sumptuously comfortable sofas and English prints. Almost everything that can be made in marble is. Parts are like a museum: there are collections of beds and cribs from many places, wall clocks of various kinds, a teapot collection and much else besides. There is also a remarkable indoor swimming pool in a vault, surrounded by plants. You can swim out one end to an outdoor pool surrounded by lawns. "The best hotel for all-round excellence in ten days' Spanish touring. Our room was lovely and everywhere there were little touches for your comfort", and "still, in my view, one of the best hotels in Spain and impossible to fault either service or *cuisine*", are two recent tributes. A visitor commends the local speciality of milk-fed lamb and adds mysteriously: "A very atmospheric dining room complete with ghostly voices – like staying in a museum of Victoriana." (*H Bramwell, R A Dubery*)

Open All year.
Rooms 9 suites, 27 double, 6 single – all with bath, telephone, air-conditioning, tea-making facilities and baby-listening.
Facilities Lift, hall, TV room, 3 salons, bar, restaurant; conference/banqueting facilities. Garden, swimming pool. English spoken. Possibly suitable for &.
Location 1.5 km S of Burgos on Madrid road.
Credit cards Amex, Visa.

Terms B&B: single 6,575pts, double 10,150pts; dinner, B&B: single 9,775pts, double 16,550pts; full board: single 11,700pts, double 20,400pts. Set lunch/dinner 3,400pts. Special meals for children.

CADIZ
Map 15

Hotel Atlántico
Tel (956) 212301
Parque Genovés 9

"Not exactly a charming little old hotel, the 173-room *Atlántico* was built in the late twenties but extensively modernised and rebuilt a few years ago; it was opened in its new incarnation by the King and Queen in 1982. We stayed in a room with a balcony looking out over the harbour entrance. Food was superb, dinner and breakfast both buffets with a magnificent choice and excellent service. The public rooms are spacious and comfortable, and a resident pianist performs in the evenings. It is a good spot in summer, as the Atlantic breeze cools the temperature. The only drawback is that nearby buildings are a bit decrepit." *(L B Pinnell)*

Open All year.
Rooms 173 double – all with bath and air-conditioning.
Facilities Salons, dining room. Pianist in evening. Sea, beaches, fishing, watersports nearby.
Location Central, next to Parque Genovés.
Restriction Probably not suitable for ♿.
Credit cards Probably some accepted.
Terms [1985 rates, excluding 5% tax] Double rooms 6,000–7,500pts. Breakfast 500pts; set lunch/dinner 1,800pts.

CALONGE Gerona
Map 15

Hostal Los Porches
Tel (972) 50

"We have spent our family summer holidays here for seventeen years. It is clean, well run, modest, cheap and an ideal base for a family that wants to eat in the evenings when tired or explore the restaurants and sights of the Costa Brava without living in the architectural monstrosities with which the coast is littered – the hotel is in the Costa Brava area but two-and-a-half miles from the sea. All its rooms are double, all have private bath (primitive tub and shower but decent plumbing by Spanish standards) and half of them have beautiful views over the elegant hotel garden and the distant hills. The hotel's restaurant, across the road, is basically Catalan but the owner/manager, Alberto Laviña, is Swiss-trained and can produce anything to order. Breakfast is first-class, usually including some cold ham. The prices are extraordinarily cheap. The pleasant town of Calonge is still more or less untouched by foreigners." *(T G Rosenthal)* This earlier report is endorsed by our inspector, who also pays tribute to the warm and relaxed reception of the Laviña family.

Open May – Sept.
Rooms 36 – all with bath and radio.
Facilities Breakfast room, restaurant (over the road). Garden.
Location 15 km SW of Palafrugell. Hotel is central.
Credit cards None accepted.
Terms [1985 rates] rooms: single 2,050pts, double 4,050pts. Breakfast 400pts.

CARMONA Seville   Map 15

Parador Nacional Alcázar del Rey Don Pedro   *Tel* (954) 14.10.10

The King and Queen of Spain formally opened this *parador* ten years ago, and it is certainly worthy of a royal opening. It has been built inside the massive walls of the ancient Moorish alcázar on the top of a hill, from which there are marvellous views over the wide green plain of the Guadalquivir valley, with mountains on the northern horizon. Although the hotel itself is new, it has been built in the Spanish renaissance manner, with Moorish influences: pierced wooden shutters and doors in the public rooms, a patio with a fountain in the middle. The walls, whitewashed or of honey-coloured brick, are sparingly punctuated with black or brown wooden and leather furniture. There is a sumptuous sitting room; the dining room is a cool, lofty hall. There is also a swimming pool – a model of good taste, with natural brick and grass surrounds; arcades to protect you from the sun; white-painted garden furniture and colourful flowers.

In short, a thoroughly superior example of the *parador* species. All our correspondents have enjoyed their visits, though there have been a few cavils: poor insulation in the bedrooms, for instance, and inadequate heating in the public rooms in March. One correspondent this year told us that he had to keep his bedroom windows closed because of the heavy lorries on the Seville/Cordoba road below, and also mentioned a pervasive smell, which he rather liked, from the nearby cattle compounds. Complaints in the past about the food have stopped, and splendid buffet breakfasts get a special commendation. (*R A Dubery, M A Goulding*)

Open All year.
Rooms 47 double, 8 single – 50 with bath, 5 with shower, all with telephone, some with balcony; some ground-floor rooms.
Facilities Lifts, hall, sitting room with TV, dining room, room for functions and banquets, air-conditioning. Patio and garden with swimming pool. English spoken. &.
Location In town centre (hotel is signposted). Parking.
Credit cards All major cards accepted.
Terms [1985 rates, excluding 5% tax] rooms: single 3,000–5,000pts, double 5,500–7,500pts. Breakfast 500pts; set lunch/dinner 1,800pts.

CHINCHÓN   Map 15

Parador Nacional de Chinchón   *Tel* (91) 89 40 836
Avenida del Generalísimo 1

"The village of Chinchón is not that far from Madrid, in lovely rolling countryside with vines and olive groves. The approach is unprepossessing, but suddenly you pass an old monastery, which is the recently converted *parador*, and enter the village square. The square is actually a circle, used as a bullring in the summer and surrounded by ancient houses with balconies. The ground floors are mostly bars selling the well-known local anis, Chinchón, sweet or dry. If your taste is for Pernod, you can have a drink in every bar (about 15).

"The *parador* is probably one of the best we stayed at in Spain – light, airy and homely. The staff were very friendly and attempted to speak

English. Reception is small, but the corridors nearby form a square around a beautiful garden with a working fountain. It rather resembles an Oxford college, being the cloisters of the old monastery. There is also a large garden at the back on several different levels with fruit trees, shrubs, benches, fountains and a swimming pool. It is very secluded and rather romantic. The bedrooms all have bathrooms, enormous single beds (no doubles) and adequate furnishings. The only drawback is that there are no carpets, only rugs laid on tiles – cold in the winter and noisy at all times. Food was superior *parador* fare, and the wine cheap, but there are also some fine restaurants up the hill." (*J & K Archer*)

Open All year.
Rooms 38 double – all with bath.
Facilities Dining room, conference room. 2 gardens, one with swimming pool. Some English spoken.
Location 46 km from Madrid. Hotel is central in village.
Restriction Probably not suitable for &.
Credit cards All major cards accepted.
Terms [1985 rates, excluding 5% tax] double rooms 5,500–7,500pts. Breakfast 500pts. Set lunch/dinner 1,800pts.

CIUDAD RODRIGO Salamanca   Map 15

Parador Nacional Enrique II   *Tel* (923) 460150
Plaza del Castillo 1

This *parador* is housed in the castle-alcázar on a hill in the heart of the town near the banks of the river Agueda. The alcázar, a Moorish fortress, is an imposing, somewhat grim-looking building, with crenellated walls and a keep. The beautiful garden mitigates the austere masonry, and the dining room has a magnificent view overlooking the river, the historic town and the countryside. A visitor this year writes: "The *parador* is approached through a maze of medieval narrow streets. Built in 1310, it is being refurbished with modern conveniences including central heating/air conditioning and sizeable bathrooms. There is a beamed and arched dining room with pleasant, middle-aged Spanish ladies waiting at table. Unusually friendly *parador* staff: the receptionist even went out to buy postcards for us when their supply ran out. Food included many regional dishes and the now ubiquitous *parador* buffet. The *parador* is well sited for forays into Portugal 50 miles to the west and to Salamanca to the east." (*H Bramwell*; also *P L Ashton*)

Open All year.
Rooms 16 double, 12 single – all with bath, telephone and air-conditioning.
Facilities Dining room, lounges. Garden. River nearby; fishing.
Location On hill in centre of town.
Restriction Probably not suitable for &.
Credit cards All major cards accepted.
Terms [1985 rates, excluding 5% tax] double rooms 4,500–6,500pts. Breakfast 500pts; set lunch/dinner 1,600pts.

When hotels fail to return their questionnaire, we have quoted 1985 prices, with a note to that effect.

CÓRDOBA Andalucia   Map 15

Parador Nacional de la Arruzafa   *Tel* (957) 27.59.00
Avenida de la Arruzafa

The *Parador*, in the hilly northern suburbs, will suit those who seek a cool retreat after a hard day's sightseeing. Rooms are large, with wide balconies looking down on the city and the mountains beyond. It is a modern building of no great distinction, and we would not put it in the first division of *paradores*. But the rooms are quiet after the hubbub of the city, and the orange groves send up marvellous scent if you are there at the right time of the year. Readers continue to endorse, with mild reservations, this earlier comment: "Although lacking the baronial splendour of some *paradores*, this was most comfortable. Its huge pool beautifully landscaped with groves of different coloured oleanders was as pleasant to look at from our big balcony as it was to swim in on a hot day." (*Mrs R B Richards*; also *Richard Oake, M A Goulding*)

Open All year.
Rooms 83 double – all with bath or shower, telephone, radio and air-conditioning, most with balcony.
Facilities Lift; lounges, bar, restaurant; conference facilities. Garden with terrace, swimming pool and tennis court. Possibly suitable for &.
Location 3½ km N of Córdoba on road to El Brillante; garage parking.
Credit cards All major cards accepted.
Terms [1985 rates, excluding 5% tax] rooms: single occupancy 4,500–5,500pts, double 6,500–7,500pts. Breakfast 500pts; set lunch/dinner 1,800pts.

DEYÁ Mallorca   Map 15

Hotel Es Molí   *Tel* (971) 63.90.00
Carretera de Valldemossa s/b   *Telex* 69007 SMOLI

"This lovely artistic village, at the foot of the Teix mountains on the rugged coast of north-west Mallorca, has one of the most perfect settings in the Mediterranean, on the beautiful coastline between Valldemossa and Soller with its sunny valleys of oranges and lemons. The hotel has beautiful air-conditioned rooms, each with its own private bathroom and most with a balcony. Summertime meals are normally taken on the terrace overlooking the magnificent gardens containing masses of brilliantly coloured flowers, fruit and shrubs. The swimming pool is bedazzling in its beauty, bright blue, with mountains at the rear and a sea view. If you do not wish to languish by the pool, sipping sangria in the very comfortable chairs, or linger on the lawns under the persimmon trees, listening to the tinkling fresh water coming down from the mountains to the seven springs of Es Molí, then the hotel provides a minibus, morning and afternoon, to its private beach (or bathing platform) at Muleta, about 20 minutes' drive away. Here there is magnificent deep-water bathing from a rocky platform. Comfortable chairs are provided in which to laze, while if one wishes to be in the shade one can ascend steps to many terraces under sweet-smelling pines. The minibus will take you back to the hotel for lunch, but if you wish to stay at this heavenly spot all day, meal vouchers are provided for an open-air restaurant a few minutes away at Muleta, where delicious seafood can be washed down by local dry white wine. Altogether a perfect hotel in a perfect setting." (*Kay Long*)

This tribute was in fact written in 1978 but there have been plenty like it since. The hotel changes little from year to year, though recently a splendid new bar has been opened on the beach. A visitor this year writes: " 'Never again,' we said in the Gatwick herding pens; 'never again,' in the aerial cattle-boat; 'nothing can be worth all this,' in the Palma baggage stampede. But we shall return to *Es Molí* and its scented garden to hear the nightingales, to look out from this terraced oasis of shady trees and cascading flowers at the surrounding semi-circle of towering crags." (*J P Berryman*) All our correspondents plan to return, but most still think the food could be improved. (*R & M Milner; Mr & Mrs J M Sennett, Conrad Dehn, Robert Heller, and others*)

Open 15 Apr – 27 Oct.
Rooms 1 suite, 60 double, 12 single – all with bath, telephone, radio, piped music and air-conditioning; most with terrace (300pts supplement); annexe with 9 rooms.
Facilities Lift; several lounges (1 with TV), 2 bars, video room, card and reading room, dining terrace, dancing by the pool weekly in summer. Large gardens with heated swimming pool, tennis court, ping-pong, pétanque. Rock beach with bar; also restaurant (not hotel's) 6 km away (free hotel minibus). English spoken.
Location 1 km from Deyá; Palma 29 km; airport 37 km. Parking in front of hotel.
Restriction Not suitable for &.
Credit cards Access, Diners, Visa.
Terms B&B: 4,500–6,400pts; dinner, B&B: 5,500–7,600pts; full board 6,500–8,600pts. Set lunch/dinner 2,000pts; full alc 3,500pts. Reduced rates for children sharing parents' room.

La Residencia
Tel (71) 63.90.11
Telex 69570 DEYA

Located in the heart of the village, this newly opened hotel is recommended as an alternative to the often fully booked *Es Molí*. It has been converted from two adjoining manor houses "at what must have been staggering expense: its faultless elegance and stylishness is almost in danger of being its only fault. The furnishings are discreet and timeless, many are antique, and the public rooms are used as a gallery to display the work of local artists. There are huge solid oak doors, small open quadrangles, a pleasingly shaped pool and well-watered gardens. The most delightful of continental breakfasts, prefaced by a tall glass of orange juice, with home-made jam, butter served in silver dishes, massive coffee pots. This is served either ceremoniously in one's room, in the breakfast room, or on the terrace where there are glorious vistas of mountains and village. At night the terrace is even more magical by candlelight. Drinks are served until quite late, and there is also a bar by the pool where food is obtainable if required. I wonder how soon I can decently return." (*Mrs Elizabeth Syrett*)

Open All year except Feb.
Rooms 7 suites, 18 double, 7 single – 29 with bath, 3 with shower, all with direct-dial telephone.
Facilities 5 salons, 3 bars, restaurant, terrace, old stone courtyard, live music, poetry readings, fashion shows etc. in summer. 32 acre grounds with olive groves, terrace and swimming pool. 5 minutes from sea (hotel's own private beach due to open in late 1986), boats, sailing, windsurfing – instructors can be arranged. Baby-sitters. Possibly suitable for &. English spoken.

Location On the edge of the town on the road to Valldemossa.
Credit cards None accepted.
Terms B&B: single 9,000–10,000pts, double 14,000–15,000pts, suites 18,000 pts. Set meals excluding service: lunch 2,500pts, dinner 2,700–3,500pts; full alc 3,500pts; reduced rates for children under 12, special meals.

ENCAMP Andorra   Map 15

Residencia Belvedere

Tel Andorra (9738) 31263
[*From France dial* (78) *instead of* (9738)]

England in high Andorra: a friendly, informal and wonderfully cheap guest-house, run by an English couple, Terry and Jo Dixon. The *Belvedere* is a quarter-mile from Encamp, above the town and just off the road to Soldeu and France. It is away from traffic and has a L-shaped sun terrace with fine Pyrenean views. In winter, people come for the skiing, and in summer for the walking. A visitor writes: "If you want a drink, you help yourself and enter it in the book. Although the hotel offers half-board, bar lunches and afternoon teas are supplied willingly. The accent is on home-cooking, and in addition to her delicious soups and egg mousse, I must mention Jo's superb packed lunches. She has a different menu for each day over a two-week period." "Welcoming proprietors, delicious dishes. Bedrooms a little spartan, but attractive and very clean." A recent visitor "endorses all accolades. Atmosphere is like a house party. Our meals were the envy of the other ski parties. The high meadows in the area are a botanist's and lepidopterist's dream, with half of the European butterfly species on view in a few square miles." (*John Ralley; also Mrs J O Nairn*)

Open 14 Dec – 13 Apr and 15 May – 15 Oct.
Rooms 9 double, 1 single – 1 ground-floor room with bath.
Facilities Lounge with open log fire, bar, dining room. Small grounds with sun terrace, lawn and terraced garden with mountain views. Convenient for ski slopes. Pony-trekking in spring, mountain walking, trout fishing; open-air swimming pool in town; winter sports nearby. English spoken.
Location 1 km from Encamp, just off road to Soldeu and France. Parking.
Restriction Probably not suitable for severely &.
Credit cards None accepted (but UK cheques accepted).
Terms B&B: £7.50–£9; dinner, B&B: single £14.50–£16.50. Set dinner (including wine and coffee) £7–£7.50. Bar snacks available at lunchtime in summer; packed lunches. Reduced rates for children sharing parents' room; high teas.

FUENTE DÉ Cantabria   Map 15

Parador Nacional Río Deva

Tel Fuente Dé (942) 73 00 01

Yet another *parador* new to the Guide, this one is magnificently sited in the Picos de Europa, a wild, mountainous region 2½ hours' drive from Santander. "It is not a difficult drive, but for the last 1½ hours the road twists up 3000 feet along the river Deva, where people were fishing for salmon. In May the wildflowers are splendid with many species rare to Europe. The road ends at the *parador*, a large modern hotel at the bottom of a 4000-foot grey rock cliff with a cable car to the top. The views from the hotel were of snow-capped peaks. The bedroom was well lit and comfortably furnished, with a small glass-enclosed balcony. The bathroom was large, the bath enormous. There was the usual magnificent *parador* buffet breakfast, excellent value and enough to set you up till dinner – three or four choices at each stage.'' (*Walter Baxter*)

Open All year.
Rooms 71 double, 7 single – most with bath and balcony.
Facilities Lounge, bar, restaurant, garden. River with fishing nearby.
Location On the N621 25 m W of Camaleno.
Restriction Not suitable for &.
Credit cards All major cards accepted.
Terms [1985 rates] rooms: 4,800–6,000pts. Breakfast 500pts; set lunch/dinner 1,600pts.

GRANADA   Map 15

Parador Nacional de San Francisco   *Tel* (958) 22.14.93
Alhambra

The *Parador Nacional de San Francisco* on the Alhambra hills is, for all practical purposes, a modern building on the site of the Franciscan monastery that was the temporary resting place of Ferdinand and Isabella, who chose to be buried at the site of what they considered to be their greatest triumph: the final extinction of Moslem rule in Spain. Their remains were later transferred to the Capilla Real adjoining the cathedral. The site of the temporary sepulchre, with its commemorative plaque, the tower and the main entrance are preserved, but very little else. Nevertheless, the architects have achieved a work of great sympathy and harmony. It has lovely formal gardens of its own and a unique view from the terrace across to the Generalife. Some people regard it as the fairest jewel in the *parador* crown, and justifying its steeper prices. "In my view, one of the best *paradores* in Spain. Food rather better than in most others, and impossible to fault rooms or service" was one recent comment. This year, however, there have been many criticisms – of the "dull, disappointing" dinners, the "overstretched" service and the "complacent" management. The *parador* may have hit a bad patch, but most correspondents, despite their reservations, were glad to have stayed in such memorable surroundings. We hope for better news next year.

Open All year.
Rooms 33 – all with bath, telephone and air-conditioning.
Facilities Lift, lounges, bar, restaurant. Garden.
Location On Alhambra hill, 3 km from city centre. Parking.
Credit cards All major cards accepted.
Terms [Excluding 5% tax] rooms: single 5,625–6,375pts, double 8,250–9,000pts. Breakfast 500pts; set lunch/dinner 1,800pts.

GUADALUPE Cáceres   Map 15

Hospedería Real Monasterio   *Tel* (927) 36.70.00
Plaza Juan Carlos I

Guadalupe is a small town about 2,000 feet up in the mountains roughly halfway between Toledo and Mérida or Cáceres. It is approached by a winding secondary road through splendid scenery. The town is picturesque: there is a main square with a fountain and cobbled narrow streets bordered by balconied houses, whose walls are clothed with flowers. The place is dominated by the monastery, both church and fortress medieval, with some marvellous 17th-century baroque rooms. The hotel is contained within the monastic buildings – in fact, in the old pharmacy. During the Middle Ages, this was a pilgrimage centre: there is a cult still of the Virgin of Guadalupe whose image is kept within the church. The present occupants of the monastery are the Franciscans who have restored the buildings inside and out during this century. There are some marvellous paintings, gorgeous decorations and many treasures.

"With hindsight, I realise that this was the best hotel we stayed in during our Spanish tour, and we should have stayed longer. We may have had better meals, better bedrooms and better views, but never at the same time – and we certainly never had better value for money. The approach from the east over the Sierras during May, when the wild flowers flood down the hills and bank up against the road, is astonishingly beautiful. You need to book in advance, and ask for a room with a view. Ours was extremely comfortable, with good bedside lighting and a large bathroom, but had frosted glass windows, presumably because we overlooked the monks' quarters. The main feature is an enormous cloister/courtyard, cool and full of plants, where you sit for coffee or drinks. The hotel is managed by Franciscan monks, but the restaurant is staffed by girls; the food is very good by Spanish standards and quite fantastic by British ones. Only criticism: the musak." (*Walter Baxter*)

Open All year except 15 Jan – 15 Feb.
Rooms 2 suites, 36 double, 2 single – all with bath and telephone.
Facilities Lift; large public rooms including entrance hall, salons, TV room, bar, restaurant, cloisters and courtyard. Possibly suitable for &.
Location Central. Parking.
Credit cards Access, Visa.
Terms [Excluding 5% tax, and service] B&B single 2,320pts, double 3,660pts; dinner, B&B single, 3,570pts, double 6,160pts; full board: single 4,420pts, double 7,840pts. Set lunch/dinner 1,250pts.

JAÉN Map 15

Parador Nacional Castillo de Santa Catalina *Tel* (953) 26.44.11

A newly modernised *parador*, a few miles outside the provincial capital of Jaén – a colossal eagle's nest of a castle perched precariously on a mountain above the town with dizzying views. Southern-facing rooms have balconies, but all have equally stunning vistas. An earlier visitor had commented: "Jaén represents the *parador* system at its best: the vision of the architect, his respect for the original structure, the harmonious, almost imperceptible blending of old and new, as well as the skill of the builders. The ante-room to the dining room has an arch springing from each of the four corners of the room to meet 60 or 70 feet above your head, and is worthy of a cathedral. The dining room itself, with its priceless tapestries, is only slightly less grand. You can easily become transported by this place, especially if, like me, you love to brood on mountain peaks. For a mountain brooder, this is the Promised

Land. Oh, for a marriage of Spanish accommodation and French cuisine, and I don't think I would ever leave the place. Still, at the price I am not complaining.'' (*J A Driver*)

Notwithstanding this encomium, the hotel was dropped after reports of unacceptable plumbing. But that was two years ago. Now a correspondent tells us that he, too, rated Jaén the best of nine *paradores* he visited: "Better food, a more exciting site and ambience, even better than at Granada. Reception unusually friendly." *(M A Goulding)*More reports welcome.

Open All year.
Rooms 36 double, 6 single – all with bath and telephone, some with balconies. 11 rooms on ground floor; bar.
Facilities Lift, 2 lounges, chess and card room, dining room, TV room, air-conditioning. Large garden with trees and seating; swimming pool. English spoken.
Location 3 km SW of Jaén.
Credit cards All major cards accepted.
Terms (Excluding tax) rooms: single 4,000–5,200pts, double 5,000–6,500pts. Breakfast 500pts; set dinner 1,600pts.

LEÓN   Map 15

Hotel San Marcos   *Tel* (987) 23.73.00
Plaza de San Marcos 7   or 23.73.50

The glory of the proud city of León, part modern, part medieval, is its great Gothic cathedral, one of Europe's finest. Its second glory, at the other end of town, is the former 16th-century Monastery of San Marcos, with a staggering renaissance facade: today part of it is an archaeological museum, and part is a *very* grand hotel (five red Michelin gables). There are three-quarters of a mile of carpeted corridors, lined on both sides with exquisite reproductions of Spanish furniture through the ages – a museum in itself. The smaller restaurant gives on to a summer terrace, with the river beyond; the main lounge, 84 feet square, has a polished marble floor and one huge painting across its ceiling. A hotel of this magnitude may not be to everyone's taste, but those ·who enjoy paradores are likely to find this *parador*-plus. Others might find it a bit formal or stuffy. (*Carol Hahn*)

Open All year.
Rooms 14 suites, 198 double – all with bath, telephone, radio and TV.
Facilities Lift, salons, restaurants, night club, conference facilities; hairdresser & beauty parlour. Garden. Archaeological museum in building.
Location Central, near river; parking.
Credit cards All major cards accepted.
Terms B&B single occupancy 6,800–7,250pts, double 10,600–11,700pts; dinner, B&B single occupancy 8,300–9,250pts, double 14,600–15,700pts; full board: single occupancy 9,900–10,350pts, double 16,800–17,900pts. Set lunch/dinner 1,700–2,000pts; full alc 2,200–2,500pts.

We ask hotels to estimate their 1986 tariffs. About a quarter of the hotels in Part Two have failed to reply, so prices in that section are more approximate in some cases than those in Part One.

Hotel Laibeny   *Tel* (91) 232.53.06 or 231.46.09
Salud 3, Madrid 28013   *Telex* 49024 LBNY

"This hotel was a real find. First, it is reasonable – 6,100 pesetas [1985] a
night for a double room. Second, it is in an excellent location, between
the Puerta del Sol and Gran Via. That means metro stops, old Madrid,
and good shopping are all close at hand. We were one block from El
Cortez Ingles, a major department store. Third, the rooms are
immaculate, comfortable and well maintained. Fourth, the staff are very
gracious. People at the front desk and the concierges all spoke English,
unusual in Spain. The hotel maintained a money exchange where we got
rates better than at most banks." (*Carol Hahn*)

Open All year.
Rooms 160 double – all with bath, telephone, colour TV and air-conditioning.
Facilities Salon, bar, restaurant.
Location Central, between Gran Via and Puerta del Sol. Garage.
Credit cards Amex, Visa.
Terms [1985 rates] double rooms 6,100pts. Breakfast 450pts; set lunch/dinner
1,100pts.

Hotel Suecia   *Tel* (91) 231.69.00
Marqués de Casa Riera 4   *Telex* 22313 SUECOTEL
Madrid 28014

"Because of its location and its excellent restaurant, the *Bellman*, it is our
favourite place to stay in Madrid," writes *Ruth Kaye* with a fresh
endorsement of this middle-sized Swedish-run hotel which has long
held favour with our readers. It is in a quiet side-street, but also in
central Madrid, between the Prado and the Puerto del Sol, usefully
placed for shops etc. It is regularly patronised by foreign journalists,
visiting opera singers and suchlike. The staff come in for special praise
from another reader: "Each and every one very well informed, cheerful
and helpful." (*Joan Williamson*)

Open All year. Main restaurant closed Sat night, Sun and Aug.
Rooms 5 suites, 59 double – all with bath/shower, telephone, air-conditioning and
mini-bar; colour TV and baby-listening on request.
Facilities Bar/breakfast room, restaurant; conference facilities. English spoken.
Location Central, but quietly situated, close to banking/commercial district, just
off Calle de Alcalá. Public parking near hotel.
Credit cards All major cards accepted.
Terms [Excluding 5% tax, 1985 rates] rooms: single occupancy 6,000–6,900pts,
double 7,500–8,500pts; suite 10,000–11,500pts. Breakfast 500pts; set lunch/dinner
2,000pts. Extra bed for child 1,600pts per night.

Hotel Villa Magna   *Tel* (341) 275.12.27
Paseo de la Castellana 22, Madrid 28046   *Telex* 22914 VIMA

A modern, fairly central hotel, with private parking (a great bonus),
"expensive, luxurious, quiet and instantly eye catching. They know
your name, book restaurants and cabs efficiently, wake you up on time,
anticipate everything without batting an eyelid. Our room was beauti-

fully designed, with a truly sumptuous bathroom and dressing room, and all in very relaxing colours. I don't normally like modern 'block' hotels but this is very different, like the *Berkeley* in London or the *Beverly Wilshire* in Los Angeles. The hotel's public rooms manage to be intimate as well as spacious, full of squelchy sofas and wide coffee tables on which to place your £8 shot of cognac. The restaurant's decor will not appeal to everyone but the breakfasts set you up for a trek through the Prado. We didn't have dinner there – *Horcher, Jockey* and *Zalacain* were all a pleasant stroll away." (*Adrian Turner; also P & J T*)

Open All year.
Rooms 10 suites, 174 double, 16 single – all with bath, telephone, radio, colour TV and air-conditioning.
Facilities Lifts; lounge, 2 bars, restaurant, banquet/conference rooms; beauty parlour, sauna, men's hairdresser, chemist, secretarial services; 24-hour room service. Garden. English spoken.
Location Central. Rooms are sound-proofed. Garage for 350 cars.
Restriction Not suitable for &.
Credit cards Amex, Diners.
Terms [Excluding 5% tax] rooms: single 16,000pts, double 26,000pts. Breakfast 970pts; set lunch/dinner 4,700pts.

MÁLAGA Andalucia   Map 15

Parador Nacional de Gibralfaro   *Tel* (952) 22.19.02
Apartado de Correos 274

A panoramic *parador* of stone arcades and terraces, on a hill above Málaga. "The position is staggering. Gibralfaro is a huge tree-covered rock, and the *parador* stands on the top, looking down on the city. The view from our bedroom terrace was incomparable – bullring to the left, busy harbour in front, while to the right even the hideous high-rise modern blocks acquire a certain grandeur at this distance. As a blood-red sun sinks behind the Sierra Mijas, the city turns pink and the lights twinkle on – magical. The bedrooms are in predictable Spanish style: roomy bathroom and bedroom with heavy carved wooden furniture. The bar is a popular place for local people to take drinks. I wish someone had warned us about the size of the set dinner – a huge plate of spinach in creamy sauce (very good), then *fourteen* small hors d'oeuvre that filled us totally, so we could only pick at the huge grilled fish and fish stew in a green herby sauce (both good), then cream and chocolate cake soaked in liqueur. Dry white Rioja, at exactly the right temperature, was excellent, and coffee was fragrant and delicious. The *parador's* atmosphere is serene and restful, save that, as in so many Spanish hotels, a huge TV set dominates the bar, blaring away deafeningly. No one appears to be watching it, but it seems to have some mystical significance." (*R and A Evans*)

Readers mostly endorse these comments. One reader offered a back-handed compliment – "The best place in Málaga, which is not saying much; a surly reception, even for Spain." Another was more generous – "A marvellous place to stay for one's arrival in the south of Spain." (*Richard Oake, J F Holman, M A Goulding*)

Do you know of a good hotel in Barcelona?

Open All year.
Rooms 12 double – all with bath, telephone and balcony.
Facilities Lift, salon with TV, bar, restaurant. Garden. Sea 4 km.
Location 3 km from town centre, on E side of city towards Almeria, in large park.
Credit cards All major cards accepted.
Terms [1985 rates] rooms: single occupancy 5,200pts, double 6,500pts. Breakfast 500pts. Set lunch/dinner 1,600pts.

MÉRIDA Badajoz   Map 15

Parador Nacional Via de la Plata   *Tel* (924) 31.38.00
Plaza Queipo de Llano 3

The *Parador* is in a sometime convent and prison built over the site of a Roman temple, in this old city of western Spain with its fine Roman remains – including amphitheatre and the best preserved Roman theatre outside Syria and Libya. One of this year's visitors enthuses about "the local museum, crammed full of Roman objects, and the Roman bridge, with 64 arches over the Guadiana, still in daily use – both within walking distance of the *Parador*". (*Blake Pinnell*) The hotel has been regularly praised over the years. "A fascinating cloistered stopover with quite delightful bedrooms, many overlooking the monastery garden. Very friendly staff (unlike some *paradores* where staff rarely smile – is it because they are all civil servants?). Used a lot by locals for meals. The table d'hôte is the best value and includes a few local specialities." "Simple, clean and comfortable. White walls, carved wooden chests, wrought-iron grilles on windows, vaulted ceilings, etc. Our room was quiet and very spacious. The place rambles eccentrically and there is no lift. Rooms are scattered about, running off landings and quaint corners. The restaurant is fairly vast and, when we were there, fairly empty. The bar at night was extremely noisy, full of slightly more affluent locals than those to be found in the town's main square. Apart from a few outdoor cafés, the *Parador* is just about the only proper restaurant in town. Service friendly but not entirely reliable. But in a decidedly out-of-the-way spot, in that searing heat, it offers a welcome blast of air-conditioning and pretty surroundings." (*Adrian Turner, H Bramwell*) Warning: requests for reservations may not be treated punctiliously.

Open All year.
Rooms 44 double, 6 single – all with bath, telephone and radio; some ground-floor rooms.
Facilities 2 salons, TV room, bar, restaurant; conference facilities. Garden with terrace. English spoken.
Location Central, just E of N630. Garage parking.
Credit cards All major cards accepted.
Terms [Excluding 6% tax] B&B: single 6,575pts, double 8,075pts; dinner, B&B: single 8,425pts, double 9,925pts; full board: single 9,630pts, double 11,130pts. Set lunch/dinner 1,850pts; full alc 2,400pts. Reduced rates and special meals for children.

In Spain, reservations for state-run establishments can be made direct or through their central booking office:
CENTRAL DE RESERVAS DE LOS PARADORES DE ESPANA.
Augustin de Bethencourt 25, 2°, MADRID 3.
Tel. 234 57 49/234 58 37/234 61 03.

MOJÁCAR Almeria Map 15

Parador Nacional Reyes Catolicos *Tel* (951) 47.82.50
Playa de Mojácar

Mojácar is in a fine position dominating the plains and the Andalucian coast. The lower slopes have not avoided the spoliation of development, but the old town retains its maze of small Moorish alleys. The *Parador* is a mile or so from the village, a modern construction just a few yards from the sea – "A really lovely place to stay, we thought. The design is pleasant and spacious, with huge terraces and gardens and a swimming pool, looking out over the sea. The large lounges were beautifully furnished with suede sofas and wood furniture. The building is designed for coolness, and bedrooms are large, comfortable and well heated. As for the food, well, one has to lower one's culinary sights when in Spain, but our simple dinner was good – tapas, gazpacho, swordfish in a caper sauce. Excellent buffet breakfast." But another winter visitor found the hotel under-heated and unkempt. (*Ray and Angela Evans*)

Open All year.
Rooms 89 double, 9 single – all with bath, telephone and air-conditioning; ground-floor rooms.
Facilities 3 lounges, bar, TV room, dining room. Garden with unheated swimming pool and tennis court; sea and golf nearby. English spoken.
Location 2.5 km from Mojácar on N340 coast road. Parking.
Credit cards All major cards accepted.
Terms [1985 rates] rooms: single 4,000–5,200pts, double 5,000–6,500pts. Breakfast 500pts; set lunch/dinner 1,600pts. Reduced rates for children sharing parents' room; special meals.

MONACHIL Granada Map 15

Parador Nacional de Sierra Nevada *Tel* (958) 48.02.00

A modern Alpine-type building (lots of wood-panelling), 2,500 metres up in a superb position facing the south-west. Most popular as a winter-skiing resort, but visitors in May felt they were getting their money's worth: "Our very comfortable room had plenty of wardrobe space, a mini-bar, lovely soft beds, spotless bathroom with large fluffy bath towels and plentiful, if rather slow-running, hot water. Breathtaking views from the plate-glass windows. The set dinner menu was a little limited, but what we chose was beautifully served and well prepared. It was made even better by a perfect view of one of the most beautiful sunsets I have ever seen. Breakfast, however, was to be the pièce de résistance. A large table was set with heated trays of bacon, sausages, potato, boiled eggs, plus platters of toast, bread, jam, fruit and various cakes and biscuits. We didn't need any lunch that day! One can imagine how full of life it must be in the winter season with skiers in residence. However, from April onwards, it must be regarded as a one-night stopover, for the beauty of the drive up from Granada and the enjoyment of a night's stay in such pleasant surroundings. There is nothing else to do here in the summer."* (Judith and Christopher Heayberd) We have no reason to believe standards have fallen but lack recent feedback. More reports please.*

Open All year except Nov.
Rooms 10 four-bedded, 22 double – 10 with bath, 22 with shower, all with telephone and mini-bar.
Facilities Salons, TV room, bar, dining room, music room, games room, terrace. Tennis court and winter sports nearby. English spoken.
Location 35 km SE of Granada, signposted from main road. Parking.
Credit cards All major cards accepted.
Terms [Excluding 5% tax] B&B: 2,600–4,600pts; dinner, B&B 4,200–6,200pts; full board 5,250–7,250pts. Set lunch/dinner 1,600pts; full alc 1,800pts. Special packages in the skiing season. Special meals for children on request.

NERJA Málaga   Map 15

Parador Nacional de Nerja   *Tel* (952) 52.00.50
Playa de Burriano-Tablazo

This *parador* continues to be controversial. It is praised unanimously for its spectacular setting – high on the cliffs overlooking the beach of Burriano on the eastern edge of Nerja. Nerja itself is described by one visitor this year as "quite ghastly, with hideous buildings and the hinterland fit only for making Westerns." Another recent visitor says, "if you *must* stay in Nerja, stay here". The large rooms have sizeable balconies with view of sea or mountains, and they are comfortably furnished with well-equipped bathrooms; all is spotlessly clean. There is a pool surrounded by a delightful garden, with trees for shade and flowers for colour, and plenty of scope for sunbathing, while a lift takes you directly to the beach below. The restaurant also overlooks the sea. Opinions are divided evenly over the quality of the food and service: "well above most other *parador* standards" is one view and "worst of all the *paradores* we've stayed in" is the other. More views please.

Open All year.
Rooms 57 double, 3 single – all with bath, telephone, tea-making facilities, air-conditioning and balcony.
Facilities Lift; bar, salons, restaurant. Garden with swimming pool; beach nearby.
Location On E edge of Nerja; signposted. Parking.
Credit cards All major cards accepted.
Terms [1985 rates – excluding 5% tax] rooms: single 4,400–6,000pts, double 5,500–7,500pts; full board 3,485pts per person; extra bed in room 1,925–2,625pts. Breakfast 500pts; set lunch/dinner 1,800pts.

OROPESA Toledo   Map 15

Parador Nacional Virrey de Toledo   *Tel* (925) 43.00.00

Oropesa is a very old little town of graceful houses, just off the main road west from Madrid to Badajoz and Lisbon. It has a feudal castle part of which has been converted into a *parador* – "You go through an archway into a flower-decked courtyard. Public rooms are best described as super-baronial. Our bedroom was enormous, and spotless, with coffee table, easy chairs; tiny wrought-iron balcony with fantastic views over wheat plains. An enormous bathroom with loads of trimmings. Dinner and wine were excellent, staff the best of eight *paradores* we visited. We booked for one night and stayed for four." "Very comfortable, fully air-conditioned and the best cooking of all the *paradores* we stayed at." (*Ann and Kelvin Price, Roy Mathias*)

Among this year's reports, one wholly endorsed the entry – "among the two or three best *paradores* in Spain" (*R A Dubery*), though another reported off-hand service and unusually poor food.

Open All year.
Rooms 2 suites, 40 double, 2 single – all with bath and telephone.
Facilities Lift; TV room, dining room, 3 conference rooms. English spoken. &.
Location Oropesa is 149 km SW of Madrid, 106 km W of Toledo. Hotel is central; parking.
Credit cards All major cards accepted.
Terms [Excluding 5% tax] B&B: single 6,200–6,700pts, double 7,400–8,400pts; dinner, B&B: single 8,000–8,500pts, double 11,000–12,000pts; full board: single 8,940–9,540pts, double 12,880–13,880pts. Set lunch/dinner 1,800pts. Special meals for children on request.

PLAYA DE FORNELLS Catalonia   Map 15

Hotel Aigua Blava   *Tel* (72) 62.20.58
Bagur, Gerona   *Telex* 57077 UNHO – Ref: HABIT

Playa de Fornells, at the northern end of the Costa Brava, is by any standard a thrillingly beautiful landscape, and the *Hotel Aigua Blava* has annexed a delicious corner of it. It occupies nooks and crannies amid trees, on rocks, at all sorts of levels, with no regard for specific order, but every regard for adaptation to the scene. "The *Aigua Blava* (which is Catalan for Blue Water) has literally grown from a fisherman's hut. Xiquet (pronounced Chickee) Sabater, who owns it, is quarter-Japanese, quarter-French, half-Spanish, and married to a local girl. He is a great charmer. Some of his first guests are still coming back after more than 30 years. The buildings have just developed round a small fishing beach and harbour – a rather random aggregation, but nothing embarrassingly picturesque. Marvellous staff – friendly and bright." (*Anne Sharpley*)

Since this report first appeared in our 1979 edition, readers have continued to write enthusiastically about "one of the best-run hotels in Spain", "the best on the Costa Brava", "a unique hotel, its excellence proved by the return year after year of enthusiastic guests". This hyperbole was confirmed by an inspector who found that the hotel is indeed of exceptional quality: that it is not only admirably run and serves good food, but that it also has the knack of creating the atmosphere of a country house party. Señor Sabater himself is clearly an anglophile: the hotel is something of a traditional British stronghold. Visitors have complained about the beds, however: "We both considered ourselves lucky not to have developed curvature of the spine after two nights", and one correspondent reported that the set menu was very dull, recommending instead the à la carte.

Open 21 Mar – 20 Oct.
Rooms 10 suites, 67 double, 8 single – 78 with bath, 7 with shower, all with telephone and air-conditioning, some with balcony; all rooms in different buildings, like a Catalan village.
Facilities 3 lounges, 2 bars, restaurant, grill room, TV room, conference and banquet rooms; boutique, hairdresser, disco. Solarium, swimming pool and paddling pools, terraces (dancing every night). Gardens with tennis and volleyball courts. Children's play area. Sand and rock beach with safe bathing, waterskiing, yacht marina and other watersports. Golf 7 km. English spoken.

Location 4 km SE of Bagur, 8 km E of Palafrugell. Garage and parking.
Restriction Not suitable for &.
Credit card Visa.
Terms [Excluding 6% tax] B&B: single 3,400–4,400pts, double 5,300–7,000pts;
dinner, B&B 4,100–6,100pts; full board 4,600–6,600pts. Set lunch/dinner 1,800pts;
full alc 3,000pts. Reductions for children under 7; special meals.

RIBADEO Lugo   Map 15

Parador Nacional de Ribadeo   *Tel* (982) 11.08.25

A *parador* new to the Guide overlooking a huge inlet of the sea on the
Galician coast, with an unusual feature: you go down by lift from the
ground floor to the bedrooms below. "Just on the outskirts of this once
quite elegant town, the *parador* offers a typical mixture of very good
rooms – large, airy and quiet on the side overlooking the bay away from
the busy road. A large balcony had a view over the lawn. The bathroom
was superb even by *parador* standards. Add to this helpful staff and
more than adequate local food. The bay of Ribadeo and the scenically
magnificent river valley with a glorious road climbing to the central
plateau make this a very attractive stop on the long north coast of
Galicia, one of the best parts of this unknown Spain." (*Angela and David
Stewart; also Walter Baxter*)

Open All year.
Rooms 41 double, 6 single – all with bath and telephone, many with balcony.
Facilities Lift, salon, dining room.
Location On outskirts of town. Parking.
Credit cards All major cards accepted.
Terms [excluding 5% tax] single: 4,400–6,000pts, double: 5,500–7,700pts; dinner,
B&B: single 6,800–8,000pts, double 10,300–11,800pts; full board: single 7,900–
9,100pts, double 12,500–14,000pts. Breakfast 600pts; set lunch/dinner 1,500pts.

SALAMANCA 37000   Map 15

Parador Nacional Salamanca   *Tel* (923) 22.87.00
Teso de la Feria 2

Salamanca, sometimes called "the Oxford of Spain", is a beautiful old
city of golden stone, narrow streets, rich facades, domes and spires; its
great university dates from 1215. The big new *Parador* lies across the
river Tormes, ten minutes' walk from the city centre over the Roman
bridge. No one has anything except abuse for its outside appearance,
but, that apart, it gives much satisfaction. "Do not expect the usual
atmospheric *parador* in ancient surroundings: this one could easily be
mistaken for a new factory or a block of flats. The essential requirement
is to ensure you have a room facing the city across the river. This aspect
is magnificent by day and stupendous by night when the two cathedrals
– the old (12th-century) and the new (16th-century) are floodlit, together
with other churches and the ancient university. Since the *parador* is so
big, you seldom need to book in advance, though business conferences
are catered for. Bedrooms are thoroughly up-to-date. There are spacious
modern lounges, but rather a disappointing dining room (apart from
that view!). A popular cafeteria adjoins the hotel, and the more
fashionable young Salamancans seem to foregather there. They are quite

charming once they know you are English." (*H Bramwell; also M Cope, Walter Baxter*)

Open All year.
Rooms 4 suites, 94 double, 10 single – all with bath and telephone.
Facilities 2 lounges, bar, TV room, restaurant. Unheated swimming pool. English spoken. &.
Location 2 km from central Salamanca. Parking.
Credit cards All major cards accepted.
Terms [1985 rates] rooms: single 5,200pts, double 6,500pts. Breakfast 500pts; set lunch/dinner 1,600pts.

SAN MIGUEL Ibiza   Map 15

Hotel Hacienda   *Tel* (971) 33.30.46
Na Xamena   *Telex* 68855
Apartado 423 Ibiza

"The island's popularity as a package destination should not deflect travellers in search of seclusion and luxury. The *Hacienda* enjoys glorious isolation on Ibiza's rugged north-west coast. The geography ensures seclusion. The hotel, under the direction of Ernesto Ramon, supplies the luxury. It perches 600 feet above the sea mid sweet-smelling pine and rosemary in its own estate at the end of a three-mile tarmac track. The bay below can only be reached with a steep climb, but the shimmering sea and wild granite hillsides provide absorbing, ever-changing views.

"The hotel is loosely based on the traditional flat-roofed Ibizenco style. White Carrara marble floors surround an open central courtyard. Dining room and bar overlook the main 50-yard kidney-shaped pool and sun terraces. Bedrooms are spacious, with large picture windows leading to totally private balconies. Bathrooms boast mosaic floors, twin sinks, bath with shower and separate lavatory and bidet. The *Hacienda* inspires repeat visits from a distinguished clientele including ambassadors and film stars. The mood is casual and unassuming. Car rental is virtually a necessity whether to reach the nearest beach at the port of San Miguel, or to make a brief foray to the exotic nightlife of Ibiza town, 15 miles away." (*Alex Finer*)

That report is more-or-less endorsed by a reader who finds the hotel "wonderful, fabulous, maddening and exhausting", and explains: "Wonderful setting up on a cliff, but walking involves exhausting treks up or down. Not suitable for the physically handicapped." She adds: "Strangest of all, no proper mirrors anywhere – I suppose the idea is for people to relax enough not to have to worry about what they look like." And another, "The hotel was certainly very good, and had the food and water been hot, it might have been appropriate to add the word 'indeed'." (*Susan Chait, R M Booth*)

Open Apr – Nov.
Rooms 10 suites, 54 double – all with bath, telephone, radio, air-conditioning, fridge, terrace; 1 room in annexe.
Facilities Lift, salon, TV room, bar, restaurant; conference facilities; indoor heated swimming pool; nightclub, hairdressing salon, shops, keep-fit room. Garden with 2 swimming pools, tennis court. Private sandy beach 2½ km. English spoken.
Location 6 km NW of San Miguel. Parking.
Restriction Not suitable for &.
Credit cards All major cards accepted.

Terms [Excluding 5% tax] B&B: single 9,075–12,265pts, double 10,450–16,830pts; dinner, B&B: single, 11,375–14,465pts, double 14,850–21,230pts; full board: single 13,200–16,390pts, double 18,700–25,080pts. Set lunch/dinner 3,000pts; barbecue/buffet 3,500pts. Reduced rates for children according to age.

SANTIAGO DE COMPOSTELA La Coruña   Map 15

Hostal de los Reyes Católicos   *Tel* (981) 58.22.00
Plaza de España 1   *Telex* 86004 HRCS

"Imagine staying at a cross between Hampton Court and All Souls, furnished with the best pieces from the Victoria and Albert Museum. If that's the sort of thing you like, it will make your heart dance. It was built at the end of the 15th century by Ferdinand and Isabella (the firm behind Columbus) for pilgrims to the shrine of St James, just a step away across the square. The hotel has four quadrangles, all different, all exquisite, so magically lit at night it would knock your eye out. There are bedrooms of varying degrees of luxury – do you have ambitions to sleep in the Cardinal's bed? Ours was simple, charming and cosy. The service is the usual first-class stuff – everywhere, immediate and unobtrusive. English is spoken. The breakfast with hot croissants, brioches, churros and tiny shiny buns is twice as much as you can manage. I liked it better than the dinner which was good but not amazing. The dining room is an enormous gracefully vaulted crypt, but you can eat much more cheaply in the elegant cafeteria. The hotel is situated in the heart of medieval Santiago. If you tire of trooping in and out of the cloisters, one hour away by car, you can walk by the ocean; best do both." (*Shelley Cranshaw*)

The above citation was written in 1979, but a hotel like *Reyes Católicos* does not change much. It is an inevitable candidate for books like *The 300 Greatest Hotels in the World*. But any hotel of its size and pretensions almost certainly has a reverse side; poor service, rude staff, dank ground-floor rooms (third and fourth floor more recommended) are some of the comments in previous issues. "Who wants to sleep in a museum at a very high price (by local standards) and then have a poor breakfast?" was one comment this year. But the royalist faction fight back: "Not so much a hotel, more an experience to be recorded in the book of one's life." (*Elizabeth Syrett*) "One of our most memorable stays." (*Carol Hahn*)

Open All year.
Rooms 3 suites, 144 double, 10 single – 105 with bath, 52 with shower, all with telephone, radio, colour TV and baby-listening; some ground-floor rooms.
Facilities Lifts, reception hall, salons, TV room, bars, dining room, cafeteria; conference facilities. Beauty parlour/hairdressing salon, boutiques, nightclub. Chapel Royal with occasional concerts. Gardens. English spoken.
Location In town centre, by cathedral. Garage parking. Special bus to station.
Credit cards All major cards accepted.
Terms Rooms: single 5,600–6,800pts, double 7,000–14,000pts; dinner, B&B: single 8,700–9,900pts, double 13,200–20,200pts; full board: single 11,200–12,400pts, double 18,200–25,200pts. Breakfast 600pts; set lunch/dinner 2,500 and 2,700pts; full alc 3,500pts. Reduced rates and special meals for children.

Please make a habit of sending a report if you stay at a Guide hotel.

Hotel Windsor   *Tel* (981) 59.28.22 or 59.29.39
República de El Salvador 16

The hotel is in the newer part of town, only five minutes' walk from the old historic quarter, and less than half the price of the *Hostal de los Reyes Católicos* (above). There is a good cheap garage around the corner, an important plus in big Spanish towns. "Excellent value for money. Though modern, it has been attractively decorated in traditional Spanish style, using wood, glass and brasswork to great effect. Our bedroom too was attractive, quiet and comfortable, though the bathroom was tiny. The Italian manager speaks English and was most friendly and helpful, as were all his staff. Even the breakfast was adjusted to suit our more substantial English palates." (*Nicolette Comport and Valerie Eden; also Walter Baxter*)

Open All year.
Rooms 40 double, 10 single – 38 with bath, 12 with shower, all with telephone, radio, tea-making facilities and baby-listening.
Facilities Lift, lounge, TV room, bar, conference facilities. Garden. English spoken.
Location Central, near the Alameida; parking.
Restriction Not ideal for &.
Credit cards None accepted.
Terms Rooms: single 1,900–2,300pts, double 3,000–3,400pts. Breakfast 250pts. (No restaurant.)

SANTILLANA DEL MAR Cantabria   Map 15

Parador Nacional Gil Blas   *Tel* (942) 81.80.00
Pl. Ramón Playo 11

One of the showplace villages of Northern Spain, Santillana is full of fine seignorial mansions and has a Collegiate Church dating from the 12th and 13th centuries. It is a convenient stop for those catching the Santander–Plymouth ferry, as Santander is only 18 miles off. It is also convenient for visiting the awesome cave paintings at Altamira, two kilometres up the road. Despite all the fine buildings – the whole place is a national monument – Santillana remains an unspoilt working town with cows wandering around the narrow cobbled streets. The *parador* is in a quiet cul-de-sac facing a cobbled square. "It is a large and well-furnished old manor house. The oak floors on the top two floors were clearly hand-made and are highly polished, and the ceilings have high oak beams and rafters. The interior has recently been refurbished to a high standard and there are paintings and tapestries. The rooms feel medieval but with 20th-century comfort. Our beds were turned down at night by a maid, the only time this has happened to us in any *parador*. The bathroom was modern with plenty of hot water. The building was rather warm without air-conditioning. There is a pleasant large dining room and the menu is perfectly adequate without being particularly imaginative. You can lunch in the enclosed garden until 4 pm and leisurely catch the 7 pm ferry, ideal for passengers with cars." (*H Bramwell, L B Pinnell*)

Open All year.
Rooms 28, mostly double – most with bath, all with telephone. 21 rooms in annexe. (Many rooms on ground floor.)

Facilities Lift, salon with TV, bar, restaurant.
Location Central; garage and private parking.
Credit cards All major credit cards accepted.
Terms [1985 rates, excluding 5% tax] double room 4,400–7,500pts. Breakfast 500pts; set lunch/dinner 1,800pts.

SANTO DOMINGO DE LA CALZADA La Rioja   Map 15

Parador Nacional Santo Domingo de la Calzada   *Tel* (941) 34.03.00
Plaza del Santo 3   *Telex* 46865 RRPP

Santo Domingo was an 11th-century anchorite who built a bridge across the Glera river and a causeway (*calzada*) to help pilgrims on their way to Santiago by the Camino Frances (French road). A town grew up at the bridge and a hostel was built for the pilgrims. The *parador* has been built around the former hostel, little of which now remains except the facade and the imposing main hall. Readers generally approve of the place: not a paragon among *paradores*, but serviceable. One report this year comments: "No luxurious extras, but clean, cool airy bedrooms with adequate bathrooms. The food was typical of *paradores* but well cooked and good value." (*Mr and Mrs K G Archer*) The Spanish hotel staff speak little English.

An earlier visitor had complained of loud bells from the campanile next door; but apparently they stop at midnight. The noise reported this year was the click-clack of people's shoes along the stone-flagged corridors, a complaint echoed at many *paradores*. The answer must be to do as the Spaniards do: dine at ten and drink plenty of excellent Rioja from the nearby vineyards.

Open All year.
Rooms 25 double, 2 single – all with bath and telephone.
Facilities Lift; 2 lounges, TV room, bar, restaurant. English spoken.
Location Central (no private parking). Town is on main Logrono/Burgos road.
Restriction Not suitable for &.
Credit cards All major cards accepted.
Terms (Excluding 5% tax) B&B: single occupancy 4,100–5,700pts, double 5,500–7,500pts; dinner, B&B: single 5,700–7,300pts, double 8,700–10,700pts; full board: single 6,745–8,345pts, double 10,790–12,790pts. Set lunch/dinner 1,600pts; full alc 1,700pts; special meals for children.

SEGOVIA 40003   Map 15

Parador Nacional   *Tel* (911) 43.04.62
Apartado de Correos 106
Carretera de Valadolid

A modern *parador* on a hill overlooking the town, with superb views of the golden cathedral and the romantic Alcázar. A visitor this year calls the hotel "an oasis in the dry interior of Spain". (*P L Asher*) "It should be ugly since it is only concrete beams and brick walls. But lines in every direction give pleasure to the eye, and the place is full of small gardens, lit by light traps from the roof to keep them flourishing. Also, since the building is cantilevered out from the hill, you have this lovely illusion that you are approaching the fabulous skyline of Segovia in an aircraft. Incidentally, the restaurants of Segovia, with their ancient Guild of Meat

Roasters, are famous all over Spain. If you say you have been to Segovia, at once you are asked whether you ate at *Candido* or *Casa Duque*. We did. Both. And it was more than memorable. If you ate only in the *Parador*, that would indeed be tragic." (*Madeleine Polland*)

In fairness to the *Parador*, we should add that one visitor who ate on the premises thought its menu offered some of the best *parador* food at a very reasonable price. Others disagree. "Dinner not very good. Dry overdone swordfish, but then it generally is in Spain. Coffee at breakfast clearly instant." (*Dr and Mrs S Cannicott*) Another recent visitor tells of an attempt to find something left to eat from the buffet breakfast at 9.15 am. A coach party had devoured it, "as if a plague of locusts had swept through". (*E D T*)

Open All year.
Rooms 5 suites, 70 double, 5 single – all with bath, and telephone; air-conditioning throughout; some ground-floor rooms.
Facilities Salon, library, TV room, bar, 2 dining rooms, conference facilities; indoor swimming pool, sauna. Garden with outdoor swimming pools. English spoken.
Location 2 km N of Segovia on N601.
Credit cards All major cards accepted.
Terms B&B: single 5,700–7,400pts, double 7,500–9,700pts; dinner, B&B: single 7,500–9,300pts, double 11,100–13,500pts; full board, single 8,685–10,540pts, double 13,470–15,980pts. Set lunch/dinner 1,900pts; full alc 3,000pts.

SEVILLE   Map 15

Hotel Alfonso XIII   *Tel* (954) 22.28.50
San Fernando 2   *Telex* 72725

Seville's grandest hotel is fairly modern (opened 1929) but was built in traditional Moorish/Andalucian style, with an inner courtyard, just near the centre of Seville. There is traffic noise and the garden is small, but it is close to the river and great parks. The public rooms are huge, the service attentive, and the atmosphere one of old-fashioned, comfortable luxury. There is a superb swimming pool in the elegant garden. We quoted a visitor last year: "Lovely big bedrooms, superbly appointed bathrooms. But the hotel has apparently been cutting back on staff, and room service has suffered accordingly. The dining room is huge and hideous, far too formal for my taste, and the food is over-elaborate and undistinguished. You do better to eat real Spanish food in one of the little restaurants of the old quarter a few yards away, the Barrio de Santa Cruz." There has been renewed criticism of the cooking this year, and reports of tepid hot water at 7 pm. Can the Alfonso justify its regal prices?

Open All year.
Rooms 19 suites, 112 double, 18 single – all with bath, telephone, radio, TV and air-conditioning; baby-listening on request.
Facilities Lift, reception hall, TV room, salons, San Fernando Bar, restaurant; convention/banqueting halls, patio. Boutiques, hairdressers, beauty parlours. Gardens with swimming pool. English spoken.
Location In town centre. Parking, underground garage.
Credit cards All major cards accepted.
Terms [1985 rates] rooms: single 8,000–9,000pts, double 10,700–12,250pts. Breakfast 520pts; set lunch/dinner 2,300pts.

> Hotels may refuse to speculate about their next year's tariff. In these cases, we give 1985 prices, with a note to that effect.

Hotel Murillo   *Tel* (954) 21.60.95
Lope de Rueda 7

"The Barrio de Santa Cruz – a medieval quarter of the city close to the Cathedral, full of tiny streets and passages – is a major tourist draw in the season. Pots of plants hang on every wall and even the tiled roofs look more alive with flowers than many English gardens. There are several restaurants, and also bars where one can sit in the tiny squares drinking vino tinto and eating *tapas*. The *Murillo* is in the heart of the Barrio, and not easy to find. The taxi drivers of Seville are used to tight squeezes down the backstreets, but even they wouldn't try to deposit you outside the *Murillo*. You wake to the sound of people, not traffic. They will probably be noisy, gabbling Spaniards who have lived in the Barrio for many years, rather than tourists who tend to opt for larger hotels further from the city centre and the bells of the cathedral (but the bells aren't loud).

"The hotel is two-star, without restaurant, and serves a cheap and efficient continental breakfast in your room – good value. Our double room was charming with windows opening on to the tiny street below. Beds were comfortable, storage space and bathroom adequate. There was constant hot water. Staff were friendly and helpful. Decoration is simple except in the foyer where there are fine examples of old Spanish carvings. I shall remember the marble floors, painted and carved wood, white walls and big wooden doors." (*Philip Lines*)

Open All year.
Rooms 14 suites, 61 rooms, mostly double – all with bath or shower and WC, telephone.
Facilities Lift; conference facilities.
Location In the Barrio de Santa Cruz, not far from the Murillo and Alcázar gardens.
Credit cards All major cards accepted.
Terms [1985 rates, excluding 5% tax] rooms: single 1,600–2,700pts, double 2,750–4,450pts. Breakfast 200pts. (No restaurant.)

TOLEDO 45000   **Map 15**

Parador del Conde de Orgaz   *Tel* (925) 22.18.50
Cerro del Emperador   *Telex* 47998 RRPT

Despite its popularity with coach parties and the omnipresence of souvenir shops selling tawdry metalware, Toledo remains a fascinating and beautiful city, full of narrow winding streets and crammed with historic buildings and churches. The *Conde de Orgaz* is one of the showpiece *paradores* of the Spanish state tourist organisation. The first impression, and it's a powerful one, is of 16th-century Spain at its most baronial: coats of arms, shields and antique weapons forged from Toledo steel abound in halls and corridors, hung with banners and portraits of grave-faced bearded grandees. In fact, it's all a big cheat, though carried out with panache. The hotel was built in 1968, and the rooms, although furnished in the old style with aged wood, wrought iron and velvet, have every modern amenity including, in the bedrooms, a well-disguised fridge stacked with drinks and cocktail snacks.

We had an entry in earlier editions, but removed it after reports of a wretched restaurant. The kitchens appear to be in good order again: one report this year claims the *parador* offered the best set menu of nine *paradores* he had visited. "The site is worth the visit alone. Perched on top of a mountain, each bedroom and balcony overlooks a deep gorge of the river Tagus flowing in a U-bend; on the opposite bank stands the magnificent city of Toledo – a truly spectacular sight." (*L B Pinnell*) Note: advance booking is essential, and even so we have had reports of reservations not honoured. Also, not all rooms have the view. More reports would be welcome.

Open All year.
Rooms 1 suite, 48 double, 8 single – all with bath, telephone, and frigo-bar.
Facilities Lift; 3 salons, TV room, restaurant, bar – all with air-conditioning.
Extensive landscaped grounds with terraces and unheated swimming pool.
Hunting and fishing nearby. English spoken.
Location 3 km S of town centre. Parking.
Restriction Not suitable for &.
Credit cards All major credit cards accepted.
Terms B&B: single 5,000pts, double 11,400pts; dinner, B&B: single 7,100pts,
double 15,600pts; full board: single 8,465pts, double 18,330pts. Set lunch/dinner
2,100pts; full alc 3,500pts.

TORDESILLAS Valladolid   Map 15

Parador Nacional de Tordesillas   *Tel* (983) 77.00.51
                                                        Telex 26215 PNDTE

One of the larger *paradores*, this was built in 1958, enlarged in 1975, and is a kilometre outside Tordesillas in pine woods, and only 30 kilometres from the university city of Valladolid (superb patio and sculptures in the San Gregoria College). It also lies close to the main highways from Madrid to Galicia and from France down into Portugal, so is a useful stopover point, but for this reason is often booked up in advance. A regular visitor to the *Parador* writes: "Staff were entirely new. It was nevertheless still excellent. In fact, the cooking had improved enormously. The '*Direccíon*' was unusually friendly. The waitresses were charming and most attentive. They laughed not at but with me when I talked Portuguese to them. The rooms were warm. The *Parador* is modern, but it is built in the traditional Spanish 18th-century style and is beautifully furnished." (*C F Colt; also E D Taylor*)

Open All year.
Rooms 65 double, 8 single – most with bath, all with phone and air-conditioning.
Facilities Lounges, bar, dining room. Garden with swimming pool.
Location 2 km from Tordesillas on N620 to Salamanca.
Credit cards All major cards accepted.
Terms [1985 rates, excluding 5% tax] rooms: single 2,200–3,000pts, double
5,000–6,000pts. Breakfast 500pts; set lunch/dinner 1,600pts.

VALVERDE Hierro, Canary Islands   Map 15

Hotel Boomerang   *Tel* (922) 55.02.00
Calle Doctor Gost 1

Quite a discovery this, for Hierro is the smallest and most remote of the Canaries, and is not yet polluted by the tourist traffic that has invaded the other islands. Its few inhabitants raise sheep and goats, make cheeses, and produce a very drinkable white wine as well as figs, tomatoes and even bananas. "Faced with only one-star *hostals* for our stay on Hierro, we were delighted to come upon the *Boomerang*, in the island's tiny inland capital, Valverde. The name derives from the fact that the owner lived in Australia for fifteen years, earning enough as a welder to return and build this attractive hotel. It is a 42-bed family-run gem – white walls, pine shutters, marble floors, all very clean. Scalding hot water from solar panels. The food was excellent in the pretty dining room, a meeting place for the local notables. The owner showed us his cellar and invited us to eat paella with him and his wife, also served delicious wine and tapas. Tourism has hardly yet touched Hierro, but this hotel could remedy this. Travel between the islands is cheap and easy. As an away-from-it-all holiday, we thoroughly recommend the *Boomerang*." (*Joan M Beckett*)

Open All year.
Rooms 2 suites, 19 double – all with bath, telephone, radio, TV; some ground-floor rooms.
Facilities Dining room; night club under construction. English spoken.
Location Hierro is 30 minutes by air from Tenerife.
Restriction Not ideal for &.
Credit cards Diners, Visa.
Terms B&B: single 2,050pts, double 3,100pts; dinner, B&B: single 2,800pts, double 4,600pts; full board: single 3,300pts, double 5,600pts. Set lunch/dinner 750pts; full alc 950pts. 10% reduction for all English-speaking visitors.

VILLAJOYOSA Alicante   Map 15

Hotel El Montiboli   *Tel* (965) 89.02.54
Apartado 8   *Telex* 67712

"Indeed an oasis amid the horrors of the Costa Blanca – it was hard to believe that Benidorm was just up the road." *El Montiboli* is only eleven kilometres from that town and three from Villajoyosa on the Alicante road, but it stands on a rocky promontory over the sea in a position of privacy and calm. It was built in 1968 and has won a first prize for the best tourist building in Spain. There are plenty of sporting facilities available at the hotel – tennis, windsurfing, sailing, waterskiing, for all of which the hotel offers coaching. There's also a sound-proof disco at weekends, and a health and beauty centre.

Since our original entry, which warmly praised the food as well as the decor and ambience, one reader has found the service a bit haphazard. Another correspondent explains the hotel's origins: "Built some 15 years ago by a former pilot and airline owner from North Africa. The location was chosen for its spectacular view, quietness and reliable climate. Built in a classic Spanish style, rather Ibizan-like, with white-washed walls, traditional tiles made at a factory in the north of the province, and with each of its rooms and suites facing the sea, so that guests can bask in the privacy of their balconies and take in the view of the turquoise sea. Terrace pool with stairs to an attractive beach club, a second pool and tennis court. The small beach has been planted out with palms. An excellent hotel well worth recommending." (*N B; also D E and C M Tomlinson, Mrs J O Nairn*)

Open Apr – Oct.
Rooms 12 suites, 35 doubles, 2 single – all with bath and shower, telephone, radio and terrace overlooking the sea; TV and baby-listening on request; 14 rooms in annexe; 4 bungalow-type rooms.
Facilities Lifts; 2 salons, 3 bars, TV room, 2 restaurants; disco in summer; conference facilities. Large garden with children's play area, 2 swimming pools (1 seawater); health and beauty centre; stairs to sandy beach with beach club, wind-surfing, sailing, water-skiing (lessons available); deep sea fishing; tennis. English spoken.
Location 3 km S of Villajoyosa on Alicante/Benidorm road.
Restriction Not suitable for &.
Credit cards Amex, Diners, Visa.
Terms [1985 rates] rooms: single 4,000–7,000pts, double 7,800–12,000pts, suites 9,500–17,000pts. Breakfast 600pts; set lunch/dinner 2,400pts. Reduced rates for children sharing parents' room; special meals on request.

YESA Navarra   Map 15

Hospedería del Monasterio de   *Tel* (948) 88.41.00
San Salvador de Leyre

"This was the find of our holiday – it was our stopover on the way back from the Pyrenees to Santander. It is 50 kilometres east of Pamplona on the road to Jaca. The setting is extraordinary. Imagine a landscape framed by red-gold mountains. The valley is filled by a turquoise-coloured lake. Perched on a hillside is a four-square monastery. It is the only building in sight and its 18th-century conventual buildings are used as a hostal. *Benedictine monks sing their offices half a dozen times a day in the lovely church, the early kings of Navarre are buried there, and the crypt is 10th-century. The* hostal *is fitted out like a* parador *– quite luxurious. The food is simple and homely. Excellent value. We have never been anywhere like it."* (R Cranshaw)

The above entry first appeared in the 1982 edition, and was endorsed by subsequent travellers. But last year, we left it out following a real stinker of a report from a seasoned traveller: "Unquestionably merits inclusion in any list of great European belvederes, but has no place in your Guide." His meal had reminded him of his barrack-room days and so had his cell; the bar looked like and smelled like a bus station . . . Now several readers beg for reinstatement: they feel the word "luxurious" in the original nomination is inappropriate, and service was "casual and mostly non-welcoming", but rooms were "spotlessly clean, very simple, and in quiet good taste". Nothing special about the food, but "this is just where a hotel is wanted, between the Plymouth/Santander crossing and the Spanish Pyrenees" (John Hills); and "an invaluable retreat (I speak as an atheist) to recover after driving swiftly across France." (David Tench) More reports please.

Open Mar–Oct.
Rooms 5 suites, 15 double, 10 single – 20 with bath, 10 with shower, all with telephone.
Facilities 2 lounges (1 with TV), dining room; facilities for parties, conferences, etc. Large grounds; 4 km from lake with beaches, waterskiing, etc. English spoken.
Location Turn N off road from Pamplona to Jaca at Yesa.
Credit card Visa.
Terms Rooms with breakfast: single 1,300pts, double 3,900pts. Set lunch 1,000pts, dinner 900pts. Reduced rates and special meals for children under 7.

Sweden

RUSTHÅLLARGÅRDEN — ARILD

ARILD 260 43 Skåne   Map 7

Rusthållargården   *Tel* (042) 462.75

The hotel is about 200 metres from the Arild harbour and high enough to
command a magnificent view of the bay. The building is old – 17th
century – but has been modernised inside and an upper floor containing
bedrooms added. None of these bedrooms is alike; each is furnished in
its own personal style and has a name of its own – Grandmother's
Room, the Major's Room, Mamselle's Room, etc. "We had the Poet's
Room and very comfortable it was too. The food is excellent, particularly
the fish, which is sent up fresh from the harbour every morning. Diners
are encouraged to talk to the chef in advance and discuss with him
exactly what they would like. The wine-cellar is good. Peter Malgren,
fourth generation of the family that owns it, has given the hotel a
friendly feeling. It is well situated for those who like outdoor life. The
whole of the peninsula from Arild to Kulla is a national park, excellent
for walking and with lovely views. There are 10 golf courses within fairly
easy reach, and the fishing village has a harbour for visiting boats. There

is bathing there, but it is only a few kilometres to good sandy beaches. We enjoyed our stay there and thought it good value for money." *(J S)* More reports would be welcome.

Open Hotel all year; restaurant Jun–Aug inclusive.
Rooms 34 double, 8 single – 4 with bath, 38 with shower, all with telephone and radio; 5 self-catering cottages.
Facilities Lounges, TV room, library, restaurant. Garden with tennis and badminton. Sauna. On seafront with bathing, sailing and fishing; golf nearby. English spoken.
Location Take main road from Helsingborg to Höganäs. After 4 km take right turn to Arild.
Restriction Not suitable for &.
Credit cards Access, Visa.
Terms B&B 225–305 Skr; half-board 90 Skr per person added. Reduced rates and special meals for children.

BORGHOLM 387 00 Öland   Map 7

Halltorps Gästgiveri   *Tel* (0485) 552.50
Hogsrum

The island of Öland is reached from the mainland by a four-mile bridge, the longest in Europe. The *Halltorps Gästgiveri* – or country inn – is about midway down the island, looking out over the Kalmarsund, and is converted from a 17th-century royal stable. "The inn may once have been an enormous barn, but it has been newly and completely refurbished. The ground floor has a dining room of *superior* quality ... A gastronomic delight. There is also a breakfast room where the morning sun streams in. Breakfast is a buffet and perfectly delicious. There are only ten rooms. Ours was two-storeyed: a sitting room and bath on the first level and our bedroom upstairs under the sloping roof with a skylight. Furniture seemed to be authentic (very comfortable beds) and the wood fairly gleamed from all the polishing." *(Marian and El Nettles)*

Open All year except 1 Jan–1 Mar and Mon in Mar, Oct and Nov.
Rooms 8 double, 2 single – 1 with bath, 8 with shower, all with telephone, radio, colour TV and mini-bar; 6 rooms have lounge and loft.
Facilities Bar, 3 restaurants. Large garden. Sandy beaches with good bathing 1 km and 15 km. English spoken.
Location 10 km S of Borgholm. Parking.
Restriction Not suitable for &.
Credit cards All major cards accepted.
Terms B&B: single 325–360 Skr, double 450–550 Skr; dinner, B&B 385–450 Skr per person; full board 455–550 Skr per person. Set lunch 70 Skr, dinner 140 Skr; full alc 225 Skr. Reduced rates and special meals for children.

GOTHENBURG 416 66   Map 7

Tidbloms Hotel   *Tel* (031) 19.20.70
Olskrotsgatan 23   *Telex* 27369 TIDBLO S

A new hotel in a turn-of-the century, turreted, red-brick house, close to the centre of Sweden's second city. "Very pleasant – stone-flagged floor and 'country style' decor. The reception is friendly and the bar welcoming, the rooms converted and comfortable. The restaurant is in a vault that was formerly a bicycle repair shop. It does a roaring lunchtime trade with simple good food." Raclette a speciality. *(David Callow)* Could we hear from some recent visitors?

Open All year.
Rooms 3 suites, 14 double, 20 single – all with shower, telephone, radio, colour TV and baby-listening; 3 rooms equipped for &.
Facilities Lift. Cocktail bar, restaurant, conference facilities. Rock and sand beach 20 minutes. English spoken.
Location In the E part of Gothenberg, 10 minutes' drive from centre. Take E3 from centre of Stockholm. Parking.
Credit cards All major cards accepted.
Terms B&B: single 250–500 Skr, double 390–650 Skr. Children under 7 sharing parents' room free.

GRYTHYTTAN 710 60 Västmanland   Map 7

Grythyttans Gästgivaregärd   *Tel* (0591) 143.10

The village of Grythyttan is off the beaten track in a region of small lakes just north of huge Lake Vanern, "but those who take the time to visit this peaceful corner of old Sweden will not regret it". Several readers have lavished praise on this unusual inn, well known in Sweden for its French-influenced gastronomy, run with showmanlike *brio* by Carl-Jan Granqvist. "The inn has arisen from the dead. Originally built in 1640 in the heart of the then flourishing iron-mining district, it fell into disuse with the arrival of the railway, and slowly decayed. In 1972 it was re-opened; Mr Granqvist bought up the surrounding 18th-century shops and cottages, converted them into comfortable bedrooms, filled the rooms with antique furniture and art, dressed the staff in period clothes, and successfully re-created the atmosphere of 150 years ago. The food is gourmet, especially on Saturday evening and Sunday lunch-time. Many of the guests are passionately interested in what they eat, and every summer a few regular clients are allowed to work in the restaurant. Service is efficient and friendly. The staff seem to take great pride in what they are doing and regard themselves as cultural pioneers rather than hotel employees." *(Nils Blythe, Rosemary McRobert)*

Open All year.
Rooms 1 suite, 56 double, 13 single – 18 with bath, 52 with shower, all with telephone, radio and baby-listening. 52 rooms in annexe. Some ground-floor rooms.
Facilities Ramps, lounges, bars, 2 TV rooms, restaurant. Dancing on Sat. 2-acre grounds with tennis court. 150 lakes in area; boats for hire, bathing and fishing. English spoken.
Location 70 km W of Orebro. In centre of village. Parking.
Credit cards All major cards accepted.
Terms B&B: 290–415 Skr; dinner, B&B: 475–600 Skr; full board 575–700 Skr. Set lunch 110–190 Skr, dinner 220–325 Skr; full alc 350 Skr. Children under 4 free; 5–12 50%.

Feedback from Scandinavia is inevitably less than from other more touristy parts of Europe. If you have been to Scandinavia and stayed in a good hotel, whether in the present Guide or not, please write and tell us.

SALTSJÖBADEN Stockholm   Map 7

Grand Hotel Saltsjöbaden   *Tel* (08) 717.00.20
Box 329, 133 03, Saltsjöbaden   *Telex* 102 10 SEAHOT

A 19th-century hotel, built with the traditional Bavarian-style stepped
roof that one sees all over northern Europe, located in a residential area
of Stockholm about 20 kilometres from the centre. The hotel housed a
great many Russian refugees after 1918 before bestowing her favours on
the likes of Harold Macmillan, Douglas Fairbanks, Mary Pickford and
the Aga Khan (what grand place hasn't *he* haunted?) "An old-fashioned
hotel by the sea. Very comfortable rooms, beautiful view from at least
half of them. Very quiet, relaxing. Excellent service, good food (wine as
unimaginative as usual in Sweden). Used a lot as a conference hotel – I
took part in a conference – but there are also plenty of other guests." *(Dr
Andrew Herxheimer)*

Open All year.
Rooms 9 suites, 50 double, 53 single – 99 with bath, 4 with shower, all with
telephone, radio, and baby-listening. Some ground-floor rooms.
Facilities Lifts. 2 TV rooms, 2 bars, restaurant, conference facilities; disco every
night, live music in bar and dining room. Large garden with mini-golf, tennis
courts, yacht harbour, beach, private island. English spoken.
Location 18 km E of centre of Stockholm on 228 road.
Credit cards All major cards accepted.
Terms B&B: single 450–695 Skr, double 630–990 Skr; dinner, B&B: single 500–785
Skr, double 730–1,040 Skr; full board: single 550–835 Skr, double 830–1,140 Skr; set
lunch 72 Skr, dinner 102 Skr; full alc 235 Skr. Reduced rates and special meals for
children. *Note:* These tariffs will increase by about 12% after April 1986.

SIGTUNA 193 00 Uppland   Map 7

Stadshotellet   *Tel* (0760) 501.00
Stora Nygatan 3

Sigtuna, an attractive old town between Stockholm and Uppsala, is said
to be the oldest in Sweden, and has ruins of very early Christian
churches. "It lies in a large lake which in March was frozen over. You
could walk across it and several men were successfully fishing through
holes in the ice. The hotel is a typical older Swedish wooden building,
recently refurbished and repainted by new owners. The bedrooms are
adequate, the restaurant with its beautiful views over the lake a delight.
Usual superb Swedish buffet breakfast." *(David Callow)*

Open All year.
Rooms 26 – all with bath or shower, telephone, radio and colour TV.
Facilities Salons, restaurant, sauna, solarium.
Location About 45 km NW of Stockholm.
Credit cards Some cards possibly accepted.
Terms [1985 rates] B&B: single from 400 Skr, double from 500 Skr. Set lunch from
30 Skr, dinner from 80 Skr. Special weekend rates.

> There are many expensive hotels in the Guide. We are keen to
> increase our coverage at the other end of the scale. If you know of
> a simple place giving simple satisfaction, please write and tell us.

STOCKHOLM   Map 7

Hotell Anno 1647   *Tel* (08) 440.480
3 Mariagränd, 116 46   *Telex* 12550

This smallish hotel takes its name from its history: in 1647 a red-brick
house was built on the site by a master tailor. "Not easy to find, but well
worth it when we did! A beautiful old house, with a small courtyard,
furnished with due regard for its period. The *pièce de résistance*, which
crowned the sense of gracious living, was the huge and magnificent
sitting room forming part of our suite (there are two of these in the
hotel). We felt like 18th-century aristocrats. There were fascinating
views from the windows over the Old Town and across the water. The
hotel has no restaurant but there is a pleasant breakfast room in the
basement. (People who find stairs a problem might be well advised to
stay elsewhere.) The staff were friendly and obliging." *(J and J W)*

Open All year.
Rooms 2 suites, 20 double, 21 single – 12 with shower, all with telephone, radio
and most with colour TV; some ground-floor rooms.
Facilities Breakfast room in basement. Sea within walking distance, fishing.
English spoken.
Location Central, in side street at Götgatan 3, by Slussen on the island of
Södermalm. Garage parking.
Restriction Not suitable for &.
Credit cards Access, Diners, Visa.
Terms (including tax and service) B&B: single 325–510 Skr, double 435–620 Skr.
(No restaurant.)

Hotel Diplomat   *Tel* (08) 63.58.00
Strandvägen 7 S-104 40

The *Diplomat*, in a fine central position overlooking the waterfront, is
described by one visitor as "expensive, fashionable and quietly distinguished", and by another as "a haven of placid bourgeois comfort, with
an air of discretion". It may not be all that discreet, for its ground-floor
tea-house is a smart Stockholm rendezvous, serving also as a breakfast
room, coffee-shop and (except on weekends in summer) an evening
restaurant; it is fresh and summery, with potted plants, white chairs,
check tablecloths. Bedrooms vary with price: the dearer ones, elegant
and modern, look on to the harbour. An inspector last year enjoyed her
lavish buffet breakfast and her prawn salad at lunch, but not so much
her beef in cherry sauce at dinner; service she found haphazard and, in
the restaurant, slow. *(S B, Tom Pocock)*

Open All year.
Rooms 5 suites (1 with private sauna bath), 70 double, 57 single – 98 with bath, 34
with shower, all with telephone, radio and colour TV.
Facilities Lounges, TV room, cocktail bar, tea-house, restaurant, open-air café,
sauna; conference facilities. English spoken.
Location 5 minutes' walk from centre. Parking.
Credit cards All major cards accepted.
Terms Rooms with breakfast: single 625–995 Skr, double 950–1,100 Skr, suites
1,500–2,800 Skr.

Hotel Esplanade   *Tel* (08) 63.07.40
Strandvägen 7 A S-114 56

"For those who require the traditional quiet bed-and-breakfast hotel in a
big city, the *Esplanade* fits the bill perfectly. Almost next door to the
National Theatre, very central, it overlooks one of Stockholm's attractive
stretches of water. The entrance is in a quiet courtyard. It is compact and
cosy; rooms are not enormous, but adequate and pleasantly furnished; a
restful sitting-room overlooks the harbour. The staff remember your
name, the floorboards creak cosily. Very reasonable." *(Murray Sutton)*

Open All year except 6 July–4 Aug.
Rooms 33 – 29 with bath or shower.
Facilities Lounge, balcony, breakfast room.
Location Central; near the National Theatre.
Credit cards Some cards possibly accepted.
Terms [1985 rates] B&B: single, 350–550 Skr, double 690–750 Skr. Weekend rates.
(No restaurant.)

Lady Hamilton Hotel   *Tel* (08) 23.46.80
Storkyrkobrinken 5, S-111 28
Lord Nelson Hotel   *Tel* (08) 23.23.90
Västerlånggatan 22, S-111 29   *Telex* 10434 (for both hotels)

Two smallish hotels of character, owned by the same small company,
and within a stone's throw of each other in the old town. "Both hotels
are sheer delight. They were made by knocking together two or three
old houses dating from the 15th century, each faithfully portraying its
theme down to the smallest detail. Nautical pictures and prints, models
of ships and embroideries done by sailors provide the backdrop. There
are also items taken from boats – coloured prows, brass rails and
wooden helms. The owners have lent some of their own antiques too."
The bedrooms are modern but not very large, and each has a traditional
wooden decorated wall cupboard that, apart from being lovely, doesn't
hold much. Readers this year recommend the *Lady Hamilton*, but warn of
street noise. The basement plunge-pool in the *Lady Hamilton* was a well
in the 15th century. *(Mr and Mrs C R Safford, D M Callow)*

Lady Hamilton Hotel
Open All year.
Rooms 3 small suites, 18 double, 13 single – 6 with bath, 28 with shower, all with
telephone, radio and colour TV.
Facilities Bar; conference facilities; sauna, plunge-pool. English spoken.
Location Central, in old town, near palace. (Front rooms can be noisy.) No
garage; parking locally.
Credit cards All major cards accepted.
Terms [1985 rates] B&B: single 740–780 Skr, double 860–920 Skr. Reduced prices
17 June–4 Aug and some weekends. (No restaurant.)

Lord Nelson Hotel
Open All year.
Rooms 9 double, 22 single – all with shower, telephone, radio and colour TV.
Facilities Rooftop terrace, sauna, conference facilities. English spoken.
Location Central, in old town, near royal palace. No garage, but parking locally.
Credit cards All major cards accepted.
Terms B&B: single 560–600 Skr, double 620–720 Skr. Reduced prices 17 June–
4 Aug and some weekends. (No restaurant.)

Sara Hotell Reisen *Tel* (08) 22.32.60
Skeppsbron 12–14, S–111 30 *Telex* 17494 REISEN

"If you like ships you will certainly like the *Reisen*, three 17th-century merchants' houses sympathetically gouged out and joined together. Not only is the decor generally maritime, but the hotel stands bang on the quayside, where ships for the archipelago come and go, and looks across to the elegant white three-master *Chapman*, permanently moored on Skeppsholmen and floodlit at night, I am told, by courtesy of the hotel. The rooms are snugly luxurious, like bedrooms in a very well-appointed shipowners' house, and if they happen to be at the side of the building are fitted with external mirrors to give you a view of the harbour anyway. Immediately behind the *Reisen* is the glorious jumble of the Old City, almost next door is the Royal Palace, a short walk away is the Opera House; but best of all, it is one of the very nicest places I know for watching the boats go by." *(Jan Morris)*

Open All year except Christmas.
Rooms 2 suites, 98 double, 26 single – all with bath, telephone, radio and TV.
Facilities Lobby, library/bar, grill restaurant. Nightly piano music in Clipper Club room. Indoor heated swimming pool, sauna. Hotel fronts on harbour with free salmon fishing. English spoken.
Location Central, in old town. (Light sleepers may be disturbed by traffic noise.) Meter parking only.
Restriction Not suitable for &.
Credit cards All major cards accepted.
Terms B&B: single 780–860 Skr, double 940–1,050 Skr; dinner, B&B 130 Skr per person added; full board 260 Skr added. Set lunch 150 Skr, dinner 250 Skr; full alc 300 Skr. Children under 15 free in parents' room.

TÄLLBERG 793 03 Dalarna Map 7

Hotel Åkerblads *Tel* (0247) 508.00

The Åkerblad family have been here since the early 18th century, and Christine and Arne Åkerblad are the 14th and 15th generations – probably the oldest reigning hotel family in Europe. They speak good English. Tällberg is halfway between Leksand and Rättvik on Lake Siljan. The hotel, the oldest part of which is a 17th-century farmhouse, is a comfortable and spacious building in the old style. It has a fine view of the lake. The bedrooms are pleasantly furnished, hardly any two being alike: they vary in size and price, the nicest being in the main building. There is a sauna and a warm brine-bath (very luxurious) all the year round, a tennis court in summer and an ice-rink in winter. Other winter attractions are good skiing, torchlit sleigh-rides through the woods and log fires in the evening. In summer there is good bathing and fishing in the lake, boats available. In the spring and autumn, the hotel runs a variety of courses: "basket-painting in the old way, slim weeks with luxury foods (not fat) and Champagne and dry wines ..."

Our inspector agreed with an earlier account that caught the charm of the place well: "We loved *Åkerblads*! We had a delightful bedroom with verandas. It felt very Swedish painted in different shades of green and orange. The atmosphere in the hotel is easy and informal. We loved the meals too – all very Swedish. Everyone helped themselves from a central table. Lunch seemed to be the main meal – often with several kinds of fish and potatoes with dill. It always ended with cake and excellent coffee in the upper hall. Local parties coming for meals often included men and women in national costume. Christina and Arne Åkerblad made us very welcome – it was a pleasant and somehow particularly Swedish experience." (J A Wainwright, S B)

Open All year except 20–27 Dec.
Rooms 4 suites, 33 double, 13 single – 45 with shower, all with telephone, radio and baby-listening; some with colour TV; 26 rooms in annexe.
Facilities 2 sitting rooms, coffee/dancing room, bar with disco. Dances once a week in winter. 2 TV rooms, 2 dining rooms; facilities for parties and functions. Large garden with tennis court, badminton, table-tennis, skating rink; bicycles; sauna, warm brine-bath, hair salon; skiing, sleigh-rides in winter; bathing at beach 400 metres away, fishing, boating in summer. English spoken.
Location 12 km from Leksand; on road between Leksand and Rättvik. Parking.
Restrictions Not suitable for ♿.
Credit cards Access, Diners, Visa.
Terms B&B: single 210–235 Skr, double 300–340 Skr. Set lunch 65–75 Skr, dinner 75–85 Skr; full alc 175 Skr. Reduced rates for children depending on age; special meals.

TANUMSHEDE 457 00 Bohuslän   Map 7

Tanums Gestgifveri

Tel (0525) 29010
Telex 5-42031

The *Gestgifveri*, which means "guesthouse", from the outside looks nothing special, a two-storey building with yellow-painted wooden walls. But it is a place of character, an inn that has been serving wayfarers since 1663. "An elegant and charming hotel with an air of sophistication unusual in Sweden. Lounge and bedrooms are in the modern hotel, restaurant in the converted 17th-century inn, close by. It is prettily furnished throughout with warm fabrics, soft lamp lighting, a profusion of prints and paintings. No two bedrooms are alike, some feminine and flowery, others plainer and more sophisticated, all comfortable. The restaurant has earned a reputation for French food, and a lot of the dishes are very rich, but of good quality. The wine list was one of the better ones I have seen in Sweden, but with high mark-ups." Another visitor points out that there is some noise, despite double-glazing, for the E6 runs close by. There are Bronze Age rock carvings in the area. (S B)

Open 7 Mar–7 Nov (closed Good Friday and 1 May).
Rooms 2 suites, 20 double, 7 single – 4 with bath, 25 with shower, all with telephone and radio, tea-making facilities and baby-listening; TV in double rooms and suites; 15 ground-floor rooms.
Facilities Lift. Lobby, salon with TV, bar, cafeteria, pool room; small sauna with dip-pool. Beach, fishing and sea bathing 4–6 km; golf 20 km. English spoken.
Location On E6 near village centre. Parking. Village is 150 km N of Göteborg.
Restriction Not suitable for ♿.
Credit cards Access, Diners, Visa.
Terms B&B: single 370 Skr, double 600 Skr; half-board: single 500 Skr, double 900 Skr; full board: single 600 Skr, double 1,100 Skr. 50% reduction for children under 10; under 2, free; special meals.

Switzerland

RHEINHOTEL FISCHERZUNFT
SCHAFFHAUSEN

AROSA 7050 Graubünden | **Map 13**

Hotel Hof Maran | *Tel* (081) 31.01.85
Telex 74329

"High above Arosa – alongside the golf course and the cross-country ski
course, depending on the season – is the very large and superbly
equipped Hof Maran, a mixture of modern hotel grafted on to the old
Swiss chalet from which it has sprung. Half-board is almost obligatory as
it is a long way down to the town, but food, as so often in Switzerland,
lacked that vital touch of imagination. Breakfast in the bedroom looking
out to distant snow-covered peaks was the best of all possible starts to
the day. The bedroom door was nearly a foot thick and totally
soundproof, closing with a gentle clunk; the bedroom furniture in
honey-gold wood veneer was superbly finished. The beds were
wonderfully hard; the bathroom beautifully fitted with all the latest
gadgets, and spotless. Dinner at 7 pm – ushered in and out with Swiss
efficiency – did mean rather a long evening, but on our second night the
small band set up and the lounge fairly rocked with music and dancing.
Surprisingly, the only thing missing was a swimming pool and sauna."
(*Angela and David Stewart*)

Open 5 Dec – Easter, 5 June – end Sept.
Rooms 52 double, 19 single – 50 with bath, 3 with shower, all with telephone,
radio, TV on request.

Facilities Lift, lounge, TV room, children's games room with ping-pong, 2 "Stübli", dining room, sun terrace on roof; conference facilities, dancing in the bar. 5 tennis courts (pro available), 9-hole golf-course. Ski-lift and ski school behind hotel.
Location Above Arosa, about 10 minutes' drive. Bus service every 20 minutes. Parking.
Restriction Not suitable for &.
Credit cards Amex, Diners, Visa.
Terms *Summer prices* B&B: single 40–100 Sfrs, double 80–220 Sfrs; half-board: single 100–135 Sfrs, double 130–270 Sfrs; *winter prices* half-board: single 110–180 Sfrs; double 210–370 Sfrs.

ASCONA 6612 Ticino   Map 13

Hotel Casa Berno   *Tel* (093) 35.32.32
                                                          Telex 846167

"The charm of Ascona is its beautiful situation facing Lago Maggiore. The wooded surroundings, the romantic attraction of the most beautiful of north Italian lakes and the limitless possibilities of excursions into the unspoilt valleys of the Ticino make up for the hustle and bustle of the village and the overcrowded city of Locarno." (*Arnold Horwell*)

Casa Berno lies on the hillside between Monte Verità and Ronco, about 30 minutes' walk from Ascona's centre. The views from the hotel's terraces and swimming pool over lake, islands and surrounding mountains are stunning. All the rooms face south, and have a balcony or terrace. The swimming pool is heated, and there are ample secluded terraced meadows for those who prefer solitary peace. This four-star hotel merits another excellent report this year: "We are not lovers of modern hotels but we thoroughly enjoyed our stay here. The public rooms are spacious and attractively furnished and our bedroom was light and airy with ample wardrobe space, large comfortable beds and even a 'mini' fridge disguised in the writing desk. The room was kept spotless and the bathroom was tidied and towels changed several times each day. Breakfast is an extensive buffet which can be taken on the terrace, and we found the *en pension* dinner to be consistently good. The staff were cheerful, helpful and efficient." (*Rosamund V Hebdon, M R*)

Open Mar–Nov.
Rooms 11 suites, 43 double, 7 single – all with phone, radio, balcony or terrace.
Facilities Lift; lounges (1 with TV), bar on roof-garden, grill room, restaurant with terrace. Sauna, massage, solarium, fitness room, ladies' hairdresser. Garden with heated swimming pool. Golf, tennis nearby. English spoken. &.
Location Between Monte Verità and Ronco; 15 minutes' downhill walk or 20–25 minutes' uphill from Ascona. Parking.
Credit card Amex.
Terms B&B: 108–130 Sfrs; half-board 120–150 Sfrs; full board 140–170 Sfrs. Set lunch 30 Sfrs, dinner 35 Sfrs; full alc 35 Sfrs. Reduced rates for children sharing parents' room; special meals.

> Wherever possible, we have quoted prices per room. Not all hotels are prepared to quote tariffs in this way. In these cases, we have given prices per person, indicating the range of prices – the lowest is likely to be for sharing a double room out of season, the highest for a single room in the high season.

BASLE Map 13

Hotel Drei Könige am Rhein
Blumenrain 8, Basle 4001

Tel (061) 25.52.52
Telex 62937

The five-star *Drei Könige* claims to have been an inn since 1026, and to be by far the oldest hostelry in Switzerland. It has a famous Golden Guest Book, bearing such name-dropping autographs as Voltaire, Dickens, Napoleon, Queen Victoria (though only when she was Princess Victoria), Farouk, and many other late and ci-devant monarchs and potentates. Today, it is one of the Leading Hotels of the World consortium, and prices are at the upper end of the tariff spectrum. "Very attractive hotel near the University. My bedroom had a delightful terrace overlooking the Rhine. The dining room similarly overlooks the Rhine. Good international cuisine. Bedrooms pleasantly furnished. A thoroughly relaxing hotel in a busy city." *(Robert Shackleton)*

Open All year.
Rooms 7 suites, 48 double, 35 single – all with bath, direct-dial telephone, radio, TV (with individual video recorder) and mini-bar; 38 rooms in annexe.
Facilities Lift, reception/sitting area, salon, bar with piano music, rotisserie, restaurant terrace overlooking the Rhine. Banquet/conference facilities; nightly disco. English spoken.
Location Central. Parking.
Restriction Not suitable for よ.
Credit cards All major cards accepted.
Terms B&B: single 162–227 Sfrs, double 254–380 Sfrs. Set lunch/dinner 17–48 Sfrs, dinner 88 Sfrs; full alc 65 Sfrs.

Hotel Merian am Rhein
Greifengasse/Rheingasse 2, Basle 4058

Tel (061) 25.94.66
Telex 63537

"Excellent value. Not luxurious but clean, friendly, efficient, central, on the bank of the Rhine, and with a superb café/restaurant. There is also an outdoor café on the river bank. My single bedroom was small but adequately furnished: a chair that fitted the well-lit desk (unusual); a comfortable bed with one of those awful duvets that everyone likes except me; a radio that worked; an adequate bathroom; a well-stocked mini-bar. And there was a fantastic view over the Rhine. That the hotel is outstanding value for money in an expensive country may be confirmed by the clientele, who were all Swiss." *(John M Sidwick)*

Open All year.
Rooms 57 – most with bath or shower and WC, all with radio, telephone and mini-bar.
Facilities Lift, bar restaurant, terrace café.
Location Central at N end of Mittlere Brücke (Central Bridge). By car go to the Schweizer Mustermesse (Swiss Industries Fair); hotel is sign-posted from there. Riverside rooms are quietest.
Credit cards Most major cards accepted.
Terms Room with breakfast: single 50–100 Sfrs, double 125 – 165 Sfrs.

> We get less feedback from smaller and more remote hotels. But we need feedback on all hotels: big and small, far and near, famous and first-timers.

DAVOS DORF 7260 Graubünden   Map 13

Hotel Flüela   *Tel* (83) 6.12.21
                                                  Telex 74347

Davos has several connections with the British. Arthur Conan Doyle
was one of the first to ski in Davos, the second person to ski from Davos
to Arosa (in 1886) over the Flüela Pass, and was largely responsible for
introducing skiing to Davos. Robert Louis Stevenson was sent to the
resort in late 1880 because of chronic lung disease, and completed
Treasure Island there. He was also responsible for introducing ice skating
and tobogganing. The British still mainly come for winter sports. The
Flüela has been in existence over a century, still managed by the Gredig
family. It is close to the Parsenn Bahn, the largest ski lift in the resort. It
is open only in the winter season. A nominator writes: "Really quite
outstanding. The hotel excels in general comfort – super lounges, with
pianist every evening, open log fire, indoor swimming pool, sauna,
solarium; and quite outstanding breakfast and dinner – really the best
food I have ever had during a skiing holiday. The service was
particularly friendly and helpful." *(Dr T J David)*

Open End Nov – end Apr.
Rooms 10 suites, 60 double, 20 single – 82 with bath, 8 with shower, all with
telephone, radio, TV.
Facilities Bar, lounge, sitting rooms, function rooms, several restaurants. Pianist
in bar-lounge. Indoor heated swimming pool with sauna, solarium, massage,
barber, hairdresser. English spoken.
Location In town centre. Parking. A few roadside rooms may be noisy.
Restriction Not suitable for &.
Credit cards All major cards accepted.
Terms B&B: single 90–170 Sfrs, double 180–340 Sfrs; dinner, B&B: single 135–215
Sfrs, double 270–430 Sfrs; full board: single 160–240 Sfrs, double 320–480 Sfrs. Set
lunch 30 Sfrs, dinner 50 Sfrs; full alc 75 Sfrs. Reduced rates and special meals for
children.

ENGELBERG 6390 Unterwalden   Map 13

Hotel Eden   *Tel* (041) 94.32.94

"We wanted a small, comfortable, friendly hotel, with no package-tour
groups, noisy bars or discos – and very good food. We found everything
in your entry to be entirely correct. Thomas and Sybil Reinhardt-Waser
speak good English and went out of their way to make sure that we were
comfortable, well looked after, and excellently fed. Thomas did all the
cooking, and in 11 nights never repeated any item on the set menu. The
locals said: 'Ah, yes, a very good kitchen!' The rooms were clean and
warm with comfortable beds and plenty of hot water, a bowl of fruit,
and efficient built-in hair dryers in the bathroom. The hotel is ideally
situated: easy walking distance from the station, ski-lift, bus-stop, new
sports centre (with an ice rink and indoor tennis courts), swimming
pool, ski-school and hire, and all the shops. People were very friendly
and helpful and there is penty to do if skiing is not possible for any
reason." *(Mr & Mrs M R M Leslie)*

Open Mid-Dec to mid-Apr; Jun–Oct.
Rooms 10 double – 8 with shower and WC, all with telephone, radio and mini-bar.
Facilities Sitting room with radio, TV room (colour), games room for children, restaurant. Garden and terrace where meals can be taken in summer. Swimming pool and sports centre nearby; close to ski-school and mountain walks. English spoken.
Location Central, near station. Garage and outdoor parking.
Credit cards All major cards accepted.
Terms B&B: single 50–65 Sfrs, double 94–110 Sfrs; dinner, B&B: single 68–83 Sfrs, double 130–146 Sfrs. Set lunch/dinner 15–18 Sfrs. Reduced rates for family holidays in summer and skiing holidays in winter (1 or 2 weeks). Reductions for children under 15; special meals.

GENEVA 1204   Map 13

Hôtel Les Armures   *Tel* (022) 28.91.72
1 Rue du Puits St-Pierre, Vieille Ville   *Telex* 421129

Not one of the grand, bland hotels with a view of the lake but a relatively small and elegant establishment in a quiet little square near the cathedral, high up in the Old Town. It is an old stone building and its restaurant, on to which it backs, is said to be the oldest in Geneva – and excellent: "from interesting experiments to just-a-salad to burgers to very good raclette". Only complaint is the noise: chiefly from kids in hot rods with radios hanging around in the Vieille Ville till the small hours. "The small reception area does not betray the treasure of comfort and perfection within. Nothing is lacking, and the service is unsurpassed, from the way your 'continental breakfast' is served in your room to the quiet execution of any of your wishes. I always ask for the quietest room in the house: it was beautifully furnished with a small roof garden/patio outside its windows, which made it impossible to hear a sound from anywhere. The finest, lightest duvet. In the perfectly equipped bathroom nothing was lacking. I am certain that had one lost one's luggage they would have been able to supply a toothbrush and nightie!" (*Mrs K M Plowden*)

Open All year. Restaurant closed public holidays.
Rooms 4 suites, 16 double, 8 single – all with bath, telephone, radio and colour TV.
Facilities Lift, lobby, salon, breakfast room, bar, lounge, restaurant, *Stüberl* (rustic bar/restaurant). English spoken.
Location Central, near St-Pierre cathedral. No special parking facilities.
Restriction Probably not suitable for &.
Credit cards All major cards accepted.
Terms B&B: single 180 Sfrs, double 230 Sfrs. Meal prices not known.

GRINDELWALD 3818   Berner Oberland   Map 13

Hotel Fiescherblick   *Tel* (036) 53.11.64

"Grindelwald, whose main street seems to contain an aimless football scrum – immaculate Japanese versus scruffy booted walkers hoping to pass as climbers – has its compensations in the beauty of the Jungfrau group and the Jungfraujoch railway. Grindelwald sports mainly characterless would-be chalet type hotels but we fell gratefully into one which while on the main street was sufficiently above the hurly-burly and directly opposite the church. The *Fiescherblick* is an old chalet, with attractive antiques to give atmosphere. The charming dining room is panelled, and the food is satisfying whether demi-pension or à la carte. I can particularly recommend emincé zürichoise. The manager told us he was in danger of losing his three-star status because of having no porter or lift – the age and structure of the building makes the latter impossible. But in a town where much is bogus we found it clean, unpretentious and good value." *(Catherine Green; also Patrick Till)*

Open 15 Dec – 15 Apr, 1 June – 20 Oct. Restaurant closed Tue.
Rooms 20 double, 3 single – 15 with bath, 8 with shower, all with telephone, radio and mini-bar, many with balcony.
Facilities Lounge, TV lounge, bar, restaurant. Garden and terrace. Winter sports and mountain climbing. English spoken.
Location Centre of village, near church. Parking.
Restriction Not suitable for &.
Credit cards Access, Diners, Visa.
Terms B&B: 46–56 Sfrs; half-board 22 Sfrs per person added. Set lunch 12–30 Sfrs, dinner 16–60 Sfrs; full alc 40–60 Sfrs. 30–50% reductions and special menus for children.

GSTAAD 3780 Berner Oberland   Map 13

Hotel Christiania   *Tel* (030) 45121
Hauptstrasse   *Telex* 922250 CHRI

More reports this year confirm earlier praise of this chalet, the smallest four-star hotel in fashionable Gstaad and located in the main street. The restaurant is small and one needs to book at weekends even when staying in the hotel. Madame's daughter is the chef and her son-in-law the head waiter. Dinner is said to be excellent, but breakfasts have disappointed. "We had a lovely welcome from Mrs Nopper, and our rooms were beautifully furnished and very comfortable. Even our walking shoes were cleaned when placed outside the door. The set meal was unusually good, the restaurant cosy and comfortable and the service discreet and efficient." *(Mr & Mrs B Williams)*

Another couple found Madame's welcome a little chilly, but she "warmed up later when we needed her help for a frozen car". They also mentioned "strangely thin towels in the bathroom which didn't match each other or the decor" and a shock at the bill stage – an extra 4% for paying by Visa.

Open All year.
Rooms 3 suites, 15 double, 8 single – all with bath, telephone, radio, colour TV, most with balcony.
Facilities Salon with fireplace, TV room, restaurant, garden where meals are served. Guests have free use of the heated swimming pool near the Palace Hotel in summer. English spoken.
Location Central, opposite the skating rink; light sleepers might find front rooms noisy. Garage. On outskirts of village, on right when coming from Saanen.
Restrictions No children under 6. Not suitable for &.
Credit card Visa.
Terms Rooms with breakfast: single 65–160 Sfrs, double 160–340 Sfrs; dinner, B&B: single 120–190 Sfrs, double 220–380 Sfrs. Set meals 34–40 Sfrs, full alc 85–100 Sfrs. Special meals for children. Christmas and New Year: no reservations of less than 15 days.

GUARDA 7575 Graubünden   Map 13

Hotel Meisser   *Tel* (084) 92188

The picturesque village of Guarda, once an important staging-post on the old main road between Munich and Milan, lies at 1600 metres, high above the Inn valley of the Lower Engadin, and splendidly isolated since 1865 when a new main road was built along the valley. "The setting is spectacular, with snow-capped mountains, panoramic views and many walking trails. Guarda is often referred to as the museum village of the Engadin valley. The houses are very old, some of the best examples of Engadin architecture that we saw in this area. Within easy driving or long walking distance are several other interesting villages, including a castle at Tarasp. We were further charmed as the bell-laden cows were herded down the narrow, cobbled main street at milking time. The hotel itself was wonderful. It is an old, nicely restored Engadin house, and we were fortunate enough to stay in what had been the upstairs living room. The room was large, and the original wooden walls and hand-carved ceiling were an unexpected pleasure. The low, carved wooden doors with their original door furniture belong in a museum. The dining room and terrace café were added where the barn was once attached to the house. The glass-enclosed restaurant section of the dining room offers breathtaking panoramas in every direction. The owners speak excellent English and were more than happy to explain the extensive menu to us. The food was delicious and the service was outstanding." *(Becky Sproviero) Arnold Horwell*, a veteran Swiss traveller, also warmly recommends the *Meisser*: "It preserves the character of an old-established Swiss hostelry, with rooms ranging from tiny garrets with shower to handsome large bedrooms with bath, and serving excellent Swiss bourgeois cuisine." (He also commends as a more modern alternative, the *"heimelig" Piz Buin*, at the upper end of the village, "in an entirely rural setting with wood-covered mountains providing a classic Alpine background".)

Open June – Oct.
Rooms 50 – most with bath or shower, all with telephone and radio.
Facilities Salon, dining room, terrace café. Garden. Winter sports, walking etc.
Location E of Davos; 2 km from Guarda station. Parking.
Credit cards Most major cards accepted.
Terms [1985 rates] Dinner, B&B: single 54–81 Sfrs, double 110–160 Sfrs; full board 12 Sfrs per person added.

HORN-AM-BODENSEE 9326 East Switzerland   Map 13

Hotel Schiff   *Tel* (071) 413040
Seestrasse 74

Horn is situated on the southern shore of the Bodensee, renowned in the warmer months for its sailing and swimming. One reader calls the *Hotel Schiff* "simple but delightful, kept spotlessly clean. Our bedroom was unexpectedly large, furnished simply, and in impeccable taste, with very comfortable beds." The main asset of this modest hotel is the garden, on the edge of the spectacular lake, where guests may take drinks and an evening meal of well-cooked fish fresh from the lake.

Another reader writes: *"Hotel Schiff* is a nice stop-gap if you need a decent place to put your head on a pillow and get a good meal after a day's drive." *(John and Elizabeth Hills, Professor H C Robbins Landon)*

Open Dates not known.
Rooms 14 beds – all rooms have shower, WC, radio-alarm and TV.
Facilities Restaurant/bar. Garden by lake.
Location On the S shore of Lake Constance. Parking.
Credit cards Not known if accepted.
Terms [1985 rates] Room with breakfast: single 40 Sfrs, double 77 Sfrs. Meals à la carte (price not known).

KANDERSTEG 3718 Berner Oberland — Map 13

Hotel Blümlisalp — *Tel* (033) 75.12.44
Telex 9221631

"The perfect introduction to Switzerland, with every kind of winter and summer activity", is one reader's comment on the resort of Kandersteg, 1,200 metres up, at the foot of the Blümlisalp range. And for those who want to be hoisted higher, whether skiers or walkers, there are chairlifts and cabin lifts. You should go up by foot, or by lift, to the serene and lovely Oeschinensee which lies just below the Blümlisalp. The eponymous hotel, down in the resort, is a middle-sized middle-priced middle-class family place, in a fine scenic position and well equipped with sporting adjuncts: an indoor swimming pool with what the hotel calls underwater massage and against-current swimming, an American bowling alley (sound-proofed) as well as a games room. In the summer the hotel organises picnic parties, walking tours and botanic trips; in winter there are sledge-drives and ski-tours at night with *Glühwein.* "Pleasant, with simple rooms, reasonable food, and very friendly helpful owners." *(Dr P Marsh)*

Open Mid-Dec to mid-Apr, mid-May to mid-Oct.
Rooms 20 double, 4 single – 8 with bath, 12 with shower, all with radio.
Facilities Lift, TV room, lounge, bar, 2 restaurants. Bowling alley, heated indoor swimming pool and whirlpool, solarium, games room, sun terrace, garden; fondue parties, garden parties. Walking, winter sports. English spoken.
Location In village main street near chairlift to Oeschinensee. Parking.
Credit cards Access, Diners, Visa.
Terms [1985 rates] B&B: 35–65 Sfrs, dinner, B&B: 46–79 Sfrs, full board 58–91 Sfrs. Full alc 28 Sfrs. Reduced weekly rates in low season; reduced rates for over-65s, and for children sharing parents' room: babies free; under 6, 50%; under 12, 30%; special meals.

Hotel Ermitage — *Tel* (033) 75.15.12

One visitor usefully compares the *Blümlisalp* (above) with the *Hotel Ermitage,* for he has stayed in both. He prefers the *Ermitage* for its more spacious rooms with TV sets and refrigerators, and because it was more friendly, had a better chef and was not on the village street. He continues: "The resort is less spoiled than many others and is an excellent walking centre. The first attraction of the *Ermitage* is that it stands half a mile from the main road, amid meadows and woods: cars can get to it, but no traffic passes here at night, so it is quiet. A pleasant walk leads in ten minutes to the village; the woods and the closeness of the mountain slopes keep the air beautifully fresh. If you love the sound of rushing water to go to sleep by, several waterfalls and a steep brook provide that. The hotel is now 12 years old and is run by Mrs Hirschi and her family – staff were among the friendliest and most helpful I have met in Switzerland. Rooms are beautifully furnished, with well-equipped bathrooms; the front-facing rooms all have large balconies with deckchairs, while at the other end is a fully-equipped kitchenette, with plenty of space in the mini-bar/fridge. Half-board terms are the norm, but out of season you can have the room with breakfast only. Breakfast is a buffet of a high standard. The hotel has a lovely garden restaurant and this was used all day long. Really excellent cakes are made on the premises and portions served were very large. The hotel's only snags: no separate lounge for guests, and bedside reading lamps badly placed. But I felt totally relaxed in this hotel and shall go back." *(Richard Pinner; warmly endorsed by Angela & David Stewart)*

Open Dec–Apr, May–Oct. Closed Mon in May, June, Sept, Oct.
Rooms 1 suite, 12 double – 6 with bath, 6 with shower, all with telephone, radio, TV and frigo-bar; many with balcony.
Facilities Restaurant, grillroom, sun terrace. Garden with restaurant. Winter sports, heated swimming pool, tennis, walking, climbing, fishing etc nearby. English spoken.
Location Turn left off road from Spiez and Thun, near Oeschinensee and chairlift. Hotel is quietly situated. Parking.
Restriction Not suitable for &.
Credit cards Access, Diners, Visa.
Terms B&B: single 40–62 Sfrs, double 70–110 Sfrs; dinner, B&B: single 60–82 Sfrs, double 112–148 Sfrs. Set lunch 9–22 Sfrs, dinner 16–24 Sfrs; full alc 30 Sfrs. Reduced rates for children.

KLOSTERS 7250 Graubünden   Map 13

Hotel Bündnerhof   *Tel* (083) 4.14.50

A visitor this year to this old-fashioned family hotel in the centre of the ski resort of Klosters writes: "Our fifth visit to this wonderfully welcoming and excellent accommodation. Very good plain cooking and plenty of food for a hungry family. I should like to reaffirm all the comments in the Guide." *(Mrs E A Budden)*

Previous visitors remarked: "Very friendly and run with typical Swiss efficiency. Bedrooms are well equipped; lovely beds. Son-in-law is an excellent chef – there is no choice but the food is plentiful and well served. Daughter supervises with an eagle eye. They speak English and love having English visitors." The sitting area is variously described as "stuffy" and "quite pleasant": anyway, there is also a pub bit where the locals come to eat and drink and Frau Anderhub, the owner, holds court. *(Arthur J Speechley, E Newall, B W Ribbons)*

Open All year except May.
Rooms 12 double, 12 single – 15 with shower.
Facilities Lift, lounge, bar, dining room. Garden with bowling and table tennis. Close to heated swimming pool, mountain cable railway, ski-lift station and skating rink. English spoken.
Location In town centre. Private parking.
Credit cards None accepted.
Terms Dinner, B&B: 57–80 Sfrs; full board 12 Sfrs per person added. Set lunch/dinner 20, 25 Sfrs; full alc 30–40 Sfrs. Reductions for children.

Hotel Chesa Grischuna   *Tel* (083) 4.22.22
                                                             Telex 74248

"An attractive old-style Swiss hotel with lots of character, right in the centre of Klosters. An ancient timber door unlatches into a bright interior that has been modernised with honey-coloured wood following the old designs, set off with furnishings in the traditional Swiss green, white and scarlet. The bright reception area is new, too, and welcoming, but the rest of the hotel is delightfully old and mellow, with floors, walls and ceilings all made of wood dark with age: on each landing stands an heirloom coffer, handsomely carved and painted. Our room on the fourth floor (no lift) was not large, but had bright rugs on the polished floor, hand-woven bedspreads, and two tiny windows. There was a washbasin (bathrooms seem scarce here); the wc was half-a-floor away. Everything was shiningly clean and the staff were pleasant and helpful. In the big dining room, the food is good, either the four-course Swiss *table d'hôte* or the *carte*, pleasantly served by girls in Klosters costume. The cellar-bar, with a real cellar look and feel, is where the young locals and the après-skiers meet: wonderful atmosphere, lively and friendly, full of noise, music and colour." *(Angela and David Stewart; endorsed by John Grenz)*

Open June – Apr.
Rooms 16 double, 10 single – 11 with bath, 4 with shower, all with telephone and radio; TV on request.
Facilities Lobby, sitting room with TV, restaurant; cellar bar with pianist in high season; bowling. Sun terrace, small garden. English spoken.
Location In centre of Klosters Platz, near the station.
Credit cards Amex, Diners, Visa.
Terms [1985 rates] dinner, B&B: single 90–165 Sfrs, double 160–310 Sfrs; full board 20 Sfrs per person added. Set lunch 32 Sfrs, dinner 48 Sfrs; full alc 75 Sfrs. Reduced rates for children.

LACHEN 8853 Central Switzerland   Map 13

Hotel Bären   *Tel* (055) 63.16.02

A couple who often stay at the *Bären* en route to Austria report: "Very simple, pleasant, clean, always with a warm welcome. Some rooms are decidedly small. The food is stunning, with the best venison I've ever eaten. And there was a splendid breakfast. Lachen is an attractive village and the hotel is a few steps from the lake." *(J & E Hills)* More reports would be helpful.

Open All year.
Rooms 11 double, 5 single – 5 with bath, 5 with shower.
Facilities Lift, TV lounge, bar, restaurant, conference/function room. Rowing, bathing and fishing. 100 metres from Lake Zurich. English spoken.
Location 25 miles E of Zürich. Central. Take Lachen exit from Zürichchur (N3) motorway. Parking.
Restriction Not suitable for &.
Terms B&B: 40 Sfrs. Set lunch 13–80 Sfrs, dinner 18–30 Sfrs; full alc 28 Sfrs. Reduced rates and special meals for children on request.

In your own interest, always check latest tariffs with hotels when you make your bookings.

LAUSANNE-JORAT 1000 Lausanne 26   Map 13

Hôtel-Restaurant Les Chevreuils   *Tel* (021) 91.61.09 or 91.63.31
Route du Jorat 80, Vers-chez-les-Blanc

A stylishly converted hunting lodge, with a garden in front and modern bedrooms in an annexe: it is in sub-alpine country about 1,000 feet above Lake Geneva, some eight kilometres north-east of Lausanne. "In a two-week business trip taking in five countries, this was easily the best hotel", a reader tells us; "it's run by an Italian manager and his wife, with a *Savoy*-trained chef whose fish specialities are excellent. Beds neither too hard nor too soft. Rooms are tastefully furnished, quiet, with good views over Lausanne and Lac Léman." This follows up earlier praise: "Lovely walks, peace and quiet; a terrace shaded by chestnut trees for meals in front; good bourgeois cooking. Views to the range of mountains opposite; behind is rolling farmland and woods. Good bus connections to Lausanne in 30 minutes or so." *(Philip Brown)*

Open All year.
Rooms 2 suites, 28 double, 1 single – all with bath or shower, telephone, radio, colour TV and mini-bar; 15 rooms in annexe.
Facilities Hall, salon, bar, bistro, restaurant, conference facilities. Large park with garden and children's play area. English spoken. ᵭ (5 rooms).
Location 8 km from village. Take Lausanne/Berne road, Chalet-à-Gobet exit. Turn right, then follow signs.
Credit cards All major cards accepted.
Terms B&B: single 70 Sfrs, double 90 Sfrs; half-board: single 95 Sfrs, double 140 Sfrs; full board: single 120 Sfrs, double 190 Sfrs. Set meals 26–38 Sfrs; full alc 35–40 Sfrs.

LUCERNE 6002 Central Switzerland

Hôtel Château Gütsch   *Tel* (041) 22.02.72
                                      Telex 72455 GUTSCH

A sophisticated exclusive luxury hotel, perched like a turreted fairytale castle on a wooded hill above Lucerne, with its own private funicular down to the city, and with magnificent views of the lake and the Alps beyond. It has its own heated swimming pool and a dressy *dîner-dansant* restaurant. Two reports recommend: "Fantastic! A step back into time. Expensive but worth it" *(Mary and Mike Dettrich)* and: "The panoramic view is magnificent. Friendly and attentive service. The furnishings are period and opulent. You can climb the narrow staircase to the tallest turret. My six-year-old was so enraptured that she didn't want to bother with the city." *(Vicki Turner)*

Open All year.
Rooms 35 double, 5 single – all with bath, telephone and radio.
Facilities Lift; salon, bar, grill, restaurant, conference/banqueting facilities. Garden with heated swimming pool and snack-bar.
Restriction Not suitable for ᵭ.
Location On hill above Lucerne (private funicular to the city). Parking.
Credit cards Most major cards accepted.
Terms [1985 rates] Rooms with breakfast: single 105 Sfrs, double 184 Sfrs; half-board add 28 Sfrs per person, full board add 40 Sfrs. Set lunch 30 Sfrs, dinner 46 Sfrs.

MURTEN 3280 Fribourg   Map 13

Hotel Weisses Kreuz   *Tel* (037) 71.26.41
Rathaugasse 31

In 1476 the Swiss defeated Charles the Bold at Murten (Morat in French –
it is near the linguistic boundary), an attractive medieval town with
ramparts and towers, on a small lake, 25 kilometres west of Berne. "Fine
room, spacious, small balcony looking out over lake and mountains.
Much interesting activity – lake steamer docking, wind-surfers, prom-
enaders, all within view of room. Big dance held downstairs but not a
sound in our room." Earlier reports praised the local freshwater fish and
the local white wines served in the restaurant. More reports welcome.
(*M S Zipp, Dr Bill and Lisa Fuerst, and others*)

Open 1 Mar–20 Dec.
Rooms 29 double, 1 single – 9 with bath (in 1986 all rooms should have bath),
10 with shower, all with telephone; 21 rooms in annexe.
Facilities Lift, lounge, restaurant, lakeside terrace. Bowling alley. English
spoken.
Location 50 metres from centre of town which is 25 km W of Berne.
Restriction Not suitable for &.
Credit cards None accepted.
Terms B&B: single 30–70 Sfrs, double 55–125 Sfrs; half-board: single 50–90 Sfrs,
double 95–165 Sfrs; full board: single 70–110 Sfrs, double 135–205 Sfrs. Set lunch
15–20 Sfrs, dinner 15–30 Sfrs; full alc 25 Sfrs. Reduced rates and special meals for
children.

NEUHAUSEN 8212 Schaffhausen   Map 13

Hotel Bellevue   *Tel* (053) 2.21.21
Bad Bahnhofstrasse 17

This aptly named hotel is splendidly situated beside the Rhine Falls, not
the highest waterfalls in Europe but the most powerful, a foaming
torrent 500 feet wide. Only two kilometres away is the attractive old
medieval town of Schaffhausen. "A pleasant hotel with a friendly
atmosphere. Our room was spacious; the bathroom was huge. Our
room, the dining room and the gardens all overlooked the falls –
spectacular views, and going to bed at night listening to the roar was a
treat. We had two outstanding dinners – excellent food and service."
(*Mr and Mrs Walt Lewis*) May we hear from other visitors here, please?

Open All year except 20 Dec–20 Jan.
Rooms 24 double, 3 single – 13 with bath, 7 with shower, all with telephone and
radio.
Facilities Lift; lounge, functions room, restaurant. Garden with terrace
restaurant. English spoken.
Location By the Rhine on outskirts of Neuhausen, 2 km from Schaffhausen.
Parking.
Credit cards Access, Amex, Visa.
Terms B&B: single 75–90 Sfrs, double 120–150 Sfrs. Alc meals 40 Sfrs. Reductions
for children's meals.

Please write and confirm an entry when it is deserved. If you
think that a hotel is not as good as we say, please write and tell us.

NYON 1260 Vaud   Map 13

Hôtel du Clos de Sadex   *Tel* (022) 61.28.31

A patrician house on Lac Léman (23 kilometres from Geneva), formerly the home of Major and Madame Louis de Tscharner, who now run it as a hotel of character and charm. The atmosphere of the aristocratic family whose seat it was (and is) is carefully preserved in the furnishing of the public rooms and the restaurant. Beautiful lakeside garden, with breakfast and lunch willingly served on the terrace overlooking the lake and French shoreline and mountains opposite. Some of the rooms are in the main building, others in a well-designed annexe. A recent report ran: "When I telephoned the hotel from England, I asked for particularly quiet rooms, and was told of their annexe. Never did I dream that an annexe could or would be superior to the main house! We lived like princesses: *each* a *huge* room, small entrance hall, perfectly equipped bathroom. This was on the ground floor. First-floor rooms are smaller. Each of our rooms was differently and beautifully furnished. Breakfast in bed was like old times. The maid was also very helpful. I viewed a room in the main house – nothing like ours in size and decor. The salon in the main house was also dark and uncosy." *(Katie Plowden)*

The Clos de Sadex *has been in the Guide since 1980. It has never lacked supporters, but strangely – we have no reason to think that standards have fallen – we have had no reports on the hotel for the past year. May we hear from recent visitors, please?*

Open All year except Feb.
Rooms 15 double, 3 single – 14 with bath, 2 with shower, all with telephone; 5 rooms in annexe; 3 ground-floor rooms.
Facilities Hall, salon with TV, restaurant, conference room. Gardens with terrace for meals, leading directly to the lake (the hotel has a small harbour); swimming, boating, waterskiing. English spoken.
Location 1 km from Nyon towards Lausanne on lake road; the hotel is on right. Parking.
Credit cards All major cards accepted.
Terms [1985 rates] rooms with breakfast: single 53–130 Sfrs, double 90–190 Sfrs; half-board: 40 Sfrs per person added to room rate; full board: 80 Sfrs added. Reduced rates for children sharing parents' room; special meals.

Hostellerie du XVIe Siècle   *Tel* (022) 61.24.41
Place du Marché

The *Hostellerie,* a five-minute walk from the railway station, is in the middle of this beautiful town, in the market square. It has an old and attractive facade, but the interior has been extensively remodelled. The rooms are large and all have modern bathrooms. There is a restaurant and an outdoor café but no public rooms. It was originally recommended for its extremely reasonable price, charm, cleanliness, location, food and service. A recent visitor endorses this, but stresses that it is essentially a modest inn. "Don't expect anything grand or very sophisticated." *(A L)*

Open All year except Christmas/New Year. Restaurant closed Sun.
Rooms 2 suites, 12 double, 4 single – all with shower and telephone.

Facilities Lift, restaurant with TV, outdoor café. English spoken.
Location 5 minutes from station, in old town. Parking in front of hotel.
Restriction Not suitable for &.
Terms B&B: single 45 Sfrs, double 70 Sfrs. Set lunch 10–13.50 Sfrs, dinner 17 Sfrs; full alc 22 Sfrs.

ST-LUC 3961 Valais   Map 13

Hôtel Bella Tola et St-Luc   *Tel* (027) 65.14.44
Telex 38194 (from summer 1986 472094 PONT)

"The sight of sunrise over the Matterhorn while breakfasting in bed" is one visitor's happiest memory of this venerable inn, in a mountain village high up the slopes of a sunny valley west of Zermatt. To those whose French is more fluent than their German, one attraction of St-Luc could be that it is just on the French side of the linguistic border. The *Bella Tola et St-Luc* dates from 1859, when it could only be reached by mule-track. The present hotel was built in 1883, and a hundred years later Olivier H Pont became its new owner and manager following three generations of Ponts before him. It has long been enjoyed by Guide readers, with particular praise for the "beautifully furnished cottage-style rooms" and good value for money. We should be glad to hear from recent visitors how the latest Pont régime is faring.

Open June – Sept, Dec – Apr.
Rooms 28 double, 14 single – 13 with bath, 8 with shower.
Facilities Lift, 3 salons (1 with TV), bar, restaurant, dining room, children's playroom. Garden, terrace. English spoken.
Location Coming from Sierre, at entrance to resort, on left. (Warning: parking is available 100 metres from the hotel, but it is right by the road and there is no security; also there is an uphill walk back to the hotel.)
Restriction Probably not suitable for &.
Credit cards Amex, Visa.
Terms [1985 rates] B&B: single 37–50 Sfrs, double 63–119 Sfrs. Set dinner 25 Sfrs. Low season 7-day package. Reduced rates for children; special meals.

ST-MORITZ 7500 Graubünden   Map 13

Hôtel Belvédère   *Tel* (082) 3.39.05
Telex 74435 BELVDMZ

Two of our most reliable regular correspondents recommend this typically St-Moritzian palace: "It belongs to the era of the great spa hotels – not in size but in atmosphere, space and quality fittings. It is beside the road halfway up the hill between the two parts of St-Moritz, and the rooms at the back (facing south) look down over the lake to the mountains. Our bedroom was unusually large, with some lovely wood panelling, ample wardrobes, well-thought-out lighting, rather Teutonically hard beds, and a well-fitted bathroom. There is an excellent swimming pool, with all possible pool-side equipment, which also has immense windows over the same view. We stayed three enjoyable days at reasonable cost. The staff were very pleasant, but we would not recommend the restaurant: there are plenty of other places at hand with delicious food at fair prices." *(David and Angela Stewart)* Thus last year's nomination. The hotel tells us that they have vastly improved their restaurant this year.

Open June – end Sept, Dec – Apr.
Rooms 2 suites, 45 double, 23 single – 46 with bath, 24 with shower, all with telephone, radio and colour TV, most with mini-bar and safe.
Facilities Lift, 2 salons, bar, games room, coffee shop, restaurant/grill room; indoor swimming pool, sauna. Terrace, garden, tennis courts. Winter sports, riding, golf. English spoken.
Location Central, on Bad-Dorf road, overlooking Lake St-Moritz; lakeside rooms are quietest. Parking.
Credit cards None accepted.
Terms Room with buffet breakfast: single 60–130 Sfrs, double 120–240 Sfrs. Children under 6 half-price; 6-12 years 30% off. Meal prices not known.

Hôtel Chesa Sur L'En   *Tel* (082) 3.31.44

"We found this gem when looking for an alternative to the solid, mid-20s spa hotels – or modern concrete and stainless steel – which make up most of St-Moritz. Glimpsed through the pines from the main road at St-Moritz Bad were the upper storeys of an archetypal Swiss chalet. A side turning led across a tiny bridge over the river Inn (En). Up a steep winding drive deep with snow, a sharp turn, and facing you is a stone tower with great overhanging eaves topped by a glassed-in watch-tower and the Swiss flag. Steps to a massive front door opened into a stone-flagged entrance hall – and beyond more massive steps to a richly panelled, ornately carved and utterly superb main hall. We were warmly welcomed by the proprietor, Herr Schwarzenbach, who spoke good English, and did his own cooking.

"The hotel is short on rooms with baths: it would be almost impossible to provide bathrooms without destroying the proportions of most of the main bedrooms. We had rooms right at the top in the watch tower which *did* include a bathroom and also had spectacular views on all four sides over the rooftops to the snow-clad mountains. Central heating was of venerable age and infirmity, but a mobile heater provided adequate back-up. The furniture here was basic, but other bedrooms had furniture to match the house, in Germanic proportions. The service was shared between a young, cheerful American girl and a more taciturn but helpful Swiss. In addition to this splendour – home for some time to ex-King Faroukh during his exile – the hotel proved remarkably reasonable in price for St-Moritz." (*Angela and David Stewart*)

Open 15 Dec – 15 Apr, 1 June – 25 Sept.
Rooms 11 double, 3 single – 2 with bath, 2 with shower, some with radio, some with mono TV.
Facilities Hall, salon with TV, breakfast room, dining room. Ski run to hotel entrance. Winter sports, indoor tennis and squash courts nearby.
Location Central; private parking.
Restriction Not suitable for &.
Credit cards Amex, Diners, Visa.
Terms B&B: 42–84 Sfrs; dinner, B&B 58–107 Sfrs. Set dinner 28 Sfrs. Minimum stay of 14 days at Christmas/New Year. 50% reduction for children in parents' room.

We asked hotels to quote 1986 prices. Not all were able to predict them in the late spring of 1985. Some of our terms will be inaccurate. Do check latest tariffs at the time of booking.

ST-NIKLAUSEN 6005 Lucerne   Map 13

Résidence St-Niklausen   *Tel* (041) 47.11.70

"Highly recommended as an alternative to a hotel – it's a home with five guest-rooms, across the street from Lucerne's lovely lake, amid an abundance of gardens and ponds. Antiques, oriental rugs, fine china and silver; private and luxurious, small and serene. Full breakfast served on the terrace under colourful umbrellas. The owner, Madame Margarethe Heer, is very friendly." (*Trudy and Neil Reid*) The ferry stop is across the road, and you can get from the village to Lucerne by boat in 20 minutes. Easy access to many paths through parklike areas and along lakeshore.

Open 1 Apr – 15 Nov.
Rooms 10 double plus guest-house – all with kitchen facilities.
Facilities Salon, dining room, 2 large partially covered sun terraces, 1 with pond. Large garden. Many paths for walks through parklike areas, woods and along lakeshore. Lake with safe bathing: 2 minutes. Fishing at the ferry stop: 1 minute (no permit required). Tennis, water sports nearby. English spoken.
Location On a peninsula, 5 km S of downtown Lucerne. Coming from Lucerne station heading towards the Richard Wagner Museum, follow the lake on the left-hand side. Look for Schönbühl shopping centre on left; within 3 km look for sign ROOMS/ZIMMER on right. Bus stop to St-Niklausen 1 min.
Credit cards None accepted.
Terms On application.

SCHAFFHAUSEN 8200 East Switzerland   Map 13

Rheinhotel Fischerzunft   *Tel* (053) 5.32.81
Quaistrasse 8

Schaffhausen is a captivating old town on the upper Rhine: it has many medieval streets, and houses with painted and richly decorated facades. The Rhine Falls, Europe's most powerful waterfall, are close by. New to the Guide last year, the *Fischerzunft* is a former fishermen's guildhouse converted into a chic – and expensive – restaurant-with-rooms. Its owner/chef, André Jaeger, met his Chinese wife Doreen in Hong Kong, and the Chinese influence is apparent in both the decor and the delicate cuisine, which wins two red toques from *Gault Millau* for such dishes as breast of duck perfumed with tea, and shrimp soup with cream. "Exquisitely decorated, this seven-guestroom masterpiece purveys personalised hospitality – and romance. Dinner by soft candlelight. Some rooms have views of the Rhine. Breakfast is served in the lovely Chinese Room. There is much sightseeing possible from Schaffhausen, including a cruise up the river to Stein-am-Rhein, another picturesque Swiss town with painted houses." (*Pamela Lechtman*)

Open All year expect 3 weeks in Feb.
Rooms 7 double – 4 with bath, 3 with shower, all with telephone, radio, colour TV and mini-bar.
Facilities 2 lounges, restaurant, conference facilities. Garden restaurant.
Location On the banks of the Rhine. Parking.
Credit cards All major cards accepted.
Terms Rooms with breakfast: single 110–140 Sfrs, double 160–190 Sfrs. Set lunch 48 Sfrs, dinner 72–88 Sfrs; full alc 90 Sfrs.

SCHÖNRIED-GSTAAD 3778 Berner Oberland   Map 13

Hotel Alpin nova   *Tel* (030) 8.33.11
Hauptstrasse   *Telex* 922230

A visitor this year nominates the three-year-old *Alpin nova* as "built in traditional Swiss Chalet style and to a very high standard. Our bedroom was of penthouse proportions with a luxurious and spotless bathroom *en suite*. Also included was a fitted kitchen, colour television and a large balcony with panoramic views of the Berner Oberland. Most impressive was the quality and cleanliness and the attention to detail. The price in low season was extremely reasonable. The dining room is small enough to feel intimate, and the standard of food and service superb. An à la carte menu is available at dinner, but our budget dictated the *en pension* menu, which was varied and delicious. The pool was beautiful. Our stay was made unforgettable, not only by the surroundings but by the friendliness and attentiveness of the staff, particularly of the proprietor, Herr Schöps. He takes a personal interest in the wellbeing of all his guests, and is obviously intent on maintaining an exceptional standard. We left feeling extremely fortunate that we could enjoy the hotel's comforts on a comparatively modest budget." (*J M Beaton*)

Open 15 Dec – 15 Apr, 15 May – 5 Nov.
Rooms 5 suites, 54 double, 5 single – 64 with bath, 6 with shower, all with telephone, radio, colour TV, tea-making and baby-listening, many with balcony or terrace; 10 rooms in annexe; some ground-floor rooms.
Facilities Lift; hall/bar, salon, 3 restaurants, conference facilities, children's playroom, heated indoor swimming pool, sauna, solarium, fitness centre; dancing, discos, videos. Salt-water swimming pool opposite hotel; winter sports, riding, fishing and walking nearby. English spoken. Probably suitable for &.
Location On N11, NE of Gstaad. Hotel is central. Parking.
Credit cards Access, Diners, Visa.
Terms B&B: single 68–154 Sfrs, double 136–243 Sfrs; dinner, B&B: single 88–174 Sfrs, double 176–283 Sfrs; full board: 15 Sfrs per person added. Set lunch 10–14 Sfrs, dinner 26–28 Sfrs; full alc 36 Sfrs. Reduced rates for children sharing parents' room. Skiing packages, flower holidays, tennis weeks.

Hotel Ermitage and Golf   *Tel* (030) 4.27.27
Telex 922213 ERMI

Surrounded by meadows and pinewoods, or unsullied snow fields, Schönried is a village in the Simmental about 180 metres above Gstaad. Although now a resort of repute, with marvellous winter sports facilities, it has preserved its character since the days when the Monaco Grimaldis built their chalet above the village. Gstaad with its smart cafés and boutiques is ten minutes away by car or little railway. In August there is also the attraction of the Festival at nearby Saanen directed by its most famous citizen, Yehudi Menuhin. "The *Ermitage*, two connected chalets, has the comforts of a first-class hotel. The new wing has the most comfortable rooms and apartments. There are three restaurants – a charcoal grill, a rôtisserie and the Restaurant Français – all really beautifully furnished in best *gemütlich* Swiss style; so are the lounge and the two well-stocked bars. There are also a sauna, a squash court, conference and 'fitness' rooms. The greatest attraction, however, is the

Solbad, a large indoor swimming pool filled with briny water heated to 35°C (95°F). Amazingly, this indoor pool opens out to an outdoor pool of similar size, heated to the same temperature. It was for us a sensational experience in December to swim outside, the body most comfortably warmed, but the head in the nippy night air of −10°C, the steam of the water rising to reveal the surrounding snow banks several metres high. The variety of the meals and a sleigh ride laid on for the guests on Christmas Eve deserve special praise." (*Dr and Mrs Lovejoy*)

"Everything was perfect – a luxurious hotel with friendly and attentive staff, a lounge with a wood-fire blazing, lunch in the midday sun on the terrace, excellent food, especially the buffet breakfasts, impeccable rooms." (*Arnold Horwell*)

Open 20 Dec – 31 Mar, 15 May – 23 Oct.
Rooms 11 suites, 24 double, 15 single – 50 with bath, all with telephone, radio and TV.
Facilities Hall, salons, 2 bars, TV room, 3 restaurants, café; terrace restaurant, conference facilities; billiards, table tennis, squash, sauna, solarium, fitness room, heated indoor and outdoor swimming pools; folk music, dances, fashion shows. Large garden with tennis court. English spoken.
Location On N11, 8 km NE of Gstaad. Underground parking.
Restriction Not suitable for &.
Credit cards All major cards accepted.
Terms B&B: 85–160 Sfrs; dinner, B&B 95–170 Sfrs; full board 110–185 Sfrs. Set lunch 20 Sfrs, dinner 35 Sfrs; full alc 50 Sfrs. Beauty weeks, tennis weeks, alpine ski weeks, *langlauf* weeks. Reduced rates for children sharing parents' room; special meals.

SCHWANDEN 3657 Berner Oberland   Map 13

Gasthof-Restaurant Rothorn   *Tel* (033) 51.11.86

Schwanden is a mountain village 1,000 metres above the resorts of Sigriswil and Gunten, and facing across the beautiful lake of Thun to the Bernese Alps. Here the *Rothorn*, a big brown chalet amid meadows, backed by pinewoods, is warmly recommended: "Wonderful. The owners, the Amstutz-Rentsch family, have an enchanting Gasthof, very modern, comfortable and reasonably priced, with attractive decor. Frau Amstutz is an excellent hostess, speaks good English. Her husband is the chef and prepares delicious meals. You can eat in the guest dining room or in the restaurant frequented by the locals. We chose the latter and were delighted with the atmosphere: local musicians sing and play. Schwanden is a peaceful and beautiful village. There are walking paths through the woods, pastures and mountains." (*Dr Bill and Lisa Fuerst*) Note: we regret that our Swiss map last year showed a different Schwanden.

Open All year except Nov. Restaurant closed Mon.
Rooms 13 double – 2 with bath, 8 with shower, some with balcony; 4 rooms in annexe.
Facilities Lounge, TV room, dining room, restaurant with occasional folk music. Overlooking mountains and lake; tennis, watersports and ski schools nearby. English spoken.
Location 20 minutes NW of Interlaken, 15 minutes NE of Thun.
Restriction Probably not suitable for &.
Credit cards None accepted.

Terms B&B: single 37–53 Sfrs, double 64–96 Sfrs; dinner, B&B: single 51–67 Sfrs, double 92–124 Sfrs; full board: single 61–77 Sfrs, double 112–144 Sfrs. Set lunch/dinner 11–15 Sfrs. Children under 6 sharing parents' room half-price, 6–12, 30% reduction.

SILS-MARIA 7514 Graubünden   Map 13

Edelweiss Hotel   *Tel* (082) 4.52.22 or 4.55.51
Dorfstrasse   *Telex* 74835

The philosopher Nietzsche used to spend his summers in a house in this village-resort of the upper Engadin valley, now turned into a small Nietzsche museum. And today the supermen and supergirls of sport and high society frequent the ski-slopes and smart cafés of nearby St-Moritz. Sils-Maria, though less grand, is also quite elegant, and lies between two crystal-blue lakes in this, one of the loveliest of Swiss mountain valleys, where the curious Romanche language is spoken. The *Edelweiss*, a sedate and confident four-starrer, dates from 1875, though most of the building is more modern and all of it is modernised. "Very clean and comfortable, food excellent, especially breakfasts; I was made to feel very much at home." "We were delighted with the menus served in the beautiful dining room, and the breakfasts were the best we have ever had on the Continent. Service efficient and courteous, management friendly. The Engadin with its profusion of wild flowers is a walker's and climber's paradise." Good skiing too. *(N Morris-Adams, C B Wilmot-Allistone)*

Open Mid-June to mid-Oct; 20 Dec to Easter.
Rooms 13 suites, 51 double, 24 single – 46 with bath, 29 with shower, all with telephone and radio; tea-making facilities in suites; 29 rooms and the suites are in annexe.
Facilities Large salon with fireplace and bar, TV room, children's games room, rôtisserie/bar with pianist, dancing in winter, bar/restaurant. Garden with tables and chairs. Winter sports. English spoken.
Location On edge of village which is 8 km SW of St-Moritz. Large car park, garages.
Credit cards Access, Diners.
Terms B&B: 60–135 Sfrs; half-board 75–150 Sfrs. Set lunch 18, 22 Sfrs, dinner 32 Sfrs; full alc 50 Sfrs. Cross-country skiing course in winter, surfing and other courses in summer. Reduced rates for children sharing parents' room; special meals.

SOGLIO 7649 Graubünden   Map 13

Hotel Stua Granda   *Tel* (082) 4.16.66

Soglio is a mountain village 1,000 metres up, reached by a narrow and steep minor road from the main highway that runs through the Bergell valley from St-Moritz to Chiavenna. A visitor this year describes it as "perhaps one of the more beautiful islands on earth. It is, of course, not an island at all, but instead sits on the green steep slopes of extreme southern Switzerland. The clear air and the magnificent views made this small town the favourite of our entire trip. And the *Stua Granda* was an impeccably maintained, totally unpretentious and absolutely charming little hotel. I wish we had been able to stay a week or a month." This commendation echoes an earlier one: "Time seems to stand still here. Chestnut trees surround the village and the air is unusually crisp and clean. The sunny terrace restaurant is a favourite meeting place for hikers and the fare is hearty and fresh. Guest rooms are beautifully furnished and spotless. High-beamed ceilings, lace curtains, soft pine, and heavenly eiderdown quilts welcome guests. Every room is different and the aroma of fresh bread and local specialities such as *bundner gerstensuppe* fill the air. Raclette is served here, along with fondue. A romantic hotel for tose who love out of the way places in beautiful settings." *Ronald Lehman, Pamela Lechtman; also Caroline Steiner)*

Open All year except Nov.
Rooms 31 double – 23 with bath, 14 with telephone and radio, some with balcony; 22 rooms in annexe, Pension Soglina.
Facilities 2 sitting rooms, restaurant. Garden terrace. English spoken.
Location On edge of village, just N of route N3 between Chiavenna (to W) and Maloja pass (to E). Nearby parking.
Credit cards None accepted.
Terms B&B: 30-37 Sfrs; half-board 53–60 Sfrs. 10% reduction for children under 12; special meals.

TEGNA 6652 Ticino   Map 13

Hotel Barbatè   *Tel* (093) 81.14.30

Tegna is a small unspoiled village in the Centovalli area of the Ticino, near Locarno at the north-east end of Lake Maggiore. It is a good centre for walking in valley, lake and mountain scenery. Just off the main street the *Barbatè* is a light and spacious modern one-storey building of character, set in a pretty garden. The decor is restful and imaginative. The lounge has books, record-player, pictures, flowers, and the atmosphere of a private house. All the bedrooms are furnished as bedsitting rooms. Most open on to their own section of the garden, so one sunbathes in peace and seclusion. As *Casa Barbatè*, it has been in the Guide since 1978, and had particularly appealed to readers because of the hospitality of the previous owner, Madame Jenny. "The *Barbatè* is still the haven of peace and quiet described in earlier editions, and I am certain the Steffens are keen to retain the honour of your recommendation. Monsieur Steffen was the host and chef, and petite Madame Steffen our considerate hostess. A small and highly personalised lodging, but the Steffens deftly managed a wide variety of guests with grace and charm. Do try the local red wine. It was an extremely pleasant surprise." *(Janet and Peter Salmon)*

Open Mid-Mar to mid-Nov.
Rooms 10 double, 2 single – 10 with bath, 2 with shower, all with telephone and tea-making facilities; some ground-floor rooms.
Facilities Lounge, restaurant; banqueting/conference facilities. Garden with sun terrace. 500 metres from river, boating; 5 km from lake with safe bathing, fishing rights, sand/rock beach. English spoken.
Location 4 km from Locarno towards Centovalli. Parking.
Credit cards None accepted.
Terms B&B: 60–85 Sfrs. Set meals 20–24 Sfrs. Reduced rates for children sharing parents' room.

THUN 3600 Berner Oberland   Map 13

Hotel Beau-Rivage   *Tel* (033) 22.22.36
Aare-Quai

The small town of Thun is the gateway to the Berner Oberland, at the western end of Lake Thun. It is far less crowded than Interlaken, at the other end of the lake, less touristy, more genuinely Swiss, and also offers a better view of the High Alps. The Beau-Rivage is an imposing turn-of-the-century building which overlooks the river Aare as it leaves the lake. The rooms facing south (the majority – but worth asking for: rooms facing north are noisy and with no outlook) have a spectacular view across the river and the Alps beyond. What readers like about the Beau-Rivage – and some readers find the place addictive and return every year – are its old-world charm, the quality of the antique furniture and rugs scattered around the rooms, the welcome of the English-speaking owner, Herr Wüthrich, the reasonable tariff, the quiet of the river-facing rooms. What people dislike are the less agreeable sides of old-worldliness: rooms, and especially beds, that have seen better days. Views about service vary from "most helpful" to "minimal". Breakfasts also tend to be mean by Swiss standards, and there is no restaurant at the hotel, only a café serving snacks. One reader reported to us – could this be true? – of a final indignity: "At 11 pm, all lights extinguished from the lounge and a surly girl told the guests: 'You must go to bed now'." More reports badly needed.

Open 1 May – 20 Oct. (Restaurant closed Mon, and Sun evening.)
Rooms 20 double, 10 single – 22 with bath, 1 with shower, all with telephone; 2 with radio.
Facilities Lift, entrance ramp; salon, TV lounge, writing room, breakfast room, bar, games (incl. video games) and fitness rooms; heated indoor swimming pool. Roof-garden; garden with coffee shop and sun terrace for meals; situated on the river, with quay; fishing, but no bathing allowed as current too fast. English spoken. &.
Location On road from Thun to Interlaken via Gunten, between town and casino, 300 metres from town centre (rooms over water quiet). Garage (7 Sfrs per night); public car park for 150 cars nearby.
Credit cards All major cards accepted.
Terms Rooms with breakfast: single 35–85 Sfrs, double 60–135 Sfrs. Plat du jour in restaurant 9.50 Sfrs. Reduced rates for children.

TRIESENBERG 9497 Liechtenstein   Map 13

Hotel Kulm   *Tel* (075) 2.87.77

Though tiny, Liechtenstein is far from twee, but very modern and go-ahead: the *Kulm* is making a strong bid to attract the business conference trade (Triesenberg has congress facilities), so you might be sharing its casual, friendly charm with fifty neat-suited executives, though the hotel also claims to extend a special welcome to children. Last year's visitors wrote of "a quiet, modern, immaculately clean small hotel in a very small town" in minuscule Liechtenstein's central valley, just south of the capital, Vaduz. "Our balcony overlooked the Rhine valley as the river curved north. With the mountains beyond, the view was superb. Food was very good; the restaurant was casual, with friendly service. Most enjoyable was the peace of the farm country and the Alps after the hassle of Vaduz." *(Mr and Mrs Walt Lewis)* Local skiing is 10 minutes away by car, with better areas 30–40 minutes away. Good summer walking. More reports, please.

Open All year.
Rooms 7 suites, 12 double, 1 single – 10 with bath, 10 with shower, all with telephone, radio, colour TV, mini-bar, baby-listening, and balcony.
Facilities Lift; lounge, bar, restaurant, conference/functions facilities. Occasional entertainment (music, dancing etc) in restaurant.
Location 5 km S of Vaduz. Hotel is central but quiet; parking.
Restriction Possibly not suitable for &.
Credit cards Amex, Visa.
Terms Rooms with breakfast: single 55–60 Sfrs, double 85–95 Sfrs; half-board: single 70–75 Sfrs, double 115–125 Sfrs; full board: single 85–90 Sfrs, double 145–155 Sfrs. Set meals 12 Sfrs; full alc 25 Sfrs. Reduced rates and special meals for children.

VEVEY 1800 Vaud   Map 13

Les Trois Couronnes   *Tel* (021) 51.30.05
49 rue d'Italie   *Telex* 451148

Vevey is a smart popular resort town on the northern shore of Lac Léman between Lausanne and Montreux; exclusive girls' finishing schools abound. *Les Trois Couronnes*, one of the town's two five-star hotels, is in the centre of Vevey. "One of the 'great' hotels of Switzerland. Of late 19th-century construction, it is old-fashioned but in a magnificent position overlooking the lake. The rooms have large French windows and balconies facing the lake, and the service and staff are beyond criticism. The food in the restaurant, a beautifully proportioned Louis XV type room, was superb and the service first-rate. There were eleven different jams to choose from at breakfast. Everything was most efficient; the hall porter was the most polite I've met in many a long day." *(N Waddington)* "A good place to stay for the view, the comfort and the peace, but don't expect quick service, outstanding food or sophisticated extras such as cocktails!" *(Kate and Steve Murray-Sykes; also Irina Ohl)*

Open All year.
Rooms 8 suites, 42 double, 30 single – all with bath and shower, telephone, radio, and colour TV; baby-listening on request.
Facilities Lift, salons, TV room, bar, restaurant, conference facilities. Pianist several evenings a week. Large terrace with open restaurant. Beach, lake, swimming, fishing nearby. English spoken.
Location Central, but quietly situated. Parking in courtyard.
Credit cards All major cards accepted.
Terms B&B: single 120–180 Sfrs, double 200–310 Sfrs; dinner, B&B: single 160–220 Sfrs, double 280–390 Sfrs; full board: single 190–250 Sfrs, double 340–450 Sfrs. Set lunch/dinner 50 Sfrs; full alc 70 Sfrs. 50% reduction for children under 12.

WEGGIS 6353 Central Switzerland   Map 13

Hotel Beau Rivage   *Tel* (041) 93.14.22
                                                 Telex 72525

The delightful resort of Weggis is 45 minutes by steamer or 30 minutes by road from the equally delightful town of Lucerne; other lake pleasures are easily accessible, as are the heights of Rigi, served by

Weggis's funicular. The *Beau Rivage* has a choice position right on the lake, a few minutes' walk from the quay. It has its own garden with swimming pool. "Weggis is A1. So is the Beau Rivage," runs a report this year. "Rooms are beautifully decorated, and bathrooms are huge, with gorgeous tile work. It's rare to find a hotel room that is large, clean, with a lovely view and where everything blends. Staff wonderful, too." *(Dr and Mrs Charles Stratton)*

Open End Mar to mid-Oct.
Rooms 3 suites, 29 double, 16 single – 33 with bath, 15 with shower, all with telephone and radio; colour TV in suites.
Facilities Lift, hall, salon, bar, garden room, restaurant, lakeside terrace. Band twice a week. Garden with swimming pool, lakeside beach, fishing. English spoken.
Location 20 km E of Lucerne; on lakeside, near quay. Garages and parking.
Restriction Some rooms not suitable for &.
Credit cards Access, Amex, Visa.
Terms B&B: single 55–95 Sfrs, double 110–190 Sfrs; half-board: single 75–125 Sfrs, double 150–250 Sfrs; full board: single 95–145 Sfrs, double 190–290 Sfrs. Set lunch 36 Sfrs, dinner 38 Sfrs; full alc 50 Sfrs.

WORB 3076 Berner Oberland　　　　　　　　　　　　　　　　**Map 13**

Gasthof Zum Löwen　　　　　　　　　　　　　　　　*Tel* (031) 83.23.03
Enggisteinstrasse 3

"The hotel and village are approximately seven kilometres from Bern and well worth the detour," writes one visitor this year. "This is a small, family-run hotel whose reputation locally is based on its excellent food – the restaurant was packed with non-residents. Dinner is chosen from a menu offering about 20 choices. Half the menu is 'two plate' where you get a second helping automatically and the rest is 'one plate'. Our double room was large, very comfortable, with a large bathroom and a mini-bar." Another visitor this year tells us that it is "a delightful place to stay, full of character and beautifully managed – for eleven generations by the same family!" and commends the "helpful jolly English-speaking staff". *(Mrs J Davidson; Mr and Mrs T E Reddish)*

Open All year except July; closed Wed & Thur until 4 pm.
Rooms 14 double – 4 with bath, 10 with shower, 7 with telephone, 7 with radio, all with baby-listening.
Facilities Lounge, bar, restaurant, conference and functions facilities, small terrace, garden with restaurant. Near swimming pool, miniature golf and tennis; winter ice skating and curling rinks. English spoken.
Location Central. Private parking facilities available.
Restriction Not suitable for &.
Credit cards All major cards accepted.
Terms B&B: single 35–70 Sfrs, double 70–115 Sfrs; set lunch/dinner 9.50 Sfrs; full alc 20–30 Sfrs. Reduced rates for children sharing parents' room; special meals.

Hotels often book you into their most expensive rooms or suites unless you specify otherwise. Even if all room prices are the same, hotels may give you a less good room in the hope of selling their better rooms to later customers. It always pays to discuss accommodation in detail when making a reservation.

ZERMATT 3290 Valais   Map 13

Hôtel Alex   *Tel* (028) 671726
                                                  Telex 472112

In this resort renowned for winter skiing and summer walking, the *Alex*
is a well-established medium-to-large hotel near the station looking out
towards the Matterhorn, and is run by a former Matterhorn guide, Alex
Perren, and his wife Gisela. "The owners are on the spot all the time.
The bar, the centre of social life in winter, is still operated by a celebrated
barman, a character. The facilities include one of the best indoor
swimming pools I have ever used, two squash courts and an indoor
tennis hall. The only criticism of the food is that the excellent set menus
really are too bit. The general service and the atmosphere can be
recommended to Guide users without any hesitation." *(J M Toogood)*

Open All year.
Rooms 30 suites, 30 double, 14 single – all with bath, telephone, radio and colour
TV; 10 rooms in annexe, some on ground floor; baby-listening on request.
Facilities Lift, bar, restaurant, 2 dancing bars (disco every night), indoor
swimming pool, solarium, sauna, squash court, tennis. Garden with sun terrace
and tennis court (tennis instructor available). English spoken.
Location Central, near the station. (No cars in Zermatt.)
Credit cards None accepted.
Terms Dinner, B&B 80–190 Sfrs. Set dinner 35–50 Sfrs; full alc 80 Sfrs; special rates
Nov – beginning Dec, Jan and Apr (minimum stay over Christmas 2 weeks);
reduced rates and special meals on request for children.

Hôtel-Garni Metropol   *Tel* (028) 67.32.31

"Excellent recommendation from the Guide. An extremely friendly
welcome, a good location and a fabulous view." *(Mr & Mrs C R Stafford)*
The *Metropol* is an unpretentious, medium-sized family establishment in
the centre of the town on the banks of the fast-flowing Vispa. A reader
who has been going to Zermatt since 1948 reports: "The hotel remains as
good as ever, with splendid rooms (sensible beds, reading lights,
spacious cupboards, well-equipped bathrooms, glass-topped writing
desk, comfortable easy chairs); the constant rush of the river next door –
so soothing at night; the excellent breakfast buffet; and, directing it all
tirelessly, the friendly Taugwalder family." *(Richard Pinner)* The Taug-
walders have now bought a meadow opposite the hotel so that its lovely
views cannot be spoiled. There are also a number of improvements:
every room now has a direct-dial telephone; shoe cleaning and laundry
services are now available; there is a separate TV room and you can also
hire a TV set for your bedroom. While main meals are available by order
only, snacks in the evenings such as omelettes and steaks are approved
of. The best bedrooms are the dozen on the south side, each with a
private bathroom, and a roomy balcony facing the Matterhorn.

Open Dec – Apr, 10 June – 10 Oct; no meals served Mon evening.
Rooms 20 double, 4 single – all with bath, shower, telephone and radio.
Facilities Lift, salon, bar, dining room, TV room, terrace; garden. English spoken.
Location Central, near station; hotel porter will fetch you. (No cars in Zermatt.)
Credit cards All major cards accepted.
Terms B&B: single 50–79 Sfrs, double 90–158 Sfrs.

Hôtel Nicoletta   *Tel* (028) 66.11.51
                                       Telex 472108

High praise from a veteran for this Guide entry, a modern four-star hotel in the centre of the resort: "We have stayed at Zermatt for skiing a good 20 times, also elsewhere in Switzerland, and five years ago we at last found a hotel with almost everything for a middle-aged couple: only idleness prevented my writing to you before. With one exception, this is much the best hotel we have stayed at in some 30 years' skiing. 1: they do not appear to overbook. 2: the reception is friendly (for a big hotel). 3: everything works. 4: the staff are clearly superbly run, unlike at some big hotels nearby. 5: the rooms have everything one could desire and are quiet. 6: there is a most pleasant bar at the top where one can dance to a piano without losing one's hearing. 7: ditto at the bottom pub for younger folk (and delete the last part of 6). 8: the waiters etc are all friendly and not all the time looking for tips; Alice who runs the bar is an institution (the manager hardly appears and the place appears to be run by a female Gorgon of tremendous efficiency). The hotel is said to be built on broken bones because it was/is owned by a retired doctor's family." 9: the hotel recommends the scenic view from its fourth-floor restaurant, bar and grill-room, as well as its fondue and raclette parties, heated indoor swimming pool, etc. *(A V Chute)*

Open All year, except probably May and Nov.
Rooms 1 apartment, 51 double, 9 single – doubles with bath, singles with shower, all with telephone and radio, colour TV (10 Sfrs per day); baby-listening on request.
Facilities Lifts, lounge, bar, TV room, children's playroom, grill room/rôtisserie, restaurant; conference facilities. Piano player in bar in winter. Small indoor swimming pool, 2 saunas, 3 solariums; tennis in summer, winter sports.
Location Central. No cars in Zermatt; parking in Täsch.
Credit cards All major cards accepted.
Terms [1985 rates] half-board: single 81–162 Sfrs, double 162–324 Sfrs; full board 15 Sfrs per person added.

ZERNEZ 7351 Graubünden   **Map 13**

Hotel Il Fuorn   *Tel* (082) 8.12.26
Am Ofenpass, Parc Naziunal

"This hotel in the Swiss National Park does not abuse its privilege. The rooms are simple but comfortable, the food is more than adequate and, on special occasions, sumptuous. Note the provision of unwrapped butter, jam and sugar for breakfast, unusual even in a Swiss hotel of this class. The view of the mountains and the walks to see the wildlife and undisturbed alpine botany are the main reasons for staying, but the facilities have the solid homely comfort that is traditionally Swiss." *(Dr O H B Gyde)* More reports on this new entry, please.

Open 10 May – 25 Oct.
Rooms 15 double, 4 single – 3 with bath, 10 with shower, all with radio.
Facilities Dining room, TV room, terraces. Walks in National Park, wildlife, trout fishing. English spoken.
Location On the St-Moritz/Merano road, 15 km E of Zernez on the Ofenpass in the middle of the Swiss National Park. Parking.
Restriction Not suitable for &.

Credit cards None accepted.
Terms [1985 rates] B&B: 36–63 Sfrs; full board 58–95 Sfrs. Reductions in low season. Reduced rates for children sharing parents' room.

ZÜRICH 8001   Map 13

Hotel Florhof   *Tel* (01) 47.44.70
Florhofgasse 4

There have been consistently good reports over the years for this well-run, friendly little hotel, in a 16th-century patrician's house with small garden. It is in a quiet residential street near the *Kunsthaus*, theatre and university. "An excellent peaceful hide-away. Very clean, simple but extremely comfortable. Receptionist could not be more charming and helpful. A good and plentiful dinner in pleasant, flowery dining room, and no noise at all at night before our prompt call and breakfast at 6.30 a.m. The efficiency was almost frightening!" The music Conservatoire is next door, so you may have Bach fugues and violin lessons for breakfast – hardly a hardship.

Open All year. Restaurant open only for breakfast Sat and Sun.
Rooms 23 double, 10 single – 23 with bath, 10 with shower, all with telephone and radio, colour TV on request; some ground-floor rooms.
Facilities Lift, small salon, restaurant. Garden with terrace for lunch and light refreshments in fine weather. English spoken.
Location Near *Kunsthaus*, theatre and university. Parking.
Restriction Not suitable for &.
Credit cards All major cards accepted.
Terms B&B: single 95–125 Sfrs, double 145–185 Sfrs. Set lunch 25 Sfrs, dinner 35 Sfrs; full alc 50–60 Sfrs.

Hotel Franziskaner   *Tel* (01) 252.01.20
Niederdorffstrasse 1   *Telex* FRHO 816431

A small hotel in the old town, close to the Limmat and not far from the main station but, the hotel tells us, away from traffic and tram noise. It is, however, in Zürich's nightlife area, and can be noisy in the evening. Zürich nightlife is said to end early, but one correspondent told us that the Niederdorffstrasse was "like midday in Calcutta, all night long." In contrast, another wrote: "A delightful hotel offering a pleasing combination of old and new. My room opened on to a flower-decked terrace that overlooked a charming square with a quaint Bernese painted fountain in the centre of it. The room itself was large, comfortably furnished and cheerfully decorated in warm shades of brown and orange. Breakfast was a self-service feast: delicious Swiss cheeses, glasses of orange juice, fresh croissants, slices of ham. All in all, good value for money and a real find." *(Donna Cuervo)* More reports please.

Open All year.
Rooms 20 double – 10 with bath, 10 with shower, all with telephone, radio, colour TV, mini-bar and safe.
Facilities Lift, foyer, bar, restaurant. Near Limmat river and Lake Zürich.
Location In Old Town, near main station. Public parking nearby.
Credit cards All major cards accepted.
Terms B&B: single 80–105 Sfrs, double 100–135 Sfrs. Set lunch/dinner 15 Sfrs; full alc 40 Sfrs. Reduced rates and special meals for children.

Turkey

KONAK OTELI — ISTANBUL

In the introduction to this section last year, we queried Turkey's low standing in the tourist charts. Indeed, for a decade or more the Western travel press has been puzzled as each season's whispered assertion that Turkey would be "The Next Place" has proved premature. The prose has been vivid: ". . . scenery as varied and exquisite as the dishes at a Sultan's table", ". . . the last empty, unpolluted and inexpensive corner of the Mediterranean", ". . . pleasures of travel and discovery now hardly to be found anywhere else in the area from Gibraltar to Lebanon". Still the rush has not happened.

Answers suggest themselves. From the time of the Crusades, the Turk's reputation for barbarity has been a commonplace of European consciousness. Shakespeare has "a malignant and a turbanned Turk" as a potent symbol of all dark threats to civilisation. More recently a film – "Midnight Express" – has been allowed to reinforce our fears. The West is of and for the Greeks. Turkey brings us out in goosebumps.

But then the Turks themselves – a race as mixed in blood as the British and with an Imperial past as full of splendour and atrocity – however warmly hospitable they may be as individuals, have been saddled with a bureaucracy that has concentrated on the country's industrial and agricultural bases and has thought the service industry rather beneath it. In 1980 the whole vast area of Turkey had about the same number of tourist beds as the island of Rhodes. Also, as Metin Munir then noted in the *Financial Times*, there were "problems of infrastructure and communications ... political instability, terrorism and a host of other disadvantages".

At least on the Turk's side the situation is changing: the fast road around the stunning south-west coast is almost complete; there is a new airport at Dalaman close to the top resorts of Bodrum and Marmaris; General Evren has put paid to terrorism and instituted a closely controlled system which seems to keep most people happy; and more money is being spent on advertising the country abroad. Facilities for the visitor are improving most quickly in the Southern Aegean and western Mediterranean areas, but the interior is often still an adventure. As far as Western prejudice is concerned, Turkophiles hope that the majority of potential visitors follow their cultural conditioning and venture no further than the Dodecanese.

There are ten new hotels with full entries this year and several more in the tentative listings at the end of this section, but once again the offering is relatively sparse. We would therefore ask travellers to Turkey to be more than usually conscientious about letting us know of establishments they find which we should be mentioning.

ALANYA

Hotel Günes   *Tel* (3231) 1918

"A delightful small bed-and-breakfast hotel literally on the attractive sandy beach of Alanya itself. The building has a distinctive character, with an abundance of pine wood. The very pleasant owner and his staff contribute greatly to its friendly ambience. Breakfast is mostly served on a shady terrace in front, where a cool drink will also alleviate the effects of too much sun (*günes* in Turkish). A new breakfast room and bar on the top floor are now operational. Most rooms have a balcony, and they all face the sea. The beach at Alanya is well equipped and the town itself offers a diversity of watersports, shops and inexpensive restaurants." (*R W*)

Open Dates not known.
Rooms 21 – all with bath or shower, most with balcony.
Facilities Bar, breakfast room, terrace. Beach with watersports.
Location On the beach at Alanya.
Credit cards Possibly some accepted.
Terms [1985 rates] B&B 2,500–4,900 TL.

Can you help us extend our coverage in Turkey?

Please make a habit of sending in a report as soon as possible after a visit when details are still fresh in your mind.

Bulvar Palas Oteli   *Tel* (41) 34.21.80
Atatürk Bulvari 141   *Telex* 42613 BLVD-TR

To establish the right mood, catch a ferry from the Galata bridge across the dusk-reddening Bosphorus to Haydarpaşa (Istanbul's Asian rail terminus); board the nine o'clock sleeper with its French-polished panelling and comfortable sofas; watch the lights along the shore of the Gulf of Nicea as you are served a four-course table d'hôte meal at a white-clothed table in the smoky, noisy dining car; return to your compartment where the bed will have been made up with starched linen sheets and soft blankets; wake again – after a night of rattles and stops – to a glass of tea at seven. Take a cab to this hotel and then breakfast off fat black olives and rose-petal jam in the flaking magnificence of the dining room under a dusty chandelier. The rest of Ankara – as is the case with so many recently adopted administrative capitals – may try to impress with its modernity, but the *Bulvar Palas* sails through still in the 'fifties, with its big bedrooms, solid plumbing and comfortable beds. Staff are efficient and abundant, meals are reasonably priced and of fair quality, but it is the atmosphere that is the thing: a 'B'-movie remake of the *Pera Palas*'s main feature (see Istanbul).

Open All year.
Rooms 177 – 167 with bath or shower, telephone, radio, TV, mini-bar and air-conditioning.
Facilities Lift, lounge, restaurant, conference facilities; hairdressing salon.
Location Central, in area called "Ministries". Next door to Belgian Ministry. Parking.
Credit cards All major cards accepted.
Terms [1985 rates] rooms: single 4,500–10,500 TL, double 6,000–14,000 TL. Breakfast (obligatory) 1,000 TL; set lunch/dinner 2,500 TL.

Keykan Oteli   *Tel* (41) 30.21.95
Fevzi Çakmak Sokak 12

On a quiet side street near Kizilay (one of the city's hubs), this friendly modern hotel has a brochure which promises "all kids [sic] of comfort". It also announces Selcuk-style architecture, but with plastic pyramid ceiling lights and an undulating concrete garden. Furniture throughout is MFI à la turque: varnished light wood, orange carpets and mirrors in curvy plastic frames. Bedrooms have large wardrobes, limited drawer-space and you can forget bedtime reading unless you are standing by the washbasin in your well-equipped bathroom. Unusually for this type of hotel (around the middle of the range although officially graded H2), they go so far as to provide small tubes of shampoo. Meals can be quite good – there is a choice of table d'hôte or grills – but one would not make a point of eating here. Rosto (baked meat with a tomato sauce) with potato purée has been excellent. Westerners may have to ask if they want olives at breakfast. This is not a hotel for a long stay, but it provides an adequate and reasonably priced base for the couple of nights – all you need to see are the Hittite Museum, Gençlik Park, Roman citadel, Baths of Carracalla, Julian Column and Temple of Augustus.

Open All year.
Rooms 50 rooms – all with bath or shower, telephone and radio, some with balcony.
Facilities Lift; restaurant; conference facilities.
Location Central on quiet side street near Kizilay. Parking.
Credit cards Some probably accepted.
Terms [1985 rates] rooms: single 8,700 TL, double 11,700 TL; full board: single 12,950 TL, double 20,200 TL. Breakfast 750 TL; set lunch/dinner 1,750 TL.

ANTALYA   Map 17

Talya Oteli   *Tel* (311) 156 00
Fevzi Çakmak Cad   *Telex* 56 111 TATA

The most luxurious five-star hotel in Antalya, and perhaps on the whole southern coast. It is just south of the old town and the splendid cliff-top park where various fairs and exhibitions are held over the summer. "The hotel is modern, very tastefully and spaciously set out and built right on the cliff top with a superb view across Antalya Bay. All rooms are double with twin beds, and it is really worth getting one with the spectacular seaview. All have private baths, air-conditioning, and a balcony where one can have breakfast. Service is excellent. All the staff are very friendly and punctilious. There is no sandy beach since these are only to be found outside the town, but the hotel has carved its own patio at the base of the cliff, complete with changing rooms, showers, diving board, steps, sunbeds and a bar. A lift goes down the side of the cliff to the beach direct from the pool. The food is also very good – a mixture of Turkish and international. The restaurant is right on the edge of the cliff bounded on three sides by the sea. Lunch can be had in the restaurant or else round the pool where there is a daily help-yourself buffet of three courses of delicious and beautifully presented food – at less than £5 a head [1984]. Two or three evenings a week they also have special dinners around the pool which is specially lighted up for the occasion. Although it has 150 rooms the hotel is not impersonally large. All in all, it was one of the best holiday hotels we have stayed in anywhere." *(Fiona Gore; also R W)*

Open All year.
Rooms 150 double – all with bath or shower, telephone, radio, TV, baby-listening, air-conditioning and balcony; 10 bungalows.
Facilities Lift; bars, restaurants, conference facilities; nightclub, hairdresser; swimming pool, tennis court. Beach patio reached by lift with swimming area and bar; waterskiing, windsurfing, boating, sailing, skin-diving off rocky beach. English spoken. &.
Location On cliff overlooking Antalya Bay, S of Old Town.
Credit cards Some may be accepted.
Terms [1985 rates] rooms: single 18,000 TL, double 26,000–36,000 TL. Breakfast 1,800–3,400 TL. Off-season reductions.

Turban Adalya   *Tel* (311) 18066
Kaleiçi yat Limani   *Telex* 56241 TBA

"The careful restoration of what was once one of the liveliest harbours in the Eastern Mediterranean has earned Antalya an international heritage award. Once again, there is life beneath the famous 'grooved' minaret, and artists, restaurateurs and shop-owners have been quick to realise the future potential of what will undoubtedly become a showplace resort. Sleek yachts are moored alongside beautifully preserved Turkish houses with their dark wooden balconies and colourful tiled roofs, while in small bars under the trees local fishermen still play backgammon from morning till late at night. The *Turban Adalya* started life in 1869 as the branch office of a bank, and was later used as a warehouse. It was eventually acquired by a former minister and lovingly converted into the most individual small luxury hotel I have come across in Turkey. The refreshing sound of running water from the fountains in the atrium-patio greets you as you walk into the welcome coolness beyond the entrance steps. The charmingly decorated bedrooms lead off from upstairs galleries. All the rooms have air-conditioning, radio, telephone and bathrooms, and there are nice little touches, like carpet slippers. There is a pleasant bar-terrace at the back overlooking the harbour, with another bar and an excellent restaurant on the top floor." *(R W, also Mike Elliott)*

Open All year.
Rooms 28 – all with bathroom, telephone, radio and air-conditioning.
Facilities Lounge, bar, snack-restaurant, patio.
Location Central; parking.
Credit cards All major cards accepted.
Terms [1985 rates] B&B: single 10,700–14,700 TL, double 14,000–19,000 TL; suite 16,600–23,000 TL for 2 people, 21,400–27,800 for 3.

BODRUM Muğla   Map 17

Manzara Pansiyon   *Tel* (6141) 1719
Kumbahçe Mah, Meteoroloji Yani

An attractive resort town opposite the Greek island of Kos and useful for boat excursions to Cnidus. "This hotel pleased us most during a three-week tour of Turkey, though oddly it is listed as a first-class *pension*. It is set a little behind the town on a hill, only about five minutes' walk fom the sea front and ten minutes from the centre of the town. The accommodation is arranged in the style of small apartments each with a terrace having table and chairs for dining outside. A living room had a further table and chairs and lounge furniture, small sink unit and, most welcome, a refrigerator. The double bedroom was comfortable and clean, if small, and had a private bathroom. There is a small heated swimming pool with an adjoining bar and small restaurant, with service throughout the day. The staff were attentive and helpful without being intrusive. Whilst we had no desire to prepare and cook our own food the facilities were available, which might suit travellers who wanted a change from the usual Turkish cooking." *(R W S Millsum)*

Open All year.
Rooms 20 double, including some suites – all with bath or shower, arranged in small apartments with living room, with sink unit and refrigerator, and terrace.
Facilities Restaurant. Terrace with swimming pool with bar.
Location On hill overlooking Bodrum.
Credit cards Some cards may be accepted.
Terms [1985 rates – excluding 3% tax] double rooms 10,500–15,800 TL. Breakfast 750 TL; set lunch/dinner 1,900 TL. 20% reductions in low season.

ÇANAKKALE   Map 17

Truva Oteli   *Tel* (1961) 1024 and 1886
Yahboyu   *Telex* 58115

A functional, modern four-star hotel convenient for Troy (32 kilometres
to the south) or for those taking the car ferry across the Dardanelles from
Asia to Europe avoiding the drive back to Istanbul. The *Truva* (Turkish
for Troy) overlooks the Hellespont, with views of passing sea traffic
from local wooden craft to huge Russian tankers, not far from where
Byron repeated Leander's legendary swim to Hero. "Wonderful position. Bedroom fair but clean. Plenty of hot water. Dinner at or after 10
pm. The staff were outstandingly friendly. They took us to a very clean
kitchen where we chose from a large choice of delicious, mainly
vegetarian, Turkish dishes. Prices very reasonable." *(C S Farrow)*

Open All year.
Rooms 3 suites, 63 double – 48 with bath, 18 with shower, all with telephone.
Facilities Lift; lobby, lounge, TV room, bar, restaurant. Garden and terrace. Near
sea.
Location 32 km N of Troy.
Credit cards None accepted.
Terms [1985 rates – excluding 15% service and 3% tax] rooms: single 2,600–6,100
TL, double 4,150–10,250 TL. Breakfast 400 TL, set lunch/dinner 1,100 TL.
Reductions for children.

ERZURUM   Map 17

Oral Oteli   *Tel* (011) 197 40
Terminal Caddesi 3   *Telex* 74117 HAVA-TR

Hearts generally sink as they enter Erzurum – a wild, bleak city at 6,000
feet where the air scarcely seems to warm even in midsummer. One
does not travel here for the ring of suburban army bases or the treeless
landscape with its wolves, bears and vultures. But there are Georgian
monasteries in the valleys, the magical northern source of the Euphrates
is a couple of hours away by jeep, and the fastest routes from Istanbul to
Ararat, Ani, Lake Van and Iran pass through. Touring the east of Turkey
often necessitates a night in Erzurum. The outside of the *Oral* – an
abrupt modern block – also often disappoints, but it is the best hotel on
this road before Tabriz and is in many ways very comfortable indeed:
well-appointed bedrooms, smart bathrooms with the area's fine fresh
water, a laundry service, comfortable seating in the lobby, highly
competent English-speaking receptionists, friendly and helpful staff.
Someone has thought about the decor long and hard and the extensive
modern wood-panelling in the public rooms is impressive. The
restaurant can be noisy if the television or tape-machine are at the usual
Turkish volume, but the food is generally excellent. *Et sote*, a local dish
of fried meat and peas, is not to be missed, also a fine cold green bean
starter – *zeytin yağli taze fasulya*, and the charcoal-grilled offal – juicy
kidneys, liver and sheep testicles (koç yumurtasi). A place like this could
never succeed entirely in a city where the electricity often cuts for hours,
but this does pretty well. Rates are extraordinarly low, perhaps reflecting a
degree of military subsisty (visiting NATO brass seem regularly to be in

residence). For more than half the year the rather banal heap of Buyuk Ejder Daği (Great Dragon Mountain) – the 10,000 footer behind the city – is snow-covered. There is a ski-lift and some long dramatic pistes – and temperatures as low as minus 40° Celsius, but the hotel has efficient heating and solid double-glazing. *(J R)*

Open All year.
Rooms 1 master-suite, 6 suites, 64 double, 19 single – all with bath, telephone and radio.
Facilities Lift, lobby/lounge area with TV, dining room; laundry service. Palandöken ski-resort nearby; 15 km from thermal springs.
Location 10 minutes' walk from centre. Hotel on left as you enter Erzurum. Parking.
Restriction Not suitable for &.
Credit cards None accepted.
Terms [excluding 10% tax] rooms with breakfast: single 6,280 TL, double 8,520 TL; half-board: single 8,890 TL, double 12,740 TL; full board: single 10,500 TL, double 15,960 TL. Set lunch/dinner 1265 TL.

FAMAGUSTA, North Cyprus   **Map 17**

Park Hotel   *Tel* (536) 65511
Salamis Road, Famagusta, Kibris,   *London representative*
c/o Mersin 10   01-493 1939

"The Park Hotel, a replica of an Austrian mountain hotel, under British management, stands on an isolated and featureless beach some six miles from Famagusta and some 500 yards from the ruins of the ancient city of Salamis. The beach is spotless, the sea is clear and provides, particularly in the vicinity of Salamis, a happy hunting-ground for snorkelling archaeologists. The use of umbrellas, beach-beds and beach-towels is free of charge, as is the use of the hotel's tennis court. Although there were quite a number of children about, the steeply sloping seabed and the sea-water pool which has no shallow end do not make this an ideal place for young children. Nor is this a place for lively teenagers – the nearest disco is a mile away. The hotel is ideal for those who seek peace (no transistors on the beach) and excellent swimming or surf-boarding. The visitors are Turkish, German and British and, particularly at weekends, there is an influx of cosmopolitan diplomats and UN personnel. The service is helpful, friendly and efficient. The air-conditioned bedrooms are well maintained, the public rooms, although hardly ever used in summer, are pleasantly furnished. The food is beautifully served but the restaurant has still some way to go before it would merit any entry in a Turkish *Good Food Guide*. There is no choice of main dish on the table d'hôte menu but, for a supplement of a few pence, one can switch to the extensive and much better à la carte selection. Turkish wines are suprisingly good and all priced at a uniform 1200 L. Many guests return to this annual seaside hotel year after year to relax, to swim and to meet interesting people." *(R E Wessely)*

Open Dates not known.
Rooms 93 – all with bath, shower and WC, telephone and air-conditioning.
Facilities Salon, restaurant. Garden with swimming pool, tennis court and beach with bar.

Location 6 m from Famagusta. (Transport via mainland Turkey – Istanbul or Izmir – and then via Cypriot Turkish Airlines. Some flights from Heathrow require a change of plane in Turkey. Taxi from airport to the hotel costs about £5.)
Credit cards None accepted.
Terms [1985 rates] double room with half-board £28. Set lunch/dinner £3.50.

IÇMELER Muğla   Map 17

Efendi Oteli   *Tel* (6121) 57
İcmeler, near Marmaris

"The Bay of Marmaris is stupendous, and Içmeler, at the western end, offers beautifully sheltered clear waters and an inviting sandy beach. The little village has several well-designed small hotels, and the authorities have been careful not to spoil its appearance. The attractions of Marmaris are a few miles along the bay, and easily accessible by cheap and frequent 'dolmus' (shared taxis). The *Efendi* is a new hotel, but the architect has given it some individual touches, with abundant use of wood in the interestingly designed balconies and windows to offset the white exterior. There is a domed Oriental sitting area with a fountain in the reception-lounge. A bar leads to the dining-terrace, and there is an outside bar as well. Evenings here are lovely, with coloured lights in the trees overhead and the twinkle of Marmaris over the waters. There are views of the bay from the balconies of the rooms, some of which have air-conditionining." *(R W)*

Open Dates not known.
Rooms 28 – all with shower and wc, some with air-conditioning, some with balcony.
Facilities Reception/lounge, 2 bars, dining terrace. Beach with watersports.
Location On the Bay of Marmaris.
Credit cards Possibly some accepted.
Terms [1985 rates] rooms 5,500–7,200 TL. Half-board 5,500–7,400 TL per person.

ISTANBUL   Map 17

Divan Oteli   *Tel* (01) 146.40.20
Cumhuriyet Cad. 2, Şişli   *Telex* 22 402 DVAN

"Smaller, quieter and less touristy than the *Hilton* and *Sheraton*. For quite a bit less money you get everything they can offer except a pool. The rooms are pleasant, clean and tastefully decorated. The staff are courteous and efficient. The restaurant is one of the finest in Istanbul. Caviar, fish, mixed grill and baklava are just about the best I've ever had. The *Divan* pastry shop makes the best Turkish delights in town – anyone in Istanbul will agree. A bountiful breakfast is served in a room that unfortunately looks like a banquet/conference room from a convention hotel. They are doing some renovation and I hope it will end up a prettier place. The other oddly decorated room is the bar – sort of 1960s modern Turkish style, but it works." *(Catherine Cuthell; also R W)*

Open All year.
Rooms 96 – mostly double – all with bath or shower, radio, TV, mini-bar and air-conditioning.
Facilities Lift. Breakfast room, restaurant, pastry shop, conference facilities.
Location Central. Parking.

Credit cards Probably some accepted.
Terms [1985 rates – excluding 15% service and 3% tax] rooms: single 12,500–
25,000 TL, double 17,000–32,000 TL. Breakfast 2,100 TL; set lunch/dinner 5,300 TL.
Reductions for children.

Harem Oteli   *Tel* (90) 1333 20 25
Ambar Sok 1, Selimye – Üsküdar   *Telex* 29420 HRM

Unlike most recommendable hotels in Istanbul, the *Harem* is on the
Asian shore, strategically located just above the Asian Otogar, looking
over the Bosphorus towards European Istanbul, 20 minutes away by
ferry. "Staggering off the overnight bus from Izmir or wherever, it is a
blessing not to have to search for a hotel. A short walk takes you to the
Harem which has a swimming pool and magnificent views over the city
and is very reasonably priced. The only snag is that the ferries from
Galata bridge now finish quite early in the evening, so that returning
from the city late can be a problem (although there may be ferries
returning later from Beşiktaş)." *(Neil Roberts)*

Open All year.
Rooms 8 suites, 76 double, 16 single – 84 with bath, 16 with shower, all with
telephone, many with balcony; some ground-floor rooms.
Facilities Lift, American bar, restaurant, conference facilities. Terrace with
swimming pool, sauna. English spoken.
Location In the Asian quarter of the city, near the Florence Nightingale Hospital.
Parking.
Restriction Probably not suitable for &.
Credit cards None accepted.
Terms [1985 rates] B&B: single 5,687 TL, double 8,899 TL; dinner, B&B: single
7,502 TL, double 12,592 TL; full board: single 9,317 TL, double 16,159 TL.

Pera Palas Oteli   *Tel* 145 22 30
Meşrutiyet Cad. 98–100   *Telex* 24 152 PERA-TR
Tepebaşi

Situated in the old diplomatic quarter of Galata just along by the
American Consulate-General, this was *the* hotel for travellers arriving on
the Orient Express, and is the grandest of the city's old hotels still in use.
It is easy to catch yourself saying Constantinople rather than Istanbul as
you take tea in the splendid central covered court, or "cin-tonik" ("c" is
pronounced like a soft English "g") at the elegant bar. Some of the
bedrooms look out over the Golden Horn; all of them are very
comfortable in a solid, 19th-century sort of way. For a literary eulogy
read the relevant chapter of Jan Morris's *Destinations*. For several years
past, unfortunately, the *Pera* seems to have been cashing in rather on its
fading glory and fame, with souvenir stall, package deals and so on. But
is is still highly atmospheric.

That was last year's citation. A reader this year comments, with
tongue firmly in cheek: "I suppose you could talk about atmosphere and
the delightful gilded cage which serves as a lift. The beds were
comfortable and the bath enormous, but the situation – we had what
purported to be one of the best rooms, with lofty ceilings (complete with
cobwebs) and imposing doors. But the noise! The street outside is
narrow, busy and uphill. The traffic in Istanbul is indescribable and we

had difficulty sleeping. The food was better than I expected, however. I am quite glad I stayed in such a historic hotel but ..." More reports would be welcome.

Open All year.
Rooms 3 suites, 95 double, 25 single – all with bath and telephone.
Facilities Lift, hall, salon, bar, restaurant. English spoken.
Location Central, near American Consulate and Galata Tower. Some parking.
Restriction Probably not suitable for &.
Credit cards All major cards accepted.
Terms [Excluding 10% tax and 15% service) B&B: single US$40, double US$60; dinner, B&B: single US$48, double US$76; full board: single US$56, double US$92. Set lunch/dinner US$8; full alc US$12.

Yeşil Konak Oteli
Sultanahmet

Tel 528.67.64 or 511.11.501
Telex 23346
(*For bookings in UK:* Savile Travel,
Maddox Street, London W1
01-499 5101)

A welcome addition to our Turkish section, a hotel of genuine character that opened its doors only in 1984. "Istanbul the magnificent is also Istanbul the exhausting – dusty, hilly and, at first, bewildering; so it is a lucky traveller who can take refuge in the *Konak*. 'Centrally situated' is almost an understatement in this case. The *Konak* is set high up in the very oldest part of the Old City, midway between Haghia Sophia and the Blue Mosque, 600 metres from the first courtyard of Topkapi Sarayi. It is an old wooden mansion (for the nervous, yes, there is a fire escape) set between a row of ever-hopeful carpet shops and a jobbing printer in a very small way of business. The 19th-century house is three storeys high, painted a fresh apple green and white. Three years ago it was derelict, but the Touring Club of Turkey has restored it lovingly. Our bedroom – one of two on the ground floor – was almost more bed than room. The well-sprung bed measured 5½ feet wide and 6½ feet long, leaving just enough room to squeeze past an armchair, a polished mahogany wardrobe and a chest of drawers. The room was high and had tall sash windows hung with lace and brocade curtains and fitted with latticed shutters giving what were basically light rooms a pleasantly secretive, Ottoman feeling. The decorations numbered an amateur oil painting of the hotel, a gilded mirror and a wonderfully kitsch light decorated with two lovebirds. Indeed, our room had no fewer than nine lamp bulbs – enough, say, for four average French hotel rooms. Communication with the outside world – and the present century – was via a brass 'candlestick' telephone made in Coventry in 1930; the switchboard operator, like all the staff, speaks enough English to be helpful and friendly. The bathroom, *en suite*, was spotlessly clean, with loo, shower, basin, and a frieze of old tiles. Soundproofing between it and the next bathroom ... well, there wasn't any.

"So far, so very good. But the walled, paved garden is the *Konak*'s happiest asset. Water splashes down from a porphyry fountain; fig and plane trees are edged with pansies and stocks, wallflowers and marigolds; roses and vines climb the walls. Somewhat too neat and municipal for some? Perhaps, and certainly the unrelenting muzak should be discouraged. Two dozen marble-topped tables with cushioned white chairs are set for breakfast, lunch, dinner or tea; there is a dining room inside for days less sunny than those we enjoyed. On one side of the garden stands a pelargonium-filled conservatory for cool evenings. The other side of the garden offers an old 'medresseh' nearing its restoration and conversion into an arts and crafts market. The food at the *Konak* is very good, typically Turkish, with a menu that is limited but with just enough variety for a week's stay, assuming that guests use other restaurants too – *Pendeli's* in the Spice Market, perhaps, or one of the shoreside fish restaurants at nearby Kumkapi.

"The *Konak* is a valuable addition to a fascinating city, and the Touring Club is to be congratulated. Those staying in the large multinational hotels, which seem less than fortunately situated in Istanbul, could at least take tea in the garden and see what local enterprise and national pride can do. And where better than here to take the last Turkish coffee of the day, turning one's gaze from the great dome of the Aghia Sophia to the six slender minarets of the Blue Mosque, with a fond glance at Sinan's elegant Baths of Roxellana in between?" *(David H M Smith; also Richard Wiersum)*
Note: Not to be confused with the Konak Oteli in Cumhuriyet Cad.

Open Dates not known.
Rooms 15 – some with bath, all with telephone.
Facilities Salon, dining room, conservatory; garden. English spoken.
Location In Old City, mid-way between Haghia Sophia and the Blue Mosque.
Credit cards Not known.
Terms [1985 rates] rooms with breakfast: single 16,445 TL, double 22,770–29,095 TL, triple 40,480 TL, "Pasha's room" 60,720 TL.

KUŞADASI Aydin   Map 17

Kismet   *Tel* (6361) 2005–9
Akyar Mevkii

The pleasant resort of Kuşadasi, convenient for Ephesus and a whole host of other remarkable antiquities, has become a fashionable marina as well as a daystop for Mediterranean cruises. The *Kismet* is by no means the largest or the most expensive hotel in town, but is by quite a margin the most sympathetic. "One of those confident, never smug, establishments which have clearly been 'discovered' for many years by those shrewd enough not to advertise its virtues. Kuşadasi is a rather chic yachting centre with a cosmopolitan air, the air clinking with the sound of rigging, rather as if the rich were ostentatiously throwing their small change to the wind. The *Kismet* is on a boss of land, above the yacht basin and far from the tavernas and carpet shops which make the evenings agreeable with colour and loud with amiable huckstering. The *Kismet's* promontory is covered with a small paradise of a garden, liberally set with lounging chairs and with a tennis court for the energetic, niched above the Aegean into which you can plunge from a private, rocky 'beach'. The sea is bracingly cool and there are some sharp rocks to be wary of, if you launch from the wrong bit. The hotel rooms are well maintained and offer remarkable value. The dining room is adequate, but we should not recommend full *pension*. However, the breakfast is self-service and there is a full vat of yoghurt on which to start the day. The *Kismet* may be expensive by Turkish standards, but it is ludicrously cheap by British ones. Nicely served afternoon teas remind one of what one is not missing, so to speak. The hotel is full, even in October, and it is essential to book." *(Frederic and Sylvia Raphael; also Sheila and Uwe Kitzinger, Catherine Cuthell)*

Open Apr–Oct.
Rooms 68, including some suites – all with bath or shower and telephone.
Facilities Lift, restaurant, bar; hairdresser. Garden with swimming pool and tennis court. Beach, waterskiing, boating.
Location On peninsula in Kuşadasi bay.
Credit cards Some cards may be accepted.
Terms [1985 rates, excluding 3% tax] rooms: single 7,800–13,050 TL, double 9,750–20,250 TL. Breakfast 750 TL; set lunch/dinner 2,250 TL.

ÖLÜDENIZ Muğla   Map 17

Meri Motel   *Tel* (1482) 1025
Ölüdeniz, near Fethiye   *Telex* 53020 MERX

"The white spit of sand curving around a turquoise lagoon that you see on all the travel posters of Turkey is Ölüdeniz. The *Meri* is on the lagoon itself at the end of the road, well away from the camping establishments on the beach outside the lagoon. The hotel's private beach is calm, with beautiful white sand. You can sit under the trees in the garden at tables or lie on wooden loungers under straw umbrellas. The rooms are built in blocks scattered up a steep ravine (the *Meri* is not for those who can't climb stairs). The views from the balconies are nice but the rooms are a little dark and the bathrooms a little the worse for wear. You must take half- or full board, depending on the season, which is a pity as the food is nothing special. At the reasonable rate however, we just ate out anyway and chalked it up to the price of the room. The restaurant, on the first floor overlooking the garden, is pleasant and breezy. The hotel has a picturesque old-style boat which goes on a tour of the lagoon every afternoon, but most people just lie on the beautiful beach or row out to the sandy spit. The clientele is a true mix – half Turkish, the rest German, English, American and French. Quite a few families. It would be a good place for kids – very safe swimming. (Note: for good fish, a pretty rooftop bar and taped jazz go to Han Camping's restaurant on the main beach.) *(Catherine Cuthell)*

Open All year.
Rooms 75 – all with shower and telephone, some with balcony. All in separate blocks.
Facilities Indoor and outdoor restaurants, bar, disco, garden with play area for children. Private beach with water sports, sailing, fishing.
Location 15 km S of Fethiye.
Restriction Not suitable for &.
Terms [1985 rates – excluding 15% service and 10% tax] rooms with breakfast: single 6,600 TL, double 11,900 TL, triple 11,175 TL. Half-board (obligatory in low season): single 8,200 TL, double 11,900 TL, triple 15,975 TL; full board (obligatory in high season): single 9,800 TL, double 15,100 TL, triple 20,775 TL. 20% reduction in low season.

Don't keep your favourite hotel to yourself. The Guide supports: it doesn't spoil.

SILIFKE İçel **Map 17**

Taştur Motel *Tel* 4590 – 290
Taşucu

A modern hotel about seven kilometres west of Silifke on the edge of a small village overlooking a rocky shoreline. "This hotel deserves an entry, and not just because it is the only hotel in its class along an extensive stretch of the coast between Antalya and Mersin. The surroundings are inauspicious. Taşucu is a small commercial port, with an ugly paper mill smoking away on its fringes and building work close to the hotel. But, once inside, you feel as if you are on a ship. Perched on a rocky cliff, the hotel is on several levels, and from all of them you look straight out to sea. Rooms are well furnished and spacious, and all have a balcony. A good swimming pool makes up for the absence of a beach (though there are plenty of secluded coves within a 20-minute drive). We spent a very relaxed 24-hour stay sun-bathing on the terraces around the pool surrounded by the odd Greek statue and attractive plants and flowers. Half-board was compulsory, but a surprisingly adventurous set menu at dinner made this little hardship. You pay over the odds for drinks at the bar, but we thought that 17,125 TL for half-board for two people made the *Taştur* good value compared with some of the much more basic but less expensive motels in nearby resorts. Service, as usual, was both efficient and friendly." *(Emma Oxford)*

Open 15 Mar–31 Oct.
Rooms 54 – all with bath and shower, telephone and balcony.
Facilities Bar, restaurant, conference facilities, terraces, swimming pool; rocky and sandy beaches nearby; excellent snorkelling.
Location 7 km W of Silifke.
Credit cards Probably some accepted.
Terms [1985 rates – excluding 15% service and 3% tax] rooms: single 7,200–11,200 TL; double 9,000–17,000 TL. Breakfast 700 TL, set lunch/dinner 1,650 TL. 15% reductions out of season.

In addition to the preceding entries, a number of other hotels have been recommended to us, though without sufficient information to provide a proper citation. We list these below – with no guarantees. The gradings are from the official listings of the Ministry of Tourism.

ABANT, Bolu Province **Turban Abant Oteli** *Tel* 04 *Telex* 42879 ABNT-TR. Graded H2. 94 comfortable rooms in a restful hotel in a beautiful area of woods, hills and lakes. Turks come here for the clear air and fine food (the country's best chefs come from Bolu). Almost the atmosphere of a spa hotel.

ALANYA **Kaptan Oteli** Iskeli Cad. 62. *Tel* 2000–1094. Graded H3. 45 rooms. Set on a slight rise a few minutes from the fine sandy beach, and close to the shops. Excellent views from the roof-top dining-terrace. Front rooms have a balcony and seaview; those at the back mostly overlook the swimming-pool.

ANTALYA **Bilgehan Oteli,** Kazim Ozalp Cad. 194 *Tel* 151 84 or 253 25. Graded H3. Just by the main bus station with a half-mile walk to the harbour, this large modern hotel (88 rooms) is comfortable if a little characterless. A good stop-over, not a resort hotel. Summer eating on the roof can afford spectacular views. Also breakfast at dawn before an early flight.

ANTALYA **Buyuk Oteli,** Cumhuriyet Cad. 57   *Tel* 114 99 or 125 43. Graded H4. Rather faded now, this used to be the city's grand hotel (a direct translation of the name). Small (42 rooms) and traditionally run, it has some good views over the harbour and tea-gardens and serves excellent breakfasts in its pastry shop.

BURSA **Akdoğan Oteli** 1. Murat Cad. 5.   *Tel* 247 55–57 *Telex* 32 229 AKOT. Graded H2. 119 Beds. Plumbing a little crude, but modest and pleasant. Its bonus is the Turkish baths in the basement. Away from the centre of town at the foot of the approach road to Mount Ulu Dag, Turkey's famous skiing resort.

BURSA **Celik Palas Oteli** Cakirge Cad. 79.   *Tel* 196 00–6 *Telex* 32 121 CEPA. Graded H2. English widely spoken. Cooking international and expensive by Turkish standards, but breakfasts remarkable value. Turkish baths, from a thermal spring, a bonus. 131 rooms. Front rooms have splendid view over Bursa plain, but are noisy. Rear rooms, looking over foothills of Ulu Dag, preferred.

INCEKUM **Alara Oteli** On a headland above an excellent sandy beach 15 miles west of Alanya, and somewhat Caribbean in its architecture. The central pavilion houses restaurant, bar, lounges and shops; the bedrooms are in separate buildings in the gardens or under pine trees. Lawns lead down to the main beach, and there is a cove beneath the hotel with its own bar. Good public transport to Side, Alanya and Antalya.

ISTANBUL **Buyuk Tarabya Oteli,** Kefelikoy Cad. Tarabya   *Tel* 162 10 00 *Telex* 26 203 HTRB-TR. Graded HL. A luxury class, 261-room hotel on a splendid stretch of the Bosphorus a few miles out of the centre. A good place for a restful holiday with excellent facilities and good views. Swimming. One of the few hotels that makes Istanbul feel like a real resort. Expensive food.

ISTANBUL **Etap Istanbul,** Meşrutiyet Cad., Tepebasi   *Tel* 144 80 80 *Telex* 24 345. Graded H1. 200 rooms. Slightly cheaper than the luxury places but with the same cosmopolitan air. A tall thin block in the heart of the old diplomatic and commercial quarter. A tiny swimming pool on the top has views from the edge over the whole city.

ISTANBUL **Olcay Oteli** Millet Cad. 187.   *Tel* 585 32 20 *Telex* 23 209 OLCA. Graded H2. Moderately priced, and close to Topkapi and the Bazaar. Popular with tour parties, but offering the bonus of a pleasant garden. 134 rooms.

IZMIR **Kismet Oteli** 1377 Sok. 9.   *Tel* 21 70 50–52. Graded H1. Beautiful decor. Quietly situated. 68 rooms.

KONYA **Başak Palace Oteli** Hükümet Mey.3.   *Tel* 113 38–39. Graded H3. In the centre of the town. Only breakfast served and few rooms have their own baths. But a remarkable place, scrupulously clean. 40 rooms.

TRABZON **Usta Oteli,** Iskele Cad, Telgrafhane Sok. 3.   *Tel* 121 95, 128 43 *Telex* 83 214 ATME-TR. Graded H3. No restaurant, but *the* place to stay here. Upper floors have views of the Black Sea. Furnishing is spartan and bathrooms are relatively primitive. Staff helpful, with some English. Good breakfasts. 72 rooms.

ÜRGÜP, Nevşehir Province **Turban Ürgüp Moteli** Graded M1. 160 beds, with chalet style blocks of 8–10 units in two-storey buildings. Attractively laid out and very clean. Expensive restaurant: eating in the village recommended.

Yugoslavia

VILLA DUBROVNIK – DUBROVNIK

BLED 64260 Slovenia   **Map 16**

Grand Hotel Toplice   *Tel* Bled (064) 77.222
                                                     Telex 34-588 TOPLICE

An oft-repeated description of this noble hotel in Yugoslavia's leading
inland resort sets the scene: "Lake Bled, as seen from the wide windows
of the *Grand Hotel Toplice*, presents a perfect picture postcard view: dense
trees mask many of the hotels which edge its shores; from the wooded
islet in the middle of the water rise the tower and tall turret of an ancient
castle and chapel; and on the horizon rise the peaks of the Julian Alps.
This area of Slovenia, just across the border from Austria, is a paradise
for fishermen, hunters, painters, and wine connoisseurs; the Riesling
here is fabulous. The *Toplice* (meaning "spa") stands right at the lake
edge, and it is in the best traditions of 19th-century Hapsburg Vienna;
but though it keeps its period elegance, mod cons have been discreetly
added. It also has its own covered swimming pool fed by a thermal
spring, and edged with columns like the Roman baths at Bath." *(George S
Jonas)*

More recent visitors have pointed out that the hotel is primarily used by tour groups, with the usual impairment of ambience. A visitor this year agrees, but adds: "It has a large, comfortable lounge with a semi-circle of picture windows overlooking beautiful Lake Bled. The dining room is vast and impressive and seems to stretch out for a hundred yards with dozens of chandeliers disappearing into the distance. We had an excellent dinner and afterwards relaxed in the bar with a Slivovitz. The bedrooms were comfortable. In the morning we swam in the hotel pool, and paid an extremely modest bill for a classic hotel." *(Gordon Bennett; also F C Parker)*

Open All year.
Rooms 14 suites, 74 double, 36 single – all with bath and telephone, most with balcony overlooking the lake; 45 rooms in annexe.
Facilities Lift, salon and cocktail bar, TV room, elegant restaurant; conference rooms, bridge room; sauna, massage, solarium, keep-fit club; indoor heated swimming pool. Dancing 6 evenings a week. Lakeside terrace and bathing beach; boats and fishing licences available; golf and tennis nearby. English spoken.
Location 55 km W of Ljubljana, near Austrian border. 200 metres from town centre. Parking. *Warning:* Rooms facing street may be noisy.
Credit cards Access, Amex, Diners.
Terms [1985 rates] rooms with breakfast: single US$20–35, double US$34–60; half-board (min 3 days): US$20–46 per person; full board (min 3 days): US$23–49 per person.

DUBROVNIK   Map 16

Villa Dubrovnik   *Tel* (050) 22.933

Of the three smart hotels on the south side of Dubrovnik, the *Excelsior*, the *Argentina* and the *Villa Dubrovnik*, it is the last which our readers seem to prefer. It is a modern medium-sized hotel, perched high on a cliff, with lovely views of the old walled town and harbour, and also over to the island of Lokrum opposite. The hotel is terraced into the cliff with lifts to all floors, except to the bathing rocks. Pine trees, flowers and blue awnings give a Riviera flavour. The bar and dining room both have superb views, and you can eat outdoors in fine weather. Most bedrooms face the front with small balconies, and are well furnished; it's well worth paying extra for sea-facing rooms. There are high standards of cleanliness. The hotel has its own "concrete" beach with rock bathing in unpolluted water; there is no nightlife on the spot, but you can wander down to the city in about twenty minutes, or take the hotel's own motor-boat, and it is easy to get a taxi back. Not recommended for the elderly or infirm, as there are steps up from the hotel entrance to the road above. More reports welcome.

Open All year.
Rooms 1 suite, 44 double, 2 single – 33 with bath, 4 with shower, all with telephone, many with sea-facing balconies.
Facilities Lifts, lounge, bar, restaurant; sub-tropical gardens; own bathing beach, mainly rock, reached by lift; sea-level bar service. English spoken.
Location On S side of Dubrovnik. Garage parking.
Restriction Not suitable for &.
Credit card Amex.
Terms [1985 rates, excluding tax] rooms with breakfast: single US$20–53, double: US$24–80; half-board (min 3 nights): US$22–61 per person; full board (min 3 nights): US$18–65 per person.

MAKARSKA 58300   Map 16

Hotel Biokovo   *Tel* (058) 612.244 or 612.125
Telex 26237 BIOMAK

The "Makarska Riviera" is a lovely necklace of towns strung along the length of the Dalmatian coast between Split and Dubrovnik. Makarska is in the geographical centre of these inexpensive jewels. "Forty-five kilometres south of Split, it is a rather understated resort: a few pretty buildings deriving from a chequered cultural history (Venetian, Turkish, Austrian) against a stunning backdrop of mountains. The *Biokovo* is to all appearances a brand-new hotel, designed with real talent. The public areas have a cool simplicity and elegance, and the bedrooms are enhanced by lace-curtained balconies and sitting rooms with comfortable chairs, a standard lamp, trailing plants and a clean, expensive-feeling modernity. Reception staff are pleasant and helpful." It is in the centre of town, so can be noisy *(Don and Di Harley)*. More reports welcome.

Open All year.
Rooms 1 suite, 54 double, 1 single – all with bath and telephone.
Facilities Salon, TV room, coffee room, restaurant, pizzeria. Terrace. Beach 100 metres. English spoken.
Location On Dalmatian coast, 45 km S of Split. Hotel is central (rooms can be noisy). Parking.
Credit cards All major cards accepted.
Terms [1985 rates] rooms with breakfast: single 38–78 DM, double 24–72 DM; half-board 22–70 DM; full board 24–78 DM. Reduced rates for children.

NOVI SAD   Map 16

Varadin   *Tel* (021) 621.811
Telex 14310

The sizeable city of Novi Sad, on the Danube 75 kilometres north-west of Belgrade, is capital of the autonomous province of Vojvodina and has Hungarian influences. "The *Varadin* came as a pleasant surprise. It is inside the fortress of Petrovaradin, on a hill on the south bank of the Danube, overlooking the city. The hotel and restaurant are stylishly decorated but my room was not over-clean. The bed however was comfortable and the plumbing in the *en suite* bathroom worked perfectly. Service at dinner was excellent despite it being a busy Saturday; breakfast was served quickly and pleasantly and the standard of *cuisine* for both meals was good for the area. The restaurant has a roof-terrace. Petrovaradin is open to the locals and obviously popular." *(F C Parker)*

Open All year.
Rooms 3 suites, 25 double, 25 single – all with bath or shower and telephone; radio and TV in suites.
Facilities Bar, restaurant; conference rooms, night club, disco; garden with terrace overlooking the Danube.
Location Inside the walls of the old city of Petrovaradin, overlooking the Danube, across the river from Novi Sad city. Parking.
Credit cards All major cards accepted.
Terms [1985 rates] rooms: single US$35, double US$31–44; half-board US$20 per person; full board US$25–28 per person.

OTOČEC OB KRKI 68222   Map 16

Grad Otočec   *Tel* (068) 21.830
Telex 35740

Imagine not just a medieval castle, but a medieval castle in medieval times, when 13th-century furniture was new and clean, the flagstones scrubbed each day, the fabrics sumptuous and far from threadbare. This is how one feels upon entering the lobby of the *Grad Otočec*, a honey-coloured stone castle converted into – by Yugoslav standards – a grand hotel. It is on an island in the lazy River Krka, reached from either side by crossing flat wooden bridges under which float swans, regally and effortlessly. On the road between Ljubljana in Slovenia and Zagreb in Croatia, the hotel is a good base for discovering just how diverse and mysterious is the "land of the South Slavs". "Excellent room, excellent meal and wine but the service is slow. This entry alone paid for the Guide," says one visitor. "Restaurant and rooms tell of better times." A slight warning: "Telephoning abroad is a drama." (*H C and Else Robbins Landon, S C Farrow; A Mc W*)

Open All year.
Rooms 2 suites, 17 double, 2 single – 10 with bath, all with telephone, 2 with TV.
Facilities Salons, bar, dining room – dancing 6 days a week – indoor swimming pool. Large park; river with bathing, boating and fishing, hunting, walks on the river banks. English spoken.
Location 7 km NE of Novo Mesto.
Restriction Not suitable for &.
Credit cards All major cards accepted.
Terms B&B: single US$15.75, double US$31.20; dinner, B&B US$14.25–18.75 per person; full board US$16.75–23.05 per person. Set lunch US$6, supper US$5.60; full alc US$10. 30% reduction for children under 7; special meals available.
Note: In addition to the castle, there is, on the northern bank of the river, a big modern hotel complex under the same management, with 164 rooms, a motel, self-catering bungalows and camping facilities.

SVETI STEFAN 81315   Map 16

Hotel Sveti Stefan   *Tel* (both hotels) (086) 41.333 or
Hotel Milocer   41.411
Telex 61188 SV STF

The area around the old walled city of Budva, in the southern part of Yugoslavia, is full of rewarding excursions. The Bay of Kotor is strikingly beautiful, and behind the town of Kotor lie the 25 hairpin bends to the former capital of the kingdom of Montenegro – Cetinje – in its mountain fastness, rich in museums and soaked in the awe-inspiring history of its fearless people. There is no shortage of hotels at Budva and along the coast, most indistinguishably commonplace. But there are exceptions.

About six miles south from Budva is a complex of three hotels. One of these, *Sveti Stefan*, is a pocket-sized island joined to the mainland by a long causeway. At the end of the war it was inhabited by a few fishermen. Then someone had the ambitious idea of converting the whole island into one big hotel, the individual cottages restored and fitted out in luxury style serving as separate suites. The result is what many claim to be the most sumptuous resort in Yugoslavia. Flowering shrubs, cacti and trees blaze between the little houses and along the narrow alleys. "As you walk around the island, which is mostly up and down stone staircases, you feel as though you are in the original town: there is absolutely no feeling of hotel about it. The restaurant was good, and meals were served on an outdoor terrace; there was also a lovely little nook for afternoon tea and pastries. Our accommodation was outstanding. Our suite had a hall (with oriental rug), a huge bathroom, a bedroom and sitting room. We had our own patio with wicker table and chairs, and relished our breakfast (room service) among the bougainvillea." (*Marian and El Nettles*)

The Milocer, on the mainland, facing the island hotel, is altogether different. Built as a summer palace by Alexander I for his wife, it was unfinished at the time of his assassination in Marseilles in 1934, but still retains an air of opulence. The central block has an exceptionally handsome, long, vine-shaded terrace where meals are served. Most of the rooms are in separate annexes set discreetly in the grounds a few minutes' walk from the hotel proper. Some readers (including the Editor) prefer the *Milocer*: "The *Sveti Stefan* is spectacularly pretty, of course, but to me claustrophobic. What is lovely about the *Milocer* is that it is very private, with big gardens, two fine (pebbly) beaches, splendid swimming and – its best feature probably – a wonderful outdoor restaurant. Not cheap by Yugoslav standards, and not as much fish as one would like, but much more varied than elsewhere in Yugoslavia. It's not a first-class hotel in the Western sense, but if you want a southern European seaside holiday, it would be very difficult to top this, both in quality and price – and charm!" (*Gitta Sereny*)

Hotel Sveti Stefan
Open May–Oct.
Rooms 1 villa, 24 suites, 76 double, 18 single – all in separate houses and all with bath/wc/bidet and telephone, radio in villa, TV on request.
Facilities Salons, cocktail bars, terrace café, restaurant; night club, casino; hairdresser, beauty salon and shops. Spacious gardens with swimming pool and mini-golf. Private sandy beach with water sports. English spoken. Possibly suitable for &.
Location 6 km S of Budva on Adriatic coast. Parking.
Credit cards All major cards accepted.
Terms B&B: US$40–70; half-board US$18 added; full board another US$18 added. Set lunch US$15–18, dinner US$20–30. Reduced rates for children sharing parents' room.

Hotel Milocer
Open Apr–end Oct.
Rooms 45 single and double, also cottage-annexes in the grounds – about half with bath or shower.
Facilities Bar, extensive terrace for meals; large secluded wooded grounds and gardens; beach nearby; tennis.
Credit cards Possibly some accepted.
Terms Not known (but cheaper than *Sveti Stefan* hotel).

Our Yugoslav section is unacceptably short. Please would travellers in Yugoslavia tell us if they come across a good hotel.

Yugoslav tariffs are in US dollars or deutschmarks.

ZAGREB   Map 16

Hotel Esplanade   *Tel* (041) 512.222
Mihanoviceva 1

This is the nostalgic report we ran last year: "We will always remember the *Esplanade*. It was elegant in the old style ... it reminded us of New York's *Savoy Plaza* of 25 years ago. Everywhere there were beautifully uniformed staff going quietly about their duties; it was the kind of hotel where you find your bed turned back and a chocolate waiting on your pillow when you reach your room of an evening. Unlike the other cold, marble hotels that we encountered, the *Esplanade* was full of warmth and flowers. I noted in my journal: 'a lovely room with all amenities ... also with round-bottomed tub in which neither sitting nor standing was safe! ... Even breakfast is a visual delight at the *Esplanade*.' The food is wholly excellent and Zagreb, our last stop, is remembered with real pleasure, thanks to the *Esplanade*." Can we hear from more recent visitors? *(Marian and El Nettles; also Brian and Margaret Aldiss)*

Open All year.
Rooms 197 – all with bath or shower, most with telephone.
Facilities Lift, hall/salon, bar, Taverna Rustica, restaurant, night club, casino; hairdresser, barber shop, beauty salon, souvenir shop; conference and private dining facilities.
Location 10 minutes' drive from town centre. Parking.
Credit cards Possibly some accepted.
Terms [1985 rates, excluding tax] rooms: single US$61–69, double US$76–122.

Report of the year competition

Once again we have awarded a dozen bottles of champagne for the best reports received during the previous year. With several thousand contenders, choosing an outright winner is far from easy. But the judges were unanimous in giving the first prize to Shelley Cranshaw of Oxford, whose nomination of the *Villa Hostilina*, Lamego, Portugal, appears in a shortened form in the main text and in full below. Short-listed and receiving a bottle apiece are: Norman Brangham, Tunbridge Wells; Gerald Campion, Hastinglea; Dr H B Cardwell, Hull; Mary McCleary Posner, Amonk, NY; Mrs R B Richards, Ware; and T C Seoh, London.

Another case of champagne will be offered next year. No special entry form is required; everything we receive in the course of the year will qualify. A winning report may be one which nominates a new hotel or comments on an existing one; a thumbs down report will qualify as much as an endorsement. And we also award champagne to those whose reports are consistently useful as well as to individually brilliant examples of the art of hotel criticism. There is no stipulation as to length: reports need not be as long as this year's winner. The essential requirement is that the communication, whether succinct or expansive, should sharply convey the particular character of the establishment.

Let me tell you what you can see from the little tiled terrace that leads off your bedroom at the *Casa Villa Hostilina,* Lamego, Portugal. Gentle hills covered with vines roll and fold into the blue distance. Immediately below is the house's own vineyard where, if you're up early enough, you can watch the workers tend the vines. It is the most peaceful prospect imaginable. Downstairs a breakfast awaits you not only generous but gorgeous to behold – figs, peaches, quince jelly, home-made jam, two kinds of bread, coffee, chocolate, tea and enormous cakes such as Alice had to divide up in *Through the Looking Glass*. The maid Julietta who sets out these dainties will train you up in the Portuguese for them if you are so minded. Thus nourished, you may set off to explore lovely Lamego, bracing yourself to be inspected in the streets for these kind people are not used to tourists. Lamego is a gem – do not miss the Cathedral cloister, the splendid little museum, the 600 steps that climb out of the centre of the town to the pilgrimage church of Nossa Senhora dos Remedios and the visit to the champagne cellars of Raposeira. Should you want to venture further, your hostess Senhora Brandao dos Santos knows things within and without the guide books that will keep your days crowded with discovery. Not in the guide books, for example, is an exquisite 13th-century Romanesque fortified bridge – also, happily enough, hard by another champagne tasting.

The villa is right on the edge of town. It is comfortable and up-to-date and the welcome is very warm. There is a gymnasium (Senhor is a karate black belt) and a swimming pool is under construction so, if you're into keeping fit, the facilities are to hand. I need not tell you that you will enjoy the wines of the area. They are many and delicious and at prices that reveal plainly that Portugal is not (yet) in the Common Market.

It has been truly observed that those who favour the north of Portugal would not readily find themselves in the south. Lamego is 2½ hours by car from Oporto – up the Douro and turn right. Fly-drive arrangements are easily accessible. If you like tranquillity, delicious food and interesting things to see, Lamego is for you. Give my love to the English labelling in the monastery church of S. João de Tarouca: it's not every day one can stand before the altar with tears of innocent merriment on the cheeks.

SHELLEY CRANSHAW

Tipping: "One of the most odious practices ever invented"

In our campaign to raise the consciousness of the public to the demeaning habit of tipping, we offer readers this eloquent indictment, written a few years ago by the formidable polemicist of the London Times, *Bernard Levin.*

An exceptionally unpleasant story not long ago, which nobody came well out of, concerned a dispute over a tip to a museum attendant; it was suggested that the tip had been solicited but not given. I say nobody came well out of the episode, but really, I have never been able to see how it is possible for anybody to come well out of the business of tipping which must be one of the most odious practices ever invented: I wish we could do away with it altogether. (A favourite traveller's tale – more exactly, fellow-travellers' tale – about the Soviet Union relates that tipping there has been abolished, but the claim is quite untrue, tips being expected and accepted in the same circumstances – restaurants, hotels, taxis – as they are elsewhere. I discovered this rapidly on my sole visit there; the only normally tippable figure who refused one was the driver of the Intourist car, and he was under the eye of my guide, who was the usual *apparatchik*. The moment her back was turned I proffered the roubles again, when they were accepted with alacrity and, I swear, a wink.)

An American once defined for me the nature of the distastefulness involved in tipping: "We never tip an equal," he said. He was right: the giving of a tip proclaims a superiority on the part of the giver, its acceptance admits an inferiority on the part of the recipient. The fact that both superiority and inferiority are imaginary is unfortunately irrelevant; it is the attitude they share that counts.

I know people who do not limit themselves, as I do, to saying that they wish that the practice did not exist; they simply refuse to bow to it. I see the point: if nobody is prepared to start. . . . But the snag lies not in fact that they are causing ill-feeling among the tippable but in the economic reality, which is that many recipients of tips rely on them for a substantial part of their income, and that indeed the income is frequently calculated on the assumption that it will be increased by tips. This must be true of taxi drivers, for instance, who do not own their own vehicles and in a general sense even of those who do; also of waiters, though I imagine the tip is not so vital a part of their income as it

749

used to be. More and more hotels and restaurants in Britain (it has long been standard practice on the Continent) put an automatic service charge on the bill, though I am afraid that I for one still feel constrained, though most uneasily, to distribute largesse none the less, and I have never yet had it refused.

I did have a tip refused in Sydney, though, and in the most encouraging circumstances. I was met at the airport by a representative of the organisation which had arranged my visit, and he accompanied me to my hotel in a taxi. After I had registered, a porter showed me upstairs, carrying my suitcase, and when I offered him money he declined it cheerfully, on the ground that "the other bloke" had fee'd him in advance. The attendant at the men's cloakroom in the old Caprice restaurant would never accept a tip, and this civilised behaviour on his part was carried out with a remarkable demeanour, which left him full of dignity without causing embarrassment in the tipper.

It is not easy to see the precise distinction between paying for goods or services we buy from a shopkeeper or other supplier and paying for the services provided by the employee of a restaurant or hotel; but I am sure that the instinct is sound which distinguishes between them, and which rightly thinks it no shame to pay for a pound of apples or the work of a window cleaner while no less rightly feeling degraded by paying a doorman for whistling up a taxi.

One problem is that the custom is so deeply embedded it seems impervious to any attempt to change it; as I say, hotels which now include a service charge are no less rife with tipping than before, but there is worse than that, for I have seen tipping going on without demur from either side of the transaction though both participants are standing beneath a sign which sternly forbids the practice altogether. And although tipping is a mark of, and reinforcement for, class divisions, it is just as widespread in countries (like Italy and United States) where class as we understand it in Britain does not exist.

No doubt some pestilent busybody will soon suggest that it should be forbidden by legislation, a cure ten times worse than the disease. My own feeling is that although pressure to abolish it must come both from the hand that proffers the money and the hand that takes it, it is in the latter that the solution lies. It is not much use icily refusing to tip if the person we would have tipped is so steeped in the attitude implied by taking a tip that he will feel resentful of the omission. After all, if the tipper insists on his superiority to the tipped, the tipped has a perfect remedy to hand: the action of refusing the tip automatically refuses the place below the salt.

Even leaving these considerations aside, the practice results in much embarrassment and confusion. For instance, a French theatre usherette expects a tip, but an English one does not; the former will be indignant and the latter bewildered if they find themselves treated like their counterparts on the wrong side of the Channel. German taxi-drivers find the practice so odd that if you tip them they simply think you have made a mistake with unfamiliar currency; if, thus encouraged, you go to New York and fail to tip a cabbie (despite the fact that no New York taxi driver knows where anything is, not excluding the Empire State Building) you will learn some extremely interesting vernacular expressions. (Although I have seen guide books so practical that they tell you what colour the telephone boxes are, I have never come across one that tells you in what circumstances to tip and in which not to.)

"You never tip an equal." That is where it begins and ends, and a pretty nasty terminus it is, too, when you think about it. For it suggests that if A has more money than B he is worth more as a human being; worse, it suggests that that view of the matter is held by B, even if it is not held by A himself. But must the human race be divided into the beggars and the begged-from? For that, put bluntly, is what the habit amounts to; a man is paid wages to serve dinner in a restaurant and when he has done the work he is paid for, he holds out his hand, metaphorically if not literally, for *baksheesh*. (In French and German, incidentally, there is a further twist to the spiral of implied contempt: the word for a tip in both languages suggests that the only thing the recipient will spend it on is drink.)

It goes back a long way, this habit: Shakespeare is full of underlings soliciting tips. And the attitude behind it is found in the oddest places; even Mr Dooley succumbed, saying: "When I give a tip 'tis not because I want to but because I'm afraid iv what th' waiter'll think." Until the waiter stops thinking it, there seems little we can do.

BERNARD LEVIN

751

What makes a good country house hotel

Nigel Corbett has been running a country house hotel – Summer Lodge, Evershot – for the past six years, and, as diligent readers of the Guide will know, has enjoyed an outstanding success. We asked him if he would set down what he considered to be the qualities needed in his work.

In one word, care! A good country house hotel should be a haven of care, good old-fashioned care, in large and generous helpings. The guests (not customers, please note) should be treated as good and revered friends. This abundance of care should be reflected in a warm welcome, guests should be met at their car and helped in with their luggage, then offered a drink – tea or whatever – to make them feel at home, regardless of the time of arrival or whether tea-making facilities are in their room anyway. This care should also be reflected by a warm and comfortable room with fresh flowers, enough pillows and blankets, decent towels, and soap of a quality that one would use oneself.

Throughout their stay, this care should be constant – not only providing delicious and sufficient food, but also being available to discuss places, shops and walks to occupy the day. When guests leave, it is important and basic good mamners to go out to the car to see them off. I would also add that I think it is poor manners when someone turns up on spec and finds the hotel full to send them away without getting them booked in somewhere else.

The staff, who should also be recipients of the owners' care so that they in turn pass it on to the guests, should be local as far as possible (nationals at least) to ensure that the atmosphere of the establishment is drawn not only from the character of the owners, but also from all who are working in the house. A brigade of excellent Italian waiters in the heart of the English countryside seems to me to be as incongruous as a large selection of French cheeses in the middle of Melton Mowbray!

In this age of computers, portion control, marketing and profit orientation, it is essential – like the clown on a tightrope appearing to be a poor acrobat when the reverse is true – that there should be a totally uncommercial air about a country house hotel. The house should have lots of nice bits and pieces as well as books and magazines lying around, possibly a pet or two, nothing locked or barred up, so that a feeling of being in a home from home prevails. Nothing ever too much trouble: on the contrary, a request should become a pleasurable opportunity to help someone.

Running a country house hotel properly and efficiently in my view is an exact science. One has to know how friendly (and possibly cheeky) to be without becoming familiar. And all is lost unless it comes from the heart – and if that lies elsewhere, then I suggest to potential owners or employees that they stick to large city hotels where everything is deputised, departmentalised and homogenised.

Finally, may I offer this definition: "A country house hotel should be an establishment where the guests forget to ask for the bill because they think that they have been staying with friends in a private house, and the proprietors cannot mention the bill for fear of spoiling the illusion that they have so painstakingly created!" Hey! Ho!

NIGEL CORBETT

Country house hotels: an opposition view

Not every one subscribes to the cult of the country house hotel. Some prefer the dependable life support systems of the hotel custom-built for the business traveller. Penny Perrick eloquently puts their case.

I had such a good time a few weeks ago staying at one of those provincial hotels built exclusively for the business traveller that I was sorry to learn from an article in *Signature* magazine called "Business women – finding it tough on the road" that I should not have done.

According to *Signature* my hotel did not look after me properly. It had booked me into a room some distance from the lift and this, said *Signature*, could have led to my being molested as I trotted along the corridor with my suit carrier. What is more, my telephone extension was the same number as my room, which, it seems, makes it easier for unsavoury callers to ring you up and go into a heavy breathing routine. Fortunately, at the time I did not know that staying in a hotel room with a spy hole in the door and an adequate lock could be as dodgy as loitering around Soho late on a Saturday night; and I spent a happy evening examining all the executive toys.

The nicest of these was the in-house movie system which at the flick of the switch screamed a newish full-length feature film starring Goldie Hawn instead of the scheduled television channel and unremitting Arthur Scargill.

By next morning when my alarm call, breakfast and news-papers all arrived at precisely the time specified I realised that this cheerfully impersonal rabbit warren, geared to the cut and thrust of sales conferences and executive training courses, was doing me far more good than an off-duty weekend spent in that newly fashionable horror, the country house hotel.

Staying at one of those establishments is supposed to be the paying equivalent of staying with rather chic friends who pride themselves on their knowledge of food, wine, flower-arranging and coordinating Laura Ashley doodahs. The writing paper always features a rather murky woodcut of the establishment and carries the legend "Marigold and Tristram look forward to welcoming you to Giddings".

Once arrived, you go through agonies trying to work out a correct code of behaviour. Are the wellingtons piled up in the hall meant to be borrowed? Is it reasonable to ask for early-morning tea even though you know that Marigold and Tristram were up till all hours cutting carrots into fan shapes and refreshing the bowls of pot-pourri in the bar?

Country-house hotel food is usually delicious, if a bit on the precious side. What mars the enjoyment is the way Tristram describes every dish as though he is introducing a Miss World contestant. There is also the unrelaxing problem of deciding whether to dress for dinner or not. It seems rude not to since Marigold's younger sister, a Constance Spry graduate, has done such unusual things for the dining room tables with a few birthday cake candles, some kitchen foil and a hollyhock, but on the other hand you feel no end of a fool sitting there in your black velvet while cries of damnation can be heard bounding off the kitchen walls.

To those grown accustomed to the efficiency of the working world, the quirky amateur charm of the country house hotel makes us rattled rather than relaxed. Which is why we are looking forward to the completion of the Luton International Hotel, now under construction.

Already it is boasting special facilities for the business classes and pleasant dreams of electric skirt presses, shoe-cleaning kits and round-the-clock room service are dancing through my head.

PENNY PERRICK

Alphabetical list of hotels

(New or readmitted ones indicated *; we are sorry that for reasons of space only countries with a considerable number of entries could be indexed)

England

Angel Bury St Edmunds 68
Appletree Holme Farm * Blawith 54
Arundell Arms Lifton 130
Ashburton House Stratford-upon-Avon 173
Ashfield House Grassington 103
Ashwick Country House * Dulverton 90
Aynsome Manor Cartmel 71
Bailiffscourt Climping 80
Basil Street London 131
Bay Tree * Burford 67
Bear Nayland 148
Beechfield House * Beanacre 48
Bell Aston Clinton 38
Bell Faringdon 96
Belle Époque * Knutsford 125
Bibury Court Bibury 51
Billesley Manor Stratford-upon-Avon 174
Black Boys * Thornage 180
Black Swan Ravenstonedale 157
Blakeney * Blakeney 53
Blakes * London 131
Boscundle Manor St Austell 162
Bowlish House * Shepton Mallet 167
Breamish House * Powburn 157
Bridgefield House * Spark Bridge 170
Buckinghamshire Arms Blickling 55
Buckland Manor Buckland 66
Burgoyne Reeth 158

Burleigh Court Minchinhampton 146
Butchers Arms Woolhope 201
Calcot Manor * Tetbury 179
Capital * London 132
Castle Taunton 177
Castle Point Salcombe 165
Cathedral Gate * Canterbury 70
Cavendish Baslow 42
Chadlington House Chadlington 72
Chedington Court Chedington 75
Cherrybrook Two Bridges 185
Chewton Glen New Milton 150
Chilvester Hill House * Calne 69
Clinchs' Chichester 77
Collin House Broadway 63
Combe House Gittisham 99
Congham Hall King's Lynn 120
Connaught London 133
Combe House Holford 113
Cormorant Golant 101
Corse Lawn Corse Lawn 83
Courtlands Hove 114
Crantock Bay Crantock 85
Crathorne Hall Crathorne 86
Dedham Hall Dedham 86
Dedham Vale Dedham 87
Devonshire Arms Bolton Abbey 57
D'Isney Place Lincoln 130
Downrew House Barnstaple 41
Duke's London 133

Dundas Arms Kintbury 122
Durrants London 134
Ebury Court London 134
Elms Abberley 33
Ettington Park Alderminster 34
Evesham Evesham 95
Fallowfields Kingston Bagpuize 122
Farlam Hall Brampton 60
Feathers Ludlow 141
Feathers Woodstock 199
Fleece * Cirencester 79
Flitwick Manor * Flitwick 98
Frog Street Farm Beercrocombe 49
Gara Rock East Portlemouth 92
George of Stamford Stamford 172
Gidleigh Park Chagford 73
Glebe Farm Diddlebury 88
Glen Rothay Rydal 160
Golden Pheasant * Burford 68
Grafton Manor Bromsgrove 65
Gravetye Manor East Grinstead 91
Halewell Withington 197
Hallam * London 135
Hall Garth Coatham Mundeville 81
Hambleton Hall Hambleton 106
Headlam Hall * Headlam 109
Heddon's Gate Heddon's Mouth 110
Highbullen Chittlehamholt 78
Higher Faughan Newlyn 150
High Fell Alston 35
Hintlesham Hall * Hintlesham 111

755

Germany

Maps

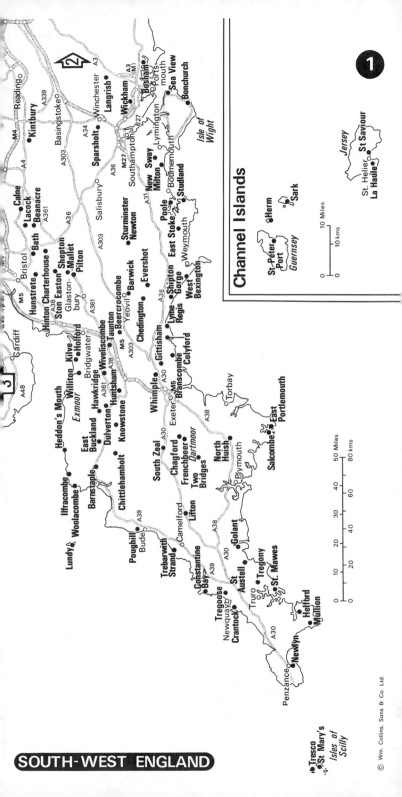

SOUTH-WEST ENGLAND

© Wm. Collins, Sons & Co. Ltd.

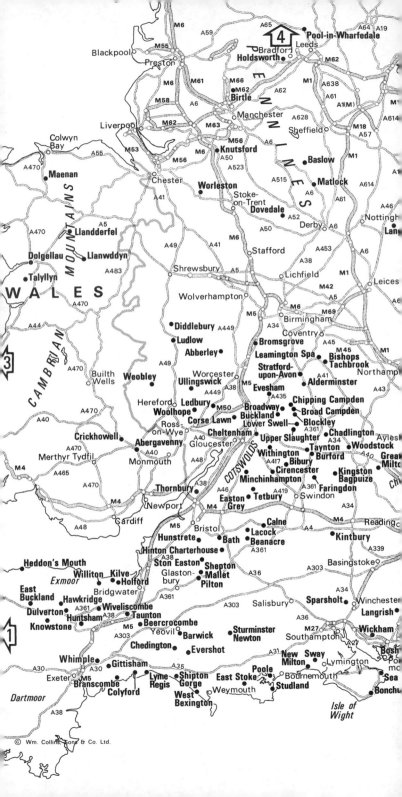

© Wm. Collins, Sons & Co. Ltd.

Kingston
upon Hull

A15

A180 ○ Grimsby

A16

A158

Lincoln

A17

A16

○ Skegness

Blakeney ●

● **Thornage**

Great ● **Blickling**
Snoring

Norfolk
Broads

A47

A47

King's Lynn ○ ● **King's Lynn**

Norwich ○

Great
Yarmouth ○

A1

nbleton
● **Stamford**

A47

A10

Peterborough ○

3

● **St. Ives**

A11

Diss ●

A12

A1

A45

A45

Cambridge ●

Bury St Edmunds ●

A45

A14

Otley ●

ton
ynes

Bedford ○

Chelsworth ● ● **Hintlesham** ● Ipswich
Nayland ●

A11

M11

Flitwick
● M1

A6

(A1(M))

Luton

A10

A11

Dedham ●

Coggeshall ●

Colchester ○

A12

on

Hertford ○

A41

A1

M11

A127

atford ○

M1

Southend-
on-Sea ○

A40

LONDON ●

M4

denhead
Vindsor

Margate ○

A3

A23

A21

A2

M2

agshot

M25

M25

M26

M20

Canterbury ●

Reigate ○

Maidstone ○

Chartham ● A2
Hatch

West Cliffe ●

Guildford ○

M23

A21

Bethersden ●

Ashford ●

A20

Godalming

East ●
Grinstead

Tunbridge
Wells ○ ● **Cranbrook**

Mersham ●

A20

Dover ○

A267

● **Wadhurst**

A259

A23

Battle ● ● **Rye**

chester A27 **Hove** ○

○ Lewes

A259

Climping ●

Brighton ●

Hastings ○

ognor
Regis

○ Eastbourne

0	10	20	30	40	50 Miles
0	20	40	60	80 kms	

CENTRAL & SOUTHERN ENGLAND

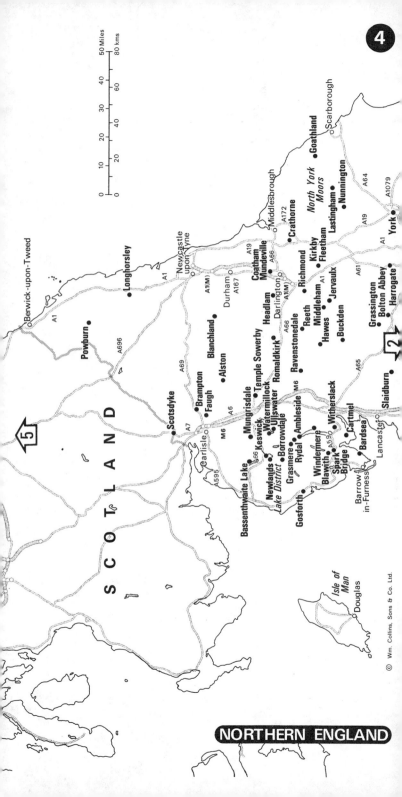

4

50 Miles
80 kms

Berwick-upon-Tweed

•Longhorsley

Newcastle upon Tyne

Middlesbrough

North York Moors

Scarborough

•Goathland

•Lastingham
•Nunnington

•Powburn

•Blanchland

Durham

Coatham
Mundeville

Headlam

Crathorne

Richmond

Kirkby
Fleetham

•Scotsdyke

•Brampton
•Faugh

•Alston

Temple Sowerby

Romaldkirk

Ravenstonedale

Reeth

Middleham
Hawes

Jervaulx

Buckden

York

Grassington
Bolton Abbey
Harrogate

S C O T L A N D

Carlisle

Mungrisdale
Keswick
Watermillock
Ullswater
Borrowdale

Newlands
Lake District

Grasmere
Rydal
Ambleside

Witherslack

Cartmel

Staidburn

Windermere
Blawith
Spark
Bridge

Bardsea

Lancaster

Gosforth

Barrow
in-Furness

*Isle of
Man*

Douglas

© Wm. Collins, Sons & Co. Ltd.

NORTHERN ENGLAND

Miles
0 10 20 30 40 50
km
0 20 40 60 80

© Wm. Collins, Sons & Co. Ltd.

Shetland Islands

Unst
Fetlar
Whalsay
Mainland
Bressay
Lerwick
Busta
Walls
Foula

◊ Fair Isle

Fraserburgh
A952
A98
Elgin
A96
A939
A95
Nairn
A96
Inverness
A9
Drumnadrochit
●**Whitebridge**
A82
Kingussie
H I G H L A N D S
A92
Aberdeen
A96

Orkney Islands

Mainland
Kirkwall
St Ola
Hoy

Wick
Thurso
A882
A9
A836
Lairg
A836
A9
A838
A838
A894
Kinlochbervie
Scourie
A838
A837
Achiltibuie
A835
Ullapool
A835
A832
A896
A890
Ardelve
A87
S U T H E R L A N D
W E S T   H I G H L A N D
Raasay
Skye
A850

O U T E R   H E B R I D E S

A857
Stornoway
A858
Lewis
A859
Timsgarry
Scarista
Harris
North Uist
Benbecula
A865
South Uist

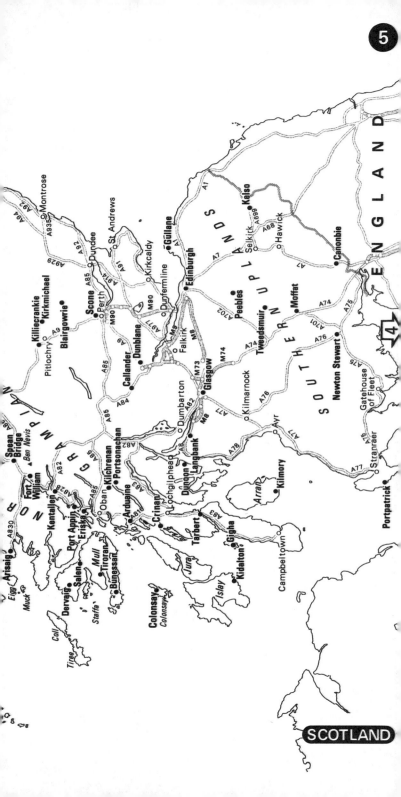

5

Montrose

A94

A935

A92

St Andrews

A929

Dundee

A92

Kirkmichael

Killiecrankie

A9

Blairgowrie

Scone

Perth

Pitlochry

Kirkcaldy

A91

A914

Dunfermline

M90

Gullane

Edinburgh

Kelso

A699

Selkirk

Hawick

A68

ENGLAND

Canonbie

A7

SOUTHERN UPLANDS

Peebles

A7

A702

Moffat

A74

A75

Tweedsmuir

A701

A76

Newton Stewart

A76

Gatehouse of Fleet

A75

Dunblane

A9

A822

Callander

A84

Falkirk

A91

M9

A9

M90

Glasgow

Kilmarnock

A71

M8

A77

Ayr

A78

A76

A77

Stranraer

A75

Portpatrick

MIDLAND

Spean Bridge

Ben Nevis

Fort William

A82

A830

A828

Kentallen

Arisaig

Eigg

Muck

Port Appin

Erisko

Salen

Tiroran

Mull

Dervaig

Staffa

Coll

Tiree

A85

Oban

A85

Kilchrenan

Portsonachan

A83

Arduaine

A816

Crinan

GRAMPIAN

Lochgilphead

Dunoon

Langbank

A82

Dumbarton

M73

M74

M8

Tarbert

Gigha

Kidalton

Kilmory

Arran

Jura

Islay

Colonsay

Colonsay

Bunessan

Campbeltown

Dundee

4

SCOTLAND

6

IRELAND

© Wm. Collins, Sons & Co. Ltd

SOUTHERN SCANDINAVIA

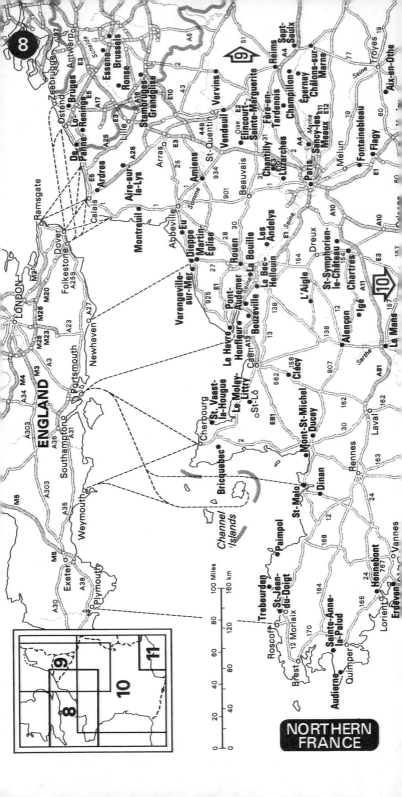

NORTHERN
FRANCE

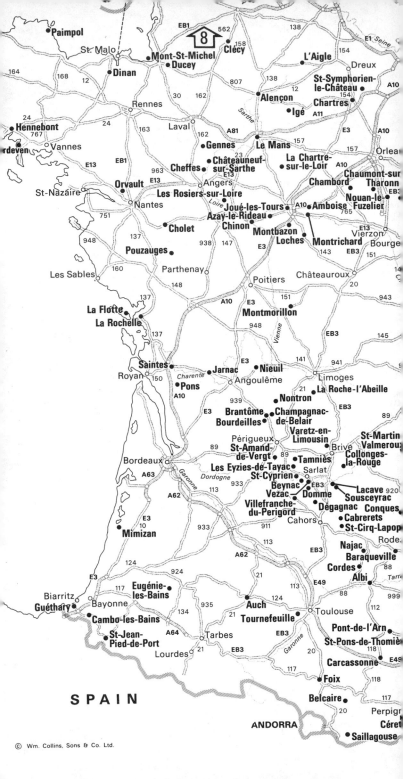

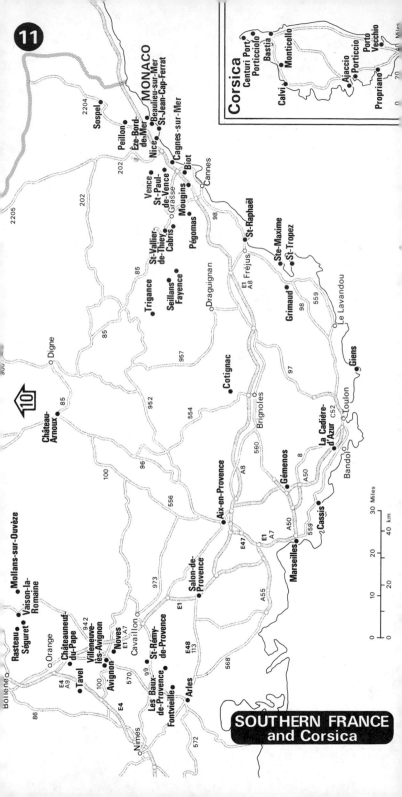

11

SOUTHERN FRANCE and Corsica

Corsica
Centuri Port
Porticciolo
Bastia
Monticello
Calvi
Ajaccio
Porticcio
Porto Vecchio
Propriano

MONACO
Beaulieu-sur-Mer
Éze-Bord-de-Mer
St-Jean-Cap-Ferrat
Nice
Cagnes-sur-Mer
Peillon
Sospel
Biot
Vence
St-Paul-de-Vence
Grasse
Mougins
Cannes
St-Vallier-de-Thiey
Cabris
Pégomas
St-Raphaël
Ste-Maxime
St-Tropez
Trigance
Seillans
Fayence
Draguignan
Fréjus
Grimaud
Le Lavandou
Digne
Cotignac
Giens
Château-Arnoux
Brignoles
Toulon
Aix-en-Provence
Gémenos
La Cadière-d'Azur
Bandol
Cassis
Marseilles
Salon-de-Provence
Mollans-sur-Ouvèze
Rasteau
Ségéret
Vaison-la-Romaine
Châteauneuf-du-Pape
Orange
Villeneuve-lès-Avignon
Noves
Tavel
Avignon
Cavaillon
St-Rémy-de-Provence
Les Baux-de-Provence
Fontvieille
Arles
Nîmes
Bollène

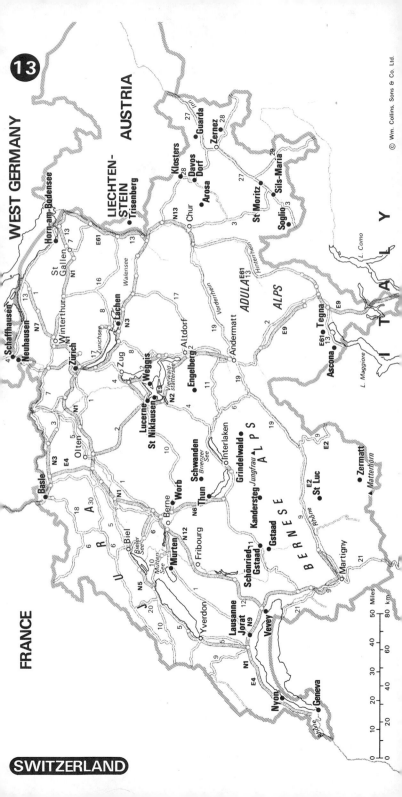

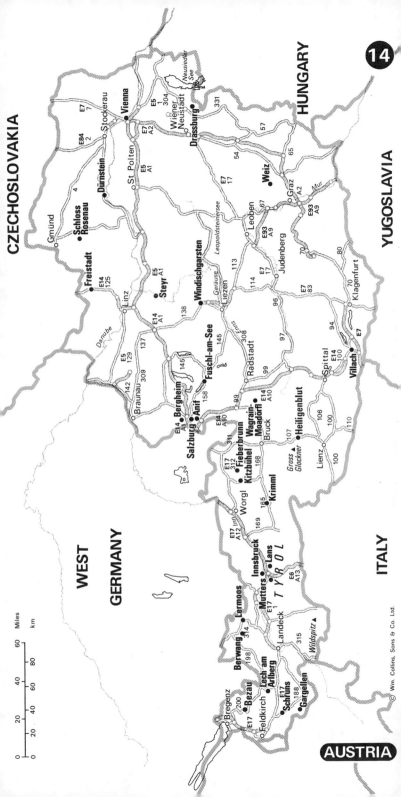

SPAIN & PORTUGAL

FRANCE

P Y R E N E E S

50
San Sebastián

8 E3
1

Pamplona

240 **Yesa**   136

ANDORRA   ● Encamp

omingo
lzada   68

15

E4
7
152 Gerona ○   ● **Playa de Fornells**

122

Ebro

240

Calonge ●

1

234

68   Zaragoza   Lérida

E4
11

Costa Brava

330

E4
2

Barcelona

E4
11

232

E26
7   ● Tarragona

Tajo

234

400   ○ Cuenca

320

E26
7

Deyá ●

Bañalbufar ● ● Palma

Minorca

E101
111   ○ Valencia

Majorca

01

BALEARIC ISLANDS

○ Albacete   430

E26
7

● **San Miguel**

Ibiza

322

301

E26
340   ○ Alicante

● **Villajoyosa**

Formentera

332

301

E26
342

● **Mojácar**

340
○ Alméria

Madeira ● **Funchal**

CANARY ISLANDS

La Palma   *Lanzarote*

Tenerife   *Fuerventura*

Las ○ Palmas

Valverde   *Gran Canaria*

0   50   100 Miles

0   50   100   150 km   © Wm. Collins, Sons & Co. Ltd

HUNGARY, ITALY & YUGOSLAVIA

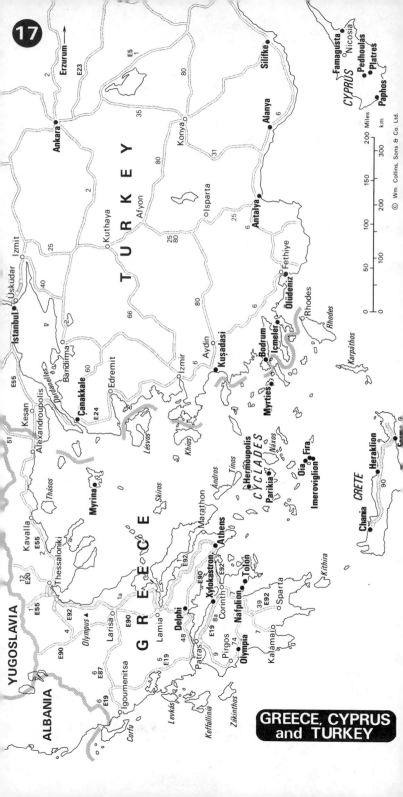

GREECE, CYPRUS and TURKEY

Exchange rates

These rates for buying currency are correct at time of printing but in some cases may be wildly awry at the time of publication. It is essential to check with banks or newspapers for up-to-date pound and dollar equivalents.

	£1 sterling	$1 US
Austria (Schillings)	27.00	20.07
Belgium (Belgian francs)	77.50	57.07
Cyprus (Cyprus pounds)	1.25	1.69
Denmark (kroner)	13.85	10.30
Finland (Finnish marks)	8.10	6.07
France (francs)	11.70	8.72
Germany (Deutschemarks)	3.83	2.86
Greece (drachmae)	178.50	133.30
Holland (guilders)	4.30	3.22
Hungary (forints)	67.00	49.55
Ireland (punts)	1.23	1.09
Italy (lire)	2,550	1,905.50
Luxembourg (Luxembourg francs)	77.5	57.62
Malta (Maltese pounds)	0.66	2.19
Norway (kroner)	11.26	8.41
Portugal, including Madeira (escudos)	228.00	169.50
Spain, Andorra, Balearics, Canaries (pesetas)	225.00	167.25
Sweden (kroner)	11.35	8.46
Switzerland, Liechtenstein (Swiss francs)	3.16	2.36
Turkey (lira)	755.00	537.25
Yugoslavia (dinar)	380.00	274.57

Hotel reports

The report forms on the following pages may be used to endorse or blackball an existing entry or to nominate a hotel that you feel deserves inclusion in next year's Guide. Either way, there is no need to use our forms, or, if you do, to restrict yourself to the space available. All nominations (each on a separate piece of paper, please) should include your name and address, the name and location of the hotel, when you stayed there and for how long. Please nominate only hotels you have visited in the past 18 months unless you are sure from friends that standards have not fallen off since your stay. And please be as specific as possible, and critical where appropriate, about the character of the building, the public rooms, the sleeping accommodation, the meals, the service, the night-life, the grounds. We should be glad if you would give some impression of the location and country as well as of the hotel itself, particularly in less familiar regions.

You should not feel embarrassed about writing at length. More than anything else, we want the Guide to convey the special flavour of its hotels; so the more time and trouble you can take in providing those small details which will help to make a description come alive, the more valuable to others will be the final published result. We mind having to pass up a potentially attractive hotel because the report doesn't really tell us enough. We are offering again this year a dozen bottles of champagne for the best report or reports of the year (see page ???).

There is no need to bother with prices or with routine information about number of rooms and facilities. We obtain such details direct from the hotels selected. What we are anxious to get from readers is information that is not accessible elsewhere. And we should be grateful, in the case of foreign hotels, to be sent brochures if you have them available. Nominations for the 1987 edition should reach us not later than 15 May, 1986. The latest date for comments on existing entries is 30 June 1986.

Please let us know if you would like more report forms. Our address is *The Good Hotel Guide*, Freepost, London W11 4BR, for UK correspondents (no stamp needed). For letters from outside the UK, the address of the Guide is 61 Clarendon Road, London W11 4JE, stamped normally.

These report forms may also be used, if you wish, to recommend good hotels in North America to our equivalent publication in the States, *America's Wonderful Little Hotels and Inns*. They should be sent adequately stamped (no Freepost to the United States), not to *The Good Hotel Guide*, but to *America's Wonderful Little Hotels and Inns*, St Martin's Press, 175 Fifth Avenue, New York, NY 10010, USA.

To: *The Good Hotel Guide*, Freepost, London W11 4BR

NOTE: No stamps needed in UK, but letters posted outside the UK should be addressed to 61 Clarendon Road, London W11 4JE and stamped normally. In appropriate cases we may share your report with *The Good Food Guide*, and, unless asked not to, we shall assume that we may publish your name if you are recommending a new hotel or supporting an existing entry.

Name of Hotel_____

Address_____

_____

Date of most recent visit   Duration of visit
☐ New recommendation   ☐ Comment on existing entry

Report:

I am not connected directly or indirectly with the management or proprietors

(Continue overleaf if you wish or use separate sheet)

Signed_____

Name and address (Capitals please)_____

_____

To: *The Good Hotel Guide*, Freepost, London W11 4BR

NOTE: No stamps needed in UK, but letters posted outside the UK should be addressed to 61 Clarendon Road, London W11 4JE and stamped normally. In appropriate cases we may share your report with *The Good Food Guide*, and, unless asked not to, we shall assume that we may publish your name if you are recommending a new hotel or supporting an existing entry.

Name of Hotel_____

Address_____

_____

Date of most recent visit   Duration of visit
☐ New recommendation   ☐ Comment on existing entry

Report:

I am not connected directly or indirectly with the management or proprietors

(Continue overleaf if you wish or use separate sheet)

Signed_____

Name and address (Capitals please)_____

_____

To: *The Good Hotel Guide*, Freepost, London W11 4BR

NOTE: No stamps needed in UK, but letters posted outside the UK should be addressed to 61 Clarendon Road, London W11 4JE and stamped normally. In appropriate cases we may share your report with *The Good Food Guide*, and, unless asked not to, we shall assume that we may publish your name if you are recommending a new hotel or supporting an existing entry.

Name of Hotel_____

Address_____

_____

Date of most recent visit   Duration of visit
☐ New recommendation   ☐ Comment on existing entry

Report:

I am not connected directly or indirectly with the management or proprietors

(Continue overleaf if you wish or use separate sheet)

Signed_____

Name and address (Capitals please)_____

_____

To: *The Good Hotel Guide,* Freepost, London W11 4BR

NOTE: No stamps needed in UK, but letters posted outside the UK should be addressed to 61 Clarendon Road, London W11 4JE and stamped normally. In appropriate cases we may share your report with *The Good Food Guide,* and, unless asked not to, we shall assume that we may publish your name if you are recommending a new hotel or supporting an existing entry.

Name of Hotel_____

Address_____

_____

Date of most recent visit   Duration of visit
☐ New recommendation   ☐ Comment on existing entry

Report:

I am not connected directly or indirectly with the management or proprietors

(Continue overleaf if you wish or use separate sheet)

Signed_____

Name and address (Capitals please)_____

_____

To: *The Good Hotel Guide*, Freepost, London W11 4BR

NOTE: No stamps needed in UK, but letters posted outside the UK should be addressed to 61 Clarendon Road, London W11 4JE and stamped normally. In appropriate cases we may share your report with *The Good Food Guide*, and, unless asked not to, we shall assume that we may publish your name if you are recommending a new hotel or supporting an existing entry.

Name of Hotel_____

Address_____

_____

Date of most recent visit   Duration of visit
☐ New recommendation   ☐ Comment on existing entry

Report:

I am not connected directly or indirectly with the management or proprietors

(Continue overleaf if you wish or use separate sheet)

Signed_____

Name and address (Capitals please)_____

_____

To: *The Good Hotel Guide*, Freepost, London W11 4BR

NOTE: No stamps needed in UK, but letters posted outside the UK should be addressed to 61 Clarendon Road, London W11 4JE and stamped normally. In appropriate cases we may share your report with *The Good Food Guide*, and, unless asked not to, we shall assume that we may publish your name if you are recommending a new hotel or supporting an existing entry.

Name of Hotel_____

Address_____

_____

Date of most recent visit   Duration of visit
☐ New recommendation   ☐ Comment on existing entry

Report:

I am not connected directly or indirectly with the management or proprietors

(Continue overleaf if you wish or use separate sheet)

Signed_____

Name and address (Capitals please)_____

_____